Costa Rica

Matthew D Firestone
Guyan Mitra, Wendy Yanagihara

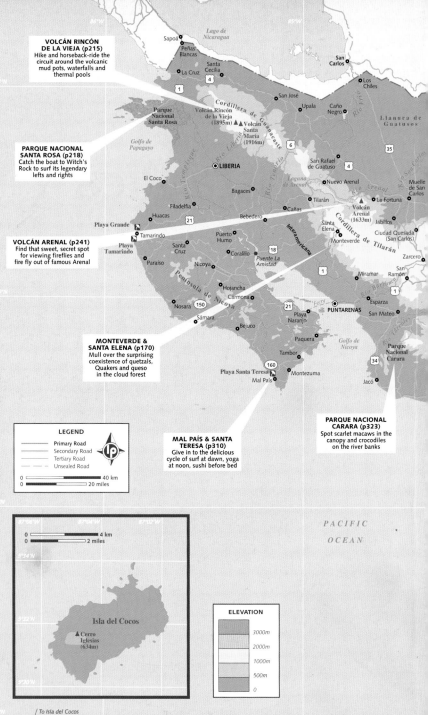

VOLCÁN RINCÓN DE LA VIEJA (p215)
Hike and horseback-ride the circuit around the volcanic mud pots, waterfalls and thermal pools

PARQUE NACIONAL SANTA ROSA (p218)
Catch the boat to Witch's Rock to surf its legendary lefts and rights

VOLCÁN ARENAL (p241)
Find that sweet, secret spot for viewing fireflies and fire fly out of famous Arenal

MONTEVERDE & SANTA ELENA (p170)
Mull over the surprising coexistence of quetzals, Quakers and queso in the cloud forest

MAL PAÍS & SANTA TERESA (p310)
Give in to the delicious cycle of surf at dawn, yoga at noon, sushi before bed

PARQUE NACIONAL CARARA (p323)
Spot scarlet macaws in the canopy and crocodiles on the river banks

LEGEND

	Primary Road
	Secondary Road
	Tertiary Road
	Unsealed Road

0 ————— 40 km
0 ————— 20 miles

ELEVATION

3000m
2000m
1000m
500m
0

Lago de Nicaragua

Sapoá
Peñas Blancas
Santa Cecilia
La Cruz
San José
San Carlos
Los Chiles
Upala
Caño Negro
Llanura de Guatusos

Cordillera de Guanacaste

Parque Nacional Santa Rosa
Volcán Rincón de la Vieja (1895m)
Volcán Santa María (1916m)

Golfo de Papagayo

LIBERIA
Bagaces
Cañas
Tilarán
Nuevo Arenal
La Fortuna
Volcán Arenal (1633m)
Muelle de San Carlos
San Rafael de Guatuso

El Coco
Filadelfia
Huacas
Playa Grande
Tamarindo
Playa Tamarindo
Santa Cruz
Paraíso
Nicoya
Hojancha
Carmona
Nosara
Sámara
Bejuco

Río Tempisque
Río Liberia
Río Tenorio

Puerto Humo
Corralillo
Puente La Amistad
Bebedero

Interamericana

Santa Elena
Monteverde
Cordillera de Tilarán
Jabillos
Ciudad Quesada (San Carlos)
Zarcero
Miramar
San Ramón
Esparza
San Mateo
PUNTARENAS
Playa Naranjo
Paquera
Tambor
Montezuma
Playa Santa Teresa
Mal País
Jacó

Península de Nicoya

Golfo de Nicoya

Parque Nacional Carara

PACIFIC OCEAN

Isla del Cocos
Cerro Iglesias (634m)

0 ————— 4 km
0 ————— 2 miles

To Isla del Cocos (300km, See inset)

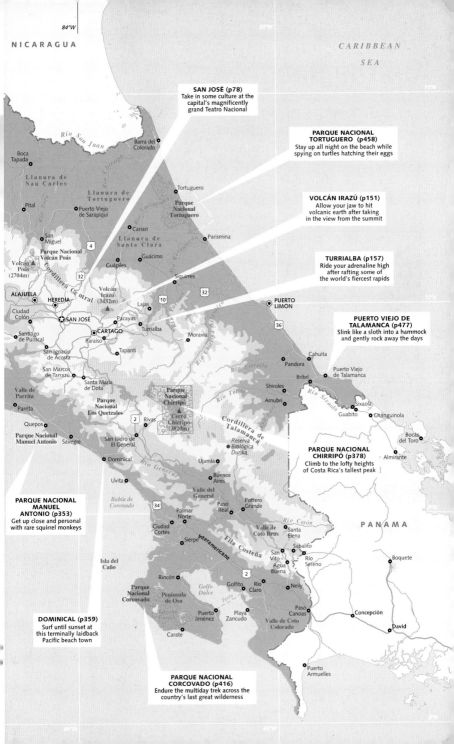

NICARAGUA

CARIBBEAN SEA

84°W

SAN JOSÉ (p78)
Take in some culture at the capital's magnificently grand Teatro Nacional

PARQUE NACIONAL TORTUGUERO (p458)
Stay up all night on the beach while spying on turtles hatching their eggs

VOLCÁN IRAZÚ (p151)
Allow your jaw to hit volcanic earth after taking in the view from the summit

TURRIALBA (p157)
Ride your adrenaline high after rafting some of the world's fiercest rapids

PUERTO VIEJO DE TALAMANCA (p477)
Slink like a sloth into a hammock and gently rock away the days

PARQUE NACIONAL CHIRRIPÓ (p378)
Climb to the lofty heights of Costa Rica's tallest peak

PARQUE NACIONAL MANUEL ANTONIO (p353)
Get up close and personal with rare squirrel monkeys

DOMINICAL (p359)
Surf until sunset at this terminally laidback Pacific beach town

PARQUE NACIONAL CORCOVADO (p416)
Endure the multiday trek across the country's last great wilderness

Boca Tapada

Llanura de San Carlos

Río San Juan

Barra del Colorado

Pital

San Miguel

Puerto Viejo de Sarapiquí

Parque Nacional Volcán Poás

Volcán Poás (2704m)

ALAJUELA

HEREDIA

Ciudad Colón

Santiago de Puriscal

San Ignacio de Acosta

SAN JOSÉ

CARTAGO

Paraíso

Tapantí

San Marcos de Tarrazú

Santa María de Dota

Valle de Parrita

Parrita

Quepos

Parque Nacional Manuel Antonio

Savegre

Parque Nacional Los Quetzales

Dominical

Uvita

Bahía de Coronado

Isla del Caño

Parque Nacional Corcovado

Península de Osa

Rincón

Carate

Puerto Jiménez

Golfo Dulce

Llanura de Tortuguero

Tortuguero

Parque Nacional Tortuguero

Cariari

Parismina

Guácimo

Guápiles

Llanura de Santa Clara

Siquirres

Volcán Irazú (3432m)

Lajas

Pacayas

Turrialba

Moravia

PUERTO LIMÓN

Cahuita

Pandora

Puerto Viejo de Talamanca

Shiroles

Bribrí

Amubri

Sixaola

Guabito

Changuinola

Bocas del Toro

Almirante

Parque Nacional Chirripó

Cerro Chirripó (3820m)

Reserva Biológica Durika

Cordillera de Talamanca

Ujarrás

Buenos Aires

Valle del General

Potrero Grande

Paso Real

Palmar Norte

Ciudad Cortés

Sierpe

Valle de Coto Brus

Santa Elena

Sabalito

San Vito

Agua Buena

Río Sereno

PANAMA

Boquete

Golfito

Río Claro

Neily

Paso Canoas

Valle de Coto Colorado

Concepción

David

Playa Zancudo

Puerto Armuelles

San Isidro de El General

Rivas

Río Coto

Río General

Interamericana

Fila Costeña

Cordillera Central

4

32

10

32

36

2

34

2

On the Road

MATTHEW D FIRESTONE Coordinating Author
I've always thought there was something surreal about suspension bridges spanning vast expanses of jungle. I guess it has something to do with my lifelong quest to be Indiana Jones. Sometimes I like to run across these kinds of bridges, pretending I'm being chased by angry savages. Then of course, I realize how stupid I look, and secretly hope that no one saw me.

GUYAN MITRA Rafting is certainly one of the coolest things you can do in Costa Rica. All I remember from our boat trip is a flurry of commands bellowed by our guide: Paddle! Get down! Faster! I ignored them all, clung to the boat and yelped like a poodle most of the way down.

WENDY YANAGIHARA After my traveling *compañero* practically veered off the road when he saw the waves at Ostional, we pulled over, he paddled out, I jotted notes, and *this* guy flipped across my towel. I walked him to the waterline and wished him long life as he was swept away.

For full author biographies see p567

COSTA RICA HIGHLIGHTS

Few travel destinations have the vast spectrum of stunning landscapes and exotic wildlife offered by Costa Rica, a tiny Central American country lodged between two great oceans. Of course, what Costa Rica lacks in size, it more than makes up for in biodiversity. In one day you can watch the sunrise over the Caribbean, and the sunset over the Pacific. Or spend the morning trekking through the highland cloud forests, and wind down in the afternoon with a cup of shade-grown brew on an organic coffee plantation. This incredible complement of landscapes is also inhabited by some of the planet's most charismatic species, including scarlet macaw and squirrel monkey in the canopy above, and jaguar and tapir on the forest floor.

National Parks

From misty rain forests and spewing volcanoes to rugged coastlines and marine reserves, Costa Rica is home to some truly mind-blowing national parks. Whether you want to explore dense jungles, or simply lounge on sun-kissed beaches, Costa Rica can serve up a range of natural landscapes to suit all sorts of travelers.

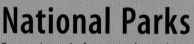

Author Tip

If you're planning some independent exploration of Costa Rica's more remote national parks, then be sure to stop by the Instituto Geográfico Nacional (National Geography Institute; see p534) in San José. Here, you can pick up some detailed topographical maps before hitting the back-country trails.

① Parque Nacional Tortuguero

This marine and terrestrial national park (p458) is regarded as one of the world's most important nesting grounds for the endangered green sea turtle. A massive wilderness area encompassing a chunk of the northern Caribbean coast, Tortuguero also protects a slew of other wildlife including manatee, monkey and sloth.

② Parque Nacional Isla del Cocos

Although you're going to have to work to access this extremely isolated tropical island (p441) in the middle of the Pacific, trust us – it's worth it. The fabled film location for *Jurassic Park*, Isla del Cocos sits alongside the Galapagos as one of the world's most ecologically diverse islands.

③ Reserva Biológica Bosque Nuboso Monteverde

This iconic cloud forest (p190) was first established by a community of Quakers who were seeking to protect their invaluable watershed. Home to such rare fauna as the resplendent quetzal, which is the Maya bird of paradise, Monteverde is partly responsible for Costa Rica's international fame as an ecotourism hot spot.

④ Parque Nacional Volcán Arenal

This red hot national park (p241) is focused on Arenal, one of the world's top 10 most active volcanoes. On a clear night when the clouds have all rolled out to sea, the skies around this towering behemoth light up as waves upon waves of lava roll down its perfectly angular slopes.

⑤ Parque Nacional Corcovado

Dubbed by *National Geographic* as the most biologically intense place on earth, this bastion of Pacific dry coastal rain forest is Costa Rica at its best. Although you will have to cross flowing rivers and bushwhack through dense jungle, an expedition across this national park (p416) will undoubtedly be the highlight of your trip.

⑥ Parque Nacional Chirripó

Costa Rica is bisected by the continental divide, a sheer spine of mountainous terrain that gives rise to much of the country's biodiversity. For a chance to scale Costa Rica's highest peak and stand upon this geological wonder, head to Cerro Chirripó, the centerpiece of this highland national park (p378).

Wildlife-Watching

For a good number of travelers, a trip to Costa Rica is synonymous with wildlife-watching. When some of the world's rarest neotropical animals can be spotted with relative ease, it's easy to see why you should touch down in Costa Rica with a pair of binoculars in hand.

Author Tip
Whether you're an aspiring birder or a seasoned veteran, be sure to pick up a copy of *A Naturalist in Costa Rica* by Dr Alexander Skutch. An icon among birders, Dr Skutch weaves his philosophies into his beautiful descriptions of flora and fauna in this enchanting memoir and natural history guide.

① Scarlet Macaw
Few canopy dwellers are as majestic as these monogamous birds, whose distinctive calls are a quick indicator to stop and look up. To maximize your chances of spotting scarlet against a backdrop of verdant green, head to Parque Nacional Carara (p323), a famous refuge for these winged beauties.

② Squirrel Monkey
Regarded as one of the country's most spectacular destinations, Parque Nacional Manuel Antonio (p353) is typified by rain-forest clad mountains sweeping down to the sea. With a little luck (and patience), you might experience a face-to-face encounter with its most famous inhabitant, the increasingly rare Central American squirrel monkey.

③ Leatherback Sea Turtle
Costa Rica is one of the few places in the world where leatherback sea turtles routinely nest. One place where you can watch these denizens of the deep roost is Playa Grande (p267), particularly when there's a full moon above the horizon. Pacific leatherbacks have laid their eggs at Playa Grande for thousands of years.

④ Jaguar
Seasoned wilderness guides spend entire lifetimes in the rain forests and jungles of Costa Rica without ever so much as catching a glimpse of this elusive feline. However, if you're keen to follow the trail of spoors and footprints left by this top predator, there's no better place than the remote and rugged Parque Internacional La Amistad (p389).

⑤ Humpback Whale
Topping the must-see list of marine animals, humpback whales are famous for their incredible breaching displays, which are very photogenic and impossible to forget. To catch a glimpse of these gentle giants on their annual migration path add Parque Nacional Marino Ballena (p365) to your itinerary.

⑥ Baird's Tapir
Something akin to a river rhinoceros, these lumbering beasts are one of the most distinctive animals in the rain forest. Although they are highly endangered due to habitat loss and illegal poaching, they are commonly sighted at the famed Sirena ranger station (p428) in Parque Nacional Corcovado.

6

Tropical Beaches

Let's get right to the point here. Costa Rica may have some of the most stunning rain forests and wildlife on the planet, but it also has some truly awesome strips of sand. Whether you're keen to body surf in the crashing spray, or just spend your days soaking up the rays, one thing is for sure – Costa Rica is a beach lover's dream.

3

Author Tip
Costa Rica has its fair share of Cancún-style party beaches, which attract lots of foreign tourists and an increasing number of resident expats. If you're not in the mood to get your drink on and dance in the sand until morning, Costa Rica is also home to plenty of wilderness beaches where you will only have to share your spot with a few passing hermit crabs.

① Playa Tamarindo
Known in most circles as Playa Tamagringo, this increasingly wealthy and touristy beach destination is home to the country's hottest ocean-side night spots. Sure, Tamarindo (p270) isn't the most authentic place in Costa Rica, but it can definitely be a lot of fun if you go with the right mindset.

② Playa Negra
As its name implies, this much-loved beach (p469) near the reggae-fueled town of Cahuita is covered in dark black sand that positively shines on a sunny day. Although the sand can get a bit warm around midday, fret not as you're never far from the turquoise waters of the Caribbean Sea.

③ Mal País & Santa Teresa
Hugging the tip of the Nicoya peninsula, these two beach towns (p310) are certainly not the easiest places to access. However, it's worth braving the bumpy roads and clouds of dust for the chance to surf along a pristine stretch of wilderness-backed beach.

④ Montezuma
Few destinations in Costa Rica attract as large a legion of devotees as Montezuma (p304), which is a classic backpacker paradise at the southern end of the Nicoya peninsula. However, you won't feel like one of the masses as there are endless miles of empty wilderness beach here for you to explore.

⑤ Playa Conchal
Arguably the most beautiful beach in Costa Rica, tiny yet never understated Conchal (p267) is covered in a fine sprinkling of crushed seashells. As you wade through crystalline water in search of a memorable souvenir, pause for a moment to reflect on how wonderful it is to be in paradise.

⑥ Manzanillo
Literally at the end of the road on the Caribbean coast, this idyllic beach town (p490) fronts a postcard-perfect beach of powder white sand. Rent a pushbike from nearby Puerto Viejo de Talamanca and cycle until you start to hear the crashing surf.

Adventure Travel

Adrenaline junkies of the world unite – Costa Rica isn't just about quiet walks in the park. On the contrary, this action-packed country is full of opportunities for extreme sports, both on land and in the water. Whether you find yourself zipping across canopies or rafting rivers, Costa Rica is all about getting your kicks.

Author Tip

Extreme sports in Costa Rica come at a price, so you're going to need a bit of cash in your wallet if you want your fix. Fortunately however, there is no shortage of cheap hostels and budget hotels around, which means that shoestringers can conserve their cash for the occasional splurge.

1 Canopy Tours

In Costa Rica, the best way to take in the lofty heights of the canopy is put on a harness, attach yourself to a zip line and soar through the tree tops on a canopy tour in the Monteverde area (p179). Although it's unlikely that you'll spot much wildlife at these speeds, we can guarantee that you'll get a whole new perspective on Mother Nature.

2 River Kayaking

River-running becomes all the more intense when you push your limits by maneuvering in and out of the rapids in a small kayak. One of Costa Rica's most legendary launches for river kayaking is the small town of Puerto Viejo de Sarapiquí (p516) in the northern lowlands near the Nicaraguan border.

3 Surfing the Caribbean

One of Costa Rica's most famous surf destinations is Salsa Brava (p478), a fierce reef break that cuts close to shore in Puerto Viejo de Talamanca. Although you're going to need some serious skills here to survive with your board (and bones) intact, a successful ride will win you some well-earned bragging rights.

4 White-Water Rafting

Costa Rica is regarded as one of the world's top white-water rafting spots. There's no better place to tackle mighty jungle rivers than Turrialba (p159). Depending on your skills, you can choose from numerous entry points on Ríos Reventazón and Pacuare.

5 Surfing the Pacific

Another one of Costa Rica's most famous surf destinations is Witch's Rock (p221), a remote break that can only be accessed by boat from Parque Nacional Santa Rosa. Regarded as something of a surf mecca among the international community, this world-class break will seriously test your surfing mettle.

6 Scuba Diving

Costa Rica may have some stunning wildlife on land, but its underwater world is impressive in its own right. One of the best ways to get a fish's-eye view is to strap on a tank and check out some of the famous dive spots scattered around the northern section of the Nicoya peninsula (p259).

Cultural Tapestries

Although Costa Rica is firmly rooted in Latin America and decidedly Spanish in character, the country is home to a surprisingly rich mix of peoples. As you explore the towns and cities of Costa Rica, you are likely to meet people from a wide spectrum of cultural and social backgrounds.

Author Tip
While in Costa Rica, talk to locals and ask them about their customs and traditions. Sometimes the best window into a local culture might be sitting next to you on the bus, drinking beside you in the bar or sharing a park bench with you – and you never know where a conversation might take you.

① Josefinos

As one of the most Westernized capitals in Central America, San José is an urban playground of international restaurants, swinging bars and all-night dance clubs. If you think you can party all night with this fun-loving lot, don't miss the city's largest club complex, the aptly named El Pueblo (p104).

② Guanacastecos

Guanacaste, a hot and dry ranching region that encompasses the Nicoya peninsula and much of northwestern Costa Rica, is a hot bed of Costa Rican cowboy culture. For a window into the Wild West, be sure to check out a *tope* (p204), which is something between a rodeo and a country fair.

③ Afro-Caribbeans

Costa Rica's Caribbean coast is largely populated by Afro-Caribbeans, who trace their ancestry to Jamaican immigrants who were brought to Costa Rica to build the railroads in the 19th century. In towns such as Puerto Viejo de Talamanca (p477), travelers are keen to feast on coconut-spiced cuisine while jamming out to calypso beats.

④ Gringos

This one-time racial slur against US citizens heading south of the border has been proudly adopted by the very community it once insulted. US retirees are now flocking to cities such as Jacó (p328) in droves, and fueling a wave of foreign investment that will inevitably transform the face of the country.

⑤ Guaymí

While much of the indigenous population has given way to the forces of Westernization, there are still pockets in the south of Costa Rica where the Guaymí (p408) continue to live a traditional lifestyle. The communities use their native tongue, wear traditional garments, and hunt and gather to subsist.

⑥ Brunka (Boruca)

The Brunka, or Boruca, is what remains of three great chiefdoms that once inhabited the Península de Osa and southern Costa Rica. Today they live in a reservation (p382) in the valley of the Río Grande de Térraba. Their annual Fiesta de los Diablitos (pictured overleaf) is an incredible spectacle that attracts attention from local and international visitors.

Contents

Regional Map Contents

Destination Costa Rica

Costa Rica is sometimes referred to as the Switzerland of Central America because of its comfortable lifestyle, peaceful democracy and overwhelming natural beauty. But is this merely the depiction on a postcard or does it have relevance for today's Tico (Costa Rican)?

Early in the 20th century, this view could rightly be called an optimistic caricature. At best, Costa Rica was an occasional democracy with widespread poverty and no discernible environmental protection policy. In the second half of the century, however, sustained economic growth created a viable middle class, a generous social welfare state and one of the world's most progressive environmental movements.

To put things in perspective, consider the fact that prior to 1950, half of the country struggled with grinding poverty, and living beyond the age of 50 was an achievement in itself. Today, less than one in five Ticos lives below the poverty line and life expectancy is on a par with the US.

As recently as 1980, Ticos lived on family farms, shopped at the neighborhood *pulpería* (corner grocery store), listened to state radio and had never visited a shopping mall. Today, urban sprawl is transforming the Central Valley, shopping at supermarkets is a matter of course, satellite TV is the norm and American-style shopping malls are all the rage.

Of course, with economic empowerment comes tremendous social change. More women have entered the workforce though opportunities in the tourist and service sectors. The divorce rate has increased and family size has shrunk. More Ticos are entering higher education, and they are doing so in Costa Rica. Migrant laborers from Nicaragua work the coffee plantations, while Tico tenants seek better jobs in the city.

Given the rise in quality of life throughout the country, Ticos are generally self-content and passive about politics. But underneath the easygoing veneer is discernable pride and support for their unarmed democracy.

As stated by recently re-elected President Oscar Arias in his Nobel Peace Prize acceptance speech, 'we seek peace and democracy together, indivisible, an end to the shedding of human blood, which is inseparable from an end to the suppression of human rights.' A unique point of view – not only in Central America, but in the whole of the world.

Lifestyle and democracy aside, Costa Rica remains mind-bendingly beautiful. Although there are certainly other countries in the world that enjoy divinely inspired natural landscapes, Costa Rica boasts a higher biodiversity than both Europe and the US combined.

In the past, the Costa Rican government viewed the rain forest as a valuable source of timber, arable land and grazing pastures. However, following a near devastating economic collapse in the 1970s, Costa Rica emerged as a global pioneer in sustainable development, providing a model in which economic and environmental interests are complementary.

But it is not without some contention. Conservation and ecotourism are administered by two powerful bureaucracies – the Ministry of Environment and Energy (Minae) and the Costa Rica Tourism Board (ICT) – who frequently clash. The San José–based eco-elite often seem removed from the concerns of local residents, who still use the land to survive. In addition, the lure of paradise has attracted foreign capital, which inflates property values and displaces the local populace.

FAST FACTS

Population: four million (USA: 300 million)

Life expectancy at birth: 78 years (USA: 78 years)

Adult literacy: 96% (USA: 99%)

Population living below the poverty line: 18% (USA: 12%)

Population using the internet: 29% (USA: 69%)

Annual carbon dioxide emissions per person: 1.6 tons (USA: 20.2 tons)

Annual coffee consumption per person: 3.9kg (USA: 4.2kg)

Passenger cars per 1000 people: 103 (USA: 478)

Protected land: 27% (USA: 16%)

Number of species of birds: 850+ (USA: 500+)

Furthermore, the success of the green revolution has created a new concern, namely the need for sustainable tourism (see p417). The increasing number of visitors to Costa Rica has led to more hotels, more transportation and more infrastructure upgrades. In addition, the tourist-driven encroachment on the rain forest inevitably places stress on the fragile ecosystem that people are flocking to see.

Of course, one of the many reasons why Costa Rica remains such a fascinating tourist destination is that it is very much unique in Latin America. Although it is certainly not without its problems, Costa Rica is one of the few places in the region where environmental issues are given a proper forum for discussion, as opposed to mere lip service.

Getting Started

Costa Rica is the most user-friendly country in Central America. Most of the tourist hotspots are well connected by cheap buses, accommodations is plentiful and decent eateries are thick on the ground in nearly every corner of the country. Unlike some other parts of the region, dining without fear for your stomach, meeting and engaging locals, and accessing the internet are all things that can be taken for granted.

Predeparture planning will usually make your trip a bit smoother, but on the whole it's unnecessary unless you're on a tight timetable, and it's usually more enjoyable to give into the idea of adventure travel. Indeed, Costa Rica has something for everyone, especially if you are an impulsive traveler seeking an adrenaline rush. Of course, if you prefer to spend some quality time with a good book on a sun-drenched beach, Costa Rica has quite a few of those, too.

See the Directory for more information on climate (p529) and festivals (p532).

For shoestringers, transport around the country is plentiful – local buses can carry you to just about every nook and cranny, and boats will pick up where buses leave off. For the more discriminating or time-pressed travelers, minivans with air-con, domestic flights and charters can reach even the most remote corners. Accommodations also range from bargain-basement cabins, campsites and hammock hotels, all the way up to 1st-class resorts loaded with every conceivable luxury.

Lodging is abundant throughout Costa Rica, and it's usually easy to find someplace to stay when you arrive in town. The exceptions to this rule are the weeks between Christmas and New Year's Day, and before and during Semana Santa (the week preceding Easter Sunday). It is also a good idea to book accommodations ahead of time during the school vacation in January and February.

Note that because Costa Rica has a high standard of living, prices here tend to be a good deal higher than those of other Central and Latin American nations. However, although your dollar may not stretch as far here as in neighboring countries, you can expect an extremely high quality of goods and services throughout Costa Rica.

WHEN TO GO

Generally, the best time to visit Costa Rica is the dry season from December through April, which locals refer to as *verano* (summer). Dry season does not mean it does not rain – it just rains less (so perhaps should be called the 'drier season'). Costa Rican schools are closed from December to February; beach towns are busy during this period, especially on weekends. Lodgings during Semana Santa are usually booked months ahead.

In May begins the rainy season, or *invierno* (winter) as it's known locally. The tourism ministry has come up with the more attractive denomination of 'green season.' The early months of the rainy season are actually a wonderful time to travel to Costa Rica: you can avoid the tourist bustle and lodging is slightly cheaper. During this time, however, rivers start to swell and dirt roads get muddy, making travel more challenging. Some more remote roads may not be accessible to public transportation, so always ask locally before setting out. Bring your umbrella and a little patience.

Because of the number of North American and European tourists, some Costa Rican towns experience a mini-high season in June and July, during the northern summer holidays. Expect to pay high-season prices in some towns at this time.

DON'T LEAVE HOME WITHOUT...

- checking the latest visa situation (p537) and government travel advisories (p530)
- insect repellent containing DEET; and if you're planning large-scale jungle adventures (or staying in budget lodging), a mosquito net
- learning at least a few basic phrases in Spanish
- Pepto-Bismol or an antidiarrheal, in case you get a bad dose of the runs
- sunblock and a hat, so you don't get cooked by the tropical sun
- clothes that you don't mind getting absolutely filthy or wet
- a swimsuit and a beach towel
- a poncho for rainy days and wet boat trips
- a pair of river sandals or reef-walkers and sturdy jungle boots
- an alarm clock for catching early-morning buses
- a waterproof, windproof jacket and warm layers for highland hiking and camping
- a flashlight (torch)
- binoculars and a field guide
- miscellaneous necessities: umbrella, padlock, matches, pocketknife
- an appetite for fresh fruit
- a thirst for cold lager
- your sense of adventure.

For surfers, the travel seasons vary slightly. For the most part, the Pacific coast sees increased swells and bigger, faster waves during the rainy season, starting in late June and peaking in the worst rainy months of September and October. The Caribbean side, however, has better waves from November through May. Some breaks are consistent year-round.

Wildlife enthusiasts may wish to plan their trip around the seasons of the critters. Turtle season on the Caribbean coast is from late February to October, with the peak season for leatherbacks in April and May, and for green turtles in August and September. On the Pacific coast, the season for leatherbacks is from October to March.

Birders will be overwhelmed by feathered friends any time of year, but the best season to spot the resplendent quetzal is between November and April. Spring (March through May) and autumn (September through November) are good times to watch the migratory flocks.

Fishing, also, is good year-round, but you might choose your season if you have your heart set on a specific fish. Anglers head to the Caribbean coast between January and May in search of tarpon, while the autumn (September through November) is the season for snook. On the Pacific coast and in the Golfo Dulce, the best time to snag that sailfish is between November and May.

COSTS & MONEY

Travel costs are significantly higher here than in most Central American countries, but cheaper than in the USA or Europe. And if you're arriving from inexpensive Central American nations, such as Nicaragua, get ready to bust that wallet wide open.

Prices in Costa Rica are frequently listed in US dollars, especially at up-market hotels and restaurants, where you can expect to pay international

HOW MUCH?

4WD rental for one week: US$250-400

Zip-line adventure through the canopy: US$40

Admission to Parque Nacional Manuel Antonio: US$7

Taxi from the international airport into central San José: US$15

Second-hand longboard from a surf shop: US$100-250

prices. Most types of tours are charged in US dollars. In fact, US dollars are widely accepted, but the standard unit of currency is still the colón.

Shoestring travelers can survive on US$25 to US$35 a day, covering just the basics of food, lodging and public transportation. The cheapest hotels start at about US$7 to US$15 per person for a bed, four walls and shared bathroom. Better rooms with private bathroom start at roughly US$15 to US$20 per person, depending on the area. It is possible to eat cheaply at the many *sodas* (lunch counters), where you can fill up on tasty casados, which are set meals, for about US$2 to US$3.

Midrange budgeters can travel comfortably for anywhere from US$50 to US$100 per day. Hotels in this category offer very good value, and double rooms come with comfortable beds, private bathroom, hot water (most of the time) and even breakfast, for US$20 to US$80 per night. Many hotels in this price range also have shared or private kitchenettes, which allows travelers the opportunity to cook – this is a great option for families. A variety of restaurants cater to midrange travelers, offering meals that range from US$5 to US$10.

Top-end visitors can find a good selection of restaurants and hotels in the touristy towns and within some of the major resorts. Luxurious beachside lodges and boutique hotels can cost from US$80 up, and offer truly world-class meals that begin at around US$15.

Lodging prices are generally higher in the dry season (December to April), and highest during holiday periods (between Christmas and New Year and during Semana Santa). During slower seasons, most hotels are eager for your business, so you can try to negotiate a lower rate. Some of the more popular tourist areas (Monteverde, Jacó, Manuel Antonio and many of the beaches on the Península de Nicoya) are also more expensive than the rest of the country.

TRAVELING RESPONSIBLY

Since our inception in 1973, Lonely Planet has encouraged its readers to tread lightly, travel responsibly and enjoy the magic independent travel affords. International travel is growing at a jaw-dropping rate, and we still firmly believe in the benefits it can bring – but, as always, we encourage you to consider the impact your visit will have on both the global environment and the local economies, cultures and ecosystems.

Sustainable tourism does not have a clear and straight-forward definition, though at its purest form it refers to striking the ideal balance between the traveler and their surrounding environment. To be a bit more specific, sustainable tourism aims to minimize the impact of the traveler on the local ecosystem and culture while simultaneously improving the local economy and generating revenue to protect the environment.

Although in theory this should be extremely easy to implement, the unfortunate reality is that competing interests and so-called 'progress' often get in the way of sound fiscal planning and responsible conservation. However, the beauty of sustainable tourism is that it starts with the individual, which means that every one of us can play our own small part in advancing these ideas.

In regard to the physical environment, travelers can aim to minimize negative environmental impacts, and to make positive contributions to the area, such as through volunteer work in conservation (see p538). Individual travelers have the power to help protect and conserve local resources.

In regard to the cultural environment, travelers can aim to respect local traditions, get involved with local events, and foster authentic interactions

TOP 10

For a small country, Costa Rica is jam-packed with sights and attractions. Hopefully the following lists will inspire you to seek out all that this beautiful country can offer.

IDYLLIC SUNSET SITES

Grab a magic moment in Costa Rica while you enjoy the last rays of the day:

1 Taking in the view from **Crestones Base Lodge** (p381) on Cerro Chirripó.

2 Looking out from **Cabinas El Mirador Lodge** (p403) in Bahía Drake.

3 Viewing the fiery Volcán Arenal from **El Castillo** (p244).

4 Sailing on the deep blue Pacific from **Tamarindo** (p270).

5 Sipping an ice-cold *cerveza* (beer) at **La Taberna** (p464) in Tortuguero.

6 Munching at **Ronny's Place** (p351), high up on the cliffs in Manuel Antonio.

7 Hiking at twilight in **Bosque Eterno de los Niños** (p176) in Monteverde.

8 Reggae-listening at **Johnny's Place** (p486) in Puerto Viejo de Talamanca.

9 Sitting on the dock in the bay at the **Banana Bay Marina** (p433) in Golfito.

10 Relaxing on colonial steps at **Plaza de la Democracia** (p90) in San José.

WORST ROADS

Conquer the dishevelled roads to uncover hidden gems and secluded spots:

1 Oldie, but goodie – the road from **Tilarán to Monteverde**.

2 The punisher – **Puerto Jiménez to Carate**.

3 Dude, where's the transmission? – bumping and grinding to the waves at **Playa Naranjo**.

4 A river runs through it – crossing the Río Ora between **Playa Carrillo and Islita**.

5 You call this a road? – **Golfito to Pavones**.

6 Bone-cruncher – **Buenos Aires to Reserva Biológica Dúrika**.

7 Car-nivore – the stretch between **Tamarindo and Avellanas** gobbles up vehicles like candy.

8 Road less traveled – the steep climb up to **Altamira and La Amistad**.

9 Keep on truckin' – swerving with the big rigs on the Interamericana between **Cañas and Liberia**.

10 Lake defect – dodging huge potholes on the road around **Laguna de Arenal**.

BEST BEACHES

With two coastlines fringed with sun-kissed beaches, Costa Rica is a beach-lover's paradise:

1 **Manzanillo** (p491) The Caribbean coast's most scenic stretch of sand.

2 **Playas San Miguel and Coyote** (p298) Abandoned beaches, backed by rugged wilderness.

3 **Playa Conchal** (p267) Crushed shells and turquoise water.

4 **Playa Grande** (p267) Sweeping blonde sand backed by mangroves, great surf.

5 **Playa Matapalo** (p358) Surfing the waves, hiking to waterfalls.

6 **Playa Montezuma** (p304) Empty white sands, rocky coves and killer sunrises.

7 **Playa Mal País** (p310) Huge, crashing surf for kilometers in each direction.

8 **Playa Negra** (p277) Dark sands and crystal clear waters.

9 **Playa San Josecito** (p436) Scarlet macaws roosting in the almond trees overhead.

10 **Playa Sámara** (p293) A destination for sophisticated beach goers and fun-loving families.

and understanding between them and their hosts. Ideally, tourism should be a two-way street whereby travelers learn just as much from locals as locals do from travelers.

Finally, travelers can ensure that their presence results in financial benefits for the host community and operates in line with the principles of fair trade. Always be aware of the power of your money, especially since many local economies throughout Costa Rica (and the world) have been adversely affected by the rise in tourism.

Common sense combined with the basic principles of sustainable travel will ensure that destinations remain desirable for both the traveler and the local. Regardless of whether you're sitting on a beach, roaming the streets, hiking through the jungle or sitting in a bar, you have the power to affect change in a positive way.

Don't be afraid to give suggestions to other travelers and to listen to theirs as well – the best advice always comes from your peers. Take only pictures. Leave only footprints. Kill only time.

TRAVEL LITERATURE

While you're in the midst of predeparture planning, check out the following recommended titles to start developing your sense of Costa Rica.

- *A Naturalist in Costa Rica* (Dr Skutch). An icon among birders, Skutch weaves his philosophies into his beautiful descriptions of flora and fauna in this enchanting memoir and natural history guide.
- *Around the Edge* (Peter Ford). A story of the author's travels along the Caribbean coast from Belize to Panama, on foot and by boat.
- *Green Dreams: Travels in Central America* (Stephen Benz). An astute analysis that questions the impact visitors are having on the region and its people.
- *Green Phoenix* (William Allen). An absorbing and inspiring account of the author's efforts, alongside American and Costa Rican scientists and activists, to conserve and restore the rain forest in Guanacaste.
- *Ninety-Nine Days to Panama* (John and Harriet Halkyard). A retired couple's detailed and entertaining account of driving an RV (complete with pet dog Brindle) from Texas to Panama.
- *So Far from God: A Journey to Central America* (Patrick Marnham). The winner of the 1985 Thomas Cook Travel Book Award gives an insightful and amusing account of a leisurely meander from Texas to Panama.
- *Traveler's Tales Central America* (eds Larry Habegger and Natanya Pearlman). A collection of striking travel essays on the region from renowned writers such as Paul Theroux and Tim Cahill.
- *Walk These Stones* (Leslie Hawthorne Klingler). This Mennonite service worker writes about her experiences living, working, praying and sharing in the small village of Cuatro Cruces.

INTERNET RESOURCES

CIA Factbook (www.cia.gov/library/publications/the-world-factbook/index.html) An excellent overview of Costa Rica's political, economic and environmental standing.

Costa Rica Guide (www.costa-rica-guide.com) Nicely organized website with detailed maps and travel information on each region.

Costa Rica Link (www.1costaricalink.com) An online directory that provides a great deal of information on transportation, hotels, activities and more.

Costa Rica Tourism Board (www.visitcostarica.com) The official website of the Costa Rica Tourism Board (known as the ICT) is a great introduction to the country. You can research your trip, and organize accomodations, tours and car rental from this site.

Guías Costa Rica (www.guiascostarica.com) Links that connect you with everything you'd ever need to know – from entertainment to health to government websites.

Lanic (http://lanic.utexas.edu/la/ca/cr) An exceptional collection of links to the websites (mostly in Spanish) of many Costa Rican organizations, from the University of Texas.

Lonely Planet (www.lonelyplanet.com) Provides information on travel in Costa Rica, links to accommodations and traveling tips from the all-important Thorn Tree bulletin board.

Tico Times (www.ticotimes.net) The online edition of Costa Rica's excellent English-language weekly newspaper.

Itineraries
CLASSIC ROUTES

THE BEST OF COSTA RICA
Two Weeks to One Month/Northwestern Costa Rica & Península de Nicoya

This route takes travelers by bubbling volcanoes, hot springs and tranquil cloud forests before hitting the sun-kissed beaches of the Nicoya.

From **San José** (p78), head north to **La Fortuna** (p230), where you can hike through forest on the flanks of **Volcán Arenal** (p241) then soak in hot springs. Come down from the mountain and hop on the jeep-boat-jeep service across Laguna de Arenal to **Monteverde** (p170) and search for the elusive quetzal at **Reserva Biológica Bosque Nuboso Monteverde** (p190).

For a change of scene, head west to the biggest party town in the Nicoya, **Playa Tamarindo** (p270), and enjoy the excellent surf in this brash town. Nature buffs will not want to miss the nesting leatherback turtles at **Playa Grande** (p267), while hardcore surfers should head straight south along a dismal dirt road to **Playas Avellanas** and **Negra** (p277).

Continuing south, don't miss the stunning beaches and cosmopolitan cuisine at **Playa Sámara** (p293) and legendary swells at **Mal País** and **Playa Santa Teresa** (p310). Wind down your trip at laidback **Montezuma** (p304) and head back to San José via **Jacó** (p328) by jet boat and bus.

For a taste of all that Costa Rica has to offer, this classic route will take you into the mountains and cloud forests of the interior before sweeping you down into the Península de Nicoya.

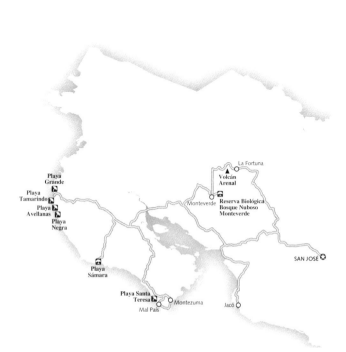

PACIFIC COASTAL EXPLORER   One to Two Weeks/Central Pacific Coast

For days on end of sun, surf and sand, head south along the central Pacific coast for back-to-back beach towns dedicated to the pursuit of hedonism.

Kick things off in the resort town of **Jacó** (p328), a heavily Americanized gringo enclave of fine dining, teeming bars and raging nightlife. In case you need a reminder that you're still in Costa Rica, backtrack a bit north up the coast to **Parque Nacional Carara** (p323), home to large populations of enchanting scarlet macaws.

Heading south along the coast, your next stop is the port town of **Quepos** (p341), which serves as a convenient base for the country's most popular national park, **Parque Nacional Manuel Antonio** (p353). Here, the rain forest sweeps down to meet the sea, providing refuge for rare animals, including the endangered Central American squirrel monkey.

Continue on south to **Hacienda Barú National Wildlife Refuge** (p359), where you can clamber on a canopy platform and sloth-spot in the trees. If you haven't had enough of the postcard-perfect Pacific coast, keep heading south to **Dominical** (p359) to catch some more waves, or to tiny and tranquil **Uvita** (p363) to escape the tourist crowds.

From Uvita, you can either continue south to the far-flung **Península de Osa** (p394), or head back to **San José** (p78) en route to the **Caribbean coast** (p444).

This excursion continues where the Best of Costa Rica route ends, and winds through the beaches and rain forests of the central Pacific region.

CARIBBEAN COASTAL EXPLORER   One to Two Weeks/Caribbean Coast

Spanish gives way to English, and Latin beats change to Caribbean rhythms as you begin to explore the 'other Costa Rica.'

Hop on the first eastbound bus out of **San José** (p78) and get off at **Cahuita** (p468), capital of Afro-Caribbean culture and gateway to **Parque Nacional Cahuita** (p475). Stick around and get your fill of this mellow little village before moving on to **Puerto Viejo de Talamanca** (p477), the Caribbean's center for nightlife, cuisine and all-round positive vibes.

From Puerto Viejo, rent a good old-fashioned pushbike and ride to **Manzanillo** (p490), from where you can snorkel, kayak and hike in the **Refugio Nacional de Vida Silvestre Gandoca-Manzanillo** (p491).

For the adventurous at heart, head north to grab a boat from **Moín** (p456) and travel the canal-lined coast to the village of **Tortuguero** (p461), where you can watch nesting green and leatherback turtles. Of course, the real reason you're here is to arrange a canoe trip through the mangrove-lined canals of **Parque Nacional Tortuguero** (p458), Costa Rica's mini-Amazon.

After spotting your fill of wildlife amidst seemingly endless watery passages, head back to San José via water taxi and bus through **Cariari** (p448) and **Guápiles** (p447).

The Caribbean coast is a world onto its own, and provides a striking and memorable contrast to time spent elsewhere in the country.

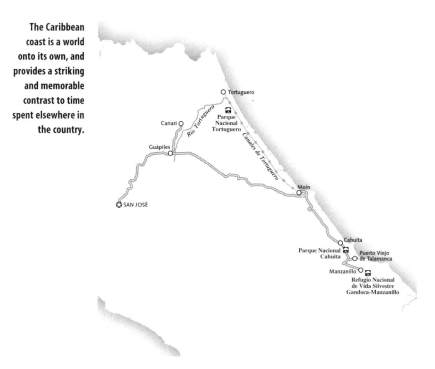

ROADS LESS TRAVELED

TREKKING ACROSS OSA   One to Two Weeks/Península de Osa & Golfo Dulce

Home to Costa Rica's most pristine nature, the Osa peninsula is an undeniable draw for anyone wanting some rugged wilderness exploration.

Either head down the Pacific coast or fly into **Puerto Jiménez** (p408), which serves as the gateway to Osa. Here, you can spend a day or so kayaking around the mangroves or otherwise soaking up the charm of this tiny town.

Next, head north to **La Palma** (p407), from where you can visit the **Reserva Indígena Guaymí** (p407) and observe firsthand the traditional lifestyle of one of Costa Rica's indigenous groups.

Next, head to **Los Patos ranger station** (p425), which will be the starting point for a trek across the spectacular **Parque Nacional Corcovado** (p416).

The first day of the trek lands you at **Sirena ranger station** (p416), one of the country's best wildlife-watching spots, especially for squirrel monkeys and Baird's tapirs. It's worth spending an extra day or so exploring the trails around this area without a pack on your back.

Finally, the last day of the hike brings you to **La Leona ranger station** (p425). In the nearby village of **Carate** (p415), catch the colectivo (small bus or shared taxi) toward Puerto Jiménez and ask to be dropped at **Cabo Matapalo** (p413), where you can chill out for as long as you like, enjoying some of the country's most beautiful beaches.

One of the highlights of any trip to Costa Rica is time spent trekking through the dense jungles of the Osa peninsula, which are positively teeming with wildlife.

RIDING RÍO SAN JUAN & SARAPIQUÍ

One to Two Weeks/Northern Lowlands & Caribbean Coast

Travel the river route through some of Costa Rica's most remote regions in the sparsely populated northern lowlands and Caribbean coast.

From **San José** (p78), bus to the tiny town of **La Virgen** (p511), a rafting and kayaking mecca where you can take a ride on the Río Sarapiquí and spend the night at the luxurious **Centro Neotrópico Sarapiquís** (p514).

As soon as you've gotten your bearings, follow the Río Sarapiquí on the bus to **Puerto Viejo de Sarapiquí** (p516), where you can wander through banana plantations, spot wildlife and mingle with busy scientists at the **Estación Biológica La Selva** (p519).

Of course, don't wait too long to leave terra firma and grab the morning boat up the Río Sarapiquí to **Trinidad Lodge** (p517), on the south bank of the Río San Juan. Stay on a working ranch, ride horses and go birding before setting out, again by boat, along the Río San Juan, with your eye to the Caribbean coast.

This river (Nicaraguan territory) offers an incredible ride, which will take you through wildlife hotspots, ranches, forest, old war zones (from when Contras inhabited the area) and the remote **Refugio Nacional de Vida Silvestre Barra del Colorado** (p465) to the village of **Barra del Colorado** (p465) and its loose assortment of lodges, where you can go sportfishing, birdwatching and croc hunting (with binoculars, not guns).

You'll have to depend upon tides, weather and independent boatworkers, but if you work it out, you'll see more wildlife and incredible scenery than you have ever imagined.

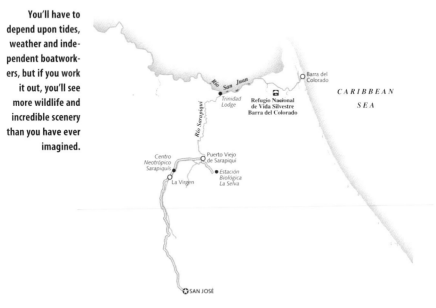

HIKING IN THE TALAMANCAS   Two to Three Weeks/Southern Costa Rica

Costa Rica's most unexplored mountainous area is home to two spectacular hikes, which can be done separately or bundled together if you've got the time.

Gear-up in **San Isidro de El General** (p374) before heading southeast through pineapple plantations to the small agricultural town of **Buenos Aires** (p381). Arrangements can be made here for transport via dirt road to the wonderfully remote **Reserva Biológica Dúrika** (p382), a self-sustaining community nestled in the Cordillera de Talamanca.

From this point, hire a local guide and trek through **Parque Internacional La Amistad** (p389), one of Costa Rica's last true wilderness areas. You can also pay a visit to the neighboring indigenous community of **Ujarrás** (p382).

If you haven't had your fill of nature yet, then head from Buenos Aires to **Altamira** (p390), where you'll find the headquarters for Parque Internacional La Amistad. From here you can take the 20km guided trek through **Valle del Silencio** (p391), one of the most isolated and remote areas in all of Costa Rica, ending up at a small refuge at the base of the **Cerro Kamuk** (p391).

From here, make the return trip through Altamira and back to the rowdy roads near the Interamericana.

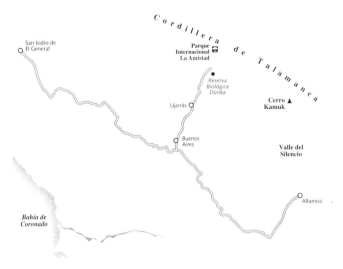

The isolated Cordillera de Talamanca is one of the most remote areas in the country and home to indigenous communities and incredible vistas.

TAILORED TRIPS

SURFING SAFARI

Costa Rican shores have been attracting surfers since *Endless Summer II* profiled some of the country's most appealing breaks.

Playa Tamarindo (p270) serves as a good base for several tasty surfing sites. You can start with a boat trip to the granddaddies of all surf breaks, Witch's Rock and Ollie's Point in the **Parque Nacional Santa Rosa** (p218).

Next, hit the isolated beaches at **Playas Avellanas** and **Negra** (p277), whose famous waves were featured in the movie. Down the coast, **Playa Guiones** (p288) is cooking all year long, and from there it's just a hop, skip and long jump to the legendary **Mal País** (p310).

The next big stop is **Jacó** (p328) and **Playa Hermosa** (p339) on the central Pacific coast, offering consistent waves, but keep moving south for good breaks at **Matapalo** (p358) and **Dominical** (p359).

Afterwards, hightail it way south to **Cabo Matapalo** (p413) on the Península de Osa, before skipping back to the mainland for one of the continent's longest left-hand breaks at **Pavones** (p439).

And don't forget the Caribbean. Catch a boat to the uninhabited **Isla Uvita** (p455) off the coast of Puerto Limón or frolic in the waves on the endless Playa Negra north of **Cahuita** (p468). Further south the famous Salsa Brava at **Puerto Viejo de Talamanca** (p477) is for experts only, while Playa Cocles has consistent waves that service surfers of all skill levels.

RAFTING SAFARI

Experience the country's world-class rivers while soaking in the sight of pristine rain forests and wildlife on a 10-day safari.

From San José head east to **Río Pacuare** (p159) for two days of enchanted Class IV white water. Move on to the nearby Pascua section of the **Río Reventazón** (p159) for 24km of heart-pumping Class IV+. Travel west to the central Pacific coast and spend a day of gentler rafting, taking in the beach-fringed rain forest of **Parque Nacional Manuel Antonio** (p353), home to more than 350 species of birds. Afterwards, suit-up for a quick half-day down the challenging **Río Naranjo** (p347), close by.

Cap it all off with two days on the largely unexplored **Río Savegre** (p347), putting in on the remote, Class IV+ upper Río División, the main tributary of the Savegre. The next day will have you continuing downstream to the bridge take-out on the Costanera, the Pacific coastal highway leading north to San José.

History

LOST COSTA RICA

The coastlines and rain forests of Central America have been inhabited by humans for at least 10,000 years. On the eve of European discovery some 500 years ago, an estimated 400,000 people were living in today's Costa Rica, though sadly our knowledge about these pre-Columbian cultures is scant. The remains of lost civilizations were washed away by torrential rains, and Spanish conquerors were more intent on subjugating rather than describing native lifestyles.

Unlike the massive pyramid complexes found throughout much of Latin America, the ancient towns and cities of Costa Rica (with the exception of Guayabo; see boxed text, p36) vanished in the jungles, never to be seen again by the eyes of the modern world. However, tales of lost cities still survive in the oral histories of Costa Rica's indigenous communities and there is hope among archaeologists that a great discovery lies in waiting. Considering that much of the country consists of inaccessible mountains and rain forests, perhaps these dreams aren't so fanciful.

The origin of earth – according to Bribrí and Cabécar creation myth – is the subject of the beautifully illustrated story *When Woman Became Sea* by Susan Strauss.

HEIRS OF COLUMBUS

On his fourth and final voyage to the New World in 1502, Christopher Columbus was forced to drop anchor near present-day Puerto Limón after a hurricane damaged his ship. While waiting for repairs, Columbus ventured into the verdant terrain, and exchanged gifts with hospitable and welcoming chieftains. He returned from this encounter, claiming to have seen 'more gold in two days than in four years in Española.' Columbus dubbed the stretch of shoreline from Honduras to Panama as Veraguas, but it was his excited descriptions of 'la costa rica' or the 'rich coast' that gave the region its lasting name.

Anxious to claim its bounty, Columbus petitioned the Spanish Crown to have himself appointed governor. But by the time he returned to Seville his royal patron Queen Isabella was on her deathbed, which prompted King Ferdinand to award the prize to Columbus' rival, Diego de Nicuesa. Although Columbus became a very wealthy man, he never returned to the New World, and died in 1506 after being worn down by ill health and court politics.

To the disappointment of his *conquistador* (conqueror) heirs, the region was not abundant with gold, and the locals were considerably less than affable. Nicuesa's first colony in present-day Panama was abruptly abandoned when tropical disease and warring tribes decimated its ranks. Successive expeditions launched from the Caribbean coast also failed as

TIMELINE

11,000 BC	2500 BC	1000 BC
The first humans occupy Costa Rica and populations quickly flourish due to the rich land and marine resources found along both coastlines.	Costa Rica is home to some of the first pottery-making villages in the Americas, such as those of the Monagrillo culture.	The Huetar power base in the Central Valley is solidified following the construction and habitation of the ancient city of Guayabo, which is continuously inhabited until its mysterious abandonment in 1400.

LIFE BEFORE THE CONQUEST

The invasion of Central America by the Spanish *conquistadores* (conquerors) brought about incalculable human suffering and loss; entire cultures and histories were erased by sword and disease alike.

What is known about pre-Columbian Costa Rica is that its early inhabitants were part of an extensive trading zone that extended as far south as Peru and as far north as Mexico. The region hosted roughly 20 small tribes, organized into chiefdoms, indicating a permanent leader, or *cacique,* who sat atop a hierarchical society that included shamans, warriors, toilers and slaves.

Adept at seafaring, the Carib dominated the Atlantic coastal lowlands, and served as a conduit of trade with the South American mainland. In the northwest, several tribes were connected to the great Mesoamerican cultures. Aztec religious practices and Maya jade and craftsmanship are in evidence in the Península de Nicoya, while Costa Rican quetzal feathers and golden trinkets have turned up in Mexico. In the southwest, three chiefdoms showed the influence of Andean Indian cultures, including coca leaves, yucca and sweet potatoes.

There is also evidence that the language of the Central Valley Huetar was known by all of Costa Rica's indigenous groups, which may be an indication of their power and influence. The Central Valley is home to the only major archaeological site uncovered in Costa Rica, namely Guayabo (p160).

Thought to be an ancient ceremonial center, Guayabo once featured paved streets, an aqueduct and decorative gold. Here, archaeologists uncovered exquisite gold ornaments and unusual life-size stone statues of human figures, as well as distinctive types of pottery and *metates,* stone platforms that were used for grinding corn. Today, the site consists of little more than ancient hewed rock and stone, though Guayabo continues to stand as a testament to a once-great civilization of the New World.

Still a puzzle, however, are the hundreds of hand-sculpted, monolithic stone spheres that dot the landscape of the Diquis Valley in Palmar (p384) and the Isla del Caño (p406). Weighing up to 16 tons and ranging in size from a baseball to a Volkswagen, the spheres have inspired many theories: an ancient calendar, extraterrestrial meddling, or a game of bocce gone terribly awry.

In recent years, Costa Ricans of all backgrounds have taken an increased interest in the pre-Columbian history of their country. A sign of increasing cultural tolerance.

In light of Costa Rica's enormous ecotourism market, indigenous communities seeking to attract tourist dollars have also jumped on the green bandwagon. For more information on sustainable travel in these highly sensitive areas, see p421.

pestilent swamps, oppressive jungles and volcanoes made Columbus' paradise seem more like a tropical hell.

A bright moment in Spanish exploration came in 1513 when Balboa heard rumors about a large sea and a wealthy, gold-producing civilization across the mountains of the isthmus – almost certainly referring to the Incan empire of Peru. Driven by equal parts of ambition and greed, Balboa scaled the continental divide, and on September 26, 1513, he became the first European

100 BC	AD 800	1502
Costa Rica becomes part of an extensive trade network that moves gold and other goods and extends from present-day Mexico down though to the Andean empires.	Indigenous production of granite spheres begins in the Diquis region, though to this day archaeologists and historians remain divided as to the spheres' intended function and significance.	Christopher Columbus docks his boat at Puerto Limón on the Caribbean coast during his fourth and final voyage to the Americas, ushering in the start of the colonial era in the New World.

to set eyes upon the Pacific Ocean. Keeping up with the European fashion of the day, Balboa immediately proceeded to claim the ocean and all the lands it touched for the king of Spain.

The thrill of discovery aside, the *conquistadors* now controlled a strategic western beachhead from which to launch their conquest of Costa Rica. In the name of God and king, aristocratic adventurers plundered indigenous villages, executed resisters and enslaved survivors throughout the Nicoya peninsula. However, none of these bloodstained campaigns led to a permanent presence as intercontinental germ warfare caused outbreaks of feverish death on both sides. Since the area was scarce in mineral wealth and indigenous laborers, the Spanish eventually came to regard it as the 'poorest and most miserable in all the Americas.'

Visit World Mysteries at www.world-mysteries .com/sar_12.htm for an investigation of Costa Rica's mysterious stone spheres.

NEW WORLD ORDER

It was not until the 1560s that a Spanish colony was firmly established in Costa Rica. Hoping to cultivate the rich volcanic soil of the Central Valley, the Spanish founded the village of Cartago (p149) on the banks of the Río Reventazón. Although the fledgling colony was extremely isolated, it miraculously survived under the leadership of its first governor, Juan Vásquez de Coronado. Preferring diplomacy over firearms to counter the indigenous threat, Vasquez used Cartago as a base to survey the lands south to Panama and west to the Pacific, and secured deed and title over the colony.

Though Vasquez was later tragically lost at sea in a shipwreck, his legacy endured: Costa Rica was an officially recognized province of the Viceroyalty of New Spain (Virreinato de Nueva España), which was the name given to the viceroy-ruled territories of the Spanish empire in North America, Central America, the Caribbean and Asia.

For roughly three centuries, the Captaincy General of Guatemala (also known as the Kingdom of Guatemala), which extended from Texas to Panama with the exception of modern-day Belize, was a loosely administered colony in the vast Spanish empire. Since the political-military headquarters of the kingdom were in Guatemala, Costa Rica became a minor provincial outpost that had little if any strategic significance or exploitable riches.

As a result of its backwater status, Costa Rica's colonial path diverged from the typical Spanish pattern in that a powerful landholding elite and slave-based economy never gained prominence. Instead of large estates, mining operations and coastal cities, modest-sized villages of small-holders developed in the interior Central Valley. According to national lore, the stoic, self-sufficient farmer provided the backbone for 'rural democracy' as Costa Rica emerged as one of the only egalitarian corners of the Spanish empire.

Equal rights and opportunities were not extended to the indigenous groups and as the Spanish settlement expanded, the local population decreased

1522	**1540**	**1562**
Spanish settlement develops in Costa Rica, though it will still be another several decades before the colonists can get a sturdy foothold on the land.	The Kingdom of Guatemala is established by the Spanish, and includes much of Central America, including Costa Rica, Nicaragua, Honduras, El Salvador, Guatemala and the Mexican state of Chiapas.	Spanish *conquistador* Juan Vásquez de Coronado arrives in Costa Rica under the title of governor, determined to moved the fringe communities of Spanish settlers to the more hospitable Central Valley.

THE LEGACY OF COLUMBUS

Despite the fact that Christopher Columbus never made landfall in what was to become the US, he is revered by the majority of Americans as a national hero. Columbus discovered the New World on October 12, 1492 and the US celebrates the discovery every year, though it's usually observed on a Monday so everyone can spend the day shopping – it's hard to pass up Columbus Day sales.

Recently, however, several cities across the US have removed the national holiday from their calendars. Claiming that Columbus' life was anything but admirable, critics view the day as a celebration of conquest and suffering. In the US Virgin Islands, Columbus Day has been replaced by Puerto Rico-Virgin Islands Friendship Day, which honors the indigenous peoples of the Caribbean who suffered under Spanish colonialism. In the state of South Dakota, Columbus Day has been replaced by Native American Day, which aims to increase awareness of the past history and modern plight of this oft-overlooked indigenous group.

The growing dissent in the US over the legacy of Columbus brings about a simple question: what did Columbus actually discover? Prior to his arrival in 1492, the US had already been 'discovered' by other explorers and immigrants, not to mention the native peoples that were living there. However, Columbus' impact on history is simply to do with the fact that his journeys came at a time when mass media was improving across Europe. By reporting what he saw to Europeans across the social spectrum, Columbus was attributed in the public eye with the discovery of the New World.

In 1828, the great American storyteller Washington Irving published a historical narrative titled *The Life and Voyages of Christopher Columbus,* which aimed to build a foundation of American folklore. His efforts propelled Columbus into the national spotlight, though adulation of the explorer peaked in 1892 when the country celebrated the 400th anniversary of his arrival in

dramatically. From 400,000 at the time Columbus first sailed, the number was reduced to 20,000 a century later, and to 8000 a century after that. While disease was the main source of death, the Spanish were relentless in their effort to exploit the natives as an economic resource. Central Valley groups were the first to fall, though outside the valley several tribes managed to survive a bit longer under forest cover, staging occasional raids. However, as in the rest of Latin America, repeated military campaigns eventually forced them into submission and slavery.

THE FALL OF AN EMPIRE

On October 27, 1807, the Treaty of Fontainebleau, which defined the occupation of Portugal, was signed between Spain and France. Under the guise of reinforcing the Franco-Spanish army occupying Portugal, Napoleon moved tens of thousands of troops into Spain. In an act of military genius, Napoleon ordered his troops to abandon the ruse and seize key Spanish fortifications. Without firing a single shot, Napoleon's

1563	1737	19th century
The first permanent Spanish colonial settlement in Costa Rica is established in Cartago by Juan Vásquez de Coronado, who chooses the site based on its rich and fertile volcanic soils.	The future capital of San José is established, sparking a rivalry between neighboring Cartago that will eventually culminate in a civil war between the two dominant cities.	Costa Rica's coffee boom takes off as the country discovers its environmental conditions are ideal for coffee cultivation. By the end of the century, coffee accounts for 80% of foreign-currency earnings.

the Americas. All across the country, monuments to Columbus were erected, while cities, towns and streets changed their names, including the capital cities of Columbus (Ohio) and Columbia (South Carolina). The admiration of Columbus was particularly embraced by Italian-American and Catholic communities, who began to view their ancestor as one of the founding fathers of the US.

The need to separate myth from reality brings about a second question: what did Columbus actually achieve? If you ask any American school child, they'll proudly tell you that Columbus proved the world was round even though everyone in Europe thought the world was flat. By defying the conventions of the time and sailing west to get to the Far East (Columbus died believing that he had arrived in the East Indies), Columbus is often hailed as a model of the American 'can-do' attitude. Of course, it is arguable that Columbus didn't actually prove that the world wasn't flat, because Portuguese explorer Ferdinand Magellan was the first person to circumnavigate the globe. (Actually, Magellan didn't circumnavigate the globe in one trip since he was killed in 1521 at the Battle of Mactan in the Philippines. Instead, it was the 18 survivors of his expedition that returned to Spain after a journey of more than three years.)

Unfortunately, history often has a way of succumbing to popular myth and lore. Since Columbus Day in the US is generally thought of as a celebration of the nation's history, there is little room for public discourse on the subject. Today, the majority of Americans do not know the full extent of Columbus' story; critics of the holiday argue that disregarding history is an injustice to the surviving indigenous communities of the New World.

Not surprisingly, this theme has been picked up by politicians across Latin America, most notably left-wing President Hugo Chávez of Venezuela, who campaigned in 2003 to wipe out Columbus Day across the Americas. Of course, it's unlikely that Chávez' message will fall on receptive ears in the US, especially given the lukewarm relationship between the two countries.

troops seized Barcelona after convincing the city to open its gates for a convoy of wounded soldiers.

Although Napoleon's invasion by stealth was successful, the resulting Peninsular War was a horrific campaign of guerrilla combat that crippled both countries. As a result of the conflict as well as the subsequent power vacuum and internal turmoil, Spain lost nearly all of its colonial possessions in the first third of the century.

In 1821, the Americas wriggled free of Spain's imperial grip following Mexico's declaration of independence for itself as well as the whole of Central America. Of course, the Central American provinces weren't too keen on having another foreign power reign over them, and subsequently declared independence from Mexico. However, all of these events hardly disturbed Costa Rica, which learned of its liberation a month after the fact.

The newly liberated colonies pondered their fate: stay together in a United States of Central America, or go their separate national ways. At first, they came up with something in between, namely the Central American

1821	April 1823	December 1823
Following a unanimous declaration by Mexico on behalf of all of Central America, Costa Rica finally gains its independence from Spain after centuries of colonial occupation.	The Costa Rican capital officially moves to San José after intense skirmishes with the conservative residents of Cartago, who take issue with the more liberal longings of the power-hungry josefinos.	The Monroe Doctrine formerly declares the intentions of the USA to be the dominant imperial power in the Western hemisphere despite protests from European powers.

Federation (CAF), though it could neither field an army nor collect taxes. Accustomed to being at the center of things, Guatemala also attempted to dominate the CAF, alienating smaller colonies and hastening its demise. Future attempts to unite the region would likewise fail.

Meanwhile, an independent Costa Rica was taking shape under Juan Mora Fernandez, first head of state (1824–33). Mora tended toward nation building, and organized new towns, built roads, published a newspaper and coined a currency. His wife even partook in the effort by designing the country's flag.

Life returned to normal, unlike the rest of the region where post-independence civil wars raged on. In 1824, the Nicoya-Guanacaste Province seceded from Nicaragua and joined its more easygoing southern neighbor, defining the territorial borders. In 1852, Costa Rica received its first diplomatic emissaries from the US and Great Britain.

> Thirty-three out of 44 Costa Rican presidents prior to 1970 were descended from just three original colonizing families.

COFFEE RICA

In the 19th century, the riches that Costa Rica had long promised were uncovered when it was realized that the soil and climate of the Central Valley highlands were ideal for coffee cultivation. Costa Rica led Central America in introducing the caffeinated bean, which remade the impoverished country into the wealthiest in the region.

When an export market was discovered, the government actively promoted coffee to farmers by providing free saplings. At first, Costa Rican producers exported their crop to nearby South Americans, who processed the beans and re-exported the product to Europe. By the 1840s, however, local merchants had already built up domestic capacity and learned to scope out their own overseas markets. Their big break came when they persuaded the captain of the HMS *Monarch* to transport several hundred sacks of Costa Rican coffee to London, percolating the beginning of a beautiful friendship.

> In the 1940s children learned to read with a text that stated, 'Coffee is good for me. I drink coffee every morning.'

The Costa Rican coffee boom was on. The drink's quick fix made it popular among working-class consumers in the industrializing north. The aroma of riches lured a wave of enterprising German immigrants to Costa Rica, enhancing the technical and financial skills in the business sector. By century's end, more than one-third of the Central Valley was dedicated to coffee cultivation, and coffee accounted for more than 90% of all exports and 80% of foreign-currency earnings.

The coffee industry in Costa Rica developed differently from the rest of Central America. As elsewhere, there arose a group of coffee barons, elites that reaped the rewards for the export bonanza. Costa Rican coffee barons, however, lacked the land and labor to cultivate the crop. Coffee production is labor intensive, with a long and painstaking harvest season. The small farmers became the principal planters. The coffee barons, instead, monopolized processing, marketing and financing. The coffee economy in Costa Rica created a wide network of high-end traders and small-scale

1824	1843	1856
The Nicoya-Guanacaste region votes to secede from Nicaragua and become a part of Costa Rica, though the region's longing for independence from both countries continues to this day.	William Le Lacheur, a Guernsey merchant and ship captain, helps to firmly establish a trade route from Europe to the Pacific coast of Central America via Cape Horn.	Costa Rica puts a damper on the expansionist aims of the war hawks in the USA by defeating William Walker and his invading army at the epic Battle of Santa Rosa.

growers, whereas in the rest of Central America, a narrow elite controlled large estates, worked by tenant laborers.

Coffee wealth became a power resource in politics. Costa Rica's traditional aristocratic families were at the forefront of the enterprise. At midcentury, three-quarters of the coffee barons were descended from just two colonial families. The country's leading coffee exporter at this time was President Juan Rafael Mora (1849–59), whose lineage went back to the colony's founder Juan Vásquez. Mora was overthrown by his brother-in-law, after the president proposed to form a national bank independent of the coffee barons. The economic interests of the coffee elite would thereafter become a priority in Costa Rican politics.

BANANA EMPIRE

The coffee trade unintentionally gave rise to Costa Rica's next export boom – bananas. Getting coffee out to world markets necessitated a rail link from the central highlands to the coast, and Limón's deep harbor made an ideal port. Inland was dense jungle and infested swamps, which prompted the government to contract the task to Minor Keith, nephew of an American railroad tycoon.

The project was a disaster. Malaria and accidents churned through workers as Tico recruits gave way to US convicts and Chinese indentured servants, who were in turn replaced by freed Jamaican slaves. To entice Keith to continue, the government turned over 800,000 acres of land along the route and provided a 99-year lease to run the railroad. In 1890, the line was finally completed and running at a loss.

Keith had begun to grow banana plants along the tracks as a cheap food source for the workers. Desperate to recoup his investment, he shipped some bananas to New Orleans in the hope of starting a side venture. He struck gold, or rather yellow. Consumers went crazy for the elongated finger fruit. By the early 20th century, bananas surpassed coffee as Costa Rica's most lucrative export and the country became the world's leading banana exporter. Unlike the coffee industry, however, the profits were exported along with the bananas.

Costa Rica was transformed by the rise of Keith's banana empire. He joined with another American importer to found the infamous United Fruit Company, soon the largest employer in Central America. To the locals, it was known as *el pulpo,* the octopus – its tentacles stretched across the region, becoming entangled with the local economy and politics. United Fruit owned huge swathes of lush lowlands, much of the transportation and communication infrastructure and bunches of bureaucrats. The company sparked a wave of migrant laborers from Jamaica, changing the country's ethnic complexion and provoking racial tensions.

For details on the role of Minor Keith and United Fruit in lobbying for a CIA-led coup in Guatemala, pick up a copy of the highly readable *Bitter Fruit* by Stephen Schlesinger and Stephen Kinzer.

1889	**1890**	**1900**
Costa Rica's first democratic elections are held, a monumental event given the long history of colonial occupation, though unfortunately blacks and women were prohibited by law to vote.	The construction of the railroad between San José and Puerto Limón is finally completed despite years of hardships and countless deaths due to diseases and accidents, such as malaria and yellow fever.	The population of Costa Rica reaches 50,000 as the country begins to develop and prosper due to the increasingly lucrative international coffee and banana trades.

BIRTH OF A NATION

The inequality of the early 20th century led to the rise of José Figueres Ferrer, a self-described farmer-philosopher and the father of Costa Rica's unarmed democracy. The son of Catalan immigrant coffee planters, Figueres excelled in school and went abroad to MIT to study engineering. Upon returning to Costa Rica to set up his own coffee plantation, he

GREAT SCOUNDRELS IN HISTORY: WILLIAM WALKER

As the Spanish empire receded, another arose. In the 19th century, the US was in an expansive mood and Spanish America looked increasingly vulnerable.

In 1853, a soldier of fortune named William Walker landed in the Mexican territory of Baja California with 45 men intending to privately conquer Mexico and Central America, establish slavery and mandate white control of the region. Walker succeeded in capturing La Paz, the capital of the territory, and declared himself the president of the new 'Republic of Lower California.'

However, less than three months after occupying the region, he was forced to retreat back to the other California due to lack of supplies and an unexpectedly strong Mexican resistance. Although he was later put on trial for conducting an illegal war, his legendary campaign won him popularity among expansionists in the conservative west and south of the US, which prompted the jury to acquit him in only eight minutes.

In 1856, Walker was back to his old tricks again, this time capitalizing on the civil war that was raging in Nicaragua. After raising a small army, he managed to sack the city of La Virgen and cripple the Nicaraguan national army. One month later, he conquered the capital of Granada and took control of the country through puppet president Patricio Rivas. Soon after, US President Franklin Pierce fully recognized Walker's regime as the legitimate government of Nicaragua.

Before long, Walker was marching on Costa Rica, though Costa Rican President Juan Rafael Mora Porras guessed Walker's intentions and managed to recruit a volunteer army of 9000 civilians. In a brilliant display of military prowess, a ragtag group of fighters surrounded Walker's army as they lay waiting in an old hacienda (estate) in present-day Parque Nacional Santa Rosa (see p218). The battle was over in just 14 minutes and Walker was forever expelled from Costa Rican soil.

During the fighting, a drummer boy from Alajuela, Juan Santamaría, was killed while daringly setting fire to Walker's defenses. The battle soon became national legend and Santamaría was exalted as a Costa Rican patriot and immortalized in statues (and in an airport) throughout the country.

After returning to Nicaragua, Walker declared himself president of the country. However, Walker's popularity was waning on all sides and soon he found himself being repatriated to the US. Of course, Walker's messianic ambitions were far from realized and after a brief hiatus he set out once again for Central America.

On his final (and ultimately fatal) expedition, Walker tried to invade Honduras, which quickly perturbed the British, who saw him as a threat to their affairs in British Honduras (present-day Belize) and the Mosquito Coast (present-day Nicaragua). After being captured by the British Royal Navy, Walker was quickly handed over to the Honduran authorities, who chose death by firing squad as a fitting punishment for trying to take over their country.

1914	1919	1940
Costa Rica is given an economic boost following the opening of the Panama Canal. The canal was forged by 75,000 laborers, many thousands of whom died during construction.	Federico Tinoco Granados is ousted as a dictator of Costa Rica in one of the few episodes of brief violence in an otherwise peaceful political history.	Rafael Ángel Calderón Guardia is elected president and proceeds to improve working conditions in Costa Rica by enacting minimum-wage laws as well as an eight-hour day.

organized the hundreds of laborers on his farm into a utopian socialist community, and appropriately named the property La Luz sin Fin, or 'The Struggle without End.'

In the 1940s, Figueres became involved in national politics as an outspoken critic of President Calderón. In the midst of a radio interview in which he badmouthed the president, police broke into the studio and arrested Figueres. He was accused of having fascist sympathies and banished to Mexico. While in exile, however, he formed the Caribbean League, a collection of students and democratic agitators from all over Central America, who pledged to bring down the region's military dictators. When he returned to Costa Rica, the Caribbean League, now 700-men strong, went with him and helped protest against the powers that be.

When government troops descended on the farm with the intention of arresting Figueres and disarming the Caribbean League, it touched off a civil war. The moment had arrived: the diminutive farmer-philosopher now played the man on horseback. Figueres emerged victorious from the brief conflict and seized the opportunity to put into place his vision of Costa Rican social democracy. After dissolving the country's military, Figueres quoted HG Wells: 'The future of mankind cannot include the armed forces.'

As head of a temporary junta government, Figueres enacted nearly 1000 decrees. He taxed the wealthy, nationalized the banks and built a modern welfare state. His 1949 constitution granted full citizenship and voting rights to women, blacks, indigenous groups and Chinese minorities. Today, Figueres' revolutionary regime is regarded as the foundation for Costa Rica's unarmed democracy.

The Last Country the Gods Made, by Adrian Colesberry, is a collection of essays and photographs, providing an overview of Costa Rican history, geography and society.

THE AMERICAN EMPIRE

Throughout the 1970s and '80s, the sovereignty of the small nations of Central America was limited by their northern neighbor, the US. Big sticks, gun boats and dollar diplomacy were instruments of a Yankee policy to curtail socialist politics, especially the military oligarchies of Guatemala, El Salvador and Nicaragua.

In 1979, the rebellious Sandinistas toppled the American-backed Somoza dictatorship in Nicaragua. Alarmed by the Sandinistas' Soviet and Cuban ties, fervently anticommunist President Ronald Reagan decided it was time to intervene. The Cold War arrived in the hot tropics.

The organizational details of the counter-revolution were delegated to Oliver North, an eager-to-please junior officer working out of the White House basement. North's can-do creativity helped to prop up the famed Contra rebels to incite civil war in Nicaragua. While both sides invoked the rhetoric of freedom and democracy, the war was really a turf battle between left-wing and right-wing thugs.

1940s	1948	1949
José Figueres Ferrer becomes involved in national politics and opposes the ruling conservatives. Figueres' social-democratic policies and criticism of the government angers the Costa Rican elite and President Calderón.	Conservative and liberal forces clash, resulting in a six-week civil war that leaves 2000 Costa Ricans dead, many more wounded and destroys much of the country's fledgling infrastructure.	Hoping to heal its wounds while simultaneously charting a bold new course for the future, the temporary government enacts a new constitution that abolishes the army, desegregates the country, and grants women and blacks the right to vote.

For a remarkably one-sided biography of Oliver North, who now works as a war correspondent for Fox News, check out www.foxnews.com /story/0,2933,50566,00 .html.

Under intense US pressure, Costa Rica was reluctantly dragged in. The Contras set up camp in northern Costa Rica, from where they staged guerilla raids. Not-so-clandestine CIA operatives and US military advisors were dispatched to assist the effort. Allegedly, Costa Rican authorities were bribed to keep quiet. A secret jungle airstrip was built near the border to fly in weapons and supplies. To raise cash for the rebels, it was reported that North neatly used his covert supply network to traffic illegal narcotics through the region.

The war polarized Costa Rica. From conservative quarters came a loud call to re-establish the military and join the anticommunist crusade, which was largely underwritten by the US Pentagon. In May of 1984, over 20,000 demonstrators marched through San José to give peace a chance, though the debate didn't climax until the 1986 presidential election. The victor was 44-year-old Oscar Arias, who despite being born into coffee wealth, was an intellectual reformer in the mold of Figueres, his political patron.

Once in office, Arias affirmed his commitment to a negotiated resolution and reasserted Costa Rican national independence. He vowed to uphold his country's pledge of neutrality and to vanquish the Contras from the territory, which prompted the US ambassador to suddenly quit his post. In a public ceremony, Costa Rican school children planted trees on top of the CIA's secret airfield. Most notably, Arias became the driving force in uniting Central America around a peace plan, which ended the Nicaraguan war, and earned him the Nobel Peace Prize in 1987.

THE GREEN REVOLUTION

In the 1970s, world coffee prices rapidly dropped due to oversupply, which plunged Costa Rica into an economic crisis. However, the unpredictable nature of the global commodity markets created a rather unusual alliance between economic developers and environmental conservationists. If wealth could not be sustained through exports, then what about imports – of tourists?

Drawing on the success of the Reserva Natural Absoluta Cabo Blanco, the country's first federally protected conservation area (see p314 for more information), Costa Rica embarked on a green revolution. In 1975, the Reserva Biológica Bosque Nuboso Monteverde recorded only 500 tourists, though it wasn't long before the rain forest was essentially paying for itself. By 1985, tourism was annually contributing US$100 million to the Costa Rican economy.

The ecotourism boom was on. By 1995, there were more than 125 government-protected sites, including national parks, forest preserves and wildlife reserves. The very same year, annual tourist revenues exceeded US$750 million and surpassed coffee and bananas as the main source of foreign currency earnings.

Success also encouraged private landholders to build reserves and today almost one-third of the entire country is under some form of environmental protection. Since 1999, Costa Rica has attracted more than one million tourists each year and continues to serve as a testament to the fact that development and conservation need not be competing interests.

1963	**1987**	**2000**
Reserva Natural Absoluta Cabo Blanco at the tip of the Nicoya peninsula becomes Costa Rica's first federally protected conservation area through the efforts of Swedish and Danish conservationists.	President Oscar Arias wins the Nobel Peace Prize for his work on the Central American peace accords, which brought about greater political freedom throughout the region.	At the start of the new millennium, the population of Costa Rica tops four million, though many believe the number is far greater due to burgeoning illegal settlements on the fringes of the capital.

COSTA RICA TODAY

In the February 2006 presidential election, Oscar Arias once again returned to office after narrowly beating Citizens' Action Party (CAP) candidate Otton Solís. After weeks of investigating potential irregularities and recounting votes, Solís conceded. Arias earned just 18,169 votes more than his opponent, winning the popular election by a 1.2% margin.

Solís' showing was significant, as his CAP was a newcomer on the political scene, founded only in 2000. Attempting to break into Costa Rica's two-party system, CAP's platform promoted citizen participation and condemned corruption – issues made relevant by the previous administration. However, the topic that dominated this particular election was the US-Central American Free Trade Agreement (Cafta).

Proponents of Cafta – including Arias – touted its economic benefits, including increased access to US markets and the prospect of job creation. Critics argued that the accord did not protect Costa Rica's small farmers and domestic industries, which would inevitably struggle to compete with the anticipated flood of cheap US products. As Solís explained, 'The law of the jungle benefits the big beast. We are a very small beast.'

Critics were also worried about Cafta's effects on the environment – always a hot issue (literally and figuratively). They feared that the international trade agreement would take precedent over local conservation laws, forcing Costa Rica to allow offshore oil drilling and open-pit mining, among other detrimental activities. However, at the time of writing, Cafta was set to go into effect from October 1, 2008 and it's near impossible to accurately predict the eventual ramifications of this accord.

Prior to his re-election, President Oscar Arias founded the Arias Foundation for Peace and Human Progress; on the web at www.arias.or.cr.

2005	**2006**	**2007**
A devastating fire at San José's Calderon Guardia hospital kills 17 patients and two nurses, a landmark event that shatters the atmosphere of a country unaccustomed to dealing with tragedy.	Nobel laureate Oscar Arias is elected president for the second time in his political career on a pro-Cafta (US-Central American Free Trade Agreement) platform despite winning by an extremely narrow margin.	A national referendum narrowly passes Cafta. Opinion is divided as to whether opening up trade with the US will be beneficial for Costa Rica.

The Culture

TICO PRIDE

Costa Ricans, or Ticos, take great pride in defining themselves by what they are not. In comparison with their Central American neighbors, they aren't poor, they aren't illiterate and they aren't beleaguered by political tumult. It's a curious line-up of negatives that somehow adds up to one big positive.

Ticos are also extremely proud of their country, from its ecological jewels, high standard of living and education levels to, above all else, the fact that it has flourished without an army for the past 50-plus years. They view their country as an oasis of calm in a land that has been continuously degraded by warfare. The Nobel Prize that Oscar Arias received for his work on the Central American peace accords is a point of pride and confirms the general feeling that they are somehow different from a grosser, more violent world. Peace is priceless.

Ticos are inevitably always well mannered and will do all they can to *quedar bien* (leave a good impression). Conversations start with a cordial *buenos días* (good morning) or *buenas tardes* (good afternoon), as well as friendly inquiries about your well-being before delving into business. Bullying and yelling will get you nowhere, but a smile and a friendly greeting goes a long way.

LIFESTYLE

A lack of war and the presence of strong exports and stronger tourism have meant that Costa Rica enjoys the highest standard of living in Central America. For the most part, Costa Ricans live fairly rich and comfortable lives, even by Western standards.

One of the main reasons for the social cohesiveness of Costa Rican society is the strength and influence of family ties. Indeed, the family unit remains the nucleus of life in Costa Rica and serves as a support network for everyone involved. Families socialize together and groups of the same clan will often live near each other in clusters. Furthermore, celebrations, weddings and family gatherings are a social outlet for rich and poor alike, and those with relatives in positions of power – nominal or otherwise – don't hesitate to turn to them for support.

Given this mutually cooperative environment, it shouldn't come as a surprise that life expectancy in Costa Rica exceeds that of the US. In fact, most Costa Ricans are more likely to die of heart disease or cancer, as opposed to the childhood diseases that tend to claim lives in many developing nations. A nationwide healthcare system and proper sanitation systems account for these positive statistics, as does a generally stress-free lifestyle, tropical weather and a healthy and varied diet.

Similar to the industrialized world, families have an average of 2.2 children. For the most part, Costa Rican youths spend ample time on middle-class worries, such as dating, music, belly-baring fashions and *fútbol* (soccer). Primary education is free and compulsory, contributing to the 97% literacy rate. Costa Rica also has a comprehensive socialized medical system and pension scheme that looks after the needs of the country's sick and elderly.

The middle and upper class largely reside in San José and the major cities of the Central Valley highlands (Heredia, Alajuela and Cartago) and enjoy a level of comfort similar to their economic brethren in Europe and the US. They live in large homes or apartments, have a maid, a car or two and, for the lucky few, a second home on the beach or in the mountains. On the outskirts of these urban areas, the urban poor have hastily constructed shanty towns, but certainly not on the scale of some other Latin American countries.

The home of an average Tico is a one-story construction made of concrete blocks, wood or a combination of both. In the poorer lowland areas, people often live in windowless houses made of *caña brava*, a local cane.

For the vast majority of *campesinos* (farmers) and *indígenas* (indigenous people), life is hard, and poverty levels are higher and standards of living are lower than in the rest of the country. This is especially true along the Caribbean coast where the descendants of Jamaican immigrants have long suffered from a lack of attention by the federal government. However, although poor families have few possessions and little financial security, every member assists with working the land or contributing to the household, which creates a strong safety net.

As in the rest of the developing world, globalization is having a dramatic effect on family ways. These days, society is increasingly geographically mobile – the Tico that was born in Puntarenas might end up managing a lodge on the Península de Osa. And, with the advent of better paved roads, cell (mobile) phones, electrification and the presence of 50,000-plus North American and European expats, change will continue to come at a steady pace for the Tico family unit.

ECONOMY

For nearly 20 years, Costa Rica's economy has remained remarkably stable thanks to strong returns on tourism, agriculture and industry. Commerce, tourism and services (hotels, restaurants, tourist services, banks and insurance) account for 60.4% of the total gross domestic product (GDP), while agriculture and industry make up 8.6% and 31% respectively.

Principle agriculture exports include pineapples, coffee, beef, sugar, rice, dairy products, vegetables, fruits and ornamental plants, while industrial exports include electronic components (microchips), food processing, textiles, construction materials, fertilizer and medical equipment.

Poverty levels have also been kept in check for more than 20 years by strong welfare programs. Although approximately 18% of the populace lives below the poverty line, beggars are few and far between, and you won't see the packs of ragged street kids that seem to roam around other Latin American capitals.

A subsistence farmer might earn as little as US$100 a year, far below the national average of US$12,500 per capita. However, even in the most deprived region, such as the Caribbean coast, most people have adequate facilities and clean drinking water. In fact, Unicef estimates that 92% of households have adequate sanitation systems, while 97% have access to potable water.

Increased legal and illegal immigration from Nicaragua has started to put a strain on the economic system. At present, there are an estimated 300,000 to 500,000 Nicaraguans in Costa Rica, who serve as an important source of mostly unskilled labor, but also threaten to overwhelm the welfare state.

Foreign investors continue to be attracted by the country's political stability, high education levels and well-developed tourism infrastructure. At the same time, the government is struggling to curb inflation, tackle its rising debts and reform its antiquated tax system. However, the current administration believes that the soon-to-be-implemented US-Central American Free Trade Agreement (Cafta) will result in an improved investment climate.

The expression *matando la culebra* (meaning 'to be idle,' literally 'killing the snake') originates with peons from banana plantations. When foremen would ask what they'd been doing, the response was, '¡Matando la culebra!'.

POPULATION

Costa Ricans call themselves Ticos (men and groups of men and women) or Ticas (females). Two-thirds of the nation's almost four million people live in the Meseta Central (Central Valley) and almost one-third is under the age of 15.

In the 1940s, Costa Rica was an overwhelmingly agricultural society, with the vast majority of the population employed by coffee and banana plantations. By the end of the century, the economy had shifted quite dramatically, and only one-fifth of the labor force was employed by agriculture. These days, industry (especially agro-industry) employs another one-fifth, while the service sector employs more than half of the labor force. Banking and commerce are prominent, but tourism alone employs more than 10% of the labor force.

Most inhabitants are *mestizo,* a mix of Spanish with Indian and/or black roots, though the vast majority of Ticos consider themselves to be white. Although it's difficult to offer a precise explanation for this cultural phenomenon, it is partly due to the fact that Costa Rica's indigenous populations where virtually wiped out by the Spanish *conquistadores* (conquerors). As a result, most Costa Ricans prefer to trace their ancestry back to the European continent and take considerable pride in the purity and clarity of their Spanish.

Indigenous Costa Ricans today make up only 1% of the total population. These groups include the Bribrí and Cabécar (p494), the Brunka (p382), the Guaymí (p408) and the Maleku (p504). For more information on their histories, see boxed text Endangered Cultures, opposite.

Get player statistics, game schedules and find out everything you ever needed to know about La Sele, the Costa Rican national soccer team, at www.fedefutbol.com (in Spanish).

Less than 3% of the population is black, the vast majority of whom are concentrated on the Caribbean coast. Tracing its ancestry to Jamaican immigrants who were brought to build railroads in the 19th century, this population speaks Mecatelio: a patois of English, Spanish and Jamaican English. It identifies strongly with its counterparts in other Caribbean countries; coconut spiced cuisine and calypso music are only a couple of elements that travelers can enjoy. In Limón, still common are the rituals of *obeah,* or sorcery, passed down from African ancestors.

Chinese immigrants (1%) also arrived in Costa Rica to build railroads in the 19th century, though there have been regular, more voluntary waves of immigration since then. In recent years North American and European immigration has greatly increased and it is estimated that roughly 50,000 North American expats live in the country.

SPORTS

The national sport is, you guessed it, *fútbol.* Every town has a soccer field (which usually serves as the most conspicuous landmark) where neighborhood aficionados play in heated matches.

The *selección nacional* (national selection) team is known affectionately as La Sele. Legions of rabid Tico fans still recall La Sele's most memorable moments, including an unlikely showing in the quarterfinals at the 1990 World Cup in Italy and a solid (if not long-lasting) performance in the 2002 World Cup. Most recently, Tico fans were celebrating La Sele's qualification to participate in the 2006 World Cup in Germany, although the team failed to progress beyond the first round. Costa Rica has also played several times in the Copa America, twice making it to the quarterfinals. Women's soccer is not followed with as much devotion, but there is a female national team. The regular season is from August to May.

Costa Rica hosts an annual tennis tournament known as La Copa del Café (The Coffee Cup).

Surfing is growing in popularity among Ticos. Costa Rica annually hosts numerous national and international competitions that are widely covered by local media.

Bullfighting is also popular, particularly in the Guanacaste region, though the bull isn't killed in the Costa Rican version of the sport. More aptly described, bullfighting is really a ceremonial opportunity to watch a drunk cowboy run around with a bull. The popular Latin American sport of cockfighting is illegal.

MULTICULTURALISM

The mix of mainstream *mestizo* society with blacks, Asians, Indians and North Americans provides the country with an interesting fusion of culture and cuisine. And while the image of the welcoming Tico is largely true, tensions always exist.

For the black population, racism has been a reality for more than a century. About 75% of the country's black population resides on the Caribbean coast, and this area has been historically marginalized and deprived of services by a succession of governments (black Costa Ricans were not allowed in the Central Valley until after 1948). Nonetheless, good manners prevail and black visitors can feel comfortable traveling around the entire country. Asian Ticos and the small Jewish population have frequently been the subject of immature jokes, though Jewish and Asian travelers alike can expect to be treated well.

It is Nicaraguans who are currently the butt of some of society's worst prejudice. During the 1980s, the civil war provoked a wave of immigration from Nicaragua. While the violence in this neighboring country has ended, most immigrants prefer to stay in Costa Rica for its economic opportunities. Many nationals like to blame Nicas for an increase in violent crime, though no proof of this claim exists (see boxed text Nica vs Tico, p229).

ENDANGERED CULTURES

The Europeans that made the long journey across the Atlantic did not come to admire the native culture. Spanish *conquistadores* (conquerors) valued the indigenous populations as an economic resource: they ruthlessly leveled tribal society, plundered its meager wealth and hunted down and enslaved the survivors. Catholic missionaries followed closely behind, charged with eradicating heathen beliefs and instilling a more civilized lifestyle. As a result, native culture in Costa Rica came close to extinction.

The remnants of a traditional native lifestyle survived at the outer margins, kept alive by isolated families beyond the reach of law and popular culture. The indigenous groups were not even encouraged to assimilate, but instead were actively excluded from Spanish-dominated society. Well into the 20th century, they were forbidden from entering populated regions and were denied fundamental political and legal rights. Indigenous peoples were not granted citizenship until the 1949 constitution, though in practice their status did not change much as a result.

In 1977, the government created the reservation system, which allowed indigenous groups to organize themselves into self-governing communities. The government, however, retained title to the land. With this change, it was now permitted to engage in traditional languages and customs – for those descendants who could still remember their roots. Ironically, this more tolerant government policy also meant access to public education and job opportunities, which accelerated native language loss and Tico acculturation.

Presently, there are 22 reservations in Costa Rica but indigenous cultures remain highly endangered. The language of the once-robust Central Valley Huetar is already extinct. In Guanacaste, the cultural inheritance of the Chorotega tribe, descendants of the rich Mesoamerican tradition, is now all but depleted. Many of the Bribrí and Cabécar who remained in the Caribbean lowlands tended to shed their native ways after finding employment on the banana plantations. The only exception is in remote pockets of the south, where some Guaymí still speak the native tongue, wear traditional garments, and hunt and gather to subsist (see boxed text Guaymí, p408).

The Brunka, also called Boruca, is what remains of three great chiefdoms that once inhabited the Península de Osa and much of the south; now they are restricted to a reservation in the valley of the Río Grande de Térraba. While their annual Fiesta de los Diablitos attracts much outside attention, their language is nearly extinct and their land is threatened by a proposal for a huge hydroelectric project (see p383).

NORTH AMERICAN IMMIGRATION

Costa Rica is currently grappling with identity issues raised by the influx of North American (and some European) settlers. Many Ticos are starting to feel that they are being discriminated against in their own country. It is not hard to see why, especially considering that more than two-thirds of all coastal property is owned by foreigners. Signs are in English, prices are in dollars and many top-end resorts are managed exclusively by foreigners, with locals serving primarily as maids and gardeners.

Some foreign hotel owners make a point of keeping their business in exclusively foreign hands. 'No Ticos,' one hotel manager on the Pacific coast said proudly. Yet another confided, 'These Latin Americans don't like to work.' This is certainly not the attitude of the majority of North American immigrants, but nobody can deny that discrimination exists. In contrast, some travelers have complained that Costa Rica is somehow a 'less authentic' destination because of the large numbers of North Americans.

But it is worth recognizing the contributions immigrants have made. Many European and North American immigrants have been responsible for organizing, supporting and financing the nation's major conservation and environmental efforts. It was two immigrants from Scandinavia who helped found the country's first national park, the Reserva Natural Absoluta Cabo Blanco (p314). On the other hand, some North American immigrants are choosing to live in gated residential communities that have little connection to the daily lives of most Ticos. Clearly, Costa Rica is in a state of cultural evolution, and it remains to be seen where the country will head in the years to come.

Indigenous populations remain largely invisible to many in Costa Rican society. Many indigenous people lead Westernized, inherently Tico, lives, and others inhabit the country's reserves and maintain a more traditional lifestyle (see boxed text Endangered Cultures, p49). Note that one translation of Indian is *indio*, which is an insulting term; *indígena* is the preferred term, meaning 'indigenous.'

In conjunction with two indigenous women, Paula Palmer wrote Taking Care of Sibö's Gifts, *an inspiring account of the intersection between the spiritual and environmental values of the Bribrí.*

MEDIA

Satellite TV is fairly ubiquitous in Costa Rica, which means that you can choose anything from Venezuelan *telenovelas* (soap operas) and Hollywood movies to Premier League football and CNN. Likewise, there is a full spectrum of radio programming, though the mix tends to skew toward reggaetón. If you read Spanish and you want to catch the latest news and politics, look no further than the daily *La Nación*.

The law guaranteeing freedom of the press in Costa Rica is the oldest in Central America, dating from 1835. While Costa Rica certainly enjoys more press freedom than most Latin American countries, do not expect a great deal of probity from its media. The outlets are limited and coverage tends to be cautious, largely due to conservative media laws.

Surprisingly, Costa Rica has a *desacato*, or insult law, on its books. This is common in most Latin American countries and allows public figures to sue journalists if their honor has been 'damaged' by the media. A 'right of response' law allows individuals who have been criticized in the media equal attention (time or space) to reply to the charges. These laws are considered to limit the freedom of the press and provide officials with a shield from public scrutiny. Indeed, in a 2003 survey, 41% of reporters polled indicated that they had left out some information due to legal concerns, while 79% said they felt some pressure to forego investigation of certain issues.

For Costa Rican news in English, check out the weekly Tico Times *at www.ticotimes.net or the tabloid* Inside Costa Rica *at www.insidecostarica.com.*

The 2001 assassination of radio journalist Parmenio Medina gave reporters another reason not to dig deep. Medina was the host of a popular investigative program called *La Patada* (The Kick). Shortly before broadcasting a series on financial irregularities at a now-defunct Catholic radio station, Parmenio Medina was shot to death outside his home in Heredia. Nine men, including a priest, were brought to trial in connection with the murder at the end of 2005, though the verdict has been delayed due to frequent appeals.

Other laws prevent journalists from doing an effective job. Libel and slander laws put the burden of proof on reporters and they are frequently required to reveal their sources in court. In July 2004, the Inter-American Court of Human Rights struck down a defamation decision against Mauricio Herrera Ulloa of *La Nación*. The Costa Rican government has promised to abide by the ruling, which called for a revision of the criminal libel laws, though progress has been frustratingly slow.

Follow current events in Costa Rica at the website of the top daily, *La Nación*, at www.nacion.com.

RELIGION

More than 75% of Ticos are Catholic (at least in principle). And while many show a healthy reverence for the Virgin Mary, they rarely profess blind faith to the dictates coming from Rome – apparently 'pure life' doesn't require being excessively penitent. Most people tend to go to church for the sacraments (baptism, first communion, confirmation, marriage and death) and the holidays.

Religious processions on holy days are generally less fervent and colorful than those found in Latin American countries such as Guatemala or Peru, though the procession for the patron virgin, La Virgen de los Ángeles, held annually on August 2, does draw penitents who walk from all over Central America to Cartago to show devotion. Semana Santa (the week before Easter) is a national holiday: everything (even buses) stops operating at lunchtime on Maundy Thursday and doesn't start up again until the afternoon of Holy Saturday.

Roughly 14% of Costa Ricans are evangelical Christians; increased interest in evangelical religions is attributed to a greater sense of community spirit within the churches. The black community on the Caribbean is largely Protestant and there are small Jewish populations in San José and Jacó. There are sprinklings of Middle Easterners and Asians who practice Islam and Buddhism, respectively.

WOMEN IN COSTA RICA

Women are traditionally respected in Costa Rica (Mother's Day is a national holiday) and since 1974, the Costa Rican family code has stipulated that husband and wife have equal duties and rights. In addition, women can draw up contracts, assume loans and inherit property; sexual harassment and sex discrimination are against the law. In 1996, Costa Rica passed a landmark law against domestic violence, one of the most progressive in Latin America.

But only recently have women made gains in the workplace, with growing roles in political, legal, scientific and medical fields. In 1993, Margarita Penon (Oscar Arias wife) ran as a presidential candidate. In 1998, both vice presidents (Costa Rica has two) were women: Astrid Fischel and Elizabeth Odio.

Despite some advances, machismo is not a thing of the past. Antidiscrimination laws are rarely enforced and women are generally lower paid and are less likely to be considered for high-level jobs. They also have more difficulty getting loans, even though their repayment record is better than that of men. In the countryside, many women maintain traditional roles: raising children, cooking and running the home.

ARTS
Literature

Few writers or novelists are available in translation and, unfortunately, much of what is written about Costa Rica and available in English (fiction or otherwise) is written by foreigners.

Carmen Naranjo (1930–) is one of the few contemporary Costa Rican writers who has risen to international acclaim. She is a novelist, poet and short-story writer who also served as ambassador to India in the 1970s, and a few years later as Minister of Culture. In 1996, she was awarded the prestigious Gabriela Mistral medal from the Chilean government. Her collection of short stories, *There Never Was a Once Upon a Time,* is widely available in English. Two of her stories can also be found in *Costa Rica: A Traveler's Literary Companion.*

Tatiana Lobo (1939–) was actually born in Chile, but has lived since 1967 in Costa Rica where her many books are set. She received the noteworthy Premio Sor Juana Inés de la Cruz for Latin American women novelists for her novel *Asalto al Paraíso* (Assault on Paradise).

José León Sánchez (1930–) is an internationally renowned memoirist. A Huetar Indian from the border of Costa Rica and Nicaragua, he was convicted for stealing from the famous Basílica de Nuestra Señora de los Ángeles (p149) in Cartago, and sentenced to serve his term at Isla San Lucas, one of Latin America's most notorious jails.

Illiterate when he was incarcerated, Sánchez taught himself how to read and write, and clandestinely authored one of the continent's most poignant memoirs: *La Isla de los Hombres Solos* (called *God Was Looking the Other Way* in the translated version). He served 20 years of his 45-year sentence and went on to produce 14 other novels and serve in several high-level public appointments.

Costa Rica: A Traveler's Literary Companion, edited by Barbara Ras, is a fine collection of 26 short stories by modern Costa Rican writers, offering a valuable glimpse of society from Ticos themselves.

Theater

The most famous theater in the country is the Teatro Nacional (p87) in San José. The story goes that a noted European opera company was on a Latin American tour but declined to perform in Costa Rica for lack of a suitable hall. Immediately, the coffee elite put a special cultural tax on coffee exports for the construction of a world-class theater. The Teatro Nacional is now the premier venue for plays, opera, performances by the national symphony orchestra, ballet, poetry readings and other cultural events. It is also an architectural work in its own right and a landmark in any city tour of San José.

Visual Arts

The visual arts in Costa Rica first took on a national character in the 1920s, when Teodórico Quirós, Fausto Pacheco and their contemporaries began painting landscapes that varied from traditional European styles, depicting the rolling hills and lush forest of Costa Rican countryside, often sprinkled with characteristic adobe houses.

The contemporary scene is more varied and it is difficult to define a unique Tico style. Several individual artists have garnered acclaim for their art work, including the magical realism of Isidro Con Wong; the surreal paintings and primitive engravings of Francisco Amighetti; and the mystical female figures painted by Rafa Fernández. Other artists incorporate an infinite variety of themes in various media, from painting and sculpture to video and site-specific installations. The Museo de Arte y Diseño Contemporáneo (p84) in San José is the top place to see this type of work and its permanent collection is a great primer.

Many art galleries are geared toward tourists and specialize in 'tropical art' (for lack of an official description): brightly colored, whimsical folk paintings depicting flora and fauna that evoke the work of French artist Henri Rousseau.

Folk art and handicrafts are not as widely produced or readily available as in other Central American countries. However, the dedicated souvenir hunter will have no problem finding the colorful Sarchí oxcarts (p135) that have become a symbol of Costa Rica. Indigenous crafts, which include intricately carved and painted masks as well as handwoven bags and linens, are also widely available.

See a stunning and comprehensive visual database on Central American contemporary art at the website for the Museo de Arte y Diseño Contemporáneo at www .madc.ac.cr/.

Music & Dance

The mix of cultures in Costa Rica has resulted in a lively music scene, incorporating elements from North and South America and the Caribbean islands. Popular dance music includes Latin dances, such as salsa, merengue, bolero and cumbia.

One Tico salsa group that has made a significant name for itself at a regional level is Los Brillanticos, which once shared the stage with Cuban legend Celia Cruz during a tour stop she made in San José. Timbaleo is a salsa orchestra founded by Ramsés Araya, who became famous as the drummer for Panamanian salsa superstar Ruben Blades. Taboga Band is another long-standing Costa Rican group that plays jazz-influenced salsa and merengue music.

San José features a regular line-up of domestic and international rock, folk and hip-hop artists, but you'll find that the regional sounds are equally vibrant, featuring their own special rhythms, instruments and styles. For instance, the Península de Nicoya has a rich musical history, most of it made with guitars, maracas and marimbas. The traditional sound on the Caribbean coast is calypso, which has roots in the Afro-Carib slave culture.

Guanacaste is also the birthplace of many traditional dances, most of which depict courtship rituals between country folk. The most famous dance – sometimes considered the national dance – is the *punto guanacasteco* (see the boxed text La Fiestas de Guanacaste, p204). What keeps it lively is the *bomba,* a funny (and usually racy) rhymed verse, shouted out by the male dancers during the musical interlude.

Food & Drink

All it takes is a quick glance at the menu to realize that Costa Rica is firmly rooted in the tropics. From exotic fruits such as mangoes, guavas and lychees and the obligatory cup of shade-grown coffee, to fillets of locally raised fish and a zesty *ceviche* (uncooked but well-marinated seafood) featuring the catch of the day, Costa Rica is just as much a feast for the palate as it for the eyes.

Of course, Costa Rica remains fiercely true to its Latin roots by featuring rice and beans prominently at most meals. Thatched country kitchens can be found all over Costa Rica, with local women ladling out basic but hearty home-cooked specials known as *comida típica* (typical food). And of course, Costa Ricans go wild for a good steak, which partially explains the abundance of cattle ranches throughout the country.

If you prefer your Tico (Costa Rican) fare a bit more upscale with a nouveau twist, the country's trendier tourist areas have seen a high level of immigration from Europe and the US, which assures a wide selection of just about anything you might want to munch on. Whether you're partial to sushi or souvlaki, this little country can go miles to satiate your appetite.

STAPLES & SPECIALTIES

If you're looking for rich and fiery *mole poblano* (meat in a rich chocolate sauce), or a perfectly crafted avocado soup, you've come to the wrong country. Sadly, the complex and varied dishes concocted in Mexico and Guatemala never made it south of the border. Costa Rican food, for the most part, is very basic and somewhat bland. The diet consists largely of rice and beans – and beans and rice – though it's fresh, hearty and honest fare.

Breakfast for Ticos is usually *gallo pinto* (literally 'spotted rooster'), a stir-fry of rice and beans. When the beans and rice are combined, the rice gets colored by the beans and the mix obtains a specked appearance. Served with eggs, cheese or *natilla* (sour cream), *gallo pinto* is generally cheap (usually a dollar or two), filling and sometimes can be downright tasty. If you plan to spend the whole day surfing or hiking, you'll find that rice and beans is great energy food. If you are not keen on rice and beans, many hotels will provide what they refer to as a 'tropical breakfast,' which is usually bread along with a selection of fresh fruits. American-style breakfasts are also available in many eateries and are, needless to say, heavy on the fried foods and fatty meats.

Most restaurants offer a set meal at lunch and dinner called a casado, or a 'married man's' lunch. This meal is always cheap, heavy on the stomach and well balanced with meat, beans, rice and salad. An extremely popular casado is the ubiquitous *arroz con pollo,* which is (as its name implies) chicken and rice that is usually dressed up with grains, vegetables and a good mix of mild spices. Also look out for *patacones,* which are mashed plantains that are fried and eaten like fries.

Food is not heavily spiced, unless you're having traditional Caribbean-style cuisine. The vast majority of Ticos have a distinct aversion to hot sauce, though most local restaurants will lay out a spicy *curtido* (a pickle of hot peppers and vegetables) or little bottles of Tabasco-style sauce for the diehards. Another popular condiment is *salsa lizano,* the Tico version of Worcestershire sauce.

Considering the extent of the coastline, it is no surprise that seafood is plentiful and fish dishes are usually fresh and delicious. Fish is often fried, but may also be grilled or blackened. While not traditional Tico fare, *ceviche*

Order gourmet Costa Rican coffee and other treats at www.cafebritt.com.

Concinando con Tia Florita is a popular Tico cooking show. Check out the recipes and meet Tia Florita herself at www.concinancdocontiaflorita.tv.

Entradas: Journeys in Latin American Cuisine, by Joan Chatfield-Taylor, has some of Costa Rica's most popular recipes – and many others.

THE GALLO PINTO CONTROVERSY

No other dish in Costa Rica inspires Ticos quite like their national dish of *gallo pinto,* that ethereal medley of rice, beans and spices. Of course, exactly what combination of this holy trinity makes up authentic *gallo pinto* is the subject of intense debate, especially since it is also the national dish of neighboring Nicaragua.

Both countries claim that the dish originated on their soil. Costa Rican lore holds that the dish and its iconic name were coined in 1930 in the neighborhood of San Sebastián, which is on the southern outskirts of San José. Nicaraguans claim that it was brought to the Caribbean coast of their country by Afro-Latinos long before it graced the palate of any Costa Rican.

The battle for the rights to *gallo pinto* doesn't stop here, especially since the two countries can't even agree on the standard recipe. Nicaraguans traditionally prepare it with small red beans, while Costa Ricans swear by black beans. And we're not even going to bore you with the subtle complexities of balancing cilantro, salt and pepper.

Much to the dismay of patriotic Costa Ricans, Nicaragua currently holds the world record for the biggest ever pot of *gallo pinto.* On September 15, 2007, a seething vat of *gallo pinto* fed 22,200 people, which firmly entrenched Nicaragua's name next to *gallo pinto* in the *Guinness Book of World Records.*

While traveling in Costa Rica, it's probably best not to mention this embarrassment. Geopolitics, complicated histories and mutual bad blood aside, Costa Ricans aren't too happy about Nicaraguans laying claim to their national dish!

is on most menus and usually contains either octopus, tilapia, dorado and/ or dolphin (the fish, not Flipper). Raw fish is marinated in lime juice with chilies, tomatoes and herbs. Served chilled, it is a delectable way to enjoy fresh seafood. Emphasis is on 'fresh' here – this is raw fish (think sushi), so if you have reason to believe it is not fresh, don't risk eating it.

The most popular foreign food in Costa Rica (at least amongst the Ticos) is Chinese. Nearly every town has a Chinese place and even if it doesn't, menus will likely include *arroz cantonés* (fried rice). Italian food is also extremely popular and pizza parlors and Italian restaurants of varying quality abound. Of course, the locally produced pizzas are sometimes heavily loaded cheese bombs.

If an establishment doesn't exactly impress you with its cleanliness, then it might be advisable not to eat fruits, vegetables or salads there. If they are improperly washed, you could be sending your stomach a little bacteria surprise, though generally speaking water from the tap in Costa Rica is of sufficient quality to drink.

DRINKS

Coffee is probably the most popular beverage in the country and wherever you go, someone is likely to offer you a *cafécito.* Traditionally, it is served strong and mixed with hot milk to taste, also known as *café con leche.* Most drinkers get *café negro* (black coffee) and for those who want a little milk, you can ask for *leche al lado* (milk on the side). Many trendier places serve cappuccinos and espressos and milk is nearly always pasteurized and safe to drink.

For a refresher, nothing beats *batidos* – fresh fruit drinks (like smoothies) made either *al agua* (with water) or *con leche* (with milk). The array can be mind-boggling and includes mango, papaya, *piña* (pineapple), *sandía* (watermelon), *melón* (cantaloupe), *mora* (blackberry), *zanahoria* (carrot), *cebada* (barley) or *tamarindo* (fruit of the tamarind tree). If you are wary about the condition of the drinking water, ask that your *batido* be made with *agua enbotellada* (bottled water) and *sin hielo* (without ice), though again, water is generally safe to drink throughout the country.

Coffee was thought to energize workers, so in 1840 the government decreed that all laborers building roads should be provided with one cup of coffee every day.

TRAVEL YOUR TASTE BUDS

Think you've got a strong palate, an iron gut and the will to travel your taste buds? Here is our list of Costa Rica's top five less-than-popular culinary oddities.

- **Mondongo (tripe soup)** Unless you grew up eating the stuff, it's difficult for most people to dig into a hot, steamy bowl of boiled intestines. Assuming you can forget about what you're eating, where they came from and what used to pass through them, flavors like chewy, stringy and spongy don't exactly get the mouth watering and the stomach grumbling.

- **Ceviche de pulpo (octopus ceviche)** Sushi aficionados the world over may disagree with us, but it takes a bit of mental preparation to put a piece of raw octopus in your mouth. Although the citric acid in the lime juice arguably cooks the octopus, it's still rubbery and hard to chew, and it's difficult to describe the feeling of the suckers sliding down your throat.

- **Vino de palma (palm wine)** The preferred firewater of rural *campesinos* (farmers) throughout Costa Rica, palm wine is the fermented sap of the *palma de corozo* tree. After burning your innards, inducing temporary blindness and killing a few million brain cells, you will be treated to one of the worst hangovers of your life.

- **Chicharrones (fried pig skin)** Although hot, salty and oily are usually good adjectives for describing a snack food, it's hard to eat pig skin if you've ever seen one rolling around in its own filth. Of course, 'pork rinds' are a popular snack food in the US, though the real thing is less like a pork-flavored potato chip and more like a greasy slab of pork-flavored fat.

- **Huevos de tortugas (turtle eggs)** Although they're rumored to increase virility, prolong erections and make you a champ in the sack, eating the eggs of endangered sea turtles is just plain wrong. Although they do occasionally appear on the menu, the taste is an earthy mix of species extinction and environmental insensitivity.

A bottled, though less-tasty alternative, is a local fruit beverage called 'Tropical.' It's sold in many stores and restaurants and the most common flavors are *mora, piña, cas* (a tart local fruit) and *frutas mixtas* (mixed fruit). Just shake vigorously before drinking or the powder-like substance at the bottom will remain intact.

Pipas are green coconuts that have a hole macheted into the top of them and a straw for drinking the 'milk' – a very refreshing and filling drink. *Agua dulce* is sugar-cane water, or in many cases boiled water mixed with brown sugar. *Horchata,* found mostly in the countryside, is a sweet drink made from cornmeal and flavored with cinnamon.

The usual brands of soft drinks are available, including some favorites you thought were long-gone, like Crush and Squirt. In rural areas, and especially on buses, don't be surprised if your soda (or your juice) is served in a plastic bag. Plastic bags are cheaper than plastic bottles or other containers, so locals fill plastic bags with a variety of beverages and sell them from coolers at the side of the road. If you are lucky, it will also have a straw, which makes it a lot easier to enjoy your drink. If it's a long bus ride, don't be surprised if a few people fill up the bags again and toss them from the window!

The most popular alcoholic drink is beer, and there are several local brands. Imperial is perhaps the most popular – either for its smooth flavor or for the ubiquitous T-shirts emblazoned with their eagle-crest logo. Pilsen, which has a higher alcohol content, is also known for its saucy calendars featuring *las chicas Pilsen* (the Pilsen girls). Both are tasty pilsners. Bavaria produces a lager and Bavaria Negro, a delicious, full-bodied dark beer. This brand is popular among the young and well-educated, but it's not so easy to find outside of the trendiest spots.

After beer, the poison of choice is *guaro*, which is a colorless alcohol distilled from sugar cane and usually consumed by the shot, though you

Are you worried that you'll head back home and dearly miss *salsa lizano* or Tropical drinks? Thankfully www.lapulpe .com sells Costa Rican products and will ship the goods to just about anywhere in the world.

can order it as a sour. It goes down mighty easily, but leaves one hell of a hangover.

As in most of Central America, the local rums are inexpensive and worthwhile, especially the Ron Centenario, which recently shot to international fame. The most popular rum-based tipple is a *cuba libre* (rum and cola), which hits the spot on a hot, sticky day, especially when served with a fresh splash of lime. Premixed cans of *cuba libre* are also available in stores, but it'd be a lie to say the contents didn't taste weirdly like aluminum.

Most Costa Rican wines are cheap, taste cheap, and will be unkindly remembered the next morning. Imported wines are available but expensive and difficult to store at proper temperatures. Chilean brands are your best bet for a palatable wine at an affordable price.

No alcohol is served on Election Day or in the three days prior to Easter Sunday.

WHERE TO EAT & DRINK

The most popular eating establishment in Costa Rica is the *soda*. These are small, informal lunch counters dishing up a few daily casados. Other popular cheapies include the omnipresent fried- and rotisserie-chicken stands.

A regular *restaurante* is usually higher on the price scale and has slightly more atmosphere. Many *restaurantes* serve casados, while the fancier places refer to the set lunch as the *almuerzo ejecutivo* (executive lunch).

For something smaller, *pastelerías* and *panaderías* are shops that sell pastries and bread, while many bars serve snacks called *bocas,* which are snack-sized portions of main meals.

Lunch is usually the day's main meal and is typically served at around noon. Dinner tends to be a lighter version of lunch and is eaten around 7pm.

Quick Eats

Street vendors sell fresh fruit (sometimes prechopped and ready to go), cookies, chips (crisps) and fried plantains. Many *sodas* have little windows that face the street and from there dispense *empanadas* (corn turnovers with ground meat, chicken, cheese or sweet fruit), tacos (usually tortillas with meat) or *enchilados* (pastries with spicy meat).

VEGETARIANS & VEGANS

If you don't mind rice and beans, Costa Rica is a relatively comfortable place for vegetarians to travel.

Most restaurants will make veggie casados on request and many are now including them on the menu. They usually include rice and beans, cabbage salad and one or two selections of variously prepared vegetables or legumes.

With the high influx of tourism, there are also many specialty vegetarian restaurants or restaurants with a veggie menu in San José and tourist towns. Lodges in remote areas that offer all-inclusive meal plans can accommodate vegetarian diets with advance notice.

Vegans, macrobiotic and raw food–only travelers will have a tougher time as there are fewer outlets accommodating those diets. If you intend to keep your diet, it's best to choose a lodging where you can prepare food yourself. Many towns have health-food stores *(macrobióticas),* but selection varies. Fresh vegetables can also be hard to come by in isolated areas, and will often be quite expensive.

EATING WITH KIDS

If you're traveling with the tots, you'll find that 'kids' meals' (small portions at small prices) are not normally offered in restaurants, though some fancy lodges do them. However, most local eateries will accommodate two children splitting a meal or can produce child-size portions on request. You can ask for

---

TOP EATS IN COSTA RICA

▪ Try Asian fusion at **Restaurante Tin-Jo** (p103) in San José.

▪ Savor spicy, delicious fish tacos from **El Loco Natural** (p485) in Puerto Viejo de Talamanca.

▪ Grab gourmet sandwiches and sweeping views at **Sun Spot** (p351) in Manuel Antonio.

▪ Sample the best woks and sushi you've ever tasted at **Wok & Roll** (p276) in Tamarindo.

▪ Try anything off the menu at **Restaurante Exótica** (p366) in Ojochal.

---

restaurant staff to bring you simple food, rice with chicken or steak cooked *a la plancha* (on the grill).

If you are traveling with an infant, stock up on formula and baby food before heading to remote areas. Avocados are safe, easy to eat, nutritious and they can be served to children as young as six months old. Young children should avoid water and ice in drinks as they are more susceptible to stomach illnesses.

Always carry snacks for long drives in remote areas – sometimes there are no places to stop for a bite.

For other tips on traveling with the tykes, see p529.

HABITS & CUSTOMS

Costa Ricans are open and informal, and treat their guests well. If you have the good fortune to be invited into a Tico home, you can expect to be served first, receive the biggest portion and perhaps even receive a parting gift. On your part, flowers or wine are both fine gifts to bring, though the best gift you can offer is extending a future dinner invitation to your hosts.

Remember that when you sit down to eat in a restaurant, it is polite to say *buenos días* (good morning) or *buenas tardes* (good afternoon) to the waitstaff and/or any people you might be sharing a table with. It is also polite to say *buen provecho*, which is the equivalent of *bon appetit*, at the start of the meal.

Costa Rican Typical Foods, by Carmen de Musmani and Lupita de Weiler, is out of print, but it is perhaps the only Tico-specific cookbook ever written.

EAT YOUR WORDS

Don't know your *pipas* from your *patacones*? A *batido* from a *bolita*? Get beneath the surface of Costa Rica's plentiful cuisine by learning the lingo. For pronunciation guidelines, see p557.

Useful Phrases

Do you have an English menu?

¿Hay una carta en inglés?	ai *oo*·na *kar*·ta en een·*gles*

I'd like ...

Quisiera ...	kee·*sye*·ra ...

I'm a vegetarian.

Soy vegetariano/a. (m/f)	soy ve·khe·te·*rya*·no/a

The bill, please.

La cuenta, por favor.	la *kwen*·ta, por fa·*vor*

Food Glossary

ON THE MENU

almojabanos	al·mo·kha·*ba*·nos	similar to *tortilla de maíz*, except hand-rolled into small sausage-sized pieces
batido	ba·*tee*·do	milkshake made with fresh fruit, sugar and milk

bocas	*bo*·kas	savory side dishes or bar snacks
bolitas de carne	bo·*lee*·tas de *kar*·ne	snack of mildly spicy meatballs
carimañola	ka·ree·man·*yo*·la	a deep-fried roll made from chopped meat and boiled yuca
carne ahumada	*kar*·ne a·hoo·*ma*·da	smoked, dried ('jerked') meat
ceviche	se·*vee*·che	marinated raw fish or shellfish
chichas	chee·*chas*	heavily sweetened fresh fruit drinks
comida corriente (casado)	ko·*mee*·da ko·ree·*en*·te ka·*sa* do	set meal of rice, beans, plantains and a piece of meat or fish
corvina	kor·*vee*·na	a flavorful white fish
empanada	em·pa·*na*·da	corn turnover filled with ground meat, chicken, cheese or sweet fruit
gallo pinto	*ga*·lyo *peen*·to	literally 'spotted rooster'; a soupy mixture of rice and black beans
hojaldres	ho·*khal*·dres	fried dough, similar to a donut; popular with breakfast
huevos fritos/ revueltos	*we*·vos *free*·tos/re·*vwel*·tos	fried/scrambled eggs
licuado	lee·*kwa*·do	shake made with fresh fruit, sugar and water
mondongo	mon·*dong*·go	tripe soup
patacones	pa·ta·*ko*·nes	green plantains cut in thin pieces, salted, pressed and then fried
pipa	*pee*·pa	coconut water, served straight from the husk
plátano maduro	*pla*·ta·no ma·*doo*·ro	ripe plantains baked or broiled with butter, brown sugar and cinnamon; served hot
raspados	ras·*pa*·dos	shaved ice flavored with fruit juice
ropa vieja	*ro*·pa *vye*·kha	literally means 'old clothes'; a spicy shredded beef combination served over rice
seco	*se*·ko	alcoholic drink made from sugar cane
tajadas	ta·*kha*·das	ripe plantains sliced lengthwise and fried
tamales	ta·*ma*·les	ground corn with spices and chicken or pork, wrapped in banana leaves and boiled
tasajo	ta·*sa*·kho	dried meat cooked with vegetables
tortilla de maíz	tor·*tee*·ya de mai·*ees*	a thick, fried cornmeal tortilla

BASICS

azúcar	a·*soo*·kar	sugar
cuchara	choo·*cha*·ra	spoon
cuchillo	choo·*chee*·lyo	knife
hielo	ee·*e*·lo	ice
mantequilla	man·te·*kee*·lya	butter
pan	pan	bread
plato	*pla*·to	plate
sal	sal	salt
servilleta	sair·vee·*lye*·ta	napkin
sopa	*so*·pa	soup
taza	*ta*·za	cup
tenedor	te·ne·*dor*	fork
vaso	*va*·so	glass

MEALTIMES

desayuno	de·sa·*yoo*·no	breakfast
almuerzo	al·*mwer*·so	lunch
cena	*se*·na	dinner

FRUITS & VEGETABLES

aguacate	a·gwa·*ka*·te	avocado
ensalada	en·sa·*la*·da	salad
fresa	*fre*·sa	strawberry
guanábana	gwa·*na*·ba·na	soursop
manzana	man·*za*·na	apple
maracuyá	ma·ra·koo·*ya*	passionfruit
naranja	na·*ran*·kha	orange
piña	*pee*·nya	pineapple
zanahoria	sa·na·o·rya	carrot
zarzamora	zar·za·*mo*·ra	blackberry

SEAFOOD

camarón	ka·ma·*ron*	shrimp
filete de pescado	fi·*le*·te de pes·*ka*·do	fish fillet
langosta	lan·*gos*·ta	lobster
langostino	lan·gos·*tee*·no	jumbo shrimp
pescado	pes·*ka*·do	fish
pulpo	*pool*·po	octopus

MEATS

bistec	bee·stek	steak
carne	*kar*·ne	beef
chuleta	choo·*le*·ta	pork chop
hamburguesa	am·boor·*gwe*·sa	hamburger
salchicha	sal·*chee*·cha	sausage

DRINKS

agua	*a*·gwa	water
bebida	be·*bee*·da	drink
café	ka·*fe*	coffee
cerveza	ser·*ve*·sa	beer
leche	*le*·che	milk
ron	ron	rum
vino	*vee*·no	wine

COOKING TERMS

a la plancha	a la pa·*ree*·lya	grilled
frito	*free*·to	fried

Environment David Lukas

THE LAND

Despite its diminutive size, 51,000-sq-km Costa Rica is a study in contrasts and contradictions. On one coast it fronts scenic Pacific shores while only 119km away lies the muggy Caribbean coast, with a range of active volcanoes and alpine peaks in between. Rich in natural resources, Costa Rica has gone from suffering the highest rates of deforestation in Latin America in the early 1990s to being a global model for tropical conservation. Now in charge of an exemplar system of well-managed and accessible parks, Costa Rica is perhaps the best place in the world to experience rain-forest habitats, while its stunning natural landscape is easily the top reason tourists visit this delightful country.

With a length of 1016km, the Pacific coastline is infinitely varied as it twists and turns around gulfs, peninsulas and many small coves. Rugged, rocky headlands alternate with classic white- and black-sand beaches and palm trees to produce an image of a tropical paradise along some stretches. Strong tidal action creates an excellent habitat for waterbirds as well as a visually dramatic crashing surf (perfect for surfers). Inland, the landscapes of the Pacific lowlands are equally dynamic, ranging from dry deciduous forests and open cattle country in the north, to lush, magnificent tropical rain forests in the south.

Monotonous in comparison, the Caribbean coastline runs a straight 212km along a low, flat plain that is inundated with brackish lagoons and waterlogged forests. A lack of strong tides allows plants to grow right over the water's edge along coastal sloughs, creating walls of green vegetation. Broad, humid plains that scarcely rise above sea level and murky waters characterize much of this region.

Running down the center of the country, the mountainous spine of Costa Rica is a land of active volcanoes, clear tumbling streams and chilled peaks clad in impenetrable cloud forests. These mountain ranges generally follow a northwest to southeast line, with the highest and most dramatic peaks in the south near the Panamanian border (culminating at the 3820m-high Cerro

Adrian Forsyth has written several colorful children's books about the rain forest, including *Journey through a Tropical Jungle* and *How Monkeys make Chocolate.*

OUT ON A REEF

Compared to the rest of the Caribbean, the coral reefs of Costa Rica are small fry. Heavy surf and shifting sands along most of the Caribbean coast produce conditions that are unbearable to corals, but on the southern coast two beautiful patches of reef are protected on the rocky headlands of Parque Nacional Cahuita and Refugio Nacional de Vida Silvestre Gandoca-Manzanillo. These diminutive but vibrant reefs are home to more than 100 species of fish and many types of coral. Countless damselfish, sergeant majors, parrotfish and surgeonfish gather to feed on abundant marine algae, while predatory barracudas come to prey on the fish. Gandoca-Manzanillo is a famous nesting ground for four species of sea turtle. Even better, turtle volunteers have been patrolling these beaches since 1986 to prevent poachers and the turtle populations are doing really well thanks to their efforts.

Unfortunately the reefs are in danger due to sediments that wash downriver from logging operations, and from toxic chemicals that wash out of nearby agricultural fields. In 1991 an earthquake lifted the reefs up as much as 1.5m, stranding and killing large portions of this fragile ecosystem.

So far the coral reefs of Costa Rica have been largely overlooked, but with these threats hanging over them, there's little time to lose.

Chirripó). The difficulties of traveling through, and farming on, these steep slopes have, until recently, saved much of this area from development and made it a haven for wildlife.

Carol Henderson's *Field Guide to the Wildlife of Costa Rica* is a handy all-in-one resource.

In the midst of the highlands is the Meseta Central – or Central Valley – which is surrounded by mountains (the Cordillera Central to the north and east and the Cordillera de Talamanca to the south). It is this fertile central plain, 1000m and 1500m above sea level with abundant rainfall and consistently mild temperatures, that contains four of Costa Rica's five largest cities and more than half of the country's population.

Like most of Central America, Costa Rica's geologic history can be traced to the impact of the Cocos Plate moving northeast and crashing into the Caribbean Plate at a rate of about 10cm every year – quite fast by geological standards. The point of impact is called a 'subduction zone,' and this is where the Cocos Plate forces the edge of the Caribbean Plate to break up and become uplifted. It is not a smooth process, and hence Central America is an area prone to earthquakes and ongoing volcanic activity (see p530). Arenal, in the north, is one of the world's most active volcanoes.

WILDLIFE

Dr Alexander Skutch is famous for the *Guide to the Birds of Costa Rica,* but he also wrote several other contemplative books about his feathered friends, including *A Naturalist in Costa Rica* and *The Minds of Birds.*

Nowhere else in the world are so many types of habitats squeezed into such a tiny area. The range of habitats in Costa Rica, a consequence of its unique geography, creates an incredibly rich diversity of flora and fauna – in fact, no other country on the planet has such variety. Measured in terms of number of species per 10,000 sq km Costa Rica tops the list of countries at 615 species, compared to a wildlife-rich country such as Rwanda that has 596, or to the comparatively impoverished US with its 104 species. This simple fact alone (not to mention the ease of travel and friendly residents) makes Costa Rica the premier destination for nature lovers from all over the world.

The large number of species in Costa Rica is also due to the relatively recent appearance of the country. Roughly three million years ago Costa Rica rose from the ocean and formed a land bridge between North and South America. As species from these two vast biological provinces started to mingle, the number of species essentially 'doubled' in the area where Costa Rica now sits.

Animals

Though tropical in nature – with a substantial number of tropical animals such as poison-dart frogs and spider monkeys – Costa Rica is also the winter home for more than 200 species of migrating birds that arrive from as far away as Alaska and Australia. So don't be surprised to see one of your familiar backyard birds feeding alongside trogons and toucans. Individual animals and insects are given more coverage in the Wildlife Guide, p193.

Two-toed sloths descend from the trees once every two weeks to defecate.

With a total of 850 species recorded in Costa Rica, it's understandable that birds are one of the primary attractions for naturalists who could stay for months and still barely scratch the surface in terms of seeing all these species. Birds in Costa Rica come in every color, from strawberry-red scarlet macaws to the iridescent jewels called violet sabrewings (a type of hummingbird). Because many birds in Costa Rica have restricted ranges, you are guaranteed to find different species everywhere you travel.

Visitors will almost certainly see one of Costa Rica's four types of monkeys or two sloths, but there are an additional 230 types of mammals awaiting the patient observer. More exotic sightings might include the amazing four-eyed opossum or silky anteater, while a lucky few might spot the elusive tapir, or have a jaguarundi cross their path.

The extensive network of national parks, wildlife refuges and other protected areas are prime places to spot wildlife. But remember that these creatures do not know park boundaries, so keep your eyes peeled in the forested areas and buffer zones that often surround these sanctuaries. Early morning is the best time to see animals because many species sleep during the hottest part of the day. Spotting one of the nocturnal species – such as Baird's tapir, the silky anteater and the kinkajou – requires going out at night with a strong flashlight (a great item to pack for your Costa Rica trip).

If you are serious about observing birds and animals, the value of a knowledgeable guide cannot be underestimated. Their keen eyes are trained to recognize the slightest movement in the forest, and they recognize the many exotic sounds. Most professional bird guides are proficient in the dialects of local birds, greatly improving your chances of hearing or seeing these species. Furthermore, a good local guide will often have an idea where certain species tend to congregate – whether it's quetzals eating fruit in an avocado tree, or American crocodiles catching fish at the mouth of a river. Through its National Biodiversity Institute, Costa Rica now trains local citizens to be professional nature guides as an alternative to letting all this skilled work go to foreign guides.

No season is a bad season for exploring Costa Rica's natural environment, though most visitors arrive during the peak dry season when trails are less muddy and more accessible. An added bonus of visiting between December and February is that many of the wintering migrant birds are still hanging around. A trip after the peak season means fewer birds, but is a stupendous time to see dried forests transform into vibrant greens and it's also when resident birds begin nesting.

> While the female scarlet macaw sits on her nest, the male regurgitates food for her to eat, and later does the same for their chicks.

> The seven species of poison-dart frog in Costa Rica are beautiful to look at but have exceedingly toxic skin secretions that cause paralysis and death.

ENDANGERED SPECIES

As expected in a country with unique habitats and widespread logging, there are numerous species whose populations are declining or in danger

LOOK BUT DON'T JUMP IN

In 2006 swimming with dolphins and whales in Costa Rica was made illegal. It is also illegal to attempt to capture or harass them. Dolphin- and whale-watching tours have become increasingly popular in recent years, leading to an explosion in the number of operators. Unfortunately, too many operators are out for a quick buck, often at the expense of the animals.

In a survey conducted by the Cetacean Society International, 17 of the operators refused to cooperate by answering survey questions, and all of the tour companies investigated made mistakes such as harassing animals, not carrying lifejackets and having motor problems. Only one company had knowledgeable guides that could provide 'reasonable natural-history information.' Lacking experience and knowledge, many operators have been conducting their tours without due attention to the integrity of the star players – the animals themselves.

In short, too much attention from tourists has caused some dolphins and whales to stress out. Research indicates that in some heavily touristed areas, dolphins are leaving their natural habitat in search of calmer seas. Some scientists believe that having humans at close proximity in the water disrupts feeding, nursing and other behavior. There is growing concern about the long-term human impact on the health of these marine mammals. The 2006 legislation banning swimming with marine mammals was enacted with their best interests in mind.

When your boat comes across these amazing creatures of the sea, do not jump in the water. From the comfort of the boat you can have an awe-inspiring and longer-lasting experience (the dolphins and whales usually swim away quickly when humans are in the water, but they might stay and swim around a boat indefinitely). And more importantly, you won't disturb the peace of these gentle giants.

DREAM OF THE BOUNTIFUL TURTLES

There are seven kinds of sea turtles, four of which frequent Costa Rica's beaches: olive ridley, leatherback, green and hawksbill. All four species are classified as endangered or critically endangered, meaning they face an imminent threat of extinction. While populations of some species are increasing, thanks to various protection programs along the Caribbean coast, the risk for these *tortugas* is still very real.

Destruction of habitat is a huge problem. With the exception of the leatherbacks, all of these species return to their natal beach to nest. That means that the ecological state of the beach directly impacts that turtle's ability to reproduce. All of the species prefer dark, undisturbed beaches, and any sort of development or artificial lighting (including flashlights) will inhibit nesting.

A devastating number of turtles are killed every year when they get caught in loglines or gill nets, which are sometimes used by commercial fisheries. The Leatherback Trust estimates that 63% of all Pacific leatherbacks get hooked by loglines, resulting in a 15% to 18% death rate.

Hunting and harvesting eggs are two major causes of declining populations. Green turtles are actually hunted for their meat. Leatherbacks and olive ridleys are not killed for meat, but their eggs are considered a delicacy – an aphrodisiac no less. The hawksbill turtles are hunted for their unusual shells, which are sometimes used to make jewelry and hair ornaments. Of course, any trade in tortoise-shell products and turtle eggs and meat is illegal, but a significant black market exists for these products.

Enforcement of hunting and harvesting bans requires lots of nighttime beach patrols during turtle-nesting season. There are many opportunities for volunteers to assist with beach patrols and education programs, see p460 for more information.

of extinction. Currently, the number-one threat to most of Costa Rica's endangered species is habitat destruction, followed closely by hunting and trapping.

The legendary resplendent quetzal – the bird at the top of every naturalist's must-see list – teeters precariously as its home forests are felled at an alarming rate. Seeing a noisy scarlet macaw could be a birding highlight in Costa Rica, but trapping for the pet trade has extirpated these magnificent birds from much of their former range. Although populations are thriving in the Península de Osa, the scarlet macaw is now extinct over most of Central America, including the entire Caribbean coast.

Sea turtles get a lot of attention in Costa Rica, and the work of several conservation groups has dramatically improved the nesting success of these turtles on Costa Rican beaches. See boxed text Dream of the Bountiful Turtles, above.

Central America's largest land mammal, the 300kg Baird's tapir, is a sought-after source of protein, making it a target for hunters. The tapir's habit of commuting between feeding patches and waterholes on distinctive 'tapir trails' makes it extremely vulnerable to hunting. Tapirs are now restricted to the least accessible wilderness areas. Similarly, the gigantic 600kg West Indian manatee is an easy victim for hunters, especially since they are placid and have no defenses. Manatees still populate the canals of Parque Nacional Tortuguero, though they are elusive.

Costa Rica's sexiest endangered species is undoubtedly the reclusive jaguar. Jaguars require a large area to support enough prey to survive. Annually, an individual jaguar needs the equivalent of 53 white-tailed deer, 18 peccaries, 40 coatis, 25 armadillos and 55 ctenosaurs. That is for one jaguar! Owing to clearing for cattle ranches and overhunting of jaguar prey, suitable habitat for viable populations of jaguars now occurs in only a handful of protected

The tale of the green turtle's rebound in Tortuguero is told in two popular books by Archie Carr: *The Windward Road: Adventures of a Naturalist on Remote Caribbean Shores* and *The Sea Turtle: So Excellent a Fishe*.

If wildlife is your thing, bring along Lonely Planet's *Watching Wildlife in Central America* by Luke Hunter and David Andrew.

The following list outlines the current endangerment levels for each of Costa Rica's turtles and the places where you can (still) see them.

Olive ridley Endangered – the world population of nesting females is estimated to be 800,000. Olive ridleys are unique in that thousands of turtles descend on one beach to nest *en masse*. This happens in Parque Nacional Santa Rosa (p218) and Refugio Nacional de Fauna Silvestre Ostional (p292) between July and November. They are also unique in that it is legal to harvest a limited number of eggs from the first laying – usually for sale in San José. The idea is to give locals a stake in protecting the nests from illegal poachers from the outside. Unfortunately, it also has the effect of encouraging illegal harvesting in other areas, as the sale is not regulated.

Leatherback Critically endangered – the world population of nesting females is estimated to be 35,000. Leatherbacks nest on the northern Caribbean coast around Parque Nacional Tortuguero (p458) and the beaches of Parismina (p456) from March to June. Pacific leatherbacks have laid eggs on Playa Grande in the Parque Nacional Marino Las Baulas de Guanacaste (p269) for thousands of years, but the number of nesting turtles has declined dramatically in recent years. In the 2005–06 season, Playa Grande attracted only 51 turtles, which is nonetheless an improvement from the previous year.

Green Endangered – the world population of nesting females is estimated to be 88,520. Green turtles nest in Parque Nacional Tortuguero (p458) and surrounding beaches from mid-June to mid-September. Green turtles represent the rare success story. Thanks to information collected by the Caribbean Conservation Corporation (see p461), scientists realized in the 1980s that fewer than 3000 female green turtles were nesting in Tortuguero annually, compared to tens of thousands in earlier decades. The alarming data helped them convince a coalition of public and private groups to initiate long-term conservation efforts geared toward bringing the turtles back. Today, more than 20,000 of the lovely ladies show up on these shores to breed during the year, and the number continues to climb.

Hawksbill Critically endangered – the world population of nesting females is estimated to be 22,900. These beauties only make rare appearances on beaches around Tortuguero between February and September, while they are more common at Parque Nacional Marino Ballena (p365) from May to November.

areas, such as Parque Nacional Corcovado (p416) and Parque Internacional La Amistad (p389).

Plants

Floral biodiversity is also high – close to 12,000 species of vascular plants have been described in Costa Rica, and more are being added to the list every year. Orchids alone account for about 1400 species.

Experiencing a tropical forest for the first time can be a bit of a surprise for visitors from North America or Europe, where temperate forests tend to have little variety. Such regions are either dominated by conifers, or have endless tracts of oaks, beech and birch. Tropical forests, on the other hand, have a staggering number of species – in Costa Rica, for example, almost 2000 tree species have been recorded. If you stand in one spot and look around, you'll see scores of different plants, and if you walk several hundred meters you're likely to find even more.

The diversity of habitats created when this many species mix is a wonder to behold – one day you may find yourself canoeing in a muggy mangrove swamp, and the next day squinting through bone-chilling fog to see orchids in a montane cloud forest. If at all possible, it is worth planning your trip with the goal of seeing some of Costa Rica's most distinctive plant communities, including rain forests, mangrove swamps, cloud forests and dry forests.

Classic rain-forest habitats are well represented in parks of the southwest corner of Costa Rica or in mid-elevation portions of the central mountains. Here you will find towering trees that block out the sky, long looping vines and many overlapping layers of vegetation. Large trees often show buttresses, wing-like ribs that extend out from their trunks for added structural support.

The tallest tree in the rain forest is usually the silk cotton tree, or the ceiba. The most famous example is a 70m elder in Corcovado.

Costa Rica's national tree is the guanacaste, commonly found on the lowlands of the Pacific slope.

COSTA RICA'S EASTER BLOSSOM

Among Costa Rica's 1400 species of orchids, the guaria morada *(Cattleya skinneri)* is celebrated with special reverence. Blooming around the time of Lent and Easter, this gorgeous orchid with dense clusters of lavender-rose flowers is prominently displayed on altars, homes and churches everywhere in Central America. In the old days these flowers grew liberally on the walls and roofs of old houses and courtyards, where they added a special charm. However, this ancient custom fell by the wayside and they are no longer a common sight.

In honor of the orchid's links to history and tradition, it was chosen as Costa Rica's national flower in 1937. Unfortunately, the plant's amazing popularity has resulted in wild populations being harvested without restraint, and an alarm was raised in 2004 that it could become extinct in the wild without immediate action. Hopefully the orchid's numbers will begin to increase again, because although they are easy to grow commercially, no quantity of orchids in a greenhouse can replace the flowers found in the wild forests of Costa Rica.

Along brackish stretches of both coasts, mangrove swamps are a world unto themselves. Growing stiltlike out of muddy tidal flats, five species of trees crowd together so densely that no boat and few animals can penetrate. Striking in their adaptations for dealing with salt, mangrove trees thrive where no other land plant dares tread. Though often thought of as mosquito-filled backwaters, mangrove swamps play extremely important roles. Not only do they buffer coastlines from the erosive power of waves, they also have high levels of productivity because they trap nutrient-rich sediment and serve as spawning and nursery areas for innumerable species of fish and invertebrates.

Most famous of all, and a highlight for many visitors, are the fabulous cloud forests of Monteverde (p190), with fog-drenched trees so thickly coated in mosses, ferns, bromeliads and orchids that you can hardly discern their true shapes. Cloud forests are widespread at high elevations throughout Costa Rica (such as the Parque Nacional Chirripó area, p378) and any of them would be worth visiting. Be forewarned, however, that in these habitats the term 'rainy season' has little meaning because it's always dripping wet from the fog.

For a complete change of pace try exploring the unique drier forests along the northwest coast. During the dry season many trees drop their leaves, creating carpets of crackling, sun-drenched leaves and a sense of openness that is largely absent in other Costa Rican habitats. The large trees here, such as Costa Rica's national tree, the guanacaste, have broad, umbrellalike canopies, while spiny shrubs and vines or cacti dominate the understory. At times, large numbers of trees erupt into spectacular displays of flowers, and at the beginning of the rainy season everything is transformed with a wonderful flush of new green foliage.

If you can't make it to one of the areas above check out the fantastic orchid gardens at Jardín de Orquídeas (p175) or Lankester Gardens (p152), which is near Cartago and home to more than 800 types of orchids.

Michael Crichton's book *Jurassic Park* is set on Isla del Cocos. In it, he refers to Ticos as 'Ticans.'

For maps and descriptions of the national parks, go to www.costarica-national parks.com.

NATIONAL PARKS

The national-park system began in the 1960s, and has since been expanded into a National Conservation Areas System with an astounding 186 protected areas, including 32 national parks, eight biological reserves, 13 forest reserves and 51 wildlife refuges. At least 10% of the land is strictly protected and another 17% is included in various multiple-use preserves. Costa Rican authorities enjoy their claim that more than 27% of the country has been set aside for conservation, but multiple-use zones still allow farming, logging and other exploitation, so the environment within them is not totally protected.

NATIONAL PARKS & PROTECTED AREAS

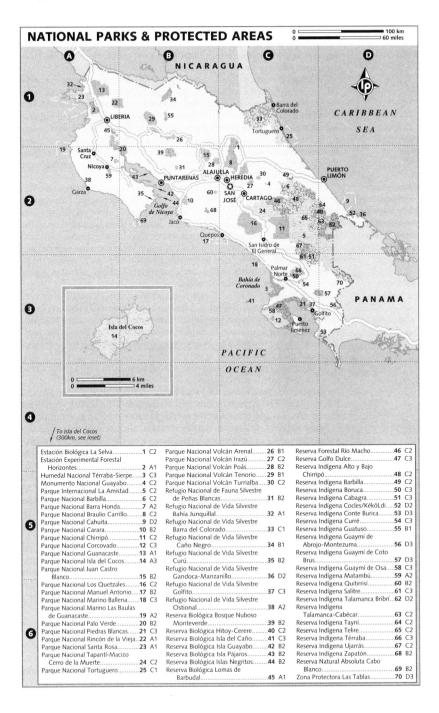

Travelers will be surprised to learn that, in addition to the system of national preserves, there are hundreds of small, privately owned lodges, reserves and haciendas (estates) that have been set up to protect the land, and many of these are well worth visiting.

Although the national-park system appears glamorous on paper, a report a few years ago from the national conservation body (Sinac; Sistema Nacional de Areas de Conservación) amplified the fact that much of the protected area is, in fact, at risk. The government doesn't exactly own all of this land – almost half of the areas are in private ownership – and there isn't a budget to buy it. Technically, the private lands are protected from development, but many landowners are finding loopholes in the restrictions and selling or developing their properties, or taking bribes from poachers and illegal loggers in exchange for access to their lands.

The fabulous limestone caves of Parque Nacional Barra Honda were formed in the remains of ancient coral reefs after they were uplifted out of the ocean.

On the plus side is a project by Sinac that links national parks and reserves, private reserves and national forests into 13 conservation areas. This strategy has two major effects. First, these so-called megaparks allow greater numbers of individual plants and animals to exist. Second, the administration of the national parks is delegated to regional offices, allowing a more individualized management approach in each area. Each conservation area has regional and subregional offices delegated to provide effective education, enforcement, research and management, although some regional offices play what appear to be only obscure bureaucratic roles.

Although many of the national parks were expressly created to protect Costa Rica's habitats and wildlife, a few parks preserve other resources such as the country's foremost pre-Columbian ruins at Monumento Nacional Arqueológico Guayabo (p160); an important cave system at Parque Nacional Barra Honda (p286); and a series of geologically active and inactive volcanoes in several parks and reserves.

Most national parks can be entered without permits, though a few limit the number they admit on a daily basis and others require advance reservations for accommodations within the park's boundaries (Chirripó, Corcovado and La Amistad). The average entrance fee to most parks is US$10 per day for foreigners, plus additional fees for overnight camping where permitted.

Many national parks are in remote areas and are rarely visited – they also suffer from a lack of rangers and protection. Others are extremely – and deservedly – popular for their world-class scenic and natural beauty, as well as their wildlife. During the '90s in the idyllic Parque Nacional Manuel Antonio (p353), a tiny park on the Pacific coast, the number of visitors reached 1000 per day in the high season and annual visitors rocketed from about 36,000 in 1982 to more than 150,000 by 1991. This number of visitors threatened to ruin the diminutive area by driving away the wildlife and polluting the beaches. In response, park visitors have since been limited to 600 per day and the park is closed on Mondays to allow it a brief respite from the onslaught.

The National Biodiversity Institute is a clearing-house of information on both biodiversity and efforts to conserve it; see www.inbio.ac.cr.

With Costa Rican parks contributing significantly to both national and local economies through the huge influx of tourist monies, there is little question that the country's healthy natural environment is important to its citizens. In general, support for land preservation remains high because it provides income and jobs to so many people, plus important opportunities for scientific investigation.

ENVIRONMENTAL ISSUES

Costa Rica is a mixed bag in terms of its environmental issues. No other tropical country has made such a concerted effort to protect the environment and in 2008 Costa Rica was ranked one of the top five nations in the world for its overall environmental performance. At the same time, as the global leader in the burgeoning ecotourism economy, Costa Rica is proving to be a case study in the pitfalls and benefits of ecological tourism.

Deforestation

Can you believe that this tropical paradise was once entirely carpeted in lush rain forests? Tragically after more than a century of clearing for plantations, agriculture and logging, Costa Rica lost about 80% of its forest cover before the government stepped in with a plan to protect what was left. Through its many programs of forest protection and reforestation, 52% of the country is forested once again – a stunning accomplishment in a mere 20 years.

> More than 30% of Costa Rica's forests were cut to raise low-grade beef that went into US fast-food hamburgers, TV dinners and pet food.

Despite protection for two-thirds of the remaining forests, cutting trees is still a major problem for Costa Rica, especially on private lands being cleared by wealthy landowners and multinational corporations. Even within national parks, some of the more remote areas are being logged illegally because there is not enough money to hire guards to enforce the law.

Apart from the direct loss of tropical forests and the plants and animals that depend on them, deforestation leads directly or indirectly to other severe environmental problems. Forests protect the soil beneath them from the ravages of tropical rainstorms; after deforestation much of the topsoil is washed away, lowering the productivity of the land and silting up watersheds and downstream coral reefs. Cleared lands are often planted with a variety of crops, including Costa Rica's main agricultural product, bananas, the production of which entails the use of pesticides and blue plastic bags to protect the fruit. Both the pesticides and the plastic bags end up polluting

POPULAR PROTECTED AREAS

Area	Features	Activities	Best Time to Visit	Page
Parque Nacional Cahuita	easily accessible hiking trail, coral reef, beaches, howler monkeys	beach walking, snorkeling	year-round	p475
Parque Nacional Chirripó	Costa Rica's highest summit, cloud forest, beautiful mountain views, diverse animal and plant life at varying altitudes	strenuous two-day hike to summit	dry season (Jan-Mar), closed in May	p378
Parque Nacional Corcovado	vast, remote rain forest: giant trees, trees, jaguar, scarlet macaw, tapir	exploring off-the-beaten path, wildlife-watching	year-round, though trails bad in rainy season (May-Nov)	p416
Parque Nacional Manuel Antonio	beautiful accessible beaches, mangrove swamp, diverse marine life, eroded rocks	beach walking, exploring	avoid peak season if possible (Jan-Mar)	p353
Parque Nacional Santa Rosa	unique dry forest: guanacaste (Costa Rica's national tree) monkey, peccary, coati	wildlife-watching, hiking	dry season (Jan-Mar) for spectacular flowering trees	p218
Parque Nacional Tortuguero	wild Caribbean coast: sea turtle, sloth, manatee, crocodile, river otter	beach walking, canoeing, turtle-watching	turtle egg-laying season, check with park for details	p458
Reserva Biológica Bosque Nuboso Monteverde	world-famous cloud forest: resplendent quetzal, epiphytes, orchid, three-wattled bellbird	bird-watching, wildlife-watching	avoid peak season if possible	p190
Reserva Natural Absoluta Cabo Blanco	scenic remote beaches, seabirds, marine life, three species of monkey	beach walking, bird-watching	year-round	p314

THE PRICE OF ECOTOURISM

Costa Rica has so much to offer the wildlife enthusiast it is no small wonder that ecotourism is growing in the country. More than 70% of foreign travelers visit one or more nature destinations, and half of these visitors come specifically to see Costa Rica's wildlife.

Such has been its popularity that 1.9 million tourists visited in 2007, which is double the figure of 20 years ago. Tourism revenues (an estimated US$1 billion) recently surpassed those of the banana and coffee industries, and prices for the traveler have risen in tandem. At first, the growth in tourism took the nation by surprise – there was no overall development plan and growth was poorly controlled. Some people wanted to cash in over the short term with little thought for the future. Unfortunately, this attitude has changed little even as pressure has grown to regulate the industry more closely.

Traditionally, tourism in Costa Rica has been on a small and intimate scale. The great majority of the country's hotels are small (fewer than 50 rooms) and staffed with friendly local people who work closely with tourists, to the benefit of both. This intimacy and friendliness has been a hallmark of a visit to Costa Rica.

But this is changing. The financial bonanza generated by the tourism boom means that new operations are starting up all the time – some are good, many are not. The big word in Costa Rica is 'ecotourism' and everyone wants to jump on the green bandwagon. There are 'ecological' car-rental agencies and 'ecological' menus in restaurants. People want tourists, they want the money that tourists carry, but unfortunately there's little infrastructure to take care that these very tourists who are interested in ecotourism don't wreck the environment or have a role in despoiling any more wilderness.

Taking advantage of Costa Rica's 'green' image, a growing number of developers are promoting mass tourism by building large hotels with accompanying environmental problems (for more

the environment. See boxed text Tallying the True Cost of Bananas, p450, for information on how this has impacted humans as well.

Because deforestation plays a huge role in global warming, there is a lot of recent interest in rewarding countries like Costa Rica for taking the lead in protecting their forests. The US recently announced a deal to forgive US$26 million of Costa Rica's debt in exchange for increased efforts to preserve rain forests. The Costa Rican government itself sponsors a program that pays landowners US$50 for each hectare of forest they set aside and is petitioning the UN for a global program that would pay tropical countries for their conservation efforts.

Few organizations are as involved in building sustainable rain forest–based economies as the Rainforest Alliance. See the website for special initiatives in Costa Rica: www.rainforest-alliance.org.

Tourism

The other great environmental issue facing Costa Rica comes from the country being loved to death, directly through the passage of more than one million foreign tourists a year, and indirectly through the development of extensive infrastructure to support this influx (see boxed text The Price of Ecotourism, above). Every year, more resort hotels and lodges pop up, most notably on formerly pristine beaches or in the middle of intact rain forest. Many of these projects are poorly planned and necessitate additional support systems, including roads and countless vehicle trips, with much of this activity unregulated and largely unmonitored. There is growing concern that many hotels and lodges are simply dumping wastewater into the ocean or nearby creeks rather than following expensive procedures for treating it. With an official estimate that only 4% of the country's wastewater is treated and with thousands of unregulated hotels in operation, there's a good chance that some hotels and lodges aren't taking care of their wastes.

The world-famous Organization for Tropical Studies runs three field stations and offers numerous classes for students seriously interested in tropical ecology. See www.ots.ac.cr.

It is worth noting, however, that many private lodges and reserves are also doing some of the best conservation work in the country, and it's really information see boxed text Clamor in Tambor, p304, and the discussion in The Papagayo Problem boxed text, p262). Apart from the immediate impacts, such as cutting down vegetation, diverting or damming rivers and driving away wildlife, there are secondary impacts such as erosion, lack of adequate waste-treatment facilities for huge hotels in areas far from sewage lines, and the building of socially, environmentally and economically inadequate 'shanty towns' to house the maids, waiters, cooks, janitors and other staff.

Another problem is that many developers are foreigners – they say that they are giving the local people jobs, but most locals don't want to spend their lives being waiters and maids while watching the big money go out of the country. We recommend staying in smaller hotels that have a positive attitude about the environment and are more beneficial to the locals, rather than the large, foreign-owned, mass-tourism destinations.

Amid all this, the government tourist board (ICT; Instituto Costarricense de Turismo) has launched mass-marketing campaigns all over the world, touting 'Costa Rica: No Artificial Ingredients,' yet hasn't followed up with the kind of infrastructure necessary to preserve those ingredients (nor does it lobby for them). Many people feel a certain degree of frustration with the ICT for selling Costa Rica as a green paradise but doing little to help preserve it.

The big question is whether future tourism developments should continue to focus on the traditional small-hotel, ecotourism approach, or turn to mass tourism, with planeloads of visitors accommodated in 'megaresorts' such as the ones in Cancún, Mexico. From the top levels of government down, the debate has been fierce. Local and international tour operators and travel agents, journalists, developers, airline operators, hotel owners, writers, environmentalists and politicians have all been vocal in their support of either ecotourism or mass tourism. Many believe that the country is too small to handle both forms of tourism properly. It remains to be seen which faction will win – or if both can coexist peacefully together.

inspiring to run across homespun efforts to protect Costa Rica's environment spearheaded by hardworking families or small organizations tucked away in some forgotten corner of the country. These include projects to boost rural economies by raising butterflies or native flowers, efforts by villagers to document their local biodiversity, or amazingly resourceful campaigns to raise funds to purchase endangered lands. The Refugio Nacional de Vida Silvestre Curú (p302), Tiskita Jungle Lodge (p441) in Pavones, La Amistad Lodge (p392) and Rara Avis (p520) near Puerto Viejo de Sarapiquí are but a few examples. Costa Rica is full of wonderful tales about folks who are extremely passionate and generous in their efforts to protect the planet's resources.

How to Help

Despite the economic benefits of tourism for Costa Rica (more than US$1 billion a year), there are many negatives. The best way to minimize the impact of your own visit is to research and be aware of your options. Have in mind the goal of finding small, locally owned businesses that have a sincere concern for their community and environment. Most of Costa Rica's problems with tourism stem from overuse of popular sites, lack of enforcement, exploitation of the local workforce, haphazard development, and culturally insensitive development projects. It's a safe bet that the vast majority of these problem issues are the product of foreign-owned companies looking to profit off of Costa Rica's lucrative tourism industry. Be particularly alert for 'greenwashing' by companies that falsely portray themselves as environmentally conscious (for more details see Green Costa Rica, p417). Check out the GreenDex, p588, for reputable green organizations in Costa Rica. If nothing else, consider joining one of the many exciting environmental volunteer programs like the **Costa Rica Conservation Trust** (www.conservecostarica.org).

Green Phoenix, by science journalist William Allen, is an absorbing account of his efforts, alongside scientists and activists, to conserve and restore the rain forest in Guanacaste.

Adventure Travel

Costa Rica's extraordinary array of national parks and reserves provides an incredible stage for the adventure traveler. Adrenaline junkies of the world unite – from mountain-biking excursions and multiday jungle treks to some of the best white water in Central America and seafaring on both the coasts – if you want it, Costa Rica's got it.

HIKING & TREKKING

Trail Source (www.trail source.com) provides information on hiking in Costa Rica. It also has info on horse riding and mountain biking. A monthly fee applies.

There is no shortage of hiking opportunities around Costa Rica, from day hikes in the countless private reserves to longer trips in some of the national parks.

Especially notable for day hikes are the fumaroles and tropical dry forest in **Parque Nacional Rincón de la Vieja** (p216), the postcard perfect beaches of **Parque Nacional Cahuita** (p476) and the cloud-forest reserves of **Santa Elena** (p202) and **Monteverde** (p191).

For those who want multiday adventures, the hikes through **Parque Nacional Corcovado** (p426) are nothing less than incredible. This last remaining strand of coastal Pacific rain forest is packed with macaws, monkeys, tapirs and peccaries, and offers totally rugged adventure. Also check out historic **Parque Nacional Santa Rosa** (p220), which offers opportunities to hike and camp in tropical dry forest.

Mountaineers will enjoy the steep and arduous hike through the *páramo* (highland shrub forests and grasslands) up **Cerro Chirripó** (p379) – the highest mountain in Costa Rica at 3820m. And for the trekker that appreciates complete solitude in absolute wilderness, there's **Parque Internacional La Amistad** (p391). This heavily forested and rarely traversed park offers some of the most breathtaking scenery in the country.

Many local companies offer guided hikes in different parts of Costa Rica; see p524.

Safety on the Trail

Costa Rica is hot and humid: hiking in these tropical conditions can really take it out of you. Overheating and dehydration are the main sources of misery on the trails, so be sure to bring plenty of water and don't be afraid to stop and rest. Make sure you have sturdy, comfortable footwear (see opposite) and a lightweight rain jacket.

Unfortunately, some readers have told us horror stories of getting robbed while on some of the more remote hiking trails. Although this is certainly not a common occurrence, it is always advisable to hike in a group for added safety. Hiring a local guide is another excellent way to enhance your experience, avoid getting lost and learn an enormous amount about the flora and fauna in your midst.

PUTTING DOWN THE GUIDE

No, we're not talking about insulting the local guy who is leading you through the rain forest. We're talking about closing this book and leaving it behind. Following your own trail, catch your own wave and paddle up your own stream. It is bound to be an adventure more memorable than the one you'll find along the gringo trail.

So put your guidebook down for a day or – even better – a week. Explore the places that are not covered in the pages of this guide and discover your own lonely planet.

THESE BOOTS WERE MADE FOR WALKING

With its ample supply of mud, streams and army ants, hiking through Costa Rica's parks can be quite an adventure – particularly for your shoes. Footwear is a personal issue, but here are some options for keeping your feet happy in the jungle.

- Do as the locals and invest in galoshes (rubber boots), especially for the rainy season. Rubber boots are indestructible, protect you from snakes and ticks, provide excellent traction and can be easily hosed off at the end of the day. The downside of the rubber boots is that they are not very comfortable. Plus, river crossings guarantee that the boots will fill up with water at some point, and then your feet are wet for the rest of the day. If you are larger than a size 44 – men's 10 in the US – consider buying them abroad. Price: approximately US$6.

- High-end sport sandals (like Chacos or Tevas) are used by climbers to scramble up boulders to the starting points for climbing routes. These are great for crossing rivers, as the water runs right off them (and your feet). However, be aware that there are lots of creepy crawlies living in the rain forest, some of which might like to make lunch out of your toes, and sandals offer little protection. Price: US$50 to US$100.

- There is something to be said for good, solid, waterproof hiking boots. You don't have to pay an arm and a leg for sturdy boots that offer strong support and keep your feet marginally dry. If you can't stand the idea of walking around with wet feet, consider tossing a pair of sandals into your pack too, and change your shoes for the river crossings. Price: US$80 to US$200.

Some of the local park offices have maps, but this is the exception rather than the rule. If you are planning to do independent hiking on long-distance trails, be sure to purchase your maps in San José in advance (see p534).

MOUNTAIN BIKING

Some cyclists claim that the steep, narrow, winding and potholed roads and aggressive Costa Rican drivers add up to a poor cycling experience. This may be true of the main roads, but there are numerous less-trafficked roads that offer plenty of adventure – from winding and scenic mountain paths with sweeping views to rugged trails that take riders through streams and by volcanoes. For information on tour operators, see p525.

DIVING & SNORKELING

There's good news and there's bad news. The good news is that Costa Rica offers body-temperature water with few humans and abundant marine life. The bad news is that the visibility is low because of silt and plankton. If you are looking for turquoise waters and plenty of hard coral, head for Belize and Honduras. However, if you're looking for fine opportunities to see massive schools of fish as well as larger marine animals such as turtles, sharks, dolphins and whales, then you have arrived in exactly the right place.

It is illegal to swim with dolphins and whales in Costa Rica.

Some of the best areas for diving and snorkeling are off the northern part of the Península de Nicoya at **Playas del Coco** (p255), **Ocotal** (p263) and **Hermosa** (p261), where you can expect to see manta rays, sharks and dozens of species of fish, all in large numbers. See also the boxed text Divers Do It Deeper, p259. Dive shops in the area provide gear and guides, as well as offer courses.

Another top dive spot is **Isla del Caño** (p406), which is home to giant schools of fish. You can organize excursions to Isla del Caño in **Bahía Drake** (p401).

The Caribbean coast offers fewer opportunities for snorkeling and diving, although **Puerto Viejo de Talamanca** (p481) and nearby **Manzanillo** (p492) are emerging centers. Most snorkel trips and dives are fairly easy and nontechnical, making this a good place for beginners.

Costa Rica is home to one world-class dive destination, namely **Isla del Cocos** (p443), which is 500km and a 36-hour ocean journey southwest of the Costa Rican mainland. Although its home to an astonishing amount of marine life, the island does not allow camping and does not provide accommodations, so you'll be spending a lot of quality time on your boat.

For practical information about diving see p523.

WHITE-WATER RAFTING & SEA KAYAKING

The waters off of Isla del Cocos are home to schooling scalloped hammerheads, countless white-tip reef sharks and even whale sharks.

Since the mid-1980s, rafting and kayaking have been major contributors to the country's ecotourism-based economy. From Class II to Class V, Costa Rica's rivers offer magical white-water experiences for both first-time runners and seasoned enthusiasts. The wildest months are from June through October, though rafting can be done year-round.

The country's most popular rafting rivers are the Pacuare and Reventazón, both located in the Central Valley town of **Turrialba** (p159). North of Turrialba, the little-known town of **La Virgen** (p512) is famous in white-water circles as a base for rafting and kayaking on the Río Sarapiquí. Several rivers near the thriving tourist mecca of **Manuel Antonio** (p347) on the central Pacific coast also offer great white water and wildlife-watching year-round.

With 1228km of coastline, two gulfs and plentiful mangrove estuaries, Costa Rica is an ideal destination for sea kayaking. Sea kayaking is a great way for beginning or expert paddlers to comfortably access remote areas and catch rare glimpses of birds and wildlife.

On the Pacific side, the Península de Nicoya's **Refugio Nacional de Vida Silvestre Curú** (p302) offers stunning paddling along palm-lined beaches, rock arch formations and estuaries teeming with birds and colorful crabs. On the central Pacific coast, **Isla Damas** (p340) and the nearby **Parque Nacional Manuel Antonio** (p354) are equally as riveting.

In the Shadow of a Sphere, by Tom Youngholm, is an imaginative – almost supernatural – novel about a young musician's adventures on Costa Rica's white water.

On the Península de Osa, the Río Agujitas in **Bahía Drake** (p401) and the mangroves around **Puerto Jiménez** (p409) are optimal for exploration by kayak.

Heading over to the Caribbean side, **Parque Nacional Tortuguero** (p459) is a coastal park that spans approximately 31,000 hectares and is well known for its amazing network of lagoons and canals.

Details on river trips and outfitters are given in the regional chapters of this book, or see p526.

SURFING

Point and beach breaks, lefts and rights, reefs and river mouths, warm water and year-round waves make Costa Rica a favorite surfing destination. See the surfer's map (p75) for an idea of what's around.

Waves are big (though not Hawaii-big) and the many reef breaks offer hollow and fast rides. For the most part, the Pacific coast has bigger swells and better waves during the latter part of the rainy season, but the Caribbean cooks from November to May. Basically, there is a wave, somewhere, waiting to be surfed at any time of the year.

If you are in the market for a good, cheap board, great places to start your search include **Jacó** (p330), **Mal País** and **Santa Teresa** (p311), and **Tamarindo** (p273). It's usually possible to buy a cheap long board for about US$250 to US$300, and a cheap short board for about US$150 to US$200. Most surf shops will buy back your board for about 50% of the price you paid.

For the uninitiated, lessons are available at almost all of the major surfing destinations. On the Pacific coast, Jacó and Tamarindo are popular places to learn.

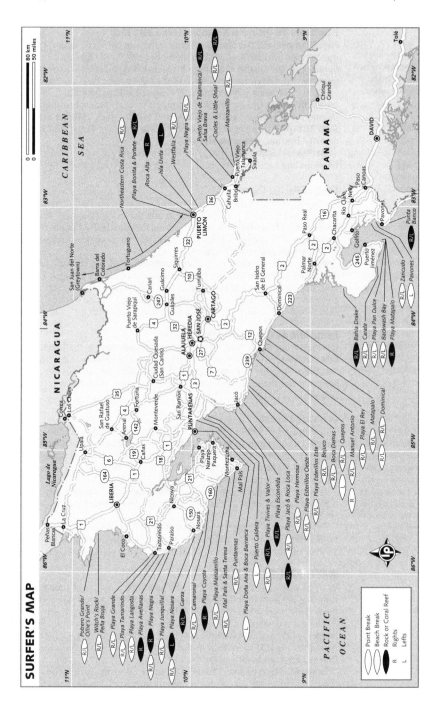

SURFER'S MAP

80 km
50 miles

0
0

CARIBBEAN SEA

PANAMA

NICARAGUA

PACIFIC OCEAN

Key locations and labels:

Tolé
Chiriquí Grande
DAVID
Paso Canoas
Neily
Río Claro
Golfito
Punta Banco
Puerto Jiménez
Pavones
Zancudo
Palmar Norte
Paso Real
Chacarita
Dominical
San Isidro de El General
CARTAGO
SAN JOSÉ
ALAJUELA
HEREDIA
Turrialba
Siquirres
Guácimo
Cariari
Guápiles
PUERTO LIMÓN
Cahuita
Bribrí
Sixaola
Puerto Viejo de Talamanca
Manzanillo
Tortuguero
Barra del Colorado
San Juan del Norte (Greytown)
Puerto Viejo de Sarapiquí
Ciudad Quesada (San Carlos)
Fortuna
San Rafael de Guatuso
Arenal
Cañas
Upala
Los Chiles
Cañas
Lago de Nicaragua
La Cruz
Peñas Blancas
El Coco
Tamarindo
Paraíso
Nosara
Nicoya
Paquera
Montezuma
Mal País
Playa Naranjo
San Ramón
Monteverde
PUNTARENAS
Jacó
Quepos
Manuel Antonio

Road numbers: 36, 32, 10, 247, 4, 33, 27, 7, 3, 1, 35, 142, 4, 19, 18, 164, 6, 21, 150, 160, 21, 12, 239, 2, 223, 245, 16, 2, 2, 2

Surf spots (with labels)

Caribbean (Northeastern Costa Rica):
- Playa Bonita & Portete — R/L
- Roca Alta — R
- Isla Uvita — L
- Westfalia — R/L
- Playa Negra — R/L
- Puerto Viejo de Talamanca/Salsa Brava — R/L
- Cocles & Little Shoal — R/L

Pacific (south):
- Bahía Drake — R/L
- Carate — R/L
- Playa Pan Dulce — R/L
- Backwash Bay — R/L
- Playa Matapalo — R
- Matapalo — R/L
- Dominical — R/L
- Playa El Rey — R/L
- Quepos — R/L
- Boca Damas — R/L
- Bejuco — R/L
- Playa Esterillos Este — R/L
- Playa Escondida — R/L
- Playa Hermosa — R/L
- Playa Jacó & Roca Loca — R/L
- Playa Tivives & Valor — R/L
- Puerto Caldera — L
- Playa Doña Ana & Boca Barranca — R/L
- Mal País & Santa Teresa — L
- Puntarenas
- Playa Manzanillo — R/L
- Playa Coyote — R
- Camaronal — R/L
- Playa Garza — R/L
- Playa Nosara — R/L
- Playa Junquillal — L
- Playa Negra — R/L
- Playa Avellanas — R/L
- Playa Langosta — R
- Playa Tamarindo — R/L
- Playa Grande — R/L
- Witch's Rock/Peña Bruja — R/L
- Potrero Grande/Ollie's Point — R/L
- Pavones — L
- Punta Banco — R/L
- Zancudo

Legend
- Point Break
- Beach Break
- Rock or Coral Reef
- R Rights
- L Lefts

Península de Nicoya & Northwestern Costa Rica

Log on to the Costa Rica Surf Report (www.crsurf .com) and check out Costa Rica's surf scene.

Playa Tamarindo (p273) is Surf City, USA. Tamarindo has been a major surfing mecca ever since Patrick and Wingnut stopped here in the film classic *Endless Summer II*. The smaller beaches in town may be good places to learn, but more-experienced surfers will appreciate the bigger, faster (and less-crowded) waves at **Playas Negra** and **Avellanas** (p277) as well as **Playa Junquillal** (p280), to the south. These are also possible jumping-off points for excursions to the infamous beach breaks at Ollie's Point and Witch's Rock in **Parque Nacional Santa Rosa** (p221). The most consistent waves are north of Tamarindo on the deserted beaches of **Playa Grande** (p267).

Mal País and **Santa Teresa** (p311) are in their second generation as surf destinations and have a groovy scene to match the powerful waves.

Central Pacific Coast

Surfing is generally better during the rainy season on the Pacific coast. But teeming **Jacó** (p330) is perhaps the exception that proves the rule, offering consistent surf year-round. If you can't stand the crowds, head south to **Playa Hermosa** (p339), where bigger, faster curls attract a more determined (and experienced) crew of wave-chasers.

Further south on the Pacific coast, **Dominical** (p360) is a laidback surfing destination with some wicked waves. It is less developed than the other Pacific coast destinations, but still has something of a scene (including one surf camp and a few places to rent boards). Nearby, **Matapalo** (p358) also offers amazing surf, though it is relatively unknown (meaning more waves for you).

Península de Osa & Golfo Dulce

On the Península de Osa, you'll find good, steady surf at the beaches of **Cabo Matapalo** (p413). Across the sweet waters of the Golfo Dulce lies the legendary long left at **Pavones** (p440). During the rainy season, die-hard surfers make the grueling four-hour journey over rocky roads to reach this world-class surf spot.

Caribbean Coast

In Search of Captain Zero, by Allen Weisbecker, recounts his adventures trying to track down his long-lost pal and a few good waves. Don't be surprised if you run into Captain Zero in Puerto Viejo.

The southern Caribbean coast is basically one long surf paradise, from Puerto Limón south to the Panamanian border. **Puerto Viejo de Talamanca** (p478) is infamous for the reef break at Salsa Brava, but it is for experts only. The slightly less intimidating beach break at Playa Cocles is also popular and excellent for learners.

If you are not into the surf scene, but still appreciate a good wave, Playa Negra in **Cahuita** (p469) is less competitive and less crowded (but the waves are still consistent).

Off the coast of Puerto Limón, **Isla Uvita** (p455) is a destination for adventurous surfers, as it is uninhabited and has no facilities. **Manzanillo** (p490) is another off-the-beaten-track destination, but bring your own board.

WATERFALL RAPPELLING

With its many pretty waterfalls, it just had to be a matter of time before someone in Costa Rica decided it'd be a good idea to rappel down one of them. This is great fun for rock-climbing types who like to get wet.

The main destination for waterfall rappelling is the area around **Puerto Jiménez** (p408) and **Cabo Matapalo** (p413) on the Península de Osa. Everyday Adventures (p413) specializes in the sport, but most of the lodges in the Jiménez area can book you on tours.

In the Monteverde area, Desafío Adventure Company (p178) also offers these types of adventures, as does Exploranatura (p157) in Turrialba.

SPORTFISHING

Fishing enthusiasts flock to both of Costa Rica's coasts for the thrill of reeling in mammoth marlins and supersized sailfish. With that said, most sportfishing companies encourage 'catch and release' practices so as not to deplete fish populations. Despite this conscientious effort, sportfishing is often the target of local criticism, mainly because of the big-spending, free-wheeling reputation of the clientele.

On the Pacific coast, both **Tamarindo** (p272) and **Quepos** (p343) offer plenty of opportunities for offshore fishing. The main attraction is the Pacific sailfish, which swims in these waters between December and April.

The Golfo Dulce is probably Costa Rica's top spot for fishing, especially for dorado, marlin, sailfish and tuna. Fishing operators work out of **Puerto Jiménez** (p410), **Golfito** (p433) and **Zancudo** (p437). The latter is also excellent for snook, which inhabit the surrounding mangrove swamps, especially from May to September.

Nearby, **Bahía Drake** (p401) claims more than 40 fishing records, including sailfish, three kinds of marlin, yellow fin tuna, wahoo, cubera snapper, Spanish and sierra mackerel and roosterfish.

There is also fishing up and down the Caribbean coast, especially in the remote northern outpost of **Barra del Colorado** (p466). Top-end fishing lodges attract world-class anglers in search of snook (September through December) and tarpon (January through June). The luxury lodges in the area go to great lengths to provide their clients with all the creature comforts, even in the far corners of Costa Rica. In **Cahuita** (p469) you'll find more barebones operations catering to simple folk who wish to drop a line.

The Big Book of Adventure Travel, by James C Simmons, is a worthwhile investment for anyone interested in the subject; it covers the entire planet, but numerous itineraries in Costa Rica are featured.

San José

Like it or loathe it, Chepe, as the capital is affectionately known by Ticos (Costa Ricans), is the beating heart of Costa Rica. Somewhat unjustly, it receives a bad rap among visitors to this part of the world. True, the rapid transformation from prewar agrarian coffee town to late-20th-century urban sprawl was somewhat unkind to the city – its architecture, especially. But it certainly isn't the offensive monstrosity some would have you believe.

San José's charm is in the raw hustle and bustle of its downtown streets. Here, vendors selling everything from handbags to hacky sacks try to out-holler the tooting horns and spluttering bus engines that provide the harmony to the city's soundtrack. The central markets are beehives of energy, where old women shuffle around squeezing mangos and inspecting fish gills. There's diversity, too: Nicaraguans, Colombians, Panamanians and others from around the continent have flocked to the city's relative prosperity, making it Central America's most cosmopolitan capital. Yet it's small enough to be covered on foot, and from every part of the city you can see the towering verdant hills around it.

San José's reputation may suffer most as a result of its surrounds: visitors come to Costa Rica for the sloth-filled rain forests, crocodile-infested backwaters and gnarly surf breaks – none of which are found in the unavoidable capital. But in a country that's somewhat culturally diluted by vast amounts of tourism, there's nowhere better to truly get in touch with the guts-and-gravel of Costa Rican culture. You'll find that most Ticos agree: to truly love Costa Rica, you must first learn to love its capital.

HIGHLIGHTS

- Ogling shiny precious objects at the **Museo de Arte y Diseño Contemporáneo** (p84) and the **Museo de Jade** (p85)

- Taking in the historic **Barrio Amón** (p86) or kicking a ball around the extensive greens of **La Sabana** (p86)

- Partying all night long in **Centro Comercial El Pueblo** (p104) and on **Calle de la Amargura** (p116)

- Sipping cocktails in **Escazú** (p122), a well-to-do San José 'burb

- POPULATION: CITY 350,000, GREATER METRO AREA OVER 1.5 MILLION
- AREA: 2366 SQ KM

HISTORY

The future capital of Costa Rica was established in 1737 as Villanueva de la Boca del Monte del Valle de Abra (New Village of the Mountain's Mouth in the Open Valley), though the name was later changed to a more manageable San José in honor of Joseph, the town's patron saint. Interestingly enough, the founding of San José was the result of an edict from the Catholic Church, which decreed that the populace must settle near a place of worship (attendance was down, times were bad and churches were cheap to build).

For much of the colonial period, San José played second fiddle to the bigger and relatively more established Cartago. Following the surprise announcement in 1821 that Spain had abandoned its colonial holdings in Central America, Cartago and San José signed a series of empty-worded accords while secretly preparing for battle. On April 5, 1823, San José defeated Cartago at the Battle of Ochomongo, and subsequently declared itself capital. (This fierce rivalry is still evident on the football field when San José's and Cartogo's teams clash.)

Although San José generously offered to rotate capital status, bitterness ensued, and on September 26, 1835, Cartago, Heredia and Alajuela joined forces in an attempt to sack the city. In a siege that became known as La Guerra de la Liga (the War of the Leagues), San José defeated its attackers and retained its status as the capital.

Recent years have been marked by a massive urban migration as Ticos (and increasingly Nicaraguans, see boxed text Nica vs Tico, p229) move to the capital in search of increased economic opportunities. Unfortunately, this has resulted in the creation of shantytowns on the outskirts of the capital, and crime is increasingly becoming a way of life for many poverty-stricken inhabitants. Ticos are quick to point fingers at the Nicaraguans (as well as the Panamanians and Colombians) for causing the degradation of their capital, and although the extreme poverty these groups are forced to live in is part of the problem, the total picture is much more complex.

ORIENTATION

The city is in the heart of a wide and fertile valley called the Meseta Central (Central Valley). San José's center is arranged in a grid with avenidas running east to west and calles running north to south. Avenida Central is the nucleus of the city center and is a pedestrian mall between Calles 6 and 9. It becomes Paseo Colón to the west of Calle 14.

Street addresses are given by the nearest street intersection. Thus, the address of the tourist office is Calle 5 between Avenidas Central and 2. Note that the map used in this book shows the streets and avenues. However, most locals do not use street addresses and instead use landmarks to guide them. Learn how to decipher Tico directions by reading the boxed text What's That Address?, p537.

The center has several districts, or *barrios*, which are all loosely defined. The central area is home to innumerable businesses, shops, bus stops and cultural sights. Perhaps the most interesting district to visitors is Barrio Amón, northeast of Avenida 5 and Calle 1, with its concentration of landmark mansions, largely converted into hotels and fine-dining establishments. Just west of the city center is La Sabana, named after the park, and just north of it is the elegant suburb of Rohrmoser. Further west again is the affluent outer suburb of Escazú. Southeast of the downtown area are the lively student areas of Los Yoses and San Pedro.

Look for maps at Lehmann's (below), Librería Universal (below) or the tourist center (p82).

INFORMATION

Bookstores

English-language magazines, newspapers and books are also available in the gift shops of the international airport and several of the top-end hotels. The following bookstores are among the most noteworthy:

7th Street Books (Map p88; ☎ 2256 8251; Calle 7 btwn Avs Central & 1; ⏲ 9am-6pm) An attractive shop with new and used books in English and other languages as well as magazines and newspapers.

Lehmann's (Map p88; ☎ 2223 1212; Av Central btwn Calles 1 & 3) It has some books, magazines and newspapers in English, and a selection of topographical and other Costa Rican maps in the upstairs map department.

Librería Francesa (Map p88; ☎ 2223 7979; Av 1 btwn Calles 5 & 7) Spanish books and magazines are available here, and there is also a selection of French, German and English titles.

Librería Universal (Map p88; ☎ 2222 2222; Av Central btwn Calles Central & 1) Situated on the 2nd floor of

SAN JOSÉ & ENVIRONS

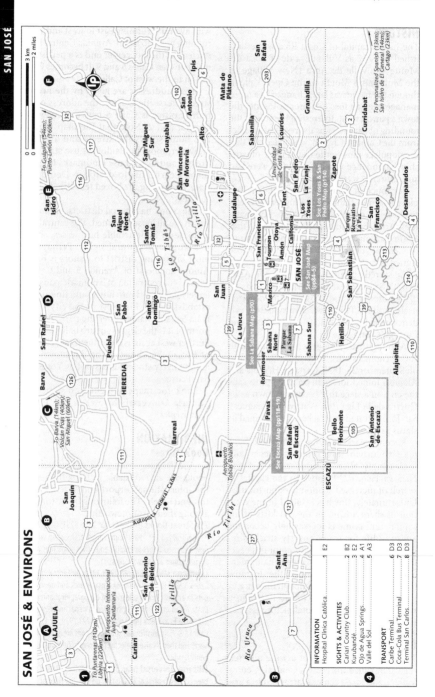

GETTING INTO TOWN

Taxis to downtown San José from Juan Santamaría international airport will cost between US$20 and US$25 depending on traffic. When leaving the airport terminal, look for the official **Taxi Aeropuerto stand** (☎ 2221 6865; www.taxiaeropuerto.com) as you exit the baggage-claim area, and pay the flat rate of US$20 in advance. The official airport taxis are orange. The ride generally lasts about 20 minutes, but may take over an hour during rush hour.

The cheapest option, however, is the red Tuasa bus (US$0.75, up to 45 minutes), which runs between Alajuela and San José, and passes the airport every few minutes from 5am to 11pm. The stop is on the far side of the parking lot outside the terminal (it's a short walk, even with luggage). Some taxi drivers will tell you there are no buses; don't believe them. The **Interbus** (☎ 2283 5573; www.interbusonline.com) is a good deal and it runs an airport shuttle service that costs US$5 per person. Reservations can be made online.

International and domestic buses all arrive at one of the many bus terminals sprinkled around the west and south of downtown San José. The downtown area is perfectly walkable provided you aren't hauling a lot of luggage. If arriving at night, take a taxi to your hotel as most bus terminals are in seedy areas; a taxi to any part of downtown costs US$1 to US$2.

Be aware that many taxi drivers in San José (and other parts of Costa Rica) are commissioned by hotels to bring them customers. In the capital, the hotel scene is so competitive that drivers will say just about anything to steer you to the places they represent. They'll tell you the establishment you've chosen is a notorious drug den, it's closed down, or that, sadly, it's overbooked. (Many owners will tell you wild stories about the horrible condition of the rooms at the competition down the street.) Do not believe everything you hear. Tell drivers firmly where it is you would like to go, and if you're still being met with resistance, get out of the taxi and try another.

---

the Universal department store, the shop has road and topographical maps, a few books in English and a small café inside.

Libro Azul (Map p88; Av 10 btwn Calles Central & 1; 🕑 8:30am-12:30pm & 1:30-5:30pm Mon-Fri, 9am-noon Sat) A tiny, well-known shop offering secondhand books, mostly in Spanish and some in English.

Mora Books (Map p88; ☎ 2255 4136, 8383 8385; Omni Center, Av 1 btwn Calles 3 & 5) Highly recommended secondhand bookstore has books mainly in English; guidebooks and comic books are a specialty.

Emergency
Emergencies (☎ 911) Ambulance, fire and police.
Fire (☎ 118)
Police (☎ 117)
Red Cross (☎ 128)
Traffic Police (☎ 2222 9330)

Internet Access
Checking email is easy in San José, where cybercafés are more plentiful than fruit peddlers. Rates are generally US$1 to US$2 per hour, though these days most hotels (even budget hostels) provide free internet access to guests.

1@10 Café Internet (Map p88; ☎ 2258 4561; www.1en10.com; per hr US$1; Calle 3 btwn Avs 5 & 7) Also serves as the gay and lesbian information center.

CyberCafé searchcostarica.com (Map p88; ☎ 2233 3310; Las Arcadas, Av 2 btwn Calles 1 & 3; per hr US$0.75; 🕑 7am-11pm) Houses a book exchange and a pizza bar.

Laundry
A do-it-yourself laundry service is hard to find in San José. Most lavanderías offer only dry-cleaning services. Many hotels and hostels offer a laundry service, but beware of top-end places that charge by the piece because this gets pricey.

Medical Services
For details of a hospital in Escazú, see p117. Note that both the Bíblica and Católica have pharmacies.

Clínica Bíblica (Map pp84-5; ☎ 2257 5252; www .clinicabiblica.com; Av 14 btwn Calles Central & 1) The top private clinic in the downtown area. Doctors speak English, French and German, and an emergency room is open 24 hours. Be prepared to pay for medical attention, though costs are generally much lower than in the USA or Europe.

Hospital Clínica Católica (Map p80; ☎ 2246 3000; www.clinicacatolica.com; Guadalupe) A private clinic located north of downtown.

Hospital San Juan de Dios (Map pp84-5; ☎ 2257 6282; cnr Paseo Colón & Calle 14) The free public hospital is centrally located, but waits are long.

Money

Any bank will change foreign currency into colones, but US dollars are by far the most accepted currency for exchange, with euros following a distant second. Upmarket hotels have exchange windows for their guests, but commissions can be steep so check before changing large sums.

Credit cards are widely accepted in San José, though Visa tends to be preferred over MasterCard and American Express. (For more information on money issues in Costa Rica, see p535.)

Banco de Costa Rica (Map p88; ☎ 2221 8143; www .bancobcr.com; Av 1 btwn Calles 7 & 9; 8:30am-6pm Mon-Fri)

Banco de San José (Map p88; ☎ 2295 9595; www .bancosanjose.fi.cr; Av 2 btwn Calles Central & 1; 8am-7pm Mon-Fri, 9am-1pm Sat) Has ATMs on the Plus and Cirrus systems.

Banco Nacional de Costa Rica Exchange House (Map p88; cnr Av Central & Calle 4; 10:30am-6pm) A good find in the event of a Sunday cash-exchange emergency since it's open seven days; expect long lines.

Compañía Financiera de Londres (Map p88; ☎ 2222 8155; cnr Calle Central & Av Central, 3rd fl; 8:15am-4pm Mon-Fri) No commission on cash transactions and accepts US and Canadian dollars, euros and yen. Will also change traveler's checks.

Credomatic (Map p88; ☎ 2295 9000; Banco de San José, Calle Central btwn Avs 3 & 5) Gives cash advances on Visa and MasterCard.

Scotiabank (Map p88; ☎ 2287 8700; www.scotiabank .com; Av 1 btwn Calles 2 & 4; 8:15am-5pm Mon-Fri) Good service, and ATMs on the Cirrus system dispense US dollars, too.

Post

Correo Central (Central Post Office; Map p88; ☎ 2223 9766; www.correos.go.cr; Calle 2 btwn Avs 1 & 3; 8am-5pm Mon-Fri, 7:30am-noon Sat) The most efficient place to send and receive mail in Costa Rica. It also offers express and overnight services. A small stamp museum is upstairs on the 2nd floor, and there's also a pleasant café.

Telephone

Local and international calls can be made from most public phones, which are all over town – several dozen are on the west side of Parque Central and around Plaza de la Cultura. Many hotels also have public phones in their lobbies. Chip and Colibrí cards are sold at souvenir shops, newsstands and Más X Menos supermarkets. Telephone directories are usually available in hotels.

For general information on phone services, see p536.

Tourist Information

Canatur (☎ 2234 6222; www.costarica.tourism.co.cr; Juan Santamaría international airport; 8am-10pm) The Costa Rican National Chamber of Tourism provides information on member services from a small stand next to the international baggage claim.

Instituto Costarricense de Turismo (ICT; ☎ 2223 1733, ext 277; www.visitcostarica.com; 9am-5pm with flexible lunch Mon-Fri); Correo Central (Map p88; Calle 2 btwn Avs 1 & 3); Plaza de la Cultura (Map p88; Calle 5 btwn Av Central & 2) The government tourism office is good for a copy of the master bus schedule and handy free maps of San José and Costa Rica.

Travel Agencies

The following are long-standing and reputable agencies. For a list of tour companies, see p93.

OTEC (Map p88; ☎ 2256 0633; www.turismojoven.com; Calle 3 btwn Avs 1 & 3) Specializes in youth travel; can also issue student discount cards.

TAM Travel Corporation (Map p88 ☎ 2256 0203; www.tamtravel.com; Calle 1 btwn Avs Central & 1) Airline ticketing, local travel and more.

DANGERS & ANNOYANCES

Street crime has been a major problem for tourists visiting San José over the last few years, and has been one of the principal reasons people have left the city with an unfavorable opinion. However, after years of hot air coming from the government buildings about what should be done to protect the much-targeted tourists, something is being done. In 2007 reported crime against tourists (most of which is petty theft) was down 36% in San José. This is largely due to the creation of the Tourist Police at the beginning of that year. However, precautions are still necessary, as the problem of street theft, such as pickpocketing, still exists. Fortunately, violent crime is still low compared to US and European cities. Like in any other city, use common sense. Always carry your money and your passport in an inside pocket or a money belt and never ever leave money, passports or important documents in the outer pocket of your backpack – you could regret it later. Also, it's a good idea to keep daypacks in front of you rather than on your back, where they can be unzipped and pilfered.

WORD ON THE STREET

Rafael Ferrera has been a taxi driver in San Jose for 12 years. He's lived in the city all his life.

What are your comments on crime and tourism? Tourists should be cautious in San José. In this city you can see a foreigner from a mile away. They stick out with their pale skin and lost look on their face. I don't understand why they need to carry so much stuff with them all the time: rucksack, money-belt, camera, sunglasses... It's no wonder they get robbed so often. The thieves must think they have too much stuff to carry and want to help them out!

Taxi drivers and tourists have lots of problems in San José. Everyone knows this. But it works both ways. Just as some taxi drivers are dishonest, some tourists are paranoid. They can be very rude and always accuse us of trying to cheat them.

I think tourists can get victimized in San José because of their attitude. A lot of tourists treat every local like a crook, so the locals in turn aren't very nice to them. They need to relax more, be more Tico. And embrace the *pura vida,* rather than be so uptight.

Unfortunately, muggings still occur in San José. If you're ever held at knifepoint or gunpoint, do not resist or fight back. Take your wallet out of your pocket slowly and calmly, and either hand it to your assailant or place it on the ground and step back. Do not try to be a hero!

The best way to prevent problems is to first find out from your hotel or other travelers about the area you're going to and, if possible, go with a friend. As a general rule, avoid wearing expensive jewelry or flashy watches in the city, and always walk confidently. If you are barhopping at night, always travel by taxi.

If you have been the victim of a crime, it is advised that you file a report in person at the **Organismo de Investigacíon Judicial** (Map pp84-5; 9am-5pm Mon-Fri) in the Supreme Court of Justice building.

The neighborhoods reviewed in this book are generally safe during the day, though you should be especially careful around the Coca-Cola bus terminal and the red-light district south of Parque Central, particularly at night. The following neighborhoods are reportedly dodgy during the day and unsafe at night: Leon XIII, 15 de Septiembre, Cuba, Cristo Rey, Sagrada Familia, México, Bajo Piuses, Los Cuadros, Torremolinos, Desamparados and Pavas. Be advised that like in most major cities, adjacent neighborhoods can vary greatly in terms of safety. If you are going to spend time in an area of the city that you are not familiar with, always inquire locally before setting out.

It is not recommended that you drive in San José, and there is very little reason to as

most car-rental agencies are located near the airport, outside of the city. However, if you have business in the city, never leave your car parked on the street – use guarded lots. And don't leave anything inside your car – even in a guarded lot. Most importantly, take care not to be swallowed up by the pit-size gutters and potholes.

Like anywhere else in the world, women traveling alone should take extra precautions. In the past, some women have complained of being harassed by taxi drivers at night – avoid taking unlicensed taxis. Also, it is not safe to walk around alone at night. (Further information for women travelers is available on p539.)

Men should beware of friendly prostitutes as they are known for their abilities to take more than their customers bargained for – namely their wallets. Also, AIDS is on the rise in Central America, and although the Costa Rican government is tolerant of prostitution, it's certainly not regulated (this isn't Amsterdam).

Finally, noise and smog are unavoidable components of the San José experience, and most central hotels are victim to a considerable amount of street noise, no matter how nice they are.

SIGHTS

The downtown area is fairly small and is best visited on foot as the streets are congested with heavy traffic and parking is difficult. Pedestrian walkways are located on Avenida Central between Plaza de la Cultura and Calle 8, and on Blvd Ricardo Jimenez south of the Parque Nacional.

SAN JOSÉ

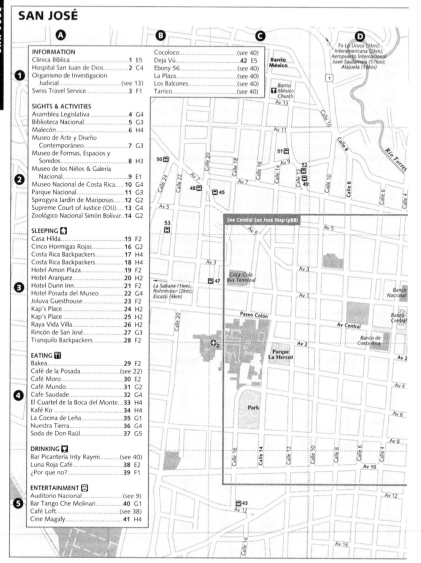

The sights here are listed in counterclockwise fashion around the city, beginning with the contemporary art museum just east of Parque España.

Museo de Arte y Diseño Contemporáneo

Commonly referred to as MADC, this **museum** (Contemporary Art & Design Museum; Map pp84-5; 2257 7202; www.madc.ac.cr; Av 3 btwn Calles 13 & 15; admission US$1; 10am-5pm Tue-Sat) is housed in the historic National Liquor Factory building, which dates to 1856. MADC primarily shows the contemporary work of Costa Rican and Central American artists, though rotating exhibitions are frequently on display here as well.

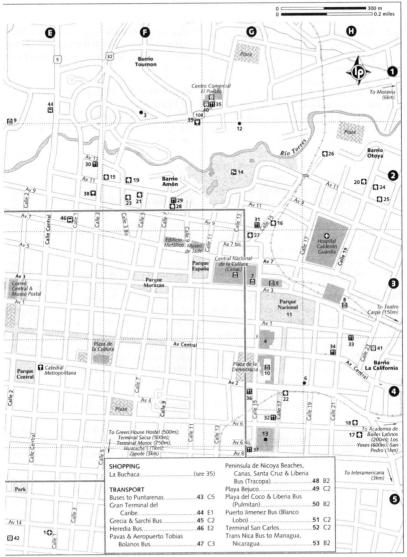

Museo de Jade

San José's most famous **museum** (Map p88;
☎ 2287 6034; Edificio INS, Av 7 btwn Calles 9 & 11, 11th
fl; adult/child 10 & under US$2/free; 🕑 8:30am-3:30pm
Mon-Fri) is on the 1st floor of the Instituto
Nacional de Seguros (National Insurance
Institute). The museum houses the world's
largest collection of American jade (say it
with us – ha-day), and is usually packed with
tour groups. But the craftsmanship of each
gemstone on display is exquisite, and the various archaeological exhibits of ceramics and
stonework are helpful in gaining an insight
to Costa Rica's pre-Columbian cultures (especially if you've already been to or you're
going to Guayabo).

Barrio Amón

This pleasant **neighborhood** (Map pp84–5) is one of the few remaining colonial districts in the city, and home to many of the city's few surviving *cafétalero* (coffee baron) mansions, which were constructed during the late-19th and early-20th centuries. Recently, many of these buildings have been converted into hotels, restaurants and offices, which makes this district perfect for a leisurely stroll. Barrio Amón, which is one of the safest areas in the city, is becoming increasingly popular with tourists, and there are currently talks of creating a pedestrian walkway and restoring many of the historic buildings. This isn't likely to happen for several years, though the crumbling mansions are presently not without a certain charm.

If you're wandering around Barrio Amón, the **Galería Andrómeda** (Map p88; ☎ 2223 3529; andromeda@amnet.co.cr; cnr Calle 9 & Av 9) is a free local art space behind the Museo de Jade. It's worth a peek to see works by emerging local artists.

Zoológico Nacional Simón Bolívar

It seems kind of absurd to have a **zoo** (Map pp84–5; ☎ 2233 6701; Av 11 btwn Calles 7 & 9; admission US$2; 8am-3:30pm Mon-Fri, 9am-4:30pm Sat & Sun) in one of the most biologically rich countries in the world, but what do we know – we just write travel guides. Readers have complained in the past of filthy cages and cramped living spaces, though a recent increase in funds has drastically improved living conditions for the animals.

Spirogyra Jardín de Mariposas

This small **butterfly garden** (Map pp84–5; ☎ 2222 2937; parcar@racsa.co.cr; adult/child/student US$6/3/5; 8am-4pm) houses over 30 species of butterflies and five species of hummingbirds in attractive enclosures. Visit during the morning to see the butterflies fluttering in top form. There is a small café that is open during the high season. The garden, 150m east and 150m south of Centro Comercial El Pueblo, can be reached on foot (about a 20- to 30-minute walk from downtown), by taxi, or by bus to El Pueblo, where there is a sign.

Museo de los Niños & Galería Nacional

The unique **Museo de los Niños** (Children's Museum; Map pp84–5; ☎ 2258 4929; www.museocr.com; Calle 4, north of Av 9; admission US$2; 8am-4:30pm Tue-Fri, 9:30am-5pm Sat & Sun) is in an old penitentiary built in 1909, and is known locally as 'La Peni.' While there are plenty of displays for the kids on science, music and geography, grown-ups will be captivated by the **Galería Nacional** (admission free), which displays modern art in old, abandoned prison cells.

Museo Postal, Telegráfico y Filatélico de Costa Rica

Go postal at the **Museo Postal** (Postal Museum; Map p88; ☎ 2223 6918; Correo Central; Calle 2 btwn Avs 1 & 3; admission free; 9am-2pm Mon-Fri), with its semi-interesting exhibit of Costa Rican stamps. It's a good way to kill time while your friends are waiting to mail some letters home.

Mercados (Markets)

Perhaps the best introduction to Latin American culture is a quick stroll through the **Mercado Central** (Map p88; Avs Central & 1 btwn Calles 6 & 8; 6am-6pm Mon-Sat). Although tame compared to the markets of countries like Perú or Guatemala (you can't find pig's heart by the kilo here – we looked), the market is nevertheless crowded and bustling, and you can buy anything from produce and fresh sausage to organic coffee beans and the obligatory *pura vida* souvenir T-shirt. In addition, some of the cheapest fresh meals in town are served here. One block away is the similar **Mercado Borbón** (Map p88; cnr Av 3 & Calle 8), which is also jam-packed with vendors.

Parque Metropolitano La Sabana

This spacious **park** (Map p90) at the west end of the Paseo Colón was once the site of the country's main airport. After an impressive landscape project, it's now the most popular retreat from the grit and the grime of the city. La Sabana is also home to two museums, a lagoon, a fountain and a variety of sports facilities, including the Estadio Nacional (National Stadium), where international and Division-1 soccer matches are played. During the day, it's a great place for a stroll, a quiet picnic or a relaxed jog.

At the west end of Paseo Colón (or the eastern entrance to the park) is the **Museo de Arte Costarricense** (Map p90; ☎ 2222 7155; www.musarco.go.cr; Parque La Sabana; admission US$1, free Sun; 10am-4pm Tue-Sun), which houses a permanent collection of Costa Rican art from the 19th and 20th centuries. The museum itself is an attractive Spanish colonial-style building that served as San José's airport until 1955, and it's next to an impressive open-air sculpture garden. Regular rotating exhibits feature works by Tico artists past and present.

Near the southwest corner of the park is the **Museo de Ciencias Naturales La Salle** (Map p90; ☎ 2232 1306; admission US$2; ⏰ 7:30am-4pm), which has an extensive collection of dusty and dated stuffed animals and butterflies. The exhibit has definitely seen better days, and although some of the animals look like they're about to fall apart, you'd be hard pressed to find a more bizarre display of taxidermy. There are also a number of exhibits on paleontology and Pre-Columbian archaeology. It's in the old Colegio La Salle (high school).

Parque Central

The city's central **park** (Map p88; Avs 2 & 4 btwn Calles Central & 2) is home to a dome-roofed bandstand that was donated to the city by former Nicaraguan dictator Anastasio Somoza. It's a bit of a controversial piece actually, though josefinos voted several years ago to keep it because, well, what else were they going to do with it?

To the east of the square is the modern, though classically inspired, **Catedral Metropolitana** (Map p88; Avs 2 & 4 btwn Calles Central & 1), which is among the city's more popular cathedrals for Sunday Mass.

On the north side of the park is **Teatro Melico Salazar** (Map p88; Av 2 btwn Calle Central & 2), which was built to serve as the poor man's alternative to the Teatro Nacional. However, it was the site of the 2002 presidential inauguration, and regularly hosts a variety of fine arts engagements and musical performances (p106).

Plaza de la Cultura

Though it's not particularly striking, virtually every Tico refers to this **plaza** (Map p88; Avs Central & 2 btwn Calles 3 & 5) as the geographic heart of Costa Rica. Coincidentally, it's also the safest place in the city as the entire plaza is the ceiling of the **Museo de Oro Precolombino**, and is considered private property (this gives security guards the right to shoo away 'unsavory' characters). It's also home to the Teatro Nacional, and there is great birding here – feral pigeons are commonly sighted.

The plaza is also home to the Instituto Costarricense de Turismo (p82), which has travel information and maps.

MUSEO DE ORO PRECOLOMBINO Y NUMISMÁTICA

Beneath the Plaza de la Cultura is this three-in-one **museum** (Map p88; ☎ 2243 4202; www.museos delbancocentral.org; basement, Plaza de la Cultura; admission US$5; ⏰ 10am-4:30pm Tue-Sun). It's owned by the Banco Central, and its architecture brings to mind all the warmth and comfort of a bank vault. The museum is a favorite of tourists as the glittering collection of pre-Columbian gold is well presented, though smaller than similar collections in Mexico and Peru. A small exhibit details the history of Costa Rican currency and another room has a temporary display space for local art.

TEATRO NACIONAL

The **Teatro Nacional** (Map p88; ☎ 2221 1329; Calles 3 & 5 btwn Avs Central & 2; admission US$3; ⏰ 9am-5pm Mon-Fri, 9am-12:30pm & 1:30-5:30pm Sat) is considered San José's most impressive public building. Built in 1897, the building features a columned neoclassical facade and is flanked by statues of Beethoven and Calderón de la Barca, a 17th-century Spanish dramatist. The lavish lobby and auditorium are lined with paintings depicting various facets of 19th-century life. The most famous is *Alegoría al café y el banano,* an idyllic canvas showing coffee and banana harvests. The painting was produced in Italy and shipped to Costa Rica for installation in the theater, and the image was reproduced on the five-colón note (now out of circulation), which you can find in some souvenir shops. However, it is clear that the painter never witnessed a banana harvest because of the way he portrayed a central man awkwardly grasping a bunch. (In case you're wondering, actual banana workers hoist the stem onto their shoulders.)

For information on performances, see p106.

There is also an excellent café (p103) here. Belonging to the national theatre is the very worthwhile **Galería García Monge** (Map p88; cnr Av 2 & Calle 5; admission free), which is located across the street and has rotating exhibitions by contemporary artists.

Museo Para la Paz

The **Museo Para la Paz** (Map p88; ☎ 2223 4664; cnr Av 2 & Calle 13; admission free; ⏰ 8am-noon & 1:30pm-4:30pm Mon-Fri) is operated by the Arias Foundation and catalogs the past efforts of President Oscar Arias, a Nobel Peace Prize laureate,

CENTRAL SAN JOSÉ

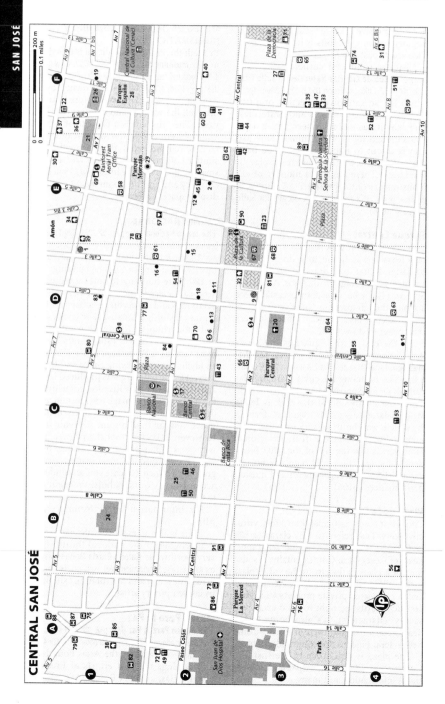

to bring peace to Central America. It also exhibits the work of other laureates, including the Dalai Lama, Jimmy Carter and Lech Walesa. There is also an interesting exhibition on the 2nd floor designed to reconstruct the history of Central America and the Arias Plan for Peace.

Museo Nacional de Costa Rica

The **Museo Nacional** (Map pp84-5; ☎ 2257 1433; Calle 17 btwn Avs Central & 2; adult/student US$4/2; ☼ 8:30am-4:30pm Tue-Sun) is located inside the Bellavista (Good View) Fortress, which served as the old army headquarters and saw fierce fighting (hence the pockmarks) in both the 1931 army mutiny and the 1948 civil war. Ironically, Bellavista was also the site where Costa Rican President José Figueres announced in 1949 that he was abolishing the country's military.

Museo Nacional de Costa Rica is the ideal place for getting a quick survey of Costa Rican history. You will find a wide range of pre-Columbian artifacts from ongoing digs at archeological sites, such as Guayabo, as well as numerous colonial objects and plenty of religious art. The natural-history wing has flora and fauna specimens, minerals and fossils.

Museo de Formas, Espacios y Sonidos

This interactive **museum** (Map pp84-5; ☎ 2222 9462; Av 3 btwn Calles 17 & 23; admission US$1; ☼ 9:30am-3pm Mon-Fri) in the old San José Atlantic train station is geared to small kids or people who want to act like them: you can clamber on an antique locomotive and traipse through old rail cars. There are also several small exhibits dedicated to the senses of sound, touch and sight.

SAN JOSÉ

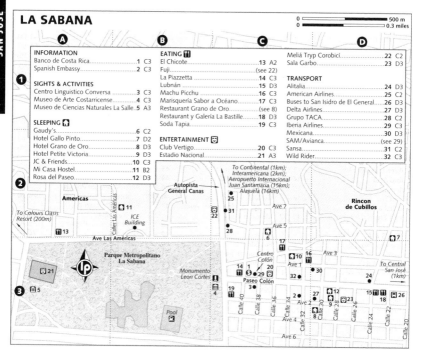

LA SABANA

0 ————— 500 m
0 ————— 0.3 miles

INFORMATION		
Banco de Costa Rica	1	C3
Spanish Embassy	2	C3

SIGHTS & ACTIVITIES		
Centro Linguistico Conversa	3	C3
Museo de Arte Costarricense	4	C3
Museo de Ciencias Naturales La Salle	5	A3

SLEEPING		
Gaudy's	6	C2
Hotel Gallo Pinto	7	D2
Hotel Grano de Oro	8	D3
Hotel Petite Victoria	9	D3
JC & Friends	10	C3
Mi Casa Hostel	11	B2
Rosa del Paseo	12	D3

EATING		
El Chicote	13	A2
Fuji	(see 22)	
La Piazzetta	14	C3
Lubnán	15	D3
Machu Picchu	16	C3
Marisquería Sabor a Océano	17	C3
Restaurant Grano de Oro	(see 8)	
Restaurant y Galería La Bastille	18	D3
Soda Tapia	19	C3

ENTERTAINMENT		
Club Vertigo	20	C3
Estadio Nacional	21	A3

Meliá Tryp Corobici	22	C2
Sala Garbo	23	D3

TRANSPORT		
Alitalia	24	D3
American Airlines	25	C2
Buses to San Isidro de El General	26	D3
Delta Airlines	27	D3
Grupo TACA	28	C2
Iberia Airlines	29	C3
Mexicana	30	D3
SAM/Avianca	(see 29)	
Sansa	31	C3
Wild Rider	32	C3

To Continental (1km);
Interamericana (2km);
Aeropuerto Internacional
Juan Santamaría (15km);
Alajuela (16km)

Autopista
General Cañas

Americas

To Colours Oasis
Resort (200m)

ICE
Building

Ave Las Américas

Parque Metropolitano
La Sabana

Monumento
Leon Cortes

Pool

Centro
Colón

Paseo Colón

Rincon
de Cubillos

To Central
San José
(1km)

A strange sight is the bust outside the museum of Tomás Guardia, who has the curious distinction of constructing the first railroad, and of being one of the only dictators in Costa Rican history.

Eastern Parks & Plazas

Numerous other green areas dot downtown San José, providing a small respite from the steel and concrete of the capital. Note that these parks are not safe after dark, and most of them become centers of prostitution during the twilight hours.

One of the nicest parks in San José is the shady, cobblestone-lined **Parque Nacional** (Map pp84-5; Avs 1 & 3 btwn Calles 15 & 19). In the center of the park is the dramatic **Monumento Nacional**, which depicts the Central American nations (with Costa Rica in the lead, of course) driving out the American filibuster William Walker.

Important buildings surrounding the park include the **Biblioteca Nacional** (National Library) to the north, the Cenac complex, which houses the modern art museum (p84), to the northwest and the **Asamblea Legislativa** (Legislative Assembly) to the south. In the Assembly's

gardens is a statue of national hero Juan Santamaría, who's best known for kicking a certain pesky gringo out of Costa Rica.

South of the Asamblea Legislativa is the stark **Plaza de la Democracia** (Map p88; Avs Central & 2 btwn Calles 13 & 15), which was constructed by President Oscar Arias in 1989 to commemorate 100 years of Costa Rican democracy. The plaza is architecturally unremarkable, though it does provide decent views of the mountains surrounding San José (especially at sunset). On its western flank, is an open-air crafts market with a good selection of gifts (see p107).

Parque España (Map p88; Avs 3 & 7 btwn Calles 9 & 11) is surrounded by heavy traffic, but manages to become a riot of birdsong every day at sunset when the local birds come here to roost. The park is bordered by the black-glass INS building to the north, which serves as the home of the Museo de Jade (p85). A block to the west is the **Edificio Metálico** (Map p88; cnr Av 7 & Calle 9), an interesting two-story yellow-and-blue metal building that was designed in France and prefabricated in Belgium. During the 1890s, the entire structure was shipped piece by piece to San José. Today, it functions as an elite school.

To the northeast of Parque España is the **Casa Amarilla** (Map p88; Av 7 btwn Calles 11 & 13), an elegant colonial house that is home to the ministry of foreign affairs (and is closed to the public). The glorious ceiba tree in front of the building was planted by John F Kennedy during his 1963 visit to Costa Rica.

To the southwest, you'll come across the slightly run-down **Parque Morazán** (Map p88; Avs 3 & 5 btwn Calles 5 & 9), which happens to be the most notorious prostitution center in the country. Tragically (or perhaps fittingly), the concrete gazebo in the center of park – commonly referred to as the **Templo de Música** (Music Temple) – is regarded by many as the symbol of San José. The park is named after General Francisco Morazán, who failed to unite the newly independent Central American countries under one flag in the 1830s.

ACTIVITIES

Parque Metropolitano La Sabana (Map p90) has a variety of sporting facilities, including tennis courts, volleyball, basketball and baseball areas, jogging paths and soccer pitches. Pick-up soccer games can be had on most days, though you'd better be good (Ticos can already sink a drop shot by age seven).

There is also an Olympic-size **swimming pool** (admission US$3; noon-2pm), though most Ticos prefer the excursion to the Ojo de Agua springs (in San Antonio de Belén, see p129), where you can swim all day.

Tennis, gym facilities and a swimming pool are also available at the **Costa Rica Tennis Club** (2232 1266) on the south side of La Sabana for US$10 per person per day. There are 11 indoor and outdoor courts, three pools, a sauna and gym facilities.

You can sign up with a local gym for about US$20 to US$40 a month. Look under 'Gimnasios' in the *Yellow Pages* directory. Or go a couple of rounds with the locals at the **Thaiboxing Center** (Map p114; 2225 7386) or **Atemi Ryu Martial Arts Center** (Map p114; 2524 0781) in San Pedro.

Golfers can lose their golf balls (and their patience) at either the **Cariari Country Club** (Map p80; 2293 3211; cariari@racsa.co.cr), the **Costa Rica Country Club** (Map pp118-19; 2228 9333, 2208 5000) or **Valle del Sol** (Map p80; 2282 9222, ext 218/219).

Adrenaline junkies can sign up for the daily bungee jumps at the nearby Río Colorado Bridge in Grecia with **Tropical Bungee** (2248 2212, 8383 9724; www.bungee.co.cr; 1st/2nd jump US$60/30). Transportation from San José is included.

WALKING TOUR

San José may not have colonial promenades and towering skyscrapers, but it sure oozes character (in a slightly seedy, film noir sort of way). This walking tour is recommended

---

WALK FACTS

Start Plaza de la Cultura
Finish Mercado Central
Distance 2km
Duration 30 minutes

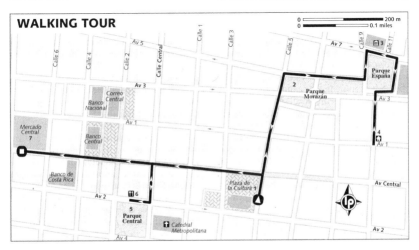

WALKING TOUR

for anyone who wants to learn about all the things that the tourist information center *won't* tell you.

Starting in the **Plaza de la Cultura** (**1**; p87), cross the street and head north for two blocks until you reach the **Parque Morazón** (**2**; p91). Sure, it's attractive enough during the day, but if you came here at night (which you shouldn't), you'd soon realize that the park also serves as an office for San José's sex workers (p100).

Before leaving the park, look toward the towering steel and glass building to the northeast. Most tourists know this building as the **Museo de Jade** (**3**; p85), but the 10 stories underneath the museum are home to the Instituto Nacional Seguros (National Insurance Institute), which is the government-owned insurance monopoly. Why should I care, you ask? Well, in case you were wondering why car rental is so expensive in Costa Rica, look no further. Curse silently under your breath. Now turn around.

The reasonably attractive pink building you're now staring at is the **Key Largo (4)**, which is mentioned here solely because some regard a visit to this club as a part of the country's wildlife experience. Ageing anglers and their slinky young Latina escorts are the most commonly sighted species. Attached to this fine establishment is the **Hotel Del Rey**, a top-end hotel that's popular with ageing anglers and their suspiciously absent wives.

Are you having fun yet? If so, let's backtrack to the Plaza de la Cultura and then walk west along the pedestrian boulevard for three blocks. When you get to the intersection, turn left and walk south for two blocks where you'll find the **Parque Central** (**5**; p87). Aside from the unlikely tribute to General Samoza, the famous Nicaraguan humanitarian whose charitable work was supported by the US government, take a moment to look at the **Food Mall (6)** on the north side of the plaza. Although this shrine of fast-food consumerism is packed on weekends with Tico families, it was once the Palace Theater, a famous art house and performance space – if you can find a more perfect symbol of globalization, let us know!

Backtrack one more time to the boulevard, and continue to head west for three more blocks where you'll see the **Mercado Central** (**7**; p107), the number-one place in San José for getting robbed. Every day, doe-eyed tour-ists armed with Nikon cameras and heavily armored wallets are vanquished by mere 'snatch-and-run' guerilla warfare. But you were smart enough to leave all your valuables at home, so jump headfirst into the consumer chaos and see if you get a good bargain on a Costa Rica snowglobe. Happy shopping!

COURSES
Dancing
If you want to improve your moves on the dance floor, then check out one of the many classes offered in the San José area. These are geared at Ticos, not tourists, but travelers who speak Spanish are welcome. You can learn all types of Latin dancing – salsa, cha-cha, merengue, bolero, tango. Classes cost around US$20 for two hours of group lessons per week. Travelers can also find dance classes by inquiring at many language schools (see opposite).

Academia de Bailes Latinos (Map pp84-5; ☎ 2233 8938; Av Central btwn Calles 25 & 27) Next to Pizza Hut in Barrio Escalante.

Kurubandé (Map p80; ☎ 2234 0682; Guadalupe)

Malecón (Map pp84-5; ☎ 2222 3214; Av 2 btwn Calles 17 & 19)

Merecumbé (Map p114; ☎ 2228 6253; Escazú)

SAN JOSÉ FOR CHILDREN
Most children will probably want to get out of San José as fast as possible – if you think the city is a little rough around the edges, imagine how they feel. But if you're spending a day – or two or three – in San José, there are a number of activities to keep the tykes busy and/or exhausted.

The **Museo de los Niños** (p86) and the **Museo de Formas, Espacios y Sonidos** (p89) are a hit with young children who just can't keep their hands off the exhibits. Interactive is what they're all about.

Both **Teatro Eugene O'Neill** (p116) and **Teatro Fanal** (p106) have children's theater groups. If your child is learning Spanish, this experience might make a vivid lesson.

Young nature lovers will enjoy getting up close and personal with butterflies at the **Spirogyra Jardín de Mariposas** (p86) or checking out the exotic animals at the **Zoológico Nacional Simón Bolívar** (p86).

Teens might dig checking each other out at the **Plaza de la Cultura** (p87), which has a number of nearby fast-food outlets and ice-cream shops. In the suburbs, **Mall San Pedro**

TALK LIKE A TICO

There are fine Spanish-language schools in the San José area. The schools listed have been operating since at least 1998 and/or they have received reader recommendations. Most of the reviewed language schools also organize volunteer placements, which is a great way to learn Spanish while giving back to those who need it most.

Unless otherwise noted, prices are given for five four-hour days of instruction, with/without a week's homestay with a local family. All prices include breakfast and dinner. Note that program fees are usually less if you study for an extended period of time.

Amerispan Unlimited (☎ in the USA & Canada 800-879 6640; www.amerispan.com; courses with/without homestay US$570/430) Offers a variety of educational travel programs, including language programs, volunteer/internship placements, academic study abroad and specialized programs, such as Salud, a medical Spanish program.

Centro Cultural Costarricense Norteamericano (Costa Rican–North American Cultural Center; Map p114; ☎ 2207 7500; www.cccncr.com; Calle 37 & Calle de los Negritos) This large school has Spanish courses, but because it operates mainly as an English school for locals, you'll be in the company of many Ticos. Monthlong programs start at $250.

Costa Rican Language Academy (Map p114; ☎ 2280 1685, in the USA 866-230 6361; www.learn-spanish .com; courses with/without homestay US$411/286) This organization also offers cooking classes and Latin dance lessons, and can provide you with enrollment information for a variety of volunteer programs. From the Subaru dealership, go 300m north and 50m west.

Institute for Central American Development Studies (Icads; ☎ 2225 0508; www.icadscr.com) This school offers monthlong programs (with/without homestay US$2100/1700) that are combined with lectures and activities focused on environmental and regional sociopolitical issues. It can also help place you in one of a variety of local volunteer positions depending on your interests. It's off the main road to Curridabat, about 1km from the center of town.

Instituto Británico (Map p114; ☎ 2225 0256; www.institutobritanico.co.cr; Los Yoses; courses with/without homestay US$305/180) This institute offers a high level of Spanish-language education that's also suited for teacher training and corporate instruction. Find it 75m south of the Subaru dealership.

Personalized Spanish (Map p80; ☎ 2278 3254; www.personalizedspanish.com; Tres Rios; courses with/without homestay US$383/488) This institute comes highly recommended by readers and is located in a beautiful suburb of the capital.

(p116) and **Multiplaza Escazú** (p123) are good for young consumers craving mall action.

To wear them out with a day of outdoor activities, there are always the swimming pools at the **Costa Rica Tennis Club** (p91), which are open to the public. For more extensive water-based activities, head northwest of San José for **Ojo de Agua** (p129).

If you're planning on spending more than a week in the city with your lovable offspring, most Spanish schools (above) offer special custom-made lessons for young *chicos y chicas* (boys and girls).

QUIRKY SAN JOSÉ

Every Sunday, the **Tico Train** (adult/child US$2/1) picks up riders from the eastern side of the Plaza de la Cultura (p87) and takes them on a 45-minute joyride through the city. The train itself looks like it was stolen from a county carnival somewhere in Iowa, though the cumbia (traditional provincial ballads) music

emanating from the train is about as Costa Rican as it gets. The Tico Train was started by the city council in an effort to inject more life and personality into the city center, and is intended to recall the days when josefinos traveled through their capital on trains. Even if you're not nostalgic for the good old days, the train ride itself is a total riot, especially when the driver overtakes cars while ringing an oversized bell.

TOURS

The city is easily navigable by independent travelers, and walking tours aren't necessary if you have a little time on your hands. If you have just a few hours and don't want to miss the key sights, Swiss Travel Service offers a recommended three-hour tour that covers the San José basics.

Calypso Tours (☎ 2256 2727; www.calypsotours.com) Does tours to the islands near Bahía Gigante by bus and 70ft motorized catamaran.

GET INVOLVED – VOLUNTEERING IN SAN JOSÉ

Volunteering can be a great way to experience and understand parts of the city that not even locals know about. There's no doubt that some people desperately need help, but be wary of the fact that many volunteers leave with the sinking feeling they've helped their egos more than the people they were supposed to be there for. Be realistic and well informed when choosing a charity. Some respected volunteer organizations include the following:

Amerispan (☎ in the USA & Canada 215-751 1100; www.amerispan.com) Has a broad range of volunteering options in San José and the rest of the country. Programs in the capital include youth work, health care, English teaching and stray-animal care.

Geo Visions (☎ in the USA & Canada 603-363 4187; www.geovisions.org) Operates placements in a San José child day-care center.

Sustainable Horizon (☎ in the USA & Canada 718-578 4020; www.sustainablehorizon.com) Arranges a wide variety of volunteering trips, from ecotourism holidays to orphanage placements.

United Planet (☎ in the USA & Canada 603-363 4187; www.geovisions.org) Runs a program in which volunteers help the elderly in San José's eastern suburbs. It also offers volunteer orphanage placements.

Volunteer Abroad (☎ in the USA & Canada 888-649 3788; www.volunteerabroad.ca) Places volunteers in the Hospital Nacional de Niños, to help with day-to-day running of the country's primary children's hospital.

World Language Study (☎ in the UK 0870 8610 423; www.worldlanguagestudy.com) Sends volunteers to teach English in schools, kindergartens and foster homes.

Costa Rica Art Tour (☎ 2288 0896, 8359 5571; www .costaricaarttour.com; tours US$95) If you're an art lover, this reader-recommended day tour goes to five different studios in the city, some of which are in artists' houses. Routes through the city change daily, so no two tours are ever the same. The tour focuses on painting, sculpting, printmaking, ceramics, jewelry-making and mixed media, and there are plenty of opportunities to purchase original art direct from artists. Lunch and hotel pick-up is included in the price. Group, senior and student discounts are available.

Lava Tours (☎ 2281 2458; www.lava-tours.com) Organizes a number of tours, including reader-recommended mountain-biking tours around the Central Valley.

Swiss Travel Service (Map pp84-5; ☎ 2221 0944) Longtime, reputable travel agency for tours all over Costa Rica. Find it 250m west of Centro Comercial El Pueblo; there is a branch office at the Radisson Europa.

Tiquicia Travel (☎ 2256 9682; www.tiquiciatravel.com; Condominios Pie Montel, La Uruca) A small agency focusing on tours to gay and gay-friendly locales around Costa Rica.

FESTIVALS & EVENTS

Festival de Arte Every even year, San José becomes host to the biennial citywide arts showcase that features theater, music, dance and film. It's held for two weeks in March. Keep an eye out for information in the daily newspapers.

Día de San José On March 19, San José marks the day for its patron saint with Masses in some churches. The day used to be a holiday, but modernization has quickly done away with that.

Festival de las Carretas (Oxcart Festival) Takes place every November, and is a celebration of the country's

agricultural heritage. The highlight is a parade of oxcarts down Paseo Colón.

Festival de Luz (Festival of Light) A month after Paseo Colón's oxcart parade is the Christmas parade, marked by an absurd amount of plastic 'snow.'

Las Fiestas de Zapote If you're in the San José area between Christmas and New Year's Eve, you absolutely have to visit this weeklong holiday celebration of all things Costa Rican (namely rodeos, cowboys, carnival rides, fried food and a whole lot of drinking). The celebration, which annually draws in tens of thousands of Ticos, takes place in the suburb of Zapote, just southeast of the city.

SLEEPING

Accommodations in San José run the gamut from grim little boxes to sumptuous world-class luxury. The cheapest hotels in the city are near the Coca-Cola bus terminal. However, this neighborhood is growing increasingly dangerous for travelers, and unless you're a die-hard fan of grunge, bustle and crime, it's recommended that you stay elsewhere.

If you want to spend the night in San José proper, the two nicest areas to stay are in Barrio Amón and La Sabana. Midrange and top-end accommodations tend to cluster in these well-to-do neighborhoods, though they are also home to the city's top budget hostels. There are also a number of good choices in central San José.

If you're looking for a quieter, more relaxed stay, consider spending the night in the city's wealthiest suburbs, namely Los Yoses and San

Pedro, and Escazú. Both neighborhoods are a few kilometers from downtown and can be easily reached by public bus or taxi.

If you're either flying in to or out of Costa Rica, it's actually more convenient to stay in Alajuela, as the city (contrary to what taxi drivers will tell you) is actually closer than San José is to the airport.

There are also several options for lodging in the suburb of Cariari, which is easy for getting to the airport (though a bit hard on the wallet).

Reservations are recommended during the high season (December through April) and the two weeks around Christmas and Semana Santa (the week before Easter Sunday). For more general information on hotels in Costa Rica, see p521. High-season prices are listed throughout.

Before reserving with a credit card, see p523 for advice.

Barrio Amón & Surrounds
BUDGET
Tranquilo Backpackers (Map pp84-5; ☎ 2223 3189, 2222 2493, 8355 5103; www.tranquilobackpackers.com; Calle 7 btwn Avs 9 & 11; dm US$10, d US$28, all incl breakfast; 🖳) Located in an old mansion in Barrio Amón, Tranquilo is one of the top reader-recommended hostels in the city, and it radiates mellow vibes and relaxing times. Big common rooms are decorated with hanging Japanese lanterns, bright murals, ample hammocks and enough mounted guitars to satisfy all your impromptu needs. There are also whimsically decorated mosaic-tile shared showers and communal kitchens, as well as free luggage storage, internet access and the famous (and universally loved) pancake breakfast. Airport transfer can be arranged.

Costa Rica Backpackers (Map pp84-5; ☎ 2221 6191; www.costaricabackpackers.com; Av 6 btwn Calles 21 & 23; dm/d US$12/26; 🅿 🖳 🛋) Located near the Supreme Court building, this extremely popular hostel is in a sprawling complex that's centered on a beautiful free-form pool surrounded by hammock-strung gardens. Chill-out music completes the laidback ambience, though you can always take things up a notch in the attached bar-restaurant, which also doubles on certain evenings as a movie theater. Rooms and shared bathrooms are well decorated with tropical-themed murals, and there are two communal kitchens and a TV lounge, as well as free luggage storage and internet access.

For a few extra bucks, the new guesthouse wing of the hostel across the road has slightly more comfortable doubles in more serene surrounds – ideal for couples looking for some peace from the party. Private parking is provided and airport transfer can be arranged.

Hotel Aranjuez (Map pp84-5; ☎ 2256 1825; www.hotelaranjuez.com; Calle 19 btwn Avs 11 & 13; s with/without bathroom US$30/23, d with/without bathroom US$40/26, all incl breakfast; 🅿 🖳) This rambling wooden hotel consists of several nicely maintained vintage homes strung together with connecting gardens and a lush backyard containing a mango tree. Spotless rooms vary in size and price, and the hosts serve a sumptuous daily breakfast buffet in the garden courtyard.

ourpick Hostel Pangea (Map p88; ☎ 2221 1992; www.hostelpangea.com; Av 7 btwn Calles 3 & 3bis; dm US$10, d with/without bathroom US$32/28; 🅿 🖳 🛋) Put simply, this is the number one hangout for backpackers in San José. Travelers swap stories round the pool by day and live it up in the bar upstairs by night. While this is very much a party hostel, the owners haven't lost sight of the fact that most guests are in San José on their way to some other part of the country. So nearly all practicalities can be taken care of by way of free internet (and wifi), free calls to North America, free luggage storage, onward travel booking service and airport pick-up (US$16).

MIDRANGE
All of the hotels listed have private hot-water showers and cable TV unless otherwise stated, and they can arrange tours throughout the country.

ourpick Kap's Place (Map pp84-5; ☎ 2221 1169; www.kapsplace.com; Calle 19 btwn Avs 11 & 13, Av 11 btwn Calle 19 & 21; s US$20-45, d US$30-55, tr US$40-65, apt from US$80; 🅿 🖳) The owner of this delightful guesthouse, Karla Arias, has individually decorated each of the 24 homey rooms in wonderfully bright colors, creating a unique, arty feel. Indian sarongs and quilted duvets are laid across the beds. Communal areas include a yucca plant–filled courtyard with hammocks strung across the perimeters and a well-stocked kitchen. Also, there's free internet, and Spanish, English and French are all spoken.

Cinco Hormigas Rojas (Map pp84-5; ☎ 2257 8581, 2255 3412; www.cincohormigasrojas.com; Calle 15 btwn Avs 9 & 11; r US$30-58; 🛋) This highly recommended traveler's refuge and artistic retreat is run by the multilingual and insanely talented Mayra, a Tica artist and naturalist who's nurtured the grounds of her small guesthouse for over 10 years. Today, 'Five Red Ants' is a micro-ecosystem that's teeming with tropical birds, and indeed it's easy to forget that you're staying in San José. The guesthouse itself has three rooms of varying sizes and amenities (if you need TV in your life, this is not the place for you), each of which is uniquely themed and displays her incredible artwork. Mayra's specialty is covering household objects in *papier-mâché*, and then sculpting and painting them into intricate designs – their originality and beauty is impossible to describe. Art is available for purchase, and every traveler leaves after breakfast with a small gift in hand.

Casa Hilda (Map pp84-5; ☎ 2221 0037; c1hilda@racsa .co.cr; Av 11 btwn Calles 3 & 3bis; s/d incl breakfast US$26/36) The Quesadas will make you feel like you're returning home at this peaceful, peach-colored inn in Barrio Amón. Rooms are very simple, but the entire property glows with domestic warmth – this is an excellent choice if you want to spend some time with a real Costa Rican family. Check out the natural spring in the center of the house that has been bubbling potable water for 90 years (even during the dry season).

Hotel Dunn Inn (Map pp84-5; ☎ 2222 3232, 2222 3426; www.hoteldunninn.com; cnr Calle 5 & Av 11; s standard/deluxe US$49/59, d standard/deluxe US$59/69, ste US$80; ☒ ☐) This pale-yellow, rambling brick-and-wood mansion was constructed in 1929 and has fully restored rooms with modern fixtures named after different words in Costa's Rica's indigenous languages (plaques in the rooms explain the words' derivations and usage). There is also a restaurant and a small bar, which stays open late. Visa is accepted.

Joluva Guesthouse (Map pp84-5; ☎ 2223 7961; www .joluva.com; Calle 3bis btwn Avs 9 & 11; s/d US$30/50; ☐) This quaint gay-operated guesthouse in Barrio Amón has seven small but well-appointed rooms (check out the massage heads on the showers) that are scattered around a number of cozy public areas. The management speaks English and can provide information on the Costa Rican gay scene.

Hotel Posada del Museo (Map pp84-5; ☎ 2258 1027; www.hotelposadadelmuseo.com; s/d/ste from US$48/55/65) This posada (country-style inn) is diagonal from the Museo Nacional, on a pedestrian street in a beautiful district of the capital. The building dates from 1928 and has a dramatic entrance, complete with a Juliet balcony overlooking the foyer. French doors line the entrances to each of the rooms, which are named after Costa Rican birds and flowers and furnished with period pieces. The Argentinean managers are multilingual (English, Spanish, French and Italian) and are committed to offering guests personalized service. The attached café is perfect for people-watching or for simply enjoying the ambience of this tranquil neighborhood.

Casa Morazan (Map p88; ☎ 2257 4187; www .casamorazan.com; cnr Calle 7 & Av 9; s/d incl breakfast US$55/65) This Art Deco mansion in Barrio Amón was built in the 1930s as the residence of John Keith, the cousin of Minor Keith, the famous banana baron who helped construct the Atlantic railroad. The house is fully furnished in period antiques, and rooms are well appointed, with bathtubs, bidets and regal beds.

Hotel Kekoldi (Map p88; ☎ 2248 0804; www .kekoldi.com; Av 9 btwn Calles 5 & 7; s/d/tr incl breakfast from US$57/69/79) The Kekoldi is in a fabulously light and airy Art Deco building in Barrio Amón that has spotless, freshly painted pastel rooms with sky-blue tiled bathrooms. There are fresh flowers in virtually every corner of the hotel, and tranquil murals of beach landscapes adorn the common areas. This hotel is gay-friendly and popular with younger travelers, and English, German and Italian are spoken. Credit cards are accepted.

Rincón de San José (Map pp84-5; ☎ 2221 9702; www.hotelrincondesanjose.com; Av 9 btwn Calles 13 & 15; s/d/tr/q incl breakfast US$56/70/86/110; ☐) This charming little hotel in a landmark colonial house in Barrio Amón is beautifully maintained and furnished with period pieces. Large rooms with polished-wood or ceramic-tile floors surround an attractive courtyard. Breakfast is served in a garden courtyard, and a small bar is open until 10pm. Credit cards accepted.

Hotel Don Carlos (Map p88; ☎ 2221 6707; www .doncarloshotel.com; Calle 9 btwn Avs 7 & 9; s/d/tr incl breakfast from US$76/87/100; ☒ ☐) This converted mansion in Barrio Amón has 33 unique rooms with colonial design schemes and huge, tiled bathrooms. The entire property is decked with artwork that ranges from Sarchí-style oxcarts to oil paintings of dead white *conquistadores* (conquerors). There is also a pre-Columbian-themed sculpture garden, bar and restaurant, as well as a sundeck with tables, a small Jacuzzi and an excellent gift shop. Rates include a welcome cocktail.

TOP END

All of the following hotels accept credit cards.

Hotel Santo Tomás (Map p88; ☎ 2255 0448; www .hotelsantotomas.com; Av 7 btwn Calles 3 & 5; d incl breakfast from US$93, extra person US$15; ☑ ☎) This early-20th-century French-colonial mansion is a Barrio Amón landmark, and once belonged to the Salazar family of *cafétaleros*. Twenty elegant rooms of varying sizes have polished wood floors, 4m-high ceilings and antique furnishings. There is a garden courtyard with a solar-heated swimming pool, a Jacuzzi and a small gym; English is spoken.

Raya Vida Villa (Map pp84-5; ☎ 2223 4168; www .rayavida.com; Calle 15, off Av 11; s/d incl breakfast US$93/110; ☑) This secluded hilltop villa is an absolute treasure of a B&B. The bedrooms and dining and sitting areas reflect the owner's interest in art and antiques, and visitors can expect to spot original works by Dalí and Toulouse-Lautrec (seriously, we're not kidding!). Rooms have been decorated to the highest possible level of luxury, straight down to the orthopedic mattresses, imported European linens and flawless bathrooms (one of which has a whirlpool tub). The house itself is an elegant colonial mansion with stained-glass windows, hardwood floors, a patio with fountain, a fireplace and a small garden. Owner Michael Long can help with reservations at other B&Bs, and can arrange for airport pick-up if you call in advance. For the taxi driver: the hotel is 100m north of Hospital Calderón Guardia on Calle 17, then 50m west on Avenida 11, then another 50m north.

Hotel Amon Plaza (Map pp84-5; ☎ 2523 4600; www .hotelamonplaza.com; Av 11; d standard/superior incl breakfast from US$150/185; ☒ ☑ ☎) This bustling downtown hotel has all the amenities you never need to leave the building. The ground-floor casino exudes the mandatory whooping and hollering, while those looking for a workout can sweat it out in the hotel gym. Rooms are bright and airy, but a little characterless for the price. The ground-floor restaurant serves reasonable international fare with street-side views of the historic neighborhood.

HOMESTAYS

Bell's Home Hospitality (☎ 2225 4752; www.homestay.thebells.org; s/d/tr incl breakfast US$30/45/50) This recommended agency is run by Vernon Bell, a Kansan who has lived in Costa Rica for more than 30 years, and his Tica wife, Marcela. The couple can arrange homestays in over 70 local homes, each of which has been personally inspected to maintain high standards of cleanliness and wholesomeness. All are close to public transportation and readers have sent only positive comments about these places. Note that there is a US$5 surcharge for one-night-only stays and for private bathrooms. The Bells can also arrange airport transfers (US$15), car rental and tours.

La Sabana & Surrounds

This section covers hotels in the neighborhoods of La Sabana, La Uruca, La Pitahaya and Rohrmoser.

BUDGET

Gaudy's (Map p90; ☎ 2258 2937; www.backpacker.co.cr; Av 5 btwn Calles 36 & 38; dm US$10, d with bathroom US$23-28; ☑) Located in a residential area east of Parque La Sabana is this homey hostel, which has been popular among shoestring travelers for years. The Colombian owners operate one of the cheapest hostels in the city, and although the design scheme is fairly basic, the service is professional and the house is well maintained. There's a communal kitchen, hot showers, a TV lounge, a hammock-strung outdoor patio and free internet. Find it 200m north and 150m east of the Banco de Costa Rica.

JC & Friends (Map p90; ☎ 8374 8246; www.jcfriends hostel.com; cnr Calle 34 & Av 3; camping per person US$7, dm US$9, r per person US$12, all incl breakfast; ☑) This recommended hostel is owned and managed by Juan Carlos (he's JC, and you're the friends), a Costa Rican–born, Spanish-raised and American-educated all-round great guy whose personal attention makes this intimate place a winner. There's a pool table, bar, TV room and outdoor hammock lounge (complete with artificial 'sand'). And here's the best part – the Tuasa airport bus conveniently stops directly in front of the hostel.

Mi Casa Hostel (Map p90; ☎ 2231 4700; www.mi casahostel.com; dm/r incl breakfast from US$8/25; ☑ ☑) This beautiful old mansion with polished wooden floors and antique furnishings has a variety of dormitories and private rooms to choose from – the nicer ones have tiled hot-water bathrooms and balconies overlooking the attractive neighborhood of La Sabana. Communal areas are well furnished, and the kitchen and hot showers are clean and comfortable. There's also free internet. It's 50m west and 150m north of the ICE Building.

MIDRANGE

All hotels have private hot showers unless otherwise stated.

Hotel Petite Victoria (Map p90; ☎ 2225 8488; victoria@amnet.com; cnr Calle 28 & Av 2; s/d incl breakfast US$25/30) This English Victorian–style house is decorated with period chandeliers and furnishings, and still retains its original colonial tiling. Unfortunately, rooms and bathrooms are a little worn, though it's still a comfortable place to spend the night.

Rosa del Paseo (Map p90; ☎ 2257 3258; www .rosadelpaseo.com; Paseo Colón btwn Calles 28 & 30; s/d ste from US$76/88/93; P ⬚) This 'Caribbean Victorian–style' mansion was built in 1897 by the Montealegre family, who were one of the first coffee exporters in Costa Rica. Today, the mansion has been converted into a highly recommended guesthouse, with much of the historic ambience intact. The original tiled floors and polished wood ceilings are preserved, and period pieces, including oil paintings and sculptures, are scattered throughout the hotel. There is also a stunning garden of heliconias and bougainvilleas, where a tropical breakfast is served each morning. Although it's hard to find the San José of yesteryear, this is one place where it's easy to imagine yourself in another epoch.

TOP END

All of the following hotels accept credit cards.

Colours Oasis Resort (☎ 2296 1880, in the USA 877-932 6652; www.colours.net; Blvd Rohrmoser, cnr of 'El Triangulo'; d/ste from US$93/140; ⬚) This self-proclaimed 'full-service gay resort' is in the quiet and elegant Rohrmoser district, and is affiliated with 'Colours Destinations International,' a collection of gay-friendly hotels throughout the world. Rooms in this sprawling Spanish-colonial complex have romantic paddle fans, modern furnishings and impeccable bathrooms. Facilities at the resort include a TV

lounge, bar-restaurant, pool, sundeck and Jacuzzi. Call ahead for directions.

ourpick Hotel Grano de Oro (Map p90; ☎ 2255 3322; www.hotelgranodeoro.com; Calle 30 btwn Avs 2 & 4; s/d/ste from US$117/122/185; P ⬚) The final word in luxury in this town. This early-20th-century mansion is located on a quiet side street from Paseo Colón, and belongs to the group of 'Small Distinctive Hotels of Costa Rica.' The 'Tropical Victorian' conversion blends wrought iron and dark wood traditional touches with Costa Rican furnishings and artwork. Private bathrooms sparkle with blue-and-white Italian tiles and gleaming base fixtures. No two rooms are alike. There is also a top-notch restaurant that's highly recommended (p102).

Central San José

Noise is a drawback at some of the following places, though you are in the center of everything (for better or worse).

BUDGET

All showers are hot unless otherwise stated.

Casa Ridgway (Map p88; ☎ 2233 6168; www .amigosparalapaz.org; casaridgway@yahoo.es; cnr Calle 15 & Av 6bis; dm/s/d US$10/12/24; ⬚) This welcoming guesthouse, on a quiet side street near the Supreme Court building, is run by the adjacent Friends' Peace Center, which promotes peace, social justice and collaboration between peoples. Rooms are immaculate, there are shared showers, the communal kitchen is spotless and the atmosphere is, well, peaceful. A lending library offers an extensive collection of books on Central American politics and society. This isn't the place for party people – there's no smoking, alcohol or drugs allowed and quiet hours are from 10pm to 6am.

Pensión de la Cuesta (Map p88; ☎ 2256 7946; www .pensiondelacuesta.com; Av 1 btwn Calles 11 & 15; s/d/tr incl breakfast US$18/28/38) Situated on a little hill behind the Asamblea Legislativa is this 1920s wooden house, which looks like it was designed and decorated by Barbie and Ken. Nine small but appealing rooms with private bathrooms share a homey TV lounge that's perfect for relaxing with the owners and guests.

Green House Hostel (Map p88; 2258 0102; www.green househostel.altervista.org; Calle 11 btwn Avs 16 & 18; dm/s/d/tr US$14/28/38/49) This very attractive hostel that recently came under the HI banner is brimming with personality – the entire building is adorned with hanging plants, historic photographs and interesting antiques. The rooms themselves are a bit more modest, though the huge perk here is that they all have private bathroom (even the dorms). Unfortunately, it's a bit pricey compared with other hostels in the city, and it's inconveniently located in Plaza Víquez, which isn't exactly the nicest of neighborhoods.

MIDRANGE & TOP END

Gran Hotel Doña Inés (Map p88; ☎ 2222 7443, 2222 7553; www.donaines.com; Calle 11 btwn Avs 2 & 6; s/d/tr incl breakfast US$45/60/60) This Italian-owned hotel is located in an old colonial home, which has a handful of quaint rooms decorated with period furniture. Rooms are set back from the street so they're fairly quiet, and they surround a small but pleasant courtyard. The staff speaks English, Spanish and Italian, and can help with travel arrangements. Credit cards are accepted.

Hotel Colonial (Map p88; ☎ 2223 0109; www.hotel colonialcr.com; cnr Calle 11 btwn Avs 2 & 6; s/d/ste US$55/67/102; 🏊) This 60-year-old Spanish-colonial mansion with distinct Moorish influences has latticed ironwork, expansive woodwork and an arched, poolside promenade. Classically accented rooms have modern furnishings, and those on the higher floors have sweeping views of the city and outlying mountains.

Gran Hotel Costa Rica (Map p88; ☎ 2221 4000; www.grandhotelcostarica.com; Calle 3 btwn Avs Central & 2; d/ste incl breakfast from US$94/160) The city's first prominent hotel was constructed in 1930 and is today recognized as a national landmark. Frequent renovations have kept the rooms modern and comfortable, though there are still subtle architectural reminders of the hotel's history, including exposed beams, molded ceilings and the dramatic entrance hall. The 24-hour alfresco Café Parisienne (p104) is one of the most popular tourist cafés in the city. There are also two restaurants, a bar and a 24-hour casino. Credit cards accepted.

Coca-Cola Bus Terminal Area

It is not recommended that you stay in this area – crime is on the increase, and travelers are easy targets, particularly at night. However, if you're just looking to crash near the station for a night, the following hotels are better than most.

BUDGET

Hotel Musoc (Map p88; ☎ 2222 9437; Calle 16 btwn Avs 1 & 3; s/d US$9/15, s/d/tr with bathroom US$12/16/18) This large building close to the Coca-Cola terminal is nicer inside than it would appear on the outside. The linoleum-tiled rooms are simple and clean, and showers are hot, but noise can be a problem with all the buses passing below. The staff speaks some English and credit cards are accepted.

Hotel Gallo Pinto (Map p90; ☎ 2257 3632; Calle 24 btwn Avs 3 & 5; dm US$12, d incl breakfast US$25) If you must stay near the Coca-Cola terminal, then this is your best bet. A family-run hostel with brightly decorated wood-floored private rooms and stone-floored dorms. Communal spaces are basic but functional, while the bathrooms with hot showers are clean. Tours and car rental can be arranged at the front desk.

By the Airport

The residential district of Cariari is located in the nether region between San José and Alajuela. It's a convenient base if you're either coming from or going to the international airport (assuming you have some dough to spare). There's no shortage of expensive hotels in this section of the city, though the following spots are particularly recommended. All of the listed hotels are easily reached by taxi. Note that these hotels are not mapped.

MIDRANGE & TOP END

Cariari Bed & Breakfast (☎ 2239 2585; www.cariaribb .com; Av de la Marina; d incl breakfast US$76-90; 🅿 💻) This charming B&B is run by a friendly North American named Laurie, and is a welcome respite from the area's absurdly priced hotels. Three suites of varying sizes and amenities (one room shares a bathroom, one has a private shower and the other a bathtub) are available for guests, though there are plenty of common areas in this stunning Spanish-colonial home, including a tropical garden, a TV lounge and a roof deck.

Hotel Herradura (☎ 2293 0033; www.hotelherradura .com; s/d/ste from US$155/170/250; 🅿 🛰 🏊) This golf resort and conference center also has privileges at the neighboring country club. Modern rooms have plush carpets and all the trimmings, though it's the amenities that you're paying for – we're talking three pools, including one with waterfalls and a swim-up bar, five Jacuzzis, a casino, a sauna, a concierge service, three restaurants and two bars.

THE CHILD SEX TRADE

Although the majority of travelers to Central America are searching for sandy beaches, tropical breezes and a Latin vibe, an increasing number of sex tourists who prey on children are also finding their way to Costa Rica.

Prostitution is legal in Costa Rica for women and men 18 years or older. Nevertheless, child prostitution is a highly visible and growing problem in the country. It is impossible to know exactly how many minors work as prostitutes in Costa Rica, but the government, police sources, and representatives of Unicef and the Human Rights Watch acknowledge that child prostitution is on the rise. The National Institute for Children (PANI) estimates that as many as 3000 children in metropolitan San José are involved in prostitution and the former executive president of Costa Rica's National Child Trust acknowledged in 2004 that there had been an accelerated increase in child prostitution in the country.

Experts have suggested many reasons for this rise in the sexual exploitation of children. First, traditional sex tourism destinations, such as Thailand and the Philippines, have in recent years enacted stricter laws and strong public awareness campaigns, which have blunted the sex industry in both countries. Second, the growth of tourism in Costa Rica has attracted a greater number of European and North American sex tourists, especially considering that adult prostitution is completely legal. Third, increased demand for child prostitutes is partly due to the mistaken belief that younger men and women are less likely to have HIV or AIDS. Fourth, the advent of the internet has made it easier for sex tourists to learn about the availability of underage sex in various destinations.

Children are often pushed into prostitution when poor families lose the ability to support themselves. Studies also show that child prostitutes are often victims of sexual and physical abuse at home, and are driven to prostitution as a means of survival. It has also been shown that drug abuse is correlated with child prostitution, and that minors often sell sex as a means of feeding their addiction.

Fortunately, there are signs that the Costa Rican government is starting to crackdown on offenders. First of all, there are stiff penalties for anyone convicted of buying sex from a minor, including hefty fines and lengthy prison sentences. At present, there are signs and leaflets in both of Costa Rica's international airports that alert arriving travelers to the penalties for having sex with a minor. Similar billboards can also be seen on major highways and at tourist sites throughout the country.

In addition, the Costa Rica Tourism Board (ICT) recently began a highly visible campaign to discourage tourists from engaging in the sex trade. It has also adopted a code of conduct to help discourage domestic workers from helping foreigners find prostitutes. For example, taxi drivers, waiters and hotel staff are often eager to help guests find prostitutes since they can usually earn a hefty commission. In an effort to combat this practice, some businesses are investing in 're-education' classes for their staff, though unfortunately, it's easy to remain skeptical of the effectiveness of this program.

There are a number of organizations fighting the sexual exploitation of children in Costa Rica, which you can contact to find out more or to report any incidents you encounter. See boxed text Preventing Child Sex Tourism in Costa Rica, p534.

Meliá Cariari Hotel (☎ 2239 0022; d/ste from US$165/275; P ✕ 🖳 🗪) This luxurious hotel has a presidential suite that isn't presidential in name only: numerous foreign leaders from around the world frequently stay here during their trips to Costa Rica. If you're not a visiting dignitary, however, there are 221 spacious, carpeted rooms and suites to choose from, all of which have air-con, cable TV and a private balcony. In addition, guests receive privileges at the neighboring Cariari Country Club.

EATING

Costa Ricans are fond of the proverb: '*Pansa llena, corazón contento,*' or 'When the stomach is full, the heart is happy.' Unsurprisingly, food is the glue that holds Costa Rican families together, and josefinos are no different. Cosmopolitan San José has an impressive number and variety of restaurants, and it's easy to find something to satisfy most tastes and budgets.

Note that approximate prices for meals are given as a guide throughout this book, though generally anything with shrimp, lobster or crab will be more expensive. Many of the better restaurants in San José get very busy (especially on evenings and weekends), so it's best to make a reservation.

Eateries in the suburbs of Escazú and Los Yoses and San Pedro are listed later in this chapter.

Supermarkets are spread throughout the city, and several are marked on each neighborhood map.

Bario Amón & Surrounds

BUDGET

Soda de Don Raúl (Map pp84-5; Calle 15 btwn Avs 6bis & 8; dishes US$2-4) This basic *soda* (small and informal lunch counter) has hearty *gallo pinto* (stir-fry of rice and beans) and abundant lunch specials (US$2.50) that attract a steady stream of suited Ticos from the nearby courts.

El Cuartel de la Boca del Monte (Map pp84-5; Av 1 btwn Calles 21 & 23; dishes US$3-6; ☺ 11:30am-2pm & 6-10pm) This popular nightclub doubles as greasy spoon during the day. Sure, the exposed-brick walls and worn-wooden floors aren't exactly the most pleasant of surroundings, but the typical fare here is cheap, filling and perfect for filling the gut before a long night of drinking.

MIDRANGE

Cafe de la Posada (Map pp84-5; ☎ 2258 1027; Calle 17 btwn Avs 2 & 4; dishes US$3-6; ☺ 11am-7pm Mon-Fri, to 5pm Sat & Sun) This Argentinean-run café, which fronts a pedestrian walkway in a quiet and scenic district of the city, is one of the few spots in San José where you can dine alfresco. The specialties here are superbly brewed coffees and authentic Argentinean-style *empanadas* (corn turnover usually filled with ground meat), though the US$5 'plate of the day' is always a good choice. The café also displays rotating exhibitions of local and international art.

Cafe Saudade (Map pp84-5; ☎ 2233 2534; Calle 17 btwn Avs 2 & 4; dishes US$4-12; ☺ 10am-6:30pm Mon-Thu, 11am-5pm Fri & Sat) This hidden gem of a place has an eclectic menu of tempting international foods, including sushi, hummus, crepes and salads, as well as your standard café offerings. It also serves as an exhibition hall for local

artists and photographers (the tables are actually display cases). Dance and yoga classes are occasionally held in the upstairs room.

La Cocina de Leña (Map pp84-5; ☎ 2223 3704, 2255 1360; Centro Comercial El Pueblo; dishes US$5-9; ☺ 11am-11pm Sun-Thu, to midnight Fri & Sat) One of the best-known restaurants in town, 'The Wood Stove' has the endearing tradition of printing its menu on brown paper bags. Typical dishes include corn soup with pork, black-bean soup, tamales, *gallo pinto* with meat and eggs, stuffed peppers, and oxtail served with yucca and fried plantain. It also serves local desserts and alcoholic concoctions, including *guaro*, which is the highly recommended local firewater. There's live marimba music on some nights.

Café Mundo (Map pp84-5; ☎ 2222 6190; cnr Av 9 & Calle 15; dishes US$5-10; ☺ 11am-11pm Mon-Fri, 5pm-12:30am Sat) A good spot if you've had enough of rice and beans and crave some European fare with a half-decent glass of Beaujolais. The restaurant is housed in a beautiful old mansion, and has a relaxing outdoor terrace that overlooks a lush garden and a bubbling fountain. This is the perfect spot for an afternoon *cafécito* (cup of coffee), though it's the Western menu of pastas, meats and salads that brings the crowds.

Kafé Ko (Map pp84-5; ☎ 2258 7453; cnr Av Central & Calle 21; dishes US$5-10; ☺ 11am-midnight Mon-Fri, 5pm-1am Sat) This hip, candlelit 'kafé' serves simple but gourmet Western-style sandwiches, quiches and salads, and during the evening it evolves into a popular nightspot. There's occasional live music during the week, though things really get going on weekends in the evening when live DJs come here to spin.

TOP END

our pick Bakea (Map pp84-5; ☎ 2248 0303; cnr Av 11 & Calle 7; dishes US$7-18; ☺ noon-midnight Tue-Fri, 7pm-midnight Sat) The trendiest restaurant in the capital is in a beautiful converted vintage home, which has numerous intimate dining rooms, a softly lit patio and a small art gallery. The menu consists of nouveau international dishes – from risotto to steak *frites* to seafood – all of it world class. Don't miss the delectable *degustación* dessert sampler. Credit cards accepted.

Café Moro (Map pp84-5; ☎ 2223 3116; cnr Calle 3 & Av 13; mains US$9-15; ☺ 11:30am-9:30pm Mon-Fri, to 10:30pm Sat) This Middle Eastern–inspired restaurant is on the ground floor of a 75-year-old

Moorish-style mansion, elaborately decorated with Arabic murals and darkly painted walls. The menu features traditional regional dishes such as kabobs, falafel, couscous and dolmades, as well as a variety of pastas, meats and fish. The coffee here is strong and potent, blending well with the honey-drenched pastries.

La Sabana & Surrounds

BUDGET

Marisquería Sabor a Océano (Map p90; ☎ 2255 0994; cnr Av 3 & Calle 34; casados US$2-6; ♙ 11am-10pm) The 'Taste of the Ocean' has a great variety of seafood dishes, including *ceviche* (local dish of uncooked but well-marinated seafood), octopus, squid, fish fillets and fish fries, none of which will break your budget.

Soda Tapia (Map p90; cnr Av 2 & Calle 42; casados US$3-4; ♙ 6am-midnight) This unpretentious spot is a local favorite – you can't go wrong with any of its featured casados, though it's worth saving some room for the sinful sundaes.

MIDRANGE

Lubnán (Map p90; ☎ 2257 6071; Paseo Colón btwn Calles 22 & 24; dishes US$5-10; ♙ 11am-3pm & 6-11pm Tue-Sat, 11am-4pm Sun) The beauty of San José is being able to find diverse places such as Lubnán, an excellent Lebanese eatery that serves Middle Eastern specialties, including shish kabobs, falafel, and lamb stews.

ourpick Machu Picchu (Map p90; ☎ 2222 7384; Calle 32 btwn Av 1 & 3; mains US$6-13; ♙ 11am-3pm & 6-10pm Mon-Sat) This highly recommended Peruvian outpost is one of the most popular restaurants in the city – and with good reason. The *ceviche* is the best in town, while the overflowing seafood platters are an absolute must. If you've never been to Peru, this is a great place to try the country's famous national cocktail, the pisco sour.

TOP END

El Chicote (Map p90; ☎ 2232 0936; mains US$8-13; ♙ 11am-3pm & 6-11pm Mon-Fri, 11am-11pm Sat & Sun) Protein fiends can go wild at this venerable steakhouse, which grills beefy sirloins in the middle of the restaurant and then serves them up with black beans and fried banana slices, along with a baked potato. A small pavement patio has seating, and the large interior is filled with flowers. El Chicote is near the northwestern corner of the park.

La Piazzetta (Map p90; ☎ 2222 7896; cnr F Colón & Calle 40; dishes US$8-18; ♙ noon-2:30pm & 6:30-11pm Mon-Fri,

6-11pm Sat) Some of the best Italian fare in the city is served to guests on a silver platter (literally). The house specialties include homemade pastas, creamy risottos, and tender cuts of veal and beef. There is an extensive list of imported wines, and several luscious desserts to choose from.

Fuji (Map p90; ☎ 2232 8122, ext 191; Calle 42, mains US$10-30; ♙ noon-3pm & 6:30-11pm Mon-Sat, noon-10pm Sun) Arguably the top Japanese restaurant in town is located in the Hotel Meliá Tryp Corobicí, 200m north of Parque La Sabana. The restaurant serves skillfully prepared sushi and traditional Japanese dishes, including *teppanyaki* and *bento*. Credit cards accepted.

Restaurant y Galería La Bastille (Map p90; ☎ 2255 4994; cnr Paseo Colón & Calle 22; dishes US$12-16; ♙ 11:30am-2pm & 6:30pm-midnight Mon-Fri, 6pm-midnight Sat) This cheerfully elegant bistro is one of San José's longest-standing French restaurants. Dishes emphasizing local meats and thick sauces are simply impeccable. The restaurant also serves as a colorful art gallery, and displays rotating exhibitions that highlight local artists.

Restaurant Grano de Oro (Map p90; ☎ 2255 3322; Calle 30 btwn Avs 2 & 4; dinner mains US$20; ♙ 6am-10pm) Foremost among small hotel-restaurants in San José is Grano de Oro, which is applauded for its historic dining area and superb international cuisine. Dishes include inventive items, such as chicken basted in coconut milk with grilled pineapple, or Chilean sea bass in orange herb sauce with macadamia nuts. The restaurant is popular, so reservations are highly recommended – even for weeknights. Guests can have their meals delivered to their rooms at no additional charge. Credit cards accepted.

Central San José & Coca-Cola Bus Terminal Area

BUDGET

Pastelería Merayo (Map p88; Calle 16 btwn Paseo Colón & Av 1; pastries US$1-2) This busy pastry shop has a wide variety of cavity-inducing goodies. The coffee is strong and it's a sweet way to pass the time if you're waiting for a bus at the Coca-Cola.

Soda Castro (Map p88; Av 10 btwn Calles 2 & 4; dishes US$2-5) The area outside is frightful, but inside it's so delightful. So it's not in the best neighborhood, but if you happen to be coming through here, Castro is a good place to feed a sweet tooth. The vast hall is an old-fashioned Tico family spot (there's a sign prohibiting public displays of affection) where you can get heaping ice-cream sundaes and banana splits.

Huarache's (Map pp84-5; Av 22 btwn Calles 5 & 7; dishes US$2-5; ☺ 11am-11pm) This bustling Mexican restaurant makes up for all the bland meals you've had in Costa Rica. Here you'll find fresh honest-to-goodness tacos, quesadillas, guacamole, tortilla soup and hot sauces that'll make you think you've died and gone to Mexico.

Vishnu (Map p88; dishes US$3-5; Av 1 Av 1 btwn Calles 1 & 3; Calle Central Calle Central btwn Avs 6 & 8) Veggies go nuts at this famous San José chain, which is known for its bounteous fare and affordable prices. A US$3 lunch special buys you soup, brown rice, veggies, a fruit drink and dessert. But it's worth coming back for dinner as well – its veggie burger and fruit-drink combo is so good it'll make your carnivorous friends jealous.

Churrería Manolo's (Map p88; churros US$0.50, meals US$3-5; ☺ 24hr; Downtown West Av Central btwn Calles Central & 2; Branch 2 Av Central btwn Calles 9 & 11) This San José institution is famous for its cream-filled churros (doughnut tubes), which draws in crowds of hungry josefinos in search of a quick sugar rush day or night. Here's a tip – the churros are the freshest around 5pm when hungry office workers beeline here straight from the office. If you're looking for something a little more filling, the Downtown West location serves killer casados, and the 2nd-floor balcony is great for spying on passers-by on the pedestrian mall below.

Chelle's (Map p88; cnr Av Central & Calle 9; dishes US$3-6; ☺ 24hr) This unpretentious spot is centrally located and serves local dishes – none of which are very exciting. Regardless, some Ticos say you haven't really experienced San José until you've had a wee-hours breakfast here after a night of drinking. (And there's even a bar in case you want to keep on going.)

Restaurant Shakti (Map p88; ☎ 2222 4475; cnr Av 8 & Calle 13; dishes US$4-6; ☺ 7am-7pm) This vegetarian restaurant is a more sophisticated version of Vishnu. The highlights of the menu are fresh-baked breads, veggie burgers, macrobiotic produce and local root vegetables. And in case your travel companions retch at the thought of eating wholesome food, the friendly staff will even cook up a chicken for your unenlightened friends.

ourpick Nuestra Tierra (Map pp84-5; cnr Av 2 & Calle 15; casados $4-6; ☺ 24hr) A glaring bull's head greets you in this ranch-style restaurant, where the theme is Costa Rican *campesino-* (peasant or farmer) style spit and sawdust. Cheery waiters whisk around heaving wooden platters spilling casados to hordes of hungry tourists and Tico families, who especially pack the place out on weekends. Portions are large, the food is good and the prices are low.

Restaurante Don Wang (Map p88; Calle 11 btwn Avs 6 & 8; dishes US$4-10; ☺ 8am-3pm & 6-11pm Mon, 8am-11pm Tue-Sat, 8am-10pm Sun) If you travel for long enough in Costa Rica, you'll be surprised to learn what passes for Chinese food in this country. At the Don Wang, you're getting the real deal, especially if you come in the morning for its Cantonese dim sum.

One of the cheapest places for a good lunch is at the **Mercado Central** (Map p88; Av Central btwn Calles 6 & 8), where you'll find a variety of restaurants and *sodas* serving casados, tamales, seafood and everything in between. One of the best spots is **ourpick Poseidon** (Map p88; dishes US$2-5), where the owner gets the best market fish every day to put on the menu. The seafood stew is one of the best dishes in town. After, stop for dessert at **Helados de Sorbetela** (Map p88; ice cream US$0.75), a real local favorite that serves up custard ice cream to the sweaty shoppers that shuffle around the market.

MIDRANGE & TOP END

Restaurante Tin-Jo (Map p88; ☎ 2221 7605; Calle 11 btwn Avs 6 & 8; ☺ 11:30am-3pm & 5:30-10pm Mon-Thu, 11:30am-3pm & 5:30 -11pm Fri & Sat, 11:30am-10pm Sun; dishes US$6-13) Certainly the best Asian food in San José; the interiors of this establishment are a riot of pan-Asian design. The menu serves a wide range of Asian fare from Indian to Indonesian (and pretty much everything in between). However, it does suffer slightly from being a jack-of-all-trades, master of none.

La Esquina de Buenos Aires (Map p88; Crn Calle 11 & Av 4; dishes US$5-20; ☺ 11:30am-3pm & 6-11pm Mon-Fri, 12-11pm Sat & Sun) Arguably the best place for a steak and glass of red in town; its tiled floors and dark-wood tables could have you believe you were in a San Telmo eatery. The Italian dishes are as good as you'll get in this part of the world, as well.

Café del Teatro Nacional (Map p88; Plaza de la Cultura; dishes US$6-8; ☺ 9am-5pm Mon-Fri, 9am-12:30pm & 1:30-5:30pm Sat) The most beautiful café in the city is, unsurprisingly, located in the most beautiful building in the city. The coffees and small sandwiches are good enough, though the real

TOP SPOTS TO EAT & DRINK FOR UNDER US$5

Eat and drink like a true on-the-go josefino, for only a few bucks:

- Slurp down a bowl of delicious seafood stew at **Poseidon** (p103).
- Get your sugar rush from the deliciously sweet and crispy doughnuts at **Churrería Manolo's** (p103).
- The thick, rich custard ice cream at **Helados de Sorbetela** (p103) is the stuff of legend for regulars to the Mercado Central.
- After a heavy night out, head straight for **Chelle's** (p103), which is where the party set shovel plates of *gallo pinto* (rice and beans) down to line their *guaro*- (local firewater) weary stomachs.

reason you're here is to soak up the ambience of the building's stunning frescoes.

Dos Gringos (Map p88; cnr Av 1 & Calle 7; dishes US$5-11; 11pm-2am) This bar and restaurant is run by two gringos, namely a Bostonian and a Floridian, and has a good mix of American dishes. During the evening, this is a popular spot for middle-age tourists, who dance to classic rock while sipping a cocktail or two.

Café Parisienne (Map p88; Plaza de la Cultura; dishes US$6-10; 24hr) Part of the Gran Hotel Costa Rica, this European-style café is the perfect place for people-watching, and you can't beat the views of the Teatro Nacional. The meals are definitely overpriced and fairly ordinary, though the waitstaff will leave you alone if you just order a coffee.

News Café (Map p88; cnr Av Central & Calle 7; dishes US$6-10; 6am-10pm) On the ground floor of Hotel Presidente is the most popular café in the city for gringo expats. The main draw is the daily selection of foreign newspapers and the free wi-fi. The attached restaurant serves a variety of American-style sandwiches, salads and recommended steaks.

Balcón de Europa (Map p88; 2221 4841; Calle 9 btwn Avs Central & 1; dishes US$6-12; 11:30am-10pm Sun-Fri) One of San José's most popular eateries, this restaurant was established in 1909 and claims to be one of the oldest in Costa Rica. The menu is heavily influenced by European culinary traditions and has a good selection of pastas, antipasto and salads, though there are plenty

of authentic Tico specialties, too, including *palmitos* (hearts of palms).

DRINKING

Whatever your poison may be (ours is a double shot of *guaro* garnished with lime), San José has plenty of options to keep you well lubricated. And there's something for everyone – from hole-in-the-wall dives to trendy lounges to gringolandia.

For listings of nightclubs and gay bars, see opposite.

For bars that also have live music, whether regular or occasional, see p106.

For more drinking options, see Los Yoses & San Pedro (p116) and Escazú (p122).

Be advised that San José is not exactly the safest city to go bar-hopping – be smart, and travel by taxi at night.

Barrio Amón & Surrounds

Centro Comercial El Pueblo (Map pp84-5; P) The recommended 'El Pueblo' is a shopping mall–type complex that's jam-packed with hip bars and clubs, including four that have live music. There is even a 24-hour ATH (A Toda Hora) ATM on the Cirrus network by the parking lot. The complex usually gets going at about 9pm and shuts down by 3am. Stringent security keeps trouble outside, so this is definitely one place in Chepe where you can kick back a few and let loose (just be careful when you leave as things do get rough outside). Bring your ID. The Peruvian-style Bar Picantería Inty Raymy has potent pisco sours, which always help start the night out right.

¿Por que no? (Map pp84-5; 2233 6622; from 5:30pm) Across the street and about 100m west of Centro Comercial El Pueblo, this is connected to Hotel Villa Tournón. Although the hotel primarily caters to business travelers, its bar is a local favorite, especially on Friday nights, when there's live music.

Luna Roja Café (Map pp84-5; 2223 2432; Calle 3 btwn Avs 9 & 11) Young, hip and trendy josefinos (leave the khakis at home and wear something black) fill this place. It has a ladies' night every Monday and even has the occasional Goth night. It charges for admission (US$2.50) most nights, though Wednesday is free.

Central San José

Nashville South Bar (Map p88; Calle 5 btwn Avs 1 & 3) A honky-tonk-style bar serves burgers, chili dogs and other fixin's to a bar full of tired-looking gringos. Still, it's a good place if you're looking to meet other gringo travelers, or if you need some time to ease into this whole 'being in a foreign country' thing. Another popular nightspot for the linguistically challenged is nearby Dos Gringos (opposite).

Chelle's (Map p88; ☎ 2221 1369; cnr Av Central & Calle 9; ❤ 24hr) If you're boozing the night away with Ticos, sooner or later they'll bring you to this 24/7 downtown landmark. In case you're feeling a little woozy, it also serves meals.

Bar Chavelona (Map p88; Av 10 btwn Calles 10 & 12; ❤ 24hr) This historic 77-year-old bar is in a somewhat deserted neighborhood south of downtown (in other words, take a taxi). The service is good, the atmosphere pleasant, and the locale is frequented by radio and theater workers, giving the place an old-world bohemian feel.

ENTERTAINMENT

Pick up *La Nación* on Thursday for a listing (in Spanish) of the coming week's nightlife and cultural events. The *Tico Times* 'Weekend' section (in English) has a calendar of theater, music, museums and events. A handy publication is the *Guía de Ciudad*, published by *El Financiero*, a free city guide featuring the latest events. It is usually available at the tourist office and at better hotels. Visit www.entretenimiento.co.cr for more up-to-date movies, bar and club listings in the San José area.

Nightclubs

Josefinos love to drink almost as much as they love to dance. Whether it's salsa, meringue, hip-hop or reggaetón, Chepe's clubs are always a hot place to be.

Clubs with live music and full-on dance floors will usually charge an admission of US$2 to US$5 depending on the night and the caliber of artist. Don't forget to bring your ID.

See also Los Yoses & San Pedro (p112) for more options in the university district.

In case you missed our first warning, here it is again – be smart, and travel by taxi at night. Most clubs open at around 10pm but don't get going until well after midnight. For the most raucous joints, closing time is at 6am.

BARRIO AMÓN & SURROUNDS

Centro Comercial El Pueblo (Map pp84–5; Ⓟ) The top nightspot in San José is a thick density of human activity on weekends. Smaller clubs come and go so follow the crowds

to see what's in, though there are a few established standards:

Cocoloco (Map pp84–5; ☎ 2222 8782) The place to be at the moment. Two dance floors are filled with a young and sexy crowd that grinds and gyrates to reggaetón beats.

Ebony 56 (Map pp84–5) This sprawling disco has no shortage of dance space, so if you don't like what's playing, move to the next room.

La Plaza (Map pp84–5; ☎ 2233 5516) This is one of the classier clubs in El Pueblo (although it's actually outside it), so dress to impress, bust out the Spanish and chat up a few josefinos.

Next door to the Luna Roja, you'll find **Café Loft** (Map pp84–5; ☎ 2221 2302; ❤ 7pm-2am), which has DJs spinning house, ambient and other types of soft electronica on a nightly basis. There's a dress code, so be spiffy or you're not getting in. Nearby Kafé Ko (p101) is also a hot spot for live modern music.

LA SABANA

Club Vertigo (Map p90; Paseo Colón btwn Calles 36 & 38) The city's premier ravers' club brings in big-name house DJs from around the world. Downstairs is an 850-person-capacity sweatbox of a dance floor, while upstairs people chill out on soft red sofas. The trick is to talk your way into the VIP room and hang out with the capital's bold and beautiful.

CENTRAL SAN JOSÉ

Ticos describe the downtown scene as being downscale (even dodgy), though there are two recommended places if you're looking for some local flavor.

El Túnel de Tiempo Disco (Map p88; Av Central btwn Calles 7 & 9) Starts pumping the techno late at night and keeps it going 'til the break of dawn.

Complejo Salsa 54 y Zadidas (Map p88; Calle 3 btwn Avs 1 & 3) Another good place to shake it, this vast 2nd-floor club is all Latin, all the time. Be prepared to cut some serious rug here – the local dancers here are expert *salseros*.

Cinemas

Many cinemas show recent Hollywood films with Spanish subtitles and the English soundtrack. Occasionally, films are dubbed over in Spanish *(hablado en español)* rather than subtitled; ask before buying a ticket. Movie tickets cost about US$3, and generally Wednesdays are two-for-one. Check the latest listings in *La Nación*, the *Tico Times* or on www.entretenimiento.co.cr.

Larger and more modern multiplexes are located in the suburbs of San Pedro and Escazú. But in town, try the following:

Cine Magaly (Map pp84-5; ☎ 2223 0085; Calle 23 btwn Avs Central & 1)

Omni (Map p88; ☎ 2221 7903; Calle 3 btwn Avs Central & 1)

Sala Garbo (Map p90; ☎ 2222 1034; cnr Av 2 & Calle 28)

Gay & Lesbian Venues

As a cosmopolitan city, San José is home to a thriving gay and lesbian scene, though it's best to remember that there is still bigotry and intolerance here toward homosexuals. For more information, see p532.

Admission is charged on weekends and special nights, with prices fluctuating between US$2 and US$5. Clubs may close on some nights and may have women- or men-only nights. To get the latest, log on to **Gay Costa Rica** (www.gaycostarica.com) for up-to-the-minute club info in English and Spanish, or drop by the 1@10 Café Internet (p81), which serves as the gay and lesbian information center.

CENTRAL SAN JOSÉ

The gay scene tends toward the periphery, so expect to find the best clubs in some of the worst areas. As always, travel by taxi at night, and if possible, bring a friend.

Bochinche (Map p88; ☎ 2221 0500; Calle 11 btwn Avs 10 & 12) An upscale gay bar that is popular among young professionals out for a night of drinking and flirting.

Deja Vú (Map pp84-5; ☎ 2223 3758; Calle 2 btwn Avs 14 & 16) This massive dance club is one of the most popular spots in the city. The club hosts a men's open-bar night on Wednesday and has go-go boys on Saturday.

La Avispa (Map p88; ☎ 2223 5343; Calle 1 btwn Avs 8 & 10) A long-standing gay establishment that has been in operation for over 25 years. La Avispa has a bar, pool tables and a boisterous dance floor that's been recommended by readers. It is most popular with gay men, though it does host a lesbian night once a month.

Los Cucharones (Map p88; ☎ 2233 5797; Av 6 btwn Calles Central & 1) This raucous place is frequented by young, working-class men for its over-the-top (and recommended) drag shows.

Live Music

Los Balcones (Map pp84-5; ☎ 2223 3704; Centro Comercial El Pueblo; **P**) A small bar specializing in live socially conscious Latin American folk music known as *nueva trova*. There are regular acoustic musicians and no admission cost.

Bar Tango Che Molinari (Map pp84-5; ☎ 2226 6904; Centro Comercial El Pueblo; **P**) An intimate Argentinean bar featuring live tango for a small admission fee.

Tarrico (Map pp84-5; ☎ 2222 1003; Centro Comercial El Pueblo; **P**) This is a popular watering hole where hard-drinking josefinos crowd the big bar and foosball table. There is frequent live music.

Theater

There is a wide variety of theatrical options in San José, provided you speak Spanish – though there are a few options in English. Local newspapers, including the *Tico Times*, list current shows. The Teatro Nacional is the city's most important theater. Most other theaters are not very large, performances are popular and ticket prices are quite reasonable. This adds up to sold-out performances, so get tickets as early as possible. Theaters rarely have performances on Monday.

Auditorio Nacional (Map pp84-5; ☎ 2249 1208; www .museocr.com; Museo de los Niños, Calle 4, north of Av 9) A grand stage for concerts, dance theater and plays – and even the site of the Miss Costa Rica pageant.

Little Theater Group (LTG; ☎ 2289 3910) This English-language theater group has been around since the 1950s and presents several plays a year; call to find out when and where the works will be shown.

Teatro Carpa (Map pp84-5; ☎ 2234 2866; Av 1 btwn Calles 29 & 33) Known for alternative and outdoor theater, as well as performances by the Little Theater Group.

Teatro Fanal (Map pp84-5; ☎ 2257 5524; Cenac Complex; Av 3 btwn Calles 11 & 15) Adjacent to the contemporary art museum, it puts on a variety of works, including children's theater – all in Spanish.

Teatro La Máscara (Map p88; ☎ 2222 4574; Calle 13 btwn Avs 2 & 6) Dance performances as well as alternative theater.

Teatro Melico Salazar (Map p88; ☎ 2233 5434; Av 2 btwn Calles Central & 2) The restored 1920s theater named after one of Costa Rica's most notable coffee barons has a variety of performances, including music and dance, as well as drama.

Teatro Nacional (Map p88; ☎ 2221 5341; Av 2 btwn Calles 3 & 5) Stages plays, dance, opera, symphony, Latin American music and other major cultural events. The season runs from March to November, although less frequent performances occur during other months. Tickets start as low as US$4. The National Symphony Orchestra (Orquesta Sínfonica Nacional) also plays here.

INDIGENOUS ART

If you want a quick education about indigenous culture in Costa Rica, **Galería Namu** (Map p88; ☎ 2256 3412; www.galerianamu.com; Av 7 btwn Calles 5 & 7; 🕙 9:30am-6:30pm Mon-Sat, 9:30am-1:30pm Sun) is a good place to start. Selected as an official site for the annual Costa Rican Arts Festival in San José, the gallery has done an admirable job of bringing together artwork and crafts from Costa Rica's small but diverse population of indigenous tribes.

Owner Aisling French regularly visits artists in remote villages around the country and can provide background information on the various traditions represented in the artwork and crafts. Boruca ceremonial masks, Guaymí dolls and dresses, Bribrí dugout canoes, Chorotega ceramics, Huetar carvings and mats, and Guatuso blankets are all among the works that can be found at the gallery.

There is also some work by contemporary urban artists, including art produced by Central American street children through a nonprofit program.

English is spoken. In the rainy season it is closed on Sunday, and shop hours may vary.

Teatro Sala Vargas Calvo (Map p88; ☎ 2222 1875; Av 2 btwn Calles 3 & 5) Known for theater-in-the-round performances.

Casinos

Gamblers will find casinos in several of the larger and more expensive hotels. Most casinos are fairly casual, but in the nicer hotels it is advisable to clean up as there may be a dress code. Be advised that casinos are often frequented by high-class prostitutes, so be suspicious if suddenly you're the most desirable person in the room.

Aurola Holiday Inn (Map p88; ☎ 2222 2424; 17th fl, cnr Calle 5 & Av 5)

Casino Club Colonial (Map p88; ☎ 2258 2807; Av 1 btwn Calles 9 & 11; 🕙 24hr)

Gran Hotel Costa Rica (Map p88; ☎ 2221 4000; Calle 3 btwn Avs Central & 2)

Meliá Tryp Corobicí (Map p90; ☎ 2232 8122; Calle 42; 🕙 6pm-2am) It's 200m north of Parque La Sabana.

Sports

International and national *fútbol* (soccer) games are played in **Estadio Nacional** (Map p90; ☎ 2257 6844) in Parque La Sabana. Call ahead for game schedules. For more information on this national passion, turn to p48.

For information on opportunities for sport around the city, see p91.

Bullfighting is also a popular Tico sport. Events are mainly held during national holidays and are the focal point of large fiestas. The largest event is held in Zapote (a southern suburb) over the Christmas period, and members of the public are encouraged to participate in the action.

SHOPPING

Whether you're looking for indigenous handicrafts or a plastic howler monkey, San José has no shortage of shops, running the gamut from artsy boutiques to shameless tourist traps. For the most part, however, the capital offers a good selection of handicraft shopping, and stores are generally cheaper here than in tourist towns. With the exception of markets, haggling is not tolerated in stores and shops – this isn't Thailand. For general information on shopping in Costa Rica, turn to p536.

Mercado Central (Map p88; Avs Central & 1 btwn Calles 6 & 8) Assuming you've dressed down and stuck a wad of extra cash in your sock, the Central Market is the best place in the city for, well, pretty much anything you'd want. If you want to do the whole tourist thing, this is the cheapest place to buy a hammock (Hecho en Nicaragua) or a '*pura vida*' T-Shirt (Made in China). For something decidedly more Costa Rican, export-quality coffee beans (we like whole-bean organic shade-grown dark roast) can be had at a fraction of the price you'll pay in tourist shops.

Mercado Artesanal (Craft Market; Map p88; Plaza de la Democracia; Avs Central & 2 btwn Calles 13 & 15) One of the best shopping experiences in the city is here, where you can browse close to 100 open-air stalls that sell everything from handcrafted jewelry and elaborate woodwork to Cuban cigars and Guatemalan sarongs.

La Casona (Map p88; Calle Central btwn Avs Central & 1; 🕙 Mon-Sat) Welcome to the number one tourist trap in Chepe! Sure, shopping in this multilevel complex is the cultural equivalent of buying art at Wal-Mart, but it's cheap and the selection is surprisingly good. This is the best place to buy all your tacky souvenirs, be they banana-leaf paper journals or tree-frog stickers. Shop around as there are some quality crafts to be had here.

La Buchaca (Map pp84-5; ☎ 2223 6773, 2253 8790; Centro Comercial El Pueblo; ❨ 4-8pm Mon-Sat) A tiny oasis in El Pueblo that carries well-made jewelry, ceramics and sculptures – all of Costa Rican origin. Of particular interest are the beautifully executed modern paintings featuring pre-Columbian motifs from around Central America.

Sol Maya (Map p88; ☎ 2221 0864; Calle 16 btwn Av Central 1; ❨ Sun-Fri) If you're looking to kill some time before getting on the bus, it's worth visiting this small shop near the Coca-Cola bus terminal. The simple but quaint store carries an impressive selection of Guatemalan textiles, and the prices are about as cheap as you'll find anywhere.

If you're in San José, it is absolutely worth the trip to go visit Biesanz Woodworks in Escazú (p123). And if you have the time and the inclination, you can also find wide selections of well-priced items in the suburb of Moravia, about 8km northeast of downtown, or by taking a day trip to the village of Sarchí, where Costa Rica's colorful oxcarts and finest woodwork are produced.

GETTING THERE & AWAY

San José is the country's transportation hub, and it's likely that you'll pass through the capital a number of times throughout your travels (whether you'd like to or not). Unfortunately, the transport system is rather bewildering to the first-time visitor, especially considering that most people get around the country by bus, yet there is no central bus terminal. Instead, there are dozens of bus stops, terminals and even an old Coca-Cola bottling plant that are scattered around the city, all serving different destinations. Efforts have been made to consolidate bus services, and the use of the Coca-Cola, San Carlo, Caribe and Musoc terminals have definitely helped the situation.

Air

There are two airports serving San José. For information on getting to them, turn to p111. If you're leaving the country, be advised that there is a departure tax of US$26.

Aeropuerto Internacional Juan Santamaría (Map p80; ☎ 2437 2626) handles international traffic from its sparkling new terminal and Sansa domestic flights from the diminutive blue building to the right of the main terminal. The airport is located near Alajuela. **Sansa** (Map p90; ☎ 2221 9414; www.flysansa.com; cnr Av 5 & Calle 42, La Sabana) also has an office in town.

Aeropuerto Tobías Bolaños (Map p80; ☎ 2232 2820; Pavas) is for domestic flights on Sansa and **NatureAir** (☎ 2220 3054; www.natureair .com). Any travel agent can book and confirm flights on both Sansa and NatureAir, although you can also make a reservation online. At the time of writing, both airlines were beginning to expand their services to other destinations in Central America.

INTERNATIONAL AIRLINES

International carriers that have offices in San José are listed here. Airlines serving Costa Rica directly are marked with an asterisk; they also have desks at the airport.

Air France (☎ 2280 0069; Curridabat) Go 100m east and 10m north from Pops.

Alitalia (Map p90; ☎ 2295 6820; cnr Calle 24 & Paseo Colón)

American Airlines* (Map p90; ☎ 2257 1266; Av 5bis btwn Calles 40 & 42, La Sabana)

Continental* (Map p90; ☎ 2296 4911; La Uruca) Next to Hotel Barceló.

COPA (Map p88; ☎ 2222 6640; cnr Calle 1 & Av 5)

Cubana de Aviación* (Map p88; ☎ 2221 7625, 2221 5881; 5th fl, Edificio Lux, cnr Av Central & Calle 1)

Delta* (Map p90; ☎ 2256 7909, press 5 for reservations; Paseo Colón) Located 100m east and 50m south of Toyota.

Grupo TACA* (Map p90; ☎ 2296 0909; cnr Calle 42 & Av 5) Located across from Datsun dealership.

Iberia* (Map p90; ☎ 2257 8266; 2nd fl, Centro Colón)

KLM* (☎ 2220 4111; Sabana Sur)

LTU (☎ 2234 9292; Barrio Dent)

Mexicana* (Map p90; ☎ 2295 6969; 3rd fl, Torre Mercedes Benz, Paseo Colón)

SAM/Avianca* (Map p90; ☎ 2233 3066; Centro Colón)

United Airlines* (☎ 2220 4844; Sabana Sur)

CHARTER AIRCRAFT

Sansa and NatureAir both offer charter flights out of San José, as do a number of aerotaxi companies. Most charters are small (three- to five-passenger) aircraft and can fly to any of the many airstrips around Costa Rica. Each listing following includes the San José airport that the company operates from.

Aero Bell (☎ 2290 0000; aerobell@racsa.co.cr; Tobías Bolaños)

Aviones Taxi Aéreo SA (☎ 2441 1626; Juan Santamaría)

Helicópteros Turísticos Tropical (☎ 2220 3940; Tobías Bolaños)

Pitts Aviation (☎ 2296 3600; Tobías Bolaños)

Viajes Especial Aéreos SA (Veasa; ☎ 2232 1010, 2232 8043; Tobías Bolaños)

Bus

The **Coca-Cola bus terminal** (Map p88; Coca-Cola; Av 1 btwn Calles 16 & 18) is a well-known landmark in San José, and an infinite number of buses leave from a four-block radius around it. Several other terminals serve specific regions. Just northeast of the Coca-Cola, the **Terminal San Carlos** (Map pp84–5; cnr Av 9 & Calle 12) serves northern destinations, such as Monteverde, La Fortuna and Sarapiquí. The **Gran Terminal del Caribe** (Caribe terminal; Map pp84–5; Calle Central, north of Av 13) serves the Caribbean coast. At the south end of town, **Terminal Musoc** (Av 22 btwn Calles Central & 1) caters for San Isidro.

Many of the bus companies have no more than a bus stop (in this case pay the driver directly); some have a tiny office with a window on the street; some operate from a terminal.

Be aware that bus schedules change regularly. Pick up the useful but not always correct master bus schedule at the ICT office (p82) or look for the helpful *Hop on the Bus*, an up-to-date brochure published by Exintur – the brochure has locations of bus terminals and covers major destinations.

At the time of writing, fuel prices were fluctuating throughout the Americas, and it's likely that the bus prices in this book will change slightly after publication.

Buses are crowded on Friday evening and Saturday morning, even more so during Christmas and Easter.

Thefts are common around the Coca-Cola terminal, so stay alert – especially at night. Theft is an increasing problem on intercity buses, so keep all valuables in your carry-on bag, and don't let it out of your sight.

An excellent way of avoiding the hassle of public buses is to book your onward travel through **A Safe Passage** (☎ 2441 7837, 8365 9678; www .costaricabustickets.com), which can purchase tickets in advance for a small fee. It also arranges airport transfers, and indeed it's possible to land in San José and then be shuttled right to your departing intercity bus.

INTERNATIONAL BUSES FROM SAN JOSÉ

Take a copy of your passport when buying tickets to international destinations. For more on border crossings, see boxed text Border Crossings, p542.

Changuinola/Bocas del Toro, Panama Panaline (Map p88; cnr Calle 16 & Av 3) US$15, eight hours, departs at 10am.

David, Panama Tracopa (Map p88; Calle 14 btwn Avs 3 & 5) US$18, nine hours, departs 7:30am.

Guatemala City Tica Bus (Map p88; cnr Calle 9 & Av 4) US$45, 60 hours, departs 6am and 7:30am.

Managua, Nicaragua Nica Bus (Map p88; Gran Terminal del Caribe) US$14, nine hours, departs at 6am, 7am and 9am; Tica Bus (Map pp84–5; cnr Calle 9 & Av 4) US$14, nine hours, departs 6am & 7:30am; Trans Nica (Map pp84–5; Calle 22 btwn Avs 3 & 5) US$14, nine hours, departs 4:30am, 5:30am and 9am; Transportes Deldu/Sirca Express (Map p88; Calle 16 btwn Avs 3 & 5) US$14, nine hours, departs 4:30am.

Panama City Panaline (Map p88; cnr Calle 16 & Av 3) US$42, 15 hours, departs 1pm; Tica Bus (Map p88; cnr Calle 9 & Av 4) US$25, 15 hours, departs 10pm.

San Salvador, El Salvador Tica Bus (Map p88; cnr Calle 9 & Av 4) US$42, 48 hours, departs 6am and 7:30am.

Tegucigalpa, Honduras Tica Bus (Map p88; cnr Calle 9 & Av 4) US$32, 48 hours, departs 6am and 7:30am.

DOMESTIC BUSES FROM SAN JOSÉ

For destinations within Costa Rica, consult the following.

To the Central Valley

Alajuela Tuasa (Map p88; Av 2 btwn Calles 12 & 14) US$0.75, 40 minutes, departs every 10 minutes from 4:20am to 11pm, every 30 minutes after 11pm.

Cartago (Map p88; Calle 13 btwn Avs 6 & 8) US$0.50, 40 minutes.

Grecia (Map pp84–5; Av 5 btwn Calles 18 & 20) US$0.50, one hour, departs every 30 minutes from 5:35am to 10:10pm.

Heredia (Map pp84–5; Calle 1 btwn Avs 7 & 9) US$0.75, 20 minutes, departs every 10 minutes from 5am to 11pm.

Sarchí (Map pp84–5; Av 5 btwn Calles 18 & 20) US$2, 1½ hours, departs every 30 minutes from 5am to 10pm.

Turrialba (Map p88; Calle 13 btwn Avs 6 & 8) US$2, two hours, departs hourly from 5:15am to 10pm.

Volcán Irazú (Map p88; Av 2 btwn Calles 1 & 3) US$4.50, two hours, departs 8am.

Volcán Poás Tuasa (Map p88; Av 2 btwn Calles 12 & 14) US$4, five hours, departs 8am.

To Northwestern Costa Rica

Cañas Tralapa (Map pp84–5; Calle 14 btwn Avs 1 & 3) US$3, 3¼ hours, departs 8:30am, 9:20am, 12:20pm, 1:40pm, 4:45pm and 6:15pm.

SAN JOSÉ

Ciudad Quesada (San Carlos) Autotransportes San Carlos (Map pp84–5; San Carlos terminal) US$2.50, 2½ hours, departs hourly 5am to 6pm.

La Fortuna (Map pp84–5; San Carlos terminal) US$4, four hours, departs 6:15am, 8:30am and 11:30am.

Liberia (Map pp84–5; Calle 24 btwn Avs 5 & 7) US$5, four hours, departs hourly from 6am to 6pm.

Monteverde/Santa Elena (Map pp84–5; Calle 12 btwn Avs 7 & 9) US$4.50, 4½ hours, departs 6:30am and 2:30pm. (This bus fills up very quickly – book ahead.)

Peñas Blancas, the Nicaragua Border Crossing Transportes Deldú (Map pp84–5; Calle 14 btwn Avs 3 & 5) US$7, six hours, departs 4:30am, 5am, 7am, 7:45am, 10:30am.

Tilarán Autotransportes Tilarán (Map pp84–5; Calle 20 & Av 3) US$4, four hours, departs 7:30am, 9:30am, 12:45pm, 3:45pm and 6:30pm.

To Península de Nicoya

Nicoya Empresas Alfaro (Map pp84–5; Av 5 btwn Calle 14 &16) US$5.25 to US$6, five hours, departs 6am, 6:30am, 8am, 10am, 10:30am, 12:30am, 1:30pm, 2pm, 3pm, 4pm, 5pm and 5:20pm.

Playa Bejuco Empresas Arza (Map pp84–5; Calle 12 btwn Avs 7 & 9) US$5.75, 5½ hours, 6am and 3:30pm.

Playa del Coco Pullmitan (Map pp84–5; Calle 24 btwn Avs 5 & 7) US$5.25, five hours, departs 8am, 2pm and 4pm.

Playa Flamingo, via Brasilito Tralapa (Map pp84–5; Calle 20 btwn Avs 1 & 3) US$6.50, six hours, departs 8am, 10:30am, 11am and 3pm.

Playa Junquillal Tralapa (Map pp84–5; Av 7 btwn Calles 20 & 22) US$8, six hours, departs 2pm.

Playa Nosara Empresas Alfaro (Map pp84–5; Calle 14 btwn Avs 3 & 5) US$5, six hours, departs 6am.

Playa Sámara Empresas Alfaro (Map pp84–5; Calle 16 btwn Avs 3 & 5) US$5, five hours, departs 12:30pm and 6pm.

Playa Panamá & Playa Hermosa Tralapa (Map pp84–5; Av 7 btwn Calles 20 & 22) US$5, five hours, departs 3:25pm.

Playa Tamarindo Empresas Alfaro (Map pp84–5; Calle 16 btwn Avs 3 & 5) US$5, five hours, departs 11am and 3:30pm.

Santa Cruz, via Tempisque bridge (Map pp84–5; Av 5 btwn Calles 14 & 16) US$5.50, departs 6:30am, 1:30pm and 3pm.

To the Central Pacific Coast

Dominical Transportes Morales (Map pp84–5; Coca-Cola) US$4.50, seven hours, departs 5:30am and 3pm.

Jacó Transportes Jacó (Map pp84–5; Coca-Cola) US$2.50, three hours, departs 7:30am, 10:30am, 1pm, 3:30pm and 6:30pm.

Puntarenas Empresarios Unidos (Map pp84–5; cnr Av 12 & Calle 16) US$2.50, 2½ hours, many buses from 4am, 6am and 7pm.

Quepos/Manuel Antonio Transportes Morales (Map pp84–5; Coca-Cola) US$4, four hours, departs 5am, 8am, 11am, 2:30pm and 4:30pm.

Uvita, via Dominical Transportes Morales (Map pp84–5; Coca-Cola) US$6, six hours, departs 6am and 3pm.

To Southern Costa Rica & Península de Osa

Ciudad Neily Tracopa (Map pp84–5; Calle 14 btwn Avs 3 & 5) US$9, eight hours, departs 5am, 10am, 1pm, 4:30pm and 6pm.

Golfito Tracopa (Map pp84–5; Calle 14 btwn Avs 3 & 5) US$8.50, eight hours, departs 7am and 3pm.

Palmar Norte Tracopa (Map pp84–5; Calle 14 btwn Avs 3 & 5) US$5, five hours, departs 5am, 7am, 8:30am, 10am, 1pm, 2:30pm and 6pm.

Paso Canoas, the Panama Border Crossing Tracopa (Map pp84–5; Calle 14 btwn Avs 3 & 5) US$9, six hours, departs 8:30am, 10:30am, 2:30pm, 7:30pm and 9pm.

Puerto Jiménez Blanco Lobo (Map pp84–5; Calle 14 btwn Avs 9 & 11) US$6.50, eight hours, departs 6am and 12pm.

San Isidro del General Tracopa (Map p88; Av 4 btwn Calles 14 & 16) US$3.75, three hours, departs hourly from 5am to 6pm; Transportes Musoc (Map p90; cnr Calle Central & Av 22) US$3.25, three hours, departs hourly from 5:30am to 5:30pm.

San Vito Empresa Alfaro (Map pp84–5; Calle 16 btwn Av 3 & 5) US$7.50, seven hours, departs 5:45am, 8:15am, 11:30am and 2:45pm.

Santa María de Dota Transportes Los Santos (Map pp84–5; Av 16 btwn Calles 19 & 21) US$2, 2½ hours, departs 7:15am, 9am, 11:30am, 12:30pm, 3pm, 5pm and 7:30pm.

To the Caribbean Coast

All of the following buses depart from the Caribe terminal (Map pp84–5):

Cahuita (Autotransportes Mepe) US$6.50, four hours, departs 6am, 10am, 12pm, 2pm and 4pm.

Cariari, for transfer to Tortuguero (Empresarios Guapileños) US$2.50, 2¼ hours, departs 6:30am, 9am, 10:30am, 1pm, 3pm, 4:30pm, 6pm and 7pm.

Guápiles (Empresarios Guapileños) US$1.75, 1½ hours, departs hourly from 5:30am to 10pm.

Puerto Limón (Autotransportes Caribeños) US$3.50, three hours, departs every 30 minutes from 5am to 7pm.

Puerto Viejo de Talamanca (Autotransportes Mepe) US$7.50, 4½ hours, departs 6am, 10am, 12pm, 2pm and 4pm.

Siquirres (Líneas Nuevo Atlántico) US$2, 1½ hours, departs 5:30am, 8am, 9:30am and 6pm.

Sixaola, the Panama Border Crossing (Autotransportes Mepe) US$9.50, six hours, departs 6am, 10am, 12pm, 2pm and 4pm.

To the Northern Lowlands

Ciudad Quesada (San Carlos) See p109.
Los Chiles, the Nicaragua Border Crossing (Map pp84-5; San Carlos terminal) US$3.75, five hours, departs 5:30am and 3:30pm.
Puerto Viejo de Sarapiquí Autotransportes Sarapiquí (Map pp84-5; Caribe terminal) US$2.50, two hours, departs 6am, 7:30am, 10am, 11:30am, 1:30pm, 2:30pm, 3:30pm, 4:30pm and 6pm.
Rara Avis (Map pp84-5; San Carlos terminal) US$4:50, four hours, departs 6:30am.
Upala Transportes de Upala (Map pp84-5; San Carlos terminal) US$6, five hours, departs 3:45pm.

TOURIST BUSES

Grayline's Fantasy Bus (☎ 2220 2126; www.grayline costarica.com) and **Interbus** (☎ 2283 5573; www.inter busonline.com) shuttle passengers from all over the San José area to a rather long and growing list of popular tourist destinations around Costa Rica. They are more expensive than the standard bus service, but they will get you there faster. Turn to p547 for more information.

GETTING AROUND

Downtown San José is extremely congested – narrow streets, heavy traffic and a complicated one-way system often mean that it is quicker to walk than to take the bus. The same applies to driving: if you rent a car, don't drive downtown – it's a nightmare! If you're in a hurry to get somewhere that is more than 1km away, take a taxi.

To/From the Airports
TO AEROPUERTO INTERNACIONAL JUAN SANTAMARÍA

You can reserve a pick-up with **Taxi Aeropuerto** (☎ 2221 6865; www.taxiaeropuerto.com), which charges a flat rate of US$12 from most parts of San José. You can also take a street taxi, but the rates may vary wildly. It should cost roughly US$12 to US$15, but this will depend largely on traffic. A cheaper option is the red **Tuasa bus** (Map p88; cnr Calle 10 & Av 2; fare US$0.60) bound for Alajuela. Be sure to tell the driver that you are getting off at the airport when you board *(Voy al aeropuerto, por favor)*. **Interbus** (☎ 2283 5573; www.interbusonline.com) runs an airport shuttle service that will pick you up at your hotel for US$5 – good value.

TO AEROPUERTO TOBÍAS BOLAÑOS

Buses to Tobías Bolaños depart every 30 minutes from Avenida 1, 150m west of the Coca-Cola bus terminal. A taxi to the airport from downtown costs about US$3.

Bus

Local buses are useful to get you into the suburbs and surrounding villages, or to the airport. They leave regularly from particular bus stops downtown – though all of them will pick up passengers on the way. Most buses run between 5am and 10pm and cost US$0.25 to US$0.75.

Buses from Parque La Sabana head into town on Paseo Colón, then go over to Avenida 2 at the San Juan de Dios hospital. They then go three different ways through town before eventually heading back to La Sabana. Buses are marked Sabana–Estadio, Sabana–Cementario or Cementario–Estadio. These buses are a good bet for a cheap city tour. Buses going east to Los Yoses and San Pedro go back and forth along Avenida 2 and then switch over to Avenida Central at Calle 29. (These buses are easily identifiable because many of them have a big sign that says 'Mall San Pedro' on the front window.) These buses start at the corner of Avenida 2 and Calle 7, near Restaurante El Pollo Campesino.

Buses to the following outlying suburbs and towns begin from bus stops at the indicated blocks. Some places have more than one stop – only the main ones are listed here. If you need buses to other suburbs, inquire at the tourist office (p82).

Escazú Avenida 6 (Map p88; Av 6 btwn Calles 12 & 14); Calle 16 (Map p88; Calle 16 btwn Avs 1 & 3)
Guadalupe (Map p88; Av 3 btwn Calles Central & 1)
Moravia (Map p88; Av 3 btwn Calles 3 & 5)
Pavas (Map pp84-5; cnr Av 1 & Calle 18)
Santa Ana (Map pp84-5; Calle 16 btwn Avs 1 & 3)
Santo Domingo (Map p88; Av 5 btwn Calles Central & 2)

Car

It is not advisable to rent a car just to drive around San José. The traffic is heavy, the streets narrow and the meter-deep curb-side gutters make parking a nerve-wracking experience. In addition, car break-ins are frequent and leaving a car – even in a guarded lot – might result in a smashed window and stolen belongings. (Never ever leave anything in a rental car.) Hire one of the plentiful taxis – available at all hours – instead.

If you are renting a car to travel throughout Costa Rica, you will not be short of choices: there are more than 50 car-rental agencies in and around San José, and the travel desks at travel agencies and upmarket hotels can all arrange rentals of various types of vehicles. *Naturally Costa Rica,* a magazine published by the ICT and Canatur (available at many hotels and the ICT office), has an extensive list of car-rental companies in the area. You can also check the local yellow pages (under Alquiler de Automóviles) for a complete listing. See p547 for general information on rental agencies.

Note that there is a surcharge of about US$25 for renting cars from rental agencies at Juan Santamaría international airport. Save yourself the expense by renting in town.

Motorcycle

Given the narrow roads, deep gutters and homicidal bus drivers, riding a motorcycle in San José is recommended only for those who are not in complete need of their appendages. But for the foolhardy – and careful – road warrior, renting a bike is an option. Rental bikes are usually small (185cc to 350cc) and rates start at about US$50 per day for a 350cc motorcycle and skyrocket from there. (Plan on paying over US$200 a day for a Harley.) These are a couple of agencies worth trying in San José.

At **Wild Rider** (Map p90; ☎ 2258 4604; www.wild -rider.com; Hotel Ritmo del Caribe, cnr Paseo Colón & Calle 32) prices start at US$350 per week for a Yamaha TT-R 250 or a Suzuki DR-350 (rates include insurance, taxes, maps and helmets). Wild Rider also has a handful of used 4WD cars that can be rented at significantly cheaper weekly rates than the big agencies. It can organize on- and off-road guided tours as well.

Harley Davidson Rentals (see p117) in Escazú rents Harleys.

Taxi

Red taxis can be hailed on the street day or night, or you can have your hotel call one for you. You can also hire taxis at any of the taxi stands at the Parque Nacional, Parque Central and near the Teatro Nacional. The most difficult time to flag down a taxi is when it's raining.

Marías (meters) are supposedly used, but some drivers will pretend they are broken and try to charge you more – especially if you're a tourist who doesn't speak Spanish. (Not using a meter is illegal.) Make sure the *maría* is operating when you get in or ne-

gotiate the fare up front. Short rides downtown cost about US$2. A taxi to Escazú from downtown will cost about US$8, while a ride to Los Yoses or San Pedro will cost less than US$4. There's a 20% surcharge after 10pm that may not appear on the *maría.*

You can hire a taxi and driver for half a day or longer if you want to do some touring around the area, but rates vary wildly depending on the destination and the condition of the roads. For a short trip on reasonably good roads, plan on spending at least US$7.50 an hour for a sedan and significantly more for a 4WD sport utility vehicle or minivan. You can also negotiate a flat fee.

AROUND SAN JOSÉ

Like most sprawling metropolitan areas, San José is home to a number of suburbs, though boundary lines have blurred in recent years due to rapid development. Although a good number of suburbs are strictly off-limits, particularly on the outskirts of the capital where shantytowns are spreading, there are a few areas that offer an appealing alternative to staying in the city proper. An easy 2km walk east of downtown are Los Yoses and San Pedro, home to a number of embassies as well as the most prestigious university in the country, the Universidad de Costa Rica (UCR). About 7km west of downtown is Escazú, which is the most elite residential area in the capital and the epicenter of a recent wave of Americanization.

Until the mid-20th century, these two suburbs were separate from San José, and were predominantly occupied by the privileged elite. Today Los Yoses, San Pedro and Escazú are contiguous with the city, though they still retain much of their historical airs. For the traveler, spending the night in these well-to-do destinations is recommended if you're looking for a safe and relaxing alternative to the urban grind.

LOS YOSES & SAN PEDRO

It shouldn't come as a surprise that this university district is brimming with the highest percentage of bars and clubs in the city. In the evenings, the under-30s crowd takes to the streets in force, and if you spend enough time partying on Calle La Amargura, you may find yourself lingering in the capital for longer than you planned. If you're not the drinking type, this area is also home to some of the nicest malls and movie theaters in the capital (perfect if you're in need of a quick Western-culture fix). And you'd be hard-pressed to find a neighborhood with better restaurants than San Pedro and Los Yoses.

These suburbs are centered on a roundabout where Avenida Central meets the road to Zapote. To the west lies Los Yoses, with the Fuente de la Hispanidad (a large fountain) and the Mall San Pedro, both serving as area landmarks. To the east lies San Pedro, anchored by a small plaza and the Iglesia de San Pedro (San Pedro church). A few blocks north of Avenida Central is the tree-lined campus of the national university.

Orientation & Information

Most streets in Los Yoses and San Pedro are unnamed, and locals rely almost entirely on the landmark method to orient themselves. (See boxed text What's That Address?, p537 for more details.) Three major area landmarks are the old ICE building *(el antiguo ICE)* and the Spoon in Los Yoses, and the old Banco Popular building *(el antiguo Banco Popular)* in San Pedro.

The neighborhood abounds with internet cafés, so there's no problem logging on. Pick up a copy of the student weekly, *Semana Universitaria*, for a comprehensive source of local events.

Internet Café Costa Rica (Map p114; ☎ 2224 7295; per hr US$0.60; ⏰ 24hr) As good a place to log on as any, 75m west of the old Banco Popular.

Librería Internacional (Map p114; ☎ 2253 9553; Barrio Dent; ⏰ 9:30am-7:30pm Mon-Sat, 1-5pm Sun) This has new books mostly in Spanish (but some in English), as well as travel and wildlife guides. It's 300m west of Taco Bell, behind Mall San Pedro.

Scotiabank (Map p114; ☎ 2280 0604; Av Central btwn Calles 5 & 7, San Pedro) Changes cash and has a 24-hour ATM on the Cirrus network.

Sights & Activities

The **Museo de Insectos** (Map p114; ☎ 2207 5318, 2207 5647; admission US$1; ⏰ 1-5pm Mon-Fri), also known as the Museo de Entomología, has a fine collection of insects curated by the Facultad de Agronomía at the Universidad de Costa Rica and housed (incongruously) in the basement of the music building (Facultad de Artes Musicales) on campus. It is claimed that this

is the only insect museum of its size in Central America. The collection is certainly extensive and provides a good opportunity to view a vast assortment of exotic – and downright alarming – creepy crawlies. The museum is signposted from San Pedro church, or you can ask for directions. Ring the bell to gain admission if the door isn't open.

If you're interested in knocking down some pins, one block south of the North American–Costa Rican Cultural Center you'll find **Boliche Dent** (Map p114; ☎ 2234 2777; cnr Av Central & Calle 23, Los Yoses; bowling per hr US$5). Just east of the rotunda in San Pedro, you can strap on the roller skates and hang out with what seems like every last teenager in San José at **Salón Los Patines** (Map p114; ☎ 2224 6821), the local roller rink.

If you're looking to pick a fight or two, check out the **Thaiboxing Center** (Map p114; ☎ 2225 7386) or **Atemi Ryu Martial Arts Center** (Map p114; ☎ 2524 0781).

Sleeping

Casa Agua Buena (Map p114 ☎ 2234 2411; www.agua buena.org/casabuena/index.html; Barrio Lourdes; r per week US$60-80) East of San Pedro, this group house, which caters to long-term renters, is very popular among international students. Its two simple peach-color homes with rooms of various sizes sit side by side on a quiet dead-end street. Houses are equipped with a common kitchen, washing machine (use of the machine is included in the rates), a lounge with cable TV and phone. Some rooms share bathrooms,

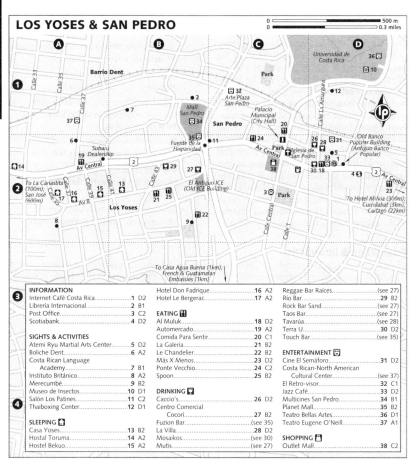

LOS YOSES & SAN PEDRO

while others have private ones – all with hot water. The house also runs the Agua Buena Human Rights Association, which is working to increase medical access for people living with HIV/AIDS. The Casa is gay-friendly.

Hostel Bekuo (Map p114; ☎ 2234 5486; www.hostel bekuo.com; dm/s/d/tr US$12/20/30/36; P ⬚) This is easily one of the most beautiful hostels in the country – unsurprisingly, one of the founding Tica owners studied interior design. The common areas of the hostel are heavily influenced by Japanese minimalist design, and have low tables, beanbag chairs and hanging lanterns. The rooms themselves are naturalist themed, and adorned with stunning mounted photography. Shared facilities include a communal kitchen, hot-water bathrooms, a recreation room with pool table and a TV lounge. Guests have free internet access (including wi-fi). It's 325m west of the Spoon.

Casa Yoses (Map p114; ☎ 2234 5486; www.casayoses .com; dm/s/d/tr incl breakfast US$12/20/28/36; P ⬚) This hostel is a winner. Dorms and private rooms with shared hot-water bathrooms are located in a 19th-century mansion, but the real appeal is the beautiful, fenced-in garden with hammocks, sun chairs and tropical plants. Guests can also rest in the comfy TV lounge, play a few pick-up games of foosball or cook a meal in the kitchen (or with the outdoor BBQ). There's also free internet (including wi-fi). The three Tico owners speak English and French (and Tico), and are all-around cool guys. It's 250m west of the Spoon.

Hostal Toruma (Map p114; ☎ 2234 8186; www.hicr.org; Av Central btwn Calles 29 & 31; dm/s/d/tr US$10/35/50/60; P 💻 🏊) The former HI hostel has recently gone under the same ownership as Hostel Pangea downtown (p95). The idea is that this is to be the more chilled and comfortable alternative to its hedonistic sibling. Toruma ticks all the boxes for your modern-day flashpacker: sun-trapped swimming pool, plasma screens and high-speed wi-fi are all features in this beautifully converted colonial home. The airy doubles are well worth busting the budget for, especially considering that they're nicer than almost anything else you'll find in the midrange options.

Hotel Milvia (Map p114; ☎ 2225 4543; www.hotelmilvia.com; s/d/tr incl breakfast US$69/80/88; 💻) This stunning Caribbean-style plantation once served as the home of Ricardo Fernández Peralta, an artillery colonel who fought in Costa Rica's 1948 civil war. It was restored to its original grandeur by his grandson, and it now operates as a small and personal hotel. Each spacious room with private hot-water bathroom combines just the right touch of modern and antique. An upstairs terrace provides incredible views of the surrounding neighborhood. Credit cards accepted. For taxi drivers: it's 100m north and 200m east of Mercado San Pedro Muñoz y Nanne.

Hotel Don Fadrique (Map p114; ☎ 2225 8166, 2224 7583; www.hoteldonfadrique.com; cnr Calle 37 & Av 8; s/d/tr incl breakfast US$68/80/95; P) This family-run hotel is decorated with a private collection of contemporary Central American and Costa Rican art, including the permanent collection of painter Florencia Urbina. Its artsy and sophisticated ambience blends well with the fresh plants and flowers peppered throughout the hotel. Continental breakfast is served on the tropical, plant-filled patio. Credit cards accepted. Take the second entrance to Los Yoses, off Avenida Central.

Hotel Le Bergerac (Map p114; ☎ 2234 7850; www.bergerac.co.cr; Calle 35, Los Yoses; s US$85-130, d US$95-145, all incl breakfast; P 💻) This boutique luxury hotel, 50m south of Avenida Central, is regarded as one of the most sophisticated places to stay in the capital. The French-colonial building is warm and inviting, though readers predominantly rave about the exceptional professionalism of the staff. Rooms of varying size are furnished with antiques and highlighted by attractive wooden accents and immaculate bathrooms. The hotel restaurant, **Restaurant L'Ile de France** (☎ 2283 5812; mains US$8-15; 🕑 6-10pm Mon-Sat), is one of the top spots in the city for French cuisine, and reservations are necessary, even if you're a hotel guest. Credit cards are accepted.

Eating

San Pedro and Los Yoses are home to some of the best restaurants in all of Costa Rica (and possibly Central America). There's no shortage of cheap student spots, but this is one area where it's worth splurging.

La Canastita (Map p114; ☎ 2221 3816; crn Avs Central & 25; dishes US$2-5; 🕑 11:30am-11pm) This strip-light-and-plastic-table sort of joint serves up delicious casados and blares out soccer to the animated punters.

Spoon (Map p114; ☎ 2253 1331; cnr Calle 43 & Av 10; dishes US$2-8; 🕑 8am-7pm Mon-Fri, 9am-5pm Sat & Sun) The Los Yoses branch of this universally adored restaurant is so famous that directions are given in relation to it! The menu is extensive, but the big breakfasts are the local favorite (especially after a long night of clubbing).

Al Muluk (Map p114; Calle 3, north of Av Central; dishes US$3-7) Although it has a great selection of traditional Lebanese and Middle Eastern dishes, you're here for the falafel, which is fresh, cheap and damn good.

Comida Para Sentir (Map p114; dishes US$4-8) Vegetarians of the world unite – this jam-packed student haunt 150m north of the church serves up cruelty-free whole-grain sandwiches with all the veggie-riffic fixings you can imagine.

Ponte Vecchio (Map p114; ☎ 2283 1810; mains US$6-15; 🕑 noon-2:30pm & 6-10:30pm Mon-Sat) This elegant Italian place vies for the 'best of' in the greater San José area and has been recognized as one of the top restaurants in Central America. Chef Antonio D'Alaimo, who once worked in New York City, makes all of his own fresh pastas and imports many of his ingredients directly from Italy. Credit cards accepted. It's 150m east of Fuente de Hispanidad and 10m north.

La Galería (Map p114; ☎ 2234 0850; Los Yoses; dishes US$7-12; 🕑 noon-2:30pm & 6:30-10:30pm Mon-Fri, 6:30-10:30pm Sat) This long-standing German-inspired eatery, 125m west of the old ICE building, is perennially listed by critics as one of the best restaurants in Central America. Its house specialties are the *schpaetzle* and strudel, and they're good enough to make any homesick German cry. Credit cards accepted.

Le Chandelier (Map p114; ☎ 2225 3980; Los Yoses; meals US$10-25; ☻ 11:30am-2pm & 6:30-11pm Mon-Fri, 6:30-11pm Sat) This is the most famous French restaurant in San José. (It even has its own line of sauces that are sold in some of the more upscale supermarkets.) The food here is predictably top-notch, and whether you're sitting next to the cozy fireplace or outside on the patio, it's hard to find a more romantic spot. Go 100m west and 100m south of the old ICE building.

The **Automercado** (Map p114; Av Central btwn Calles 39 & 41, Los Yoses) and the **Más X Menos** (Map p114; Av Central, San Pedro) are large, modern supermarkets that offer plenty of options for self-caterers.

Drinking

Río Bar (Map p114; cnr Av Central & Calle 39, Los Yoses) Just west of the fountain, this popular bar has live bands on some nights and a pyro-technic house drink called the *la cucaracha* (the cockroach). There are two-for-one drink specials on Monday night.

Centro Comercial Cocorí (Map p114; south of Av Central, Los Yoses) The nightlife hub, further east and just south of Los Antojitos Cancún. Most of the places here get started after 9pm and run late (till the last customer leaves). Rock Bar Sand is the regular watering hole for local rockers, as is Mutis out front. Around the back, Reggae Bar Raíces draws in the Rasta crowd, while Taos Bar, next door, is slightly mellower, but still gets packed.

Calle La Amargura (Street of Sorrow; Map p114; San Pedro) This is what Calle 3 is known as, to the north of Avenida Central. However, it should be called Calle de la Cruda (Street of Hangovers) because it has perhaps the highest concentration of bars of any single street in town, many of which are packed with customers even during daylight hours. Terra U, Mosaikos, Caccio's and Tavarúa are raucous, beer-soaked places packed with a steady stream of rowdy young customers. A more relaxed (and slightly grown-up) place is La Villa, located in a distinctive wood house with a candlelit back patio. There is live music some weekends.

Mall San Pedro (Map p114; ☎ 2283 7516) This is northwest of Fuente de la Hispanidad and has two popular bars, especially among mall rats who aren't quite ready to go home when the sun goes down. Fuzion Bar alternates between hip hop and reggae, while Touch Bar, as its name implies, is a flirtatious lounge that's great for meeting (and chatting up) people.

Entertainment

Cinemas are plentiful in the neighborhood. **Multicines San Pedro** (Map p114; ☎ 2283 5715/6; top level, Mall San Pedro; admission US$4) has 10 screens showing the latest Hollywood flicks. Better yet, head to **Cine El Semáforo** (Map p114; ☎ 2253 9126; www.cineselsemaforo.com; admission US$3; ☻ 11am-8pm), a hip little theater showing Spanish and Latin American movie classics every day. (It's Spanish only, so it's great if you want to come to practice.) It's beside the train tracks, east of Calle 3.

If live theater is your bag, there are a couple of choices in the area. **Teatro Eugene O'Neill** (Map p114; ☎ 2207 7554; www.cccncr.com; cnr Av Central & Calle 37, Los Yoses) has performances sponsored by the Centro Cultural Costarricense Norteamericano (Costa Rican–North American Cultural Center). On the east side of the Universidad de Costa Rica campus is the **Teatro Bellas Artes** (☎ 2207 4327), which has a wide variety of pro-gramming, including works produced by the university's fine arts department.

Jazz Café (Map p114; ☎ 2253 8933; ☻ 6pm-2am) is the destination in San Pedro for live music, with a different band every night. Cover charges vary, depending on the prominence of the musical act, but usually fluctuate between US$4 and US$6 for local groups. It's 50m west of old Banco Popular.

For a full-blown dance party, hit **Planet Mall** (Map p114; ☎ 2280 4693; ☻ 8pm-2:30am Thu-Sat), one of San José's most expensive nightclubs. The enormous, warehouse-size disco has a couple of levels, several bars, and is situated on the 4th and 5th stories of Mall San Pedro, where you can admire the twinkling lights of San José from its oversize windows. Admission here can fluctuate depending on who is spin-ning or performing, but can easily creep up to US$10 on any given night.

One of the hippest spots in the area is **El Retro-visor** (Map p114; Arte Plaza San Pedro; ☻ 6pm-2am), an Argentinean-owned retro café that's adorned with 1980s pop culture memo-rabilia. It's very popular among trendy UCR students.

Shopping

Both **Mall San Pedro** (Map p114; ☎ 2283 7516; north-west of Fuente de la Hispanidad) and the **Outlet Mall**

(Map p114; Av Central) offer ample opportunities for mall rats looking to shop till they drop. It's east of the road to Zapote.

Getting There & Away

From the Plaza de la Cultura in San José, take any bus marked 'Mall San Pedro.' A taxi ride from downtown will cost US$1.50 to US$2.

ESCAZÚ

Packed with gringo expats and moneyed Tico aristocrats, the affluent suburb of Escazú is spread out on a hillside overlooking San José and Heredia. The area is really comprised of the three adjoining neighborhoods of San Rafael de Escazú, Escazú Centro and San Antonio de Escazú, each of which has its own unique character and flair.

San Rafael, which is one part Costa Rica, two parts USA, is dotted with strip malls, car dealerships, nice homes, nicer cars and chain restaurants that print their menus largely in English. (The US ambassador lives in this area in a very secure-looking white-walled compound.) Escazú Centro thankfully retains a more unhurried Tico ambience, with its narrow streets and numerous shops and *sodas*. And the area around San Antonio remains almost entirely residential, though it does have a handful of hotels with spectacular views of the valley.

For the traveler, staying in Escazú is an excellent choice as it's well connected to downtown by public buses, it's brimming with some of the best restaurants in the city and there are some truly top-notch accommodations to choose from.

Information

Banco Nacional de Costa Rica (Map pp118-19; cnr Calle 2 & Av 2, Escazú Centro; ⊙ 8:30am-3:45pm) On the main plaza, can change money and traveler's checks, and it even has a drive-thru window.

Banex (Map pp118-19; Centro Comercial Guachipelín, Carretera JF Kennedy, San Rafael) On the northwestern end of the Centro Comercial Guachipelín you'll find a 24-hour ATM.

Escazú Internet (Map pp118-19; ground fl, Centro Comercial Plaza Escazú, Escazú Centro; per hr US$0.50; ⊙ 8:30am-10pm Mon-Sat, 9am-9pm Sun) Email access.

Hospital CIMA (Map pp118-19; ☎ 2208 1000; www .hospitalsanjose.net) Medical care – emergency or otherwise. This is 500m west of the Próspero Fernández toll booth in the area of Guachipelín, on the west side of Escazú, and is one of the most modern hospitals in the greater San José metropolitan area. It is affiliated with Baylor University Medical Center in the USA and is recommended.

Librería Internacional (Map pp118-19; ☎ 2201 8320; Multiplaza Escazú; ⊙ 10am-8pm Mon-Sat, to 7pm Sun) A branch of the bookshop chain.

Scotiabank (Map pp118-19; Carretera JF Kennedy, San Rafael) Has a Cirrus ATM.

Activities

You can arrange motorcycle tours or rent bikes at **Harley Davidson Rentals** (Map pp118-19; ☎ 2289 5552; www.mariaalexandra.com), which has an office inside the Apartotel María Alexandra. Riders have to be more than 25 years of age and have a valid motorcycle driving license. Rates start at US$80 per bike per day and include helmet, goggles and unlimited mileage (insurance and tax not included). The agency can deliver bikes to other destinations at an extra charge.

Reputable **Swiss Travel Service** (Map pp118-19; ☎ 2282 4898; www.swisstravelcr.com; Autopista Próspero Fernández, 300m west of Cruce de Piedeades de Santa Ana) offers tours all over Costa Rica.

Those who want to practice their golf swing can head to the **Costa Rica Country Club** (Map pp118-19; ☎ 2228 9333, 2208 5000; www.costarica countryclub.com), which has a nine-hole course. There are also tennis courts and a pool. In Santa Ana, west of Escazú, is **Valle del Sol** (Map pp118-19; ☎ 2282 9222, ext 218/219; www.vallesol.com; green fees US$7, golf carts US$20), inside a community of the same name, which has a new 18-hole (7000yd, par 72) public course.

If you're looking for something more adrenalin-pumping in this slow-paced suburb, you can always play soldiers in the hills at the local paintballing outfit, **Paintball Arena** (☎ 2560 0400; www.paintball.co.cr, per person US$10).

Festivals & Events

On the second Sunday of March, Escazú celebrates **Día del Boyero**, which is a celebration in honor of oxcart drivers. Dozens of *boyeros* from all over the country decorate the traditional, brightly painted carts and form a colorful (if slow) parade.

Sleeping

Escazú has a variety of accommodations – all in the midrange to top-end categories. Street addresses aren't given here – refer to the map or call the hotel for directions (which are invariably complicated). All of

ESCAZÚ

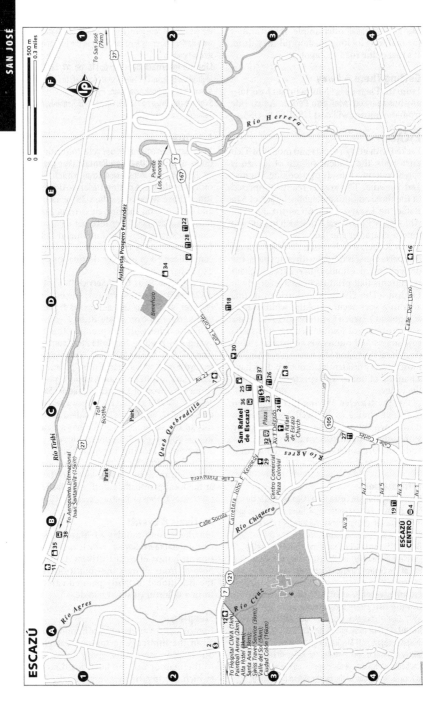

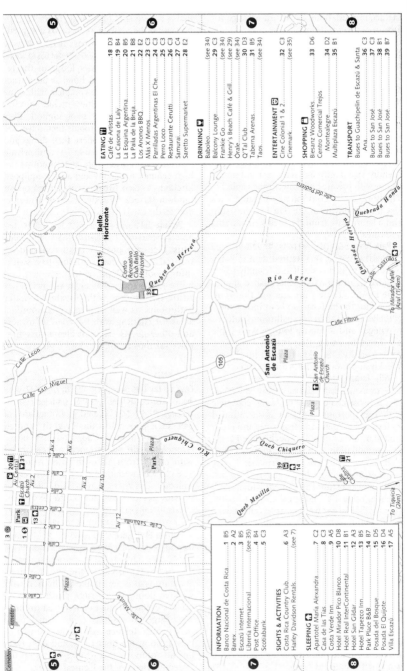

the accommodations listed can arrange for airport transportation.

Escazú is dotted with a fine selection of B&Bs that offer a homey alternative to chain hotels. They are listed first.

MIDRANGE

Hotel Tapezco Inn (Map pp118-19; ☎ 2228 1084; info@ tapezco-inn.co.cr; Calle Central btwn Avs 2 & 4; s/d incl breakfast US$45/55; P ☎) Located near the Escazú church and on the town plaza, this is the best budget option in the entire area. The brightly painted yellow-and-blue hotel is managed by a friendly Tico family, and has clean and simple rooms with private hot showers and cable TV. The hotel is also conveniently situated – it's less than 100m from the San José bus stop and a short walk from the area's restaurants and cafés.

Park Place B&B (Map pp118-19; ☎ 2228 9200; s/d incl breakfast US$55/60; P) Retired dentist Barry Needman runs this small and friendly place, situated in an attractive whitewashed alpine-style house. (There's no sign out the front, so look for the high eaves.) Four immaculate guest bedrooms share two bathrooms, kitchen privileges and a roomy lounge with cable TV. Every morning, Barry cooks a heaping, American-style breakfast for all his guests. Weekly and monthly rates are available.

Villa Escazú (Map pp118-19; ☎ 2228 7971; www .hotels.co.cr/vescazu.html; s/d/tr incl breakfast US$45/65/80; P) A Swiss chalet–type building, complete with a wraparound veranda, is surrounded by terraced gardens and fruit trees and is patrolled by a very friendly pooch named Felíz. Accommodation is in six quaint wood-paneled rooms that have local artwork, comfy couches and shared hot-water bathrooms. There is also a studio apartment with a small kitchen, cable TV and good-size tiled bathroom (US$250 per week) – an excellent deal. English is spoken.

Hotel Mirador Pico Blanco (Map pp118-19; ☎ 2228 1908, 2289 6197; pblanco@costarica.net; s/d US$48/68, ste US$64/70, cottage US$81; P) This countryside hotel is located high in the hills about 3km southeast of central Escazú, and has staggering views of the Central Valley from its balconied rooms. The 15 spacious units have painted stone walls, queen-size beds, cable TV and hot showers. There are also three cottages (which lack views) that sleep up to six and are rented on a monthly basis. There is a small restaurant (dishes US$4 to US$8)

that is a good spot for slowing down and appreciating the views. Credit cards accepted.

Costa Verde Inn (Map pp118-19; ☎ 2228 4080; www .costaverdeinn.com; s/d/tr US$60/75/82, apt US$70, all incl breakfast; P ☎) The sister lodge of the famous Manuel Antonio hotel is an attractive, country-style home complete with some fairly impressive amenities, including a hot tub, lighted tennis court, pool, sundeck, BBQ area and fireplace. The rooms themselves are well decorated with modern furnishings and have a king-size bed, cable TV and private hot shower. Larger loft apartments have high ceilings, a balcony and a fully equipped kitchen. A Tico breakfast is served on an outdoor terrace. Weekly rates are available, and credit cards are accepted.

Posada del Bosque (Map pp118-19; ☎ 2228 1164; posada@amerisol.com; d incl breakfast US$75; P ✗ ☎) This Tico-run posada is surrounded by tropical gardens that are home to a swimming pool, BBQ pit, a tennis court and horse-riding trails. The eight-room inn has rustic-style rooms with private hot-water bathrooms, as well as plenty of communal areas for chatting with the friendly owners and other guests. There is also a cozy fireplace for those cool, San José nights.

TOP END

Casa de las Tías (Map pp118-19; ☎ 2289 5517; www .hotels.co.cr/casatias.html; Calle León; s/d/tr incl breakfast US$71/95/107; P ✗) Located in a quiet area of San Rafael, rooms in this brightly painted yellow-and-turquoise Cape Cod–style house (complete with picket fence) are decorated with crafts from all over Latin America. The place is special, however, because of the welcoming owners, Xavier and Pilar, who provide personalized service to all of their guests. Breakfast is served in the lovely backyard, which even has an artificial stream.

Posada El Quijote (Map pp118-19; ☎ 2289 8401; www.quijote.co.cr; s/d/tr incl breakfast from US$89/99/124; P ✗ ☎) This hillside posada rates as one of the top B&Bs in the San José area. Standard rooms are simple yet homey, with wooden floors, throw rugs, plush bedding, cable TV and private hot-water bathrooms, while larger rooms have either a small patio or a private terrace. All guests are free to take a nip at the honor bar, and then relax on the outdoor patio while soaking up the sweeping views of the Central Valley.

DAY TRIPPER: ESCAZÚ TO CIUDAD COLÓN

Need a city break? There's an interesting day trip to be had if you have your own wheels. From Escazú, head 3km west to the town of **Santa Ana**, which is a local artisan center for traditional as well as contemporary pottery. Continuing west for another 5km, you'll reach the small village of **Piedades**, which is centered on a historic colonial church that's worth checking out for its beautiful stained-glass windows. Continuing west for another 8km, you'll reach the town of **Ciudad Colón**. Here, you'll find the **Julia & David White Artists' Colony** (☎ 2249 1414; www.forjuliaanddavid.org), which was established in 1998 as a refuge for writers, visual artists and composers, and regularly offers a number of workshops and classes.

Just 5km southwest of Ciudad Colón is the **Reserva Forestal el Rodeo**, a 350-hectare private reserve that protects the last stretch of primary forest in the Central Valley. The reserve is a part of the **Hacienda el Rodeo** (☎ 2249 1013; ☷ 10am-6pm Sat & Sun), which has a small restaurant, **Restaurante del Abuelo** (meals US$4-8), which serves country fare on weekends. If you're looking to prolong your city escape, consider spending the night at **Albergue El Marañon** (☎ 2249 1271; www.cultourica.com/frameseteng.html; s/d/tr US$35/49/77; ℗), located a few kilometers west of Santa Ana in the village of La Trinidad. This quaint 11-room country guesthouse is surrounded by a fruit orchard and has stunning views of the Central Valley that span as far as Volcán Poás.

Apartotel María Alexandra (Map pp118-19; ☎ 2228 1507; www.mariaalexandra.com; cnr Calle 3 & Av 23; d US$105; ℗ ❐ ❑) This clean, quiet and centrally located apartment hotel in San Rafael de Escazú is a good option of you're looking for fully furnished accommodations. Though clean and well maintained, the apartments are completely ordinary, but the bedrooms are totally separate from the kitchen and living areas. Facilities include a sauna, private parking, VCR rental, and a washer and dryer. Maid service is included and there are weekly and monthly rates available. Book well ahead in high season. The apartment hotel is home to Harley Davidson motorbike tours and rentals (see p117).

Hotel San Gildar (☎ 2289 8843; www.hotelsangildar.com; Carretera JF Kennedy; d/tr US$118/145; ℗ ❐ ❑) Just northwest of the Costa Rica Country Club is this trendy hotel in a Spanish hacienda–style building. The hotel aims to rejuvenate and relax its guests with comfortable, soothing rooms and a picturesque garden-fringed pool. The hotel's chic bar-restaurant (open 6am to 10pm, mains US$7 to US$12) serves continental cuisine and is locally popular.

Alta Hotel (Map pp118-19; ☎ 2282 4160; www.thealtahotel.com; d/ste from US$165/195; ℗ ❐ ❑) On the road between Escazú and Santa Ana is one of the country's premier boutique hotels, the Alta, which is highly recommended for its professional service, stunning location, and top-notch rooms and amenities. The hotel itself is an immaculately sculpted Spanish

Mediterranean–style villa, from where, on a clear day, there are views as far as the Pacific.

Hotel Real InterContinental (Map pp118-19; ☎ 2289 7000; www.interconti.com; r US$250, ste US$400-1000; ℗ ❐ ❑ ❑) About 2km northwest of Escazú is this branch of the well-respected InterContinental hotel chain. The five-story building has 260 deluxe air-con rooms with all the usual upscale business-hotel amenities and an impressive list of facilities, including a pool, spa, gym, three restaurants, two bars, a convention and business center, concierge service and a small gift shop. The country's largest shopping mall, the Multiplaza, is across the street.

Eating

There are a few inexpensive local *sodas* in Escazú Centro, though for the most part, Escazú is home to expensive, cosmopolitan eateries. If you just can't bear the thought of being separated from all of your favorite American chain eateries, there's everything from a Tony Roma's to a TGI Friday's in San Rafael.

BUDGET

La Casona de Laly (Map pp118-19; cnr Av 3 & Calle Central; US$1-5; ☷ 11am-12:30am) In the heart of Escazú Centro is this much-loved *soda*, which specializes in traditional country-style Tico fare. In the evenings, locals pack the joint for their cheap *bocas* (savory bar snacks) and ice-cold beers.

La Paila de la Bruja (Map pp118-19; dishes US$2-5; 4pm-midnight Mon-Thu, noon-midnight Fri-Sun) This rustic *soda* in San Antonio de Escazú is a famous institution that prepares traditional Tico specialties using outdoor brick ovens. The terrace is bustling in the evenings, and the dramatic views of the Central Valley make this a memorable spot.

La Esquina Argentina (Map pp118-19; cnr Av Central & Calle L Cortés; 7am-2pm Mon-Fri; dishes US$2-7) This popular roadside stand sells piping-hot *empanadas* to hungry locals, though the outdoor patio is a good spot to linger over a cup of coffee and spend an hour or two people-watching.

Perro Loco (Map pp118-19; Centro Comercial El Cruce, cnr Calle L Cortés & Carretera JF Kennedy; dishes US$3-5; noon-8pm Mon-Tue, to 4am Wed-Sat, 4-10pm Sun) If you've been boozing it up a little too much, this greasy spoon is just what you need. The menu at the 'Crazy Dog' consists of 10 internationally themed hot dogs, all of which are served with plentiful toppings (our favorite is the Chihuahua dog, which comes loaded with fresh guacamole).

Self-caterers can try Más X Menos in San Rafael de Escazú or the Saretto Supermarket near the Autopista Próspero Fernández.

MIDRANGE & TOP END

Café de Artistas (Map pp118-19; 2228 6045, 2288 5082; dishes US$4-8; 8am-6pm Tue-Sat, to 4pm Sun) This intimate café displays rotating exhibitions of local art (some for sale) on its walls and shelves, which makes for a charming and light-hearted meal. The coffees and homemade pastries are excellent, and there's also a heartier selection of vegetarian dishes, sandwiches and salads. Come here for the Sunday brunch, which is accompanied by live music.

Parrilladas Argentinas El Che (Map pp118-19; Calle L Cortés; mains US$6-10; noon-midnight) Whether you spend the afternoon hours sitting on the outdoor patio and cradling a cold beer, or stop by for dinner and feast on a huge Argentine-style steak, you're going to like the relaxed atmosphere at this popular local restaurant, south of Carretera JF Kennedy.

Tiquicia (Map pp118-19; 2289 5839; mains US$6-10; 5pm-midnight Tue-Fri, 1pm-2am Sat, 11am-6pm Sun) This typical upmarket restaurant gives a sophisticated spin on traditional Costa Rican dishes by emphasizing fresh produce and high-quality meats and fish. The restaurant is 5km south of central Escazú on a well-paved

road, and has a relaxed, rustic setting with spectacular views of the Central Valley – it's worth the drive here. There is frequently local music on weekends. Call ahead for directions as it's tricky to find.

Los Anonos BBQ (Map pp118-19; 2228 0180; dishes US$7-12; noon-3pm & 6-10pm Tue-Sat, 11:30am-9pm Sun) On the road between San José and Escazú is this BBQ shack, which has been in operation since the early 1960s. The entire restaurant is constructed of polished wood, and there are historic photos of Costa Rica along all the walls. Los Anonos caters to hungry carnivores, and the extensive selection of meats includes both locally raised animals and imported USDA-approved cuts of meat. Credit cards accepted.

Mirador Valle Azul (Map pp118-19; 2254 6281; dishes US$8-12; 4pm-midnight Mon-Sat) A tough, steep drive takes you to the aptly named Mirador Valle Azul (Blue Valley Lookout), from where the views of the San José valley are breathtaking – get there before sunset. The cuisine is European inspired, and features a wide selection of pastas, meats and seafood as well a few Costa Rican standards. On Saturday and Sunday evenings, there's a good chance there will be live music here. It's 700m south and 700m west from Hotel Mirador Pico Blanco.

Samurai (Map pp118-19; 2228 4124; Calle L Cortés; dishes US$9-25; noon-3pm & 6:30-10pm) Sushi is all the rage these days in Escazú, though this upscale Japanese eatery, complete with tableside hibachis, also offers authentic *teppanyaki*, as well as mixed fish and seafood grills. If you're a traditionalist, the sushi here is about as good as it gets, and though it's pricey, the quality is undeniable.

Restaurante Cerutti (Map pp118-19; 2228 4511, 2228 9954; Calle L Cortés; dishes US$10-20; noon-2:30pm & 6-11pm Wed-Mon) This restaurant, south of Carretera JF Kennedy in San Rafael de Escazú, is regarded as one of the best Italian restaurants in the capital. The food here is predictably top-notch, and features hand-selected seafood and delectable homemade pastas. The ravioli with ricotta and mushrooms (US$15) is a local favorite, though you can't go wrong with its big list of risottos. Credit cards accepted.

Drinking

The hottest nightspot in the most exclusive district of San José is the **Centro Comercial**

Trejos Montealagre, a more upscale version of El Pueblo (p104). This complex is packed on weekends with the trendiest scenesters in the capital, and there's no shortage of dance spots to show off all the new threads that daddy's money bought you. The most established clubs are Baboleo, Taos and Frankie Go, though like all things fashionable, this is likely to change. At the time of writing the hottest beats were the Puerto Rican–inspired reggaetón, though again, like all things fashionable, this is likely to change. A recommended spot in Trejos Montealagre is Órale, which serves Tex-Mex fare that's popular among pre-partiers, though things really get hopping on Friday nights when there's cheap drink specials.

An Escazú institution, **Taberna Arenas** (Map pp118-19; Escazú Centro; from 4pm) is a delightful, old-fashioned Tico bar, diagonal from the Shell gas station. Arenas has exceptional *bocas* (US$1) and a good selection of domestic and imported beers. Owner Don Israel is a true charmer, and has his photos with various heads of state on the walls, among the agricultural implements that are de rigueur in any decent country bar.

Two hearty drinking options are in the Plaza San Rafael shopping center a few hundred meters east of the soccer field. **Balcony Lounge** (Map pp118-19; Carretera JF Kennedy; noon-1am) is an upscale bar and gringo hangout that specializes in well-crafted martinis, while the more laidback (but equally gringo) **Henry's Beach Café & Grill** (Map pp118-19; Carretera JF Kennedy; 11-2:30am) is your best spot for partying it up on the dance floor.

On the road into town from San José, you'll find the **Q'tal Club** (Map pp118-19; Calle L Cortés; 6pm-2am), which is a sophisticated lounge complete with its own house band. There are frequent live jazz performances here; there is a US$5 admission price.

Entertainment

For first-run Hollywood movies, check out the **Cine Colonial 1 & 2** (Map pp118-19; 2289 9000; ground fl, Plaza Colonial Escazú, San Rafael; admission US$3) or the **Cinemark** (Map pp118-19; 2288 1111; Multiplaza Escazú; admission US$3).

Shopping

Biesanz Woodworks (Map pp118-19; 2289 4337; www.biesanz.com; 8am-5pm Mon-Fri, Sat & Sun by appointment) You'll find delicate and high-quality wood craftsmanship in the traditional pre-Columbian style at this showroom in Bello Horizonte. A variety of bowls and other decorative containers are all beautifully produced, the majority using a traditional crafting method in which the natural lines and forms of the wood determine the shape and size of the bowl. This makes every piece unique. The products are expensive (starting at US$50 for a palm-size bowl), but they are well worth it.

Multiplaza Escazú (Map pp118-19; 2289 8984; www.multiplazamall.com; 10am-8pm Mon-Sat, to 7pm Sun) A full-scale suburban-style mall that has just about everything you need (or don't) – from clothes to eyeglasses to shoes. There is also a good food court. Of particular interest to travelers is the **Cemaco** (2289 7474), a sort of Wal-Mart-style department store that sells basic fishing and camping supplies, including propane gas for your portable stove. If you're coming from San José, the mall can be reached by taking any bus that is marked with 'Escazú Multiplaza.' (See p111 for more information on these buses.)

Getting There & Away

Frequent buses between San José and Escazú cost US$0.25 and take 25 minutes. All depart San José from east of the Coca-Cola bus terminal and take several routes: buses labeled 'San Antonio de Escazú' go up the hill to the south of Escazú and end near San Antonio de Escazú church; those labeled 'Escazú' end in Escazú's main plaza; and others, called 'Guachipelín' go west on the Carretera John F Kennedy and pass the Costa Rica Country Club. All go through San Rafael.

Central Valley & Highlands

The rolling verdant valleys of Costa Rica's midlands have traditionally only been witnessed during travelers' pit stops on their way to the country's more established destinations. The area has always been famous for being one of the globe's major coffee-growing regions, and every journey involves twisting and turning through lush swooping terrain with infinite coffee fields on either side. You'll also find misty rain forests and brooding volcanoes here, which you'll rarely have to share with more than a handful of other tourists.

Only Alajuela and Turrialba have really featured on the tourist radar to date. As a result of Alajuela's proximity to the airport, visitors have been opting to stay in the tranquil town before moving on to the beach, thus bypassing San José's urban grime. The cascading rapids outside Turrialba, meanwhile, are top of the list for white-water rafters and kayakers the world over, and should not be missed by any thrill-seeking visitors.

The area is fantastic for self-drive exploration. Roll the top down and drive through the winding roads, using distant volcano peaks as a compass when the local road maps inevitably let you down. Those who give the region more than the standard half hour at the roadside restaurant will discover that unknown beauty, culture and charm are sitting in the country's heartland and, surprisingly, right under the nose of the nation's capital.

This chapter is arranged in a roughly west–east sequence of the four major population centers – Alajuela, Heredia, Cartago and Turrialba.

HIGHLIGHTS

- White-knuckle riding down the swooping and diving rapids of the **Río Reventazón** and **Río Pacuare** (p159)

- Tentatively peering into the mammoth craters of the area's live volcanoes, **Volcánes Irazú** (p151), **Poás** (p139) and **Turrialba** (p162)

- Driving through the lush coffee fields in the **Valle de Orosi** (p152)

- Going back in time at the country's major archaeological site, **Monumento Nacional Arqueológico Guayabo** (p160)

- Not sleeping for a week at Costa Rica's largest fiesta in **Palmares** (p137)

★ Volcán Poás

Monumento
Nacional
★ Palmares   Arqueológico
    Volcán Turrialba ★   Guayabo
    Volcán Irazú ★   ★

    Río Reventazón ★
    Valle de Orosi ★   Río
             Pacuare ★

History

Of the 20 or so tribes that inhabited pre-Hispanic Costa Rica, it is thought that the Central Valley Huetar Indians were the most dominant. But there is very little historical evidence from this period, save for the archeological site at Guayabo. Tropical rains and ruthless colonization have erased most of pre-Columbian Costa Rica from the pages of history.

In 1561 the Spanish pitched their first permanent settlement at Garcimuñoz, in the western Central Valley. Two years later, real colonization got under way. Cartago was founded and the Spanish began farming the land and enslaving the indigenous population. The rich fertile lands of the volcanic valleys led to increasing numbers of settlements, and Heredia, San José and Alajuela all sprang up in the 18th century.

It wasn't until the beginning of the 19th century that the area really began to prosper, due to its enormous coffee-growing revenues. The planting of the 'golden bean' brought riches to the local community, and encouraged the development of a large and powerful agrarian middle class. More recently, the decrease in the value of coffee has seen agriculture become more diversified, but the region's educated and well-to-do community remains a heavy influence on the rest of the country.

Climate

For this part of the world, the weather is surprisingly mild. Year-round the mercury hovers around 25°C/77°F. The elevated altitude and landlocked location mean the heat that most of the country endures doesn't pose a problem. From June to December, it's not uncommon for a light afternoon shower, but the sun usually pokes through after an hour of rain, so nothing to fret about.

Parks & Reserves

Watch wildlife and explore volcanic landscapes in some of the Central Valley's magnificent national parks.

Los Angeles Cloud Forest Reserve (p137) This away-from-the-crowds activity-based reserve offers the chance to whiz through the leaves on the zip-line canopy tour or trot through the branches on the horseback trails.

Los Jardines de la Catarata la Paz (p141) Offers 3.5km of hiking trails through rich wildlife-filled rain forest, with a hummingbird garden, serpentarium, frog exhibit, trout lake and the world's largest butterfly enclosure.

Monumento National Arqueológico Guayabo (p160) The country's only significant archaeological site isn't quite as impressive as anything found in Mexico or Guatemala, but the rickety outline of forest-encompassed villages will still spark your inner Indiana Jones.

Parque Nacional Tapantí-Macizo Cerro de la Muerte (p155) This park receives more rainfall than any other part of the country, so it is full of life. Jaguars, ocelots and tapirs are some of the more exciting species.

Parque Nacional Volcán Irazú (p151) One of the few lookouts on earth that affords views of both the Caribbean and the Pacific, Irazú also lays claim to being the country's highest live volcano.

Parque Nacional Volcán Poás (p139) A shimmering crater lake and surrounding cloud forest make this one of the prettiest volcanoes in the region. The steaming geysers sometimes get so aggressive that the park has to close down.

Dangers & Annoyances

While the area is generally considered to be very safe and welcoming, there have been reports of car break-ins, particularly in the larger towns like Alajuela. Try and secure off-street parking and never leave valuables in your car.

Getting There & Around

It makes sense to hire a car to seek out all the hard-to-find corners of this part of the country. All the towns are well connected by regular buses from San José, but getting between them by public transport can be a pain. Locals (and the odd gung ho Lonely Planet author) occasionally wave down passing cars. If you do this, beware that there are risks (see p549), and always offer to help with gas costs.

ALAJUELA & THE NORTH OF THE VALLEY

Cradled by the gentle undulations of coffee fincas and tamed jungle parks, the provincial capital of Alajuela lies about 18km northwest of San José. Originally known as Villa Hermosa, it's still a very 'pretty city,' not to mention the country's second largest, with a population of more than 185,000. And, contrary to what most taxi drivers will tell you, Alajuela is only 3km from Juan Santamaría

CENTRAL VALLEY & HIGHLANDS

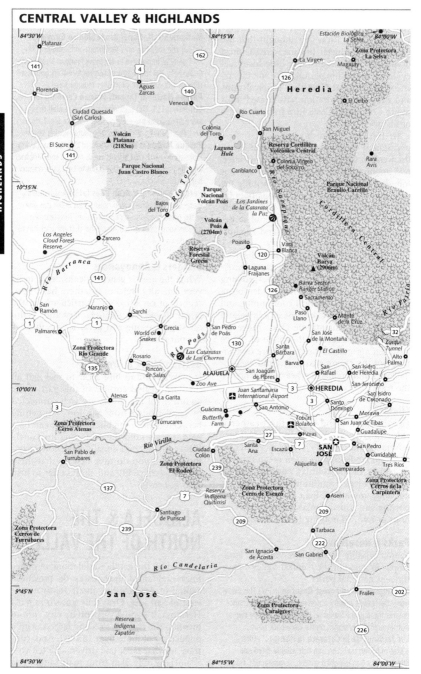

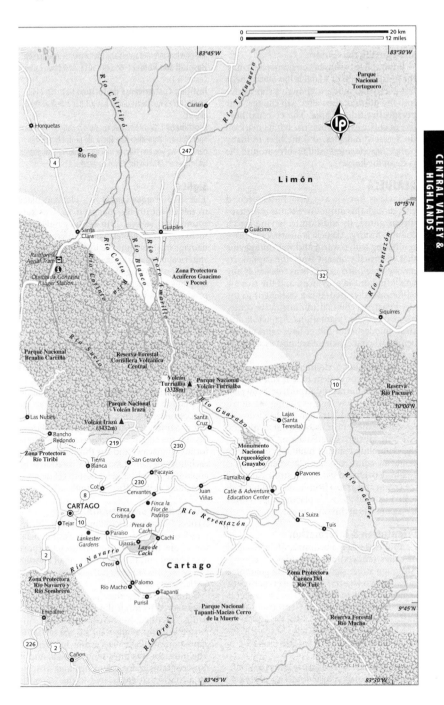

international airport, and is rapidly becoming the preferred base for travelers leaving and entering the country.

From coffee barons to conglomerate banks, the pulse and ebb of Alajuela has always been fast paced and modern, though a short drive into the north of the valley will change your perspective on the area. The colonial heyday of coffee exportation has left its mark on the terraced hillsides, and the lives of many *campesinos* (farmers) still revolve around the cycle of the harvest.

ALAJUELA

Alajuela is known as Costa Rica's second city, though this diminutive status is perhaps unwarranted. In addition to having a rich colonial history, Alajuela is an attractive place resonating with a warm and welcoming vibe that is virtually absent from the capital. Its mango-tree-lined center is as relaxed as any you'll find in the provinces, and the soaring whitewashed cathedral is a testament to the city's past as a colonial administrative center for nearby coffee plantations. Alajuela is also clean, modern and full of hard-working urbanites who take their jobs almost as seriously as their football.

Alajuela is not a 'destination' for tourists, though it's a convenient base if you're flying into or out of the nearby airport, or if you plan on spending a few days exploring the north of the valley. And although Costa Rican cities are nowhere near as beautiful as historic cities in Mexico, Guatemala or Nicaragua, the crumbling colonial buildings in the city center are attractive, especially when the sun is beaming overhead. So, take a stroll, eat some ice cream and grab a beer if the local football team Liga Alajuelense is playing (especially if it's against its archrival Saprissa!).

Orientation & Information

Central Alajuela is a pedestrian-friendly grid of calles (streets) and avenidas (avenues). Although street signs are never a guarantee in Costa Rica (see p537), Alajuela is fairly well signed and easy to navigate. The city center is at the intersection of Calle Central and Av 1.

BYTE (☎ 2441 1142; cnr Calle 3 & Av 1, 2nd fl; per hr US$0.75; ⏲ Mon-Sat) Internet access.

Clínica Norza (☎ 2441 3572; Av 4 btwn Calles 2 & 4; ⏲ 24 hr) Basic medical services.

Goodlight Books (☎ 2430 4083; Av 3 btwn Calles 1 & 3) If you've got a long trip (or flight) ahead of you, stop by and

visit the friendly and always helpful owner, Larry. In addition to selling used and new books, Larry also runs a small café and provides internet access and useful tourist information.

Hospital San Rafael (☎ 2441 5011; Av 9 btwn Calles Central & 1)

Instituto Costarricense de Turismo (ICT; ☎ 2442 1820) There's no tourist office, but ICT has a desk at the airport.

Scotiabank (☎ 2443 2168; cnr Av 3 & Calle 2; ⏲ 8am-5pm Mon-Fri, 8am-4pm Sat) There are probably a dozen banks where you can change money, including Scotiabank, which has an ATM on the Cirrus network.

Sights

The shady **Parque Central** is a pleasant place to relax beneath the mango trees. It is surrounded by several 19th-century buildings, including the **cathedral**, which suffered severe damage in an earthquake in 1991. The hemispherical cupola is unusually constructed of sheets of red corrugated metal. The interior is spacious and elegant rather than ornate; two presidents are buried here.

A more baroque-looking church (though it was built in 1941) is the **Iglesia La Agonía**, six blocks east of Parque Central.

Two blocks south of the park is the rather bare **Parque Juan Santamaría**, where there is a statue of the hero (see below) in action, flanked by cannons.

Three kilometers southeast in Río Segundo de Alajuela is **Flor de Mayo** (☎ 2441 2658), a very successful green and scarlet macaw breeding program. Run by Richard and Margot Frisius, the botanical garden is an early home for infant macaws and has three aviaries that each house a pair of macaws. Visitation is by appointment only, and it's best to get detailed directions as it's difficult to find.

MUSEO JUAN SANTAMARÍA

Alajuela's main claim to fame is as the birthplace of national hero Juan Santamaría, for whom the nearby international airport was named and to whom this small **museum** (☎ 2441 4775; cnr Av 3 & Calle 2; admission free; ⏲ 10am-6pm Tue-Sun) is devoted.

Santamaría was the drummer boy who volunteered to torch the building that was being defended by North American filibuster William Walker in the war of 1856. Santamaría died after succeeding in his quest. The museum was once the town jail, and it now contains maps, paintings and historical artifacts that are related to the war with

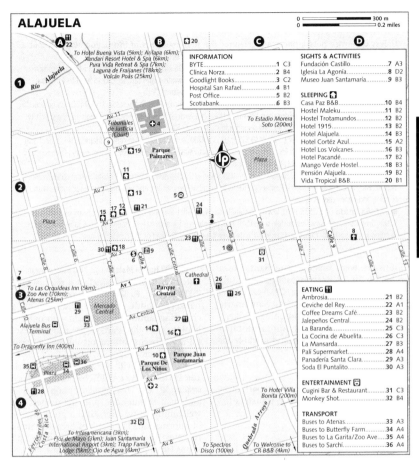

ALAJUELA

CENTRAL VALLEY & HIGHLANDS

Walker, as well as a rotating art exhibition. There is a small auditorium where performances are occasionally staged.

OJO DE AGUA

About 6km south of Alajuela are the **Ojo de Agua** (☎ 2441 2808; admission US$2; ☼ 8am-5pm) springs, a picturesque working-class resort that's packed on weekends with folks from San José and Alajuela. Approximately 20,000L of water gush out from the spring each minute, filling swimming pools and an artificial boating lake before being piped down to Puntarenas, for which the springs are a major supply of water. There are also snack stands, game courts and a small gymnasium. From San José, drivers can take the San Antonio de Belén exit off the Interamericana; Ojo de Agua is just past San Antonio.

Courses

Slightly more tranquil than the capital, Alajuela is a lovely spot to base yourself and do a Spanish course, and there are a number of choices for schools. See boxed text Spanish Schools in the Central Valley, p130, as well as boxed text A Natural Education, p148, for more details.

Festivals & Events

The anniversary of the **Battle of Rivas**, April 11, is particularly celebrated in Alajuela, the hometown of the battle's young hero, Juan Santamaría. After William Walker and the

---

SPANISH SCHOOLS IN THE CENTRAL VALLEY

Unless otherwise noted, prices are given for five four-hour days of instruction, with/without a week's homestay with a local family. All prices include breakfast and dinner.

Adventure Education Center (Map p158; ☎ 2556 4609, 2556 4614; www.adventurespanishschool.com; US$415/315) Folks who want to combine Spanish classes and, say, white-water rafting, should head to Turrialba, where this cool school also offers courses tailored for medical professionals.

Finca la Flor de Paraíso (☎ 2534 8003; www.la-flor-de-paraiso.org; with homestay US$370) On an organic farm – see boxed text A Natural Education (Part II), p153 – not far from Cartago, vegetarian meals are the specialty and your cultural experiences could include seeing traditional Costa Rican farming techniques.

Fundación Castillo (Map p129; ☎ 2440 8771; US$310/200) A few blocks from central Alajuela, this school also offers courses in business Spanish for a bit extra. There are activities and field trips around town every afternoon, and students get a discount at a local Latin dance school.

Intercultura (Map p142; ☎ 2260 8480, in the USA 800-552 2051; www.spanish-intercultura.com; US$370/260) This Heredia school also arranges volunteer positions throughout the country, and your new language comes with cooking and dance classes included.

Montaña Linda (☎ 2533 3640; www.montanalinda.com; with homestay US$155) All classes are one-on-one at this Orosi outpost, also a fine hostel (see p154). The rate given is for homestays, though you can save money by sleeping in the hostel or camping. Classes are only three hours a day, instead of the customary four.

Filibusters were ousted from Santa Rosa on March 20, 1856, the Costa Rican militia chased them into Nicaragua. On April 11 the Battle of Rivas climaxed when Santamaría was shot and killed after torching Walker's stronghold. The event is commemorated with a parade, civic events and a whole lot of firecrackers.

Sleeping

Since Alajuela is so close to the airport, most hotels and B&Bs can arrange transfers for a small fee.

BUDGET

There are some great budget hotels and hostels in Alajuela. All hotels have hot water.

Casa Paz B&B (☎ 2431 2691; casa-paz@mail.com; Calle 2 btwn Avs 2 & 4; d US$15-45; P 💻) As the name (House of Peace) implies, this place is totally mellowed out with pastel paints and friendly management. There is a variety of different room sizes for different budgets, but you'll probably agree that the biggest room (complete with a huge balcony overlooking Parque Juan Santamaría) is worth the splurge – go on, treat yourself!

Hostel Trotamundos (☎ 2430 5832; www.hosteltrotamundos.com; Av 5 btwn Calles 2 & 4; dm incl breakfast US$10, d US$25-30; P 💻) This reader-recommended hostel is a winner – we're talking cheap dorms, a communal kitchen, TV lounge, free internet and plenty of communal space for hanging out with other travelers.

our pick Hostel Maleku (☎ 2430 4304; www.maleku hostel.com; Av 9 btwn Calles Central & 2; dm/s/d/tr US$12/25/30/40; P 💻) This sweet little backpackers' abode is clean and run by a charming family who can help with onward bookings to other parts of the country (useful if you're just off the plane). Free airport transfers included.

Hotel Pacandé (☎ 2443 8481; www.hotelpacande .com; Av 5 btwn Calles 2 & 4; s US$27-50, d US$28-50, all incl breakfast; P 💻) This popular option is spick-and-span throughout, plus the owners are welcoming to travelers and a great source of information. The outdoor breakfast nook is a great spot to have a morning brew and some fresh pineapple. Shared and private bathrooms are available.

Hotel Cortéz Azul (☎ 2443 6145; Av 5 btwn Calles 2 & 4; s/d/tr US$15/30/45; P) The owner, Eduardo Rodríguez, is a talented artist who displays his unique work (we're talking about surreal vases growing out of cement walls) throughout the property. Homey rooms are comfortable, with polished wood floors, and there's a fine common area and two kitchens (check out the mural of the Last Supper). Original art is available for purchase at reception.

Mango Verde Hostel (☎ 2441 6330; mirafloresbb@ hotmail.com; Av 3 btwn Calles 2 & 4; s/d US$15/30, with bathroom US$20/40) This popular hostel has bare and basic rooms, though there's a nice kitchen, plenty of hammocks and enough lounge space to strike up a conversation.

Pensión Alajuela (☎ 2441 6251; www.pension alajuela.com; Av 9 btwn Calles Central & 2; s/d US$25/35, with bathroom US$30/40; **P** 🏢 🖳) Another great option, as attractive rooms are centered on a 'jungle lounge,' where you chat up other travelers and give (or get) advice on your trip. There's a communal kitchen, optional air-con (US$10) and wi-fi internet.

Arilapa (☎ 2443 6941; www.arilapa.com; dm/s/d/tr US$8/30/35/45; **P** 🖳) Just outside of town, this is a great option if you want to go straight from the airport to nature. Set in a delightful orange grove, the rural getaway is run by a lovely couple, Arnold and Ileana, who throw in free airport pick-ups and tortilla-making lessons in the in-house bakery.

Welcome to CR B&B (☎ 2265 6563; www.welcometocr .com; dm/d US$14/35; **P** 🖳) This solid backpacker option is about 5km east of the airport on the road to San Joaquín. The American-Tico owners spent years managing the famous Toruma Hostel in San José, and now they've finally got a place of their own. The colonial town of San Joaquín is a pleasant alternative to Alajuela, and the hostel itself is newly constructed and full of nature-loving travelers. Rates include breakfast and airport transfer (if there are two people or more).

MIDRANGE

For a few dollars more, there are some lovely B&Bs to choose from.

Hotel Alajuela (☎ 2441 1241; alajuela@racsa.co.cr; Calle 2 btwn Avs Central & 2; d US$30-45; **P** 🖳) Fifty simple rooms make up this hotel. Some of the rooms at the front are a little dingy: it's worth having a look around the various rooms before deciding. There's also a nice little plant-filled patio for reading and relaxing.

Hotel Los Volcanes (☎ 2441 0525; www.montezuma expeditions.com/hotel.htm; Av 2 btwn Calles Central & 2; s/d incl breakfast US$30/45; **P** 🏢 🖳) This 1920s refurbished home, which has been converted into an intimate six-room B&B, definitely aims to please. Rooms are furnished with period pieces and have hardwood accents and a combination of private and shared bathrooms.

Vida Tropical B&B (☎ 2443 9576; www.vidatropical.com; s/d incl breakfast US$30/45; **P** 🖳) In a quiet residential neighborhood just north of downtown is this Colombian-American-run B&B (the owners also own the recommended Jalapeños Central restaurant, see p132). The entire house is awash in bright murals, and the backyard garden is perfect for getting some sun. There

are also plenty of hammocks, comfy couches and the warm company of the owners.

Dragonfly Inn (☎ 2443 4152; www.dragonflyinncr.com; s/d incl breakfast US$45/65; **P** 🖳) About 1km west of downtown, in a quiet residential neighborhood northwest of Parque La Trinidad, this charming inn is run by a North American couple named Dawn and Michael. Bright and airy rooms in this two-story, white colonial home share two immaculate bathrooms (one of which has a Jacuzzi), and the upstairs balcony and 'business center' is perfect for relaxing (or checking your email).

our pick **Hotel 1915** (☎ 2441 0495; www.1915hotel .com; Calle 2 btwn Avs 5 & 7; s/d US$45/55, s/d/tr with air-con US$50/65/75; **P** 🏢) This highly recommended hotel is in one of the most beautiful buildings in Alajuela. Although it looks closed from the outside (and, indeed, taxi drivers will tell you the same), the interior of the 101-year-old Spanish-colonial-style hotel is breathtaking, and it's easy to feel as if you've been transported to a different era.

Hotel Villa Bonita (☎ 2441 0239; www.hotelvilla bonita.com; Av 8, Calle 9; s/d US$47/57; **P** 🖳) A charming and homey hotel, on the outskirts of the town centre. Rooms are comfy, with plump white pillows and deep mattresses. The main draw is the floral garden where guests lounge on the manicured lawn and swing away the afternoon in hammocks.

TOP END

Hotel Buena Vista (☎ 2442 8595; www.hotelbuena vistacr.com; d US$75-130; **P** ✖ 🏢 🖳 🕱) About 5km north of Alajuela on the road to Poás, this whitewashed Mediterranean-style hotel is perched on a mountaintop and has panoramic views of the nearby volcanoes, particularly from the balconies of the more expensive rooms. Rooms are fully equipped and come in a variety of shapes and sizes, though everyone can walk around the expansive grounds and soak up the dizzying views.

Las Orquídeas Inn (☎ 2433 9346; www.orquideas inn.com; d US$79-99, ste US$99-150, apt US$140; **P** ✖ 🏢 🕱) About 5km west of Alajuela on the road to San Pedro de Poás is this stately Spanish-colonial mansion. Standard rooms are decked out with Guatemalan bedspreads and are just steps from the pool, while the varied suites are lavish (our favorites are the geodesic domes). The restaurant and bar are both well known: the first for its gourmet cuisine, and the second for its full-on Marilyn Monroe paraphernalia.

our pick **Trapp Family Lodge** (☎ 2431 0776; www .trappfam.com; d US$110; P 🖵 🞇) This is certainly the comfiest option within reach of the airport landing strip. Each of the 20 terra-cotta-tiled rooms have two queen-size beds, the best of which have balconies overlooking the lovely pool and garden. Free airport transfers provided.

Pura Vida Retreat & Spa (☎ 8392 8099, in the USA 888-767 7375; www.puravidaspa.com; d US$165-185, 7-day package per person US$1465; P 🗙 🞇) Rates include two daily yoga classes, which is your first clue that this is a very different resort. A renowned yoga and alternative-health center that's a destination in itself, the retreat puts guests up in plush but zen 'tentalows' or more comfortable indoor suites, and offers classes and organized outings that usually include a spiritual or alternative-healing angle. It's about 7km north of Alajuela on the road to Carizal, signed from the Estadio.

Xandari Resort Hotel & Spa (☎ 2443 2020; www .xandari.com; d villa US$192-280; P 🗙 🞇 🞇) Set in a coffee plantation overlooking the Central Valley, about 6km north of Alajuela, this relaxed resort seems like it would make for an even better chick trip than a romantic holiday. Rooms are predictably plush and views are postcard perfect, with 3km of private trails and waterfalls running through them. But the Xandari also offers visitors fitness classes and full spa packages, from facials and pedicures to exotic massages, plus two swimming pools, a Jacuzzi and, the real clincher, a gourmet restaurant that specializes in low-fat and vegetarian meals.

Eating

Soda El Puntalito (cnr Calle 4 & Av 3; snacks US$1-3) Do as the locals do and grab a bar stool at this dirt-cheap, unassuming roadside stand.

Panadería Santa Clara (Av 1 btwn Calles 6 & 8; items US$1-3) Follow your nose to this outstanding bakery, which is stocked with all types of homemade breads as well as eye-popping pastries and cakes.

Coffee Dreams Café (Calle 1 btwn Avs 1 & 3; dishes US$2-5) This adorable café is a great place to sample the local blend, but it's worth bringing your appetite along, too, as the tamales here are hot and heavenly.

La Cocina de Abuelita (Cnr Av Central, btwn Calles 1 & 3; meals US$2-5; 🕙 11am-3pm) A real locals' haunt,

this place serves up a buffet of such Tico treats as pork stew and fried plantains. It's as cheap, hearty and authentic as a farmer's cackle.

Ceviche del Rey (☎ 2442 3977; Calle 2 north of Río Alajuela; meals US$3-6; 🕙 11am-11pm) It's definitely worth the trek to the northern outskirts of town to get the best *ceviche* (uncooked but well-marinated seafood) in the area, which is served up by boisterous Peruvian waiters.

Jalepeños Central (☎ 2430 4027; Calle 1 btwn Avs 3 & 5; dishes US$3-6; 🕙 11:20am-9pm Mon-Sat) Don't leave Alajuela without eating here! Run by an animated Colombian-American from Queens, New York, this Tex-Mex spot provides the much needed spice in your life.

La Baranda (Av Central btwn Calles 1 & 3; dishes US$3-7) Though this *soda* (inexpensive eatery) caters to tourists, it's still packed with locals in search of hearty casados and fresh *ceviche*.

La Mansarda (☎ 2441 4390; Calle Central btwn Avs Central & 2, 2nd fl; meals US$4-9; 🕙 11am-11pm) The top place in town for Costa Rican fare is this wonderfully casual balcony restaurant overlooking the street milieu. Fresh seafood dishes and grilled meats can be complemented by something special from the wine list.

Head to the enclosed **Mercado Central** (Calles 4 & 6 btwn Avs 1 & Central; 🕙 7am-6pm Mon-Sat) for lots of *sodas*, produce stands and much, much more. If you're having a little bit of culture shock, all of your favorite fast-food chains are conveniently located downtown. Self-caterers can stock up on groceries at the **Palí supermarket** (cnr Av 2 & Calle 10; 🕙 8am-8pm).

Entertainment

The perennial Costa Rican soccer champions, Alajuela's own La Liga, play at the Estadio Morera Soto at the northeast end of town on Sundays during soccer season. If you can't get seats, stop by **Cugini Bar & Restaurant** (☎ 2440 6893; cnr Av Central & Calle 5; 🕙 noon-midnight Mon-Sat) and you can catch the game over a brew or two.

There's no shortage of dive bars in Alajuela, and there's a good chance that karaoke will be on offer after 10pm (there's nothing like a bunch of drunken Ticos mumbling *Let It Be*). If this is your first night in Costa Rica, we recommend the Guaro Cacique. Bottoms up!

If you're looking to experience the melodic monotony that is reggaetón, check out **Monkey Shot** (Calle 4), a huge indoor-outdoor bar that sometimes has male and female strippers. Or head to **Spectros Disco** (Calle 2 btwn

Avs 10 & 12), which has the biggest dance floor in the city.

Getting There & Away

For details of flights to Aeropuerto Internacional Juan Santamaría, see p108 and p545. You can take a taxi (US$3) to the airport from Parque Central.

There are several bus stops in Alajuela, the largest being the **Alajuela bus terminal** (Calle 8 btwn Avs Central & 1) for buses to San José, the international airport, Volcán Poás and other destinations.

Atenas US$0.50, 30 minutes, depart from the corner of Calle 6 and Avenida Central every 30 minutes from 6am to 9pm.

Butterfly Farm US$0.50, 30 minutes, depart from the corner of Calle 8 and Avenida 2 at 6:20am, 9am, 11am and 1pm.

Heredia US$0.50, 30 minutes, depart from Alajuela bus terminal every 15 minutes from 5am to 11pm.

La Garita/Zoo Ave US$0.50, 30 minutes, depart from the corner of Calle 10 and Avenida 2 every 30 minutes from 6am to 9pm.

Laguna de Fraijanes US$0.50, 30 minutes, depart from Alajuela bus terminal at 9am, 1pm, 4:15pm and 6:15pm.

San José (Tuasa) US$0.75, 45 minutes, depart from Alajuela bus terminal every 10 minutes from 5am to 11pm.

Sarchí US$0.50, 30 minutes, depart from Calle 8 between Avenidas Central and 2 every 30 minutes from 5am to 10pm.

BUTTERFLY FARM

Built in 1983, back when tourism was just a small sector of the country's economy, the **Butterfly Farm** (☎ 2438 0400; www.butterflyfarm.co.cr; adult/child 5-12yr/student US$15/7/10; ☷ 8:30am-5pm) originally opened as the first commercial butterfly farm in Latin America. In the wild it's estimated that less than 2% of caterpillars survive to adulthood, while breeders at the farm boast an astounding 90% survival rate. This ensures a steady supply of pupae for gardens, schools, museums and private collections around the world. If you visit on a Monday or a Thursday from March to August, you can watch thousands of pupae being packed for export.

The butterflies are busiest when it's sunny, particularly in the morning, so try to get there early. Your entrance fee includes a guided two-hour tour, where you can learn about the stages of the complex butterfly life cycle, and the importance of butterflies in nature. Tours in English, German, Spanish or French run three times daily, more often when it's busy.

The complex also has other attractions, primarily gardens devoted to bees, orchids and other tropical species, and you can take a traditional oxcart ride.

The Butterfly Farm also offers several one-day package tours (adult/child/student US$63/48/53) that include transportation from any San José hotel, lunch and a tour of the farm, plus a Coffee Tour at the Café Britt Finca (see p144) and any number of other side trips.

Drivers can reach the Butterfly Farm by heading 12km south of Alajuela to the village of La Guácima; it's almost in front of the well-signed El Club Campestre Los Reyes. The farm provides a round-trip shuttle service from San José hotels for US$10 per person, or you can take a direct bus from Alajuela (see left).

WEST TO ATENAS

The road west from Alajuela to Atenas (25km) is a pleasant day trip for anyone who's even remotely interested in corn, though the perfect climate and rural atmosphere are reasons enough to linger.

La Garita

This pilgrimage-worthy destination for folks who really appreciate corn is 11km west of Alajuela. At La Garita you can stop for a quick bite at a number of 'corny' restaurants (sorry, we couldn't resist!), as well as visiting the largest collection of birds in Central America.

Zoo Ave (☎ 2433 8989; www.zooave.org; adult/child US$9/1; ☷ 8:30am-5pm), 10km west of Alajuela, just before La Garita, has more than 80 Costa Rican species of birds on colorful, squawking display in a relaxing parklike setting – this is a great stop for families. All four Costa Rican species of monkey as well as other critters are on view, though the 'zoo' is actually a breeding center that aims to reintroduce native species into the wild. There are volunteer opportunities here as well, especially if you have experience handling animals.

SLEEPING & EATING

Martino Resort & Spa (☎ 2433 8382; www.hotelmartino .com; d standard/deluxe US$187/244; ⒫ ⓧ ⓧ ⓧ ⓧ) Couples who can't decide between Las Vegas and Central America can compromise here amid over-the-top, Roman-style luxury, complete with 'Costa Rica's most elegant casino.' Gourmet organic Italian meals, a bird sanctuary, an outrageous spa, huge pools, sauna and full gym are also on offer. It's 2km north of the Alajuela exit from the Interamericana, about 15 minutes from the airport.

Scientists from around the world come to Costa Rica's corn breadbasket to study maize. Everyone else comes to dine at one of a number of unusual restaurants to do their own tasty investigation.

La Fiesta del Maíz (☎ 2487 7057; mains US$1-5; ♥ 6am-9:30pm) This understated spot is famed for its wide variety of corn concoctions, as well as fried pork skins.

Delicias del Maíz (☎ 2433 7206; mains US$3-9; ♥ 8am-9:30pm) Delicias is decidedly more upmarket, with its rustic dining room and grill, and also adapts just about every possible recipe to include corn. Iowa, eat your heart out.

La Casa del Viñedo (☎ 2487 6086; mains US$4-15; ♥ 11am-11pm) Dare we say it – if corn is not your thing, visit this vineyard on the edge of La Garita, which produces small batches of seven different wines. You can sample them alongside the recommended steaks, Argentine or American style.

GETTING THERE & AWAY

Buses (US$0.75, 30 minutes) run between Alajuela and La Garita, via Zoo Ave, every half hour. If you're driving, take the Atenas exit off the Interamericana, then go 3km east to Zoo Ave.

Atenas

This small village is on the historic *camino de carretas* (oxcart trail) that once carried coffee beans as far as Puntarenas, though it's best known as having the most pleasant climate in the world, at least according to a 1994 issue of *National Geographic*. It's not too heavy on sights, though springtime is always in the air.

Follow the signs to **El Cafetal Inn B&B** (☎ 2446 5785; www.cafetal.com; s/d from US$80/90; P), a sweeping coffee plantation 5km north of Atenas, where you can stay the night or simply stop by to sample the local specialty – that'd be coffee. There's a large garden (with two easy trails to waterfalls), a pool and several attractive rooms that vary in size and amenities, but that all have lots of light and great country views. The onsite café **Mirador del Cafetal** (dishes US$1-5; ♥ 7am-5pm) sells its own brand of coffee, La Negrita – as beans or in an outstanding selection of beverages, drunk hot or cold while gazing across the entire Central Valley.

The **Rancho Típico La Trilla** (☎ 2446 5637; mains US$3-8), 75m east of the gas station, serves rustic-style casados and is a popular tourist stop where you can opt for the caffeine theme at the 'coffee mill' (the restaurant's name refers to an old mill, nearby).

Frequent buses connect Atenas to San José and Alajuela.

NORTHWEST TO SARCHÍ

Scattered across the carefully cultivated hills to the northwest of Alajuela are the small towns of Grecia (22km), Sarchí (29km), Naranjo (35km) and Zarcero (52km), which are popular romantic getaways for josefinos in search of flowering trees and fresh country air. In addition to its charming atmosphere, the region also boasts excellent coffee and a subdued collection of eccentric attractions, including the country's most famous topiary bushes and its arts-and-crafts capital.

Grecia

Centered on the incongruous, bright-red metal **Catedral de la Mercedes**, which was boxed up in Belgium and shipped to Costa Rica in 1897, Grecia is a modern town spiced up with a fair dash of Costa Rican folklore. The small **Casa de Cultura** (☎ 2444 6767) has the official version, with Spanish-colonial artifacts, articles about Grecia's 'Cleanest Little Town in Latin America' award and an impressive insect collection.

INFORMATION

Theoretically, **Minae** (Ministry of Environment and Energy; ☎ 2494 0065; ♥ 8am-4pm Mon-Fri) has information about the surrounding parks. The town has several simple *sodas* and bars, plus banks with 24-hour ATMs and a post office.

SIGHTS

Check out the **18th-century rock bridge** south of town connecting the hamlets of Puente de Piedra and Rincón de Salas. Grecians say that the only other rock bridge like this is in China, and some tales have it that it was built by the devil. In 1994 it was declared a National Site of Historical Interest.

The premier attraction, however, is **World of Snakes** (☎ 2494 3700; adult/child US$12/7; ♥ 8am-4pm), 1.5km southeast of the town center, a well-run attraction with an endangered-snake breeding program. More than 150 snakes (40 species in all) are displayed in large cages as

'Snakes of the World' or 'Snakes of Costa Rica.' Informative tours in English, German or Spanish may include the chance to handle certain snakes if there's time. Any bus to Grecia from Alajuela can drop you at the entrance.

Mariposario Spirogyra (adult/child US$5/3; 8am-5pm), 150m from the church, is a small but pretty butterfly garden with a few informative plaques. Guided tours are included with the price.

About 5km south of Grecia, toward Santa Gertrudis, are **Las Cataratas de Los Chorros** (admission US$4; 8am-5pm), two gorgeous waterfalls and a swimming hole surrounded by picnic tables. It's a popular spot for weekending couples.

ACTIVITIES

Is Costa Rica's safe and peaceful image just not doing it for you? Live dangerously at **Tropical Bungee** (2290 5629; www.bungee.co.cr; 1st/2nd jump US$60/30), where you can hurl yourself off the 75m bridge that spans the Río Colorado. Your impending doom is 2km west of the turnoff for Grecia.

SLEEPING & EATING

Healthy Day Country Inn Resort (2444 5903; d incl breakfast US$45; P) Although the crumbling, jungle facade adorning the entrance looks like it's seen better days, this Tico resort is a great city break, especially if you're looking to slim down. Rooms with shared bathrooms are great value considering guests have access to the on-site tennis court, gym and Jacuzzi, as well as less taxing weight-loss opportunities like homeopathic therapies, massages and macrobiotic meals. It's 800m northeast of the church on the main road.

ourpick Vista del Valle Plantation Inn (2450 0800; www.vistadelvalle.com; s/d US$100/120, ste incl breakfast US$155-200; P) In the village of Rosario, about 7km southwest of Grecia as the parrot flies, this choice property with a regular airport shuttle may well be one of the swankiest jungle lodges in Costa Rica. Elegant garden cottages scattered throughout the luxuriously landscaped botanical garden have balconies that overlook the Río Grande, various volcanoes and even San José city lights. Trails lead past a 90m-high waterfall into the adjoining Zona Protectora Río Grande, a cloud-forest reserve at about 800m. Horseback tours and massage therapy are available, and there is also a pool and Jacuzzi for soaking off the hike.

There are a few well-stocked markets, bakeries and basic *sodas* in town.

GETTING THERE & AWAY

The bus terminal is about 400m south of the church, behind the *mercado* (market).

San José US$0.50, one hour, depart every 30 minutes from 5:30am to 10pm.

Sarchí, connecting to Naranjo US$0.25, one hour, depart every 25 minutes from 4:45am to 10pm.

Sarchí

There's just one problem with vacationing in Costa Rica: lousy souvenir shopping. Blame the whole ecotourism thing – it just seems wrong to buy a plastic bauble commemorating your visit to some of the last untouched rain forests in the world. But here it is, the end of your trip, and you've got to face jealous friends and family who won't care that you spotted a rare three-wattled bellbird while trekking through waist-deep mud. Nope, they want presents.

Welcome to Sarchí, Costa Rica's most famous crafts center, where artisans showcase the country's deeply ingrained woodworking tradition. The pretty town is a jumble of bungalow-size stalls, surrounded by undulating coffee-growing valleys. Unfortunately, a 45-minute stop in town (especially if you're on a tour bus) is likely to give you the impression that you've landed in a tourist trap, albeit one with free coffee. But keep in mind that there are more than 200 workshops peppered around the nearby countryside, and if you're a little bit independent it's often possible to meet different artists, and even custom-order your own creation or arrange a lesson or two.

ORIENTATION & INFORMATION

Sarchí is divided by the Río Trojas into Sarchí Norte and Sarchí Sur, and is rather spread out, straggling for several kilometers along the main road from Grecia to Naranjo. In Sarchí Norte you'll find the main plaza with the typical twin-towered church, a hotel and some restaurants. There is a **Banco Nacional** (2454 4262; 8:30am-3pm Mon-Fri) for changing money.

SLEEPING & EATING

Cabinas Mandy (2454 2397; s/d US$10/15; P) Close to the fire station in Sarchí Norte is the best budget option in town. Small but well-kept rooms have cable TV and private hot showers.

A SHOPPERS GUIDE TO SARCHÍ

Elegantly polished or brightly painted, Sarchí work is unmistakable. Although the range of crafts available for purchase is extensive, most travelers are interested in *carretas*, the elaborately painted oxcarts that are the unofficial souvenir of Costa Rica (and official symbol of the Costa Rican worker).

Painting the elaborate mandala designs requires a steady hand and active imagination, and is a process well worth watching. Though pricier models are ready for the road (oxen sold separately), most are scaled-down versions designed for display in gardens and homes, while others have been customized to function as indoor tables, sideboards and minibars. Smaller models are suitable for every budget and backpack.

In addition to *carretas*, shoppers in the know come to Sarchí for leather-and-wood furniture, specifically rocking chairs that collapse Ikea style for shipping. Other items you won't find elsewhere include gleaming wooden bowls and other tableware, some carved from rare hardwoods (which you should think twice about buying unless you want to contribute to further deforestation). Most of the hardwoods sculpted in Sarchí are grown locally on plantations, though it's best to inquire about a piece if you're feeling unsure.

What makes Sarchí so much more than another stop on the tourist circuit is that the top artisans are part of renowned woodworking families, many of whom are very welcoming to inquisitive travelers. If you're interested in commissioning a custom piece, artisans will be happy to listen to your ideas as well as to offer suggestions, and prices are generally fair and reasonable. There are also plenty of opportunities in Sarchí for taking woodworking classes or organizing an apprenticeship – talk to different artisans, ask for a few prices and work out a deal that makes everyone happy.

Workshops are usually open from 8am to 4pm daily, and they accept credit cards and US dollars. Below is a listed of recommended spots, though with over 200 places to choose from, it pays to shop around and enjoy the experience.

Fábrica de Carretas Joaquín Chaverri (☎ 2454 4411) The oldest and best-known factory in Sarchí Sur. This is a good spot for watching artisans from the old school of transportation aesthetics emblazon those incredible patterns on oxcarts by hand.

Los Rodríguez (☎ 2454 4097), **La Sarchiseño** (☎ 2454 3430) and **El Artesano** (☎ 2454 4304) All are located along the main road, and specialize in rocking chairs and other furniture.

Pidesa Souvenirs (☎ 2454 4540) By the main plaza, this spot specializes in hand painting local souvenirs Sarchí style, including full-size milk cans.

Plaza de la Artesanía (☎ 2454 3430) In Sarchí Sur, this is the top choice for connoisseurs of kitsch. It's a shopping mall with more than 30 souvenir stores selling everything from truly beautiful furniture to mass-produced key chains.

Taller Lalo Alfaro Two blocks north of the church is Sarchí's oldest workshop, where they still make working oxcarts using machinery powered by a waterwheel.

Hotel Daniel Zamora (☎ 2454 4596; d US$35; P) On a quiet street east of the soccer field, this is a slightly more upmarket choice. Rooms have cable TV and private hot showers, and are large and nicely furnished.

Las Carretas (☎ 2454 1636; mains US$5-10; ⏱ 11am-9pm) The most popular restaurant in town for tour buses and locals alike serves up Tico classics in an elegant dining room adorned with local woodwork.

A great farmers market is held on Fridays behind Taller Lalo Alfaro, where you can grab homemade snacks, palmetto cheese and lots of produce.

GETTING THERE & AROUND

If you're driving, you can take the unpaved road northeast from Sarchí to Bajos del Toro and on through Colonia del Toro to the northern lowlands at Río Cuarto. The main attraction of this route is the beautiful water-fall north of Bajos del Toro. Look for local signs for the 'Catarata.'

Alajuela (Tuasa) US$0.75, 30 minutes, depart every 30 minutes from 6am to 11pm.

Grecia US$0.50, 20 minutes, depart every 30 minutes from 6am to 11pm.

San José US$2, 1½ hours, depart at 6am, 1pm and 4:05pm.

PALMARES

Palmares' claim to fame is the annual **Las Fiestas de Palmares**, a 10-day beer-soaked extravaganza that takes place in mid-January and features carnival rides, parades, a *tope* (horse parade), fireworks, discotheques, big-name bands, small-name bands, exotic dancers, fried food, Guaro Cacique tents and the highest proportion of drunken Ticos you've ever seen. Unsurprisingly, it's one of the biggest events in the country, and is widely covered on national TV.

For the other 355 days of the year, Palmares is a bit of a tumbleweed town, where what little life exists is centered on the ornate stained-glass church in the central plaza.

During festival time, crowds can reach upwards of 10,000 people. Over the 10-day period, the fiesta continues unabated virtually day and night, and you won't believe how hard Ticos can party until you've seen it for yourself. If you're traveling in Costa Rica in January, look for posters advertising the festival, which will detail what events are taking place on which days.

Give up any plans you have of staying in Palmares unless you know someone with a house in the area. Buses run continuously from San José to Palmares throughout the festival, though it's common for groups of Ticos to rent private shuttles. If you're driving, the road from Sarchí continues west to Naranjo, where it divides – head south for 13km to reach Palmares.

SAN RAMÓN

The colonial town of San Ramón is no wall-flower in the pageant of Costa Rican history. The 'City of Presidents and Poets' has sent five men to the country's highest office, including ex-president Rodrigo Carazo, who built a tourist lodge a few kilometers to the north at the entrance to the Los Angeles Cloud Forest (see right).

Stories of the former presidents, plus poets and more, can be found on plaques around town or at the **Museo de San Ramón** (☎ 2437 9851; admission free; ⏱ 8:30-11am Wed-Sat, 1-5pm Mon-Fri) on the north side of the park. It's worth working around the museum's schedule to see life-size dioramas depicting colonial Costa Rica and well-done exhibits on the area's impressive history.

At the center of San Ramón are the twin spires of the ash-gray **Iglesia de San Ramón**, which soar high above the town and give it a dignified air. In front of the church is **Parque Central**, which is surrounded by a few colonial buildings and has a bizarre collection of lime-green *torii,* the traditional Japanese gates found at the entrance to a Shinto shrine.

The best time to come is on Saturday for the weekly farmers market, when all manner of cheeses and chorizo are on display and the area's old women do their weekly shopping and gossiping.

Sleeping & Eating

There are a few inexpensive places to stay in town, as well as two upscale lodges in the nearby Los Angeles Cloud Forest Reserve (see p138).

Hotel Gran (☎ 2445 6363; s/d US$10/15; P) Three blocks west of the park is this decent budget option, which has completely standard rooms that surround a courtyard and come with private hot-water bathrooms and cable TV.

Hotel la Posada (☎ 2445 7359; s/d incl breakfast US$30/40) Spend the extra money and upgrade to this executive-worthy hotel, which has seriously plush rooms complete with beautiful wooden furniture and huge TVs. Private bathrooms have steaming-hot showers that will make you realize what you've been missing!

Il Giardino (dishes US$4-8) On the southwestern corner of the central park, Il Giardino specializes in wood oven–fired pizzas and thick, juicy steaks.

The Saturday farmers market is a big one, with smaller markets on Wednesday and Sunday.

Getting There & Away

There are hourly buses to San José as well as frequent buses to Ciudad Quesada via Zarcero. Buses depart from Calle 16 between Avenidas 1 and 3.

LOS ANGELES CLOUD FOREST RESERVE

This **private reserve** (☎ 2661 1600; per person US$18), about 20km north of San Ramón, is centered on a lodge and dairy ranch that was once owned by ex-president Rodrigo Carazo. Some 800 hectares of primary forest have a short boardwalk and longer horse and foot trails that lead to towering waterfalls and misty cloud-forest vistas. The appeal of this cloud forest (which is actually adjacent to the reserve at Monteverde, see p190) is that it is comparatively untouristed, which means you will have a good chance of observing wildlife (jaguars and ocelots are occasionally spotted), and the birding here is simply fantastic. Although quetzals do not roost in the reserve, other trogons are commonly sighted.

Bilingual naturalist guides are available to lead hikes (per person US$25) and you can also rent horses (per hour US$20) or take to the zip lines on a canopy tour (per person US$40). Tours of the reserve are arranged through Villablanca Cloud Forest Hotel & Spa (below), though guests of the hotel can enter for free. A taxi to the reserve and hotel costs US$10 from San Ramón, and the turnoff is well signed from the highway.

Sleeping

Villablanca Cloud Forest Hotel & Spa (☎ 2228 4603; www.villablanca-costarica.com; d US$135-175) The large main lodge, restaurant and about 30 white-washed, red-tiled, rustic adobe *casetas* (huts) here are surrounded by the Los Angeles Cloud Forest Reserve. Comfortable cabins have refrigerators, bathtubs and fireplaces, and there's a fine onsite restaurant and spa. The big perk here, however, is free and easy access to the adjacent reserve.

Valle Escondido Lodge (☎ 2231 0906; s/d US$70/94) The lodge's collection of luxurious cabinas are adjacent to another private reserve featuring 20km of cloud-forest trails and a working ornamental-plant and citrus-fruit farm. Nonguests can pay US$8 for day use of the trails. There is also a pool, Jacuzzi and a locally popular restaurant with Italian specialties. It's about halfway between Hotel Villablanca and the village of La Tigra.

ZARCERO

North of Naranjo, the road winds for 20km until it reaches Zarcero's 1736m perch at the western end of the Cordillera Central. The mountains are gorgeous and the climate is famously fresh, but the reason you've come is evident as soon as you pull into town.

Parque Francisco Alvarado, in front of the already off-kilter pink-and-blue 1895 Iglesia de San Rafael, was just a normal plaza until the 1960s (of course), when gardener Evangelisto Blanco suddenly became inspired to shave the ordinary, mild-mannered bushes into bizarre abstract shapes and, over the years, everything from elephants to bull fights (the latest creation is a double tunnel of surreal, melting arches).

Today the trippy topiary is certainly the town's top sight, but space-age trees aren't the only thing growing in Zarcero – this is a center for Costa Rica's organic-farming movement. You can find unusual varieties of pesticide-free goodies all over town, and the surrounding mountains are just perfect for an afternoon picnic.

Activities

The roads around Zarcero are lined with small stores selling picnic supplies – be on the lookout for *queso palmito*, a locally made cheese that has a delicate taste and goes well with fresh tomatoes and basil. Once you've packed your picnic basket, explore the surrounding countryside and find your own grassy spot beneath the shade of a Guanacaste tree.

If you brought your swimsuit, stop into **Piscinas Apamar** (☎ 2463 3674; per person US$2; ☼ 7am-4pm Mon-Sat), 500m west of the park on the road to Guadalupe, where there's not only a huge swimming pool but also three hot tubs and a Jacuzzi.

Sleeping

Hotel Don Beto (☎ 2463 3137; www.hoteldonbeto .com; d without/with bathroom US$28/33, tr US$35; [P]) Just north of the town church is this hotel, which has homey rooms with either shag rugs or hardwood floors and private balcony. The Tico owners treat everyone as if they were visiting family, and they're a great resource for organizing trips throughout the area, especially to nearby Los Angeles Cloud Forest Reserve and Parque Nacional Juan Castro Blanco.

Getting There & Away

Hourly buses traveling between San José and Ciudad Quesada stop at Zarcero, though some buses may be full by the time they reach Zarcero, particularly on weekends. There are also buses from Alajuela and San Ramón.

PARQUE NACIONAL JUAN CASTRO BLANCO

This 143-sq-km **national park** (admission US$6, camping US$2) was created in 1992 to protect the slopes of Volcán Platanar (2183m) and Volcán Porvenir (2267m) from logging. The headwaters for five major rivers originate here as well, making this one of the most important watersheds in the entire country.

The park is in limbo, federally protected but still privately owned by various plantation families – only those parts that have already been purchased by the government are technically open to the traveler. As yet, there is almost no infrastructure for visitors, though there is a **Minae office** (☎ 2460 7600) in El Sucre, next to the only official entrance, where you can pay fees for camping or day use. However, the office is usually closed, and fees are rarely collected.

The park is popular among anglers as each of the five rivers is brimming with trout, and the difficult access means that the park is nearly always abandoned. Also, the lack of infrastructure and tourist traffic means that your chances of spotting rare wildlife are very high. However, since there are no facilities and few marked trails in the park, it's recommended that you hire a guide, which can be arranged at any of the hotels in the area.

PARQUE NACIONAL VOLCÁN POÁS

Just 37km north of Alajuela by a winding and scenic road is the most heavily trafficked **national park** (admission US$7; ◷ 8am-3:30pm) in Costa Rica. However, there are few places in the world where you can peer into an active volcano – without the hardship of actually hiking up one. The centerpiece of the park is, of course, Volcán Poás (2704m), which had its last blowout in 1953. This event formed the eerie and enormous crater, which is 1.3km across and 300m deep. There are also two other craters, one of which contains a lake, that serve as evidence of the volcano's violent past.

Poás continues to be active to varying extents with different levels of danger. The park was briefly closed in May 1989 after a minor eruption sent volcanic ash spouting more than 1km into the air, and lesser activity closed the park intermittently in 1995. In recent years, however, Poás has posed no imminent threat, though scientists are still worried – the water level of the lake has dropped dramatically in the past decade, which is a major warning sign of an impending eruption (see boxed text Feelin' Hot, Hot, Hot!, p243).

In the meantime, the most common hazard for visitors is the veil of clouds that the mountain gathers around itself almost daily (even in the dry season), starting at around 10am. Even if the day looks clear, get to the park as early as possible or you won't see much.

But, crowds and clouds aside, the sight of the bubbling and steaming cauldron is truly astonishing, especially when it belches sulfurous mud and steaming water hundred of meters into the air.

Information

Some 250,000 people visit the park annually, making Poás the most packed national park in the country – visiting on weekends in particular is best avoided. The visitors center has a coffee shop, souvenirs and informative videos hourly from 9am to 3pm. A small museum offers explanations in both Spanish and English. There's no camping at the park.

The best time to visit is during the dry season, especially early in the morning before the clouds roll in and obscure the view. Even if the summit is clouded in, don't despair! Take a hike to the other craters and then return to the cauldron later – winds change rapidly on the summit, and sometimes thick cloud cover is quickly blown away.

Be advised that overnight temperatures can drop below freezing, and it may be windy and cold during the day, particularly in the morning. Also, Poás receives almost 4000mm of rainfall each year. Dress accordingly.

Hiking

From the visitors center, there is a wheelchair-accessible paved road that leads directly to the crater lookout. Because of the toxic sulfuric-acid fumes that are emitted from the cauldron, visitors are prohibited from descending into the crater.

From the crater, there are two trails that branch out – to the right is **Sendero Botos**, to the left **Sendero Escalonia**. Sendero Botos is a short, 30-minute round-trip hike that takes you through dwarf cloud forest, which is the product of acidic air and freezing temperatures. Here you can wander about looking at bromeliads, lichens and mosses clinging to the curiously shaped and twisted trees growing in the volcanic soil. Birds abound, especially the magnificent fiery-throated hummingbird, a high-altitude specialty of Costa Rica. The trail ends at **Laguna Botos**, a peculiar cold-water lake that has filled in one of the extinct craters.

Sendero Escalonia is a slightly longer trail through taller forest, though it gets significantly less traffic than the other parts of the park. While hiking on the trail, look for other highland specialties, including the sooty robin, black guans, screech owls and even the odd quetzal (especially from February to April). Although mammals are infrequently sighted in the park, coyotes and the endemic montane squirrel are present.

Tours

Numerous companies offer daily tours to the volcano, but readers frequently complain that they're an overpriced affair. Typically, they cost US$40 to US$100, and the kicker is that you usually arrive at the volcano around 10am – right when the clouds start rolling in. Also, readers complain that they're often rushed off the crater, though there always seems to be time for stopping at a few souvenir stores on the way back.

As always, it's important to shop around and ask questions. Generally, the cheaper tours are large-group affairs providing only transportation, park entrance and limited time at the crater. The more expensive tours feature smaller group sizes, bilingual naturalist guides and lunch. However, just remember that it's possible to visit the volcano quite easily using public transportation from San José, and it's definitely cheaper for two people to rent a car for the day and drive themselves.

Sleeping

ON THE ROAD TO POÁS

Lo Que Tu Quieres Lodge (☎ 2482 2092; s/d/tr cabins US$19/25/30; P) About 5km before the park entrance, the name of this place translates to 'Whatever You Want Lodge.' This is a good budget option as cabinas are all equipped with heaters and hot water, and the owners will usually let you camp for a few dollars. There is a small restaurant (dishes US$3 to US$8) on the grounds that serves simple, typical food.

Lagunillas Lodge (☎ 2448 5506; d/tr US$25/30, cabinas US$30-40; P) The closest accommodation to the volcano is recommended for its stellar views and the warm welcome you'll get on arrival. Rooms and larger cabinas, which can accommodate up to six people, have hot-water showers and heaters, and all are surrounded by good hiking trails. There's also a fish pond out back where you can catch dinner, and the restaurant (mains US$4 to US$10) will prepare it – with side dishes. To get here, a signed turnoff about 2km before the park entrance sends you along a steep 1km dirt road that may require a 4WD – call ahead.

AROUND POÁS

Poás Volcano Lodge (☎ 2482 2194; www.poasvolcano lodge.com; s/d US$45/55, with bathroom US$55/75, ste US$90-115; P □) About 16km east of the volcano near Vara Blanca, a high-altitude dairy farm frames this attractive stone building, which blends architectural influences from Wales, England and Costa Rica (the original owners were English farmers). Trails radiate from the eclectically decorated rooms, and common areas include a billiard room ('pool' doesn't do it justice). There's a sitting area with a sunken fireplace, and books and board games to while away a stormy night.

Bosque de Paz Rain/Cloud Forest Lodge & Biological Reserve (☎ 2234 6676; www.bosquedepaz .com; s/d/tr incl 3 meals US$121/196/279; P) Tastefully decorated in rustic luxury, this 1000-hectare biological reserve offers access to what forms a wild corridor between Parque Nacional Volcán Poás and Parque Nacional Juan Castro Blanco: not your average lodge grounds. There are 22km of trails, sometimes used by researchers from all over the world, and the owners can arrange guided hikes. If driving north from the Interamericana through Zarcero, take a right immediately after the church and head north about 15km. The reserve will be on your right, just before the last bridge to Bajos del Toro.

Eating

On sunny days the road to Poás is lined with stands selling fruit, cheese and snacks – it's worth picking up picnic supplies because the coffee shop at the visitors center has a limited menu. Bring your own bottled water, as proximity to primordial seepage has rendered the tap water undrinkable.

Colbert Restaurant (dishes US$5-10) About 2km east of the Poás Volcano Lodge (above), on a ridge overlooking the volcano, this reader-recommended rustic French restaurant highlights localy produced cheeses in traditional, continental dishes.

Getting There & Away

You can take a taxi to the park for around US$80 from San José, US$40 from Alajuela. If you're driving, the road from Alajuela to the volcano is well signed. Most visitors using public buses come from San José. Get to the terminal early.

From San José (US$4, three hours) Tuasa buses depart 8:30am daily from Avenida 2 between Calles 12 and 14, stopping in Alajuela at 9:30am and returning at 2:30pm.

LOS JARDINES DE LA CATARATA LA PAZ

La Paz Waterfall Gardens (☎ 2265 0643; www.water fallgardens.com; adult/child & student US$25/15; ⏱ 8:30am-5:30pm) are built around an almost impossibly scenic series of waterfalls formed as Río La Paz drops 1400m in less than 8km down the flanks of Volcán Poás. The lowest, whose name means 'Peace Waterfall,' is one of the most loved (and photographed) sights in Costa Rica.

Visitors, many on tours from San José, follow 3.5km of well-maintained trails that wind past a butterfly conservatory (the largest in the world), a hummingbird garden and a rare orchid display before plunging down alongside five cascading waterfalls. Small children, city slickers and active seniors won't have any problems with this adventure, especially since there is a shuttle bus at the bottom of the falls that brings hikers back up to the visitors center.

The gardens are administered by the **Peace Lodge** (☎ 2482 2720; www.waterfallgardens .com; d US$185-215), one of six 'Small Distinctive Hotels of Costa Rica.' Take a long, hard look at your travel companion – if you love him or her in the slightest way (and money isn't an option), you'll change your plans and spend the night here. Standard rooms are a work of art with waterfall showers that gush at the slightest turn of a knob, manicured-stone fireplaces for those cool, crisp nights and exotic design schemes that will bring all of your rain forest fantasies to life. Deluxe rooms are all this and more (we're talking two Jacuzzis for all your indoor and outdoor soaking pleasures).

Even if you're not staying in the hotel, you can still visit the lodge's buffet (adult/child US$10/5), where you can dine alongside a huge fireplace that provides welcome respite from the weather on a rainy day.

HEREDIA AREA

Despite outward appearances and a convenient location, Heredia (population 33,000) isn't just a suburb of San José. Since the late 1990s the city has come into its own as the high-tech capital of Costa Rica – microchips produced here have become the country's most important export. Career opportunities make Heredia a magnet for this highly educated nation's tech heads, and considering that the historic coffee center also produces some of the world's strongest brews, programmers have little excuse to stop coding. Ever.

But there's much more to this province than its well-to-do capital. The Heredia area retains its heritage as a coffee-production center, and indeed it's possible to visit the headquarters of the most famous roaster in the country, Café Britt Finca (p144). The town itself has a very young vibe, particularly around the western edge of town, where students lounge around the cafés and bars at all hours of the day. The area is also home to one of Costa Rica's largest swaths of rain forest, Parque Nacional Braulio Carrillo (p146).

HEREDIA

During its colonial heyday, la Ciudad de las Flores (the City of the Flowers) was home to the Spanish aristocracy, who made their fortunes by exporting Costa Rica's premium blend. Over the years, the Spanish built an attractive colonial city on an orderly grid, and although Heredia grew in both size and prominence, it managed to retain its charming elegance and small-city feel. Following the independence of Costa Rica, Heredia was even considered for the seat of federal government.

Although it is only 11km from San José, Heredia is a world away from the grit and grime of the capital. The cosmopolitan bustle comes courtesy of the multinational high-tech corporations that have their Central American headquarters here, while more bohemian stylings radiate from the National University, whose local bars are abuzz with young folk idling away afternoons. Heredia's historic center is one of the most attractive in the country, with a lovely, leafy main square that is overlooked by the stocky cathedral. From a tourist perspective, the city serves as a convenient base for exploring the diverse attractions of the province.

Information

Though there's no tourist office, most other services are readily available. The university district is full of copy places, internet cafés, cell phone shops, and music and video stores.

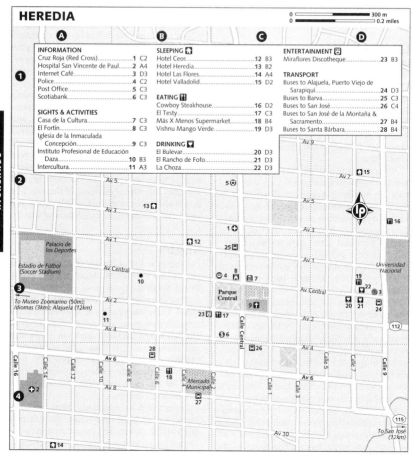

HEREDIA

Hospital San Vicente de Paul (☎ 2261 0001; Av 8 btwn Calles 14 & 16)

Internet Café (Av Central btwn Calles 7 & 9; per hr US$0.75) For 24-hour access to the web.

Scotiabank (☎ 2262 5303; Av 4 btwn Calles Central & 2; ☺ 8am-5pm Mon-Fri, 8am-4pm Sat) The only place that changes money, it has a 24-hour ATM that dispenses US dollars.

Sights

Heredia was founded in 1706, and in true Spanish-colonial style it has several interesting old landmarks arranged around **Parque Central**. To the east is **Iglesia de la Inmaculada Concepción**, built in 1797 and still in use. Opposite the church steps you can take a break and watch old men playing checkers at the park tables

while weddings and funerals come and go. The church's thick-walled, squat construction is attractive in a Volkswagen Beetle sort of way. The solid shape has withstood the earthquakes that have damaged or destroyed almost all the other buildings in Costa Rica that date from this time.

To the north of the park is an 1867 guard tower called simply **El Fortín**, which is the last remaining turret of a Spanish fortress and the official symbol of Heredia. This area is a national historic site, but passageways are closed to the public.

At the park's northeast corner, **Casa de la Cultura** (☎ 2262 2505; cnr Calle Central & Av Central; www.heredianet.co.cr/casacult.htm, in Spanish; admission free; ☺ hours vary), formerly the residence of

President Alfredo González Flores (1913–17), now houses permanent historical exhibits as well as rotating art shows and other events.

The campus of **Universidad Nacional**, six blocks east of Parque Central, is a great place for doing a little guerrilla learning – strap on your backpack (the small one) and follow the student crowds. While you're on campus, keep an eye out for posters advertising cultural offerings and special events happening around the city. Also, check out the marine biology department's **Museo Zoomarino** (☎ 2277 3240; admission free; ✆ 8am-4pm Mon-Fri), where more than 2000 displayed specimens give an overview of Costa Rica's marine diversity. The Museo Zoomarino is not on campus, but located about 1km west of the university.

Courses

There are three Spanish-language schools in town: **Centro Panamericano de Idiomas** (☎ 2265 6306; www.cpi-edu.com), **Intercultura** (☎ 2260 8480, in the USA 800-552 2051; www.spanish-intercultura.com) and **Instituto Profesional de Educación Daza** (☎ 2238 3608; www.learnspanishcostarica.com). See also boxed text Spanish Schools in the Central Valley, p130, for more details.

Sleeping

Most travelers prefer to stay in nearby San José, though there are plenty of budget hotels in town that cater to students – if you like paper-thin walls. Plenty have cheap monthly rates.

Hotel Las Flores (☎ 2261 8147; www.hotel-lasflores.com; Av 12 btwn Calles 12 & 14; s/d/tr US$12/24/36; P) Though it's a bit of a walk from downtown, this hotel has a warm, welcoming management and bright, sunny rooms complete with steamy showers and thick mattresses.

Hotel Ceos (☎ 2262 2628; cnr Calle 4 & Av 1; s/d/tr US$20/30/40; P) This is another good option as newly furnished rooms have private solar-heated showers, cable TV and a large communal balcony – perfect for those Imperial-swigging nights. Check out the old photos that adorn the walls of the ground floor.

Hotel Heredia (☎ 2238 0880; Calle 6 btwn Avs 3 & 5; s/d/tr US$20/30/40; P) This adorable white-and-blue house features sparkling rooms with private solar-heated showers and cable TV, not to mention plenty of green space for lounging about.

Hotel Valladolid (☎ 2260 2905; valladol@racsa.co.cr; cnr Calle 7 & Av 7; s/d incl continental breakfast US$80/93/107; P ✆) Fully equipped rooms at the most established hotel in town caters primarily to discerning business travelers. It's a good choice if you're looking for a few added comforts, namely a sauna, Jacuzzi and top-floor solarium.

Eating

In the grand tradition of university towns worldwide, Heredia offers plenty of spots for pizza slices and cheap vegetarian grub, not to mention one branch of every fast-food outlet imaginable.

El Testy (Cnr Calle 2 & Av 2; dishes US$1-5) Here it is folks, your one-stop shopping for burritos, ravioli, hamburgers, tacos, chicken and fries. Feeling indecisive? It also sells ice cream, candy, cookies and snacks!

Vishnu Mango Verde (Calle 7 btwn Avs Central & 1; dishes US$3-5; ✆ 9am-6pm Mon-Sat) This branch of the famous San José chain is the top spot in town for cheap and healthy vegetarian fare – your stomach (and your karma) will thank you.

Cowboy Steakhouse (Calle 7 btwn Avs 3 & 5; dishes US$4-9; ✆ 5-11pm Mon-Sat) A rough-and-ready all-wood shack that serves up the best cuts of beef in town. As the title suggests, steak is the focal point, making it a meat-lovers' must. But the hearty salads are worth a nibble as well.

You can fill up for a few hundred colones at the **Mercado Municipal** (Calle 2 btwn Avs 6 & 8; ✆ 6am-6pm), with *sodas* to spare and plenty of very fresh groceries. **Más X Menos** (Av 6 btwn Calles 4 & 6; ✆ 8:30am-9pm) has everything else.

Drinking & Entertainment

With a thriving student body, there's no shortage of live music, cultural events and the odd happening. For info on what's going on, look for fliers near the campus or ask a student to fill you in on the scene.

The university district is hopping most nights of the week (Tico students live it up like you wouldn't believe). **La Choza** (Av Central btwn Calles 7 & 9), **El Bulevar** (cnr Calle 7 & Av Central) and **El Rancho de Fofo** (Av Central btwn Calles 5 & 7) are three popular student spots.

After a few rounds of beers and *bocas* (savory bar snacks), the party really kicks off at the **Miraflores Discotechque** (Av 2 btwn Calles Central & 2), on the southern edge of the Parque Central. Stay aware, however: Heredia can get dodgy

---

'NO TLC'

No doubt you'll see the graffiti sign 'No TLC' on almost every corner. This is in reference to the free trade agreement, DR-Cafta (known as TLC in Costa Rica), which was narrowly passed in October 2007. The whole country was divided down the middle on the issue. And it's still a sensitive subject not to be brought up lightly, especially in this industrious part of the country where the agreement has the most impact. We spoke to two politics students from Heredia to give us the opposing arguments:

Si

Juande Catarini: Whether we like it or not, we need free trade with the US. Regardless of their political actions over the years, we can't afford not to be affiliated with them. We're too small. Also, internally, there is one major reason we needed to approve the TLC, and that's competition. For too long, major sections of the market had become monopolized by government-backed institutions. The best example of this is the national telecommunications company, ICE, which has been running an inefficient service for way too long. ICE was at the center of the debate because they had the major monopoly for all of Costa Rica's telecommunications. While I don't expect costs to change dramatically under the influx of foreign competitors, I do expect the quality of service to improve greatly. This will benefit the country in every angle of commerce, and it will finally allow us to compete in the global call-center market, in which we have been lagging behind.

If we had opted out of TLC, our formerly leading, but now slow-paced, technology industry would have been left eating the dust of our competitor countries. In the early '90s we were light years ahead of the rest of Central America in technological infrastructure, but we have rested

---

at nighttime, though there is an established police presence.

Getting There & Away

There is no central bus terminal, and buses leave from bus stops near Parque Central and market areas. Buses for Barva leave from near **Cruz Roja** (Red Cross; Calle Central btwn Avs 1 & 3). Buses to San José de la Montaña and Sacramento, with connections to Volcán Barva in Parque Nacional Braulio Carrillo, leave from Avenida 8 between Calles 2 and 4. Ask around the market for information on other destinations.

Alajuela US$0.75, 20 minutes, depart from corner of Avenida Central and Calle 9 every 15 minutes from 6am to 10pm.

Barva US$0.50, 20 minutes, depart from Calle Central between Avenidas 1 and 3 every 30 minutes from 5:15am to 11:30pm.

Puerto Viejo de Sarapiquí US$2, 3½ hours, depart from the corner of Avenida Central and Calle 9 at 11am, 1:30pm and 3pm.

San José US$0.50, 20 minutes, depart from Avenida 4 between Calles Central and 1 every 20 to 30 minutes from 4:40am to 11pm.

Santa Bárbara US$0.50, 20 minutes, depart from Avenida 6 between Calles 6 and 8 every 10 to 30 minutes from 5:15am to 11:30pm.

Taxis are plentiful and can take you to San José (US$5) or the airport (US$8).

BARVA

Just 2.5km north of Heredia is the historic town of Barva, which dates from 1561 and has been declared a national monument. The town center is packed with 17th- and 18th-century buildings, and is centered on the towering **Iglesia San Bartolomé**. With its scenic mountainside location and colonial ambience, the town is a popular residence among the Costa Rican elite – Cleto González Víquez, twice president of Costa Rica, used to live here. The town is perfect for a lazy afternoon stroll, and although Barva proper doesn't have any lodgings, some truly spectacular luxury hotels are just outside of town.

Sights

The most famous coffee roaster in Costa Rica, **Café Britt Finca** (☎ 2277 1600; www.coffeetour .com, www.cafébritt.com; adult with/without lunch US$30/20, student US$27/18; ☼ tours 11am year-round, 9am & 3pm in high season) is headquartered just 1km south of Barva. Although the tour is a bit pricey, it comes highly recommended by readers. For 90 minutes, bilingual guides will walk you through the plantation and the process-on our laurels since then and we certainly can't afford to stay in our dreamy elevated bubble any longer. The momentum is with our progressive neighbors, and we don't want to lose our business to them.

We also have to look beyond our neighbors. How can we hope to trade and compete with rising world leaders such as China and India if we can't do the same with states on our own doorstep? Now we have to heal the bitter wounds, caused in large part by the old-fashioned unions, that this heated debate has inflicted on our country.

No

Carlos Angulo: If there's one glaringly obvious fact that has come to light from historical and contemporary international politics of late, it is that the US looks after its own interests and will pay any price to protect them. Granted, that's their prerogative, but all you have to do is look at the increasing unemployment in El Salvador, Nicaragua and Mexico to see that free trade with the US doesn't benefit Central American countries. Even Canada is at loggerheads with, and is constantly involved in international tribunals against, the US.

As a nation we have created a position of being the most socially developed country in Central America, and this is because historically we have maintained an independent position and rejected these treaties. While we don't want to go to their political extremes, both Venezuela and Cuba are proving that it's possible to prosper without favorable US trade. We will lose our sovereignty and become another pawn state that will be subject to the political and economical agenda of the US. In Costa Rica we have a certain way of going about business. It isn't always motivated or measured by profit margins, but by respect and trust. These values will be forgotten if we involve ourselves with the hyper-capitalism that TLC will encourage.

ing center where you can learn the difference between regular and organic coffee-growing processes, as well as the history of coffee production in Costa Rica. And don't worry – there are plenty of free samples. For an extra US$5, you can combine your tour with a one-hour trip to the *benefico* (processing plant), where you can learn about the wonders of coffee-bean harvesting. Café Britt operates a daily shuttle that will pick you up from San José – call for a reservation. If you drive or take the bus, you can't miss the signs between Heredia and Barva.

Located in Santa Lucía de Barva, about 1.5km southeast of Barva, the **Museo de Cultura Popular** (☎ 2260 1619; admission US$2; ☺ 9am-4pm) recreates colonial Costa Rica in a century-old farmhouse, restored with period pieces and ingenious tools. If you're lucky, docents in period costumes may use the beehive-shape ovens to make typical Tico foods, which you can purchase anytime at the **garden café** (dishes US$2-5; ☺ 11am-2pm).

INBio (☎ 2507 8107; www.inbio.ac.cr/en/default2 .html; adult/child/student US$15/8/12; ☺ 7:30am-4pm), the El Instituto Nacional de Bioversidad (the National Biodiversity Institute), is a private research center that was formed in 1989 to catalog the biological diversity of Costa Rica

and promote its sustainable use. Visitors to the center spend their time at **INBioparque**, a high-quality collection of attractions, including biodiversity exhibition halls, wildlife-viewing stations, a butterfly garden, an aquarium, a working farm, medicinal plant garden and sugar mill. However, the center functions primarily as a biodiversity management center, and if you have an appropriate background, there are great volunteer opportunities here.

Festivals & Events

Each July and August, the Hotel Chalet Tirol (below) is the site of the **International Music Festival**, which, true to the hotel's Austrian motif, is heavy on the classical music.

Sleeping

More affordable accommodations can be found in nearby Heredia (p143), but each of the following luxury hotels comes highly recommended.

Hotel Chalet Tirol (☎ 2267 6222; www.costarica bureau.com/hotels/tirol.htm; d chalet US$80; P ⭐) Between Monte de la Cruz and Club Campestre El Castillo, you'll find this quaint country hotel, formerly the residence of Costa Rican president Alfredo González Flores. The cloud-forest enclave is rustic-chic, with comfy

Austrian-style chalets arranged around open-air common spaces, including a pizza parlor where you can relax and watch the mist drift by. The hotel plays host to an international music festival in the summertime.

Hotel Bougainvillea (☎ 2244 1414; www.hb.co.cr; s/d/tr/ste US$102/110/122/133; P ☐ ☒) In the town of Santo Domingo de Heredia, on the road between Heredia and San José, this luxury property is situated among stately coffee fincas, old-growth trees and stunning flowers. Wood-accented rooms and suites have dramatic balconies that overlook either the nearby mountains or the flickering lights of San José. Several private trails wind through the jungle and fruit orchards, passing the swimming pool, restaurant and tennis courts en route to the hills. Best of all, this rural wonderland comes with free hourly shuttles to downtown San José.

Finca Rosa Blanca (☎ 2269 9392; www.fincarosa blanca.com; d US$250-350; P ☐ ☒) Just outside Santa Bárbara, this honeymoon-ready confection of gorgeous garden villas and architecturally outstanding suites, cloaked in fruit trees that shade trails and cascading rivers, ranks as one of the most exclusive hotels in Costa Rica. Rooms with balconies overlooking the rain forest are individually and lavishly appointed; one tops a tower with a 360-degree view, reached by a winding staircase made from a single tree trunk. Shower in an artificial waterfall, take a moonlight dip in the sculpted garden pool and hot tub, or have a romantic dinner.

Getting There & Around

Half-hourly buses travel between Heredia and Barva (US$0.75, 20 minutes), and pick up in front of the church.

PARQUE NACIONAL BRAULIO CARRILLO

Thick virgin forest, countless waterfalls, swift rivers and deep canyons – it will be difficult to believe that you are only 30 minutes north of San José when you're walking around this underexplored national park. Braulio Carrillo has an extraordinary biodiversity attributable to the steep range of altitudes, from the misty 2906m cloud-forest camp sites atop massive Volcán Barva to the lush, humid 50m lowlands stretching toward the Caribbean Sea.

The park's creation was the result of a unique compromise between conservation-

ists and developers. For more than a century, San José's only link to Puerto Limón was limited to the crumbling railway and a slow rural road. In the 1970s, however, government and industry agreed that a sleek modern highway was required to link the nation's capital to its most important port. But the only feasible route was through a low pass between Volcán Barva and Volcán Irazú, which was still virgin rain forest – conservationists were not happy campers.

The compromise was simple – Parque Nacional Braulio Carrillo (named after Costa Rica's third president, who conceived the cultivation of coffee) was established in 1978, off-limits to development beyond a single major highway to bisect it. Conservationists rejoiced in the creation of a nearly 48,000-hectare national park (we're talking the size of Rhode Island!) that was comprised of 85% primary forest, and protected the watershed for San José. Government and industry rejoiced in the creation of the San José–Guápiles highway, which was completed in 1987, effectively cutting the park into two smaller preserved areas (though it's still administered as a single unit).

Driving through the park will give you an idea of what Costa Rica looked like prior to the 1950s – rolling hills cloaked in mountain rain forest. About 75% of Costa Rica was rain forest in the 1940s, while today less than one quarter of the country retains its natural vegetative cover.

Orientation & Information

The two most popular hiking areas can be accessed from the San José–Guápiles highway. At the southern end of the park is the **Zurquí ranger station** (☎ 2257 0992; admission US$6; ☉ 7am-4pm), 19km northeast of San José, while **Quebrada González ranger station** (☎ 2233 4533; admission US$6; ☉ 7am-4pm) is at the northeast corner, 22km past the Zurquí tunnel. There is a guarded parking lot, toilets and well-marked trails.

People who want to climb Volcán Barva on a day trip or camp overnight can stop by the **Barva Sector ranger station** (☎ 2261 2619; ☉ 7am-4pm), in the southwest of the park, 3km north of Sacramento.

There are also two remote outposts, El Ceibo and Magasay, in the extreme northwest corner of the park.

Temperatures can fluctuate drastically in the park, and annual rainfall can be as high as

8000mm. The best time to go is the supposedly 'dry' season (from December to April), but it is liable to rain then, too. Bring warm clothing, appropriate wet-weather gear and good hiking boots.

Wildlife-Watching

Birding in the park is excellent, and commonly sighted species include parrots, toucans, hummingbirds and even quetzals at higher elevations. Other rare but sighted birds include eagles and umbrella birds.

Mammals are difficult to see due to the lushness of the vegetation, though deer, pacas, monkeys and tepezcuintle (the park's mascot) are frequently seen. Pumas, jaguar and ocelots are present but rare.

Hiking

From Zurqui, there is a short but steep 1km trail that leads to a viewpoint. You can also follow the **Sendero Histórico**, which follows the crystal-clear Río Hondura to its meeting point with the Río Sucio (Dirty River), whose yellow waters carry volcanic minerals.

From Quebrada González, you can follow the 2.8km **Sendero La Botella** past a series of waterfalls into Patria Canyon. There are several other unmarked trails that lead through this area, including a few places where you are permitted to camp, although there are no facilities.

Keep an eye out for the distinctive huge-leafed Gunnera plants, which quickly colonize steep and newly exposed parts of the montane rain forest. The large leaves can protect a person from a sudden tropical downpour – hence the plant's nickname *sombrilla del pobre* (poor folks' umbrella).

Climbing Volcán Barva

Climbing Volcán Barva is a good four- to five-hour round-trip adventure along a well-maintained trail. Because of its relative inaccessibility, there is a good chance you can commune with the volcano solo. Begin on the western side of the park at the Sacramento entrance, north of Heredia. From there the signed track climbs to the summit at a leisurely pace. Trails are often muddy, and you should be prepared for rain any time of the year.

The track leads to three lagoons – Lagos Danta, Barva and Copey – at the volcano's summit, and several spur trails lead to water-

> **WARNING**
> Unfortunately, there have been many reports of thefts from cars parked at entrances to some trails in Parque Nacional Braulio Carrillo, as well as armed robbers accosting tourists hiking on the trails or walking along the highway. Readers have reported hearing shots fired on the trails, and hitchhikers have reported being told it is a dangerous area. Stay alert. Don't leave your car parked anywhere along the main highway. As a general rule, you should always register at a station before setting out on a hike. When possible, it's also advised that you either hike with a park ranger or arrange for a guide through any of the stations. You can also visit the park as part of a tour, which is usually arranged in San José.

falls and other scenic spots along the way. If you wish to continue from Barva north into the lowlands, you will find that the trails are unmarked and not as obvious. It is possible, regardless, to follow northbound 'trails' (overgrown and unmaintained) all the way through the park to La Selva (p519) and La Virgen (p511). A Tico who has done it reported that it took him four days, and it is a bushwhacking adventure only for those used to roughing it and able to use a topographical map and compass.

If you're visiting on a day trip, get there as early as possible as the mornings tend to be clear and the afternoons cloudy. The nighttime temperatures can drop to several degrees below freezing. Camping is allowed at the basic **campsites** (per person US$2) near the chilly but impossibly scenic summit, though you will need to bring your own drinking water.

Getting There & Away

Both Zurqui and Quebrada González stations are on Hwy 32 between San José and Guápiles. Buses between San José and either Guápiles or Puerto Viejo can drop you off 2km from the entrance, but pick-up on the major freeway will be dangerous and difficult.

Barva station can be reached by following the decent paved road north from Heredia through Barva and San José de la Montaña to Sacramento, where a signed, 3km-long, 4WD-only trail leads north to the entrance.

El Ceibo and Magasay can be accessed via rough roads from La Virgen (p511).

RAINFOREST AERIAL TRAM

The brainchild of biologist Don Perry, a pioneer of rain forest canopy research, the **Rainforest Aerial Tram** (☎ 2257 5961; www.rainforest tram.com; adult/student & child US$50/27.50) is a highly recommended splurge to the heights of the cloud forest in an airborne gondola.

The pricey entrance fee is worthwhile, as it includes a trained guide who can point out all the small and important things you'd otherwise miss, and who also leads the (optional) hike through the 400-hectare reserve, contiguous with Parque Nacional Braulio Carrillo. Although the area is rich with wildlife, the sheer density of the vegetation makes observing animals difficult.

The 2.6km aerial tram ride takes 40 minutes each way, affording a unique view of the rain forest and unusual plant-spotting and birding opportunities. Amazingly, the whole project was constructed with almost no impact on the rain forest (canopy tour operators could learn a thing or two; see boxed text Canopy Fighting, p178). A narrow footpath follows the tram, and all 250,000kg of construction material was carried in on foot or by a cable system to avoid erosion, with the exception of the 12 towers supporting the tram that were brought in by helicopter by the Nicaraguan Air Force (needless to say, pacifist Costa Rica is decidedly lacking in air support).

From the parking lot a truck takes you about 3km to the tram-loading point, where there is a small exhibit area, restaurant and gift shop. Here you can see an orientation video, and there are short hiking trails that you can use for as long as you want. Tram riders should be prepared for rain – although the cars have tarpaulin roofs, the sides are open to the elements.

Driving from San José, the well-signed turnoff to the tram is just past the national-park entrance, on your right. To get here by public transport from San José, take the bus for Guápiles from Terminal Caribe (US$1.50, 1¼ hours), departing hourly from 6:30am to 7pm, and ask the driver to let you out at the *teleférico*. Tram staff will help you flag down a return bus.

MORAVIA

Just 6km northeast of San José, Moravia was an important center for Costa Rica's coffee fincas. Workers hauled sacks of ruby-red fruit down hillsides and into the town, where the beans were packed on oxcarts and transported to nearby *beneficos*. After being milled and dried, the beans were then shipped to cafés throughout Europe and North America.

The coffee industry has sadly moved on, though Moravia remains in the spotlight as a famous production center for handicrafts, including leather, ceramics, jewelry and wood. A visit here is a popular day trip from San José, and perfect for filling up on souvenirs before heading home.

Around and nearby the spacious Parque Central are several stores. Some started as saddle shops but now sell a variety of leather

---

A NATURAL EDUCATION

The **Cerro Dantas Wildlife Refuge** (www.cerrodantas.co.cr) is a research center and education facility that works with scientists, teachers and students to promote environmental conservation. In addition to protecting rare fauna, including jaguars, tapirs and quetzal, Cerro Dantas runs a variety of educational programs aimed at students, teachers and researchers. Day and long-term visitors are welcome.

Programs are varied, but the emphasis is on various facets of the ecosystem, including endangered-species preservation, environmental protection, rain forest ecology and global warming. Basic rates are quoted on individual bases, with or without meals, while special rates are available for students, teachers and researchers. It is advised that you make reservations 30 days in advance as space is often limited.

Cerro Dantas is headquartered in Monte de la Cruz, and is a part of the large Parque Nacional Braulio Carrillo. For more information on the programs offered, visit the website or contact the refuge at pavoreal@racsa.co.cr.

and other goods. Look for **Artesanía Bribrí**, which sells work made by the Bribrí people of the Caribbean slope, and the pleasant **Mercado de Artesanías Las Garzas**, a festive complex with arts and crafts stores, a few *sodas* and clean toilets. It's 100m south and 75m east of the *municipio* (town hall).

Local buses to San Vincente de Moravia depart San José from Avenida 3 between Calles 3 and 5.

CARTAGO AREA

The stunning riverbank setting of the city of Cartago was handpicked by Spanish Governor Juan Vásquez de Coronado, who said that he had 'never seen a more beautiful valley.' Cartago was founded as Costa Rica's first capital in 1563, and Coronado's successors endowed the city with the country's finest Spanish colonial architecture. However, as things tend to happen in Costa Rica, Cartago was destroyed during the 1723 eruption of Volcán Irazú, with remaining landmarks taken care of by earthquakes in 1841 and 1910.

Although the city was relegated to backwater status when the seat of government was moved to San José in 1823, the surrounding area, particularly the Orosi Valley, flourished during the days of the coffee trade. Today this tradition continues to leave its mark on the landscape, and although Cartago is merely a provincial capital, it is an important commercial hub and continues to retain the most important religious site in the country.

CARTAGO

After the rubble was cleared, nobody bothered to rebuild Cartago (population 127,000) to its former quaint specifications – though it is an attractive modern city, in a heavily reinforced sort of way. One exception is the bright white Basílica de Nuestra Señora de los Ángeles, which is visible from any part of the city and stands out like a snow-capped mountain above the plane of one-story edifices. It is considered to be the holiest shrine in Costa Rica and has been religiously rebuilt after each of the city's trials and tribulations.

The city is thrown briefly into the spotlight each year on August 2, when pilgrims from every corner of the country descend on the basilica to say their most serious prayers. The remainder of the year, Cartago exists mainly as a bustling commercial and residential center, though the beauty of the surrounding mountains helps to take the edge off modern life.

Orientation & Information

The city is based around the standard Latin American grid system. As always, street signs are infrequent and sometimes inaccurate. If in doubt, look for the ever-present cathedral and use that as your bearing. There is no tourist office in Cartago.

Banco Nacional (cnr Av 4 & Calle 5) Several banks downtown change money, including Banco Nacional.

Hospital Max Peralta (☎ 2550 1999; Av 5 btwn Calles 1 & 3) Offers emergency health care.

Internet Alta Velocidad (Calle 1 btwn Avs 1 & 3; per hr US$1; ☼ 9am-9pm) Check your email here, 50m east of Las Ruinas.

Sights

The most important site in Cartago is the **Basílica de Nuestra Señora de los Ángeles** (cnr Av 2 & Calle 16), which has a formal Byzantine grace and an airy spaciousness, with fine stained-glass windows and a polished-wood interior. This latest version is the result of a 1926 makeover that followed its near-total destruction in the 1910 earthquake. Though the outer walls have crumbled numerous times since 1635, La Negrita (a famed holy 'Black Virgin' statue) has miraculously remained intact, and she continues to sit on a golden altar beset with precious stones. The basilica is absolutely jammed during pilgrimages and holy days, but it's the perfect atmosphere for experiencing the aura of La Negrita.

Las Ruinas de la Parroquia (cnr Av 2 & Calle 2), or Iglesia del Convento, was built in 1575 as a shrine to St James the Apostle, destroyed by the 1841 earthquake, rebuilt a few years later and then destroyed again in the 1910 earthquake. Today only the outer walls of the church remain, but 'the Ruins' are a popular spot for picnicking and people-watching.

For an insight into Costa Rica's pre-Columbian cultures, there are two local museums worth visiting. The **Elias Leiva Museum of Ethnography** (☎ 2551 0895; Calle 3 btwn Avs 3 & 5; ☼ 7am-2pm Mon-Fri) has a few displays of historical artifacts, while the **Kirieti Indian History**

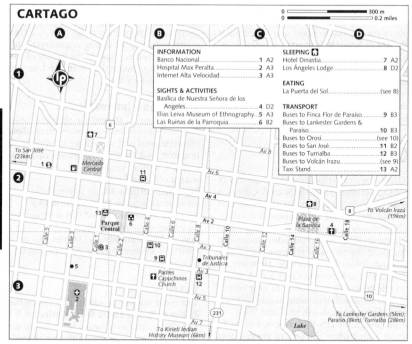

CARTAGO

INFORMATION
Banco Nacional..............................**1** A2
Hospital Max Peralta.....................**2** A3
Internet Alta Velocidad................**3** A3

SIGHTS & ACTIVITIES
Basílica de Nuestra Señora de los
   Angeles......................................**4** D2
Elias Leiva Museum of Ethnography...**5** A3
Las Ruinas de la Parroquia.............**6** B2

SLEEPING
Hotel Dinastía...............................**7** A2
Los Ángeles Lodge.......................**8** D2

EATING
La Puerta del Sol......................(see **8**)

TRANSPORT
Buses to Finca Flor de Paraíso..........**9** B3
Buses to Lankester Gardens &
   Paraíso....................................**10** B3
Buses to Orosi.........................(see **10**)
Buses to San José........................**11** B2
Buses to Turrialba......................**12** B3
Buses to Volcán Irazu.............(see **9**)
Taxi Stand.................................**13** A2

Museum (☎ 2573 7113; ☉ 10am-4pm Mon-Fri), 6km southwest of Cartago in Tobosi, emphasizes history through documentation.

Sleeping & Eating

Lodging options are limited and your best bet for food is to stroll along Avenidas 2 and 4 downtown, where *sodas* and bakeries can be found.

Hotel Dinastía (☎ 2551 7057; Calle 3; d without/with bathroom US$13/16) The cheap price and private hot-water bathrooms balance out the thin walls and aging rooms.

Los Ángeles Lodge (☎ 2551 0957, 2591 4169; Av 4 btwn Calles 14 & 16; s/d incl full breakfast US$30/35; ⓟ ⌘) With its balconies overlooking the Plaza de la Basílica, this comfy B&B stands out with spacious and comfortable rooms, hot showers and a big breakfast made to order by the cheerful owners.

La Puerta del Sol (Av 4 btwn Calles 14 & 16; mains US$3-6; ☉ 8am-midnight) This *soda* opposite the basilica is a good choice for its attractive dining room and good variety of cooked-to-order dishes.

Getting There & Away

While Cartago may not be a hotbed of excitement, the surrounding areas provide plenty to do – from botanical gardens, serene mountain towns and organic farms to an active volcano – all easy to reach via local buses and never more than an hour or two away. Most buses arrive along Avenida 2 and go as far as the basilica before returning to the main terminal on Avenida 4. The following buses serve destinations in the area:

Finca la Flor de Paraíso (US$1) Take a La Flor/Birrisito/ El Yas bus from in front of Padres Capuchinos church, 150m southeast of Las Ruinas. Get off at the pink church in La Flor; the entrance to the finca is 100m to the south.

Paraíso & Lankester Gardens (US$0.75, depart from the corner of Calle 4 and Avenida 1 hourly from 7am to 10pm) For the gardens, ask the driver to drop you off at the turnoff. From there, walk 750m to the entrance.

Orosi (US$0.75, 40 minutes, depart from the corner of Calle 4 and Avenida 1 hourly from 8am to 10pm Monday to Saturday) The bus will stop in front of the Orosi Mirador.

San José US$0.75, 45 minutes, depart from Avenida 4 between Calles 2 and 4, north of Parque Central every 15 minutes.

CENTRAL VALLEY & HIGHLANDS

Turrialba US$1.50, 1½ hours, depart from Avenida 3 between Calles 8 and 10, in front of Tribunales de Justicia, every 45 minutes from 6am to 10pm weekdays, 8:30am, 11:30am, 1:30pm, 3pm and 5:45pm weekends.

Volcán Irazú (US$5, one hour) Depart only on weekends from Padres Capuchinos church, 150m southeast of Las Ruinas. The bus originates in San José at 8am, stops in Cartago at about 8:30am and returns from Irazú at 12:30pm.

PARQUE NACIONAL VOLCÁN IRAZÚ

Looming quietly (though not too quietly) 19km northeast of Cartago, Irazú, which derives its name from the indigenous word *ara-tzu* (thunderpoint), is the largest and highest (3432m) active volcano in Costa Rica. In 1723 the Spanish governor of Costa Rica, Diego de la Haya Fernández, watched helplessly as the volcano unleashed its destruction on the city of Cartago. Since then 15 major eruptions have been recorded, and although Diego de la Haya Fernández never restored Cartago to its former grandeur, his name was bestowed upon one of Irazú's craters.

The volcano's most recent major eruption on March 19, 1963, welcomed the visiting US president John F Kennedy with a rain of hot volcanic ash that blanketed most of the Central Valley (it piled up to a depth of more than 0.5m). During the two-year eruption, agricultural lands northeast of the volcano were devastated, while clogged waterways flooded the region intermittently. In 1994 Irazú unexpectedly belched a cloud of sulfurous gas, though it quickly quieted down. At the time of writing, Irazú was slumbering peacefully aside from a few hissing fumaroles, though it's likely that farmers will be reminded again why the soil in the Central Valley is so rich. For more information on predicting a volcanic eruption, see boxed text Feelin' Hot, Hot, Hot!, p243.

The national park was established in 1955 to protect 2309 hectares around the base of the volcano. The summit is a bare landscape of volcanic-ash craters. The principal crater is 1050m in diameter and 300m deep; the Diego de la Haya Crater is 690m in diameter, 100m deep and contains a small lake; and the smallest, Playa Hermosa Crater, is slowly being colonized by sparse vegetation. There is also a pyroclastic cone, which consists of rocks that were fragmented by volcanic activity.

Information

There's a small **information center** (☎ 2551 9398; admission to park & center US$7; ☑ 8am-3:30pm) and basic café but no accommodations or camping facilities. Note that cloud cover starts thickening, even under the best conditions, by about 10am, about the same time that the weekend bus rolls in. If you're on one of those buses, do yourself a favor and don't dally – head straight for the crater. Folks with cars will be glad that they made the extra effort to arrive early.

From the summit it is possible to see both the Pacific and the Caribbean, but it is rarely clear enough. The best chance for a clear view is in the very early morning during the dry season (January to April). It tends to be cold, windy and cloudy on the summit, and there's an annual rainfall of 2160mm – come prepared with warm and rainproof clothes.

Although not nearly as crowded as Volcán Poás (p139), Irazú is still one of the most popular destinations in the Central Valley.

Hiking

From the information center, a 1km trail leads to a viewpoint over the craters; a longer, steeper trail leaves from behind the toilets and gets you closer to the craters (note that this trail is intermittently closed). While hiking, be on the lookout for high-altitude bird species, such as the volcano junco.

Tours

Tours are arranged by a variety of San José operators and cost US$30 to US$60 for a half-day tour, and up to US$100 for a full day combined with lunch and visits to the Lankester Gardens and the Orosi Valley.

Tours from hotels in Orosi (US$25 to US$40) can also be arranged – these may include lunch and visits to the basilica in Cartago or sites around the Orosi Valley.

Eating

Restaurant 1910 (☎ 2536 6063; mains US$4-9) It's worth stopping here for lunch or dinner to see its collection of old photographs documenting the 1910 earthquake that completed the destruction of colonial Cartago. Cuisine is standard Tico fare, though there are a few European-style dishes available. It's about 500m north of the Pacayas turnoff.

CENTRAL VALLEY & HIGHLANDS

Getting There & Away

Barring a 20km hike, there are three ways to get here on weekdays: an organized tour; a US$30 to US$40 taxi from Tierra Blanca, which includes the driver waiting for you at the park for a few hours; or by car. Drivers can take Hwy 8 from Cartago, which begins at the northeast corner of the plaza and continues 19km to the summit.

Frustratingly, the only public transport to Irazú departs from San José (US$4.50, 1½ hours) on Saturday and Sunday. It stops in Cartago (US$4, one hour), departing at about 8:30am. The bus departs from Irazú at 12:30pm.

VALLE DE OROSI

This river valley and renowned road trip southeast of Cartago is famous for its mountain vistas, colonial churches (one in ruins), hot springs, orchid garden, lake formed by a hydroelectric facility, its truly wild national park, and coffee – lots and lots of coffee. A 60km scenic loop of the valley winds through a landscape of rolling hills terraced with shade-grown coffee plantations and expansive valleys dotted with pastoral villages. If you're lucky enough to have a rental car (or a good bicycle), you're in for a treat, though it's still possible to navigate most of the loop via public buses.

ROAD-TRIP PIT STOPS

Get out of the car and stretch your legs at some of the best pit stops in the Central Valley:

- Pick up some famous Turrialban Cheese for an on-the-road snack, either at the weekly Turrialban Farmers Market or at **La Castellana** (p160).
- Park at the area's most spectacular lookout point at **Mirador Orosi** (right).
- After a long and winding drive through endless coffee fields, recharge you batteries by getting a cup o' joe straight from the source at **Finca Cristina** (right) organic coffee farm.
- Soothe your pedal-weary feet in the hot springs at **Los Balnearios** (opposite).
- Fill the boot up with all kinds of tat at one of the woodwork shops in **Sarchí** (p136).

The loop road starts 8km southeast of Cartago in Paraíso, and then heads south to Orosi (opposite). At this point you can either continue south to Parque Nacional Tapantí-Macizo Cerro de la Muerte (p155) or loop back to Paraíso via Ujarrás (p156).

Paraíso

The town of Paraíso has been absorbed into the urban sprawl of the provincial capital, only 8km away, and fails to capture the attention of travelers. Although the concrete-block houses lining the road into town are hardly picturesque, the Orosi Valley emerges just outside of Paraíso. A few kilometers further along the road to Orosi is the **Mirador Orosi**, which is the official scenic overlook, complete with toilets, a parking lot and plenty of great photo opportunities. There are also two noteworthy sights near Paraíso that are definitely worth visiting before heading into the valley.

The University of Costa Rica now runs the exceptional **Lankester Gardens** (☎ 2552 3247; jbl@cariari.ucr.ac.cr; admission US$3.50; 🕑 8:30am-4:30pm), which was started by British orchid enthusiast Charles Lankester in 1917. Orchids are the big draw, with 800 at their showiest from February to April. In addition, you can see lush areas of bromeliads, palms, secondary tropical forest, heliconias and other tropical plants from the paved trails winding through the gardens.

With many plant species labeled and informative plaques throughout the unbelievable grounds, this is a shady introduction to Costa Rica's wealth of flora before you hit the wilder (and unlabeled) national parks. This is also one of the very few places where foreigners can legally purchase orchids to take home. Guided walks through the gardens are offered on the half hour from 8:30am to about 2:30pm daily. The entrance to the gardens is well signed, 5km west of Paraíso on the road to Cartago.

Two kilometers east of Paraíso on the road to Turrialba is **Finca Cristina** (☎ 2574 6426; www.cafecristina.com; admission US$10), a working organic coffee farm that is open to visitors by appointment only (call ahead for a reservation). Linda and Ernie have been farming in Costa Rica since 1977, and a 90-minute tour of their *microbenefico* (miniprocessing plant) is a fantastic introduction to the processes of organic-coffee growing, harvesting and roast-

---

A NATURAL EDUCATION (PART II)

The **Finca la Flor de Paraíso** (www.la-flor-de-paraiso.org) is a nonprofit organic farm operated by the Association for the Development of Environmental and Human Consciousness (Asodecah). The farm operates an 'Alternative Spanish Institute,' which combines formal Spanish-language education alongside the themes of environmental conservation and community development.

The farm also operates a volunteer-work program that emphasizes organic agriculture, reforestation, animal husbandry, medicinal-herb cultivation, construction, arts and crafts, community outreach and childhood education. Volunteers can rotate between projects, and are housed in onsite guesthouses and dormitories.

The cost for one week at the Alternative Spanish Institute, including 20 hours of classes, a local homestay and three daily vegetarian meals, is US$370. Prices for the volunteer-work programs, including full room and board, are US$15 daily for the first two weeks and US$12 after the first two weeks. Prices for visitors on vacation, including private accommodation and guided hikes, are US$22 for a day visit, US$35 for two days and US$210 for six days. All profits are invested directly into a number of community-development initiatives.

Finca la Flor de Paraíso is 7km northeast of Paraíso on the road to El Yas, and can be reached via buses from Cartago. For more information on the programs offered, visit the website or contact Asodecah at asodecah@racsa.co.cr.

---

ing. Finca Cristina also sells its product to guests at wholesale prices.

The most beautiful places to stay are just outside of town. On the road from Paraíso to Orosi stands **Orosi Valley Farm** (☎ 2533 3001; www .orosivalleyfarm.com; r incl breakfast US$45; **P**), a picturesque old farmhouse with a trickling creek flowing through the grounds and jaw-dropping views of the lush green valley.

About 2km south of Paraíso, **Sanchirí Mirador** (☎ 2574 5454; www.sanchiri.com; s/d/tr incl breakfast US$47/60/70 **P** 🖳) is a delightful, family-run hotel that offers as good a reason as any to break up your trip. Older wooden cabins and newer concrete rooms are fairly basic, but it's wonderful to be able to linger amid the beauty of the natural surroundings. Even if you're not staying here, stop by the open-air restaurant (dishes US$4 to US$7), which faces out toward the valley and is a good consolation prize if you're pressing on. The complex is also home to a **butterfly garden** (adult/child US$5/3), a picnic area and a system of trails that can be explored either on foot or horseback.

Orosi

This town was named for a Huetar chief who lived here at the time of the conquest. Spanish colonists quickly became enamored of the town's wealth of water – from lazy hot springs to bracing waterfalls – perfect climate and rich soil. So, in the typical fashion of the day, they decided to take property off Orosi's hands.

Orosi is one of the few colonial towns to survive Costa Rica's frequent earthquakes, which have left the whitewashed 1743 **Iglesia de San José Orosi** the oldest church still in use in Costa Rica. The roof of the church is a combination of thatched cane and ceramic tiling, while the altar is carved entirely out of wood and adorned with religious paintings of Mexican origin. Adjacent to the church is a small **museum** (☎ 2533 3051; admission US$0.50; 🕙 9am-noon & 2-5pm Tue-Fri, 9am-5pm Sat & Sun) with some interesting examples of Spanish-colonial religious art and artifacts.

And while the attractive town has thus far managed to avoid the more rattling aspects of living in a volcanic region, it's got two big perks, namely the hot springs at **Los Balnearios** (☎ 2533 2156; admission US$2; 🕙 7:30am-4pm), on the southwest side of town next to the Orosi Lodge, and **Los Patios** (☎ 2533 3009; admission US$2; 🕙 8am-4pm Tue-Sun), 1.5km south of town. Los Balnearios is more convenient as it's in town, but Los Patios is a larger complex with a few more springs. Both, however, are modest affairs with simple pools of warm water that are popular with locals and a few foreigners in the know.

INFORMATION

Orosi Tourist Information & Arts Café (Otiac; ☎ 2533 3640; 🕙 9am-4pm Mon-Sat), two blocks south of the park, is run by the multilingual Toine and Sara, two long-term residents who have collected a wealth of information and advice on

CENTRAL VALLEY &
HIGHLANDS

HIGHER GROUNDS

In 1779 Spanish colonists discovered that the cool climate and rich volcanic soil of the Central Valley were perfectly suited for the cultivation of coffee, and began to terrace the hillsides with massive plantations. Since dried beans are relatively nonperishable and thus easy to ship, coffee quickly surpassed cacao, tobacco and sugar in importance, and became the major source of revenue for the colony as early as 1829. By the late 19th century (thanks to a strong push by the young independent government), Costa Rican coffee was being served in cafés throughout Europe, and became famous for its high caffeine content and acidic, multidimensional flavor.

In the past 20 years, however, the Costa Rican coffee market has suffered greatly. Following a collapse in the world quota cartel system, the world coffee price plummeted nearly 40% in just a few years. Although the market eventually stabilized in 1994, this was the same year that Vietnam entered the world market following the lifting of the US trade embargo. Since the market rewarded the efficiency of Vietnamese coffee suppliers, many coffee-exporting nations (Costa Rica included) lost a large percentage of their traditional market share.

Today, Costa Rican coffee continues to be grown in the provinces of Alajuela, Heredia and Cartago. Harvesting occurs primarily in the dry season, and is dependent on cheap, seasonal labor (predominantly Nicaraguan migrant workers). Once picked, the ripened berries are transported to *beneficos*, where they are separated from the fruit and dried in the sun. Green coffee beans are then vacuum sealed to retain their characteristic acidity, and shipped to roasters throughout the world.

In recent years, it's ironic that the price of green coffee beans has plummeted at the same time that the price of a cup of coffee has skyrocketed. While coffee suppliers like Starbucks continue to run lucrative enterprises, coffee farmers (not to mention migrant workers) are receiving an absurdly small percentage of the profits. This phenomenon initiated a push for fair trade, which is an economic (and increasingly political) term referring to the unhindered flow of goods and services between countries. When a coffee advertises itself as fair trade, it is usually sold at a sustainable price to ensure that profits are more evenly distributed.

With Cafta (or TLC as it's locally known) on the horizon, trade barriers are about to be redefined throughout the Americas. However, since Costa Rica is a comparatively small player in Latin America, it is difficult to say whether this legislation will be enough to secure a market niche in light of the growing production capabilities of countries like Brazil (see p144).

---

the valley. They organize a variety of outings to surrounding volcanoes and hot springs for the traveler on a budget, as well as guided walks (US$10), camping and overnight stays at the private **Monte Sky Reserve** (per person incl meals US$25).

In addition to providing the usual tourist services, Otiac functions as a cultural hall, town center and café. It's also a great place for interacting with both travelers and locals. If you're looking for information on volunteering, teaching English or becoming involved in environmental conservation or community development, Otiac is an invaluable resource.

PC Orosi (☎ 2533 3302; per hr US$1; ☒ 8am-7pm) has a reasonably fast internet connection.

COURSES
Toine and Sara also run **Montaña Linda** (☎ 2533 3640; www.montanalinda.com), one of the most affordable Spanish schools in the country. For more information, see boxed text Spanish Schools in the Central Valley, p130.

SLEEPING
Montaña Linda (☎ 2533 3640; www.montanalinda.com; camping per person US$3.50, dm US$6.50, s/d with shared bathroom US$10.50/17, d with private bathroom US$25; P ☒) Two blocks south and three blocks west of the bus stop is this great budget option, which has a festive hostel environment, hot showers and kitchen privileges (US$1) or excellent cheap home-cooked meals (US$1 to US$3). Accommodations are in dorms, but there are a few doubles for couples.

Hotel Reventazón (☎ 2533 3838; d incl breakfast US$35-55; P) Clean, modern rooms sleeping three are two blocks west of Otiac, and come with a nice collection of creature comforts: cable TV, hot-water shower and fridge. The onsite restaurant (dishes US$4 to US$8) is definitely touristy, but it does whip up a good casado.

Orosi Lodge (☎ 2533 3578; www.orosilodge.com; d US$52; P) This peaceful hotel is run by a friendly German couple and has simple and intimate rooms with excellent views of the valley. Rooms include a private hot shower, a wet bar with minifridge and a shared balcony or patio – the perfect combination for a sundowner. A small garden separates the rooms from the reception area, which is in the highly recommended Cafetería Orosi (mains US$4 to US$8, open from 7am to 7pm). The cafetería serves the dreamy coffee you keep smelling in the air as well as a mix of homemade pastries, salads and sandwiches. Los Balnearios hot springs is just a few steps away.

GETTING THERE & AWAY
All buses stop about three blocks west of the *fútbol* (soccer) field; ask locally about specific destinations. Buses from Cartago (US$0.50, 40 minutes) depart hourly from Calle 6, between Avenidas 1 and 3, close to the church.

Cachí Dam & Ruinas US$0.50, 20 minutes, depart every 30 minutes from 6am to 9pm.

Cartago US$0.75, 40 minutes, depart every 45 minutes from 5am to 9pm.

South of Orosi
If you're continuing south toward Parque Nacional Tapantí-Macizo Cerro de la Muerte rather than looping back via Ujarrás to Paraíso, you'll follow a rough road that slices through coffee plantations while passing the rural villages of Río Macho, Palomo and Purisil (13km). From Purisil, a dirt road leads a few more kilometers to **Parque Purisil** (☎ 2228 6630; ⏰ 8am-5pm), where nature lovers can take a guided three-hour hike (US$10) into the nearby cloud forests and anglers can catch dinner at the well-stocked trout pond (price per kilo US$3). The onsite restaurant prepares your catch to order.

Note that buses from Cartago to Orosi occasionally continue as far south as Purisil, though you need to check with the driver to make sure.

Parque Nacional Tapantí-Macizo Cerro de la Muerte
Despite its unwieldy name, this **park** (admission US$7; ⏰ 6am-4pm) protects the rain-forested northern slopes of the Cordillera de Talamanca, and boasts a rainy claim to fame – this is the wettest park in the entire country. In 2000 the park was expanded to 583 hectares, and now includes the infamous Cerro de la Muerte (p373). The 'Mountain of Death' marks the highest point on the Interamericana as well as the northernmost extent of the *páramo*, a highland shrub and tussock grass habitat that's commonly found throughout the Andes and is home to a variety of rare bird species.

On the other hand, Tapantí (as it's locally known) protects wild and mossy country that's fed by literally hundreds of rivers. Waterfalls abound, vegetation is thick and the wildlife is prolific, though not easy to see since the terrain is rugged and the trails are few. Nevertheless, Tapantí is a popular destination for dedicated bird-watchers, and opens at 6am to accommodate its avian-searching needs.

INFORMATION
There is an **information center** (⏰ 6am-4pm) near the park entrance and a couple of trails leading to various attractions, including a picnic area, a swimming hole and a lookout with great views of a waterfall. Rainfall is about 2700mm in the lower sections but reaches more than 7000mm in some of the highest parts of the park – pack an umbrella. Fishing is allowed in season (from April to October; permit required), but the 'dry' season (from January to April) is generally considered the best time to visit.

WILDLIFE-WATCHING
Quetzals are said to nest on the western slopes of the valley, where the park information center is located. More than 300 other bird species have also been recorded in the park, including hummingbirds, parrots, toucans, trogons and eagles.

Though rarely sighted due to the thick vegetation, monkeys, coatis, pacas, tayras and even pumas, ocelots and oncillas are present.

HIKING
There are three signed trails leading from the information center, the longest a steep 4km round-trip, while a well-graded dirt road that is popular with mountain bikers runs through the northern section of the park. Unfortunately, the Tapantí is not open to backcountry hiking, and some visitors walk

away feeling as if they only caught a glimpse of the park. However, the birding here is legendary, and most people are satisfied simply being able to spot a large variety of birds in such a small area.

SLEEPING & EATING

There is a basic but adequate **guesthouse** (dm US$5) with a shared kitchen and bathrooms at the ranger station. Cooked meals (US$1 to US$3) are available with prior notice.

On the road between Purisil and Tapantí, **Kiri Lodge** (☎ 2592 0638; s/d incl breakfast US$25/35), has six rustic cabins with private hot showers resting on 50 mossy hectares of land. There are also expansive trails leading into the Río Macho Forest Preserve, which is adjacent to Tapantí and inhabited by much of the same wildlife. The restaurant (mains US$3 to US$6, open from 7am to 9pm) specializes in trout, which can be caught in the well-stocked pond and then served up anyway you like it.

GETTING THERE & AWAY

If you have your own car, you can take a good gravel road passable to all vehicles from Purisil to the park entrance.

Buses are a bit trickier. From Cartago, take an Orosi-bound bus (though make sure it's going to Purisil). From there, it's a 5km walk to the entrance. Or, you can take a **taxi** (☎ 2771 5116, 2551 2797) from Orosi to the park for about US$12 one way.

Orosi to Paraíso

From Orosi, the loop road heads north and parallels the Río Orosi before swinging around the artificial **Lago de Cachí**. The lake was created following the construction of the **Cachí Dam** (the largest in the country), which supplies San José and the majority of the Central Valley with electricity. Buses run from Orosi to the dam and nearby ruins, though this stretch is best explored by car or bicycle.

About 2km south of the Cachí Dam is the **Casa del Soñador** (Dreamer's House; ☎ 2577 1186; admission free; ☺ 8am-6pm), a whimsical house designed and built by the renowned Tico carver Macedonio Quesada. Every detail of the construction, built largely of coffee branches and bamboo, is elaborately chiseled to divine effect. Quesada's sons, who have managed the workshop since Macedonio's death in 1995, continue the family wood-

working tradition, and carvings of local *campesinos* (peasants or farmers), religious figures and other characters, some life-size, are on display. Some of them are available for purchase.

Past the dam, you'll find the small village of **Ujarrás** at the bottom of a long, steep hill – a couple of stores with the word 'Ujarrás' tell you that you've arrived. Turn right at a sign for Restaurant La Pipiola to head toward the old village (about 1km), which was damaged by a flood in 1833 and abandoned.

The waters have since receded, revealing the ruins of the 1693 **Iglesia de Nuestra Señora de la Limpia Concepción**, once home to a miraculous painting of the Virgin discovered by a local fisherman. Using similar tactics as La Negrita, the relic refused to move, forcing area clerics to build the church here. In return, the Virgin helped locals defeat a group of marauding British pirates in 1666. After the floods and a few earthquakes, however, the painting conceded to move to Paraíso, leaving the ruins to deteriorate photogenically in an overgrown park. Every year, usually on the Sunday closest to April 14, there is a procession from Paraíso to the ruins, where Mass, food and music help celebrate the day of **La Virgen de Ujarrás**. The church's grassy grounds are a popular picnicking spot on Sunday afternoons.

After Ujarrás, the road continues for a few more kilometers before returning to Paraíso.

SLEEPING & EATING

Cabañas de Montaña Piedras Albas (☎ 2577 1462; www.cabinas.co.cr/costa_rica1.htm; s/d US$46/53; ᴾ) If you're looking to slow down and enjoy the scenery, stay at these well-equipped cabins. You can pretend you're roughing it on the private trails, then relax in front of the cable TV, take a hot shower, fix some dinner in the kitchen and perhaps arrange a tour at the desk. The cabinas are on a signed turnoff just past La Casona.

La Casona del Cafetal Restaurant (☎ 2533 3280; mains US$5-15; ᴴ 11am-6pm) This restaurant is about 3km southeast of the dam, where you can enjoy a really fresh cup of coffee or a meal while watching the next batch of beans being picked (November to March). It's popular on Sunday, when families with kids go for short horseback or horse-drawn cart rides, also available here.

TURRIALBA AREA

At an elevation of 650m above sea level, the Río Turrialba flows into the Río Reventazón and gouges a mountain pass through the Cordillera Central. In the 1880s this hydrogeological quirk allowed the 'Jungle Train' between San José and Puerto Limón to roll through, and the mountain village of Turrialba grew prosperous from the coffee trade. Later, the first highway linking the capital to the coast exploited this same quirk. Turrialba thrived.

However, things changed in 1991 when an earthquake shut down the nation's rail system, and the smooth and straight (read as boring) Hwy 32 was completed. Suddenly, Turrialba (population 70,000) found itself off the beaten path, but no one cared to move away – it's too gorgeous here.

Today Turrialba is a low-key agricultural town that's renowned for its mountain air, strong coffee and Central America's best white water. It's also situated in the wake of the undertouristed Volcán Turrialba and close to the country's most important cultural site, Guayabo (p160).

TURRIALBA

The residents of Turrialba are a proud people, and following the relegation of their city to backwater status in 1991, folks here humbly returned to their coffee-cultivating roots. Railways and highways come and go, but life must always go on.

By this time, rafters the world over were already whispering about Turrialba, a modest mountain town with access to some of the best white water on the planet. Tourism was suddenly on the rise, and residents were happy to share their town's charms with curious travelers. However, when the ICE (the national power company) began making good on plans to dam the scenic waterways, the town united with conservation groups and put up a fierce fight (see boxed text Damming the Rivers?, p161). Fair enough – Turrialba has sacrificed enough to the bulldozers of progress. So far, it seems as if the residents are winning the battle, though it's always a very fine line between conservation and capitalism in Costa Rica.

Information

There's no official tourist office, but better hotels and most white-water rafting outfits can organize tours, accommodations and transportation throughout the region.

Banco Popular (9am-5pm Mon-Fri) Has a 24-hour ATM.

Dimension Internet (per hr US$0.75; ✆ 9am-9pm) Check your email here, on the northeast corner of Parque Central.

Sights

About 4km east of Turrialba, and known throughout Costa Rica by its acronym of Catie (which is just as well), **Centro Agronómico Tropical de Investigación y Enseñanza** (Catie; Center for Tropical Agronomy Research & Education; ✆ 2556 6431; www.catie.ac.cr; admission free; ✆ 7am-4pm) consists of about 1000 hectares dedicated to tropical agricultural research and education. Agronomists from all over the world recognize this as one of the most important agricultural stations in the tropics. You need to make reservations for a guided tour of the various agricultural projects, including one of the most extensive libraries of tropical-agriculture literature anywhere in the world, laboratories, greenhouses, a dairy, herbarium, seed bank and experimental plots. Or you can pick up a map and take a self-guided tour through the gardens to the central pond, where waterbirds such as the purple gallinule are a specialty. Another good birding area is the short but steep trail descending from behind the administration building to the Río Reventazón. You can walk to Catie or get a taxi (US$2) from Turrialba.

About 10km east of Turrialba, in the village of Pavones (500m east of the cemetery), **Parque Viborana** (✆ 2538 1510; admission US$3; ✆ 9am-4pm Mon-Fri) is known for its serpentarium. Here you can see a variety of Costa Rican snakes, including some unusual albino specimens and several boas, one of which weighs as much as a good-size person. The serpentarium has a rustic visitors area with educational exhibits.

Tours

The following operators all offer either kayaking or rafting, and most can arrange tours throughout the area.

Aventuras de Turrialba (✆ 8363 4539; kayakers@latinmail.com) Specializes in kayaking, though it can arrange put-ins and pick-ups.

Costa Rica Ríos (✆ in the USA 888-434 0776; www.costaricarios.com) Offers weeklong rafting trips that must be booked in advance. It's 25m north of Parque Central.

Exploranatura (✆ 2556 4932; www.costaricacanyoning.com) Also runs a reader-recommended canyoning course and waterfall rappelling trips.

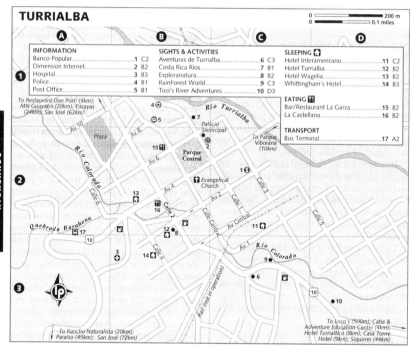

Loco's (☎ 2556 6035; riolocos@racsa.co.cr) A local company that works with small groups.

RainForest World (☎ 2556 0014; www.rforestw .com/welcome2.cfm) Offers an overnight in the Cabécar Indigenous Reserve while running the river.

Tico's River Adventures (☎ 2556 1231; www.tico river.com) A local company that also offers a trip down the Class IV Río Chirripó from June through November.

Sleeping

TURRIALBA

Whittingham's Hotel (☎ 2550 8927; Calle 4 btwn Avs 2 & Central; s/d US$6/8) Seasoned budget travelers won't mind the cool, clean (just like the showers) and cavernous rooms with private bathroom.

Hotel Interamericano (☎ 2556 0142; www.hotel interamericano.com; Av 1; r per person without/with bathroom US$11/18; (P) (🖳)) On the south side of the old train tracks is this hotel, which is regarded by kayakers and rafters as *the* meeting place in Turrialba. Rooms with big windows and shared hot-water bathrooms are well maintained. However, the real reason to stay here is to meet up with like-minded white-water enthusiasts, and to take advantage of the hotel's

(white-water) shuttle services. There is also a bar, restaurant and very professional staff.

Hotel Turrialba (☎ 2556 6654; Av 2 btwn Calles 2 & 4; d without/with air-con US$26/30; (P)) This is great value, as small and standard rooms with attractive wood accents are well equipped with air-con, cable TV and private hot shower. The onsite restaurant (dishes US$3 to US$5) whips up a tasty casado.

Hotel Wagelia (☎ 2556 1566; www.hotelwagelia.com; Av 4 btwn Calles 2 & 4; s/d incl breakfast US$55/69; (P) (🧺)) The most established hotel in town is a good choice if you're looking for a bit more comfort in your life. Standard but well-furnished rooms have air-con, private (steaming) hot shower, a huge cable TV and a sitting area for, well, all your sitting needs.

AROUND TURRIALBA

There are some stellar hotels around the Turrialba area. All hotels have private hot-water bathrooms, and can arrange tours and rafting trips.

Hotel Turrialtico (☎ 2538 1111; www.turrialtico.com; s/d US$52/62) On the old highway to Siquirres and Limón, 8km from town, this Tico-run

WHITE-WATER RAFTING (AND KAYAKING) 101

Let's start at the beginning. There are two major rivers in the Turrialba area that most rafters are interested in – the Río Reventazón and the Río Pacuare. The following is a quick guide to the ins, outs, ups and downs of each river, as well as tips on how to organize a trip and estimated costs.

Río Reventazón

The Cachí Dam across the Río Reventazón created the artificial lake, Lago de Cachí, from which the river now tumbles, starting at 1000m above sea level and running down the eastern slopes of the mountains to the Caribbean lowlands. The river is a favorite and is one of the most difficult runs in the country. With more than 65km of rapids, you can get as hard-core as you like.

Tour operators divide the river into four sections between the dam and take-out in Siquirres. **Las Máquinas** (Power House) is a Class II-III float that's perfect for families, while **Florida**, the final and most popular segment, is a scenic Class III with a little more white water to keep things interesting. The **Pascua** section, with 15 Class IV rapids featuring names like 'The Abyss,' is considered to be the classic run. The Class V **Peralta** segment is the most challenging white water in the country, and tour operators will not always run this section due to safety concerns.

Water levels stay fairly constant year-round because of releases from the dam. Note that there are no water releases from the dam on Sunday and, although the river is runnable, this is considered the worst day.

Río Pacuare

The Río Pacuare is the next major river valley east of the Reventazón, and has arguably the most scenic rafting in Costa Rica, if not Central America. The river plunges down the Caribbean slope through a series of spectacular canyons clothed in virgin rain forest, through runs named for their fury and separated by calm stretches that enable you to stare at the near-vertical green walls towering hundreds of meters above – a magnificent and unique river trip.

The Class III-IV **Lower Pacuare** is the more famous and more accessible run: 28km through rocky gorges and isolated canyons, past an indigenous village, untamed jungle and lots of wildlife curious as to what the screaming is all about. The **Upper Pacuare** is also classified as Class III-IV, but there are a few sections that can go to Class V depending on conditions. It's about a two-hour drive to the put-in, though it's worth it – you'll have the prettiest jungle cruise on earth all to yourself.

The Pacuare can be run year-round, though June to October are considered the best months. The highest water is from October to December, when the river runs fast with huge waves. In March and April the river is at its lowest, and though waves aren't as big, the river is still challenging.

Organizing Trips

Agencies in Turrialba (p157) can organize trips. Children must be at least nine years old for most trips, older for tougher runs.

Day trips usually raft the Class III-IV Lower Pacuare or Class III segments of Río Reventazón, which both have easy-access put-ins that reduce your travel time. There are other runs, however, including the less accessible (and less crowded) Upper Pacuare and Pascua segment of Reventazón, which folks willing to spend more time in a van will find rewarding. These should be arranged in advance. Most operators also offer rafting on other rivers, including Río Sarapiquí (p512), the Class IV Río Chirripó and white-water-free Río Pejibaye (perfect for families).

Two-day trips are offered by almost every operator, usually including a very comfortable campsite or a fairly plush lodge, guided hikes and borderline gourmet meals.

Prices

For day trips, you can expect to pay anywhere from US$80 to US$120 depending on transportation and accessibility. Generally, the cheapest trips leave from Turrialba, and put-in on the Lower Pacuare or Class III segments of the Reventazón. For two-day trips, prices vary widely depending on amenities, but expect to pay around US$175 to US$300 per person.

CENTRAL VALLEY & HIGHLANDS

lodge has been owned and managed by the García family since 1968. There are 14 wood-paneled rooms in an old farmhouse that have locally sewn bedspreads and paintings from local artists. The restaurant (dishes US$4 to US$10) shows off the family's woodworking prowess, though it's hard to beat the dramatic views (and the fresh fish).

Casa Turire Hotel (☎ 2531 1111; www.hotelcasaturire .com; d US$156, ste US$165-330; P ✕ 🖳 ➘) This elegant three-story mansion belongs to the group of 'Small, Distinctive Hotels of Costa Rica,' and recalls the colonial heyday of gracious plantation living. The hotel has 12 deluxe rooms and four suites with lofty ceilings and private verandas, from where you can gaze wistfully at the sweeping fields of sugar cane, coffee beans and macadamia nuts.

ourpick Rancho Naturalista (☎ 2297 4134; www .costaricagateway.com/lodges/index1.php; s/d incl 3 meals US$175/350, 7-day package per person with 3 meals US$1138; P 🖳) Located 20km southeast of Turrialba near the village of Tuis (4WD needed), this Spanish-style, five-bedroom lodge with accompanying cabins is legendary among birdwatchers. The North American owners are avid birders who have recorded over 400 species in the area – over 200 species have been recorded from their balcony alone. Hundreds of species of butterflies can be found on the grounds as well, and there is an expansive trail system leading through the nearby rain forest.

Eating

There are several *sodas*, Chinese restaurants, bakeries and grocery stores in town.

La Castellana (Cnr Calle 2 & Av 4; snacks US$1-3; ☯ 7am-7pm Mon-Sat) Follow your nose to the soft warm smell of this bakery that serves up cakes, *empanadas* (corn turnovers filled with ground meat, chicken, cheese or sweet fruit) and local cheese.

Bar/Restaurant La Garza (Cnr Av 6 & Calle Central; mains US$3-6; ☯ 10am-10pm) This Turrialba institution has been serving good seafood, chicken and beef to happy customers, tourists and locals alike for as long as anyone can remember.

Restaurant Don Porfi (☎ 2556 9797; mains US$4-8; ☯ 10am-10pm) Four kilometers north of town on the road to San José is this reader-recommended spot, which is regarded by locals as one of the top eats in the Turrialba area. Portions of European-influenced dishes are sizable, delicious and best when accompa-

nied by a glass of wine. The delightful owner, Sergio, will even arrange transportation for you if you don't have a car.

Getting There & Away

The bus terminal is on the western edge of town off Hwy 10. In addition to the services listed below, there are also frequent local buses to the villages of La Suiza, Tuis and Santa Cruz.

Monumento Nacional Guayabo US$0.75, one hour, depart at 11:15am, 3:10pm and 5:20pm.
San José US$2, two hours, depart hourly from 5am to 9pm.
Siquirres, for transfer to Puerto Limón US$1.50, 1¾ hours, depart almost hourly.

MONUMENTO NACIONAL ARQUEOLÓGICO GUAYABO

The largest and most important archaeological site in the country is 19km northeast of Turrialba. Although Guayabo is not nearly as breathtaking as Maya and Aztec archaeological sites (don't expect pyramids), excavations have unearthed sophisticated infrastructure and mysterious petroglyphs. Polychromatic pottery and gold artifacts found here are exhibited at the Museo Nacional (see p89) in San José.

The most impressive find at Guayabo is the aqueduct system, which may have served more than 20,000 people in AD 800, the height of the city's prominence. It uses enormous stones hauled in from far-off Río Reventazón along an 8km road that's still in pretty good shape, by Costa Rican standards. The extra effort was worth it – the cisterns still work, and (theoretically) potable water remains available onsite, which you can enjoy among various unearthed structures and unexcavated but suspicious-looking mounds.

The site, which may have been occupied as early as 1000 BC, was mysteriously abandoned by AD 1400 – the Spanish *conquistadors* (conquerors), explorers and settlers left no record of having found the ruins. Though underfunded archaeologists continue to hypothesize about Guayabo's significance, most believe it was an important cultural, religious and political center. However, it's unfortunate that no written records have been recovered from Guayabo, and it's difficult to credit a particular group with having built the site.

In 1968 Carlos Aguilar Piedra, an archaeologist with the University of Costa Rica, began the first systematic excavations of

DAMMING THE RIVERS?

Considered one of the most beautiful white-water rafting trips in the world, the wild Río Pacuare became the first federally protected river in Central America in 1985. Two years later, Instituto Costarricense de Electricidad (ICE), Costa Rica's national energy and communications provider, unveiled plans to build a 200m gravity dam at the conveniently narrow and screamingly scenic ravine of Dos Montañas.

This dam would be the cornerstone of the massive Siquirres Hydroelectric Project, proposed to include four dams in total, linked by a 10km-long tunnel that would divert water from the Río Reventazón to the Río Pacuare. If built, rising waters on the Pacuare would not only flood 12km of rapids, up to the Tres Equis put-in, but also parts of the Awari Indigenous Reserve and a huge swath of primary rain forest where some 800 animal species have been recorded.

When the project was first proposed, ICE was in debt and struggling to keep up with rapidly increasing power demands (tourists, after all, must have their air-conditioning). Costa Rica uses fossil fuels only for vehicles; all other power is generated using renewable resources, including geothermal, solar and wind energy, with a whopping 81% of its power produced by a dozen hydroelectric dams. Technically, this is a renewable resource, but in practice, dams not only interrupt rivers and wash away ecosystems, they have long-term impacts that are not completely understood.

As the project moved from speculation toward construction, a loose coalition of local landowners, indigenous leaders, conservation groups and, yep, white-water rafting outfits were already organizing a resistance movement. They filed for the first Environmental Impact Assessment (EIA) in history, an independent audit of such projects that the Central American Commission for Environment and Development first proposed in 1989. The paper shuffling didn't come to much legally, but it stalled the dam's construction and earned international attention for the Río Pacuare's plight.

Today Costa Rica is a net exporter of electricity (not including oil), primarily to Panama and Nicaragua. Because of new geothermal plants built since the dam was proposed, as well as coordinated national efforts to reduce electricity usage, the dam is not currently needed. For now.

Plans for the project have not been abandoned, not by a long shot. Siquirres would be relatively easy to build, and could generate a tremendous amount of income and electricity in a country modernizing more rapidly than most. However, pressure from international conservation groups is holding ICE at bay, while growth in white-water rafting has helped the Pacuare prove its worth on a spreadsheet somewhere in San José, protecting it for another day.

The neighboring Río Reventazón, however, has not been so lucky: the (in)famous Peralta section has already lost one-third of its Class V rapids due to the first phase of the Siquirres Project. Don't put your white-water rafting trip off until the next time you make it down to Costa Rica.

Guayabo. As its importance became evident, the site was declared a national monument in 1973, with further protection decreed in 1980. Although the site only occupies 232 hectares, most of the ruins are waiting to be uncovered, and there are hopes that future excavations will reveal more about the origins of Guayabo.

Information

There's an information and **exhibit center** (☎ 2559 1220; admission US$4; ⏱ 8am-3:30pm), but many of the best pieces are on display at the Museo Nacional in San José. Excavations are ongoing during the week, and some sections may be closed to visitors at certain times. Guided tours are not currently available, but it's worth asking around in Turrialba or at the ranger station about independent local guides.

Camping (per person US$2) is permitted, and services include latrines and running water. Keep in mind that the average annual rainfall is about 3500mm; the best time to go is during the January to April dry season – though it might still rain.

Wildlife-Watching

The site currently protects the last remaining premontane forest in the province of

Cartago, and although mammals are limited to squirrels, armadillos and coatis, there are good birding opportunities here. Particularly noteworthy among the avifauna are the oropendolas, which colonize the monument by building sacklike nests in the trees. Other birds include toucans and brown jays – the latter are unique among jays in that they have a small, inflatable sac in their chest, which causes the popping sound that is heard at the beginning of their loud and raucous calls.

Getting There & Away
The last 3km of the drive to the monument may be passable to normal cars, if it's dry and you're careful, though your life will be made much easier with a 4WD. Buses from Turrialba (US$0.75, one hour) depart at 11:15am, 3:10pm and 5:20pm, and return at 12:45pm and 4pm. Buses and most taxis (about US$10 one way from Turrialba) drop you at the turnoff to the park, from where it's a 4km hike.

PARQUE NACIONAL VOLCÁN TURRIALBA
This rarely visited active volcano (3328m) was named Torre Alba (White Tower) by early Spanish settlers, who observed plumes of smoke pouring from its summit. Since 1866, however, Turrialba has slumbered quietly, and today the summit is considered safe enough to explore. For more information on predicting a volcanic eruption, see boxed text Feelin' Hot, Hot, Hot!, p243.

Turrialba was declared a national park in 1955, and protects a 2km radius around the volcano. Below the summit, the park consists of mountain rain and cloud forest, dripping with moisture and mosses, full of ferns, bromeliads and even stands of bamboo. Although small, these protected habitats shelter 84 species of birds and 11 species of mammals.

In 2001 the volcano showed its first signs of activity in 135 years, though so far it's been limited to fumaroles and microtremors. While hiking the summit, you can peer into the **Central Crater**, which has minor fumarole activity consisting of bubbling sulfurous mud. The **Main Crater**, which last erupted in 1866, is starting to spew jets of sulfur and steam again, and is thus closed to the public. The smaller **Eastern Crater** lacks fumarole activity, though

moisture is present in the crater during the rainy season.

Although the craters are not nearly as dramatic as Poás or Irazú, the lack of infrastructure (and tourists) gives the summit a wild and natural feeling that is absent from more-touristed volcanoes.

Information
At the time of writing, there was neither a ranger station nor admission fee, though there are frequently rangers at the top of the summit. The average temperature up here is only about 15°C/59°F, so dress accordingly.

Volcán Turrialba Lodge arranges a variety of guided hikes and horseback rides through the park.

Hiking
From the end of the road, there are trails heading to the Eastern Crater and the Central Crater, though they are unmarked (rangers can usually show you in which direction to head). Be advised that the summit is not developed for tourism, so you need to keep your distance from the craters and be especially careful around their edges – they are very brittle and can easily break.

From the rim there are views of Irazú, Poás and Barva volcanoes – weather permitting. Although your hiking options are limited, you can explore the edges of the summit without having to navigate the tourist crowds. The hike up the volcano from Santa Cruz is likely to be a solitary slog through montane forest.

Sleeping
Volcán Turrialba Lodge (☎ 2273 4335; www.volcan turrialbalodge.com; s/d with 3 meals US$70/140; P) About 14km northwest of Santa Cruz (accessible by 4WD only), this mountain lodge and working cattle ranch is perched between the Turrialba and Irazú volcanoes, and recommended for travelers looking for some highland adventure. Cozy rooms with electric heaters, great views and some with wood stoves are augmented by interesting, well-guided hikes and horseback rides to Volcán Turrialba. The rustic hotel has a blazing wood stove in the bar-restaurant and sitting room, with TV and board games.

Getting There & Away
The volcano is only about 15km northwest of Turrialba as the crow flies, but more than twice as far by car than foot. From the village

of Santa Cruz (which is 13km from Turrialba and connected via public buses), an 18km road climbs to the summit. The road is paved for the first 10km, and then becomes increasingly rough – a 4WD is necessary to reach the summit. You can also get a 4WD taxi from Santa Cruz for about US$20 each way (you can arrange for the taxi to wait or pick you up later). There are signs along the way, and this is the official route into the national park.

Another approach is to take a bus from Cartago to the village of San Gerardo on the southern slopes of Volcán Irazú. From here a rough road continues to Volcán Turrialba – it's further than from Santa Cruz, but San Gerardo, at 2400m, is a higher starting point than Santa Cruz is at 1500m. The rough road goes about 25km, then there are a few kilometers of walking, but this route is unsigned.

CENTRAL VALLEY & HIGHLANDS

Northwestern Costa Rica

Iconic Costa Rica lives in the northwest. Whether it's for a glimpse of Volcán Arenal spitting fiery lava, the flash of green from a quetzal's wing or the perfect barrel ride at Witch's Rock, this region is heavily traveled for these and a wealth of other reasons. The landscape ranges from the blazing, dry beaches of the Guanacaste coast to the mist-shrouded heights of Volcán Miravalles (2028m) along the region's chain of volcanoes. The number and diversity of national parks and reserves alone sums up northwestern Costa Rica's classic ecodestination status.

Many visitors make Arenal and Monteverde their first and last stop in the region, but if you have more time, it's worth seeking out the smaller, less-visited spots for a taste of something more authentic. Fumaroles and bubbling mud pots, impossibly aquamarine waterfalls and jewel-toned frogs and toucans add unexpected wonder to swaths of tropical wet forest and the humid slopes of the Cordillera de Guanacaste. At lower elevations, the open stretch of big-sky country along the Interamericana is lined with fincas (farms) and the odd guanacaste tree, for which the province is named. Just short of the Nicaraguan border, a detour west off the Interamericana leads to out-of-the-way bays, some kick up consistent wind for kiteboarding addicts while others shelter tranquil sands for unruffled sunbathers.

While the hot spots in the northwest are undoubtedly well traveled, the infinitude of natural attractions and remote destinations means that the experience can be as small, or as sprawling, as you want to make it. Backroads abound, offering independent travelers endless opportunities to explore the lesser-known, tucked-away treasures of the region.

HIGHLIGHTS

- Watching lava light the night above the peak of **Volcán Arenal** (p241) from viewpoints in La Fortuna or El Castillo
- Waking early to hike in the magical mists of **Reserva Biológica Bosque Nuboso Monteverde** (p190) and **Reserva Santa Elena** (p201) before the busloads arrive
- Satisfying your need for speed on windy **Bahía Salinas** (p227) with a kitesurfing course, or taking the chance to bronze on a deserted bay
- Trekking the circuit of waterfalls, thermal pools and volcanic vents of **Volcán Rincón de la Vieja** (p215) by foot and horseback
- Hiking out to the otherwordly cerulean-blue waters of the Río Celeste at **Parque Nacional Volcán Tenorio** (p205)
- Watching wildlife at Costa Rica's largest wetland sanctuary, **Parque Nacional Palo Verde** (p208)

★ Bahía Salinas

Volcán Rincón de la Vieja ★

Parque Nacional ★ Volcán Tenorio

Parque Nacional Palo Verde ★   Reserva Santa Elena ★

★ Volcán Arenal

★ Reserva Biológica Bosque Nuboso Monteverde

History

The first occupants of Guanacaste are believed to have been the Chorotega, who occupied large tracts of land throughout Costa Rica, Honduras and Nicaragua in the 8th century BC. Unfortunately, our knowledge about the group is incomplete due to the lack of extensive ruins typical of populations in other parts of Central America. For more information on the Chorotega, see boxed text, p285.

Although their civilization prospered for over 2000 years, the Chorotega were wiped out by warfare and disease during the Spanish colonial period. During this era, the Spanish systematically clear-cut large tracts of dry tropical rain forest as the table-flat landscape was perfect for growing crops and raising cattle.

Following the independence of Central America from Spain, the newly independent provinces formed the Central American Federation. At the time, Guanacaste was part of Nicaragua, although border disputes resulted in skirmishes with Costa Rica. But on July 25, 1824, Guanacastecos voted to separate and join Costa Rica. Contemporary Guanacastecos take pride in their unique origin and culture, and it's not uncommon to see flags proclaiming an independent Guanacaste.

Climate

The climate in northwestern Costa Rica varies widely from the heat of Guanacaste to the peaks of the chain of volcanoes in the region. As Costa Rica's driest province, Guanacaste gets little to no rain during the months of November through April, in sharp contrast to the rest of the tropical country. At higher elevations that range from dry tropical forest to the famous misty cloud forests, temperatures are significantly cooler (averaging at around 18°C/65°F year-round), and places like Monteverde modulate between humid and rainy.

Parks & Reserves

Northwestern Costa Rica has a wealth of parks and reserves, ranging from little-visited national parks to the highlight on many visitors' itineraries, Monteverde.

Parque Nacional Guanacaste (p222) One of the least-visited parks in Costa Rica, the land transitions between dry tropical forest to humid cloud forest.

Parque Nacional Palo Verde (p208) Stay at the research station here and take a guided tour to see some of the 300-plus bird species that have been recorded in this rich wetland.

Parque Nacional Rincón de la Vieja (p215) Peaceful, muddy isolation can be found just outside of Liberia, where bubbling thermal activity abounds.

Parque Nacional Santa Rosa (p218) Access legendary surf, hike through the largest stand of tropical dry forest in Central America and visit an historical battle site.

Parque Nacional Volcán Arenal (p241) Centered on the perfect cone of Volcán Arenal, the clouds will sometimes disperse to reveal red-hot lava or a plume of smoke.

Refugio Nacional de Fauna Silvestre Peñas Blancas (p168) If you're self-sufficient, it's possible to visit this wild refuge in the southern Cordillera de Tilarán.

Refugio Nacional de Vida Silvestre Bahía Junquillal (p221) Another small, peaceful protected site, this refuge has a beach backed by mangrove swamp and tropical dry forest.

Reserva Biológica Bosque Nuboso Monteverde (p190) Costa Rica's most famous cloud forest, Monteverde receives a steady stream of visitors without having lost its magic.

Reserva Biológica Lomas de Barbudal (p209) If you're here in March, you might be lucky enough to catch the yellow blooms of the *corteza amarilla* tree in this tropical dry forest reserve.

Reserva Santa Elena (p201) Slightly less crowded and at a higher elevation than Monteverde, this is also a good spot to seek a quetzal sighting.

Dangers & Annoyances

While foreign women generally have no problems traveling in Costa Rica, they may sense a whiff of *machismo* in Guanacaste, most often if traveling alone, and usually in the form of harmless hissing or catcalls. This constant annoyance may become exasperating (especially when combined with heat and humidity), and the best way to combat it is simply to ignore it.

Getting There & Around

More and more visitors are flying directly into Liberia, a convenient international airport that makes for quick escapes to both northwestern Costa Rica and the beaches of the Península de Nicoya. Liberia is also a major transport center for buses traveling the Interamericana, from the border with Nicaragua to San José. Regular buses also serve the Península de Nicoya to hubs such as Santa Cruz and Nicoya and coastal points beyond. The most unusual mode of transport in the area is the jeep-boat-jeep transfer between Monteverde and La Fortuna, but it's also possible to do the trip on horseback.

NORTHWESTERN COSTA RICA

NORTHWESTERN COSTA RICA

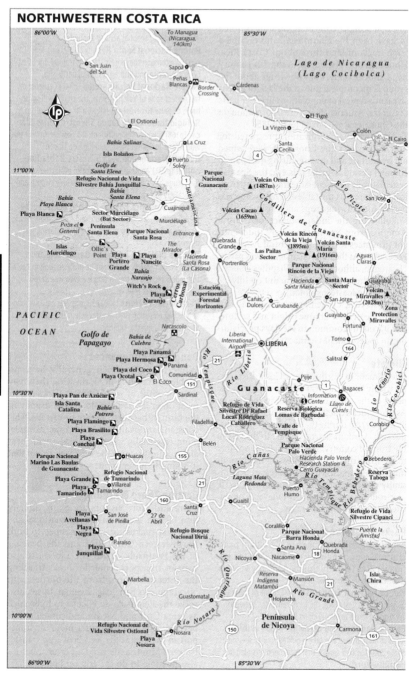

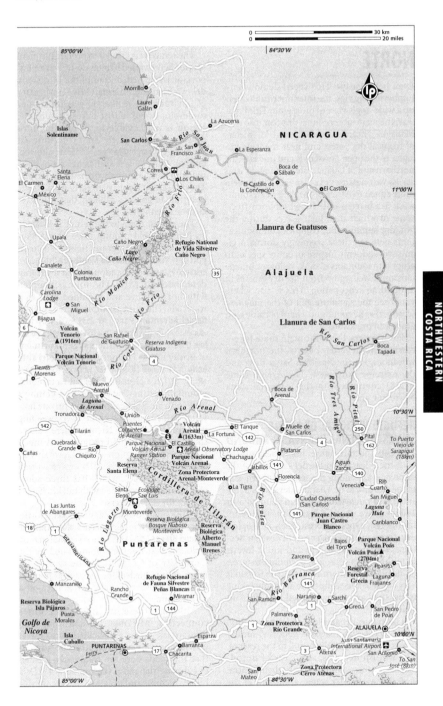

INTERAMERICANA NORTE

Even between the Tico speed demons and lumbering big rigs, the Interamericana offers up a wide-angle view of the region. This highway, the main artery connecting San José with Managua, Nicaragua, runs through kilometers of tropical dry forest and neat roadside villages, to the open grasslands and fincas of the northern end of Guanacaste Province. Vistas across vast expanses of savannah, which seem more suited to Africa or the American southwest, are broken only by windblown trees, some of which shed their leaves during the hot, dry summer. But complex communications between these seemingly dormant giants will suddenly inspire an entire species to erupt into fountains of pink, yellow or orange blossoms, welling up from the dry grasses in astounding syncopation. This is also where you'll see the signature gait of the *sabanero* (cowboy) as he rounds up a herd of cattle with grace and precision.

For travelers, this is the main route for accessing Monteverde, Liberia, the northern volcanoes, Parque Nacional Santa Rosa and the extreme northwest. The Arenal route (p228) connects with the Interamericana Norte in Cañas.

REFUGIO NACIONAL DE FAUNA SILVESTRE PEÑAS BLANCAS & AROUND

This 2400-hectare refuge, not to be confused with the Nicaraguan border crossing of the same name, is along the steep southern arm of the Cordillera de Tilarán. Elevations in the small area range from less than 600m to over 1400m above sea level, variations that result in different types of forest, such as tropical dry forest in the lower southwestern sections, semideciduous dry and moist forests in middle elevations, and premontane forest in the higher northern sections. The terrain is very rugged, and while there are some hiking trails, they are unmaintained and difficult to follow.

The name Peñas Blancas (White Cliffs) refers to the diatomaceous deposits, similar to a good-quality chalk, found in the reserve. The whitish deposits, remnants of unicellular algae once common here when Central America was under water, are found in the steep walls of some of the river canyons in the refuge.

The refuge was created to protect the plant species in the varied habitats as well as an important watershed, and until the Ministerio del Ambiente y Energía (Minae; Ministry of Environment & Energy) gets the money to develop some tourist infrastructure, the region is inaccessible to all but the most diligent visitors. There are no facilities at the refuge. **Camping** (per person US$2) is allowed, but you must be self-sufficient and in good shape to handle the very demanding terrain. The dry season (January to early April) is the best time to go – it's unlikely that you'll see anyone else there.

The closest town to the refuge is **Miramar**, an historic gold-mining town about 8km northeast of the Interamericana. In town you can visit **Las Minas de Montes de Oro** (guided tour US$79), an old, abandoned gold mine that dates back to 1815. The tour is coupled with horse riding and a guided hike to a waterfall. The mine is administered by **Finca Daniel Adventure Park** (☎ 2639 9900; www.finca -daniel.com; 2hr horse riding tour US$45, waterfall canopy tour US$89), which has the usual assortment of pricey tours. The onsite lodge, **Hotel Vista Golfo** (s/d/tr standard US$64/67/82, with view US$75/78/94; ⓟ ▣ ☎), is a pleasant hotel with a tranquil, mountain setting that's perfect for getting a little fresh air. Rustic rooms have private hot-water bathrooms, and some have sweeping views of the Golfo de Nicoya. There's also a shady pool and a good restaurant. A much more personal option is the German-run **Finca El Mirador B&B** (☎ 2639 8774; www.finca-mirador .com; d US$60; ⓟ ▣), which has three adorable bungalows equipped with full kitchens – perfect for self-caterers.

In the small town of Zapotal, 18km northeast of Miramar, is the **Reserva Biológica Alberto Manuel Brenes** (☎ 2437 9906; resbiol@cariari.ucr.ac.cr), a cloud-forest reserve administrated by the University of Costa Rica. The park is famous among birders for its quetzal population, and travelers usually arrive here on a private tour.

Although there are infrequent buses connecting Miramar to San José and Puntarenas, this is a difficult area to travel in without your own car. Also, be advised that the roads here are frequently washed out during the rainy season, so a 4WD is highly recommended.

COSTA DE PÁJAROS

The 40km stretch of road between Punta Morales in the south and Manzanillo in the north is famous for its mangrove-lined shores, which attract countless varieties of birds (and birders). The most famous sight in the area is **Isla Pájaros** (Bird Island), which lies less than 1km off the coast at Punta Morales. There are no facilities on the 3.8-hectare islet, which protects a rare colony of brown pelicans. It also acts as a refuge for various seabirds, and the island is a virtual forest of wild guava trees. Aside from becoming an ornithologist, you can visit the island on an organized tour (from US$30), which can be arranged at La Ensenada Lodge.

Popular among the birding population, **La Ensenada Lodge** (☎ 2289 6655; www.laensenada.net; s/d/tr/q US$49/62/76/84; P ⧓) is a 380-hectare finca and working cattle ranch, salt farm and papaya orchard. Comfortable villas, which face out onto the Golfo de Nicoya, have private bathrooms heated by solar panels and private patios with hammocks – perfect for watching sunsets (or birds). There's also a pool, restaurant and tennis courts, and you can help out with reforestation projects or on the farm.

JUNTAS

Las Juntas de Abangares (its full name) is a small town on the Río Abangares that was once the center of the gold-mining industry in the late 19th and early 20th centuries. Juntas was once the premier destination in Costa Rica for fortune seekers and entrepreneurs from all over the world, who wanted a part of mine-owner Minor Keith's other golden opportunity. Today, it's simply a pleasant mountain town full of ranchers and farmers.

With the gold boom over, Juntas is trying to reel in travelers by flaunting its ecomuseum and a recently constructed hot-springs resort. Most travelers aren't making special detours here on their way to or from Monteverde, but Juntas makes for a pleasant enough stop if you've got your own wheels. If it's starting to get dark, it's a good place to spend the night rather than misguidedly attempting the muddy slip-and-slide commonly known as the road to Monteverde.

Orientation & Information

The town of Juntas is centered on the Catholic church, which has some very nice stained glass, and the small but bustling downtown is about 300m north of the church, with a Banco Nacional and several *sodas* (inexpensive eateries) and small markets. The Ecomuseo is 3km from the main road.

Sights

OK, so the terms 'eco' and 'mining' don't exactly sing 'chocolate and peanut butter' to us either, but it's still worth visiting the small **Ecomuseo de las Minas de Abangares** (☎ 2662 0310; suggested donation US$2; ⧗ 8am-5pm Tue-Fri), which has a few photographs and models depicting the old mining practices of the area. In the grounds outside the museum are a picnic area and children's play area, and there's a good system of trails that pass by old mining artifacts, such as bits of railway. There's also good **birding** (and iguana-ing) along the trails, and monkeys are occasionally sighted.

From the Interamericana, take the paved road 100m past the Parque Central, turn left, cross a bridge, then turn right at the 'Ecomuseo 4km' sign. About 2km past Juntas, the road forks – a sign indicates a road going left to Monteverde (30km) and to the right to the Ecomuseo (3km).

Tours

Mina Tours (☎ 2662 0753; www.minatours.com; ⧗ 8am-5pm Mon-Fri), behind the church, is a family-run tour outfit that can arrange transportation and accommodations reservations, and offers several gold-themed tours, including the Ecomuseo and abandoned mines, beginning at about US$30 per person for day trips and more for overnight excursions.

Sleeping & Eating

Cabinas Las Juntas (☎ 2662 0153; s/d US$6/10; P ⧓) The cheapest bed in town is perfectly acceptable if you're just looking to get a bit of shuteye before heading to Monteverde. Basic but clean, small, tiled rooms with a cold private shower and cable TV. América, the proprietor, will fix breakfast for US$2 extra. It's 200m south of the gas station.

Centro Turístico Cayuco (☎ 2662 0868; d with/without air-con US$15/10; P ⧓ ⧓) This is a popular option with vacationing Ticos as there's an onsite pool, hot spring, restaurant and bar, all 200m north of the mining statue. Unfortunately, the pool barely looks swimmable, and the hot spring is a concrete dish that's fed by a pipe bearing 'springwater' of dubious origins. The rooms, however, are decent, and have cable TV and private bathrooms with cold water.

Pueblo Antiguo Lodge & Spa (☎ 2662 0033; www .puebloantiguo.com; s/d incl breakfast US$32/61; P ✕ ⚊) This rustic mountain getaway next to the Ecomuseo caters to tourists looking for a rejuvenating escape; and its onsite hot springs, swimming pool, Jacuzzi, sauna, nature trails and restaurant ensure you will be sufficiently entertained (and relaxed). Ten rooms in wooden cabins have private bathrooms and scenic mountain views, and there's a good chance wildlife will appear on your front doorstep. The friendly staff members also arrange tours to the nearby Ecomuseo and gold mines.

Restaurante Los Mangos (☎ 2662 0410; mains US$3-6; ☯ 11am-2am Tue-Sun) The nicest restaurant in town (we know it's run-down, but there aren't exactly a lot of options here) is on the main road, and does your standard mix of casados (set meals), *ceviche* (local dish of uncooked but well-marinated seafood) and fried chicken, and it'll get you liquored up at night.

Getting There & Away

Buses from Cañas (US$0.50, 45 minutes) depart at 9:30am and 2:15pm. There are no buses to the Ecomuseo, but a taxi will cost about US$4 one way.

Drivers can take the turnoff from the Interamericana, 27km south of Cañas at a gas station called **La Irma** (☎ 2645 5647), where you can also catch buses between Liberia and San José. Monteverde is 30km from Las Juntas on a rough dirt road, though it's passable to normal cars in the dry season; buses taking the 2½-hour route to Monteverde stop at La Irma around 2:30pm.

MONTEVERDE & SANTA ELENA

Strung between two lovingly preserved cloud forests is this slim corridor of civilization, which consists of the Tico village of Santa Elena and the Quaker settlement of Monteverde. A 1983 feature article in *National Geographic* described this unique landscape and subsequently billed the area as *the* place to view one of Central America's most famous birds – the resplendent quetzal. Suddenly, hordes of tourists armed with tripods and telephoto lenses started braving Monteverde's notoriously awful access roads, which came as a huge shock to the then-established Quaker community. In an effort to stem the tourist flow, local communities lobbied to stop developers from paving the

roads. And it worked. Today, the dirt roads leading to Monteverde and Santa Elena have effectively created a moat around this precious experiment in sustainable ecotourism.

The cloud forests near Monteverde and Santa Elena are Costa Rica's premier destination for everyone from budget backpackers to well-heeled retirees. On a good day, Monteverde is a place where you can be inspired about the possibility of a world where organic farming and alternative energy sources help to salvage the fine mess we've made of the planet. On a bad day, Monteverde can feel like a cross between a natural reserve and Disneyland. But the upside is that the local community continues to maintain the fragile balance of this ecopark and fight against the threat of overdevelopment.

History

The history of these settlements dates back to the 1930s when a few Tico families left the gold-mining settlement of Juntas, and headed up the mountain to try to make a living through logging and farming. In a completely unrelated turn of events, four Quakers (a pacifist religious group also known as the 'Friends') were jailed in Alabama in 1949 for their refusal to be drafted into the Korean War. Since Quakers are obligated by their religion to be pacifists, the four men were eventually released from prison. However, in response to the incarceration, 44 Quakers from 11 families left the US and headed for greener pastures – namely Monteverde.

The Quakers chose Monteverde (Green Mountain) for two reasons – a few years prior, the Costa Rican government had abolished its military and the cool, mountain climate was ideal for grazing cattle. The Quakers found their isolated refuge from the ills of the world, and adopted a simple, trouble-free life of dairy farming and cheese production amid a newfound world of religious freedom.

But the story doesn't end there. In an effort to protect the watershed above its 1500-hectare plot in Monteverde, the Quaker community agreed to preserve the mountaintop rain forests. When ecologists arrived in the area years later to investigate the preserve, they discovered that the cloud forests were actually two different ecosystems that straddled both sides of the continental divide. In the Reserva Biológica Bosque Nuboso Monteverde (p190), the warm, moisture-laden trade winds from the Caribbean sweep up the slopes of the divide where they then cool and condense to form clouds. These clouds also pass over the Reserva Santa Elena (p201), though the absence of the trade winds means that the forests here are a few degrees warmer than in Monteverde. As a result, each ecosystem boasts several distinct species (most of which you probably won't be able to see, however).

Orientation

Driving from either of the Interamericana's first two turnoffs to the region, you'll first arrive in Santa Elena, a bustling little community with lots of budget hotels, restaurants and attractions. A road beginning at the northern point of the triangle leads to Juntas and Tilarán, with a turnoff to Reserva Santa Elena. From the westernmost point of the triangle (to the right as you enter town) you can access a scenic and heavily rutted 6km road to the Monteverde reserve.

This road forms the backbone of a spread-out community, and is lined with hotels and restaurants of varying degrees of attractiveness. About 2km from Santa Elena, the neighborhood of Cerro Plano has a neat nucleus of cute businesses centered on Casem and the Monteverde Cheese Factory. Almost 5km from town, a turnoff leads a steep 3km to the Ecolodge San Luis and research station and San Luis Waterfall. Roads are generally paralleled by pedestrian trails.

Information

BOOKSTORES

Librería Chunches (☎ 2645 5147; Santa Elena; ❧ 8am-7pm Mon-Fri, 8am-6pm Sat) A bookstore and coffee shop with a fine selection of books (many in English), including travel and natural history guides and some US newspapers. There's laundry service (US$6 to wash and dry up to 4kg) and its bulletin board is a good source of information. Also see Bromelias Books (p189).

EMERGENCY

Police (☎ 2645 5127; Santa Elena)

INTERNET ACCESS

Internet access is widely available around Santa Elena and many hotels.

Hotel Camino Verde (☎ 2645 6304; www.exploring monteverde.com/hotel-camino-verde; ❧ 6:30am-10pm) Has a busy internet café in front, with international internet calling available; across from the Santa Elena bus terminal.

Internet Pura Vida (☎ 2645 6419; www.internet Puravida.com; per hr US$2; ❧ 9am-10pm) Across from Banco Nacional in Santa Elena; they'll also do laundry.

Tree House Restaurant & Café (☎ 2645 5751; www .canopydining.com; ❧ 6:30am-10pm) Has a few terminals downstairs that you can use for free (!) for half an hour.

MEDICAL SERVICES

Consultorio Médico (☎ 2645 7778, 8304 2121; ❧ 24hr) Across the intersection from Hotel Heliconia.

Red Cross (☎ 2645 6128; ❧ 24hr) Just north of Santa Elena.

MONEY

Euros, US dollars and traveler's checks can be exchanged at Hotel Camino Verde (left), although you can expect to pay a fairly hefty commission.

Banco de Costa Rica (☎ 2645 5519; ❧ 8am-4pm Mon-Fri, 8am-noon Sat) Has a 24-hour ATM; up the same driveway as Hotel El Sapo Dorado.

Banco Nacional (☎ 2645 5027; Santa Elena; ❧ 8:30am-3:45pm)

TOURIST INFORMATION

Cámara de Empresarios Turísticos y Afines de Monteverde (CETAM; ☎ 2645 6565; www.monteverdecr .com; Santa Elena; ❧ 8am-8pm) As the local chamber of commerce, this office only promotes hotels and tour companies that pay the membership fee, so come in with the understanding that you'll get biased information.

Monteverde Treehouse Tourist Center (☎ 2645 7070; www.monteverdeinfo.com; ❧ 8am-10pm) Long a great source of information online, now staff will also happily book you as well. Based at the Tree House Restaurant & Café (p187).

Pensión Santa Elena (p180; www.pensionsantaelena .com) A better option than the tourist office, even if you're not staying at this place, talk to its friendly staff or check out its comprehensive website.

Sights

Ecotourism is big business in Monteverde and Santa Elena, so it's unsurprising that there are a number of ecoriffic attractions scattered around both towns. And if there's a certain critter you're itching to see, there are plenty of places where your view won't be obscured by all those pesky trees.

As places possessed of such sublime beauty are apt to do, the Santa Elena–Monteverde corridor is attracting an impressive array of art, and there are a growing number of galleries scattered throughout the cloud forest. One specialty here is woodwork, but not at

MONTEVERDE & SANTA ELENA

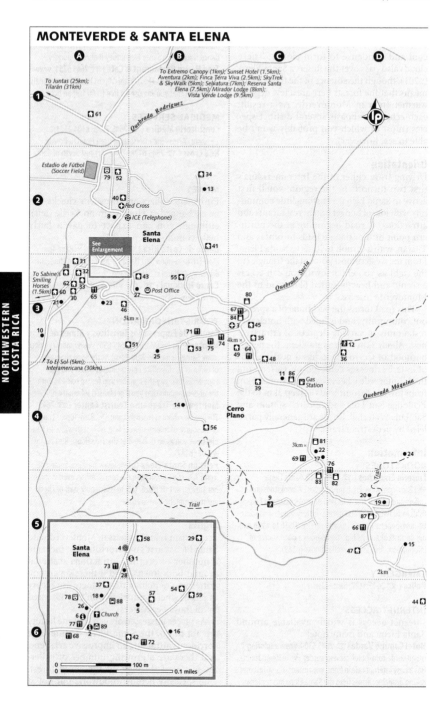

To Juntas (25km);
Tilarán (31km)

To Extremo Canopy (1km); Sunset Hotel (1.5km);
Aventura (2km); Finca Terra Viva (2.5km); SkyTrek
& SkyWalk (5km); Selvatura:(7km); Reserva Santa
Elena (7.5km); Mirador Lodge (8km);
Vista Verde Lodge (9.5km)

Quebrada Rodríguez

Estadio de Fútbol
(Soccer Field)

Red Cross

ICE (Telephone)

Santa
Elena

See
Enlargement

To Sabine's
Smiling
Horses
(1.5km)

Post Office

Quebrada Sucia

5km

To El Sol (5km);
Interamericana (30km)

Gas
Station

Quebrada Máquina

Cerro
Plano

3km

Trail

Trail

2km

Santa
Elena

Church

0   100 m
0   0.1 miles

```
0 _____ 500 m
0 _____ 0.3 miles
```

INFORMATION
Banco de Costa Rica.......................(see 41)
Banco Nacional..................................**1** B5
Bromelias Books..............................(see 82)
Cámara de Empresarios Turísticos y
  Afines de Monteverde (CETAM).....**2** A6
Consultorio Médico.........................**3** C3
Internet Access...................................(see 6)
Internet Access.................................(see 37)
Internet Pura Vida...........................**4** A5
Librería Chunches............................**5** B6
Monteverde Tree House Tourist
  Center..**6** A6
Pensión Santa Elena.......................(see 57)
Police..(see 68)
Preserve Entrance & Visitor Center.....**7** F5
Reserva Santa Elena Office...............**8** A2

SIGHTS & ACTIVITIES
Aerial Adventures & Natural
  Wonders Tram...............................(see 25)
Bat Jungle.......................................(see 22)
Bosque Eterno de los Niños Trailhead.**9** C5
Caballeriza El Rodeo.......................**10** A3
Café Monteverde Tours....................(see 83)
Centro Panamericano de Idiomas....**11** C4
Cerro Amigos Trailhead...................**12** D3
Cloud Forest School.........................**13** B2
Desafío Adventure Company...........(see 68)
El Jardín de las Mariposas...............**14** B4
Friends Meeting House & School......**15** D5
Jardín de Orquídeas........................**16** B6
Meg's Riding Stables........................**17** C4
Monteverde Canopy Tour Office.....**18** A6
Monteverde Cheese Factory (La
  Lechería).....................................**19** D5
Monteverde Institute.......................**20** D5
Monteverde Studios of the Arts......(see 20)
Mundo de Los Insectos...................**21** A3
Original Canopy Tour......................(see 34)
Paseo de Stella...............................**22** C4
Ranario..**23** A3
Reserva Sendero Tranquilo..............**24** D4
Santuario Ecológico........................**25** B3
Selvatura Office..............................**26** A6
Sendero Valle Escondido.................(see 56)
Serpentario.....................................**27** B3
SkyTrek & SkyWalk Office...............**28** A5
Valle Escondido Trailhead...............(see 56)

SLEEPING 🏠
Arco Iris Ecolodge..........................**29** B5
Cabinas Eddy..................................**30** A3
Cabinas El Pueblo...........................**31** A3
Cabinas Mar Inn..............................(see 40)
Cabinas Vista al Golfo.....................**32** A3
Casa Tranquilo.................................**33** A3
Cloud Forest Lodge.........................**34** B2
El Establo Mountain Resort.............**35** C3
Hotel Bellbird..................................(see 86)
Hotel Belmar...................................**36** D3
Hotel Camino Verde........................**37** A6

Hotel Claro de Luna........................**38** A3
Hotel de Montaña Monteverde.......**39** C4
Hotel Don Taco...............................**40** A2
Hotel El Sapo Dorado......................**41** B2
Hotel El Sueño.................................**42** B6
Hotel Finca Valverde.......................**43** B3
Hotel Fonda Vela............................**44** D6
Hotel Heliconia...............................**45** C3
Hotel Poco a Poco...........................**46** A3
La Colina Lodge..............................**47** D5
Los Pinos Cabañas y Jardines..........**48** C3
Manakin Lodge................................**49** C3
Mariposa B&B..................................**50** E6
Monteverde Backpackers.................(see 32)
Monteverde Lodge & Gardens.........**51** B3
Monteverde Rustic Lodge................**52** A2
Nidia Lodge....................................**53** B3
Pensión Colibrí...............................**54** B6
Pensión Flor de Monteverde...........**55** B3
Pensión Monteverde Inn..................**56** B4
Pensión Santa Elena........................**57** B6
Pensión Sinaí..................................**58** B5
Quetzal Inn.....................................**59** B6
Reserve Dormitories........................(see 70)
Sleepers Sleep Cheaper Hostel........**60** A3
Swiss Hotel Miramontes..................**61** A1
Tina's Casitas..................................**62** A3
Trapp Family Lodge.........................**63** F6

EATING 🍴
Chimera...**64** C3
Coop Santa Elena............................(see 83)
Dulce Marzo....................................(see 84)
Flor de Vida....................................(see 67)
Kaffá El Café...................................**65** A3
La Cocina de Leña de Doña Flory....**66** D5
La Pizzería de Johnny......................(see 67)
Moon Shiva Restaurant....................**67** C3
Morpho's Restaurant........................**68** A6
Panadería Jiménez..........................(see 73)
Pizzería Tramonti............................**69** C4
Reserve Restaurant.........................**70** F5
Restaurant de Lucía........................**71** B3
Restaurante Campesino....................**72** B6
Restaurante Mar y Tierra.................**73** A3
Sabores..**74** B3
Sofía...**75** B3
Stella's Bakery.................................**76** D4
Supermercado La Esperanza.............**77** A6
Tree House Restaurant & Café..........(see 6)

ENTERTAINMENT 🎭
Amigos Bar.....................................**78** A6
Bromelias Music Garden..................(see 82)
Galeron Cultural Aspinall Murray ..(see 67)
Taberna Los Valverde......................(see 43)
Unicornio Discotec.........................**79** A2

SHOPPING 🛍
Alquimia Artes................................(see 83)
Art House..**80** C3
Atelier Simbiogénesis......................**81** C4
Bromelias Books..............................**82** D5
Casem...**83** C5
Complej Atmosphera.......................**84** C3
Flor de Vida....................................(see 67)
Hummingbird Gallery......................**85** F5
Luna Azul..**86** C4
Río Shanti.......................................**87** D5

TRANSPORT
Bus Terminal & Ticket Office...........**88** A6
Taxis...**89** A6

Cerro Amigos ▲
(1842m)

Cordillera de Tilarán

Reserva Biológica
Bosque Nuboso
Monteverde

Monteverde

Río Guacimal

1km

Trail

To Ecolodge San Luis (3km);
Cataratas San Luis (6km)

NORTHWESTERN COSTA RICA

E · F · G · H
1 · 2 · 3 · 4 · 5 · 6

THE FABLE OF THE GOLDEN TOAD

Once upon a time, in the cloud forests of Monteverde, there lived the golden toad (Bufo periglenes), also known as the *sapo dorado*. Because this bright-orange, exotic little toad was often seen scrambling amid the Monteverde leaf litter – the only place in the world where it appeared – it became something of a Monteverde mascot. Sadly, the golden toad has not been seen since 1989 and is now believed to be extinct.

In the late 1980s, unexplained rapid declines in frog and toad populations all over the world spurred an international conference of herpetologists to address these alarming developments. Amphibians once common were becoming rare or had already disappeared, and the scientists were unable to agree upon a reason for the sudden demise of so many amphibian species in so many different habitats.

Several factors may be to blame for these declines, including the fact that amphibians breathe both with primitive lungs and through their perpetually moist skin, which makes them susceptible to airborne toxins. Their skin also provides little protection against UV light, which studies have shown can result in higher mortality rates to amphibian embryos and damaged DNA that in turn causes deformities. Pesticides also have been proven to cause deformities and hermaphroditism; and then there's the global issue of habitat loss. If all that didn't tell a bleak enough story, scientists have since discovered that the worldwide spread of chytridiomycosis disease (caused by the fungus *Batrachochytrium dendrobatidis*, in case you were wondering) has decimated amphibian populations everywhere.

According to the Global Amphibian Assessment, an entire 39% of New World amphibians (that would be 1187 species) are currently threatened with extinction. In response to this dire statistic, an international coalition of zoos and wildlife conservation organizations have jointly established **Amphibian Ark** (www.amphibianark.org), an attempt to 'bank' as many species as possible in the event of further die-offs. We may never know what happened to the golden toad, but as one of the first warning signs that the ecosystem is off balance, its mysterious disappearance might have given a chance for survival – and a happy ending? – to other amphibian species.

all like that of the Sarchí scene – sculpture, figurative and fluid, is a local art movement worth checking out. Artists from all over the country also display their work in town.

EL JARDÍN DE LAS MARIPOSAS

One of the most interesting activities is visiting the **El Jardín de las Mariposas** (Butterfly Garden; ☎ 2645 5512; adult/student US$9/6; ☼ 9:30am-4:30pm). Admission entitles you to a naturalist-led tour (in Spanish, English or German) that begins with an enlightening discussion of butterfly life cycles and the butterfly's importance in nature. A variety of eggs, caterpillars, pupae and adults are examined. Visitors are taken into the greenhouses, where the butterflies are raised, and on into the screened garden, where hundreds of butterflies of many species are seen. The tour lasts about an hour, after which you are free to stay as long as you wish. There's also a theater that presents an informational video in English, Spanish, French, Dutch or German. It's best to visit in the morning when the butterflies are most active. There are good volunteer opportunities available here.

RANARIO

Monteverde's cloud forest provides a heavenly habitat for amphibians, which, if you're lucky, you'll see in the park. But no need for luck at the **Ranario** (Frog Pond; ☎ 2645 6320; www .ranario.com; adult/student or child US$9/7; ☼ 9am-8:30pm), where about 30 species of Costa Rica's colorful array of frogs and toads reside in terraria lining the winding indoor-jungle paths. Sharp-eyed guides lead informative tours in English or Spanish, pointing out frogs, eggs and tadpoles with flashlights. You'll get to see the brilliantly fake-looking red-eyed tree frog (*Agalychnis callidryas*), the glass frog (*Hyalinobatrachium fleischmanni*) and a variety of poison-dart frogs.

If you're lucky, your guide may also imitate frog calls, or give you the lowdown on local folklore (tips are always appreciated). Many resident amphibians are more active by night, so it's best to visit during the evening;

your ticket allows you to return for free in the evening.

SERPENTARIO
Biologist Fernando Valverde has collected about 40 species of snake, plus a fair number of frogs, lizards, turtles and other cold-blooded critters at his **serpentario** (serpentarium; ☎ 2645 6002; adult/student/child US$7/5/3; ☺ 8:30am-8pm). Sometimes it's tough to find the slithering stars of the show in their comfy, foliage-filled cages, but guides are available in Spanish or English for free tours. The venomous snake displays are awesome, and you'll get to see your first (and hopefully last) fer-de-lance.

BAT JUNGLE
Learn about echolocation, bat-wing aerodynamics and other amazing facts about the (incredibly cute) flying mammal, the bat. The stellar **Bat Jungle** (☎ 2645 6566; www.paseodestella .com; adult/child US$8/6; ☺ 9:30am-8:30pm), a labor of love realized by biologist Richard Laval, has terrific exhibits including a free-flying bat habitat, beautiful sculptures and a lot of bilingual educational displays. The Bat Jungle makes up part of the new Paseo de Stella visitors center, a modern hacienda-style building that also houses a café specializing in Argentinean chocolate, a museum of Monteverde history and an art gallery. The wide terrace of the building is a wonderful spot to stop for coffee and a handmade truffle.

MUNDO DE LOS INSECTOS
The **Mundo de los Insectos** (World of Insects; ☎ 2645 6859; klatindancer@hotmail.com; adult/student US$8/6; ☺ 9am-7pm) goes beyond just butterflies with its collection of creepy cloud-forest crawlies, from hermaphroditic walking sticks to notoriously venomous banana spiders. Other insects featured here include water cockroaches, scorpions and various arachnids, all explained on tours in Spanish or English. It's better to visit at night, when the insects are more active, but these days the displays are looking a bit worse for wear and may not measure up to the price of admission.

JARDÍN DE ORQUIDEAS
This sweet-smelling **Jardín de Orquideas** (Orchid Garden; ☎ 2645 5510; www.monteverdeorchidgarden.com; adult/child US$5/3; ☺ 8am-5pm) has shady trails winding past more than 400 types of orchid organized into taxonomic groups. Guided tours in Spanish and English are included with admission, on which you'll see such rarities as *Plztystele jungermannioides*, the world's smallest orchid, and several others marked for conservation by the Monteverde Orchid Investigation Project. And if you have orchids at home, you might also learn some tips and tricks for organic care.

CAFÉ MONTEVERDE
Coffee lovers will be excited to find some of the finest coffee in the world right here at **Café Monteverde** (☎ 2645 5901; www.cafemonteverde .com; ☺ 7:30am-6pm), where you can sample six roasts free of charge. Better yet, make reservations in advance for a three-hour **tour** (www .monteverdecoffeetour.com; per adult/student US$30/25) of the coffee fincas, which use entirely organic methods to grow the perfect bean. You can help pick some beans, after which you'll be brought to the *beneficio* (coffee mill), where you can watch as the beans are washed and dried, roasted and then packed. Of course, you'll also get to taste the final product with a snack. Late April is the best time to see the fields in bloom, while the coffee harvest (done entirely by hand) takes place from December to February. Anytime is a good time to see how your favorite beverage makes the transition from ruby-red berry to smooth black brew.

MONTEVERDE CHEESE FACTORY
Until the recent upswing in ecotourism, Monteverde's number-one employer was this **cheese factory** (☎ 2645 5522; tours adult/child US$8/6; ☺ 7:30am-4pm Mon-Sat, to 12:30pm Sun), also called La Lechería (the Dairy). Reservations are required for the two-hour tour of operations, where you'll see old-school methods used to produce everything from a creamy Gouda to a very nice sharp, white cheddar, sold all over the country, as well as other dairy products such as yogurt and, most importantly, ice cream. If you've got a hankering for something sweet, our favorite treat is the coffee milk shake.

Stop by for a cone of soft-serve scrumptiousness here or at a few other select locations around town, including Sabores (p186). The small attached shop also sells deli meats, homemade granola and other picnic goodies, and you can watch cheese being made through the big window Monday to Friday.

SELVATURA

The makers of ecofun really went all out at **Selvatura** (☎ 2645 5929, 2645 5757; www.selvatura.com; admission hummingbird garden US$5, hanging bridges US$20, canopy tour US$40, exhibition US$10; ☒ 7:30am-4pm), a huge ecocomplex 150m from Reserva Santa Elena complete with butterfly and hummingbird gardens, a canopy tour (p179) and a series of hanging bridges, though the star attraction is the slightly overwhelming **Jewels of the Rainforest Exhibition**. This exhibition houses the majority of the Whitten Entomological Collection, a mind-boggling collection of the strangest and most stunning insects you've ever seen. The entire exhibition is the life's work of Richard Whitten (with a little help from his wife, Margaret), and is masterfully presented using a combination of art, video and music. If you only have time for one sight in Monteverde, this is the one. Check the website for package deals.

FRIENDS MEETING HOUSE

The Quakers (or more correctly, the Society of Friends) who settled in Monteverde played a direct role in preserving the cloud forest (p170), and they remain extremely active in the local community, though they're not recognizable by any traditional costume (you know what we mean). Quakerism began as a breakaway movement from the Anglican Church in the 1650s, founded by the young George Fox, who in his early 20s heard the voice of Christ, and claimed that direct experience with God was possible without having to go through the sacraments. Today, this belief is commonly described by Quakers as the 'God in everyone,' and the community continues to lead a peaceful lifestyle in the Monteverde area.

If you're interested in learning more about the Society of Friends, prayer meetings at the **Friends Meeting House** in Monteverde are held on Sunday at 10:30am and Wednesday at 9am. If you're willing to give at least a six-week commitment, there are numerous volunteer opportunities available. For more information, contact the **Monteverde Friends School** (www.mfschool.org).

Activities

Don't forget your hiking boots, bug spray and a hat – there's plenty to do outdoors around here, including lots of action either on horseback or in the jungle canopy.

HIKING

The best hikes are at the two cloud-forest reserves bookending the main road, Reserva Biológica Bosque Nuboso Monteverde (see p190) and Reserva Santa Elena (see p201).

If you've ever felt cynical about schoolchildren asking for money to save the rain forest, then you really must stop by **Bosque Eterno de los Niños** (Children's Eternal Forest; ☎ 2645 5003; www.acmcr.org; adult/student day use US$7/4, guided night hike US$15/10; ☒ 7:30am-5:30pm) and see what they purchased with all that spare change. Keep in mind, however, that this enormous 22,000-hectare reserve, which dwarfs both the Monteverde and Santa Elena reserves, is largely inaccessible. The international army of children who paid the bills decided that it was more important to provide a home for local wildlife among the primary and secondary forest (and to allow former agricultural land to be slowly reclaimed by the jungle) than to develop a lucrative tourist infrastructure. Kids today, what can you do?

The effort has allowed for one fabulous trail that hooks into a system of unimproved trails that are primarily for researchers, the 3.5km **Sendero Bajo del Tigre** (Jaguar Canyon Trail), which offers more open vistas than do those in the cloud forest, so spotting birds tends to be easier. The reason is that a good portion of the surrounding area was clear-cut during the mid-20th century, though there has been significant regrowth since it was granted protected status. The resulting landscape is known as premontane forest, which is unique in Costa Rica as most things that are cut down stay cut down. Visitors also report that wildlife-watching tends to be better here than in the reserves at Monteverde or Santa Elena since the tourist volume is considerably lower.

Make reservations in advance for the popular night hikes, which set off at 5:30pm for a two-hour trek by flashlight (bring your own) through a sea of glowing red eyes. The San Gerardo Biological Station at the end of the trail has dorm beds for researchers and students, but you may be able to stay overnight with prior arrangements. If you're looking for a good volunteer program, the administration of the Bosque Eterno de los Niños is always looking for help.

Offering hikes of varying lengths, **Santuario Ecológico** (Ecological Sanctuary; ☎ 2645 5869; admission adult/student/child US$9/7/5, guided night tour US$15/12/10; ☒ 7am-5:30pm) has four loop trails (the longest takes about 2½ hours at a slow pace) through private property comprising premontane and secondary forest, coffee and banana plantations, and past a couple of waterfalls and lookout points. Coati, agouti and sloth are seen on most days, and monkey, porcupine and other animals are also common. Birding is also good. Guided tours are available throughout the day, but you'll see even more animals on the guided night tours (adult/student US$14/9, 5:30pm to 7:30pm).

An 81-hectare private reserve, **Reserva Sendero Tranquilo** (Tranquil Path Reserve; ☎ 2645 5010; admission US$20; ☉ tours 7:30am & 1pm) is located between the Reserva Biológica Bosque Nuboso Monteverde and the Río Guacimal. Trails here are narrow to allow for minimal environmental impact, and the group size is capped at six people, which means you won't have to worry about chattering tourists scaring away all the animals. The trails pass through four distinct types of forest, including a previously destroyed area that's starting to bud again.

Sendero Valle Escondido (Hidden Valley Trail; ☎ 2645 6601; day use US$5, night tour adult/child US$15/10; ☉ 7am-4pm) begins behind the Pensión Monteverde Inn and slowly winds its way through a deep canyon into an 11-hectare reserve. In comparison with the more popular reserves, Valle Escondido is quiet during the day and relatively undertouristed, so it's a good trail for wildlife-watching. However, the reserve's two-hour guided night tour (at 5:30pm) is very popular, so it's best to make reservations for this in advance.

Take a free hike up **Cerro Amigos** (1842m) for good views of the surrounding rain forest and, on a clear day, of Volcán Arenal, 20km away to the northeast. Near the top of the mountain, you'll pass by the TV towers for channels 7 and 13. The trail leaves Monteverde from behind Hotel Belmar and ascends roughly 300m in 3km. From the hotel, take the dirt road going downhill, then the next left. Note that this trail does not connect to the trails in the Monteverde reserve, so you will have to double back.

Another popular (but strenuous) hike is to visit the **Catarata San Luis**, a gorgeous ribbon of water streaming from the cloud forests into a series of swimming holes just screaming for a picnic. The distance from the parking area to the falls is only a few kilometers, but it's steeply graded downhill, and the rocky, mud-filled terrain can get very slick. Readers report that their entire families have been OK on the trail, but it's important to go slow and turn back if it becomes too difficult. However, your efforts will be worth it as the waterfall is simply breathtaking.

Drivers will need 4WD to ford the little river and climb the muddy road out. You can park (US$6 per car) at a private farm, which is next to the trailhead. Several horseback-riding companies offer excursions to the falls (US$50 per person), but note that much of the road is now paved and this is hard on the horses' knees. A taxi from town to the falls will cost about U$12.

CANOPY TOURS

Wondering where the whole canopy tour craze was born? Santa Elena is the site of Costa Rica's first zip lines, today eclipsed in adrenaline by the nearly 100 imitators who have followed, some of which are right here in town. You won't be spotting any quetzals or coatis as you whoosh your way over the canopy, but this is the best way to burn your holiday buck.

Before you tighten your harness and clip in for the ride, you're going to have to choose which canopy tour will get your hard-earned cash – this is more challenging than you'd think. Much like the rest of Costa Rica, Monteverde works on a commission-based system, so be skeptical of the advice that you're given, and insist on choosing the canopy tour that you want. We provide basic information on the five major players in town (p179), though it's good to talk to the friendly, unbiased staff at the Pensión Santa Elena if you want the full scoop (see p180).

HORSEBACK RIDING

Until recently, this region was most easily traveled on horseback, and considering the roads around here, that's probably still true. Several operators offer you the chance to test this theory, with guided horse rides ranging from two-hour tours to five-day adventures. Shorter trips generally run about US$15 per hour, while an overnight trek including meals and accommodations runs between US$150 and US$200.

Some outfitters also make the trip to La Fortuna, an intriguing transportation option with several caveats (US$60 to US$100; see boxed text, p188), including only going in the dry season. Though a few operators will

CANOPY FIGHTING

All is not well in the world of zip-line operators. As competition has come to a boil between the nearly 100 canopy-tour operators around the country, the founder of the Original Canopy Tour decided to patent his concept and the words 'canopy tour' with Costa Rica's National Registry. After receiving the title, Darren Hreniuk, the Canadian behind the tour, has claimed that all other operators are running 'pirate tours' and has demanded that they pay him licensing fees or shut down.

The title has been largely ignored by other operators, who insist that the idea of crossing trees on a cable-and-pulley system is hardly a new one. (There is a painting dating back to 1858 in the Museo Nacional de San José that shows people transporting themselves on ropes tied between trees.) Hreniuk insists otherwise. 'I am the inventor of the canopy tour,' he told the *Tico Times* in August 2003. 'If people like that or not, it is irrelevant.'

The National Registry supported his claim and provided Hreniuk with a cease-and-desist order that demanded that all other tours close up shop. Armed with this, Hreniuk visited more than a dozen tour sites in April and December 2003 and attempted to shut them down. Since then, the government annulled the patent in 2005, and while Hreniuk has probably not given up the ghost on that one, he has moved on to develop a (patent-pending!) double-line for added safety.

Locally, Hreniuk's legal moves were poorly regarded. Many Ticos viewed his patent and subsequent enforcement of it as an attempt to create a foreign monopoly on an activity that more than a quarter of all tourists who go to Costa Rica participate in. This is the kind of legal wrangling that can take all the fun out of traveling, in our opinion, and we can only hope that the person who 'invented' rafting doesn't try to do the same.

As an aside, another criticism of canopy tours is that their environmental impact may be greater then previously believed. Specifically, canopy tours can contribute to ground erosion, the disruption of vegetation and damage to tree trunks, though this varies widely from operator to operator. And an increase in the number of screaming gringos flying across the rain-forest canopy can't be good for nearby birders and wildlife-watchers. Regardless, it's likely that at some point during your travels in Costa Rica, you'll probably give in to the temptation and sign up for a quick adrenaline fix. The point is simply to inquire about the environmental impact of a particular canopy tour before you fork out your cash, and to be happy that Costa Rica has a good system of patent law in place.

charge less, remember you (or more likely, the horse) get what you pay for.

Caballeriza El Rodeo (☎ 2645 5764, 2645 6306; elrodeo@racsa.co.cr) Does local tours on private trails, as well as trips to San Luis Waterfall and a sunset tour to a spot overlooking the Golfo de Nicoya.

Desafío Adventure Company (☎ 2645 5874; www .monteverdetours.com) Does local treks for groups and individuals around town, day trips to San Luis Waterfall (six hours, per person including admission US$60) and several multiday rides. This established outfitter will arrange rides to La Fortuna for US$75, usually on the Lake Trail. The company also arranges white-water rafting trips on the Ríos Toro, Sarapiquí and others, and can help with transport and hotel reservations.

Meg's Riding Stables (☎ 2645 5560, 2645 5052) Takes folks on private trails nearby plus treks to San Luis Waterfall. Kid-sized saddles and gentle horses are also available. The horses are well looked after, and this is the longest-established operation in Monteverde.

Mirador Lodge (p182; ☎ 2645 5354; Monteverde to Arenal ride US$70) The Quesada family at this isolated cloud-forest lodge takes riders on horseback tours as well as to Arenal, starting from the lodge. If the weather and trail conditions are not perfect, they will arrange a taxi-boat-taxi transfer as an alternative.

Sabine's Smiling Horses (☎ 2645 6894, 8385 2424; www.horseback-riding-tour.com) Run by Sabine, who speaks English, French, Spanish and German, Smiling Horses offers a variety of treks, from US$15-per-hour day trips to specialty tours, including a Full Moon Ride (per person US$50, three hours). Several multiday treks are also on offer, and Sabine may also take experienced riders on the Castillo Trail, weather permitting. This outfitter has been highly recommended by readers year after year.

TRAMS & HANGING BRIDGES

OK, so you're too scared to zip through the canopy on a steel cable, but fear not as the makers of ecofun have something special for you – trams and hanging bridges, the safe and slightly less expensive way to explore the tree tops.

Aerial Adventures & Natural Wonders Tram (☎ 2645 5960; naturalwonders@racsa.co.cr; tram adult/child US$15/8, hike US$7, tram & hike US$20) is essentially a ski lift, offering a 1.5km journey in electrically propelled gondola chairs on rails attached to towers; heights reach 12m. The ride lasts an hour, and you have the option of pausing your car briefly to look around. You can also rent golf carts (US$30) that hold up to three people for cruising around the trails afterward – a great choice for folks with limited mobility who want to get out in the woods on their own.

Selvatura, SkyWalk (owned by SkyTrek) and Aventura (see Tours, right) have systems of hanging bridges across which you can traipse and live out your Indiana Jones fantasies. There are subtle differences between all of them (some are fat, some are thin, some are bouncy, some are saggy), though you're going to enjoy the views of the canopy regardless of which one you pick. They're all priced around US$20 for adults and US$15 for students.

Festivals & Events
The **Monteverde Music Festival** is held annually on variable dates from late January to early April. It's gained a well-deserved reputation as one of the top music festivals in Central America. Music is mainly classical, jazz and Latin, with an occasional experimental group to spice things up. Concerts are held on Thursday, Friday and Saturday, at different venues all over town and at Monteverde Institute, which sponsors it (see right). Some performances are free, but most events ask US$5 to US$15 – proceeds go toward teaching music and the arts in local schools.

The **Sol y Música** festival is sponsored by Bromelias Books (p189), with weekly shows happening from February through April at its amphitheater. In July and August it also hosts the **Gotas y Notas** festival to keep spirits afloat during the wet season; ask around town about shows during your visit.

Courses
Centro Panamericano de Idiomas (CPI; ☎ 2265 6306; www.cpi-edu.com; classes with/without homestay US$465/315; ☒ 8am-5pm) Specializes in Spanish-language education, with some courses geared to teenagers, medical professionals or social workers. Also has locations in Heredia

and Playa Flamingo, with the opportunity to transfer from campus to campus.

Monteverde Institute (☎ 2645 5053; www.mvinstitute .org) A nonprofit educational institute, founded in 1986, that offers interdisciplinary courses in tropical biology, conservation, sustainable development and Spanish, among other topics. Courses are occasionally open to the public, as are volunteer opportunities in education and reforestation – check the website. Monthly intensive Spanish courses are offered for US$790, while short courses (US$800 to US$1800, two weeks) teach both high-school and college students about conservation and land use in the Monteverde area. Long courses (US$4000, 10 weeks) are university-accredited programs for undergraduates and they emphasize tropical community ecology.

Monteverde Studios of the Arts (☎ 2645 5053) Administered by Monteverde Institute, this offers a variety of classes and workshops, sometimes open to visitors, covering everything from woodworking to papermaking, with a special emphasis on pottery.

Tours
Aventura (☎ 2645 6388; www.monteverdeadventure .com; adult/student US$40/30; ☒ 7am-4pm) Aventura has 16 platforms that are spiced up with a Tarzan swing and a 15m rappel. It's about 3km north of Santa Elena on the road to the reserve, and transportation from your hotel is included in the price.

Extremo Canopy (☎ 2645 6058; www.monteverde extremo.com; adult/student/child US$37/27/25; ☒ 8am-4pm) The newest player on the Monteverde canopy scene, this outfit runs small groups and doesn't bother with extraneous attractions if all you really want to do is fly down the zip lines.

Original Canopy Tour (☎ 2645 6950; www.canopy tour.com; adult/student/child US$45/35/25; ☒ 7:30am-4pm) On the grounds of Cloud Forest Lodge, this has the fabled zip lines that started an adventure-tourism trend of questionable ecological value (see boxed text, opposite). These lines aren't as elaborate as the others, but with 14 platforms, a rappel through the center of an old fig tree and 5km of private trails worth a wander afterward, you can enjoy a piece of history that's far more entertaining than most museums.

Selvatura (☎ 2645 5929; www.selvatura.com; adult/child US$40/30; ☒ 7:30am-4pm) One of the bigger games in town, Selvatura has 3km of cables, 18 platforms and one Tarzan swing through primary forest. The office is across the street from the church in Santa Elena.

SkyTrek (☎ 2645 5796; www.skywalk.co.cr; adult/student US$44/37; ☒ 7:30am-5pm) If you're not buying the whole 'eco' element of canopy tours, then this is definitely for you. This seriously fast canopy tour consists of 11 platforms attached to steel towers that are spread out along a road. We're talking about some serious speed here, which is probably why SkyTrek is the only canopy tour that has a real brake system.

Sleeping

During Christmas and Easter, many hotels are booked up weeks in advance. During the January-to-April busy season and also in July, reservations are a good idea, though you can almost always find somewhere to stay. Note that Monteverde can get very cool at night, so don't be surprised if your room doesn't have a fan (but do be if it doesn't have a warm blanket!).

The rates given are high-season rates, but low-season rates could be as much as 30% to 40% lower.

BUDGET

Competition has kept costs low and budget spots usually offer warm showers.

Pensión Sinai (☎ 2645 6252; lucreciajc@yahoo.com; r per person with/without bathroom US$10/6; **P** **Q**) Tiled rooms in this homey family-owned *pensión* are pristine, and readers rave about the friendly staff and the warm communal feel. Showers have warm water, and there is a communal kitchen available.

Cabinas Mar Inn (☎ 2645 5279; cabmarin@racsa.co.cr; d incl breakfast with/without bathroom US$12/10; **P**) On a hill about 50m north of the high school, this is a great option as the managers are welcoming, the breakfasts are filling and there's a nice outdoor patio overlooking the town. Wood-paneled rooms are rustic and airy, and the quiet location means a restful night's sleep.

Hotel Bellbird (☎ 2645 5026; www.hotelbellbird.com; r per person with/without bathroom & incl breakfast US$12/10; **P** **Q**) On the road toward Monteverde next to Centro Panamericano de Idiomas is this cute wooden hotel surrounded by a small garden. The friendly Tico owner, Alexis, offers simple, homey rooms and a quiet environment. The common area upstairs has comfy chairs and excellent views.

Casa Tranquilo (☎ 2645 6782; www.casatranquilo hostel.com; r per person incl breakfast with/without bathroom US$15/12; **P** **Q**) This wonderful little hotel is owned and managed by a delightful Tico couple, David and Elena (and their little one, Josue). Some of the wood-paneled rooms have skylights and views of the gulf. Check out the great upstairs terrace, perfect for a few late-night ballads on the guitar. There's also a communal kitchen, free internet (and wi-fi), free coffee and tea, CD burning and printing,

and a buffet breakfast with granola, bread, eggs and fruit.

our pick **Pensión Santa Elena** (☎ 2645 5051; www .pensionsantaelena.com; camping per person US$3, dm US$5, r without bathroom US$7-28, r with bathroom US$15-18, cabinas US$25-50; **P** **Q**) This full-service shoe-stringer's hostel is a perennial favorite, right in central Santa Elena. Ran and Shannon, the brother-sister duo from Austin, Texas, are committed to offering budget travelers top-notch, five-star service. They offer the most unbiased tourist information in town and will take the time to explain all the options to travelers. They're also environmentalists at heart, and work with the local community on projects such as the reduction of gray water by installing septic tanks. Each room is different, with something to suit everyone – take a look at several, as quality and cleanliness also vary. Amenities include hot showers, cozy front porch, message board, excellent shared kitchen, free internet (wi-fi too), and free coffee and tea all day. The Costa Rican staff is also fully bilingual, extremely professional and altogether charming.

Cabinas Eddy (☎ 2645 6635; www.cabinas-eddy.com; d with/without bathroom US$25/14; **P** **Q**) This reader-recommended budget spot continues to get raves for its delightful, English-speaking staff and the marimba-playing owner and manager Eddy. Breakfast is an extra US$3, but there's a shared kitchen. The balcony is a great place to relax with a cup of free coffee and take in the view.

Sleepers Sleep Cheaper Hostel (☎ 2645 6204; www.sleepershostel.blogspot.com; dm US$6, s with/without bathroom US$20/15, d US$25/15, all incl breakfast; **P** **Q**) Run by the friendly Ronny and his darling family, this hostel is a terrific deal, with free internet access, tea and coffee, and a great shared kitchen. Rooms are simple but comfortable, with hot-water shower, and there's a convivial atmosphere.

Tina's Casitas (☎ 2645 5641; www.tinascasitas.de; s with/without bathroom US$20/10, d US$25/18; **P**) The casitas (cottages) at this funky German-run spot are a great value. The rooms are well maintained, featuring firm beds and hand-carved furniture of Tina's own design. There's also a shared kitchenette.

Monteverde Backpackers (☎ 2645 5844; www .monteverdebackpackers.com/home.html; dm US$10, s/d/ tr/q US$20/30/39/44, all incl breakfast; **Q**) Another branch from the guys running Pangaea in San José, this new budget spot in Monteverde is just down the road from Supermercado La Esperanza and has been getting good reviews from travelers.

Cabinas El Pueblo (☎ 2645 6192; www.cabinaselpueblo.com; s with/without bathroom US$15/10, d US$24/15, all incl breakfast; **P** 🖳) These pleasant cabinas are run by an attentive Tico couple who will do everything possible to make your stay memorable. Well-furnished rooms have firm mattresses and private hot-water showers, and there's a fully equipped kitchen and a garden out back.

Pensión Colibrí (☎ 2645 5682; r per person with/without bathroom US$25/6; **P**) Another popular budget option, this small, family-run *pensión* is on a quiet lane and feels like it's perched among the trees. The larger rooms with private bathroom are worth the money as they have balconies overlooking the woods, which are perfect for breathing in the cool, mountain air. There's also a small communal kitchen.

Quetzal Inn (☎ 2645 6076; www.quetzalinn.com; s/d US$15/30; **P** 🖳) Up the same quiet alley as Pensión Colibrí is this lovely little lodge. With wood-plank walls, high sloped ceilings and green surroundings, this family-run inn embodies the perfect combination of central location, thoughtfully designed accommodations and a personable, hospitable ambience.

Pensión Flor de Monteverde (☎ 2645 5236; flormonteverde@racsa.co.cr; s/d/tr/q incl breakfast US$20/30/45/60; **P**) Though it's definitely further out than other hotels, you'll be glad you came to this sheltered hideaway. Owner Eduardo Venegas Castro is a font of information. In the past, he worked at both the Monteverde and Santa Elena reserves, and was director of the latter. Rooms are basic but comfortable. Tours and transportation can be arranged.

Hotel El Sueño (☎ 2645 5021; www.hotelelsuenocr.com; s/d incl breakfast US$25/40; **P**) This Tico-run hotel has huge wooden rooms with private hot showers. Upstairs rooms are airier, though the best ones are toward the back. There's a great balcony with sweeping views of the area.

Cabinas Vista al Golfo (☎ 2645 6321; www.cabinasvistaalgolfo.com; s with/without bathroom US$17/12, d US$29/17; **P**) This is a very comfortable locale run by a congenial Costa Rican family. Rooms are well kept, the showers are hot and the owners will make you feel right at home. The upstairs balcony has great views of the rain forest and, on a clear day, the Golfo de Nicoya. There's a small, communal kitchen.

Manakín Lodge (☎ 2645 5080, 2645 5835; www.manakinlodge.com; r per person incl breakfast standard/superior US$15/20; **P** 🖳) This simple Tico family-run lodge in Cerro Plano has a friendly, laidback feel. All rooms have homey furnishings, wi-fi and private hot-water showers, though the 2nd-floor superior rooms have better views of the forest and TV and fridge.

Pensión Monteverde Inn (☎ 2645 5156, 2645 6601; r per person incl breakfast US$20; **P**) In a tranquil corner of Cerro Plano is this small inn, next to the trailhead for the Sendero Valle Escondido (p177). Spartan rooms have private hot showers, and its remote location means lots of peace and quiet. The owners can pick you up at the bus stop if you have a reservation.

MIDRANGE

ourpick Arco Iris Ecolodge (☎ 2645 5067; www.arcoirislodge.com; s US$25-55, d US$35-120, honeymoon ste US$180; **P** 🖳) This clutch of pretty cabins is on a little hill overlooking Santa Elena and the surrounding forests, and has the privacy and intimacy of a mountain retreat. The lodge features a system of private trails that wind throughout the property, including one that leads to a lookout point where you can see the Pacific on a clear day. There are a variety of different room sizes and styles to choose from, so you can either go rustic or live it up. If you're traveling in a group, the four-to-five-person split-level cabin (US$95 to US$200) is highly recommended – it's adorned with rich tapestries and features volcanic rock-laden showers. The multilingual German owners are delightful, and they make excellent meals that sometimes feature organic vegetables grown on the grounds. Breakfast is an additional US$6.50.

Mariposa B&B (☎ 2645 5013; vmfamilia@costarricense.cr; s/d incl breakfast US$25/40; **P**) Just 1.5km from the Monteverde reserve, this friendly family-run place has simple but very nice rooms with private hot showers, all nestled into the forest. In addition to breakfast (a *real* breakfast of fruits, pancakes, eggs and tortillas), there's also a little balcony for observing wildlife, because nothing is cuter than a passel of *pizotes* (coatimundis).

Finca Terra Viva (☎ 2645 5454; www.terravivacr.com; d US$40, extra person US$5, 3 meals extra US$14, caseta US$60; **P**) This 135-hectare finca 2.5km or so out on the road toward Reserva Santa Elena is being gradually returned to the forest; about 60% is already there. In the meantime, cattle,

NORTHWESTERN COSTA RICA

pigs, goats, horses and chickens offer guests a typically Costa Rican rural experience – kids love this place. Each of the six rustic, wooden rooms sleeps up to four and has a private hot shower; a few free-standing *casetas* (huts), each sleeping four and fitted with kitchenette, are available for those desiring more privacy. Owner Federico is a well-known naturalist and guide who has long envisioned living in a finca that combines education, conservation and farming – this is the result. Horse riding can be arranged, and you can try your hand at milking cows and making cheese at the organic dairy.

Sunset Hotel (☎ 2645 5228; s/d/tr incl breakfast US$30/40/55; **P**) About 1.5km out of Santa Elena toward Reserva Santa Elena, this intimate guesthouse is in a secluded location with great views of the Golfo de Nicoya and ample opportunities for bird-watching on private trails. Clean, standard rooms with porches have two little luxuries: real hot showers (not suicide machines) and toilets with enough pressure to flush paper. German and English are spoken.

La Colina Lodge (☎ 2645 5009; www.lacolinalodge .com; camping per person US$5, d with/without bathroom incl breakfast US$52/44; **P**) This is the former Flor Mar opened in 1977 by Marvin Rockwell, one of the area's original Quakers, who was jailed for refusing to sign up for the draft in 1949 and then spent three months driving down from Alabama. Nowadays, the gringo owners John and Kim are as gracious and unpretentiously welcoming as the lodge itself. All of the rambling rooms on this peaceful property are hand-painted in cheery colors with unique furniture and décor, and the kitchen and communal areas provide either shade or sun, and always a relaxed vibe.

Swiss Hotel Miramontes (☎ 2645 5152; www.swiss hotelmiramontes.com; s/d US$47/58, d chalet US$87, all incl breakfast; **P**) Just outside Santa Elena on the road to Juntas is this charming European-inspired retreat, well situated in a grove of pine trees and tropical flowers. Eight rooms of varying size come with fabulous private hot-water bathrooms, while the two chalets have a little more breathing space, and a private porch where you can kick off your shoes. Kids love the expansive landscaped grounds, with trails through the well-stocked orchid garden (US$5 for nonguests) and everyone enjoys the huge, pretty chalets. The restaurant (mains US$4 to US$10, open 1pm to

10pm) specializes in Swiss treats, and as this is a Swiss-run Costa Rican hotel, staff speak English, German, French and Spanish.

Hotel Don Taco (☎ 2645 5263; www.cabinasdontaco .com; d standard/cabina incl breakfast US$29/47, cabaña US$58; **P**) The name sounds a little silly, but with big porches, great murals and an outdoor dining and chill-out area, this spot is fabulous. Cabañas come with TV, refrigerator and a balcony overlooking the Golfo de Nicoya. It's just north of Santa Elena proper, so you can rest easy at night.

Monteverde Rustic Lodge (☎ 2645 6256; www .monteverderusticlodge.com; s/d/tr incl breakfast US$35/52/ 68; **P**) The tree-branch posts and tree-trunk table tops play along with the theme, but the rooms are spotless, comfortable and not at all rustic. Rooms have private hot-water showers and tile floors and open onto the garden. It's a short walk from the center of Santa Elena and the Tico owners will happily arrange tours for you.

Nidia Lodge (☎ 2645 5236, 2645 6082; www.nidia lodge.com; s/d standard US$45/60, deluxe US$65/80, junior ste US$80/100, all incl breakfast; **P** **⌨**) The proprietor of Pensión Flor de Monteverde, Eduardo Venegas Castro, has a beautiful new inn named for his wife. The area is peaceful and just steps away from the Santuario Ecológico, so there's a good chance that wildlife will grace your front doorstep and the motmots will hang out in the trees out back. First-rate accommodations feature hot water and private balconies upstairs, with free wi-fi to boot. There's a nice restaurant where breakfast is served. Nidia provides a super-chill presence around the inn, and Eduardo, an expert naturalist, clearly revels in offering guided walks of the area's forests.

Mirador Lodge (☎ 2645 5354; www.miradorlodge .com/home.html; s/d/tr incl breakfast US$70/90/130; **P** **⌨**) About 9km north of Santa Elena, the Quesada family has established this 55-hectare private reserve in the mists of virgin cloud forest. With views of Arenal, the wooden cabins have gas-heated water, and some have wood-burning stoves. There's generator-powered electricity, but candles are provided as a backup, and it's advisable to bring a flashlight. The lodge provides free transfers from town, and transportation in the area for a small fee. The owners also run reputable horseback tours (p177).

Cloud Forest Lodge (☎ 2645 5058, toll-free 877-2623 3198; www.cloudforestlodge.com; s/d/tr/q US$81/93/105/116;

(P) (🖳) (♿) Simple, wood-walled rooms at this hilltop lodge have hot-water showers, but lack extras like satellite TV. Instead, there are trails to walk, birds and sometimes sloths to be seen in the garden and surrounding cloud forest, and views of the Golfo de Nicoya. The helpful staff can arrange tours. It's a pleasant walk into town, but you might want a car to get around.

Los Pinos Cabañas y Jardines (☎ 2645 5252; www .lospinos.net; cabaña standard/family/junior ste US$65/80/120; (P)) Eleven free-standing cabañas (cabins) are scattered around the peaceful, forested gardens of this nine-hectare property, which once formed a part of the family finca. Each cabaña affords a sense of privacy, with plenty of space between each one, and has a fully equipped kitchen and small terrace. It's a superb setting for those seeking a little solitude in easy walking distance of restaurants and shops around Cerro Plano. Though all of the cabañas are very comfortable and cozy, junior suites are the largest and are outfitted with hair dryers, cable TV and more upscale furnishings.

Hotel Claro de Luna (☎ 2645 5269; www.hotelclaro deluna.com; s standard/deluxe US$60/67, d standard/deluxe US$70/79, all incl breakfast; (P)) This sweet mountain chalet just southwest of Santa Elena is the perfect getaway for lovers. If you squint your eyes just a bit while staring at the hotel's Swiss-inspired architecture, you could convince yourself you're summering high up in the Alps. All nine rooms have hardwood floors and ceilings, and feature luxurious, hot-water bathrooms with regal tiles.

El Sol (☎ 2645 5838; www.elsolnuestro.com; d small/ large cabin US$60/80; (P) (♨)) Located 5km outside of Santa Elena near Guacimal is this 'sunny' spot. This small farm with two guest cabins is at a lower elevation than Santa Elena – the climate is drier and the sun is warmer. The owners of this highly recommended accommodations, Elisabeth and Ignacio, are a German-Spanish couple who will pamper you with strong massages and delicious home cooking. Their teenage son, Javier, is a great guide around the private trails on foot or on horseback.

Hotel Finca Valverde (☎ 2645 5157; www.mont everde.co.cr; d standard/cabin/superior US$87/93/111, extra person US$17-23; (P)) Just outside Santa Elena, this working coffee farm is a great choice if you're looking for something a bit different. Cabins each have two bare units with private hot-water showers, an upstairs loft and a balcony,

though the real reason you're here is to soak up the rural atmosphere. Junior suites are only slightly more expensive, though they have full bathrooms and cable TV. A simple but pleasant restaurant (mains US$4 to US$11, open 6am to 9:30pm) serves good fish and meat dishes as well as vegetables from the backyard garden. The attached bar is locally popular.

Hotel Poco a Poco (☎ 2645 6000; www.hotelpocoapoco .com; s/d/tr incl breakfast US$81/93/105; (P) (🗶) (🖳)) A short walk from Santa Elena will bring you to this funky property, which is adorned with ceramic mushrooms, tree frogs and other Costa Rican critters. Yellow-stuccoed rooms sleep three, and they have some great perks – full bathtubs, free wi-fi, big cable TVs and a DVD library (rental US$3) to dip into during those rainy nights. The best draw, however, is the excellent restaurant (mains US$6 to US$11, open 6:30am to 9am and noon to 9:30pm), also open to the public, which specializes in reader-recommended BBQs.

TOP END

Many of the pricier hotels are experimenting with alternative technologies, from solar-heated showers to elaborate gray-water systems. Owners are usually more than happy to offer impromptu tours with full explanations of how these technologies work, and can offer suggestions to folks who'd like to implement similar systems back home.

Monteverde Lodge & Gardens (☎ 2257 0766; www.costaricaexpeditions.com; s/d/tr/q US$99/136/150/173; (P) (🗶) (🖳) (🛏)) A progressive recycling strategy, a solar-energy system and a huge solar-powered – but nice and hot – Jacuzzi are among this nonsmoking hotel's noteworthy environmentally sound practices. Large rooms with full bathrooms and wraparound picture windows have garden or forest views. The large lobby is graced by a huge fireplace, and there's an impeccable bar that looks down on the huge Jacuzzi. The grounds are attractively landscaped with a variety of native plants, emphasizing ferns, bromeliads and mosses, and a short trail leads to a bluff with an observation platform at the height of the forest canopy, with good views of the forest and a river ravine. Most folks are here on all-inclusive package deals that include three meals, served à la carte and featuring quality international cuisine, as well as guided tours and transportation from San José.

ourpick Hotel Belmar (☎ 2645 5201; www.hotel belmar.net; s/d/tr standard US$98/110/126, chalet US$87/98/ 110, all incl breakfast; P 🖳 🖳) Despite being a 'real' ecoresort, the Hotel Belmar admirably doesn't flaunt this in its name. Rooms here are definitely upscale, though even their design scheme is commendable as all the artwork is from Casem (see p188). Minibars in the rooms, a TV lounge, and transportation from the bus stop are all part of the deal, but the biggest bonus is right out back: this is the trailhead for Cerro Amigos (p177). And you can be sure that the management works continuously to minimize its environmental impact – even the excess water from the mountainside Jacuzzi and pool is reused in the organic gardens, which itself makes for some great dishes at the onsite restaurant (with tremendous views of cloud forest and the gulf).

Hotel Fonda Vela (☎ 2645 5125; www.fondavela.com; s/d US$109/120, junior ste US$120/141, extra person US$9; P ✕ 🖳 🖳) With a convenient location near the Monteverde reserve, unique architectural styling, 14 hectares of trail-laden grounds and a private stable, this classy retreat is a sophisticated home base for enjoying the pleasures of the area. Standard rooms are spacious and light, with wood accents and large windows; and the suites are among the nicest rooms in town, featuring bathtubs, balconies and sitting rooms with huge TVs. Many rooms are wheelchair accessible. The restaurant (mains US$8 to US$16, open 6:15am to 9am, noon to 2pm and 6:30pm to 8:30pm) is open to the public, and recommended for its excellent food that emphasizes fresh, local ingredients. The hotel is owned by the two sons of Paul Smith, who first arrived in Monteverde in the 1950s and is a well-known local artist whose work graces the walls.

Hotel Heliconia (☎ 2645 5109; www.hotelheliconia .com; d standard/junior ste/family ste/master ste incl breakfast US$99/111/134/151; P 🖳 🖳) In Cerro Plano, this attractive, wooden, family-run hotel consists of the main lodge and several bungalows that are spread out across a mountainside. Standard rooms have breezy views while junior suites are ridiculously luxurious with two double beds, full bathrooms and stained-glass windows. The two master suites, which can each accommodate up to six people or be connected for a party of 12, are downright palatial with huge sitting areas, whirlpool tubs and outdoor terraces overlooking the Golfo de Nicoya. Owners arrange all the usual tours,

and operate a spa and aesthetic center where you can soak your stresses away in the Jacuzzi, or indulge in an endless list of beauty treatments. The onsite Restaurante Mediterráneo (mains US$8 to US$12, open 6:30am to 9pm) offers innovate Italian and seafood specialties as well as a smattering of typical Costa Rican dishes.

Trapp Family Lodge (☎ 2645 5858; www.trapp fam.com; d superior/ste US$93/111, extra person US$17; P ✕ 🖳) The closest lodge to the reserve entrance (just under 1km away) has 20 spacious rooms with high wooden ceilings, big bathrooms and fabulous views from the picture windows (which overlook either gardens or cloud forest). Suites come complete with TV and refrigerator, and there's no smoking anywhere, so you can breathe easy. There's a homey restaurant (mains US$10 to US$16) for guests only; a bar and sitting room with cable TV is open till 10pm. The emphasis here is on creating a family atmosphere, so bring the kids along and teach them a thing or two about nature.

Hotel El Sapo Dorado (☎ 2645 5010; www.sapo dorado.com; s/d incl breakfast US$120/142, extra person US$30; P ✕ 🖳) This hotel is owned by the Arguedas family, which first settled in the Monteverde area 10 years prior to the Quakers. Today the family is extremely active in the community, and they're regular promoters of the virtues of sustainable tourism. The 'Golden Toad' has 30 spacious rooms mostly in duplex cabins. All have two queen-size beds, a table and chairs, and private hot showers. Various deluxe suites have minibars, refrigerators and French doors that open to private terraces with views of the Golfo de Nicoya. The private forest behind the hotel has an extensive system of trails, and the restaurant (mains US$10 to US$20, open 6:30am to 9am, noon to 3pm and 6pm to 9pm) is renowned for its use of locally grown produce and wide range of vegetarian dishes.

Vista Verde Lodge (☎ 8380 1517; www.vista -monteverde.com; s/d standard US$93/107, junior ste US$102/115, extra person US$14, all incl breakfast; P) When you really want to get away from it all, take the signed side road just east of Selvatura and head 2.5 rough kilometers (4WD only) to this marvelous lodge, where you'll fall asleep to the sounds of the surrounding rain forest. Wood-paneled rooms with picture windows take in views of Volcán Arenal, and the current direction of the lava flow means that on a clear night you will see plenty of fireworks.

There's also a great common area where you can unwind in front of the TV and warm your feet beside the fire. Some 4km of trails through the primary forest surrounding this gorgeous spot can be explored on horseback. Staff can pick you up from the airport with advance notice, and they provide a shuttle service into Santa Elena. If you're expecting luxury at this price, look elsewhere (plus generator power can mean dim lights and quickly cooling showers), but solitude you'll find in spades.

Hotel de Montaña Monteverde (☎ 2645 5046; www .monteverdemountainhotel.com; standard/superior US$73/132; P ☐) Opened in 1978 as the first high-end accommodations in Monteverde, this hotel has had a recent renovation to show off its expansive lobby views to better advantage; though the rooms didn't benefit from any added character, they're still perfectly comfortable. Standard rooms have wood accents, thick mattresses and cable TV, and they can

sleep up to three people. The superior rooms can accommodate up to four people, and they have a huge bathtub, a private balcony and a minibar. The spacious gardens and forests of the 15-hectare property are pleasant to walk around, and there's also a sauna and Jacuzzi.

El Establo Mountain Resort (☎ 2645 5110; www .hotelelestablo.com; d deluxe/ste incl breakfast US$187/237; P ☒ ☐ ☒) This is a seriously upscale lodge offering a variety of rooms, which are among the most luxurious that the Monteverde–Santa Elena area has to offer. Deluxe rooms have an orthopedic mattress, cable TV, fridge, safe and hair dryer. Junior suites have all of those amenities in addition to split bathrooms and sitting areas, while the open-plan suites are A-frame lofts with private terraces. Some of the suites have Jacuzzi tubs facing wonderful views, while others have private flagstone terraces. Since this is Monteverde, you'll be happy to know that the deluxe property comes

INSPIRATION IN THE CLOUD FOREST

Born and raised in Monteverde, Marco Tulio Brenes moved to San José at age 18, where he worked with established artists. He ran the gallery Éxtasis for a decade, lived in the US, and exhibited his work there in group and solo shows, and found inspiration for recent work in his travels through Europe and Turkey. He's been an artist – or at least wished to be one – since he was very small. Now he is dedicated to working mostly in sculpture and painting in his open studio, Simbiogénesis (p188), in the cloud forest.

What are your artistic influences? In my sculptures I always find that nature is my biggest influence, and when I saw the works of Henry Moore, they also influenced me for some time. In painting, my primary influence was the Surrealists, especially Dalí; after some time, I discovered that the true influence for my work I found inside myself, through the investigation of the intense colors and organic shapes of the tropics.

How would you describe your style, and in what media do you work? It's difficult for me to describe my own style. It's imaginative, visionary art. In painting, I work in oil and acrylic on canvas. And in sculpture, I work in stone, ceramics and principally in clay. Stone and clay are my favorite media.

Can you tell me about the arts world in Monteverde? I live in Monteverde because it's the place that brings me the most inspiration, with its marvelous forests and its spectacular views of the Pacific. Furthermore, it's a place where I meet good artists working in different media, and who live the artistic life very intensely, and with a dedication to diverse cultural activities. For this reason it's a great place where I can show the public my work in my studio and at the same time demonstrate my process.

What is it like being an artist in Monteverde? I think that Monteverde is a unique place to feel and live art. There's a definite feeling of a dedicated artistic community, whose art manifests itself in diverse media – music, poetry, sculpture, yoga, photography, makers of musical instruments… There are quite a few arts events here, but the artists and the art-appreciating community always wish there were more events and opportunities to share artistic experiences.

complete with solar power, gray-water systems, a well-insulated underground electrical network and a good restaurant where buffet-style meals usually include locally grown produce. It's a steep hike to the best rooms, but the resort runs a shuttle on request.

Eating

The top-end hotels in town often have good restaurants, most of which are open to the public. Santa Elena has most of the budget eateries in the area.

Restaurante Mar y Tierra (mains US$3-7; 8:30am-9pm) In the heart of downtown Santa Elena, this spot serves top-quality typical food, including casados featuring the usual suspects from land and sea.

Dulce Marzo (2645 6568; pastries US$1.50-3; 10am-6pm) Yummy homebaked sweets, wraps, sandwiches, good espresso drinks and a favorite-café feel make this one of those places to linger over a late-morning coffee as you skim the paper or your guidebook. Foreign magazines scatter the tables and there's also a book exchange if you need reading material for the next leg of your trip.

Sabores (2645 6174; cones US$1-3; 11am-8pm) With longer hours than La Lechería, this place serves Monteverde's own brand of ice cream, plus coffee and a variety of homemade desserts. It's the perfect place for a civilized scoop after a morning hike through primitive forest.

Stella's Bakery (2645 5560; mains US$2-5; 6am-6pm) Order your choice of sandwich on delicious homemade breads with a convenient order form (one side is in English), and don't skimp on the veggies, many of which are locally grown (and organic). You can also get soups, salads, quiches and lots of tempting sweet pastries.

La Cocina de Leña de Doña Flory (2645 5306; mains US$4-6; 8am-8pm Sun-Fri) On a tiny turnoff close to La Colina Lodge, this 'Restaurante Rustico' is owned by Flory Salas and her husband Marvin Rockwell, one of the area's original Quaker settlers. Not surprisingly, food at this outdoor soda is simple yet healthy and filling, and it probably has the best tamales in town as well as its own special stew on Sunday.

Restaurante Campesino (mains US$2-8; 9am-11pm) Relax beneath about 80 stuffed animals won from machines by the dexterous owner, who also serves up amazing casados, salads

and a variety of sublime *ceviche* with a smile. The blue shopfront also has our favorite mural in town, and we've never seen toilet cozies quite like these.

Panadería Jiménez (2645 5035; 6am-6pm Mon-Sat, 6-10am Sun) This bakery has the best goods in town, like whole-wheat breads, pastries and coffee for folks booked on the early bus.

Chimera (2645 6081; tapas US$3-9; noon-10pm) Latin-infused tapas are complemented by an excellent wine list featuring robust reds like Chilean syrah-cabernets and crisp whites like pinot grigio. Dine alfresco at the trellis patio or the big-windowed dining room with beautiful jungle views. Charming staff will lay out a spread of cocktails (like kiwi caipirinhas, with lime, sugar and rum) and tapas like sea bass with passion-fruit cream and spicy mayo, or fried yuca with chipotle garlic aioli, all on white tablecloths.

Kaffá El Café (2645 6335; mains US$3-10; noon-10pm) Where else in Monteverde can you sit at a bar in a swing? Nowhere, that's where. There are tables for regular dining, if you feel like having a sweet *tres leches* (as dairy-licious as it sounds), chicken in parchment paper, or a vegetarian quesadilla stuffed with fresh veggies. Or find a comfortable spot in one of the lounge rooms in back, with low tables and cushions heaped invitingly on the floor. On Thursday and Friday nights you'll often find a great DJ or live music in the main room.

Morpho's Restaurant (2645 5607; mains US$4-10; 7:30am-9:30pm) This romantic, downtown restaurant spices up typical Costa Rican food by adding a gourmet flair. Casados feature a variety of European-influenced sauces (think sea bass in a fruity demiglaze), and are served with a traditional *batido* (fruit shake) or a more sophisticated glass of wine. The menu also has a good variety of vegetarian dishes.

La Pizzería de Johnny (2645 5066; www.pizzeria dejohnny.com; mains US$4-10; 11am-10pm) Wood-fired, thin-crust pizzas will warm you right up after a long hike through the cloud forests (or up the hill from Santa Elena). The warm atmosphere and lovely dining area make it feel as though you are having a nice dinner out without paying the price.

Pizzería Tramonti (2645 6120; mains US$5-11; noon-9pm, closed Mon in low season) It's worth the trip out here if you hanker for authentic Italian, as the pizzas are baked in a wood-fired oven, and the pastas and seafood are consistently fresh. The atmosphere is also relaxed yet romantic, and the picture windows are perfect for admiring the cloud forest and passers-by.

Tree House Restaurant & Café (☎ 2645 5751; www .canopydining.com; mains US$5-13; ⏰ 6:30am-10pm) Built around a half-century-old *higuerón* (fig) tree, this hip café serves up your favorite Mexican dishes from burritos to huevos rancheros (eggs served with tortillas and a tomato sauce), but also has a healthy selection of salads and sandwiches. The burlap-bag ceiling and jungle-themed murals painted on the yellow stucco walls surround the airy atrium. It's a cool, lively space to have a bite, linger over wine and sometimes catch good live music.

Moon Shiva Restaurant (☎ 2645 6270; www.moon shiva.com; mains US$10-14; ⏰ 11am-10pm) We get a lot of readers' mail about this Israeli-run bohemian eatery. By day, Moon Shiva is a good spot for Mediterranean- and Middle Eastern–inspired dishes. By night it turns into the hippest spot in town for live music. Look for flyers in town advertising different shows and events, as this is *the* place for everything from rock and jazz to salsa and electronica.

Flor de Vida (☎ 2645 6328; www.flordevida.net; mains US$8-15; ⏰ 7am-9pm) The emphasis at this Argentinean-run spot is on homemade international food, made with an artistic and loving hand. The menu features many vegetarian options, including spicy lentil stews or polenta layered with vegetables and cheese, as well as substantial burgers and lasagna. The sweet-toothed should save room for carrot cake or heavenly tiramisu. Even better, this is the only place in town with excellent, dense bagels shipped from San José.

Restaurant de Lucía (☎ 2645 5337; www.costa -rica-monteverde.com; mains US$7-15; ⏰ 11am-9pm) On the same road as El Jardín de las Mariposas, this Chilean-owned place is Monteverde's most famous restaurant. Chef José Belmar, who speaks more languages then you and your friend put together, regularly chats up guests and asks for feedback on the cuisine, and dishes (a good mix of Italian and South American specialties) are always flawless (and reasonably priced).

Sofia (☎ 2645 7017; mains US$10-18; ⏰ 5-10pm) Sofia has established itself on the Monteverde restaurant scene as one of the best places in town with its *nuevo Latino* cuisine – a modern fusion of traditional Latin American cooking styles. The ambience is flawless – soft lighting, hip music, picture windows, romantic candle settings, sloping wooden ceilings, pas-

tel paintwork and potent cocktails to lighten the mood.

Try **Supermercado La Esperanza** (☎ 2758 7351; ⏰ 7am-8pm) in Santa Elena for organic groceries. **Coop Santa Elena** (⏰ 7:30am-6pm) in Cerro Plano has a smaller selection, but profits are reinvested in the community.

Entertainment

Monteverde and Santa Elena nightlife generally involves a guided hike into one of the reserves, but since this misty green mountain draws artists and dreamers, there's a smattering of regular cultural offerings. When and if there's anything going on, you'll see it heavily advertised around town with flyers. Look for events at Galeron Cultural Aspinall Murray (left) or Bromelias Music Garden (p189), the long-running and constantly metamorphosing haven for the arts in Monteverde.

If you desire aural pleasure, pop into the Tree House Restaurant & Café (left), Moon Shiva (left) or Kaffá El Café (opposite) to see if anyone's playing live music – you'd be surprised at the quality of local music you might hear.

Unicornio Discotec is an almost exclusively local hangout near the northern end of the soccer field; it's the only place in town that has Imperial on tap (pro), but also has karaoke (con). Two popular bars that usually have a good mix of locals and tourists are Amigos Bar, a great place to drink and shoot pool, and the Taberna Los Valverde (at Hotel Finca Valverde; see p183), which has a dance floor made for shaking your moneymaker.

Shopping

These are some local galleries, listed in order from Santa Elena to Monteverde reserve.

Flor de Vida (☎ 2645 6328; www.flordevida.net; ⏰ 10am-7pm) One of the best galleries in the area, this small space packs a lot of punch. The restaurant owner and her daughter both have work here, of the batik-silk variety, but there's also a high-quality collection of photographs, paintings, wearable textiles, jewelry and handmade musical instruments. Most artists exhibiting here are from the area.

Art House (Casa de Arte; ☎ 2645 5275; www.monte verdearthouse.com; ⏰ 9am-6:30pm) Several rooms stuffed with colorful Costa Rican artistry is what you'll find at the Art House. There's jewelry, ceramic work, Boruca textiles and paintings. Though styles here differ quite a bit, it's more along the crafty end of the artsy-craftsy spectrum. It's a great place to find a unique local souvenir.

Compleja Atmosphera (☎ 2645 6555; complejoat-mosphera@yahoo.com.mx; ☺ 10am-8pm) An upscale Cerro Plano gallery that specializes in wood sculpture created by artists from all over Costa Rica. Several are from the Monteverde area, and the pieces run the gamut of style and function. They're also priced accordingly, from about US$25 to US$5000. If you fall in conflicted love with some sinuous piece here, may we suggest you think it over with a massage (US$50 to US$60) at the in-house natural spa.

Luna Azul (☎ 2645 6638; lunaazulmonteverde@gmail.com; ☺ 9am-6:30pm) This funky boutique is decked out in celestial murals, and it's a relaxing spot to do a little souvenir shopping for your friends…or yourself. There's a great variety of clothing, handmade jewelry and local art up for grabs as well as various aroma-therapy products. Check out the fused glass jewelry – some of our favorite pieces here.

Río Shanti (☎ 2645 6121; www.rioshanti.com; ☺ 10am-5pm) The real reason to come here is for a spa treatment, massage or yoga class (be sure to call ahead for an appointment or schedule), but this calming space on the road into Monteverde also has a gallery of local art for sale.

Atelier Simbiogénesis (☎ 2645 5567; ☺ 11am-5pm Mon-Sat) A working studio where you can browse the gallery and also roam upstairs to watch the artists at work, this art is a bit more experimental and an intriguing look into the contemporary scene fostered by the magi-cal Monteverde atmosphere (see also boxed text, p185).

Alquimia Artes (☎ 2645 5847; www.alquimiaartes.com; ☺ 10am-5pm) Has work that is a tad more affordable than some other places (check out the jewelry by Tarsicio Castillo from the Ecuadorian Andes), but this doesn't mean its collection of wood sculpture, paintings and prints by Costa Rican artists isn't astounding.

Casem (Cooperativa de Artesanía Santa Elena Monteverde; ☎ 2645 5190; www.casemcoop.org; ☺ 8am-5pm Mon-Sat, 10am-4pm Sun high season) Begun in 1982 as a wom-en's cooperative representing eight female artists, today Casem has expanded to include almost 150 local artisans, eight of whom are men. Embroidered and hand-painted cloth-ing, polished wooden tableware, handmade cards and other work, some priced even for budget souvenir shoppers, make for an eclectic selection.

TO RIDE OR NOT TO RIDE?

Though the top two tourist destinations in the region, La Fortuna and Monteverde–Santa Elena, are only about 25km apart, there are a few roadblocks that have thus far stopped anyone from paving a direct route between them: an erupting volcano, the country's largest lake, seven rivers and the Cordillera de Tilarán for starters, not to mention mountains of bureaucratic red tape in San José. Currently, it takes several very bumpy hours by bus to make the trip.

In the mid-1990s, local entrepreneurs began offering transportation on horseback between the towns, calling it 'the shortest and most convenient connection.' The idea enchanted tourists and quickly became a booming business; as demand for the scenic trip grew, so did the number of outfitters. The result was severe price cutting, and someone had to suffer for the savings. It was usually the horses.

Unethical practices such as buying cheap old horses and literally working them to death were reported; Lonely Planet received scores of horrified letters describing thin, diseased mounts that could barely make it through the mud; at least one overworked animal died on the Castillo Trail. Author Rob Rachowiecki wrote about the problem, angering local businesspeople who com-plained that his 'job was to write a guidebook, not harass them.' But the letters kept coming, so Rachowiecki kept reporting. Many companies went out of business.

Today, standards are high for reputable operators, in part (we like to think) because of informed tourists who asked hard questions and insisted on examining their horses before setting out – two precautions we still ask you to take. Although incidents of abuse are still reported, these are happily the exception rather than the rule. Costs have risen, the advertising revolves around how healthy the horses are, and most operators offer mellower alternatives.

Bromelias Books (☎ 2645 6272; www.bromelias musicgarden.com; ☟ 10am-5:30pm) Don cute felt shoes before entering this bookstore, with its polished-wood Cerro Plano expanse of local arts and crafts, including some intricate batik. There are also books about the region, in particular natural history, in English and Spanish, plus lots of excellent Costa Rican and Central American music. The small amphitheater outside the bookstore has regular theater and musical performances – be on the lookout for posters advertising events.

Hummingbird Gallery (☎ 2645 5030; ☟ 8:30am-5pm) This gallery just outside Monteverde reserve has beautiful photos, watercolors, art by the indigenous Chorotega people and, best of all, feeders that constantly attract several species of hummingbird. Great photo ops include potential hot shots of the violet sabrewing (Costa Rica's largest hummer) and the coppery-headed emerald, one of only three mainland birds endemic to Costa Rica. An identification board shows the nine species that are seen here. If you'd like a closer look, slides and photographs of the jungle's most precious feathered gems (and other luminous critters) by renowned British wildlife photographers Michael and Patricia Fogden are on display; the smaller prints are for sale.

Getting There & Away

The government has been planning to build a series of bridges across the several rivers that feed Laguna de Arenal's southwestern shore for about 20 years. If completed, this would provide a road connection between Monteverde and La Fortuna, which would probably be the end of the ecoparadise formerly known as Monteverde. There are always a few scattered spots where some construction work is going on but, fortunately, for the time being, they're not making too much progress.

BUS

All intercity buses stop at the **bus terminal** (☎ 2645 5159; ☟ 6-11am & 1:30-5pm Mon-Fri, closes 3pm Sat & Sun) in downtown Santa Elena, and most continue on to the Cheese Factory in Monteverde. On the trip in, keep an eye on your luggage, particularly on the San José–Puntarenas leg of the trip, as well as on the Monteverde–Tilarán run.

Purchase tickets to the Monteverde and Santa Elena reserves at Hotel Camino Verde (p171), which can also make reservations for pricier trips with private companies. Destinations, bus companies, fares, journey times and departure times are as follows:

There are now three main routes: the gorgeous and infamous **Castillo Trail** (three hours on horseback), also called the 'Mountain Trail' or 'Mirador Trail,' crosses the fierce Caño Negro three times. It's still in use, but should only be done during the dry months (if then) from mid-March through May (assuming that it's actually dry) by experienced riders. Some businesses offer the trek year-round, as it saves operators about US$25 per person in transport costs compared to other options – but don't do it in the rainy season, no matter what your operator says.

The **Chiquito Trail** (3½ hours on horseback) is still scenic and slippery, but doesn't require crossing the deepest rivers. This trail should also be avoided during wet weather, particularly by inexperienced riders. Finally, the flat and somewhat-less-scenic **Lake Trail** (5½ hours on horseback) is fine year-round, great for newbies, and basically skirts Laguna de Arenal between the boat taxi and jeep taxi that provide the actual transportation.

A good operator will never guarantee these or any other horseback trip, particularly along the Castillo Trail, as safety for both you and the horse depends completely on the weather. If they aren't offering some kind of refund in the event of rain, and/or an alternate lake trail or jeep-boat option, something's wrong. Also note that some hotels will imply that they are booking you through an established operator, but actually deliver you to a pal's independent company: ask if anything seems fishy.

And yes, budget travelers, you can find cheaper rides or even bargain reputable operators down by a few dollars in the low season. It's your choice. But consider this: when you save US$5, it's got to come out of someone's hide. Whose do you think it will be?

If you happen to witness any instance of horse abuse, talk to the equine-loving folks at the Pensión Santa Elena (p180) – they know the scene well, and will make sure that the complaint reaches the right people.

Las Juntas US$2, 1½ hours, departs from bus station at 4:30am. Buses to Puntarenas and San José can drop you off in Las Juntas.

Managua, Nicaragua (Tica Bus) US$13, eight hours; a small shuttle bus (US$1.50) departs from the bus station at 6am and brings you to the Interamericana in Lagartos, where you can pick it up.

Puntarenas US$3, three hours, departs from the front of Banco Nacional at 6am.

Reserva Monteverde US$0.50, 30 minutes, departs from front of Banco Nacional at 6:30am, 7:30am, 9:30am, 11:30am, 1pm and 2:30pm, returns 6:40am, 8am, 10:40am, noon, 2:10pm and 3pm.

Reserva Santa Elena US$2, 30 minutes, departs from front of Banco Nacional at 6:30am, 8:30am, 10:30am, 2:30pm and 3:30pm, returns 11am, 1pm and 4pm.

San José (TransMonteverde) US$3.90, 4½ hours, departs from La Lechería at 6:30am and 2:30pm, with pick-up at the bus station in Santa Elena.

Tilarán, with connection to La Fortuna US$2, seven hours, departs from the bus station at 5:30am. This is a long ride as you will need to hang around for two hours in Tilarán. If you have a few extra dollars, it's recommended that you take the jeep-boat-jeep (see right) option to La Fortuna.

CAR

While most Costa Rican communities regularly request paved roads in their region, preservationists in Monteverde have done the opposite. All roads here are shockingly rough, and 4WD is necessary all year, especially in the rainy season. Many car-rental agencies will refuse to rent you an ordinary car during the rainy season if you admit that you're headed to Monteverde.

There are four roads from the Interamericana: coming from the south, the first turnoff is at Rancho Grande (18km north of the Puntarenas exit); a second turnoff is at the Río Lagarto bridge (just past Km 149, and roughly 15km northwest of Rancho Grande). Both are well signed and join one another about a third of the way to Monteverde. Both routes boast about 35km of steep, winding and scenic dirt roads with plenty of potholes and rocks to ensure that the driver, at least, is kept from admiring the scenery.

A third road goes via Juntas (p169), which starts off paved, but becomes just as rough as the first two roads a few kilometers past town, though it's about 5km shorter than the previous two options. Finally, if coming from the north, drivers could take the paved road from Cañas via Tilarán (p251) and then take the rough road from Tilarán to Santa Elena.

HORSE

There are a number of outfitters that offer transportation on horseback (five to six hours, per person US$65 to US$100) to La Fortuna, usually in combination with jeep rides. The Castillo Trail has long been the source of some hand-wringing on the part of animal lovers and guidebook writers, but today there are three different trails available of varying difficulty. Use your own best judgment (see boxed text, p188).

JEEP-BOAT-JEEP

The fastest route between Monteverde–Santa Elena and La Fortuna is a jeep-boat-jeep combo (around US$30, three hours), which can be arranged through almost any hotel or tour operator in either town. A 4WD jeep taxi takes you to Río Chiquito, meeting a boat that crosses Laguna de Arenal, where a taxi on the other side continues a few to La Fortuna. This is increasingly becoming the primary transportation between La Fortuna and Monteverde as it's incredibly scenic, reasonably priced and saves half a day of rough travel.

RESERVA BIOLÓGICA BOSQUE NUBOSO MONTEVERDE

When Quaker settlers first arrived in the area, they agreed to preserve about a third of their property in order to protect the watershed above Monteverde. By 1972, however, encroaching squatters began to threaten the region. The community joined forces with environmental organizations such as the Nature Conservancy and the World Wildlife Fund to purchase 328 hectares adjacent to the already preserved area. This was called the Reserva Biológica Bosque Nuboso Monteverde (Monteverde Cloud Forest Biological Reserve), which the Centro Científico Tropical (Tropical Science Center) began administrating in 1975.

In 1986 the Monteverde Conservation League (MCL) was formed to buy land to expand the reserve. Two years later it launched the International Children's Rainforest project, which encouraged children and school groups from all over the world to raise money to buy and save tropical rain forest adjacent to the reserve. Today the reserve totals 10,500 hectares.

The most striking aspect of this project is that it is the result of private citizens working for change rather than waiting around for a national park administered by the government. The reserve relies partly on donations from the public (see Information, right). Considering that the ridiculously underfunded Minae struggles to protect the national-park system, enterprises like this are more important than ever for maintaining cohesive wildlife corridors.

Visitors should note that some of the walking trails are very muddy, and even during the dry season (late December to early May) the cloud forest is rainy (hey, it's a rain forest – bring rainwear and suitable boots). Many of the trails have been stabilized with concrete blocks or wooden boards and are easy to walk on, though unpaved trails deeper in the preserve turn into quagmires during the rainy season.

Because of the fragile environment, the reserve allows a maximum of 160 people at any time. During the dry season this limit is almost always reached by 10am, which means you could spend the better part of a day waiting around for someone to leave. The best strategy is to get there before the gates open, or better (and wetter) to come during the off season, usually May through June and September through November.

There are a couple of important points to consider, so read carefully. If you only have time to visit either the Monteverde or Santa Elena reserve, you should know that Monteverde gets nearly 10 times as many visitors, which means that the infrastructure is better and the trails are regularly maintained, though you'll have to deal with much larger crowds. Also, most visitors come to Monteverde (and Santa Elena) expecting to see wildlife. However, both reserves cover large geographic areas, which means that the animals have a lot of space to move around in. Taking a night tour or staying overnight in one of the lodges deep within the reserve will maximize your chances of spotting wildlife; still, it's best to enter the parks without any expectations. The trees themselves are primitive and alone worth the price of admission, though a lot has changed since the quetzal-spotting days of 1983. The animals have adapted to the increased tourist volume by avoiding the main trails, but most people who visit either reserve are more than satisfied with the whole experience.

Information

The **visitor center** (☎ 2645 5122; www.cct.or.cr; park entry adult/child under 6yr/student US$15/7.50/6.50; ☼ 7am-4pm) is adjacent to the reserve gift shop, where you can get information and buy trail guides, bird and mammal lists, and maps. The shop also sells T-shirts, beautiful color slides by Richard Laval, postcards, books, posters and a variety of other souvenirs, and rents binoculars (US$10); you'll need to leave your passport. The annual rainfall here is about 3000mm, though parts of the reserve reportedly get twice as much. It's usually cool (high temperatures around 18°C/65°F), so wear appropriate clothing.

It's important to remember that the cloud forest is often cloudy (!) and the vegetation is thick – this combination cuts down on sound as well as vision. Also keep in mind that main trails in this reserve are among the most trafficked in Costa Rica. Some readers have been disappointed with the lack of wildlife sightings. The best bet is, as always, to hire a guide.

Donations to the **Friends of Monteverde Cloud Forest** (www.friendsofmonteverde.org) are graciously accepted at the following address: PO Box 1964, Cleveland, OH 44106, USA.

If you're looking for a great volunteer opportunity, the **Cloud Forest School** (☎ 2645 5161; www.cloudforestschool.org) is a kindergarten-through-11th-grade bilingual school locally known as the Centro de Educación Creativa. The school was founded in 1991 to increase educational opportunities for a growing population of school-age children in the area. This independent school offers creative, experiential education to 220 students with an emphasis on integrating environmental education into all aspects of the school. For more information about volunteering as well as a few intern positions, you can contact the Volunteer Coordinator at opportunities@cloudforestschool.org.

Activities
HIKING

There are 13km of marked and maintained trails – a free map is provided with your entrance fee. The most popular of the nine trails, suitable for day hikes, make a rough triangle (El Triángulo) to the east of the reserve entrance. The triangle's sides are made up of the popular **Sendero Bosque Nuboso** (1.9km), an interpretive walk (booklet US$0.75 at gate) through the cloud forest that begins at the ranger station, paralleled by the more open, 2km **El Camino**, a favorite of bird-watchers. The **Sendero Pantanoso** (1.6km) forms the far side of El Triángulo, traversing swamps, pine forests and the continental divide. Returning to the entrance, **Sendero Río** (2km) follows the Quebrada Cuecha past a few photogenic waterfalls.

Bisecting the triangle, the gorgeous **Chomogo Trail** (1.8km) lifts hikers 150m to 1680m, the highest point in the triangle, and other little trails crisscross the region, including the worthwhile **Sendero Brillante** (300m), with bird's-eye views of a miniature forest. There's also a 100m suspension bridge about 1km from the ranger station. However, keep in mind that despite valiant efforts to contain crowd sizes, these shorter trails are among the most trafficked in the country, and wildlife learned long ago that the region is worth avoiding unless they want a good look at hominids.

There are also more substantial hikes, including trails to the three backcountry shelters (p201) that begin at the far corners of the triangle. Even longer trails, many of them less developed, stretch out east across the reserve and down the Peñas Blancas river valley to lowlands north of the Cordillera de Tilarán and into the Bosque Eterno de los Niños. If you're strong enough and have the time to spare, these hikes are highly recommended as you'll maximize your chances of spotting wildlife, and few tourists venture beyond the triangle. If you're serious about visiting the backcountry shelters, you should first talk to the park service as you will be entering some fairly rugged terrain, and a guide is highly recommended and, at times, essential. Camping is normally not allowed.

For advice on deep-jungle trekking and reputable local guides, contact trekking guide **Andres Vargas** (www.euforiaexpeditions.com), a socially responsible, superknowledgeable adventure specialist.

WILDLIFE-WATCHING

Monteverde is a birding paradise, and though the list of recorded species tops out at over 400, the one most visitors want to see is the resplendent quetzal. The Maya bird of paradise is most often spotted during the March and April nesting season, though you could get lucky anytime of year.

For mammal-watchers, the cloud forest's limited visibility and abundance of higher primates (namely human beings) can make wildlife-watching quite difficult, though commonly sighted species (especially in the backcountry) include coati, howler, capuchin, sloth, agouti and squirrel (like squirrel-squirrel, not the squirrel monkey).

Tours & Guides

Although you can hike around the reserve on your own, a guide is highly recommended, and not just by us but by dozens of readers who were inspired by their adventures to email Lonely Planet. The park runs a variety of guided tours: make reservations *at least* one day in advance. As size is limited, groups should make reservations several months ahead for dry season and holiday periods. Guides speak English and are trained naturalists, and proceeds from the tours benefit environmental-education programs in local schools.

The reserve offers guided **natural history tours** (☎ reservations 2645 5112; tours excl entry fee US$15) at 7:30am daily, and on busy days at 8:30am as well. Participants meet at the Hummingbird Gallery (p189), where a short 10-minute orientation is given. A half-hour slide show from renowned wildlife photographers Michael and Patricia Fogden is followed by a 2½- to three-hour walk. Once your tour is over, you can return to the reserve on your own, as your ticket is valid for the entire day.

The reserve also offers recommended two-hour **night tours** (incl entry fee with/without transportation US$15/13) at 7:15pm nightly. These are by flashlight (bring your own for the best visibility), and offer the opportunity to observe the 70% of regional wildlife with nocturnal habits.

Guided **birding tours** (5hr tour incl entry fee per person US$40-50) in English begin at Stella's Bakery (p186) at 6am, and usually sight more than 40 species. There's a two-person minimum and six-person maximum. Longer tours go on by request at a higher fee, and usually more than 60 species are seen.

Several local businesses can arrange a local to guide you within the reserve or in some of the nearby surrounding areas. Staff can also recommend **private guides** (guide@monteverdeinfo .com), or ask at your hotel or tour operator.

The reserve can also recommend excellent guides, many of whom work for it, for a

(Continued on page 201)

Wildlife
Guide

A flamboyant red-eyed tree frog makes a colorful statement

A morpho butterfly flashes electric blue wings

TOM BOY

Costa Rica has some of the most diverse wildlife in the world. From stunning, colorful birds to fleeting glimpses of rare mammals, it is a land of surprises and enchantment.
This guide includes a fraction of the common species that you might see in Costa Rica. Wildlife enthusiasts are encouraged to bring one of the many excellent wildlife books (listed throughout the Environment chapter, p61) and to hire local guides where possible.

INSECTS

More than 35,000 species of insects have been recorded in Costa Rica, but thousands remain undiscovered. Butterflies and moths are so abundant that Costa Rica claims 10% of the world's butterfly species. In excess of 3000 species have been recorded in Parque Nacional Santa Rosa (p218) alone.

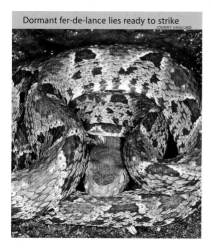

Dormant fer-de-lance lies ready to strike

JOHNNY HAGLUND

The distinctive morpho butterfly, with its electric-blue upper wings, lazily flaps and glides along tropical rivers and through openings in the forests across Costa Rica. When it lands, though, the wings close and only the mottled brown underwings become visible, an instantaneous change from outrageous display to modest camouflage.

AMPHIBIANS

The 160 species of amphibian includes the tiny and colorful poison-dart frog, in the family of Dendrobatidae. Some are bright red with black legs, others are red with blue legs, and still others are bright green with black markings. Several species have skin glands exuding toxins that can cause paralysis and death in many animals, including humans. Dendrobatids, which are widespread in tropical areas, were traditionally used by forest Indians as a poison for the tips of their hunting arrows.

REPTILES

More than half of the 220-plus species of reptile in Costa Rica are snakes. Snakes are rarely seen, but keep an eye out for the fer-de-lance and bushmaster, two deadly poisonous snakes. Both have broadly triangular heads and are widespread at lower elevations. The fer-de-lance, which can be anything from olive to brown or black in color, has a pattern of Xs and triangles on its back. The bushmaster is usually tan colored with dark diamond-shaped blotches.

Of the country's lizards, the most frequently seen is the abundant ameiva lizard, which has a white stripe running down its back. Also common is the bright-green basilisk lizard, noted for the huge crest running the length of its head, body and tail, which gives it the appearance of a small dinosaur almost 1m in length. It is common along watercourses in lowland areas. Seen in the same areas is the stocky green iguana, which is regularly encountered draping its 2m-long body across a branch over water.

BIRDS

The wealth of Costa Rica's world-famous avifauna is one of the top reasons visitors choose to travel here. The country hosts more bird species (approximately 850) than huge areas such as Europe, North America or Australia. The sheer numbers and variety are somewhat baffling and overwhelming and, in patches of healthy rain forest, the din of countless birds all calling at once will leave a lasting impression on even the most hardened travelers.

In addition to diverse forest birds, Costa Rica also hosts spectacular seabirds, including the magnificent frigatebird. This distinctive black bird, with an inflatable red throat pouch,

Proud basilisk shows off his prehistoric figure

MARK NEWMAN

Does my nose look big in this? The chestnut-mandibled toucan in profile

TOM BOY

is large, elegant and streamlined. It makes an acrobatic living by aerial piracy, harassing smaller birds into dropping their catch and then swooping to catch their stolen meal mid-air. Frigatebirds are found along both coasts but are more common along the Pacific.

Larger species of herons include the boat-billed heron, a stocky, mostly gray bird with a black cap and crest, and distinctively large, wide bill. The yellow-crowned night-heron is quite common in coastal areas and has an unmistakable black-and-white head with a yellow crown. Despite its name, it's mainly active by day.

The descriptively named roseate spoonbill is mostly seen in the Palo Verde (p208) and Caño Negro (p506) areas. It has a white head and a distinctive spoon-shaped bill, and feeds by touch. The spoonbill swings its open bill back and forth, submerged underwater, while stirring up the bottom with its feet, until it feels food and then snaps the bill shut.

A favorite waterbird for many visitors is the northern jacana, which has extremely long, thin toes that enable it to walk on top of aquatic plants, earning it the nickname 'lily-trotter.' It is common on many lowland lakes and waterways. At first glance its brown body, black head, yellow bill and frontal shield seem rather nondescript, but when disturbed the bird stretches its wings to reveal startling yellow flight feathers.

Of the 16 species of parrot recorded in Costa Rica, none is as spectacular as the scarlet macaw – unmistakable for its size (84cm long), bright red body, blue-and-yellow wings, long red tail and white face. Macaws are seen flying overhead, in pairs or small flocks, calling raucously to one another. Recorded as common in 1900, it is now rare to see them outside of Parque Nacional Carara (p323) and Corcovado (p416) due to deforestation and poaching for the pet trade.

Over 50 species of hummingbird have been recorded – their delicate beauty is matched only by their extravagant names. Largest is the violet sabrewing (found in mid-elevations), which has a striking violet head and body with dark green wings. Over 20 species may be seen at local feeders, including the purple-throated mountain-gem and crowned woodnymph.

The most famous of Costa Rica's 10 species of trogon is the resplendent quetzal (ket-*sal*), easily the most dazzling and culturally important bird in Central America. It had great ceremonial significance to the Aztecs and the Mayas and is the national bird and symbol of Guatemala. It is extremely difficult to keep in captivity, where it usually dies quickly, which is perhaps why it became a symbol of liberty to Central Americans during the colonial period. The male lives up to its name with glittering green plumage set off by a crimson belly, and white tail feathers contrasting with bright-green tail coverts that stream over 60cm beyond the bird's body. The head feathers stick out in a spiky green helmet through which the yellow bill peeks coyly. The quetzal is found from 1300m to 3000m in forested or partially forested areas. Locals usually know where to find one; good places

A resplendent quetzal shakes a tail feather
TOM BOYDEN

to look are in Reserva Biológica Bosque Nuboso Monteverde (p190) and the namesake Parque Nacional Los Quetzales (p372). Quetzals hang around slightly lower altitudes like Monteverde for nesting season (March to June), but are easily spotted at higher altitudes between November and April. At other times they are less active and quite wary, as are all the trogons.

Toucans are classic rain-forest birds and six species are found in lowland forests in Costa Rica. Huge bills and flamboyant plumage make species such as the chestnut-mandibled toucan and keel-billed toucan hard to miss. The chestnut-mandibled toucan is mainly black with a yellow face and chest, red under the tail and a bicolored bill – yellow above and chestnut below. The keel-billed toucan is similarly plumaged but the bill is multicolored. But with toucans, even smaller species such as the collared aracari are notable.

About half of Costa Rica's birds are passerines, a sprawling category that includes warbler, sparrow, finch and many other types of birds. Nearly limited to the tropics, however, are tanager and cotinga. The blue-gray tanager is common in Costa Rica and a resident of open, humid areas up to 2300m. The male scarlet-rumped tanager is jet black with a bright-scarlet rump and lower back – a flashy and unmistakable combination.

The male red-headed barbet is striking with its bright-red head and chest, yellow bill, green back and yellow belly. It forages in trees at mid-elevations. The white-fronted nunbird

A roseate spoonbill stretches its wings
LUKE HUNTER

A blue-gray tanager surveys the area
RALPH HOPKINS

is an upright-perching black bird of the Caribbean lowlands. It's immediately identified by its red bill with white feathers at the base.

Cotinga are even more dramatic in appearance – two species are pure white and two are a sparkling blue color. One of the strangest cotinga is the three-wattled bellbird, a highlight for visitors to Monteverde reserve (p190) because of its penetrating metallic *bonk!* and eerie whistling calls (not to mention the male's odd appearance).

MARINE ANIMALS

Long famous are the giant sea turtles of Costa Rica, impetus for the establishment of Tortuguero and several other coastal national parks. With a shell up to 1.6m long, the massive 360kg leatherback turtle is a stunning creature. The smaller olive ridley is legendary for its remarkable synchronized nesting, when tens of thousands of females emerge from the sea on the same night. All sea turtles are highly endangered and the conservation efforts on their behalf are some of the most important projects in Costa Rica.

In a few of the rivers, estuaries and coastal areas (especially around Parque Nacional Tortuguero, p458) you may glimpse the endangered West Indian manatee, a large marine mammal (up to 4m long and weighing 600kg, though usually smaller), which feeds on aquatic vegetation. There are no seals or sea lions in Costa Rica, so a manatee is easy to recognize.

'With a shell up to 1.6m long, the massive 360kg leatherback turtle is a stunning creature'

Costa Rica has one of the most biologically diverse marine ecosystems in the world and an astounding variety of marine mammals. Migrating whales arrive from both the northern and southern hemispheres. Deep-water upwellings are constant year-round, making these waters extremely productive and creating ideal viewing conditions at any season. Humpback whales are seen almost every month, while common, bottle-nosed and spotted dolphins are year-round residents. Seeing more than a dozen other species of dolphin and whale is possible, including orca, blue and sperm whale, and several species of relatively unknown beaked whale. All of these animals are best seen on guided boat tours along both coasts.

LAND MAMMALS

Five species of sloth are found in the neotropics, and the two species widespread in Costa Rica are the brown-throated three-toed sloth and Hoffman's two-toed sloth. The diurnal three-toed sloth is often sighted, whereas the nocturnal two-toed sloth is seen less often. Both are 50cm to 75cm in length with stumpy tails. Sloths hang motionless from branches or slowly progress upside down along a branch toward leaves, which are their primary food.

Anteaters lack teeth and use a long, sticky tongue to slurp ants and termites. There are three species in Costa Rica, including the giant anteater, which reaches almost 2m in length and has a tongue that protrudes an astonishing 60cm up to 150 times a minute!

Two species of armadillo inhabit Costa Rica. The best known is the nine-banded armadillo. Despite its name, there can be from seven to 10 bands. These armadillos grow up to 1m long (one-third is tail). Largely nocturnal, they eat insects, fruit, fungi and carrion.

A white-faced capuchin ventures hesitantly out of the undergrowth

ALFREDO MAIQUEZ

Costa Rica has four monkey species and in some places you can see all four at the same location. The Central American spider monkey is named for its long and thin legs, arms and tail, which enable it to pursue an arboreal existence in forests throughout Costa Rica. Spider monkeys swing from arm to arm through the canopy, and can hang supported just by their prehensile tail while using their long limbs to pick fruit. They rarely descend to the ground and require large tracts of unbroken forest. Logging, hunting and other disturbances have made them endangered.

The loud vocalizations of a male mantled howler monkey can carry for more than 1km even in dense rain forest. Variously described as grunting, roaring or howling, this crescendo of noise is one of the most characteristic and memorable of all rain-forest sounds. Inhabiting wet lowland forests, howlers live in small groups. These stocky blackish monkeys with coiled prehensile tails reside high in the canopy so they can be hard to spot.

The small and inquisitive white-faced capuchin is the easiest to observe in the wild. It has a prehensile tail that is typically carried with the tip coiled. Capuchins occasionally descend to the ground where foods such as corn and even oysters are part of their diet. Their meticulous foraging and prying into leaves, litter and bark makes them a joy to watch.

The diminutive Central American squirrel monkey persists only in isolated areas of the south Pacific coastal rain forests, including Manuel Antonio (p353) and Corcovado (p416) national parks, where it travels in small to medium-size groups during the day, squealing or chirping noisily and leaping and crashing through vegetation in search of insects and fruit in the middle and lower levels of lowland forests.

The white-nosed coati is the most frequently seen member of the raccoon family. It is brownish and longer, but slimmer and lighter, than a raccoon. Its most distinctive features are a long, mobile, upturned whitish snout with which it snuffles around on the forest floor looking for insects, fruit and small animals; and a long, faintly ringed tail held straight up in the air when foraging. Coatis are found country-wide in all types of forest up to 3000m.

Lacking the facial markings and ringed tail of its cousins, the cuddly kinkajou is a raccoon relative found in lowland forests. It is an attractive reddish-brown color and is hunted both for food and the pet trade. Nocturnal and mainly arboreal, it jumps from tree to tree searching for fruits (especially figs), which comprise most of its diet.

The southern river otter lives in and by fast-moving lowland rivers, but is infrequently seen. It is a rich brown color with

White-nosed coati preens his lustrous coat
LUKE HUNTER

whitish undersides and has the streamlined shape of an aquatic weasel. The similarly shaped tayra is more easily spotted; it is blackish brown, with a tan head, and is territorial and arboreal. It is more than 1m long (the tail is about 40cm) and found in forests up to 2000m.

It is every wildlife-watcher's dream to see a jaguar in the wild. However, these big cats are extremely rare and well camouflaged, so the chance of seeing one is remote. Jaguars have large territories and you may see their prints or droppings in large lowland parks with extensive forest such as Corcovado (p416). Occasionally you may hear them roaring – a sound more like a series of deep coughs. There's no mistaking this 2m-long yellow cat with black spots in rosettes and a whitish belly. Good luck seeing one.

Other Costa Rican felids include the ocelot, a little more than 1m in length with a short tail and a pattern of many beautiful rosettes. Though it is the most common of the Costa Rican cats, it is shy and rarely seen. It adapts well to a variety of terrain, wet and dry, forested and open, and has been recorded in most of the larger national parks.

The widespread collared peccary lives in a variety of habitats. An adult is about 80cm long and weighs around 20kg, and has coarse gray hair and a light collar. The larger white-

Young spider monkey goes out on a limb
RALPH HOPKINS

lipped peccary is darker and lacks the collar but has a whitish area on the lower chin. Peccaries are noisy and aggressive with audible tooth gnashing and clicking.

Large rodents are among the most commonly seen rain-forest mammals. The Central American agouti is diurnal and terrestrial and found in forests up to 2000m. It looks like an oversized cross between a rabbit and a squirrel, with a very small tail and short ears. The closely related paca looks similar, except it has white stripy marks on its sides and is twice the size of an agouti. It is common but nocturnal.

David Lukas is an expert in natural history.

(Continued from page 192)

private tour. Costs vary depending on the season, the guide and where you want to go, but average about US$60 to US$100 for a half-day. Entrance costs may be extra, especially for the cheaper tours. Full-day tours are also available. The size of the group is up to you – go alone or split the cost with a group of friends.

Sleeping & Eating

Near the park entrance are **dormitories** (☎ reservations 2645 5122; www.cct.or.cr; dm adult/student US$37/33) with 43 bunks and shared bathrooms. These are often used by researchers and student groups but are often available to tourists – make reservations. Full board can be arranged in advance.

There are also three **backcountry shelters** (dm US$5), with drinking water, showers, propane stoves and cooking utensils. You need to carry a sleeping bag, candles, food and anything else (like toilet paper) you might need. El Valle (6km, two hours) is the closest; Alemán Hut (8km, four hours) is near a cable car across Río Peñas Blancas; and Eladios Hut (13km, six hours) is the nicest, with separate dorm rooms and a porch. Trails are muddy and challenging, scenery mossy and green, and the tourist hordes that inundate the day hikes a far-off memory. This may be the best way to appreciate the reserve. Reservations are highly recommended, and they can be made at the park office prior to setting out on your hike.

There is a small **restaurant** (plates US$2-5; ⏰ 7am-4pm) at the entrance to the reserve, which has a good variety of healthy sandwiches, salads and typical dishes.

Getting There & Away

Public buses (US$2, 45 minutes) depart the Banco Nacional in Santa Elena at 6:30am, 7:30am, 9:30am, 11:30am, 1pm and 2:30pm daily. Buses return from the reserve at 6:40am, 8am, 10:40am, noon, 2:10pm and 3pm. You can flag down the buses from anywhere on the road between Santa Elena and the reserve – inquire at your hotel about what time they will pass by. Taxis are also available for around US$5.

The 6km walk from Santa Elena is uphill, but lovely – look for paths that run parallel to the road. There are views all along the way, and many visitors remark that some of the best birding is on the final 2km of the road.

RESERVA SANTA ELENA

Though Monteverde gets all the attention, this exquisitely misty reserve, at 310 hectares just a fraction of the size of that other forest, has plenty to recommend it. You can veritably hear the canopy, draped with epiphytes, breathing in humid exhales as water drops onto the leaf litter and mud underfoot. The odd call of the three-wattled bellbird or low crescendo of a howler monkey punctuates the higher-pitched bird chatter and chirps.

While Monteverde Crowd…er…Cloud Forest entertains almost 200,000 visitors annually, Santa Elena sees fewer than 20,000 tourists each year, which means its dewy trails through mysteriously veiled forest are usually far quieter. It's also a bit cheaper and much less developed; plus your entry fee is helping support another unique project.

This cloud-forest reserve was created in 1989 and opened to the public in March 1992. It was one of the first community-managed conservation projects in the country, and is now managed by the Santa Elena high school board and bears the quite unwieldy official name of Reserva del Bosque Nuboso del Colegio Técnico Profesional de Santa Elena. You can visit the **reserve office** (☎ 2645 5693; ⏰ 8am-4pm Wed-Fri) at the high school.

The reserve is about 6km northeast of the village of Santa Elena. This cloud forest is slightly higher in elevation than Monteverde, and as some of the forest is secondary growth, there are sunnier places for spotting birds and other animals throughout. There's a stable population of monkey and sloth, many of which can be seen on the road to the reserve. Unless you're a trained ecologist, the old-growth forest in Santa Elena is fairly similar in appearance to Monteverde, though the lack of cement blocks on the trails means that you'll have a much more authentic (note: muddy) trekking experience.

This place is moist, and almost all the water comes as fine mist, and more than 25% of all the biomass in the forest are epiphytes – mosses and lichens – for which this place is a humid haven. Though about 10% of species here won't be found in Monteverde, which is largely on the other side of the continental divide, you can see quetzal here too, as well as Volcán Arenal exploding in the distance – theoretically. Rule No 407 of cloud forests: it's often cloudy.

Information

You can visit the **reserve** (☎ 2661 8290; www .monteverdeinfo.com/reserve-santa-elena-monteverde; adult/ student US$8/4.50; ☺ 7am-4pm) on your own, but a guide will enhance your experience tenfold (see below).

There's also a simple restaurant, coffee shop and gift store. Note that all proceeds go toward managing the reserve and to environmental-education programs in local schools. Donations are graciously accepted.

If you have some extra time, there's a good volunteer program here – possible projects include trail maintenance, surveying, administration and biological research. You're expected to make at least a one-week commitment, and very basic (no electricity, very cold showers) dorm-style accommodations are available free to volunteers, though all but the most rugged will prefer a US$10-per-day homestay, including three meals. Although at times it's possible to simply show up and volunteer, it's best to contact the reserve in advance.

Activities

More than 12km of trails are open for hiking, featuring four circular trails offering walks of varying difficulty and length, from 45 minutes to 3½ hours (1.4km to 4.8km) along a stable (though not 'concrete-blocked') trail system. Rubber boots (US$1) can be rented at the entrance. Unlike Monteverde, Santa Elena is not developed enough to facilitate backcountry hiking, and at the time of writing it was not possible to overnight in the reserve.

Tours & Guides

The reserve offers guided **daylight tours** (3hr tours excl admission per person US$15) at 7:30am and 11:30am daily; try to make the earlier hike. Popular **night tours** (1½hr tour excl admission per person US$13) leave at 7pm nightly. Tours have a two-person minimum and six-person maximum, so reservations are recommended for both tours during the dry season. The reserve can also arrange three-day private tours through various guides for US$20.

Getting There & Away

A daily shuttle (US$1 each way) between the village of Santa Elena and the reserve departs from the Banco Nacional in town at 6:30am, 8:30am, 10:30am and 2:30pm, and returns at 11am, 1pm and 4pm. A taxi from Santa Elena costs US$8.

ECOLODGE SAN LUIS & RESEARCH STATION

Formerly a tropical-biology research station, this facility now integrates research with ecotourism and education, and is administrated by the University of Georgia. The 70-hectare site is on the Río San Luis and adjoins the southern part of the Monteverde reserve. Its average elevation of 1100m makes it a tad lower and warmer than Monteverde, and birders have recorded some 230 species attracted by the slightly nicer weather. There are also a number of trails into primary and secondary forest, and there's a working farm with tropical fruit orchards and a coffee harvest from November to March.

A variety of comfortable accommodations at the **lodge** (☎ 2645 8049; www.ecolodgesanluis.com; dm US$65, s/d cabin US$85/160; Ⓟ) are available for anyone interested in learning about the cloudforest environment and experiencing a bit of rural Costa Rican life. Rates include all meals and most activities. There are a host of day and night hikes guided by biologists, as well as slide shows, seminars, horse rides and even an introduction to research activities. Discounts can be arranged for students, researchers, large groups and long stays.

The ecolodge also runs a resident naturalist volunteer program, though there is a preference for University of Georgia students and graduates, and a six-month commitment is required. The position entails running a number of teaching workshops and guided walks, as well as participating in development projects on the station and in the community. Training, room and board are provided.

From the main road between Santa Elena and Monteverde, it's a steep 3km walk from the signed road where the bus will drop you off. A 4WD taxi from town costs about US$12 each way, and the lodge can also arrange transportation from San José in advance.

PUENTE LA AMISTAD

About 23m south of Cañas on the Interamericana is a turnoff, continuing for another 25km to the Puente La Amistad. Prior to debut of the 'Friendship Bridge,' constructed with the help and funding of the Taiwanese government, drivers had to ferry across the Río Tempisque. The bridge has greatly reduced travel time to and from the beaches in Nicoya.

CAÑAS

If you're cruising north on the Interamericana, Cañas (population 25,000) is the first town of any size in Costa Rica's driest province, Guanacaste. *Sabanero* culture is evident on the sweltering and quiet streets, where full-custom pick-up trucks share the road with wizened cowboys on horseback, fingering their machetes with a swagger you just don't see outside the province. It's a dusty, typically Latin American town, where everyone walks slowly and businesses shut down for lunch, all centered on the Parque Central and Catholic church – which are most definitely not typical.

You're better off basing yourself in livelier Liberia, which has more traveler-oriented services. That said, Cañas is a good place for organizing rafting trips on the nearby Río Corobicí or for exploring Parque Nacional Palo Verde. And if you need to stop here for gas, there are a couple of interesting sights to check out.

Information

You can find public phones, a post office, library and a Banco Nacional, as well as many simple *sodas* and hotels here.

Emergency clinic (☎ 2669 0092; cnr Av Central & Hwy 1; 🕒 7am-4pm Mon-Fri) Has 24-hour on-call service.

Internet Ciberc@ñas (☎ 2663 5232; Av 3 btwn Calles 1 & 3; per hr US$1.25; 🕒 8:15am-9pm Mon-Sat, 2-9pm Sun) Has fast computers, air-con and, if you get here at 8:15am, two hours for the price of one.

Minae/ACT office (☎ 2669 0533; Av 9; 🕒 8am-4pm Mon-Fri) Has limited information about nearby national parks and reserves.

Sights & Activities

Though most visitors simply use the town as a base for visits to nearby **Parque Nacional Palo Verde** (p208) or rafting the **Río Corobicí**, it's worth the trip just to see the Catholic church's **psychedelic mosaics** designed by famed local painter Otto Apuy. Sinewy vines and colorful starbursts that have enveloped the modern church's once clean lines are enhanced by jungle-themed stained glass that's completely different from anything on offer at the Vatican. In **Parque Central** opposite, park

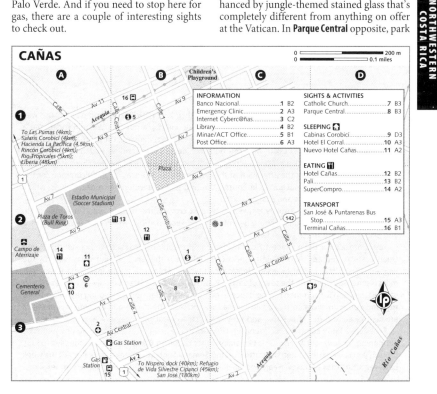

CAÑAS

INFORMATION		SIGHTS & ACTIVITIES	
Banco Nacional................1 B2		Catholic Church................7 B3
Emergency Clinic..............2 A3		Parque Central................8 B3
Internet Cyberc@ñas.......3 C2		
Library...............................4 B2		SLEEPING
Minae/ACT Office............5 B1		Cabinas Corobicí...............9 D3
Post Office........................6 A3		Hotel El Corral................10 A3
		Nuevo Hotel Cañas........11 A2
		EATING
		Hotel Cañas....................12 B2
		Pali................................13 B2
		SuperCompro...................14 A2
		TRANSPORT
		San José & Puntarenas Bus
		Stop............................15 A3
		Terminal Cañas...............16 B1

Children's Playground

To Las Pumas (4km);
Safaris Corobicí (4km);
Hacienda La Pacífica (4.5km);
Rincón Corobicí (4km);
Río Tropicales (5km);
Liberia (48km)

Plaza

Estadio Municipal
(Soccer Stadium)

Plaza de Toros
(Bull Ring)

Campo de
Aterrizaje

Cementerio
General

Gas Station

Gas
Station

To Níspero dock (40km); Refugio
de Vida Silvestre Cipancí (45km);
San José (180km)

Río Cañas

benches and the pyramid-shaped bandstand are equally elaborate.

LAS PUMAS

Directly behind the office of Safaris Corobicí is **Las Pumas** (☎ 2669 6044; admission by donation; ☒ 8am-5pm), a wild-animal shelter started in the 1960s by Lilly Hagnauer, a Swiss woman, and said to be the largest shelter of its kind in Latin America. Pumas, jaguars, ocelots and margays – plus peccaries and a few birds that were either orphaned or injured – are taken care of here and it has clearly been a labor of love to save and raise them. Lilly died in 2001, but the shelter is still managed by her family. Las Pumas is not officially funded and contributions are crucial to offsetting the high costs of maintaining the shelter; you may also be able to volunteer here by contacting it beforehand.

REFUGIO DE VIDA SILVESTRE CIPANCÍ

New in 2001, this small wildlife refuge is at the confluence of the Ríos Tempisque and Bebedero, at the southern end of Parque Nacional Palo Verde. It's a good spot for **birding** and **fishing**, though it's virtually untouristed. Local fishers offer passenger boats for tours on these two rivers. A three-hour guided tour costs around US$20 per person (US$150

minimum), and can usually be arranged at the docks; show up early.

The Minae/ACT office in Cañas has more information on the park. Boats leave from the Níspero dock, just north of the Tempisque ferry.

RAFTING

Gentle rafting trips down the Río Corobicí can be made with **Safaris Corobicí** (☎ 2669 6191; www .nicoya.com; Km 193 Interamericana Hwy; ☒ departures 7am-3pm). Bookings can be made at its office on the Interamericana about 4.5km north of Cañas. The emphasis is on wildlife observation rather than exciting white-water rafting. The river is Class I-II (in other words, pretty flat) but families and nature lovers enjoy these trips. Swimming holes are found along the river. Per person, based on a two-person minimum, a two-hour float costs US$35/17.50 per adult/child under 14 years, a three-hour birding float covering 12km costs US$45/22.50, and a half-day 18km float including lunch costs US$60/30. The company also rents out a little guesthouse nearby.

A branch office of the popular **Rio Tropicales** (☎ 2233 6455; www.riostropicales.com/english.htm; ☒ departures 7am-3pm) operates out of the Rincón Corobicí restaurant (opposite).

LAS FIESTAS DE GUANACASTE

Guanacastecos love their horses, almost as much as they love their fiestas. And what better way to get the best of both worlds than with a *tope* (horse parade), a mix of a Western rodeo and a country fair complete with a cattle auction, food stalls, music, dancing, drinking and, of course, bull riding? Fortunately, in Costa Rica the bulls are never killed, and so watching the insane helmetless, bareback, bucking bronco action is exciting and (usually) gore-free. Even better than watching the bull riding is the aftermath of the rider getting tossed, as it's fairly common for the local drunks and young machos to jump into the ring to act as volunteer rodeo clowns, which is simultaneously hilarious and scary.

Though the bull riding usually draws the biggest crowds, the main event is the *tope* itself, where you can see the high-stepping gait of the *sabanero* (cowboy), which demands endurance and skill from both horse and rider.

Topes are also a great place to catch the region's traditional dance, known as the Punto Guanacasteco. Perhaps the showiest aspect of the dance is the long, flowing skirts worn by the women. This skirt is meant to resemble an oxcart wheel, which is a traditional Costa Rican craft most often associated with the town of Sarchí. Punto Guanacasteco traditionally served as a means of courtship, and it's common for the dance to be frequently interrupted by young men who shout rhyming verses in order to try to win over a love interest. The dance and accompanying music are fast paced and full of passion, and they're similar to most other Central American styles.

Topes are a fairly common occurrence in Guanacaste, so ask a local about where one might be happening, or look out for posters. Generally, *topes* occur on Costa Rican civic holidays (p533), though you can bet on finding big parties during Semana Santa (the week before Easter), the week between Christmas and New Year, and on July 25, the anniversary of Guanacaste's annexation.

Sleeping

Cañas is a cheaper place to stay than Liberia, though the following places cater more to truckers than travelers. Rooms have cold showers unless otherwise stated.

Cabinas Corobicí (☎ 2669 0241; cnr Av 2 & Calle 5; r per person US$10; **P**) At the southeastern end of town, this is a good budget option as the friendly management maintains comfortable, good-sized rooms with warmish private showers, and the area is fairly quiet at night.

Hotel El Corral (☎ 2669 1467; s/d US$17/32; **X**) Right on the Interamericana, ask for your absolutely standard room (some with air-con, hot shower and/or TV) in the back, away from the highway noise. The attached restaurant (mains US$2 to US$5, open 6am to 10pm) overlooks the Interamericana, so you can watch (and smell) the big rigs blast by while enjoying your casado.

Nuevo Hotel Cañas (☎ 2669 5118; hotelcanas@racsa .co.cr; Av 3 btwn Calle 4 & Hwy 1; s/d US$30/45; **P** **X** **≋**) This is by far the best option in town, and although it's a bit pricey, the Nuevo Hotel Cañas is consistently packed with vacationing Ticos who adore the swimming pool and Jacuzzi. All rooms have air-con, cable TV and private hot shower, so you're definitely getting bang for your buck here.

Hotel Capazuri (☎ 2669 6280; capazuri@racsa.co.cr; camping US$5, d incl breakfast with/without air-con US$50/45; **P** **X** **≋**) Inconveniently located about 2.5km northwest of Cañas on the Interamericana, this is the place to stay if you have your own transport. This small Tico resort has rather frilly rooms, most sleeping three, with TV and private hot-water bathroom. There's also a festive, onsite restaurant and, best of all, a huge pool (admission US$1.25 for nonguests). The friendly management will also let you pitch a tent on the well-maintained grounds.

Eating

Hotel Cañas (☎ 2669 0039; cnr Calle 2 & Av 3; mains US$3-8; 🕐 6am-9pm Mon-Sat, 7am-2pm Sun) You can count on the most reliable quality at this hotel restaurant, serving up a number of Western dishes, including chicken cordon bleu and beef stroganoff. Dine here if you're pretty sure you can't stomach another casado.

Rincón Corobicí (☎ 2669 1234; www.nicoya.com /rincon; mains US$3-10; 🕐 8am-6pm) This attractive Swiss-run restaurant is 4km north of Cañas on the banks of the Río Corobicí, and is a great lunch stop for authentic fondue. A terrace provides river and garden views, and a short trail follows the riverbank where you can take a cool dip. English, French and German are spoken here, and you can book tours with Rio Tropicales for the Río Corobicí or other destinations in Costa Rica.

Hacienda La Pacífica (☎ 2669 6050; mains US$5-12; 🕐 7am-9pm) Once a working hacienda and nature reserve, this elegant restaurant is 4.5km north of Cañas on the Interamericana and is now part of a private hotel for researchers. Many of the ingredients are grown right here on experimental organic plots, including the only large-scale organic rice cultivation site in the country.

Many of the restaurants in town shut down on Sundays, but luckily there's an enormous **SuperCompro** (🕐 8am-8pm) right on the Interamericana and a **Palí** (🕐 8am-8pm) just around the corner.

Getting There & Away

All buses arrive and depart from **Terminal Cañas** (🕐 8am-1pm & 2:30-5:30pm) at the northern end of town. There are a few *sodas* and snack bars, and you can store your bags (US$0.50) at the desk. There's also a taxi stand in front.

Juntas US$0.50, 1½ hours, departs 9am and 2:15pm.

Liberia US$1.20, 1½ hours, departs 5:30am, 6:45am, 7:30am, noon, 1:30pm, 4:30pm and 5:30pm.

Puntarenas US$2, two hours, departs 6am, 6:40am, 9:30am, 10:30am, 11:30am, 12:30pm, 1:45pm, 3:30pm and 4:30pm.

San José US$3, 3½ hours, departs 4am, 4:50am, 5:40am, 9am, 12:15pm and 1:30pm.

Tilarán US$0.75, 45 minutes, departs 6am, 8am, 9am, 10:30am, noon, 1:45pm, 3:30pm and 5:30pm.

Upala US$2, two hours, departs 4:30am, 6am, 8:30am, 11:15am, 1pm, 3:30pm and 5:15pm.

VOLCÁN TENORIO AREA

A paved road 6km northwest of Cañas branches off the Interamericana and heads north to Upala, passing between Volcán Miravalles to the west and Volcán Tenorio (1916m) to the east. **Parque Nacional Volcán Tenorio**, among Costa Rica's newest national parks and part of the Area de Conservación Arenal (ACA), is one of the highlights of northwestern Costa Rica, especially since the dearth of public transportation and park infrastructure contribute to the lack of tourists. However, if you have your own transport, the park entrance is just a few kilometers south of Bijagua, and the park is an easy day trip from either Liberia or Cañas.

The trail system is relatively undeveloped. Grab a map at the **ranger station** (☎ 2200 0135; admission US$10; ☺ 7am-4pm), which outlines one of the finest short hikes in Costa Rica. On the northeast flanks of the volcano, the **Río Celeste**, just 1.5km from the ranger station, is famed for the blue created by many minerals dissolved in its waters. After navigating a winding trail through secondary forest, you'll find yourself in front of an impossibly milky-blue **waterfall** that cascades down the rocks into a fantastically aquamarine pool. If after seeing the falls you're wondering what the thermal headwaters look like, continue along the trail for a few hundred more meters until you reach the confluence of two rivers, where the brown co-mingles with the deeper turquoise and forms an unusual variation of colors. Another 3km hike through epiphyte-laden cloud forest takes you past a series of hot springs and boiling mud pots – take great care not to scald yourself when you're exploring the area.

Since volcanic activity at Tenorio is limited to fumaroles, hot springs and mud pots, it's possible to hike to the top of the crater on a two-day trek where you can camp next to a small lake that will make your evening surreally beautiful. The trail system here is unmarked and passes through rough terrain, so you'll need the services of a local guide, who can be hired either at the ranger station or at any of the lodges.

Sleeping & Eating

There are a few simple *sodas* in Bijagua, but other than that, you'll probably be eating at your lodge.

Rio Celeste Lodge (☎ 8365 3415; www.riocelestelodge .com; camping US$2, r per person US$20) This simple set of rustic cabinas is the cheapest accommodations in the area, and is a good option if your day trip suddenly turns into an overnight stay. Rooms have fans and warm showers, and the lodge is conveniently located on the hill near the trailhead. Staff can also arrange horseback riding and guided hikes.

Posada Cielo Roto (☎ 8352 9439, 2466 8692; r per person incl 3 meals & horse rides US$45; ⓟ) On expansive grounds with horse stables and several kilometers of private trails, owner Mario Tamayo, who speaks English, has built several lovely, rambling houses with shared kitchens that are just perfect for groups. Some rooms are doubles, but most are dorm style, all with private bathrooms and lots with big windows

overlooking the stunning scenery. There's no electricity, but kerosene lamps and candles are provided. Mario accepts walk-ins, but it's better to make reservations so he can bring in food, ice and whatnot for your stay.

La Carolina Lodge (☎ 8380 1656; www.lacarolina lodge.com; s/d incl 3 meals & horse rides from US$75/130; ⓟ ⌂) This isolated lodge run by a gracious North American named Bill is on a working cattle ranch on the slopes of the volcano, and is highly recommended for anyone looking for a beautiful escape from the rigors of modern life. The remote location means there's limited electricity – but candlelight only adds to the ambience. Amazing meals (organic beans, rice, fruits, cheeses, chicken and pork from the farm), cooked over an outdoor wood-burning stove, are a treat, as is soaking in the wood-fired hot tub. Rooms with hot showers are basic, but you'll be spending most of your time in the nearby hot springs, swimming holes or on the riverside (where you can lounge, swim, fish or go birding). The lodge is about 12km north of Bijagua and 7km east of the highway on the road toward the village of San Miguel.

VOLCÁN MIRAVALLES AREA

Volcán Miravalles (2028m) is the highest volcano in the Cordillera de Guanacaste, and although the main crater is dormant, the geothermal activity beneath the ground has led to the rapid development of the area as a hot-springs destination. As more travelers land in Liberia, they're starting to discover this nearby refuge from the ubiquitous cold shower.

Volcán Miravalles isn't a national park or refuge, but the volcano itself is afforded a modicum of protection by being within the Zona Protectora Miravalles. You can also take guided tours of the government-run Proyecto Geotérmico Miravalles, north of Fortuna, an ambitious project inaugurated in 1994 that uses geothermal energy to produce electricity, primarily for export to Nicaragua and Panama, but also producing about 18% of Costa Rica's electricity. A few bright steel tubes from the plant snake along the flanks of the volcano, adding an eerie touch to the remote landscape. But the geothermal energy most people come here to soak up comes in liquid form. Note that all of the listed hot springs are north of Fortuna.

Thermo Manía (☎ 2673 0233; www.thermomania.net; adult/child US$6/4; ☺ 8am-10pm) is the biggest com-

---

HERE'S MUD IN YOUR EYE

Actually…you'll want to keep thermal mud *out* of your eyes. To get the most out of your mud bath, local hot-springs devotees suggest this general regimen.

If there's a sauna, start with a nice steam for about 15 minutes to open your pores; otherwise, have a few minutes' soak in a warm pool. Then get dirty – squish your hands into the basin of gray volcanic mud (never directly from the pools themselves, which could ruin the experience by burning the flesh off your hands) and apply liberally, avoiding the eye area. Find a spot to relax and let the mud dry on your skin for 10 to 15 minutes before rinsing off under a hot shower and/or having a good soak in the hot pools (the recommended duration depends on the location of the hot springs). Ending with a brave dip in a cold pool, if there is one, not only recharges you in a big way but also sends a healthy jolt of blood to your internal organs.

Before getting into hot water – the thermal kind, at least – remove any silver jewelry to prevent it from oxidizing and turning black.

---

plex in the area, with seven thermal pools that are connected by all manner of waterslides, heated rivers, waterfalls and faux-stone bridges. There are also a playground, soccer field and picnic tables; the busy restaurant-bar (mains US$4 to US$10) is housed in a 170-year-old colonial cabin furnished with museum-worthy period pieces. Guests who stay in the log-cabin rooms (per person adult/child US$22/11) have free access to the pools during their stay, with TV and cold-water bathrooms (neatly counterbalancing the lack of cold-water pools).

El Guayacán (☎ 2673 0349; www.termaleselguayacan .com; adult/child US$4/2), whose hissing vents and mud pots (absolutely stay on the trail!) are on the family finca, lie just behind Thermo Manía. With its five thermal pools and one cold pool in front of its simple, cold-water cabinas (adult/child US$18/11), this unpretentious place has a mellow, family vibe to it. There's an onsite restaurant (mains US$2 to US$6).

Nearby **Yökö Hot Springs** (☎ 2673 0410; www .yokotermales.com; adult/child US$5/3; 7am-11pm) has four hot springs with a small waterslide and waterfall, set in an attractive meadow at the foot of Miravalles. The 12 elegant cabinas (single/double with breakfast US$50/77) have huge bathrooms and gleaming wood floors. Extra amenities include a Jacuzzi, sauna and a relaxed restaurant (mains US$2 to US$10) serving everything from burgers to filet mignon.

For some local flavor, the more far-flung **Thermales Miravalles** (☎ 8358 4586, 8305 4072; adult/ child US$2.50/1.50) has two pools and lies along a thermal stream. The owners have set up a small restaurant and offer camping (per person US$6) on the property. They're usually open on weekends year-round, and daily during high season.

On the southern slopes of Miravalles, **Las Hornillas** (☎ 8839 9769; www.lashornillas.com; admission US$15; 9am-5pm) is the center of volcanic activity in the area. The entrance fee includes an informative tour around the small crater (again, stay on the trail, kids) and allows you to soak in the thermal pools. This wonderfully isolated, family-run spot also offers hiking tours (US$25) via hanging bridges to a waterfall, including lunch and access to the mud and pools.

Near the base of the volcano is the newly opened **Centro de Aventuras** (☎ 2673 0697; www .volcanoadventuretour.com), which has a number of offerings including a canopy tour (without/ with lunch US$20/28), rappelling (US$10), horse riding (US$25 to US$50), and a guided tour through a nearby macadamia-nut farm (US$40). The clean, brightly painted cabinas (double US$30) have private hot-water bathrooms and are centered on a pool that's fed by mountain springwater; camping (US$5) is also available, with access to showers and bathrooms. This is a good place to inquire about local guides who can take you on independent tours, eg a two-day hike to the summit of Miravalles.

Volcán Miravalles is 27km northeast of Bagaces and can be approached by a paved road that leads north of Bagaces through the communities of Salitral and Torno, where the road splits. From the left-hand fork, you'll reach **Guayabo**, with a few *sodas* and basic cabinas; to the right, you'll find **Fortuna** (not to be confused with La Fortuna), with easier access to the hot springs. Both towns are small population centers, and are not of much interest to travelers. The roads reconnect north of the two towns and toward Upala, and also make a great scenic loop. Though the region is relatively remote, it's well served by buses from Bagaces.

BAGACES

This small town is about 22km northwest of Cañas on the Interamericana, and is the headquarters of the **Area de Conservación Tempisque** (ACT; ☎ 2200 0125; ⓨ 8am-4pm Mon-Fri), which, in conjunction with Minae, administers Parque Nacional Palo Verde, Reserva Biológica Lomas de Barbudal, and several smaller and lesser-known protected areas. The office is on the Interamericana opposite the signed main entry road into Parque Nacional Palo Verde. The office is mainly an administrative one, though sometimes rangers are available. Any buses between Cañas and Liberia can drop you off in Bagaces. If you're heading to Miravalles, there are hourly local buses to both Fortuna and Guayabo.

If you have your own car, 3km south of Bagaces on the road to Palo Verde is the turnoff for **Llano de Cortés**, a hidden waterfall that's free to enter and perfect for an afternoon swim. Follow the dirt road for about 1.5km until you reach the small parking area.

PARQUE NACIONAL PALO VERDE

The 18,417-hectare Parque Nacional Palo Verde is a wetland sanctuary in Costa Rica's driest province that lies on the northeastern banks of the mouth of Río Tempisque at the head of the Golfo de Nicoya. All of the major rivers in the region drain into this ancient intersection of two basins, which creates a mosaic of habitats, including mangrove swamps, marshes, grassy savannahs and evergreen forests. A number of low limestone hills provide lookout points over the park, and the park's shallow, permanent lagoons are focal points for wildlife.

The park derives its name from the *palo verde* (green tree), which is a small shrub that's green year-round and abundant within the park. The park is also contiguous in the north with the 7354-hectare Refugio de Vida Silvestre Dr Rafael Lucas Rodríguez Caballero and the Reserva Biológica Lomas de Barbudal (opposite), which, along with Parque Nacional Barra Honda (p286), make up part of the **Area de Conservación Tempisque**, a large conservation area containing some of the remaining strands of dry tropical forest. A recent addition to this project was Refugio do Vida Silvestre

Cipancí, which protects the corridors linking the various parks from being clear-cut by local farmers.

Palo Verde has the greatest concentrations of waterfowl and shorebirds in Central America, and over 300 different bird species have been recorded in the park. Birders come particularly to see the large flocks of heron (including the rare black-crowned night heron), stork (including the endangered jabirú stork), spoonbill, egret, ibis, grebe and duck, and forest birds, including scarlet macaw, great curassow, keel-billed toucan, and parrot are also common. Frequently sighted mammals include deer, coati, armadillo, monkey and peccary, as well as the largest population of jaguarundi in Costa Rica. There are also numerous reptiles in the wetlands including crocodiles that are reportedly up to 5m in length.

The dry season, from December to March, is the best time to visit as flocks of birds tend to congregate in the remaining lakes and marshes and the trees lose their leaves, thus allowing for clearer viewing. However, the entire basin swelters during the dry season, so bring adequate sun protection. There are also far fewer insects in the dry season, and mammals are occasionally seen around the water holes. Take binoculars or a spotting scope if possible. During the wet months, large portions of the area are flooded, and access may be limited.

Orientation & Information

The **park entrance** (☎ 2200 0125; admission US$6; ⓨ 8am-4pm) is 28km along the turnoff from the Interamericana near the town of Bagaces. However, your best source of information on the park is the Hacienda Palo Verde Research Station (opposite). There is a fairly extensive system of roads and hiking trails that originate from the park entrance and lead to a series of lookout points and observation towers.

Tours

To fully appreciate the size and topography of the park, it's worth organizing a boat trip. Travelers recommend the **guided tours** (2/3/4 people half-day US$35/60/75) that can be arranged through the Hacienda Palo Verde Research Station. The station also offers **birding tours** (half-/full day per person US$38/30) through the park. Tour operators in San José and La Fortuna run package tours to

Palo Verde, but you'll save money by arranging everything yourself.

Sleeping & Eating

Overnight visitors should make reservations and must also pay the US$6 entry fee.

Camping (per person US$4) is permitted near the Palo Verde ranger station, where toilets and hot-water showers are available. Meals and box lunches (US$12) are available at the OTS research station by advance arrangement.

Hacienda Palo Verde Research Station (☎ 524-0607; www.ots.ac.cr; s/d incl meals US$65/124) Run by the Organization of Tropical Studies (OTS), this station conducts tropical research and teaches university graduate-level classes. Researchers and those taking OTS courses get preference for dormitories with shared bathrooms. A few two- and four-bed rooms with shared bathrooms are also available. The rates for visitors include a guided hike. The research station is on a well-signed road 8km from the park entrance.

Getting There & Away

The main road to the entrance, usually passable to ordinary cars year-round, begins from a signed turnoff from the Interamericana, opposite Bagaces. The 28km gravel road has tiny brown signs that usually direct you when the road forks, but if in doubt, take the fork that looks more used. Another 8km brings you to the limestone hill, Cerro Guayacán (and the Hacienda Palo Verde Research Station), from where there are great views; 2km further are the Palo Verde park headquarters and ranger station. You can drive through a swampy maze of roads to the Reserva Biológica Lomas de Barbudal without returning to the Interamericana.

Buses connecting Cañas and Liberia can drop you at the ACT office, opposite the turnoff to the park. If you call the ACT office in advance, rangers may be able to pick you up in Bagaces. If you're staying at the Hacienda Palo Verde Research Station, the staff can also arrange to pick you up in Bagaces.

RESERVA BIOLÓGICA LOMAS DE BARBUDAL

The 2646-hectare Lomas de Barbudal reserve forms a cohesive unit with Palo Verde, and protects several species of endangered trees, such as mahogany and rosewood, as well as the common and quite spectacular *corteza*

amarilla. This tree is what biologists call a 'big bang reproducer' – all the yellow cortezes in the forest burst into bloom on the same day, and for about four days the forest is an incredible mass of yellow-flowered trees. This usually occurs in March, about four days after an unseasonal rain shower.

Nearly 70% of the trees in the reserve are deciduous, and during the dry season they shed their leaves as if it were autumn in a temperate forest. This particular habitat is known as tropical dry forest, and occurs in climates that are warm year-round, though characterized by a long dry season that lasts several months. Since plants lose moisture through their leaves, the shedding of leaves allows the trees to conserve water during dry periods. The newly bare trees also open up the canopy layer, enabling sunlight to reach ground level and facilitate the growth of thick underbrush. Dry forests were once common in many parts of the Pacific slopes of Central America, but little remains. Dry forests also exist north and south of the equatorial rainforest belt, especially in southern Mexico and the Bolivian lowlands.

Lomas de Barbudal is also known for its abundant and varied wasps, butterflies, moths and other insects. There are about 250 different species of bee in this fairly small reserve – representing about a quarter of the world's bee species. Bees here include the Africanized 'killer' bees – if you suffer from bee allergies, this is one area where you really don't want to forget your bee-sting kit.

There are more than 200 bird species, including the great curassow, a chickenlike bird that is hunted for food and is endangered, as well as other endangered species including the king vulture, scarlet macaw and jabirú stork. Much like Palo Verde, Lomas de Barbudal is also home to a variety of mammal species as well as some enormous crocodiles – you might want to leave your swim trunks at home.

Orientation & Information

At the reserve entrance, there's a small **information center** (☎ 2671 1029, 2237 7039; reserve admission US$2; ☉ 7am-4pm), though the actual reserve is on the other side of the Río Cabuyo, behind the museum. The infrastructure of the park is less geared to tourists than at Palo Verde, though there is a small network of hiking trails that radiates from the information center. A small map is provided. It is not possible to

overnight in the park and backcountry hiking
is not permitted.

Getting There & Away
The turnoff to Lomas de Barbudal from the
Interamericana is near the small community
of Pijije, 14km southeast of Liberia or 12km
northwest of Bagaces. It's 7km to the entrance
of the reserve. The road is unpaved, but open
all year – some steep sections may require
4WD in rainy season. Buses between Liberia
and Cañas can drop you at the turnoff to
the reserve.

LIBERIA
Well, the secret's out. Before the boom in
Costa Rican tourism, deciphering the bus
timetables and fighting your way through
the crowds at the Coca-Cola terminal in San
José was a rite of passage for the uninitiated
traveler. Even just a few years ago, getting to
the beaches on the Península de Nicoya took
determination, patience and – depending on
the state of Costa Rica's dreadful roads – a
little luck. These days, though, travelers are
getting their first glimpse of *pura vida* Costa
Rica at Liberia's own Aeropuerto Internacional
Daniel Oduber Quirós, which is roughly the
size of a Wal-Mart parking lot, but more of a
breeze to exit.

Previously, the sunny capital of Guanacaste
served as a transportation hub connecting
Liberia with both borders, as well as the standard bearer of Costa Rica's *sabanero* culture
(see boxed text, p204). Even today, a large part
of the greater Liberia area is involved in ranching operations, but tourism is fast becoming
a significant contributor to the economy.
Liberia has long been a base for visiting the
nearby volcanoes, national parks and beaches,
and nowadays the sight of gringos heading for
their second homes in Tamarindo, or surfers
toting their boards, is commonplace.

For now, Liberia is a much safer and surprisingly chill alternative to San José, although
the government is looking to expand the airport in several years, with an eye to accommodating as much traffic, or more, as Juan
Santamaría airport. A brand-new Hilton was
slated to open by this book's publication, and
the Guanacaste Country Club, complete with
18-hole golf course and a gated community,
is also under construction.

Liberia is still a great base for exploring
the attractions in the northwest and the
beaches of the Península de Nicoya. And,
though most of the historic buildings in
the city center are a little rough around the
edges and in desperate need of a paint job,
the 'white city' is a pleasant one, with a good
range of accommodations and services for
travelers on all budgets.

Information
INTERNET ACCESS
Cyberm@nia (☎ 2666 7240; Av 1 btwn Calles 2 & Central; per hr US$1; ☺ 8am-10pm) With the friendliest staff
ever, this spot is also good for cheap long-distance calls,
charging US$0.25 a minute to most parts of the world.
Planet Internet (☎ 2665 3737; Calle Central btwn
Avs Central & 2; per hr US$1; ☺ 8am-10pm) Has speedy
machines in a spacious, frigidly air-conditioned room; also
offers internet calls.

MEDICAL SERVICES
Hospital Dr Enrique Baltodano Briceño (☎ 2666
0011, emergencies 2666 0318) Behind the stadium on the
northeastern outskirts of town.

MONEY
Most hotels will accept US dollars, and may
be able to change small amounts. If not,
Liberia probably has more banks per square
meter than any other town in Costa Rica.
BAC San José (☎ 2666 2020; Centro Comercial Santa
Rosa; ☺ 9am-6pm Mon-Fri, 9am-1pm Sat) Changes
traveler's checks; try this 24-hour ATM if others won't
accept your card.
Banco de Costa Rica (☎ 2666 2582; cnr Calle Central
& Av 1) Has a 24-hour ATM.
Banco Nacional (☎ 2666 0191; Av 25 de Julio btwn
Calles 6 & 8; ☺ 8am-3:45pm Mon-Fri, 9am-1pm Sat) Has
a 24-hour ATM.

TOURIST INFORMATION
**Sabanero Art Market & Tourist Information
Center** (☎ 2666 2183; www.elsabanero.8k.com; Calle 2
btwn Avs Central & 2) Travelers seeking guidance will be
best off here. It has bus schedules, information on tours
and lodging, and will arrange taxi pick-ups.
Tourist office (☎ 2666 4527; cnr Av 6 & Calle 1) Has
hours that remain a mystery. One local explained it this
way: 'Sometimes it's open. Sometimes it's closed.'

Sights & Activities
Though there's not much of historical or
cultural interest in town, the lack of sights
gives you an excuse to relax in one of the
local restaurants or bars as you plan your
next trip to a beach or volcano.

The tourist office has a tiny **museum** of local ranching artifacts – cattle-raising is a historically important occupation in Guanacaste. There has also been talk of reopening a museum of *sabanero* culture in **La Gobernación**, the old municipal building at the corner of Avenida Central and Calle Central.

In the meantime, a **statue** of a steely eyed *sabanero*, complete with an evocative poem by Rodolfo Salazar Solórzano, stands watch over Avenida 25 de Julio, the main street into town. The blocks around the intersection of Avenida Central and Calle Central contain several of the town's oldest houses, many dating back about 150 years.

The pleasant Parque Central frames a modern church, **Iglesia Inmaculada Concepción**

de María. The park is also the seasonal hangout of the Nicaraguan grackle, a tone-deaf bird that enjoys eating parrot eggs and annoying passers-by with its grating calls.

Walking six blocks northeast of the park along Avenida Central brings you to the oldest church in town, popularly called **La Agonía** (although maps show it as La Iglesia de la Ermita de la Resurrección). Strolling to La Agonía and around the surrounding blocks makes a fine walk.

Tours

Hotel Liberia and La Posada del Tope (p212) are great budget hotels that can organize trips and tours throughout Costa Rica. La Posada del Tope has the best deals on rental cars.

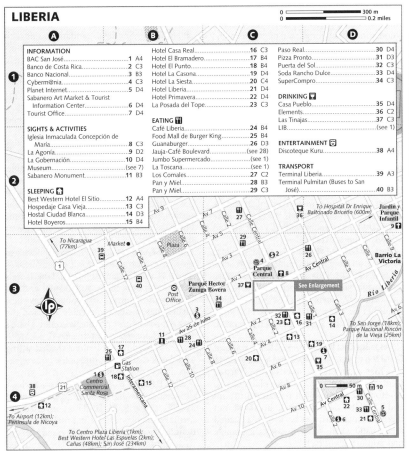

LIBERIA

0 _____ 300 m
0 _____ 0.2 miles

INFORMATION
BAC San José....................................1 A4
Banco de Costa Rica.........................2 C3
Banco Nacional.................................3 B3
Cyber@nia..4 C3
Planet Internet..................................5 D4
Sabanero Art Market & Tourist
    Information Center..........................6 D4
Tourist Office....................................7 D4

SIGHTS & ACTIVITIES
Iglesia Inmaculada Concepción de
    María..8 C3
La Agonía...9 D2
La Gobernación...............................10 D4
Museum.......................................(see 7)
Sabanero Monument........................11 B3

SLEEPING
Best Western Hotel El Sitio...............12 A4
Hospedaje Casa Vieja.......................13 C3
Hostal Ciudad Blanca.......................14 D3
Hotel Boyeros..................................15 B4

Hotel Casa Real...............................16 C3
Hotel El Bramadero..........................17 B4
Hotel El Punto..................................18 B4
Hotel La Casona..............................19 D4
Hotel La Siesta.................................20 C4
Hotel Liberia....................................21 D4
Hotel Primavera...............................22 D4
La Posada del Tope..........................23 C3

EATING
Café Liberia.....................................24 B4
Food Mall de Burger King................25 B4
Guanaburger....................................26 D3
Jauja-Café Boulevard...................(see 28)
Jumbo Supermercado...................(see 1)
La Toscana...................................(see 1)
Los Comales....................................27 C4
Pan y Miel.......................................28 B3
Pan y Miel.......................................29 C3

Paso Real...30 D4
Pizza Pronto.....................................31 D3
Puerta del Sol..................................32 D4
Soda Rancho Dulce..........................33 D4
SuperCompro...................................34 C3

DRINKING
Casa Pueblo.....................................35 D4
Elements..36 C2
Las Tinajas.......................................37 C3
LIB..(see 1)

ENTERTAINMENT
Discoteque Kuru..............................38 A4

TRANSPORT
Terminal Liberia...............................39 A3
Terminal Pulmitan (Buses to San
    José)...40 B3

Sleeping

Liberia is at its busiest during the dry season – reservations are strongly recommended over Christmas, Easter, Día de Guanacaste and on weekends. During the wet season, however, most of the midrange and top-end hotels give discounts.

Note that although streets are labeled on the map, very few of them are signed, especially once you get away from Parque Central (see boxed text, p537).

BUDGET

Hotel Liberia (☎ 2666 0161; www.hotelliberia.com; Calle Central btwn Avs Central & 2; s with/without bathroom US$19/11, d with/without bathroom US$22/18; P) Rooms in this rambling, century-old building surround an outdoor lounge complete with TV, hammocks, and jet-lagged backpackers chatting about their past and present travel plans. Rooms are tidy and bright but pretty basic, and a buffet breakfast is available for US$3. The hotel is recommended for its vibrant atmosphere that's in part created by the Peruvian manager Beto, who's an absolute riot.

La Posada del Tope (☎ 2666 3876; www.posada deltope.com; Calle Central btwn Avs Central & 2; r per person US$5-17; P ✗ 🖳) This budget hotel is housed in an attractive mid-19th-century house that's decorated with old photos, antiques and mosquito nets, and has a bit of an old-plantation feel to it. Rooms have shared bathrooms and are fairly basic, though the hotel is recommended as the bilingual Tico owner, Denís, is a wealth of information. The annex across the street, Hotel Casa Real, has slightly nicer rooms with TV, set around a lovely little courtyard.

Hotel La Casona (☎ 2666 2971; casona@racsa.co.cr; cnr Calle Central & Av 6; s/d with fan US$16/24, with air-con US$20/30; P 🖳) This pink, wooden house has simple rooms with private bathrooms and cable TV. There's no hot water (which shouldn't be an issue), and there is also an apartment at the same rates per person as the rooms.

Hospedaje Casa Vieja (☎ 2665 5826; Av 4 btwn Calles Central & 2; s/d with fan US$18/22, with air-con US$36/44; 🖳) Just a couple of blocks from Parque Central, this quiet, home-like place has 10 comfortable rooms with private bathroom and TV. Rates do not include breakfast, but there's a small yard out back with a shaded raised patio where you can enjoy the granola that you bring yourself.

MIDRANGE & TOP END

Hotel Primavera (☎ 2666 0464; Av Central btwn Calles Central & 2; s/d with fan US$30/42, with air-con US$34/47; P 🖳) Just off Parque Central but set back from the street a bit, rooms at this small hotel are a little worn, but they have attractive wood accents and come furnished with microwave, cable TV and private cold showers. Not the best value in town, but perfectly OK.

Hostal Ciudad Blanca (☎ 2666 3962; Av 4 btwn Calles 1 & 3; s/d with fan US$30/40, with air-con US$35/45; P 🖳) One of Liberia's most attractive hotels is in a historic colonial mansion that has been completely refurbished. Tree-shaded rooms have air-con, fan, cable TV, nice furnishings and private hot-water bathroom. The charming little restaurant-bar downstairs is perfect for a nightcap – or a game of pinball.

Hotel La Siesta (☎ 2666 0678; lasiestaliberia@hot mail.com; Calle 4 btwn Avs 4 & 6; s/d incl breakfast US$40/50; P 🖳 🖳 🖳) Spotless, standard rooms with cable TV and private cold showers are arranged around a pretty poolside garden. Rooms upstairs are slightly larger, but all are very quiet and the place has a relaxed feel. The real reason to stop by, however, is the attached restaurant (meals US$4 to US$7), which is regarded by locals as having the best casado in town.

Hotel El Bramadero (☎ 2666 0371; www.hotel elbramadero.com; cnr Interamericana & Hwy 21; s/d US$40/58; P 🖳 🖳 🖳) El Bramadero is a comfortable, midrange hotel that has well-appointed rooms with air-con, hot showers and cable TV. It has a *sabanero* theme, so it follows that the restaurant (meals US$10 to US$16) has some of the thickest and juiciest steaks you've ever feasted on.

Hotel Boyeros (☎ 2666 0722, 2666 0809; www.hotel boyeros.com; cnr Interamericana & Av 2; s/d/tr US$56/68/74; P ✗ 🖳 🖳) The largest hotel in Liberia feels like a cross between a dude ranch and the Holiday Inn. Immaculate rooms all have new furnishings, air-con and cable TV, and the upstairs rooms have private balconies. There's also a 24-hour restaurant, free wi-fi, pool with waterslide, kiddie pool and a shaded sitting area. Look for the sculpture of the *boyero* (oxcart driver) out front.

Hotel El Punto (☎ 2665 2986; www.elpuntohotel.com; Interamericana btwn Avs 25 de Julio & 2; s/d/tr/q incl breakfast US$70/90/100/110; P 🖳 🖳) This converted elementary school is now a chic hotel, and would definitely feel more at home in trendy Miami than in humble Guanacaste. The saturated tropical colors of the loft apartments manage also to be understated and minimalist. All rooms have beautifully tiled bathrooms, kitchenettes, hammocks, free wi-fi and colorful modern art. The common area features low outdoor sofas and even crayons for the kids, and unsurprisingly, the bilingual architect-owner Mariana is charm personified.

Not one, but two, Best Western Hotels are available for all your overpriced chain-hotel needs.

Best Western Hotel Las Espuelas (☎ 2666 0144; espuelas@racsa.co.cr; s/d incl breakfast US$70/81, ste US$151; P ✗ ✗ ⬚ ⬚ ⬚) About 2km south of Liberia, this has all the standard amenities and generic rooms you'd expect.

Best Western Hotel El Sitio (☎ 2666 1211; htlsitio@ racsa.co.cr; s/d incl breakfast US$70/81; P ✗ ✗ ⬚ ⬚ ⬚) On the road to Nicoya, this one is closer to town.

Eating

Food Mall de Burger King (cnr Interamericana & Hwy 21; 7am-1pm) Yearning for the gringo-style fast-food you left behind? Don't worry, it's followed you to Costa Rica: this food mall houses Burger King, Church's Chicken, Papa John's Pizza, Subway, TCBY and Pizza Hut.

Café Liberia (☎ 2665 1660; www.cafeliberia.com; Calle 8 btwn Avs 25 de Julio & 2; snacks US$1-3; 8:30am-7:30pm Mon-Fri, 10am-6pm Sat & holidays; ✗ ⬚) Run by a sweet Tica named Radha, this hip spot is a dream, serving organic juices, Costa Rican coffee, fresh sandwiches, pastries, wines and lots of vegetarian items. Plus, there's free wi-fi and sometimes live music.

Guanaburger (cnr Calle 3 & Av 1; burger, fries & drink combo US$2.50; noon-2:30pm & 5:30-10pm) This famous homegrown institution packs in the locals with its US$2.50 bargain combo.

Soda Rancho Dulce (Calle Central btwn Avs Central & 2; mains US$2-4; breakfast, lunch & dinner) Sometimes a casado is more than a casado, and this outstanding open-air soda, with groovy wooden tables and good batidos, serves some of the best.

Los Comales (Calle Central btwn Avs 7 & 5; plates US$2-5; 6:30-9pm) This convivial, popular local spot is run by a women's collective, and serves native Guanacaste dishes as well as typical cuisine. The specialty is chicken and salsa, but the casados are just as tasty.

Pan y Miel (☎ 2666 0718; Av 25 de Julio btwn Calles 10 & 8; mains US$2-5; 6am-6pm) The best breakfast in town can be had at this branch of the local bakery, which serves its excellent

bread as sandwiches and French toast, as well as offering a buffet line with casado fixings, pastries and fresh fruit. There's a surlier bakery-only branch a block north of Parque Central.

Jauja-Café Boulevard (☎ 2665 2061; Calle 25 de Junio btwn Calles 10 & 8; mains US$3-9; breakfast, lunch & dinner) A German bakery with beautifully flaky croissants, a respectably authentic sushi counter doing what it can with the local rice and an international kitchen turning out Euro-style numbers can all be found at this corner spot. The patio is also a great place for a beer under the canopy of the huge guanacaste tree.

Pizza Pronto (☎ 2666 2098; cnr Av 4 & Calle 1; mains US$5-9; lunch & dinner) Situated in a handsome 19th-century house, this romantic pizzeria is in a class of its own. You can choose from a long list of toppings for your wood-fired pizza, including fresh, local seafood or pineapple; the pastas are just as tasty.

ourpick Puerta del Sol (cnr Calle Central & Av 2; mains US$5-7; noon-3pm & 6-10pm) Peruvian-style ceviche is the bomb at this four-table establishment, done up in blue and deliciousness. In addition to the specialty of the house, there are interesting corn-based desserts and drinks, like the refreshing, nonalcoholic chicha morada. And if you're with someone special, you might consider one of the aphrodisiac dishes, like the leche de tigre (tiger's milk), made from seafood and tantalizingly secret ingredients.

La Toscana (☎ 2665 0653; Centro Comercial Santa Rosa; mains US$4-13; noon-11pm; ✗) Satisfy those pangs for gnocchi or spaghetti carbonara at one of the most authentically Italian restaurants in the region. Tuscan wine, tablecloths and tiramisu await.

Paso Real (☎ 2666 3455; Av Central btwn Calles Central & 2; mains US$6-20; 11am-10pm) Liberia's most famous restaurant has a breezy balcony overlooking Parque Central, and is locally known for its inventive cuisine, like sea bass served in a cream sauce of puréed spinach.

Liberia has many inexpensive sodas, or you could grab groceries at the **SuperCompro** (Av Central btwn Calles 4 & 6; 8am-8pm Mon-Fri, to 6pm Sat & Sun). For a good selection of international groceries, including tahini, Argentinean wine and curry paste, stop by the **Jumbo Supermercado** (Centro Comercial Santa Rosa), conveniently located at the intersection, to load up on supplies before heading to the beach.

lonelyplanet.com

Drinking

Despite the recent tourist influx, Liberia is short on nightlife. There are a number of local spots where you can get hammered for under US$10.

Las Tinajas (Calle 2 btwn Avs Central & 1; ☺ lunch & dinner) Sip a cold beer and nosh on some greasy fries at this parkside pub, an ideal place to people-watch the happenings in Parque Central. It occasionally has live music.

Casa Pueblo (Calle Central btwn Avs 6 & 8; ☺ 5:30-10pm) This cool little bar is housed in an old Spanish colonial building, and is a good place to meet the local hipsters.

Elements (Calle 3 btwn Avs 5 & 3) Probably the priciest and definitely the sleekest bar in Liberia, the theme is based on the four elements (earth, wind, alcohol and lounge sofas…no, wait…).

LIB, housed upstairs in the Centro Comercial Santa Rosa, is a newish hot spot attracting locals and tourists. It occasionally hosts live music, and you may have to pay admission on weekends.

Entertainment

Cultural offerings are unfortunately slim to none in Liberia. Your best chance of seeing Punto Guanacasteco is to be in town for a *tope* (p204).

Cinema (Centro Plaza Liberia) If you're looking for your Hollywood fix, this has a decent offering of mainstream American films.

Discoteque Kuru (Av 25 de Julio) Across from the Best Western El Sitio, lets the DJs do their thing Thursday through Sunday nights.

Getting There & Away

AIR

Since 1993, Aeropuerto Internacional Daniel Oduber Quirós (LIR), 12km west of Liberia, has served as the country's second international airport, providing easy access to all those beautiful beaches without the hassle of dealing with the lines and bustle of San José. It's a tiny airport, jam-packed with increasing traffic; all international flights are through the USA, though there's talk of starting direct flights to Europe.

NatureAir and Sansa both make multiple daily runs between Liberia and San José, with connections all over the country, for about US$90 one way, US$185 round-trip.

There are no car-rental desks at the airport; make reservations in advance, and your company will meet you at the airport with a car. You'll find a money-exchange, café and gift shop. Taxis to Liberia cost US$10.

At the time of writing the first six airlines listed were the only ones that flew direct into and out of Liberia from the USA.

American Airlines (☎ 800-421 7300; www.aa.com) Flights to/from Miami, Florida.

Continental (☎ 800-231 0856; www.continental.com) To/from Houston, Texas.

Delta (☎ 800-241 4141; www.delta.com) To/from Atlanta, Georgia.

NatureAir (☎ 2220 3054; www.natureair.com) To/from San José.

Northwest Airlines (☎ 800-800 1504; www.nwa.com) To/from Minneapolis, Minnesota.

Sansa (☎ 2668 1047; www.flysansa.com) To/from San José.

United Airlines (☎ 800-538 2929; www.united.com) To/from Chicago, Illinois.

US Airways (☎ 800-622 1015; www.usairways.com) To/from Charlotte, North Carolina.

BUS

Buses arrive and depart from **Terminal Liberia** (Av 7 btwn Calles 12 & 14) and **Terminal Pulmitan** (Av 5 btwn Calles 10 & 12). Routes, fares, journey times and departures are as follows:

Cañas US$1.20, 1½ hours, departs Terminal Liberia 5:30am, 6:45am, 7:30am, noon, 1:30pm, 4:30pm and 5:30pm. It's quicker to jump off the San José–bound bus in Cañas.

La Cruz/Peñas Blancas US$1.25, 1½ to two hours, departs Pulmitan 5:30am, 8:30am, 9am, noon, 1pm, 3pm, 5pm and 6:30pm.

Managua, Nicaragua US$10, five hours, departs Pulmitan 8:30am, 9:30am and 1pm (buy tickets one day in advance).

Nicoya, via Filadelfia & Santa Cruz US$1.15, 1½ hours, 15 departures from Terminal Liberia from 6:30am to 7:30pm.

Playa del Coco US$0.75, one hour, departs Pulmitan 5:30am, 7am, 9:30am, 11am, 12:30pm, 2:30pm, 4:30pm and 6:30pm.

Playa Hermosa, Playa Panamá US$1.30, 1¼ hours, departs Terminal Liberia 5:30am, 7:30am, 11:30am, 1pm, 3:30pm, 5:30pm and 7:30pm.

Playa Tamarindo US$0.90, 1½ to two hours, departs Terminal Liberia 3:50am, 6:10am, 8:10am, 10am, 11:10am, 12:45pm and 4:10pm.

Puntarenas US$2.25, three hours, seven services from 5am to 3:30pm. It's quicker to jump off the San José–bound bus in Puntarenas.

San José US$3.70, four hours, 11 departures from Pulmitan from 4am to 8pm.

CAR

Liberia lies on the Interamericana, 234km north of San José and 77km south of the Nicaraguan border post of Peñas Blancas. Hwy 21, the main artery of the Península de Nicoya, begins in Liberia and heads southwest. A dirt road, passable to all cars in dry season (4WD is preferable), leads 25km from Barrio la Victoria to the Santa María entrance of Parque Nacional Rincón de la Vieja; the gravel road to the Las Pailas entrance begins from the Interamericana, 5km north of Liberia (passable to regular cars, but 4WD is recommended).

There are several rental-car agencies in the region (none of which have desks at the airport) that charge about the same amount as those in San José. Most can arrange pick-up in Liberia and drop-off in San José, though they'll try to charge you extra. Rental agencies are on Hwy 21 between Liberia and the airport, but should be able to drop off your car in town. La Posada de Tope (p212) arranges the cheapest car rental in Liberia. At last count, there were upwards of 30 car-rental agencies in Liberia, but here are a few of the more popular ones:

Adobe (☎ 2667 0608; www.adobecar.com)
Avis (☎ 2668 1196; www.avis.co.cr)
Budget (☎ 2668 1024; www.budget.com)
Dollar (☎ 2668 1061; www.dollarcostarica.com)
Economy Rent-A-Car (☎ 2666 2816; www.economy rentacar.com)
Europcar (☎ 2668 1023; www.europcar.co.cr)
Hola (☎ 2667 4040; www.hola.net)
Mapache (☎ 2665 4444; www.mapache.com)
National (☎ 2666 5595; www.natcar.com)
Payless (☎ 2667 0511; www.paylesscr.com)
Toyota Rent a Car (☎ 2666 8190; www.carrental -toyota-costarica.com)
Tricolor (☎ 2665 5555; www.tricolorcarrental.com)

PARQUE NACIONAL RINCÓN DE LA VIEJA

Given its proximity to Liberia – really just a hop, skip and a few bumps away – this 14,161-hectare national park feels refreshingly uncrowded and remote. Named after the active Volcán Rincón de la Vieja (1895m), the steamy main attraction, the park also covers several other peaks in the same volcanic range, including the highest, Volcán Santa María (1916m). The park breathes geothermal energy, which you can see for yourself in its multihued fumaroles, hot springs, lively *pailas* (mud pots) bubbling and blooping clumps of

ashy gray mud, and a young and feisty *volcancito* (small volcano). All these can be visited on foot and horseback on well-maintained but sometimes-steep trails.

The park was created in 1973 to protect the 32 rivers and streams that have their sources within the park, an important watershed. Its relatively remote location means that wildlife, rare elsewhere, is out in force here, with the major volcanic crater a rather dramatic backdrop to the scene. Volcanic activity has occurred many times since the late 1960s, with the most recent eruption of steam and ash in 1997. At the moment, however, the volcano is gently active and does not present any danger – ask locally for the latest, as it's in their nature for volcanoes to act up.

Elevations in the park range from less than 600m to 1916m, so visitors pass through a variety of different habitats as they ascend the volcanoes, though the majority of the trees in the park are typical of those found in dry tropical forests throughout Guanacaste. One interesting tree to look out for is the strangler fig, a parasitic tree that covers the host tree with its own trunk and proceeds to strangle it by competing for water, light and nutrients. The host tree eventually dies and rots away, while the strangler fig survives as a hollow, tubular lattice. The park is also home to the country's highest density of Costa Rica's national flower, the increasingly rare purple orchid *(Cattleya skinneri),* locally known as *guaria morada.*

Most visitors to the park, however, are here for the hot springs, where you can soak to the sound of howler monkeys overhead. Many of the springs are reported to have therapeutic properties, which is always a good thing if you've been hitting the Guaro Cacique a little too hard. Several lodges just outside the park provide access and arrange tours. You can also book transportation and tours directly from Liberia.

Orientation & Information

Each of the two main entrances to the park has its own ranger station, where you sign in and get free maps. Most visitors enter through **Las Pailas ranger station** (☎ 2661 8139; admission US$6; ☼ 7am-5pm, no entry after 3pm, closed Mon) on the western flank. Trails to the summit and the most interesting volcanic features begin here. Note that on the way to Las Pailas, you must pay a fee of US$1.50 for the privilege of passing through the private property of Hacienda Guachipelín. The fee is ostensibly for road maintenance but is fairly ludicrous considering its hotel rates.

The **Santa María ranger station** (☎ 2661 8139; admission US$6; ⊙ 7am-5pm, no entry past 3pm, closed Mon), to the east, is in the Hacienda Santa María, a 19th-century ranch house with a small public exhibit that was reputedly once owned by US President Lyndon Johnson. It's closest to the sulfurous hot springs and also has an observation tower and a nearby waterfall.

Activities

WILDLIFE-WATCHING

The wildlife of the park is extremely varied. Almost 300 species of bird have been recorded here, including curassow, quetzal, bellbird, parrot, toucan, hummingbird, owl, woodpecker, tanager, motmot, dove and eagle.

Insects range from beautiful butterflies to annoying ticks. Be especially prepared for ticks in grassy areas – long trousers tucked into boots and long-sleeved shirts offer some protection. A particularly interesting insect is a highland cicada that burrows into the ground and croaks like a frog, to the bewilderment of naturalists.

Mammals are equally varied; deer, armadillo, peccary, skunk, squirrel, coati and three species of monkey make frequent appearances. Tapir tracks are often found around the lagoons near the summit. Several of the wild cat species have been recorded here, including the jaguar, puma, ocelot and margay, but you'll need patience and good fortune to observe one of these.

HIKING

A circular trail east of Las Pailas (about 3km in total) takes you past the boiling mud pools (Las Pailas), sulfurous fumaroles and a *volcancito* (which may subside at any time). About 700m west of the ranger station along the **Sendero Cangreja** is a swimming hole, which is prescribed for lowering your body temperature after too much time in the hot springs. Further away along the same trail are several waterfalls – the largest, **Catarata La Cangreja**, 5km west, is a classic, dropping straight from a cliff into a small lagoon where you can swim. Dissolved copper salts give the falls a deep blue color. This trail winds through forest, then onto open grassland on the volcano's flanks, where you can enjoy views as far as the Golfo de Nicoya. The slightly smaller **Cataratas Escondidas** (Hidden Waterfalls) are 4.3km west on a different trail.

The longest and most adventurous hike in the area is the 16km round-trip trek to the summit of Rincón de la Vieja and to nearby **Laguna de Jilgueros**, which is reportedly where you may see tapirs – or more likely their footprints, if you are observant. The majority of this hike follows a ridge trail, and is known for being extremely windy and cloudy – come prepared for the weather. It's also advised

---

HOTTEST SPOTS FOR THERMAL POOLS & MUD POTS

Costa Rica's volcano-powered thermal pools and mud pots provide plenty of good, *clean* fun for beauty queens and would-be mud wrestlers alike.

- On the slopes of Volcán Rincon de la Vieja, **Simbiosis Spa** (opposite) has several pools, a wood sauna and quiet vibe, all in a jungle setting.

- While some hot spots around Arenal charge outrageous fees to soak in sparkly surrounds, **Eco-Termales** (p233) maintains its sense of elegance by limiting guest numbers.

- **Las Hornillas** (p207) keeps it real on the southern slope of Volcán Miravalles, with a steaming, bubbling crater you can pick your way around before taking the plunge in its mud pots and hot pools.

- The pinnacle of luxury dirt exists in the remote heights of Rincón de la Vieja at **Hotel Borinquen** (opposite), where, if mineral mud is not your thing, you can opt instead for a wine or chocolate skin treatment.

- Tico-run and family-friendly, **El Guayacán** (p207) has a waterslide, several thermal pools, a trail encircling bubbling mud pots and inexpensive cabinas so you can take your time enjoying it all.

that you hire a guide from the ranger station or a nearby hotel as the trail is dotted with sulfurous hot springs and geysers, and hikers have been severely burned (and occasionally boiled) in the past.

From the Santa María ranger station, a trail leads 2.8km west through the 'enchanted forest' and past a waterfall to sulfurous **hot springs** with supposedly therapeutic properties. Don't soak in them for more than about half an hour (some people suggest much less) without taking a dip in one of the nearby cold springs to cool off. An observation point is 450m east of the station.

SIMBIOSIS SPA

Affiliated with Hacienda Guachipelín, this **spa** (☎ 2666 8075; www.simbiosis-spa.com; admission US$15; ☯ 9am-5:30pm) is also open to the public. With spring-fed hot pools, volcanic mud, a sauna, showers and lounge chairs, all in a natural outdoor setting, this is a lovely place to unwind. You can also arrange massages and spa treatments (US$35 to US$75) on the spot, though it recommends reserving ahead.

Tours

All of the tourist lodges can arrange a number of tours, including horse riding (US$25 to US$35), mountain biking (US$10 to US$30), guided waterfall and hot-springs hikes (US$15 to US$25), rappelling (US$20 to US$50), rafting and tubing on the lesser-known Río Colorado (US$45 to US$60), hanging bridges (US$15 to US$20) and everyone's favorite cash-burner, canopy tours (US$30 to US$50). Rates vary depending on the season, and there are a number of package deals available. If you're staying in Liberia, it's possible to organize these activities in advance either through your hotel, or by contacting the lodges directly.

Sleeping & Eating

INSIDE THE PARK

Both ranger stations have camping (per person US$2). Each campground has water, pit toilets, showers, tables and grills. There is no fuel available, so bring wood, charcoal or a camping stove. Mosquito nets or insect repellent are needed in the wet season, as is a strategy to keep your food secure from persistent, marauding raccoons and coatis.

Camping is allowed in most places within the park, but you should be self-sufficient

and prepared for cold and foggy weather in the highlands – a compass is very useful. The wet season is very wet (October is the rainiest month), and there are plenty of mosquitoes then. Dry-season camping in December, March and April is recommended. January and February are prone to strong winds.

OUTSIDE THE PARK

Note that all of the following are a long way from any eateries, so you're stuck with paying for (usually pricey) meals at your hotel restaurant.

our pick **Rinconcito Lodge** (☎ 2200 0074; www .rinconcitolodge.com; camping per person US$3, s/d/tr/q US$20/35/47/57; **P**) Just 3km from the Santa María sector of the park, this recommended budget option has attractive, rustic cabins with private warm-water showers, and is surrounded by some of the prettiest pastoral scenery imaginable. Meals are available for around US$5 and breakfast isn't complimentary, but it's worth paying for as your eggs and milk come straight from the lodge's farm. Since it primarily caters to budget travelers, it also offers inexpensive local tours. Shuttles travelers to and from Liberia (one way US$20).

Rincón de la Vieja Mountain Lodge (☎ 2200 0238; www.rincondelaviejalodge.net; standard s/d incl breakfast US$45/65, bungalow US$55/75; **P** 🖳 🖭) Closest to the Las Pailas entrance, this rustic hacienda is on 400 hectares of protected land and has 49 spacious standard rooms, some with wildly painted walls or exposed-beam roofs, and even larger cottages with balconies. The electricity is produced by water falling into a turbine, but the ecofriendly power goes out after 10pm (candles are thoughtfully provided). Staff here are utterly charming.

Hacienda Guachipelín (☎ 2666 8075; www.gua chipelin.com; standard s/d/tr incl breakfast US$51/73/93, superior US$66/83/107; **P** 🖳 🖭) On the road to Las Pailas, this appealing, 19th-century working cattle ranch is on 1200 hectares of primary and secondary forest, and has over 100 attractively designed, spacious rooms and suites with private hot-water bathrooms and porches. It has a garden-fringed pool, receives guests at check-in with a welcome drink and has free wi-fi. The only downside (aside from charging all and sundry to cross its property) is that it feels like a factory farm, catering largely to package-tour clientele.

our pick **Hotel Borinquen** (☎ 2690 1900; www.borin quenresort.com; s incl breakfast US$175-357, d US$204-374;

P X 🚼 🛏 🍽 &) If you want to splurge, wallow here. The most luxurious resort in the area features plush, fully air-conditioned bungalows with private deck, minibar and satellite TV. The onsite hot springs, mud baths and natural saunas are beautifully laid out and surrounded by greenery, but a treatment at the unbelievable Anáhuac Spa (treatments US$35 to US$100, open 10am to 6pm), suspended over the river and jungle, is the icing on this decadent mud pie.

Cropping up on the road to the park is an eclectic collection of truly lovely lodges that are worth considering if you've got your own wheels. The following are listed in the order you'll encounter them from Liberia.

Rancho Curubandé Lodge (☎ 2665 0375; www .rancho-curubande.com; s/d/tr incl breakfast US$35/45/55, villa d US$70; P 🚼) Quiet, peaceful finca setting with garden rooms; also has horses for hire.

Canyon de la Vieja Lodge (☎ 2665 5912; www .canyonlodgegte.com; standard s/d/tr/q incl breakfast US$48/69/90/105, bungalows US$65/80/100/120; P 🚼 🍽) Riverside rooms surround a *palapa* (shelter with a thatched, palm-leaf roof and open sides) bar and pool, and the attractive accommodations are a comfortable place to crash after a day of adventure tours.

Posada El Encuentro Lodge (☎ 8848 0616; www .posadaencu.com; r incl breakfast US$75-85, cottage US$105; P 🚼 🍽) A few stylish rooms in the cozy house, plus a stand-alone cottage with five beds; has expansive ocean and volcano views from its isolated orchard locale.

El Sol Verde (☎ 2665 5357; www.elsolverde.com; camping US$5, camping incl tents & bedding US$18, r US$40-60; P) The sweet Dutch couple here in Curubandé village have three lovely stone-floored, wood-walled rooms and a camping area with shared outdoor kitchen.

Casa Rural Aroma de Campo (☎ 2665 0008; www.aromadecampo.com; s/d/tr/q incl breakfast US$55/68/92/111; P 🍽) This serene, epiphyte-hung, hammock-strung oasis has elegantly designed rooms with polished clay floors, open bathrooms, mosquito nets and classy rural sensibility.

Buena Vista Lodge (☎ 2690 1414; www.buenavista lodgecr.com; s/d/tr US$44/59/73, incl breakfast US$51/75/95; P 🍽) On the way to Borinquen, this friendly finca lodge has spring-fed pools, a herpetarium, great views and loads of activities.

Getting There & Away

The Las Pailas sector is accessible via a good, 20km gravel road that begins at a signed turnoff from the Interamericana 5km north of Liberia; a private road is needed to reach the park and costs US$1.50 per person. The Santa

María ranger station, to the east, is accessible via a rougher road beginning at Barrio La Victoria in Liberia. Both roads are passable to regular cars throughout the dry season, but a 4WD is required during the rainy season and is highly recommended at all other times (or it will take you twice as long). There's no public transportation, but any of the lodges (see p217) can arrange transport from Liberia for around US$15 per person each way (two or three people minimum). Alternately, you can hire a 4WD taxi for about US$25 to Las Pailas, or US$45 to Santa María, each way.

PARQUE NACIONAL SANTA ROSA

Among the oldest (established in 1971) and largest national parks in Costa Rica, Santa Rosa's sprawling 38,674 hectares on the Península Santa Elena protects the largest remaining stand of tropical dry forest in Central America, and some of the most important nesting sites of several species of sea turtle. Santa Rosa is also famous among Ticos as a symbol of historical pride – Costa Rica has only been invaded by a foreign army three times, and each time the attackers were defeated in Santa Rosa.

The best known of these events was the Battle of Santa Rosa, which took place on March 20, 1856, when the soon-to-be-self-declared President of Nicaragua, an American named William Walker, invaded Costa Rica. Walker was the head of a group of foreign pirates and adventurers known as the 'Filibusters' that had already seized Baja and southwest Nicaragua, and were attempting to gain control over all of Central America. In a brilliant display of military prowess, Costa Rican President Juan Rafael Mora Porras guessed Walker's intentions, and managed to assemble a ragtag group of fighters that proceeded to surround Walker's army in the main building of the old Hacienda Santa Rosa, known as La Casona. The battle was over in just 14 minutes, and Walker forever driven from Costa Rican soil.

Santa Rosa was again the site of battles between Costa Rican troops and invading forces from Nicaragua in both 1919 and 1955. The first was a somewhat honorable attempt to overthrow the Costa Rican dictator General Federico Tinoco, while the second was a failed coup d'état led by Nicaraguan dictator Anastasio Somoza. Today, you can still see Somoza's abandoned tank, which lies in a ditch beside the road just beyond the entrance to the park. However, the military history surrounding the park didn't end with Somoza, as Santa Rosa was later used as a staging point for the US military during the Sandinistas-Contra War.

Although the park was established mainly due to historical and patriotic reasons, in a surprising coincidence Santa Rosa has also become extremely important to biologists. With its acacia thorn trees and tall *jaragua* grass, first impressions of the park are likely to make you believe you've suddenly landed in the African savannah, though closer inspection reveals more American species of plants, including cacti and bromeliads. Santa Rosa is also home to Playa Nancite, which is famous for its *arribadas* (mass nesting) of olive ridley sea turtles that sometimes number up to 8000 at a single time.

However, a good number of travelers are here for one reason – the chance to surf the near-perfect beach break at Playa Naranjo, which is created by the legendary offshore monolith known as Witch's Rock (also known locally as Roca Bruja). The park is also home to another break of arguably equal fame, namely Ollie's Point, which was immortalized in the film *Endless Summer II,* and is named after US Marine Lieutenant Colonel Oliver North. North is most famous for illegally selling weapons to Iran during the Reagan Era, and using the profits to fund the Contras in Nicaragua – Ollie's Point refers to the nearby troop staging area that everyone but the US Congress knew about.

Difficult access means that Santa Rosa is fairly empty, though it can get reasonably busy on weekends in the dry season when Ticos flock to the park in search of their often-hard-to-find history. In the wet months from July through December, particularly September and October, you'll often have the park virtually to yourself.

Orientation & Information

Parque Nacional Santa Rosa's entrance is on the west side of the Interamericana, 35km north of Liberia and 45km south of the Nicaragua border. The Santa Rosa Sector **park entrance** (☎ 2666 5051; admission US$6, camping per person US$2; ◷ 8am-4pm) is close to the Interamericana, and it's another 7km to park headquarters, with the administrative offices, scientists' quarters, an information

center, a basic campground, museum and nature trail. This office administers the Area de Conservación Guanacaste (ACG).

From this complex, a very rough track leads down to the coast to Playa Naranjo, 12km away. Even during the dry season, this road is only passable to a high-clearance 4WD, and you must sign a waiver at the park entrance stating that you willingly assume all liability for driving this road. The park also requires that you be completely self-sufficient should you choose to undertake the trip, which means bringing *all* your own water and knowing how to do your own car repair. The rangers simply do not have the resources to bail you out or perform vehicle repair if you get into trouble. During the rainy months (May to November), the road is open to hikers and horses but closed to all vehicles; if you want to surf here, it's infinitely easier to gain access to the beach by hiring a boat from Playa del Coco or Tamarindo, further south. Be aware that rangers can and will shut down Playa Nancite to all visitors during the turtle nesting season. From the campsite at Playa Naranjo, it's a 5km hike to the beach. Playa Nancite is generally closed to visitors unless you have permission from the park office.

The park's Sector Murciélago (Bat Sector) encompasses the wild northern coastline of the Península Santa Elena, and is not accessible from the main body of the park. From the Interamericana, continue north past the entrance to the Santa Rosa sector for 10km and then turn left once you pass through the police checkpoint. Continue on this road for a few more kilometers until you reach the village of Cuajiniquíl and then bear left. Continue on this road for another 15km, which will bring you past such historic sights as the former hacienda of the Somoza family (it's currently a training ground for the Costa Rican 'police') and the old airstrip that was used by Oliver North to 'secretly' smuggle goods to the Nicaraguan Contras in the 1980s. Just after the airstrip is the **park entrance** (admission US$6; camping per person US$2; ◷ 8am-4pm), which is in the village of Murciélago. From here, it's another 16km to the isolated white-sand beach of Playa Blanca and the trailhead for the Poza el General watering hole, which attracts birds and animals year-round.

Ollie's Point in Playa Portero Grande is in this sector of the park and can only be reached by boat from Playa del Coco or

Tamarindo. Or you can do as Patrick and Wingnut did in *Endless Summer II* and crash-land your chartered plane on the beach (not actually recommended).

Sights

The historic **La Casona**, the main building of the old Hacienda Santa Rosa, is near the park headquarters in the Santa Rosa sector. Unfortunately, the original building was burnt to the ground by arsonists in May 2001, but was rebuilt in 2002 using historic photos and local timber. The battle of 1856 was fought around this building, and the military action, as well as the region's natural history, is described with the help of documents, paintings, maps and other displays (mostly in Spanish). If you remember your dictionary, this will be an inspiring (and perhaps humbling) history lesson in how not to invade a country – you'd think the US government would have learnt by now.

The arson was set by a local father-son team of poachers who were disgruntled at being banned from hunting here by park rangers. They were caught and sentenced to 20 years in prison for torching a building of national cultural and historical value. Unfortunately, poaching continues in the park since it's difficult for rangers to effectively patrol such a large landmass.

Activities

WILDLIFE-WATCHING

The wildlife is certainly both varied and prolific, especially during the dry season when animals congregate around the remaining water sources and the trees lose their leaves. More than 250 bird species have been recorded, including the raucous white-throated magpie jay, unmistakable with its long crest of maniacally curled feathers. The forests contain parrot and parakeet, trogon and tanager, and as you head down to the coast, you will be rewarded with sightings of a variety of coastal birds.

Bats are also very common; about 50 or 60 different species have been identified in Santa Rosa. Other mammals you have a reasonable chance of seeing include deer, coati, peccary, armadillo, coyote, raccoon, three kinds of monkey, and a variety of other species – about 115 in all. There are also many thousands of insect species, including about 4000 moths and butterflies – bring insect repellant.

Reptile species include lizards, iguanas, snakes, crocodiles and four species of sea turtle. The olive ridley sea turtle is the most numerous, and during the July to December nesting season tens of thousands of turtles make their nests on Santa Rosa's beaches. The most popular beach is Playa Nancite, where, during September and October especially, it is possible to see as many as 8000 of these 40kg turtles on the beach at the same time. The turtles are disturbed by light, so flash photography and flashlights are not permitted. Avoid the nights around a full moon – they're too bright and turtles are less likely to show up. Playa Nancite is strictly protected and entry restricted, but permission may be obtained from park headquarters to observe this spectacle; call ahead.

The variety of wildlife reflects the variety of habitat protected within the boundaries of the park. Apart from the largest remaining stand of tropical dry forest in Central America, habitats include savannah woodland, oak forest, deciduous forest, evergreen forest, riparian forest, mangrove swamp and coastal woodland.

HIKING

Near Hacienda Santa Rosa is **El Sendero Indio Desnudo**, a 1km trail with signs interpreting the ecological relationships among the animals, plants and weather patterns of Santa Rosa. The trail is named after the common tree, also called *gumbo limbo*, whose peeling orange-red bark can photosynthesize during the dry season, when the trees' leaves are lost (resembling a sunburned tourist…or naked Indian, as the name implies). Also seen along the trail is the national tree of Costa Rica, the guanacaste (*Enterolobium cyclocarpum*). The province is named after this huge tree species, which is found along the Pacific coastal lowlands. You may also see birds, monkeys, snakes, iguanas and petroglyphs (most likely pre-Columbian) etched into some of the rocks on the trail.

Behind La Casona a short trail leads up to the **Monumento a Los Héroes** and a lookout platform. There are also longer trails through the dry forest, including a gentle 4km hike to the Mirador, with spectacular views of Playa Naranjo, which is accessible to hikers willing to go another 9km along the deeply rutted road to the sea. The main road is lined with short trails to small waterfalls and other photogenic natural wonders as well.

From the southern end of Playa Naranjo, there are two hiking trails – **Sendero Carbonal** is a 20km trail that swings inland and then terminates on the beach at Cerros Carbonal, while **Sendero Aceituno** parallels Playa Naranjo for 13km and terminates near the estuary across from Witch's Rock. There's also a 6km hiking trail that starts where the northern branch of the access road terminates – this leads to the biological research station at Nancite; you'll need prior permission to access this beach.

Although it's not officially recommended by the park service, the opportunities for long-distance beach hiking abound, especially if you're an experienced hiker who's prepared to carry large quantities of food and water. Inquire locally about the feasibility of long-distance trekking (especially in regards to permanent water sources). We have heard a rumor that it's possible to hike from Santa Rosa to Playa del Coco (if you make it, let us know!).

SURFING
The surfing at Playa Naranjo is truly world-renowned, especially near Witch's Rock, a beach break famous for its fast, hollow 3m rights (although there are also fun lefts when it isn't pumping). Beware of rocks near the rivermouth, and be careful near the estuary as it's a rich feeding ground for crocodiles during the tide changes. The surfing is equally legendary at Ollie's Point off Playa Portero Grande, which has the best right in all of Costa Rica with a nice, long ride, especially with a south swell. The bottom here is a mix of sand and rocks, and the year-round offshore is perfect for tight turns and slow closes. Shortboarding is preferred by surfers at both spots.

Sleeping & Eating
There's a shady developed **campground** (per person US$2) close to the park headquarters, with picnic benches, grills, flushing toilets and cold-water showers. Playa Naranjo has pit toilets and showers, but no potable water – _ bring your own. Other camping areas in the park are undeveloped. There's a 25-person, two-night maximum for camping at Playa Naranjo. There's also a small campsite with pit toilets and showers near the ranger station in the Sector Murciélago, though you'll have to carry in your own food and water.

Make reservations in advance to stay at the **research station** (dm US$15); eight-bed bunkrooms have cold showers and electricity. Researchers get priority, but there's usually some room for travelers. Good meals (US$3 to US$7) are available, but you must make arrangements the day before.

Getting There & Away
The well-signed main park entrance can be reached by public transport: take any bus between Liberia and the Nicaragua border and ask the driver to let you off at the park entrance; rangers can help you catch a return bus. You can also arrange private transportation from the hotels in Liberia for about US$15 per person round-trip.

To get to the northern Sector Murciélago, go 10km further north along the Interamericana, then turn left to the village of Cuajiniquíl, with a couple of *sodas* and a *pulpería* (corner grocery stores), 8km away by paved road. Keep your passport handy, as there may be checkpoints. The paved road continues beyond Cuajiniquíl and dead-ends at a marine port, 4km away – this isn't the way to Sector Murciélago but goes toward Refugio Nacional de Vida Silvestre Bahía Junquillal. It's about 8km beyond Cuajiniquíl to the Murciélago ranger station by poor road – 4WD is advised, though the road may be impassable in the wet season. You can camp at the Murciélago ranger station, or continue 10km to 12km on a dirt road beyond the ranger station to the remote bays and beaches of Bahía Santa Elena and Bahía Playa Blanca.

REFUGIO NACIONAL DE VIDA SILVESTRE BAHÍA JUNQUILLAL
This 505-hectare wildlife refuge is part of the ACG, administered from the park headquarters at Santa Rosa. There is a **ranger station** (☎ 2679 9692; admission incl Parque Nacional Santa Rosa US$6, camping per person US$2; ☉ 7am-4pm) in telephone and radio contact with Santa Rosa.

The quiet bay and protected beach provide gentle swimming, boating and snorkeling opportunities, and there is some tropical dry forest and mangrove swamp. Short trails take the visitor to a lookout for marine birding and to the mangroves. Pelicans and frigate birds are seen, and turtles nest here seasonally. Volcán Orosí can be seen in the distance. Campers should note that during the dry season especially, water is at a premium and is turned on for only one hour a day. There are pit latrines.

NORTHWESTERN
COSTA RICA

To get here from Cuajiniquíl, continue for 2km along the paved road and then turn right onto a signed dirt road. Continuing 4km along the dirt road (passable to ordinary cars) brings you to the entrance to Bahía Junquillal. From here, a poorer 700m dirt road leads to the beach, ranger station and camping area.

PARQUE NACIONAL GUANACASTE

This newest part of the ACG was created on July 25 (Guanacaste Day), 1989. The park is adjacent to Parque Nacional Santa Rosa, separated from it by the Interamericana, and is only about 5km northwest of Parque Nacional Rincón de la Vieja.

The 34,651 hectares of Parque Nacional Guanacaste are much more than a continuation of the lowland habitats found in Santa Rosa. In its lower western reaches, the park is indeed composed of the dry tropical rain forest characteristic of much of Guanacaste, but the terrain soon begins to climb toward two volcanoes – Volcán Orosí (1487m) and Volcán Cacao (1659m). Here the landscape slowly transitions to the humid cloud forest that's found throughout much of the highland Cordillera de Guanacaste. This habitat, which is similar in function to Parque Nacional Carara, provides a refuge for altitudinal migrants that move between the coast and the highlands. Thus the national park allows for the ancient migratory and hunting patterns of various animal species to continue as they have for millennia.

However, this ecosystem is more the domain of biologists than tourists (it's among the least visited parks in Costa Rica), and there are three major research stations within the borders of the park. In addition to observing animal migratory patterns, researchers are also monitoring the pace of reforestation as much of the park is composed of ranch land. Interestingly enough, researchers have found that if the pasture is carefully managed (much of this management involves just letting nature take its course), the natural forest will reinstate itself in its old territory. Thus crucial habitats in the national park are not just preserved, but in some cases they are expanded.

For information on this park, contact the **ACG headquarters** (☎ 2666 5051) in Parque Nacional Santa Rosa.

Sights & Activities

The three research stations within the park borders are open to tourists, and they're great spots for wildlife observation. If you have a relevant background in biology or ecology, volunteer positions are available, though it's best to contact ACG well in advance of your arrival.

MARITZA BIOLOGICAL STATION

This is the newest station and has a modern laboratory. From the station, at 600m above sea level, rough trails run to the summits of Volcán Orosí and Volcán Cacao (about five to six hours). There is also a better trail to a site where several hundred petroglyphs have been found that are chipped into volcanic rock. As with most indigenous sites in Costa Rica, little is known about the origins of the petroglyphs, though the area was believed to be inhabited by the Chorotega (p165). There is also another trail that leads to the Cacao Biological Station.

To get there, turn east off the Interamericana opposite the turnoff for Cuajiniquíl. The station is about 17km east of the highway along a dirt road that may require a 4WD vehicle, especially in the wet season.

CACAO BIOLOGICAL STATION

High on the slopes of Volcán Cacao (about 1060m), this station offers access to rough trails that lead to the summit of the volcano and to Maritza Biological Station. Cacao Biological Station is reached from the southern side of the park. At Potrerillos, about 9km south of the Santa Rosa park entrance on the Interamericana, head east for 7km on a paved road to the small community of Quebrada Grande (marked 'Garcia Flamenco' on many maps). A daily bus leaves Liberia at 3pm for Quebrada Grande. From the village plaza, a 4WD road that is often impassable during the wet season heads north toward the station, about 10km away.

PITILLA BIOLOGICAL STATION

This station lies on the northeast side of Volcán Orosí, which is on the eastern side of the continental divide. The surrounding forests here are humid, lush and atypical of anything you'll find in the rest of Guanacaste.

To get to the station, turn east off the Interamericana about 12km north of the Cuajiniquíl turnoff, or 3km before reaching

A WHOPPER OF A PROBLEM

Although there is a long history of deforestation in Costa Rica, massive clear-cutting of the rain forests (particularly in Guanacaste) intensified during the 1970s. Currently, there is much debate regarding the causes of this wide-scale deforestation, but research suggests that a shift in governmental philosophy likely sparked the event. Specifically, national policies were implemented at the time that promoted increased land use relating to agriculture, wood production, pasture land creation and improved transit infrastructure. It is argued that these initiatives were aimed at speeding up the country's economic development, especially in response to the decrease in the international demand for Costa Rican coffee.

Clearly, development is a double-edged sword as it's impossible to argue that the philosophies of the 1970s did not in fact improve the quality of life in Costa Rica. Today, Guanacaste is one of the richest provinces in Costa Rica, and the country as a whole is often regarded as the gem of Central America. Quality of life in Costa Rica is among the highest in Latin America, and Ticos have never had to starve like their neighbors to the north and south. However, cattle ranchers in Costa Rica produce an abundance of meat, much of which is destined for the international fast-food market. Thus the devastation of the rain forest is not solely a product of national improvement.

The body of evidence supporting these claims is astounding, and consists of everything from court testimonials to recorded data on imports and exports. Officially, most fast-food companies maintain that they are in favor of rain-forest preservation, and that they do not use hamburger meat of foreign origin in their products. However, although imported beef is only a small portion of the total meat consumed in the USA, this accounts for a significant percentage of Central American beef production. One documented problem is that when Central American beef arrives at a US point of entry, it is often marked as 'US inspected and approved,' which disguises the origin of the product. Furthermore, since the meat in a single burger can be derived from multiple cows, it's difficult to verify that a product is in fact free of foreign beef.

As a consumer, it's virtually impossible to ensure that you're not eating beef that's been raised on recently deforested areas, aside from boycotting the major fast-food retailers. At the time of writing, Costa Rica had just received an extension on passing laws that would allow it to participate in the Central American Free Trade Agreement (Cafta), which will likely mean increases in Central American beef exports. Fortunately, Western diets are shifting away from beef and processed meats, and several fast-food companies have started adopting healthier menus (though much of this is attributable to recent declines in profits). And you can take comfort in knowing that researchers in Costa Rica are hard at work investigating the natural processes of reforestation (for more information, see Parque Nacional Guanacaste, opposite).

the small town of La Cruz. Follow the paved eastbound road for about 28km to the community of Santa Cecilia. From there, a poor dirt road heads 11km south to the station – you'll probably need 4WD. (Don't continue on the unpaved road heading further east – that goes over 50km further to the small town of Upala.)

Hiking

Hiking trails in the national park are among the least developed in the entire country, and are principally used by researchers to move between each of the stations. It's advisable to talk to the staff before setting out on any of the hikes, as infrastructure in the park is almost nonexistent. If you're interested in summit-ting Volcán Cacao, it's strongly recommended that you hire a guide, which can be arranged through any of the biological stations or at Hacienda Los Inocentes (p224).

Sleeping & Eating

INSIDE THE PARK

You can **camp** (per person US$2.50) near the stations, but there aren't any facilities.

If there's space, you may be able to reserve dorm-style accommodations at **Maritza or Cacao Biological Stations** (☎ 2666 5051; dm US$20). The stations are both quite rustic, with room for about 30 people, and shared cold-water bathrooms. Meals are also available for US$3 to US$7, and should be arranged in advance.

HEADING NORTH OF THE BORDER

Peñas Blancas is a busy border crossing, open 6am to 8pm daily. You won't be charged to exit or enter Costa Rica, but leaving Nicaragua costs US$2. The fee to enter Nicaragua is US$7; your car will cost another US$22 (note that most car-rental companies in Costa Rica won't allow you to cross borders; be sure to ask before you sign your contract). Banks on either side will change local colones and córdobas for dollars, but inconveniently, not for each other. Independent moneychangers will happily make the exchange for you – at whatever rates they feel like setting.

The border posts, are about 1km apart; if you're in the mood you can hire a golf cart (US$2) to make the run. Hordes of totally useless touts will offer to 'guide' you through the simple crossing – let them carry your luggage if you like, but agree on a fee beforehand. You may be charged US$1 to enter the state of Rivas, but this fee is voluntary. Should you have any hard currency left at this point, there's a fairly fabulous duty-free shop, with fancy makeup and lots of liquor, waiting for you in Sapoá, the Nicaraguan equivalent of Peñas Blancas.

Relax with your purchases on the 37km bus ride (US$0.75, 45 minutes), departing every 30 minutes, to Rivas. The city is a quiet, transport hub, though its well-preserved 17th-century center is worth exploring (think a more run-down version of Granada without all the crowds).

If you're good at bargaining (and you will have to bargain hard), there are a number of taxis waiting on the Nicaraguan side of the border to whisk you to Rivas (US$8).

San Juan del Sur

After standing in line in the hot sun and negotiating the chaos of crossing the border, all you might feel up for is collapsing on a beach with a shot of Flor de Caña in hand – if your answer to that is 'sí, por favor,' then make tracks to San Juan del Sur. This fishing village has geared itself to tourism, so you can pick up a used novel, go surfing, diving or deep-sea fishing, and then party in the evening with other travelers and local expats. Buses and water taxis also make trips to some of the stunning beaches north and south of San Juan.

There are several places to stay along the market street where the buses pull in. The beachfront is lined with breezy cafés, and you'll find lots of cheap eateries at San Juan's market.

■ **Casa Oro** (☎ 505-568 2415; www.casaeloro.com; dm US$5-6, r with/without bathroom US$18/12) This well-run hostel is deservedly popular and always heavily booked. Quieter upstairs rooms have more space and private bathrooms.

■ **Hotel Estrella** (☎ 505-568 2210; r per person US$5) On the beach strip, this place was probably once quite elegant. Now it's a pretty basic budget flophouse, but some rooms have little balconies, and there's a nice lounge area, book exchange, and a beautiful café out front.

■ **El Gato Negro** (☎ 505-828 5534) Stake out a table here for a good shot of espresso and treats like fresh sandwiches.

■ **El Timón** (☎ 505-568 2243; dishes US$5-10) This excellent beach restaurant is the place to go for a more upmarket seafood dinner, with professional service and delicious seafood; the *pulpo al vapor* (steamed octopus with a tasty garlicky sauce) is highly recommended.

Buses to and from Rivas (US$0.60, 45 minutes), with connections to the border, depart every 30 minutes or so from 3:30am to 7pm. Taxis from Sapoá to San Juan del Sur cost about US$10.

Isla de Ometepe

One of Nicaragua's highlights, Isla de Ometepe is like something from a fantasy landscape. The island's twin volcanoes – **Concepción** (1610m above the lake) and **Maderas** (1394m) – rise dramatically from Lago de Nicaragua and are connected by an isthmus formed by lava flow.

OUTSIDE THE PARK

Hacienda Los Inocentes (☎ 2679 9190; www.losinocenteslodge.com; d with/without 3 meals US$70/45) This former cattle ranch on the northern edge of the park was the former property of the Inocente family, who used to own nearly one-third of Guanacaste. Today, it's part biological research station, part ecolodge, and the principal aim is to convert much of the 1000-hectare ranch from pasture land to rain forest. The

Parts of Ometepe are still covered in primary forest, which shelters abundant wildlife, including howler monkey and green parrot. The island is also famous for its ancient Chorotega stone statues and petroglyphs.

It's possible to hike both volcanoes, though these are serious, eight- to 12-hour treks that are best attempted with a local guide. There are also great beaches for sunning and swimming all around the island. The most popular beach, **Playa Santo Domingo**, is on the isthmus and has plenty of places to stay and eat. Many local accommodations have horses, bikes or kayaks to hire at reasonable rates.

The island's two major settlements, Altagracia and Moyogalpa, both offer accommodations and restaurants, but to experience the true charms of Ometepe, travel further out: Charco Verde, Playa Santo Domingo, Balgüe and Mérida all offer lovely settings amid the island's rich biodiversity.

The fastest way of reaching Ometepe is via San Jorge near Rivas, from where boats make the 15km crossing to Moyogalpa on Ometepe. There are two types of boat: significantly more comfortable car/passenger ferries (San Jorge–Moyagalpa 1st/2nd class US$3.30/2.20, departures 7:45am, noon, 2:30pm, 4:30pm and 5:30pm) and fairly basic *lanchas* (small motorboats; US$1.60, departures at 9am, 9:30am, 10:30am, 11:30am, 1:30pm and 3:30pm). Taxis from Sapoá to the San Jorge ferry will run about US$10 if you bargain hard.

Granada

The lovely colonial city of Granada is a sight for sore eyes after the brutally bland architecture of Costa Rica. The carved colonial portals, elegant churches and fine plaza, as well as its location on Lago de Nicaragua, have enchanted visitors for centuries since the city was founded in 1524. And not only is it a beautiful city to enjoy for a few days, it also makes a convenient launching point for Nicaragua's other attractions. Stop by the **Intur office** (☎ 505-552 6858; granada@intur.gob.ni; Calle Arsenal; 8am-noon & 2-5pm Mon-Fri, 8:30am-12:30pm Sat & Sun), across from the San Francisco church, to pick up a good map of the city's historic buildings.

A few blocks northeast of Parque Central is the striking light-blue facade of the **Convento y Iglesia de San Francisco** (Calle Cervantes). It fronts a complex that was initiated in 1585, burned to the ground by William Walker in 1856, and rebuilt in 1867–68. It houses the city's must-see **museum** (admission US$2; 8:30am-5:30pm Mon-Fri, 9am-4pm Sat & Sun). Admission includes a bilingual guided tour.

Some recommended places to stay:

- **Hostal Esfinge** (☎ 505-552 4826; Calle Atravesada; dm US$3.30, s/d US$6.60/10, with bathroom US$10/13.90; P) A gracious, old-style ambience pervades this gorgeous historic building. Rooms surround a large courtyard, and guests have access to a communal kitchen.

- **Posada Don Alfredo** (☎ 505-552 4455; alfredpaulbaganz@hotmail.com; Calle 14 de Septiembre; r US$20-28, with bathroom US$35, with air-con US$40;) The disordered, homey colonial elegance of this lovely old building give this place great character; spacious rooms vary widely and mostly share bathrooms.

- **Patio del Malinche** (☎ 505-552 2235; www.patiodelmalinche.com; Calle El Caimito; s/d incl breakfast US$57/67;) This lovingly restored colonial home is one of Granada's most appealing places to stay. The personal attention and delicious, massive breakfasts make it feel more like a guesthouse than a hotel.

Buses from Rivas (US$1, 1½ hours) depart eight times daily until mid-afternoon. Taxis from Sapoá can take you to Granada for around US$30.

ranch has a very attractive location below the Volcán Orosí, and nearly two-thirds of the property has returned to secondary forest (not surprisingly, there are great opportunities here for wildlife-watching). The hacienda building itself is a very attractive, century-old wooden house, and has 11 spacious wooden bedrooms with private (but separate) bathroom, plus several larger separate cabins. The upper floor is surrounded by a beautiful, shaded, wooden veranda with hammocks and also volcano views – a good spot for sunset/moonrise. The staff can arrange guided hikes throughout the park as well as to the top of Volcán Cacao.

The hacienda is 15km east of the Interamericana on the paved road to Santa Cecilia. Buses from San José to Santa Cecilia pass the lodge entrance at about 7:30pm, returning at around 4:15am. Taxis from La Cruz charge about US$10.

LA CRUZ

La Cruz is the closest town to the Peñas Blancas border crossing with Nicaragua (see boxed text, p224), and it's the principal gateway to Bahía Salinas (opposite), one of Costa Rica's premier windsurfing and kitesurfing destinations. Although La Cruz itself is a fairly sleepy provincial town, its hilltop location is awash with scenic views of the coastline, and you can easily bus down to several stunning, isolated white-sand beaches on Bahía Salinas. An underrated place to spend the night before heading to Nicaragua.

Information

Changing money at the border post often yields a better exchange rate than in town.

Banco Nacional (☎ 2679 9296) At the junction of the short road into the town center and the Interamericana; has a 24-hour ATM.

Banco Popular (☎ 2679 9352) In the town center, has an ATM.

Cruz Roja (☎ 2679 9004, emergency 2679 9146) There is a small clinic just north of the town center on the road toward the border.

Internet Café (☎ 2679 8190, 8838 8128; per hr US$1; ☼ approximately 8am-7pm Mon-Sat)

Sleeping

Hotel Bella Vista (☎ 2679 8060; per person fan/air-con US$7/10; P ✜ ✜) With a lovely mosaic-bottomed pool and breezy restaurant at the top of the hill, this Dutch-run hotel is a great place for a beer in the evenings. Although it was a bit run-down when we visited, the owner's son had plans to clean up the still-decent rooms. All rooms have private hot-water bathrooms, and those upstairs are a bit brighter with partial views of the bay. There's also an attached restaurant (open breakfast, lunch and dinner), where breakfast will set you back US$3.

Cabinas Santa Rita (☎ 2679 9062; s/d with bathroom US$9/13, with air-con US$15/23; P ✜) The best budget option in town has clean, though dark, rooms

with shared bathrooms and is popular with migrant workers. Across the street, the newer annex has frillier rooms with private bathroom, cable TV, hot showers and air-con.

our pick Amalia's Inn (☎ 2679 9618; s/d US$20/35; P ✜ ✜) By far the best place in La Cruz to kick back with a cool drink at sunset, the shared terra-cotta terraces at Amalia's look out onto huge, stupendous bay views. The white stucco house on a cliff isn't a bad place to spend the night, either – cozy, homey rooms are decorated with anything from white wicker to modular leather, each with private hot-water bathroom and air-con. Walls in the meandering house are hung with modernist paintings by Amalia's late husband Lester Bounds. Amalia's niece is now the lady of the house, and short of offering meals, she'll make you feel right at home.

Eating

La Cruz might possibly have the most *helader-ías* (ice-cream shops) per capita in Costa Rica, for which you'll be glad when the mid-afternoon heat smites you. Pick up groceries at the neighboring Almacen Super Único and SuperCompro La Cruz, on the east side of the plaza.

Soda Candy (mains US$2-5; ☼ 6am-8pm) There's no menu at this basic *soda* across from the bus terminal, but in addition to casados and *gallos* (tortilla sandwiches) 'made with a lot of love,' Candy knows all the bus schedules by heart and can fill you in if the station happens to be closed.

Pollo Rico Rico (mains US$2-5; ☼ 10am-10pm) Folks who love fried chicken should stop by this spot, right on the park, or try the roasted chicken, which is even tastier (and a whole lot better for your poor arteries).

Soda Herbol (☎ 2679 8360; mains US$2-6; ☼ 6am-7pm) This *soda* doesn't have a menu, either, but staff will make your casado to order, and the friendly owner speaks a bit of English while the resident green parakeet Ana narrates her adventures on the curtains.

Getting There & Away

A **Transportes Deldú counter** (☼ 7am-1pm & 3-5:30pm) sells tickets and stores bags. To catch a TransNica bus to Peñas Blancas, you'll need to flag a bus down on the Interamericana. Buses to the beaches depart just up the hill from Hotel Bella Vista; a taxi to the beach costs about US$12.

Liberia (Transportes Deldú) US$1, two hours, departs 6:15am, 7:30am, 9:30am, 11:30am, 3:15pm, 3:30pm, 5:30pm and 6:30pm.
Peñas Blancas US$1, 45 minutes, departs 5am, 7am, 7:45am, 10:45am, 1:20pm and 4:10pm.
Playa Jobó US$1, 30 minutes, departs at 11am and 4pm.
San José (Transportes Deldú) US$5, five hours, departs 5:45am, 8am, 10am, 11am, 12:20pm, 2pm and 4:15pm.

BAHÍA SALINAS

Bahía Salinas is the second-best place in all of Costa Rica (only after Laguna de Arenal) for windsurfing, and is arguably the best place in the country for kiteboarding because the vegetation around Arenal can be quite dangerous for kiters in the air. The bay otherwise happens to be a bit under the radar, so you'll often find that you have an entire jungle-edged crescent of white-sand beach to yourself. The bay is also home to Isla Bolaños, which protects a large colony of seabirds, including the endangered brown pelican (from January to May).

Sights & Activities

A dirt road (normally passable to cars) leads down from the lookout point in La Cruz past the small coastal fishing community of **Puerto Soley** and out along the curve of the bay to the consistently windy beaches of **Playa Papaturro** and **Playa Copal**. If wind isn't your thing but sunbathing is, head around the point to **Playa Jobó**, a perfect horseshoe of a bay with calm water, or **Playa Rajada** just beyond. Boats can be rented in the village of El Jobó or at one of the local resorts to visit **Isla Bolaños** (visits are restricted to April through November to avoid disturbing nesting seabirds). Or try contacting **Frank Schultz** (☎ 8827 4109; franksdiving@costaricense.co.cr), who also organizes fishing and diving trips.

WINDSURFING & KITEBOARDING

The strongest and steadiest winds blow from November through March, but the wind is pretty consistent here year-round. The shape of the hills surrounding the bay funnels the winds into a predictable pattern, and the sandy, protected beaches make this a safe place for beginners and experienced windsurfers and kiteboarders alike. It's important to remember that there are inherent dangers to kiteboarding (namely the risk of losing a limb – yikes!), so it's best to seek professional instruction if you're not an experienced kiteboarder. Responsible instructors recommend

at least two days of lessons before you can safely go out on your own. Windsurfing rentals and lessons can be found at **Ecoplaya Beach Resort** (☎ 2676 1010; www.ecoplaya.com).

If windsurfing is too tame for you, then enroll at **Kitesurf School 2000** (☎ 8826 5221; www.suntoursandfun.com/kite_surfing.htm), a sporty combination of wind and waves (which school instructors insist is much easier to learn than regular surfing) where you are attached to a large kite, then pulled across the bay by the breeze, allowing more advanced students to do flips and other aerial acrobatics above the froth and swells – way cool. If you want to give this a try, make reservations a couple of days in advance for two days of lessons (US$240) or just equipment rental (basic gear per day US$69).

Another reputable kitesurfing school is **Cometa Copal** (☎ 2676 1192; lguardbl@gmail.com), run by Bob Selfridge, who not only offers kitesurfing lessons with PASA (Professional Air Sports Association) certified instructors, but is himself an instructor, lifeguard *and* emergency medical technician.

Sleeping & Eating

Most hotels in Bahía Salinas offer transfers from San José or Liberia airports.
La Sandia Cabinas & Activities (☎ 8370 4894; www.lasandia-costarica.com; r US$20; **P**) Stay at these colorful cabinas, and the owners can help arrange windsurfing, kitesurfing, horseback riding and all manner of activities around the bay.
Blue Dream Hotel (☎ 2676 1042, 8826 5221; www.bluedreamhotel.com; dm US$15, s/d US$28/36; **P** 🖥 🛜) Home base of Kitesurf School 2000, this friendly little hotel looks out over Playa Papaturro from its terraced hillside, with simple, comfortable tiled rooms at the top of the hill. Along with the hammock-strung garden, there's a yoga terrace, Mediterraneo restaurant (open breakfast, lunch and dinner) serving local and Mediterranean food, and spa services to boot, all run by Italian kiteboarding instructor Nicola and his Tica wife Katya.
Cometa Copal (☎ 2676 1192; lguardbl@gmail.com; villas from US$65; **P** 😼) In addition to organizing kitesurfing lessons and rentals, the friendly American couple running Cometa Copal also rents gear and beachfront villas for the short- or long-term. Bob and Kirsten offer sweet extras like shiatsu massage, overnight kite repairs and home-baked goodies.

Bolaños Bay Resort (☎ 2676 1163; hotelbolanosbay@ gmail.com; s/d incl breakfast US$50/70; P ⚙ ☐ ⚋) This older, low-key resort on Playa Coyotera is being revived after being left to wither. It has sort of an appealing castaway feel to it, and the staff is very friendly, but don't expect any flashy amenities. There's a pleasant pool area above the deserted beach, and an onsite restaurant with a huge bar area.

Proyecto Pura-Vida (☎ 2676 1055, 8389 6784; www .progettopuravida.com; apt & house per night US$30-100) Though geared toward long-term stays, this Italian-owned agency rents several wicker-furnished apartments and houses, priced according to size and amenities, which may include a pool or, perhaps, a bidet. Smaller apartments accommodate up to four people, while the larger villas can house seven. Each property is reasonably spaced from the others, and overlooks a pristine stretch of white sand. Weekly and monthly discounts are available.

Ecoplaya Beach Resort (☎ 2676 1010; www.ecoplaya .com; r & villa US$116-250; P ✗ ⚙ ☐ ⚋ ☷) About 16km from La Cruz, Ecoplaya efficiently delivers a luxury resort experience. Rooms and bungalows range from elegant studios, complete with kitchenettes and sustainable-teak furniture, to full luxury suites containing minibar, sitting room and air-con in every room. All rooms have DirecTV and private terrace or balcony. Opt for the full American plan (adult/ child additional US$78/39), and all meals are included, as are all drinks from 10am to 10pm (you read that right). The hotel's stretch of white-sand beach is picture perfect, and the pool with swim-up bar perfectly self-indulgent. The hotel also offers plenty of activities, including kayaking, mountain biking, fishing, diving, windsurfing and horseback riding.

Restaurant Copal (☎ 2676 1006; mains US$4-7; ☯ lunch & dinner) This glassed-in *palapa* on a hilltop has little competition here in Playa Copal, but it still turns out excellent Italian food, and the romantic locale can't be topped. Stop by on Thursday nights for wood-fired pizza.

Getting There & Away
Buses (US$1) along this road depart the La Cruz bus terminal at 5am, 11am and 4pm daily and return approximately one hour later. A taxi to the beaches will cost about US$12, and you can usually catch a colectivo (small bus; US$3.50) from La Cruz, close to the taxi stand, though you may have to wait a while for it to fill up.

ARENAL ROUTE

If you've got your own wheels and you've got a little time, take the road from Ciudad Quesada to the Arenal area – you are in for one beautiful ride. With the backdrop of Volcán Platanar behind you, the road winding through this green, river-rich agrarian region passes through prosperous, quaint towns bright with bougainvillea. In front of you, if the weather cooperates, the smoking peak of Arenal will loom in the distance.

Past La Fortuna, the paved road (beware of potholes) hugs the north bank of Laguna de Arenal. On either side of the road, up the green slope and down on the lake side, turn-outs and driveways for lovely inns, kooky ersatz Austrian mini-villages, hip coffee houses and eccentric galleries appear invitingly like pictures in a pop-up book. Scattered in between, you can't help but notice the scads of real-estate signs offering lots for sale, but the area is bucolic and not overdeveloped, and each stop feels far enough away from the next to give a sense of isolation.

Heading back around the western edge of the lake, you'll pass through the lakeside Nuevo Arenal and down to the pleasant mountain town of Tilarán before descending back toward the Interamericana. If you don't have your own vehicle, the route is well served by public transportation.

CIUDAD QUESADA (SAN CARLOS)
The official name of this small city is Ciudad Quesada (sometimes abbreviated to 'Quesada'), but all the locals know it as San Carlos, and local buses often list San Carlos as the destination. It's long been a bustling ranching and agricultural center, known for its *talabaterías* (saddle shops), where some of the most intricately crafted leather saddles in Costa Rica are made and sold; a top-quality saddle can cost US$1000. The city is also home to the **Feria del Ganado** (cattle fair and auction), which is held every April and accompanied by carnival rides and a *tope*.

Although San Carlos is surrounded by pastoral countryside, the city of 31,000 has developed into the commercial center of the region – it's also gritty and congested, and driving here can be harrowing for the uninitiated driver. Fortunately, there's no real

NICA VS TICO

Ticos have a well-deserved reputation for friendliness, and it's rare for travelers of any sex, race or creed to experience racism in Costa Rica. However, it's unfortunate and at times upsetting that the mere mention of anything related to Nicaragua is enough to turn your average Tico into a hate-spewing bigot (NB, even the term 'Nica' is used by *some* Ticos in a somewhat derogatory manner, so watch your language). Despite commonalities in language, culture, history and tradition, Nica vs Tico relations are at an all-time low, and rhetoric (on both sides) of *la frontera* isn't likely to improve anytime soon.

Why is there so much hostility between Nicas and Ticos? The answer is as much a product of history as it is of misunderstanding, though economic disparities between both countries are largely to blame.

Though Nicaragua was wealthier than Costa Rica as little as 25 years ago, decades of civil war and a US embargo quickly bankrupted the country, and today Nicaragua is the second-poorest country in the western hemisphere (after Haiti). For example, the 2007 CIA World Factbook lists the GDP per capita purchasing-power parity of Costa Rica as US$13,500, while Nicaragua is listed at only US$3200. The main problem facing Nicaragua is its heavy external debt, though debt relief programs implemented by the IMF and the pending free-trade zone created by the Central American Free Trade Agreement (Cafta) are both promising signs.

In the meantime, however, Nica families are crossing the border in record numbers, drawn to Costa Rica by its growing economy and impressive education and health systems. Unfortunately, immigration laws in Costa Rica make it difficult for Nicas to find work, and the majority end up living in shantytowns. Also, crime is on the rise throughout Costa Rica, and though it's difficult to say what percentage is actually attributable to Nica immigrants, Ticos are quick to point the finger.

It's difficult to predict whether or not relations will improve between both countries, although current signs are fairly negative. Costa Rica, whose civil guard is better funded than most country's militaries, has a bad habit of being caught on the river San Juan with a patrol boat of fatigued combat troops brandishing M16s. Nicaragua, which has the power to simultaneously defuse Tico racism and promote tourism, recently passed a law requiring all visiting Ticos to be in possession of a valid visa. Like all instances of deep-rooted prejudice, the solution is anything but clear.

NORTHWESTERN COSTA RICA

reason to enter the city, except to either change buses or visit one of the area's fine hot springs.

Check your email at the **internet café** (per hr US$1; 8am-9pm Mon-Sat, 3-7pm Sun), 100m north of Parque Central. Banco de San José, 200m north of Parque Central, and the Mutual de Alajuela across the street both have ATMs on the Cirrus and Plus systems.

If you're not staying at one of the two private hot-springs resorts, you can visit the budget-friendly **Aguas Termales de la Marina** (2460 1692; admission US$2). The springs, on the outskirts of town, are referred to locally as 'El Tucanito' (El Tucano is the name of the most expensive resort in town).

Sleeping

Hotel del Norte (2460 1959; s/d US$6/9, with bathroom US$9/13) Small, clean rooms with TV have ridiculously thin walls (so pray that you like what your neighbor is watching), although the excellent security and professional staff make

this the best budget option in town. It's 200m north of Banco Nacional.

Hotel Don Goyo (2460 1780; s/d US$15/25; P) This is the most established hotel in San Carlos proper, and has small, pleasant, salmon-colored rooms with private hot showers. The attached restaurant (mains US$4 to US$10) is well respected for its high-quality food, including traditional Tico favorites and a good variety of Western dishes. It's 100m south of Parque Central.

Termales del Bosque (2460 4740; www.termales delbosque.com; s/d incl breakfast US$49/61; P) Several airy cottages are arranged around the jungle-like grounds at this recommended resort designed with Tico tourism in mind, though it's popular with foreigners who don't want to fork out the cash at nearby El Tucano. Luxury here is low-key with therapeutic soaking taking place in seven natural hot- and warm-water springs (adult/child US$10/5), which are arranged on the riverbank in a forested valley populated by morpho butterflies.

To reach the resort, turn right behind the cathedral and continue for 7km to the east; you will see a sign on the left.

Hotel Occidental El Tucano (☎ 2460 6000; www.1 costaricalink.com/eng/hotels/hota/tucano/home.htm; d incl breakfast US$152-215; P ⊠ ⊠) This posh Mediterranean-style resort, 8km northeast of Ciudad Quesada, is in primary forest and comes complete with an Italian restaurant, swimming pool, Jacuzzi, spa and sauna, plus various sports facilities ranging from tennis courts to miniature golf. The real draw is the nearby thermal springs, which are tapped into three small warm pools that are perfect for soaking away your ills.

Eating

San Carlos has gone urban – chain restaurants abound throughout the city, though there are a few decent local spots on or near the park.

Restaurant Los Geranios (☎ 2460 0553; mains US$2-6; ⊗ lunch & dinner) On a 2nd-story terrace 100m south of the cathedral, overlooking the bustling street below, this popular meeting spot for the city's 20-somethings has cheap casados and cold beer – a perfect combination.

Restaurant El Parque (☎ 2460 0938; mains US$3-6; ⊗ lunch & dinner) If you're looking for a break from the standard rice and beans, head to this small *soda* 50m north of the *parque*, which specializes in Italian pastas.

Restaurante Don Goyo (☎ 2460 1780; Hotel Don Goyo; mains US$4-9; ⊗ breakfast, lunch & dinner) This San Carlos institution is the place to go when you really need a burger – they're big, juicy and oh-so-cheap.

Getting There & Away

The Terminal Quesada is about 2km from the center of town. Taxis (US$1) and a twice-hourly bus (US$0.25) make regular runs between town and the terminal. Walking there is fine if you don't mind hauling your luggage uphill. Popular bus routes (and their bus companies) from Ciudad Quesada:

La Fortuna (Coopatrac) US$0.75, 1½ hours, departs 6am, 10:30am, 1pm, 3:30pm, 5:15pm and 6pm.

Los Chiles (Chilsaca) US$3, two hours, departs 12 times daily from 5am to 7:15pm.

Puerto Viejo de Sarapiquí (Empresarios Guapileños) US$1.50, 2½ hours, departs 4:40am, 6am, 9:15am, 10am, 3pm and 5:30pm.

San José (Autotransportes San Carlos) US$2.50, 2½ hours, 11 departures from 5am to 6pm.

Tilarán (Transportes Tilarán) US$4, 4½ hours, departs 6:30am and 4pm.

LA FORTUNA & AROUND

The influx of tourism has altered the face, fame and fortunes of this former one-horse town; still, La Fortuna has not quite become just an overdeveloped gateway to Volcán

---

SCAMS

If you're taking the bus to La Fortuna, they start before you even get there, boarding a few kilometers out of town, then working the crowd: 'That hotel is overpriced, but I have a friend…' You know this scam, right? But it gets worse.

In addition to steering travelers to poor hotels, which discredits reputable hoteliers who meet the bus because they can't afford flashy brochures and still charge US$5 per room, there's a family in La Fortuna who'll also book you on 'half-price tours.' Usually you'll just show up for your tour and learn that your receipt is invalid, though we've also heard about folks taken to pricey hot springs, then abandoned without transportation or their entry fees paid as promised. In a disturbing recent development, we've even heard of touts selling vouchers for phony tours in such far-flung locales as Monteverde and Caño Negro.

After milking a batch of tourists, family members trade off between La Fortuna, Monteverde and other hot spots for a couple of weeks; it's worked hassle-free for years. Why haven't the police done anything? That's a good question, but basically it comes down to the fact that no one wants to wait around for months to bring these folks to trial. Any police report you file will be for insurance purposes only – period.

It's worth going through a reputable agency or hotel to book your tours around here. You may pay twice as much, but at least you'll get to go. On the bright side, the recent upswing in tourism in the La Fortuna area has brought promises from the Instituto Costarricense de Turismo (ICT) that there will be a crackdown on touts, though remember that the government is in the business of making promises it can't keep. Don't believe us – just look at the state of the roads!

Arenal. It's true that tour operators have set up shop on every block, and that arriving visitors need to steel themselves for the onslaught of touts and hawkers as they step off their buses, but that's because tourism drives the local economy. La Fortuna has managed to retain an underlying, small-town *sabanero* feel to it, with all the bustling action still centered on the attractive church and Parque Central. Stroll beyond the park and you'll quickly hit dirt roads and mom-and-pop cabinas away from the hustle and traffic flow.

Prior to 1968, La Fortuna was a sleepy agricultural town, 6km from the base of Cerro Arenal (Arenal Hill). However, on the morning of July 29, 1968, Arenal erupted violently after nearly 400 years of dormancy, and buried the small villages of Pueblo Nuevo, San Luís and Tabacón – yes, Tabacón Hot Springs (right) is in fact in the eruption path. Suddenly, like moths to the flame, tourists from around the world started descending on La Fortuna in search of fiery night skies and the inevitable blurry photo.

Since then, La Fortuna has served as the principal gateway for visiting Volcán Arenal, and it's one of the top destinations for travelers in Costa Rica. The town is well connected by public transport to San José, and many travelers arrive from or head out to Monteverde via the scenic and unusual jeep-boat-jeep transfer. If you have your own transport, however, consider staying at the Arenal Observatory Lodge (p242) or in the small town of El Castillo (p245) as you'll be rewarded with less crowds and better views of the lava flows.

Orientation & Information

Streets in La Fortuna are named, but there are few street signs and most locals will provide better directions using landmarks. The town is centered on a small park, which is adjacent to the bus stop and taxi stand.

INTERNET ACCESS
Expediciones (Map p232; ☎ 2479 9101; per hr US$1.55; ☼ 7am-10pm Mon-Sat) Most tour operators in town also provide internet access, but if you're not interested in hearing a sales pitch, there are no hassles here.

LAUNDRY
Lavandería Alice (Map p232; ☎ 2479 7111; per kg US$3; ☼ 7am-10pm) Here you get the full fluff-and-fold treatment, 100m north of the park.

Lavandería La Fortuna (Map p232; ☎ 2479 9547; per 4kg US$7, internet per hr US$1; ☼ 8am-9pm Mon-Sat) DIY, or it will wash and dry, all while you surf the internet.

MEDICAL SERVICES
Clínica Fortuna (Map p232; ☎ 2479 9461; Calle 3 btwn Avs Volcán & Fort; ☼ 8am-5pm Mon-Fri)

MONEY
Banks listed below have 24-hour Atms.
BAC San José (Map p232; ☎ 2295 9797; cnr Av Fort & Calle 3) Can change traveler's checks.
Banco de Costa Rica (Map p232; ☎ 2479 9113; Av Central)
Banco Nacional (Map p232; ☎ 2479 9355; Calle 1)

TOURIST INFORMATION
Unsurprisingly, there is no unbiased tourist information center in La Fortuna, though any tour operator or hotel front desk will be happy to give you information out of enlightened self-interest.
Lunatíca (Map p232; ☎ 2479 8255; lunaticarte2@ice.co.cr; ☼ 8:30am-8pm) For cultural offerings in La Fortuna area, information on events and happenings, which unfortunately are infrequent to rare. The store, across from the school, also displays the work of local artists, including baskets, masks and jewelry made by Maleku Indians.

Sights
HOT SPRINGS
What's the consolation prize if you can't actually see the volcano? Why, hot springs, of course, and La Fortuna has some doozies.

If Spielberg ever needed a setting for the Garden of Eden sequence in Genesis, **Tabacón Hot Springs** (Map p234; ☎ 2519 1900; www.tabacon.com; adult/child US$60/20, after 7pm US$45/20; ☼ 10am-10pm), 13km west of La Fortuna, would be it. Enter through the gratuitously opulent ticket counter, flanked by an outrageous buffet (US$15 extra) on one side and glittering gift shop on the other. Then, with a thundering announcement, rare orchids and more florid tropical blooms part to reveal, oh yes, a 40°C/104°F waterfall pouring over a cliff, concealing naturalish-looking caves complete with camouflaged cup holders. And lounged across each well-placed stone, in various stages of sweat-induced exhaustion, relax reddening tourists all enjoying what could be called a hot date.

This hedonism comes at a price – on top of the exorbitant price of admission, that is. The spa is actually on the site where a volcanic eruption ripped through in pretourist

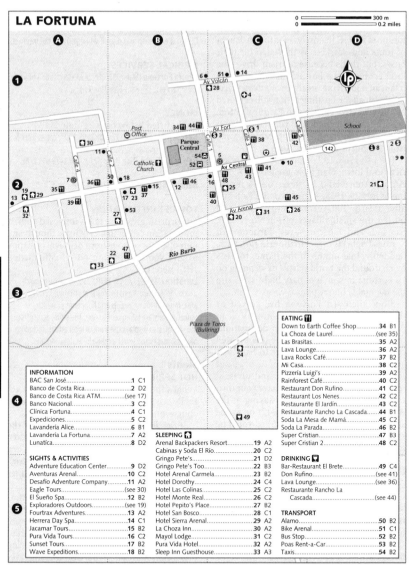

LA FORTUNA

0 ——————— 300 m
0 ——————— 0.2 miles

INFORMATION
BAC San José......................................**1** C1	
Banco de Costa Rica.........................**2** D2	
Banco de Costa Rica ATM..........(see 17)	
Banco Nacional..................................**3** C2	
Clínica Fortuna..................................**4** C1	
Expediciones......................................**5** C2	
Lavandería Alice................................**6** B1	
Lavandería La Fortuna......................**7** A2	
Lunatíca...**8** D2	

SIGHTS & ACTIVITIES
Adventure Education Center.............**9** D2	
Aventuras Arenal............................**10** C2	
Desafío Adventure Company..........**11** A2	
Eagle Tours...................................(see 30)	
El Sueño Spa...................................**12** B2	
Exploradores Outdoors.................(see 19)	
Fourtrax Adventures.......................**13** A2	
Herrera Day Spa..............................**14** C1	
Jacamar Tours.................................**15** B2	
Pura Vida Tours..............................**16** C2	
Sunset Tours...................................**17** B2	
Wave Expeditions...........................**18** B2	

SLEEPING
Arenal Backpackers Resort.............**19** A2	
Cabinas y Soda El Río.....................**20** C2	
Gringo Pete's..................................**21** D2	
Gringo Pete's Too............................**22** B3	
Hotel Arenal Carmela.....................**23** B2	
Hotel Dorothy.................................**24** C4	
Hotel Las Colinas...........................**25** C2	
Hotel Monte Real...........................**26** C2	
Hotel Pepito's Place.......................**27** B2	
Hotel San Bosco.............................**28** C1	
Hotel Sierra Arenal.........................**29** A2	
La Choza Inn...................................**30** A2	
Mayol Lodge...................................**31** C2	
Pura Vida Hotel...............................**32** A2	
Sleep Inn Guesthouse....................**33** A3	

EATING
Down to Earth Coffee Shop............**34** B1	
La Choza de Laurel......................(see 35)	
Las Brasitas....................................**35** A2	
Lava Lounge....................................**36** A2	
Lava Rocks Café.............................**37** B2	
Mi Casa...**38** C2	
Pizzeria Luigi's...............................**39** A2	
Rainforest Café...............................**40** C2	
Restaurant Don Rufino...................**41** C2	
Restaurant Los Nenes.....................**42** C2	
Restaurante El Jardín......................**43** C2	
Restaurante Rancho La Cascada.....**44** B1	
Soda La Mesa de Mamá..................**45** C2	
Soda La Parada...............................**46** B2	
Super Cristian.................................**47** B3	
Super Cristian 2.............................**48** C2	

DRINKING
Bar-Restaurant El Brete...................**49** C4	
Don Rufino...................................(see 41)	
Lava Lounge................................(see 36)	
Restaurante Rancho La	
Cascada....................................(see 44)	

TRANSPORT
Alamo...**50** B2	
Bike Arenal....................................**51** C1	
Bus Stop...**52** B2	
Poas Rent-a-Car.............................**53** B2	
Taxis...**54** B2	

1975, killing one local, and several times a year the resort is evacuated whenever Arenal has a bit of indigestion and decides to belch some poisonous gas (and we haven't even told you about the threat of sudden avalanches). Chances are you'll be fine, but remember that as an active volcano, Arenal always poses the risk of unpredictably acting up.

Baldi Termae Hot Springs (Map p234; ☎ 2479 9651; www.arenal.net/baldi-hot-springs.htm; with/without buffet US$45/28; ☉ 10am-10pm) sports concrete Roman pillars and a Maya pyramid sprouting waterslides; the ambience of these springs 5km west of La Fortuna falls somewhere between Caesar's Palace and Epcot Center. The 16 thermal pools here can only be considered understated in comparison to Tabacón, but despite the high prices, the swim-up bars and techno music attract younger visitors.

Across the street is an unsigned gate that leads to the recommended **Eco-Termales** (Map p234; ☎ 2479 8484; adult/child US$24/16; ☼ 10am-9pm) hot-spring complex, which is by reservation only. The theme here is minimalist elegance, and everything from the natural circulation systems in the pools to the soft, mushroom lighting is understated yet luxurious. Just 100 visitors per four-hour slot are welcomed at 10am, 1pm and 5pm, and you can phone ahead, make a reservation next door at Hotel el Silencio del Campo (p238), or take your chances by just showing up. During the evening session, guests have the option to choose from one of three set menus (US$15/17/23), which feature home-style food served in earthenware pots.

We're certainly not going to let out the secret, but there are several free **hot springs** in the area that any local can take you to.

DAY SPAS

El Sueño Spa (Map p232; ☎ 2479 8261; massages US$35-60; ☼ 9am-9pm) offers massages, facials and reflexology treatments in its peaceful little salon just across from the south side of Parque Central. It also sells volcanic mud so you can relive the spa experience at home.

Herrera Day Spa (Map p232; ☎ 2479 9016; massages US$20-85; ☼ 9am-10pm), 200m northeast of Parque Central, has an intimate, European atmosphere and sells its own line of homemade beauty products.

WATERFALLS

Even if you can't see Arenal, La Fortuna has another natural wonder that pales only in comparison with an erupting volcano: **La Catarata de la Fortuna** (Map p234; admission US$8; ☼ 8am-5pm), a sparkling 70m ribbon of clear water pouring through a sheer canyon of dark volcanic rock arrayed in bromeliads and ferns. It's photogenic, and you don't have to descend the canyon – a short, well-maintained and almost-vertical hike paralleling the river's precipitous plunge – to get the shot, though you do have to pay the steep entry fee.

It's worth the climb out (think Stairmaster with a view) to see the rare world at the jungle floor. Though it's dangerous to dive beneath the thundering falls, a series of perfect swimming holes with spectacular views tiles the canyon in aquamarine – cool and inviting after the hike or ride here. Keep an eye on your backpack.

From the turnoff on the road to San Ramon, it's about 4km uphill to the falls. If you decide to walk up, you'll enjoy spectacular views of Cerro Chato as you hike through pastures and past the small hotels lining the road. You might appreciate a stop at **Neptune's House of Hammocks** (Map p234; ☎ 2479 8269; hammocks US$50-150), which sells soft drinks and hammocks (cat-sized models also available) that you can try out while you take a breather.

You can also get to the *catarata* on horseback (US$25 to US$35 per person) or by car or taxi (US$5 one way); several outfits offer overpriced tours that include a shuttle. A handful of snack and souvenir stands are at the entrance to the falls, but it's worth packing your own lunch and making a day of it.

The falls are also the trailhead for the steep, five- to six-hour **Cerro Chato** climb, a seriously strenuous but rewarding trek to a beautiful lake-filled volcanic crater, where you can have a swim once you summit Cerro Chato. Starting from here, you'll have to pay a US$10 fee for crossing the finca leading to Cerro Chato; a slightly cheaper (though you'll still pay a fee) and less physically taxing alternative would be to hike up the other side from Arenal Observatory Lodge (p242).

Can't handle the hike? Just past the turnoff to the *catarata*, at the third bridge as you leave La Fortuna for San Ramón, there's a short trail on the left leading to a pretty **swimming hole** just under the road, with a rope swing and little waterfall of its own, thank you very much.

ECOCENTRO DANAUS

The reader-recommended **Ecocentro Danaus** (ecological center; Map p234; ☎ 2460 8005; www.ecocentrodanaus.com; admission US$5; ☼ 8am-3:30pm), 3km east of town then 500m on a dirt road, has a well-developed trail system that's good for birding, and there are frequent sightings of sloth, coati and howler monkey. The price of admission also includes a visit to a butterfly garden, a ranarium featuring poison-dart frogs and a small lake containing caiman and turtles. Various tour operators in town run guided night tours (US$25) to the ecological center.

NORTHWESTERN COSTA RICA

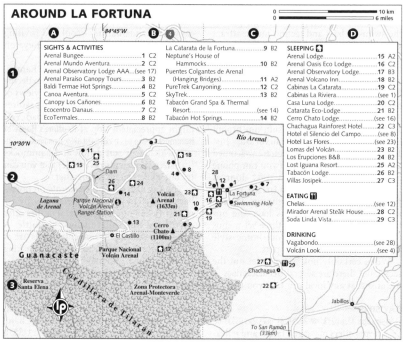

AROUND LA FORTUNA

SIGHTS & ACTIVITIES		
Arenal Bungee..........................**1** C2		
Arenal Mundo Aventura..............**2** C2		
Arenal Observatory Lodge AAA....(see 17)		
Arenal Paraíso Canopy Tours........**3** B2		
Baldi Termae Hot Springs............**4** B2		
Canoa Aventura.......................**5** C2		
Canopy Los Cañones..................**6** B2		
Ecocentro Danaus.....................**7** C2		
EcoTermales...........................**8** B2		

La Catarata de la Fortuna............**9** B2		
Neptune's House of		
Hammocks........................**10** B2		
Puentes Colgantes de Arenal		
(Hanging Bridges)...............**11** A2		
PureTrek Canyoning...................**12** C2		
SkyTrek...............................**13** B2		
Tabacón Grand Spa & Thermal		
Resort............................(see 14)		
Tabacón Hot Springs.................**14** B2		

SLEEPING		
Arenal Lodge..........................**15** A2		
Arenal Oasis Eco Lodge..............**16** C2		
Arenal Observatory Lodge...........**17** B3		
Arenal Volcano Inn...................**18** B2		
Cabinas La Catarata..................**19** C2		
Cabinas La Riviera...................(see 16)		
Casa Luna Lodge......................**20** C2		
Catarata Eco-Lodge..................**21** B2		
Cerro Chato Lodge...................(see 16)		
Chachagua Rainforest Hotel........**22** C3		
Hotel el Silencio del Campo.........(see 8)		
Hotel Las Flores.....................(see 23)		
Lomas del Volcán....................**23** B2		
Los Erupciones B&B.................**24** B2		
Lost Iguana Resort...................**25** A2		
Tabacón Lodge.......................**26** B2		
Villas Josipek........................**27** C3		

EATING		
Chelas...............................(see 12)		
Mirador Arenal Steāk House........**28** C2		
Soda Linda Vista.....................**29** C3		

DRINKING		
Vagabondo..........................(see 28)		
Volcán Look.........................(see 4)		

Activities

There's no shortage of things to do around La Fortuna, but it's going to cost you.

ATV RIDING

Ecotourism and ATV riding go together like topless sunbathing and the Middle East, but whatever – to each their own. There are a surprising number of companies, though **Fourtrax Adventures** (Map p232; ☎ 2479 8444; www .fourtraxadventure.com; Av Central; 3-hr tour US$75) is the most established operator, on the western edge of town. The three-hour tour brings you to the base of the Arenal; a second passenger on one ATV costs an extra US$30.

BUNGEE JUMPING

It was bound to spring up here sometime – **Arenal Bungee** (Map p234; ☎ 2479 7440; www .arenalbungee.com; jump US$39; ☼ 9:30am-9:30pm) lets you fling yourself through the air from its 'Extreme Machine' structure in several ways, including launching upwards from the ground. Confused? Try it for yourself at this outfit, safety-certified by the North American Bungee Association.

CANOEING

Highly recommended, **Canoa Aventura** (Map p234; ☎ 2479 8200; www.canoa-aventura.com; ☼ 6:30am-9:30pm) is about 1.5km west of town on the road to Arenal and specializes in canoe and float trips led by bilingual naturalist guides. Most are geared toward wildlife-watching, with birds (green macaw, roseate spoonbill, honeycreeper etc) being the focus of various tours. Popular paddles include the full-day trip to Caño Negro (US$105, including breakfast and lunch) and an overnight (US$250) to the northern rain forest for an opportunity to spot the great green macaw.

CANOPY TOURING

Try **Arenal Paraíso Canopy Tours** (Map p234; ☎ 2460 5333; www.arenalparaiso.com; adult/student or child US$45/35) for two-hour tours along 12 zip lines. On the other side of La Fortuna, **Canopy Los Cañones** (☎ 2461 1818; adult/child US$45/35) is based at the Hotel Los Lagos, with 15 cables over the rain forest. You can also do canopy tours inside the park itself with SkyTrek, see p244. Then there's **Arenal Mundo Aventura** (Map p234; ☎ 2479 9762; www.arenalmundoaventura;

adult/child canopy tour US$60/30), an ecological park where you can take a canopy tour, go rappelling and catch Maleku performances all in one go.

CANYONING
The reputable **Puretrek Canyoning** (Map p234; ☎ 2479 9940, 2461 2110; www.puretrek.com; ☉ 7am-10pm) leads guided rappels down four waterfalls, one of which is 50m in height. The four-hour tour costs US$85 and includes transportation and lunch. Find it 500m west of town.

HORSEBACK RIDING
Desafío Adventure Company (Map p232; ☎ 2479 9464; www.desafiocostarica.com; ☉ 6:30am-9pm) treats its horses well and has been recommended for the trek to Monteverde (US$75), with a couple of caveats (see boxed text, p188). Along with horseback riding trips, the company also organizes adventure tours rappelling down waterfalls, and community-based tours visiting a local women's recycling collective and animal rescue shelter.

KITESURFING & WINDSURFING
You're only a short drive from the premier spot in Costa Rica for wind sports – Laguna de Arenal (p245).

WHITE-WATER RAFTING & KAYAKING
Desafío Adventure Company (Map p232; ☎ 2479 9464; www.desafiocostarica.com; ☉ 6:30am-9pm) is also recommended for its expertise in river rafting. White-water rafting and kayaking on the Ríos Toro, Peñas Blancas and Sarapiquí are convenient day trips from La Fortuna, and rapids ranging from Class I to Class IV cater to all skill levels. Depending on access and the difficulty of the rapids, trips cost between US$45 and US$100.

Another company that has appeared on the scene is **Wave Expeditions** (Map p232; ☎ 2479 7263; www.waveexpeditions.com; ☉ 7am-9pm), running fun, professional river trips for all experience levels. Prices are competitive, and readers have raved about the excellent staff running these trips.

Festivals & Events
The big annual bash is **Fiestas de la Fortuna**, held in mid-February and featuring two weeks of Tico-rules bullfights, colorful carnival rides, greasy festival food, craft stands and unusual gambling devices. It's free, except for the beer (which is cheap) and you'll have a blast trying to decide between the temporary disco with go-go dancers getting down to reggaetón or the rough and wild tents next door with live ranchero and salsa.

Courses
The **Adventure Education Center** (Map p232; ☎ 2479 8390; www.adventurespanishschool.com; 1 week with/without homestay US$440/315) is an unusual Spanish school that includes outdoor healthy and safety courses as well as various guided hikes and adventures in the curriculum (most adventures cost a little extra). Specialized courses include programs for children, and others teaching medical Spanish. There are other campuses in Turrialba and Dominical.

Tours
You could have someone blindfold you and spin you around on Avenida Central and chances are you'd manage to stumble right into a tour-operator's desk – unless a tout got a hold of you first. While exploding development in La Fortuna means there's a lot of healthy competition, you'll need to shop around, compare prices and not buy your tour from some friendly dude on the street. This is one place where the freedom of having your own wheels can save you money and hassles.

There's usually a two-person minimum for any trip, and groups can work out discounts in advance with most outfitters. If you don't want to deal with the tour operators, most hotels can arrange trips for you, though you will probably be charged a US$5-per-person commission. It's also becoming standard practice in La Fortuna to sell tourists pricey tours to distant destinations, such as Caño Negro. If you're turned off by the idea of public transportation, this is a fine option, though you'll save yourself a ton of money (and probably have a much better experience) if you actually go to these places on the local bus and then organize a tour upon arrival.

Most tourists are interested in taking the obligatory trip to Volcán Arenal, which is generally an afternoon excursion to either the national park or a private overlook to appreciate the mountain by day, combined with a trip to one of the hot springs and usually dinner. Then it's off to another overlook in the evening, where lucky souls will see some lava. Prices vary widely, but generally run US$25 to US$65 per person. Make sure your tour includes entry fees to the park and hot springs, which could easily add another US$25 to the total. Also remember that there's a better-than-even chance that Arenal will remain demurely wrapped in cloud cover for the duration of your trek. There are no refunds if you can't see anything, but nighttime soaks in the hot springs are pretty damn great anyway.

Most agencies in town can also arrange jeep-boat-jeep transportation to Monteverde (see p241), which is the easiest, most scenic way to visit the cloud forests.

The tour operators listed below are a few of the more established agencies, but this list is by no means exhaustive.

Aventuras Arenal (Map p232; ☎ 2479 9133; www .arenaladventures.com; ☯ 6:30am-9pm) Has been around for 15 years, organizing a variety of local day tours via bike, boat and horseback.

Eagle Tours (Map p232; ☎ 2479 9091; www.eagle tours.net; ☯ 6:30am-9pm) Budget travelers rave about this professionally run tour agency, with an office about 150m west of the church.

Exploradores Outdoors (Map p232; ☎ 2479 7500; www.exploradoresoutdoors.com; ☯ 6am-10pm) Specializing in rafting trips on the Río Pacuare, it has a desk at Arenal Backpackers Resort.

Jacamar Tours (Map p232; ☎ 2479 9767; www.arenal tours.com) Recommended for its incredible variety of naturalist hikes.

Pura Vida Tours (Map p232; ☎ 2479 9045; www.pura vidatrips.com; ☯ 7:30am-9pm)

Sunset Tours (Map p232; ☎ 2479 9800; www.sunset tourcr.com; ☯ 6:30am-9pm) This is La Fortuna's most established tour company, recommended for high-quality tours with bilingual guides.

Sleeping

Costa Rican holidays call for merrymaking and explosions, and what better fireworks show is there than the famous lava of La Fortuna? Visitors both foreign and domestic are drawn to La Fortuna for the chance to see the volcano spit some magma, particularly on weekends and holidays, so for those times try to make advance reservations.

There are a bajillion places to stay in town, and we've only listed a handful. The great thing about La Fortuna is the number of small, family-run places, usually a few simple rooms with electric showers and maybe a private bathroom, offering meals by arrangement and good conversation. You may hear about them through word of mouth or just by roaming

around for a few minutes. These places will help arrange local tours and are a good way to help locals cash in on the tourism boom. Hotel touts meet the buses and can be more strong-armed than in most of Costa Rica; not all are trustworthy (see boxed text, p230).

If you're driving, consider staying on the pastoral road to Cerro Chato, a few kilometers south of town, where several appealing hotels have cropped up. Note that hotels west and south of town are listed separately.

Rates given are high-season prices, but low-season rates plummet by as much as 40%.

IN TOWN
Budget
Prices are quoted here with taxes excluded, since paying in cash usually means no taxes.

Gringo Pete's (Map p232; ☎ 2479 8521; gringo petes2003@yahoo.com; camping per person US$2, dm US$3, r per person with/without bathroom US$5/4; ℗) With a clean and cozy vibe, it's hard to believe that this purple hostel, 100m south of the school, is so cheap! Whether you're in the comfy dorms sleeping four or your own private room, you'll flock to the breezy covered common areas, which are great spots to chat with other backpackers. Pete, from Washington State, can point you toward cut-rate tours and store your bags for you while you're on them. There's also a book exchange, and lockers in every room. If it's full, stroll about 750m along the river toward Arenal and see if there's room at Gringo Pete's Too.

our pick Arenal Backpackers Resort (Map p232; ☎ 2479 7000; www.arenalbackpackers.com/home.html; Av Central; camping US$6, dm US$10, d/tr/q US$50/60/72; ℗ ✕ ☐ ⊒) This self-proclaimed 'five-star hostel' 300m west of the church is among the cushier hostels in Costa Rica. Dorm rooms have private hot-water bathrooms, and you'll sleep easy on the thick, orthopedic mattresses. Private rooms definitely cater to midrange travelers, though with flat-screen TVs and tiled-bathrooms, they're worth the splurge. But the real draw is the landscaped pool where backpackers spend lazy days lounging with a cold beer. Other amenities include wi-fi, a professional-quality shared kitchen and pool table. Some readers have complained of impersonal service here.

Sleep Inn Guesthouse (Map p232; ☎ 8394 7033; mis terlavalava@hotmail.com; Av Arenal; r with/without bathroom per person US$7/5) If you're looking for a welcoming Tico family to stay with, you've found them – Cándida will invite you into her home, 250m west of MegaSuper, as if it were yours, and Carlos, whose nickname is Mr Lava-Lava Man, guarantees you'll see lava (or you get to go again for free), and his tours (US$25) are the cheapest in town.

Hotel Dorothy (Map p232; ☎ 2479 8068; www.hotel dorothy.com; r per person incl breakfast downstairs/upstairs US$8/10; P ▣) Although it's a bit far from town, at 300m south next to the bullring, and a little rough around the edges, this spot is highly recommended simply because Noel, the bilingual Limónese owner, is positively beaming with Caribbean warmth. Noel is also something of a local hero – upon noticing that the nearby bullring was on fire, Noel alerted the fire department, saving the scores of undocumented Nicaraguan workers who were being detained inside.

La Choza Inn (Map p232; ☎ 2479 9091; www.la chozainnhostel.com; Av Fort btwn Calles 2 & 4; dm US$5, s/d/tr US$8/10/15, with bathroom & air-con US$20/30/40; P ▣ ▣) This popular budget inn 100m west of Parque Central has a great variety of rooms, a well-stocked communal kitchen, an extremely personable staff and is consistently packed with discriminating travelers. The on-site location of the recommended Eagle Tours (opposite) is a huge bonus.

Mayol Lodge (Map p232; ☎ 2479 9110; www.mayol lodge.com; Av Arenal; s/d with fan US$18/30, with air-con US$30/45; P ▣) Small, bright rooms done up in cheery blue-and-yellow tile are centered on a cool, refreshing pool with volcano views. It's 200m southeast of Parque Central.

Cabinas La Riviera (Map p234; ☎ 2479 9048; Av Fort; camping per tent US$6, s/d/tr incl breakfast US$20/30/40; P ▣) A pretty 10-minute walk east from town, this recommended spot has nine basic, fan-cooled cabinas scattered around absolutely fantastic gardens, where fruit trees attract all manner of birds.

Cabinas y Soda El Río (Map p232; ☎ 2479 9341; Av Arenal; r with fan/air-con US$25/35; ▣) Next to the river and run by a friendly family, rooms here are secure, homey and comfortable. Plus there's the *soda* out front, open 6am to 9pm.

Midrange
All of the listed accommodations have private bathrooms with hot water.

Pura Vida Hotel (Map p232; ☎ 2479 9495; www.hotel puravida.net; s/d/tr US$25/35/50; P ▣) Although Pura Vida is nothing too out of the ordinary, it's reasonably priced and extremely

comfortable with features like good shower pressure and firm mattresses. The Chinese family that owns the hotel also runs a – wait for it – Chinese restaurant (US$3 to US$10) downstairs.

Hotel Las Colinas (Map p232; ☎ 2479 9305; www .lascolinasarenal.com; Calle 1 btwn Avs Central & Arenal; s/d/ tr/q incl breakfast from US$29/42/60/75; ▣ ▣) The su-perfriendly owners of Las Colinas have com-pletely remodeled this hotel, creating modern, airy rooms and a 2nd-story terrace with great views of the volcano. All rooms have cable TV and solar-generated hot water, but rates increase with amenities like air-con, minibar and sitting rooms.

Hotel Pepito's Place (Map p232; ☎ 2479 9238; Calle 2; s/d US$30/40; P ▣ ▣) A cute family-run choice with flowerpots on the balconies, this is a good deal on the lower end of this price range. Find it 100m south of the church.

Hotel Sierra Arenal (Map p232; ☎ 2479 9751; Av Central; s/d/tr incl breakfast US$40/50/60; P ▣ ▣) Everything you're looking for is right here – hot showers, good mattresses, cable TV, internet access, private balconies and some of the best volcano views in town. Rooms upstairs have better volcano views and cost about US$10 extra. The Tico owners are laidback and really helpful.

Hotel Monte Real (Map p232; ☎ 2479 9357; www .monterealhotel.com; Av Arenal btwn Calles 3 & 5; d US$50-75; P ▣ ▣) Next to the Río Burío with a pool in the middle of the landscaped grounds, this comfortable hotel is run by an attentive Tico couple named Francisco and Nury. Pricier rooms are larger and have balconies with river or volcano views, and the setting means that you'll sometimes see sloths hanging out in the hotel trees.

Hotel San Bosco (Map p232; ☎ 2479 9050; www .arenal-volcano.com; Av Volcán; s/d incl breakfast US$66/77; P ▣ ▣ ▣) The most established hotel in town is also the priciest, though the perks include free wi-fi in all the spotless rooms, free coffee and tea all day, a guarded parking lot, lovely pool and superfriendly staff.

Hotel Arenal Carmela (Map p232; ☎ 2479 9010; www.hotelarenalcarmela.com; Av Central; s/d incl breakfast US$50/60; P ▣ ▣ ▣) They've crammed quite a few rooms into this small area – if any-one's on the balcony while you take a dip in the pool, you may feel like a performing seal. But the rooms are modern and clean, if on the small side, and as it's just across from the church it's right in the center of town.

WEST OF TOWN

There are a few recommended places to stay along the road to Arenal, some of which have more character than others. Note that hotels are listed according to their distance from La Fortuna.

Hotel Las Flores (Map p234; ☎ 2479 9307; camping per person US$5, s/d/tr incl breakfast US$20/30/40; **P** 🔀) This is a great budget option! Attractive, wood-paneled cabinas 2.5km west of town with hot-water bathrooms are pleasantly located on a quiet farm, which is a world away from La Fortuna. If you have a tent, feel free to pitch it here.

Cerro Chato Lodge (Map p234; ☎ 2479 9522; www .cerrochato.com; r incl breakfast US$30-60; **P** 🖳) Owned by Miguel Zamora, an avid naturalist who delights in leading tourists on nature tours. Rooms here are simple and sweet, with hot-water bathrooms and great views of the volcano. About 1.5km west of La Fortuna, you'll see the lodge's turnoff, after which it's another 800m to the lodge. Miguel can pick you up for free from La Fortuna.

Los Erupciones B&B (Map p234; ☎ 2460 8000; s/d incl breakfast US$65/75; **P** 🔀) The colorful cabinas at this appealing B&B are adorned with ornamental tiles and windows facing the volcano. And each one comes with its own private patio with chairs, looking onto the green scenery or the volcano. There's even a Jacuzzi at this sweet spot, 9km west of La Fortuna.

Arenal Oasis Eco Lodge (Map p234; ☎ 2479 9526; www.arenaloasis.com; s/d/tr incl breakfast US$50/65/80; **P** 🖳) The Rojas Bonilla family, which operates a sustainable farm, has five cute cabins about 800m south of the highway. All are equipped with hot water and bathtubs, and the family is warm and hospitable. There are walking trails through the surrounding rain forest, and the property itself is set in a beautiful botanic garden.

Arenal Volcano Inn (Map p234; ☎ 2461 2021; www .arenalvolcanoinn.com; s/d/tr incl breakfast from US$82/95/107; **P** 🔀 🖳) The beautifully landscaped grounds of this quaint inn surround a pool and bungalow-style rooms, about 6.5km from La Fortuna. The tiled rooms are simple but include kitchenette and cable TV, and the management do all they can to make your stay relaxing and comfortable.

Lomas del Volcán (Map p234; ☎ 2479 9000; www.lomas delvolcan.com; s/d/tr/q incl breakfast US$95/100/120/140; **P** 🔀 🖳 🖳) Although Lomas del Volcán is one of the original resorts lining this stretch of road, it's recommended because of its quiet location (you can hear monkeys in the trees) and stunning volcano views (especially when you're soaking in the outdoor hot tub). Comfy, hardwood cabins have private hot-water bathrooms with stained-glass accents, and there are plenty of opportunities for hiking through the surrounding primary forest. Find it about 2km west of La Fortuna and then another signposted 1.5km down a dirt road.

Hotel el Silencio del Campo (Map p234; ☎ 2479 7055; www.hotelsilenciodelcampo.com; d/tr/q incl breakfast US$119/134/149; **P** 🔀 🖳 ♿) This lovely resort 4km west of town was built by the same owners as Eco-Termales and reflects the same understated elegance that makes its hot springs so memorable. Cabins here are luxurious without being showy, and have attractive tiling, plush bedding and soft lighting. Bonus: if you stay here, you get a discount at Eco-Termales. When last we checked, there was a hideous hotel rudely putting up walls right next to the property, but hopefully it won't affect the peaceful atmosphere here.

Tabacón Lodge (Map p234; ☎ 2256 1500; www .tabacon.com; d incl breakfast US$302-466; **P** 🔀 🔀 🖳 🖳) Guests staying at Tabacón have unlimited access to the hot springs, which is where you'll want to spend most of your time if you stay here. Though the rooms are adequate for a higher end, they do not justify these over-the-top rates. But, if you're going to blow the cash to stay here, do it right and book a suite. The resort is 13km west of La Fortuna.

SOUTH OF TOWN

Just a few kilometers south of town, a mostly dirt road trundles up to the base of Cerro Chato, and hotels now dot either side of the path where before there were fincas. A few of these hotels are listed in order of distance from the main road.

Even further flung is the village of Chachagua, about 8km south along the road to San Ramón. Crisscrossed by local rivers, this area is a quiet place in the rain forest, away from the touristy brouhaha of La Fortuna.

Cabinas La Catarata (Map p234; ☎ 2479 9753; s/d US$25/30; **P**) About 1km further up the road, you'll see a few places offering cabinas; of these, this riverside, family-run spot is by far the best value. Though the wood-walled cabins are simple, they're spotlessly clean and come with fully equipped kitchen, TV and hot water. Some sleep up to eight people, and the setting is peaceful and rustic.

Catarata Eco-Lodge (Map p234; ☎ 2479 9522; www.cataratalodge.com; s/d incl breakfast US$35/54; P ⬜) Well, they do recycle and don't automatically throw your linens in the wash every day; apart from that the 'eco' of this lodge extends to simply caring about the environment. But it has a gorgeous setting at the base of Cerro Chato, and the staff takes beautiful care of the garden, pool and guests.

Villas Josipek (Map p234; ☎ 2430 5252, 2479 9555; www.costaricavillasjosipek.com; d/tr US$60/75; P 🐾) In the village of Chachagua, these immaculate, simple wooden cabins with volcano views are surrounded by private rain forest trails that penetrate the Bosque Eterno de los Niños. All eight of the cabins have full kitchens, and the largest sleeps up to 12. There's a well-kept pool on the quiet, jungle-fringed property, and the family can arrange tours in the region.

Chachagua Rainforest Hotel (Map p234; ☎ 2468 1010; www.chachaguarainforesthotel.com; s/d incl breakfast US$82/92; P ✗ 🐾) This hotel is a naturalist's dream, situated on a private reserve that abuts the Bosque Eterno de Los Niños. Part of the property is a working orchard, cattle ranch and fish farm, while the rest is humid rain forest that can be accessed either through a series of hiking trails or on horseback. Request the older, Frank Lloyd Wright-esque wooden cabins, which have low windows for watching the birds. There's also a pool within the exquisitely lush grounds, as well as two restaurants (meals US$8 to US$16) that feature some produce and meats raised on the premises. The 2km dirt road forking off the main road may require 4WD in the rainy season.

Casa Luna Lodge (Map p234; ☎ 2479 7368; www.casalunalodge.com; r incl breakfast US$95; P ✗ ⬜ 🐾 ♿) Wooden doors open into elegant rooms tiled in terra-cotta. Some rooms are wheelchair-accessible, and all of which have large orthopedic beds. There's wi-fi access and secure parking, and the pleasant pool area is edged with landscaped garden walkways leading to an open-air restaurant. It's 1.5km from the main road, on the right.

Eating

BUDGET

Mi Casa (Map p232; ☎ 2479 7115; Calle 3; pastries US$1-2; ⌚ 7am-6pm Mon-Sat, 7am-5:30pm Sun) This European-style café, rounded out with plenty of Tico charm, has a good variety of strong coffees, *batidos* and supersweet homemade pastries. It's 200m east of Parque Central.

Rainforest Café (Map p232; ☎ 2479 7239; Calle 1 btwn Avs Central & Arenal; pastries US$1-5; ⌚ 7am-8:30pm) Superb coffee and espresso is served in what feels like an industrial tent, all glass walls and aluminum bathroom door. There's a dash of urban coffeehouse atmosphere as well, in the burlap coffee bags on the floor and coffee beans under the glass tabletops. The pastry case is a marvel, and the menu has some sandwich-type items along with specialty coffee drinks.

Soda La Mesa de Mamá (Map p232; ☎ 2479 9727; Av Arenal btwn Calles 3 & 5; mains US$2-5; ⌚ 6am-10pm) Probably the best casados in La Fortuna are served here – judge for yourself, but try to arrive before or after the noontime feeding frenzy.

Soda Linda Vista (Map p234; ☎ 2468 0660; mains US$2-5; ⌚ 8am-10pm) Down in Chachagua, this roadside *soda* with fabulous views is about 500m south of Villas Josipek. The nice ladies running this place serve typical Costa Rican dishes.

Lava Rocks Café (Map p232; ☎ 2479 9222; Av Central; mains US$2-7; ⌚ 7am-10pm) This popular café dishes out big breakfasts, hearty casados and fresh salads, and has breezy, open-air seating in the shade. It's a magnet for tourists, who can also book tours from the desk here.

Restaurante El Jardín (Map p232; ☎ 2479 9360; cnr Av Central & Calle 3; mains US$2-7; ⌚ 5am-1pm) You can either relax over a shrimp pizza in this bustling eatery 100m east of the Parque Central, or grab a chair beneath the Pollo Pito Pito sign and snack on a few pieces of greasy (but delicious) fried chicken.

Chelas (Map p232; ☎ 2479 9594; mains US$3-7) This popular, open-air spot next to Valle Cocodrilo has great *bocas* (small, savory dishes), including *chicharrones* (stewed pork) and *ceviche de pulpo* (raw octopus marinated in lemon juice). The bar stays open until 1am, so wash your meal down with a cold Imperial (or four).

Soda La Parada (Map p232; ☎ 2479 9547; Av Central; mains US$2-8; ⌚ 24hr) Facing Parque Central and all the street action, this popular *soda* serves great steak casados, decent pizza and a couple of bizarre Tico health drinks – *chan* (slimy) and *linaza* (good for indigestion) – to after-hours revelers and folks waiting for their buses.

Down to Earth Coffee Shop (Map p232; ☎ 2479 7328; godowntoearth.org; Av Fort; ☺ 9am-8pm) Owner Matías Zeledón's family has been growing coffee since 1883, and this gregarious guy is happy to share his knowledge of the heavenly bean as well as other Costa Rican specialties. Not only can you kick back with a cup of his homegrown, pair it with a great sandwich, take home a pound of his organic beans (or chocolate-covered peaberries, mmm) *and* have him explain the etymology of Tico slang. He runs a socially responsible company – ask him about the golden rules.

For groceries, stop by the well-stocked **Super Cristian 2** (Map p232; cnr Av Central & Calle 1; ☺ 7am-9pm) on the southeast corner of Parque Central; there's another **branch** (Map p232; cnr Av Arenal & Calle 2; ☺ 7am-9pm) down by the river.

MIDRANGE & TOP END

La Choza de Laurel (Map p232; ☎ 2479 9231; www.la chozadelaurel.com; mains US$4-9; ☺ 6:30am-10pm) This place serves good, reasonably priced *comida típica* (typical food), and it always seems to be bustling. Live large and order a banana split, served on the half-shell of a pineapple.

Lava Lounge (Map p232; ☎ 2479 7365; Av Central btwn Calles 2 & 4; mains US$4-11; ☺ 11am-10:30pm) One of the newer restaurants in cuisine-poor Fortuna, this hip, open-air restaurant is a breath of fresh air when you just can't abide another casado. There's pasta, fish and a fair selection of other such well-executed international standbys, brought to you by friendly waiters.

Restaurante Rancho La Cascada (Map p232; ☎ 2479 9145; Av Fort; mains US$4-15; ☺ 7-11am & 6pm-2am) This thatched-roof landmark is probably a better bet for an evening beer or cocktail as dishes are pricey and unmemorable. But if you've got the cash, it's got a decent list of imported wines.

Mirador Arenal Steak House (Map p234; ☎ 2479 9023; mains US$5-12; ☺ 6:30am-10pm) Go West, young (wo)man! If you're craving a good *churrasco* (steak), that is. This *sabanero*-themed steakhouse has the grilling technique down pat.

Restaurant Los Nenes (Map p232; ☎ 2479 9192; Calle 5; mains US$5-15; ☺ 10am-11pm) This classic La Fortuna establishment 200m east of Parque Central is adored by locals and tourists alike. If you're in the mood for fine dining, and the seafood platters here can't be beat, and the *ceviche* (US$3) is as good as it gets.

Las Brasitas (Map p232; ☎ 2479 9819; Av Central; mains US$5-15; ☺ 11am-11pm) Sometimes you just need some good Mexican food – nothing against

Lizano sauce, but there's just no burn. Check out this breezy but elegant open-air spot 200m west of Parque Central, with good fajitas (US$6) and something called a *choriqueso* (sort of like a sausage fondue). Hey, if you're going to have a heart attack, go happy.

Pizzería Luigi's (Map p232; ☎ 2479 9909; cnr Av Central & Calle 4; breakfast US$5, dinner US$6-15; ☺ 7-9:30am & 11am-11pm) This spacious, Italian restaurant 200m west of Parque Central is formal enough to justify buttoning up your shirt and putting on a little lipstick (or at least washing your hair for once). The buffet breakfast is a popular option if you've got a long day of hiking ahead of you, though the pizzas, calzones and pastas are a better bet. The bar-casino stays open till 3am or so.

Restaurant Don Rufino (Map p232; ☎ 2479 9997; www.donrufino.com; cnr Av Central & Calle 3; mains US$3-30; ☺ 10am-11pm) Continental cuisine with judiciously applied Tico flavor makes up the menu here – skip the dressed-up casado, and opt instead for seafood with garlic and cognac, or maybe the prime rib. Half-in and half-out, the bar is also a prime place to chill with a cocktail (as late as 2:30am, if you're in that kind of mood).

Drinking & Entertainment

Despite the tourist influx, La Fortuna unfortunately remains a cultural wasteland. Occasionally, offerings are advertised at Lunatíca (p231), though entertainment in the area tends to be more of the liquid kind, and is aimed more at locals looking to get hammered and hopefully score with a gringa.

Volcán Look (Map p234; ☎ 2479 9690; ☺ 8pm-2:30am Wed-Sat) This club is reportedly the biggest discotheque in Costa Rica outside of San José. It's about 5km west of town, though it's virtually abandoned except on weekends and holidays, but don't bother showing up until after 11pm unless you want to dance cumbia alone.

Lava Lounge (Map p232; ☎ 2479 7365; Av Central btwn Calles 4 & 2; ☺ until 10:30pm) On the west side of town, this cool spot has a few romantic tables at which you can gaze over your margarita into someone's eyes – but also, the food's good, the ambience is lively and it's a welcome addition to evenings in La Fortuna.

Vagabondo (Map p234; ☎ 2479 9565; ☺ 8:30pm-late) Has a small disco bar that's popular with travelers and Ticos working in the tourist industry. It's 1.5km west of La Fortuna, and if you're out this way, it also makes wood-fired pizza and good pasta dishes.

Don Rufino (Map p232; cnr Av Central & Calle 3; 🕑 until 2:30am) Mingle with locals and other travelers at this inviting streetside bar.

Restaurante Rancho La Cascada (Map p232; ☎ 2479 9145; Av Fort; 🕑 until 2am) This is one of La Fortuna's more established places to have a beer at night; occasionally it transforms into a disco or movie theater.

Bar-Restaurant El Brete (Map p232; ☎ 2479 9982; 🕑 11am-late) Just south of town on the road to San Ramón, this bar has ladies' nights and other specials on cheap beer.

Getting There & Away
BUS
All buses currently stop at Parque Central, though a real bus terminal is currently in the works.

Keep an eye on your bags, particularly on the weekend San José run.

Ciudad Quesada (Auto-Transportes San José-San Carlos) US$1, one hour, departs 5am, 8am, noon and 3pm.

Monteverde US$2, six to eight hours, departs 8am (change at Tilarán at 12:30pm for Monteverde).

San José (Auto-Transportes San José-San Carlos) US$3, 4½ hours, departs 12:30pm & 2:30pm.

Tilarán (Auto-Transportes Tilarán) US$1.85, 3½ hours, departs 8am and 12:30pm.

HORSEBACK
Several companies also make the trip partially by horseback, including Desafío Adventure Company (p235). There are a few other options, one of which is not always recommended. See boxed text, p188, for a full description of the trip.

JEEP-BOAT-JEEP
The fastest route between Monteverde–Santa Elena and La Fortuna is the sexy-sounding jeep-boat-jeep combo (US$13 to US$20, three hours) – the 'jeep' is actually a mini-van with the requisite yellow 'turismo' emblazoned on the side. Jeep or not, it's a terrific transportation option and can be arranged through almost any hotel or tour operator in either town. The minivan from La Fortuna takes you to Laguna de Arenal, meeting a boat that crosses the lake, where a 4WD taxi on the other side continues to Monteverde. This is increasingly becoming the primary transportation between La Fortuna and Monteverde as it's incredibly

scenic, reasonably priced and it'll save you half a day of travel over rocky roads.

Getting Around
BICYCLE
Some hotels rent bikes to their guests, though **Bike Arenal** (Map p232; ☎ 2479 9454; www.bikearenal.com; Av Volcán; half-/full day US$52/75) has the best-maintained mountain and road bikes in town. It also offers guided bike tours, including beautiful rides to El Castillo and around Laguna de Arenal. Note that cycling after dark is illegal in La Fortuna.

The classic mountain-bike trip to La Catarata (about 7km from town) climbs to a fairly brutal, if nontechnical, last few kilometers, although we've heard stories of hardy pack-a-day smokers who've made it (just barely).

CAR
La Fortuna is easy to access by public transportation, but nearby attractions such as the hot springs, Parque Nacional Volcán Arenal and Laguna de Arenal require a bit more of an effort without internal combustion. Luckily, you can rent cars at **Alamo** (Map p232; ☎ 2479 9090; www.alamocostarica.com; cnr Av Central & Calle 2; 🕑 7:30am-6pm) or **Poas Rent-a-Car** (Map p232; ☎ 2479 8418; www.carentals.com; Calle 2), 100m west of the church, for similar rates to those you will find in San José or in Liberia. We really think it's worth having your own wheels while you're here.

PARQUE NACIONAL VOLCÁN ARENAL
Arenal was just another dormant volcano surrounded by fertile farmland from about AD 1500 until July 29, 1968, when something snapped. Huge explosions triggered lava flows that destroyed three villages, killing about 80 people and 45,000 cattle. The surrounding area was evacuated and roads throughout the region were closed. Eventually, the lava subsided to a relatively predictable flow and life got back to normal. Sort of.

Although it occasionally quietens down for a few weeks or even months, Arenal has been producing menacing ash columns, massive explosions and streamers of glowing molten rock almost daily since 1968. Miraculously, the volcano has retained its picture-perfect conical shape despite constant volcanic activity, though its slopes are now ashen instead of green.

The degree of activity varies from year to year and week to week – even day to day. Sometimes there can be a spectacular display of flowing red-hot lava and incandescent rocks flying through the air; at other times the volcano subsides to a gentle glow. During the day, the lava isn't easy to see, but you might still see a great cloud of ash thrown up by a massive explosion. Between 1998 and 2000, the volcano was particularly active (which is when many of those spectacular photos you see in tourist brochures were taken), and while the lava of late hasn't been quite that photogenic, it's still an awe-inspiring show.

The best nighttime views of the volcano these days are from its southwestern side, which you can appreciate by taking a night tour or by spending the night at either the Arenal Observatory Lodge (right) or one of several accommodations in El Castillo (see p245). However, be aware that clouds can cover the volcano at any time, and on rainy days a tour can be a miserably cold affair – thank goodness for all those hot springs!

Orientation & Information

The **ranger station** (☎ 2461 8499; admission to the park US$6; ☼ 8am-4pm) is on the western side of the volcano. Most people arrive as part of a group tour, but you can reach it independently. Drivers (who have at least a half-tank of gas!) can head west from La Fortuna for 15km, then turn left at the 'Parque Nacional' sign and take a 2km dirt road to the entrance. You can also take an 8am bus toward Tilarán (tell the driver to drop you off at the park) and catch the 2pm bus back to La Fortuna.

From the 'Parque Nacional' sign off the main road, a 2km dirt road leads to the ranger station, information center and parking lot. From here, trails lead 3.4km toward the volcano. Rangers will tell you how far you are allowed to go. At the time of writing, this area was not in a danger zone.

From the ranger station and information center, the road splits – head left unless you want to go back to the main highway or to the park headquarters. After heading right for about 5.5km, you'll come to another split in the road – left will bring you to Arenal Observatory Lodge (about 9km), right will bring you to the village of El Castillo (about 4km). Even in the dry season, this is most definitely 4WD country. A taxi to either the lodge or to El Castillo will run about US$20.

Sights & Activities

Arenal was made a national park in 1995, and it is part of the Area de Conservación Arenal, which protects most of the Cordillera de Tilarán. This area is rugged and varied, and the biodiversity is high; roughly half the species of land-dwelling vertebrates (birds, mammals, reptiles and amphibians) known in Costa Rica can be found here.

Birdlife is very rich in the park, and includes such specialties as trogons, rufous motmots, fruitcrows and lancebills. Commonly sighted mammals include howlers, white-faced capuchins and surprisingly tame coatis (though tempting, don't feed the wild animals; see boxed text, p355).

ARENAL OBSERVATORY LODGE

The **Arenal Observatory Lodge** (☎ reservations 2290 7011, lodge 2479 1070; www.arenalobservatory lodge.com; day use US$7; Ⓟ) was built in 1987 as a private observatory for the University of Costa Rica. Scientists chose to construct the lodge on a macadamia-nut farm on the south side of Volcán Arenal due to its proximity to the volcano (only 2km away) and its relatively safe location on a ridge. Since its creation, volcanologists from all over the world, including researchers from the Smithsonian Institute in Washington, DC, have come to study the active volcano. Today, the majority of visitors are tourists, though scientists regularly visit the lodge, and a seismograph in the hotel continues to operate around the clock. The lodge is also the only place inside the park where you can legally bed down.

The lodge offers massages (from US$60), guided hikes and all the usual tours at good prices. You can swim in the pool, wander around the macadamia nut farm or investigate the pine forest that makes up about half of the 347-hectare site. You can also rent horses for US$8 per hour.

A tiny **museum** (admission free) on the old observation deck has a seismograph and some cool newspaper clippings.

HIKING

From the ranger station (which has trail maps available), you can hike the 1km circular **Sendero Los Heliconias**, which passes by the site of the 1968 lava flow (vegetation here is slowly sprouting back to life). A 1.5km-long path branches off this trail and leads to an overlook, though the view here

---

FEELIN' HOT, HOT, HOT!

Volcanoes are formed over millennia as a result of the normal shifting processes of the earth's crust. For example, when oceanic crust slides against continental crust, the higher-density oceanic crust is pushed into a deep region of the earth known as the asthenosphere. This process, along with friction, melts the rocky crust to form magma, which rises through weak areas in the continental crust due to its comparatively light density. Magma tends to collect in a chamber below the Earth's crust until increasing pressure forces it upward through a vent and onto the surface as lava. Over time, lava deposits can form large, conical volcanoes with a circular crater at the apex from which magma can escape in the form of gas, lava and ejecta.

Although our understanding of volcanoes has greatly progressed in the past few decades, scientists are still unable to predict a volcanic eruption with certainty. However, it is possible to monitor three phenomena – seismicity, gas emissions and ground deformation – in order to predict the likelihood of a volcanic eruption. Seismicity refers to the ongoing seismic activity that tends to accompany active volcanoes. For example, most active volcanoes have continually recurring low-level seismic activity. Although patterns of activity are difficult to interpret, generally an increase in seismic activity (which often appears as a harmonic tremor) is a sign that an eruption is likely to occur.

Scientists also routinely monitor the composition of gas emissions as erupting magma undergoes a pressure decrease that can produce a large quantity of volcanic gases. For example, sulfur dioxide is one of the main components of volcanic gases, and an increasing airborne amount of this compound is another sign of an impending eruption. Finally, scientists routinely measure the tilt of slope and changes in the rate of swelling of active volcanoes. These measurements are indicators of ground deformation, which is caused by an increase in subterranean pressure due to large volumes of collecting magma.

Since Volcán Arenal is considered by scientists to be one of the 10 most active volcanoes in the entire world, comprehensive monitoring of the volcano occurs daily. Although there is constant activity and frequent eruptions, nothing has thus far rivaled the deadly 1968 eruption. In recent years, the lava flow switched directions to the southwest (much to the chagrin of hotel owners in La Fortuna), though scientists are predicting that the flow might reverse itself in years to come.

---

is foreshortened (but the explosions sure do sound loud!).

The **Sendero Las Coladas** also branches off the Heliconias trail, and wraps around the volcano for 2km past the 1993 lava flow before connecting with the **Sendero Los Tucanes**. This trail extends for another 3km through the tropical rain forest at the base of the volcano. To return to the car-parking area, you will have to turn back. You'll get good views of the summit on the way back since you're now at a better angle to view it.

From the park headquarters (not the ranger station), there is also the 1.2km **Sendero Los Miradores**, which leads you down to the shores of the lake, and provides a good angle for viewing the volcano.

Every once in a while, perhaps lulled into a sense of false security by a temporary pause in the activity, someone tries to climb to the crater and peer within it. This is very dangerous – climbers have been killed and maimed by explosions. The problem is not so much that the climber gets killed (that's a risk the foolhardy insist is their own decision) but rather that the lives of Costa Rican rescuers are placed at risk.

If you're not staying at Arenal Observatory Lodge, it's worth visiting as there are 6km of **trails** in total, and it's only US$7 to enter. A handful of short hikes include views of a nearby waterfall, while sturdy souls could check out recent lava flows (2½ hours), old lava flows (three hours) or the climb to Arenal's dormant partner, Volcán Chato, whose crater holds an 1100m-high lake only 3km southeast of Volcán Arenal (four hours). For the best nighttime views, a guided hike is suggested. Maps and local English-speaking guides are available for these hikes. The lodge also has a 4.5km bike trail that winds through secondary forest, as well as a 1km sidewalk trail that is completely wheelchair accessible.

Note that camping is not allowed inside the park, though people do camp (no facilities) off some of the unpaved roads west of the volcano by the shores of the lake.

Sleeping & Eating

Arenal Observatory Lodge (Map p234; ☎ reservations 2290 7011, lodge 2692 2070; www.arenalobservatorylodge .com; s/d/tr/q incl breakfast La Casona US$68/81/95/111, standard r US$95/108/116/136, Smithsonian r US$128/142/151/162, junior ste US$155/163/172/182, White Hawk Villa 8 people US$495; ☐ ☒ ☐ ☒) Although most of the lava flows are on the southwest side of Arenal (the lodge is positioned to the west), the views of the eruptions are excellent, and the constant rumbling is enough to make you sleep a bit uneasily at night. The lodge has a variety of rooms spread throughout the property, five of which are wheelchair accessible (along with the pool and several trails – this lodge hasn't slouched). Rates include a buffet breakfast and guided hike. La Casona is about 500m away in the original farmhouse. It now houses four rustic double rooms sharing two bathrooms; there are volcano views from the house porch. Standard rooms, adjacent to the main lodge, were originally designed for researchers but have been renovated to acceptably plush standards. Smithsonian rooms, accessible via a suspension bridge over a plunging ravine, are the best and have the finest views. The White Hawk Villa, with a kitchen and several rooms, is perfect for groups.

The restaurant (lunch/dinner US$10/25), though overpriced, has a good variety of international dishes and is decorated with jars of venomous snakes in formaldehyde.

EL CASTILLO

The tiny mountain village of El Castillo is a wonderful alternative to staying in La Fortuna – it's bucolic, untouristed and perfectly situated to watch the southwesterly lava flows. There are also some delightful accommodation options, a number of worthwhile sights and a promising ecotourism venture that will bring a tear of hope to the most jaundiced eye (see boxed text, below).

On the road to El Castillo, **SkyTrek** (Map p234; ☎ 2645 7070; www.skytrek.com; adult/student/child tram only US$55/44/28, canopy tour US$66/52/42; ☒ 7:30am-4pm) runs canopy tours on the south side of Arenal. This canopy tour gives stellar views of Laguna de Arenal, the volcano and the lush

---

RANCHO MARGOT

This 152-hectare **ranch** (☎ 2479 7259, 8302 7318; www.ranchomargot.org), which is just past El Castillo in the village of Pueblo Nuevo, is home to one of the most exciting development projects in the entire country (see also boxed text, p246). According to Juan, the Chilean mastermind behind this incredible venture, Rancho Margot is 'a sustainable, self-sufficient working ranch.' Indeed, you only need to speak with Juan for a moment to grasp the beauty and depth of his grand vision.

At the ranch, electricity is produced by turbines, dairy cows are raised for cheese and milk, orchards and organic gardens are sown for produce, pigs and chickens are being raised for food, biodigestors are converting animal waste into energy to heat thermal pools, native fish species are being reintroduced into the waters (the list goes on and on).

And, as if this wasn't impressive enough, Juan also flexes his muscle in the local community, and has already paid off school debts, purchased shuttle buses, reforested hillsides, and built an animal rescue center, veterinary hospital and a ranger station. Although the ranch is still a work in progress, it is already attracting students, researchers, farmers, horticulturists, backpackers and high-end tourists alike.

If you're interested in spending the night on the ranch (and we highly recommend that you do!), Juan offers immaculate **bunkhouses** (per night US$40) complete with orthopedic mattresses and handmade wooden fixtures, as well as elegantly crafted **bungalows** (s/d US$100/130, extra person US$30) that are perched dramatically on the hillsides. Guests are also invited for **meals** (lunch/dinner US$15/17), which prominently feature locally raised meats and produce grown on the ranch.

As this is a working ranch, Juan can also organize a variety of horseback **riding trips** (from US$35) into the surrounding rain forest. If you're looking for holistic healing, the ranch is also home to a stunning **yoga center** that is built on stilts over a babbling brook.

If you don't have your own transportation, Juan can arrange free bus pick-up to and from La Fortuna as well as private hotel transfers (US$25) with prior arrangement.

rain forest. A silent gondola (the SkyTram) slowly conveys visitors up above the canopy, and at the top you can either tram it back down or fly down the zip lines.

On the only road in town, you'll find two noteworthy ecological attractions. The **El Castillo-Arenal Butterfly Conservatory** (☎ 2479 1149; www.butterflyconservatory.org; with/without guide US$10/8; ☻ 8am-5pm) is run by an American expat named Glenn, whose conservation project far exceeds your normal butterfly garden. He is seeking to understand life cycles and hatching times for different species, and routinely works with students and volunteers to rigorously catalog every scrap of data. Here you'll find seven different gardens pertaining to each habitat as well as a rana-rium, an insect museum, a medicinal herb garden, botanic garden trails and a river walk. The conservatory has one of the largest butterfly exhibitions in Costa Rica, and is one of the few places that raises all of the butterflies and frogs on exhibit. The center proportionally releases these species for re-populating habitats within the area. Glenn is also actively involved in local reforestation programs, and is always looking for a few good volunteers.

Next door is the **Jardín Zoológico de Serpientes del Arenal** (☎ 8358 6773; admission US$8; ☻ 8:30am-5:30pm), where local snake-handler Victor Hugo Quesada will introduce you to six species of frog, four species of turtle, 35 species of snake and a fair number of lizards and iguanas.

Sleeping & Eating

Majestic Lodge (☎ 8350 7431; www.arenalmajesticlodge .com; r incl breakfast US$35-50; P ☒) On the road to Rancho Margot, this gringo-run lake-view lodge has DirecTV in its small, spotless guest rooms. The attractive wood deck is perfect for stargazing and socializing. Creative dinners are sometimes thrown together for guests, and the small balconies provide private nooks for when you're not feeling so social.

Cabanitas El Castillo Dorado (☎ 2692 2065; s/d US$40/55; P) Here you'll find simple cabins with private warm-water bathrooms and vol-cano views through enormous picture windows. The onsite restaurant (mains US$2 to US$6) is recommended for its fresh tilapia and, needless to say, great vistas.

Hotel Linda Vista del Norte (☎ 2692 2090, 8380 0847; www.hotellindavista.com; s/d incl breakfast standard US$63/73, ste US$95/105; P ☒ ☒) The first accom-

modations you'll pass on the road into town is a lodge consisting of 11 simple rooms with smashing views, perched high on a mountain-top (though only some of the rooms look onto the volcano). Even better is the restaurant-bar (mains US$10 to US$15), which is lined with picture windows and has spectacular views of the lava flows from Arenal.

Nido del Colibrí (☎ 8835 8711; www.humming birdnestbb.com; s/d incl breakfast US$50/75; P) At the entrance to town, you'll see a small path that leads up the (steep) hill to one of our favorite B&Bs in all of Costa Rica. It's owned by Ellen, a former Pan Am stewardess and all-round world traveler who has finally found a small slice of paradise to call her own. Her quaint little home has two guest bedrooms with pri-vate hot showers and enough frilly pillows to make you miss home – but that's not even the best part! In her immaculately landscaped front garden, you can soak the night away in a huge outdoor Jacuzzi while watching the lava flow down Arenal. You can even arrange to have a massage (US$45) while watching the lava. Ellen (who's also charming and full of grace) is active in the local schools, and is a good person to talk to about volunteering in the area.

Café Jardín Escondido (☻ lunch & dinner) On the road from the Majestic Lodge, look for the sign leading to this lovely pizzeria, where John, a friendly American, also whips up delicious homemade ice cream.

LAGUNA DE ARENAL AREA

About 18km west of La Fortuna, you'll arrive at a 750m-long causeway across the dam that created Laguna de Arenal, an 88-sq-km lake that is the largest in the country. Although a number of small towns were submerged during the lake's creation, the lake currently supplies valuable water to Guanacaste, and produces hydroelectricity for the region. High winds also produce power with the aid of huge, steel windmills, though windsurfers and kitesurfers frequently steal a breeze or two.

If you have your own car (or bicycle), this is one of the premier road trips in Costa Rica. The road is lined with odd and elegant busi-nesses, many run by foreigners who have fallen in love with the place, and the scenic views of lakeside forests and Volcán Arenal are about as romantic as they come. Strong winds and high elevations give the lake a temperate feel, and you'll be forgiven if you suddenly imagine

NORTHWESTERN COSTA RICA

JUAN SOSTHEIM ON RANCHO MARGOT

Juan Sostheim, the visionary behind Rancho Margot, is aiming to reshape the very definition of sustainable tourism. Over a sifter glass of fine rum, Juan shared his vision for a greener Costa Rica.

What is the driving concept behind Rancho Margot? The big message is that we are a working ranch that aims to educate and inspire our guests about the consequences of their lifestyle. Although we don't subscribe to any particular dogma, Rancho Margot is all about awareness. We hope that all of our guests come here with an open mind, and leave fully aware of the impact of their actions on this planet. Ultimately, I envision turning this ranch into a life-skills university where people can come and learn about topics such as alternative energies, organic farming and reforestation.

What is your definition of sustainable tourism? The big problem in Costa Rica is that words like sustainable, green and eco are often abused. To me, the fundamental idea behind these terms is that an individual must have the least possible impact on the natural environment. For example, all of the building materials that we are using here on the ranch are locally derived. We are strictly using lumber that has been raised for the purpose of milling, ceramic tiles that have been recovered from old houses and caña brava, a bamboo-type plant that quickly regenerates when you cut it.

How do Costa Ricans view Rancho Margot? As a Chilean living in Costa Rica, I believe that it is my responsibility to set a positive example for others to follow. When Costa Rican families visit us here, they are almost always struck by the tremendous beauty of their natural patrimony. When they see how much love and care we give to this place, we hope that they will be inspired by our actions, and perhaps take better care of their own environment. It's easy to point your finger

yourself in the English Lakes District or the Swiss countryside.

But (you already know what's coming), things are changing – quickly. Baby boomers, lured to the area by the cool climate and premier fishing, are snapping up every spot of land with a 'For Sale' sign on it. The problem is that Costa Rican law does not require would-be-realtors to possess a valid real-estate license, and these days it seems like every other schmoe is looking to speculate in the hopes of turning a quick buck. Costa Ricans are not happy about the impending loss of their lakeside paradise, and it doesn't seem likely that the construction boom is going to slow.

Most of the road is paved and in decent condition, though you'll encounter some big potholes. Buses run about every two hours, and hotel owners can tell you when to catch your ride. If you're heading to Monteverde via the jeep-boat-jeep transfer, you're in for a lovely ride.

Dam to Nuevo Arenal

This beautiful stretch of road is lined on both sides with cloud forest, and there are a number of fantastic accommodations strung along the way.

AROUND THE DAM

Unlike the fly-by view you'll get on a zip-line canopy tour, a walk through **Puentes Colgantes de Arenal** (Arenal Hanging Bridges; Map p234; ☎ 2479 9686; www.hangingbridges.com; adult/student/child under 12yr US$22/12/free; ☼ 7:30am-4:30pm) allows you to explore the rain forest and canopy from trails and suspended bridges at a more natural and peaceful pace. Reservations are required for guided birding tours (three hours, from 6am) or informative naturalist tours (8am and 2pm).

The bridges are easily accessible by car and well signed, though most tourists arrive on a package tour from La Fortuna. The Tilarán bus can drop you off at the entrance, but it's a 3km climb from the bus stop.

If you want to stay in the area, **Arenal Lodge** (Map p234; ☎ 2460 1881; www.arenallodge .com; s/d incl breakfast standard US$83/91, junior ste US$145/152, chalet US$150/159, matrimonial ste US$184/191; P ⚓ ⚐) is 400m west of the dam, at the top of a steep 2.5km, though the entire lodge is awash with views of Arenal and the sur-

and blame others for the problems of the world, but the bottom line is that if you want to have an impact, you have to first change your own ways.

What kind of people are you seeking to attract? Rancho Margot operates as a community where everybody contributes in their own unique way. We invite people to come here, and to foster a particular skill set, while simultaneously developing as an individual. For the most part, our guests are mature and well-educated people who have the sensibility to understand what is going on in the environment, and feel compelled to do something about it. The type of visitor that is not for Rancho Margot is the package holidaymaker arriving here on a tour, or the checklist traveler who just wants to rush in and rush out.

Why do you think interest in the ranch is increasing? The beauty of what we're doing here is that anyone, regardless of their age, can take part in our ongoing social experiment. Rancho Margot is equally attractive to baby boomers who have the time to think about what their lives have meant, as well as backpackers who are in the process of forming their own identities. The common link between all of our guests is that they question some of the old wisdoms, and are willing to support a place that can provide them with a small measure of truth.

Are you optimistic about the potential impact of this project? When you hear someone proclaim that they want to influence the way people live their lives, it is certainly an enormous mouthful to swallow. Although some people may think that my dreams are hollow, I believe that I have the right intentions. Of course, I don't always get the right results, but the possibility of a greener Costa Rica is a goal that we should all be striving to achieve. In the end, my deepest hope is that my children and my children's children will learn from and follow my example.

rounding cloud forest. Standard rooms are just that, but junior suites are spacious, tiled and have wicker furniture, a big hot-water bathroom and a picture window or balcony with volcano views. Ten chalets sleep four and have kitchenette and good views. The lodge also has a Jacuzzi, a billiards room, a sophisticated restaurant (mains US$6 to US$15), complimentary mountain bikes and private stables.

Alternatively, **ourpick Lost Iguana Resort** (Map p234; ☎ 2461 0122; www.lostiguanaresort.com; r/ste US$215/297, villa US$460-535, all incl breakfast; P ☒ ☑) is easily the area's most stylish place to lay your head. This resort occupies a serene mountainside that affords phenomenal volcano views, sequestered far from the activity in La Fortuna. Even the standard rooms have private balconies looking out on Arenal, beds boasting Egyptian cotton sheets, satellite TV, and an invaluable sense of peace and privacy. Surrounded by rain forest, the rooms are tastefully decorated with bamboo furniture, open-beamed ceilings and large windows. Reception and restaurant areas are romantic enough to appeal, even if leaving your cozy casita seems a tragedy.

UNIÓN AREA

A serene, German-run escape, **La Ceiba Tree Lodge** (☎ 2692 8050, 8814 4004; www.ceibatree-lodge .com; d US$49; P) is 21km west of the dam and centered on a 500-year-old ceiba tree. Its five spacious, cross-ventilated rooms are entered through Maya-inspired carved doors and decorated with original paintings. Views of Laguna de Arenal, the lush, tropical gardens and utterly lovely dining-hangout area make this mountaintop spot a tranquil retreat from whatever ails you. A small apartment (price negotiable) is also available for rent

You can't miss **Hotel Los Héroes** (☎ 2692 8012/3; www.hotellosheroes.com; d with/without balcony US$65/55, tr US$85, apt US$115, all incl breakfast; P ☑), a slightly incongruous alpine chalet 14km west of the dam, complete with carved wooden balconies and Old World window shutters – and that's just on the outside. Large, immaculate rooms with wood paneling and private hot bathrooms are decorated with thickly hewn wood furniture that may make Swiss-Germans a little homesick, particularly when viewing paintings of tow-headed children in lederhosen smooching innocently. There are also three apartments (each sleeps up to six) with full kitchen, huge bathroom and balcony overlooking the lake. Facilities include a Jacuzzi, swimming pool, a church complete with Swiss chimes, and a restaurant (mains US$5 to US$12, open 7am to 3pm and 6pm to 8pm) that gets Swiss folks on the road too long to indulge in authentic *Zürcher Geschnetzeltes* (Zurich-style veal served over potatoes) and fondues. The owners have even built a miniature train (US$10) that brings you up a hill to an underground station beneath the Rondorama Panoramic Restaurant (mains US$8 to US$15), a revolving restaurant (seriously!) that's reportedly one-of-a-kind in Mexico and Central America. There's also a hiking trail that leads to the restaurant and is great for wildlife-watching.

Another accommodation option is **Villa Decary B&B** (☎ 2694 4330, 8383 3012; www.villadecary .com; s/d US$90/107, caseta with kitchen US$164, extra person US$15, all incl breakfast; **P**), an all-round winner with bright, spacious, well-furnished rooms, delicious full breakfasts and fantastic hosts. Five rooms have private hot showers, a queen and a double bed, bright Latin American bedspreads and artwork, and balconies with excellent views of the woodland immediately below and the lake just beyond. There are also three separate *casetas* with a kitchenette. Paths into the woods behind the house give good opportunities for birding and wildlife-watching, and there's a good chance that howlers will wake you in the morning. Guests can borrow binoculars and a bird guide to identify what they see. Jeff, one of the US owners, has gotten the bird bug and can help out with identification. His partner, Bill, is a botanist specializing in palms (Decary was a French botanist who discovered a new species of palm). Come prepared – credit cards are not accepted.

A few kilometers past Villa Decary on the left-hand side of the highway is **Nuevo Arenal** (camping per tent US$5), a small lakeside park with campsites, cold showers and bathrooms.

Rates for the simply gorgeous two-person cottages – works of art, really – at **La Mansion Inn Arenal** (☎ 2692 8018; www.lamansionarenal.com; cottages incl breakfast US$204-640; **P** 🌐 🖭) also include a champagne breakfast, fruit basket, welcome cocktail, canoe access and horse rides, all conspiring with the magnificent views to make this the most romantic inn in the region. The cottages feature huge split-level rooms with private terraces, lake views, high

ceilings, Italianate painted walls and arched, bathroom doors. There's also an ornamental garden featuring Chorotega pottery, an infinity swimming pool that appears to flow into the lake, a pool table, a formal restaurant (four-course dinner excluding wine US$35) and a cozy bar shaped like the bow of a ship. It's 17km west of the dam.

For an espresso and heavenly macadamia chocolate brownies try **Toad Hall** (☎ 2592 8001, 2692 8020; www.toadhall-gallery.com; mains US$3-8; ⊙ 8am-5pm). The restaurant, 16km west of the dam, overlooks the forest and lake and serves a short, delicious and beautifully presented menu that tends toward California cuisine, incorporating homegrown organic veggies and homemade focaccia; take some time to enjoy a bite and one of its fruit drinks outdoors. While there, you can browse the bookstore and art gallery, which has a high-quality collection of local and indigenous art and jewelry, and hosts an artist-in-residence program. Just beyond Toad Hall, a dirt road to the right goes to the Venado Caves, which can be explored with guides.

If you're a gourmand suffering from a lack of memorable cuisine, make absolutely sure to book dinner reservations at the new **our pick Gingerbread Hotel & Restaurant** (☎ 2694 0039, 8351 7815; www.gingerbreadarenal.com; r incl breakfast US$100; ⊙ 5-8pm Tue-Sat, lunch by reservation only), arguably the best restaurant in northwestern Costa Rica (if not the entire country). Better yet, stay at the charming boutique hotel, where the beds are sumptuous and the rooms adorned with murals by renowned local artists – this way, you'll get homemade preserves and pastries at breakfast. With the freshest local fare providing the foundation of his weekly menus, Chef Eyal turns out transcendent meals (mains US$11 to US$20, wines US$30 to US$200) and is choosy about his wine list, emphasizing top Chilean and Spanish vino. And yet there's no pretension in this very cozy, out-of-the-way, lake-view dining room with walls covered in paintings by artists in the community (including manager Coryn). A word to the wise: do not pass up dessert.

Nuevo Arenal

The only good-sized town between La Fortuna and Tilarán is the small Tico settlement of Nuevo Arenal, which is 29km west of the dam. In case you were wondering what happened to the old Arenal (no, it wasn't wiped out by the volcano, but good guess), it's about 27m below the surface of Laguna de Arenal. In order to create a large enough reservoir for the dam, the Costa Rican government had to make certain, er, sacrifices, which ultimately resulted in the forced relocation of 3500 people. Today, the humble residents of Nuevo Arenal don't seem to be fazed by history, especially since they now own premium lakeside property.

Nuevo Arenal is something of a rest stop for travelers heading to Tilarán and points beyond, though it's certainly a pleasant (and cheap) place to spend the night. The tiny downtown also has a gas station, a Banco de Costa Rica, SuperCompro and a bus stop near the park.

SLEEPING & EATING

Cabinas Rodríguez (☎ 2694 4237; r per person with bathroom US$6) Near the soccer field, this is pretty much the cheapest place you're going to find in the whole Laguna de Arenal region. Rooms are clean though a bit dark, and guests can share the kitchenette.

Cabinas Catalina (☎ 8819 6793; d US$20; P) Find these budget digs across from the gas station (where you should enquire about rooms if no one's around the cabinas), which consist of sterile cabinas with concrete walls and warmish showers that will do in a pinch.

Hotel Lago de Arenal (☎ 2694 4319; www.hotellago arenal.com; s/d/tr incl breakfast US$70/79/87; P 🛇 🖳 🖼) Considering its hillside location with expansive lake views, this hotel feels like it could be so much more, but is simply too tired to fulfill its full potential (le sigh). But if you must stop in Nuevo Arenal for the night, it's infinitely more comfortable than the town's budget options. It's a bumpy 1.5km from the main road.

Bar y Restaurant Bambú (☎ 2694 4048; mains US$2-4; 🕑 6am-10pm) In addition to doing good casados and gallos (not to mention another round of beer on Friday night when there's live music), the owner has tourist information and can arrange tours, including fishing trips, guided hikes and horse rides.

Lava Java (☎ 2694 4753; per hr US$1; 🕑 6am-8:30pm) Check your email here on the main road as you sip a fresh smoothie or slurp down a quick coffee.

Restaurant La Casa de Doña Celina (☎ 2694 4609; mains US$4-8; 🕑 7am-9pm) This is just your basic soda, next door to Lava Java, but the views make your lunch taste better, as do the retro

diner tables on the patio, and you can work up your appetite with a game of pinball.

Tom's Pan (☎ 2694 4547; mains US$1-6; 🕑 7am-4pm Mon-Sat; P) This German bakery is a famous rest stop for road-trippers heading to Tilarán. Its breads, strudels and cakes are all homemade and delicious, though heartier eaters will rave over the big German breakfasts, goulash with homemade noodles, and a deli stocking Leiberkäs and Weisswurst. Behind the restaurant, there is a cozy double room for rent (US$55 per night, with breakfast) with huge windows and an outdoor Jacuzzi.

After you've had your fill, browse **Ellen's Indigenous Souvenir Shop** (☎ 2694 4582; ellenssouvenir .de; 🕑 10am-7pm) next door, where the goods are '100% not made in China.'

Nuevo Arenal to Tilarán

Continue west and around the lake from Nuevo Arenal, where the scenery becomes even more spectacular just as the road gets progressively worse. Tilarán is the next 'big' city, with a reasonable selection of hotels and restaurants, plus roads and buses that can take you to Liberia, Monteverde or beyond.

SLEEPING & EATING

La Rana de Arenal (☎ 2694 4031; www.dorislake arenal.com; s/d incl breakfast US$30/45; P) Watch out for the hairpin turnoff at the driveway to La Rana, a quaint German-run spot with seven comfortable rooms. The restaurant (mains US$6 to US$11, open 11am to 10pm) serves good international food, with an emphasis on German cuisine, in an airy upstairs pub-style dining room. There are tennis courts on the property, which is excellent for bird-watching, and the staff can arrange horseback and boat tours.

Chalet Nicholas (☎ 2694 4041; www.chaletnicholas .com; d incl breakfast US$79, extra person US$15; P 🛇) This attractive mountain chalet 2km west of Nuevo Arenal is owned by Catherine and John Nicholas, though their co-owners, five very playful Great Danes (don't be alarmed when they come bounding out to greet you), really know how to steal the show. Two downstairs rooms have private bathroom, while the upstairs loft has two linked bedrooms (for families or groups) and shares a downstairs bathroom. On clear days, all rooms have views of the volcano at the end of the lake. The owners enjoy natural history and have a living collection of dozens of orchids, which

WORLD-CLASS WIND

Some of the world's most consistent winds blow across northwestern Costa Rica, and this consistency attracts windsurfers from all over the world. Laguna de Arenal is rated one of the three best windsurfing spots in the world, mainly because of the predictability of the winds. From December to April, the winds reliably provide great rides for board sailors who gather on the southwest corner of the lake for long days of fun on the water. Windsurfing is possible in other months, too, but avoid September and October, which are considered the worst.

Although there are plenty of fly-by-night operators, there are really only two places you should consider for all your surfing needs. The best company for windsurfing is **Tico Wind** (☎ 2695 5387; www.ticowind.com; rentals incl lunch half-/full day US$38/68), which sets up a camp on the western shores of the lake each year from December 1 to April 15. It has state-of-the-art boards and sails that are replaced every year. There are 50 sails to allow for differing wind conditions, experience and people's weights, but it rents only 12 at a time so that surfers can pick and choose during the day as conditions change – a class act. Staff will arrange nearby hotel accommodations. Serious surfers book boards weeks ahead of time; newbies and those wishing to improve their skills can take lessons. Tico Wind also offers rentals and lessons through Ecoplaya Beach Resort (p228) on the Bahía Salinas, Costa Rica's second windsurfing destination.

Hotel Tilawa (below) has emerged as a popular destination for windsurfers (and increasingly kitesurfers, too), and has an excellent selection of sailboards for rent at comparable rates. Although some folks think that the high winds, waves and world-class conditions are too much for a beginner to handle, the folks at Tilawa disagree. They run a reader-recommended **windsurfing and kitesurfing school** (half-/full day US$100/150), and if you don't enjoy your first day of lessons, which takes place on land using stationary boards, they'll refund your money. After the first day, lessons become more expensive (US$60 per hour) and cater to all skill levels – once you've learned the basics, self-motivated practice with short instructional periods is the best way to learn. If you're staying at the hotel, you can also take advantage of discount rates on rental equipment (half-/full day US$45/55).

It gets a little chilly on Laguna de Arenal, and rentals usually include wet suits, as well as harnesses and helmets (serious boarders bring their own for the best fit, just renting the board and sail). For a warm change, head down to Bahía Salinas on Costa Rica's far northwestern coast. Resorts here offer windsurfing year-round, and though the wind may not be quite as world class as at Laguna de Arenal, it comes pretty close. The seasons are the same as for the lake.

attract numerous species of birds. This place has many repeat guests.

Lago Coter Ecolodge (☎ 2440 6768; www.ecolodgecostarica.com; s/d/tr standard US$76/87/99, cabin US$93/105/122, all incl breakfast; P ☒) This environmentally friendly lodge caters mostly to visitors that come on a complete package, including meals, rental equipment and guided naturalist hikes. Standard rooms with private hot showers are in a handsome wood-and-stone lodge that has a large fireplace and a relaxation area with billiards, TV and a small library. There are also 14 larger cabins that have picture windows overlooking the lake. Go 5km west of Nuevo Arenal then turn 3km down an unpaved road.

Mystica Resort (☎ 2692 1001; mystica@racsa .co.cr; s/d incl breakfast US$76/81, villa US$163; P) This Mediterranean-style retreat lies on a hill 1km after the Tierras Morenas turnoff, and is an-

other good midrange option. The resort has several comfortable, colorful rooms with blue tiles, vibrant woven bedspreads, hot showers and volcano views. Even if you're not staying here, it's a great place to stop for a wood-fired pizza lunch (mains US$5 to US$10, open noon to 9pm). The Essence, a yoga and meditation center, is on the grounds for all your holistic-healing needs.

Hotel Tilawa (☎ 2695 5050; www.hotel-tilawa.com; d US$68-98; P ☒ ☒ ☐ ☒) It's something of a legend among windsurfers and kitesurfers, and whether you're semiprofessional or just starting out, you'll find a great community of wind warriors here. As for the rooms, well, they're definitely spacious and they cater to different budgets, though the Grecian theme – frescoes and all – is sort of over-the-top. Tilawa also has the best collection of amenities on the lake, including a huge skateboard park, pool, tennis courts and free bike rental.

Lucky Bug B&B and Caballo Negro Restaurant (☎ 2694 4515; www.luckybugcr.com; r incl breakfast US$79-140; P) Set on a rain-forest lagoon, the bungalows at the Lucky Bug are not only blissfully isolated but feature unique art and decorative details by local artisans. The Caballo Negro (Black Horse; mains US$3 to US$10, open 8am to 8pm) serves excellent organic, vegetarian and European fare handcrafted by owner Monica, who speaks English and German and makes a mean schnitzel. Also here is the fabulously quirky Lucky Bug Gallery, which features high-quality work from local and national artisans, not least of whom are Monica's triplets Kathryn, Alexandra and Sabrina. The artistry really is outstanding, and should you fall in love with a painting of a bug or something bigger, they can ship it for you. It's 3km west of Nuevo Arenal.

Café y Macadamia de Costa Rica (☎ 2692 2000; cafeymacadamia@yahoo.com; mains US$2-8; 7:30am-5pm) Pull over for a cup of coffee – and maybe a salad or Thai chicken curry, and leave room for a tasty pastry – all best savored along with the spectacular views of the lake (or clouds and fog, as the weather dictates). The gigantic, wood-floored room and equally large outdoor terrace alone make it worth a stop to stretch your legs.

Equus Bar-Restaurant (mains US$4-8; 11am-close) This lakeside spot 13km west of Nuevo Arenal is perennially popular among windsurfers looking to brag about their exploits over a cold Imperial. There's a good mix of Costa Rican and Western dishes, and on some nights there's live music here.

TILARÁN

Near the southwestern end of Laguna de Arenal, the small town of Tilarán has a prosperous air to it – probably because it has served as a regional ranching center since long before there was a lake to speak of. Every year, this tradition is honored on the last weekend in April with a rodeo that's popular with Tico visitors, and on June 13 with a bullfight-filled fiesta that's dedicated to patron San Antonio.

Because it's situated on the slopes of the Cordillera de Tilarán, this little hub is a much cooler alternative (in climate and atmosphere) to, say, Cañas, and makes a pleasant stop between La Fortuna and Monteverde.

Check email while waiting for your bus at **Cybercafé Tilarán** (☎ 2695 9010; per hr US$1.25; 9am-10pm Mon-Sat), which has computers with speedy connections, 25m west of the bus terminal.

Sleeping & Eating

All of the hotels listed following have private warm(ish) showers.

Hotel Tilarán (☎ 2695 5043; r shared/private bathroom US$6/10; P) If you can get one of the rooms toward the back, this is a decent budget choice on the west side of Parque Central. The tiny rooms have cable TV and are clean enough to lay your head for a night.

Hotel Mary (☎ 2695 5479; d US$25; P) On the south side of Parque Central, Hotel Mary is an excellent option with clean rooms that feature the kind of linens your grandma would love. Plan on street noise in the parkside rooms, or just enjoy it from the balcony. The attached restaurant (mains US$3 to US$6, open 6am to midnight) has a mix of some Tico and Chino favorites.

Hotel El Sueño (☎ 2695 5347; s/d standard US$20/30, with balcony US$25/35) Near the bus terminal, this beautiful hotel (in an ageing, baroque sort of way) has antique decorated rooms, but it's worth splurging for the balcony where you can bask in the faded glory. Downstairs is Restaurante El Parque (☎ 2695 5425, mains US$3 to US$5, open 7am to 11pm) with a selection of *bocas* that discriminating barflies also appreciate.

Hotel Guadalupe (☎ 2695 5943; www.hotelguadalupe cr.com; s/d incl breakfast US$25/40; P) Quiet, clean rooms with cable TV are arranged around the secure parking area at this well-maintained hotel a block-and-a-half southeast of the park. The downstairs cafeteria (mains US$2 to US$6, open 6am to 9pm Monday to Friday, 7am to 5pm Saturday) is consistently packed with hungry locals.

Hotel La Carreta (☎ 2695 6593; s/d incl breakfast US$40/55; P &) Owners Rita and Ed have beautifully refurbished these skylit rooms, installing orthopedic beds, reading lights and hand-painted murals by local artists. In addition to the indoor dining area, there's a pleasant garden terrace for sipping coffee and reading something you've picked up from the book exchange in the front room. Breakfasts feature homemade pastries, and nonguests can also stop by for lunch. Look for the painted *carreta* (oxcart) out front, 150m south of Banco de Costa Rica.

Restaurant Casa Antigua (☎ 2695 6053; mains US$5-14; ⊗ 7am-9:30pm Mon-Sat, 3-9:30pm Sun) This stylish blue-and-white café creates an elegant ambience with its dark-wood interior and espresso bar. Serving pastas, salads and steaks alongside the usual *comida típica*, this is a great place for a romantic supper. Find it kitty-corner to the gas station in town.

Cheap meals can be found in the *mercado* (market), beside the bus terminal, or pop into the **SuperCompro** (⊗ 8am-8pm), just across from the park, for groceries.

Getting There & Away

Tilarán is usually reached by a 24km paved road from the Interamericana at Cañas. The route on to Santa Elena and Monteverde is unpaved and rough, though ordinary cars can get through with care in the dry season.

Buses arrive and depart from the bus terminal, which is half a block west of Parque Central. Be aware that Sunday-afternoon buses to San José may be sold out by Saturday. The route between Tilarán and San José goes via Cañas and the Interamericana, not the Arenal–La Fortuna–Ciudad Quesada route. Regular services go to the following locations:

Cañas US$0.50, 30 minutes, departs 5am, 6:40am, 7:30am, 8am, 10am, 11:30am and 3:30pm.

Ciudad Quesada, via La Fortuna US$2.50, four hours, departs 7am and 12:30pm.

Nuevo Arenal US$0.75, 1¼ hours, departs 5am, 6am, 8am, 9am, 10am, 11am, 1pm, 2:30pm and 3:30pm.

Puntarenas US$2.50, two hours, departs 6am and 1pm.

San José (Auto-Transportes Tilarán) US$3.50, four hours, departs 4:45am, 7am, 9:30am, 2pm and 5pm.

Santa Elena US$1.75, three to four hours, departs 12:30pm.

Península de Nicoya

The allure of the Península de Nicoya needs no explanation. Archetypal tropical beaches edge this jungle-trimmed rich coast, whose shores have been imprinted on the memories of the millions of marine turtles who return to their birthplaces to nest. So, too, do travelers descend on these beaches, seeking to witness such magical patterns of nature for themselves. Humans, however, make more of an environmental impact than the leatherbacks do.

Development is the name of the game at the moment, and Nicoya is the high-stakes playing field. That field is in danger of being paved over – is, in fact, in that very process in various parts of the peninsula – but it's difficult to call an outcome. Optimists will point out that Costa Rica is one of the most eco-conscious nations on the planet – President Oscar Arias has grand plans to make the country the first carbon-neutral nation by 2021 – and grassroots community activism led by both Ticos (Costa Ricans) and foreigners is leading to instances of government enforcement of sustainable development. The next moves will require a sustained effort to maintain the peninsula's intrinsic wildness, but we are betting on the Ticos and local expats to rise to the occasion.

Easy accessibility to all this beauty may be to blame for its exploitation, but who can be blamed for wanting to play, beckoned by waves that never seem to close out, tropical forests teeming with wild things, the slow, sane pace of *la vida costariccense* and what lies beyond that next turn down a potholed dirt road?

HIGHLIGHTS

- Catching the morning swell and perfecting afternoon asanas in **Nosara** (p287)
- Taking the gringo trail and observing the contrasts between **Playa Tamarindo** (p270) and mellow **Montezuma** (p304)
- Hiking to the tip of the peninsula at **Reserva Natural Absoluta Cabo Blanco** (p314), Costa Rica's first wildlife park
- Surfing uncrowded breaks at **Playas Grande** (p267), **Avellanas** and **Negra** (p277)
- Kayaking to Isla Chora for a morning snorkel at **Playa Sámara** (p293)
- Fording rivers on the bumpy route to the 'bad country' and good waters of **Mal País** (p310)

★ Playa Grande
★ Playa Tamarindo
★ Playa Avellanas
★ Playa Negra
★ Nosara
★ Playa Sámara
Montezuma ★
Mal País ★ Reserva Natural Absoluta Cabo Blanco

History
Following the independence of Central America from Spain, the peninsula (along with northwestern Costa Rica) comprised the bulk of Guanacaste, a province of the newly formed country of Nicaragua. However, on July 25, 1824, Guanacastecos voted to secede and join Costa Rica, creating yet another grievance between Nicas and Ticos (p229). Today, some in the region still hold on to the dream of independence, and it's not uncommon to see the Guanacaste flag flying high – sometimes higher than the national one. Tellingly, the Guanacaste coat of arms states, 'De la Patria por Nuestra Voluntad': literally, 'Of the Country of our Will.'

Climate
The northern Península de Nicoya has one of the driest climates in Costa Rica, with its coastline mostly characterized by dry tropical forest. Moving further south, as the peninsula transitions from dry tropical forest to tropical rain forest, the amount of moisture increases. Rainfall gradually increases during the green season in the southern Nicoya, typically wettest in September and October and making some regions impassible due to dirt roads being washed out and rivers too swollen to ford.

Parks & Reserves
Most of Nicoya's parks and reserves lie along the shoreline, with several stretching out to sea to protect marine turtles and their nesting sites.

Parque Nacional Barra Honda (p286) Best in the dry season, you can go spelunking in the limestone caves of this underground wonderland.

Parque Nacional Marino Las Baulas de Guanacaste (p269) Crucial to the survival of the leatherback turtle, this park protects one of the turtle's major Pacific nesting sites.

Refugio Nacional de Fauna Silvestre Ostional (p292) Olive ridleys nest and sometimes have *arribadas* (mass nestings) at Ostional.

Refugio Nacional de Vida Silvestre Camaronal (p297) This out-of-the-way refuge has good surf and protects the nesting grounds of four marine turtle species.

Refugio Nacional de Vida Silvestre Curú (p302) The small area of this privately owned reserve is an unexpected oasis of diverse landscapes.

Reserva Natural Absoluta Cabo Blanco (p314) Costa Rica's first protected wilderness area is at the southern tip of the Península de Nicoya.

Getting There & Around
Now that more international air traffic flies directly to Liberia, the Península de Nicoya is even easier to access. Small airstrips serving Tamarindo, Nosara, Sámara, Punta Islita and Tambor are host to daily flights, so you can bypass tough (or impossible) drives on bad roads.

Most popular destinations are served by public buses; Santa Cruz and Nicoya are the region's hubs. Private shuttles run to those destinations not regularly served by public transportation. Sámara and Montezuma are good places to arrange onward travel to more remote places on the southwestern coast.

To drive the roads less traveled, it's mandatory to have a 4WD, but be aware that during the rainy season many roads in the southern peninsula are impassable. Always ask locally about conditions before setting out.

NORTHERN PENINSULA

The northern Nicoya coastline in a snapshot: white-sand beaches, wild green yonder, azure waters. It's no wonder that this is some of the most coveted real estate in the country. What it means when you zoom in is bustling construction of resorts and retirement properties among the trees behind the high-tide line. On the ground it doesn't take super-sharp focus to pick out the high gringo-to-Tico ratio round these parts.

Though the dry forests of the northern peninsula have been cut down over the generations to be transformed into farms and pastureland, these days trees are being felled – more selectively, sure – to put up second homes. Costa Rican lifestyles here have traditionally revolved around the harvest and the herd, but today Ticos live by the tourist season. Each year from December to April, when the snow falls on Europe and North America, Guanacaste experiences its dry season and tourists descend en masse.

While the booming tourism buoys the economy, local Ticos and expats alike are becoming increasingly aware of the tricky balance of development and conservation. But even as construction goes up, the waves keep rolling in and the sun continues to smile on the beaches of the northern peninsula.

PENÍNSULA DE NICOYA

The main artery into this region, Hwy 21, runs from Liberia southwards, with coastal access roads branching out from the small towns of Comunidad, Belén and Santa Cruz.

PLAYA DEL COCO

Thirty-seven kilometers west of Liberia and connected by good roads to San José, Playa del Coco is the most easily accessible of the peninsula's beaches. Its name is derived from the cocoa-colored sand that lies between its two rocky headlands, though it can appear, well, dirty. While nearby Tamarindo has become the enclave of moneyed foreigners, Playa del Coco is more the party destination for young Ticos on weekends and the domain of sportfishers and divers during the week. Though slick development continues its creep, El Coco retains a languid, slightly trashy charm.

Although most travelers either pass through quickly or skip Coco in favor of beaches further south, the town is a growing scuba diving center and a preferred jumping-off point for surfers heading to the celebrated Witch's Rock and Ollie's Point (see p218).

Information

The police station and post office are both on the southeast side of the plaza by the beach. The Banco Nacional, south of the center on the main road into town, exchanges US dollars and traveler's checks. The few people arriving at Playa del Coco by boat will find the *migración* (immigration) office near the Banco Nacional.

Internet Juice Bar (per hr US$2; 8am-9pm) Surf the internet, get your laundry done (US$2 per kg), drink fresh juice (US$2) or rent a mountain bike (per day US$8).

Internet Leslie (☎ 2670 0156; per hr US$1.50; 7:30am-8pm) Email access and English-language newspapers are available.

Activities

DIVING & SNORKELING

The following agencies are thoroughly recommended.

Deep Blue Diving Adventures (☎ 2670 1004; www.deepblue-diving.com) Inside the Coco Bay Hotel & Casino (Map p258), this outfitter runs two-tank boat dives for US$70, including snacks.

Rich Coast Diving (☎ 2670 0176, in the USA & Canada 800-434 8464; www.richcoastdiving.com) On the main street, this American-owned dive shop has a trimaran for overnight diving trips.

Summer Salt (☎ 2670 0308; www.summer-salt.com) This friendly little Swiss-run dive shop has professional, bilingual staff who are as interested in showing you a good time as they are in your safety. Two-tank dive trips are US$70 with snacks included.

SWIMMING

Travelers are generally dissatisfied with the quality of the beach at Playa del Coco, but it's just a 4km drive or walk along the paved road to Playa Ocotal (p263), which is clean, quiet and perfect for swimming and snorkeling.

SURFING

There's no surf in Playa del Coco, but the town is a jumping-off point for Costa Rica's most legendary surf destinations: Witch's Rock and Ollie's Point, which are inside Parque Nacional Santa Rosa (p218). The best way to reach them is by boat, and boat operators *must* be licensed by Minae (Ministry of Environment and Energy) to enter the park.

Roca Bruja Surf Operation (☎ 2670 0952; www.costaricasurftrips.com) is a local licensed operator, offering an eight-hour tour to both breaks for US$270 (for up to five people). It also rents boards and runs sportfishing and snorkeling trips.

Several surf shops in Tamarindo (p273) also run trips to Santa Rosa.

OTHER ACTIVITIES

Sportfishing, sailing and sea kayaking are other popular activities. Many places will rent sea kayaks, which are perfect for exploring the rocky headlands to the north and south of the beach as well as the nearby beaches.

Papagayo Marine Supply (☎ 2670 0774; papagayo@infoweb.co.cr) has bounteous information and supplies for anglers. Nearby, **R & R Tours** (☎ 2670 0573) offers fishing charters and runs day trips to Parque Nacional Palo Verde (p208) for US$65.

Festivals

In late January the town hosts a **Fiesta Cívica**, with bullfights, rodeos, dancing and plenty of drinking. But the biggest festival in Coco is the **Fiesta de la Virgen del Mar**, celebrated in mid-July with a vivid religious-themed boat procession in the harbor and a horse pageant.

Sleeping

BUDGET

The following lodgings have cold-water showers and fans unless otherwise noted,

PENÍNSULA DE NICOYA

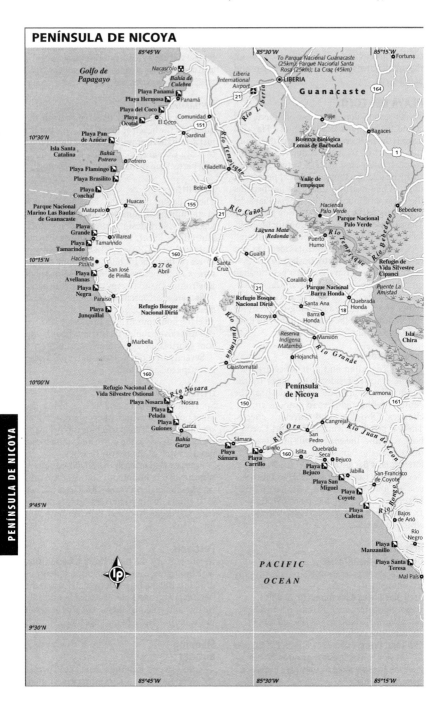

and primarily cater to Tico weekenders. It's popular for Ticos to camp near the beach, though you need to be careful as things can get dodgy when the clubs let out.

Camping Chopin (☎ 8391 5998; per person US$5; **P**) Camping isn't allowed on the beach, but this is the next best thing, and includes bathroom facilities.

Cabinas Jivao (☎ 2670 0431; r per person US$10; **P**) This is a solid choice as these homey cabinas are super-clean and in a quiet part of town. Each cabina has a private bathroom and a small outdoor deck with a table and hammocks.

Cabinas Marimar (☎ 2670 1212; s/d US$14/30; **P**) Across the road from the beach are these simple fan-cooled rooms in a wooden stilt building. It's no-frills but friendly, and hey, it's beachfront, baby.

Cabinas Catarino (☎ 2670 0156; cabinascatarino@hotmail.com; r per person US$15; **P** 🖳) Conveniently (or inconveniently) located near the discotheque, rooms here were being remodeled when we visited and looked to be cleaning up nicely.

MIDRANGE

Laura's House B&B (☎ 2670 0751; www.laurashousecr.net; s/d incl breakfast US$50/60; **P** 🕸 🖳 🖳) The eight spotless rooms at this homey B&B overlook a small pool and have wi-fi access and cable TV. The place has a friendly, family vibe and is a short walk to the center of town.

La Luna Azul (☎ 2670 0313; www.la-luna-azul.com; r incl breakfast with/without air-con US$65/55; **P** 🕸) This tiny newcomer has two rooms that share a bath, set in a well-kept garden about 300m from the beach. The owners provide transfers to Liberia airport (US$30) and generally create a warm atmosphere for their guests.

Pato Loco Inn (☎ 2670 0145; www.costa-rica-beach -hotel-patoloco.com; s/d US$58/64; **P** 🕸 🖳 🖳) This small inn is one of Coco's most pleasant places to stay, if you don't mind forgetting you're in Costa Rica. It's run by an American whose daughter has covered the walls with colorful murals. Each room has a design motif and range of amenities depending on your budget, and the bar in front is a welcoming spot to hang with a beer and shoot the breeze with the other (most likely American) guests. The backyard surrounds a pool, and the small restaurant (dishes US$4 to US$8) specializes in fresh pastas.

Villa del Sol B&B (☎ 2670 0085, in the USA 866-815 8902, in Canada 866-793 9523; www.villadelsol.com; s/d/tr

PENINSULA DE NICOYA

incl breakfast US$58/70/81; P ⊠ ▯ ⊠) This quiet French-Canadian-run place is 1km north of the town center and has a good mix of spotless, well-furnished rooms and studio apartments. There are also six pricey villas that sleep up to 16, though these cater primarily to long-term renters. The hotel is about 100m from the beach, which isn't as crowded at this end.

Flor de Itabo (☎ 2670 0438; www.flordeitabo.com; bungalow US$58, s/d US$81/99, apt US$186-210; P ⊠ ▯ ⊠) If you're into sportfishing, this is your spot, as the owners have a reputation for catching big game and can organize expeditions throughout Nicoya and the Pacific coast. All rooms have air-con, satellite TV, phone and fridge, while deluxe rooms also have whirlpool tubs. Apartments, with full kitchens, sleep four or six. There's a restaurant serving Italian and international food, a casino and a bar.

Hotel Coco Palms (☎ 2670 0367; www.hotelcocopalms.com; s/d US$75/104; P ⊠ ▯ ⊠) This low-key resort hotel has a variety of rooms and apartments with free wi-fi. The hallways are light and airy with high ceilings, but some of the cheaper interior rooms are a little

dark. There's a pleasant outdoor deck and pool, and the small sushi bar (sushi US$5 to US$10) and bigger international restaurant keep guests well fed. The great market here sells wine and imported goods in addition to the usual groceries.

Hotel La Puerta del Sol (☎ 2670 0195; hotelsol@sol.racsa.co.cr; s/d/tr/ste incl breakfast US$76/93/122/128; P ⊠ ⊠) A five-minute walk from town, this unpretentiously luxurious Mediterranean-inspired hotel has two large suites and eight huge pastel-color rooms, each with its own private terrace. The well-manicured grounds have a pool and trellis-shaded gym, and the excellent Sol y Luna Restaurant & Bar (see p260) is one of the best eats in town.

TOP END

In addition to the hotels listed here, see also the listings under Playa Ocotal (p263), 4km to the south, and Playa Hermosa (p261), 5.5km to the north.

Casa Vista Azul (☎ 2670 0678; www.hotelvistaazul.com; r incl breakfast US$105, apt US$140; P ⊠ ⊠) This new hotel has seven rooms and two apartments, all of which have air-con and pri-

PLAYA DEL COCO

0 _____ 500 m
0 _____ 0.3 miles

PENÍNSULA DE NICOYA

Plaza

Soccer Field

Church

See Enlargement

PACIFIC OCEAN

To Ocotal Beach Resort (4km); Playa Ocotal (4km)

Quebrada San Francisco

To Casa Vista Azul (500m); Rancho Armadillo (500m); Playa Hermosa (5.5km); Sardinal (7.5km); Santa Cruz (48km)

DIVERS DO IT DEEPER

The northern area of the peninsula is one of the best and most easily accessible sites in the country for diving. As beach diving in this area isn't the greatest, dives are made either around volcanic rock pinnacles near the coast, or from a boat further off at **Isla Santa Catalina** (about 20km to the southwest) or **Isla Murciélago** (40km to the northwest, near the tip of Península Santa Elena).

Diving here is not like diving the Caribbean – do not expect to see colorful hard coral on the scale of Belize. Conditions can be mediocre from a visibility standpoint (9m to 15m visibility, and sometimes up to 20m), but the sites make up for it in other ways: namely, their abundant marine life. The richness, variety and sheer number of marine animals is astonishing. This is the place to see large groupings of pelagics, like manta rays, spotted eagle rays, sharks, whales, dolphins and turtles, as well as moray eels, starfish, crustaceans and huge schools of native tropical fish. Most of the dive sites are less than 25m deep, allowing three dives a day. Keep in mind, however, that since February 2006 it is now illegal to swim in close proximity to dolphins and whales.

The Papagayo winds blow from early December to late March and make the water choppy and cooler, cutting down on visibility, especially for the four days around the full moon. June and July are usually the best months for visibility.

Isla Santa Catalina and Isla Murciélago both have a rich variety of marine life living and cruising around these rocky outcrops. Manta rays have been reported from December to late April, and at other times you can expect to spot eagle rays, eels, Cortez angelfish, hogfish, parrot fish, starfish, clown shrimp and other bottom dwellers. The far point of Murciélago is known for its regular sightings of groups of bull sharks, which can be a terrifying sight if you're not an experienced diver. Divers also head to **Narizones**, which is a good deep dive (about 27m), while **Punta Gorda** is an easy descent for inexperienced divers.

The good thing about scuba diving is that the sheer cost of starting and maintaining a dive center discourages fly-by-night operators from setting up shop. As a general rule, though, it's good to feel out a dive shop before paying for a trip – talk to the divemaster, inspect the equipment and make sure you're comfortable with everything before heading out (you should never feel pressured into diving!).

If you haven't been scuba diving before, consider taking a 'Discovery Course,' which costs about US$125 and will teach you all the basics. If you're interested in getting your Open Water Diver certification, which allows you to dive anywhere in the world, a three- to four-day course is about US$400. Compared to what these courses can cost in either North America or Europe, this price is a bargain.

vate bathroom and are flooded with light and wide-open ocean views. There's also a breezy rooftop dining area, and the owner can help you arrange tours. To get there, head west off the main road, just south of Flor de Itabo, and follow the signs to Casa Vista Azul.

Rancho Armadillo (☎ 2670 0108; www.rancho armadillo.com; d/tr incl breakfast US$170/232; P ☒ ☒) Near the entrance to town, this private estate is on a hillside about 600m off the main road (all paved). The view from the common areas is the best in Playa del Coco, and it's a perfect retreat from the heavily touristed coastline. The seven rooms are light, spacious and nicely decorated with individually crafted furniture. Suites sleep four; some have two bathrooms and two entrances. There's a pool, outdoor gym and plenty of decorative armadillos, though the location itself makes for a relaxing, meditative stay. The American owners arrange fishing, sailing, diving and surfing trips. Gourmands will enjoy comparing recipes with chef-owner Rick Vogel and using the fully equipped professional kitchen.

Cafe de Playa (☎ 2670 1471, 2670 1621; www .cafedeplaya.com; d incl breakfast US$197; P ☒ ☒ ☒) Several elegant rooms at this beach club, adorned with gallery-worthy contemporary art, look on to the pool area and provide easy access to the beach, open-air sushi bar and beachfront restaurant. It's about 15 minutes' walk into the town center, but you may not feel the need to leave.

Eating

Soda Teresita (sandwiches US$2-4; ☺ lunch & dinner) On the west end of the soccer field, this popular pink *soda* (basic eatery) is your best bet for a *torta* (sandwich) and some chitchat with the locals.

Coco Coffee Company (☎ 2670 1055; mains US$3-6; ☺ 7am-4pm Mon-Sat) Next door to Papagayo Seafood, this coffee joint draws the gringos with its siren call of bagels with cream cheese, fresh sandwiches, espresso drinks and tasty homemade pastries.

Jardín Tropical (☎ 2670 0428; mains US$3-9; ☺ 7am-8:30pm) Also on the soccer field, this well-established, neat and efficient *soda* has a wide selection of menu items, including filling pizzas and freshly caught fish. It's also a great place for a big breakfast by the beach.

Zouk Cafe (☎ 2670 0191; www.zouksantana.com; mains US$3-10; ☺ 7am-2am; ☐) Most definitely the hippest place to eat in Coco, you won't be surprised to know it's Italian owned. Breakfast offerings include brioche and espresso, and as the day moves on, so goes the menu, with green salads to cool you in the heat of afternoon, and a kitchen serving fusion cuisine late into the night to fuel your second wind at the downstairs bar.

Sushi Playa (☎ 2670 1621, 2670 1471; sushi US$3.50-7; ☺ 11:30am-2pm & 6:30-10pm) With cool breezes coming off the ocean and the low light of its open-air terrace, the sushi bar at Cafe de Playa has a low-key ambience conducive to properly appreciating the nuances of the *maguro* (tuna) melting on your tongue.

Papagayo Seafood (☎ 2670 0298; mains US$5-8; ☺ lunch & dinner) Seafood is the name of the game here, clearly, and you can find the day's catch either blackened, pan-fried or *a la veracruzana* (in a tomato, onion and olive sauce) – whichever way, you can't go wrong.

Louisiana Bar & Grill (☎ 2670 0319; mains US$6-9; ☺ lunch & dinner) Put some heat back into your diet with spicy Cajun classics, including jambalaya, seafood gumbo and po'boys. But if you're not feeling it, you can opt instead for fish cooked a dozen ways – from seared with Asian ginger-sesame sauce to grilled with macadamia pesto. Either way, try to get one of the balcony tables to check out the street scene.

Sol y Luna Restaurant & Bar (Hotel La Puerta del Sol; dishes US$6-9; ☺ dinner) Dine on authentic Italian pasta while soaking up the Mediterranean atmosphere at this restaurant at the Hotel La Puerta del Sol (p258). But make sure you save room for a slice of the heavenly homemade tiramisu.

Tequila Bar & Grill (☎ 2670 0741; mains US$6-11; ☺ noon-11pm) This popular nightspot has traditional (though pricey) Mexican favorites, including burritos, tacos and fajitas, though most people here prefer the margarita liquid dinner, of which there are over 20 varieties.

There's a Super Luperón market for self-caterers, and the well-stocked **Coco Palms Supermercado** (☎ 2670 0367; ☺ 6am-11pm).

Drinking

Playa del Coco has a boisterous mix of Ticos looking to get toasted and sunburned sportfishers cooling their heels and swapping fish stories. If you're looking for entertainment that doesn't involve drinking, you've gone to the wrong town.

The restaurants surrounding the plaza double as bars, with the Bar El Ancla de Oro being a beachside favorite. The open-air Bar El Roble is preferred by heavy drinkers, while the **Lizard Lounge** (☺ 3pm-2am) attracts a livelier crowd of dancers. It's a nice place to start out the evening with a game of pool, a cocktail and a *boca* (the Costa Rican equivalent of tapas) on the streetside terrace. Tequila Bar & Grill (see above) is the spot for slamming a few pitchers of margaritas, but if you're looking for a more stylish venue, head to **Zouk Santana** (☎ 2670 0191; www.zouksantana.com; ☺ 5pm-2am), where there's an open seating area, dance floor and streetside bar.

Boogie till the break of dawn at **Discoteca CocoMar** (☺ 8pm-2am) on the beach, which is the biggest (and sweatiest) dance-fest around. Keep the party moving at **La Vida Loca** (☎ 2670 0181; ☺ 5pm-2am).

Getting There & Away

All buses arrive and depart from the main stop on the plaza, across from the police station.

Filadelfia, for connection to Santa Cruz US$0.75, 45 minutes, departs at 11:30am and 4:30pm.

Liberia US$1.25, one hour, departs at 5:30am, 7am, 9am, 11am, 1pm, 3pm, 5pm and 6pm.

San José (Pulmitan) US$5.25, five hours, departs at 4am, 8am and 2pm.

A taxi from Liberia to Playa del Coco costs US$30. Taxis between Playa del Coco and

PENÍNSULA DE NICOYA

Playas Hermosa or Ocotal cost between US$7 and US$9.

Note that there's no gas station in town; the nearest one is in Sardinal, about 9km inland from Playa del Coco.

PLAYA HERMOSA

If you're looking for the legendary surf beach, see p339. For those of you still with us, Playa Hermosa is a gently curving and tranquil gray-sand beach that stretches for about 2km. Although it's only 7km (by road) north of Playa del Coco, and development is springing up rapidly along this entire coastline, Hermosa feels less dissipated and more dignified than Coco. The hillsides may be up for sale, but they're still pretty green and the locals not so jaded.

If you are keen to get in the water, **Bill Beard's Diving Safaris** (☎ 2453 5044, in the USA & Canada 877-853 0538; www.billbeardcostarica.com) at the Villas Sol Hotel have been scuba diving and snorkeling since 1970. Or **Aqua Sport** (☎ 2672 0050) has boats for fishing, water tours and snorkeling.

From the main road, there is a southern and northern access road leading to Hermosa.

Sleeping

Do it the Tico way and camp for free under a few shady spots near the main beach, but don't expect any facilities.

The second (or northern) entrance to the beach is lined with a variety of hotels and inns should none of the following options pan out.

Iguana Inn (☎ 2672 0065; s/d US$20/30; ⊠) Set 100m back from the beach, this rambling bi-level terra-cotta inn has 10 simple, slightly beat-up rooms with private bathroom, though the price is definitely right. The Tico owners are also super laidback, which makes for a relaxing, worry-free stay.

Cabinas La Casona (☎ 2672 0025; gaviotalouise@ hotmail.com; s/d US$30/45; P) The seven cutesy cabinas here with whitewashed rooms, small kitchenettes, TV and private hot-water bathrooms are ideal for self-caterers, and they're just steps from the beach.

Playa Hermosa Inn (☎ 2672 0063; www.costa-rica -beach-hotel.com; s/d incl breakfast US$45/70; P ⊠) Centered on a gigantic tree right on the beach, this B&B has a certain decaying appeal to it; though it seemed a bit neglected when we stopped by, it does have character and a quiet, beachfront location. You'll find it at the end of the dirt road on the left of the northern access road as you head toward the beach.

Hotel El Velero (☎ 2672 0036, 2672 1017; www .costaricahotel.net; d US$92; P ⊠ ⊠) Just steps from the beach, this resort hotel has 22 spacious and fully equipped rooms decorated with woodwork and colorful bedspreads. The complex has a pool, patio lounge and American-style restaurant and bar, though the real draw is the owner's 38ft sailboat. Guests are invited on a number of cruises through the crystal-blue waters of the Bahía Culebra, including daily sunset cruises (US$40 per person, minimum four people).

Hotel Playa Hermosa (☎ 2672 0046; www.hotel playahermosa.com; r US$99, deluxe s/d US$134/169; P ⊠ ⊠ ⊠ ⊠) 'Hermosa' would be the simplest way to describe this lovely hotel after a recent renovation. On the southern end of the beach via the first entrance road, the luxurious rooms are screened by branches and greenery of the property's old-growth trees. The well-appointed rooms, with cable TV, comfortable furniture and a simple, tropical aesthetic, ring around a pool and beautifully landscaped garden. There's wi-fi access in the central area.

Villas Sol Hotel (☎ 2672 0001; www.villassol.com; d US$212, villa US$316; P ⊠ ⊠) If an all-inclusive resort deal sounds attractive, this hillside is your place. Standard rooms are equipped with everything you'd want, and the views of the gulf are breathtaking. The villas are definitely pricier, but they have three bedrooms, a kitchen and a private pool option, so gather a few of your rich friends and live it up. There are also tennis courts, a restaurant and a bar, and the owners can arrange all types of activities. Bill Beard's Diving Safaris is based here. Credit cards accepted.

Eating & Drinking

Whether you're just passing through Playa Hermosa or spending the night, there are some great spots to eat here. Food and other basic supplies are available at Mini Super Cenizaro, on the paved road into town.

Restaurant Pescado Loco (☎ 2672 0017; mains US$5-14; ⏱ 9am-1am) The 'Crazy Fish' serves up some of the freshest seafood around, including Costa Rican standards like red snapper and *ceviche* (uncooked, marinated seafood), though we got excited about the *pulpo de gallego* (Galician octopus). The restaurant is between the first and second entrances to Playa Hermosa.

Ginger (☎ 2672 0041; mains US$15-20; ☼ dinner Tue-Sun) If you're driving north, look to the hills on the right and you'll see this stunner of an open-air restaurant (it was designed by the famous Costa Rican architect Victor Cañas). The chic ambience, which feels more NYC than CR, is complemented by a gourmet list of Asian- and Mediterranean-inspired tapas.

Monkey Bar (☎ 2672 0267; ☼ 5pm-midnight) For all your liquid needs visit this huge tree house between the first and second entrances to Playa Hermosa, where you can sip a sundowner to the tune of howlers bleating overhead.

Getting There & Away

There is a daily bus from San José, but you can always take a bus to Liberia and switch there for more frequent buses to Playa Hermosa. A taxi from Liberia costs about US$15, and a taxi from Coco about US$5. If you're driving from Liberia, take the signed turnoff to Playa del Coco. The entire road is paved.

THE PAPAGAYO PROBLEM

If anyone reading this right now thinks that Costa Rica is a virtual ecoparadise where environmental conservation always takes precedence over capitalist gains, sit down and listen to the not-so-pretty side of the story.

In the mid-1970s the Costa Rican Tourism Board, known as the ICT (whose slogan, by the way, is 'No Artificial Ingredients'), hatched a long-term development plan for the Gulf of Papagayo, focusing particularly on the Nacascolo peninsula, a tiny, beautiful strip of land that juts out into the Bahía de Culebra. The idea was to use Costa Rica's image as a happy, sloth-hugging tropical wonderland to lure package tourists away from traditional resort destinations, like Cancún.

The project took off during the administration of President Rafael Calderón, who adamantly backed the development proposal. Soon after, the Grupo Papagayo conglomerate was formed, headed by Mexico's Grupo Situr (which was reportedly investing US$2.5 billion in the project). Although no environmental impact studies were done, the group unveiled plans to raze most of the peninsula's dry tropical forest to make way for 20,000 hotel rooms, two golf courses, a marina, racetrack, athletic center and (of course) condos. Developers never stopped to consider the availability of fresh drinking water, let alone the pre-Columbian archaeological sites that dotted the peninsula.

However, when an independent commission appointed by Calderón expressed concerns that the Papagayo project was, to put it bluntly, an environmental disaster, it really hit the fan. The tourism minister was indicted on charges of corruption, and all of the ICT was embroiled in scandal (it didn't help much that bulldozers were occasionally turning up pre-Columbian sites). In a quick scramble, Calderón seized control of the entire peninsula, while Grupo Papagayo put on a fresh coat of PR paint by changing its name to Ecodesarollo Papagayo (Papagayo Eco-development). For a quick lesson in what it actually means to be 'eco,' see boxed text How to Know if a Business is Really Ecofriendly, p346.

The company went bankrupt, and development stalled until a group of North American investors seized the straggled remains of the project in 1999, led by Tico developer Alan Kelso. In 2004 the Four Seasons Resort opened up for business, and in 2009 the first phase of the huge 350-slip Marina Papagayo is slated to make its debut. Currently, there are a number of high-end resorts along the bay, but there's new dirt plaguing Papagayo: the human kind. In February 2008, after being investigated by Minae nine months prior for improper waste management, the 300-room Hotel Occidental Allegro Papagayo was shut down by the government for dumping its waste into a nearby estuary and neighboring communities (whose grassroots investigation and protest helped instigate the closure). Soon thereafter, the Occidental Grand Papagayo, another resort owned by the same group, was investigated for allegedly pumping its waste directly into the ocean at Playa Buena, where there's a fragile coral reef offshore.

If you'd like to stay at one of the upscale resorts at Papagayo, do a little environmental investigation of your own before booking something. You can make a positive impact on green development in Costa Rica by creating demand for it, and by putting your hard-earned bucks there when you find it.

Buses to Liberia and San José depart from the main road on the northern end of the beach and make a stop in Sardinal.

Liberia US$0.75, 1¼ hours, departs at 5:30am, 7am, 9:30am, 11am, 12:30pm, 2:30pm, 4:30pm and 6:30pm.

San José (Empresa Esquivel) US$5, six hours, departs at 5am.

PLAYA OCOTAL

This small but attractive gray-sand beach with tidal pools on both ends is 4km southwest of Playa del Coco by paved road. Aside from a few privately owned villas (which are mostly rented as vacation houses), there isn't an actual town here, though it's close enough to Coco that you can either drive or take a leisurely stroll here along the road. Although it's a fairly quiet beach, Ocotal can get mobbed on weekends by Ticos looking to escape the Coco scene.

If you feel like diving, **Ocotal Beach Resort** (☎ 2670 0321; www.ocotalresort.com) offers dive packages, such as an eight-day, seven-night deal including accommodations, breakfast, and six days of boat and beach diving (per person US$1095 based on double occupancy). It also offers fishing charters (it has six boats) and kayak rentals. Complete fishing packages are also available.

Sleeping & Eating

Los Almendros de Ocotal (☎ 2670 1560, 2670 1744; www.losalmendrosrentals.com; studio/apt/villa US$60/180/235; P ✱ ☐ ☎) Perched on the hillside just above Playa Ocotal, these apartments are a great deal for self-caterers or longer-term visitors. They're quiet, have superb views, and are well maintained and comfortable. Apartments sleep four, while villas sleep six, and some units have private pools and terraces.

Villa Casa Blanca (☎ 2670 0518; www.hotelvillacasablanca.com; d/ste incl breakfast US$145/163, additional person US$10; P ✱ ☐ ☎) Between Playa del Coco and Ocotal, this attractive villa is perched on a pleasant hilltop just a few minutes' walk from the beach. The rooms are beautifully decorated with either Victorian motifs or more modern accents. Three honeymoon suites are larger and feature a step-up bathtub and ocean views. The pool has a swim-up bar, and there's wi-fi access. The hotel was for sale when we visited.

Ocotal Beach Resort (☎ 2670 0321; www.ocotalresort.com; s/d incl breakfast from US$175/200; P ✱ ☐ ☎) This beachside resort on the bay has a relaxed ambiance and is a great choice for divers and sportfishers. There are several swimming pools, tennis courts, and a notable Mediterranean-fusion restaurant whose chef was trained at the Cordon Bleu. Suites (US$378) are a bit cramped with gigantic beds, but they have ocean views and Jacuzzi tubs, while duplex-style bungalows (US$175) share small private pools. All rooms include the creature comforts you'd expect.

Father Rooster Bar & Grill (☎ 2670 1246; www.fatherrooster.com; mains US$5-16; ☽ 11am-11pm) This awesome beachside eatery serves up a good variety of grilled dishes, including fish, snacks and burgers, and you cannot beat the location: sit in the coolness of the restaurant, on the shaded wooden terrace or under the palms on the beach. The bartenders make a good margarita as well as a killer frozen Tica Linda, whose knockout punch is naturally Guaro Cacique.

BEACHES SOUTH OF PLAYA OCOTAL

Although they're next to one another, Playas Pan de Azúcar, Potrero, Flamingo, Brasilito and Conchal have relatively nothing in common. The beaches range from gray sand to white sand to crushed seashells, while the range of development is also a seemingly random pattern.

Although it's tempting to take the 'road' from Sardinal to Potrero, there's a reason why locals call this route the 'monkey trail.' The first 9km of dirt road leading to the small town of Artola isn't so bad, but the second half is pretty brutal, and should only be tackled if you have a 4WD (and after you've talked to a few locals).

If you want to avoid the rough roads, return to the main peninsular highway then head south through Filadelfia and on to Belén (a distance of 18km), from where a paved road heads 25km west to Huacas (where there's a gas station). Then take the road leading north until you hit the ocean at the village of Brasilito. Turn right and head north: you'll pass Playa Flamingo and Bahía Potrero before reaching Playa Pan de Azúcar. If you make a left instead and head south, you will end up at Playa Conchal.

Buses from San José, Liberia or Santa Cruz can also get you to most of the beaches. If you're into sea kayaking, the proximity of the beaches to one another makes for some great day trips.

PENÍNSULA DE NICOYA

In the small village of Artola you can take the **Congo Trail Canopy Tour** (☎ 2666 4422; US$45) if you're looking for adventure *sans* broken axles.

Playa Pan de Azúcar

Although the buses stop at Potrero, those with their own ride (it'd better be a 4WD in the rainy season) can head 3km north on a rough dirt road to 'Sugar Bread Beach,' which derives its name from the crystalline strip of white sand that's protected at both ends by rocky headlands. Difficult access and the lack of cheap accommodations create an atmosphere of total seclusion, and the ocean here is calm, clear and perfect for snorkeling.

Although the beach is fronted by the Hotel Sugar Beach, don't be afraid to walk down to the shore as beaches are public property in Costa Rica.

Luxury at the **Hotel Sugar Beach** (☎ 2654 4242; www.sugar-beach.com; d from US$145; P ❄ 🖳 🏊) is simple and understated, which is the right approach considering how difficult it is to compete with the natural beauty of the beach. The 22 lovely rooms are brightly painted and entered via elaborately hand-carved wooden doors. Deluxe rooms are slightly larger and have stunning ocean views. There are also four two-bedroom apartments, two beach houses (with two or three bedrooms sleeping 10 to 12) and a small restaurant. But the real reason you're here is to slow down and linger on one of the most isolated beaches in all of Costa Rica.

Bahía Potrero

This stretch of bay is separated from Playa Flamingo by a rocky headland. Although the overdeveloped eyesore that is Playa Flamingo can be seen across the bay, monkeys can still be heard in the trees here. The hillsides and shoreline are seeing development, and tourists in quad caravans kick up dust along the roads, but the bay has a decidedly lower-key – and shall we say, classier – scene.

Several undeveloped beaches are strung along the bay. The black-sand beach is **Playa Prieta**, the white-sand beach is **Playa Penca** and **Playa Potrero**, the biggest, is somewhere in between. (These names, it should be noted, are used loosely.) The rocky islet 10km due west of Playa Pan de Azúcar is **Isla Santa Catalina**, a popular diving spot (see boxed text Divers Do

It Deeper, p259). Hotels on the beaches rent water-sports equipment.

There's a small community at **Potrero**, just beyond the northern end of the beach. This is where the bus line ends, and the beaches here don't get the weekend rush found at Brasilito.

SLEEPING & EATING

If you're looking for budget accommodation, consider staying 7km south in Brasilito (p266).

Mayra's (☎ 2654 4213, 2654 4472; camping per person US$6, s/d US$18/36; P) Right on the southern beach, this friendly, tranquil place has shady camping with beach showers and five rustic rooms with refreshing cold showers, fridge and kitchenette. Mayra is helpful and friendly, and her husband, Álvaro, a retired journalist, is well stocked with stories.

Cabinas Isolina (☎ 2654 4333; www.isolinabeach .com; d/tr/q incl breakfast from US$64/76/87, d/tr/q villa incl breakfast US$99/111/134; P ❄ 🖳 🏊) These attractive yellow buildings are set back from the northern end of the beach and completely surrounded by huge bushes of fragrant hibiscus. Rooms have tiled hot showers, cable TV and air-con, while larger villas have two bedrooms and a fully equipped kitchen. There's wi-fi access outside, and the attached restaurant serves up some Tico-Mediterranean specialties.

Bahía Esmeralda (☎ 2654 4480; www.hotelbahia esmeralda.com; s/d/q incl breakfast from US$70/81/108, apt/villa US$157/215; P ❄ 🖳 🏊) A short walk from the beach, this Italian-owned resort offers super-comfortable accommodations at a bargain price. Standard rooms are a little on the small side, though the relaxed atmosphere, pool and excellent Italian restaurant (open for breakfast and dinner, meals from US$3 to US$12) more than make up for it. The apartments sleeping up to four have fold-out futons and a kitchen, while larger villas sleep six. Credit cards accepted. The property was for sale at the time of writing.

Bahía del Sol (☎ 2654 4671, 2224 7290; www.potrero bay.com; d/ste incl breakfast from US$163/227; P ❄ 🖳 🏊) With a prime beachfront location at Playa Potrero (by the cute baby-turtle sign admonishing quad drivers to stay off the beach), this luxurious resort gets high marks for laidback elegance. Large, tiled rooms and suites have all the amenities you would want (suites include fully equipped kitchens and private terraces) and surround a lovely garden with a spa area. Out front, there's a pool with waterfall and swim-up bar, and a lawn leading out to the beach is peppered with *palapas* (shelter with a thatched, palm-leaf roof and open sides).

Las Brisas Bar & Grill (☎ 2654 4047; casados US$3.75) There are a number of *sodas* in Potrero if you're looking for cheap eats, and this local favorite is at the far end of the bay past the village. Villagers pack the joint nightly for *bocas,* beers and brilliant sunsets. The pool table here is probably the most exciting entertainment offering in town.

GETTING THERE & AWAY
Many buses begin their route in Potrero on the southeast corner of the soccer field. See Playa Flamingo (p266) for schedules. Ask locally before setting out as not every bus goes all the way into Potrero.

Playa Flamingo
The crescent strip of white sand known as Playa Flamingo is postcard-worthy, which is probably why it was billed decades ago as Costa Rica's most sophisticated beach destination. These days the beach has gone completely upscale, though the scene ain't so pretty. The hills above the bay are lined with private villas and expensive condos, and the area has a reputation for rampant cocaine use, high-end prostitution and more dirty old men than you can shake a cigar at. Package tourists and sportfishers still frequent the old resorts that line the bay, but there are definitely better places to spend your time and money. That said, the white-sand shoreline itself is a blue-flag beach, making it a lovely place to while away a free hour or two.

The original name of the beach was Playa Blanca; it changed its name in the 1950s to coincide with the construction of the area's first major hotel, the Flamingo Beach Resort. Funnily enough, flamingo season here runs from never to never.

Across from the Flamingo Marina Resort, **Banco de Costa Rica** (☎ 2654 4984) can exchange US dollars and traveler's checks. Super Massai, on the main north–south road, is good for all kinds of food supplies and toiletries.

ACTIVITIES
At the entrance to Playa Flamingo, the **Edge Adventure Company** (☎ 2654 4946; www.theedge

adventure.com) has a range of rentals and tours. A two-tank dive is US$75, and snorkeling gear, bikes and body boards are available for rent. Fishing charters are also available.

Samonique III (☎ 2654 5280, 8388 7870; www.costa-rica-sailing.com) is a 15.5m ketch available for sunset cruises for US$60 per person (minimum four). Overnight tours are available by arrangement. You can find the office at the Mariner Inn.

Spanish classes are operated by **Centro-Panamericano de Idiomas** (☎ 2265 6306; www.cpi-edu.com; classes with/without homestay US$415/285), which also has locations in Heredia (p143) and Monteverde (p179), with the opportunity to transfer from campus to campus.

SLEEPING & EATING
Budget options are nonexistent in Playa Flamingo. If you want to visit the beach but save a few bucks, consider staying in nearby Brasilito (p266).

Mariner Inn (☎ 2654 4081; marinerinn@racsa.co.cr; s/d US$34/45; P ❄ ☐ ☒) Just next to the marina, the Mariner Inn has a sweet terrace bar with beautiful views of the bay where you can have a cocktail before turning in. Rooms downstairs are on the small side but very comfortable, with air-con, hot water, cable TV and some with fridge.

Guanacaste Lodge (☎ 2654 4494; www.guanacaste lodge.com; s/d incl breakfast US$60/70; P ❄ ☒) Another affordable option in town is a good choice as the spacious, well-furnished rooms with air-con, cable TV and private hot showers are surrounded by shady, tropical grounds. There's a nice pool, and the attached restaurant (dishes US$3 to US$6) has good casados and grilled meats.

Flamingo Beach Resort (☎ 2654 4444; www.resort flamingobeach.com; r US$120-300; P ❄ ☐ ☒) The Flamingo is the granddaddy of the area's resorts, with 91 rooms, tennis courts, a pool and a wide restaurant terrace that looks out on the beautiful beach out back. It has a 1950s Vegas look and feel, with no dearth of amenities or gaudy aesthetic.

Marie's (☎ 2654 4136; meals US$6-24; ⏱ 6:30am-9:30pm) One of the longest-established eateries in town has a breezy round dining terrace, and such offerings as yogurt, granola and fruit at breakfast, avocados stuffed with shrimp, and spinach-and-ricotta ravioli. The pancakes, burgers and rotisserie chicken are locally famous.

GETTING THERE & AWAY

Air
You can fly to Tamarindo (p277), which has regular scheduled flights and is about 8km away by paved road.

Bus
Buses depart from the Flamingo Marina on the point and travel through Brasilito on the way out. Schedules change often, so ask locally about departure times as well as the best place on the road to wait for the bus.

Liberia US$1.50, two hours, departs at 5:30am and 2:30pm.

San José (Tralapa) US$6.50, five hours, departs at 2:45am, 9am and 2pm Monday to Saturday, 10:30am on Sunday.

Santa Cruz US$1.50, one hour, eight buses departs from 5:45am to 10pm.

Playa Brasilito
Brasilito has managed to avoid the overdevelopment that's plagued much of northern Nicoya. It might be that the gray-sand beach here isn't as pretty as nearby strips of palm-fringed white sand, and the lack of resorts and big hotels gives the town a laidback atmosphere. Playa Brasilito is popular with weekending Ticos and travelers 'in the know,' who are drawn here for the relaxed beach scene, pleasant swimming, cheap accommodations and spectacular Pacific sunsets.

Brasilito Excursiones (☎ 2654 4237; www.brasilito .com), which operates out of Hotel Brasilito, can book horseback rides, sunset sails and two-tank dives.

Internet is available (US$2 per hour) at Rancho Nany.

SLEEPING
The town of Brasilito consists of a few small stores and *sodas*, as well as some great mid-range accommodations.

Cabinas Gloria (☎ 2654 4878; camping adult/child under 6yr US$3/free, tr US$50; P 🅿 📶 🖵) Run by an amiable Tico named Santos, these spruced-up rooms with air-con, cable TV and free wi-fi are a great deal if you're traveling trio. This place is definitely a bit upmarket, even though the modest, painted-black sign on the road looks pretty budget. It's 200m south of the plaza.

Cabinas Ojos Azules (☎ 2654 4346; www.cabinas ojosazules.com; dm/d US$5/50; P 🅿) The best budget option in town is a somewhat ramshackle collection of rooms featuring big, comfy beds complete with saucy mirrored headboards.

Fancy doubles are upstairs, and simpler downstairs quarters fit up to eight people. All units have private bathrooms with hot water, and there's a small shared kitchen. It's 200m south of the plaza.

Hotel Brasilito (☎ 2654 4237; www.brasilito.com; r with/without air-con US$47/40; P) On the beach side of the plaza, this recommended hotel is the perfect place to slow down and chill out for a few days. The rooms are simple and clean, though you'll scream with joy when you take a steamy shower with some serious pressure. If it's available, splurge for the sea-view room in the front that has a private hammock-strung patio that's ideal for soaking up the sunset, after which you can hang at the popular restaurant. The friendly owners speak German, English, Spanish and French, and will help arrange tours. Credit cards accepted.

Rancho Nany (☎ 2654 4320; d/q US$50/90; P 🅿 🖵 🖥) Between Playas Brasilito and Conchal, Rancho Nany is an impressive Tico-run complex complete with its own internet café, steakhouse, supermarket, swimming pool and cabinas. Large rooms here are painted in cheerful tropical colors, and come with cable TV, air-con and warm showers. The hotel is managed by the López family, who have been in the area for four decades.

Conchal Hotel (☎ 2654 9125; www.conchalhotel .com; d incl breakfast US$90; P 🅿 🖵 🖥) Rooms at this recommended hotel are simply stunning – white-washed walls are offset by exposed wooden beams, ceramic tiling and elegant bathrooms. Don't judge it by the characterless terra-cotta wall in front. Simon, the owner, and his staff make every effort to make your holiday comfortable and memorable.

EATING & DRINKING
Indira Bar y Restaurant (☎ 2654 4028; dishes US$3-10; 🕑 lunch & dinner) Come to this large beachfront spot for a great vibe, especially in the evening when its outdoor tables are packed with tourists and locals alike. The *ceviche* here is killer, especially when it's washed down with an Imperial (or four).

Roy's Place (mains US$3-6; 🕑 breakfast, lunch & dinner Thu-Tue) The super-friendly owner of this sweet little *soda* makes the casados, *ceviche* and salads taste even better than they would standing alone. Pull up a chair, sip on a *batido* (fruit shake) and watch the day's dramas on the little plaza.

Il Forno Restaurant (☎ 2654 4125; meals US$5-12; ⓨ lunch & dinner) This recommended Italian restaurant is in a romantic garden, and has such delightful menu items as thin-crust pizza, homemade pastas and risottos, and enough fresh eggplant dishes to keep vegetarians happy and healthy.

Outback Jack's Roadkill Café (☎ 2654 5463; mains US$4-12; ⓨ 6am-11pm) A good spot for a beer, this open-air restaurant-bar attached to the Hotel Brasilito looks out on the beach. Though its Ozzie-themed decor would have you believe otherwise, the cuisine is more about international basics with a Tico accent.

GETTING THERE & AWAY

Buses to and from Playa Flamingo travel through Brasilito; see opposite for details.

Playa Conchal

Just 2km south of Brasilito is Playa Conchal, which is widely regarded as *the* most beautiful beach in all of Costa Rica. The name comes from the billions of *conchas* (shells) that wash up on the beach, which are gradually crushed into a coarse sand. The ocean water is an intense turquoise blue, which is indeed a rarity on the Pacific coast. If you have snorkeling gear, this is the place to bust it out.

The beach is bounded on the north by an expansive resort that can make beach access frustratingly difficult. However, it's easy enough to stay in nearby Brasilito (opposite) and then simply walk south along the road for 2km.

Why is it that the most expensive resorts always seem to have the most ridiculous names? With 285 hectares of property, including an over-the-top free-form pool and a championship golf course, it's not like **Paradisus Playa Conchal Beach & Resort** (☎ 2654 4123; www.paradisusplayaconchal.travel; d US$350-630; P ⚇ ⚐) really needs a fancy name to compensate for any inadequacies. Guests have got it all here, and everything from the marble columns to the gold-trimmed toothbrush holder is a class act. Needless to say, the whole shebang is about as *un*–Costa Rican as you can get.

GETTING THERE & AWAY

If you're staying in Conchal, it's probably best to catch buses in Brasilito; see opposite for details.

PLAYA GRANDE

From Huacas, the southwesterly road leads to Playa Grande, a beach that's famous among conservationists and surfers alike. By day, the offshore winds create steep and powerful waves, especially at high tide and in front of the Hotel Las Tortugas. By night, an ancient cycle continues to unfurl as leatherback sea turtles bearing clutches of eggs follow the ocean currents back to their birthplace.

Since 1991 Playa Grande has been part of the Parque Nacional Marino Las Baulas de Guanacaste (p269), which bars beachfront development to ensure that one of the most important leatherback nesting areas in the world is preserved for future generations. However, this is not to say that Playa Grande is pristine. The park's official boundary ends 50m from the high-tide line, and government agencies have been lax about permitting real estate development that is technically within the boundaries of the park. In 2007, the Supreme Court of Costa Rica restated a 2005 moratorium on all construction within park boundaries; meanwhile, conservation groups are lobbying to prevent development near the central beach, where turtles can still nest undisturbed by lights and the presence of development.

Currently, neat subdivided lots are for sale by the dozen in Playa Grande, and several of the hotels listed here are in a 33-hectare gated community (open to the public). Though Playa Grande is still far from overdevelopment, and the essential wildness and beauty of the place remains largely intact, it will take the continued efforts of concerned conservationists (like Louis Wilson; see the listing for Hotel Las Tortugas, p268) and scrupulous developers to adhere to a high standard of environmental integrity to keep it that way. It's not hyperbolic to say that the survival of the leatherback turtle depends on it.

Although Playa Grande does have a few accommodations near the beach, they are set back from the shoreline and carefully managed to ensure that ambient light is kept to a minimum.

Activities

Surfing is most people's motivation for coming to Playa Grande, and if you don't know how, there are people who will happily teach you.

Frijoles Locos (☎ 2652 9235; www.frijoleslocos.com; ⓨ 9am-5pm) On the road into town, the friendly Ian and

PENÍNSULA DE NICOYA

Corynne Bean rent and sell surfboards (US$15 to US$20 per day), give lessons (US$45 for one person, US$60 for two), and offer massage therapy and naturopathic treatments.

Matos Films Surf Store (☎ 2652 9227; www.matos films.com; ☻ 8am-7pm) This Tico-run surf shop rents surfboards (US$20 per day), mountain bikes and beach cruisers (US$10) and has free internet access for customers. You can even do a weekly rental arrangement for US$100 per week, swapping out boards from their quiver as often as you like.

Playa Grande Surf Camp (below) Gerry and his cohorts will rent you shortboards or longboards ($20 per day), and show you how to ride 'em.

Sleeping & Eating

Hotels are well signed from the main road into Playa Grande. It's a good idea to bring a flashlight for walking around at night, as the roads are necessarily dark (and uneven!).

Playa Grande Surf Camp (☎ 2653 1074; www.playa grandesurfcamp.com; r per person with/without air-con US$25/15; P ☒ ☒) Next to El Manglar is this great budget option, run by surfing brothers Gerry and Patrick. The three A-frame cabinas with thatch roofs and two stilt cabinas (each sleeps four) with private hammock-strung porches all have private bathrooms, and are just steps from the beach. Heads up, surfer girls – some staff here can be a bit overfriendly.

El Manglar (☎ 2653 0952; www.hotel-manglar.com; d standard/deluxe US$45/70; P ☐ ☒) Near the southern end of the beach is this funky, friendly spot with brightly painted stuccoed rooms and lush, tropical grounds. Standard rooms have private cold showers, while deluxe rooms have hot water and slightly more space.

Villa Baula (☎ 2653 0644, 2653 0493; www.hotelvilla baula.com; d/tr US$66/77, bungalow with/without air-con US$138/132; P ☒ ☒) Across from the estuary near the southern end of the beach, this rustic beachfront hotel emits virtually no ambient light at night. All rooms have private hot-water bathrooms, while more expensive bungalows have air-con and optional kitchens. There's an attractive pool, and this end of the beach is much quieter as it's further from the best surfing.

Rip Jack Inn (☎ 2653 0480; www.ripjackinn.com; d/cabina US$87/111; P ☒ ☐ ☒) Just south of Las Tortugas on the inland road, this comfy, convivial inn has a handful of clean, modern rooms with private bathrooms and air-con. There's also a beautiful open-air bar-restau-

rant with stunning ocean views, plus regular yoga classes on offer.

Playa Grande Inn (☎ 2653 0719; www.playagrandein .com; r/ste US$58/87; P ☒ ☒) Around the corner from the Rip Jack Inn, air-conditioned rooms at this laidback place are decked out with polished stained-wood floors, ceilings and walls, and have cable TV and hot water. There's also a cozy bar area and small pool.

Hotel Las Tortugas (☎ 2653 0423; www.lastortugas hotel.com; s/d/ste US$58/93/140, apt US$29-116; P ☒ ☐ ☒) The owner of this hotel, Louis Wilson, is a local hero as he was instrumental in helping to designate Playa Grande as a national park. Although his hotel is near the beach, it was carefully designed to keep ambient light away from the nesting area, and to block light from development to the north. Eleven spacious rooms with air-con have private bathrooms with hot water, plus thick walls and small windows to enable daytime sleep after a night of turtle-watching. The hotel also has two apartments with kitchens for rent up the hill. Surfboards, body boards, sea kayaks, snorkels and horses can be rented. There's a pool, Jacuzzi and a popular restaurant, and all tours can be arranged.

La Marejada Hotel (☎ 2653 0594; www.lamarejada .com; r US$81 incl breakfast; ☒ ☒) This new, bamboo-fenced hotel has a few elegantly understated rooms around a small pool area. A palm-shaded common area is strung with hammocks and leads to the Mar Bar in front.

Hotel Bula Bula (☎ 2653 0975; www.hotelbulabula .com; s/d incl breakfast US$93/128; P ☒ ☐ ☒) A few hundred meters inland near the Tamarindo estuary is this recommended hotel, owned by two Americans (one of whom is a professional chef). The rooms are exquisite, with full amenities and original artwork on all the walls, and the landscaped grounds and free-form pool are perfect for relaxing after a hard day of surfing. But one of the biggest draws is The Great Waltini's (dishes US$9 to US$16), the onsite restaurant that serves up only the freshest local seafood and some truly excellent grilled meats.

Kike's Place (☎ 2653 0834; www.kikesplace.com; ☻ breakfast, lunch & dinner) On the road into town, take note of Kike's (it's 'KEE-kays,' so's you know), the friendly local bar and restaurant where you can shoot some pool, eat some *ceviche* and let your hair down.

Aside from eating at the hotels, try tasty **Los Malinches** (☎ 2653 0236; mains US$5-9; ☻ 8am-9pm

Mon-Sat), where you can dine on good, fresh seafood underneath a giant *palapa*. Next door, the **supermercado** (7:30am-noon & 3-7pm Mon-Sat) sells produce, booze and other staples. It also rents a few cute, clean **cabinas** (s/d US$20/25) with air-con.

Getting There & Away

There are no buses to Playa Grande. You can drive to Huacas and then take the paved road to Matapalo, followed by a 6km dirt road to Playa Grande. If you don't have your own car and are staying in Playa Grande, call ahead and the hotel owners can arrange for a pick-up from the Matapalo turnoff (where the bus from San José can drop you off).

Alternatively, you can cut your travel time in half by catching a boat across the estuary from Tamarindo to the southern end of Playa Grande (around US$1.25 per person).

PARQUE NACIONAL MARINO LAS BAULAS DE GUANACASTE

Playa Grande is considered one of the most important nesting sites in the entire world for the *baula* (leatherback turtle). In 1991 the entire beach and adjacent land (379 hectares), along with 22,000 hectares of ocean, was designated as Marino Las Baulas National Park. This government act followed a 15-year battle between conservationists and various self-motivated parties, including poachers, developers and tour operators.

However, lest you think that the Costa Rican government was particularly concerned about the welfare of the turtles, the actual impetus for the creation of the national park came from the owner of the Hotel Las Tortugas (see opposite). In fact, the sole stipulation for designating Playa Grande as a protected area was that the beach needed to generate revenue based on tourism. Fortunately, tourists perennially pay the park fees to watch the turtles nest, and local guides ensure that the beach (and their economic livelihood) stays intact.

The ecology of the park is primarily composed of mangrove swamp, and it's possible to find here all of the six mangrove species native to Costa Rica. This habitat is ideal for caiman and crocodile, as well as numerous bird species, including the beautiful roseate spoonbill. Other creatures to look for when visiting are howler monkey, raccoon, coati, otter and a variety of crab. But, as is to be expected, the main attraction is the nesting of the world's largest species of turtle, which can weigh in excess of 400kg. Nesting season is from October to March, and it's fairly common for three or four leatherbacks to lay their eggs here on any given night.

The leatherback is critically endangered from overhunting, a lack of protected nesting sights and coastal overdevelopment (beachside lights disorient the turtles when they come up to nest). Despite increased conservation efforts, fewer and fewer leatherbacks are nesting on Playa Grande each year. In 2004 an all-time low of 46 leatherbacks visited the beach, which was a vast departure from the estimated 1000 turtles that nested here in the 1990s. While it's easy to point fingers at developers in Tamarindo, park rangers attribute the decline in nesting turtles to longline commercial fishing, though the construction of high-rise apartments and beachside fast-food joints certainly isn't helping.

In an effort to protect the dwindling leatherback population, park rangers collect the eggs daily and incubate them to increase their chances of survival. Even so, sea turtles must hatch on the beach and enter the water by themselves, otherwise memory imprinting does not occur, and the hatchlings will never return to their birthplace to nest. It's estimated that only 10% of hatchlings will survive to adulthood, though leatherbacks can live over 50 years, and females can lay multiple clutches of eggs during a single nesting season.

During the day, the beach is free and open to all, which is a good thing as the breaks off Grande are fast, steep and consistent. During the nighttime, however, it is only possible to visit the beach on a guided tour, which is also a good thing as it ensures that the nesting cycles of the leatherback will continue unhindered.

Turtle-Watching

The **park office** (2653 0470; admission incl tour US$13) is by the northern entrance to Playa Grande. Reservations for turtle-watching can be made up to seven days in advance, and they're highly recommended as there are a limited number of places each evening. If you phone ahead, you will be promised a spot within a week, though there is usually a vacancy within a day or two. You can also show up in the evening as there are frequent no-shows, though this is less likely on weekends and during the busy winter holiday season.

CAMERA SHY

A picture might be worth a thousand words, but sometimes it's better to say nothing at all. Take, for instance, the miracle of birth – who would want to share that with random gawkers and paparazzi? This is not to poke fun of a serious situation. One of the reasons why turtles no longer nest on Playa Tamarindo is that they're extremely sensitive to ambient light. You can see why a string of beachside bars might deter a turtle from laying her clutch of eggs on that particular beach. So at the beaches where endangered turtles still do return to nest, you'll understand why flash photography is strictly verboten.

When you take a turtle tour, the rangers will politely ask that you refrain from photographing or filming the turtles, but we'd just like to underscore the fact that by experiencing it in the moment and not committing it to film, you are helping to maintain a fragile cycle that has renewed itself continually for millions of years.

Many hotels and tourist agencies in Tamarindo can book tours that include transport to and from Playa Grande, admission to the park and the guided tour. The whole package costs about US$35. If you don't have your own transport, this is the best way to go. When making a reservation, passport numbers and full names are required as this prevents big hotels in Tamarindo from reserving blocks for their guests.

The show kicks off anytime from 9pm to as late as 2am, though there is no guarantee that you will see a turtle – this is nature, not the San Diego Zoo. This also means that you may only have to wait for 10 minutes before a turtle shows up, or you could be there for five hours. A small stand at the exhibit sells snacks and *sodas,* but bring a (thick) book or a deck of cards for entertainment. It could be a very long night – but well worth it. While you're waiting, a good way to begin your tour is with a visit to **El Mundo de la Tortuga** (☎ 2653 0471; admission US$5; ⏰ 4pm-dawn), a small and informative self-guided exhibit about leatherback turtles near the northern end of the park.

To minimize the impact of viewing the turtles, guidelines for the tours are very strict; see boxed text Camera Shy, above. Tourists are not allowed on the beach until the turtles have made it to dry sand. Guards with two-way radios are posted on the beach and they will alert your guide when a turtle is ready for its close-up. As a group, you will be accompanied by a guide to a designated viewing area, though photography, filming or lights of any kind are *not* allowed. Over the span of one to two hours, you can watch as the turtle digs its nest, lays about 150 silver shiny eggs and then buries them in the sand (while grunting and groaning the whole time).

If you're looking for a worthwhile volunteer project, the park office usually accepts volunteers to help monitor and catalog each nesting.

PLAYA TAMARINDO

Well, they don't call it Tamagringo for nothing. Call it what you will, but its accessibility from Liberia and decades-long status as one of Costa Rica's must-stop surf spots has made it the last word for many expats who have settled here, as well as the next wave of non-surfing gringos who have snapped up coastal property like there's no tomorrow – which there may not be, if real estate development continues at the pace it's going. Luckily, Tamarindo residents who care about the community and the ecosystem are attempting to put a stop to the insanely unsustainable construction (see boxed text Saving Tamarindo, opposite for more information). Despite the boutiques on the strip and the condos lining the coast, Tamarindo forms a part of the Parque Nacional Marino Las Baulas de Guanacaste (p269). Visitors have long flocked here for a reason, and the beach and surf themselves retain their inherent allure. But forget about finding any 'real' Costa Rica here – it's more like a slice of San Diego. So drop your pretenses, drop in on some fun waves and drop a few colones worth of Jägermeister shots at one of the beachside bars, because that's why you're in Tamarindo.

Orientation

Once a sleepy fishing village that turned into a little surf town, Tamarindo now channels the spirit of rush hour in southern California on the weekends, when traffic gridlocks along the two-lane main drag. Just before the main street dead-ends into a cul-de-sac at the south-eastern end of the beach, a road branches off to the left and passes the new Plaza Conchal mall. If you turn left again where that road forms a Y, you'll find several hotels along the dirt road. Turn right and you'll be headed for Playa Langosta, where the coast is crowded with condos and villas, a casino resort and a couple of exquisite little inns.

Amazingly, even though Tamarindo is possessed of frozen yogurt, yoga studios and air-conditioned malls, there's no gas station. For that, you'll have to drive 15 paved kilometers to Huacas – from Tamarindo, make a left at the intersection in Villareal, drive to Huacas, hang a right and go up the hill. The gas station is 4km up the road, on the right.

Information

Tourist information is available from any of the tour operators in town, or your hotel. Keep up on the local haps by picking up a copy of the *Tamarindo News*, available all over town or online at www.tamarindonews.com. For a cheerily jaundiced look at the state of modern Tamarindo, pick up a copy of the local zine *Flyswatter*.

BAC San José (☎ 2653 1617; ☺ 8:30am-3:30pm) Has an ATM, and exchanges US dollars and traveler's checks.
Coastal Emergency Medical Service (☎ 2653 0611, 2653 1974; ☺ 24hr) It does house calls! Can you say that about your hometown doc?
Internet Café del Mar (☎ 2653 1740; www.cafedelmarinternet.com; per hr US$1.50; ☺ 8am-8pm)
Jaime Peligro (☎ 8820 9004; ☺ 9am-8pm Mon-Sat, noon-5pm Sun) A local spot for new and used foreign-language books and the best Central American CDs and DVDs.

Dangers & Annoyances

The tourist invasion has left Tamarindo with a growing drug (and prostitution) problem. Vendors openly ply their wares (and women) on the main road by the rotunda, and some bars can get rough at closing time.

Theft is a problem. Leave your hotel room locked, use room safes and don't leave valuables on the beach. If you're driving, never leave anything in your car.

Activities
BIKING
The local expert on mountain biking, distance cycling and repairs is **Blue Trax** (☎ 2653 1705; www.bluetraxcr.com; ☺ 8:30am-6:30pm Mon-Sat). And if multiday mountain-biking tours are not your thing, it can also rent you a beach cruiser (US$10 per day).

DIVING
Agua Rica Diving Center (☎ 2653 0094; www.aguarica.net), the area's scuba-diving expert, offers snorkeling and an assortment of dives, including diving certification classes.

GOLF
Just outside Tamarindo, near the village of San José de Pinilla, lies a residential development project that boasts one of the finest golf courses in Central America. **Hacienda Pinilla** (☎ 2680 3000; www.haciendapinilla.com) has a 7500yd par-72 course that was designed

PENINSULA DE NICOYA

SAVING TAMARINDO

The price of blithely disregarding the pressure on Tamarindo's environment is coming due. At the end of 2007, Playa Tamarindo lost its Bandera Azul Ecológica (Ecological Blue Flag) designation, which marked it as a community with high water quality, safety and environmental responsibility. Frankly, it was about time the flag got pulled, as it was an open secret that the water quality had been deteriorating, due in part to appalling practices like a certain hostel draining its raw sewage into open trenches on the street.

Losing the Bandera Azul, and watching the alarming spate of high-density construction rising in the middle of tiny Tamarindo, has raised red flags for local business owners and residents. The town is teetering on the brink of sustainability; if the exploitation of the land continues, Tamarindo not only loses its luster for visitors, but it displaces wildlife, irreparably damages the local ecology and becomes another sad story of greed trumping the well-being of a community. But many in Tamarindo recognize this pivotal moment and are acting up.

At the time of writing, organizers of the **Save Tamarindo Campaign** (www.savetamarindo.com) were putting forward a new urban development plan that would curb high-density development and require stricter government regulation.

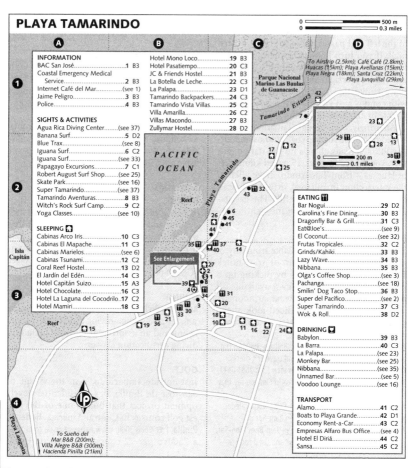

PLAYA TAMARINDO

INFORMATION
BAC San José..............................**1** B3
Coastal Emergency Medical
  Service...................................**2** B3
Internet Café del Mar..............(see 1)
Jaime Peligro............................**3** B3
Police.......................................**4** B3

SIGHTS & ACTIVITIES
Agua Rica Diving Center........(see 37)
Banana Surf..............................**5** D2
Blue Trax...............................(see 8)
Iguana Surf...............................**6** C2
Iguana Surf............................(see 33)
Papagayo Excursions.................**7** C1
Robert August Surf Shop.......(see 25)
Skate Park.............................(see 16)
Super Tamarindo...................(see 37)
Tamarindo Aventuras................**8** B3
Witch's Rock Surf Camp............**9** C2
Yoga Classes.........................(see 10)

SLEEPING
Cabinas Arco Iris.....................**10** C3
Cabinas El Mapache.................**11** C3
Cabinas Marielos....................(see 6)
Cabinas Tsunami.....................**12** C2
Coral Reef Hostel....................**13** D2
El Jardín del Edén...................**14** C3
Hotel Capitán Suizo.................**15** A3
Hotel Chocolate......................**16** C3
Hotel La Laguna del Cocodrilo..**17** C2
Hotel Mamiri...........................**18** B3

Hotel Mono Loco.....................**19** B3
Hotel Pasatiempo.....................**20** C3
JC & Friends Hostel.................**21** B3
La Botella de Leche..................**22** C3
La Palapa.................................**23** D1
Tamarindo Backpackers.............**24** C3
Tamarindo Vista Villas.............**25** C2
Villa Amarilla...........................**26** C2
Villas Macondo.......................**27** B3
Zullymar Hostel.......................**28** D2

EATING
Bar Nogui................................**29** D2
Carolina's Fine Dining.............**30** B3
Dragonfly Bar & Grill...............**31** C3
Eat@Joe's..............................(see 9)
El Coconut............................(see 32)
Frutas Tropicales.....................**32** C3
Grinds/Kahiki..........................**33** B3
Lazy Wave...............................**34** B3
Nibbana..................................**35** B3
Olga's Coffee Shop..................(see 3)
Pachanga...............................(see 18)
Smilin' Dog Taco Stop.............**36** B3
Super del Pacifico....................(see 2)
Super Tamarindo.....................**37** C3
Wok & Roll..............................**38** D2

DRINKING
Babylon..................................**39** B3
La Barra..................................**40** C3
La Palapa..............................(see 23)
Monkey Bar..........................(see 25)
Nibbana.................................(see 35)
Unnamed Bar.........................(see 5)
Voodoo Lounge......................(see 16)

TRANSPORT
Alamo.....................................**41** C2
Boats to Playa Grande.............**42** D1
Economy Rent-a-Car................**43** C2
Empresas Alfaro Bus Office......(see 4)
Hotel El Diriá...........................**44** C2
Sansa.....................................**45** C2

PACIFIC OCEAN

Parque Nacional Marino Las Baulas de Guanacaste

To Airstrip (2.5km); Café Café (2.8km); Huacas (15km); Playa Avellanas (15km); Playa Negra (18km); Santa Cruz (22km); Playa Junquillal (29km)

Tamarindo Estuary

See Enlargement

Isla Capitán

Reef

Reef

To Sueño del Mar B&B (200m); Villa Alegre B&B (300m); Hacienda Pinilla (21km)

by noted architect Mike Young. Greens fees are US$125/165 per person during the low/high season.

SAILING

For sunset and daylong sailing excursions, book in advance via phone or online with one of the following outfits:

Blue Dolphin Sailing (☎ 2653 0867, 8842 3204; www.sailbluedolphin.com) Reader-recommended trips on Captain Jeff's catamaran include a sunset sail (US$60) and snorkel-and-sunset sail (US$75).

Mandingo Sailing (☎ 2653 0623, 8831 8875; www .tamarindosailing.com) Runs a gaff-rigged schooner for sunset cruises (US$65) and a sleek speedboat for snorkeling trips (US$50).

SKATEBOARDING

If you happen to have your deck with you, there's a fun little one-bowl **skate park** behind the Voodoo Lounge.

SPORTFISHING

None of the following outfitters have offices, so you'll have to book excursions by phone or online. All practice catch-and-release policies on billfish.

Capullo Sportfishing (☎ 2653 0048, 8829 8891; www.capullo.com) Has a 10.8m custom Topaz and a 6.6m Boston Whaler; both inshore and offshore trips are available for half-day (US$400 to US$700) and full-day (US$525 to US$1200) charters.

Lone Star Sportfishing (☎ 2653 0101; www.lonestar sportfishing.com) Bilingual captains Juan Mungia and

Alonso Gonzalez run trips aboard a 9m Palm Beach boat available for half-day/full-day (US$500/800) charters.
Tantrum Sportfishing (☎ 2653 1020, 8845 8562; www.tamarindofishingcharters.com) Captain Philip Leman has a 7.8m Boca Grande custom sportfisherman available for half-day/full-day (US$450/725) charters.

SURFING

The most popular wave in Tamarindo is a medium-sized right that breaks directly in front of the Diria Hotel. The waters here are full of virgin surfers learning to pop up, most of whom can't help but play aquatic bumper cars. There is also a good left that's fed by the river mouth, though be advised that crocodiles are occasionally sighted here, particularly when the tide is rising (which is coincidentally the best time to surf). You'll have to get a local to let you in on some of their favorite spots, as we're not going to ruin it for them.

More advanced surfers will appreciate the bigger, faster and less crowded waves at **Playas Langosta** (on the other side of the point), **Avellanas** and **Negra** (p277) and **Junquillal** (p280) to the south, and **Playa Grande** (p267) to the north. Note that the best months for surfing coincide with the rainy season.

A number of surf schools and surf tour operators line the main stretch of road in Tamarindo. Surf lessons hover at around US$30 for 1½ to two hours and most operators will let you keep the board for a few hours beyond that to practice. All outfits can organize daylong and multiday excursions to popular breaks, rent equipment and give surf lessons.
Banana Surf (☎ 2653 1270; www.bananasurfclub.com; ☺ 8am-6pm) This Argentinean-run outfit has the fairest prices in town on new and used boards, and is reminiscent of the way surf shops used to be (ie before they rented space in shopping malls).
Iguana Surf (☎ 2653 0148; www.iguanasurf.net; ☺ 8am-6pm) Operates a surf taxi service to neighboring beaches (US$10 per person to Playa Grande, US$25 per person to Playa Negra). Two locations (at either end of town) conveniently at your service.
Robert August Surf Shop (☎ 2653 0114; rasurf shop@yahoo.com; ☺ 9am-5pm) The august Robert August, having put Tamarindo on the map, now offers his name-brand boards, lessons and surf trips from his shop. Based at Tamarindo Vista Villas.
Witch's Rock Surf Camp (☎ 2653 0239; www.witchs rocksurfcamp.com; ☺ 8am-8pm) Board rentals, surf camps, lessons and regular excursions to Witch's Rock and Ollie's Point are available, though they're pricey. There

are beachside accommodations for surfers who sign up for multiday packages.

YOGA

Daily yoga classes are offered at the Cabinas Arco Iris (p274).

Tours

Boat tours, ATV tours, snorkeling trips and scooter rentals can be arranged through the various tour agencies in town. Many also rent equipment. The most reputable ones include the following:
Brisa del Mar (☎ 8868 0947; pitbest11@gmail.com) A true man of the sea, Pit (pronounced Pete) runs personalized tours emphasizing fishing, surfing, snorkeling and coastline cruising. He also speaks English, Spanish and Italian, and is a true entertainer in any language – drop him an email a few days before arriving in town for a good time!
Papagayo Excursions (☎ 2653 0254; www.papagayo excursions.com) The longest-running outfitter in town organizes a variety of tours, including visits to turtle-nesting sites.
Tamarindo Aventuras (☎ 2653 0108; www.tamarindo adventures.net; scooters per 4hr US$25, ATVs per 4hr US$60, dirt bikes per 4hr US$34) Also rents water-sports equipment, including kayaks, snorkeling gear and surfboards.

Sleeping

The rates given are high-season rates; low-season rates can be about 25% lower.

BUDGET

Note that we constantly receive complaints about hotels in Tamarindo, so choose your accommodations wisely. All the following hotels have cold water (and you won't mind a bit).
our pick La Botella de Leche (☎ 2653 0189; labo telladeleche@racsa.co.cr; dm/s/d US$10/12/24; P 🕸 🖳) With a relaxed vibe and over-the-top cow theme, this Argentinean-run spot is highly recommended for its warm and attentive management, fully air-conditioned rooms and dormitories, and quiet location at the eastern edge of town. Facilities include a shared kitchen, surfboard racks, big-screen-TV lounge and free bike use. The lovely owner will even lend you a spare umbrella if you're here in the rainy season!
Tamarindo Backpackers (☎ 8385 3501; www.tam arindobackpackers.com; dm US$12) At the time of writing, the ribbon was just about to be cut at this soon-to-be all-star backpackers spot, brought to you by the same guys who run Hostel Pangea in San José (p95). With an outdoor

swimming pool, central air–cooled rooms, a fully equipped kitchen and what promises to be a great vibe, you will most likely enjoy yourself here.

JC & Friends Hostel (camping/dm/r per person US$5/10/14; 🖥 🕹) This newer hostel near Grinds/Kahiki has unique amenities like an indoor pool, camping area and free internet access, but we've heard mixed reports from travelers – it's a bit dark and not the cleanest, but the staff is very friendly and helpful. Hopefully with time they'll work the bugs out.

Cabinas Tsunami (☎ 2653 0280; s/d from US$18/22; P) Tsunami houses a lot of longer-stay surfer types, as it's right across from the 50m path to the river mouth. Front rooms are a bit smaller, with that classic concrete-block ambience, while larger rooms in back have fridge and a shared terrace festooned with bougainvillea. There's also a shared outdoor kitchen.

Coral Reef Hostel (☎ 2653 0291; s/d US$20/30; P 🖥) The 10 rooms here are clean and fairly basic, with shared bathrooms. Though it's on a noisy section of the road, the guys running the place are friendly and offer a variety of services, like surfboard rental, internet access and a BBQ area.

MIDRANGE
All the hotels below have private hot-water bathrooms unless otherwise stated.

Cabinas Marielos (☎ 2653 0141; www.cabinasmarielos cr.com; d with/without air-con US$40/30; P 🕹) Rooms at this well-priced place have firm beds, private bathrooms and share a kitchen with the biggest fridge ever. Some of the rooms face the garden, and the place is decorated with Sarchi-style accents.

Cabinas El Mapache (☎ 2653 0882; r with/without air-con US$40/30; P 🕹 🖥) Away from the main road, these colorful, simple cabinas circle a garden with a communal kitchen. The shared patio is hung with hammocks, and all rooms have wi-fi.

Villa Amarilla (☎ 2653 0038; carpen@racsa.co.cr; d with/without bathroom US$45/30, additional person US$10; 🕹) This quaint, French-owned inn is one of the safest beachfront hotels you'll find in Tamarindo. There are four rooms with private bathroom, air-con and cable TV, as well as three cheaper units that have shared hot-water showers. All have a fridge and safe, and share an outdoor kitchen. Credit cards are accepted.

Hotel Mamiri (☎ 2653 0079; www.hotelmamiri.com; s/d US$36/41, apt US$59-75; P 🕹) This delightful open-air hotel is decorated with memorabilia from the Italian owners' travels through Asia and Central America. Each room is unique, and some feature attractive volcanic stone tiling on the floors and walls. The relaxed and breezy grounds are strung up with hammocks, and there's a well-equipped communal kitchen for all your self-catering needs. The attached restaurant, Pachanga, is one of the top spots to dine in town.

Zullymar Hostel (☎ 8846 4500; laualbro@yahoo.com; s/d US$20/50; P 🖥) Not to be confused with the hotel of the same name, this place is located just before the roundabout – it's down a walkway housing spa services and opens on to a pleasant courtyard. Rooms are simple and slightly aged, though tidy, with fridge and private bathroom. There's wi-fi access, laundry, lockers and a communal kitchen.

Hotel Mono Loco (☎ 2653 0238; elmonoloco@racsa .co.cr; d with fan/air-con US$36/45; 🕹 🕹) This quiet hotel is on the road into Playa Langosta, so you can definitely sleep soundly at night. The hotel itself is a yellow stucco and thatched-roof building that surrounds a beautifully landscaped pool. Bright and airy rooms have cable TV and optional air-con. The onsite restaurant serves reasonably priced Costa Rican fare all day long.

ourpick Villas Macondo (☎ 2653 0812; www.villas macondo.com; s/d/tr US$41/47/58, s/d/tr with air-con US$64/76/87, 2-/4-person apt US$122/169, additional person US$10; P 🕹 🖥 🕹) Although it's only 200m from the beach, this German-run establishment is an oasis of serenity in an otherwise frenzied town – it's also one of the best deals around. Beautiful modern villas with private hot showers and hammock-strung patios surround a solar-heated pool and tropical garden, while larger apartments are equipped with cable TV, a full kitchen and air-con. Credit cards accepted.

Cabinas Arco Iris (☎ 2653 0330; www.hotelarcoiris .com; s/d/tr US$45/50/60, deluxe d/tr/q US$60/70/80; P 🕹 🖥) A cluster of garden cabinas makes up this wonderfully reclusive Italian-owned place. Every unit is simply decorated with bamboo and wood, and its hillside location creates a sense of peace and relaxation. The hotel offers weekday yoga (and occasional martial arts) classes in the shaded 'dojo-gym.' Guests can also use the communal open-air kitchen, and there's wi-fi available.

La Palapa (☎ 2653 0362; www.lapalapa.info; s/d/tr/q incl breakfast US$70/80/90/100; [P] [⌘]) Despite the attached bar-restaurant being one of the most popular places for a sunset cocktail, this little beachfront hotel is surprisingly quiet and secluded. All six stylish rooms have loft beds, ocean views and big-screen TVs with DVD players, and the terra-cotta-tile floors lead to shaded terraces directly on the beach. Though it's only 20m from the roundabout, the hotel's size makes it feel intimate and relaxed.

Hotel Chocolate (☎ 2653 1311; www.thechocolate hotel.com; r/ste US$87/105; [⌘] [□] [▣]) Up the same road as the 'Milk Bottle' hostel, this sweet little hotel has several well-appointed rooms done up in dark wood and terra-cotta tile floors, with orthopedic mattresses on the beds. Rooms upstairs have higher ceilings and get more light, but all are elegant and comfortable and surround the garden-fringed pool. One suite has a fully equipped kitchen. The lovely young family running the place will make you feel at home.

Hotel La Laguna del Cocodrilo (☎ 2653 0255; www .lalagunadelcocodrilo.com; r US$87-99, ste US$151; [P] [⌘]) A beachfront location blesses this charming French-owned hotel, with luxurious, well-kept rooms overlooking either the shady grounds or the ocean and estuary. Adjacent to a crocodile-filled lagoon (hence the name), the hotel has a private trail leading to the beach. There's also a restaurant specializing in seafood, but lovers of pastry will be most delighted with the sublime items from the onsite French bakery. Credit cards accepted.

TOP END

All hotels can arrange tours in the area, and all accept credit cards.

Tamarindo Vista Villas (☎ 2653 0114; www.tam arindovistavillas.com; d/ste incl breakfast from US$104/185; [P] [⌘] [□] [▣]) Perched on a hill overlooking the entrance to Tamarindo, this hotel is one of the most popular places in town for well-to-do travelers, and the 33 rooms and suites have all the amenities (and institutionalized blandness) you associate with the Best Western chain. But, it does have an ocean-view pool, the popular Monkey Bar, a dive shop, the Robert August Surf Shop and a tour desk.

Hotel Pasatiempo (☎ 2653 0096; www.hotel pasatiempo.com; d US$115-127, ste US$150, additional person US$15; [P] [⌘] [▣]) This well-established Tamarindo landmark is known for its popular live-music nights at the bar-restaurant, though it's also a great place to stay. Rooms are awash in tropical-themed murals, and have comfortable beds, modern bathroom, air-con and a private hammock-strung patio. Suites have a living room with fold-out couch, which is perfect if you're traveling with the offspring. Though breakfast isn't included, there's free coffee and pastries offered in the morning.

El Jardín del Edén (☎ 2653 0137; www.jardindel eden.com; d/apt/ste incl breakfast from US$157/192/256; [P] [⌘] [□] [▣]) On a hill overlooking Tamarindo, this luxurious French-run hotel has 36 exquisite rooms, each with a sitting area and private patio or balcony (and some of Tamarindo's best views). Rooms are gorgeously designed according to one of four themes: Balinese, Japanese, African and Tunisian. There are also two apartments (sleeping five) with kitchenette, plus a Jacuzzi, pool with swim-up bar and Mediterranean-inspired bar-restaurant.

Villa Alegre B&B (☎ 2653 0270; www.villaalegre costarica.com; r US$170-185, villa US$230, all incl breakfast; [P] [⌘] [□] [▣] [♿]) This beachside B&B in nearby Playa Langosta has five rooms of various sizes, each decorated with memorabilia from the owners' world travels (you can choose from the Caribbean, USA, California, Guatemala or Mexico rooms). Or stay in the Japan or Russia villas, which are equipped with full kitchens. There's an honor bar, a comfortable guest living room and plenty of games for children. Bounteous breakfasts are served on the deck, and your hosts Barry and Suzye make their home as sunny and welcoming as they are.

our pick **Sueño del Mar B&B** (☎ 2653 0284; www .sueno-del-mar.com; d US$195-295, casitas US$220-240; [P] [⌘] [□] [▣]) This stunning Spanish-style posada (country-style inn) in nearby Playa Langosta is run by lovely innkeepers Ashton and Tui, and decorated with handcrafted rocking chairs, hammocks and a cozy living room that's perfect for relaxing with the other guests. The six rooms have four-poster beds, artfully placed crafts and open-air garden showers, while the romantic honeymoon suite has a wraparound window with sea views. There's private beach access beyond the pool and tropical garden, and a priceless, pervasive atmosphere of seclusion and beauty…so, no children under 12 allowed.

Hotel Capitán Suizo (☎ 2653 0075; www.hotelcapitan suizo.com; r with/without air-con US$227/204, bungalow with/without air-con US$320/274, additional person US$47, all incl breakfast; [P] [⌘] [□] [▣]) On the southern end of the beach is this Swiss-run hotel, which belongs to the group of 'Small Distinctive Hotels of Costa Rica.' The 22 rooms and 18 larger, thatched-roof bungalows are decorated with natural stone floors, polished hardwoods and soft, pastel hues. The entire complex is centered on a free-form pool that's shaded by expansive gardens, and all units are just steps from a quiet strip of sand. There's also a six-person beachfront apartment (US$500).

Eating

You can't have sophisticated modern living without boutique gourmet eateries, so it's unsurprising that Tamarindo has some of the best restaurants in Costa Rica. But be prepared to pay – a cheap meal in this town is about as common as a nesting turtle.

If you're self-catering, the Super Tamarindo is well stocked with international groceries, as is the Super del Pacífico.

Olga's Coffee Shop (☎ 8395 5838; www.olgascoffee shop.com; snacks US$1-3; ☷ 7am-4pm) In a new corner location with floor-to-ceiling windows, this sleek Russian-owned café serves up organic Costa Rican coffee and homemade pastries – the outside terrace is the perfect place to hang in the morning as you let the caffeine do its thing.

Café Café (☎ 2653 1864; mains US$3-5; ☷ 8am-3pm Mon-Sat) About 3km outside of town, this super-friendly café is a great place to pick up an espresso, smoothie or panini on your way into or out of town.

Frutas Tropicales (mains US$2-6; ☷ breakfast, lunch & dinner) One of the few places you can get a good, inexpensive casado, this friendly spot serves up tasty local food…at a local pace.

Smilin' Dog Taco Stop (mains US$2.50-7; ☷ lunch & dinner) Those hankering for Mexican grub will appreciate the quality of offerings at this popular eatery while shoestringers will revel in the generous portions and low prices.

Bar Nogui (☎ 2653 0029; mains US$3-11; ☷ 6am-9:30pm Thu-Tue) This beachside restaurant offers upscale casados with grilled fish, mixed meats and unbelievable shrimp and lobster. It's consistently popular with locals and tourists alike, so come early for dinner or be prepared to wait at the bar for a couple of Imperiales with the rowdy regulars.

Eat@Joe's (☎ 2653 1262; mains US$4-9; ☷ 7am-late) The best snack in town is at this American-run surf camp, where you can order the famous 'nachos as big as your ass' (or sushi rolls) while sucking down cold ones on the outdoor deck until 2am.

Wok & Roll (☎ 2653 0156; mains US$4-10; ☷ noon-9:30pm Mon-Sat) Korean-American owner Kandice routinely inspires fear in local fishermen throughout the Nicoya. She is famous for scrutinizing daily tuna and mahi-mahi catches, and will only buy the freshest of fish. The result: some of the best sushi we've ever eaten. Her woks and Vietnamese spring rolls are also popular.

Grinds/Kahiki (☎ 2653 3816; www.kahikirestau rant.com; mains US$6-12; ☷ 6am-late Tue-Sun) In the mornings, you can get breakfast grinds like giant pancakes and bottomless cups of coffee. Dinner is another story, with good Hawaiian-influenced fusion dishes emphasizing the local catch. The bar is a cool place to hang if you don't feel like eating, with a long and intriguing cocktail menu.

El Coconut (☎ 2653 0086; mains US$7-20; ☷ dinner Tue-Sun) Another recommended choice for seafood and pasta dishes. You can get a special dinner here without having to get formal about it. The ambience is laidback but elegant, with a tropical flair and a dessert menu that begs you to save room.

Nibbana (☎ 2653 0447; www.nibbana-tamarindo .com; US$6-15; ☷ lunch & dinner) One of the nicest beachfront dining areas in town, Nibbana has tables scattered underneath the palms. It serves great pizza at lunch, and Tico-flavored continental cuisine, like shrimp, lemon and basil risotto, or grilled tuna with a fresh mint-and-tomato compote. It also has free wi-fi access.

Carolina's Fine Dining (☎ 2653 0091; mains US$10-25; ☷ 6-11pm Thu-Tue) This is one place worth the splurge. Sophisticated continental cuisine highlights skillfully prepared sauces, tender cuts of meat, delectable fish and an impressive selection of imported wines. To truly appreciate the culinary experience, opt for the five-course tasting menu with a full wine tasting (US$70).

Lazy Wave (☎ 2653 0737; meals US$10-25; ☷ 6-10pm Sat-Thu) Dine at a table if you must, but the best place to enjoy your meal and glass of wine is on the covered pavilion, where you can curl up amid pillows in cushy lounge chairs. If you're out to woo that hot thing you met last night, this hip nightspot, built around a huge tree, is a good place to start the evening. There's a solid wine list, good mix of cocktails and Asian- and Euro-influenced *bocas*, as well as a full menu.

Dragonfly Bar & Grill (☎ 2653 1506; www.dragon flybarandgrill.com; mains US$10-25; ☺ dinner Mon-Sat) Dragonfly is a local favorite, probably not just for its refined menu, but also for its lovely atmosphere in the festive tent-like structure of the dining room. The menu has a Californian bent, featuring fresh items like pork chop with chipotle-apple chutney and the Thai-style crispy fish cake with curried corn. Linger a while over your wine and perhaps you can also find room for a divine dessert.

Pachanga (☎ 2653 0021, 8368 6983; prix fixe dinner US$23; ☺ 6-10pm Mon-Sat) Don't leave town without eating here – it may be the best meal you have in Costa Rica. The Israeli chef Shlomy serves innovative dishes with Mediterranean accents that change daily depending on the availability of local ingredients. The restaurant is understated yet elegant, which focuses your attention on the perfection of Shlomy's cuisine.

Drinking
In Tamarindo, all you really have to do is follow the scene wherever it happens to be on that night. On weekends especially, cruising the main drag has the festive feel of a mini Mardi Gras or spring break.

But, for a start, the Monkey Bar inside the Tamarindo Vista Villas is usually a good bet, and it has a ladies' night on Fridays. Also recommended is the Tuesday-night live-music jam at the Hotel Pasatiempo, Wednesday-night Latin dancing at La Barra and Thursday reggae night at Babylon. Any night of the week you can expect the music to be pumping *loudly* at the unnamed bar, even if no one is there.

There's often live music on the weekends at Voodoo Lounge, which has a great outdoor bar and stage in the back. Nibbana and La Palapa are good beachside spots to have a quiet getting-to-know-you cocktail.

Getting There & Away
AIR
The airstrip is 3km north of town; a hotel bus is usually on hand to pick up arriving passengers or you can take a taxi. During high season, Sansa has seven daily flights to and from San José (one way/return US$89/178), while NatureAir has three (US$96/192).

Sansa (☎ 2653 0012) has an office on the main road, and the travel desk at Hotel El Diriá can book trips on NatureAir. The airstrip belongs to the hotel and all passengers must pay a US$3 departure tax to use it.

BUS
Buses from San José (US$6, six hours) depart from the Empresas Alfaro office next to the police station at 3:30am, 5:45am and 12:30pm.

Catch the following buses across the street from Zullymar Hostel:
Liberia US$1.50, 2½ hours, departs at 5:45am, 7:30am, 8:50am, 11:20am, 1pm and 2:15pm.
Santa Cruz US$0.75, 1½ hours, departs at 6am, 9am, noon, 2:30pm and 4:15pm.

CAR & TAXI
If driving to Tamarindo, the better road is from Belén to Huacas and then south. It's also possible to drive from Santa Cruz to 27 de Abril on a paved road and then northwest on a dirt road for 19km to Tamarindo – this route is rougher, though passable for ordinary cars. A taxi from Santa Cruz costs about US$20, and it's twice that from Liberia.

Getting Around
Boats on the northern end of the beach can be hired to cross the estuary for daytime visits to the beach at Playa Grande. The ride is roughly US$1.25 per person, depending on the number of people.

Many visitors arrive in rental cars. If you get here by air or bus, you can rent bicycles and dirt bikes in town (see p271). There's no gas station, but you can buy expensive gas from drums at the hardware store near the entrance to town. (It's cheaper to fill up in Santa Cruz or at the gas station in Huacas.) Cars can be rented from **Alamo** (☎ 2653 0727) or **Economy Rent-a-Car** (☎ 2653 0752).

PLAYAS AVELLANAS & NEGRA
These popular **surfing beaches** have some of the best, most consistent waves in the area, made famous in the surf classic *Endless Summer II* (one of the breaks off Avellanas is known as 'Pequeño Hawaii'). The beaches begin 15km south of Tamarindo and are reached by dismal dirt roads requiring 4WD most times of the year (in the wet season there are three rivers to cross). Though the difficult access keeps the area refreshingly

PENINSULA DE NICOYA

WHAT TO DO IF YOU'RE CAUGHT IN A RIPTIDE

Riptides account for the majority of ocean drownings, though a simple understanding of how these currents behave can save your life. Rip currents are formed when excess water brought to shore by waves returns to the sea in a rapidly moving depression in the ocean floor. They are comprised of three parts: the feeder current, the neck and the head.

The feeder current consists of rapidly moving water that parallels the shore, though it's not always visible from the beach. When this water reaches a channel, it switches direction and flows out to sea, forming the neck of the rip. This is the fastest-moving part of the riptide, and can carry swimmers out to sea at a speed of up to 10km/h. The head of the riptide occurs past the breakers where the current quickly dissipates.

If you find yourself caught in a riptide, immediately call for help as you only have a few seconds before being swept out to sea. However, it's important to conserve your energy and not to fight the current – this is the principal cause of drownings. It's almost impossible to swim directly back to shore. Instead, try one of two methods for escaping a rip. The first is to tread water and let yourself be swept out past the breakers. Once you're in the head of the rip, you can swim out of the channel and ride the waves back to shore. Or you can swim parallel or diagonally to the shore until you're out of the channel.

Rip currents usually occur on beaches that have strong surf, though temporary rips can occur anywhere, especially when there is an offshore storm or during low tide. Fortunately, there are indicators, such as the brownish color on the surface of the water that is caused by swept-up sand and debris. Also look for surface flattening, which occurs when the water enters a depression in the ocean floor and rushes back out to sea. If you're ever in doubt about the safety of a beach, inquire locally about swimming conditions.

Remember, rips are fairly survivable as long as you relax, don't panic and conserve your energy.

---

uncrowded, growth here is inevitable. But concerned locals have taken steps to create a plan for sustainable growth *before* development has a chance to get out of hand, forming the **Association of Playa Avellanas** (www .avellanas.org) to that end.

Avellanas is a long stretch of white sand backed by mangroves, and Negra, a few kilometers further south, is a darker, caramel-color beach broken up by rocky outcrops. At Avellanas, **Little Hawaii** is a powerful and open-faced right at medium tide, while **Beach Break** barrels at low tide (though the surfing is good any time of day). Negra has a world-class right that barrels, especially with a moderate offshore wind. In between is the community of **Playa Lagartillo**, with a few cabinas and *sodas* scattered along the road.

If you're not coming from Tamarindo, head west on the paved highway from Santa Cruz, through 27 de Abril to Paraíso, then follow signs or ask locals. (This is a confusing area to drive through as road signs sometimes face only one direction).

While you're at the beach, be absolutely certain that nothing is visible in your car as professional thieves operate in this area, and they will remove your window even for a broken flip-flop or moldy sarong.

Café Playa Negra (☎ 2652 9351; www.playanegracafe .com; ⏱ 7am-9pm) has a laundry service (per load US$6), internet access (per hour US$2) and a small book exchange.

Sleeping & Eating
PLAYA AVELLANAS
The following places to stay and eat are very spread out around Playa Avellanas.

Casa Surf (☎ 2652 9075; r per person US$10; P) Look for the sign for the *panadería* (bakery) across from Cabinas Las Olas, and pull over – if not for espresso and yummy banana bread, then for a clean, quiet place to stay. Run lovingly by a Tico-Swiss surfer couple, this place has three simple rooms with shared bathroom and a full kitchen. They also rent surfboards and bikes for US$10 per day.

Rancho Iguana Verde (☎ 2652 9045; r per person US$10; P) About 50m from the beach on the road toward Playa Negra, these six cabinas are a bit dark but reasonably clean, and share cold-water showers. The owner Josué also runs a great *soda* here, serving up excellent, inexpensive casados.

Las Avellanas Villas (☎ 2652 9212; www.lasavellanas villas.com; d/tr/q US$64/76/87) Stunningly designed by Costa Rican architect Victor Cañas, these four casitas (cottages) are covetable as permanent residences. With an aesthetic balancing the interior environment with the exterior, they have sunken stone floors crossed by wooden bridges, open-air showers, and large windows looking out on front and back terraces. The casitas have full kitchens, but dinner is available, and the grounds are just 300m from the beach.

Mauna Loa Surf Resort (☎ 2652 9012; www.mauna loa.it; s/d US$76/81; P ⊠ ▣ ⅃) This pleasant Italian-run spot is a great place for families, with a secure location that's a straight shot to the beach. Paths lead from the pool area through a well-tended garden, and the cute bungalows have orthopedic beds and hammocks hanging on the terraces.

Cabinas Las Olas (☎ 2652 9315; www.cabinaslasolas .co.cr; s/d/tr US$81/93/105; P) On the road from San José de Pinilla into Avellanas, this pleasant hotel is set on spacious grounds only 200m from the beach. Ten airy, individual bungalows have shiny woodwork, stone detailing, hot-water showers and private decks. There's a restaurant, and a specially built boardwalk leads through the mangroves down to the beach (good for wildlife-spotting). Kayaks and surfing gear are available for hire.

Lola's on the Beach (☎ 2658 8097; meals US$5-10; ⏰ breakfast, lunch & dinner Tue-Sun) Lola's is the place to hang, in low-slung plank chairs on a palm-fringed stretch of Avellanas sand, if the water is looking a bit glassy. Try the amazing *poke* (Hawaiian raw-fish salad) or green papaya salad with a beer. Oh, and in case you're curious, Lola is the owner's massive, happy pet pig. And no, she doesn't surf (they get this question all the time!).

Soda El Mapache (☎ 2652 9114; snacks US$2-5; ⏰ 9am-7pm) This sweet little *soda* serves fruit shakes, waffles and the only real ice cream for miles. Stop in for some sugar after your surf session.

PLAYA NEGRA

In Playa Negra there are a variety of surfer-oriented places.

Kontiki (☎ 2652 9117; kontikiplayanegra@yahoo.com; dm US$10) Along the road from Avellanas, this low-key Peruvian-run place has a rambling collection of tree-house dorms on stilts that are frequented by both surfers and howlers. In

the middle of it all is a rickety pavilion where guests hang out in hammocks and benches. There's a small restaurant serving up traditional Peruvian dishes.

Aloha Amigos (☎ 2652 9023; r with/without bathroom from US$25/15; P) Friendly, self-described 'haole from Hawaii' Jerry and his son Joey keep basic, screened cabinas with shared cold-water bathrooms and more expensive doubles with private hot-water bathrooms. There's a spacious shared kitchen in the center of the grassy grounds, and the atmosphere is about as chilled as it gets.

Cabinas Doña Paulina (☎ 2652 9158; r per person US$20; P ⊠ ▣) Great breezy patio with hammocks, hot water, wi-fi, just a short walk to Playa Negra.

Piko Negro (☎ 2652 9369; s/d US$35/50; P ⊠) Just down the road from its sister operation El Mapache, Piko Negro has a few comfortable cabinas and a mellow restaurant-bar in Playa Lagartillo.

Mono Congo Surf Lodge (☎ 2652 9261; www.mono congolodge.com; r/ste from US$64/87; P ⊠ ▣) This large, open-air, Polynesian-style tree house lodge is surrounded by howler-filled trees and is the pinnacle of tropical luxury in Playa Negra. High-ceilinged, polished wood rooms are exquisite, and private bathrooms have hot water and Spanish tiles. A patio has hammocks, and a star-watching deck on the roof provides 360-degree views of the area. A variety of international meals are available from the gourmet kitchen (mains US$7 to US$18). Rates include coffee and fresh fruit in the morning.

Hotel Playa Negra (☎ 2652 9134; www.playanegra .com; s/d/tr/q US$81/93/105/116; P ▣) This charming hotel, right on the beach at Playa Negra's reef break, is a collection of 10 spacious, circular bungalows with thatched roofs, bright tropical colors and traditional indigenous-style tapestries and linens. Each cabin has a queen-size bed, two single beds, and a private bathroom with hot water and roomy showers.

ourpick Café Playa Negra (☎ 2652 9351; www .playanegracafe.com; r per person US$18 incl breakfast; ⏰ 7am-9pm; P ▣) This small hotel has a handful of sparkling-clean rooms upstairs from the café at street level. Ranging in size to accommodate pairs or small groups, these stylish, minimalist digs have cool, polished concrete floors, elevated beds neatly covered with colorful bedspreads and open-door bathrooms. The shared deck facing the road has lounge sofas and big pillows, and amenities include laundry service, internet access and a free continental breakfast with homemade baguettes – a superb deal for these prices. The café serves Tico/Peruvian food (mains US$3 to US$6).

Restaurant Oasis (☎ 2652 9082; pizzas US$4-8; ⊙ 6-9pm Tue-Sun) Along the main road in Playa Negra, this oasis is a good spot for a slice of thin-crust pizza or Mexican comfort food like burly burritos. The spacious, high-ceilinged rancho is also a good place to watch surf videos with a cold beer in the evenings. Oasis was for sale when we visited.

La Ventana (☎ 2652 9197; mains US$3-7; ⊙ breakfast & lunch) An unexpectedly urbane café-gallery off the main road, La Ventana is run by a lovely American woman who makes amazing peanut butter–cup cookies, internationally influenced wraps and sandwiches (jerk chicken, tahini and hummus, eggplant parmigiana) and espressos, teas, juices and smoothies. The generously windowed gallery space features work by local Tico and expat artists, and there's free wi-fi. Heading away from the beach, it's up the road veering to the left, past the small commercial center.

Getting There & Away
The daily bus to Playa Negra leaves Santa Cruz at 8am; the bus for Santa Cruz departs at 1:30pm from the V on the main road (US$0.60, 1½ hours). There's no public transportation to Avellanas, but surf outfitters in Tamarindo (p273) organize trips. Just about every local in town is willing to give you and your board a ride – bargain hard.

PLAYA JUNQUILLAL
Junquillal is a 2km-wide gray-sand wilderness beach that's absolutely stunning and mostly deserted – probably because the surf is high and the rips are fierce (for information on riptides, see boxed text, p278). It's best to leave your swimming trunks at home, though there are clean lefts and rights when the waves drop a bit in size. Olive ridley turtles nest here from July to November, with a peak from August to October, though in smaller numbers than at the refuges; Junquillal is also an important nesting site for leatherbacks. Though Junquillal is not a protected area, conservation groups have teamed up with local communities to protect the nesting sites and eliminate poaching.

The nearest village is 4km inland at **Paraíso**, which has a few local *sodas* and bars. Accommodations are spread out along the beach.

Sleeping & Eating
Camping Los Malinches (☎ 2658 8429; per person US$5) Just south of the Iguanazul, this pretty campground has toilets, showers, electricity until 9pm and ocean views.

El Castillo Divertido (☎ 2658 8428; www.costarica-adventureholidays.com; s/d US$24/30, s/d with ocean view US$28/35; P) On a hilltop about 500m down the road, you'll find the entrance to this quirky inn owned by an affable German/Tica couple and son. The hotel's rooftop bar has panoramic views – a breezy place to laze in a hammock. Paulo, one of the owners, plays his guitar for guests during sunsets. Tiled rooms are clean and have private hot showers, and it's worth splurging for the ones with ocean views. The restaurant (dishes US$3 to US$10) has good breakfasts and dinners with plenty of German favorites.

Hotel Hibiscus (☎ 2658 8437; s/d/tr incl breakfast US$40/50/60; P 🛜) This charming Nica/German-run hotel has five spotless rooms with private bathrooms and hammock-strung patios overlooking the palm-fringed garden. There's a small restaurant that has a good variety of international cuisine, and the breakfasts are immense and delicious.

Villa Roberta (☎ 2658 8127; dietzcon@racsa.co.cr; d incl breakfast US$58, apt US$87; P 🛜) This hospitable two-room B&B is intimate, quaint and full of personality. The rooms are fairly simple, but the house has beautiful stone floors and vaulted ceilings, and its location in the trees makes it feel tranquil in the extreme.

Guacamaya Lodge (☎ 2658 8431; www.guacamayalodge.com; s/d US$58/64, apt s/d/tr/q US$81/87/93/99, villa US$140; P 🛜 🖳 🛜) Next door to El Castillo, this quiet Swiss-run place has six quaint bungalows, a two-bedroom villa with a kitchen and an apartment with balcony views. There's also a pool, tennis courts and a restaurant-bar with ocean views and a smattering of Swiss delicacies. The warm and wonderful brother and sister owners speak a remarkable seven languages. Credit cards accepted.

Hotel Tatanka (☎ 2658 8426; www.crica.com/tatanka; s/d US$58/76; P 🛜 🛜) Ten rancho-style rooms with private hot-water bathrooms are pretty in pink and have rustic wooden furnishings. There's an inviting pool as well as an open-air pizzeria that serves authentic wood-fired pizza pies (US$4 to US$7) in the evenings. Credit cards accepted.

Hotel Iguanazul (☎ 2658 8124; www.iguanazul.com; s/d/tr US$70/81/93, s/d/tr with air-con from US$93/100/116, all incl breakfast; P ⊠ □ ▣) Don't let the gaudy fountain out front put you off; the aesthetics at this well-established resort hotel are much more relaxed and attractive. The 24 brightly painted and cool, tiled rooms have garden or ocean views. Amenities include a pool, pool table, volleyball and a restaurant-bar with killer views.

Villa Serena (☎ 2658 8430; www.land-ho.com/villa /index2.html; d/tr US$175/210; P ⊠ □ ▣) Owned by a friendly couple who also runs a restaurant in Cape Cod, this is the most luxurious digs in Junquillal. Large, airy rooms have an open design and roomy bathrooms. Turn left down the beachfront road and you'll find a shaded lawn, tennis courts, shaded pool area and a glass-walled gym. The excellent restaurant (mains US$10 to US$20) serves classic American fare like burgers and grilled fish along with nightly specials. Guests have free use of kayaks, snorkeling equipment and boogie boards.

Aside from the hotel restaurants, your best option for cheap eats is to head to nearby Paraíso, though there a few small spots on the beach, including the locally popular **Bar y Restaurant Junquillal** (dishes US$3-6) and **Rudy's** (☎ 2658 8114; mains US$3-7; ⓧ breakfast, lunch & dinner), a mellow little bar and restaurant serving Tico standbys and casual fare.

Getting There & Away
Buses arrive and depart from Hotel Playa Junquillal on the beach. Daily buses to Santa Cruz (US$0.60, 1½ hours) depart at 5:45am, noon and 4pm.

If you're driving, it's about 16km by paved road from Santa Cruz to 27 de Abril, and another 17km by unpaved road via Paraíso to Junquillal. From Junquillal, you can head south by taking a turnoff about 3km east of Paraíso on a road marked 'Reserva Ostional.' This is for 4WD only and may be impassable in the rainy season. There are no gas stations on the coastal road and there is little traffic, so ask before setting out. It's easier to reach beaches south of Junquillal from Nicoya.

A taxi from Santa Cruz to Junquillal costs about US$30.

SANTA CRUZ
A stop in Santa Cruz, a *sabanero* town typical of inland Nicoya, provides some of the local flavor missing from foreign-dominated beach towns. Unfortunately, there aren't any attention-worthy sights in town, so most travelers' experience in Santa Cruz consists of changing buses and buying a mango or two. It doesn't help much that Santa Cruz (with Liberia a close second) holds the dubious title of being the hottest city in Costa Rica (we're talking temperature, not sex appeal). However, the town is an important administrative center in the region, and serves as a good base for visiting Guaitil (see boxed text, p282). And if you're here for lunch, don't miss a casado at CoopeTortilla.

About three city blocks in the center of Santa Cruz burned to the ground in a devastating fire in 1993. An important landmark in town is a vacant lot known as the **Plaza de Los Mangos**, which was once a large grassy square with three mango trees. However, soon after the fire the attractive and shady **Parque Bernabela Ramos** was opened up 400m south of Plaza de Los Mangos.

Information
Kion, on the southwest plaza corner, is a Wal-Mart-style department store selling English-language newspapers and more. There's a gas station off the main intersection with the highway.

Banco de Costa Rica (☎ 2680 3253) Change money at this bank, three blocks north of Plaza de Los Mangos.

Ciberm@nia (☎ 2680 4520; per hr US$2; ⓧ 9am-9pm) Check your email here, 100m north of Parque Ramos.

Festivals & Events
There is a rodeo and fiesta during the second week in January and on July 25 for **Día de Guanacaste** (see p204). At these events, you can check out the *sabaneros*, admire prize bulls and drink plenty of beer while listening to eardrum-busting music.

Santa Cruz is considered the folklore center of the region and is home to a long-time marimba group, Los de la Bajura. The group plays traditional *bombas*, a combination of music with funny (and off-color) verses. Keep an eye out for wall postings announcing performances or ask hotel staff for information.

PENÍNSULA DE NICOYA

GUAITIL

An interesting excursion from Santa Cruz is the 12km drive by paved road to the small pottery-making community of Guaitil. Attractive ceramics are made from local clays, using earthy reds, creams and blacks in pre-Columbian Chorotega style. Ceramics are for sale outside the potters' houses in Guaitil and also in San Vicente, 2km beyond Guaitil by unpaved road. If you ask, you can watch part of the potting process, and local residents would be happy to give you a few lessons for a small price.

If you have your car, take the main highway toward Nicoya and then follow the signed Guaitil road to the left, about 1.5km out of Santa Cruz. This road is lined by yellow corteza amarilla trees and is very attractive in April when all of them are in bloom. There are local buses from Santa Cruz, though they're infrequent and unreliable. However, a round-trip taxi should only cost about US$10 to US$15, depending on how long you stay.

If you don't have time to get to Guaitil, visit the small *depósito* (outlet) selling ceramics on the peninsular highway, about 10km north of Nicoya on the eastern side of the road. Be aware that if you take a tour to Guaitil, you may be taken to one particular shop on a commission basis; try to browse other shops in town and share the wealth.

Sleeping & Eating

Any directions that mention the 'plaza' are making reference to Plaza de Los Mangos. All showers are cold, though you'll wish they were even colder.

Pensión Isabel (☎ 2680 0173; r per person US$8) The cheapest beds in town are housed in bare whitewashed rooms, though they're reasonably firm, the shared bathrooms are acceptable and the owner's quite friendly. It's southeast of the plaza.

Hotel Diriá (☎ 2680 0080, 2680 0402; hoteldiria@ hotmail.com; s/d US$30/45; P ⊠ ⊇) Though once in grander shape, this long-standing hotel 500m north of the plaza is looking a little tired lately – the restaurant was shuttered and the swimming pools not quite full when we stopped by. But rooms come with air-con, private bathroom and cable TV, and the pleasant shared terraces have lovely rattan rocking chairs. Credit cards accepted.

Hotel La Pampa (☎ 2680 0586; d with/without air-con US$58/39; P ⊠) A good midrange option, 50m west of the plaza, this terra-cotta-color building houses 33 simple and clean modern rooms, all with private bathroom and cable TV.

La Calle de Alcalá (☎ 2680 0000, 2680 1515; hotela-lcala@hotmail.com; s/d US$54/73; P ⊠ ⊇) With its stucco arches and landscaped garden around a pool with swim-up bar, this inn gets points for design details. Carved wooden doors open into cool, tiled rooms with amenities like hair dryers, wicker furniture and window seats. A pleasant alfresco restaurant-bar rounds out the picture.

CoopeTortilla (casados US$3; ⊗ 5:30am-5pm) Feast on tasty, inexpensive casados at this busy place 700m south of the plaza. Also referred to as 'la tortillera,' it's a huge corrugated-metal barn with big windows lined with plants. Seat yourself at long, wooden communal tables, and eat whatever's available – all of it cooked right in front of you on an enormous wood-fired clay stove, and all served with a side of house-made tortillas. Try a glass of the tamarindo juice, perfect on a parched Santa Cruz afternoon.

El Milenio (☎ 2680 3237; mains US$3-6; ⊗ 9am-9pm) With a notable Chinese population, Santa Cruz has its share of Chinese food – El Milenio tops them all with its colossal portions of fried rice, decent stir-fries, big-screen TV and blessed air-con. It's 100m west of the plaza.

Among the several supermarkets in town, the SuperCompro, just east of the Empresas Alfaro station, is the biggest.

Getting There & Away

Santa Cruz is 57km from Liberia and 25km south of Filadelfia. It's on the main peninsular highway and is often an overnight stop for people visiting the peninsula. A paved road leads 16km west to 27 de Abril, from where dirt roads continue to Playa Tamarindo, Playa Junquillal and other beaches.

Some buses depart from the terminal on the north side of Plaza de Los Mangos. For Empresas Alfaro buses, buy tickets at the Alfaro office, 200m south of the plaza, but catch the bus on the main road north of town.

Liberia (La Pampa) US$1, 1½ hours, departs every 30 minutes from 5:30am to 7:30pm.
Nicoya (La Pampa) US$0.50, one hour, departs every 30 minutes from 5:30am to 9:20pm.
San José US$5.50, 4½ hours, seven buses from 3:30am to 5pm (Tralapa); eight buses from 3am to 4:30pm (Empresas Alfaro).

Other local buses leave from the terminal 400m east of the plaza. These schedules fluctuate constantly, so ask around.
Bahía Potrero US$1.50, 1¼ hours, departs every two to three hours.
Playa Brasilito US$1.50, one hour, departs in the morning and afternoon.
Playa Flamingo US$1.50, one hour, departs afternoon.
Playa Junquillal US$2, 1½ hours, departs in the afternoon.
Playa Tamarindo US$2, 1½ hours, departs every two to three hours.

CENTRAL PENINSULA

Long the political and cultural heart of Guanacaste, the inland region of the central peninsula looks and feels palpably more 'Costa Rican' than the beach resorts of the northern coast. Over the generations, the dry tropical forest has been cut down to make way for the *sabaneros'* cattle, but stands of forest remain, interspersed between fincas and coastal villages, sometimes backing stretches of wild, empty beaches.

Hwy 21 snakes through the higher elevations of the interior, from the population center of Santa Cruz down through Nicoya, where Hwy 151 branches southward toward Sámara in a winding road through the forest.

Development in the region is considerably less than in the north of the peninsula, though the areas around Sámara and Nosara are growing slowly. Most foreigners who are drawn to the rugged coastal landscapes of the central peninsula are actively committed to its conservation. This part of the coast is rife with secluded beaches, small villages where authenticity reigns, and endless possibilities for getting off the map.

NICOYA

Situated 23km south of Santa Cruz, Nicoya was named after an indigenous Chorotega chief, who welcomed Spanish *conquistador*

(conqueror) Gil González Dávila in 1523 (a gesture he regretted; see boxed text, p324). In the following centuries, the Chorotegas were wiped out by the colonists, though the distinctive facial features of the local residents is a testament to their heritage.

Although Nicoya is in fact a colonial city, very little still remains of the original architecture, and what is left is usually in a state of disrepair. However, Nicoya is one of the most pleasant cities in the region, and the bright buildings and bustling streets contribute to the welcoming atmosphere.

For travelers, Nicoya primarily serves as a transportation hub for the region, though the city serves as a good base for exploring Parque Nacional Barra Honda (p286). It's also a good base for visiting **Puerto Humo**, a small town about 27km northeast on the road past Coralillo that has good opportunities for birding.

Information
Area de Conservación Tempisque (ACT; ☎ 2685 5667; ☺ 8am-4pm Mon-Fri) The office of the ACT can help with accommodations and cave exploration at Parque Nacional Barra Honda.
ATH ATM (A Toda Hora ATM) This 24-hour ATM accepts cards on the Cirrus system.
Banco de Costa Rica (☺ 8:30am-3pm Mon-Fri) Exchanges US dollars.
Banco Popular (☺ 9am-4:30pm Mon-Fri, 8:15-11:30am Sat) Also exchanges US dollars.
Ciber Club (☎ 2685 4182; per hr US$1; ☺ 8am-10pm Mon-Sat, 10am-9pm Sun) Has air-con and roughly a dozen terminals with very good connections.
Clínica Médica Nicoyana (☎ 2685 5138) For lesser illnesses, visit this clinic.
Hospital La Anexión (☎ 2685 5066) The main hospital on the peninsula is north of town.
Nicoya Netcafé (☎ 2686 8090; per hr US$1; ☺ 8am-8pm) Make international internet calls at this conveniently located café.

Sights
In Parque Central, a major town landmark, is the attractive white colonial **Iglesia de San Blas**, which dates back to the mid-17th century. The appealingly peaceful, wood-beamed church is under continuous restoration, and its mosaic tiles are crumbling, but it can be visited when Mass is not in session. Have a look at the wooden Jesus with articulated joints and bleeding stigmata. Or attend a **Mass** (☺ 6pm Mon & Fri, 7am Tue, 7am & 7pm Thu). It

PENÍNSULA DE NICOYA

has a small collection of colonial religious artifacts. The park outside is an inviting spot to people-watch from one of the shady stone benches.

On the opposite side of the park is **La Casa de la Cultura**. This small exhibit area has cultural exhibits a few times a year and features work by local artists. The exhibit schedule and hours of operation are erratic, but it's worth a peek if the doors are open.

Festivals & Events

The town goes crazy for **Día de Guanacaste**, on July 25, so expect plenty of food, music and beer in the plaza to celebrate the province's annexation from Nicaragua. The Festival de La Virgin de Guadalupe (see boxed text A Brief History of the Chorotega, opposite) is one of the most unique festivals in Costa Rica.

Sleeping & Eating

All showers are cold unless otherwise stated.

Hotel Chorotega (☎ 2685 5245; s/d with bathroom US$17/22, without bathroom US$6/12; ❄) Next to the Río Chipanzo and run by a pleasant family that keeps bare-bones rooms that could use a face-lift but are reasonably clean and neat. You won't find a cheaper bed elsewhere.

Hotel Las Tinajas (☎ 2685 5081; s/d US$11/17; P) This hotel is decent and mercifully far from the noise of the plaza, though it's on a relatively busy road. The 28 rooms are clean (though rough around the edges), with cable TV and private bathrooms.

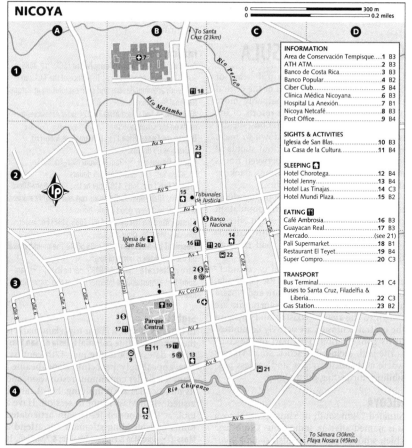

NICOYA

0 — 300 m
0 — 0.2 miles

INFORMATION
Area de Conservación Tempisque.....**1** B3
ATH ATM..**2** B3
Banco de Costa Rica............................**3** B3
Banco Popular.......................................**4** B2
Ciber Club..**5** B4
Clínica Médica Nicoyana.....................**6** B3
Hospital La Anexión.............................**7** B1
Nicoya Netcafé.....................................**8** B3
Post Office...**9** B4

SIGHTS & ACTIVITIES
Iglesia de San Blas...............................**10** B3
La Casa de la Cultura...........................**11** B4

SLEEPING 🛏
Hotel Chorotega....................................**12** B4
Hotel Jenny..**13** B4
Hotel Las Tinajas...................................**14** C3
Hotel Mundi Plaza................................**15** B2

EATING 🍴
Café Ambrosia.......................................**16** B3
Guayacan Real.......................................**17** B3
Mercado...(see 21)
Palí Supermarket...................................**18** B1
Restaurant El Teyet...............................**19** B4
Super Compro..**20** C3

TRANSPORT
Bus Terminal..**21** C4
Buses to Santa Cruz, Filadelfia &
  Liberia..**22** C3
Gas Station...**23** B2

To Santa Cruz (23km)

Río Perico

Río Matambo

Río Chipanzo

Av 9
Av 7
Av 5
Av 3
Av 1
Av Central
Av 2
Av 4
Av 6

Calle Central
Calle 1
Calle 2
Calle 3
Calle 4
Calle 5
Calle 6

Tribunales de Justicia

Banco Nacional

Iglesia de San Blas

Parque Central

To Sámara (30km);
Playa Nosara (45km)

A BRIEF HISTORY OF THE CHOROTEGA

Although there were several pre-Columbian populations in the Nicoya peninsula, the most prominent were the Chorotega, which translates as 'Fleeing People.' The Chorotega arrived on the peninsula around the 8th century BC, and are believed to be descendants of the Olmec in Mexico. They were also contemporaries of the Maya, and a part of a cultural link extending from Mexico through Central America to the Andes.

Unlike their contemporaries, however, the Chorotega were not prolific builders. As a result, most of our understanding of the group is based on the representations that appear in their artwork. The Chorotega are best known for their elaborate jade work, though they were also talented potters and sculptors.

Archaeologists believe that the Chorotega were a hierarchical and militaristic society that kept slaves and regularly practiced both cannibalism and human sacrifice. It's also believed that shamanism, fertility rites and ritualistic dance played an important role in their society, though little is actually known about their belief structure.

Although their civilization survived for over 2000 years, the Chorotega were wiped out by warfare and disease during the Spanish colonial period, though their artisan tradition is still evident among the surviving indigenous populations of Península de Nicoya (see boxed text Guaitíl, p282). The December 12 **Festival de La Virgin de Guadalupe** in the city of Nicoya incorporates the Chorotega legend of *La Yequita,* which relates how a little mare stopped two brothers from killing one another over the love of a princess. The celebration blends Catholic and Chorotega elements by parading a statue of the Virgin to the tune of indigenous music and loud fireworks, while revelers drink copious amounts of *chicha*, a traditional liquor of fermented corn and sugar that's served in hollowed gourds.

Hotel Jenny (☎ 2685 5050; s/d/tr/q US$16/24/28/36; 🗶) This is one of the best deals in town – all 24 spic-and-span rooms have air-con, cable TV and private bathrooms. Try to get a room in the cooler, darker halls rather than the noisier ones facing the street.

Hotel Mundi Plaza (☎ 2685 3535; hotelmundiplaza@ yahoo.com; s/d US$26/36; 🅿 🗶) The Mundi Plaza has clean, bland, comfortable rooms with air-con and cable TV, and some have balconies as well. The staff here does nothing to improve on the indifferent atmosphere, however. Credit cards accepted.

Restaurant El Teyet (mains US$2-5; 🕑 lunch & dinner) Chinese restaurants such as this are some of the tastiest and cheapest spots to eat in the city. Grab a seat on the patio or in the air-conditioned interior and feast on huge portions of chow mein and other noodle dishes.

Guayacan Real (mains US$2-4; 🕑 lunch & dinner) The best place for a drink and delicious *bocas* is the consistently packed Guayacan Real. The *ceviche* and *patacones* (fried plantain with bean dip) are exceptional – and there is cable TV.

Café Ambrosia (☎ 2685 4251; mains US$5-8; 🕑 8:30am-7pm Mon-Sat) Excellent espresso drinks, pasta carbonara, gnocchi and fresh sandwiches and salads are the specialties of the house. They also dish out ice cream, for which you'll be thankful if the air-conditioned room isn't doing enough for you. They even accept credit cards.

Super Compro and Palí supermarkets provide food and supplies for self-caterers. There are also a number of cheap *sodas* in the *mercado* (market) that are good for a quick bite, as well as all your favorite Costa Rican fast-food chains.

Getting There & Away

Most buses arrive at and depart from the bus terminal southeast of Parque Central.

Liberia US$1.40, 2½ hours, departs every 30 minutes from 3am to 8pm.

Playa Naranjo, connects with ferry US$1.75, three hours, departs at 5am, 9am, 1pm and 5pm.

Playa Nosara US$1.25, 2½ hours, departs at 5am, 10am and 2pm.

Puntarenas US$2.75, 2½ hours, departs at 7:35am and 4:20pm.

Sámara US$1, two hours, departs at 6am, 7:45am, 10am, noon, 3pm, 4:20pm and 5pm.

San José, via Liberia (Empresas Alfaro) US$6, five hours, departs five times daily.

San José, via Río Tempisque bridge US$6, four hours, departs seven times daily from 3am to 5:20pm (Empresas Alfaro), and five times daily from 3:20am to 1:45pm (Tralapa).

PENINSULA DE NICOYA

Santa Ana, for Barra Honda one hour, US$1.25, departs at 8am, 11:30am and 4pm Monday to Saturday.

Other buses for Santa Cruz, Filadelfia and Liberia depart every 30 minutes from 3:50am to 8:30pm from the terminal northeast of the park.

If you need a taxi, try calling **Cootagua** (☎ 2686 6490, 2686 6590) or **Taxis Unidos de Nicoya** (☎ 2686 6857).

PARQUE NACIONAL DIRIÁ
Since 2004, **Parque Nacional Diriá** (☎ 2680 1820; admission US$6; ☼ 8am-4pm) covers 5424 hectares, 1500 of which are primary tropical dry forest and river basins of the Ríos Diriá, Enmedio, Tigre and Verde. At its higher altitudes are stands of tropical humid forest, as well. In addition to protecting these vital watersheds, the park is also a refuge for wildlife, such as howler monkey, deer, anteater and over 100 species of bird.

Two trails, El Venado and El Escabel, lead through the forest and to the lovely Brasil waterfall.

It's possible to stay in a basic bunkhouse here, which has running water and electricity, but you'll have to be otherwise self-sufficient. Call the Santa Cruz Minae office (at the number listed above) to make arrangements.

The park is 14km southwest of Santa Cruz; there is no public transportation.

PARQUE NACIONAL BARRA HONDA
Situated about halfway between Nicoya and the mouth of the Río Tempisque, this 2295-hectare national park protects a massive underground system of more than 40 caves and is one of the most unusual (and also highly memorable) national parks in all of the country. The caverns, which are composed of soft limestone, were carved by rainfall and erosion over a period of about 70 million years. Speleologists have discovered just more than 40 caverns, with some of them reaching as far as 200m deep, though to date only 19 have been fully explored. There have been discoveries here of pre-Columbian remains dating back to 300 BC.

The caves come with the requisite cave accoutrements: stalagmites, stalactites and a host of beautiful formations with intriguing names such as fried eggs, organ, soda straws, popcorn, curtains, columns, pearls, flowers and shark's teeth. However, unlike caverns in your own country perhaps, Barra Honda is not developed for wide-scale tourism, which means that the caves here feel less like a carnival attraction and more like a scene from *Indiana Jones*. So, don your yellow miner's hat, put on some sturdy boots and be prepared to get down and dirty.

Information
The dry season is the only time that tourists are allowed to enter the caves, though hiking is good any time of year. In the dry season, carry several liters of water and let the rangers know where you are going. Two German hikers died at Barra Honda in 1993 after getting lost on a short hike – they had no water, and succumbed to dehydration. Sneakers or preferably boots are necessary if you will be caving.

The **ranger station** (☎ 2659 1551; ☼ 8am-4pm) in the southwest corner of the park takes the US$7 admission fee and provides information. Plan to arrive by noon to tour the caverns, as tours last three to four hours and guides won't start tours much later than that.

Sights
You can only explore the **caves** with a guide from the Asociación de Guías Ecologistas de Barra Honda, which can be arranged in the national park offices in **Nicoya** (☎ 2686 6760), **Santa Cruz** (☎ 2680 1920) or **Bagaces** (☎ 2671 1455). A guide charges about US$14 for up to four people, including equipment (US$2 per additional person). The descent involves using ladders and ropes, so you should be reasonably fit and you must be at least 12 years of age.

A guide service is available for hiking the trails within the park and also for descending into the most popular caves. Guides speak Spanish, though a few of the rangers speak some English.

The only cave with regular access to the public is the 62m-deep **La Terciopelo**, which has the most speleothems – calcite figures that rise and fall in the cave's interior. The best known of these is **El Órgano**, which produces several notes when lightly struck. Scientists and other visitors are required to have permits from the park service to enter other caves. These include **Santa Ana**, the deepest (249m); **Trampa** (Trap), 110m deep with a vertical 52m drop; **Nicoya**, where early human remains were found; and, our favorite, **Pozo Hediondo**, or Fetid Pit, which is famous for its huge piles of bat droppings. Note that caves cannot be entered after 1pm.

Activities
While **wildlife-watching** underground, you'll have the chance to see such fun-loving creatures as bat, albino salamander, blind fish and a variety of squiggly little invertebrates. On the surface, howler and white-faced monkey, armadillo, coati, kinkajou and white-tailed deer are regularly spotted, as are striped hog-nosed skunk and anteater.

For **hiking**, the Barra Honda hills have a few trails through deciduous, dry tropical rain forest that lead to waterfalls (in the rainy season) adorned with calcium formations. It's also possible to hike to the top of Cerro Barra Honda, which has a lookout with a view that takes in the Río Tempisque and Golfo de Nicoya. Since this national park is comparatively undertouristed and undeveloped, it is advised that you either inquire about the state of the trails before setting out, or hire the services of a guide.

Sleeping & Eating
At the entrance to the park, there is a **camping area** (per person US$2) with bathrooms and showers. There is also a small park-administered area that has three basic dorm-style **cabins** (per person US$12), each with a shower and six beds. Meals can be prearranged (breakfast US$2.50, lunch and dinner US$5). Reserve accommodations and meals through the **ACT office** (☎ 2685 5667) in Nicoya or by calling the ranger station. Spanish is necessary.

Getting There & Away
The easiest way to get to the park is from Nicoya. No bus goes directly to the park; however, buses to Santa Ana (1km away) will get you close. These leave Nicoya at 8am, 11:30pm and 4pm. Return buses leave Santa Ana at noon and 4:30pm. There are no buses on Sunday. The better option is to take a taxi from Nicoya, which will cost about US$12. You can arrange for your driver to pick you up later at a specified time.

If you have your own vehicle, take the peninsular highway south out of Nicoya toward Mansión and make a left on the access road leading to Puente La Amistad. From here, continue another 1.5km and make a left on the signed road to Barra Honda. The dirt road will take you to the village of Barra Honda and

will then wind to the left for another 6km before ending up at the entrance to the national park. The community of Santa Ana is passed en route. The road is clearly marked, and there are several signs along the way indicating the direction of the park. After the village of Barra Honda, the road is unpaved, but in good condition. However, there is no telling what the next rainy season will do to it, so ask locally before setting out.

If you are coming to the park from Puente La Amistad you will see the access road to Barra Honda signed about 16km after leaving the bridge. From this point, follow the above directions.

PUENTE LA AMISTAD
Once made exclusively by ferry (car and passenger), the trip over the Río Tempisque has been completely transformed by the recent construction of a brand-new 780m bridge, now the largest in Costa Rica (but tiny by US standards). The Puente La Amistad (Bridge of Friendship) was built with Taiwanese financial support and opened in July 2003. There is a small parking area and observation platform on the western side of the river so that you can admire it and take photos (as the locals proudly do).

NOSARA AREA
The attractive beaches near the small Tico village of Nosara are backed by a pocket of luxuriant vegetation that attracts birds and wildlife. The area has seen little logging, partly because of the nearby wildlife refuge, and partly because of real-estate development – an unlikely sounding combination.

There are a few hundred foreigners living permanently in the Nosara area (mainly North Americans), the majority of them keen on protecting the rain forests. One resident describes the area as 'sophisticated jungle living,' and indeed blending retirement with conservation is an interesting experiment. However, Ticos remain hostile to the development of the area, mainly because land prices have been driven through the roof in just under a decade.

The Nosara area is a magical destination as you can sometimes see parrot, toucan, armadillo and monkey just a few meters away from the beaches. There are three distinct beaches here. North of the river is **Playa Nosara**, which is difficult to access and primarily used by fishermen. Further south is **Playa Pelada**, a small crescent-shaped beach with an impressive blowhole that sends water shooting through the air at high tide. The southernmost beach is **Playa Guiones**, a 7km stretch of sand that's one of the best surf spots on the central peninsula.

Orientation

The Nosara area is spread out along the coast and a little inland (making a car a bit of a necessity). Nosara village, where you'll find supplies and gas, and the airport are 5km inland from the beach. The main areas with accommodations, restaurants and beaches are Playa Pelada to the north and Playa Guiones to the south. There are many unidentified little roads, which makes it hard to get around if you don't know the place – look for hotel and restaurant signs, and ask for help. Log on to Nosara Travel's website (www.nosaratravel.com/map.html) for a handy map.

Information

There is a public phone by Café de Paris; you'll find one gas station on the road between Playa Pelada and Nosara village, and another in the village.

Banco Popular (☎ 2682 0267, 2682 0011; ☉ 9am-3pm Mon-Fri) Changes US dollars and traveler's checks, and gives cash advances on Visa cards only; the ATM also only accepts Visa cards.

Café de Paris (☎ 2682 0087, 2682 1035; internet per hr US$6) Check your email at the air-conditioned internet café in this hotel or get a password to use its wireless access.

Nosaranet & Frog Pad (☎ 2682 4039; www.thefrog pad.com; internet per hr US$6; ☉ 9am-8pm) The going rates for internet use are pretty astronomical in Nosara. The Frog Pad also has used books for sale, and DVDs, bikes and surfboards for rent.

Nosara Travel (☎ 2682 0300; www.nosaratravel.com; ☉ 9am-3pm Mon-Fri) In Playa Guiones, this office books air tickets, arranges car rentals and books hotel reservations or vacation homes.

Police (☎ 2682 0317) Next to the Red Cross and post office on the southeast corner of the soccer field in the village center.

Post office (☉ 7:30am-noon & 1-6pm)

Super Nosara (☉ 8am-7pm Mon-Sat, 8am-3pm Sun) Super Nosara, southwest of the soccer field, will change US dollars and traveler's checks. This is also a good place to stock up on supplies – it's cheaper than anything by the beaches.

Activities

CANOPY TOUR

Miss Sky (☎ 2682 0969; www.missskycanopytour.com; adult/child US$60/30; ☉ 7am-5pm) has brought a canopy tour to Nosara. It's the longest in the world – at least for now – with a total length of 11,000m, above a pristine, private reserve. The zip lines don't go from platform to platform, but from mountainside to mountainside, and have double cables for added safety. When last we heard, plans were afoot to build the last zip line to a bar. Tours leave twice daily, at 8am and 2pm.

HIKING

The **Reserva Biológica Nosara** behind the Lagarta Lodge (p290) has private trails leading through a mangrove wetland down to the river (five minutes) and beach (10 minutes). This is a great spot for birding, and there's a good chance you'll see some reptiles as well (look up in the trees as there are occasionally boa constrictors here). Nonguests can visit the reserve for US$6.

SURFING

Check out **Playa Guiones** for the best beach break in the central peninsula, especially when there is an offshore wind. Although the beach is usually full of surfers, there are fortunately plenty of take-off points.

At the main intersection in Guiones, the surf shop **Coconut Harry's** (☎ 2682 0574; www .coconutharrys.com; ☉ 7am-5pm) offers private surfing lessons (US$35 per hour), board rental (US$20 per day) and repair, and long-term board storage (US$90 per year).

From here, turn left on the main road into Guiones past Café de Paris and you'll find **Nosara Surf Shop** (☎ 2682 0186; www.nosarasurfshop .com; ☉ 7am-6pm). It rents surfboards (US$15 to US$20 per day) and ATVs (US$35 to US$50), does board repairs and arranges surf lessons (US$40) and tours.

TURTLE-WATCHING

Most hotels in the area can arrange guided tours to Refugio Nacional de Fauna Silvestre Ostional (p292), where you can watch the mass arrivals of olive ridley turtles.

YOGA

In the hills near Playa Guiones is the famous **Nosara Yoga Institute** (☎ 2682 0071, toll-free 866-439 4704; www.nosarayoga.com). The institute offers regular classes, open to the public, as well as workshops, retreats and instructor training courses. To practice in such a beautiful jungle setting, in airy studios ventilated by ocean breezes, is a wonderful experience for beginners or yogis (and yoginis) alike.

Sleeping & Eating

Playa Pelada lies to the north of the Nosara area, while Playa Guiones is to the south.

PLAYA GUIONES

Rancho Congo (☎ 2682 0078; rcongo@racsa.co.cr; r incl breakfast US$20-50; P) This three-room B&B is a sweet, German-run retreat with big rooms, hammocks and a quiet garden setting just off the main road.

ourpick Kaya Sol (☎ 2682 0080; www.kayasol.com; dm US$10, d US$41-93, cabins US$47-58; ⚟) The heart of this sprawling surfer-and-seeker retreat (formerly Blew Dogs) is the dorm-style accommodations in the 'flop house,' though the shared bathrooms are spotless and the pool, with waterfall shower, is perfect for cooling off. There are also a few rooms and private cabins with hot-water bathroom in the back of the property, as well as a beach house (US$757 per week). A restaurant serves American-style food, and the bar is *the* place to hang out at night. It's down the road toward the beach on the right-hand side, just before the Mini Super Delicias.

La Banana (☎ 2682 4082; d/tr US$47/58; P) Approaching the area from the south, you'll see the new French-run La Banana on your right, just before Nosara Yoga Institute. Rooms have private bathroom and are breezy and simple, with wood floors, muted shades of tropical fruit, and jute curtains. The bar, raised on stilts, looks like it could become a gathering place for relaxed evenings.

Casa Romántica (☎ 2682 0272; www.casa-romantica .net; d incl breakfast from US$71; P ⚟ ⚟ ⚟) Right next to Playa Guiones is this recommended Spanish colonial mansion with several rooms with private bathrooms. They've all been recently renovated, and have views of the manicured gardens surrounding the pool. There is also private beach access, a small restaurant featuring international cuisine and well-being services (yoga and massage). Tours can be arranged. Credit cards are accepted.

Giardino Tropicale (☎ 2682 0258; www.giardino tropicale.com; s/d from US$64/76; P ⚟) On the main road, north of Marlin Bill's, this collection of

white-walled cabins offers various sizes and views. The pleasant quarters with solar-heated showers all look out on to a lawn shaded by a huge tree, and there's a pool for taking a cool dip. Deluxe rooms include kitchens (sans stove). There's also a rambling, rustic restaurant (dishes US$5 to US$9) that's popular for its thin-crust pizzas.

Harbor Reef Lodge (☎ 2682 0059; www.harborreef .com; d US$111-122, Pelada/Guiones ste US$150/173, casas per week from US$1664; P ⚟ ⚟ ⚟) These cool, tiled rooms with private bathroom, air-con, hot water and fridge have wood detailing and attractive Latin American textiles. Suites are located on Playas Pelada and Guiones, and are much more expansive and have full kitchens. There are also two- and three- bedroom casas, and suites within casas, available for rent. They are pristine, secluded and guests can use the hotel's facilities. Credit cards accepted. To get here, continue beyond Nosara Surf Shop to where the road bends to the left as it hits the shore.

Harmony Hotel (☎ 2682 4114; www.harmonynosara .com; d US$186, 2-person bungalow US$262, 4-person ste US$402; P ⚟ ⚟ ⚟) Designed with clean lines and fostering a tranquil, happy atmosphere, this effortlessly stylish hotel lives up to its name in look and feel. Better, it also strives for harmony with the environment, employing a full-time sustainability coordinator and involving itself with the community and environmental initiatives. Simple but luxurious rooms have spacious, private decks with outdoor showers and hammocks, and bungalows afford even more privacy and space. Using fresh, organic ingredients as much as possible, the restaurant and bar (mains US$11 to US$20) are worth a visit if you're not staying here (reservations recommended).

Café de Paris (☎ 2682 0087, 2682 1035; www.cafede paris.net; d/tr US$80/92; P ⚟ ⚟ ⚟) This pleasant hotel is located at the corner of the main road and the first access road that leads to Playa Guiones. Shiny, clean rooms have plenty of polished woodwork, a private bathroom and air-con, while larger bungalows and villas are great deals if you're traveling in a group. The bakery-restaurant turns out heavenly French breads and pastries and is an excellent place to eat or pick up a lovely brioche.

ourpick Robin's (☎ 2682 0617; mains US$5-7; ⚟ 7:30am-7pm Mon-Fri, 7:30am-5pm Sat & Sun) Perfectly suited to the health-conscious yoga practitioners and surfers who live in and visit Nosara,

Robin offers a welcome menu of salads, wraps and sandwiches on homemade, whole-wheat focaccia. But she also caters to the indulgent side as well, with dessert crêpes and sublime homemade ice cream and sorbet. The tree-canopied patio is a lovely spot for lunch.

Marlin Bill's (☎ 2682 0548; meals US$6-14; ☼ 11am-2:30pm & 6pm-late Mon-Sat) Across the main road is this popular bar-restaurant with fantastic ocean views. It's worth grabbing lunch here when the menu is cheaper, though it's worth the price anytime for a hearty filet of blackened tuna and a slab of key lime pie.

Gilded Iguana Bar & Restaurant (☎ 2682 0259; www.gildediguana.com; d US$52-87; P ☒ ☒) Down the second access road to Guiones, this long-standing hotel for anglers and surfers has well-furnished, tiled rooms of varying sizes with private hot-water bathrooms and refrigerators. Fishing charters can be arranged, and kayaking, snorkeling and nature tours are also offered. The tasty restaurant will grill your catch for you, and the attached bar is a popular gringo hangout. Credit cards accepted.

Mini Super Delicias del Mundo (☎ 2682 0291; ☼ 8:45am-1pm & 2:30-6:15pm) Groceries are available here, on the second access road to Playa Guiones.

On the road between Playas Guiones and Playa Pelada are two hillside retreats worth checking out.

Vista del Mar (☎ 2682 0633; www.lodgevistadelmar.com; s/d incl breakfast US$36-48/44-56, apt from US$90; P ☒ ☒) Run by a super-friendly gringo named Gale, this is a great option for long-term surf bums and swimmers, as it has a 25m lap pool.

Vista del Paraíso (☎ 2682 0637; www.paradiseviewvillas.com; d US$76-175; P ☒ ☒) Small, family-run (and family-friendly) lodge with drop-dead stunning views from the top of the mountain.

PLAYA PELADA

Refugio del Sol (☎ 2682 0287; www.refugiodelsol.com; s/d/tr US$35/47/52, d with kitchen US$55; P) Five cozy rooms surround a garden courtyard at this small hotel across from Pancho's. It's a very mellow place to stay, and just a short stroll down to Playa Pelada from here.

Nosara B&B (☎ 2682 0209; www.nosarabandb.net; s/d/tr incl breakfast US$39/49/64) Further north, on a signed access road, this cute, clean and very quiet option is set back in the trees near a quiet strand of beach. All of the homey rooms have private hot-water bathroom and simple decorative motifs.

Rancho Suizo Lodge (☎ 2682 0057; www.nosara.ch; s/d incl breakfast US$41/58; P ☒) From Pancho's, take a right instead of heading toward the beach and follow the road to the left for another 200m to the end to get to Rancho Suizo. It's only a few minutes' walk from Playa Pelada and is run by René and Ruth, a charming Swiss couple. Rustic, tiled bungalows all have private hot-water bathrooms, and there's an inviting pool and whirlpool. There's a good restaurant and bar, and transfers to and from the airport are free.

Villa Mango B&B (☎ 2682 0130; www.villamangocr .com; s/d US$69/79; P ☒) You can't help but relax at this tiny B&B in the trees, with ocean views and hosts who enjoy chatting with their guests. While there's a pool on the property, you can also take a short stroll down to an isolated stretch of beach.

Pancho's Resort (☎ 2682 0591; www.panchosresort.com; bungalow US$76-145; P ☒ ☐ ☒) On the main road between Playa Pelada and Nosara village, this large property has it all: supermarket, bar, restaurant and cabinas. Comfortable bungalows sleeping four to six people have private hot-water bathrooms along with attractive tile floors, high ceilings, lofts and kitchenettes. To top it off, Pancho and his bilingual family are all incredibly nice.

Lagarta Lodge (☎ 2682 0035; www.lagarta.com; s/d/tr US$72/79/86; P ☐ ☒) Further north, a road dead-ends at this six-room hotel, a recommended choice high on a steep hill above the private 50-hectare Reserva Biológica Nosara. Birding and wildlife spotting is good here – and you can watch from the comfort of the hotel balcony or see many more species if you go on a hike. Large rooms have high ceilings, hot showers and small private patios or balconies. The balcony restaurant (breakfast and lunch US$4 to US$7, dinner US$9 to US$15; closed Tuesday) is worth a visit just for the spectacular view and sunsets, though the rotating menu of international and Tico specialties is equally appealing.

our pick Hotel Playas de Nosara (☎ 2682 0121; s/d US$70/85; P ☒) Follow the Playa Pelada road to the left and all the way to the point, where you'll dead-end at this fantastic Nosara landmark, perhaps the most unusual hotel in Costa Rica. With its whitewashed minaret-style tower and unique rambling architecture, it's somewhere between *1001 Nights* and a Salvador Dalí painting.

TOP SPOTS FOR A SPECTACULAR SMOOCH

The Península de Nicoya is blessed with endless romantic beaches, but if you're looking for a dramatic backdrop for that cinematic kiss, here's where to set the scene.

▣ The 360-degree view from the domed observation terrace at **Hotel Playas de Nosara** (opposite) is pretty swoony by itself.

▣ Perched high on a bluff, **Restaurant Mirador Barranquilla** (p298) is stunning at sunset with the Pacific at your feet.

▣ Wake early and hike up to the **Montezuma Waterfall** (p306) to have the pools to yourself.

▣ After dark, nestle into sumptuous pillows at the **Lazy Wave** (p276), where low lighting and low tables invite canoodling over cocktails.

▣ Pack picnic provisions, rent kayaks in the morning and paddle away from **Sámara** (p294) to play castaway on uninhabited Isla Chora.

Balconied rooms offer beautiful beach views, with trail access to beaches on either side of the point. There's a good restaurant and pool, and the owner-designer's daughter is bringing it back to its proper glory.

Olga's Bar & Restaurant (casados US$3; ⌣ breakfast, lunch & dinner) A few hundred meters to the north of La Luna, on a separate side road, lies this perennially popular beachside institution. The Tico-owned joint whips up cheap, yummy casados and very reasonable fish dinners (US$6).

La Luna (☎ 2682 0122; dishes US$9-12; ⌣ lunch & dinner) On the beach, to the right of the Hotel Playas de Nosara, you'll find this impressive stone building that houses a trendy restaurant-bar. The eclectic menu has Asian and Mediterranean flourishes, and the views (and cocktails) are intoxicating. Call ahead for reservations.

NOSARA
Rancho Tico (☎ 2682 0006; dishes US$4-6; ⌣ lunch & dinner) The best casados are served here, at the western end of town, or try the catch of the day, which is usually farm-raised tilapia or red snapper.

There are a few grocery stores in town as well as a number of small *sodas*.

Drinking & Entertainment

Aside from the bars and restaurants previously listed, there are a few spots in the village of Nosara.

Near the soccer field are two Tico-riffic spots – Tropicana, which is a great place for showing off your salsa moves, and Bar Bambú, another hot spot for Saturday nights.

The bar at Kaya Sol (p289) sometimes has live music and always a good vibe.

Getting There & Away
AIR
Both Sansa and NatureAir have one daily flight to and from San José for about US$93 each way.

BUS
Local buses depart from the *pulpería* (corner grocery store) by the soccer field. Traroc buses depart for Nicoya (US$1.25, two hours) at 6am, 12:15pm and 3pm. Empresas Alfaro buses going to San José (US$6, five to six hours) depart from the pharmacy by the soccer field at 12:30pm.

For US$0.25, any of these buses will drop you off at the beach. To get to Sámara, take any bus out of Nosara and ask the driver to drop you off at *la bomba de Sámara* (Sámara gas station). From there, catch one of the buses traveling from Nicoya to Sámara. It's also easy to hitch at this point (see p549 for tips).

CAR
From Nicoya, a paved road leads toward Playa Sámara. About 5km before Sámara (signed), a windy, bumpy (and, in the dry season, dusty) dirt road leads to the village (4WD recommended). It's also possible to continue north (in the dry season), to Ostional, Paraíso and Junquillal, though you'll have to ford a few rivers. Ask around before trying this road in the rainy season, when the Río Nosara becomes all but impassable.

PENINSULA DE NICOYA

TRACKING TURTLES

Looking to give back before heading home? Since 1998 Programa Restauracíon de Tortugas Marinas (Pretoma; Marine Turtle Restoration Program) has collaborated with locals to monitor turtle nesting activity and the operation of hatcheries in order to guarantee the efficient protection of nesting sea turtles and the production of hatchlings. Members of the community are hired as field assistants, and environmental education activities are held with the children in town. The project also involves tagging, measuring and protecting nesting turtles, which has resulted in a drastic reduction in poaching levels.

At the time of writing, Pretoma was operating projects in Playa Ostional, Playa San Miguel, Playa Costa de Oro (on the Central Pacific Coast) and Punta Banco, near the border with Panama. For more information on volunteering, visit the website at www.tortugamarina.org.

REFUGIO NACIONAL DE FAUNA SILVESTRE OSTIONAL

This 248-hectare coastal refuge extends from Punta India in the north to Playa Guiones in the south, and includes the beaches of Playa Nosara and Playa Ostional. It was created in 1992 to protect the *arribadas,* or mass nesting of the olive ridley sea turtles, which occurs from July to November with a peak from August to October. Along with Playa Nancite in Parque Nacional Santa Rosa, Ostional is one of two main nesting grounds for this turtle in Costa Rica.

The olive ridley is one of the smallest species of sea turtle, typically weighing around 45kg. Although endangered, there are a few beaches in the world where ridleys nest in large groupings that can number in the thousands. Scientists believe that this behavior is an attempt to overwhelm predators, which contributes to increased species survival.

Prior to the creation of the park, coastal residents used to harvest eggs indiscriminately (drinking raw turtle eggs is thought to increase sexual vigor). However, an imaginative conservation plan has allowed the inhabitants of Ostional to continue to harvest eggs from the first laying, which are often trampled by subsequent waves of nesting turtles. By allowing locals to harvest the first batches, the economic livelihood of the community is maintained, and the villagers in turn act as park rangers to prevent other poachers from infringing on their enterprise.

Rocky **Punta India** at the northwestern end of the refuge has tide pools that abound with marine life, such as sea anemone, urchin and starfish. Along the beach, thousands of almost transparent ghost crabs go about their business, as do the bright-red Sally Lightfoot crabs. The vegetation behind the beach is sparse and consists mainly of deciduous trees, and is home to iguana, crab, howler monkey, coati and many birds. Near the southeastern edge of the refuge is a small mangrove swamp where there is good birding.

Activities

Mass arrivals of **nesting turtles** occur during the rainy season every three or four weeks and last about a week (usually on dark nights preceding a new moon), though it's possible to see turtles in lesser numbers almost any night during nesting season. In the dry season, a fitting consolation prize is the small numbers of leatherback and green turtles that also nest here. Many of the upmarket hotels and tour operators in the region offer tours to Ostional during nesting season, though you can also visit independently.

Aside from turtle-watching, **surfers** can catch some good lefts and rights here just after low tide, though the beach is notorious for its strong currents and huge, crashing surf – it's definitely not suitable for swimming unless you're green and have flippers.

Sleeping & Eating

Camping (per person US$3) is permitted behind the centrally located Soda La Plaza, which has a portable toilet available. The *soda* is open for breakfast, lunch and dinner.

Cabinas Guacamaya (☎ 2682 0430; r per person with/without bathroom US$8/6; P) In the village of Ostional, this place has several small and dark rooms with shared cold showers, though you'll be thrilled to spend the night here as demand is high during nesting season. The same folks run the attached *pulpería,* which can sell you basic supplies.

Cabinas Ostional (☎ 2682 0428; s/d/q US$10/16/28; P) The rooms are slightly better here, with private cold-water shower and a cozy garden. It, too, fills up quickly.

Rancho Brovilla (☎ 2280 4919, 8821 5910; www .brovill.com; r US$33-66, apt US$120-200, casas US$250-280; P 🖳 🖭) In the hills, 2km north of town, Rancho Brovilla is an upscale lodge that's a world away from the more modest accommodations in Ostional. Rooms are adorned with stained-wood accents and come equipped with private hot-water bathrooms. There's also a restaurant-bar (dishes US$6 to US$10) featuring international food.

Getting There & Away

Ostional village is about 8km northwest of Nosara village. During the dry months there are two daily buses from Santa Cruz (times change, so ask around), but at any time of the year the road can get washed out by rain. Hitching from Nosara is reportedly easy.

If you're driving, plan on taking a 4WD as a couple of rivers need to be crossed. From the main road joining Nosara beach and village, head north and cross the bridge over the Río Nosara. After the bridge, there's a T-junction after about 2km; take the left fork (which is signed) and continue on the main road north to Ostional, about 6km away. There are several river crossings on the way to Ostional, so ask locally about conditions before setting out.

Beyond Ostional, the dirt road continues on to Marbella before arriving in Paraíso, northeast of Junquillal. Ask carefully before attempting this drive and use 4WD.

PLAYA SÁMARA

The crescent-shaped strip of pale-gray sand at Sámara is one of the most beloved beaches in Costa Rica – it's safe, tranquil, reasonably developed and easily accessible by public transportation. Not surprisingly, it's popular with vacationing Tico families, backpackers, wealthy tourists, snorkelers and surfers alike (even President Oscar Arias has a vacation house near here).

In recent years the village has undergone a bit of a transformation. Sámara is becoming increasingly more sophisticated, and Tico and expat residents are giving facelifts to tired-looking shops, restaurants and storefronts. Although the village is trying to hang on to the authenticity of its relaxed vibe, Sámara is one of the more sophisticated destinations on the central peninsula.

Information

Go to www.samarabeach.com to get the skinny on Samara.

Banco Nacional (☎ 2656 0086; ⏰ 9am-5pm Mon-Fri) Change money at this bank behind the church; there's also an ATM.

Sámara Beach Travel Center (☎ 2656 0920; www .samara-tours.com; ⏰ 9am-9pm) On the main road, this place has an internet café, and can book flights and Interbus tickets and arrange tours. Also rents bicycles (US$12 per day) and scooters (US$35 per day).

Se@net Internet Café & Tours (☎ 2656 0302; per hr US$2; ⏰ 9am-6pm Mon-Sat) Check your email here, 100m east of the main road.

Activities

BIKING

Ciclo Sámara (☎ 2656 0438) rents bicycles for US$2.50 an hour or US$12 per day. It's 100m west of Cabinas Arenas.

CANOPY TOUR

The local zip-line operator is **Wing Nuts** (☎ 2656 0153; adult/child US$55/35), on the eastern outskirts of town off the main paved road.

FLIGHTS

Several kilometers west, in Playa Buenavista, the **Flying Crocodile** (☎ 2656 8048; www.flying-croco dile.com) offers ultralight flights (20-minute tour US$75).

SWIMMING

Though the surf can pick up just before high tide, Sámara is safe for swimming.

SNORKELING & DIVING

When the water's calm and visibility high, snorkelers should check out the coral reef in the center of the bay. Divers can go to **Pura Vida Dive Center** (☎ 2656 0643, 8843 2075), which arranges trips to nearby sites. Find the dive center 200m west of Banco Nacional.

SURFING

Experienced surfers will probably be bored with Sámara's inconsistent waves, though beginners can have a blast here.

The experienced and personable Jesse at **Jesse's Sámara Surf School** (☎ 2656 0055; www .samarasurfschool.com) has been teaching wannabe surfers for years, as does his daughter Sunrise. Their friendly, expert instruction is highly recommended by readers (private one-hour lesson US$40). Jesse also arranges custom surfing safaris to secret spots all over the coast.

Another great choice is the **C&C Surf School & Adventure Center** (☎ 2656 0628; www.samarasurf camp.com) at the northern end of town, which gives one-hour private lessons for US$40; the fee includes another hour of board rental afterwards, and the school donates US$3 from every surf lesson to a local children's school and a turtle conservation project. It also rents kayaks and surfboards and arranges a variety of tours and trips throughout Costa Rica.

Courses

Centro de Idiomas Intercultura (☎ 2656 0127, 2260 8480; www.interculturacostarica.com) has a campus right on the beach. Language courses begin at US$270 a week without homestay.

Tours

Tío Tigre (☎ 2656 0098; www.samarabeach.com/tiotigre), around the corner from the Super Sámara, offers all kinds of excursions: snorkeling, dolphin-watching, turtle-watching, kayaking and horseback riding.

Sleeping

BUDGET

Showers are all cold unless otherwise noted. High-season prices are listed.

Camping Los Coco (☎ 2656 0496; camping per person US$5) On the eastern edge of the beach, this attractive site has well-maintained facilities but can sometimes be absolutely packed. There are several other campsites along this road if Los Coco has no space.

Hotel Playa Sámara (☎ 2656 0190; www.hotelplaya samara.com; r per person US$12; P) Off the soccer field, this is the number one choice for Tico travelers (who must be completely immune to the sound of the nightclub next door). Clean lime-green rooms with private bathroom are yours for a cheap price, but don't expect to get much sleep here.

Cabinas Kunterbunt (☎ 2656 0235; www.cabinas -villa-kunterbunt.com; s/d without bathroom US$20/25, s/d/tr with bathroom US$30/40/50; P ⚓ ⚓) Tommy and Antje, the German owners, have built a beachfront house and 'multicolored' (in case you were wondering what Kunterbunt meant) cabinas right beside a peaceful section of beach. From the communal outdoor kitchen to the lawn area leading on to the beach, the place has a bare-bones, ma-

rooned-on-a-desert-island feel. It's 3km from town, so you'll want your own wheels.

Bar Olas (☎ 2656 1100, 8830 2414; camping per person US$5, s/d cabins US$20/30; P) This beachside place is about 200m west of Soda Sheriff Rustic, and offers the most unusual accommodations in town: thatched huts with private bathroom. There are no screens, so bring bug repellent – and it's next to the bar, so plan on drinking yourself to oblivion or bring earplugs. You can also camp here.

La Locanda (☎ 2656 0036; www.locandasamara.com; d with/without bathroom US$35/30, d with air-con US$70, apt US$110-150; P ⚓) These clean, bright rooms are right on the beach, and there's a bar and café out front. Rooms that have air-con also have fridge and cable TV, and the hotel has secure parking.

Hotel Casa del Mar (☎ 2656 0264; www.casadelmar samara.com; d incl breakfast with/without bathroom US$79/30; P ⚓ ⚓) Just east of the Super Sámara and close to the beach is this agreeable American-run hotel, which has a good mix of rooms for travelers of all budgets. If you don't need your own bathroom, rooms here are a steal (and you can still use the Jacuzzi), though those with private bathroom are bright, airy and well worth the money.

MIDRANGE & TOP END

All showers are hot unless otherwise stated.

Bungalows Casa Valeria (☎ 2656 0511; casavale ria_af@hotmail.com; d/tr/q from US$35/52/81; P ⚓) This intimate little inn is right on the beach about 100m east of the main road. The rooms and bungalows vary in size and are fairly simple, though it's the hammock-strung palm trees and tranquil garden setting that make this place a winner. A communal kitchen is available.

Posada Matilori (☎ 2656 0291, 8817 8042; posad amatilori@racsa.co.cr; d/tr US$41/52; P ⚓) With four brand-new rooms in a cozy and secure home, the extremely friendly Italian-Tica couple running this inn provide every comfort – orthopedic beds, free laundry, free coffee and tea, free use of the boogie boards, a fully equipped kitchen (with a waffle iron!) and lots of comfy hammocks. The house is absolutely spotless and on a quiet side street just 100m from the beach.

Entre Dos Aguas B&B (☎ 2656 0998; www .hoteldosaguas.com; s/d/tr/q incl breakfast US$45/50/55/65; P ⚓ ⚓) This fantastic little inn, on the way into town, is what one reader accurately describes as 'Mercedes Benz accommodations on a Toyota budget.' Seven brightly colored rooms have private stone showers and vibrant woven linens. A well-manicured garden surrounds the pool, and the common courtyard is invitingly strung with hammocks and set with heavy tables. There's an outdoor wood-fired oven if you're inspired to grill your supper.

Tico Adventure Lodge (☎ 2656 0628; www.tico adventurelodge.com; s/d/apt US$29/52/128; P ⊠ ⚛) The American owners are proud of the fact that they built this lodge without cutting down a single tree, and they have every reason to be – it's stunning. Nine double rooms with private bathrooms and wood accents are surrounded by lush vegetation and old-growth trees while the tree-top apartment for four lets you swing on the patio hammock from three stories high. Or you can stay in the poolside house for five (US$151) with a fully equipped kitchen and dining room and dream about a life in the tropics. Cheaper weekly and monthly rates are available.

Casa Paraiso (☎ 2656 0741; s/d incl breakfast US$29/58; P) This comfortable B&B run by a pleasant Tico family is on the road to Playa Carrillo. Rooms with private bathrooms are basic, though the owners fill the place with warmth, and the freshly cooked breakfasts are a great way to start your day.

Hotel Belvedere (☎ 2656 0213; www.samara-costarica .com; s/d/tr/q US$45/65/75/85, bungalow US$75, all incl breakfast; P ✗ ⊠ ⚛) Set in a breezy garden with nice views at the northern end of town, the Hotel Belvedere has 10 whitewashed rooms with exposed wooden beams, solar-heated private shower, cable TV and a small private terrace. Two larger bungalows include a kitchenette – perfect for self-caterers looking for a quiet spot in town. The German owners also speak English. Credit cards are accepted.

Sámara Tree House Inn (☎ 2656 0733; www .samarabeach.com; bungalow incl breakfast from US$111; P ⊠ ⚛ ⚛) These five stilt treehouses for grown-ups are so appealing that you might not want to move out. Fully equipped kitchens have pots and pans hanging from driftwood racks, the cable TVs spin on lazy Susans to face whichever room you're in, and there's wi-fi throughout. Even the bathroom tile is gorgeous. Huge windows let in light and breezes, and hammocks are hung underneath the raised bungalows.

Hotel Rancharlo (☎ 2656 0573; www.rancharlo.com; s/d US$41/47, with bathroom US$47/76, all incl breakfast;

P ⊠ ⚛) New, very clean rooms here have a modern Mediterranean flavor to them, though they're a bit on the small side. The atmosphere is low-key and friendly, with a pool, bar and Italian restaurant.

Villas Pepitas (☎ 2656 0747; www.villaspepitas.com; d/tr/q apt US$116/140/163, d/tr/q villa US$128/151/175; P ✗ ⊠ ⚛) On the west side of town, just before crossing the river, these cheery yellow villas are like a sunny slice of Italy in a tropical garden setting. It's quiet on this road, but just a short walk into town and to the beach. The owner is friendly but completely respectful of guests' privacy and comfort.

Hotel Mirador de Sámara (☎ 2656 0044; www .miradordesamara.com; tr incl breakfast US$105, apt US$122; P ⚛) Perched on a hill on the northern edge of town is this architecturally unusual hotel, complete with looming towers that offer dizzying views of the area. The 'sky rooms' can accommodate up to three, while the large apartments with kitchens can sleep up to six. There's also a small private restaurant with panoramic views of the entire area. Credit cards accepted.

Eating

Out with the old and in with the new is the name of the game in Sámara. There are still some simple *sodas* left in town, but with each passing year the restaurant scene is reinventing itself to cater to a more sophisticated palate. Self-caterers can stock up on supplies at the Super Sámara Market, east of the main road.

Panadería Café Sámara (☎ 2656 0811; pastries US$1.50-3; ◷ 6am-6pm Wed-Mon) Around the corner from Super Sámara and Casa del Mar (opposite), this heavenly little bakery turns out excellent, light German pastry, great breads and baguettes, and the patio is a wonderfully minimalist place to have coffee and breakfast.

Soda Sheriff Rustic (dishes US$2-5; ◷ breakfast, lunch & dinner) One of a few classic *sodas* in town, the beachside location sells itself, though the filling breakfasts, killer casados and low, low prices aren't too bad either.

Restaurante Jardín Marino (mains US$4-8; ◷ lunch & dinner) This large, airy *soda* is always packed, and if you sit yourself down and order something here, you'll see why. The typical food is fresh and of high quality – a *casado de pescado* here means grilled fish, not a deep-fried filet. It's on the main road leading to the beach.

Shake Joe's (☎ 2656 0252; mains US$4-10; 🕙 11am-late) This hip beachside spot is awash with chilled-out electronica and cool, calm travelers lounging on the huge wooden outdoor couches. You can grab a burger here after your surf session, but the ambience is tops when the sun goes down and the drinks start to flow.

El Dorado (☎ 2656 0145; mains US$5-10; 🕙 5-10pm, closed Thu) It's not hard to have the best Italian food in Sámara when all your pasta is homemade, your meats and cheeses are imported directly from Italy, and you have the Pacific Ocean in your backyard.

Restaurant Las Brasas (☎ 2656 0546; dishes US$7-12; 🕙 noon-late) This upscale Spanish restaurant on the main street has all the signature dishes including tortillas, paellas and roast suckling pig. It also has a well-stocked wine cellar, and the upstairs balcony is perfect for people-watching.

Drinking & Entertainment

The coolest nightspot in town is La Vela Latina, on the beach, which serves sophisticated *bocas* and perfectly blended cocktails and sangría to guests sitting on wooden seats or rocking in comfy leather chairs. To settle in for the evening with some *bocas* and beers with the locals, check out Pablito's Bar way on the west side of town.

On the main road, La Gondola is also a fun late-night spot for drinks, pool and darts – check out the full-on mural of Venice. Shake Joe's (see above) really gets going in the evenings with low lighting and trendy tunes. Tutti Frutti Discotheque (on the beach) keeps the music pumping late most weekends of the year, and is perennially popular with Ticos. Bar Olas (p294) is a good place to get started with an Imperial on a beach log.

Shopping

Numerous vendors sell crafts and hand-made jewelry at stands along the main road.

Koss Art Gallery (☎ 2656 0284) Visit Jaime at his outdoor studio on the beach, where he frequently displays his richly hued works in the high season. Call ahead for a viewing.

Galería Dragonfly (☎ 2656 0964; www.samaraarte.com) You'll see Leonardo Palácios' mural as you walk the main street; the gallery inside houses uniquely wrought jewelry in all sorts of media like leather and seashells, along with sculpture, paintings and decorative pieces in a very organic style.

Also worth a stop is Mama Africa, which sells beautiful beaded leather sandals from Kenya. The Italian owners work directly with a Maasai collective that crafts the sandals, and purchases support this work.

Getting There & Away

The beach lies about 35km southwest of Nicoya on a well-paved road.

AIR

The airport serving Playa Sámara is nearer to Playa Carrillo (and is often referred to as Carrillo). Sansa flies daily to and from San José (one way/round-trip US$89/178). Book flights at Sámara Beach Travel Center (see p293).

BUS

Empresas Alfaro has a bus to San José (US$6, five hours) that departs from the main road at 4:30am, 8:30am and 3pm. Only the 8:30am bus runs on Sundays.

Traroc buses to Nicoya (US$1.25, two hours) depart 11 times daily from the *pulpería* by the soccer field; there's a more limited schedule on Sundays.

PLAYA CARRILLO

About 4km southeast of Sámara, this lazily curving beach with its palm-fringed boulevard is quieter and less developed. With its clean sand, rocky headlands and backdrop of jungle, Carrillo is a postcard-perfect tropical beach. During weekends and holidays, the boulevard is lined with cars and the beach crowded with Tico families camped out festively beneath the palms.

The little town is on a hillside above the beach and attracts a trickle of surfers working their way down the coast, as well as schools of American sportfishers chasing billfish.

Activities

SPORTFISHING

Kingfisher Sportfishing (☎ 2656 0091; www.costaricabillfishing.com) is a well-known local outfit, offering full-day offshore excursions for US$950.

Kitty Cat Sportfishing (☎ 2656 0170; www.sportfishcarrillo.com) is another reputable operation with competitive prices; call to charter a trip.

SURF CASTING

You don't have to drop big bucks to catch some nice-sized fish – do as the Ticos do and try your hand at surf casting. Most hotels and tour outfitters can set you up for a few dollars.

SURFING
Surfing here is better than at nearby Playa Sámara, though it's nothing great. Mid-to high tide is when you can catch some decent waves.

Tours
Popos (☎ 2656 0086; www.poposcostarica.com) offers exciting, well-orchestrated and reasonably priced kayak tours, including a few designed for families. Prices start at US$55.

Carrillo Tours (☎ 2656 0543; www.carrillotours.com; ⊙ 8am-7pm), on the road up the hill, organizes snorkeling, dolphin-watching, kayaking, horseback riding and trips to Palo Verde (p208).

Sleeping & Eating
Camping Mora (☎ 2656 0118; per person US$5; P)
At the western end of the beach, this campsite has showers, bathrooms, electricity and potable water.

All of the following hotels are at the eastern end of the beach on a hill. The beach is a five- to 10-minute walk down from most of these places.

Casa Buenavista (☎ 2656 0385; www.samarabeach .com/casabuenavista; d incl breakfast US$45-55; P) A sweet Italian couple runs this two-room B&B. Each basic but homey room has its own hot-water bathroom, porch and entrance, and there's a small shaded yoga terrace in the garden.

Cabinas El Colibrí (☎ 2656 0656; www.samarabeach .com/elcolibri; s/d/tr incl breakfast US$50/60/70; P ❄) These Argentinean-run cabinas are high on the hilltop, and come fully equipped with private hot-water bathrooms; mini-apartments with kitchenettes are the same price but don't include breakfast. It's a relaxed and comfortable spot, and you'll be well fed at the attached restaurant (open from 5pm to midnight, dishes US$4 to US$10), which serves traditional Argentinean *parrilladas* (grilled meats) and *empanadas* (corn turnovers with minced meat).

Carrillo Club (☎ 2656 0316; www.carrilloclub.com; s/d/tr/q incl breakfast US$55/85/95/105, apt US$85; P ❄ 💺) This pretty yellow inn on the hillside has a clutch of comfortable cabinas with private terraces and hot-water bathrooms. The two-person apartments are equipped with

kitchens. There's a pool with ocean views, and the beach is a short walk downhill. Taking breakfast on the big terrace in front is a treat, with beautiful, big views of Playa Carrillo below.

Hotel Arena Blanca (☎ 2656 2025; www.arena blancahotel.com; d incl breakfast US$111; P ❄ 💺 🔇) Designed like a modern-day hacienda, this hotel employs rustic detail with contemporary polish. Backed by trees, the low-lying building circles a pool area, and the beach is only 150m away. Staff can arrange tours.

Hotel Esperanza (☎ 2656 0564; www.hotelesperanza .com; s/d incl breakfast US$110/120; P ❄ 💺) Cheerful rooms at this newly remodeled hotel are set back from a columned promenade and open on to the pool area. The rooms are a bit small, but packed with amenities like cable TV, DVD players, hair dryers and tropical artwork.

There are a number of small *sodas* along the road and soccer field.

Getting There & Away
Regularly scheduled Sansa flights to and from San José (one way/round trip US$89/178) use the airstrip just northwest of the beach. Some Traroc buses from Nicoya to Sámara continue on the well-paved road to Playa Carrillo – check with the driver first.

ISLITA AREA
The coast southeast of Playa Carrillo remains one of the most isolated and wonderful stretches of coastline in the Nicoya, mainly because it's largely inaccessible and lacking in accommodations. Regardless, if you're willing to tackle some rugged roads or venture down the coastline in a sea kayak (or possibly on foot), you'll be rewarded with abandoned beaches backed by pristine wilderness and rugged hills.

There are a few smaller breaks in front of the Hotel Punta Islita. Another good beach break lies north of Punta Islita at **Playa Camaronal**. This beach also happens to be a protected nesting site for leatherback, olive ridley, hawksbill and black turtles, and is officially known as **Refugio Nacional de Vida Silvestre Camaronal**.

Playa Corzalito and **Playa Bejuco** to the south of the Punta Islita are both backed by mangrove swamps, and offer good opportunities for birding and wildlife-watching.

Also worth a visit is the small town of **Islita**, which is home to the Museo de Arte

Contemporáneo al Aire Libre, an open-air exhibition of contemporary art featuring mosaics, murals, carvings and paintings that adorn everything from houses to tree trunks. This project was organized by the Hotel Punta Islita, which sells local art in its gift shops and invests proceeds in the community. If you're interested in helping with the project, inquire at the hotel about volunteer possibilities in the community.

Sleeping & Eating

You can camp on the beaches (without facilities) if you have a vehicle and are self-sufficient.

Hotel Punta Islita (☎ 2661 4044; www.hotelpunta islita.com; d/ste incl breakfast US$349/489, casitas from US$559; P ✗ ▢ ▨) This luxury resort should serve as an example of how to ethically operate a hotel in Costa Rica. In addition to organizing community arts projects, the hotel has sponsored the construction of various public buildings, including a new church, and is consistently working to integrate the rural community of Islita into its development. The hotel is on a hilltop, and has 40 fully equipped rooms with staggering ocean views; spend up for a suite (with private outdoor Jacuzzis). The infinity pool and surrounding grounds are simply stunning, and the staff can arrange any tour you desire.

Restaurant Mirador Barranquilla (mains US$3-5; ✆ 11am-midnight Wed-Mon) On the crest of a hill about 2km southeast of the hotel, the Mirador Barranquilla has breathtaking 180-degree views of Punta Islita and Playas Bejuco and San Miguel, and is the top place in the area for a sunset beer.

Cambute (mains US$4-8; ✆ lunch & dinner) For something more low-key, this dressed-up *soda* serves excellent *ceviche* and casados in a relaxed, riverside setting.

1492 Restaurant (☎ 2661 4044; mains US$10-25; ✆ breakfast, lunch & dinner) The movie *1492* was shot on location in Punta Islita, and some of the set pieces adorn the restaurant. The cuisine here, which is a fusion of Costa Rican and international food, is top quality – and the view is superlative.

Getting There & Away

AIR

NatureAir and Sansa each fly once daily between San José and Punta Islita (one way/round-trip around US$94/188).

BUS

The closest you can get to Islita by bus is Empresa Arza's two daily buses from San José that go through San Francisco de Coyote and on to Playas San Miguel and Bejuco. Keep in mind, though, that from Bejuco there is still a long uphill hike to Islita – and hitching is almost impossible due to the lack of traffic.

CAR

Although Punta Islita is less than 10km by road southeast of Playa Carrillo, the road is wicked and requires some river crossings that are impossible in the wet season. See boxed text, p310 for more information. The 'easiest' route is for you to head inland from Playa Carrillo through the communities of San Pedro and Cangrejal, which is also known as Soledad, and then down to Bejuco on the coast. From there, you can head to Islita (to the northwest).

PLAYAS SAN MIGUEL & COYOTE

Just south of Playa Bejuco are arguably two of the most beautiful and least visited beaches in Costa Rica. Playa San Miguel, to the north, and Playa Coyote, to the south, are wilderness beaches of fine, silver-gray sand that are separated by the mouth of the Río Jabillo. Despite opportunities for great surfing, kayaking and just about anything else you want to do on a sandy strip of paradise, the beaches are nearly always abandoned (the lack of reliable public transportation is probably to blame). As if there weren't enough reasons to visit, San Miguel and Coyote also serve as nesting grounds for olive ridley turtles.

There are no coastal villages to speak of, though a number of in-the-know foreigners have settled in the area and have built some beautiful accommodations near the shoreline. The nearest village is **San Francisco de Coyote**, which is 4km inland and has a few small *sodas* and cabinas.

Activities

You can revel in the crowd-free beach breaks to **surf** off San Miguel, particularly when the tide is rising. At Coyote there is an offshore reef that can be surfed at high tide.

If **swimming**, you are advised to take precautions as the surf can pick up, and there are not many people in the area to help you in an emergency.

If you have your own sea kayak, these beaches (as well as nearby Islita) are perfect for coastal exploration.

Sleeping & Eating

You can camp on both beaches if you're self-sufficient, as there are no services.

Soda Familiar y Cabinas Rey (☎ 2655 1055; s/d/tr US$6/15/20; P 🖳) For those taking the more direct (and treacherous) route to Mal País, this Tico-run *soda* in the village of San Francisco de Coyote is a good place to stock up on provisions and get some local advice. If it's getting late, you might want to stay here as there are simple cabinas with private cold showers for rent. Believe it or not, this is a wi-fi hot spot.

Blue Pelican (☎ 2655 8046; www.thebluepelicaninn .com; s/d incl breakfast from US$25/35; P 🖳) Near the center of Playa San Miguel is this quirky, purple wooden house. There's a variety of rooms suited for singles to groups, including a great upstairs suite with ocean views and a private terrace. Just steps from the beach, the inn has an outdoor shower and board storage racks. The bar-restaurant (dishes US$4 to US$12) has international dishes emphasizing fresh seafood, and the beer is cold.

Flying Scorpion (☎ 2655 8080; rossi@escorpionvolador .com; d incl breakfast US$45, apt US$75; P) Turn right at the Blue Pelican and continue on the dirt road along the beach for a few hundred meters to find this mellow inn with a handful of clean, very comfortable rooms with new teak beds and an assortment of eclectic folk art. It has direct beach access for long days of surfing, and you'll be happy to come back to the bar-restaurant's homemade bread, pasta and ice cream. Run by an amiable couple and their pack of Weimeraners, this is a great spot to zone out for a few days or weeks.

Casitas Azul Plata (☎ 2655 8209; www.casitasazul plata.com; d/tr apt US$70/80; P 🖳 🖳) This homey, German-run spot has a couple of two-bedroom apartments with full kitchens, cable TV and hot-water showers. It's a great choice for families, located on a quiet hillside.

Hotel Arca de Noé (☎ 2655 8065; www.hotelarcadenoe .com; dm US$10, d incl breakfast US$70, additional person US$10; P 🖳 🖳) Inland from the beach, this pleasantly landscaped, critter-friendly complex has 10 attractive doubles with private hot showers and air-con. It grows many of its own fruits and herbs, has a dairy that provides the milk and cheese for the restaurant and has begun a community recycling program in the area.

Casa Caletas (☎ 2289 6060; www.casacaletas.com; d/ste incl breakfast US$192/233; P 🖳 🖳) Down at the end of the road before turning toward Mal País, this beautiful little boutique hotel sits on the bank of the Río Coyote and feels blissfully isolated. There's an airy *palapa* restaurant, cushy rooms and an infinity pool overlooking river and ocean. The beach is accessible by crossing the river or via trails, and the hotel can arrange horseback rides, kayaking and fishing trips. To get here, take the road from San Francisco de Coyote toward Mal País and follow the signs for the hotel.

Bar.Co Nico (☎ 2655 1205; www.barco-nico.com; bocas US$3-10; 🕙 10am-late; 🖳) A few kilometers past the village on the turnoff for Costa de Oro, this German-run beachfront restaurant (which looks like a giant ship) has reinstated the old Tico tradition of giving away a free *boca* with every beer. The beer is cold and the *bocas* are delicious – what are you waiting for? There's also free wi-fi, and Nico now rents a few simple cabinas.

Getting There & Away

BUS

Empresa Arza (☎ 2650 0179) has two daily buses from San José that cross the Golfo de Nicoya on the Puntarenas ferry and continue through Jicaral to San Francisco de Coyote, and on to Playa San Miguel and Bejuco. Buses depart San José at 6am and 3:30pm, pass through San Francisco de Coyote at about 11:30am and 10pm, and arrive at Playa San Miguel at noon and 10:30pm. Return buses leave Bejuco at 2:15am and 12:30pm, pass through Playa San Miguel at around 3am and 1:45pm, and San Francisco de Coyote at 3:30am and 2:15pm. This service is sketchy in the rainy season and the trip may take longer if road conditions are bad.

There aren't any other bus services frequenting this area from Nicoya – or from any other of the peninsula towns, for that matter.

In addition, there is no bus service (because there is barely an actual road) along the coast between Playa Coyote and Mal País.

CAR

See opposite for valuable information about heading north along the coast from here. Also consult the boxed text Along the West Coast by 4WD, p310, for details on how you could *possibly* travel further south along the coast.

PENÍNSULA DE NICOYA

SOUTHEASTERN PENINSULA

At the very southern tip of the Nicoya penín-sula lies the first and one of the most pristine natural reserves in Costa Rica – and there's a reason it has remained so untouched. An arduous drive down the rugged southeastern coastal route crosses several rivers through the thick rain forest before dropping back down toward the beach at Mal País, just north of the reserve. From the other side, it used to require hours of dusty bus rides and sluggish ferries from the mainland to access this tropical land's end, but these days more roads in the region are slowly being paved and regular shuttles are dropping tourists right into Mal País and Montezuma, mak-ing Cabo Blanco a day trip from either burgeoning base.

Word has spread about the miles of surf breaks in Mal País and the chill vibe of hippie outpost Montezuma – and trans-port options have sprung up to meet the demands of surfers and wanderers steadily streaming in to the southeastern peninsula. Growth is somewhat limited by geography in Montezuma and the pulse there beats at the same relaxed pace, but Mal País is pumping. The beauty and wildness on either side of the peninsula can hold you under its thrall, so give yourself the luxury of time here.

As in the rest of the peninsula, Ticos in this region primarily live rural lives centered on agriculture and ranching, though the re-cent influx of travelers has created a number of jobs in the tourism market.

PLAYA NARANJO

This tiny village next to the ferry terminal is nothing more than a few *sodas* and small hotels that cater to travelers either waiting for the ferry or arriving from Puntarenas. There really isn't any reason to hang around, and thankfully you probably won't have to, as the ferries tend to run reasonably on time.

If you get stuck at the port for a night, the **Hotel El Ancla** (☎ 2661 3887; d with/without air-con US$64/52; P ⊠ ⊛) is just 200m from the pier. Rooms with cold-water bathrooms seem a bit pricey, but there's a pool, bar and restaurant to help kill the time.

There's a small *soda* next to the ferry port, as well as a few vendors selling shaved ice and other goodies.

Getting There & Away
All transportation is geared to the arrival and departure of the Puntarenas ferry, so don't worry – if either is running late, the other will wait.

BOAT
The **Coonatramar ferry** (☎ 2661 1069; passenger US$1.50, car US$10.50) to Puntarenas operates daily at 8am, 12:30pm, 5:30pm and 9pm, and can accommodate both cars and passengers. The trip takes 1½ hours. If traveling by car, get out and buy a ticket at the window, get back in your car and then drive on to the ferry. You cannot buy a ticket on board. Show up at least an hour early on holidays and busy weekends, as you'll be competing with a whole lot of other drivers to make it on.

BUS
Buses meet the ferry and take passengers to Nicoya (US$1.75, three hours). Departures are at approximately 7am, 10:50pm, 2:50pm and 7pm.

Regular buses ride from Paquera to Monte-zuma, though there are none that go southeast from here.

CAR & TAXI
It's possible to get to Paquera via a scenic, bumpy and steep dirt road with some great vistas of Bahía Gigante. For this, a 4WD is recommended, especially in the rainy season when there are rivers to cross. The only public transportation is 4WD taxi – about US$25, depending on the number of passengers and road conditions.

ISLANDS NEAR BAHÍA GIGANTE
The waters in and around the isolated Bahía Gigante, 9km southeast of Playa Naranjo, are studded with rocky islets and deserted islands, 10 large enough to be mapped on a 1:200,000 map. Since there is no public transportation here, and a 4WD is a necessity almost year-round, the area feels quiet and unhurried (read: completely abandoned).

However, travelers are drawn to this off-the-beaten-path destination for its range of activities, namely sportfishing, snorkeling, diving and kayaking, which can all be arranged through hotels and travel agencies in the area. There are also plenty of opportunities for some serious adventure here: kayak between the islands, camp on a deserted island or explore the crumbling ruins of an island prison – the choice is yours.

Isla San Lucas

The largest island in Bahía Gigante (just more than 600 hectares) is about 5km off the coast from Playa Naranjo, and from a distance seems like a beautiful desert island. On the contrary, the 'Island of Unspeakable Horrors' has a 400-year history as one of the most notorious jails in Latin America. The island was first used by Spanish *conquistadors* as a detention center for local tribes in the 16th century. In 1862 the job of warden was inherited by the Costa Rican government, which used the island to detain political prisoners up until 1992. The prison was also the inspiration for Costa Rica's most internationally famous memoir: *La isla de los hombres solos* (available in English as *God Was Looking the Other Way*) by José León Sánchez, who was imprisoned on the island for stealing *La Negrita* from the cathedral in Cartago.

Visitors to the island can expect to see the 100-year-old overgrown remains of the prison. Although there are still guards living on the island, their primary purpose is to discourage poachers, which means that travelers are usually permitted to wander freely through the prison grounds and even camp on the island.

Isla Gigante

In the middle of Bahía Gigante is the 10-hectare Isla Gigante, which is shown on most maps as Isla Muertos (Island of the Dead) because it is home to a number of Chara burial sites (and believed by locals to be haunted).

The island once served as a rustic resort for yachters, but is now completely abandoned and covered with cacti. Isla Gigante is an interesting place to explore, especially since most Ticos are afraid to set foot on the island (good luck trying to convince anyone to spend the night).

Isla Guayabo, Islas Negritos & Los Pajaros

This cluster of islands was recently established as a biological reserve to protect nesting seabird populations, including the largest breeding colony of brown pelicans in Costa

Rica along with frigate birds, boobies, egret, peregrines and petrels. Although they're not geographically close to one another, the islands are managed as a single unit. For the protection of the birds, no land visitors are allowed except researchers with permission from the park service. However, the reserves can be approached by boat, and the bird populations are large enough to be visible from the ocean.

Isla Tortuga

Isla Tortuga, which consists of two uninhabited islands just offshore from Curú, is widely regarded as the most beautiful island in Costa Rica. The white-sand beaches feel like baby powder, there are gargantuan coconut palms overhead, and the coral reef is perfect for snorkeling. Unfortunately, Tortuga receives heavy boat traffic from tour operators in Montezuma and Jacó, but if you can visit during the week in low season it can be a magical place.

Tours

Most travelers arrange tours either through the hotels listed below or with an operator in Montezuma (p306) or Jacó (p332). However, this is one region where independence (and language skills) can make for a good adventure – inquire locally to find out if someone with a boat is willing to take you where you want to go for a fair price.

The most luxurious excursion is with **Calypso Tours** (☎ 2256 2727; www.calypsocruises.com). The company transports passengers to Isla Tortuga in a luxurious 21m motorized catamaran called the *Manta Raya*. It's all flash with this boat, which has air-con, a couple of outdoor Jacuzzis and an underwater viewing window. The cost is US$99 – not a bad deal considering the price includes transportation from Quepos or Manuel Antonio, food and drinks.

Sleeping

Hotels come and go quickly in these parts, though there are two recommended places that have stood the test of time. Both are located on the road between Naranjo and Paquera.

Hotel Maquinay (☎ 2641 8011; s/d US$30/35; P ▣) In Playa Naranjo, this quaint hacienda-style hotel is a great deal, with comfortable fan-cooled rooms and shared terraces that look on to a tropical garden and swimming pool.

CALLING ALL COSTA RICAN CAT CONSERVATIONISTS

Since 1992 Programa para la Conservación de Felinos (Profelis; Feline Conservation Program) has taken care of confiscated felines that were given to the center by Minae. The project concentrates on smaller felines, including the margay, ocelot and jaguarundi, and aims to rehabilitate and, when possible, reintroduce animals into the wild. In addition, a large component of the program involves the environmental education of the public.

Profelis is headquartered in Hacienda Matambú, a private wildlife reserve in San Rafael de Paquera, about 5km west of Paquera. Volunteers are sought after, especially if you have experience in either keeping animals or veterinary science. For more information on volunteering, visit the website at www.grafischer.com/profelis or contact **Profelis** (☎ 2641 0644, 2641 0646; profelis@racsa.co.cr).

Hotel Bahía Luminosa Resort (☎ 2641 0386; tropics@racsa.co.cr; d with fan/air-con US$52/70, q US$105; P ⊠ ⊠) Set back in the hills and overlooking the bay is this 15-room resort complex with well-appointed rooms, attractive hammock-strung gardens and an inviting pool. This is also a good spot for organizing tours around the bay.

Getting There & Away

There is no public transportation in the area. The dirt road from Playa Naranjo to Paquera requires 4WD for most of the year.

PAQUERA

The tiny village of Paquera is about 25km by road from Playa Naranjo and 4km from the ferry terminal. Paquera is more of a population center than Playa Naranjo, though there's little reason to stay here longer than you have to.

Banco Popular (⊗ 8:15am-4pm), on the side street, can change US dollars and traveler's checks. On the main road, across from the gas station, you'll find the new **Turismo Curú** (☎ 2641 0004; www.curutourism.com; ⊗ 7am-9pm), operated by the knowledgeable Luis Schutt of the Curú refuge (right). Luis offers a tour that combines a visit to Curú and a snorkeling trip to Isla Tortuga for US$25 per person (a great deal!).

There are a number of cabinas in the village, though the best option is **Cabinas & Restaurant Ginana** (☎ 2641 0119; s/d/tr/q US$33/37/44/51; P ⊠ ⊠), which has 28 simple and clean rooms with private bathroom and optional air-con. There's also a good restaurant (dishes US$3 to US$5) in case you need a bite to eat before getting on the ferry.

Getting There & Away

All transportation is geared to the arrival and departure of the Puntarenas ferry. If either is running late, the other will wait.

BOAT

Ferry Naviera Tambor (☎ 2641 2084; passenger US$1.50, car US$9) operates daily at 8am, 9:30am, 12:30pm, 2:30pm, 6pm and 9pm (the last ferry doesn't run in the low season). The trip takes about an hour. Buy a ticket at the window, reboard your car and then drive onto the ferry; you can't buy a ticket on board. Show up at least an hour early on holidays and busy weekends.

BUS

Buses meet passengers at the ferry terminal and take them to Paquera, Tambor and Montezuma. The bus can be crowded, so try to get off the ferry fast to get a seat.

Most travelers take the bus from the terminal directly to Montezuma (US$2.25, two hours). Many taxi drivers will tell you the bus won't come, but this isn't true. There are no northbound buses.

TAXI

Getting several travelers together to share a taxi is a good option since the ride will take half as long as the bus. The ride to Montezuma is about US$7 per person and to Mal País it's about US$10 – provided you can get enough people together.

A 4WD taxi to Playa Naranjo costs about US$25.

REFUGIO NACIONAL DE VIDA SILVESTRE CURÚ

This small 84-hectare **refuge** (day fee US$8; ⊗ 7am-3pm), which is now part of a larger protected area of almost 1500 hectares, is a wilderness gem in the largely deforested peninsula. Situated at the eastern end of the peninsula and only 6km south of Paquera, the tiny Curú holds a great variety of landscapes, including dry tropical forest, semideciduous forest and five types of mangrove swamp. The rugged coastline is also home to a series of secluded coves and white-sand beaches that are perfect for snorkeling and swimming.

The refuge is privately owned by the Schutts, a Tico family whose roots in the area go back more than 70 years. They have long been active in environmental efforts, and were instrumental in having the area designated a wildlife refuge. Currently, they are working to reintroduce species to the area, including the scarlet macaw and the rare *mono tití*, or squirrel monkey.

The entrance to the refuge is clearly signed on the paved road between Paquera and Tambor (it's on the right-hand side). Day visitors can show up anytime during operating hours and pay the day fee to hike the trails and visit the reserve. In addition, a variety of tours are available – from horseback riding and kayaking through the estuary to snorkeling and guided hikes. The Schutts can arrange transport to the reserve from Paquera, and travel agencies in Montezuma (p306) can arrange guided day tours.

Seventeen well-marked, easy to moderate trails take visitors through the different ecosystems; maps are available at the entrance. Readers recommend hiring a guide as it greatly increases your chances of spotting wildlife. The forested areas are the haunts of deer, monkey, agouti and paca, and three species of cat have been recorded. Iguana, crab, lobster, chiton, shellfish, sea turtle and some other marine creatures can be seen on the beaches and in the tide pools. Birders have recorded more than 232 species of bird throughout the reserve, though there are probably more.

Camping is not allowed in the reserve, though there are six rustic **cabinas** (r per person with 3 meals US$35) with private cold showers. Stays must be arranged in advance either through the office in Paquera, your tour operator or at the entrance. There is no electricity, so take a flashlight and batteries.

PLAYAS POCHOTE & TAMBOR

These two mangrove-backed gray-sand beaches are protected by Bahía Ballena, the largest bay on the southeastern peninsula, and are surrounded by a few small fishing communities. In the past 15 years, however, the area has slowly been developed as a resort destina-tion; the outcome has been less than green (see boxed text Clamor in Tambor, p304). Fortunately, there are a few good choices for accommodations in the area, and for the most part Pochote and Tambor are un-dertouristed, providing plenty of opportu-nities for hiking, swimming, kayaking and even whale-watching.

The beaches begin 14km south of Paquera, at the community of Pochote, and stretch for about 8km southwest to Tambor – they're divided by the narrow and wadeable estuary of the Río Pánica.

Activities

Both beaches are safe for **swimming**, and there are occasional **whale sightings** in the bay. The gentle waters also make this a good spot for **kayaking**. Although the mangroves are not set up for hiking, Curú (opposite) is just down the road.

Sleeping

There are a number of all-inclusive, very ex-pensive, environmentally questionable resorts around here – if you want more information, talk to your travel agent.

Hotel Dos Lagartos (☎ 2683 0236; aulwes@cos tarica.net; d with/without bathroom US$30/20; **P**) At the southern end of the bay, in the village of Tambor, this clean, simple American-run hotel has beach views, a nice restaurant and a pleasant garden. Seventeen tidy rooms share clean bathrooms, while five pricier units have private bathrooms.

Cabinas El Bosque (☎ 2683 0039; s/d/tr/q US$17/23/27/29; **P**) A short walk to the beach, this is a good, cheap option. Rooms are neatly tiled, and though they're on the small side, they're quiet and have private cold-water bathrooms.

Cabinas Cristina (☎ 2683 0028; s/d/tr US$17/23/27; **P** ⚄) These recommended cabinas are run by the always-welcoming Eduardo and Cristina, a Tico couple who are eager to show you the *real* beauty of the area. Rooms are simple and spotless, and accommodate travel-ers of all budgets. There's also a small restau-rant, and the owners can give you good advice about booking tours in the area.

Hotel Costa Coral (☎ 2683 0105; www.costacoral.com; d incl breakfast with/without air-con US$70/58, additional person US$19; **P** ⚄ ⚄) Slightly more upscale (though you don't have to wear those ridicu-lous bracelets), the Costa Coral's 10 colorful

CLAMOR IN TAMBOR

Few sites are better examples of how *not* to be environmentally sustainable than Playa Tambor. In 1991 Spanish hotel chain Grupo Barceló began the construction of a massive beachside resort on this tranquil bay that was to include 2400 hotel rooms, a golf course and a marina. The following year, Barceló and the regional government overseeing the project were challenged by grassroots groups alleging environmental violations – from the draining of mangrove swamp to the removal of sand and gravel from a nearby riverbed (causing erosion). The hotel chain was ultimately fined the paltry sum of US$14,000 for its actions. The project proceeded – though the plans were significantly scaled down – and Hotel Barceló Playa Tambor opened its doors to the public in 1992. Ironically, the hotel's website now touts the resort as ideal for 'nature lovers.'

The small fine outraged Noemi Canet, a Costa Rican biologist who was active in Ascona (Costa Rican Association for the Protection of Wildlife), an organization that helped lead the charge against Barceló. But for her, the main issue shouldn't be one hotel chain's alleged actions but the compliant attitude of her own government, which in turn opens the door for other developers to do the same thing.

Canet says that a number of things need to improve. For one, all tourism projects should require an environmental impact study conducted by a biologist knowledgeable about the area. In addition, she reports that the permit process is so Byzantine that sometimes it's difficult to know who is in charge of what, much less enforce environmental laws. Unfortunately, groups such as Ascona are fighting a continuing battle – one that pits the influence of money against the interests of local communities. 'This belongs to the people of Costa Rica,' says Canet of the country's natural wonders. 'It's a national treasure – we should start treating it as such.'

As the massive developments at the equally controversial Papagayo project (p262) continue on the northern Península de Nicoya, it's easy to be skeptical about whether this will happen soon enough.

For more information on the Costa Rican Tourism Institute's sustainable tourism program, visit www.turismo-sostenible.co.cr/en/home.shtml.

Spanish-colonial villas accommodate up to four people and have hot-water bathroom, cable TV, kitchenette and optional air-con. There's a pool and Jacuzzi, and there's also a small bar-restaurant. Credit cards are accepted.

Getting There & Away

The airport is just north of the entrance to Hotel Barceló Playa Tambor. Hotels will arrange pick-up at the airport for an extra fee. Between them, Sansa and NatureAir (one way/round-trip US$72/144) have about six daily flights to San José.

Paquera–Montezuma buses pass through here.

CÓBANO

Cóbano has a post office, gas station, clinic and **Banco Nacional** (☎ 2642 0210; ☼ 8:30am-3:45pm Mon-Fri, 9am-1pm Sat), making it the only real 'city' (it's hardly even a town) in the southeastern peninsula. Although there are a few hotels and restaurants here, there's no reason to stay since Montezuma is only 5km away.

Paquera–Montezuma buses pass through here, and a 4WD taxi to Montezuma costs about US$6.

MONTEZUMA

Up until the late 1990s, a traffic jam in Montezuma was getting off your bike to shoo some cows off the road, a tourist was someone who left after only a month, a night out was rolling a spliff on the beach instead of in your hammock, a good time was – OK, you get the idea. Montezuma was one of the original 'destinations' in Costa Rica, and its remote location and proximity to Costa Rica's first nature reserve, Cabo Blanco (p314), attracted hippies, artists and dreamers alike. You had to work to get here, and no one had plans to leave quickly.

Montezuma is still a charming village, and foreign travelers continue to be drawn here by the laidback atmosphere, cheap hotels and sprawling beaches. And while nothing ever stays the same, Montezuma has managed to hang on to its tranquil appeal. Typical touristy offerings, like canopy tours and ATV rentals, do a brisk trade here, but you'll see – in the yoga classes, the volunteer opportunities, the arts festivals and the vegan food – that the town stays well in touch with its hippie roots.

Information

The nearest bank is in Cóbano (opposite). For money exchange, tour operators in town will take US dollars, euros or traveler's checks, though you can expect to pay a heavy commission. Laundry service is available at most hotels for about US$3 per kg. A couple of good web resources are www.nicoyapeninsula.com and www.playamontezuma.net.

El Sano Banano (☎ 2642 0638; per hr US$2) Internet access.

Librería Topsy (☎ 2642 0576; ☉ 8am-4pm Mon-Fri, 8am-noon Sat & Sun) Has American newspapers and magazines, and a large lending library with books in several languages. It also serves as the unofficial post service, selling stamps and making regular mail drops at Cóbano's post office.

Sights & Activities

BEACHES

Picture-perfect white-sand beaches are strung out along the coast, separated by small rocky headlands and offering great beachcombing and tide-pool studying. Unfortunately, there are strong rips along the entire coastline, so inquire locally before going for a swim and take care. For more information on riptides see boxed text, p278.

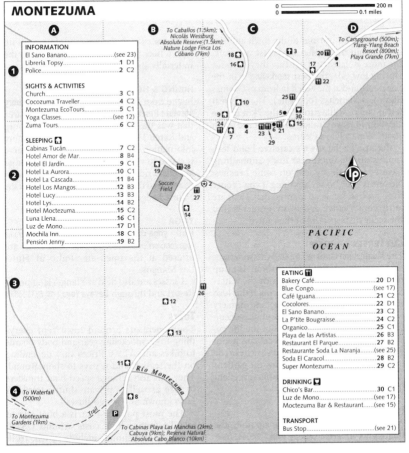

MONTEZUMA

0 ——— 200 m
0 ——— 0.1 miles

INFORMATION
El Sano Banano..........................(see 23)
Librería Topsy................................**1** D1
Police..**2** C2

SIGHTS & ACTIVITIES
Church...**3** C1
Cocozuma Traveller........................**4** C2
Montezuma EcoTours......................**5** C1
Yoga Classes..............................(see 12)
Zuma Tours....................................**6** C2

SLEEPING
Cabinas Tucán...............................**7** C2
Hotel Amor de Mar.........................**8** B4
Hotel El Jardín...............................**9** C1
Hotel La Aurora............................**10** C1
Hotel La Cascada.........................**11** B4
Hotel Los Mangos........................**12** B3
Hotel Lucy...................................**13** B3
Hotel Lys.....................................**14** B2
Hotel Moctezuma.........................**15** C2
Luna Llena...................................**16** C1
Luz de Mono................................**17** D1
Mochila Inn.................................**18** C1
Pensión Jenny.............................**19** B2

To Caballos (1.5km);
Nicolás Wessburg
Absolute Reserve (1.5km);
Nature Lodge Finca Los
Cóbano (7km)

To Campground (500m);
Ylang-Ylang Beach
Resort (800m);
Playa Grande (7km)

PACIFIC
OCEAN

Soccer
Field

Río Montezuma

To Waterfall
(500m)

To Montezuma
Gardens (1km)

Trail

To Cabinas Playa Las Manchas (2km);
Cabuya (9km); Reserva Natural
Absoluta Cabo Blanco (10km)

EATING
Bakery Café..................................**20** D1
Blue Congo...............................(see 17)
Café Iguana.................................**21** C2
Cocolores....................................**22** D1
El Sano Banano...........................**23** C2
La P'tite Bougraisse.....................**24** C2
Organico.....................................**25** C1
Playa de las Artistas.....................**26** B3
Restaurant El Parque....................**27** B2
Restaurante Soda La Naranja.......(see 25)
Soda El Caracol...........................**28** B2
Super Montezuma........................**29** C2

DRINKING
Chico's Bar..................................**30** C1
Luz de Mono............................(see 17)
Moctezuma Bar & Restaurant......(see 15)

TRANSPORT
Bus Stop...................................(see 21)

PENÍNSULA DE NICOYA

THE MONTEZUMA WATERFALL

A 20-minute stroll south of town takes you to a set of three scenic waterfalls. The main attraction here is to climb the second set of falls and jump in. Though countless people do this every day, be aware that even though there is a warning sign, about half a dozen people have died attempting this.

The first waterfall has a good swimming hole, but it's shallow and rocky and not suitable for diving. From here, if you continue on the well-marked trail that leads around and up, you will come to a second set of falls. These are the ones that offer a good clean leap (from 10m up) into the deep water below. To reach the jumping point, continue to take the trail up the side of the hill until you reach the diving area. Do *not* attempt to scale the falls. The rocks are slippery and this is how most jumpers have met their deaths. From this point, the trail continues up the hill to the third and last set of falls. Once again, these aren't that safe for jumping. However, there is a rope swing that will drop you right over the deeper part of the swimming hole (just be sure to let go on the out-swing!).

A lot of travelers enjoy the thrill, but as with anything of this nature, you undertake it at your own risk. To get there, follow the main Montezuma road south out of town and then take the trail to the right after Hotel La Cascada, past the bridge. You'll see a clearly marked parking area for visitors (US$2.50 per car) and the beginning of the trail that leads up.

The beaches in front of the town are nice enough, but the further northeast you walk, the more isolated and pristine they become. During low tide, the best **snorkeling** is in the tide pools, and at the beach in front of Cabinas Playa Las Manchas (opposite). There's great **surf** if you're willing to walk the 7km up the coastline to Playa Grande, or if you head south about 3km to Playa Cedros.

Because of the town's carefree boho feel, topless and (sometimes) nude sunbathing have become de rigueur on some beaches. No one is likely to say anything if you choose to go topless, but keep in mind that Ticos are fairly conservative and many residents find the scene disrespectful of their town.

BUTTERFLY GARDEN

The **Montezuma Gardens** (☎ 8888 4200; www.monte zumagardens.com; ☼ 8am-4pm) are about 1km up the hill toward Cóbano, alongside the waterfall trail, you can take a tour through this lush *mariposario* (butterfly garden) and nursery where the mysterious metamorphosis occur. On your walk, you'll learn about the life cycles and benefits of a dozen local species, of which you'll see many colorful varieties. The lovely Oregonian family running the gardens also have a B&B here and offer excellent live-work opportunities.

CANOPY TOUR

After you've flown down nine zip lines, the **Montezuma Waterfall Canopy Tour** (☎ 2642 0808;

www.montezumatraveladventures.com; US$45) winds up with a hike down – rather than up – to the waterfalls. Bring your swimsuit.

HIKING & HORSEBACK RIDING

Inland from Montezuma is the **Nicolás Wessburg Absolute Reserve**, a private conservation area that was the original site of Olof Wessburg and Karen Mogensen's homestead (for more information, see p314). Although the reserve is closed to visitors, you can either hike or go horseback riding along its perimeter – tours can be arranged through operators in town or at the Nature Lodge Finca Los Caballos (p308).

YOGA

Daily **yoga classes** (☎ 8811 7582; www.montezuma yoga.com; per person US$12, private session US$40) are offered at the open-air studio at Hotel Los Mangos.

Classes are also held at Ylang-Ylang Beach Resort and through **Devaya Yoga** (☎ 8833 5086).

Tours

Tour operators around town rent everything from snorkeling gear and body boards to bikes and ATVs. Prices vary depending on the season, and it pays to shop around. They can also arrange speed-boat transfers to Jacó as well as private shuttle transfers (also known as 'Gringo Buses').

The most popular tour is a boat trip to Isla Tortuga, which costs around US$40 a person and should include lunch, fruit, drinks and snorkeling gear. Although the island is certainly beautiful, travelers complain that the whole outing feels like a tourist circus, especially during high season when the entire island is full of boat tours.

Another popular excursion is to take a guided hike (US$55) or a half-day horseback ride (US$50) to nearby Cabo Blanco.

The following three tour operators are recommended:

Cocozuma Traveller (☎ 2642 0911; www.cocozuma .com; ⏲ 24hr)

Montezuma EcoTours (☎ 2642 0467; www.playa montezuma.net/ecotours/agency.htm; ⏲ 8am-9pm)

Zuma Tours (☎ 2642 0024; www.zumatours.net; ⏲ 24hr)

Festivals & Events

Keep an eye out for posters advertising special events, as there always seems to be something going on in town.

Festival de Arte Chunches de Mar (www.chunches demar.com) This arts festival brings together artists and musicians to camp on the beach for one month – dates change every year, but is usually during high season – and create art together from found objects.

Montezuma International Film Festival (www .montezumafilmfestival.com) Usually held in November, this is a great excuse to celebrate the arts in Montezuma before high season kicks in.

Sleeping

The high season gets crowded, though with so many hotels dotting such a small town you're bound to find something. High-season prices are listed throughout.

BUDGET

All the following hotels have shared cold-water showers unless otherwise stated. Also, be careful with your stuff – travelers frequently complain of thefts from hotel rooms in Montezuma.

Camping is illegal on the beaches, though some travelers seem to have not had a problem outside the town limits. If you want to play it safe, there is a small, shaded **campground** (per person US$3) with bathrooms and cold showers only a 10-minute walk north of town.

Mochila Inn (☎ 2642 0030; d US$15, d/tr cabins from US$20/25; **P**) On a quiet hillside north of town, this secluded inn is brimming with wildlife and is silent (except for the sounds of the rain forest) at night. There are a variety of

rooms available that cater to different budgets, though everyone can use the outdoor toilets, which offer only a thin curtain between you and nature. (Bring binoculars and watch nature from the throne.)

Cabinas Playa Las Manchas (☎ 2642 0415; www .beach-hotel-manchas.com; d with kitchenette US$40, without US$17-30, casitas US$140; **P**) About 2km south of the bridge, this low-key Italian-run spot is a fabulous deal. The wooden cabinas are simple and comfortable (despite having thin walls); one has its own kitchenette. The breezy common area (with pool table) opens to the romantic terrace restaurant in front, which serves authentic Italian specialties with hints of Asian influences. Best of all, it's directly across from the small beach Playa Las Manchas – a wonderful place for a sunrise snorkel.

Cabinas Tucán (☎ 2642 0284; s/d US$10/20) Just north of the soccer field, the Tucán is attentively managed by the crotchety Doña Marta. Rooms are spotless, as are the communal showers.

Pensión Jenny (r per person US$10) This lovely white-and-blue country house north of the soccer field is a bit removed from the action, which makes it a good option if you want a quiet night's sleep.

Hotel Lucy (☎ 2642 0273; s/d US$10/24; **P**) This beachside pension is popular with shoestring travelers, and was the first budget place to open up in town. It's an excellent deal in this price range, with hammocks, tables and chairs on the shared terraces. There's free coffee and fruit in the mornings and a communal fridge, but no kitchen. Ask for a room upstairs – the ocean views and verandas make all the difference.

Luna Llena (☎ 2642 0390; www.playamontezuma.net /lunallena/index.swf; dm/s/d/tr from US$10/18/28/35; **P**) On the northern edge of town at the base of the hills is this delightful German-run budget option that's terrific value. Eight rooms at the edge of the forest share kitchens and four hot-water bathrooms, but if you can, snag the honeymoon suite, an incredible pavilion that overlooks the bay. If not, the gorgeous shared blue-tile and wood-floored aerie boasts its own stunning ocean view.

Hotel Moctezuma (☎ 2642 0058; www.playa montezuma.net/ecotours.htm; s/d US$15/30) This hotel right in the center of town has 21 worn-out rooms containing private warm-water bathrooms, though the loud (and we mean very

L-O-U-D) bar next door won't allow for any beauty rest.

Hotel Lys (☎ 2642 0642; www.hotellysmontezuma.net; camping US$6, r per person US$16) This recommended beachside budget hotel is run by a group of funky Italians who are bursting with creativity. In addition to creating a laidback vibe that's perfect for slowing down and reflecting on your travels, the owners have also launched a project known as Libre Universidad de Montezuma, or LUDM. This rapidly evolving concept is based on communication through artistic expression, and the aim is for travelers to bring an idea to the resident artisans and explore a part of their personality that may not have been previously expressed. Past 'graduates' have studied music, sculpture, painting, cooking, photography and fashion, though the founders believe that the possibilities are endless as long as you arrive with an open mind.

MIDRANGE
Montezuma
All hotels have private hot-water showers.

Hotel Los Mangos (☎ 2642 0076; www.hotellosmangos.com; d with/without bathroom US$70/35, tr bungalow US$93; P 🞄) This is a charming hotel offering bright, clean yellow-and-blue doubles with shared bathroom in the main building and bungalows with private bathrooms scattered around the mango-dotted gardens. There is also a small wooden pavilion near the base of the hills where daily yoga classes (p306) take place.

Hotel La Cascada (☎ 2642 0057; www.playamontezuma.net/cascada.php; d US$45, additional person US$15; P) By the river en route to the waterfalls, this classic Montezuma hotel has 19 simple wooden rooms with ocean views and a 2nd-floor deck that's fully strung with cozy hammocks – perfect for swinging or snoozing.

Hotel Amor de Mar (☎ 2642 0262; www.amordemar.com; d US$58-111, houses from US$210; P) At the southern end of town, this charming, serene place has a well-manicured lawn strewn with palms and strung with luxurious hammocks, all fronting a beautiful beach with a tide pool big enough to swim in. There are 11 rooms of different shapes and sizes that have varying amenities depending on your budget.

Hotel La Aurora (☎ 2642 0051; www.playamontezuma.net/aurora.htm; s/d from US$47/58, additional person US$5; P 🞄) La Aurora has been around for more than 20 years. and the pretty, vine-covered yellow building has an assortment of 15 comfortable rooms with fan, orthopedic bed and mosquito net; others have varying degrees of cold or hot water and air-con. There's a communal kitchen and plenty of hammocks for chilling out. Credit cards accepted.

Luz de Mono (☎ 2642 0090; www.luzdemono.com; d/ste US$81/93, casitas from US$140, all incl breakfast; P 🞄 🞄) Between the beach and the forested hills, this hotel has a variety of rooms and casitas, though they're all well appointed with solar-heated showers, ceramic tiles and wooden accents (it's worth the splurge to have a private outdoor Jacuzzi). The bar-restaurant Blue Congo (dishes US$5 to US$12) serves a good mix of international and Tico dishes, but the real reason you're here is to try the restaurant's wine (who knew grapes grew in the tropics?). It's bottled under its own label, and it's called – wait for it – 'monkeyshine.' Credit cards accepted.

Hotel El Jardín (☎ 2642 0074; www.hoteleljardin.com; d US$85-95, 4-person villa US$135; P 🞄 🞄) This hillside hotel has 15 luxurious stained-wood cabinas of various sizes and amenities (some have stone bathrooms and ocean views). The grounds are landscaped with tropical flowers and lush palms, and there's also a pool and Jacuzzi for soaking your cares away.

Around Montezuma
Nature Lodge Finca Los Caballos (☎ 2642 0124; www.naturelodge.net; d incl breakfast US$100-160, additional person US$23; P 🞄) North of Montezuma on the road to Cóbano, this 16-hectare ranch is adjacent to the Nicolás Wessburg Absolute Reserve. The lodge has a variety of rooms around the property with either jungle or ocean views. The Canadian owner prides herself on having some of the best looked-after horses in the area, and there are great opportunities here for riding on the trails around the reserve. You can also rent bikes, go hiking, have a meal in the restaurant or splash around the infinity pool.

Ylang-Ylang Beach Resort (☎ 2642 0636; www.ylangylangresort.com; d bungalow US$186, beachfront r/ste US$204/244, beachfront bungalow US$274-308, all incl breakfast & dinner; 🞄) About a 15-minute walk north of town along the beach is this resort catering to holistic holiday-seekers. Here you'll find a collection of beautifully appointed rooms, suites and polygonal bungalows with private hot showers (some open-air), as well as a palm-fringed swimming pool, yoga center, gourmet restaurant and spa. Oh, and you can't actually drive here, though staff will pick you up in their custom beach cruisers. Credit cards are accepted.

Eating

Self-caterers should head to the Super Montezuma for fresh food.

Bakery Café (☎ 2642 0458; sanforest@hotmail.com; dishes US$1-3; ☺ 6am-4pm) Grab a chair on the outdoor patio of this homey vegetarian restaurant and feast on homemade banana bread and French toast – or get some tasty wholegrain bread for a picnic on the beach (or on the ferry).

La P'tite Bougraisse (crêpes US$3-5; ☺ 5-10pm Wed-Sun) Run by a lovely Montreal native, this wonderful crêperie has low-lit seating in which to enjoy your made-to-order savory and sweet crêpes as you watch the world walk by.

Restaurante Soda La Naranja (☎ 2642 1001; mains US$3-5; ☺ 7:30am-10pm Mon-Sat) Typical food on the main strip, this *soda* has a nice shaded patio next to Organico and reasonably priced eats.

Restaurant El Parque (dishes US$3-6; ☺ breakfast, lunch & dinner) For beachside ambience and cheap seafood, this small *soda* is a good choice.

Organico (www.organicomontezuma.com; smoothies US$4; ☺ 8am-6pm) When they say 'pure food made with love,' they mean it – this healthy new café turns out homemade, nondairy ice creams, vegan pastries, *batidos* (fruit smoothies) and other tasty treats you can feel good about.

Soda El Caracol (dishes US$4-6; ☺ 11am-7pm) Although the building looks like it's seen better days, don't let appearances fool you – the casados here are tops.

Café Iguana (dishes US$4-6; ☺ 6am-9pm) In the center of town is this vegetarian-friendly spot, where you can get hummus sandwiches, veggie lasagna, healthy salads and fresh *batidos*.

El Sano Banano (☎ 2642 0638; dishes US$4-12; ☺ breakfast, lunch & dinner) This restaurant is way overpriced for simple dishes – nine bucks for a casado? But it's worth showing up in the evening when the restaurant shows nightly films for US$6 minimum consumption.

Cocolores (☎ 2642 0348; dishes US$5-12; ☺ 2-9:30pm) One of the best restaurants in Montezuma, Cocolores has a pleasant patio for candle-lit dinners and heaping portions of French-influenced cuisine, as well as some Tico-fusion standards.

Playa de las Artistas (☎ 2642 0920; mains US$8-12; ☺ 10:30am-10:30pm) This artfully decorated beachside spot is the most adored restaurant in town. The international menu with heavy Mediterranean influences changes daily depending on locally available ingredients, though you can always count on fresh seafood and impeccable culinary sophistication.

Drinking & Entertainment

There are a few bars in town, and you can stop by El Sano Banano to check out which movie it's screening that night.

Chico's Bar is a sprawling complex of bars, tables, beach chairs and dance space with the music turned up loud – making it party central most nights. If you can score a table outside, it can be sort of romantic.

Luz de Mono has an open-air discotheque that plays house music on Thursday and reggae on Saturday (smoke 'em if you got 'em).

Moctezuma Bar & Restaurant at Hotel Moctezuma has an excellent location on the beach and two cool terraces.

Getting There & Away

BOAT

Travelers are increasingly taking advantage of the jet-boat transfer service that connects Jacó to Montezuma. Several boats per day cross the Gulf of Nicoya, and the journey only takes about an hour. At US$30 it's not cheap, but it'll save you about a day's worth of travel. Wear shoes you can use for a beach landing.

PENÍNSULA DE NICOYA

ALONG THE WEST COAST BY 4WD

If you are truly adventurous, have a lot of time on your hands and have some experience driving in places where there is nary a road in sight, then you might be ready to take on the southern Pacific coast of Península de Nicoya. Make sure that you have a 4WD with high clearance though, as well as a comprehensive insurance policy. Do *not* attempt this drive during the rainy season.

Mal País, Montezuma and Cabo Blanco are most frequently reached by the road that follows the eastern part of the peninsular coast and connects with the ferry from Puntarenas in Playa Naranjo. However, if you're looking for some adventure in your life, it's possible to take a 4WD from Playa Carrillo along the southeast coast to Islita, Playa Coyote, south to Mal País and points beyond. Again, don't even think of trying to do any of this in a regular car.

As the crow flies, it's about 70km of 'road' from Playa Carrillo to Mal País, though you should allow at least five hours for the trip (provided you encounter no delays). Several rivers have to be forded, including the Río Ora about 5km east of Carrillo, which is impassable at high tide during the dry season – even to 4WDs; check tide schedules.

From Playa Coyote, drivers will cross a few more rivers, including the Río Bongo and Río Arío, and pass by Playas Caletas, Arío and Manzanillo (you can camp on any of these beaches if you're self-sufficient). There are some pretty hairy river crossings throughout this stretch, so it certainly helps to talk to locals before setting out. In some cases the road doesn't cross directly through the river, and you'll have to drive up the river a bit to find the egress. In these cases, it is best to walk the river first, double-check the egress and then drive in so that you don't plunge your rental car into thigh-deep mud or onto a pile of rocks. Many a rental vehicle has been lost to this stretch of road, so it definitely pays to be cautious (see boxed text Driving Through Rivers, p548).

From Playa Manzanillo head inland to Cóbano (p304), which is well connected to Montezuma, Mal País and Cabo Blanco by reasonable dirt roads.

For the majority of the trip, there are no facilities, a couple of villages and few people that can help you if you get stuck. Also, the roads are unsigned, so getting lost will be part of the deal, though you can always navigate with a compass and the sun. Take a jerry can of gas, your favorite snack foods and plenty of water – if you break down, plan on spending some quality time on your own or with your traveling companion.

For very good reason, Costa Rica's tourist office recommends against undertaking this journey.

BUS

Buses depart Montezuma from in front of Café Iguana. Buy tickets directly from the bus driver.

Cabo Blanco US$1, 30 minutes, departs at 8:15am, 10:15am, 2:15pm and 6:15pm.
Paquera US$2, 1½ hours, departs at 5:30am, 8am, 10am, noon, 2pm, 4pm and 6pm.
San José US$10, nine to 12 hours, departs at 4:45am.
Santa Teresa US$1.25, 45 minutes, departs at 10:30am and 2:30am.

CAR & TAXI

During the rainy season, the stretch of road between Cóbano and Montezuma is likely to require a 4WD. In the village itself, parking can be a problem, though it's easy enough to walk everywhere.

A 4WD taxi is able to carry five people, and can take you from Montezuma to Cóbano (US$6), Cabo Blanco (US$12), Tambor (US$30), Mal País (US$35) or Paquera (US$30).

Montezuma Expeditions (www.montezumaexpeditions .com) runs private shuttles to San José (US$35), Mal País and Santa Teresa (US$35).

MAL PAÍS & SANTA TERESA

Mal País (Bad Country) refers to the southwestern corner of Nicoya that's famous among surfers for its consistent waves. The area lies more or less north to south along the coastline, with Santa Teresa being the largest village in the area. Further south is the smaller village of Playa Carmen, and more southerly still is Mal País, the village. ¿*Comprende*? Don't worry if it doesn't make sense at first; the villages have pretty much merged into one surf community lining the coast, and are collectively known as Mal País.

The legendary waves at Mal País have been attracting surfers since the 1970s, so it's not surprising that many of them grew up and decided to stay. In the last several years, this once isolated corner of the peninsula has become something of the backpacker's version of Nosara – surf session in the morning, yoga in the afternoon and cruising at night. Widespread development is rapidly carving up the beachfront, and at press time, the dust on the coastal road was swirling as the road was being prepared for paving. Considering the speed of these changes and the busloads of international neo-hippies and surfers arriving by the day, it's looking like the next big thing – a big thing like Jacó or Tamarindo.

Mal País is not for everyone. If you're an experienced surfer looking for a 'scene,' throw away your itinerary because you're going to get stuck here. But if you're looking for an authentic Costa Rican beach town and are not so stoked on surf culture, skip the trip.

Orientation & Information

The road from Cóbano meets the beach road next to Frank's Place (see p312), on the western side of the peninsula. To the left (south) lies Mal País and to the right (north) there's Santa Teresa.

Across the intersection from Frank's Place is the new Centro Comercial Playa El Carmen, where you'll find a branch of **Banco Nacional** (☎ 640-0598; ⏰ 1-7pm) that can change US dollars if it doesn't accept your ATM card. Super Santa Teresa (300m north of Frank's Place), on the road to Santa Teresa, will change US dollars and traveler's checks.

You can find internet access all over Mal País, but for a start, try Frank's Place on the main intersection and **Beach Break Surf Hotel** (☎ 2640 0612; www.beachbreakcr.net; ⏰ 7am-10pm) in Santa Teresa.

A useful website for local info is www.malpais.net.

Activities

Surfing is usually the be-all and end-all for most visitors to Mal País, but the beautiful beach stretches north and south for kilometers on end – many accommodations can arrange horseback riding tours and fishing trips.

SURFING

The following beaches are listed from north to south. If you choose a lodge that has 'surf camp' in its name, chances are it's right in front of a good break. At the very least, it can point you to the best nearby spots.

About 8km north of the intersection, **Playa Manzanillo** is a combination of sand and rock that's best surfed when the tide is rising and there's an offshore wind.

The most famous break in the Mal País area is at **Playa Santa Teresa**, and is characterized as being fast and powerful. This beach can be surfed virtually any time of day, though be cautious as there are scattered rocks.

Playa El Carmen, which is at the end of the road leading down from the main intersection, is a good beach break that can also be surfed anytime.

The Mal País area is saturated with surf shops, and competition has kept prices low – this is a good place to pick up an inexpensive board, and you can probably make most of your money back if you sell it elsewhere. Most of the local shops also do rentals and repairs, and may let you in on some good surf spots. This is by no means an exhaustive list.

Alex Surf Shop (☎ 2640 0364) Rent or buy a board here, or take a lesson; 250m north of the intersection.

Corduroy to the Horizon (☎ 2640 0173; ⏰ 8am-6pm) Shapers Andy and Aaron create custom epoxy boards and also do ding repairs. Find their shop 50m west of Frank's Place.

Jobbie's Surf Camp (www.surfjobbie.com) Not a shop, per se, but kooky local Canuck Josh (aka 'Jobbie') is a brand in and of himself, and he gives surfing lessons.

Shit Hole (☎ 8887 9144) Yep, that's really what it's called, 200m north of the main intersection. It rents and sells boards as well as gives lessons – also, it claims to make crêpes.

Tuanis (☎ 2640 0370) Has internet access, various gifts and sundries, and can help book taxi services around the area. It's 2km north of Frank's.

YOGA

Yoga naturally complements surfing – at the very least, if you haven't been in the water for awhile, the stretching can be the perfect antidote to sore paddling arms.

Casa Zen (p312) Offers three- to seven-day yoga retreats; the instructor here teaches a variety of styles, from Ashtanga to Vinyasa.

Horizon Yoga Hotel (☎ 2640 0524; www.horizon-yogahotel.com) Offers three classes daily, in a serene environment overlooking the ocean.

Milarepa (p313) Offers classes in Hatha yoga, Swasthya yoga and partner yoga for all levels of practice.

PENÍNSULA DE NICOYA

Sleeping & Eating

We've listed these places in relation to the main intersection in Playa Carmen, where Frank's Place (below) occupies the corner. For simplicity's sake, though the nomenclature isn't technically accurate, listings north of the intersection appear in the Santa Teresa section. Listings around and south of the intersection we'll call Mal País.

SANTA TERESA

You'll find all of the following places heading north into Santa Teresa – they're listed below according to their distance from Frank's Place.

Frank's Place (☎ 2640 0096, 2640 0071; s with shared bathroom US$25, bungalow US$60, d US$70; P ☒ ☐ ☒) Coming into town from Cóbano, the first place you'll see is this local landmark and historic surfer outpost, which has taken over the entire corner with lots of rooms and an internet café. Spacious, tiled cabinas are comfortable, and the shared bathrooms and communal kitchen are well kept. This place is always full of travelers, and the free-form pool, whirlpool and restaurant are great places to hang out and get the latest surf report.

Las Piedras (☎ 2640 0453; mains US$3-7; ☒ lunch & dinner) This Argentinean-run chicken shack proclaims that, 'Our chicken is the sh%t.' One bite and you'll agree – its chicken really is the sh%t.

Tranquilo Backpackers (☎ 2640 0589; www.tranquilo backpackers.com; dm US$10, d/tr with shared bathroom US$30/45, d with private bathroom US$35, 4-/5-person loft apt US$60/75, all incl breakfast; P ☐) One of the best budget options in the area. Everything here has been designed to be smart, hip and functional – you can even flush the toilet paper. The owners know exactly how to create happy campers who get to eat their fill of free pancakes every morning and have access to the shared kitchen, shared hot-water bathrooms, free internet and free surfboards to borrow. Bikes can be rented for US$3 per day, and if it's full (or you're almost broke), they'll let you sleep in a hammock (US$7).

Hotel Buenos Aires (☎ 2640 0254; www.buenosaires malpais.com; d with/without air-con US$65/45; P ☒ ☒) The eight rooms at this awesome hillside hotel have either hammocks or comfy chairs on its shared terraces, and private hot-water showers. There's a pool as well, but best of all is the restaurant, serving international food (mains US$5 to US$11) on a terrace with some of the

area's best views. Not a bad place for a few romantic drinks in the evening, either.

Luz de Vida (☎ 2640 0568; www.luzdevida-resort.com; d/tr/q US$93/105/116, bungalow d/tr/q US$111/122/134; P ☒ ☒) The light of life is an apt name for this bright tropical refuge. All of the rooms and bungalows have air-con and private bathroom, and the common areas have a pool and cozy *palapa* bar.

Casa Zen (☎ 2640 0523; www.zencostarica.com; dm US$12, d with shared bathroom US$24-45, apt from US$55; P) This recommended Asian-inspired guesthouse is decked out in Zen art, celestial murals and enough happy Buddha sculptures to satisfy all your belly-rubbing needs. The owner, Kelly, is committed to helping guests 'chill and recreate on their own time.' She also runs an eclectic restaurant (dishes US$3 to US$7) that has everything from veggie sandwiches and burgers to fresh sushi and Thai curries. Casa Zen also offers a variety of yoga retreats; check the website for current offerings.

Trópico Latino Lodge (☎ 2640 0062; www.hotel tropicolatino.com; d/tr/q US$100/115/130, bungalow from US$140; P ☒ ☒) Beautifully decorated with dark wood and deep, saturated colors, the roomy bungalows here are peppered around a tropical garden and along the beach, and feature air-con, king-size beds, hammock-strung patios and private hot-water bathrooms (one bungalow also has a full kitchen). There's a dreamy pool fringed with palms and heliconia, and a surfside restaurant (dishes US$4 to US$8) that specializes in Italian food.

Hostal Brunela (☎ 2640 0321; hostalbrunela.com; dm US$12; P) This big hostel feels very homey, maybe because there are so many long-term surf slaves living here, or because the owner has a kind, paternal air about him, or the lounge area feels like a giant living room with, uh, *sleepy* surfers sprawled out watching TV. Comfortable, colorful rooms each have four beds, lockers and a private bathroom. The kitchen is huge and fully equipped – with free coffee – and the place is right next to a great surf break.

Don Jon's (☎ 2640 1938; grupodonjons@gmail.com; dm/d/apt from US$12/35/50; P ☒) This basic spot is run by a couple of Tico brothers who offer clean rooms for various budgets, some with fridges and air-con. The two-bedroom apartment has a full kitchen and is roomy enough for four or five.

Funky Monkey Lodge (☎ 2640 0272; www.funky -monkey-lodge.com; dm/ste US$12/99, 4-person bungalow

US$93, 8-person bungalow US$163; (P) (X) (L) (R)) Up the hill from Tuanis (p311), this funky lodge is situated at the top of a natural rock hill, and has sweet, rustic-style bungalows built out of bamboo. Each has an open-air shower, and the larger ones have a fully equipped kitchen. A popular bar-restaurant (sushi rolls US$4 to US$8) packs in the crowds with good international food and excellent sunsets.

Point Break Hotel (☎ 2640 0190; www.surfing -malpais.com; casita with/without bathroom from US$50/40; (P)) Down a quiet dirt road, these cute wooden casitas are a great deal, and about 50m to a beautiful beach break. The bigger casitas are raised on stilts, have full kitchens and lofts – perfect if you're on a surf trip with a few buddies.

ourpick Cuesta Arriba (☎ 2640 0607; www.santateresa hostels.com; dm US$12; (P)) Up a hill across from one of Santa Teresa's best surf breaks, this Argentinean-run hostel is a gem – each bright, colorful room sleeps four and has a private bathroom. There's a big, beautiful kitchen area with a breezy wood-floored terrace upstairs with a flat-screen TV and DVDs. It also has boards for rent, laundry service, coffee and toast in the morning, and secure parking. There are hammocks in the garden, lots of places to lounge, and the vibe is happy and relaxed.

Milarepa (☎ 2640 0023; www.milarepahotel.com; bungalow from US$198; (P) (R)) This self-proclaimed 'small hotel of luxurious simplicity' has Asian-inspired bungalows constructed of bamboo and Indonesian teak. Each is furnished with four-poster beds draped in voluminous mosquito nets, and comes complete with a shower open to the sky. The restaurant (mains US$6 to US$9) serves international cuisine that emphasizes the fresh local seafood. The owners can arrange tours and activities and offer several types of yoga classes (see p311 for details).

Florblanca (☎ 2640 0232; www.florblanca.com; villa incl breakfast US$675-1050; (P) (X) (L) (R)) The most sumptuous hotel in Santa Teresa is truly in a class of its own – not surprisingly, it belongs to the group of 'Small Distinctive Hotels of Costa Rica.' Ten romantic villas are scattered around 3 hectares of land next to a pristine white-sand beach. Each villa is lit by warm hues, with indoor-outdoor spaces such as open-air sunken bathtubs and living areas. Complimentary yoga and Pilates classes are offered, as are free use of bikes, surfboards

and snorkeling equipment. Transfers to and from Tambor airport are included in the rates. Its Asian-fusion restaurant, Nectar (dishes US$7 to US$20), is open to the public and is highly recommended for its innovative dishes and unbelievably fresh sushi. Credit cards accepted; children under 13 are not allowed.

On the beach, **Roca Mar** (☎ 2640 0250; per person US$6; (P)) and **Zeneida's** (☎ 2640 0118; camping per person US$6; (P)) offer secure parking and lots of space to camp, as well as toilets and cold showers, but no kitchen.

MAL PAÍS

Frank's Place (opposite) marks the spot – this is the main intersection, where shuttles will drop you off and pick you up.

Umi Sushi (☎ 2640 0968; sushi US$3-10; ⏲ noon-10pm) In the courtyard of the Centro Comercial Playa El Carmen, this sushi bar has a pleasant dining room and tables outside. If you're lucky, it will have a surf movie projected on the outside wall while you savor your Mal País roll. Beer drinkers beware: it only serves Japanese beers, at exorbitant prices.

Palma Real (☎ 2640 1913; mains US$3-8; ⏲ noon-9pm) On the road back toward Cóbano, past Frank's Place, pull up a chair at this family-run spot for fresh *ceviche*, fish tacos and fried yuca. It does typical Tico food as well, but if you're craving a taco, this is where you want to be. It is open daily during the hours listed, *más o menos*.

You'll find all of the following places heading south from the intersection into Mal País.

Ritmo Tropical (☎ 2640 0174; ritmotropical_mp@ yahoo.com; s/d US$58/64; (P) (R)) Clean, tropical-themed cabins with airy rooms, hot showers and shady verandas dot the simple grounds of this peaceful, family-run place. There's an on-site bar-restaurant (dishes US$3 to US$7) that does pancakes and *gallo pinto* (beans and rice) in the morning, and Italian-inspired dishes for lunch and dinner.

The Place (☎ 2640 0101; www.theplacemalpais .com; d incl breakfast US$68-230, additional person US$12; (P) (X) (R)) Cheaper rooms in this Swiss-run guesthouse are air-conditioned and have private hot-water bathrooms, but it's absolutely worth it to splurge on the more expensive bungalows – each one is creatively decorated according to a different theme (check the website for pictures). Rooms ring a small

PENÍNSULA DE NICOYA

pool amid the somewhat random landscaping. The owners can arrange surfing lessons and tours, and the small restaurant serves Mediterranean-style seafood by candlelight in the evenings.

Malpaís Surf Camp & Resort (☎ 2640 0061; www .malpaissurfcamp.com; camping per person US$7, cabina US$41, r US$64, villa US$111; P 🌀 🖭) Whether you're looking for a breezy bunkhouse or poolside villa, this 'surfer's lodge' caters to travelers of all budget levels. However, regardless of how much you're paying each night, you can wander the landscaped tropical grounds, swim in the lavish pool or grab a cold beer in the open-air bar-restaurant.

Soda Piedra Mar (☎ 2640 0069; mains US$3-7; 🕑 breakfast, lunch & dinner) This is one of the best local places to eat in Mal País, with generous portions of fresh seafood and, as the name suggests, a rocky location right on the ocean.

Blue Jay Lodge (☎ 2640 0089; www.bluejaylodge costarica.com; s/d incl breakfast US$50/65, additional person US$20; P) These charming stilt bungalows are built along a forest-covered hillside, each with its own hot-water bathroom and huge, screened-in veranda with hammocks. The bamboo-and-wood bungalows sleep three, and though they're a bit on the rustic side, the luxury is in their spaciousness and openness to their surroundings. The lodge is 200m from the beach.

Star Mountain Eco Resort (☎ 2640 0101 www .starmountaineco.com; s/d/tr incl breakfast US$65/95/110; P 🌀 🖭 🖳) This intimate and secluded lodge was built without cutting down a single tree, and today the grounds of the resort abound with wildlife. There are trails leading through the property that have good birding, and a viewpoint overlooks both sides of the peninsula. There are four hillside rooms, each simply and thoughtfully decorated in muted tropical colors. Only the casita (US$130) has air-con and wi-fi access. The resort is off the rough road (4WD only) between Mal País and Cabuya, alongside the Cabo Blanco reserve (follow the signs), 5.5km south of Frank's Place. It's closed in September and October.

Getting There & Away
From Mal País, there's a bus to Cóbano at 7am. From Santa Teresa there are buses at 6:45am and 11am. A taxi to these areas from Cóbano costs about US$18, depending on road conditions.

CABUYA
This tiny village is scattered along a dirt road about 9km south of Montezuma. Although it's rather uninteresting, it's worth visiting the town **cemetery**, which is on Isla Cabuya to the southeast and can only be reached at low tide. Here you'll find a few modest graves marked by crosses, though make sure you keep an eye on the tides!

Aside from the cemetery, most travelers either pass through Cabuya on their way to Cabo Blanco or use the town as a base for exploring Cabo Blanco.

Coming from Montezuma, the first hotel you'll come to is the Belgian-owned **Hotel Celaje** (☎ 2642 0374; www.celaje.com; s/d incl breakfast US$70/82; P 🌀 🖭 🖳), which has a collection of beautiful A-frame, thatched bungalows that sleep four. Neatly standing beside a nice pool and Jacuzzi, each lovely bungalow has its living quarters above, and an open ground floor with its own hammock. Real Belgian beer is readily available.

The Dutch-owned **Ancla de Oro** (☎ 2642 0369; www.cabloblancopark.com/ancla; d US$22, d/tr bungalow US$35/42; P) was one of the original places to stay in the area and is looking a little overgrown. There are simple rooms catering to budget travelers, but it's worth springing for the 'jungalows,' which are raised bungalows like the others in Cabuya – but the most rustic of the lot.

Turning down the signed side road, you'll find the Tica-run **Howler Monkey Hotel** (☎ 2642 0303; www.cabloblancopark.com/howler; bungalow US$60; P 🖳). These are cute A-frame bungalows with kitchenettes. In price and condition, they strike a happy medium between Hotel Celaje and Ancla de Oro. They are perfectly clean and comfortable, and the place is right on a slice of very quiet, rocky beach.

For everything else, make a pit stop at **Café Coyote** (dishes US$5-6; 🖳). The owners serve up pizza, seafood and veggie meals, and offer internet access.

RESERVA NATURAL ABSOLUTA CABO BLANCO
Just 11km south of Montezuma is Costa Rica's oldest protected wilderness area. Cabo Blanco is comprised of 1272 hectares of land and 1700 hectares of surrounding ocean, and includes the entire southern tip of the Península de Nicoya. The moist microclimate present on the tip of the peninsula fosters the growth

of evergreen forests, which are unique when compared with the dry tropical forests typical of the Nicoya. The park also encompasses a number of pristine white-sand beaches and offshore islands that are favored nesting areas for various species of bird.

The park was originally established by a Danish-Swedish couple, the late Karen Mogensen and Olof Wessberg, who settled in Montezuma in the 1950s and were among the first conservationists in Costa Rica. In 1960 the couple was distraught when they discovered that sections of Cabo Blanco had been clear-cut. At the time, the Costa Rican government was primarily focused on the agricultural development of the country (see boxed text A Whopper of a Problem, p223), and had not yet formulated its modern-day conservation policy. However, Karen and Olof were instrumental in convincing the government to establish a national park system, which eventually led to the creation of the Cabo Blanco reserve in 1963. The couple continued to fight for increased conservation of ecologically rich areas, but tragically Olof was murdered in 1975 during a campaign in the Osa Peninsula. Karen continued their work until her death in 1994, and today they are buried in the Nicolás Wessburg Absolute Reserve, which was the site of their original homestead.

Cabo Blanco is called an 'absolute' nature reserve because prior to the late 1980s visitors were not permitted. Even though the name has remained, a limited number of trails have been opened to visitors, though the reserve remains closed on Monday and Tuesday to minimize environmental impact.

Information

The **ranger station** (☎ 2642 0093; admission US$8; ☟ 8am-4pm Wed-Sun) is 2km south of Cabuya at the entrance to the park, and trail maps are available. It is not possible to overnight in the park, though there are plenty of options in nearby Cabuya (opposite) or Montezuma

(p307). Bring drinks and snacks as there is no food or water available.

The average annual temperature is about 27°C/80°F and annual rainfall is some 2300mm at the tip of the park. Not surprisingly, the trails can get muddy, so it's best to visit from December to April – the dry season.

Activities
WILDLIFE-WATCHING
Monkey, squirrel, sloth, deer, agouti and raccoon are usually present, and armadillo, coati, peccary and anteater are occasionally sighted.

The coastal area is known as an important nesting site for brown booby, which are mostly found 1.6km south of the mainland on **Isla Cabo Blanco** (White Cape Island). The name 'Cabo Blanco' was coined by Spanish *conquistadores* when they noticed that the entire island consisted of guano-encrusted rocks. Other seabirds in the area include brown pelican and magnificent frigatebird.

HIKING
From the ranger station, the **Swedish Trail** and **Danish Trail** lead 4.5km down to a wilderness beach at the tip of the peninsula. Note that both trails intersect at various points, and it's possible to follow one down and return on the other. Be advised that the trails can get very muddy (especially in the rainy season), and are fairly steep in certain parts – plan for about two hours in each direction. From the beach at the end of the trails it's possible to follow another trail to a second beach, though check first with park rangers as this trail is impassable at high tide.

Getting There & Away
Buses depart from the park entrance for Montezuma at 7am, 9am, 1pm and 4pm.

A 4WD taxi (for six passengers) from Montezuma to the park costs about US$12. You can prearrange for a pick-up.

PENÍNSULA DE NICOYA

Central Pacific Coast

Stretching from the rough and ready port city of Puntarenas to the tiny town of Uvita on the shores of Bahía Drake, the central Pacific coast is home to both wet and dry tropical rain forests, sun-drenched sandy beaches and a healthy dose of rare wildlife. On shore, national parks protect endangered animals, such as the squirrel monkey and the scarlet macaw, while off-shore waters are home to migrating whales and pods of dolphins.

With so much biodiversity packed into a small geographic area, it's no wonder the central Pacific coast is often thought of as Costa Rica in miniature. Given its close proximity to San José and the Central Valley, and its well-developed system of paved roads, the region has traditionally served as a weekend getaway for sun-worshippers, tree-huggers and fishermen.

Sadly, the picture isn't entirely rosy, especially given the fierce battle between the forces of development and conservation that is playing out in the region. Up and down the entire coast, towering residential blocks, gated communities and endless condo developments are transforming the coastline into a vast suburb of moneyed North American and European expats. The sad result is that a region once favored by Tico holidaymakers is now starting to look more and more like a foreign enclave.

These days, it's frustrating to see rampant construction along the coastline with seemingly few plans for sustainable development. However, it's important to see the bigger picture, namely the stunning nature that first put the central Pacific coast on the map. Although at times it can be hard to look beyond the towering cranes, spotting a troop of monkeys swinging through the canopy will quickly renew your faith in the natural beauty of Costa Rica.

HIGHLIGHTS

- Watching squirrel monkey troops scamper along the beaches at **Parque Nacional Manuel Antonio** (p353)

- Listening to squawking pairs of rare scarlet macaws flying overhead at **Parque Nacional Carara** (p323)

- Surfing the breaks at **Dominical** (p359), **Playa Hermosa** (p339) and **Matapalo** (p358)

- Spotting pods of breaching humpback whales at **Parque Nacional Marino Ballena** (p365)

- Clambering up the canopy platforms at **Hacienda Barú National Wildlife Refuge** (p359)

Parque Nacional Carara

Playa Hermosa

Parque Nacional Manuel Antonio

Matapalo

Hacienda Barú National Wildlife Refuge

Dominical

Parque Nacional Marino Ballena

History

Prior to the tourism boom in Costa Rica, the central Pacific coast – particularly the Quepos port area – was historically one of the country's largest banana-producing regions. However, in response to the 1940 banana blight that affected most of Central America, the United Fruit Company (also known as Chiquita Banana) introduced African palms to the area. Native to West Africa, these palms are primarily cultivated for their large, reddish fruits, which are pressed to produce a variety of cooking oils.

Although the banana blight finally ended in the 1960s, the palm plantations were firmly entrenched and starting to turn a profit. Since palm oil is easily transported in tanker trucks, Quepos was able to close its shipping port in the 1970s, which freed up resources and allowed the city to invest more heavily in the palm-oil industry. In 1995, the plantations were sold to Palma Tica, which continues to operate the plantations today. With the exception of commercial fishing and tourism, the palm-oil plantations serve as the primary source of employment in the Quepos area.

In more recent years, this stretch of the Pacific has grown increasingly popular with the North American package-holiday crowd, as it's easy to squeeze in a one-week retreat and be back to work on Monday. Unable to resist the draw of paradise, a good number of baby boomers nearing retirement have also begun snatching up beachfront property.

As a result, beach towns like Jacó that were once the exclusive enclaves of vacationing Tico families are now quickly being colonized by American-style strip malls, gated communities and 4x4 car dealerships. Foreign investment blessed this region with continuous development and solid infrastructure, though Ticos are starting to wonder if they will soon feel like tourists in their own backyard.

Things are indeed changing quickly, and it's difficult to say which interests will win out in the end. A new marina at Quepos will bring in a larger volume of tourists visiting Costa Rica on cruise ships, though it's difficult to imagine that the authenticity of the coastal fishing villages and palm-oil plantations could ever be lost.

Climate

West of the Cordillera Central, rains fall heavily during the months between April and November. The hillsides are particularly lush and green during this time, while in summer (December to March) little rain falls, leaving the countryside dry and barren looking.

Parks & Reserves

The central Pacific is home to a number of parks and reserves, including the most-visited national park in Costa Rica.

Hacienda Barú National Wildlife Refuge (p359) A small reserve that encompasses a range of tropical habitats, and is part of a major biological corridor that protects a wide range of species.

Parque Nacional Carara (p323) Home to no less than 400 different species of birds, including the rare scarlet macaw, which is amazingly a commonly sighted species in the park.

Parque Nacional Manuel Antonio (p353) The pristine beaches, rain forest–clad mountains and dense wildlife never fail to disappoint in Costa Rica's most touristed national park.

Parque Nacional Marino Ballena (p365) This is a vitally important marine park, which is the country's premier destination for both whale- and dolphin-watching.

Getting There & Around

The best option for exploring the coast in-depth is to have your own form of private transportation. With the exception of the unpaved stretch of road between Quepos and Dominical, the central Pacific coast has some of the country's best roads.

Major cities and towns along the coast, such as Puntarenas, Jacó, Quepos, Dominical and Uvita, are serviced by regular buses. Generally speaking, public transportation is frequent and efficient, and is certainly more affordable than renting a car.

Both **NatureAir** (www.natureair.com) and **Sansa** (www.sansa.com) service Quepos, which is the base town for accessing Manuel Antonio. Prices vary according to season and availability, though you can expect to pay a little less than US$75 for a flight from San José or Liberia.

PUNTARENAS TO QUEPOS

This increasingly populated stretch of coastline extends from the maritime port of Puntarenas, a historic shipping hub that has fallen on harder times, to the booming town of Quepos, which is a gateway to

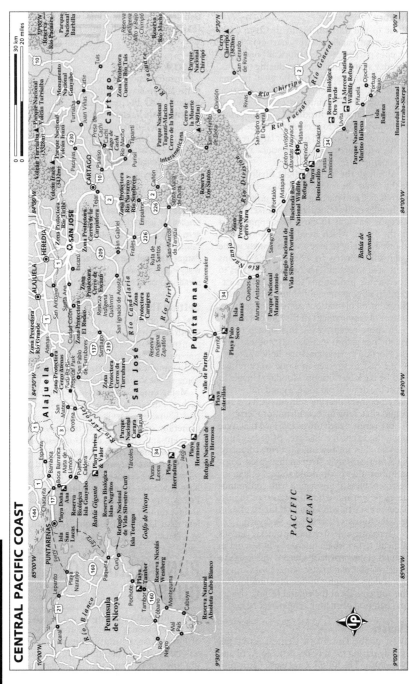

CENTRAL PACIFIC COAST

Parque Nacional Manuel Antonio. Centered on the epicenter of 'gringolandia,' namely the North American colony of Jacó, this region is experiencing rapid growth and development in response to wave upon wave of foreign investment. However, while there are some places where foreigners outnumber Ticos by a long shot, others are home to little more than forested hillsides, wilderness beaches and large concentrations of remarkable wildlife.

PUNTARENAS

Port cities the world over have a reputation for polluted waters, seedy environs and slow decay, which is pretty much a good way to sum up Costa Rica's gateway to the Pacific. As the closest coastal town to San José, Puntarenas has long been a popular escape for landlocked Ticos, especially since it takes just a few hours to reach here from San José and surrounding environs. However, although the town council has done a commendable job in cleaning the beaches and renovating the boardwalk, it's hard to escape the feeling that you're bathing and/or sunning yourself in a container yard.

In the years to come, visitor numbers to Puntarenas will likely drop, as the new San José–Orotina Hwy (see p326) pulls the traffic further south. In the meantime, Puntarenas is struggling to reap the benefits of increased tourism, though sadly failing to capture the interest (or the dollars) of foreign investors. With that said, the city's ferry terminal does serve as a convenient way to access the more pristine beaches further south in southern Nicoya, though few travelers are keen to spend any more of their time here than it takes to get on and off the boat.

History

Prior to the mid-20th century, Puntarenas was the largest and most significant open-water port in Costa Rica. Some of the finest coffees to grace European tables and coffee cups were carried to the continent on Puntarenas-registered freighters, and the steady flow of capital back into the city transformed Puntarenas into the 'Pearl of the Pacific.' However, after the construction of the railway leading from the Central Valley to Puerto Limón in 1890, the establishment

---

FIVE AGAINST THE SEA

In January 1988 five fishermen from Puntarenas set out on a trip that was meant to last seven days. Just five days into the voyage, their small vessel was facing 30ft waves triggered by northerly winds known as El Norte. Adrift for 142 days, they would face sharks, inclement weather, acute hunger and parching thirsts. They were finally rescued – 7200km away – by a Japanese fishing boat. *Five Against the Sea* by American reporter Ron Arias recounts in gripping detail the adversities they faced and how they survived.

---

of a more direct shipping route to Europe initiated the city's decline in importance, though Puntarenas did manage to remain a major port on the Pacific coast.

Orientation

Situated at the end of a sandy peninsula (8km long but only 100m to 600m wide), Puntarenas is Costa Rica's most significant Pacific coastal town, and is just 110km west of San José by paved highway. The city has 60 calles (streets) running north to south, but only five avenidas (avenues) running west to east at its widest point. As in all of Costa Rica, street names are largely irrelevant, and landmarks are used for orientation (see p537).

Information

INTERNET ACCESS

Coonatramar (☎ 2661 9011, 2661 1069; cnr Calle 31 & Av 3; per hr US$1.50; ☺ 8am-5pm)

MEDICAL SERVICES

Hospital Monseñor Sanabria (☎ 2663 0033; 8km east of town)

MONEY

The major banks along Avenida 3, to the west of the market, exchange money and are equipped with 24-hour ATMs.

Banco de San José (cnr Av 3 & Calle 3) is connected to the Cirrus network.

TOURIST INFORMATION

Puntarenas tourism office (Catup; ☺ 8am-5pm Mon-Fri) Opposite the pier on the 2nd floor above the Báncredito. It closes for lunch.

CENTRAL PACIFIC COAST

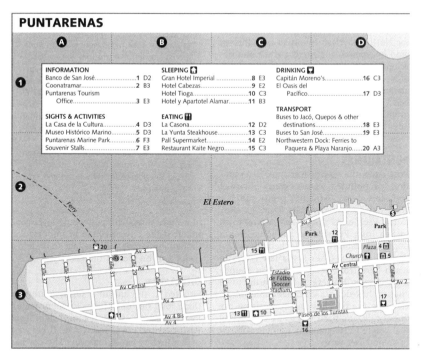

PUNTARENAS

INFORMATION
Banco de San José.....................1 D2
Coonatramar...........................2 B3
Puntarenas Tourism
    Office................................3 E3

SIGHTS & ACTIVITIES
La Casa de la Cultura................4 D3
Museo Histórico Marino............5 D3
Puntarenas Marine Park............6 F3
Souvenir Stalls.......................7 E3

SLEEPING 🏠
Gran Hotel Imperial 8 E3
Hotel Cabezas..........................9 E2
Hotel Tioga...........................10 C3
Hotel y Apartotel Alamar..........11 B3

EATING 🍴
La Casona.............................12 D2
La Yunta Steakhouse................13 C3
Palí Supermarket.....................14 E2
Restaurant Kaite Negro............15 C3

DRINKING 🍷
Capitán Moreno's.....................16 C3
El Oasis del
    Pacífico..........................17 D3

TRANSPORT
Buses to Jacó, Quepos & other
    destinations......................18 E3
Buses to San José....................19 E3
Northwestern Dock: Ferries to
    Paquera & Playa Naranjo......20 A3

Sights & Activities

La Casa de la Cultura (☎ 2661 1394; Av Central btwn Calles 3 & 5; ☽ 10am-4pm Mon-Fri) has an art gallery with occasional exhibits as well as a performance space offering seasonal cultural events. Behind the Casa is the **Museo Histórico Marino** (☎ 2661 5036, 2256 4139; admission free; ☽ 8am-1pm & 2-5pm Tue-Sun). The museum describes the history of Puntarenas through audiovisual presentations, old photos and artifacts.

The **Puntarenas Marine Park** (adult/child under 12yr US$7/1.50; ☽ 9am-5pm Tue-Sun) has an aquarium that showcases manta rays and other creatures from the Pacific. The park sits on the site of the old train station and has a tiny splash pool, snack bar, gift shop and information center.

You can stroll along the beach or the aptly named **Paseo de los Turistas** (Tourist's Stroll), a pedestrian boulevard stretching along the southern edge of town. Cruise ships make day visits to the eastern end of this road, and a variety of **souvenir stalls** and *sodas* (lunch counters) are there to greet passengers.

For information on sights around Puntarenas, see p322.

Tours

Coonatramar (☎ 2661 9011, 2661 1069; www.coonatramar .com; cnr Av 3 & Calle 31) can organize tours to the islands in and around Bahía Gigante as well as fishing charters. Prices vary depending on the size of your party and the nature of your trip.

Festivals & Events

Puntarenas is one of the seaside towns that celebrate the **Fiesta de La Virgen del Mar** (Festival of the Virgin of the Sea) on the Saturday closest to July 16. Fishing boats and elegant yachts are beautifully bedecked with lights, flags and all manner of fanciful embellishments as they sail around the harbor, seeking protection from the Virgin as they begin another year at sea. There are also boat races, a carnival, and plenty of food, drink and dancing.

Sleeping

There's no shortage of accommodation in Puntarenas, though like most port cities the world over, finding a secure place that doesn't charge by the hour isn't always an easy proposition. However, we have tried to list places that we would be comfortable bring-

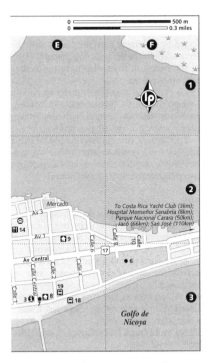

narrowest portion of the peninsula, this somewhat historic yacht club caters to members of both local and foreign yachters as well as the public. Considering that wealthy yachters are fairly discerning when it comes to accommodation, rooms at the club are surprisingly plain. However, Cocal is a vastly different world than Puntarenas, especially since the grounds are home to an attractive maritime-themed restaurant-bar as well as a luxurious pool. If you're traveling in a group, the modern villas can easily accommodate a gaggle of five yachties.

Hotel Tioga (☎ 2661 0271; Paseo de los Turistas btwn Calles 17 & 19; d standard/deluxe/balcony incl breakfast from US$65/85/100; P ⊠ ⊠) Opened in 1959, this is the most established hotel in Puntarenas, and arguably the best place in the city to lie down for the night. Prices vary according to the room, though it's worth spending a few extra dollars for the larger ones, which have sweeping views of the sea. However, you really can't go wrong as all of the rooms feature modern amenities and generally good vibes.

Hotel y Apartotel Alamar (☎ 2661 4343; cnr Paseo de los Turistas & Calle 31; d/tr/q standard US$75/95/115, d/q apt US$125/150; P ⊠ ⊠) If you're looking for a bit more space to stretch your legs, this upmarket hotel (for Puntarenas at least) offers enormous family-style rooms and apartments at surprisingly affordable prices. Rooms are all spotless, with attractive tiled floors and tropical flourishes scattered about, while apartments have fully equipped kitchens with everything you could want to whip up a feast. As family fun is the theme of the Alamar, there are two pools (one for kiddies) where guests congregate.

Eating

The cheapest food is available in the small stands and restaurants near the Palí supermarket. This area is also inhabited by sailors, drunks and prostitutes, but it seems raffish rather than dangerous – during the day, at least. Restaurants along the Paseo de los Turistas are, predictably, filled with *turistas* (tourists).

There's a row of fairly cheap *sodas* on the beach by the Paseo de los Turistas, between Calle Central and Calle 3. They are good for people-watching, and serve snacks and non-alcoholic drinks. You'll also find a collection of Chinese restaurants on Avenida 1 east of the church.

ing our own mother to, so you can sleep easy knowing that there won't be any unwanted midnight visitors.

Hotel Cabezas (☎ 2661 1045; Av 1 btwn Calles 2 & 4; s/d from US$12/22; P) In a city where most hotels charge by the hour, this no-nonsense budget option is an excellent choice. Pastel-painted rooms have functional overhead fans and screened windows, which means you'll sleep deeply without needing air-con. Although you certainly shouldn't leave your valuables strewn about, this hotel is fairly safe and secure.

Gran Hotel Imperial (☎ 2661 0579; Paseo de los Turistas btwn Calles Central & 2; s/d from US$14/24; P) Well situated near the bus stations, this dilapidated and rickety wooden structure still manages to retain a little Old World charm. Cavernous rooms (some with spacious balconies) are cool and clean, and have subtle colonial flourishes, such as wooden furniture and dated paintings to help set the atmosphere. A beer cooler of Imperial (Costa Rica's favorite beer) greets you when you enter.

Costa Rica Yacht Club (☎ 2661 0784; s/d from US$35/45, villa with air-con US$115; P ⊠ ⊠ ⊠) Some 3km east of downtown in Cocal at the

La Casona (cnr Av 1 & Calle 9; casados US$3-6) This bright yellow house is marked with a small, modest sign, but it's an incredibly popular lunch spot, attracting countless locals who jam onto the large deck and into the interior courtyard. Portions are heaped, and soups are served in bathtub-sized bowls – bring your appetite.

Restaurant Kaite Negro (☎ 2661 2093; cnr Av 1 & Calle 17; dishes US$2-9) On the north side of town, this rambling restaurant is popular with locals, and serves good seafood and a good variety of tasty *bocas*. If you really want to see the place swinging, the open-air courtyard comes to life on weekends with live music and all-night dancing.

La Yunta Steakhouse (☎ 2661 3216; Paseo de los Turistas btwn Calles 19 & 21; meals US$6-10) Your culinary mecca for every imaginable cut of meat has professional service, great ocean views and enough hunks of dead animal to arouse your doctor's anger.

Drinking & Entertainment

Entertainment in the port tends to revolve around boozing and flirting, though the occasional cultural offering does happen at La Casa de la Cultura (see p320). If you're looking for the more traditional liquid entertainment, do as the Ticos do and head for the countless bars that line Paseo de los Turistas. A time-honored spot for shaking some booty is **Capitán Moreno's** (Paseo de los Turistas at Calle 13), which has a huge dance floor right on the beach. Another popular spot is **El Oasis del Pacífico** (cnr Paseo de los Turistas & Calle 5), which has a lengthy bar and a warehouse-sized dance floor. Hey – it's not Cancún, but you can definitely have a bit of fun here if you go with the right mindset.

Getting There & Away

BOAT

Car and passenger ferries bound for Paquera and Playa Naranjo depart several times a day from the **northwestern dock** (Av 3 btwn Calles 31 & 33). (Other docks are used for private boats.) If you are driving and will be taking the car ferry, arrive at the dock early to get in line. The vehicle section tends to fill up quickly and you may not make it on. In addition, make sure that you have purchased your ticket from the walk-up ticket window *before* driving onto the ferry. You will not be admitted onto the boat if you don't already have a ticket.

Schedules are completely variable, change seasonally (or even at whim), and can be affected by inclement weather. Check with the ferry office by the dock for any changes. Many of the hotels in town also have up-to-date schedules posted.

To Playa Naranjo (for transfer to Nicoya and points west), **Coonatramar** (☎ 2661 1069; northwestern dock) has several daily departures (passenger/car US$3/10, two hours).

To Paquera (for transfer to Montezuma and Mal País), **Ferry Peninsular** (☎ 2641 0118; northwestern dock) also has several daily departures (passenger/car US$3/10, two hours).

BUS

Buses for San José depart from the large navy-blue building on the north corner of Calle 2 and Paseo de los Turistas. Book your ticket ahead of time on holidays and weekends.

Buses for other destinations leave from across the street, on the beach side of the paseo.

Jacó US$1.50, 1½ hours, 5am, 11am, 2:30pm and 4:30pm.

Liberia US$2, two hours, 4:40am, 5:30am, 7am, 8:30am, 9:30am, 11am, 2:30pm and 3pm.

Nicoya, Santa Cruz & Filadelfia US$2.75, three to five hours, 6am and 3:45pm.

Quepos US$3, 3½ hours, 5am, 11am, 2:30pm and 4:30pm.

San José US$2.50, 2½ hours, every hour from 4am to 9pm.

Santa Elena, Monteverde US$2.50, three to four hours, 1:15pm and 2:15pm.

Getting Around

Buses marked 'Ferry' run up Avenida Central and go to the ferry terminal, 1.5km from downtown. The taxi fare from the San José bus terminal in Puntarenas to the northwestern ferry terminal is about US$2.

Buses for the port of Caldera (also going past Playa Doña Ana and Mata de Limón) leave from the market about every hour and head out of town along Avenida Central.

AROUND PUNTARENAS

The road heading south from Puntarenas skirts along the coastline, and a few kilometers out of town you'll start to see the forested peaks of the Cordillera de Tilaran in the distance. Just as the port city fades into the distance, the water gets cleaner, the air crisper and the vegetation more lush. At this point, you should take a deep breath and heave a sigh of relief – the Pacific coastline gets a whole lot more beautiful as you head further south.

About 8km south of Puntarenas is **Playa San Isidro**, the first 'real' beach on the central Pacific coast. Although this is popular with beachcombers from Puntarenas, surfers prefer to push on 4km south to **Boca Barranca**, which boasts what is reportedly the third-longest left-hand surf break in the world. Conditions here are best at low tide, and it is possible to surf here year-round. However, be advised that there aren't much in the way of services out here, so be sure that you're confident in the water and seek local advice before hitting the break.

Just beyond the river mouth is a pair of beaches known as **Playas Doña Ana & El Segundo**, which are relatively undeveloped and have an isolated and unhurried feel to them. Surfers can find some decent breaks here, too, though like Playa San Isidro, they are more popular for Tico beachcombers on day trips from Puntarenas, especially during weekends in high season. Day-use fees for the beach are US$1.50/0.75 per adult/child and the beach is open 8am to 5pm. There are snack bars, picnic shelters and changing areas, and supervised swimming areas.

The next stop along the coast is **Mata de Limón**, a picturesque little hamlet that is situated on a mangrove lagoon, and locally famous for its birding. If you arrive during low tide, flocks of feathered creatures descend on the lagoon to scrounge for tasty morsels. Mata de Limón is divided by a river, with the lagoon and most facilities on the south side.

The major port on the Pacific coast is **Puerto Caldera**, which you pass soon after leaving Mata de Limón. There aren't any sights here (unless you've ever wondered what a container yard looks like), and the beach is unremarkable unless you're a surfer, in which case there are a few good breaks to be had here (though be careful as the beach is rocky in places).

Buses heading for Caldera Port depart hourly from the market in Puntarenas, and can easily drop you off at any of the spots listed above. If you're driving, the break at Boca Barranca is located near the bridge on the Costanera Sur (South Coastal Highway), while the entrance to Playa Doña Ana and El Segundo is a little further south (look for a sign that says 'Paradero Turístico Doña Ana.') Also, the turnoff for Mata de Limón is located about 5.5km south of Playa Doña Ana.

TURU BA RI TROPICAL PARK & AROUND

The **Turu Ba Ri Tropical Park** (☎ 2250 0705; www .turubari.com; adult/student US$60/55; ⏱ 9am-5pm) is a collection of botanical gardens reflecting each of the topographic zones native to Costa Rica. As you walk along impeccably manicured trails, you'll pass through palm forests, pasture lands, herbariums, cactus fields, bamboo groves, bromeliad gardens, orchid beds and a loma canopy. The gardens are accessed by an aerial cable car, which is included in the price of admission.

If you're an adrenaline junkie, there is also a canopy tour (adult/student US$60/55) that has you swinging through the trees, as well as opportunities for horseback riding and rock climbing. If you're traveling with the little ones, they'll be content for hours either playing in the two hedge mazes or checking out the exhibits in the reptile house.

Although there is no accommodation in the park, there is a wonderfully intimate bed and breakfast in the nearby town of San Pablo de Turrubares, namely **Ama Tierra** (☎ 2419 0110; www.amatierra.com; s/d with breakfast US$127/149; P ⏱ 🖳 🖳). Accommodation is in a handful of warm and wooden *casetas* that are scattered along landscaped trails and manicured gardens, though the highlight is its onsite holistic center, yoga studio and organic restaurant. If you're interested in detoxing the body and clearing the mind, Ama Tierra offers a number of multiday packages that are dedicated to improving your well-being. San Pablo de Turrubares is located approximately 10km east of Orotina on the road to Santiago de Puriscal – once in town, follow signs for the B&B.

The park is easily accessed by buses from Orotina (US$0.50, 30 minutes), which depart at 5:30am, noon and 4:30pm. However, most tourists organize private transportation to the park either from Puntarenas or San José. If you're driving, look for a road to the east, just south of Orotina signed 'Coopebaro, Puriscal.' This road goes over an Indiana Jones–worthy wooden suspension bridge to the park. The park is about 9km beyond the bridge, and half the road is paved.

PARQUE NACIONAL CARARA

Straddling the transition between the dry forests of Costa Rica's northwest and the sodden rain forests of the southern Pacific lowlands,

CENTRAL PACIFIC COAST

GARABITO

The area encompassed by Parque Nacional Carara (see p323) was once home to a legendary indigenous hero, a local *cacique* (chief) named Garabito. Commanding a vast area from the Golfo de Nicoya to the Central Valley, he led a fierce struggle against the Spanish.

A favorite tactic of the Spanish to weaken native resistance was to decapitate tribal leadership – literally. In 1560, the Guatemalan high command dispatched a military force to arrest Garabito. The wily chieftain used the forest to elude capture, but the Spanish managed to seize his wife, Biriteka, as a hostage. Garabito countered by having one of his followers dress up as the chieftain who allowed himself to be captured. While the camp celebrated catching who they thought was Garabito, the real Garabito escaped with his wife.

Garabito's ploy, however, was the exception. The more common fate of captured *caciques* was to star in an imperial morality play. In Act One, the shackled chief sat through a trial at which his numerous transgressions against God and king were expounded. The chief responded to the charges, then was sentenced to death. In Act Two, a public execution was staged, whereby the guilty chief had his eyes and tongue cut out, was shot with a crossbow, was beheaded with an axe, had his severed head displayed on a pike, and finally had his body burned to ashes. The End.

---

this **national park** is a biological melting pot of the two. Acacias intermingle with strangler figs, and cacti with deciduous kapok trees, creating a heterogeneity of habitats with a blend of wildlife to match. The significance of this national park cannot be understated – surrounded by a sea of cultivation and livestock, it is one of the few areas in the transition zone where wildlife finds sanctuary.

Carara is also the famed home to one of Costa Rica's most charismatic bird species, namely the scarlet macaw. While catching a glimpse of this tropical wonder is a rare proposition in most of the country, macaw sightings are virtually guaranteed at Carara. And of course, there are more than 400 other avian species flitting around the canopy, as well as Costa Rica's largest crocodiles in the waterways – best to leave your swim trunks at home!

Orientation

Situated at the mouth of the Río Tárcoles, the 5242-hectare park is only 50km southeast of Puntarenas by road or about 90km west of San José via the Orotina highway. The dry season from December to April is the easiest time to go, though the animals are still there in the wet months. March and April are the driest months. Rainfall is almost 3000mm annually, which is less than in the rain forests further south. It's fairly hot, with average temperatures of 25°C/77°F to 28°C/82°F – but it's cooler within the rain forest. An umbrella is important in the wet season and occasionally needed in the dry

months. Make sure you have insect repellent. According to the park rangers, the best chance of spotting wildlife is at 7am when the park opens.

Dangers & Annoyances

Increased tourist traffic along the Pacific coast has unfortunately resulted in an increase in petty theft. Vehicles parked at the trailheads are routinely broken into, and although there may be guards on duty, it is advised that drivers leave their cars in the lot at the Carara ranger station and walk along the Costanera Sur for 2km north or 1km south. Also, be sure to travel in a group and don't carry unnecessary valuables as muggings are reported here occasionally. Alternatively, park beside the Restaurante Ecológico Los Cocodrilos (see opposite).

Sights

With the help of a hired guide, it's possible to visit the archaeological remains of various indigenous **burial sites** located within the park, though they're tiny and unexciting compared to anything you might see in Mexico or Guatemala. At the time of the Europeans' arrival in Costa Rica, these sites were located in an area inhabited by an indigenous group known as the Huetar (Carara actually means 'crocodile' in the Huetar language). Unfortunately, not much is known about this group, as little cultural evidence was left behind. Today, the few remaining Huetar are confined to several small villages in the Central Valley. For more on the area's indigenous history, see boxed text Garabito, opposite.

If you're driving from Puntarenas or San José, pull over to the left immediately after crossing the Río Tárcoles bridge, also known as **Crocodile Bridge**. If you scan the sandbanks below the bridge, you'll have a fairly good chance of seeing as many as 30 basking crocodiles. Although they're visible year-round, the best time for viewing is low tide during the dry season. Binoculars help a great deal.

Crocodiles this large are generally rare in Costa Rica as they've been hunted vigorously for their leather. However, the crocs are tolerated here as they feature prominently in a number of wildlife tours that depart from Tárcoles. And of course, the crocs don't mind as they're hand-fed virtually every day. Please people, we're asking you nicely – don't feed the animals.

Activities

WILDLIFE-WATCHING

The most exciting bird for many visitors to see, especially in June or July, is the brilliantly patterned scarlet macaw, a rare bird that is common to Parque Nacional Carara. Their distinctive call echoes loudly through the canopy, usually moments before a pair of these soaring birds appears against the blue sky. If you're having problems spotting them, it may help to inquire at the ranger's station, which keeps tabs on where nesting pairs are located.

Dominated by open secondary forest punctuated by patches of dense, mature forest and wetlands, Carara offers some superb birding. Over 400 different species of birds inhabit the reserve, though your chances of spotting rarer species will be greatly enhanced with the help of an experienced guide. Some commonly sighted species include orange-billed sparrow, five kinds of trogons, crimson-fronted parakeet, blue-headed parrot, golden-naped woodpecker, rose-throated becard, gray-headed tanager, long-tailed manikins and rufous-tailed jacamar (just to name a few!).

Birds aside, the trails at Carara are home to several mammal species, including red brocket, white-tailed deer, collared peccary, monkey, sloth and agouti. The national park is also home to one of Costa Rica's largest populations of tayra, a weasel-like animal that scurries along the forest floor. And, although most travelers aren't too keen on stumbling

upon an American crocodile, some truly monstrous specimens can be viewed from a safe distance at the nearby Crocodile Bridge (see left).

HIKING

Some 600m south of the Crocodile Bridge on the left-hand side is a locked gate leading to the **Sendero Laguna Meándrica** trail. This trail penetrates deep into the reserve and passes through open, secondary forest and patches of dense, mature forest and wetlands. About 4km from the entrance is Laguna Meándrica, which has large populations of heron, smoothbill and kingfisher. If you continue past the lagoon, you'll have a good chance of spotting mammals and the occasional crocodile, though you will have to turn back to exit.

Another 2km south of the trailhead is the **Carara ranger station** (admission US$8; ☉ 7am-4pm), where you can get information and enter the park. There are bathrooms, picnic tables and a short nature trail. Guides can be hired for US$15 per person (two minimum) for a two-hour hike. About 1km further south are two loop trails. The first, **Sendero Las Araceas**, is 1.2km long and can be combined with the second, **Sendero Quebrada Bonita** (another 1.5km). Both trails pass through primary forest, which is characteristic of most of the park.

Sleeping & Eating

Camping is not allowed, and there's nowhere to stay in the park. As a result, most people come on day trips from neighboring towns and cities such as Jacó (p328).

Restaurante Ecológico Los Cocodrilos (☎ 2428 9009; d from US$24) Located on the north side of the Río Tárcoles bridge, this is the nearest place to stay and eat. Rooms are unexciting, though it's a cheap and convenient base for getting to the park before the tour buses arrive. Its restaurant has meals for US$4 to US$6, and is extremely popular with travelers stopping to check out the crocodiles. It is open from 6am to 8pm. If you're nervous about leaving your car at the trailhead, there is secure parking here in a guarded lot.

Getting There & Away

There are no buses to Carara, but any bus between Puntarenas and Jacó can leave you at the entrance. You can also catch buses headed north or south in front of the Restaurante

SUPERHIGHWAY TO THE COAST

Regardless of which side of the development-conservation debate you gravitate toward, both sides can agree that the story of a sleepy little town being turned into a booming international city is something of a cliché here in Costa Rica. Indeed, places like Jacó and Tamarindo were little more than beach villages a decade ago, though today they're international destinations that are slowly being transformed by waves upon waves of foreign investment.

Although the question regarding where and when the next great destination will spring up is a popular one in Costa Rica, it's a good bet that it might be the relatively unknown coastal town of Orotina. Of course, if a town lies near the terminus of a proposed superhighway linking San José to the central Pacific coast, it doesn't take a professional gambler or a math whiz to tell you that the odds are in your favor.

As of early 2008, the Costa Rican government was well underway in its plans to construct a new superhighway between San José and the Caldera Port. When the much-anticipated road is finished in 2011 (or possibly before), Orotina will be a mere 45-minute drive from the capital (it's currently two hours' drive sans traffic).

The town will also emerge as the major gateway to destinations further south along the coast, such as Jacó, Dominical and Quepos. And, considering that Orotina is already linked to the Interamerican Hwy, which grants easy access to the Nicoya peninsula, the superhighway to the coast will be the final spoke in the transport link between the capital of San José and Guanacaste.

And, if you're still not convinced that change is on the horizon, all you need to do is look at the numbers. Ten years ago, a square meter of land in Orotina cost US$60, though the going rate as of early 2008 was well over US$500. Of course, the land is being sold off in bulk and snatched up for a lot less than this amid reports that large Korean, Chinese and Israeli developers are unfurling plans to create vast office parks and commercial centers.

Even tax officials in Orotina are batting their eyes in confusion. According to figures printed in the *Tico Times* newspaper, property tax revenues have been soaring through the roof. A few years back, annual property tax revenues in Orotina were no more than US$30,000, though the canton collected a whopping US$134,800 in 2007. In fact, much of this money was the result of the 1.5% transfer tax that must be paid every time property is bought and sold.

Of course, all of this brings about the one simple question that fails to get asked so often in Costa Rica: is Orotina ready for change? Depending on who you ask, be it aspiring realtors and businesspeople or farmers and small-business owners, you will get drastically different answers. However, one thing is for certain: infrastructure in terms of water, electricity and sewage is still years behind the intended development boom.

Fortunately, the municipality in Orotina is aware of these hurdles, and has announced on several occasions that it is working hard to devise a zoning plan that addresses all of these fundamental concerns. With that said, there are a fair share of skeptics about that are beginning to wonder whether the cliché of a sleepy little town being turned into a booming international city mirrors reality just a little too often.

Ecológico Los Cocodrilos. This may be a bit problematic on weekends, when buses are full, so go midweek if you are relying on a bus ride. If you're driving, the entrance to Carara is right on the Costanera and is clearly marked.

TÁRCOLES & AROUND

The small, unassuming town of Tárcoles is little more than a few rows of houses strung along a series of dirt roads that parallel the ocean. As you'd imagine, this tiny Tico town isn't exactly a huge tourist draw, though the surrounding area is perfect for fans of the superlative, especially if you're interested in seeing the country's tallest waterfall and its largest crocodiles. Here, intrepid hikers can penetrate virgin forest in search of remote swimming holes and ample wildlife, while aspiring crocodile hunters can get an up-close and personal view of these exquisite predators. Seek local advice to ensure the water is crocodile free before you take a dip.

Orientation

About 2km south of the Carara ranger station is the Tárcoles turnoff to the right (west) and the Hotel Villa Lapas turnoff to the left. To get to Tárcoles, turn right and drive for 1km, then go right at the T-junction to the village.

Sights & Activities

A 5km dirt road past Hotel Villa Lapas leads to the primary entrance to the **Catarata Manantial de Agua Viva** (☎ 8831 2980; admission US$10; ☼ 8am-3pm), which is a 200m-high waterfall and claims to be the highest in the country. From here, it's a steep 3km climb down into the valley, though there are plenty of benches and viewpoints where you can rest. Be sure to keep an eye out for the beautiful, but deadly, poison-dart frog as well as the occasional scarlet macaw. The falls are more dramatic in the rainy season when they're fuller, though the serene rain-forest setting is beautiful any time of year. At the bottom of the valley, the river continues through a series of natural swimming holes where you can take a dip and cool off. A camping area and outhouse are located at the bottom. Local buses between Orotina and Bijagual can drop you off at the entrance to the park.

Although the man at the top of the waterfall might tell you that he operates the only entrance to Manatial de Agua Viva, you can also access the trails by heading 2km further up the road to the 70-hectare **Jardín Pura Vida** (☎ 2637 0346; admission US$15; ☼ 8am-5pm) in the town of Bijagual. Although it costs a few more dollars here to enter the waterfall, the admission price also includes access to a private botanical garden that is impeccably manicured, and offers great vistas of Manatial de Agua Viva cascading down the side of a cliff. There is a small restaurant on the grounds, and you can also arrange horse riding and tours through the area.

Before leaving Jardín Pura Vida, be sure to stop by the small kiosk near the parking lot to say hi to Lauri and Howard, a charming American–South African couple who roast small batches of Tarrazu coffee under the brand name **Costa Rica Coffee Roasting Company**. Lauri and Howard will delight in explaining the intricacies of the coffee-roasting process, and they certainly know how to make a powerful brew. Lauri and Howard live in Jacó, and are the owners of a delightful guesthouse called Sonidos del Mar (p336).

Tours

If you want to get the adrenaline pumping, check out a crocodile tour on the mudflats of the Río Tárcoles. Bilingual guides in boats will take you out in the river for croc spotting and some hair-raising croc tricks. And you know it's going to be good when the guide gets *out* of the boat and *into* the water with these massive beasts – it's *Crocodile Hunter* without the Australian accent. Both **Crocodile Man** (☎ 2637 0426; crocodileman@hotmail.com) and **Jungle Crocodile Safari** (☎ 2637 0338; www.junglecrocodilesafari .com) have offices in Tárcoles. The tours leave from town or you can arrange for them to pick you up at your hotel.

Unfortunately, although the tours are definitely a spectacle to behold, it's frustrating to watch the crocodiles being hand-fed by the tour guides. Furthermore, several travelers report that these tours may not be worth it if you've already been to Tortuguero (p458). Tours usually cost US$25 per person for two hours.

Sleeping & Eating

Accommodation in the Tárcoles area is limited to the pricey Hotel Villa Lapas. However, if you don't have the cash (or the interest) to stay at this all-inclusive resort, there is a good variety of hotels and hostels in nearby Jacó (p333).

Hotel Villa Lapas (☎ 2221 5191; www.villalapas.com; all-inclusive from US$200; P ⊠ ⊠) Located on a private reserve comprised both of secondary rain forest and expansive tropical gardens, this all-inclusive resort is a classy retreat for anyone who wants their ecofun served up in a fruity cocktail with an umbrella on top. With a modest number of rooms housed in an attractive Spanish colonial–style lodge, guests can unwind in relative comfort in between guided hikes, birding trips, canopy tours and the obligatory soak in the infinity pool. If this kind of luxury is your cup of shade-grown coffee, then check out the website as discounted packages are available if you book in advance.

Getting There & Away

There are no buses to Tárcoles, but any bus between Puntarenas and Jacó can leave you at the entrance. If you're driving, the entrance to the town is right on the Costanera and is clearly marked. If you're staying at Hotel Villa Lapas, then it's possible to arrange a

CENTRAL PACIFIC COAST

BIG SPLURGE: HOTEL VILLA CALETAS

Located on the tiny headland of Punta Leona about halfway between Tárcoles and Jacó on the Costanera, the **Hotel Villa Caletas** (☎ 2637 0505; www.hotelvillacaletas.com; r US$165-425; P ⊠ ☎) is one of only eight hotels in all of Costa Rica belonging to the 'Small Distinctive Hotels of Costa Rica Group' – from the moment you enter the property you'll understand why.

Since it's perched high on a dramatic hillside, you'll first have to navigate a 1km-long serpentine driveway adorned with cacti and Victorian lanterns. The drive will be worth it as upon entering the property, you'll be rewarded with panoramic views of the Pacific coastline. But, what makes the hotel truly unique is its fusion of architectural styles, incorporating elements as varied as tropical Victorian, Hellenistic and French colonial. Unlike most luxury hotels, Villa Caletas is solely comprised of 35 units, each sheltered in a tropical garden and dense foliage that gives the appearance of total isolation. The interiors of the rooms are individually decorated with art and antiques, but nothing is nearly as magnificent as the views you'll have from your room. There is also a French-influenced restaurant, an inviting infinity pool and a private 1km trail leading to the beach.

Even if you're not staying at the hotel, it's worth stopping by to have a drink at the amphitheatre, which is built according to Grecian specifications and is carved into the hillside facing the ocean. For a few dollars, you will be rewarded with what may be the best Pacific sunset you've ever seen.

---

pick-up from either San José or Jacó with an advance reservation.

PLAYA HERRADURA

Until the mid-1990s, Playa Herradura was a rural, palm-sheltered beach of grayish-black sand that was popular mainly with campers. In the late 1990s, however, the beach was thrown into the spotlight when it was used as the stage for the movie *1492*. As with all things 'discovered,' rapid development ensued, and soon Playa Herradura had a marina, several condominium complexes and one of the most expensive hotels in the country, namely the Los Sueños Marriott Beach & Golf Resort. Today, the beach is starting to look like one giant construction site, and few people aside from local Ticos and rich North American investors are keen on spending much time here.

The **Los Sueños Marriott Beach & Golf Resort** (☎ 2630 9000; www.lossuenosresort.com; r from US$250; P ⊠ ▯ ☎) is a US$40 million hotel, marina and condo project that has completely transformed this once-secluded bay into Costa Rica's most exclusive destination for the rich and powerful. The centerpiece of the project is a 250-berth yacht marina that unfolds onto a lush golf course, upscale shopping center, resort hotel and multimillion-dollar residential development.

The entire Spanish colonial complex is the epitome of unchecked luxury and hedonism,

though many concerned conservationists are quick to use Los Sueños as an example of a future where economic interests crush environmental aims. With that said, the experience of staying here is something along the lines of a night in Dubai – it certainly lacks any amount of Costa Rican authenticity.

The Herradura turnoff is on the Costanera Sur, 3.5km north of the turnoff to Jacó. From here, a paved road leads 3km west to Playa Herradura. There are frequent local buses (US$0.75, 20 minutes) connecting Playa Herradura to Jacó.

JACÓ

Few places in Costa Rica generate as broad a range of opinions and emotions as the beach town of Jacó. In one camp, you have the loyal surfing contingent, resident North American expats and international developers who bill Jacó as the ultimate central Pacific destination, and one of the country's most rapidly developing cities. Truth be told, the surfing is excellent, the restaurants and bars are cosmopolitan, and a skyline of future high-rise apartments and luxury hotels is rapidly being constructed.

However, there is also another camp of dissatisfied tourists, concerned environmentalists and marginalized Ticos who would urge you to steer clear of Jacó, and make an effort to spread the word to others. Again, truth be told, there is a burgeoning drug and prostitution problem, questions of sustainability and the fear that Ticos will be priced out of their homes.

Like all cases concerning the delicate balance between conservation and development, Jacó is steeped in its fair share of controversy. However, it's probably best to ignore the hype and the stereotypes alike, and make your own decisions about the place. Although the American-style cityscape of shopping malls and gated communities may be off-putting to some, it's impossible to deny the beauty of the beach and the surrounding hillsides, and the consistent surf that first put the beach on the map is still as good as it ever was.

History

Jacó has a special place in the hearts of Ticos as it is the quickest ocean-side escape for landlocked denizens of the Central Valley. Many josefinos recall fondly the days when weekend shuttle buses would pick up beach-seekers in the city center and whisk them away to the undeveloped Pacific paradise of Jacó. With warm water, year-round consistent surf, world-class fishing and a relaxed, beachside setting, it was hard to believe that a place this magical was only a short bus ride away from San José.

The secret got out in the early 1990s when Canadians on package tours started flooding Jacó, though for the most part tourism remained pretty low-key. Things picked up a bit in the late 1990s when surfers and anglers from North America and Europe started visiting Costa Rica en masse, though Jacó remained the dominion of Central Valley Ticos looking for a little fun and sun. However, things changed dramatically as soon as retiring Baby Boomers in search of cheap property began to colonize this once tiny Costa Rican beach town.

In only a few years time, Jacó became the most rapidly developing town (some would argue city) in all of Costa Rica. Plots of land were subdivided, beachfronts were cleared, hillsides were leveled and almost overnight Jacó became the exclusive enclave of moneyed expats. Ticos were happy that development brought coveted Western institutions like paved roads and fast-food restaurants, but as the initial flash of cash and glitz started to fade, some began to wonder if they had inadvertently sold the door mat beneath their feet.

Truth be told, it's hard to know where the future of Jacó lies. Optimists point out that the town is simply experiencing growing pains, and argue that the drugs and prostitution will subside just as soon as the infrastructure stabilizes and the town residents begin to clamp down on illicit vices. However, pessimists are quick to retort that wealth attracts opportunism, especially of the illicit kind, and that the problems in Jacó are just getting started. Regardless of which camp you fall into, one thing is for certain, all of Costa Rica is casting a watchful eye on Jacó, and will ultimately point to the city as an example of either unchecked development gone awry, or a success story of wealth creation.

Orientation

Playa Jacó is about 2km off the Costanera, 3.5km past the turnoff for Herradura. The beach itself is about 3km long, and hotels and restaurants line the road running behind it. The areas on the northern and southern fringes are the most tranquil and attractive, and are the cleanest.

In an effort to make foreign visitors feel more at home, the town has placed signs with street names on most streets. These names are shown on the map, but the locals continue to use the traditional landmark system (see boxed text What's That Address?, p537).

Information

Jacó is relatively expensive, and during the high season it's jam-packed with tourists, so reservations are recommended, especially around the winter holidays.

There's no unbiased tourist information office, though several tour offices will give information. Look for the free monthly *Jacó's Guide*, which includes tide charts and up-to-date maps, or go to www.jacoguide.com. The free monthly magazine *Central Pacific Way* has information on tourist attractions up and down the coastline.

Banco de San José (Map p332; Av Pastor Díaz, north of Calle Cocal; ⏰ 8am-5pm Mon-Fri, 8am-noon Sat) Has a Cirrus ATM open during bank hours on the 2nd floor of the Il Galeone shopping center.

Banco Popular (Map p332; Av Pastor Díaz at Calle La Central) Exchanges US dollars and traveler's checks.

Books & Stuff (Map p332; Av Pastor Díaz btwn Calles Las Olas & Bohío) Has books in several languages as well as US newspapers.

Mexican Joe's (Map p332; Av Pastor Díaz btwn Calles Las Olas & Bohío; per hr US$0.75; ⏰ 9am-9pm Mon-Sat,

10am-8pm Sun) The best place to check email; has multiple computers with high-speed connections and air-con.

Red Cross (Map p332; ☎ 2643 3090; Av Pastor Díaz btwn Calles Hicaco & Las Brisas) Medical clinic.

Dangers & Annoyances

Aside from occasional petty crime such as pick-pocketing and breaking into locked cars, Jacó is certainly not a dangerous place by any stretch of the imagination. However, the high concentration of wealthy foreigners and comparatively poor Ticos has resulted in a thriving sex and drug industry. It is almost guaranteed that at some point during your stay in Jacó, you will be approached by a dealer and/or a pimp, whether you're looking for it or not.

We're not your mother, and it's entirely up to you how you want to spend your time in Costa Rica. Assuming the working girl is over 18 (which is not always a given), prostitution is 100% legal in Costa Rica. However, before you start flashing the Benjamins and expecting to score, you might want to check out the boxed text, opposite. In regards to drugs, you also might want to familiarize yourself with

the law, and the repercussions of breaking it (see Got Drugs, will Travel, p334), before puffing away at a seemingly innocent joint.

Activities
SWIMMING

Jacó is generally safe for swimming, though you should avoid the areas near the estuaries, which are polluted. Be advised that the waves can get crowded with beginner surfers who don't always know how to control their boards, so be smart and stay out of their way. Riptides do occasionally occur (see boxed text, p278), especially when the surf gets big, so enquire about local conditions and keep an eye out for red flags marking the paths of rips.

SURFING

Although the rainy season is considered best for Pacific coast surfing, Jacó is blessed with consistent year-round breaks. Although more advanced surfers head further south to Playa Hermosa, the waves at Jacó are strong, steady and a lot of fun. Jacó is also a great place to start a surf trip as it's easy to buy and sell boards here. If you're looking to rent a board

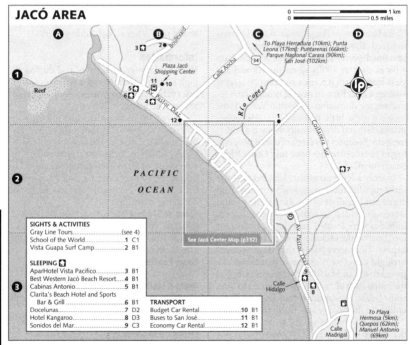

JACÓ AREA

0 —————— 1 km
0 —————— 0.5 miles

To Playa Herradura (10km); Punta
Leona (17km); Puntarenas (66km);
Parque Nacional Carara (90km);
San José (102km)

Reef

Plaza Jacó
Shopping Center

PACIFIC

OCEAN

See Jacó Center Map (p332)

Calle
Hidalgo

To Playa
Hermosa (5km);
Quepos (62km);
Manuel Antonio
(69km)

Calle
Madrigal

SIGHTS & ACTIVITIES	
Gray Line Tours	(see 4)
School of the World	1 C1
Vista Guapa Surf Camp	2 B1

SLEEPING	
AparHotel Vista Pacifico	3 B1
Best Western Jacó Beach Resort	4 B1
Cabinas Antonio	5 B1
Clarita's Beach Hotel and Sports Bar & Grill	6 B1
Docelunas	7 D2
Hotel Kangaroo	8 D3
Sonidos del Mar	9 C3

TRANSPORT	
Budget Car Rental	10 B1
Buses to San José	11 B1
Economy Car Rental	12 B1

GIRLS GONE WILD

Jacó is rife with stories of girls gone wild, but none are as scandalous as those surrounding *Las Dormilonas* or the Sleepyheads, three prostitutes whose exploits where splashed across the tabloids in early 2008. According to law enforcement officials who broke the case, the three women normally charged US$200 per 'session,' though decided to lure three men at once by offering a discount price of only US$500.

Here is where things get interesting: instead of actually performing the dirty deed, the women instead drugged the men with massive quantities of benzodiazepine (commonly known as Valium), and then robbed them blind while they were sleeping. All told, the three women had racked up nearly US$80,000 from only 15 victims (mostly rich gringos) prior to being arrested.

Although it's hard not to be impressed by their highly lucrative scam, their arrest is no laughing matter as it highlights Jacó's worsening image problem, as well as the naiveté of some of the city's resident expats and sex tourists. Interestingly, some of the suspected women were engaged, perhaps they were just making a bit of extra cash to put toward their big day!

---

for the day, shop around as the better places will rent you a board for US$15 to US$20 for 24 hours, while others will try to charge you a few dollars per hour.

There are too many surf shops to list, and it seems like every store in town does ding repair and rents long boards. Six-time national surf champion Alvaro Solano runs the highly respected **Vista Guapa Surf Camp** (Map p330; ☎ 2643 2830, in the USA 409-599 1828; www.vistaguapa.com), which comes recommended by readers. Weekly rates including full board start at around US$800.

SURFCASTING
Several shops in town rent fishing gear and sell bait for a few dollars each, and there are plenty of spots along the beach where you can crack a beer and try your luck. Surfcasting is extremely popular with locals, so dust off your Spanish vocab and strike up a conversation or two.

HIKING
A popular local pastime is following the trail up Miros Mountain, which winds through primary and secondary rain forest, and offers spectacular views of Jacó and Playa Hermosa. The trail actually leads as far as the Central Valley, though you only need to hike for a few kilometers to reach the viewpoint. Note that the trailhead is unmarked, so ask a local to point it out to you.

HORSE RIDING
Readers have reported incidents of horse abuse in Jacó, specifically operators using malnourished and mistreated animals. However, one recommended company is **Discovery Horseback**

Tours (☎ 8838 7550; www.horseridecostarica.com; from $60), which is run by an English couple, and offers an extremely high level of service and professionalism.

KAYAKING
If you're interested in organizing kayaking and sea canoeing trips that include snorkeling excursions to tropical islands, contact **Kayak Jacó Costa Rica Outriggers** (☎ 2643 1233; www.kayakjaco.com), which offers a wide variety of customized day and multiday trips.

CANOPY TOURS
In Jacó there are two competing companies offering similar products: **Canopy Adventure Jacó** (☎ 2643 3271; www.adventurecanopy.com; tours US$55) and **Waterfalls Canopy Tour** (☎ 2632 3322; www.waterfallscanopy.com; tours US$55).

SPAS
A branch of the exceedingly professional **Serenity Spa** (Map p332; ☎ 2643 1624; Av Pastor Díaz, east of Calle Bohio) offers the full range of spa services.

Courses
City-Playa Language Institute (Map p332; ☎ 2643 2123; www.spanishschool-costarica.com; Av Pastor Díaz btwn Calle Las Palmeras & Calle Las Olas) offers inexpensive courses in Spanish for as little as US$80 per week.

School of the World (Map p330; ☎ 2643 1064; www.schooloftheworld.org; 1-4 week packages US$645-2045; P ☑) is a popular school and cultural-studies center offering classes in Spanish, surfing, art and photography. The sweet new building also houses a café and art gallery. Rates include kayaking and hiking field trips and

CENTRAL PACIFIC COAST

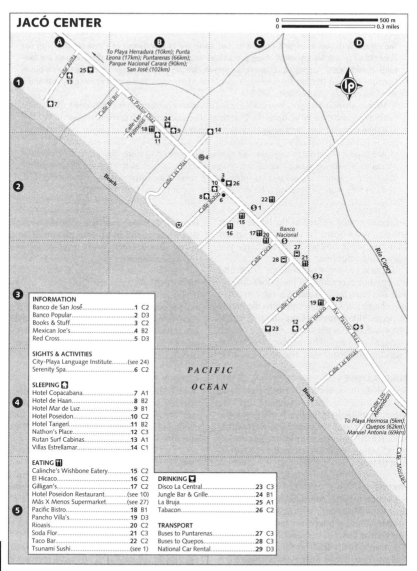

JACÓ CENTER

0 _____ 500 m
0 _____ 0.3 miles

To Playa Herradura (10km); Punta
Leona (17km); Puntarenas (66km);
Parque Nacional Carara (90km);
San José (102km)

Beach

PACIFIC
OCEAN

Banco
Nacional

Río Copey

To Playa Hermosa (5km);
Quepos (62km);
Manuel Antonia (69km)

INFORMATION
Banco de San José.................................**1** C2
Banco Popular.......................................**2** D3
Books & Stuff.......................................**3** C2
Mexican Joe's.......................................**4** B2
Red Cross...**5** D3

SIGHTS & ACTIVITIES
City-Playa Language Institute........(see 24)
Serenity Spa...**6** C2

SLEEPING
Hotel Copacabana................................**7** A1
Hotel de Haan.....................................**8** B2
Hotel Mar de Luz................................**9** B1
Hotel Poseidon..................................**10** C2
Hotel Tangerí.....................................**11** B2
Nathon's Place...................................**12** C3
Rutan Surf Cabinas.............................**13** A1
Villas Estrellamar...............................**14** C1

EATING
Calinche's Wishbone Eatery...............**15** C2
El Hicaco..**16** C2
Gilligan's...**17** C2
Hotel Poseidon Restaurant.............(see 10)
Más X Menos Supermarket............(see 27)
Pacific Bistro......................................**18** B1
Pancho Villa's....................................**19** D3
Rioasis..**20** C2
Soda Flor...**21** C3
Taco Bar..**22** C2
Tsunami Sushi................................(see 1)

DRINKING
Disco La Central..................................**23** C3
Jungle Bar & Grille.............................**24** B1
La Bruja...**25** A1
Tabacon...**26** C2

TRANSPORT
Buses to Puntarenas............................**27** C3
Buses to Quepos.................................**28** C3
National Car Rental.............................**29** D3

onsite lodging. Spanish and surfing are the
most popular programs.

Tours

Tours around the area include visits to Parque
Nacional Carara (from US$45) as well as
longer-distance trips around the country.
Another popular destination is Isla Damas –

you can organize tours here or in Quepos,
further south. Isla Damas is not 100% an island, but the tip of a pointed mangrove forest
that juts out into a small bay just south of
Parrita. During high tide, as the surrounding
areas fill with water, this point becomes an
island – offering an incredible opportunity for
birders and other wildlife watchers. Boating

tours can be arranged from Jacó for around US$65 per person, but more avid adventurers can opt for a sea-kayaking expedition with Amigo Tico Complete Adventure Tours in Quepos (p343).

Virtually every shop, hotel and restaurant in town books tours, as Jacó operates on a lucrative commission-based system. As you'd imagine, it's hard to actually know who is greasing whose palms and who is actually running tours, though usually it all works out – assuming you use your judgment and book from places that look reliable. Needless to say, you shouldn't book anything from touts on streets, and if an offer from a vendor seems too good to be true, then most likely it is.

One long-standing agent that receives good reviews from readers is **Gray Line Tours** (Map p330; ☎ 2220 2126; www.graylinecostarica.com; Best Western, Av Pastor Díaz), which books tours throughout the country as well as private inter-city transportation.

Sleeping

The center of town, with its many bars and discos, can mean that noise will be a factor in where you choose to stay. The far northern and southern ends of town have more relaxed and quiet accommodations. Reservations are highly recommended on weekends in the dry-season and become critical during Easter and the week between Christmas and New Year's Eve.

The rates given are high-season rates, but low-season rates could be as much as 30% to 40% lower. If you plan on a lengthy stay (more than five days), ask about long-term rates. Hotels below are listed from north to south.

BUDGET
There is no shortage of cheap budget hotels scattered around the Jacó area, though we constantly receive reports from travelers of theft from accommodations in Costa Rica. With that said, sometimes it's worth spending a few extra dollars for the safety and peace of mind that comes with having a secure room. In keeping with this theme, we list places that meet our high standards; however, you should always be vigilant about locking up your valuables (even at top-end places), and never give anyone a reason to wonder what you're keeping inside your room.

Rutan Surf Cabinas (Map p332; ☎ 2643 3328; www.cabinasrutan.com; Calle Anita; dm & r per person US$11-

15; P ⛌ ⛆) Formerly known as Chuck's Cabinas, this location has proudly served the international surf community for years. Now under Californian ownership, and sporting a new name and a fresh look and feel, Rutan Surf Cabinas is the best-valued accommodation in town. Don't let the rock-bottom prices fool you – dorms and rooms of varying sizes and shapes feature tile floors, solid mattresses and plenty of decorative flourishes, though the same vibes that first put this place on the map are still in heavy supply.

Cabinas Antonio (Map p330; ☎ 2643 3043; cnr Av Pastor Díaz & Boulevard; r from US$15; P ⛆) Something of an institution among shoestringers and local Tico families, this clutch of cabins at the northern end of Jacó is one of the best deals in town. Fairly uninteresting rooms are certainly nothing to write home about, but they are clean and cozy, and come with private cold showers and cable TV. And of course, when you're just steps from the surf, it's hard to be too fussy about your surroundings.

Nathon's Place (Map p332; ☎ 8355 4359; www.nathonshostel.com; Calle Hicaco; dm/d/tr US$10/25/30; P ⛌ ⛆) The cheapest proper hostel in town, this surfer shack radiates good vibes thanks to the charismatic owner and manager, self-proclaimed 'Texas guitar-legend Nathon Dees.' In keeping with the good-times theme, Nathon dishes out plenty of surf advice alongside killer tunes. The building is fairly basic, but it's hard not to have a good time here when you're surrounded by like-minded travelers.

MIDRANGE
Jacó is chock-a-block with midrange hotels, and our brief list is by no means comprehensive. However, we have tried to select places that have a certain je ne sais quoi, while still offering safety, security and comfortable surroundings to slightly more discerning travelers.

Clarita's Beach Hotel and Sports Bar & Grill (Map p330; ☎ 2643 3327; www.claritashotel.com; western end of Boulevard; r US$25-65; P ⛌ ⛆) Straddling the border between budget and midrange accommodation, Clarita's attracts a broad range of guests with varying wallet sizes, though everyone can quickly agree that the beachfront location is difficult to top. Basic rooms with cutesy flourishes are a bargain at US$25, especially if you can sleep easy with just a fan at night, while more expensive rooms come with 'luxuries,' such as hot-water shower, cable TV

GOT DRUGS, WILL TRAVEL

Drugs are plentiful in Costa Rica, and a good number of tourists would never give a second thought to lighting up a joint on the beach (or, more recently, blowing a line of coke in a discotheque). However, drugs are 100% illegal in Costa Rica, and if you are charged with possession you can be fined and imprisoned depending on the severity of the offense. There are currently foreigners serving out terms, and occasionally a big drug bust will make the headlines. The bad news is that there is little that your embassy can do on your behalf. The good news is that as far as Latin American penal systems are concerned, there are places a hell of a lot worse than a Costa Rican prison.

The reality is that most police officers would rather collect a bribe or confiscate a joint and smoke it themselves than send a bunch of backpackers to jail. Unlike other destinations on the hippie trail, like Morocco, Thailand and India, Costa Rica has a squeaky-clean, ecofriendly image that it needs to uphold, and the last thing the tourist board wants is the mugs of a bunch of American teenagers plastered on the front page of *USA Today*. However, things are changing rapidly, and as more gringos start packing their bags and heading to Costa Rica, you can expect that the supply will meet the demand.

The main problem with the market in Costa Rica right now is that a greater number of hard drugs are becoming readily available for purchase. On beaches with a growing international scene like Jacó and Tamarindo, it's possible to buy just about any drug on any street corner in any language. The drug of choice in the bars is quickly becoming cocaine, and although there's no guarantee you're actually getting ecstasy, backpackers are popping pills in the clubs like they were Tic-Tacs.

Ticos will tell you that the Colombians, Jamaicans, Panamanians and just about every other nationality are to blame for importing drugs into their country, but the truth is that they share an equal amount of blame. An eight-ball of cocaine yields a much larger profit than a wood-carving of a tree frog, and most backpackers are happy to pay in US dollars for a dime-bag of dubious quality.

The moral of the story is that at some point during your travels in Costa Rica, there is a good chance that you will be offered drugs. And there's a good chance that if you're reading this right now, you might say yes. So, remember to use your judgment, consider the consequences and don't say that we didn't warn you.

and air-con. The attached sports bar and grill is a fun and friendly open-air joint that serves up your typical beer and nachos fare.

Hotel Kangaroo (Map p330; ☎ 2643 3351; www.hotel -kangaroo.com; dm US$12, d with/without air-con US$45/35; P ⊠ 🖳 🕿) This much-loved hostel, which is located just 100m from one of the quietest and most beautiful strips of sand, is seriously chilled out thanks to the pair of French surfers who run the place. Vibrant rooms here are draped in Nepali prayer flags and adorned with huge dream catchers, and come with either fan or air-con depending on your budget. Extra amenities include free breakfast, 24-hour free internet, a shared kitchen and a refreshing pool (check out the awesome mural!). If you're arriving by bus, the owners will pay for a taxi from the center of town.

Hotel de Haan (Map p332; ☎ 2643 1795; www.hotel dehaan.com; Calle Bohío; dm/d/tr US$12/35/45; P 🖳 🕿) This Dutch/Tico outpost is one of the top budget bets in town, and is perennially popular with backpackers from around the world. Freshly tiled rooms with steamy hot-water showers are clean and secure, and there's a shared kitchen with fridge, a pool and free internet around the clock. The highlight of the property, however, is the upstairs balcony where you can congregate with fellow backpackers, and swap travel stories over a few cans of Imperial until the wee hours of the morning.

AparHotel Vista Pacifico (Map p330; ☎ 2643 3261; www.vistapacifico.com; top of the hill off Boulevard; d incl breakfast from US$55, additional person US$10; P ⊠ 🕿) Located on the crest of a hill just outside Jacó, this Canadian-run hotel is an absolute gem that is worth seeking out. The views of the coastline from here are phenomenal, particularly at sunset when you'll have panoramic vistas of a fiery sky, and the mountain-top location also means that it's a few degrees cooler (and a whole lot quieter) than neigh-boring Jacó. Homey rooms of varying sizes and shapes cater to all budgets, and are made all the better by the warm and caring hosts – there is even a BBQ pit where you can grill up some killer eats while chatting up other guests.

Hotel Poseidon (Map p332; ☎ 2643 1642; www.hotel -poseidon.com; Calle Bohío; d from US$65; **P** **⚡** **⚲**) It's hard to miss the huge Grecian wood carvings that adorn the exterior of this small European-run hotel. On the inside, sparkling rooms are perfectly accented with elegant furniture and mosaic tiles, though the highlight of the property is the elegant open-air restaurant that specializes in fresh fish – it's one of the best spots in town. There's a pool, with a con-venient swim-up bar, as well as a small Jacuzzi for getting to know your neighbors.

Hotel Copacabana (Map p332; ☎ 2643 1005; www .copacabanahotel.com; Calle Anita; r from US$70; **P** **⚡** **⚲**) This three-story resort hotel gets good marks for offering a variety of rooms and suites to meet the size and needs of your party. If you're traveling either by yourself or with your sig-nificant other, fairly modern standard rooms are well priced considering the hotel's conven-ient beachfront location and rich offerings of amenities, including an attractive pool and hot tub. Of course, the hotel really packs in the value with its larger suites that come equipped with well-stocked kitchenettes and spacious private balconies from where you can get a personal view of the Pacific sunset.

Villas Estrellamar (Map p332; ☎ 2643 3102; www .estrellamar.com; eastern end of Calle Las Olas; r US$65, 1-/2-bedroom villa US$71/111; **P** **⚡** **⚲**) While the spa-cious rooms at the Estrellmar are certainly good value considering they boast massive bathrooms and private balconies, it really is worth paying the small bit of extra cash for your own personal villa. Depending on the size of your party, you can choose from one-and two-bedroom villas that have full kitchens and plenty of space for stretching out after a day out at the beach or a night out on the town. Regardless of which accommodation option you choose, be sure to take a relaxing swing in the hammock pavilion, and keep an eye out for the huge iguanas that live on the grounds and feed off the mango tree.

Hotel Mar de Luz (Map p332; ☎ 2643 3259; www .mardeluz.com; Av Pastor Díaz btwn Calles Las Palmeras & Los Olas; d/tr/q incl breakfast US$75/80/95; **P** **⚡** **⚲**) This adorable little hotel with Dutch-inspired

murals of windmills and tulips has tidy and attractive air-con rooms that are perfect for a little family fun in the sun. Since it can be difficult sometimes to appease the little ones, the friendly Dutch owners (who also speak Spanish, English, German and Italian) offer two swimming pools, several BBQ grills and plenty of useful information on how to best enjoy the area. The owners are also extremely committed to fighting drugs and prostitution in Jacó, and are at the forefront of an admira-ble campaign to clean up the city.

TOP END

Jacó is in the midst of going upscale, though it's still going to be a few years before some of the proposed top-end resorts and hotels open up to the tourist masses. In the mean-time, however, there are a number of all-in-clusive–style resorts and a few boutique hotels and guesthouses where your dollars can buy you a nice slice of luxury.

Hotel Tangerí (Map p332; ☎ 2643 3001; www.hotel tangeri.com; Av Pastor Díaz btwn Calles Las Palmeras & Las Olas; r from US$120, villa from US$180; **P** **⚡** **⚲**) This low-key resort complex is smack-dab in the middle of it all, but surprisingly manages to remain tranquil despite the ensuing craziness surrounding it. The tropical-infused grounds are extremely well manicured, and home to no less than three pools where you can soak up the rays while floating the daylight away. Rooms are fairly standard, though they do boast ocean views and are brightened up a bit by the colorful linens. However, if you have a bit of extra cash to burn, larger villas with full kitchens are certainly worth the splurge, and help you make the necessary transition to resort living.

Best Western Jacó Beach Resort (Map p330; ☎ 2643 1000; www.bestwestern.com; Av Pastor Díaz btwn Boulevard & Calle Ancha; r from US$125; **P** **⚡** **⚲**) Despite whatever preconceived notions you may have about the Best Western, this particular establishment in the famous American chain is the original full-service beach resort in Jacó. With that said, dark and dingy rooms are certainly showing their age, though you can't beat the impres-sive grounds, convenient beach access and the laundry-list of resort activities on offer. Of course, these days gringos prefer to bed down in some of the newer top-end resorts, though the Best Western does attract a loyal Tico-family following. If you're planning on spending the night here, it pays to check the internet for special discount rates.

Docelunas (Map p330; ☎ 2643 2277; Costanera Sur; d/junior ste incl breakfast US$130/150; P ☒ ☒ ☐ ☒) Situated in the foothills across the highway, 'Twelve Moons' is a heavenly mountain retreat consisting of only 20 rooms sheltered in a pristine landscape of tropical rain forest. Each teak-accented room is intimately decorated with original artwork that's available for purchase, and the luxurious bathrooms feature double sinks and bathtubs. Yoga classes are given daily, there's a full spa that uses the hotel's own line of beauty products and you can dip in a free-form pool that's fed by a waterfall. The open-air restaurant serves everything from marlin *ceviche* (raw but well-marinated seafood) to vegan delicacies. To reach the hotel, make a left off the Costanera between the two entrances for Playa Jacó.

Sonidos del Mar (Map p330; ☎ 2643 3924, 2643 3912; www.sonidosdelmar.com; Calle Hidalgo; house US$250; P ☒ ☒) Howard and Lauri, a South African–American couple, will welcome you to their guesthouse as if you were family. And, when you see their house, you'll wish you were! Set within a mature garden at the bend of a river, 'Sounds of the Ocean' may be one of the most beautiful guesthouses in Costa Rica. Lauri is a skilled artist and a collector who has lovingly filled each room with original paintings, sculptures and indigenous crafts. The house itself is impeccable, incorporating stylistic elements such as vaulted Nicaraguan hardwood ceilings and black, volcanic rock showers. Guests have free use of kayaks and surfboards, and the beach is only 50m away. Full spa services are also available. The house can accommodate up to six people, and cheaper weekly and monthly rates are available.

Eating

Plenty of restaurants busily cater to the crowds, and new ones open (and close) every year. Hours can fluctuate wildly, especially in the rainy season, so it's best to eat early. Generally speaking, the quality of fare in Jacó is surprisingly good, which shouldn't be too much of a surprise as gringos have a reputation as being finicky eaters! To be fair though, there are still a few local spots that have weathered the storm of change, and the city does boast the most eclectic offering of international cuisine on the central Pacific coast.

Soda Flor (Map p332; Av Pastor Díaz, north of Calle La Central; casados US$3-5) This Jacó institution is a perennial favorite of locals and budget travelers alike. Remarkably, the menu hasn't changed in years despite the fact that nearly every other place in town is now offering everything from sushi to sirloin. Food is fresh, tasty, cheap and 100% Costa Rican, which is a good thing, as portions here are huge.

Pancho Villa's (Map p332; cnr Av Pastor Díaz & Calle Hicaco; dishes US$4-8) The greasy food here certainly isn't gourmet by any stretch of the imagination, but you'll probably end up here since the kitchen is open until the wee hours. It's also located downstairs from a rowdy club, so you know you're bound to see some interesting characters hanging about.

Taco Bar (Map p332; mains US$5-10) As the sign advertises, this is your place for 'Fish, Shakes + Salads.' Smoothies here come in gargantuan 1L sizes, and the salad bar has over 20 different kinds of exotic and leafy combinations. And of course, there's the obligatory fish taco, which may be one of the planet's greatest food combinations.

Rioasis (Map p332; cnr Calle Cocal & Av Pastor Díaz; pizza US$6-10) There's pizza, and then there's *pizza* – this much-loved pizzeria definitely falls into the latter category, especially considering that there are more than 30 different kinds of pies on the menu. Of course, considering that each one emerges from an authentic wood-fired oven, and is topped with gourmet ingredients from both Costa Rica and abroad, you really can't go wrong here.

Calinche's Wishbone Eatery (Map p332; Av Pastor Díaz, south of Calle Bohío; meals US$6-12) Overseen by the charming Calinche, this is the most famous restaurant in town, and has been so for years and years. The eclectic menu includes pizza, pitas, stuffed potatoes, pan-seared seabass and tuna-sashimi salads, though its justifiable fame comes from the fact that everything is quite simply fresh, delicious and good value.

Gilligan's (Map p332; Av Pastor Díaz, north of Calle Cocal; breakfast US$3-5, mains US$8-12) The best place in town if you're feeling homesick for your mom's meatloaf, though you'll be equally happy if you turn up for breakfast and find yourself sitting in front of a short stack of pancakes or French toast. After all, sometimes it's OK to momentarily forget your surroundings and dig into a bit of comfort food.

Tsunami Sushi (Map p332; Av Pastor Díaz, north of Calle Cocal; sushi US$8-15) If you've got a hankering for raw fish, don't miss Tsunami, a modern and lively restaurant that serves up an exquisite assortment of sushi, sashimi and Californian-style rolls. The Far East may be a long way away, but the nearby Pacific is home to some seriously tasty sports fish, such as dolphin fish, tuna and wahoo.

Pacific Bistro (Map p332; Av Pastor Díaz, south of Calle Las Palmeras; mains US$8-15) This deservedly popular place is run by a gourmet chef from California who specializes in Pan Asian–style fusion dishes. Whether you're partial to Indonesian-style noodles and fiery Thai curries, or more refined Japanese soba and fish fillets topped with exotic Chinese sauces, one thing is for certain: this gem of a restaurant really hits the spot, especially if you've been craving fine Asian cuisine.

Hotel Poseidon Restaurant (Map p332; ☎ 2643 1642; Calle Bohío; dishes US$10-20) One of the most

---

LOSE TUMMY, SAVE MONEY

The concept of medical tourism isn't new to Costa Rica, especially since Americans have grown accustomed to seeking medical care overseas in light of soaring medical costs at home. Indeed, the concept is brilliantly conceived, especially since it's possible to save money on expensive treatments while simultaneously enjoying a foreign holiday.

Medical tourists in Costa Rica are typically interested in cosmetic surgical practices, such as tummy tucks, breast implants, face lifts and other elective procedures that generally aren't covered by domestic insurance policies. Furthermore, these procedures on average cost 40% to 70% less outside the US, especially given that Costa Rican doctors aren't required to carry large malpractice insurance plans.

Historically, medical tourism destinations in Costa Rica were Jacó, Tamarindo and San José, though the flow of wealth into the country has brought this lucrative industry elsewhere. In fact, there are currently a large number of upscale hotels throughout the country that advertise all-inclusive medical tourism package deals alongside traditional ecoholidays!

Given this ever-expanding industry, it's surprising to find in Costa Rica an increasing number of medical tourists, a good number of which fall outside the traditional target bracket, namely aging wealthy Americans. The medical tourism industry has also started targeting image-conscious Europeans hailing from countries with socialized medical systems, as well as younger travelers who have a bit of disposable cash to burn.

Needless to say, the issue regarding the merits of increased medical tourism in Costa Rica is just as complicated as any of the others facing the country. On one hand, hospitals in Costa Rica certainly operate at a much lower cost than comparative institutions overseas, and the standard of medical care throughout the country is certainly rising. However, the safety and quality of cosmetic procedures in comparison to more developed countries remains the principle issue of concern in most peoples' minds.

Supporters of an expanded medical tourism industry in Costa Rica point out that the medical system in America is limited by expensive human resources and medical supplies, a high demand for services and the ever-present fear of litigation. They also point out that Costa Rican doctors and nurses are among the best-trained medical professionals in Latin America, and that the growing demand has allowed for increased investment in the industry.

Of course, regardless of how much money it's possible to save on an elective procedure, at the end of the day it's impossible to argue that medical standards and training in Costa Rica are at par with more developed countries. Furthermore, there is little recourse in the event that a procedure goes wrong, and it's worth pointing out that cosmetic surgery can be fatal if improperly performed.

As with anything involving the safety and security of your body, it pays to always exert common sense. Regardless of what you may read and hear, you should only go through with something if you have 100% confidence in the skills and reputation of the medical service provider. Conduct detailed research, ask for references and most importantly don't rush into anything. After all, you only have one body, and there are plenty of ways to enjoy it in Costa Rica that don't involve a surgeon's scalpel.

CENTRAL PACIFIC COAST

sophisticated restaurants in town, the specialty here is fresh seafood served up with an Asian flare. Sauces are inventive, the staff professional and the atmosphere upscale yet relaxing. A good bet for top-quality food and refined European-style dining that consistently receives good marks from travelers.

our pick **El Hicaco** (Map p332; ☎ 2643 3226; dishes US$15-30) Generally regarded as the top dining experience in Jacó, it's hard not to be impressed by the innovative offerings at this ocean-side spot brimming with casual elegance. Although the menu is entirely dependent on seasonal offerings, both from the land and the sea, the specialty of the house is seafood, prepared with a variety of special sauces highlighted by Costa Rica's tropical produce.

If you're counting your colones, or just prefer to skip out entirely on the restaurant scene, self-caters go ga-ga at the Western-style **Más X Menos** (Map p332; Av Pastor Díaz), which is pronounced 'mas por menos' and means 'more for less.' Más X Menos has an impressive selection of fresh produce, local and international culinary items and a surprisingly good outdoors section.

Drinking & Entertainment

Jacó is something of a wasteland in regards to cultural offerings, but it's a great place to get hammered and do something you'll most likely regret in the morning. There are several dance clubs, though in this fast-changing town, it's worth asking around to find the latest hot spots. Be advised that a good portion of Jacó nightlife revolves around prostitution, so be wary of suddenly being the most attractive guy in the bar.

All of these places (unless otherwise stated) are located on Avenida Pastor Díaz and only cross-street information is provided.

Tabacon (Map p332; at Calle Bohío) Definitely one of the more respectable night spots in town – there's a good chance there will be live music here on most nights of the week.

Jungle Bar & Grille (Map p332; south of Calle Las Palmeras) The second-story terrace gives you a good vantage point for sizing up your prey, which is a good thing as this place can turn into a meat market.

La Bruja (Map p332; south of Calle Anita) This old standby offers a mellow atmosphere for downing a few beers. Try the Maudite – it's the best beer you'll ever taste.

Disco La Central (Map p332; Calle La Central) This disco sets the volume at 11, whether or not there's anyone on the dance floor, though good fun can be had here if you're properly inebriated prior to walking in.

Getting There & Away
BOAT
Travelers are increasingly taking advantage of the jet-boat transfer service that connects Jacó to Montezuma. Several boats per day cross the Golfo de Nicoya, and the journey only takes about an hour. At US$30 it's definitely not cheap, but it'll save you about a day's worth of travel. Reservations can be made at most tour operators in town. It's a beach landing, so wear the right shoes.

BUS
Buses for San José (US$2.50, three hours) stop at the Plaza Jacó mall (Map p330), north of the center, and depart at 5am, 7:30am, 11am, 3pm and 5pm.

The bus stop for other destinations is opposite the Más X Menos supermarket (Map p332). (Stand in front of the supermarket if you're headed north; stand across the street if you're headed south.) Buses to Puntarenas (US$1.50, 1½ hours) depart at 6am, 9am, noon and 4:30pm. Buses to Quepos (US$2, 1½ hours) depart at 6am, noon, 4:30pm and 6pm. These are approximate departure times since buses originate in Puntarenas or Quepos. Get to the stop early!

Getting Around
BICYCLE & SCOOTER
Several places around town rent bicycles, mopeds and scooters. Bikes usually cost about US$3 an hour or US$8 a day, though prices can change depending on the season. Mopeds and small scooters cost from US$35 to US$50 a day (many places ask for a cash or credit card deposit of about US$200).

CAR
There are several rental agencies in town, so shop around for the best rates.
Budget (Map p330; ☎ 2643 2665; Plaza Jacó mall; ⏰ 8am-6pm Mon-Sat, 8am-4pm Sun)
Economy (Map p330; ☎ 2643 1719; Av Pastor Díaz, south of Calle Ancha; ⏰ 8am-6pm)
National (Map p332; ☎ 2643 1752; Av Pastor Díaz at Calle Hicaco; ⏰ 7:30am-6pm)

GOING TOPLESS?

Though it's the cultural norm for European women and American college girls on spring break, going topless is heavily frowned upon in Costa Rica. This of course shouldn't be surprising as more than 75% of Ticos are practicing Catholics. Sure, if you bare it all the guys on the beach will hoot and holler, but remember Costa Rican beaches are often frequented by families. If the temptation to get a little extra sun is too much to bear, please be considerate and move to an isolated stretch of sand. And remember, if you're spending your spring break in Costa Rica, be generous with the sunscreen.

Just for the record, there is one place in the central Pacific where topless sunbathing is tolerated, namely La Playita in Manuel Antonio. However, it's worth mentioning that this beach is predominantly a pick-up scene for gay men on vacation – for more information, see p348.

TAXI

Taxis to Playa Hermosa from Jacó cost about US$3 to US$5. To arrange for a pick-up, call **Taxi 30-30** (☎ 2643 3030), or negotiate with any of the taxis along Avenida Pastor Díaz.

PLAYA HERMOSA

While newbie surfers struggle to stand up on their boards in Jacó, a few kilometers south seasoned veterans are thrashing their way across the faces of monster waves at Playa Hermosa. Regarded as one of the most consistent breaks in the country, Playa Hermosa serves up some serious surf, though you really need to know what you're doing in these parts as the huge waves and strong rip tides here are unforgiving.

If you don't think you can hack it with the aspiring pros, you might want to give this beach a miss. However, consider stopping by in August when local and international pro surfers descend on Hermosa for the annual **surf competition**. Dates vary, though the event is heavily advertised around the country, especially in neighboring Jacó.

The following places to stay and eat are listed from north to south.

The most famous hotel on Playa Hermosa is **Terraza del Pacífico** (☎ 2643 3222; www.terrazadel pacifico.com; r/ste from US$100/160; P ☒ ☒), which has prime beachfront property overlooking some seriously killer breaks. Of course, with Spanish colonial accents, spacious tile-floored rooms and a whole list of impressive amenities, this Hermosa establishment is strictly for upscale surfers.

If your wallet is a bit thinner, then head a bit further south to **Brisa del Mar** (☎ 2643 2076; d US$35-50; P ☒), a Floridian-run hotel that is decidedly more budget friendly. Brisa del Mar has a few rooms of varying size with air-con,

private hot shower and cable TV, as well as a communal kitchen where you can self-cater while saving a few extra bucks.

For a bit more European flair, head further south to the **Costanera B&B** (☎ 2643 1942; d incl breakfast US$35-55; P), an Italian-run B&B that boasts a slightly more sophisticated ambience. Five rooms of various sizes and shapes have vaulted wooden ceilings and beachfront terraces, though the real highlight is the authentic pasta served in the onsite restaurant each evening.

Further south still is **Las Olas Hotel** (☎ 2643 3687; www.lasolashotel.com; r US$35-60; P ☒), a distinctive three-story A-frame building home to the awesome 'skybox room.' If heights aren't your thing, you can also rent one of several beachside bungalows that come equipped with kitchenettes, and sleep several people comfortably.

If you're looking for a quick bite between sets, the **Jungle Surf Café** (dishes US$3-5; ☒ 7am-3pm & 6-10pm Thu-Tue) is a local institution that offers everything from burritos to kebabs, though locals swear by the seriously gourmet fish tacos.

Located only 5km south of Jacó, Playa Hermosa can be accessed by any bus heading south from Jacó. As a result, most travelers choose to stay in Jacó since there is a better variety of accommodations, and taxis (with surf racks) are abundant (see left).

PLAYA ESTERILLOS

Just 22km south of Jacó is this beautiful stretch of gray sand, which can easily be reached by short side-roads from the Costanera. Although the beach is relatively undiscovered and little visited, there are a few great surf spots here, which should be evident once you see the small groups of surfers camping

CENTRAL PACIFIC COAST

underneath the trees at the northern edge of the beach.

For anyone not keen on exposing themselves to the elements, there's always the longstanding **Pélican Hotel** (☎ 2778 8105; www .pelicanhotelcr.com; r from US$65; P ☒ ☒), a homey, beachfront spot that has a handful of rustic rooms, and is only steps away from the surf. And of course, there are plenty of hammocks onsite – perfect for lounging – as well as free surfboards, body boards and bikes for guests.

If it's possible for you to stretch your budget for a night or two, do not miss the chance to stay at the brand-new **ourpick** **Xandari by the Pacific** (☎ 2778 7070; www.pelicanhotelcr .com; villa US$235-370; P ☒ ☐ ☒), a visually stunning resort that is aiming to put Playa Esterillos on the map. There is no shortage of attractive resorts along this stretch of the Pacific, but what makes Xandari so unique is the incredible architectural scheme that is evident from the moment you step foot on the property. Each individually designed villa encompasses a range of intriguing design elements including wooden-lattice ceilings, sheer walls of glass framing private gardens, concrete-poured furniture done up with custom leather work and impossibly intricate mosaic tile-work. As if all of this wasn't enough to make you postpone your onward travel plans, there is also an onsite restaurant specializing in gourmet and organic healthy fare, as well as an immaculate palm-fringed infinity pool that faces out toward the crashing surf. Welcome to paradise, where you can check in any time you like, but it's damn hard to leave!

The Playa Esterillos area can be a little confusing to navigate as there are three towns with access to the beach: Esterillos Oeste, Esterillos Centro and Esterillos Este. These towns are all off the Costanera about 22km, 25km and 30km southeast of Jacó, respectively, and can all be reached by any bus heading south from Jacó.

PARRITA

Parrita, a bustling town on a river of the same name, is home to a tremendous palm oil processing plant. If the wind is blowing right, the plant can be smelled from several kilometers away, though the odor is somewhat pleasant if you're a fan of fried foods. Although palm oil doesn't have the immediate recognition as olive oil perhaps, the product finds its way into just about everything, from Snickers bars and french fries to baked goods and snack foods.

While you're driving through the area, watch the workers in the fields on the sides of the road as the **palm oil** industry is a fascinating one. In terms of day-to-day maintenance, workers spend hours keeping the palms clear of insects, which is accomplished by clearing growth on the forest floor and applying poison to the trunks. In addition, fronds must be regularly clipped in order to encourage fruit growth and to provide easy access to the pod. Workers must also collect mature pods and transport them to processing plants where the fruits are separated and pressed. This last step is perhaps most evident in the huge big-rig trucks stacked full of reddish fruit that come flying down this relatively poor stretch of the Costanera – be careful if you're on the road out there!

The primary reason for visiting Parrita (aside from learning about palm oil!) is to visit **Playa Palo Seco**, a quiet, unhurried gray-sand beach located near mangrove swamps that provide good opportunities for birding. A 6km dirt road connects the eastern edge of town to the beach. Another popular excursion is to visit **Isla Damas**, which is actually the tip of a mangrove peninsula that becomes an island at high tide. Most people arrive here on package tours from Jacó and Quepos, though you can hire a boat to bring you to and from the island for around US$5.

If you're looking to stay on Playa Palo Seco, **Beso del Viento B&B** (☎ 2779 9674; d/q US$70/150; P ☒) has four modest but comfortable apartments for rent that have private tiled bathrooms, fully stocked kitchens and breezy grounds. Kayaks, bikes and horses can be rented if you're interested in exploring this off-the-beaten-path area. The French owners are extremely warm and accommodating, and go out of their way to make guests feel more like visiting family.

Parrita is about 40km south of Jacó, and can be reached by any bus heading south from Jacó. After Parrita, the coastal road dips inland through more African palm-oil plantations on the way to Quepos. If you're driving, the road is a mix of a badly potholed pavement and stretches of dirt, with several rickety one-way bridges.

RAINMAKER AERIAL WALKWAY

Rainmaker was the first **aerial walkway** through the forest canopy in Central America, though it is still regarded as one of the region's best. From its tree-to-tree platforms, there are spectacular panoramic views of the surrounding primary and secondary rain forest, as well as occasional vistas out to the Pacific Ocean. The reserve is also home to the full complement of tropical wildlife, which means that there are myriad opportunities here for great birding as well as the occasional monkey sighting.

Tours with naturalist guides leave hotels in Manuel Antonio and Quepos daily except Sunday; reservations can be made at most hotels or by calling the **Rainmaker office** (☎ in Quepos 2777 3565; www.rainmakercostarica.org). Standard tours cost US$65 and include a light breakfast and lunch, though there are also birding (US$90) and night tours (US$60) available. Binoculars are invaluable for watching wildlife, as are water and sun protection for staying hydrated and sunburnt free.

Rainmaker also offers opportunities for volunteers to participate for two weeks to one month in one of the four departments needed to run and preserve the project. There are also opportunities to work with local schools and various community outreach programs. Fees are US$1250 for a two-week placement and US$2400 for one month.

From the parking lot and orientation area, visitors walk up a beautiful rain-forest canyon with a pristine stream tumbling down the rocks. A wooden boardwalk and series of bridges across the canyon floor lead to the base of the walkway. From here, visitors climb several hundred steps to a tree platform, from which the first of six suspension bridges spans the treetops to another platform. The longest span is about 90m, and the total walkway is about 250m long. At the highest point, you are some 20 stories above the forest floor.

In addition, there are short interpretive trails that enable the visitor to identify some of the local plants, and some long and strenuous trails into the heart of the 2000-hectare preserve. Keep your eye out for poison-dart frogs, which are very common along the trails!

A large colorful sign marks the turnoff for Rainmaker on the Costanera at the northern end of Pocares (10km east of Parrita or 15km west of Quepos). From the turnoff, it is 7km to the parking area.

QUEPOS & MANUEL ANTONIO

The sleepy, provincial town of Quepos never had ambitions of being anything more than a community of fishermen, merchants and plantation workers. However, as the international spotlight began to shine on nearby Parque Nacional Manuel Antonio, Quepos suddenly found itself with an opportunity to cash in on something even more lucrative than fish and palm oil: tourism. With rain-forested hills sweeping down to the sea, Manuel Antonio is a stunning destination worthy of the tourist hype, while decidedly more relaxed Quepos is admirably maintaining its roots despite increased foreign investment.

Note that this section is divided into Quepos proper, the road from Quepos to Manuel Antonio, the village of Manuel Antonio and the national park itself.

QUEPOS

Located just 7km from the entrance to Manuel Antonio, the small town of Quepos serves as the gateway for the national park, as well as a convenient base for travelers in need of goods and services. While a good number of visitors to Manuel Antonio prefer to stay outside of Quepos, accommodation is generally cheaper in town, though you will need to organize transportation to the national park and the beaches.

However, Quepos can be an appealing place to stay, especially since it exudes an attractive small-town charm that is absent from much of the central Pacific coast. Although the tourism boom is rapidly transforming the Manuel Antonio area, Quepos remains a relatively authentic Tico town that provides a more low-key alternative to the tourist-packed gringo trail beyond.

History

This town's name was derived from the indigenous Quepoa, a subgroup of the Borucas, who inhabited the area at the time of the Conquest. As with many indigenous populations, the Quepoa declined because of European diseases and slavery. By the end of the 19th century, no pure-blooded Quepoa were left, and the area began to be colonized by farmers from the highlands.

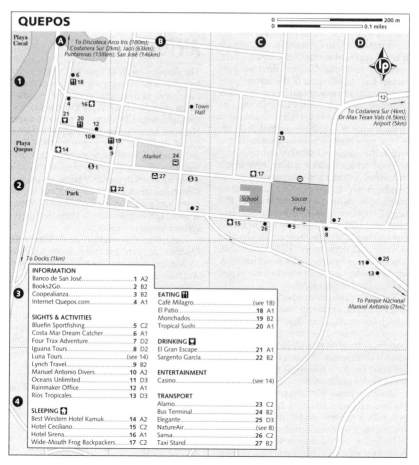

QUEPOS

To Discoteca Arco Iris (100m); Costanera Sur (2km); Jacó (63km); Puntarenas (138km); San José (146km)

To Costanera Sur (4km); Dr Max Teran Vals (4.5km); Airport (5km)

To Docks (1km)

To Parque Nacional Manuel Antonio (7km)

Playa Cocal

Playa Quepos

Town Hall

Market

School

Soccer Field

Park

Quepos first came to prominence as a banana-exporting port in the early 20th century, though crops declined precipitously in subsequent decades due to disease and labor issues (underpaid workers had the gall to demand raises). African oil palms, which currently stretch toward the horizon in dizzying rows around Quepos, soon replaced bananas as the major local crop, though unfortunately they generated a lot less employment for the locals.

But the future is looking bright for locals as tourists are coming to Manuel Antonio by the boatload, and the construction of the new marina in the next few years means that cruise liners will no longer have to dock at Puntarenas. More visitors means more jobs in

the area's rapidly expanding tourist market, though the question of sustainability and the need for balanced growth is weighing heavy on most people's minds. The Pez Vela Marina is scheduled to open by this book's publication, but it is too early to tell what effect this will have on this humble town.

Information
BOOKSHOP
Books2Go (☎ 2777 1754, 8371 3476; tours2go@racsa .co.cr; internet per hr US$2; ☼ 10am-6pm) Susan runs a quaint little bookshop that also serves as a traveler's meeting place. You can post messages, store your bags, burn photos onto CDs, check the internet, or just hang out and read a good book. Susan also books tours in the area, and guarantees that she has the lowest prices around.

INTERNET ACCESS
Internet Quepos.com (per hr US$2; 8am-8pm Mon-Sat) You can check email here on several computers with decent connections.

MEDICAL SERVICES
Dr Max Teran Vals (2777 0200) A hospital that provides emergency medical care for the Quepos and Manuel Antonio area. It's on the Costanera Sur en route to the airport. However, this hospital doesn't have a trauma center and seriously injured patients are evacuated to San José.

MONEY
Banco de San José and Coopealianza both have 24-hour ATMs on the Cirrus and Plus systems. Other banks will all change US dollars and traveler's checks.

TOURIST INFORMATION
Quepolandia (www.quepolandia.com) The latest happenings are listed in this free English-language monthly magazine, found in many of the town's businesses.

Dangers & Annoyances
The town's large number of easily spotted tourists has attracted thieves. In response, the Costa Rican authorities have greatly increased police presence in the area, but travelers should always lock hotel rooms and never leave cars unattended on the street – use guarded lots instead. The area is far from dangerous, but the laidback atmosphere should not lull you into a false sense of security.

In addition, women should keep in mind that the town's bars attract rowdy crowds of plantation workers on weekends. So walking around town in your swimsuit will most certainly garner the wrong kind of attention.

Note that the beaches in Quepos are polluted and not recommended for swimming. Go over the hill to Manuel Antonio instead.

Activities
SPORTFISHING
Sportfishing is big in the Quepos area. Offshore fishing is best from December to April, when sailfish are being hooked. Some of the main charter outfits are listed following. Not all charters have offices in Quepos, so it's usually best to call ahead. If you don't have a reservation, any hotel in the area can help put you in contact with a charter outfit. You can expect to pay upwards of US$1000 to hire out a boat for the day.

Bluefin Sportfishing (2777 1676, 2777 2222; www.bluefinsportfishing.com) Across from the soccer field.
Costa Mar Dream Catcher (2777 0725; www.costamarsportfishing.com) Next to Cafe Milagro.
Luna Tours (2777 0725; www.lunatours.net) In Best Western Hotel Kamuk.

DIVING
The dive sites are still being developed in the Quepos and Manuel Antonio area, though the following operators have both been recommended by readers. The dive sights are away from the polluted beaches, so water pollution is not a problem when diving.
Manuel Antonio Divers (2777 3483; www.manuelantoniodivers.com)
Oceans Unlimited (2777 3171; www.oceansunlimitedcr.com)

Tours
There are numerous reputable tour operators in the Quepos area.
Amigo Tico Complete Adventure Tours (2777 2812; www.puertoquepos.com) Offers a range of tours, including rafting, walks in national parks, mountain biking and fishing. A full day of rafting on the Savegre is US$95 and this outfit also offers boat and kayaking tours of Isla Damas. Amigo Tico doesn't have an office in Quepos; book by phone or through your hotel.
Four Trax Adventure (2777 1825; www.fourtraxadventure.com) Four-hour ATV tours are US$95 per person.
Iguana Tours (2777 1262; www.iguanatours.com) An adventure-travel shop offering river rafting, sea kayaking, horse rides, mangrove tours and dolphin-watching excursions.
Lynch Travel (2777 1170; www.lynchtravel.com) From airline reservations to fishing packages and rainforest tours, this travel shop has it all.
Ríos Tropicales (2777 4092; www.riostropicales.com) The venerable Costa Rican rafting company has an office in Quepos.

Sleeping
Staying in Quepos offers a cheaper alternative to the sky-high prices at many lodges on the road to Manuel Antonio. It can also be more convenient, as all the banks, supermarkets and bus stops are in Quepos. Reservations are recommended during high-season weekends and are necessary during Easter and the week between Christmas and New Year's Eve.

For more accommodation options, see the Quepos to Manuel Antonio section, p347 as well the Manuel Antonio Village section, p352.

CENTRAL PACIFIC COAST

X MARKS THE SPOT

Locals have long believed that a treasure worth billions and billions of dollars lies somewhere in the Quepos and Manuel Antonio area waiting to be discovered. The lore was popularized by the English pirate John Clipperton, who befriended the coastal Quepoa during his years of sailing to and from the South Pacific. Clipperton's belief stemmed from a rumor that in 1670, a number of Spanish ships laden with treasure escaped from Panama City moments before it was burned to the ground by Captain Henry Morgan. Since the ships were probably off-loaded quickly to avoid being raided at sea, a likely destination was the San Bernadino de Quepo Mission, which had a strong loyalty to the Spanish crown.

John Clipperton died in 1722 without ever discovering the legendary treasure, and the mission closed permanently in 1746 as most of the Quepoa had succumbed to European diseases. Although the ruins of the mission where discovered in 1974, they were virtually destroyed and were long since looted. However, if the treasure was indeed as large as it's described in lore, then it is possible that a few gold doubloons could still be lying somewhere, waiting to be unearthed.

---

ourpick **Wide-Mouth Frog Backpackers** (☎ 2777 2798; www.widemouthfrog.org; dm US$9, d with/without bathroom US$34/24; P ⊠ 🖥 🖳) This backpacker outpost is run by a welcoming British–New Zealand couple who are determined to make their little spot one of the best accommodations in Costa Rica – and so far, they've done everything right. Brightly tiled rooms are centered on an inviting pool with plenty of lounge chairs where backpackers can congregate and swap stories. There's also a communal kitchen with a huge dining area, a TV lounge with a free DVD rental library and free internet. But what makes this place so memorable is the generally good vibes that radiate throughout the premises, especially in the evenings when everyone unwinds and lets loose over a few drinks.

Hotel Ceciliano (☎ 2777 0192; d from US$25; P) There is no shortage of budget hotels in Quepos catering primarily to Tico travelers, though this family-friendly spot gets good marks for its comfortable rooms and welcoming owners. Although the Ceciliano isn't the newest hotel on the block, everything here is kept spic-and-span, and the welcoming staff ensure that Costa Rican hospitality reigns true during the entirety of your stay.

Hotel Sirena (☎ 2777 0572; www.lasirenahotel .com; s/d/tr US$55/65/75; P 🖳) This intimate boutique hotel is a warm and welcome addition to the Quepos scene, and is easily the best midrange option in town. Whitewashed walls with soft pastel trim are subtly lit by blue Tiffany lamps, which give the hotel a soothing, Mediterranean ambience that is a world away from the rough-and-ready Quepos street scene. The hotel is also perfectly accented with potted plants and original artwork, and is highlighted by a quaint tiki bar overlooking a tranquil swimming pool.

Best Western Hotel Kamuk (☎ 2777 0379; www .kamuk.co.cr; r from US$85; P ⊠ 🖳) This upmarket Quepos stalwart bears the somewhat stale Best Western brand name, though in reality the Hotel Kamuk is a surprisingly refreshing historic building that provides excellent value. The Best Western label ensures that service is professional from check-in to check-out, though once you get past reception, the hotel is anything but American in ambiance. In fact, the core of the hotel is a winding wooden staircase that fans out to breezy hallways adorned with colonial flourishes. Rooms are a bit on the small side, though they're equipped with modern amenities, and you can always head to the attractive pool or Western-style restaurant if you want a bit more breathing space. If you're planning on staying here, check the internet as discount rates are sometimes available.

Eating

For a small Tico town (albeit on the edge of a major tourist attraction), Quepos is home to a surprising number of international eateries.

For more eating options, see the Quepos to Manuel Antonio section, p351 as well the Manuel Antonio Village section, p352.

Café Milagro (dishes US$2-5; ⏱ 6am-10pm Mon-Fri) Serving some of the country's best cappuccino and espresso, this is a great place to perk up in the morning – try the *perezoso* (lazy or a sloth), which is a double espresso poured into a large cup of drip-filter coffee. Or, if you want to simply relax and read the English-language newspapers that are available, you can indulge in a baked good or a freshly made deli sandwich.

Monchados (dishes US$7-12; ⊗ 5pm-midnight) Something of a Quepos institution, this long-standing Mex-Carib spot is always bustling with dinner-goers who line up to try tradi-tional Limónese dishes and Mexican stand-ards. Food here is eclectic, innovative and never bland, a theme that is also reflected in the vibrant decorations and fairly regular live music.

Tropical Sushi (rolls US$1-3; ⊗ 5-10pm) Quepos has gone cosmopolitan – for authentic Japanese (yes, the sushi chef is from Japan!), try this colorfully decorated restaurant, which has an all-you-can-eat special for just US$15. If you're a purist, you can stick to the tuna sashimi spreads, though it's worth venturing out a bit and sampling some of the local Costa Rican–style rolls.

El Patio (mains US$8-15; ⊗ 6am-10pm) This Nuevo Latino spot is adored by locals and tourists alike, in part because its menu changes daily yet never fails to entice and surprise. The unspoken rule here is fresh and local, which means that meats, seafood and produce are always of the highest quality, and always prepared in a way that highlights their natural flavors. If you're a fan of.tapas, sample a few dishes here, though go slow, and enjoy your meal over a few glasses of imported wine.

Drinking & Entertainment

Nightlife in Quepos is a good blend of locals and travelers, and it's cheaper than anything you'll find in the Manuel Antonio area. If you are looking for something a bit more sophisticated, however, it's easy enough to jump in a taxi.

The fishermen-friendly **El Gran Escape** (☎ 2777 0395; ⊗ 6am-11pm) is good for a beer and chit-chat, as is the American-themed **Sargento García** (☎ 2777 2960; ⊗ 9am-11pm). If you feel like giving away your cash, there's the casino at the Best Western Hotel Kamuk, and the indus-trial-sized **Discoteca Arco Iris** (⊗ 10pm-late), north of town, brings out the locals with thumping dance beats.

Getting There & Away
AIR
Both **NatureAir** (www.natureair.com) and **Sansa** (www.sansa.com) service Quepos, which is the base town for accessing Manuel Antonio. Prices vary according to season and availability, though you can expect to pay a little less than US$75 for a flight from San José or Liberia. Flights are packed in the high season, so book (and pay) for your ticket well ahead of time and reconfirm often.

Lynch Travel (☎ 2777 1170; www.lynchtravel.com) can book charter flights to and from the Quepos area.

The airport is 5km out of town, and taxis make the trip for US$3 to US$5 (depending on traffic).

BUS
All buses arrive and depart from the main terminal in the center of town. Buy tick-ets for San José well in advance at the **Transportes Morales ticket office** (☎ 2777 0263; ⊗ 7-11am & 1-5pm Mon-Sat, 7am-1pm Sun) at the bus terminal. Buses from Quepos depart for the following destinations:

Jacó US$1.50, 1½ hours, 4:30am, 7:30am, 10:30am and 3pm.

Puntarenas US$3, 3½ hours, 8am, 10:30am and 3:30pm.

San Isidro, via Dominical US$3, three hours, 5am and 1:30pm.

San José (Transportes Morales) US$4, four hours, 5am, 8am, 10am, noon, 2pm, 4pm and 7:30pm.

Uvita, via Dominical US$4, 4½ hours, 10am and 7pm.

Getting Around
BUS
Buses between Quepos and Manuel Antonio (US$0.25) depart roughly every 30 minutes from the main terminal between 6am and 7:30pm, and less frequently after 7:30pm. The last bus departs Manuel Antonio at 10:25pm. There are more frequent buses in the dry season.

CAR
The following car-rental companies operate in Quepos; reserve ahead and reconfirm to guarantee availability:

Alamo (☎ 2777 3344; ⊗ 7:30am-noon & 1:30-5:30pm)

Elegante (☎ 2777 0115; ⊗ 7:30am-5pm Mon-Fri)

TAXI
Colectivo taxis between Quepos and Manuel Antonio will usually pick up extra passen-gers for about US$0.50. A private taxi will cost about US$5. Call **Quepos Taxi** (☎ 2777 0425/734) or catch one at the taxi stand south of the market.

CENTRAL PACIFIC COAST

HOW TO KNOW IF A BUSINESS IS REALLY ECOFRIENDLY

Ecotourism means big business in Costa Rica, and sometimes it can seem like every hotel, restaurant, souvenir stall, bus company, surf shop and ATV tour operator is claiming to be a friend and protector of Mother Earth. It's certainly easy to dupe your average package tourist with business cards printed on recycled paper and a bunch of tree-frog stickers plastered on an office wall, but sometimes in Costa Rica it's difficult even for the discerning traveler to know whether a business is truly 'eco.' Sure, you didn't cut down a single tree when you built your canopy tour, but can you explain why your gray water trickles down the hillside into the stream below?

The guiding principle behind ecotourism is striking a balance between the positive and negative impacts of tourism, specifically traveling in a manner that is sensitive to the conditions of your destination while simultaneously minimizing negative impacts on the environment. Unfortunately, the problem is that it is becoming increasingly popular for destinations to label themselves as 'ecodestination,' yet there are no universal guidelines dictating exactly what it means to be 'eco.' However, there are various environmental, economic and sociocultural aspects of running an ecofriendly business that every traveler should be aware of.

Since most ecotourism destinations are located in areas where the natural environment is relatively untouched, it is important for a business to adhere to strict conservation guidelines. At the bare minimum, an ecofriendly business should participate in recycling programs, effectively manage their wastewater and pollutants, implement alternative energy systems, use natural illumination whenever possible and maintain pesticide-free grounds using only native plants. When it is possible, a business should also participate in environmental conservation programs as well as be an active member of regional or local organizations that work on solving environmental problems.

The economics of an ecotourist destination is a major issue concerning tourists, local communities and developers as the misdistribution of economic benefits generated by a business can have harmful consequences on the sustainability of an area. This is especially important as tourists are increasingly interested in visiting the most undeveloped areas possible, which is a problem as the individuals living in these locales are relatively removed from the greater economy. An ecofriendly business can address these realities by hiring a majority of its employees from the local population, associate with locally owned businesses, provide places where native handicrafts can be displayed for sale, serve foods that support local markets and use local materials and products in order to maintain the health of the local economy.

The sociocultural aspect of ecotourism refers to the ability of a community to continue functioning without social disharmony as a result of its adaptation to an increased volume of tourists. Although tourism contributes to the loss of cultural integrity, it can also alleviate poverty and help maintain natural resources that might otherwise be exploited. An ecofriendly business can achieve these goals by fostering indigenous customs; protecting sites of historical, archaeological and/or spiritual importance; educating visitors about local customs and practices; regulating the tourist flow to indigenous areas; and, when possible, donating a portion of profits to the local community.

Tourism will never be a completely harmless venture, but there are ways of minimizing its damage and distributing its benefits to local communities. Travel responsibly, think green and be critical the next time you see the word 'eco.'

QUEPOS TO MANUEL ANTONIO

From the port of Quepos, the road swings inland for 7km before reaching the beaches of Manuel Antonio Village and the entrance to the national park. The serpentine road passes over a number of hills awash with picturesque views of forested slopes leading down to the palm-fringed coastline. Of course, this narrow stretch of road isn't exactly pristine and idyllic as it is lined with the vast majority of tourist-oriented hotels, restaurants and shops in the Quepos and Manuel Antonio area.

Although competition for the tourist dollar is fierce, generally speaking there is an extremely high-standard of service in these parts. With that said, the area isn't cheap, but if you shop around and avoid the obvious tourist traps, your cash will go a long way. And, there are truly are some world-class hotels and restaurants here where you can bed down and dine out in the lap of luxury.

Orientation

Note that the road to Manuel Antonio is steep, winding and very narrow. Worse, local bus drivers love to careen through at high velocities, and there are almost no places to pull over in the event of an emergency. At all times, you should exercise caution and drive and walk with care, especially at night.

Information

INTERNET ACCESS

Cantina Internet Café (per hr US$2)
El Chante Internet (per hr US$2)

MONEY

Banco Promerica (8am-5pm Mon-Fri, 9am-1pm Sat) Has a 24-hour ATM on the Cirrus network and can exchange US dollars.

TOURIST INFORMATION

La Buena Nota (☎ 2777 1002; buennota@racsa.co.cr; Manuel Antonio) A good source of tourist information for this area.
Rafiki Safari Lodge (☎ 2777 2250; www.rafikisafari .com) The booking and information office for this lodge (p357) offers white-water rafting, horseback riding, hiking and birding tours.

Sights & Activities

You can relax after a day's activities at the **Serenity Spa** (☎ 2777 0777, ext 220; Si Como No hotel), a good place for couple's massages, sunburn-relief treatments, coconut body scrubs and tasty coffee.

Also belonging to the Si Como No hotel and situated just across the street is **Fincas Naturales** (www.butterflygardens.co.cr; admission US$15), a private rain-forest preserve and butterfly garden. About three dozen species of butterfly are bred here. The garden has a sound-and-light show at night (US$40 per person) and is surrounded by nature trails.

Amigos del Rio (☎ 2777 1084; www.adventuremanuel antonio.com) runs white-water rafting trips for all skill levels on the Savegre and Naranjo rivers. Prices vary depending on the size of the party and the nature of your trip.

Courses

Escuela de Idiomas D'Amore (☎ 2777 1143, in the USA 310-435 9897, 262-367 8589; www.escueladamore.com) has

Spanish immersion classes at all levels; local homestays can be arranged. Two-week classes without/with homestay start at US$845/995, though significant discounts are available for longer periods of study. This institute comes recommended by a large number of readers for its high level of service and professionalism.

Sleeping

This stretch of winding, forested road has mostly top-end hotels, but there are a few midrange and budget options as well. High-season rates are provided throughout, and reservations are a must for weekends. Low-season rates can be as much as 40% lower in some hotels. Hotels listed here are in the order they're passed traveling from Quepos to Manuel Antonio.

For more accommodation options, see the Quepos section, p343 as well the Manuel Antonio Village section, p352.

Hotel Plinio (☎ 2777 0055; www.hotelplinio.com; d with/without air-con US$75/65, 2-/3-story ste US$85/110, jungle house US$100; P) This cozy hotel is nestled on the verdant edge of the rain forest, and is the perfect retreat from all of your stresses. Rooms have super-high ceilings, which create a tranquil, relaxed atmosphere. Larger suites are two and three stories tall, and have great polished-wood decks for lounging, while groups of up to five can live it up in the jungle house. The grounds boast 10km of trails into the forest, where you'll find a 17m-high lookout tower (open to the public).

Mimo's Hotel (☎ 2777 2217; www.mimoshotel .com; d US$65, junior ste US$85; P) Run by a delightful Italian couple, this whitewashed and wood-trimmed hotel has spacious, clean, terra-cotta-tiled rooms that are positively lit up with bright, colorful murals. Highlights here include the palm-fringed swimming pool, a fiber-optically lit Jacuzzi and restau-rant-bar serving Italian-influenced dishes. The owners speak half a dozen languages, and can share with you a wealth of knowledge about Costa Rica.

Hotel Mono Azul (☎ 2777 2572; www.monoazul.com; s/d/tr from US$55/60/65, child under 12yr free; P) This is a great family option as the entire hotel is decorated with animal murals and rain-forest paraphernalia, not to mention the three pools and games room. You'll also sleep well at night knowing that your money is going to a good cause. The Mono Azul is home to 'Kids Saving the Rainforest' (KSTR), started by

GAY GUIDE TO MANUEL ANTONIO

For jet-setting gay men the world over, Manuel Antonio is regarded as something of a dream destination…

Homosexuality has been decriminalized in Costa Rica since the 1970s, which is indeed a rarity in machismo-fueled conservative Central America. As a result, gays and lesbians have had Costa Rica on their travel wish-list for decades, though the blossoming gay scene in Manuel Antonio is unlike any other in the country.

It's not hard to understand why Manuel Antonio first started attracting gay men, especially since the area is stunningly beautiful, and has long attracted liberal-minded and tolerant individuals. The area also has a burgeoning artist community, a sophisticated restaurant scene and one of the country's few nude beaches.

So, without further adieu, here is your concise gay guide to Manuel Antonio:

Sights & Activities

During the daylight hours, the epicenter of gay Manuel Antonio is the famous **La Playita** (Map p349), one of the few beaches in Costa Rica where nude sunbathing and skinny dipping are tolerated. Although there are a few women here, who come to sunbathe topless in relative safety and comfort, La Playita is a playful pick-up scene for gay men on the prowl.

Sleeping

Manuel Antonio's most famous gay-friendly spot is **La Plantación** (Map p349; ☎ 2777 1332, 2777 1115, in the USA & Canada 800-477 7829; www.bigrubys.com; r from US$149; P 🌂 🖳 🖵), part of the international 'Big Ruby's' hotel network. If you're a gay man, welcome to paradise! The sophisticated and all-together impeccable rooms at 'the Plantation' are cool, light and spacious, with regal bathrooms, unforgettable views and highly memorable mosquito nets romantically draped over king-sized beds. And, let's not forget the pool and clothing-optional sundeck where you can chat up fabulous men from around the world while sipping on an expertly crafted cocktail.

Eating & Drinking

The nearby Hotel Casitas Eclipse is home to the **our pick** **Restaurant Gato Negro** (Map p349; ☎ 2777 0408, 2777 1738; dishes US$12-35), one of the glitziest restaurants in Manuel Antonio. Although dinner here comes with a huge price tag, it's one of the hippest spots in the area to be seen out and about. And, it's worth pointing out that the European-influenced food is consistently flawless, and every detail from the presentation of the meat to the thickness of the sauce is simply perfect. The upstairs bar at the 'Black Cat' is also consistently packed with stylish gay men, so dress your best and be ready to impress.

two local schoolchildren who were concerned about the endangered *mono tití* (Central American squirrel monkey) – 10% of hotel receipts are donated to the organization.

La Colina (☎ 2777 0231; www.lacolina.com; r with breakfast US$59-95; P 🌂 🖳) This pleasant B&B is tucked away in a peaceful, forest setting that's almost as magnificent as the ocean views you'll have from your room.

our pick **Hostal Vista Serena** (☎ 2777 5162; www .vistaserena.com; dm/d US$12/50; P 🖳) In an area that is hopelessly overpriced, it's a relief to find such a great budget hostel. Perched scenically on a quiet hillside, this memorable hostel allows guests to enjoy spectacular, ocean sunsets from a hammock-filled terrace.

Unsurprisingly, most travelers find themselves getting stuck here for longer than they planned, especially when you can spend your days hiking down from the hostel through a farm to a remote wilderness beach. Catering to the needs of the backpacker, Vista Serena offers spic-and-span white-tiled dorms with shared bathroom, a communal kitchen and a TV lounge, as well as affordable private rooms for couples who want a bit more privacy. Sonia and her son Conrad, the super-helpful Tico owners, speak fluent English.

BaBaLoo Inn (☎ 2777 3461; www.babalooinn.com; d standard/king US$89/145; P 🌂 🖳) This American-run establishment offers standard rooms overlooking a lush, tropical garden with a private

MANUEL ANTONIO AREA

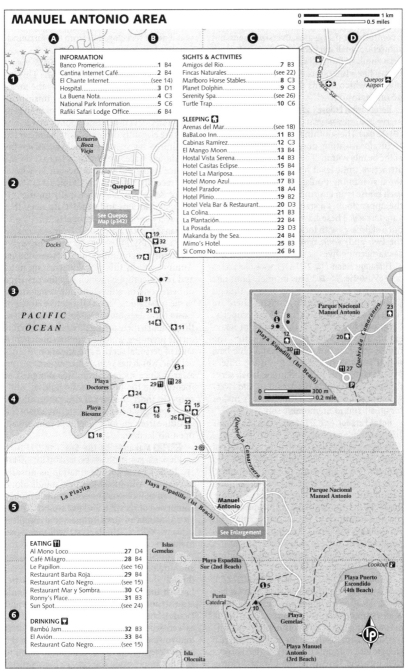

0 — 1 km
0 — 0.5 miles

INFORMATION
Banco Promerica..............................1 B4
Cantina Internet Café.......................2 B4
El Chante Internet......................(see 14)
Hospital..3 D1
La Buena Nota.................................4 C3
National Park Information.................5 C6
Rafiki Safari Lodge Office.................6 B4

SIGHTS & ACTIVITIES
Amigos del Rio................................7 B3
Fincas Naturales.......................(see 22)
Marlboro Horse Stables.....................8 C3
Planet Dolphin.................................9 C3
Serenity Spa............................(see 26)
Turtle Trap....................................10 C6

SLEEPING
Arenas del Mar.........................(see 18)
BaBaLoo Inn...................................11 B3
Cabinas Ramírez.............................12 C3
El Mango Moon...............................13 B4
Hostal Vista Serena.........................14 B3
Hotel Casitas Eclipse.......................15 B4
Hotel La Mariposa...........................16 B4
Hotel Mono Azul.............................17 B3
Hotel Parador.................................18 A4
Hotel Plinio....................................19 B2
Hotel Vela Bar & Restaurant............20 D3
La Colina.......................................21 B3
La Plantación.................................22 B4
La Posada......................................23 D3
Makanda by the Sea........................24 B4
Mimo's Hotel.................................25 B3
Si Como No....................................26 B4

EATING
Al Mono Loco.................................27 D4
Café Milagro...................................28 B4
Le Papillon...............................(see 16)
Restaurant Barba Roja.....................29 B4
Restaurant Gato Negro................(see 15)
Restaurant Mar y Sombra................30 C4
Ronny's Place.................................31 B3
Sun Spot..................................(see 24)

DRINKING
Bambú Jam....................................32 B3
El Avión..33 B4
Restaurant Gato Negro................(see 15)

Estuario Boca Vieja

Quepos

See Quepos Map (p342)

Docks

PACIFIC OCEAN

Playa Doctores

Playa Biesanz

Parque Nacional Manuel Antonio

Playa Espadilla (1st Beach)

Quebrada Camaronera

0 — 300 m
0 — 0.2 mile

Islas Gemelas

Manuel Antonio
See Enlargement

Playa Espadilla (1st Beach)

La Playita

Quebrada Camaronera

Parque Nacional Manuel Antonio

Playa Espadilla Sur (2nd Beach)

Punta Catedral

Playa Gemelas

Lookout

Playa Puerto Escondido (4th Beach)

Playa Manuel Antonio (3rd Beach)

Isla Olocuita

Costanera Sur

Quepos Airport

balcony. However, we're partial to the larger king rooms featuring dramatic ocean views, a comfortable sitting area, oversized beds and showers, a small kitchenette and enough room for a family of four. All rooms come with small extras, like a fully stocked mini-bar and DVD players, which means that there is plenty to do on a rainy day.

Hotel Casitas Eclipse (☎ 2777 0408, 2777 1738; www .casitaseclipse.com; standard/ste/casita from US$125/170/300; P 🄿 🅂) The soothing curves of this architecturally arresting, pure-white complex hint at the beauty within. The hotel consists of nine attractive, split-level houses spread around three swimming pools. The bottom floor of each house is an enormous junior suite, while the upper floor is a standard room with private terrace. These have a separate entrance but a staircase (with lockable door) combines the two and, *voilà*, you have a sumptuous casita sleeping five.

El Mango Moon (☎ 2777 5323; www.mangomoon .net; r US$150-350; 🅂 🄿) This intimate boutique hotel is run by an American couple, though it obviously has a woman's touch – there are fresh flowers in every corner of the property, luxurious linens on all the beds and heavenly bathrooms with steaming hot water. The rooms also face out onto a crystal-blue bay, which you can hike down to on the hotel's private trail. True to its boutique label, service here is extremely personalized and overwhelmingly accommodating, which makes for an all-round memorable stay.

Hotel Parador (☎ 2777 1411, in the USA 800-648 1136; www.hotelparador.com; r US$185-950; P 🅂 🄿) This hotel, which was created for admirers of lavish excess – a la *Lifestyles of the Rich and Famous* – is a 68-room, 10-suite complex, complete with a private helicopter landing pad, outdoor and indoor Jacuzzis, infinity pools with swim-up bars, a European-style spa and health club, tennis courts, minigolf etc (you get the idea!). Splendiferous rooms ranging from huge to ridiculously huge, are, needless to say, absurdly posh and brimming with every conceivable amenity.

Si Como No (☎ 2777 0777, in the US 800-237 8201; www.sicomono.com; r US$190-310, child under 6yr free; P 🅂 🄿 🄿) This flawlessly designed hotel is an example of how to build a resort while maintaining your environmental sensibility. Rooms are insulated for comfort and use energy-efficient air-con units; water is recycled into the landscape, and solar-heating panels are used to heat the water. The rooms feature picture windows and balconies, so you'll never feel closed in from the surrounding rain forest.

Hotel La Mariposa (☎ 2777 0355/456; www.la mariposa.com; r from US$205-440; P 🅂 🄿) This internationally acclaimed hotel was the area's first luxury accommodation, so unsurprisingly it snatched up the best view of the coastline. Fifty-seven pristine rooms of various sizes are elegantly decorated with hand-carved furniture – big spenders should check out the penthouse suite, which has a Jacuzzi on the terrace facing out toward the sea. This hotel was recently listed in the book *1000 Places to See Before you Die*, principally for the immaculate gardens and world-class views that hug every corner of the property.

Arenas del Mar (☎ 2777 2777; www.arenasdelmar .com; r from US$220-580; P 🅂 🄿) The newest luxury accommodation in the Manuel Antonio area is this visually arresting hotel and resort complex, which has the privilege of being one of only eight hotels belonging to the prestigious 'Small Distinctive Hotels of Costa Rica.' Despite the extent and breadth of the grounds, there are no more than 40 rooms on the premises, which ensures an unmatched level of personal service and attention. Arenas del Mar, which has won numerous ecotourism awards since its inception, was designed to incorporate the beauty of the natural landscape. In short, the overall effect is breathtaking, especially when you're staring down the coastline from the lofty heights of your private open-air Jacuzzi.

our pick Makanda by the Sea (☎ 2777 0442; www.makanda.com; studio/villa incl breakfast US$265/400; P 🅂 🄿) Even in a destination as upscale as Manuel Antonio, Makanda stands alone in a class of its own. The entire hotel is solely comprised of six villas and five studios, which give Makanda an air of intimacy and complete privacy. Villa 1 (the largest) will take your breath away – the entire wall is open to the rain forest and the ocean. The other villas and studios are air-conditioned and enclosed, though draw upon the same minimalistic, Eastern-infused design schemes. The grounds are also home to a beautiful infinity pool and Jacuzzi, both offering superb views out to sea, as well as a series of flawless Japanese gardens that you can stroll through and reflect on the beauty of your surroundings. And, if you're still not impressed, you can access a private

QUINTESSENTIAL EATS & DRINKS

The Quepos and Manuel Antonio area is home to some of the country's most spectacular restaurants and bars. With that said, choosing the best of the best is no easy task, though the following top picks are recommended simply for their unique atmosphere.

- **ourpick El Avión** (☎ 2777 3378; dishes US$5-7) This unforgettable airplane bar was constructed from the body of a 1954 Fairchild C-123. Here is where the story gets interesting – the plane was originally purchased by the US government in the '80s for the Nicaraguan Contras, but it never made it out of its hangar in San José because of the ensuing Iran-Contra scandal that embroiled Oliver North and his cohorts in the US government. (The plane is lovingly referred to as 'Ollie's Folly.') In 2000 the enterprising owners of El Avión purchased it for US$3000, and then proceeded to cart it piece by piece to Manuel Antonio. It now sits on the side of the main road, where it looks as if it had crash-landed into the side of the hill. It's a great spot for a beer, guacamole and a Pacific sunset, and on evenings in the dry season there is live music.

- **Ronny's Place** (☎ 2777 5120; mains US$5-12; ⏱ 7:30am-10pm) Head 800m west from the main drag, on the good, well-signed dirt road opposite Manuel Antonio Experts – it's worth the trip as the view here won't disappoint. Ronny, the bilingual Tico owner, has worked hard to make his reststop a favorite of locals and travelers alike. Feast on a big burger or some fresh seafood, and then wash down your meal with some of the best sangría in the country while enjoying views of two pristine bays and 360° of primitive jungle. While plenty of places along this stretch of road boast similar views, nowhere else can you enjoy them in such a laidback and carefree surrounding.

- **Sun Spot** (☎ 2777 0442; Makanda by the Sea; dishes US$10-25) OK, so your budget won't allow you to stay at Makanda by the Sea, though trust us – it's worth checking out the exclusive little poolside restaurant here for its breathtaking rain-forest and ocean views. The kitchen whips up delicious seafood, sandwiches and salads, though the real reason you're stopping by is to soak up the atmosphere of one of the most beautiful hotels on the Pacific coast. After all, just because you can't afford to lie down in the lap of luxury doesn't mean you can't sit on it from time to time.

- **ourpick Le Papillon** (☎ 2777 0355/456; Hotel La Mariposa; lunch US$10-20, dinner US$20-40) The featured restaurant at Manuel Antonio's landmark luxury hotel is perfectly perched to take in daily sunset over the vast expanse of the Pacific Ocean. As you'd imagine, you're paying for the view at this world-class institution, though when the sun dips below the horizon and lights up the sky, you'll stop caring about the price. The food is largely continental cuisine that takes advantage of Costa Rica's rich bounty of fresh seafood and tropical produce – if you're pinching your pennies, the lunch menu is a good deal.

beach by taking the 552 steps down the side of the mountain – bliss!

Eating & Drinking

Many hotels mentioned earlier have good restaurants open to the public. Reservations are recommended in the high season.

For more eating options, see the Quepos section, p344 as well the Manuel Antonio Village section, p352.

Café Milagro (breakfast US$3-4, sandwiches US$4-6) The sister café to the one in Quepos is an obligatory stop on the way to the park as its coffee is pure, black gold. Breakfast and sandwiches are reasonably priced and filling, and will put that extra spring in your step, which you'll certainly need once you hit the trails.

Restaurant Barba Roja (☎ 2777 0331; dishes US$8-15; ⏱ 4-10pm Mon, 10am-10pm Tue-Sun) A longstanding Manuel Antonio institution, the Barba Roja has undergone several changes over the years, though currently offers an excellent mix of American standards with a bit of Mexican flair. After a long day on the trails, recoup over a heaping bowl of nachos and a smooth but potent margarita.

Bambú Jam (Hotel Mirador del Pacífico) Although most nightlife in Manuel Antonio tends to involve a quiet cocktail or beer in the hotel bar, this is a popular music and drinking spot, especially on Friday nights when there are live

CENTRAL PACIFIC COAST

bands and plenty of guests looking to unwind on the dance floor.

Getting Around

Many visitors who stay in this area arrive by private or rented car. Drive carefully on this narrow, steep and winding road – and keep an eye out for pedestrians. There's no shoulder, so everyone walks in the street.

Buses between Manuel Antonio and Quepos (US$0.25) operate up and down the main road and run every 30 minutes between 6am and 7:30pm, and less frequently after 7:30pm. The last bus departs Manuel Antonio at 10:25pm.

Colectivo taxis between Quepos and Manuel Antonio will usually pick up extra passengers for about US$0.50. A private taxi will cost about US$5 – call **Quepos Taxi** (☎ 2777 0425/734).

MANUEL ANTONIO VILLAGE

Here's an analogy for you – Mainstreet USA is to Walt Disney World as Manuel Antonio Village is to the national park (minus the mouse ears, of course!). Run the tourist gauntlet of roadside vendors selling stuffed monkeys (Made in China) and commemorate your trip to the rain forest with a tree-frog sarong (Hecho en Guatemala). Indeed, things have certainly changed in Manuel Antonio, so if you're coming here expecting deserted beaches frequented by hundreds of monkeys, you're in for a surprise.

Of course, the tourist hordes descend on this tiny village with good reason – it marks the entrance to Parque Nacional Manuel Antonio, one of the country's most stunningly beautiful national parks. True, it may be getting increasingly difficult to have a quiet moment to yourself, though the environs here truly are stunning. And, if you can convince those around you to keep their voices down, you really can get up close and personal with some marvelous wildlife.

Information

La Buena Nota (☎ 2777 1002; buennota@racsa.co.cr), at the northern end of Manuel Antonio Village, serves as an informal information center. It sells maps, guidebooks, books in various languages, English-language newspapers, beach supplies and souvenirs; it also rents body boards. You can inquire here about guesthouses available for long-term stays.

Look for a free copy of the English-language *Quepolandia*, which details everything to see and do in the area.

Sights & Activities

There's a good beach near the entrance to the park, namely **Playa Espadilla**, though you need to be wary of rip currents (for more information see boxed text, p278). There are however some lifeguards working at this beach, though not at the others in the area. At the far western end of Playa Espadilla, beyond a rocky headland (wear sandals) is **La Playita**, a gay beach frequented primarily by young men and offering nude sunbathing (use lashings of sunscreen). This point is inaccessible one hour before and after the high tide, so time your walk well or you'll get cut off. Don't be fooled – you do not need to pay to use the beaches as they're outside the park.

Snorkeling gear, body boards and kayaks can be rented all along the beach at Playa Espadilla. If you're looking to surf, the gentle ankle-slappers here are perfect for getting your sea legs, and **Manuel Antonio Surf School** (☎ 2777 4842) and **Monkey Surf** (☎ 2777 5240) both have kiosks near the beach.

Steve Wofford at **Planet Dolphin** (☎ 2777 2137; www.planetdolphin.com; Cabinas Piscis) offers dolphin- and whale-watching tours; starlight sailing cruises are also available. Outings start at US$65 for four hours, including lunch and snorkeling. The Tico-run **Marlboro Horse Stables** (☎ 2777 1108) rents horses, and can organize trips through the rain forest.

White-water rafting and sea kayaking are both popular in this area – see p343 for details of companies that offer these and other options.

Sleeping & Eating

The village of Manuel Antonio is the closest base for exploring the national park, though reservations are a must for the high season, especially on weekends, and lengthy advance planning is needed for Easter week.

For more accommodation options, see the Quepos section, p343 as well the Quepos to Manuel Antonio section, p347.

For more eating options, see the Quepos section, p344 as well the Quepos to Manuel Antonio section, p351.

Cabinas Ramirez (☎ 2777 5044; r per person US$10, camping per person US$3; **P**) In the real estate game, there's only three simple rules: location, location and location. Taking this theme to heart, Cabinas Ramirez offers budget accommodation that is literally steps from the beach, and within easy walking distance of the national park. Of course, the entire property is somewhat reminiscent of a trailer park, and the nearby disco may discourage sleep, though what do you expect for 10 bucks a night!

Hotel Vela Bar & Restaurant (☎ 2777 0413; www .velabar.com; s/d US$40/50; P ⌘) The Hotel Vela is primarily known in these parts for its justifiably famous bar and restaurant, which serves up some of the freshest seafood in the Manuel Antonio area. Meals cost between US$7 and US$15. But, the Hotel Vela is also a surprisingly affordable spot to post up for a night or two – rooms here are fairly basic, but it's hard to beat the price considering that you can literally wake up, have your morning coffee and stroll over to the entrance to the national park before your caffeine perk sets in.

La Posada (☎ 2777 1446; www.laposadajungle.com; bungalows US$115-225; P ⌘) Your private jungle bungalow can accommodate you and several of your friends, though you might have some furry visitors as – quite literally – you're on the edge of the national park. From the comfort of your fully equipped home away from home, which is jam-packed with modern amenities, including a fully stocked kitchen, you can view wildlife as it scurries across your front yard (or across your rooftop in the middle of the night!).

Al Mono Loco (casados US$6) Just north of the rotunda, Al Mono Loco sits under a thatched rancho (small house or house-like building) and serves Tico and international specialties. If you find yourself up early, and can't bare to hit trails without a good breakfast, look no further – the *gallo pinto* here really hits the spot in the wee hours of the morning.

Restaurant Mar y Sombra (casados US$3-5, fish dinners US$6-10) This seriously chilled-out beach bar isn't exactly the most gourmet spot on the block, but you can't beat the feeling of eating next to the sea. On weekends, however, the restaurant turns into a discotheque that's pretty much the most happening spot in the town.

Getting There & Away

Buses depart Manuel Antonio for San José (US$4, four hours) at 6am, 9:30am, noon and 5pm. These will pick you up in front of your hotel if you are on the road to flag them down or from the Quepos bus terminal, after which

there are no stops. Buy tickets well in advance at the Quepos bus terminal. This bus is frequently packed and you will not be able to buy tickets from the driver. Buses for destinations other than San José also leave from the main terminal in Quepos, see p345.

PARQUE NACIONAL MANUEL ANTONIO

Parque Nacional Manuel Antonio was declared a national park in 1972, preserving it (with minutes to spare) from being bulldozed and razed to make room for a crucial development project – namely an all-inclusive resort and beachside condominiums. Although Manuel Antonio was enlarged to its present-day size of 1625 hectares in 2000, it remains the country's second-smallest national park. Of course, as one of Central America's top tourist destinations, you're going to have to share your idyllic spot of sand with the rest of the camera-clicking hordes.

With that said, Manuel Antonio is absolutely stunning, and on a good day at the right time, it's easy to convince yourself that you've died and gone to a coconut-filled paradise. The park's clearly marked trail system winds through rain-forest backed tropical beaches and rocky headlands, and the views across the bay to the pristine outer islands are unforgettable. And, as if that wasn't enough of a hard sell, add to the mix iguanas, howlers, capuchins, sloths and squirrel monkeys, which may be the gosh-darn cutest little fur balls you've ever seen.

Orientation & Information

Visitors must leave their vehicles in the parking lot near the park entrance; the charge is US$3. However, the road here is very narrow and congested and it's suggested that you leave your car at your hotel and take an early-morning bus to Manuel Antonio and then walk in. The **park entrance** (admission US$7; ☉ 7am-4pm Tue-Sun) is a few meters south of the rotunda. Count your change as many tourists complain about being ripped off. Here you can hire naturalist guides to take you into the park; see Tours p354.

To reach the entrance, you'll have to wade through the Camaronera estuary, which can be anywhere from ankle to thigh deep, depending on the tides and the season. However, in an impressive display of opportunism, there are boaters here to transport you 100m for the small fee of US$1.

SAVING THE SQUIRREL MONKEY

With its expressive eyes and luxuriant coat, the *mono tití* (Central American squirrel monkey) is one of the most beautiful of Costa Rica's four monkey species. Unfortunately, it is also in danger of extinction. Roughly 1500 of these charming animals are left in the Manuel Antonio area, one of their last remaining habitats. Unfortunately, the area is in constant environmental jeopardy due to overdevelopment. To remedy this problem, the folks at **Ascomoti** (Asociación para la Conservación del Mono Tití, Association for the Conservation of the Titi Monkey; ☎ 2224 5703; www .ascomoti.com) have begun to take measures to prevent further decline.

The organization is creating a biological corridor between the hilly Cerro-Nara biological protection zone in the northeast and the Parque Nacional Manuel Antonio, which lies on the Pacific coast. To achieve this, they are reforesting the Río Naranjo, a key waterway linking the two locations. Already more than 10,000 trees have been planted along 8km of the Naranjo. This not only has the effect of extending the monkeys' habitat, but also provides a protected area for other wildlife to enjoy. Scientists at the Universidad Nacional de Costa Rica have mapped and selected sites for reforestation and the whole project is supported financially by business owners in the area. (Ascomoti's website has a list of all of the local businesses supporting this valuable effort.)

If you want to volunteer, Ascomoti is looking for individuals interested in planting trees or tracking monkey troops. Volunteers must be able to devote at least one month. The cost is US$350 per person per month to cover room and board. Inquire months ahead of your desired travel date as opportunities are not always immediately available.

The ranger station and **national park information** center (Map p349; ☎ 2777 0644) is just before Playa Manuel Antonio. Drinking water is available, and there are toilets, beach showers, picnic tables and a refreshment stand. There is no camping and guards will come around in the evening to make sure that no one has remained behind.

The beaches are often numbered – most people call Playa Espadilla (outside the park) 'first beach,' Playa Espadilla Sur 'second beach,' Playa Manuel Antonio 'third beach,' Playa Puerto Escondido 'fourth beach' and Playa Playita 'fifth beach.' Some people begin counting at Espadilla Sur, which is the first beach in the park, so it can be a bit confusing trying to figure out which beach people may be talking about. Regardless, they're all pristine, and provide ample opportunities for snorkeling or restful sunbathing. There is a refreshment stand on Playa Manuel Antonio.

The average daily temperature is 27°C/ 80°F and average annual rainfall is 3875mm. The dry season is not entirely dry, merely less wet, so you should be prepared for rain (although it can also be dry for days on end). Make sure you carry plenty of drinking water, sun protection and insect repellent. Pack a picnic lunch if you're spending the day.

Tours

Hiring a guide costs US$20 per person for a two-hour tour. The only guides allowed in the park are members of Aguila (a local association governed by the park service), who have official ID badges, and recognized guides from tour agencies or hotels. This is to prevent visitors from getting ripped off and to ensure a good-quality guide – Aguila guides are well trained and multilingual. (French-, German-, or English-speaking guides can be requested.) Visitors report that hiring a guide virtually guarantees wildlife sightings.

Sights & Activities
HIKING

After the park entrance, it's about a 30-minute hike to **Playa Espadilla Sur**, where you'll find the park ranger station and information center; watch for birds and monkeys as you walk. West of the station, follow an obvious trail through forest to an isthmus separating Playas Espadilla Sur and Manuel Antonio. This isthmus is called a *tombolo* and was formed by the accumulation of sedimentary material between the mainland and the peninsula beyond, which was once an island. If you walk along Playa Espadilla Sur, you will find a small mangrove area. The isthmus widens into a rocky peninsula, with a forest in the center. A trail leads around the peninsula to **Punta Catedral**, from where there are good views of the Pacific Ocean and various rocky islets that are bird reserves and form part of the national park. Brown boobies and pelicans are among the seabirds that nest on these islands.

You can continue around the peninsula to **Playa Manuel Antonio**, or you can avoid the peninsula altogether and hike across the isthmus to this beach. At the western end of the beach, during the low tide, you can see a semicircle of rocks that archaeologists believe were arranged by pre-Columbian Indians to function as a **turtle trap**. (Turtles would swim in during high tide, but when they tried to swim out after the tide started receding, they'd be trapped by the wall.) The beach itself is an attractive one of white sand and is popular for swimming. It's protected and safer than the Espadilla beaches.

Beyond Playa Manuel Antonio, the trail divides. The lower trail is steep and slippery during the wet months and leads to the quiet Playa Puerto Escondido. This beach can be more or less completely covered by high tides, so be careful not to get cut off. The upper trail climbs to a **lookout** on a bluff overlooking Puerto Escondido and Punta Serrucho beyond – a stunning vista. Rangers reportedly limit the number of hikers on this trail to 45.

The trails in Manuel Antonio are well marked and heavily traversed, though there are some quiet corners near the ends of the trails. Off-trail hiking is not permitted without prior consent from the park service.

Watch out for the *manzanillo* tree (*Hippomane mancinella*) – it has poisonous fruits that look like little crab apples, and the sap exuded by the bark and leaves is toxic, causing the skin to itch and burn. Warning signs are prominently displayed beside examples of this tree near the park entrance.

WHITE-WATER RAFTING & KAYAKING
While not as popular as Turrialba (p159), Manuel Antonio is something of an emerging white-water rafting and sea kayaking center. Although you shouldn't expect the same level of world-class runs here as in other parts of the country, there are certainly some adrenaline kicks to be had. For more information, see Tours, p343.

WILDLIFE-WATCHING
Increased tourist traffic has taken its toll on the park's wildlife as animals are frequently driven away or – worse still – taught to scavenge for tourist handouts. To its credit, the park service has reacted by closing the park on Monday and limiting the number of visitors to 600 during the week and 800 on weekends and holidays.

Even though visitors are funneled along the main access road, you should have no problem seeing animals along here, even as you line up at the gate. White-faced capuchins are very used to people, and normally troops feed and interact within a short distance of visitors – they can be encountered anywhere along the main access road and around Playa Manuel Antonio.

DON'T FEED THE MONKEYS! DAMMIT WE'RE SERIOUS!
We at Lonely Planet respect the environment, so you can imagine how irate we become when we hear that tourists (and Ticos alike) are feeding the monkeys their left-over Cheetos. Sure, they're cute, and you may think that you're doing them a favor, but you're not. Really.

Here are a few reasons why:
- Monkeys are susceptible to bacteria transmitted from human hands.
- Irregular feeding leads to aggressive behavior and creates a dangerous dependency.
- Bananas are NOT their preferred food, and can cause serious digestive problems.
- Increased exposure with humans facilitates illegal poaching.

This list could go on and on. Please people, we're on our hands and knees. Don't feed the monkeys, and if you see someone else doing so, be responsible and say something. The problem has become so bad in Manuel Antonio that an initiative has been started in which the names (and sometimes photos) of violators are published in the local press. To report an irresponsible soul, call ☎ 2777 2592.

ANDRES POVEDA ON COSTA RICAN PRIDE

Andres Poveda, the founder of the Costa Rican Hostel Network, has spent the last several years raising the bar for backpacker haunts throughout the country. Over an ice-cold Imperial lager and a bowl of nachos, Andres shared his thoughts on being Costa Rican.

How did you end up owning backpacker hostels? That's a good story, especially since the honest truth is that I always dreamed of becoming a lawyer. As a kid I used to get into a lot of trouble, so I thought that I should probably learn how to properly defend myself! Anyway, after finishing law school and landing a high-powered job with the government, I learned that wearing a suit and dealing with papers wasn't the kind of life that I wanted. So, together with my identical twin brother Adrian, we decided to create a place where travelers could experience the real side of Costa Rica. Today, we are proud of the fact that we are one of the few Costa Rican–owned businesses in this country catering exclusively to backpackers from around the world.

What does it mean to be Costa Rican? If you want to understand what it means to be Costa Rican, all you need to do is spend some time hanging out with us Costa Ricans, or as we prefer to call ourselves, Ticos. I think one of the most infectious qualities of Ticos is that we don't think too much about the future, and instead prefer to have a great time and simply enjoy the moment for what it is. Ticos are also extremely family orientated, which means that we are really quick to treat friends as if they were our own kin. You know, almost immediately upon arriving in this country, travelers are greeted with the words *'pura vida,'* which really is a catch-all phrase for Ticos. Although it directly translates as 'pure life,' *pura vida* really is a philosophy of living that all of us strive to uphold.

What makes Costa Rica so unique? Costa Rica is such a tiny country with only a few million people, so you would think that it would be hard for us to have a strong identity. On the contrary, there are so many unique things about Costa Rica that give us Ticos a strong sense of pride and love for our country. For instance, everyone knows that our country is home to some of the world's most virgin rain forest, and that we haven't had a standing army for decades. To me, however, what makes this country so unique is that we are honest people who work hard for what we have. The reality is that we will never be one of the world's largest economies, though people here are extremely satisfied with their lives, which is why we are so passionate about having fun!

What is the best way for travelers to experience Costa Rica? The great thing about this country is that it has a youthful spirit, so you don't have to be 18 or 21 to have a good time here. In Costa Rica, the great social equalizer is beer, so all you have to do is grab a bottle and just interact with the people around you.

What is the best part of being in the hostel business? The answer is definitely meeting backpackers from all around the world, and knowing that at the end, we are all human beings. When you work in an international environment like a hostel, it's a daily affirmation to learn that we all share the same wants, needs and desires.

What is the most challenging part of the hostel business? Keeping it real, keeping it Costa Rican. This is the way our business has always been, the way it is, and the way that it will always be. Others may be motivated by profit, but for me, it's about sharing my pride in being Tico with every single backpacker that steps foot through the front door.

Costa Rican Hostel Network accomodations: Hostel Pangea (p95), Hostel Toruma (p115), Arenal Backpackers Resort (p236), Monteverde Backpackers (p180) and Tamarindo Backpackers (p273).

You'll probably also hear mantled howler monkeys soon after sunrise and, like capuchins, they can be seen virtually anywhere inside the park and even along the road to Quepos – watch for them crossing the monkey bridges that were erected by several local conservation groups.

Agoutis and coatis can be seen darting across various paths, and both three-toed and two-toed sloths are also common in the park. Guides are extremely helpful in spotting sloths as they tend not to move around all that much.

However, the movements of the park's star animal and Central America's rarest primate, namely the Central American squirrel monkey, are far less predictable. These adorable monkeys are more retiring than capuchins, though they are occasionally seen near the park entrance in the early morning, they usually melt into the forest well before opening time. With luck, however, a troop could be encountered during a morning's walk, and they often reappear in beachside trees and on the fringes of Manuel Antonio Village in the early evening.

Offshore, keep your eyes peeled for pantropical spotted and bottlenose dolphins, as well as humpback whales passing by on their regular migration routes. Other possibilities include orcas (killer whales), false killers and rough-toothed dolphins.

Big lizards are also something of a featured sighting at Manuel Antonio – it's hard to miss the large ctenosaurs and green iguanas that bask along the beach at Playa Manuel Antonio and in the vegetation behind Playa Espadilla Sur. To spot the well-camouflaged basilisk, listen for the rustle of leaves along the edges of the trails, especially near the lagoon.

Manuel Antonio is not usually on the serious birders' trail of Costa Rica, though the bird list is respectable nevertheless. The usual suspects include the blue-gray and palm tangers, great-tailed grackles, bananaquits, blue dacnises and at least 15 different species of hummingbirds. Among the regional endemics to look out for include the fiery-billed aracaris, black-hooded antshrikes, Baird's trogons, black-bellied whistling-ducks, yellow-crowned night-herons, brown pelicans, magnificent frigate birds, brown boobies, spotted sandpipers, green herons and ringed kingfishers.

Getting There & Away

The entrance and exit to Parque Nacional Manuel Antonio lies in Manuel Antonio Village – for more information, see p353.

QUEPOS TO UVITA

South of Quepos, the well-trodden Central Pacific gringo trail slowly tapers off, though this certainly shouldn't deter you from pushing on to more far-flung locales. In fact, this stretch of coastline is a great place to get a feel for the Costa Rica of 10 years ago, and if you're an intrepid traveler, you can have your pick of any number of deserted beaches and great surf spots. The region is also home to a great bulk of Costa Rica's African palm oil industry, which should be immediately obvious after the few dozen kilometers of endless plantations lining the sides of the Costanera.

RAFIKI SAFARI LODGE

Nestled into the rain forest, with a prime spot right next to the Río Savegre, the **Rafiki Safari Lodge** (☎ 2777 2250, 2777 5327; www.rafikisafari .com; s/d/ste incl 3 meals US$168/287/402, child under 5yr free; P ☒) combines all the comforts of a hotel with the splendor of a jungle safari – all with a little bit of African flavor. The owners, who are from South Africa, have constructed nine luxury tents on stilts equipped with private bathroom, hot water, private porch and electricity. All units are screened in, which allows you to see and hear the rain forest without actually having creepy-crawlies in your bed. There's a spring-fed pool with a waterslide and ample opportunity for horse riding, birdwatching (more than 350 species have been identified), hiking and white-water rafting. And of course, South Africans are masters on the *braai* (BBQ), so you know that you'll eat well alongside other guests in the rancho-style restaurant.

The entrance to the lodge is located about 15km south of Quepos in the small town of Savegre. From here, a 4WD dirt road parallels the Río Savegre and leads 7km inland, past the towns of Silencio and Santo Domingo,

---

SO WHAT'S THE DEAL WITH THE ROAD?

About 4km south of Quepos, the paving on the Costanera Sur suddenly stops. Most travelers never give this much thought, though they later scratch their heads when they reach Dominical and realize that the paving starts up again. Curious? So were we.

The reason (are you ready for this one?) is that this stretch of road is owned by the Quepos regional government, and the last thing they want is tourists dividing their time between Manuel Antonio and points further south. Sure, backpackers could care less about a couple of potholes, but most tour buses wouldn't dare proceed. Isn't feudalism great?

Of course, the real losers in this sad state of affairs are the local Ticos who perennially beg the government to pave the road, though the somewhat fortunate consequence is that the overdevelopment of the coastline slows down south of Quepos.

---

to the lodge. However, if you don't have private transportation, the lodge has an office on the Quepos to Manuel Antonio road (see Map p349), and can arrange all of your transportation.

MATAPALO

Although we don't want to be the ones who let the secret out, Matapalo is one of the best, yet least-known surf destinations on the entire central Pacific coast. With two river mouth breaks, a smattering of reasonably priced accommodation and some wicked, wicked waves, the fact that Matapalo hasn't blown up is a bit of a mystery.

Of course, it's worth pointing out that surfing in Matapalo is not for the inexperienced, especially since the beach is infamous for having some of the country's most dangerous transient rips (for more information on riptides, see boxed text, p278).

Just south of Matapalo are the **Terciopelo Waterfalls**, which are famous for their swimming pools. The falls are located a few kilometers south of Rió Hatillo Viejo, though it's best to ask someone to point out the trailhead for you as it's tough to find.

The first hotel you'll see after turning off the Costanera is the German-run **El Coquito del Pacífico** (☎ 2787 5028, 8384 7220; www.elcoquito .com; s/d/tr/q US$70/80/90/100; P ⊠ ⊠), which consists of a small batch of bungalows highlighted by their beaming white-washed walls and rustic furnishings. The entire complex is attractively landscaped with shady gardens of almond and mango trees, and centered on an open-air bar and restaurant serving up the obligatory traditional German specialties.

Just down the road on the beach side is **Dos Palmas B&B** (☎ 2787 5037; d US$60, additional person

US$5; P), a tiny, bright-yellow inn with some of the best views of the crashing surf in town. The owners are a charming Canadian couple, and since there are only two rooms on the premises, you'll feel incredibly welcome from the moment you check-in. Your hosts are also a great source of information on the area, and can help you plan out your next stop along the coast.

The American-owned **Jungle House** (☎ 2787 5005, 2777 2748; www.junglehouse.com; d from US$65; P ⊠) provides the epitome of relaxation, with five polished-wood quarters decorated with a good smattering of rustic knick-knacks. If you're traveling with your better half, the bamboo 'honeymoon' cabin in the back is a large open-air unit with incredible views of the distant hills. Charlie, the friendly owner, is active locally and supports local education initiatives and trash pick-up efforts on the beach.

The most upscale lodging on the beach is **Dreamy Contentment** (☎ 2787 5223; www.dreamy contentment.com; bungalow/house US$125/200; P ⊠), a beautiful, Spanish colonial property with impressive woodworking and towering trees throughout. The bungalows are equipped with functional kitchenettes, though the real star attraction is the main house, which has the kitchen of your dreams, a beachfront veranda and a princely bathroom complete with hot tub.

If you're looking for a bite to eat, **Tico Gringo** (☎ 2787 5023; dishes US$3-10) is owned by an American expat and his Tica wife who've lived in Matapalo for decades. Seafood, burgers and wings are the standard here, though the real draw is the display of old black-and-white photos of Costa Rica.

Buses between Quepos and Dominical can drop you off at the turnoff to the village; from there it's a couple of kilometers to the beach.

HACIENDA BARÚ NATIONAL WILDLIFE REFUGE

Located on the Pacific coast 3km northeast of Dominical on the road to Quepos, this wildlife refuge (☎ 2787 0003; www.haciendabaru.com; admission US$6, each subsequent day US$2) forms a key link in a major biological corridor called 'the Path of the Tapir.' It is comprised of more than 330 hectares of private and state owned land that has been protected from hunting since 1976. The range of tropical habitats that may be observed there include pristine beaches, river banks, mangrove estuaries, wetlands, selectively logged forests, secondary forests, primary forests, tree plantations and pastures.

This diversity of habitat plus its key position in the Path of the Tapir Biological Corridor accounts for the multitude of species that have been identified on Hacienda Barú. These include 351 birds, 69 mammals, 94 reptiles and amphibians, 87 butterflies and 158 species of trees, some of them over 8.5m (27.5ft) in circumference. Ecological tourism provides this wildlife refuge with its only source of funds with which to maintain its protected status, so guests are assured that money spent there will be used to further the conservation of tropical rain forest.

There is an impressive number of guided tours (US$20 to US$60) on offer. You can experience the rain-forest canopy in three different ways – a platform 36m above the forest floor, tree climbing and a zip line called 'the Flight of the Toucan.' In addition to the canopy activities, Hacienda Barú offers bird-watching tours, hiking tours, and two overnight camping tours in both tropical rain forest and lowland beach habitats. Hacienda Barú's naturalist guides come from local communities and have lived near the rain forest all of their lives.

For people who prefer to explore the refuge by themselves, there are 7km of well-kept and marked, self-guided trails, a bird-watching tower, 3km of pristine beach, an orchid garden and a butterfly garden.

The **Hacienda Barú Lodge** (d US$60, additional person US$10, children under 10yr free) consists of six clean, two-bedroom cabins located 350m from Barú Beach. The red-tile roofed, open-air restaurant (meals US$6 to US$10) serves a variety of tasty Costa Rican dishes.

The Quepos–Dominical–San Isidro bus stops outside the hacienda entrance. The San Isidro–Dominical–Uvita bus will drop you at the Río Barú bridge, 2km from the hacienda office. A taxi from Dominical costs about US$5.

If you're driving, the El Ceibo gas station, 50m north of the Hacienda Barú Lodge, is the only one for a good way in any direction. Groceries, fishing gear, tide tables and other useful sundries are available, and there are clean toilets.

DOMINICAL

With monster waves, a chilled vibe and a reputation for reefer madness, Dominical is the kind of place where travelers get stuck for longer than they intended, so long as the surf's up and the spliff isn't out. Although Dominical is definitely gringo-fied, development is being kept in check by locals and concerned resident expats alike, all of whom are determined to keep the town from becoming the next Jacó. As a result, Dominical is one of the most laidback destinations on the Pacific coast for surfers, backpackers and do-nothings alike.

BATTLING THE BLOOD SUCKERS

Whether you call them skeeters, mozzies or midges, everyone can agree that fending off mosquitoes is one of the most annoying parts of traveling in the tropics. Although the scientific evidence surrounding effective mosquito-bite prevention is circumstantial at best, the following is a list of road-tested combat strategies for battling the blood suckers.

- Wear socks, trousers and a long-sleeve shirt, especially at dusk when mosquitoes feed.
- Eat lots of garlic (not recommended if you're traveling with your significant other).
- Fill your room with the smoke of the ever-present burnable Costa Rican mosquito coils.
- Invest in a good-quality mosquito net, preferably one that has been chemically treated.
- Never underestimate the power of spraying yourself with vast quantities of DEET.

CENTRAL PACIFIC COAST

Dominical recalls to mind the mystical 'old Costa Rica,' namely a time when the legions of international tourists had yet to jump onto the ecotourism bandwagon. Indeed, while in Dominical, it's best to just slow down, take things as they come, and try to strike the difficult balance between getting stoked on surf and stoned on pot.

Orientation & Information

Difficult access has spared Dominical from the fate suffered by other beaches on the central Pacific coast. Development remains low-key, the few roads around the village are still dusty and potholed, and the majority of the beach is fronted by forests not fast food.

The main Costanera highway bypasses Dominical; the entrance to the village is immediately past the Río Barú bridge. There's a main road through the village, where many of the services mentioned are found, and a parallel road along the beach.

There are no banking facilities, but San Clemente Bar & Grill will exchange both US dollars and traveler's checks. It has a postal service upstairs.

Dominical Internet (per hr US$2; ☻ 9:30am-7pm Mon-Sat) Check email here, above the San Clemente Bar & Grill.
Police (☎ 2787 0011)

Dangers & Annoyances

Waves, currents and riptides in Dominical are very strong and many people have drowned here (don't smoke and swim!). Watch for red flags (which mark riptides), follow the instructions of posted signs and swim at beaches that are patrolled by lifeguards.

MOVIES IN THE JUNGLE

Every Friday night, a resident expat named Toby in the nearby town of Escaleras invites locals and travelers to watch his favorite flicks. **Cinema Escaleras** is built on a hilltop with panoramic views of jungle-fronted coastline and features state-of-the-art projection equipment and surround sound. Seriously, this guy loves his movies! Films are shown every Friday at 6pm, and a small donation to pay for the projector bulbs is requested. To get to the cinema, follow the first entrance to Escaleras a few hundred meters up the mountain and look for a white house on the left-hand side.

Because of the heavy-duty party crowd Dominical is attracting, there is a burgeoning drug problem, and some of the bars can get rough at night. A little pot never hurt anyone, but keep in mind that there are much harder drugs getting passed around town these days.

Sights

Just north of the turnoff for Dominical is the junction for San Isidro – if you turn left toward San Isidro and travel for about 10km, you'll see an entrance to the right that leads to **Centro Turístico Cataratas Nauyaca** (☎ 2787 0198, 2771 3187; www.ecotourism.co.cr/nauyacawaterfalls/index.html). This Costa Rican–family owned and operated tourist center is home to a series of wonderful waterfalls that cascade through a protected reserve of both primary and secondary forest.

There's no vehicle access to this tourist center, but you can hire horses for a guided ride to two waterfalls that plunge into a deep swimming hole. With advance notice, a tour can be arranged, including the guided ride, swimming and country meals with the local family. Tours leave at 8am, take six to seven hours and cost US$40 per person. A campground with dressing rooms and toilets is available. Accommodations in Dominical can also arrange tours to the falls.

Another worthwhile diversion is the aptly named **Parque Reptilandia** (☎ 2787 8007; www.cr reptiles.com; admission adult/child US$10/1; ☻ 9am-4:30pm), also located 10km outside of Dominical in the town of Platanillo. If you're traveling with kids who love slick and slimy reptiles, or you yourself just can't get enough of these prehistoric creatures, then don't miss the chance to get face to face with Costa Rica's most famous reptiles. The animal park is home to everything from alligators and crocodiles to turtles and dart frogs. Of course, our favorite section is the viper section, home to such infamous critters as the deadly fer-de-lance. For an added bonus, stop by on Friday for feeding time – we promise you won't be disappointed.

Activities

Dominical owes its fame to its seriously sick point and beach breaks, which attract jetsetting surfers the world over. Conditions here are variable, though in general it pays to have a bit of board experience, as you can really get trashed out here if you don't know what you're doing. With that said, the nearby beach of Domincalito is a bit more tame for anyone who still has training wheels on their board.

Of course, one great way to get a bit more experience under your belt is by heading to the reader-recommended **Green Iguana Surf Camp** (☎ 8815 3733; www.greeniguanasurfcamp.com). Located on a side road leading to the beach, this camp is run by experienced surfers Jason and Karla Butler, and offers a variety of surf lessons and tours, as well as seven- to 10-day surfing camps.

Dominical has emerged as something of a base for day trips to Parque Nacional Corcovado (p416) and Parque Nacional Marino Ballena. Get details at **Southern Expeditions** (☎ 2787 0100; www.dominical.biz/expeditions) at the entrance to the village. The staff can also organize trips to the Guaymí indigenous reserve near Boruca and the tours can be customized to meet your interests.

Courses

Adventure Spanish School (☎ 2787 0023, in the USA & Canada 800-237 730; www.adventurespanishschool.com) runs one-week Spanish-language programs starting at US$315, without homestay. Private lessons are available, as are discounts for longer periods of study.

Sleeping

Dominical is home to the majority of the area's budget accommodation, while a handful of midrange and top-end places are located on the outskirts of the town. The rates given are for high season, but low-season rates could be as much as 30% to 40% lower.

Note that there are additional accommodation options in the nearby mountaintop village of Escaleras (p362).

IN TOWN

Antorchas Camping (☎ 2787 0307; camping per person US$5, r from US$10; P) Just a few meters from the beach, this campground is one of the most secure in town, though you should still be extremely diligent about locking up your valuables in the provided lockers. Campers can take advantage of basic amenities, including cold showers and a share kitchen, while more finicky shoestringers can bed down in Spartan dorms for a few extra dollars a night.

Cabinas San Celemete (☎ 2787 0158; bed US$10-30; P) Backpackers gravitate to this classic Dominical spot, which is actually comprised of a variety of different accommodation op-

tions. The highlights of the property are the private beach houses that are just steps from the surf, though more budget conscious travelers can choose from either shiny wooden cabinas or simple dorm rooms at the adjacent Dominical Backpackers Hostel.

Tortilla Flats (☎ 2787 0033; s/d US$20/30, with air-con US$30/40; P) Another popular option, this budget hotel contains 20-odd rooms of varying shapes and sizes, though all feature hot-water showers as well as hammock-strung patios and terraces – a nice option considering the cheap price tag. The downstairs restaurant can get a bit noisy at night, but on the other hand it serves up one of the town's best breakfasts.

Hotel Domilocos (☎ 2787 0244; s/d US$30/50; P) The newest addition to the Dominical hotel scene is this Italian-run spot, which offers surprisingly swish rooms despite the modest price tag. The orthopedic mattresses are thick and comfortable, the water is hot and steamy and the air-con will make you forget you're in the tropics. And, as if all of this wasn't enough of an incentive to stay here, there's even a plunge pool, a European-influenced restaurant and a mellow cocktail bar.

Hotel DiuWak (☎ 2787 0087; www.diuwak.com; r US$85-110, ste US$135-175; P) This proper resort complex is the most upscale accommodation in town, though the emphasis is on low-key luxury as opposed to unchecked hedonism. With that said, the grounds surrounding the waterfall-fed pool are palm fringed, which makes for relaxing days of idle laziness, and there are some great onsite amenities, including bars, restaurants, a fitness center and health spa. Inquire about the size of the room as some are larger than others, and can easily accommodate you and a few of your friends.

AROUND DOMINICAL

Albergue Alma de Hatillo B&B (☎ 8850 9034; www.cabinasalma.com; r US$60; P) One of the most loved B&Bs on the entire Pacific Coast, this hidden gem is run by Sabina, a charming Polish woman who has legions of dedicated fans the world over. If you're looking for a quiet base from which to explore the Dominical area, this tranquil spot is home to immaculate cabins spread among several hectares of fruit trees. Guests rave about the organic produce on offer at Sabina's restaurant, as well as the daily yoga classes in her

Zen-inducing outdoor studio. Alma de Hatillo is located about 6km north of town.

Hotel y Restaurante Roca Verde (☎ 2787 0036; www.rocaverde.net; r US$85; P ⊠ ⚑) Overlooking the beach about 1km south of town, this chic and stylish American-owned hotel is decorated with hardwoods, tile mosaics, festive murals and rock inlays. The 12 tropical-themed rooms are superbly comfortable places to unwind, though the real action takes place in the festive communal areas, which include an open-air bar and infinity pool. On certain nights, the hotel turns into a theater when local theater groups and dancers perform in the hotel lobby.

Eating & Drinking

Soda Nanyoa (dishes US$2-5) The cheapest eatery in town is consistently packed with hungry surfers snatching up cheap and tasty Costa Rican favorites for a few bucks a plate. After all, you can work up quite an appetite while surfing, which is good as *gallo pinto* (rice and beans) packs quite the caloric punch.

Thrusters Bar (Cabinas Thrusters) The local party people congregate here for beer and skateboarding around the pool tables. Next door is a small sushi bar that's definitely worth checking out, as raw fish and tap beer are a blissful combination indeed.

San Clemente Bar & Grill (dishes US$3-8) This classic Dominical watering hole complete with broken surfboards on the walls serves up big breakfasts and Tex-Mex dishes. With that said, it's more popular as a place to get tanked with travelers from around the world.

Maracutú (dishes US$5-10) The self-proclaimed 'world-music beach bar and Italian kitchen' serves up an eclectic culinary offering that is highlighted by some delicious vegetarian and vegan fare. Each night of the week here features a different genre of music, a good amount of which is live.

Restaurant Wachaca (dishes US$6-12) Regarded as the best restaurant in Dominical, this Limónese-inspired Caribbean spot dishes up innovative cuisine emphasizing fresh fish and tropical flavors. Dishes are served up in an open-air courtyard underneath a giant, old ceiba tree.

Getting There & Away
BUS
Buses pick-up and drop-off along the main road in Dominical.
Palmar US$2.50, 2½ hours, 4:30am and 10:30am.
Quepos US$3, three hours, 7:30am, 8am, 10:30am, 1:45pm, 4pm and 5pm.
Uvita US$1, one hour, 4:30am, 10:30am, noon and 6:15pm.

TAXI
Taxis to Uvita cost around US$15, while the ride to San Isidro costs US$25 and to Quepos is US$55. Cars can accommodate up to five people and can be hailed in town from the main road.

ESCALERAS
Escaleras, a small community scattered around a steep and narrow dirt loop-road that branches off the Costanera, is famed for its sweeping views of the coastline and the crashing surf. Of course, if you want to make it

up here, you're going to need a 4WD to navigate one of the country's most notoriously difficult roads. Needless to say, the locals weren't kidding when they named the place *escaleras* (staircase). Aside from the scenic views, travelers primarily brave the road to either have a relaxing, mountain retreat in any of the places listed following, or to catch a 'Movie in the Jungle' (see boxed text, p360).

The first entrance to Escaleras is 4km south of the San Isidro turnoff before Dominical, and the second is 4.5km past the first. Both are on the left-hand side of the road and poorly signed.

One of the first places you'll come to along the main road is the **Bellavista Lodge & Ranch** (☎ 3888 0155, in the USA 800-909 4469; www.bella vistalodge.com; r/cabin US$55/75; P), a remote farm owned by long-time resident Woody Dyer. The lodge itself is in a revamped farmhouse (surrounded by a balcony providing superb ocean views) that contains four shiny-wood rooms with private, solar-heated shower. The grounds are also home to a two-floored private cabin with a full kitchen and living room and enough space to comfortably accommodate six. Rates include breakfast or an evening snack of beer and chips, and there are tasty home-cooked meals (and pies!) available. If you don't have a 4WD, Woody will pick you up in Dominical for a small fee.

About another 1km up the Escaleras road, **Villa Escaleras** (☎ 8823 0509, in the USA 773-279 0516; www.villa-escaleras.com; villa for 4/6/8 people US$240/280/320; P ⚡ ⚡) is a spacious four-bedroom villa accented by cathedral ceilings, tiled floors, colonial furnishings and a palatial swimming pool. Twice-weekly maid service and a wraparound balcony awash with panoramic views make the setting complete. If you're planning on staying here long-term, inquire about discounted weekly and monthly rates.

Located on a different access road that's 1.2km south of the first entrance is **Pacific Edge** (☎ 2531 8000; www.pacificedge.com; cabin/bungalow US$50/75; P ⚡ ⚡). The owners are a worldly North American–British couple who delight in showing guests their slice of paradise. Four cabins are perched on a knife-edge ridge about 200m above sea level, while larger family-friendly bungalows accommodate up to six and have fully stocked kitchen. Of course, if you're not one for cooking, there

is a wonderful onsite restaurant specializing in international cuisine.

Escaleras is best accessed by private vehicle, though any of the accommodations listed previously can arrange a pick-up service with advanced notice. If you're coming for Movies in the Jungle, a taxi from Dominical shouldn't cost more than US$10.

UVITA

As the most southerly destination on the central Pacific coast, Uvita is the last major population center before entering the country's far-flung corner, namely the Osa peninsula. Of course, this little hamlet just 17km south of Dominical is really nothing more than a loose straggle of farms, houses and *sodas*, which should give you an idea of what Costa Rican beach towns looked like before the tourist boom. With that said, Uvita does serve as the base town for visits to Parque Nacional Marino Ballena, a pristine marine reserve famous for its migrating pods of humpback whales as well as its virtually abandoned wilderness beaches.

Unfortunately, the secret is out about the Brunca coast, and the recent paving of the Costanera Sur has seen an influx of developers and speculators. Real-estate offices are popping up over town, and there is talk of developing the town along similar lines as Dominical, Quepos and even Jacó. However, thus far the pace of development has been extremely slow, which is a hopeful sign that the small-town charm of Uvita will continue unabated, at least for a few more years.

Orientation & Information

The area off the main highway is referred to locally as Uvita, while the area next to the beach is called Playa Uvita and Playa Bahía Uvita (the southern end of the beach).

The beach area is reached through two parallel dirt roads that are roughly 500m apart. The first entrance is just south of the bridge over the Río Uvita and the second entrance is in the center of town. At low tide you can walk out along Punta Uvita, but ask locally before heading out so that you don't get cut off by rising water.

Sights & Activities

Uvita serves as a perfect base for exploring Parque Nacional Marina Ballena (p365), which is home to some truly spectacular beaches that don't see anywhere near the number of tourists that they should attract. Then again, perhaps this is a good thing as you'll have plenty of space to sprawl out and soak up the sun without having to worry about someone stealing your beach chair.

Surfers passing through the area tend to push on to more extreme destinations further south, though there are occasionally some swells at **Playa Hermosa** to the north and **Playa Colonia** to the south. However, if you've just come from Dominical, or you're planning on heading to Pavones (p439), you might be a bit disappointed with the mild surfing conditions on offer here.

The **Jardín de Mariposas** (admission US$4; 8am-4pm) on Playa Uvita (just follow the signs) is a Tico-run outfit raising butterflies for export and education, and this is a good opportunity to get up-close-and-personal with breeds such as the morpho. Go early in the morning when butterflies are at their most active. Admission includes a guided tour.

A few kilometers before Uvita, you'll see a signed turnoff to the left on a rough dirt road (4WD only) that leads 3.5km up the hill (look over your shoulder for great views of Parque Nacional Marino Ballena) to **Reserva Biológica Oro Verde** (2743 8072, 8843 8833). This private reserve is on the farm of the Duarte family, who have lived in the area for more than three decades. Two-thirds of the 150-hectare property is rain forest and there are guided hikes, horse-riding tours and birding walks (departing at 5am and 2pm).

Opposite the turnoff to Oro Verde is **La Merced National Wildlife Refuge**, a 506-hectare national wildlife refuge (and former cattle ranch) with primary and secondary forests and mangroves lining the Río Morete. Here, you can take guided nature hikes, horseback tours to Punta Uvita and birding walks. You can also stay at La Merced in a 1940s **farmhouse** (r per person incl 3 meals US$60), which can accommodate 10 people in double rooms of various sizes.

Sleeping & Eating

The main entrance to Uvita leads inland, east of the highway, where you'll find the following places. For more accommodation options, also check out Parque Nacional Marino Ballena (p365).

Toucan Hotel & Hostel (2743 8140; www.tucanhotel.com; tent US$5, hammock US$6, dm US$10, treehouse US$12, d US$25-30; P X) Located 100m inland of the main highway in Uvita, this is the most popular hostel in Uvita – and with good reason. Run by a delightful family that has made some major changes here in the last few years, the Toucan is home to a variety of accommodations to suit all budgets, from simple tents and hammocks to dormitories, private rooms and the lofty treehouse. Even though the beach is right down the road, most guests never escape the evil clutches of the hammock movie theatre, a spectacular creation that needs to be treated with respect unless you want to defer your future travel plans.

Cabinas Los Laureles (2743 8235; s/d US$18/22; P) About 200m up the road you'll find this pleasant, locally run spot which has eight clean, polished-wood cabins that are set in a beautiful grove of laurels. If you're looking for a bit of local flavor and authentic Costa Rican hospitality, this is a good choice. The friendly and accommodating family can arrange horse-riding tours and any other activities you might be interested in.

Cascada Verde (2743 8191; www.cascadaverde.org; dm US$10, shared loft per person US$8, r US$14-16; P) About 2km inland and uphill from Uvita, this organic permaculture farm and holistic retreat attracts legions of dedicated alternative lifestylers, who typically spend weeks here searching for peace of mind and sound body. Accommodation is extremely basic and somewhat exposed to the elements, though there is ample outdoor communal space for yoga and quiet meditation, and you'll sleep deeply at night if you've spent any time here working on the farm. Cascada Verde is also home to a restaurant that serves vegetarian and raw-food specialties that take advantage of produce grown on the property. A taxi here will cost about US$3 from the highway area.

Balcón de Uvita (2743 8034; www.exploringcostarica.com/balcon/uvita.html; bungalow US$62; P) About 1km inland on a 4WD access road across from the gas station and run by a Dutch-Indonesian couple, this secluded spot is home to a lovely collection of rustic, stone-walled bungalows featuring huge, walk-in solar-powered showers. Drawing on the owners' heritages, the restaurant here is highly recommended for its Thai and Indonesian delicacies, as well as a few European standards.

There are a number of small *sodas* on the Costanera in Uvita where you can get a good meal for a few bucks. Of course, most visitors to the Uvita area are happy to keep eating at **Soda Salem** (casados US$3-5), a small cantina located across the street from Hotel Tucan – just sit at the counter and ask what's cooking.

Getting There & Away
Most buses depart from the two sheltered bus stops on the Costanera in the main village.
Palmar US$2, 1½ hours, 4:45am and 10:30am.
San Isidro de El General US$2, 1½ hours, 6am and 2pm.
San José US$6, six hours, 5am, 6am and 2pm.

Parque Nacional Marino Ballena is accessed from Uvita either by private vehicle or a quick taxi ride – inquire at your accommodation for the latter.

PARQUE NACIONAL MARINO BALLENA
This stunner of a **marine park** protects coral and rock reefs surrounding Isla Ballena. Although the confines of the marine park are fairly modest, the importance of this area cannot be overstated, especially since it protects migrating humpback whales, pods of dolphins and nesting sea turtles, not to mention colonies of sea birds and several terrestrial reptiles.

Although Ballena is essentially off-the-radar screens of most coastal travelers, this can be an extremely rewarding destination for beach lovers and wildlife watchers alike. The lack of tourist crowds means that you can enjoy a quiet day at the beach – something that is not always possible in Costa Rica. And, with a little luck and a bit of patience, you just might catch a glimpse of a humpback breaching or a few dolphins gliding through the surf.

Orientation & Information
From Punta Uvita, heading southeast, the park includes 13km of sandy and rocky beaches, mangrove swamps, estuaries and rocky headlands. All six kinds of Costa Rican mangrove occur within the park. There are coral reefs near the shore, though they were heavily damaged from sediment run-off from the construction of the coastal highway.

The **ranger station** (☎ 2743 8236; admission US$3) is in Playa Bahía, the seaside extension of Uvita. While there's a set admission, the guards at the gate will often charge less because of the limited number of visitors. The station is run by Asoparque (Association for the Development of the Ballena Marine National Park), a joint protection effort launched by local businesses

in conjunction with Minae. It has worked hard at installing services, so be considerate and don't litter, cook with driftwood and use biodegradable soap when bathing.

Sights & Activities
The beaches at Marino Ballena are a stunning combination of golden sand and polished rock. All of them are virtually deserted and perfect for peaceful swimming and sunbathing. And, the lack of visitors means you'll have a number of quiet opportunities for good birding.

From the station, you can walk out onto Punta Uvita and snorkel (best at low tide). Boats from Playa Bahía to Isla Ballena can be hired for US$30 per person for a two-hour snorkeling trip, though you are not allowed to stay overnight on the island.

If you're looking to get under the water, **Mystic Dive Center** (☎ 2788 8636; www.mysticdivecenter .com; Playa Ventanas) is a PADI operation that offers scuba trips in the national park.

There is also some decent surfing near the river mouth at the southern end of Playa Colonia.

WILDLIFE-WATCHING
Although the park gets few human visitors, the beaches are frequently visited by a number of different animal species, including nesting seabirds, bottle-nosed dolphins and a variety of lizards. And, from May to November with a peak in September and October, both olive ridley and hawksbill turtles bury their eggs in the sand nightly. However, the star attractions are the pods of humpback whales that pass through the national park from August to October and December to April.

Scientists are unsure as to why humpback whales migrate here, though it's possible that Costa Rican waters may be one of only a few places in the world where humpback whales mate. There are actually two different groups of humpbacks that pass through the park – whales seen in the fall migrate from California waters, while those seen in the spring originate from Antarctica.

Sleeping & Eating
The park is home to a free campground just 300m from the entrance, which has toilets and showers but no electricity. Keep in mind that the campsite is not secure, so do not leave any valuables lying around inside your tent.

In addition to the accommodations listed here, there are also several other options in nearby Uvita (p363).

Finca Bavaria (☎ 8355 4465; www.finca-bavaria.de; standard/superior US$75/85; ⓟ ☒) On the inland side of the road, you'll see a signed dirt road leading to this quaint German-run inn, home to a handful of pleasing rooms with wood accents, bamboo furniture and romantic mosquito-net draped beds. The lush grounds are hemmed by forest, though you can always ascent to the hilltop pool and take in the sweeping views of the open ocean. And of course, there's plenty of great German beer served by the stein.

La Cusinga (☎ 2770 2549; www.lacusingalodge.com; Finca Tres Hermanas; dm incl three meals US$73, s/d with breakfast US$107/134; ⓟ) About 5km south of Uvita is this beachside ecolodge, which is admirably powered by the hydroelectric energy provided by a small stream, and centered on a working organic farm. Accommodation is in simple but functional wooden rooms and dormitories, though guests tend to spend most of their time on boat trips to the national park, hiking and birding on the onsite network of trails, and snorkeling and swimming in the national park. If you work up an appetite, head to the farmhouse and dine on rural Tico-style food that includes locally raised chicken, fresh seafood and organic produce.

Whales & Dolphins Ecolodge (☎ 2770 3557; www .whalesanddolphins.net; d standard/ste US$105/125; ⓟ ☒ ☒ ☒) Located on a hilltop overlooking Playa Hermosa, this understated ecolodge is one of the few top-end accommodations in the area, though its emphasis is on low-key luxury as opposed to overwhelming opulence. Rooms are attractively decorated in tropical motifs, and the entire property is brimming with amenities. However, its main appeal is the stunning location, which provides constant whale-watching opportunities.

our pick Restaurante Exótica (☎ 2786 5050; meals US$10-25) Located in the nearby town of Ojochal, this phenomenal gourmet restaurant is a hidden gem that is worth seeking out. Despite the humble exterior, the menu features a mind-blowing array of internationally inspired dishes, each emphasizing a wide breadth of ingredients that are brought together in masterful combinations. Defying classification, perhaps the best way to describe the food here is simply 'exotic.'

Getting There & Away

Parque Nacional Marino Ballena is accessed from Uvita either by private vehicle or a quick taxi ride – inquire at your accommodation for the latter.

Southern Costa Rica

In southern Costa Rica, the Cordillera de Talamanca descends dramatically into agricultural lowlands that are carpeted with sprawling plantations of coffee beans, bananas and African palms. Here, *campesinos* (farmers) work their familial lands, maintaining an agricultural tradition that has been passed on through the generations. While the rest of Costa Rica adapts to the recent onslaught of package tourism and soaring foreign investment, life in the southern zone remains constant, much as it has for centuries.

In a country where little pre-Columbian influence remains, southern Costa Rica is where you'll find the most pronounced indigenous presence. Largely confined to private reservations, the region is home to large populations of Bribrí, Cabécar and Boruca, who are largely succeeding in maintaining their traditions while the rest of the country races toward globalization.

Costa Rica's well-trodden gringo trail seems to have bypassed the southern zone, though this isn't to say that the region doesn't have any tourist appeal. On the contrary, southern Costa Rica is home to the country's single largest swath of protected land, namely Parque Internacional La Amistad. Virtually unexplored, this national park extends across the border into Panama and is one of Central America's last true wilderness areas.

And while Monteverde is the country's most iconic cloud forest, southern Costa Rica offers many equally enticing opportunities to explore this mystical habitat. If you harbor any hope of spotting the elusive resplendent quetzal, you can start by looking in the cloud forest in Parque Nacional Los Quetzales. Or, if you want to stand on top of the Cordillera Central, you can climb the cloudcapped heights of Cerro Chirripó (3820m), Costa Rica's highest peak.

HIGHLIGHTS

- Wondering why you're the only one around in the pristine but under-touristed **Parque Internacional La Amistad** (p389)

- Catching a glimpse of the Maya bird of paradise in **Parque Nacional Los Quetzales** (p372)

- Trekking to the top of Costa Rica's highest summit at **Cerro Chirripó** (p378)

- Getting a history lesson at the vibrant Fiesta de los Diablitos at the **Reserva Indígena Boruca** (p382)

- Following the footsteps of one of Costa Rica's greatest ornithologists at **Los Cusingos Bird Sanctuary** (p376)

History

Upon arriving in Costa Rica, the Spanish *conquistadores* (conquerors) began to level tribal society, plunder its meager wealth and enslave indigenous survivors. The few outposts that did survive were later subjugated by Catholic missionaries, who wiped out traditional beliefs in an attempt to bring 'civilization' to the region.

Even as late as the 20th century, indigenous groups were kept on the fringes and were actively excluded from the Spanish-dominated society. In fact, citizenship was not granted to the indigenous population until 1949 and reservations were not organized until 1977.

In the last three decades, indigenous groups have been allowed to engage in their traditional languages and customs. However, an increasing number of indigenous youths are finding themselves unable to subsist on their ancestral lands, and are instead choosing to shed their native ways in favor of employment in the agricultural sector.

Climate

Given its geographic diversity, the climate varies considerably throughout the southern zone. In the lowlands, it remains hot and humid year-round, with marked rainfall from mid-April through mid-December. In the highlands however, you can expect much cooler temperatures year-round (getting as low as 40°F at times).

Parks & Reserves

The parks and reserves of southern Costa Rica offer great opportunities for wildlife-watching and hiking.

Cloudbridge Nature Preserve (p377) A tiny private reserve on the slopes of Cerro Chirripó that is operated by two New Yorkers, and is the site of an ongoing reforestation project.

Parque Internacional La Amistad (p389) This enormous bi-national park is shared with Panama and protects a biological corridor of incredible ecological significance.

Parque Nacional Chirripó (p378) Home to Costa Rica's highest and most famous peak, which offers views of both the Pacific and the Caribbean on a clear day.

Parque Nacional Los Quetzales (p372) Costa Rica's newest national park is extremely rich in birdlife and offers a good chance of spotting the quetzal in all of its resplendent glory.

Reserva Biológica Dúrika (p382) This private reserve within Parque Internacional La Amistad is home to an independent, sustainable community that is committed to conservation.

Getting There & Around

The best way to explore the peninsula in depth is with your own form of private transportation, though you will have to leave your wheels behind if you plan on trekking through La Amistad or scaling Chirripó. Note that this chapter refers to the numbered posts along the Interamericana, which count the kilometers from San José.

Major towns in the southern zone are serviced by regular buses, though public transportation can get sporadic once you leave these major hubs.

Both **NatureAir** (www.natureair.com) and **Sansa** (www.sansa.com) service Palmar, which is a jumping off point for the Osa peninsula. Prices vary according to season and availability, but usually you can expect to pay a little less than US$75 for a flight from San José or Liberia.

THE ROAD TO CHIRRIPÓ

Scaling the lofty heights of Chirripó is undoubtedly the highlight of any trip into the southern zone, though the road to the mountain passes through stunning countryside of redolent coffee plantations and cool cloud forests. The first major area of interest is the Zona Santa or 'Saint's Zone,' a collection of highland villages that famously bear sainted names: San Pablo de León Cortés, Santa María de Dota, San Marcos de Tarrazú, San Cristóbal Sur and San Gerardo de Dota. Further south in the Valle de El General, family-run fincas dot the fertile valley, though the action tends to centre on San Isidro de El General, southern Costa Rica's largest town and major transportation hub.

SANTA MARÍA & VALLE DE DOTA

Centered on a green, grassy soccer field and surrounded by lavish plantations, Santa María de Dota is a charming Tico (Costa Rican) town that merits at least a quick stop. As you'd imagine, coffee production is the economic lifeblood of Santa María, especially since the Coopedota processing facility employs much of the town.

Coopedota (☎ 2541 2828; www.coopedota.com) can give you the complete picture of where your caffeine fix comes from: the Coffee Experience is a half-day tour (US$12) that takes guests to an organic coffee farm, visits the production facility and – most importantly – offers tastings of several different kinds of coffee. The co-founder and manager of the café previously won third place in a national barista competition and is locally famous for her signature coffee drinks.

A true tree-hugger's paradise, **Actividades Arboreales** (☎ 8352 0597; www.treewalking.com; Providencia de Dota; 6hr tour for 2 people US$60) offers all sorts of adventures in the treetops. The farm, La Cabana, is rigged with treetop platforms, linked by suspension bridges and slack lines, creating a 'canopy maze.' For the purist, this place is also great for good old-fashioned tree climbing (or not so old-fashioned, like climbing up the *inside* of a 30m strangler fig). The price includes transportation from Copey de Dota or Ojo del Agua. Otherwise, if you have your own vehicle, drive east from Santa María and continue 12km past El Toucanet Lodge. Coming from the south, turn off the Interamericana at Ojo del Agua; drive about 10km south and west.

A great place to spend the night is at **El Toucanet Lodge** (☎ 2541 3131; www.eltoucanet.com; Copey de Dota; s/d incl breakfast US$50/65; **P**) a lovely country lodge that is perched at 1850m and offers seven rustic hardwood cabins with wonderful views of Valle de Dota. The valley and the surrounding cloud forest are excellent for birding and co-owner Gary leads daily tours – fruit birds are commonly sighted, as well as the resplendent quetzal and the namesake toucanet. The Flintstones-style hot tub is an excellent place to recover from the day's activities. To reach the lodge, drive east from Santa María or turn off the Interamericana at Km 58.

Located in the center of Santa María, **Artesanías Café Amanecer** (☎ 2541 1616; ☺ sporadic) has homemade ice cream and specialty coffee drinks, as well as some handicrafts made by the local women's association. It's a treat if you happen to be here when it's open.

If you are traveling south on the Interamericana, **Los Santos Café** (Interamericana Km 52; ☺ 10:30am-5:30pm), is a convenient place to stop and sample the fruits of the region, including fancy espresso drinks. Incidentally, the gas station at this intersection is the last place to fill your tank before San Isidro de El General.

Getting There & Away

Most drivers take the Interamericana south to Empalme, almost 30km from Cartago. Just south of the station a signed turnoff leads west on a paved road and turns to Santa María de Dota (10km away), San Marcos de Tarrazú (7km beyond) and San Pablo (4km further). Six daily buses (US$2, 2½ hours) connect these towns to San José.

SAN GERARDO DE DOTA

Birders flock to this small town, no pun intended – the area surrounding San Gerardo de Dota is famed for attracting high-altitude species. In fact, the elusive quetzal is such a celebrity in these parts that the government recently named a national park after him, Parque Nacional Los Quetzales. Indeed, San Gerardo is the easiest access point to Costa Rica's newest national park – for more information, see p372.

History

The banks of the Río Savegre were long protected by the steep flanks of the Talamanca mountains, prohibiting settlement in this area. It was not until 1952 that Efrain Chacón and his brothers – driven by drought – made their way south from Copey de Dota and established a farm on the western slopes of Cerro de la Muerte – which would become the village of San Gerardo.

In the early days, they planted *cubano* beans, a typical subsistence crop in this region. That's as far as the Chacón family followed the typical trend, however. Eschewing coffee (which would not thrive at these high altitudes) and beef cattle (which would destroy the surrounding cloud forest), the Chacón family instead raised dairy cattle.

Later, they supplemented dairy-farm activity by stocking their streams with trout and planting apple orchards and other fruit trees. The former had the effect of attracting anglers from San José, while the latter (along with the abundant wild avocado trees) attracted the resplendent quetzal, in turn attracting birders.

As tourism in Costa Rica flourished, so did San Gerardo. Today, this little farming village has become famous for highland birding. Quetzals are spotted frequently every April and May (during breeding season) and are fairly common throughout the rest of the year.

SOUTHERN COSTA RICA

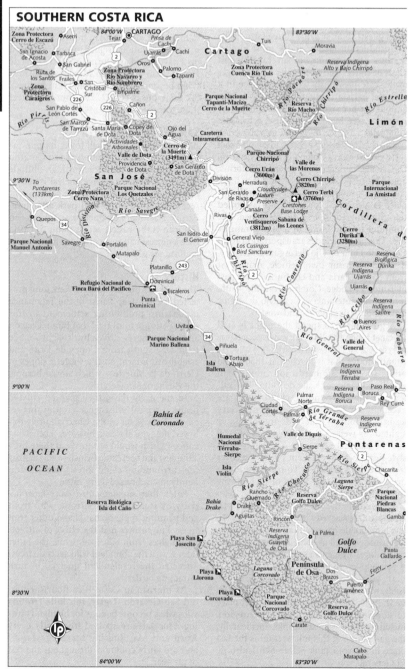

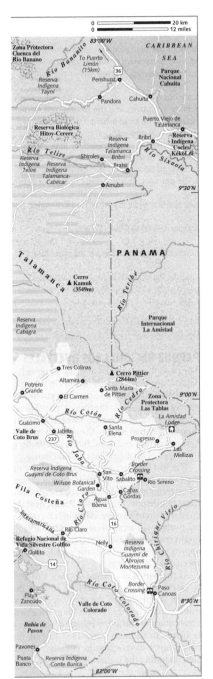

Activities

SPORTFISHING

The trout fishing in the Río Savegre is excellent: May and June is the time for fly-fishing and December to March for lure-fishing (see boxed text, p372 for more information). And the Chacón family, now several generations deep, operates the well-established Savegre Hotel de Montaña (see below) on the grounds of their productive farm, while other facilities have sprung up around the village.

BIRD-WATCHING & HIKING

The best place to go birding and hiking in the area is Parque Nacional Los Quetzales. Unfortunately there are no information facilities for tourists in the park, so inquire at the lodges in San Gerardo before you set out. For information on the park, see p372.

Sleeping & Eating

All of the following places offer access to the Parque Nacional Los Quetzales and are along the road from the Interamericana.

Ranchos La Isla & Restaurant Los Lagos (☎ 2740 1038; camping per person US$4; P) If you're heading to Chirripó then you're probably prepared to do a little bit of camping, which is a good thing as this attractive property offers a handful of shady campsites alongside a small river. The accommodating Chinchilla family also go all out to make sure their guests are entertained by guiding hikes to nearby waterfalls in the hope of spotting the elusive quetzal. If you're looking for a hot meal (US$3 to US$5), the onsite restaurant is a modest affair serving up wholesome, country-style casados, or set meals.

ourpick Dantica Cloud Forest Lodge (☎ 8352 2761; www.dantica.com; s/d incl breakfast US$132/146; P) Definitely the slickest place in San Gerardo, if not the whole southern zone, this upscale lodge consists of beautiful natural wood and stone cabins that are bedecked with artwork from the owner's native Colombia. The kicker though is the wall of picture windows that provides extraordinary vistas over the cloud forest. A romantic breakfast is served each morning on your private terrace, which will most likely be frequented by countless species of tropical birds.

ourpick Savegre Hotel de Montaña (☎ 2740 1028; www.savegre.co.cr; d/ste incl 3 meals US$161/217; P) Set on a 160-hectare orchard and reserve, this justifiably famous lodge has been owned and

TALAMANCA TROUT FISHING

While most sportfishers flock to the coast for the thrill of the big catch, the mountain rivers of the Cordillera de Talamanca offer a different kind of fishing experience. The crystal-clear waters and the cool air of the cloud forest are a delightfully tranquil setting, and the fish – here, rainbow trout – are no less tasty.

Interestingly, the trout that populate these rivers are not endemic. Supposedly, they were first introduced to Central American rivers by the US military in Panama and the healthy fish made their way north into Costa Rican waters. The most popular spot for trout fishing is the Río Savegre, although the nearby Río Blanca and Río Dota also attract local anglers.

In order to maintain healthy populations, fishers are strongly encouraged to limit stream fishing to catch and release. If you want to take home your trout for dinner, fish in one of the local spring-fed ponds, which are well stocked with 30cm to 50cm trout. Success is guaranteed and you just pay for what you take home (about US$4 per kilo). This is a great option for kids and folk with poor fishing karma.

Finca Madre Selva (☎ 2224 6388; Copey de Dota) A popular local fishing spot that is home to a well-stocked trout pond as well as hiking trails – good for a full day of fun.

Pesca Deportiva Río Blanca (☎ 2541 1818, 2541 1816; Copey de Dota) Near Santa María de Dota, this is another local spot that is popular among Tico families.

Ranchos La Isla (☎ 2740 1038; San Gerardo de Dota) Borrow equipment to fish in the river and ponds, then bring your catch back and have the staff fry it up for dinner.

Savegre Hotel de Montaña (☎ 2740 1028; San Gerardo de Dota) This lodge provides equipment and guides for fly-fishing in Río Savegre, or you can fish in the picturesque pond and pay for what you catch. See p371 for more info.

operated by the Chacón family since 1957. It's now something of a Costa Rican institution, especially among birders keen to catch a glimpse of the quetzal. Of course, this isn't a difficult proposition in these parts, especially since the edges of the grounds are lined with avocado trees, the favorite perch of the bird of paradise. If you have the cash to burn, the Savegre suites are gorgeous: wrought-iron chandeliers hang from the high wooden ceilings, while rich wooden furniture surrounds a stone fireplace.

La Comida Tipica Miriam (meals US$3-6; P) One of the first places you will pass in San Gerardo (about 6km from the Interamericana) is the cozy house advertising comida tipica, or 'typical meals.' Eating is almost like receiving a personal invitation to dine in a Tico home: the food is delicious and abundant and the hospitality even more so. Miriam also rents a few cabins (US$30) in the woods behind the restaurant, which are a modest but comfortable place to spend a night or two.

Getting There & Away

The turnoff to San Gerardo de Dota is near Km 80 on the Interamericana. From here, the dirt road descends 8km to the village. The road is very steep: be careful if you're in an ordinary car. Buses between San José and

San Isidro de El General can drop you off at the turnoff.

PARQUE NACIONAL LOS QUETZALES

The park, formerly known as the Reserva Los Santos, was made official in 2005 in honor of the Maya bird of paradise that first put this region of Costa Rica on the tourist map. Spread along both banks of the Río Savegre, at an altitude of 2000m to 3000m, the park covers 5000 hectares of rain and cloud forest that lie along the slopes of the Cordillera de Talamanca.

The Río Savegre, which starts high up on the Cerro de la Muerte, feeds several mountain streams and glacial lakes at a range of altitudes before pouring into the Pacific near the coastal town of Savegre. Although it covers a relatively small area, this region is remarkably biodiverse – the Savegre watershed contains approximately 20% of all the registered bird species in Costa Rica.

As the park's new name implies, this area is extremely rich in birdlife – indeed the quetzal is only one of the many species that call this park home. Trogon, hummingbird, great tinamou and sooty robin are some bird favorites. In addition to the rare quetzal, the park is home to several other endangered species, including the jaguar, Baird's tapir, black guan and squirrel monkey.

While hiking through the higher altitudes, take notice of the fact that the flora is very different from what you will see in the lowland forests. The park, which is classified as montane and premontane forests (the latter being the second-most endangered life zone in Costa Rica), is home to massive oak trees and alpine plants.

The park does not have any facilities for tourists, although all of the lodges around San Gerardo de Dota offer hiking and birding tours. If you wish to explore on your own, follow the road to San Gerardo to its end, from where a trail will lead you through lush forest to a spectacular waterfall. With that said, it's worth inquiring locally for more specific directions before you set out as the going can get difficult in these parts.

CERRO DE LA MUERTE

Along the stretch between Empalme and San Isidro de El General, the highway passes the highest point along the Interamericana, the famed **Cerro de la Muerte** (3491m). The so-called 'Mountain of Death' received this moniker before the road was built, though the steep, fog-shrouded highway, which climbs into the clouds, is still considered one of the most dangerous in Costa Rica. When the fog clears however, this area offers exquisite panoramic views of the Cordillera de Talamanca – but only for a moment, as the fog undoubtedly rolls back in almost immediately.

Cerro de la Muerte also marks the northernmost extent of the *páramo*, a highland shrub and tussock grass habitat typical of the southern zone. This Andean-style landscape is extremely rich in wildlife and is home to many of the same species found in nearby Parque Nacional Chirripó (p378).

Orientation

The road itself is paved and smooth, but it twists and turns around the mountain, which can make overtaking treacherous and potentially life-ending. During the rainy season, landslides may partially or completely block the road. As in most places in rural Costa Rica, it's best to avoid driving at night.

This area is actually part of the Parque Nacional Tapantí-Macizo Cerro de la Muerte, which is easily accessible when traveling from the Central Valley. For more information, see p155.

Sleeping & Eating

All the lodges in this area offer access to hiking trails and opportunities for birding.

Iyök Ami (☎ 8387 2238, 2772 0222; www.ecotourism .co.cr/iyokami/index.htm; Interamericana Km 71; r per person US$30-40; P) Meaning 'Mother Earth' in the Bribrí language, Iyök Ami is a remote cloud-forest reserve (admission US$5), rustic lodge and quaint coffee shop, all in one. Considering that everything is run by one Tica woman, this is an extremely impressive operation that is certainly worthy of your support. Guests also have access to 6km of trails that lead to a picturesque lake, as well as delicious homemade Tico-style meals (US$10 for three meals a day).

Mirador Vista del Valle (☎ 8384 4685, 8836 6193; www.ecotourism.co.cr/vistadelvalle; Interamericana Km 119; s/d US$41/47, extra person US$12; P) Aptly named, the 'View of the Valley Lookout' boasts a windowed-restaurant (meals US$3 to US$6) that offers panoramic views that perfectly complement local specialties like fried trout fillet, and fresh-brewed coffee. Below the restaurant, ecofriendly cabins built entirely from cultivated wood are brightened by colorful indigenous tapestries. Guests can take advantage of nearly 11km of onsite trails that allow for excellent bird-watching.

Bosque del Tolomuco (☎ 8847 7207; www.bosquedel tolomuco.com; Interamericana Km 118; d incl breakfast US$70; P ☄) Named for the sly tayra (tree otter) spotted on the grounds, this relative newcomer is run by a lovely, loquacious Canadian couple. There are four spacious, light-filled cabins, the most charming of which is the secluded 'Hummingbird Cabin.' The grounds offer 5km of hiking trails, ample opportunities to indulge in bird-watching and some magnificent views of Los Cruces. A made-to-order gourmet dinner is also available with advance notice.

Mirador de Quetzales (☎ 2771 8456; www.exploring costarica.com/mirador/quetzales.html; Interamericana Km 70; cabin per person incl 2 meals US$45; P) Commonly known as Eddie Serrano's farm, this excellent-value lodging option is located about 1km west of the Interamericana. Painted wood walls and colorful curtains brighten up the eight cozy cabins that line the farm's ridge (and electric heaters warm them up). Prices also include an early-morning 'quetzal walk' – these bright beauties reside in these forested hills year-round, but sightings are virtually guaranteed between November and April.

Getting There & Away

Frequent buses running between San José and San Isidro de El General can drop you off at any of the lodges listed p373.

SAN ISIDRO DE EL GENERAL

Considering that most settlements in the southern zone are mere mountain villages, it doesn't take much in these parts to be called a 'big city.' Indeed, with a population of only 45,000, San Isidro de El General is little more than a large town, though it does boast a western supermarket, a McDonald's and a surprising concentration of gas stations. As you'd imagine, there is little here to draw in the tourists, though residents of the southern zone can't help but flock to the bright city lights.

With that said, 'El General' is the region's largest population center and major transport hub, so it's likely that you'll pass through here at some point in your travels. If you do happen to get stuck here for longer than you intended, fret not as there are some interesting attractions in the surrounding area (see boxed text, p376). And, if it's any consolation, the women of San Isidro de El General are widely regarded as Costa Rica's finest – must be all that mountain air and fresh coffee!

Orientation

The heart of San Isidro is the network of narrow streets that are clustered around the recently renovated Parque Central. An uncharacteristic but impressive cathedral lords over the eastern end of this square.

Note that locals sometimes refer to San Isidro as Pérez – the surrounding county is Pérez Zeledón. Though labeled on the map, streets are poorly signed and everyone uses landmarks to orient themselves (see boxed text What's That Address?, p537).

Information

Banco Coopealianza Avenida 2 (btwn Calles Central & 1); Avenida 4 (btwn Calles 2 & 4) Both branches have 24-hour ATMs on the Cirrus network.

Brunc@Net Café (☎ 2771 3235; Av Central btwn Calles Central & 1; per hr US$1; ⏰ 8am-8pm Mon-Sat, 9am-5pm Sun)

BTC Internet (☎ 2771 3993; Av 2 btwn Calles Central & 1; per hr US$1; ⏰ 8:30am-9pm Mon-Fri, to 8pm Sat, 10am-4pm Sun)

Ciprotur (☎ 2770 9393; www.ecotourism.co.cr; Calle 4 btwn Avs 1 & 3; ⏰ 7:30am-5pm Mon-Fri, 8am-noon Sat) Tourist office with information about the southern Pacific region.

Clínica El Labrador (☎ 2771 7115, 2771 5354; Calle 1 btwn Avs 8 & 10) This medical service has private doctors in a variety of specialties.

Minae park service office (Sinac; ☎ 2771 3155; aclap@sinac.go.cr; Calle 2 btwn Avs 2 & 4; ⏰ 8am-noon & 1-4pm Mon-Fri) Dispenses a minimal amount of information about Parque Nacional Chirripó. Here is where you can make reservations for the mountaintop hostel at Chirripó – see p381 for details.

Post office (Calle 1 btwn Avs 6 & 8)

Selva Mar (☎ 2771 4582, 2771 4579; www.exploring costarica.com; Calle 1 btwn Avs 2 & 4; ⏰ 8am-noon & 1:30-6pm) Useful for booking area hotels and buying plane tickets. Also houses offices for Costa Rica Trekking Adventures.

Tours

Pieter Westra runs **Aratinga Tours** (☎ 2770 6324; www.aratinga-tours.com) and specializes in bird tours in his native Dutch, but he is fluent in English, Spanish and many dialects of bird. His website provides an excellent introduction to birding in Costa Rica. It is based at Talari Mountain Lodge (opposite).

Sleeping

IN TOWN

Hotel Chirripó (☎ 2771 0529; Av 2 btwn Calles Central & 1; s/d/tr/q from US$15/20/25/30; P) Popular with discerning budget travelers, here you'll find bare, whitewashed rooms that are utterly barren but surprisingly dirt- and grime-free. A few flowering plants and a festive mural in the lobby brighten otherwise stark surroundings, though you'll sleep easy at night knowing that you can pinch a few pennies and keep on traveling for a little while longer.

Hotel Los Crestones (☎ 2770 1200, 2770 1500; Calle Central at Av 14; s/d US$30/40, with air-con US$40/45, extra person US$10; P ✷) This sharp motor court is decked with blooming flowerboxes and climbing vines outside, which is indeed a welcome sight to the road-weary traveler. Inside, functional rooms feature modern furnishings and fixtures, which are made all the better by the attentive staff that keep this place running efficiently.

Hotel Diamante Real (☎ 2770 6230; cnr Av 3 & Calle 4; d/tr/q/ste US$35/55/60/75; P ✷ ▢ ⟨) 'Executive Elegance' is the boast of this upscale business hotel, which is surprisingly swish considering that San Isidro is fairly understated as far as business destinations go. Indeed, all the expected amenities are here, including telephones with voice mail and wi-fi access, which makes staying in touch easy even in this far flung corner of Costa Rica. The classy quarters are painted bright yellow and fitted with shiny black lacquer furniture to complete the executive package.

AROUND SAN ISIDRO

Hotel La Princesa (☎ 2772 0324; www.laprincesahotel .com; San Rafael; d/q US$35/45; P) If sitting in the hot tub watching the sun drop behind the Talamancas sounds appealing, La Princesa is for you, especially if you're looking for affordable luxury and quieter surrounds than downtown San Isidro. Eight sparkling rooms are decorated with wood furniture and bright linens, while lovely gardens are filled with blooms and birds. To reach the property, turn off the Interamericana 5km north of San Isidro in the barrio (district) of San Rafael.

Talari Mountain Lodge (☎ 2771 0341; www.talari .co.cr; Rivas; s/d/tr incl breakfast US$39/59/79; P 🖳) This secluded mountain lodge exudes an incredible amount of charm, as does the Dutch-Tica couple who run the place. They are ever-accommodating, also offering arrangements for treks to Chirripó and customized bird tours – Pieter Westra of Aratinga Tours in San Isidro is their son. Accommodations are in simple wooden cabins on the edge of the forest, though the real attraction here is the prolific birdlife on the grounds, as well as the 2km of trails that wind through the forest. To get here, drive 7km south of San Isidro on the road from San Gerardo de Rivas.

Eating & Drinking

Taquería México Lindo (☎ 2771 8222; Av 2 btwn Calles Central & 1; dishes US$3-5; 🕙 10am-8:30pm) For a welcome change of pace, stop by this *taquería* (taco shop) for tasty tacos as well as burritos, nachos and fajitas, not to mention homemade guacamole and several kinds of salsa. Photos of Mexico and festive *piñatas* will send you south – er, north – of the border.

SAN ISIDRO DE EL GENERAL

DAY TRIPS AROUND SAN ISIDRO DE EL GENERAL

Not to disparage El General, but there's no point in hanging around town if you don't have to. The following day trips are great ways to fill a free day in the area.

- **Fudebiol Reserve** (☎ 2771 4131; admission US$2; ☉ 8am-4pm Tue-Sun) North of El General, Fudebiol is a community reserve along the Río Quebradas. Its 750-hectare grounds include extensive hiking trails, some with rewarding lookout spots, a cooling pond and a butterfly farm (always a treat for kids). Fudebiol offers volunteer opportunities for travelers who want to live with a local family and work at the reserve; this educational facility also has lodging for visiting groups. For information, contact Ciprotur (p374).

- **Los Cusingos Bird Sanctuary** (☎ 2200 5472; www.cct.or.cr; Quizarrá; adult/child US$10/5; ☉ 7am-4pm Tue-Sun) This sanctuary and museum are on the grounds of the farm that was once home to the great ornithologist Dr Alexander Skutch. Author of the birder's bible, *A Guide to the Birds of Costa Rica*, Dr Skutch enjoyed a long and fruitful career studying the birds of the tropics. Much of his work took place at this 78-hectare reserve, which is now open to the public. The grounds are wonderful for watching wildlife, wandering the trails and meditating on the mysteries of nature, as Dr Skutch often did. The great scientist's home is due to open as a museum dedicated to his life and work. To get to Los Cusingos, drive 8km north on the road to San Gerardo de Rivas. Turn right at Rivas and continue 5km through General Viejo, then turn east to Quizarrá. Aratinga Tours leads birding walks here (p374).

- **Rancho La Botija** (☎ 2770 2146, 2770 2147; www.rancholabotija.com; Rivas; admission US$5; ☉ 8:30am-5pm Tue-Sun) A great option for families with kids, this is a working coffee and sugar farm. Trails traverse the grounds, and a daily guided hike departs at 9am and leads to the famous 'Indian Rock,' an ancient stone carved with pre-Columbian petroglyphs. There is entertainment for all ages, whether you paddle a kayak around the lake or a raft around the swimming pool. A restaurant and a few cabins (double including breakfast US$61; wheelchair accessible) are onsite. The rancho is 7km from the Interamericana along the road to San Gerardo de Rivas.

Restaurant/Bar La Cascada (☎ 2771 6479; cnr Calle 2 & Av 2; dishes US$4-8; ☉ 11pm-late) Pleasant restaurant by day, trendy bar by night. The well-stocked bar, massive TV screens showing music videos, and an extensive menu of pub grub attract plenty of local youth, who spend quality time getting to know the beer, the burgers and each other.

ourpick **Kafe de la Casa** (Av 3 btwn Calles 2 & 4; meals US$4-10; ☉ 7am-8pm) Set in an old Tico house, this bohemian café features brightly painted rooms decorated with eclectic artwork, an open kitchen and shady garden seating. With a menu featuring excellent breakfasts, light lunches, gourmet dinners and plenty of coffee drinks, this funky place receives a stream of regulars.

Travelers watching their colones should head for the inexpensive *sodas* (lunch counters) in the **Mercado Central** (Av 4 btwn Calles Central & 2), while self-caterers can shop at the **Supermercado Central** (Ave 6 btwn Calles Central & 2; ☉ 7am-9pm Mon-Sat, 8am-2pm Sun), one block south.

Getting There & Away

BUS

In San Isidro the local bus terminal is on Avenida 6 and serves nearby villages. Long-distance buses leave from various points near the Interamericana and are frequently packed, so buy tickets early.

From Tracopa Terminal

You will find **Tracopa bus terminal** (☎ 2771 0468) on the Interamericana, just southwest of Avenida Central.

Neily US$5, six hours, depart 4:45am, 7:30am, 12:30pm and 3pm.

Palmar Norte US$2.75, three hours, depart 4:45am, 7:30am, 12:30pm and 3pm.

Paso Canoas US$4.50, five hours, depart 8:30am, 10:30am, 2:30pm, 4pm, 7:30pm and 9pm.

San José US$2.75, three hours, depart 7:30am, 8am, 9:30am, 10:30am, 11am, 1:30pm, 4pm, 5:45pm and 7:30pm.

San Vito US$2.75, three hours, depart 5:30am and 2pm.

From Terminal Quepos

Terminal Quepos (☎ 2771 2550) is on the side street south of the Tracopa terminal.

Dominical US$2.50, 2½ hours, depart 7am, 8am, 1:30pm and 4pm.

Palmar Norte US$2.75, three hours, depart 6:30am and 3pm.

Palmar Norte/Puerto Jiménez US$4.50, five hours, depart 6:30am and 3pm.

Quepos US$3, three hours, depart 7am and 1:30pm.

Uvita US$1.50, 1½ hours, depart 8:30am and 4pm.

From Other Bus Stops

The following buses all originate in San Isidro.

Buenos Aires (Gafeso) US$1.50, one hour, depart hourly 5am to 5pm from north of Terminal Quepos.

San Gerardo de Rivas, for Parque Nacional Chirripó US$2.50, 2½ hours, depart from Parque Central at 5am and from the local terminal on Avenida 6 at 2pm.

TAXI

A 4WD taxi to San Gerardo de Rivas will cost between US$20 and US$25 depending on your final destination.

SAN GERARDO DE RIVAS

If you have plans to climb to the summit of Chirripó, then fear not – the tiny but tranquil town of San Gerardo de Rivas marks the entrance to the national park. Here, you can make reservations for accommodations within the park, pick up a few last minutes supplies and (perhaps most importantly) get a good night's rest and/or a hot meal before the trek.

Although hikers are understandably keen to press on to the park as quickly as possible, San Gerardo has its own merits. The backdrop to this village scene is the rushing Río Chirripó and the rocky peak of the same name, which is characterized by breathtaking alpine scenery and bountiful birdlife. And of course, you don't have to climb the mountain to be able to walk around with your head in the clouds – Cloudbridge Nature Preserve (right) is a perfect alternative for those who don't have the time (or energy) to go all the way to the summit.

Orientation & Information

The road to San Gerardo de Rivas winds its way 22km up the valley of the Río Chirripó. The road is paved for the first 10km or so; after the town of Rivas however, it is a gravel road that is bumpy, narrow and steep. The

'center' of San Gerardo – as it is – consists merely of the soccer field and the *pulpería* (corner grocery store) opposite. Otherwise, there's not much to this village – just the family-run farms and cabinas that are strung along this road.

The **Chirripó ranger station** (Sinac; ☎ 2200 5348; ☺ 6:30am–noon & 1-4:30pm) is located about 1km below the soccer field on the road from San Isidro. Stop by here (the earlier the better) to check for space and availability at Los Crestones mountaintop hostel (p381), and to confirm and pay your fee before setting out.

Sights & Activities

About 2km past the trailhead to Cerro Chirripó you will find the entrance to the mystical, magical **Cloudbridge Nature Preserve** (☎ in the USA 212-362 9391; www.cloudbridge.org; admission by donation; ☺ sunrise-sunset). Covering 182 hectares on the side of Cerro Chirripó, this private reserve is an ongoing reforestation and preservation project, spearheaded by New Yorkers Ian and Genevieve Giddy. A network of trails traverses part of the property, which is easy to explore independently; maps are available. Hike to two waterfalls, including the magnificent **Catarata Pacifica**, which is close to the entrance. You are bound to see some amazing birdlife, including the vibrant emerald toucanet, the endangered black guan and many other cloud-forest species. Also, be sure to inquire if you are interested in volunteering on the reforestation program at Cloudbridge. You can drive up here if you have a 4WD; otherwise it's a steep but rewarding hike.

If you can't stand the thought of going for another hike, you will undoubtedly appreciate a soak in the **thermal hot springs** (☎ 8391 8107; Herradura; admission US$3; ☺ 7am-6pm) that are about 2km north of San Gerardo. Just above the ranger station the road forks; take the left fork and walk for about 1km on a paved road. Turn right and take the rickety suspension bridge over the river. A switchback trail will lead you another 1km to a house with a *soda*, which is the entrance to the springs.

Sleeping & Eating

our pick **Hotel y Restaurant Roca Dura Café** (☎ 2262 7218; camping per person US$5; r from US$25-40; **P**) Conveniently located in the center of town just opposite the soccer field, this hip hostelry is built right into the side of a giant boulder, lending a Flintstones ambience to the quarters. Wall murals brighten the smallest stone rooms, while pricier rooms have tree-trunk furniture and fixtures and views of forested hillsides. Even if you're not staying here, the upstairs restaurant is a popular pit stop for locals looking for a night out on the town, er, village.

Albergue Urán (☎ 8388 2333, 2771 1669; dm/d from US$10/25; P) Just 50m below the trailhead, this no-nonsense youth hotel is something of an institution for hikers heading to/from Chirripó. Budget-friendly rooms of varying shapes and sizes are perfect for a restful snooze, while the onsite restaurant, grocery store and laundry facility all cater to the backpacker set. The affable and accommodating owner loves sending hikers off on their way to Chirripó, so feel free to pick his brain before hitting the slope.

Hotel El Pelicano (☎ 8382 3000; d/tr with bathroom US$30/60, r per person without bathroom US$10; P 🏊) About 300m below the ranger station, this simple but functional budget lodge has a collection of spartan but spotless rooms that overlook the river valley. The highlight of the property however is the gallery of the owner, a late-blooming artist who sculpts whimsical wood pieces. If you're looking for a modest meal, there is a small bar and restaurant onsite that whips up fairly tasty casados for US$4 to US$8.

Talamanca Reserve (☎ 2772 1715; d from US$85; P 🖥) This sprawling 1600-hectare private reserve caters to guests who want their creature comforts, even at 2500m. Ominous Talamanca Indian sculptures pose among the spacious stone cabins, which are furnished with lacquered wood, American-style bathrooms and picture windows. This full-service lodge also lures in nonguests with its decidedly modern restaurant that is surprisingly gourmet, as well as its impressive network of hiking trails. The entrance is about 1km south of the trailhead for Chirripó.

Getting There & Away

Buses to San Isidro depart from the soccer field at 7am and 4pm (US$1, two hours). Any of the hotels can call a taxi for you.

Driving from San Isidro, head south on the Interamericana and cross the Río San Isidro at the southern end of town. About 500m further cross the unsigned Río Jilguero

and take the first, steep turn up to the left, about 300m beyond the Jilguero. Note that this turnoff is not marked.

The ranger station is about 18km up this road from the Interamericana. The road is paved as far as Rivas but beyond that it is steep and graveled. It is passable to ordinary cars in the dry season, but a 4WD is recommended. If you are driving past the village of San Gerardo de Rivas, to Albergue Urán or to Cloudbridge Nature Preserve, you will need a 4WD.

PARQUE NACIONAL CHIRRIPÓ

Costa Rica's mountainous spine runs the length of the country in four distinct *cordilleras* (ranges) of which the Cordillera de Talamanca is the highest, longest and most remote. While most of the Talamanca highlands are difficult to access, Costa Rica's highest peak, Cerro Chirripó, at 3820m above sea level, is the focus of this popular **national park**. Of course, while Chirripó is the highest and most famous summit in Costa Rica, it is not unique: two other peaks inside the park top 3800m and most of its 502 sq km lie above 2000m.

Like a tiny chunk of the Andes, Chirripó National Park is an entirely unexpected respite from the heat and humidity of the rain forest. Above 3400m, the landscape is *páramo*, which is mostly scrubby trees and grasslands, and supports a unique spectrum of highland wildlife. Rocky outposts, such as the unmistakable facade of Los Crestones, punctuate the otherwise barren hills and feed a series of glacial lakes that earned the park its iconic name (Chirripó means 'eternal waters').

The bare *páramo* contrasts vividly with the lushness of the cloud forest, which dominates the hillsides between 2500m and 3400m. Oak trees (some more than 50m high) tower over the canopy, which also consists of evergreens, laurels and lots of undergrowth. Epiphytes – the scraggy plants that grow up the trunks of larger trees – thrive in this climate. However, the low-altitude cloud forest is being encroached by agricultural fields and coffee plantations in the areas near San Gerardo de Rivas.

The only way up to Chirripó is by foot. Although the trekking routes are long and challenging, watching the sun rise over the Caribbean from such lofty heights is an undeniable highlight of Costa Rica. You will have to be prepared for the cold and at times wet slog to the top, though your efforts will be rewarded with some of the most sweeping vistas that Costa Rica can offer.

ORIENTATION

The dry season (from late December to April) is the most popular time to visit Chirripó. February and March are the driest months, though it may still rain. On weekends, and especially during holidays, the park is crowded with Tico hiking groups and the mountaintop hostel is often full. The park is closed in May, but the early months of the rainy season are still good for climbing as it usually doesn't rain in the morning. In any season, temperatures can drop below freezing at night, so warm clothes (including hat and gloves), rainwear and a three-season sleeping bag are necessary. In exposed areas, high winds make it seem even colder. The ranger station in San Gerardo de Rivas is a good place to check on the weather conditions.

The maps available at the ranger station are fine for the main trails. However, more detailed topographical maps are available from the Instituto Geográfico Nacional in San José (p534). Frustratingly, Chirripó lies at the corner of four separate 1:50,000-scale maps, so you need maps 3444 II *San Isidro* and 3544 III *Dúrika* to cover the area from the ranger station to the summit of Chirripó, and maps 3544 IV *Fila Norte* and 3444 I *Cuerici* to cover other peaks in the massif.

INFORMATION

It is essential that you stop at the **Chirripó ranger station** (Sinac; ☎ 2200 5348; ⏰ 6:30am-noon & 1-4:30pm) at least one day before you intend to climb Chirripó so that you can check availability at the mountaintop hostel and pay your entry fee (US$15 for two days, plus US$10 for each additional day). Space at the hostel is limited, so it's best to arrive early – first thing in the morning – to inquire about space on the following day. Even if you have a reservation, you must stop here the day before to confirm (bring your reservation and payment confirmation). You can also make arrangements here to hire a porter (about US$25 for 14kg) or to store your luggage while you hike.

WILDLIFE-WATCHING

The varying altitude means an amazing diversity of fauna in Parque Nacional Chirripó. Particularly famous for its extensive birdlife, the national park is home to several endangered species, including the harpy eagle and the resplendent quetzal (especially visible between March and May). Even besides these highlights, you might see highland birds including the three-wattled bellbird, black guan and tinamou. The Andean-like *páramo* guarantees volcano junco, sooty robin, slaty finch, large-footed finch and the endemic volcano hummingbird, which is found only in Costa Rica's highlands.

In addition to the prolific birdlife, the park is also home to some unusual high-altitude reptiles, such as the green spiny lizard and highland alligator lizard. Mammals include puma, Baird's tapir, spider monkey, capuchin and – at higher elevations – Dice's rabbit and the coyotes that feed on them.

Although spotting rarer animals is never a guaranteed proposition, here are few tips to maximize your chances: pumas stick to the savannah areas and use the trails at dawn and dusk to move about; Baird's tapir gravitate to various highland lagoons, mainly in the rainy season, so stake out the muddy edges at dawn or dusk if you see recent tracks; at nighttime, coyote can be seen feeding at the rubbish bins near Crestones Base Lodge.

HIKING
Climbing Chirripó

The park entrance is at San Gerardo de Rivas, which lies 1350m above sea level; from here the summit is 2.5km straight up! An easy-to-follow 16km trail leads all the way to the top and no technical climbing is required.

Allow seven to 14 hours to cover the 10km from the trailhead to the hostel, depending on how fit you are: the recommended departure time is 5am or 6am. The trailhead lies 50m beyond Albergue Urán in San Gerardo de Rivas (about 4km from the ranger station). The main gate is open from 4am to 10am to allow climbers to enter; no one is allowed to begin the ascent after 10am. Inside the park the trail is clearly signed at every kilometer.

CHIRRIPÓ CHECKLIST

Costa Rica might be in the tropics, but Chirripó lies at some chilly altitudes. Don't get caught without the necessities when hiking Costa Rica's highest mountain. Check the Chirripó checklist before you head off:

- water bottle (there is one water stop between the trailhead and the base camp)
- food (including snacks for the hike)
- warm jacket, gloves and hat (temperatures can dip below freezing)
- good sleeping bag (also available to rent at the lodge)
- rain gear (even when it's not raining, the summit is misty)
- plastic bags (to protect your clothing and personal items from the rain)
- sunblock (it may be chilly but the sun is powerful, and much of the route is not shaded)
- flashlight (there's no electricity for much of the evening at the mountaintop hostel)
- compass and map (especially if you are planning to hike one of the lesser-used trails)
- camera (photographic evidence that you reached the top!).

The open-sided hut at **Llano Bonito**, halfway up, is a good place for a lunch break. There is shelter and water, but it is intended for emergency use, not overnight stays.

About 6km from the trailhead, the **Monte Sin Fe** (which translates as 'Mountain without Faith'; this climb is not for the faint of heart) is a preliminary crest that reaches 3200m. You then enjoy 2km with gravity in your favor, before making the 2km ascent to the Crestones Base Lodge at 3400m.

Reaching the hostel is the hardest part. From there the hike to the summit is about 6km on relatively flatter terrain (although the last 100m is very steep): allow at least two hours if you are fit, but carry a warm jacket, rain gear, water, snacks and a flashlight just in case. From the summit on a clear day, the vista stretches to both the Atlantic and the Pacific Oceans. The deep-blue lakes and the plush-green hills carpet the Valle de las Morenas in the foreground. Readers recommend leaving the base camp at 3am to arrive in time to watch the sunrise from the summit.

A minimum of two days is needed to climb from the ranger station in San Gerardo to the summit and back, leaving no time for recuperation or exploration. It is definitely worthwhile to spend at least one extra day exploring the trails around the summit and/or the base lodge.

Other Trails

Most trekkers follow the main trail to Chirripó and return the same way, but there are several other attractive destinations that are accessible by trails from the base camp. An alternative, longer route between the base lodge and the summit goes via **Cerro Terbi** (3760m), as well as **Los Crestones**, the moonlike rock formations that adorn many postcards. If you are hanging around for a few days, the glorious, grassy **Sabana de los Leones** is a popular destination that offers a stark contrast to the otherwise alpine scenery. Peak-baggers will want to visit **Cerro Ventisqueros** (3812m), which is also within a day's walk of Crestones. These trails are fairly well-maintained, but it's worth inquiring about conditions before setting out.

For hardcore adventurers, an alternative route is to take a guided three- or four-day loop trek that begins in Herradura and spends a day or two traversing cloud forest and *páramo* on the slopes of Fila Urán. Hikers ascend **Cerro Urán** (3600m) before the final ascent of Chirripó and then descend through San Gerardo. This trip requires bush camping and you must be accompanied by a local guide at all times. Costa Rica Trekking Adventures (see below) can make arrangements for this tour. Alternatively, contact the **guides' association** (☎ 2771 1199) in Herradura, which is run through the local *pulpería*.

TOURS

Most travelers prefer to access the park either independently or by hiring a local guide, though **Costa Rica Trekking Adventures** (☎ 2771 4582; www.chirripo.com) is highly recommended if you prefer organized adventure. This well-established company offers several different guided excursions around Chirripó, ranging from a one-day trek to Llano Bonito to a four-day trek around the Urán loop. Note that prices are negotiable, and ultimately dependant on the size of the party and the time of year.

SLEEPING & EATING

The only accommodation in Parque Nacional Chirripó is at **Crestones Base Lodge** (dm US$10), housing up to 60 people in dorm-style bunks. The basic stone building has a solar panel that provides electric light from 6pm to 8pm and sporadic heat for showers. The lodge rents a variety of gear including sleeping bags, blankets, cooking equipment and gas canisters for a few dollars per day.

Reservations are absolutely necessary at Crestones Base Lodge. Your tour company will likely make reservations for you; but for those traveling independently, it is virtually impossible to make reservations before your arrival in Costa Rica. Once in Costa Rica however, it is necessary to contact the **Minae office** (☎ 2771 3155; fax 2771 3297; aclap@sinac.go.cr) in San Isidro. If space is available, you will be required to pay by credit card in order to confirm the reservation. You must present your reservation and payment confirmation at the ranger station in San Gerardo de Rivas on the day before you set out.

Fortunately, the lodge reserves 10 spaces per night for travelers who show up in San Gerardo and are ready to hike on the following day. This is the more practical option for most travelers, although there is no guarantee that there will be space available on the days you wish to hike. Space is at a premium during holiday periods and on weekends during the dry season. The ranger station opens at 6:30am – the earlier you arrive, the more likely you will be able to hike the following day.

Crestones Base Lodge provides drinking water, but no food. Hikers must bring all of their own provisions. Camping is allowed only at a special designated area near Cerro Urán – not at Crestones or anywhere else in the park.

GETTING THERE & AROUND

See details under San Gerardo de Rivas (p377) for directions on how to get here. From opposite the ranger station, in front of Cabinas El Bosque, there is free transpor-

tation to the trailhead at 5am. Also, several hotels offer early-morning trailhead transportation for their guests.

THE ROAD TO LA AMISTAD

From San Isidro, the Interamericana winds its way southeast through some glorious geography of rolling hills and coffee plantations backed by striking mountain facades, towering as much as 3350m above. Along this stretch, a series of narrow, steep, dirt roads lead to some of the country's most remote areas – some nearly inaccessible due to the prohibitive presence of the Cordillera de Talamanca. Of course, it's worth enduring the thrilling road for the chance to visit Parque International La Amistad, a true wilderness of epic scale.

BUENOS AIRES

All it takes is a quick glance at the town's Del Monte processing plant to realize that pineapples are big business in Buenos Aires. Of course, unless you're interested in getting a good price on a truckload of sweetened pineapple rings, there is little reason to give the town more than a passing glance, though Buenos Aires does serve as an administrative center for the Ujarrás, Salitre and Cabagra indigenous groups.

If you're planning on visiting any of the reserves, a good starting point is the **Asociacíon Regional Aborigen del Dikes** (Aradikes; ☎ 2730 0289; www.aradikes.org), a local organization that works to increase the capacity of indigenous communities in the Buenos Aires region. Efforts range from reforestation to cultural tourism to activism against the Boruca hydroelectric project (p383). Another good place to stop is the **Fundación Dúrika Office** (☎ 2730 0657; www.durika.org), which helps travelers make reservations to stay at the Reserva Biológica Dúrika (see p382).

If you get stuck for the night, you can always grab a room at **Aradikes** (☎ 2730 0289; r from US$15; P 🛇), which also serves as something of a makeshift-business hotel comprised of several whitewashed cabins surrounding a thatch-roof rancho. Cheap and hearty meals are also available on the premises, as are cold beers to help beat the tropical heat.

Buses that travel between Palmar Norte, San Vito, San Isidro and San José pass by without stopping in Buenos Aires, though you can flag them down on the Interamericana. However, there is no marked bus shelter, so be sure that you are visible otherwise the bus driver won't stop for you.

If you have your own transportation, Buenos Aires can be reached by turning off the Interamericana just south of the Del Monte plant – a paved road leads 3km north to Buenos Aires. This main road into town forks about 1km south of town: the left fork passes the Fundación Dúrika Office and heads into the center of town, near the Parque Central; the right fork bypasses the center and heads to Aradikes.

RESERVA BIOLÓGICA DÚRIKA
A perfect example of sustainable tourism in action, this 7500-hectare biological reserve is home to a small but thriving community of Ticos and resident foreigners who are committed to local conservation, natural medicine and the preservation of indigenous culture. Since 1992, Dúrika has opened its arms to any travelers interested in partaking in their inspiring social experiment.

Tours of the working farm demonstrate the principles and processes of organic agriculture that Dúrika employs, such as fertilizer made from chili peppers. Guests can also arrange short hikes into the reserve, daylong forays to the Cabécar indigenous village of **Ujarrás**, and/or multiday treks. Travelers with a strong interest in indigenous cultures or medicinal plants should inquire about the **Shaman Tour**, a week-long journey that visits several communities, and focuses on traditional healing methods.

Visitors are also welcome to stay closer to home, participating in the life of the farm, checking out local waterfalls (which fuel the community's hydroelectric power) and otherwise exploring the grounds. Accommodation (from US$35 per person) is also available in cabins of various sizes sleeping two to eight people. As an added bonus, rates include organic vegetarian meals made from locally grown foods. Note that discounted rates are available for large groups and students, and volunteer opportunities are available.

Reservations and information are available from the **Fundación Dúrika office** (☎ 2730 0657; www.durika.org) in Buenos Aires. If possible, it is advised that you make reservations as early as possible since accommodation fills up quickly in the high season. Although it is possible to drive to Dúrika in a 4WD, the office can easily arrange transport to the reserve (US$30 for up to five passengers) and watch over your car while you're staying at the reserve.

RESERVA INDÍGENA BORUCA
The picturesque valley of the Río Grande de Térraba is the setting for the indigenous reserve of Brunka (Boruca) peoples. Historians believe that the present-day Brunka have evolved out of several different indigenous groups, including the Coto, Quepos, Turrucaca, Burucac and Abubaes, whose territories stretched all the way to the Península de Osa in pre-Columbian times. Today however, the entire Brunka population is largely confined to the small villages of Rey Curré, which is bisected by the Carretera Interamericana, and Boruca, 8km north.

At first glance, it is difficult to differentiate these towns from a typical Tico village, aside from a few artisans selling their handiwork. In fact, these towns hardly cater to the tourist trade, which is one of the main reasons why traditional Boruca life is continuing on without much distraction. In any case, please be particularly sensitive when visiting indigenous communities – always dress modestly and avoid taking photographs of people without asking permission. Although they can be incredibly interesting places to visit, indigenous villages are not human zoos, but rather living communities struggling to maintain their culture amidst a changing world.

Orientation & Information
Rey Curré (usually just 'Curré' on maps) is about 30km south of Buenos Aires, right on the Interamericana. Drivers can stop to visit a small **cooperative** (☺ 9am-5pm Mon-Fri, 2-5pm Sat) that sells handicrafts. In Boruca, local artisans post signs outside their homes advertising their handmade balsa masks and woven bags. Exhibits are sometimes on display in the **museo**, a thatch-roof rancho 100m west of the *pulpería*.
Asociación Regional Aborigen del Dikes (Aradikes; ☎ 2730 0289; www.aradikes.org; Buenos Aires) Inquire about homestays and local tour guides.
Galería Namu (☎ 2256 3412; www.galerianamu.com; Av 7 btwn Calles 5 & 7, San José; per person per day

---

THE BORUCA DAM

Rey Curré is the proposed site of a huge hydroelectric project, specifically, a 220m dam across the Río Grande de Térraba that if completed, would reportedly be the largest dam in Central America. Needless to say, the proposal for the Boruca dam has caused quite the controversy, especially since it would flood 25,000 hectares of land as well as displace thousands of residents, the majority of which are members of the Brunka indigenous group.

The Brunka have strong ties to their land, not only due to their subsistence from agriculture and dependence on plants for medicinal use, but also due to the presence of ancestral burial grounds. Furthermore, the Brunka recognize that relocation would inevitably result in the physical division of their community, something they have already experienced – to a smaller degree – with the construction of the Interamericana.

In theory, the hydroelectric project cannot go forward without the consent of the residents, but many of the Brunka feel helpless and hopeless in the face of the ICE: a government-owned electricity company that has an incredible amount of weight and capital behind them. As a result, organizations like the **Asociacíon Regional Aborigen del Dikes** (Aradikes; see p381) have been actively campaigning against the ICE's initiative, though the odds are clearly stacked against them.

At the time of research, it was difficult to say which side was winning. According to the official spokesperson of the ICE, the project was steadily moving forward, with plans to have the dam functional by 2015. On the other hand, there is little evidence that construction is even close to commencing and the ICE has acknowledged that it can't proceed without making a concrete proposal to the Brunka.

Like all issues centered on the fine line between economic development and environmental conservation, there is no cut-and-dry answer that will appease both parties. Hopefully this politically and emotionally charged issue will be handled with both competence and dignity.

US$45) This San José gallery – which specializes in indigenous art – can arrange tours to Boruca, which include homestay, hiking to waterfalls, handicraft demonstrations and storytelling. Transportation to Boruca is not included. For more information, see p107.

Festivals & Events

The **Fiesta de los Diablitos** is a three-day Brunka event that symbolizes the struggle between the Spanish and the indigenous population. Sometimes called the Danza de los Diablitos, or 'dance of the little devils,' the culmination of the festival is a choreographed battle between the opposing sides. Villagers wearing wooden devil masks and burlap costumes play the role of the natives in their fight against the Spanish conquerors. The Spaniards, represented by a man in a bull costume, lose the battle. This festival is held in Boruca from December 31 to January 2 and in Curré from February 5 to 8.

Many outsiders descend on Boruca and Curré during these events. While the Brunka welcome visitors, they request that guests respect their traditions. Tourists are generally required to pay a fee for the right to take photographs or video. No flash photography or artificial lighting is allowed, and tourists are not allowed to interfere with the program.

The lesser-known **Fiesta de los Negritos**, held during the second week of December, celebrates the Virgin of the Immaculate Conception. Traditional indigenous music (mainly drumming and bamboo flutes) accompanies dancing and costumes.

Sleeping & Eating

The only regular place to stay in the area is at the Tico-owned **Bar Restaurante Boruca** (☎ 2730 2454; d from US$10) in Boruca, which consists of five basic rooms with private cold-water bathrooms.

However, for a more in-depth understanding of the Brunka culture and lifestyle, it's recommended that you arrange a home-stay through **Pedro Rojas Morales** (☎ 506-362-2545; saribu@yahoo.com; prices negotiable). A soft-spoken Brunka artist who is certainly a local expert, Señor Morales can help you arrange a wide range of activities on the reservation.

Shopping

The Brunka are celebrated craftspeople and their traditional art plays a leading role in the survival of their culture. While most people make their living from agriculture, some indigenous people have begun producing fine handicrafts for tourists. The tribe is most famous for its ornate masks, carved from balsa or cedar, and sometimes colored with natural dyes and acrylics. Brunka women also use pre-Columbian backstrap looms to weave colorful, natural cotton bags, placemats and other textiles.

Getting There & Away

Buses (US$1.75, 1½ hours) leave the central market in Buenos Aires at noon and 3:30pm daily, traveling to Boruca via a very poor dirt road. The bus returns the following morning, which makes Boruca difficult for a day trip relying on public transportation. A taxi from Buenos Aires to Boruca is about US$20.

Drivers will find a better road that leaves the Interamericana about 3km south of Curré – look for the sign. In total, it's about 8km to Boruca from Curré, though the going is slow, and a 4WD is recommended.

PALMAR

At the intersection of the country's two major highways, the unremarkable village of Palmar is a transportation hub that serves as a gateway to the Osa peninsula and Golfo Dulce (for more information, see p394). Although the town also serves as an important banana-growing center, for the average traveler, there is little reason to spend any more time here than it takes to get off the plane or change buses.

Palmar is actually split in two – to get from Palmar Norte to Palmar Sur, take the Interamericana southbound over the Río Grande de Térraba bridge, then take the first right beyond the bridge. Most facilities are in Palmar Norte, clustered around the intersection of the Carretera Interamericana and the Costanera Sur (Pacific Coast Hwy), while Palmar Sur is the locale of the airstrip. In Palmar Norte you can grab some cash at the **Banco Coopelianza** (🕐 8am-5pm Mon-Fri, 8am-noon Sat) or **Banco Popular** (☎ 2786 7033), both on the Interamericana.

Lack of charm aside, Palmar is one of the best sites in the country to see the **granite spheres**, or *esferas de piedra,* a legacy of pre-Columbian cultures – some of which exceed 2m in diameter. They are scattered all over town, including at the airstrip – some of the largest and most impressive are in front of the peach-colored *el colegio* (school) on the Interamericana.

You'll not want to linger in Palmar, but if you miss a connection, a good option is the **Brunka Lodge** (☎ 2786 7944; brunkalodge@costarricense .cr; s/d/tr US$25/30/35; 🅿 🅢). Accommodation is in sun-filled, clean swept bungalows that are clustered around a swimming pool and a pleasant open-air restaurant. The **Panadería Palenquito** (Transportes Térraba bus stop) is a useful breakfast spot if you are catching an early morning bus.

Getting There & Away

AIR

Departing from San José, **NatureAir** (www.natureair .com) and **Sansa** (www.sansa.com) have daily flights to the Palmar airstrip. Prices vary according to season and availability, though you can expect to pay around US$100 to/from San José.

Taxis meet incoming flights and charge about US$3 to Palmar Norte and US$15 to Sierpe. Otherwise, the infrequent Palmar Norte–Sierpe bus goes through Palmar Sur – you can board it if there's space available.

BUS

Buses to San José and San Isidro stop on the east side of the Interamericana. Other buses leave from in front of Panadería Palenquito or Supermercado Térraba a block apart on the town's main street. The bus ticket office is inside the Palenquito.

Neily (Transportes Térraba) US$1.25, 1½ hours, depart 5am, 6am, 7am, 9:30am, noon, 1pm, 2:20pm & 4:50pm.

San Isidro (Tracopa) US$2.75, three hours, depart 8:30am, 11:30am, 2:30pm and 4:30pm.

San José (Tracopa) US$5, five hours, 5:25am, 6:15am, 7:45am, 10am, 1pm, 3pm and 4:45pm.

Sierpe US$1, one hour, depart 4:30am, 7am, 9:30am, 11:30am, 2:30pm and 5:30pm.

NEILY

Although it is southern Costa Rica's second-largest 'city,' Neily has retained the friendly atmosphere of a rural town. Much like Palmar, Neily is a major transport hub and agricultural center that is decidedly lacking in tourist appeal.

Neily sits on the west bank of the Río Corredor, on the north side of the

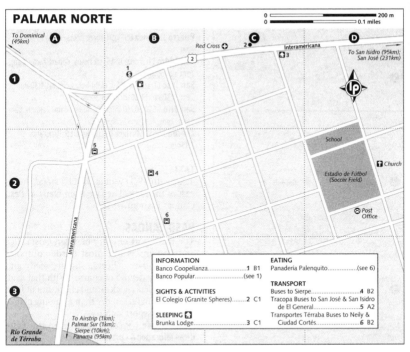

PALMAR NORTE

0 _____ 200 m
0 _____ 0.1 miles

INFORMATION	
Banco Coopelianza	1 B1
Banco Popular	(see 1)

SIGHTS & ACTIVITIES	
El Colegio (Granite Spheres)	2 C1

SLEEPING ⌂	
Brunka Lodge	3 C1

EATING	
Panaderia Palenquito	(see 6)

TRANSPORT	
Buses to Sierpe	4 B2
Tracopa Buses to San José & San Isidro	
de El General	5 A2
Transportes Térraba Buses to Neily &	
Ciudad Cortés	6 B2

Interamericana. From here the Interamericana continues 17km to Panama, while Rte 16 makes a beeline north to the attractive mountain village of San Vito.

About 15km north of Neily on the road to San Vito, **Las Cavernas de Corredores** are a network of little-explored caverns on a private banana plantation. Besides the huge, impressive stalactites, several species of bats are also in the caves. It's not geared toward tourists, but it is usually possible to visit.

William Hidalgo is a **local guide** (☎ 2770 8225) who leads travelers through the cavern. If you have a 4WD, turn off about 15km north of Neily, just before the school. The small *pulpería* (look for the 'telefono publico' sign) has more information. Otherwise, you can hire a 4WD taxi from Neily for about US$10.

In Neily there is a **Banco Coopealianza**, southwest of the *mercado* (market), that has a 24-hour ATM on the Cirrus network. Alternatively, **Banco de Costa Rica** (⌚ 8am-3pm Mon-Fri) changes traveler's checks. If you need to check your email try **Technoplanet Internet** (☎ 2783 4744; per hr US$1; ⌚ 9am-5pm).

Few people have reason to stick around town, though you can always grab a clean room and a hot meal at **Centro Turistico Neily** (☎ 2783 3031; r from US$30; P X R), a low-key resort in a quiet residential part of town. The faux-colonial decorations create a relaxed ambiance, as does the tranquil open-air restaurant overlooking the grounds.

Getting There & Away
AIR
Departing from San José, **NatureAir** (www.natureair .com) and **Sansa** (www.sansa.com) have daily flights to the Neily airstrip. Prices vary according to season and availability, though you can expect to pay around US$100 to/from San José.

BUS
The following buses leave from the main terminal on the east side of town:

Airport US$0.50, 30 minutes, depart 7:30am, 9:15am, 11:30am, 1:15pm, 3:15pm, 5:30pm and 6pm.

Golfito US$0.50, 1½ hours, depart hourly from 6am to 7:30pm.

Palmar US$1.25, 1½ hours, depart 4:45am, 9:15am, noon, 12:30pm, 2:30pm, 4:30pm and 5:45pm.

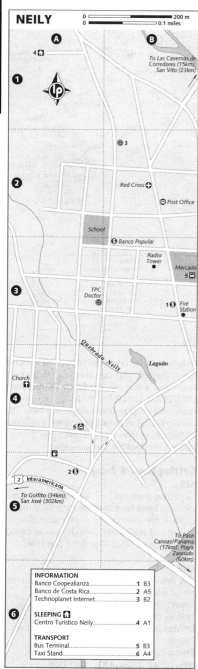

NEILY

To Las Cavernas de
Corredores (15km);
San Vito (23km)

Red Cross ✚

✚ Post Office

School

Ⓢ Banco Popular

Radio
Tower

Mercado
5 ⌂

TPC
Doctor
@

1 Ⓢ *Fire
Station*

Quebrada Neily

Laguito

Church

6 ⌂

2 Ⓢ

2 *Interamericana*

To Golfito (34km);
San José (302km)

To Paso
Canoas/Panama
(17km); Playa
Zancudo
(60km)

Paso Canoas US$0.50, 30 minutes, depart every half hour from 6am to 6pm.

Puerto Jiménez US$3.50, three hours, depart 7am and 2pm.

San Isidro (Tracopa) US$5, six hours, depart 7am, 10am, 1pm and 3pm.

San José (Tracopa) US$9, eight hours, depart 4:30am, 5am, 8:30am, 11:30am and 3:30pm.

San Vito US$0.50, 30 minutes, depart 6am, 7:30am, 9am, noon, 1pm, 4pm and 5:30pm.

Zancudo US$1.50, three hours, depart 9:30am and 2:15pm.

TAXI

Taxis with 4WD wait at the taxi stand southeast of the park. The fare from Neily to Paso Canoas is about US$6.

PASO CANOAS

The main port of entry between Costa Rica and Panama is like most border outposts the world over – hectic, slightly seedy and completely devoid of charm. With that said, most travelers check-in and check-out of Paso Canoas with little more than a passing glance at their passport stamp.

Báncredito (☒ 8am-4:30pm), near the **Costa Rican Migración & Customs** (☒ 6am-11pm), changes traveler's checks and there is an ATM on the Visa Plus system near the border. Rates for converting excess colones into dollars are not good, but they will do in a pinch. Colones are accepted at the border, but are difficult to get rid of further into Panama.

The **Instituto Panameño de Turismo** (☎ 2727 6524; ☒ 6am-11pm), in the Panamanian immigration post, has information on travel to Panama. If you are arriving in Costa Rica, you'll find sparse tourist information at the Costa Rican Tourist Information office in Costa Rican Migración and Customs.

The hotels in Paso Canoas aren't particularly inviting, but **Cabinas Romy** (☎ 2732 2873; r from US$10; Ⓟ) will do if necessary. Set around a pleasant courtyard, shiny rooms are decked with pastel-colored walls, wooden doors and floral bedspreads, which add a surprising bit of warmth to an otherwise drab town.

Tracopa buses leave for San José (US$9, six hours) at 4am, 7:30am, 9am and 3pm. The **Tracopa bus terminal** (☎ 2732 2201), or window really, is north of the border post, on the east side of the main road. Sunday-afternoon buses are full of weekend shoppers, so buy tickets as early as possible. Buses for Neily (US$0.50, 30

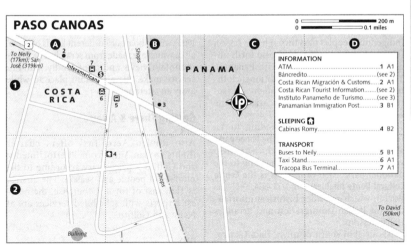

PASO CANOAS

| 0 | 200 m |
| 0 | 0.1 miles |

INFORMATION	
ATM	1 A1
Báncredito	(see 2)
Costa Rican Migración & Customs	2 A1
Costa Rican Tourist Information	(see 2)
Instituto Panameño de Turismo	(see 3)
Panamanian Immigration Post	3 B1

| SLEEPING | |
| Cabinas Romy | 4 B2 |

TRANSPORT	
Buses to Neily	5 B1
Taxi Stand	6 A1
Tracopa Bus Terminal	7 A1

minutes) leave from in front of the post office at least once an hour from 6am to 6pm. Taxis to Neily cost about US$6 and to the airport about US$8.

For more information on border crossing specifics, see boxed text, p390.

WILSON BOTANICAL GARDEN

About 6km south of San Vito is this world-class **botanical garden** (☎ 2773 4004; www.esintro .co.cr; Las Cruces Biological Station; admission US$6, guided tours US$15; ☒ 8am-4pm). Covering 12 hectares and surrounded by 254 hectares of natural forest, the garden was established by Robert and Catherine Wilson in 1963 and thereafter became internationally known for its collection.

In 1973 the area came under the auspices of the Organization for Tropical Studies (OTS) and today the well-maintained garden – part of Las Cruces Biological Station – holds more than 1000 genera of plants from about 200 families. As part of the OTS, the garden plays a scientific role as a research center. Species threatened with extinction are preserved here for possible reforestation in the future.

The gardens are well laid out, many of the plants are labeled and a trail map is available for self-guided walks, featuring exotic species like orchids, bromeliads, palms and medicinal plants. The many ornamental varieties are beautiful, but the tours explain that they are useful too (such as the delicate cycad, used by Cabécar and Bribrí indigenous people as a treatment for snakebites). The gardens are

especially popular among bird-watchers, who may see scarlet-thighed dacni, silver-throated tanager, violaceous trogon, blue-headed parrot, violet sabre-wing hummingbird and turquoise cotinga.

If you want to stay overnight at the botanical gardens, make your reservations well in advance: facilities are often filled with researchers and students. Accommodation is in comfortable cabins (single/double including meals US$88/164) in the midst of the gorgeous grounds. The rooms are simple, but they each have a balcony with an amazing view of the surrounding flora. Rates include entry to the gardens.

Buses between San Vito and Neily pass the entrance to the gardens. Make sure you take the bus that goes through Agua Buena as buses that go through Cañas Gordas do not stop here. A taxi from San Vito to the gardens costs US$3.

SAN VITO

Founded by Italian immigrants in the 1950s, San Vito is home to a large Italian community that has retained their language and culture (not to mention their cuisine!). Of course, this is no small feat considering that this remote mountain town is located on the edge of Parque Internacional La Amistad, one of Central America's last great wilderness areas.

In addition to the descendants of the original Italian founders, San Vito is also home to a large population of Guaymí people.

The proximity of the town to the Reserva Indígena Guaymí de Coto Brus means that indigenous peoples pass through this region (Guaymí enclaves move back and forth undisturbed across the border with Panama). You might spot women in traditional clothing – long, solid-colored *pollera* dresses trimmed in contrasting hues – riding the bus or strolling the streets.

If you're planning on heading to La Amistad, San Vito is home to the **Minae parks office** (☎ 2773 3955; ☒ 9am-4pm), which can help you get your bearings before heading to the national park. Also of interest is the **Centro Cultural Dante Alighieri** (☎ 2773 4934; ☒ 1-7pm Mon-Fri), which provides historical information on Italian immigration and arranges Italian lessons.

About 3km south of town, **Finca Cántaros** (☎ 2773 3760; admission US$1; ☒ 9:30am-5pm Tue-Sun) is a recreation center and reforestation project. The 10 hectares of grounds – which used to be coffee plantations and pasture land – are now a lovely park with garden trails, picnic areas and a dramatic lookout over the city. The reception is housed in a pretty, well-maintained cabin that contains a small but carefully chosen selection of local and national crafts.

The best option in town is the **Hotel El Ceibo** (☎ 2773 3025; s/d/tr US$25/35/45; ☒), conveniently located about 100m west of the main intersection. Here, you can sleep easy in simple but functional rooms (some with forest views) and dig into some truly authentic Italian pastas and wines.

Another great spot for Italian fare is the **Pizzería Restaurant Lilliana** (pizzas US$3-5; ☒ 10:30am-10pm), which boasts 15 different kinds of pizza, all of which are made from scratch. The lovely mountain views and the friendly, familiar service make this a pleasant place to while away an afternoon.

Getting There & Away
AIR
Alfo Romeo Aero Taxi offers charter flights to San Vito from Puerto Jiménez and Golfito – prices vary according to the number of people and season. The airstrip is 1km east of town. Otherwise, the nearest airports with scheduled services are at Neily and Golfito.

BUS
The main **Tracopa bus terminal** (☎ 2773 3410) is located on the northern end of the main street.

San Isidro US$2.75, three hours, depart 6:45am and 1:30pm.

San José US$7.50, seven hours, depart 5am, 7:30am, 10am and 3pm.

A local bus terminal on the northwest end of town runs buses to Neily and other destinations.

Neily US$1.25; two hours; depart 5:30am, 7am, 7:30am, 9am, 11am, noon, 2pm and 5pm.

Río Sereno US$1; 1½ hours; depart 7am, 10am, 1pm and 4pm.

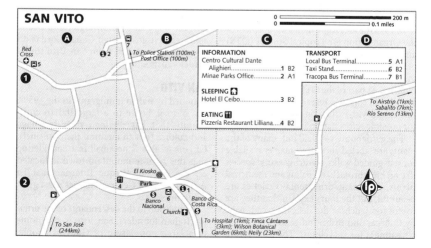

SAN VITO

0 ___ 200 m
0 ___ 0.1 miles

INFORMATION
Centro Cultural Dante
  Alighieri.............................1 B2
Minae Parks Office.............2 A1

SLEEPING ⌂
Hotel El Ceibo.....................3 B2

EATING 🍴
Pizzería Restaurant Lilliana....4 B2

TRANSPORT
Local Bus Terminal.................5 A1
Taxi Stand.............................6 B2
Tracopa Bus Terminal.............7 B1

To Police Station (100m);
Post Office (100m)

To Airstrip (1km);
Sabalito (7km);
Río Sereno (13km)

Red Cross

El Kiosko
Park
Banco Nacional
Church
Banco de Costa Rica

To San José (244km)

To Hospital (1km); Finca Cántaros (3km); Wilson Botanical Garden (6km); Neily (23km)

RAIN-FOREST MEDICINE

Indigenous groups use tropical flowers, herbs and plants to treat all kinds of illnesses, from diabetes to a slipped disk. Here are a few of our favorites, courtesy of Paradise Tropical Garden (see below):

- Most doctors treat stomach ulcers with antibiotics, but natural-medicine connoisseurs recommend the seeds from the spiny red annatto pod. Remove the seeds from the pod and wash away the red paste. You can eat the seeds straight from the pod, or dry them and grind them into your food.

- The leaves of the avocado tree are said to cure high blood pressure. Just boil them for three minutes and let them steep for another three. Strain the murky drink and store it in the fridge. Apparently you should drink three cups a day, but beware: this brew is a diuretic.

- If you suffer from a slipped disk, you might try this natural remedy, made from the bracts of the beautiful red plume ginger (*Alpinia purpurata*), which is bountiful in the rain forest. The bracts are the small leaves at the base of the bloom. Pull them off the stem of the ginger and stuff as many as you can fit into a small bottle, then fill the bottle with rubbing alcohol. Let it sit for three days, before rubbing this tincture onto your sore back. This remedy should ease your pain within a few days.

If you would like to learn more, pay a visit to the **Paradise Tropical Garden** (☎ 2789 8746; http://paradis-garden.tripod.com; Río Claro; admission by donation; ☺ 6am-5pm) where Robert and Ella Beatham have created a wonderfully sensual introduction to tropical fruits and rain-forest remedies that they call the 'Tropical Fruit See, Smell, Taste & Touch Experience.' Besides this interactive display, visitors also learn about the production of African palm oil and how it came to be the dominant crop of this region following the collapse of the banana industry. Robert and Ella are wonderful hosts, but you should call a day in advance if you want their full attention. The gardens are located just west of the town of Río Claro – follow the Interamericana for 1km, cross the Río Largarto and turn right at the end of the bridge. From here, the garden is just 200m beyond.

CAR

The drive north from Neily is a scenic one, with superb views of the lowlands dropping away as the road winds up the hillside. The paved road is steep, narrow and full of hairpin turns. You can also get to San Vito from San Isidro via the Valle de Coto Brus – an incredibly scenic and less-used route with fantastic views of the Cordillera de Talamanca to the north and the lower Fila Costeña to the south.

PARQUE INTERNACIONAL LA AMISTAD

This 407,000-hectare international park was established jointly in 1988 by Panama and Costa Rica – hence its name, La Amistad (Friendship). It is by far the largest protected area in Costa Rica, and stands as a testament to the possibilities of international cooperation in the name of environmental conser-

vation. In 1990, La Amistad was declared a Unesco World Heritage Site and later became part of the greater Mesoamerican Biological corridor, which protects a great variety of endangered habitats.

The backbone of this park is the Cordillera de Talamanca, which not only includes the peaks of the Chirripó massif, but also numerous other mountains higher than 3000m. At this altitude, the landscape is characterized by the shrubby, stunted vegetation of the *páramo*, while slightly lower altitudes yield impressive oaks and the thick vegetation of the cloud forest. The lowlands of the Talamanca valley are fertile rain forest – a canopy of cedar, cypress and oak trees, with a thick undergrowth of palms, ferns and epiphytes. This diversity of altitude and habitat creates unprecedented biological diversity, thus attracting the attention of ecologists and conservationists worldwide.

Although most of the park's area is high up in the Talamanca mountains and remains virtually inaccessible, there is no shortage of

GETTING TO PANAMA

To David

On the Carretera Interamericana, Paso Canoas is the major border crossing with Panama. Although it is conveniently open 24 hours, it is crowded and confusing, especially during holiday periods, when hordes of Ticos arrive for shopping sprees. Note that it's very easy to walk across the border without realizing it. No harm done, but don't go too far without getting the proper stamps in your passport.

Costa Rican *migración* (immigration) is on the eastern side of the highway, north of the Tracopa bus terminal. After securing an exit visa, walk 300m east to the Panamanian immigration post, in the huge new yellow cement block. Here you can purchase the necessary tourist card (US$5 for US citizens) to enter Panama. You might be asked for an onward ticket and evidence of financial solvency (presenting a credit card does the trick). From here dozens of minivans go to the city of David (US$2, 1½ hours).

If you are in a private vehicle, you must have your car fumigated (US$4). Keep a copy of the fumigation ticket as roadside checkpoints often request it. Note that you cannot cross the border in a rental vehicle.

To Río Sereno

East of San Vito a little-transited road leads to the border crossing at Río Sereno, from where you can continue on to the village of Volcán near Parque Nacional Volcán Barú in Panama. Río Sereno is a tranquil, pleasant place – atypical of border towns. The crossing here is hassle-free.

Migración (☉ 8am-6pm) is beside the police station. Panamanian immigration officials may require an onward ticket, plus US$500 (or bank and credit cards) to show solvency. The latter isn't usually demanded if you have a passport from a first-world country and look reasonably affluent.

US passport holders will need to purchase a tourist card (US$5), which is sold at the bank, about 100m past the *migración* office. Officials can direct you there. Note that the bank is closed on Sundays and Saturday afternoons.

There are no facilities on the Costa Rican side, but Río Serena in Panama has a decent hotel, a good pizza place and internet access. Note that the banking facilities at the border do not handle foreign exchange, so it's best to bring US dollars, which function as the Panamanian currency (known as *balboas*). Once across the border, buses depart Río Sereno hourly to David via Volcán.

---

hiking and camping opportunities available for intrepid travelers. However, tourist infrastructure within the park is almost nonexistent, which means trekkers are limited to specific areas and/or the services of guides.

While tourists flock to Costa Rica's more well-known parks in the hopes of having an 'eco-adventure,' La Amistad exists as one of the country's last true wilderness areas. Tackling this pristine yet potentially treacherous environment is no easy task, though La Amistad is brimming with possibilities for rugged exploration – if you're afraid of growing old in an urban jungle, spend some time in this verdant one.

ORIENTATION & INFORMATION

Limited information is available at local **Minae offices** (Buenos Aires ☎ 2730 0846; San Isidro ☎ 2771 3155, 2771 4836, 2771 5116; Calle 2 btwn Avs 4 & 6; San Vito ☎ 2773 4090). They are all minimally helpful.

To make reservations to camp or to stay in a refuge, it's better to call directly to park headquarters at **Altamira** (☎ 2200 5355; park fee per person per day US$5). This is the best-developed area of the park, with a camping area, showers and drinking water, electric light and a lookout tower. A group of parataxonomists studying insects in this area has created a small display of butterflies and moths.

The thickly forested northern Caribbean slopes and southern Pacific slopes of the Talamancas are protected in the park, but it is only on the Pacific side that ranger stations are found. Besides the headquarters at Altamira, there are additional, little-used ranger stations at **Potrero Grande** (☎ 2742 8090), north of Paso Real, and Santa María de Pittier on the slopes of Cerro Pittier (2844m). While there is an extremely basic hostel with toilets and fresh water at Santa María, these stations are not really set up to accommodate tourists.

ACTIVITIES
Wildlife-Watching
Although most of Parque Internacional Amistad is inaccessible terrain high up in the Talamanca, the park is home to a recorded 90 mammal species and more than 400 bird species. The park has the nation's largest population of Baird's tapirs (see boxed text, p428), as well as giant anteaters, all six species of neotropical cats – jaguar, puma (mountain lion), margay, ocelot, oncilla (tiger cat) and jaguarundi – and many more-common mammals.

In excess of 500 bird species (49 unique) have been sighted – more than half of the total in Costa Rica – including the majestic but extremely rare harpy eagle (see p392). In addition, the park protects 115 species of fish, 215 different reptiles and amphibians, as well as innumerable insect species.

Visiting Indigenous Groups
Besides the countless animal species, La Amistad is also home to five different indigenous reservations for the Cabécar and Bribrí groups. These tribes originally inhabited lands on the Caribbean coast (and many still do), but over the past century, they have migrated west into the mountains and as far as the Pacific coast. It is possible to visit the Cabécar via the Reserva Biológica Dúrika (p382) and the Bribrí via ATEC (p481) in Puerto Viejo de Talamanca.

With that said, the reserves see few foreign visitors and it's unlikely that the cruise ship circuit will swing this way anytime soon. As a result, the Cabécar and Bribrí tend to view tourists with equal parts respect and awe, and at times you will be amazed at the hospitality of your hosts. Although they are tough people that have made a life for themselves in an unforgiving habitat, the Cabécar and Bribrí have smiles that could melt gold.

Of course, you should still make an effort to respect the sensibilities of your hosts. Although some men and women still walk around topless in the village, these are still fairly conservative societies, and it's recommended that you cover up as a sign of respect. In regards to photography, most villagers will be happy to pose for a photo, but you should always ask before sticking your camera where it doesn't belong. Generally speaking, you will not be asked to pay for a photo, though it's best to ask your guide what is expected from you.

Tourism has a long way to develop in the region, which is one reason why a visit to a Cabécar or Bribrí village is so refreshing. Inquire locally about proper conduct in La Amistad.

Hiking
Behind Altamira station, **Los Gigantes del Bosque** is a short 3km circuit that is named for the 40m trees along the way. Signposts in Spanish provide simple explanations of some of the flora, although they are clearly designed for kids. Nonetheless, the trail is an easy means of seeing some ancient rain forest. It passes two lookout points, one on the edge of the primary forest, and the other overlooking the rural landscape outside the park. Note that this trail is marked, but it is not well maintained. Be prepared to climb over fallen branches and wade through high grass. More importantly, make sure you bring plenty of water and snacks and pay close attention to the markers. Normally the loop takes two hours, but it can be much longer if you lose the trail.

The longest trail (approximately 20km) – known as the **Valle del Silencio** – departs from the Estación Altamira and winds its way through pristine and hilly primary forest before ending up at a camping area and refuge at the base of **Cerro Kamuk** (3549m). The walk takes anywhere from eight to 12 hours, provided you are in very good physical condition. It is reportedly spectacular and traverses one of the most isolated areas in all of Costa Rica.

A local guide is required to make the journey. Contact the association of guides **Asoprola** (☎ 2743 1184) in Altamira to inquire about these arrangements. Asoprola can also provide food and lodging in the village of Altamira, just below the park headquarters.

Hardy adventurers can also hike to the summit of Cerro Kamuk from the village of Potrero Grande or Tres Colinas. This journey requires three days to ascend and two days to descend and – again – the services of a guide. Lodging is in tents and hikers must transport all of their own supplies and provisions. Contact the **Tres Colinas guides' association** (☎ 8814 0889) for more information.

THE MOTHER OF ALL EAGLES

The harpy eagle, Central America's most striking raptor, is considered by many to be the most powerful bird of prey in the world. Unfortunately, opportunities to see the bird in the wild are limited as they are rare throughout most of their range and are hard to spot in the canopy even when they are present. Fortunately, you're in La Amistad, which is home to a healthy nesting population. Although the chances of spotting one are still low, your chances are better here than anywhere else in Costa Rica.

Harpy eagles are enormous birds with a wingspan of 2m and a height of 1.5m – they are immediately recognizable. Adults tend to have white breasts with a broad black chest band and faint leg barring as well as gray upperparts. They also have piercing yellow eyes that can be seen from the forest floor, as well as powerful yellow talons and a hooked bill.

Anyone who has had the privilege to watch a harpy eagle hunt will tell you that it is simply awesome. For instance, a harpy seen with a large male howler writhing in her grip will shift her talons with a resounding 'pop' in order to crush the monkey's skull and carry it back to the nest unhindered. With massive claws as big as a grizzly bear's and legs as big as man's wrist, the harpy is an undeniable killing machine.

A female harpy can weigh up to nine kilograms, and such a large predator obviously has high energy requirements. As a result, harpies hunt all but the largest forest mammals, as well as other large birds and a whole slew of snakes and lizards. As an apex predator (like the jaguar), the harpy eagle probably never occurred in high densities, though deforestation has removed much of its prey base and its habitat. Furthermore, its habit of perching for long spells, even when people approach, makes it vulnerable to poachers.

Harpies rarely soar above the treetops and usually hunt by rapidly attacking prey through the canopy. Monkeys are plucked from the foliage, unwary birds are taken from limbs and snakes are swept off the forest floor. However, the majority of the harpy's diet consists of sloths, which are extremely vulnerable in the morning when they are basking in the sun. A harpy will sit nearby – sometimes for days – until it is hungry, and then snatch the sloth at its leisure.

SLEEPING & EATING

Besides the options listed here, see also the Reserva Biológica Dúrika (p382), which is contained within the borders of the park.

All of the ranger stations, such as Altamira, have **camping facilities** (per person US$5). There are **basic hostels** (per person US$6) at Santa María de Pittier and at the base of Cerro Kamuk. These camps and hostels offer drinking water and toilets, and – in the case of Altamira – electricity. All food and supplies must be packed in and out.

Asoprola (☎ 2743 1184) can make arrangements for lodging in local homes in the village of Altamira. For an intimate look at the lives of people living on the fringes of the rain forest, there is no better way than to arrange a homestay.

West of Santa María de Pittier, in the village of El Carmen, **Soda La Amistad** (El Carmen; r per person US$6) has simple cabins with cold-water showers. The cabins are useful if you want one last night's rest before heading in or out of the park.

Situated about 3km by poor dirt road from the village of Las Mellizas, **La Amistad Lodge** (☎ 2200 5037, in San José 2289 7667; www.laamistad.com; s/d/tr US$96/168/240; P) sits on 100 sq km of wilderness and organic farmland that constitutes Costa Rica's third-largest reserve. Since 1940, the congenial Montero family has operated this organic coffee farm, and has long worked to balance the needs of development with protecting the environment. The main lodge has tropical hardwood cabins with hot water and electricity provided by a low-impact hydroelectric plant. Four additional jungle camps have been built at different altitudes and habitats, allowing visitors to do a multiday trek around the area without leaving the comforts of a solid bed and good cooking. The staff will transport your belongings from one site to another and provide meals at each camp, which have full-sized walk-in tents, toilets and running water. The extensive network of trails (40km) is excellent for birding and horseback riding. Guests are also invited to participate in the harvesting and processing (and drinking) of the homegrown coffee.

Rates include three meals a day (and lots of fresh-brewed coffee), as well as the entry fee into the park. Buses to Las Mellizas can get you close to the lodge, but the owners will come get you if you call ahead.

GETTING THERE & AWAY

To reach Altamira, you can take any bus that runs between San Isidro and San Vito and get off in the town of Guácimo (often called Las Tablas). From Guácimo buses depart at noon and 5pm daily and travel the 16km to the town of El Carmen; and if the road conditions permit, they continue 4km to the village of Altamira. From the village of Altamira, follow the Minae sign (near the church) leading to the steep 2km hike to the ranger station. To return to Guácimo, buses depart from Altamira at 5am and 2:30pm daily.

Vehicles with 4WD go all the way to Altamira station. In theory, it is possible to hire a 4WD taxi to bring you here, either from San Vito or from Buenos Aires. Keep in mind, however, that the roads are grueling, and bad conditions can make it pretty tough for anyone to get there. If you are driving here, inquire about road conditions prior to your departure.

Península de Osa & Golfo Dulce

This remote enclave in the extreme southwestern corner of the country is regarded by locals and tourists alike as the most picturesque, the most pristine and the most perfect spot in Costa Rica. Centered on Parque Nacional Corcovado, which contains one of the continent's last remaining patches of Pacific rain forest, and shaped by the serene waters of the wildlife-rich Golfo Dulce, the entire peninsula operates as a vast biological corridor. Not surprisingly, *National Geographic* famously labeled Osa as 'the most biologically intense place on earth.'

Although much of the rain forest in Costa Rica is protected by the national park system, no other region of the country can offer the breadth and extent of wildlife found in Osa. In Corcovado, it's sometimes possible to see all four native species of monkey swinging in the canopy overhead, while rare animals such as Baird's tapir can become commonly spotted finds. Indeed, the Osa peninsula is Costa Rica at its finest, and striking evidence that there is an intrinsic value and beauty of the rain forest that is worth saving.

Beyond Corcovado, the Osa peninsula captivates travelers with its abandoned wilderness beaches, world-class surf and endless opportunities for rugged exploration. In a country where adventure is all too often downgraded and packaged for tourist consumption, Osa is the real deal. Simply put, it's a place for travelers with youthful hearts, intrepid spirits and a yearning for something truly wild. If you've been growing old in a concrete jungle, spend some time in this verdant one – just be sure to bring a good pair of boots, a sturdy tent and some serious quantities of bug spray!

HIGHLIGHTS

- Testing your survival skills by trekking across **Parque Nacional Corcovado** (p416), the country's premiere wilderness experience

- Exploring the dense jungles that fringe the crystalline waters of **Bahía Drake** (p399)

- Catching a ride on the world's longest left break at the undiscovered surfing paradise that is **Pavones** (p439)

- Watching the sun rise over the Golfo Dulce and the sun set over the Pacific from the deserted beaches on **Cabo Matapalo** (p413)

- Diving off the coastlines of the far-flung **Isla del Cocos** (p441), the onscreen location of *Jurassic Park*

History

While the Guaymí were the earliest inhabitants of the Osa (for more information see boxed text, p408), the vast majority of the peninsula was never populated or developed by Ticos. In fact, because of the remoteness of the region, commercial logging was never a threat until the early 1960s.

Although this tumultuous decade saw the destruction of much of Costa Rica's remaining primary forests, Osa was largely spared. By 1975 however, international companies were greedily eyeing the peninsula's natural resources, namely its vast timber and gold reserves. Fortunately, these ill-conceived ambitions were halted when researchers petitioned President Daniel Oduber to establish a national park. Following the creation of Parque Nacional Corcovado, Oduber received the Albert Schweitzer Award from the Animal Welfare Institute for his much applauded actions.

In recent years, the peninsula has attracted the attention of gringos who want to trade in their workaday world for a piece of paradise. Prime real estate is being snatched up, and it's inevitable that things are set to change in Osa as they have in the rest of Costa Rica. However, there is hope that development will be more sustainable in this part of the country, particularly since there is a vested interest in keeping the peninsula green. For a local's perspective on the changes in the region, see p438.

Climate

The Osa peninsula has two drastically different seasons: the rainy season and the dry season. During the rainy season (mid-April to mid-December), the amount of precipitation is astounding, with most months boasting more than 500mm. Even in the dry season, better described as the 'less rainy season,' you can expect a good downfall every now and again, especially while trekking through Corcovado.

Parks & Reserves

As the country's premier ecotourism destination. The Península de Osa is home to a plethora of parks, reserves and wildlife refuges.

Humedal Nacional Térraba-Sierpe (p397) Approximately 33,000 hectares of protected mangrove wetlands that is home to numerous species of aquatic birds.

Parque Nacional Corcovado (p416) This park occupies a great bulk of the peninsula, is Osa's crown jewel and one Costa Rica's last true wilderness areas.

Parque Nacional Isla del Cocos (p441) The island from *Jurassic Park* is equally as difficult to access as it is visually stunning and utterly pristine.

Parque Nacional Piedras Blancas (p435) Formerly known as Parque Nacional Esquinas, this contains one of the last remaining stretches of lowland rain forest in the country.

Refugio Nacional de Fauna Silvestre Golfito (p432) This tiny 2810-hectare reserve surrounding the town of Golfito is home to rare cycads, or living plant fossils.

Reserva Biológica Isla del Caño (p397) A tiny marine and terrestrial park in Bahía Drake that is a popular destination for snorkelers, divers and biologists.

Reserva Forestal Golfo Dulce (p407) On the northern shore of Golfo Dulce, this is an important biological corridor for migrating wildlife.

Reserve Indígena Guaymí (p407) This reserve is home to the vast majority of the peninsula's indigenous communities, though most of the reserve is not open to tourism.

Dangers & Annoyances

The greatest hazard in the Osa is the difficult environment, particularly in Parque Nacional Corcovado. Trails are generally well marked, but it can be difficult going at times, especially if you're not accustomed to wilderness navigation. Also, the many large rivers that run through the park create their own hazards, especially if they're running swift in the rainy season. Any help at all, much less medical help, is very far away – if you get lost out here, you have a serious problem on your hands.

To minimize these risks, it's recommended that you explore Corcovado either as part of an organized tour or with the help of a local guide. Hiring a knowledgeable guide will also provide up-to-date information on potential hazards, and it provides safety through numbers.

Areas of Corcovado are also prime territory for the deadly fer-de-lance snake. The chance of getting a snakebite is remote, but you should be careful – always wear boots while walking in the forest. Although they don't carry Lyme Disease, ticks are also everywhere in Corcovado. In reality, they're nothing more than nuisance, though you'd be wise to bring a good pair of tweezers and a few books of matches. If you're not traveling with a buddy, a pocket mirror will also help as these little buggers have a habit of turning up in some rather uncomfortable places.

PENÍNSULA DE OSA & GOLFO DULCE

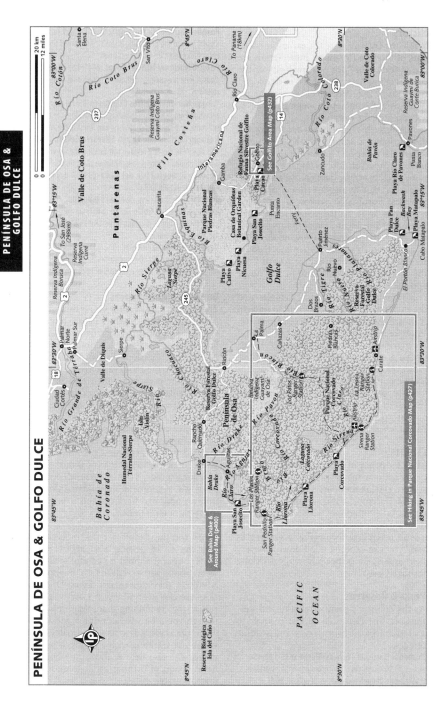

Getting There & Around

The best option for exploring the peninsula in depth is to have your own form of private transportation. However, you will need to bring a spare tire (and plenty of patience): roads in Osa are extremely poor, as most of the peninsula is still off the grid.

Major towns in Osa such as Golfito and Puerto Jiménez are serviced by regular buses, though public transportation can get sporadic once you leave these major hubs. Unpaved roads can also make for a long and jarring bus ride, so it's probably best to bring a rolled-up fleece for your bottom and an MP3 player for your sanity.

If you're planning on hiking through Corcovado or visiting one of the lodges in Bahía Drake, another excellent option is to fly. Both **NatureAir** (www.natureair.com) and **Sansa** (www.sansa.com) service the Osa peninsula, namely Bahía Drake, Puerto Jiménez and Golfito. Prices vary according to season and availability, though you can expect to pay around US$100 to/from San José.

Alfa Romeo Aero Taxi (☎ 2735 5353) offers charter flights connecting Puerto Jiménez, Drake and Golfito to Carate and Sirena. Flights are best booked at the airport in person, and one-way fares are typically less than US$100.

TO CORCOVADO VIA BAHÍA DRAKE

The first of two principal overland routes to Parque Nacional Corcovado, the Bahía Drake route starts in the Valle de Diquis at the northern base of the Península de Osa, which is named for the indigenous group of this area. From here, the valley stretches west to the basin of the Río Grande de Térraba and south to Sierpe, from where the Río Sierpe flows out to Bahía Drake. The route also takes in the Humedal Nacional Térraba-Sierpe, a vast reserve that protects an amazing array of jungle swampland and overgrown mangroves.

SIERPE

This sleepy village on the Río Sierpe is the gateway to Bahía Drake, and if you've made a reservation with any of the jungle lodges further down the coast, you will be picked up here by boat. With that said, there is little reason to spend any more time here than it takes for your captain to arrive, though fortunately you won't have to if you time the connection right.

The **Centro Turistico Las Vegas** (⏲ 6am-10pm), next to the boat dock, has become a sort of catch-all place for tourist information, distributing a wide selection of maps and brochures. It also offers internet access and serves a broad range of food to waiting passengers.

If you get stuck for the night, the best option in town is the **Hotel Oleaje Sereno** (☎ 2786 7580; oleajesereno@racsa.co.cr; r from US$40; P ⚇). This surprisingly stylish little motel has a prime dockside location overlooking the Río Sierpe, and is home to 10 spick-and-span rooms with wood floors, sturdy furniture and crisp, mismatched linens. The open-air restaurant is one of the Sierpe's most welcoming, with linen tablecloths and lovely river views. If you make prior arrangements with the manager, you can safely and conveniently leave your car here when you continue on to Drake.

Getting There & Away

AIR

Scheduled flights and charters fly into Palmar Sur (see p384), 14km north of Sierpe.

BOAT

If you are heading to Bahía Drake, your lodge will make arrangements for the boat transfer. If for some reason things go awry, there is no shortage of water taxis milling about, though you will have to negotiate to get a fair price.

BUS & TAXI

Buses to Palmar Norte (US$0.50, 30 minutes) depart from in front of the Pulpería Fenix at 5:30am, 8:30am, 10:30am, 12:30pm, 3:30pm and 6pm. A taxi to Palmar costs about US$15.

HUMEDAL NACIONAL TÉRRABA-SIERPE

The Ríos Térraba and Sierpe begin on the southern slopes of the Talamanca mountains and flow toward the Pacific Ocean. Once near the sea, however, they form a network of channels and waterways that weave around the country's largest mangrove swamp. This **river delta** comprises the Humedal Nacional Térraba-Sierpe, which protects approximately 33,000 hectares of wetland and is home to red, black and tea mangrove species. The reserve also protects a plethora of birdlife, especially water birds such as herons, egrets and cormorants.

Information

The Térraba-Sierpe reserve has no facilities for visitors, though the lodges listed below can organize tours to help you explore the wetlands.

Sleeping & Eating

Eco Manglares Sierpe Lodge (☎ 2786 7414; ecosiepa@ racsa.co.cr; 2km north of Sierpe along the road to Palmar; s/d from US$50/60; P ⊠) Owned and managed by a longtime resident Italian family (which explains the excellent pizzas and homemade pastas), this secluded lodge is accessible by a narrow metal suspension bridge – it looks dodgy but it will support your car! Ten spacious, thatch-roof cabins are nicely furnished and have artistic cane and mangrove pieces.

Estero Azul Lodge (☎ 2786 7422; esteroazul@hotmail .com; 2km north of Sierpe along the road to Palmar; r per person incl meals US$80; P ⊠) Named for the peaceful flowing river, the Estero Azul Lodge is set on several hectares of primary forest along the road to Palmar. Safari-style rooms have hardwood floors, screened porches and tile bathrooms, while delectable gourmet meals highlight fresh river fish and local seafood.

Río Sierpe Lodge (☎ 2253 5203, 8384 5595; www .riosierpelodge.com; 4-day package incl meals & tours per person from US$385) The Río Sierpe's namesake lodge is nestled in this remote spot near where the river meets the sea. Breezy rooms with hardwood floors overlook the waterways that wind through the Sierpe delta, while hiking trails radiate from the lodge into the surrounding primary forest. Transportation from Sierpe is included in the price as the lodge is only accessible by boat.

Sábalo Lodge (☎ 2770 1457; www.sabalolodge.com; s/d US$65/110, 4-day package incl meals & tours US$475) Accepting only 12 guests at a time in order to maximize the chance of getting up close and personal with wildlife, this highly personalized wilderness lodge has received rave reviews since new management took over in 2006. Guests are treated to a variety of activities, including guided hikes, horseback riding and ocean kayaking. The lodge is only accessible by boat, and transportation from Sierpe is included in the package price.

Getting There & Away

Eco Manglares Sierpe Lodge and Estero Azul Lodge are 2km north of Sierpe along the road to Palmar, and can easily be reached by car. If you don't have private transportation, ring the lodges and arrange for a pick-up.

FLOATING FOREST

As many as seven different species of mangrove, or *manglar,* thrive in Costa Rica. Comprising the vast majority of tropical coastline, mangroves play a crucial role in protecting it from erosion. Mangroves also serve as a refuge for countless species of animals, especially fish, crab, shrimp and mollusks, and as a sanctuary for roosting birds seeking protection from terrestrial predators.

Mangroves are unique amongst plants in that they have distinct methods for aeration (getting oxygen into the system) and desalination (getting rid of the salt that is absorbed with the water). Red mangroves, which are the most common species in Costa Rica, use their web of above-ground prop roots for aerating the plant's sap system. Other species, such as the black mangrove, have vertical roots that stick out above the mud, while buttonwood mangroves have elaborate buttresses.

The most amazing feature of the mangrove is its tolerance for salt, which enables the plant to thrive in brackish and saltwater habitats. Some species, like the Pacific coast black mangrove, absorb the salinated water, then excrete the salt through their leaves and roots, leaving behind visible crystals. Other species filter the water as it is absorbed – the mangrove root system is so effective as a filter that the water from a cut root is drinkable!

Despite their ecological importance, mangrove habitats the world over are being increasingly threatened by expanding human habitats. Furthermore, mangrove wood is an easily exploitable source of fuel and tannin (used in processing leather), which has also hastened their destruction. Fortunately in the Humedal Nacional Térraba-Sierpe, this fragile yet vitally important ecosystem is receiving the respect and protection that it deserves.

Río Sierpe Lodge and Sábalo Lodge are only accessible by boat; make prior arrangements to be picked up in Sierpe.

BAHÍA DRAKE

Parque Nacional Corcovado aside, the jungle-fringed crystalline waters of Bahía Drake is arguably Osa at its best. As one of the peninsula's (and the country's) most isolated destinations, Bahía Drake is a veritable Lost World of tropical landscapes and abundant wildlife. In the rain-forest canopy, howlers greet the rising sun with their haunting bellows, while pairs of macaw soar between the treetops, filling the air with their cacophonous squawking. Offshore in the bay itself, schools and pods of migrating dolphins flit through turquoise waters.

Of course, one of the reasons why Bahía Drake is brimming with wildlife is that it remains largely cut off from the rest of the country. With little infrastructure beyond dirt roads and the occasional airstrip, most of the area remains off the grid. However, Bahía Drake is home to a number of stunning wilderness lodges, which all serve as ideal bases for exploring this veritable ecological gem. And of course, if you're planning on visiting Sirena ranger station in Corcovado (p416), you can trek south along the coastline and enter the park at San Pedrillo ranger station.

History

The bay is named for Sir Francis Drake himself, who visited this area in March 1579, during his circumnavigation in the *Golden Hind*. History has it that he stopped on the nearby Isla del Caño, but locals speculate that he probably landed on the continent as well. A monument at Punta Agujitas (on the grounds of the Drake Bay Wilderness Resort, p403) states as much.

Orientation

The shores of Bahía Drake are home to two settlements: Agujitas, a tiny town of 300 residents that is spread out along the southern shore of the bay, and Drake, a few kilometers to the north, which is little more than a few houses alongside the airstrip.

Agujitas is a one-road town (and not a very good road, at that). It comes south from Rincón and past the airstrip in Drake. At the T, the right branch dead-ends at the water, where the *pulpería* (grocery store), clinic

and school constitute the heart of Agujitas; the left branch heads out of town southeast to Los Planes. From the eastern end of Agujitas, a path follows the shoreline out of town. A swinging, swaying pedestrian bridge crosses the Río Agujitas to Punta Agujitas. From here, the trail picks up and continues south along the coast, all the way to Parque Nacional Corcovado.

The only way to get around the area is by boat or by foot. Fortunately, both forms of transportation are also recreation, as sightings of macaw, monkey and other wildlife are practically guaranteed

Information

It's not easy to visit Bahía Drake if you're a backpacker since only a few shoestring options exist in Agujitas. Also, supplies, food and just about everything else are shipped in, which is reflected in local prices. However, Bahía Drake is one destination where parting with a bit of cash can greatly improve the quality of your experience.

Activities

HIKING

All of the lodges offer tours to Parque Nacional Corcovado (p416), usually a full-day trip to San Pedrillo ranger station (from US$75 to US$100 per person), including boat transportation, lunch and guided hikes. Indeed, if you came all the way to the Península de Osa, it's hard to pass up a visit to the national park that made it famous.

Some travelers, however, come away from these tours disappointed. The trails around San Pedrillo station attract many groups of people, which inhibit animal sightings. Furthermore, most tours arrive at the park well after sunrise, when activity in the rain forest has already quieted down.

Considering their hefty price tag, these tours are not necessarily the most rewarding way to see wildlife. The lodges strongly encourage their guests to take these tours (because they are obviously money-makers), but you have other options.

The easiest and most obvious one is the long, coastal trail that heads south out of Agujitas and continues about 10km to the border of the national park. Indeed, a determined hiker could make it all the way to San Pedrillo station on foot in three to four hours (make sure you reserve a spot at the ranger station if you intend to spend the night). From here, you can follow the coastal tour south to wildlife-rich Sirena ranger station, which is undoubtedly the highlight of Corcovado.

Of course, if you don't have the time (or the inclination) for this challenging trek, you can take comfort in the fact that most of the same species that inhabit the park are frequently spotted in the surrounding buffer zone. In fact, macaw, monkey and other exotic species travel this trail as often as humans!

In addition to Corcovado, other popular day trips include nearby **Playa San Josecito** (p436), a stunningly remote beach where you can slow down and soak up the beauty of the bay. If you want to head inland, you can also explore the **Punta Río Claro Wildlife Refuge** (also called the Marenco Rain Forest Reserve; p405), which can be accessed from the Río Claro Trail or from Playa San Josecito.

When hiking without a guide, make sure that somebody knows when and where you are going. Should you get lost, try to find a

river or stream, which you can follow to the ocean and then re-establish your bearings.

SWIMMING & SNORKELING

Isla del Caño (p406) is commonly considered the best place for snorkeling in this area. Lodges and tour companies all offer day trips to the island (US$75 to US$100 per person), which usually includes the park fee, snorkeling equipment and lunch, as well as a guided island hike in the afternoon. As is the case anywhere, the clarity of the water and the variety of the fish fluctuate according to water and weather conditions: it's worth inquiring before dishing out the cash for a tour.

There are other opportunities for snorkeling on the coast between Agujitas and Corcovado. **Playa San Josecito** attracts scores of colorful species, which hide out among the coral reef and rocks. Another recommended spot is **Playa Las Caletas**, just in front of the Corcovado Adventures Tent Camp, and **Playa Cocalito**, a small, pretty beach that is near Agujitas and is pleasant for swimming and sunbathing.

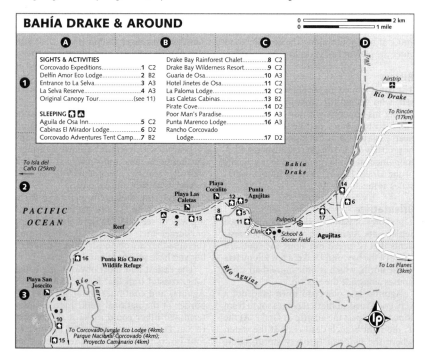

BAHÍA DRAKE & AROUND

SIGHTS & ACTIVITIES		Drake Bay Rainforest Chalet..............8 C2
Corcovado Expeditions.....................1 C2		Drake Bay Wilderness Resort............9 C2
Delfín Amor Eco Lodge.....................2 B2		Guaria de Osa.................................10 A3
Entrance to La Selva........................3 A3		Hotel Jinetes de Osa......................11 C2
La Selva Reserve.............................4 A3		La Paloma Lodge............................12 C2
Original Canopy Tour.................(see 11)		Las Caletas Cabinas........................13 B2
		Pirate Cove....................................14 D2
SLEEPING		Poor Man's Paradise........................15 A3
Aguila de Osa Inn.............................5 C2		Punta Marenco Lodge.....................16 A3
Cabinas El Mirador Lodge.................6 D2		Rancho Corcovado
Corcovado Adventures Tent Camp....7 B2		Lodge..17 D2

PENÍNSULA DE OSA & GOLFO DULCE

A DUMMY'S GUIDE TO PARQUE NACIONAL CORCOVADO

If you're confused about the best way to access Parque Nacional Corcovado, don't be. With a little prior planning, and a good idea as to the kind of trip you're interested in, you'll find yourself trekking through the rain forest, fording rivers and (hopefully!) spotting tapirs in no time at all!

For starters, it helps to know that there are two major centers where tourists tend to organize their expeditions: Bahía Drake (p399) and Puerto Jiménez (p410). Both of these areas are home to hotels, lodges and tour operators where you can arrange your onward plans, hire guides and purchase supplies.

Each area has its own unique flair and tourist draws, though for the most part travelers choose Puerto Jiménez since it's closer to the famed Sirena ranger station, where most of the wildlife action happens. However, staying in a remote jungle lodge along the coastline of Bahía Drake is truly one of the highlights of Osa.

If you start the trek from Bahía Drake, your entry into the park will most likely be at San Pedrillo ranger station, from where you easily trek to either Sirena or the more remote Los Planes ranger station. If you start the trek from Puerto Jiménez, your entry into the park will most likely be at either La Leona or Los Patos ranger station, both of which are good bases for accessing Sirena.

A third option for accessing the park is to fly direct to the air strips in either Carate or Sirena, see p431 for details on how to fly from Puerto Jiménez or Drake to Carate or Sirena. This option is certainly more expensive, but it can be a huge time-saver if you're dealing with a time-crunched itinerary.

Be advised that if you're planning on sleeping in Corcovado, you must register in advance with the park headquarters in Puerto Jiménez. This can be done either in person, by phone or often through your tour operator.

For information on the Bahía Drake route, see p404. For information on the Puerto Jiménez route, see p407. For information on the park itself, see p416.

SCUBA DIVING

About 20km west of Agujitas, **Isla del Caño** is one of Costa Rica's top spots for diving, with attractions including intricate rock and coral formations and an amazing array of underwater life, teeming with colorful reef fish and incredible coral formations. Divers report that the schools of fish swimming overhead are often so dense that they block the sunlight from filtering down.

While the bay is rich with dive sites, a local highlight is undoubtedly the **Bajo del Diablo** (Devil's Rock), an astonishing formation of submerged mountains that attracts an incredible variety of fish species, including jack, snapper, barracuda, puffer, parrotfish, moray eel and shark.

A two-tank dive runs from US$100 to US$150 depending on the spot, or you can do an open-water course for US$325 to US$400. Most of the upscale lodges in the area either have onsite dive centers or can arrange trips and courses through a neighboring lodge.

KAYAKING & CANOEING

A fantastic way to explore the region's biodiversity is to paddle through it. The idyllic **Río**

Agujitas attracts a huge variety of birdlife and lots of scaly reptiles. The river conveniently empties out into the bay, which is surrounded by hidden coves and sandy beaches ideal for exploring in a sea kayak. Paddling at high tide is recommended because it allows you to explore more territory.

Most accommodations in the area have kayaks and canoes for rent. Another option is to arrange a guided tour through Corcovado Expeditions.

HORSE RIDING

The **coastal trail** running between Agujitas and Corcovado is perfect for horse riding, especially if you relish the idea of galloping wildly across deserted beaches while the waves crash below you. **Los Planes** is another popular destination for horse riders, with ample opportunities for wildlife-watching along the way. Again, most of the upscale lodges in the area offer guided rides (from US$65), or can arrange trips through a neighboring lodge.

SPORTFISHING

Bahía Drake claims more than 40 fishing records, including sailfish, marlin, yellowfin tuna, wahoo, cubera snapper, mackerel and roosterfish. Fishing is excellent year-round, although the catch may vary according to the season. The peak season for tuna and marlin is from August to December. Sailfish are caught year-round, but experience a slow-down in May and June. Dorado and wahoo peak between May and August. Other species are abundant year-round, so you are virtually assured to reel in something. Many lodges can arrange fishing excursions, but you need to be prepared to pay heavily – half-/full-day excursions cost around US$550/800.

DOLPHIN- & WHALE-WATCHING

As of 2006, swimming with dolphins and whales is illegal in Costa Rica. These measures are a result of an increase in tourist activity, often led by inexperienced guides who did not respect the best interests of these amazing creatures. However, dolphin- and whale-watching tours still provide opportunities to get up close and personal with these sea creatures – but only from the comfort and safety of the boat.

Bahía Drake is rife with marine life, including more than 25 species of dolphin and whale that pass through on their migrations throughout the year. This area is uniquely suited for whale-watching: humpback whales come from both the northern and the southern hemispheres to calve, resulting in the longest humpback whale season in the world. Humpbacks can be spotted in Bahía Drake year-round (except May), but the best months to see whales are late July through early November.

Several of the lodges are involved with programs that protect and preserve marine life in Bahía Drake, as well as programs that offer tourists a chance for a close encounter. Tours generally cost about US$100 per person.

The program at Drake Bay Wilderness Resort (see opposite), is highly recommended. Marine biologist Shawn Larkin has an infectious enthusiasm about marine mammals. He spends his time researching and filming dolphins and whales for his educational organization, the **Costa Cetacea Research Institute** (www.costacetacea.com).

Delfín Amor Eco Lodge (☎ in the USA 831-345 8484; www.divinedolphin.com) specializes in educational marine tours, with an excellent website detailing the species of dolphin and whale and their migratory patterns. Under the auspices of the nonprofit **Fundación Vida Marina** (www.vidamarina.org), staff are involved in collecting data to work towards establishing a protected marine sanctuary in this area. They use an amazing 'Flying Inflatable Boat' to track and monitor dolphins, whales and commercial fishing in the area.

Tours

Corcovado Expeditions (☎ 8818 9962, 8833 2384; www.corcovadoexpeditions.net) Competitively priced tours to Corcovado and Caño Island, as well as specialty hikes to look for birds (per person US$25) and poison-dart frogs (per person US$25). Corcovado Expeditions also rents mountain bikes (per hour/day US$10/35) and leads biking tours (half/full day US$35/50).

Night Tour (☎ 8382 1619; www.thenighttour.com; admission US$35; ☾ 7:45-10pm) Tracie the 'Bug Lady' and her spotting partner, Victor, have created quite a name for themselves with this fascinating nighttime walk in the jungle. Tracie is a walking encyclopedia on bug facts. Participants use night-vision scopes as an added bonus. Make reservations well in advance.

JUNGLE NIGHTS

As night falls in the jungle, an amazing transformation takes place. That is, all the birds that were squawking all day long are suddenly quiet. And a whole new host of noises fills the air. The sounds of crickets, cicadas and other tropical bugs, awakening at dusk, are utterly overwhelming: the buzz emanates from all sides, vibrating throughout the forest. This is also when the aptly named vesper bats come out, seemingly flying circles around your head.

As the darkness engulfs you, your other senses are heightened. That is the only way to explain the amazing otherworldly quality of the exotic night sounds, like the mournful coo of the puraque calling his mate, or the scream of fighting coatis in the distance.

Most of the night tours in Bahía Drake focus on finding nocturnal critters like river shrimps, frogs, spiders and insects. But many mammals are nocturnal: night tours around Sirena station in Corcovado (p416) are the best way to spot Baird's tapir, kinkajou and skunk, as well as American crocodile. It doesn't happen often, but if you're going to see a feline it will likely be at night.

Original Canopy Tour (☎ 8371 1598; admission US$55; ☺ 8am-4pm) Bahía Drake's only such facility is located at Hotel Jinetes de Osa. Nine platforms, six cables and one 20m observation deck provide a new perspective on the rain forest. Reservations are recommended.

Sleeping & Eating

This area is off the grid, so many places do not have electricity (pack a flashlight) or hot water. Reservations are recommended in the dry season (mid-November to the end of April). High-season rates are quoted; prices are per person, including three meals, unless otherwise stated.

Note that three daily meals are also included in the price at all midrange and top-end lodges because stand-alone eating options are virtually nonexistent in this part of the peninsula. At budget places, affordably priced food is available onsite at the restaurant/cantina. Most hotels and lodges also have small shops that sell snacks and drinks. If you're planning on hiking, be sure to stock up on lots of fresh water as well as your favorite form of trail mix – once you're out on the trail, options are decidedly limited.

All of the midrange and top-end accommodations listed in this section provide transport (sometimes free, sometimes not) from either Agujitas or the airstrip in Drake with prior arrangements.

For other accommodations, check out the stretch of coastline from Bahía Drake to Corcovado (p405).

BUDGET & MIDRANGE

Rancho Corcovado Lodge (☎ 2786 7903; camping without meals US$10, cabins US$45; Ⓟ) This decidedly low-key family-run lodge is amazingly secluded, considering its location in the middle of the village. Fruit trees and coconut palms shade the grounds, which face a wide stretch of sandy beach, and the two sets of rustic cabins here afford both beach and mountain views.

Cabinas El Mirador Lodge (☎ 8836 9415; www.mirador drakebay.com; r US$42; Ⓟ) High on a hill at the northern end of Agujitas, El Mirador (Lookout Point) lives up to its name, offering spectacular views of the bay from its eight cozy cabins – catch the sunset from the balcony, or climb to the lookout that perches above. The hospitable Vargas family ensure all guests receive a warm welcome, as well as three square meals a day of hearty, home-cooked Costa Rican fare.

Hotel Jinetes de Osa (☎ 8371 1598, 2236 5637, in the USA 800-317 0333; www.costaricadiving.com; r standard/ superior from US$60/80) The affordably priced Jinetes de Osa boasts a choice bayside location that is literally a few steps from the ocean – you can sip your morning coffee (it's delivered!) from your hotel room while staring out across the bay. Jinetes also has Bahía Drake's only canopy tour, as well as one of the peninsula's top PADI dive facilities, which means that guests have plenty of adrenaline-soaked activities on the roster.

TOP END

Pirate Cove (☎ 2234 6154; www.piratecovecostarica.com; r from US$80) Breezy, tent-like bungalows and spacious hardwood cabins both offer an element of laidback luxury at the appropriately named Pirate Cove (Sir Francis Drake wasn't exactly the most honorable of captains!). With private terraces that are strung up with hammocks, most guests seem content to just swing the day away, though there are 2km of deserted beach in front of the property to explore.

Corcovado Jungle Eco Lodge (☎ 2770 8209; www .corcovadojungleecolodge; 3-/5-night package per person from US$325/630) Surrounded by miles and miles of primary rain forest, this jungle lodge is inland from Bahía Drake on the northern edge of the Parque Nacional Corcovado. Standard accommodations are clean and comfortable cabinas (and one fun tree house), while more upscale ranchos are accessible only by a series of wooden walkways and elevated observation platforms. A network of trails crosses the 100-hectare private reserve, providing ample opportunities for wildlife-watching and hiking.

ourpick **Drake Bay Wilderness Resort** (☎ 2770 8012; www.drakebay.com; 4-day package from US$695; ☒) Sitting pretty on Punta Agujitas, this relaxed resort occupies the optimal piece of real estate in all of Bahía Drake. Naturalists will be won over by the lovely landscaping, from flowering trees to the ocean-fed pool, while history buffs will appreciate the memorial to Drake's landing. Accommodations are in comfortable cabins, which have mural-painted walls and private patios with ocean views, while family-style meals feature ingredients from your congenial host's organic farm.

Aguila de Osa Inn (☎ 2296 2190; www.aguiladeosa .com; 2-/3-/4-/5-night package from US$514/769/948/1128) On the east side of the Río Agujitas, this swanky lodge consists of roomy quarters with shining wood floors, cathedral ceilings and private decks overlooking the ocean. The vast centerpiece of the lodge, however, is the comfortable yet elegant open-air rancho (small house-like building), which serves up signature cocktails and innovative *bocas* (savory bar snacks) throughout the day and into the evening.

La Paloma Lodge (☎ 2239 7502; www.lapalomalodge .com; 3-/4-/5-day package from US$1100/1245/1390; ⊠) Perched on a lush hillside, this exquisite lodge provides guests with an incredible panorama of ocean and forest, all from the comfort of the sumptuous, stylish quarters. Rooms have shiny hardwood floors and queen-size orthopedic beds, draped in mosquito netting, while shoulder-high walls in all the bathrooms offer rain-forest views while you bathe. Each room has a large balcony (with hammock, of course) that catches the cool breeze off the ocean.

ourpick **Drake Bay Rainforest Chalet** (☎ 8382 1619; www.drakebayholiday.com; 3-/4-/5-/6-/7-day package from US$1150/1275/1400/1525/1650) Set on 18 hectares of pristine rain forest, this jungle getaway is a remote, romantic adventure. Huge French windows provide a panoramic view of the surrounding jungle, enjoyed from almost every room in the house. Sleeping quarters have a king-size bed with giant mosquito net, flanked by a luxurious tiled bathroom with a sunken shower and a decadent two-person hot tub. In an innovative twist on luxury, the Moroccan-themed kitchen is fully stocked for self-catering, though chef service is available for the culinary impaired.

Getting There & Away
AIR
Departing from San José, **NatureAir** (www.nature air.com) and **Sansa** (www.sansa.com) have daily flights to the Drake airstrip, which is 2km north of Agujitas. Prices vary according to season and availability, though you can expect to pay around US$100 to/from San José.

Alfa Romeo Aero Taxi (☎ 2735 5353) offers charter flights connecting Drake to Puerto Jiménez, Golfito, Carate and Sirena. Flights are best booked at the airport in person, and one-way fares are typically less than US$100.

Most lodges provide transportation to/from the airport, which involves a jeep or a boat or both, but advanced reservation is necessary.

BOAT
All of the hotels offer boat transfers between Sierpe and Bahía Drake with prior arrange-

ments. The trip to Drake is scenic and – at times – exhilarating. Boats travel along the river through the rain forest and the mangrove estuary. Captains then pilot boats through tidal currents and surf the river mouth into the ocean. Most hotels in Drake have beach landings, so wear the appropriate footwear.

If you have not made advanced arrangements with your lodge for a pick-up, you can always grab a private water taxi in Sierpe at a negotiable price.

BUS & CAR
A rough dirt road links Agujitas to Rincón, from where you can head south to Puerto Jiménez or north to the Interamericana. A 4WD is recommended for this route, especially from June to November, as there are several river crossings. The most hazardous crossing is the Río Drake, and locals fish many a water-logged tourist vehicle out of the river – see boxed text, p548 for some tips on not destroying your rental.

Once in Agujitas, you will likely have to abandon your car as most places are accessible only by boat or by foot. As theft or vandalism is always a very real possibility in Costa Rica, you should park your car in a secure place, and pay someone to watch it for a few days. There are several small *pulperías* where the management would be happy to watch over your 4WD for a nice tip.

If you are hiking through Parque Nacional Corcovado, but you want to avoid the arduous San Pedrillo trail, you can hire a 4WD vehicle to La Palma (US$50) and start the hike there. In theory, a bus also goes to La Palma (US$5), departing Drake at 4am during the dry season only, but it's best to inquire locally as it's not reliable.

HIKING
From Bahía Drake, it's a four- to six-hour hike along the beachside trail to San Pedrillo ranger station at the north end of Corcovado. If you are heading into the park, make sure you have reservations to camp at the ranger stations – for more information, see p416.

BAHÍA DRAKE TO CORCOVADO
This craggy stretch of coastline is home to sandy inlets that disappear at high tide, leaving only the rocky outposts and luxuriant rain forest. Virtually uninhabited and undeveloped beyond a few tourist lodges, the setting here

is magnificent and wild. If you're looking to spend a bit more time along the shores Bahía Drake before penetrating the depths of Parque Nacional Corcovado, consider a night or two in some of the country's most remote accommodations.

Orientation & Information

A public trail follows the coastline for the entire spectacular stretch. It's easy to follow and wonderful for wildlife. Among the multitude of bird species, you're likely to spot (and hear) squawking scarlet macaw, often traveling in pairs, and the hooting chestnut-mandible toucan. White-faced capuchin and howler monkey inhabit the treetops, while eagle-eyed hikers might also spot a sloth or a kinkajou.

The only way to get around the area is by boat or by foot, which means that travelers are more or less dependent on their lodges.

Sights & Activities

This entire route is punctuated by scenic little inlets, each with a wild, windswept beach. Just west of Punta Agujitas, a short detour off the main trail leads to the picturesque **Playa Cocalito**, a secluded cove perfect for sunning, swimming and body surfing. With no lodges in the immediate vicinity, it's often deserted. **Playa Las Caletas**, in front of the Corcovado Adventures Tent Camp, is excellent for snorkeling.

Further south, the Río Claro empties out into the ocean. Water can be waist deep or higher, and the current swift, so take care when wading across. This is also the start of the Río Claro trail, which leads inland into the 400-hectare **Punta Río Claro Wildlife Refuge** (formerly known as the Marenco Rain Forest Reserve) and passes a picturesque waterfall along the way. Be aware that there are two rivers known as the Río Claro: one is located near Bahía Drake, while the other is inside Corcovado near Sirena station.

South of Río Claro, the **Playa San Josecito** is the longest stretch of white sand beach on this side of the Península de Osa. It is popular with swimmers, snorkelers and sunbathers, though you'll rarely find it crowded.

From here you can access another private reserve, **La Selva**. A short, steep climb leads from the beach to a lookout point, offering a spectacular view over the treetops and out to the ocean. A network of trails continues

inland, and eventually connects La Selva to the Río Claro reserve. Be advised that La Selva does not have any facilities: the trails are not labeled; there is no water or maps; you'll likely meet nobody along the way. If you choose to continue past the lookout point, make sure you have food, water and a compass.

The border of Parque Nacional Corcovado is about 5km south of here (it takes three to four hours to hike the entire distance from Agujitas to Corcovado). The trail is more overgrown as it gets closer to the park, but it's a well traveled route.

Sleeping & Eating

Reservations are recommended in the dry season (mid-November to the end of April). High-season rates are quoted; prices are per person, including three meals, unless otherwise stated. Many places in this area don't have electricity (pack a flashlight) or hot water. Stand-alone eating options are virtually nonexistent in this part of the peninsula.

With prior arrangements, all of the accommodations listed in this section provide transport (free or for a charge) from either Agujitas or the airstrip in Drake.

Las Caletas Cabinas (☎ 8381 4052, 8326 1460; www .caletas.co.cr; r from US$65; ▯) This adorable little hotel is set on the picturesque beach of the same name and consists of five cozy wooden cabins that are awash with sweeping views. The Swiss-Tico owners are warm hosts who are passionate about environmental sustainability, which means you can rest easy knowing that solar and hydroelectric power provides electricity around the clock.

Corcovado Adventures Tent Camp (☎ 8384 1679; www.corcovado.com; r US$70, 4-day package US$355) Less than an hour's walk from Drake brings you to this fun, family-run spot. It's like camping, but comfy: spacious, walk-in tents are set up on covered platforms and fully equipped with sturdy wood furniture. Twenty hectares of rain forest offer plenty of opportunity for exploration, and the beachfront setting is excellent for water sports.

Poor Man's Paradise (☎ 2771 4582; www.mypoor mansparadise.com; 5-day package tent/ranch/cabin US$426/449/495) Sportfishing can be an expensive prospect, but local fisherman Pincho Amaya aims to make it more accessible. Here at the aptly named Poor Man's Paradise, guests can take advantage of Bahía Drake's most reasonably priced fishing excursions. Accommodation is in large canvas tents, which are elevated on sturdy wooden platforms to protect you from the cold, wet ground. You can also choose rooms in the rustic ranch houses and cabins, which have private en suite facilities.

Proyecto Campanario (☎ 2258 5778; www.camp anario.org; 4-day package US$427) Run by a former Peace Corps volunteer, this biological reserve is more of an education center than a tourist facility, as evidenced by the dormitory, library and field station. Behind the main facility, five spacious platform tents with 'garden' bathrooms offer a bit more privacy and comfort. Ecology courses and conservation camps are scheduled throughout the year, but individuals are also invited to take advantage of the facilities. The whole place is set on 150 hectares of tropical rain forest, which provides countless opportunities for exploration and wildlife observation.

Punta Marenco Lodge (☎ 2234 1308, 2234 1227; www.puntamarenco.com; 3-day package US$339) This intimate family-run lodge shares access to the Punta Río Claro Wildlife Refuge, providing excellent opportunities for independent hiking and wildlife-watching. Accommodation is in thatch-roof cabañas in the style of the Boruca indigenous peoples and have private terraces, ocean views and 360 degrees of screened windows, which affords a wonderful cross-breeze.

Guaria de Osa (☎ 2235 4313, in the USA 510-235 4313; www.guariadeosa.com; 3-day package US$395) Cultivating a new-age ambiance, this Asian-style retreat center offers yoga, tai chi and all kinds of massage, along with the more typical rain forest activities. The lovely grounds include an ethnobotanical garden, which features exotic local species used for medicinal and other purposes. The architecture of this place is unique: the centerpiece is the Lapa Lapa Lounge, a spacious multi-story pagoda, built entirely from reclaimed hardwood.

our pick **Casa Corcovado Jungle Lodge** (☎ 2256 3181, in the USA 888-896 6097; www.casacorcovado.com; 5-day package from US$1244; 🏊) A spine-tingling boat ride takes you to this luxurious lodge on 175 hectares of rain forest bordering the national park. Each bungalow is tucked away in its own private tropical garden, each with a hammock. Artistic details – such as Mexican tiles and stained glass – make the Casa Corcovado one of this area's classiest accommodation options. On site, the Margarita Sunset Bar lives up to its name,

serving up 25 different 'ritas and great sunset views over the Pacific.

Getting There & Away
BOAT
All of the hotels offer boat transfers between Sierpe and Bahía Drake with prior arrangements. If you haven't made advance arrangements with your lodge for a pickup, grab a private water taxi in Sierpe for a negotiable price.

HIKING
From Bahía Drake, it's a four- to six-hour hike along the beachside trail to San Pedrillo ranger station at the north end of Corcovado. If you're heading into the park, make sure you have reservations to camp at the ranger stations – for more information, see p416.

RESERVA BIOLÓGICA ISLA DEL CAÑO
The centerpiece of this biological reserve is a 326-hectare island that is the tip of numerous underwater rock formations. Along the rocky coastline, towering peaks soar as high as 70m, which provide a dramatic setting for anyone who loves secluded nature.

The submarine rock formations are among the island's main attractions, drawing divers to explore the underwater architecture. Snorkelers can investigate the coral and rock formations along the beach right in front of the ranger station. The water is much clearer here than along the mainland coast, though rough seas can cloud visibility. Fifteen different species of coral have been recorded, as well as threatened animal species that include the Panulirus lobster and the giant conch. The sheer numbers of fish attract dolphins and whales, which are frequently spotted swimming in outer waters. Hammerhead sharks, manta rays and sea turtles also inhabit these waters.

A steep but well-maintained trail leads inland from the ranger station. Once the trail plateaus, it is relatively flat, winding through evergreen forest to a lookout point at about 110m above sea level. These trees are primarily milk trees (also called 'cow trees' after the drinkable white latex they exude), believed to be the remains of an orchard planted by pre-Columbian indigenous inhabitants. Near the top of the ridge, there are several pre-Columbian granite spheres.

Archaeologists speculate that the island may have been a ceremonial or burial site for the same indigenous tribes.

Camping is prohibited, and there are no facilities except a ranger station by the landing beach. Most visitors arrive on tours arranged by the nearby lodges – admission is US$8 per person, although this fee is usually included in your tour price.

TO CORCOVADO VIA PUERTO JIMÉNEZ

The second of two principal overland routes to Parque Nacional Corcovado, the Puerto Jiménez route on the eastern side of the peninsula is much more 'developed.' Of course, as this is Osa, developed means a single road and a sprinkling of villages along the coast of Golfo Dulce. The landscape is cattle pastures and rice fields, while much of the inland area is protected by the Reserva Forestal Golfo Dulce. The largest settlement in the area is the town of Puerto Jiménez, which has transitioned from a boom town for gold miners to an emerging ecotourism hot spot.

RESERVA FORESTAL GOLFO DULCE

The northern shore of the Golfo Dulce is home to this vast forest reserve, which links Parque Nacional Corcovado to the Parque Nacional Piedras Blancas. This connecting corridor plays an important role in preserving the biodiversity of the peninsula, and allowing the wildlife to migrate to the mainland. Although much of the reserve is not easily accessible, there are several area lodges that are doing their part to preserve this natural resource by protecting their own little pieces of this wildlife wonderland.

Sights & Activities

About 9km southeast of Rincón, the town of **La Palma** is the origin of the rough road that turns into the trail to the Los Patos ranger station. If you're hiking across Corcovado, this will likely be the starting point or ending point of your trek. Before heading out however, don't miss the chance to get some sun at the beautiful sand and coral beach, known as **Playa Blanca**, at the east end of town.

The **Reserva Indígena Guaymí** is southwest of La Palma, on the border of Parque Nacional Corcovado.

About 8km south of La Palma, the Tico-run **Köbö Farm** (☎ 8351 8576; www.kobofarm.com; 3-hr tour in Spanish/English US$20/30) is a chocolate-lover's dream come true. In fact, *köbö* means 'dream' in Guaymí. The 50-hectare finca is dedicated to organic cultivation of fruits and vegetables and – the product of choice – cacao. Tours give a comprehensive overview of the life cycle of cacao plants and the production of chocolate (with dégustation!). To really experience life on the farm, you can stay in simple, comfortable teak **cabins** (r per person US$15, meals from US$6).

Just before entering Puerto Jiménez, a turnoff in the road leads 16km to the hamlet of **Río Nuevo**, also in the forest reserve. A good trail network leads to spectacular mountain viewpoints, some with views of the gulf. Birding is excellent in this area: you can expect to see the many species that you would find in Corcovado. Most of the following lodges offer daylong excursions in this area.

Sleeping

Danta Corcovado Lodge (☎ 8378 9188, 8819 1860; www.dantacorcovado.net; s/d/tr US$25/35/40, camping per person US$6) Conveniently located midway between Los Patos and La Palma, this low-key lodge is set on the finca of the congenial Sanchez family. Rustic wood cabins are painted in warm hues and furnished with handcrafted pieces. The highlight of the lodge, however, is the family's traditional wood stove, which fires up some delicious, home-cooked meals.

Suital Lodge (☎ 8826 0342; www.suital.com; 15km east of Rincón; s/d/tr US$45/62/70; (P)) Lots of love has gone into the construction of this tiny clutch of cabinas on the northern shores of Golfo Dulce. Situated on 30 hectares of hilly, forested property (not a single tree has been felled), guests can take advantage of a network of trails that winds through the property and down to the beach.

Río Nuevo Lodge (☎ 2735 5411, 8365 8982; www.rionuevolodge.com; s/d US$65/100) Who knew that former gold-miners would be so friendly? The Aguirre family now owns and operates this popular tent lodge set on a forested mountainside 2km west of Río Nuevo. This is camping made easy: guests sleep in comfortable, furnished tents on covered platforms, with access to shared

GUAYMÍ

The earliest inhabitants of Costa Rica's far southern corner were the Guaymí, or Ngöbe, who migrated over generations from neighboring Panama. The Guaymí inhabit indigenous reserves in the Valle de Coto Brus, on the Osa peninsula and in southern Golfo Dulce, though they retain some semi-nomadic ways and are allowed to pass freely over the border into Panama. This occurs frequently during the coffee harvesting season, when many Guaymí travel to work on plantations.

The Guaymí have been able to preserve – to some degree – their customs and culture, and it is not unusual to see women wearing traditional dress. These vibrant, solid-color *pollera* dresses hang to the ankles, often trimmed in contrasting colors and patterns. Unlike other indigenous groups, the Guaymí still speak their native language and teach it in local schools.

The Guaymí traditionally live in wooden huts with palm roofs and dirt floors, although most families have now upgraded to wooden houses on stilts. However, they still live off the land, cultivating corn, rice and tubers, while fruit and palmitos grow in the wild.

The Guaymí reserves are largely inaccessible, which may be one reason why the culture persists. However, as tourism filters into the farthest corners of the country, there is a growing interest in indigenous traditions and handicrafts, and this demand may actually encourage their preservation. But, the reserves are also at a precipitous point – without proper management and community participation, an influx of tourists (and tourist dollars) can also lead to cultural dilution.

The best way to visit the reserve is through the **Tamandu Lodge** (☎ 8821 4525; www.tamandu-lodge .com; r per person US$45), which is run by the Carreras, a Guaymí family. This unique lodge provides a rare chance to interact directly with an indigenous family and experience firsthand the Guaymí lifestyle. This is hands-on stuff: gather crabs and fish with palm rods; hunt for palmito or harvest yucca; learn how to prepare these specialties over an open fire. Accommodations are in rustic, wooden houses, built on stilts with thatch roofs. Home-cooked meals are included in the price. A member of the Carrera family will meet you in La Palma, from where it is a two-hour journey on horseback to the lodge – getting there is half the fun!

cold-water facilities. Tasty meals (included) are served family style in a traditional thatch-roof rancho.

Bosque del Río Tigre (☎ in Puerto Jiménez 2735 5062, 8824 1372, in the USA 888-875 9453; www.osaadventures .com; Dos Brazos; s/d US$149/258, 4-day package per person from US$500; ⓟ) On the edge of the Reserva Forestal Golfo Dulce, in the midst of a 13-hectare private reserve, this off-the-beaten-track ecolodge is a birder's paradise. Four well-appointed guest rooms and one private, open-air cabaña have huge windows for viewing the feathered friends that come to visit. In case you want to brush up on your taxonomy, the lodge contains a library well stocked with wildlife reference books.

Villa Corcovado (☎ 8817 6969; www.villacorcovado .com; 500m Este Parada, Rincón; s/d incl meals US$289/376; ⓟ ⌨) Rincón seems an unlikely setting for a brand new top-of-the-line resort, but you'll understand when you glimpse the 30 hectares of exquisite, unspoiled rain forest and the magnificent unobstructed vista of the Golfo Dulce. Eight light-filled, luxurious villas have private porches, wood-beamed ceilings and hardwood floors, not to mention classy, contemporary decor. Gourmet meals (included) feature organic produce straight from the garden; you can request yours packed in a picnic to enjoy on a nearby deserted beach.

Getting There & Away

The easiest way to travel the eastern coast of the peninsula is by car. Otherwise, frequent buses ply the sole road between La Palma and Puerto Jiménez (US$0.50, 30 minutes). La Palma can be reach from Neily (US$3, three hours), San Isidro (US$5, four hours) and San José (US$8, nine hours).

PUERTO JIMÉNEZ

Puerto Jiménez is something of a natural wonder in itself. Sliced in half by the swampy, overgrown Quebrada Cacao, and flanked on one side by the emerald waters of the Golfo Dulce, this untamed environment is shared equally by local residents and wildlife. While walking through the dusty streets of Port Jim (as the gringos call it), it's not unusual to spot scarlet macaw roosting on the soccer field, or white-faced capuchin swinging in the treetops adjacent to the main street.

Then again, it's not too hard to understand why Puerto Jiménez is brimming with wild-life, mainly because the town lies on the edge of Parque Nacional Corcovado (p416). As the preferred jumping-off point for travelers heading to the famed Sirena ranger station, the town is a great place to organize an expedition, stock up on supplies and get a good night's rest before hitting the trails.

History

Although it appears on maps dating to 1914, Puerto Jiménez was little more than a cluster of houses built on a mangrove swamp. With the advent of logging in the 1960s and the subsequent discovery of gold in the local streams, Jiménez became a small boomtown. The logging industry still operates in parts of the peninsula, but the gold rush has quieted down in favor of the tourist rush.

Even so, the town retains a frontier feel. Now, instead of goldminers descending on the town's bars on weekends, it's outdoors and fishing types who come to have a shot of *guaro* (local firewater) and brag about the snakes, sharks and alligators they've allegedly tousled with.

Parts of Puerto Jiménez are currently being threatened by seemingly indiscriminate enforcement of maritime zone laws. As in coastal areas around the country, townsfolk are rallying against the municipality's threats to demolish some 200 odd homes that are built within the zone.

Information

Banco Nacional de Costa Rica (8:30am-3:45pm Mon-Fri)

Cafenet El Sol (2735 5719; www.soldeosa.com; per hr US$3; 7am-10pm) Internet access is painfully slow (and often nonexistent).

Colectivo Transportation (2735 5539; Soda Deya, 200m south of the bus station) Will exchange US dollars and euros when the bank is closed.

Oficina de Área de Conservación Osa (2735 5036, 2735 5580; 8am-noon & 1-4pm Mon-Fri) Information about Corcovado, Isla del Caño, Parque Nacional Marino Ballena and Golfito parks and reserves. Make reservations to camp in Corcovado.

Osa Tropical (2735 5062, 2735 5722; www.osaviva .com) Doña Isabel is the NatureAir agent and the best and

most reputable source of local travel information. She handles hotel and transportation arrangements of all kinds and has a radio that reaches all the lodges on the peninsula and in the Golfo Dulce areas.

Red Cross (2735 5109) For medical emergencies.

Sights & Activities

About 5km east of town, the secluded – and often deserted – **Playa Platanares** is excellent for swimming, sunning and recovering from too much adventure. The nearby mangroves of Río Platanares are a paradise for kayaking and bird-watching.

On the east side of the airstrip, **Herrera Gardens & Conservation Project** (2735 5267; admission US$4, guided tour US$15-30; 6am-5pm) is a 100-hectare reserve with beautiful botanical gardens. This innovative, long-term reforestation project offers an ecologically and economically sustainable alternative to cattle-grazing. Visitors can explore the 5km of garden trails or 15km of well-marked forest trails. Guided tours focus on birding, botany or even tree climbing! Stop by Jagua Arts & Crafts (p412) to buy a map or arrange your tour.

If you prefer to tour the rain forest at high speed, the thrilling **Aventuras Bosquemar Canopy** (2735 5102; Miramar; admission US$75) is the first zip-line canopy tour on this side of the peninsula.

DAY TRIPPER

You've got a free day in Port Jim and you don't want to hang around town? Here's what you can do:

■ Catch a wave and you're sittin' on top of the world. Check out the point break at Playa Pan Dulce in **Cabo Matapalo** (p413).

■ Indulge your sweet tooth. See (and taste) where chocolate comes from at **Köbö Farm** (p407).

■ Slow down and get some sun. Have a picnic on the deserted wilderness beach of **Playa Blanca** (p407).

■ Get a bird's eye view from the top of a 60m ficus tree. Tree-climbing tours offered by **Everyday Adventures** (p413).

■ Experience tropical paradise among the orchids, bromeliads and heliconia at **Casa de Orquídeas** (p436).

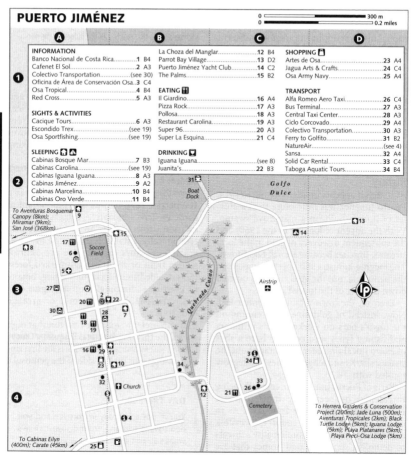

PUERTO JIMÉNEZ

0 ———————— 300 m
0 ———————— 0.2 miles

INFORMATION
Banco Nacional de Costa Rica...........**1** B4
Cafenet El Sol.................................**2** A3
Colectivo Transportation................(see 30)
Oficina de Área de Conservación Osa..**3** C4
Osa Tropical......................................**4** B4
Red Cross...**5** A3

SIGHTS & ACTIVITIES
Cacique Tours....................................**6** A3
Escondido Trex.............................(see 19)
Osa Sportfishing............................(see 19)

SLEEPING
Cabinas Bosque Mar...........................**7** B3
Cabinas Carolina............................(see 19)
Cabinas Iguana Iguana........................**8** A3
Cabinas Jiménez.................................**9** A2
Cabinas Marcelina............................**10** B4
Cabinas Oro Verde.............................**11** B4

La Choza del Manglar......................**12** B4
Parrot Bay Village............................**13** D2
Puerto Jiménez Yacht Club..............**14** C2
The Palms.......................................**15** B2

EATING
Il Giardino......................................**16** A4
Pizza Rock......................................**17** A3
Pollosa...**18** A3
Restaurant Carolina.........................**19** A3
Super 96...**20** A3
Super La Esquina.............................**21** C4

DRINKING
Iguana Iguana................................(see 8)
Juanita's...**22** B3

SHOPPING
Artes de Osa...................................**23** A4
Jagua Arts & Crafts..........................**24** C4
Osa Army Navy...............................**25** A4

TRANSPORT
Alfa Romeo Aero Taxi......................**26** C4
Bus Terminal...................................**27** A3
Central Taxi Center..........................**28** A3
Ciclo Corcovado..............................**29** A4
Colectivo Transportation..................**30** A3
Ferry to Golfito...............................**31** B2
NatureAir.....................................(see 4)
Sansa...**32** A4
Solid Car Rental..............................**33** C4
Taboga Aquatic Tours......................**34** B4

Golfo
Dulce

Boat
Dock

To Aventuras Bosquemar
Canopy (8km);
Miramar (9km);
San José (368km)

Soccer
Field

Airstrip

Quebrada Cacao

Church

Cemetery

To Herrera Gardens & Conservation
Project (200m); Jade Luna (500m);
Aventuras Tropicales (2km); Black
Turtle Lodge (5km); Iguana Lodge
(5km); Playa Platanares (5km);
Playa Preci-Osa Lodge (5km)

To Cabinas Eilyn
(400m); Carate (45km)

Five lines stretch between five platforms, winding 600m through primary forest. It's about 8km from Jiménez near the village of Miramar – prices include transportation from Puerto Jiménez.

Boat tours around the Golfo Dulce are becoming increasingly popular. The all-day outing often includes a mangrove tour, snorkeling excursion and dolphin watch. Remember that it is illegal to swim with the dolphins, despite your tour guide's best intentions.

Tours

Aventuras Tropicales (☎ 2735 5195; www.aventuras tropicales.com) A Tico-run operation that offers all sorts of tropical adventures.

Cacique Tours (☎ 8815 8919; www.lasosas.org) The affable Oscar Cortés offers a variety of wildlife tours, his specialty being an early-morning bird walk.

Escondido Trex (☎ 2735 5210; www.escondidotrex.com) Specializes in kayak tours, including mangrove paddles, night paddles, sunset tours and kayak-snorkel combos.

Osa Sportfishing (☎ 2735 5675; www.costa-rica -sportfishing.com; Restaurant Carolina) Transplanted Florida fishers who organize sportfishing vacations and dolphin- and whale-watching on the 50ft double-decker *Delfin Blanco*.

Sleeping
BUDGET

Puerto Jiménez is one of the few places on the Península de Osa with a good selection of budget accommodations. All rooms have private cold-water bathrooms and fans, unless otherwise stated.

Cabinas Iguana Iguana (☎ 2735 5158; r per person US$15; P ⅏) Wood cabins are set on quiet and shady grounds here on the northern edge of town. The rooms are slightly dank, and the swimming pool bears a striking resemblance to a frog swamp, but the overall atmosphere is pleasant. The onsite bar is among the town's hottest spots on weekend nights so light sleepers should probably stay elsewhere.

Cabinas Oro Verde (☎ 2735 5241; r per person US$15) Simple and central: this is what you are looking for in a budget hotel. Rooms are clean, if a little musty, and the bars on the windows are not pretty, but at least you know the place is safe. All in all, this is a good place to stumble back to late at night, but don't be surprised if you're woken up in the morning by early-bird shoppers.

Cabinas Jiménez (☎ 2735 5090; r US$30-60; P ⅏) The efforts of the new American ownership are evident at this long-standing clutch of cabinas. All of the rooms have jungle scenes painted on the walls and underwater murals in the hot-water bathrooms. Refrigerators and safes are practical, while details like carved wooden furniture, woven textiles and batik curtains add an elegant flair. The pricier rooms have fantastic views of the lagoon.

Cabinas Marcelina (☎ 2755 5286; d with/without air-con US$40/30; P ⅏) Marcelina's place is a long-standing favorite among budget travelers looking for a peaceful night of sleep. The concrete building is painted salmon pink and surrounded by blooming trees, lending it a homey atmosphere that invites good dreams. Rooms have modern furniture, fluffy towels and tile bathrooms, which are certainly a welcome sight at this price range.

The Palms (☎ 2735 5012; r US$30-60; P ⅏ ▯) Arguably the best-value accommodation in Port Jim, the former Brisas del Mar has been completely renovated by its new American owners. Rooms of varying sizes and shapes have artsy touches – from the hand-painted sinks and murals to the soft lighting and fine linens. There are also hot-water bathrooms. Of course, the biggest draw is what has always made this place special, namely the cooling breezes that sweep through the waterside property.

Campers should head to **Herrera Gardens & Conservation Project** (☎ 2735 5267; camping per person US$6-8) or the ironically named **Puerto Jiménez Yacht Club** (☎ 2735 5051; camping per person US$3).

MIDRANGE

All hotels listed have private bathrooms with hot water.

Cabinas Carolina (☎ 2735 5696; d with air-con US$35; ⅏) The lack of windows makes this low-priced stalwart feel something like a concrete prison, but at least it's got air-conditioning and a central location. The attached *soda*, Restaurant Carolina, is a Jiménez institution, so even if you're looking for something in a higher price bracket, don't miss the stellar casados on offer here.

Cabinas Bosque Mar (☎ 2735 5681; d with air-con US$40; P ⅏) This hot-pink motel-style building is one of the best bargains in Jiménez, especially considering that all the rooms are large and airy. Although the atmosphere is nothing to write home about, there is a decent onsite restaurant for those feeling too lazy to head into town, as well as a helpful onsite tour agency.

Cabinas Eilyn (☎ 2735 5465; r US$40; P ⅏) Hospitality is a family affair at these quiet quarters on the edge of town. High ceilings, tile floors and a comfy porch enhance the decor of the four cozy cabinas that are attached to the Tico owners' home. Prices include a home-cooked breakfast of hearty *gallo pinto* (rice and beans) and fresh fruit.

La Choza del Manglar (☎ 2735 5002; www.man glares.com; r US$40-90; P ⅏ ▯) Set on the edge of the mangrove swamp, this tropical inn is – as it claims – 'a *very* natural place.' Wildlife sightings are de rigueur on these beautifully landscaped grounds – from crocodiles to kinkajous, monkeys to macaws. Bright and airy rooms have hand-carved furniture and mural-painted walls, as well as large windows overlooking the lush surroundings.

Playa Preci-Osa Lodge (☎ 8818 2959; www.playa -preciosa-lodge.de; r US$68-100; P) All of the options at this romantic beach lodge on nearby Playa Platanares offer excellent value: four spacious thatch-roof bungalows have a sleeping loft and plenty of living space (great for families), while eight screened platform tents are set in the secluded garden. The grounds are filled with fruit trees and flowering plants that attract loads of birdlife, monkeys and iguanas, while the ocean is literally a few feet from your doorstep.

TOP END

Black Turtle Lodge (☎ 2735 5005; www.blackturtle lodge.com; Playa Platanares; cabinetta s US$85-110, d US$140-170; **P**) A peaceful retreat along Playa Platanares, this ecolodge offers the choice of two-story cabinas, which have magnificent views over the treetops to the Golfo Dulce, and the less spacious *cabinettas* (small cabins) which are nestled into the tropical garden below. All have bamboo furniture and hard-wood floors, but the *cabinettas* share hot-water bathrooms. Gourmet meals (included) receive rave reviews from readers.

Parrot Bay Village (☎ 2735 5180, 2735 5748; r US$125; **P** 🐾) With the beach on one side and the mangrove swamp on the other, Parrot Bay Village enjoys a prime locale and a laidback beach-bum atmosphere. Eight spacious, screened cabins are clustered loosely around an open-air restaurant. Each is exquisitely deco-rated with ceramic tile floors, uniquely carved doors and polished hardwood detailing.

Iguana Lodge (☎ 2735 5205; www.iguanalodge .com; Playa Platanares; casitas/villas US$155/450; **P**) This luxurious lodge fronting Playa Platanares has the most architecturally alluring cabins in the area: four two-story bungalows have huge breezy decks, bamboo furniture, orthopedic beds draped in mosquito netting and lovely stone bathrooms with garden showers. Rates include three delectable meals a day: the crea-tive cuisine is a highlight. If you're traveling in a large group, consider renting the three-room Villa Villa Kula, a charming tropical colonial house with a fully stocked kitchen.

Eating & Drinking

Stock up on food items, bug repellent and other necessities at the Super La Esquina or the smaller Super 96.

Restaurant Carolina (dishes US$3-8) This is *the* hub in Puerto Jiménez. Expats, nature guides, tourists and locals all gather here for food, drinks and plenty of carousing. The food is famous locally and the fresh-fruit drinks and cold beers go down pretty easily on a hot day.

Pollosa (☎ 2735 5667; meals US$4-8; 🕑 noon-9pm Sun-Fri) Pollosa is renowned among locals for juicy, delectable rotisserie chicken, but it also has a good selection of salads, sandwiches and spaghetti. Carry-out is available, so this is an excellent option for picnicking.

Pizza Rock (pizzas US$5-8; 🕑 6-10pm) Sizzling piz-zas come straight out of the wood-burning oven and onto your plate at this informal, open-air diner. If you're heading to, or coming back from, Corcovado, a cheesy slice is exactly the kind of indulgence you're looking for.

Il Giardino (☎ 2735 5129; meals US$10-12; 🕑 10am-2pm & 5-10pm) The specialties of the house at Il Giardino are homemade pasta and fresh seafood. Considering that you're on the edge of the wilderness in a far-flung corner of Costa Rica, there is a fair measure of Italian authenticity here.

our pick **Jade Luna** (☎ 2735 5735; meals US$15-25; 🕑 6-9pm Mon-Sat) A delectable dining experi-ence, starting with the linen napkins and candlelit tables, and ending with tropical-flavored homemade ice cream. Not to gloss over what comes in between: the menu var-ies, but always features fresh Cajun-style fish and garlicky jumbo shrimp straight from the gulf, plus a host of appetizers and salads pre-pared with the freshest organic produce.

Drinking

You can get greasy Mexican food at **Juanita's** (🕑 5pm-2am), but it's better to stick to the beer and passable margaritas (happy hour is 4pm to 6pm). **Iguana Iguana** (🕑 4pm-midnight), at the cabins of the same name, is a popular watering hole, especially on weekends when the locals join in the action.

Shopping

Artes de Osa (☎ 2735 5429) This cutesy souve-nir shop has the usual tourist knick-knacks in addition to some attractive handcrafted furniture and hand-painted pottery.

Jagua Arts & Crafts (☎ 2735 5267; 🕑 6:30am-5pm) A great collection of art and jewelry by local and expat craftspeople, including some amazing painted masks.

Osa Army Navy (🕑 8am-7pm Mon-Sat, 9am-4pm Sun) Your one-stop shop for sportswear, boogie boards, fishing gear, bug nets, knives, back-packs and other outdoor gear.

Getting There & Around
AIR

NatureAir (www.natureair.com) and **Sansa** (www.sansa .com) have daily flights to/from San José; one-way flights are approximately US$100.

Alfa Romeo Aero Taxi (☎ 2775 5353) has light aircraft (three and five passengers) for char-ter flights to Golfito, Carate, Drake, Sirena, Palmar Sur, Quepos and Limón. Prices are dependant on the number of passengers, so it's best to try to organize a larger group if you're considering this option.

BICYCLE
Rent a bike at **Ciclo Corcovado** (☎ 2735 5429; per hr US$1; 🕒 8am-5pm).

BOAT
Two passenger ferries travel to Golfito (US$2, 1½ hours), departing at 6am and 10am daily. Note that these times are subject to change; in this part of the country, schedules often fall prey to the whims of the captain.

A better option than chugging away on the ferries is to hire a private water taxi to shuttle you across the bay. You will have to negotiate, but prices are generally reasonable considering that you'll be free of having to rely on the ferry. Fortunately, waters in the Golfo Dulce are sheltered and generally calm, though it's still good to have a reasonable degree of faith in the seaworthiness of both your captain and their ship before you set out.

Taboga Aquatic Tours (☎ 2735 5265) runs water taxis to Zancudo for US$35.

BUS
Most buses arrive at the new peach-color terminal on the west side of town. All of these pass La Palma (23km away) for the eastern entry into Corcovado. Buy tickets to San José in advance.

Neily US$3.50, three hours, 5:30am and 2pm.
San Isidro US$4.50, four hours, 1pm.
San José, via San Isidro (Autotransportes Blanco Lobo) US$6.50, eight hours, 5am and 11am.

CAR & TAXI
Colectivo Transportation (☎ 8837 3120, 8832 8680; Soda Deya) runs a collective jeep-taxi service to Matapalo (US$3) and Carate (US$6) on the southern tip of the national park. Departures are from the Soda Deya at 6am and 1:30pm, returning at 8:30am and 4pm.

Otherwise, you can call and hire a 4WD taxi from **Taxi 348** (☎ 8849 5228; taxicorcovado@racsa .co.cr) or from the **Central Taxi Center** (☎ 2735 5481). Taxis usually charge US$60 for the ride to Carate, US$25 for the ride to Matapalo and US$100 for the overland trek to Drake.

You can also rent a vehicle from **Solid Car Rental** (☎ 2735 5777; per day US$75).

CABO MATAPALO
The tip of the Osa peninsula and the entrance to Golfo Dulce lies just 17km south of Puerto Jiménez, but this heavily forested and beach-fringed cape is a vastly different world. A network of trails traverses the foothills, which are uninhabited except for migrating wildlife from the Reserva Forestal Golfo Dulce. Along the coastline, miles upon miles of beaches of pristine wilderness are virtually abandoned, except for handfuls of surfers in the know.

Although facilities in this remote corner are extremely limited, Cabo Matapalo is home to a number of luxurious lodges that cater to travelers searching for peace and seclusion. Of course, it's hard to feel lonely out here given the breadth of animals about: scarlet macaw, brown pelican and all breeds of heron are frequently sighted on the beaches, while four species of monkey, sloth, coati, agouti and anteater roam the woods.

Sights & Activities
Cabo Matapalo is an attractive destination for adventurers who wish to go it alone. All of the lodges have easy access to miles of **trails** which you can explore without a guide. Indeed, you are likely to spot a good selection of wildlife just walking along the Cabo's tree-lined dirt road. A fantastic and easy hiking destination is **King Louis**, a magnificent, 28m waterfall which can be accessed by trail from **Playa Matapalo**. For ocean adventures, most of the lodges also offer **kayaks**; and the wild, beautiful beach – surrounding on three sides – is never more than a short walk away.

These pristine beaches around Cabo Matapalo offer three breaks that are putting this little peninsula on the surfing map. **Playa Pan Dulce** is a double point break. The inside break is a small wave that is ideal for beginners; experts can find the point on the outside break and ride it all the way into shore. **Backwash Bay** offers a nice beach break at low tide. The steep beach makes it excellent for long-boarding. **Playa Matapalo** also has an A-plus right break, with the biggest and best waves in the area. Conditions are usually good with a west swell; surfing season coincides with the rainy season, which is April to October.

Tours
Naturalist Andy Pruter runs **Everyday Adventures** (☎ 8353 8619; www.everydaycostarica.com),

which offers all kind of adventures in Cabo Matapalo. His signature tour is tree-climbing (US$55 per person): scaling a 60m ficus tree, aptly named 'Cathedral'. Also popular (and definitely adrenaline inducing) is waterfall-rappelling (US$75) down cascades ranging from 15m to 30m.

Sleeping

This area is off the grid, so many places do not have electricity around the clock or hot water. Reservations are recommended in the dry season (mid-November to the end of April). High-season rates are quoted; prices are per person, including three meals, unless otherwise stated.

Ojo del Mar (☎ 2735 5531; www.ojodelmar.com; s/d incl breakfast US$55/90; P) Tucked in amid the windswept beach and the lush jungle, this is a little plot of paradise. The four beautifully handcrafted bamboo bungalows are entirely open-air, allowing for all the natural sounds and scents to seep in (thatch roofs and mosquito nets provide protection from the elements). Solar power provides electricity in the *casa grande* (main house). Hammocks swing from the palms, while howler monkeys swing above. Rates include breakfast, but Niko – co-owner and cook – also serves an excellent, all-organic dinner (US$15). Look for this gem on the road to Carate, just before the Buena Esperanza Bar.

Ranchos Almendros (Kapu's Place; ☎ 2735 5531; http://home.earthlink.net/~kapu/; Cabo Matapalo; 2-/3-/4-person cabañas US$90/160/225; P) This is the end of the line on the Cabo Matapalo, where the road stops pretending and turns into a sandy beach path. The property includes three cozy cabañas that are equipped with solar power, large, screened windows, full kitchens and garden showers. As per the name, 'Almond Tree Ranch' is part of an ongoing project dedicated to the reforestation of Indian almond trees to create habitat for the endangered scarlet macaw.

El Remanso Rain Forest Beach Lodge (☎ 2735 5569; www.elremanso.com; road to Carate, 18km; cabins per person US$95-155; P ⚡) Set on 56 hectares of rain forest, El Remanso is another tropical paradise. Constructed entirely from fallen tropical hardwoods, the secluded, spacious and sumptuous cabins have shiny wood floors and beautifully finished fixtures. Several units have folding French doors that

open to unimpeded vistas of the foliage and the ocean in the distance.

Casa Bambú (www.casabambu.addr.com; Cabo Matapalo; 2-/3-/4-person cottages without meals US$195/205/215; P) This property on the pristine Playa Pan Dulce has three secluded *casas*. All have solar power, bamboo-and-hardwood construction and screen-free half-walls, allowing nothing to come between you and the ocean breezes (except maybe a mosquito net). Fully equipped kitchens and twice-weekly maid service make this an excellent option for longer-term guests who want to get back to nature (weekly rates available). Meals are not included; kayaks, boogie boards and other beach toys are.

Bosque del Cabo (☎ 8381 4847, in Puerto Jiménez 2735 5206; www.bosquedelcabo.com; road to Carate, 18km; s US$195-205, d US$300-330; P ⚡) Nine quaint cabins are perched on a bluff here overlooking the ocean. Modern bathrooms, garden showers and personal hammocks in lush surroundings are the norm; deluxe cabins have added perks like king-size beds, dressing rooms and wraparound porches. Explore the surrounding 200 hectares of rain forest at canopy level (by zip line or by suspension bridge) or at ground level (on miles of marked trails).

Lapa Ríos (☎ 2735 5130; www.laparios.com; road to Carate, 17km; s/d US$425/590; P ⚡) A few hundred meters beyond El Portón Blanco along the road to Carate, this top-notch all-inclusive wilderness resort combines the right amount of luxury with a rustic, tropical ambience. Scattered over the site are 16 spacious, thatch bungalows, all decked out with queen-sized beds, bamboo furniture, garden showers and private decks with panoramic views. An extensive trail system allows exploration of the 400-hectare reserve, while swimming, snorkeling and surfing are at your doorstep.

Eating & Drinking

About 1km before El Portón Blanco, you'll find the trendy, tropical **Buena Esperanza Bar** (☎ 2735 5531; road to Carate, Carbonera; meals US$5-10; ✌ 9am-midnight), a festive, open-air tropical bar on the east side of the road. The limited menu includes lots of sandwiches and vegetarian items, plus a full bar. It's Cabo Matapalo's only place to eat or drink, and so often attracts a decent crowd of locals, resident expats and tourists.

Most hotels and lodges also have small shops that sell snacks and drinks. If you're planning on hiking, be sure to stock up on lots of fresh water as well as your favorite form of trail mix – once you're out in the woods or on the beach, options are decidedly limited.

Getting There & Away

From the Puerto Jiménez–Carate road, the turnoff for the Cabo Matapalo is on the left-hand side, through a white cement gate (called 'El Portón Blanco'). If you are driving, a 4WD is highly recommended – even in the dry season – as roads frequently get washed out. Otherwise, the transport colectivo will drop you here; it passes by at about 6:30am and 2pm heading to Carate, and 10am and 5:30pm heading back to Jiménez. A taxi will come here from Port Jim for about US$30.

CARATE

About 45km south of Puerto Jiménez, the dirt road that rounds the peninsula comes to an abrupt dead end in the village of Carate, which is literally nothing more than an airstrip and a *pulpería*. Needless to say, Carate doesn't exactly rate high on the list of Osa's top tourist destinations, but it does serve as the southwestern gateway for anyone hiking into Sirena ranger station (p416) in Parque Nacional Corcovado.

With that said, there are a handful of recommended wilderness lodges in the area, any of which can provide a good night's rest for travelers heading to/from Corcovado. The ride from Puerto Jiménez to Carate is also an adventure in itself as the narrow, bumpy dirt road winds its way around dense rain forest, through gushing rivers and across windswept beaches. Birdlife and other wildlife are prolific along this stretch: keep your eyes peeled and hang on tight.

Sleeping & Eating

Many places in Carate don't have 24-hour electricity or hot water. Reservations are recommended in the dry season – communication is often through Puerto Jiménez, so messages may not be retrieved every day. High-season rates are quoted; prices are per person, including three meals, unless otherwise stated.

West of Carate is the national park, so if you're planning on hiking into Corcovado, you must be self-sufficient from here on out. The *pulpería* is the last chance you have to stock up on food and water.

Corcovado Lodge Tent Camp (☎ in San José 2227 0766, 2222 0333; www.corcovadolodge.com; tent with/without meals US$70/20) On the beach south of Parque Nacional Corcovado, 1.7km west of the *pulpería*, this long-established lodge is owned and operated by Costa Rica Expeditions. Twenty platform tents have two single beds, clean linens and access to shared bathrooms (but no electricity). The grounds are sort of stark, but a steep trail leads into a 160-hectare private reserve, which is ripe for exploration. A highlight of the reserve is the canopy platform – high up in a 45m guapinol tree – where you can spend the day bird- and wildlife-watching (US$70) or the night under the stars (US$125).

Lookout Inn (☎ 2735 5431; www.lookout-inn .com; r from US$125; P ⏚ 🖵) Another isolated wilderness retreat, the Lookout has comfortable quarters with mural-painted walls, hardwood floors, beautifully carved doors and – you guessed it – unbeatable views. Accommodation is in 'tiki huts,' which are open-air, A-frame huts that are accessible only by a wooden walkway winding through the giant Joba trees (prime birding territory). Behind the inn, 360 steps – known as the 'stairway to heaven' – lead straight up the side of the mountain to four observation platforms and a waterfall trail.

La Leona Eco-Lodge & Tent Camp (☎ 2735 5704; www.laleonalodge.com; s/d with shared bathroom US$80/140, with private bathroom US$106/180; 🖵) On the edge of Parque Nacional Corcovado 2km west of the *pulpería*, this friendly, family-run lodge offers all of the thrills of camping, without the hassles. Sixteen comfy forest-green tents are nestled between the palm trees, with decks facing the beach. All are fully screened and comfortably furnished; solar power provides electricity in the restaurant. Behind the accommodations, 30 hectares of virgin rain-forest property offer opportunities for waterfall hiking, horseback riding and wildlife-watching.

Laguna Vista (☎ 2735 5062; www.lagunavistavillas .com; s/d US$100/170; P 🖵) As the name suggests, this isolated lodge is perched up on a hillside, overlooking the picturesque Laguna Pejeperrito, 2.5km east of the Carate airstrip. Three uniquely designed villas are built in a Mediterranean style, with stucco walls, red-tile roofs and European design accents. Thanks to carefully planned construction, all units have both sunrise and sunset views from the comfort of your king-size beds.

Luna Lodge (☎ 8380 5036, in the USA 888-409 8448; www.lunalodge.com; s/d tents US$105/170, haciendas US$155/250, bungalows US$235/330; Ⓟ) A steep road goes through the Río Carate and up the valley to this enchanting mountain retreat, located about 2km north of the *pulpería*. Taking full advantage of the vista, the high-roofed, open-air restaurant is a marvelous place to indulge in the delights of the gardens and orchards on the grounds. Seven spacious, thatch-roof bungalows each have a huge garden shower and private patio. The open-air meditation studio is nothing less than inspirational.

Getting There & Away
Transportation Colectivo (US$6, 2½ hours) departs Puerto Jiménez for Carate at 6am and 1:30pm, returning at 8:30am and 4pm. Note that the colectivo often fills up on its return trip to Puerto Jiménez, especially during the dry season. Arrive at least 30 minutes ahead of time or you might find yourself stranded.

Alternatively, catch a taxi from Puerto Jiménez (US$60). If you are driving, you'll need a 4WD – even in the dry season as there are a couple of river crossings. Assuming you don't have valuables in sight, you can leave your car at the *pulpería* (per night US$5), and hike to La Leona station (1½ hours) or either of the tented camps listed above.

PARQUE NACIONAL CORCOVADO

This **national park** is the last great tract of tropical rain forest in Pacific Central America. The bastion of biological diversity is home to Costa Rica's largest population of scarlet macaw, as well as countless other endangered species, including Baird's tapir, the giant anteater and the world's largest bird of prey, the rare harpy eagle. Its amazing biodiversity has long attracted the attention of tropical ecologists, as well as a devoted stream of visitors who come from Bahía Drake and Puerto Jiménez to explore the remote location and spy on a wide array of rare and enchanting wildlife.

HISTORY
Because of its remoteness, Corcovado remained undisturbed until loggers invaded in the 1960s. The destruction was halted in '75 when the area was established as government-administered parklands. The early years were a challenge, as park authorities, with limited personnel and resources, sought to deal with illegal clear-cutting, poaching and gold-mining, the latter of which was causing severe erosion in the park's rivers and streams. By 1986, the number of gold miners had exceeded 1000, which promptly caused the government to evict them and their families entirely from the park.

Unfortunately, poaching remains a severe problem in Corcovado to this day. The highest-profile victims are the highly endangered Central American jaguar and its main food source, the white-lipped peccary. Heavily armed hunters gun down peccaries en masse and sell their meat, resulting in a drastic decline in their populations in the last five years. Jaguars, suffering from a diminishing food supply, prey on domestic animals in the area, making them a target of local residents (not to mention the fact that jaguar pelts and bones fetch hefty sums, as well). Minae has stepped up its police patrols, but has been unable to curb the poaching.

On the bright side, illegal logging has all but subsided, primarily since increased tourism has lead to an increased human presence in the park. Furthermore, in an effort to control hunting, agencies such as Conservation International, The Nature Conservancy and the World Wildlife Fund, as well as various other NGOs and charities, have banded together to help organize and fund the park's anti-poaching units.

ORIENTATION & INFORMATION
The 42,469-hectare park is nestled in the southwestern corner of the Península de Osa, and protects at least eight distinct habitats, ranging from mangrove swamps to primary and secondary rain forest to low altitude cloud forest. The most accessible and visible habitat is the 46km of sandy coastline.

Information and maps are available at the **Oficina de Área de Conservación Osa** (☎ 2735 5036, 2735 5580; park fee per person per day US$10; ⏱ 8am-4pm) in Puerto Jiménez. Contact this office to make reservations for lodging and meals at all of the ranger stations and to pay your park fee. Be sure to make these arrangements a few days in advance as facilities are limited, and they do fill up on occasion in the dry season.

Park headquarters are at **Sirena ranger station** on the coast in the middle of the park.

(Continued on page 425)

Green
Costa Rica

An endangered baby sea turtle steps toward a brighter future

Buying organic coffee beans protects both the local economy and the rain forest

JORDI CAMÍ/ALAMY

top five
WAYS TO SAVE THE RAIN FOREST

Plant a tree
At Selva Bananito Lodge (p469) on the Caribbean coast, you can help reforest a former banana plantation while learning about the conservation philosophy from the lodge's conscientious owners, the Stein family.

Drink organic, shade-grown coffee
Organic coffee-growing avoids the use of chemical pesticides and fertilizers, minimizing their impact on flora and fauna. Shade-grown coffee ensures the survival of old-growth forests and is planted under shade plants that produce nitrogen and improve the quality of both the soil and the coffee crop.

Educate the masses
Work on a community education program with the Fundación Corcovado (p425), a grassroots organization dedicated to preserving one of Costa Rica's last true frontiers – Parque Nacional Corcovado.

Say no to beef
The number-one reason for forest clearing in Central America is to make way for cattle pasture – mostly to feed the export market. If you can't bypass that burger, make sure you know where your cow came from. Consider indulging in grass-fed beef, which is better for your health and better for the environment.

Give a donation
Money talks, especially when it's in the hands of the **Monteverde Conservation League** (www .monteverdeinfo.com/monteverde_conservation_league .htm), a charitable organization that is dedicated to preserving the Bosque Eterno de los Niños (Children's Eternal Rainforest; see p176).

As the world's most iconic eco-tourism destination, Costa Rica spoils travelers with a never-ending assortment of environmentally friendly activities.

Animal lovers can help baby sea turtles scamper out to sea, while tree huggers can help plant new life in the forest floor. Green thumbs can try their hand at organic agriculture, while nature lovers can explore some of the planet's most pristine landscapes. Indeed, few tourist spots so easily combine wildlife-watching, adventure travel, volunteering and environmental conservation in one Earth-friendly package.

However, the greatest challenge to travelers in Costa Rica is preserving the purity of this destination for future generations. The secret is out, the tourism industry is booming, and travelers are leaving behind a larger footprint on the country than ever before. As a result, each of us bears the responsibility to minimize the impact of our stay in Costa Rica and to travel in the most sustainable way possible. Fortunately, it's not too hard to think green while in Costa Rica.

HOW TO PROTECT THE ENVIRONMENT

The following tips cover how to protect the environment in Costa Rica and beyond:

- **Drink tap water** Fill up your bottle from a rain water-collection system, and purify natural water sources while hiking. Reuse plastic bottles.

- **Recycle** When you arrive in a new town, ask around to see if there are any recycling programs. If a system is in place, spread awareness among your fellow travelers.

- **Pick up garbage** While walking along a beach or a trail, pick up any garbage you see – your actions might inspire another person to do the same.

- **Respect the land** Stick to the trails as this reduces the erosion caused by human transit. Likewise, don't damage plants, and always observe wildlife from a distance.

- **Respect the sea** Always follow the basic snorkel and scuba guidelines, keep garbage out of the water, and remember not to eat or purchase endangered or undersized seafood.

- **Don't feed animals** Feeding the animals interferes with their natural diets and makes them susceptible to bacteria transferred by humans or pesticides contained within fruit.

- **Use your head** When in doubt, remember that common sense and awareness are always your best guides, regardless of where you are in the world.

WHAT IS SUSTAINABLE TOURISM?

When backpackers started blazing the 'hippie trail' across the old Silk Road during the 1960s and '70s, sustainability was an implicit concept that few people needed to give much thought to. Travel at the time was nearly always slow, overland and utterly dependent upon local economies.

Things change however, and sometimes in dramatic ways. Today, travel is one of the world's fastest growing industries, and global economists predict that the industry is expanding as much as 6% annually. The advent of cheap budget airlines, improved tourist infrastructure and wider profiles for exotic, distant destinations, has made travel a consumable good for the mass market.

The continuous growth of the travel industry has brought incredible economic success to countries throughout the world, Costa Rica being a notable example. However, while this growth has had positive impacts it has also placed enormous stress on both biological and cultural habitats, and threatens to destroy the very destinations that tourists are seeking out.

In recent years, the term 'sustainable tourism' has emerged as a buzz word in the industry, though few people have a clear idea of exactly what this concept entails. In its purest form, sustainable tourism simply refers to striking the ideal balance between the traveler and their surrounding environment.

Stick to the trail when hiking to reduce your impact on the fragile forest
YADID LEVY/ALAMY

Costa Rica is home to some of the most biodiverse rain forests on Earth

CHRISTER FREDRIKS

PROTECTING LOCAL ENVIRONMENTS

It's impossible to deny the beauty and fragility of the natural world while traveling through Costa Rica. From verdant rain forests and soaring jungled peaks to white-sand beaches and clear-blue tropical seas, nature in its full glory is everywhere. Fortunately, the vast majority of Costa Rica's natural spaces are protected, though the system is not without its faults and travelers play a part in helping to protect the country's rich natural environment.

One of the simplest things you can do before going to Costa Rica is learn about the local conservation and environmental issues – see the Environment chapter p61) for more information. While in Costa Rica, don't be afraid to ask questions – usually the best source of information about an area is a local.

Although the temptation to follow the herds can be strong, try not to visit conservation areas that are saturated by travelers. On the contrary, do support tourism companies and environmental groups that promote conservation initiatives and long-term management plans. For a list of ecofriendly businesses in Costa Rica, see the GreenDex (p588).

TOP FIVE ECOLODGES

It's easy to lie down for the night in a hotel when you know that your stay isn't negatively impacting the environment. Although there is certainly no shortage of ecolodges in Costa Rica, the following lists some of our favorites:

- **Esquinas Rainforest Lodge** (p435) A private reserve that is managed by 'Rainforest for the Austrians,' a group that helped establish Piedras Blancas national park.
- **Punta Mona** (p493) This remote retreat on the edge of the Caribbean is a working experiment in organic permaculture farming.
- **Rancho Margot** (p244) 'A sustainable, self-sufficient dude ranch' that is aspiring to be a life-skills university.
- **Si Como No** (p350) This ecotourism pioneer is a testament to the fact that luxury and sustainability are not incompatible.
- **Tiskita Jungle Lodge** (p441) Set on 100 hectares of orchards, this jungle lodge has more than 100 varieties of tropical fruit from around the world.

SHOP SUSTAINABLY

The most immediate change brought by increased tourism in Costa Rica is the creation of a thriving consumer market for indigenous arts and crafts. If purchased directly from the source, arts and crafts generate income from the ground up and encourage communities to maintain their traditional practices. Spend your money where it counts and help ensure a culture's future.

In Costa Rica, there are also a number of cooperatives that purchase indigenous crafts from villages around the country, sell them at a premium, and return the profits to the artisan. An excellent example of this commendable practice is Galería Namu (p107) in San José, which is regarded as the premier indigenous art boutique in the country.

Although it should go without saying, never purchase endangered animal products or rare hardwoods no matter how important it may be to the local economy. Supporting this trade hastens species and habitat destruction, and despite the assurances of the salesperson, there is virtually no way to guarantee that these products were collected in an ecologically sensible or legal manner.

Generating income from the ground up: an indigenous craftsman weaves a basket to sell

ROBERT FRIED/ALAMY

PRESERVING LOCAL COMMUNITIES

One of the most important tenets of sustainable tourism is the notion of respecting local communities. Cultural ruin of a destination is irreversible, but community preservation is one area where travelers can make a big difference.

While in Costa Rica, talk to locals and ask them about their customs and traditions. An eagerness to learn on the part of the traveler may reassure a local that their customs are valued by others, even if everything is changing around them. In fact, the best window into a local culture might be sitting next to you on the bus, drinking on the stool next to you in the bar or sharing a park bench with you. And, you never know where a conversation will take you, whether it be a new adventure or a new friendship.

A growing interest in Costa Rica's indigenous cultures – mostly on the part of foreign tourists – is beginning to draw a bit of attention to these long-ignored groups. The indigenous groups are responding with varying degrees of receptivity, but many recognize the economic benefits of encouraging tourism.

The indigenous villages throughout Costa Rica can accommodate visitors who are curious to get a glimpse of a traditional lifestyle, or who want to learn the healing powers of medicinal forest plants. Costa Rica has a history of disparagement and neglect of indigenous peoples, so a better understanding of the native cultures is a welcomed practice. For more information on indigenous populations in Costa Rica, see boxed text Endangered Cultures, p49.

THE ESSENTIAL RAIN FOREST

Why should humans become more serious about saving the rain forest? Even though most of us don't encounter them in our daily lives, rain forests affect every one of us in more ways than we realize. The future survival of rain forests is essential for a number of reasons:

Carbon Sink Effect

One of the most common media buzzwords these days is 'climate change' or 'global warming,' particularly in regard to humans negatively impacting the health and sustainability of the planet. As developing nations continue to modernize, global carbon emissions rise and evidence of the greenhouse effect can be felt across the planet.

One of the best defenses humans have against rising carbon dioxide (CO_2) levels is the tropical rain forest. Tropical rain forests limit the greenhouse effect of global warming by storing carbon and hence reducing the amount of CO_2 in the atmosphere – they act as a 'carbon sink.' Unfortunately, our best defense against climate change is rapidly being destroyed the world over. In a frightening example of the interconnectedness of environments, the deforestation of Latin American rain forests is impacting global ecosystems, such as the Sahel in Africa, where desertification has increased as deforestation in Latin America increases.

Unfortunately, the total picture is even bleaker. In 2004, scientists made an announcement following a 20-year study in the Amazon, claiming the world's tropical forests may become less able to absorb CO_2. In some areas of the forest scientists discovered that bigger, quicker-growing species were flourishing at the expense of the smaller ones living below the forest canopy. Since plant growth is dependent upon CO_2, the team hypothesized that the bigger plants in tropical rain forests were getting an extra boost from rising levels of global emissions.

As a result of changing rain-forest dynamics, specifically the decline of densely wooded subcanopy trees, the ability of tropical rain forests to act as a carbon sink is in jeopardy. The reality that CO_2 levels are increasing, however frightening it may be, and it affects us all.

Bioprospecting

In October 2003, the scientific journal *Ecological Society of America* published an article on one of the most fascinating scientific research projects ever undertaken in the tropics – one that could have long-lasting implications for rain-forest conservation around the globe.

Several US scientists developed a program in Panama of 'bioprospecting,' or scouring the rain forest for compounds that may one day become new drugs. They set up six labs and hired Panamanian cell biologists and chemists to develop and run experiments. Although the labs have far less funding than similar labs in the US and Europe, researchers have already started to produce remarkable results and have published their findings in a number of academic journals.

The success of bioprospecting places a great deal of importance on the rain forest's biodiversity, especially since further research – and by necessity, conservation – potentially equals cures for widespread diseases. Bioprospecting is slowly attracting the attention of large pharmaceutical companies, which could lead to a huge investment to help unlock the mysteries of rain forests and consequently preserve them. Ultimately, this would make conservation both the end and the means.

Intrinsic Value

Climate change and bioprospecting aside, a simple argument for saving the rain forest is that its intrinsic value is enough to warrant increased conservation efforts. Costa Rica's natural vegetation was originally almost all forest, though during the past few generations much of this has been cleared to create pastures and agricultural land. The destruction of the rain forest has wiped out countless flora and fauna species that will now never be known. Beyond the plants and animals that inhabit the forests, deforestation also negatively impacts migratory animals that pass through the forests annually, such as bats, butterflies and birds.

Deforestation and habitat destruction have also threatened the traditional cultures of Costa Rica's indigenous populations, who have lived in the rain forest for generations. While humans the world over lament the destruction of this crucial ecosystem, it is the original denizens of the rain forests who have already lost the most.

If you're thinking about visiting an indigenous community, consider how you go about doing it. Revenue from tourism can play a vital role in the development of the region, particularly if you are buying locally produced crafts or paying for the services of a guide to take you through the rain forest. Be sensitive to indigenous groups by inquiring locally about proper conduct and protocols when visiting indigenous reservations. Generally speaking, conservative dress, moderate camera use and a willingness to buy crafts will earn you a great deal of respect.

FOSTERING LOCAL ECONOMIES

One of the most immediate benefits of tourism is a strong financial boost to the local economy. Keeping this in mind, if the opportunity arises to spend money at a locally run business or vendor, give a little back.

Enjoy the flavors at a local restaurant. If there is a kid selling an *empanada* (corn turnover filled with ground meat) out of his shoulder satchel, don't worry about your stomach – just buy one. Enjoy the creativity of a local artisan. If you spot a piece on display that catches your eye, buy it instead of saying you'll come back later. In all cases, you'll be surprised how far your dollar can stretch.

A great way of stimulating local economies in a sustainable manner is to frequent businesses that are dedicated to these aims. For a list of ecofriendly businesses in Costa Rica, see the GreenDex on p588.

A farmer husks coconuts at a market: shopping locally fosters local economies

NIK WHEELER/ALAMY

Volunteers excavate turtle hatchlings in an effort to increase the dwindling turtle population

JAN CSERNOCH/ALAMY

VOLUNTEERING IN COSTA RICA

One of the best ways to have a truly unique experience in Costa Rica is to spend a portion of your travels in a rewarding volunteer position. Not only is volunteering a great way to help foster local economies in a sustainable way, but it also opens the doorway to a potentially life-changing travel experience.

Costa Rica is justifiably famous as a leading 'voluntourism' destination, particularly because there is a wide range of programs on offer. Depending on your particular needs and interests, you can choose a program in a variety of fields ranging from environmental conservation to community action.

For a complete list of volunteer programs in Costa Rica, see p538.

top five

VOLUNTOURISM EXPERIENCES

Teach English
Although you may take your mother tongue for granted, English opens doors throughout the world. To gain valuable teaching experience while potentially changing someone's life, check out the programs offered by **World Language Study** (www .worldlanguagestudy.com).

Save the turtles
Baby sea turtles are just about the gosh darn cutest little things you've ever laid your eyes on, though there are tragically less and less of them with each passing year. For a chance to help give these little guys a fighting chance, consider a volunteer placement with **Pretoma** (www.tortugamarina.org).

Help kids
Few things in life are as rewarding as putting a smile on the face of a child, especially one who is in desperate need of your help. If you want to get involved in youth work, a good point of contact is **Amerispan** (www.amerispan.com).

Protect the forest
If you're an aspiring forester, or simply want to feel good about saving the rain forest, consider a placement with the **Bosque Eterno de los Niños** (Children's Eternal Forest; www.acmcr.org). There are opportunities here to learn about trail maintenance, surveying, administration and wildlife management.

Go organic
Organic farming is the wave of the future, so why not take some time to learn how to grow a better tomato. One of the country's best volunteer-run farms is **Finca la Flor de Paraíso** (www.la-flor-de-paraiso.org), which offers training in a variety of agrarian disciplines.

(Continued from page 416)

Other ranger stations are located on the park boundaries: **San Pedrillo station** in the northwest corner on the coast; the new **Los Planes station** on the northern boundary (near the village of the same name); **La Leona station** in the southeast corner on the coast (near the village of Carate); and **Los Patos ranger station** in the northeast corner (near the village of La Palma). Always check with rangers before setting out about trail conditions and possible closures (especially during the wettest months, from June to November).

ACTIVITIES
Wildlife-Watching
The best wildlife-watching in Corcovado is at Sirena, but the coastal trails have two advantages: they are more open, and the constant crashing of waves covers the sound of noisy walkers. White-faced capuchin, red-tailed squirrel, collared peccary, white-nosed coati and northern tamandua are regularly seen on both trails.

On the less traveled San Pedrillo trail, Playa Llorona is a popular nesting spot for marine turtles, including leatherback, olive ridley and green turtles. Nesting turtles attract ocelot, jaguar and other predators, though they are hard to spot.

Both coastal trails produce an endless pageant of birds. Pairs of scarlet macaws are guaranteed, as the tropical almond trees lining the coast are a favorite food. The sections along the beach shelter mangrove black hawk by the dozens and numerous waterbird species. The little rock island opposite Salsipuedes serves as a roost for hundreds of birds, including the magnificent frigate bird and brown booby.

The Los Patos trail attracts lowland rain forest birds such as great curassow, chestnut-mandibled toucan, fiery-billed aracari, turquoise cotinga and rufous piha; trogon, hummingbird and wood creeper are plentiful. Encounters with mixed flocks are common. Mammals are similar to those sighted on the coastal trails, but Los Patos is better for primates and white-lipped peccary.

For wildlife-watchers frustrated at the difficulty of seeing rain forest mammals, a stay at Sirena ranger station is a must. Topping the list, Baird's tapir are practically assured – that is a statement that can be made at few other places in the world. This endangered and distant relative of the rhinoceros is frequently spotted grazing along the airstrip after dusk. Sirena is excellent for other herbivores, particularly red brocket (especially on Sirena trail) and both species of peccary. Agouti and tayra are also common.

The profusion of meat on the hoof means there are predators aplenty, but they are not nearly as confiding. Jaguar are occasionally sighted near the airstrip in the very early morning (midnight to 4am). While spotlighting at night you are more likely to see kinkajou and crab-eating skunk (especially at the mouth of the Río Sirena). Ocelot represents your best chance for observing a cat, but again, it's difficult.

Corcovado is the only national park in Costa Rica with all four of the country's

---

GREEN GRASSROOTS

The impressive **Fundación Corcovado** (☎ 2297 3013; www.corcovadofoundation.org) is a network of local businesspeople – mostly hoteliers – who have teamed up to raise both money and awareness to support their most valuable resource: the biodiversity of the national park. Through their own fund-raising efforts, they have hired additional rangers to crack down on poaching, implemented various community education programs and worked toward establishing a sustainable-tourism code for local businesses.

Fundación Corcovado has also been spearheading an increasingly high-profile campaign to designate Parque Nacional Corcovado as a Unesco World Heritage Site. However, due to ongoing reports of uncontrolled poaching, the process has been frustratingly slow.

The Fundación Corcovado invites volunteers to work in the community and in the park. Tasks might include teaching about waste management and conservation at local schools, maintaining trails and bridges in the park, patrolling beaches and collecting data during turtle season, and providing assistance and expertise to visiting tourists. The daily fee of approximately US$25 for volunteers includes transportation from San José as well as room and board with a local family. Note that there is a two-week minimum commitment for all service projects.

POISON DARTS & HARMLESS ROCKETS

Traversed by many streams and rivers, Corcovado is a hot spot for exquisitely beautiful poison-dart frogs. Two species here, the granular poison-dart frog and the Golfo Dulce poison-dart frog, are Costa Rican endemics – indeed, the latter only occurs in and around Corcovado. A search of the leaf litter near Sirena ranger station readily turns up both species, as well as the more widespread green and black poison-dart frog.

You might also find some other members of the family that have one important difference: they're not poisonous! Called rocket frogs because of their habit of launching themselves into streams when disturbed, they are essentially poison-dart frogs without the poisonous punch.

Why the difference? It probably arises from their diets. Poison-dart frogs have a diet dominated by ants, which are very rich in alkaloids, and are thought to give rise to their very formidable defenses. Rocket frogs also eat ants, but in far lower quantities, and rely instead on their astounding leaps to escape predation. They also lack the dazzling warning colors of their toxic cousins, but it's safer (and kinder to the frog) to observe, rather than handle, any species you might encounter.

primate species. Spider monkey, mantled howler and white-faced capuchin can be encountered anywhere, while Sirena trail is best for the fourth and most endangered species, the Central American squirrel monkey. Sirena also has fair chances for the extremely hard-to-find silky anteater, a nocturnal animal that frequents the beachside forests between the Río Claro and the station.

The Río Sirena is a popular spot for all kinds of heron, as well as waders like ruddy turnstone and western sandpiper. You may be more excited to spot the other riverside regulars, which include the American crocodile, three-toed sloth and bull shark.

Here's a good tip: the abundant banana trees along the coastal trails are not indigenous to Costa Rica (bananas are Asian in origin), but they serve as huge magnets for wildlife. In addition to the more obvious visitors, namely monkeys, there are a few other interesting species to be on the lookout for. For instance, hermit crab dine on the fallen fruit, while rufous-tailed hummingbird build their nest under banana leaves. Thomas' fruit-eating bat also snip the supporting veins of the leaves to create their awning-like tents.

Hiking
Paths are primitive and the hiking is hot, humid and insect-ridden; but the challenge of the trek and the interaction with wildlife at Corcovado are thrilling. Hiring a local guide is highly recommended. Obviously, your guide will know the trails well, thus avoiding the unmitigated disaster of getting lost; furthermore, he or she will have a keen eye for spotting and identifying wildlife.

Otherwise, travel in a small group. Bring a compass, as it is impossible to navigate using the sun or stars underneath the rain forest canopy. Carry plenty of food, water and insect repellent. And always verify your route with the rangers before you depart.

The most popular route traverses the park from Los Patos to Sirena, then exits the park at La Leona (or vice versa). This allows hikers to begin and end their journey in or near Puerto Jiménez, offering easy access to La Leona and Los Patos. The trek between Sirena and San Pedrillo is more difficult, both physically and logistically. The travel times listed are conservative: fit hikers with light packs can move faster, unless you spend a lot of time birding or taking photos.

Hiking is best in the dry season (from December to April), when there is still regular rain but all of the trails are open. It's still muddy, but you won't sink quite as deep.

SIRENA TO SAN PEDRILLO
The route between Sirena and San Pedrillo is the longest trail in Corcovado, covering 23km in 10 to 15 hours. The first 18km of this hike are along the beach, which means loose sand and little shade – grueling, especially with a heavy pack. One local guide recommends doing this portion of the hike at night to avoid the hot sun.

Another tricky factor is the three river crossings, which become very difficult or impossible at high tide. As a result, the time of departure from Sirena station depends on the tides; the recommended departure time is about two hours before low tide.

The first river crossing – Río Sirena – is about 1km north of Sirena. The largest river on the hike, it is the neighborhood hangout for sharks and crocodiles, so cross with caution. The final river, the cascading Río Llorona, also marks the end of the beach trail.

This trail is only open from December through April, since heavy rains can make the Río Sirena impassable. Due to the complexity of this route, taking a guide is strongly recommended.

SIRENA TO LA LEONA

The 16km hike from Sirena to La Leona is another sizzler, following the shoreline through coastal forest and along deserted beaches. It involves one major river crossing at Río Claro, just south of Sirena station.

The journey between Sirena and La Leona takes six or seven hours. You can camp at La Leona; otherwise, it takes another hour to hike the additional 3.5km to Carate, where you can stay in a local lodge or catch the collective taxi to Puerto Jiménez.

SIRENA TO LOS PATOS

The route to Los Patos goes 18km through the heart of Corcovado, affording the hiker an opportunity to pass through plenty of primary and secondary forest. The trail is relatively flat for the first 12km. You will hike through secondary forest and wade through two river tributaries before reaching the Laguna

PENINSULA DE OSA & GOLFO DULCE

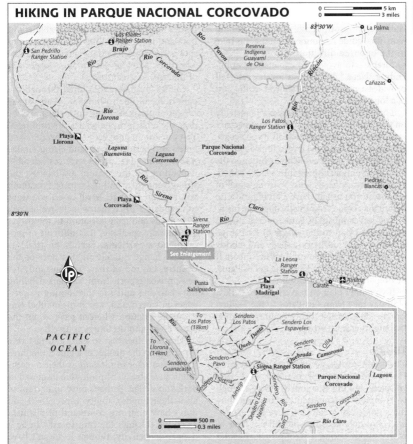

HIKING IN PARQUE NACIONAL CORCOVADO

BAIRD'S TAPIR PROJECT

The Baird's Tapir Project has been studying the populations of Baird's tapir around Sirena station since 1994 in the hope of enhancing conservation efforts. Scientists use radio telemetry (that's radio collars to us) to collect data about where the tapirs live, how far they wander, whom they associate with and how often they reproduce. So far, 28 tapirs around Sirena are wearing collars, which allows scientists to collect the data without disrupting the animals.

Sirena station is an ideal place to do such research, because there is no pressure from deforestation or hunting, which gives researchers the chance to observe a healthy, thriving population. The animals' longevity and slow rate of reproduction mean that many years of observation are required before drawing conclusions.

So, what have we learned about these river rhinos so far? The nocturnal animals spend their nights foraging – oddly, they prefer to forage in 'disturbed habitats' (like along the airstrip), not in the dense rain forest. They spend their days in the cool waters of the swamp, out of the hot sun. Tapirs are not very social, but a male-female pair often shares the same 'home range,' living together for years at a time. Scientists speculate that tapirs may in fact be monogamous – who knew these ungainly creatures would be so romantic!

Corcovado. From this point, the route undulates steeply (mostly uphill!) for the remaining 6km. One guide recommends doing this hike in the opposite direction – from Los Patos to Sirena – to avoid this exhausting, uphill ending. Near Los Patos, a lovely waterfall provides a much-needed shower at the end of a long trek.

The largest herds of peccary are reportedly on this trail. Local guides advise that peccary sense fear, but they will back off if you act aggressively. Alternatively, if you climb about 2m off the ground you'll avoid being bitten in the unlikely event of running into a surly bunch. Hint – peccary herds emit a strong smell of onions, so you usually have a bit of head's up before they come crashing through the bush.

You can camp at Los Patos, or continue an additional 14km to the village of La Palma. This four-hour journey is a shady and muddy descent down the valley of the Río Rincón. If you are traveling from La Palma to Los Patos, be prepared for a steep climb.

If you don't plan on traversing the park, a 6km day hike from Los Patos to the Laguna Corcovado is feasible. (This requires spending two nights at Los Patos.)

TOURS

The main routes across Parque Nacional Corcovado are well marked and well traveled, making this journey easy enough to complete independently. However, hiring a guide can greatly enhance this experience, not only because you will not have to worry about taking a wrong turn. Besides

their intimate knowledge of the trail, local guides are amazingly knowledgeable about flora and fauna, including the best places to spot various species. Many guides also carry telescopes, allowing for up-close inspection of the various creatures.

Guides are most often hired through the park office in Puerto Jiménez, at any of the ranger stations heading into the park, or near the airstrip in either Carate or Sirena. You can also inquire with tour operators and hotels in Puerto Jiménez and Bahía Drake. As you'd imagine, prices vary considerably depending on the season, availability, the size of your party and the type of expedition you want to arrange. In all cases, you want to negotiate a price that is inclusive of park fees, meals and transportation to the park.

Generally speaking, it is difficult to recommend a particular agency or guide as things change quickly in this part of the country. On top of that, we constantly receive mixed reports from travelers detailing life-changing and life-threatening experiences in Corcovado, which means that this is one destination where it pays to put the book down and do things yourself.

Although there is no hard and fast rule for sizing up the quality of a guide, the three things you want to measure is their a) communicative ability, b) professionalism and c) park knowledge. Perhaps most important of all is their English ability, especially if you don't have a strong command of Spanish. Trekking through the rain forest can be a dangerous activity, though it doesn't have to be if both you and your guide stay in constant communication.

Professionalism is best assessed by using your common sense – simply put, ask yourself whether or not this is the kind of person you would trust your life with. Professional guides are also usually outfitted with modern and well-maintained gear, and are quick to reassure travelers of the length and breadth of their experience.

On that note, the final factor in choosing a guide is park knowledge. No matter how many guidebooks you've read or maps you've studied, Corcovado can be a tricky place to access. Before choosing your guide, talk to them about your intended route, and be sure that they are knowledgeable about the trek ahead.

Finally, don't stress – Corcovado is truly a world-class trekking destination, and so long as you're comfortable with your guide, you're guaranteed to have an amazing experience here.

SLEEPING & EATING

Camping costs US$5 per person per day at any station; facilities include potable water and latrines. Sirena station has a covered platform, but other stations have no such luxuries. Remember to bring a flashlight or a kerosene lamp, as the campsites are pitch black at night. Camping is not permitted in areas other than the ranger stations.

Simple dormitory lodging (US$10) and meals (breakfast US$8, lunch or dinner US$11) are available at Sirena station only. Food and cooking fuel have to be packed in, so reserve at least 15 to 30 days in advance through the **Oficina de Área de Conservación Osa** (☎ 2735 5036) in Puerto Jiménez. Scientists and researchers working at the Sirena biological station get preference over travelers for

---

CORCOVADO WILDLIFE

As one of the most biologically intense places on Earth, Parque Nacional Corcovado is absolutely teeming with wildlife. Just to get you excited for the trek ahead, we've prepared a few top picks for the best (and worst) of Corcovado wildlife.

Wish List

- **Jaguar** These elusive felines sit at the top of nearly everybody's rain forest wish list, though you're going to need an incredible amount of luck to spot one in the wild.
- **Ocelot** Of Corcovado's feline predators, these medium-sized cats are the most spotted – they're largely ground-lovers, and tend to stick to the trails.
- **Tapir** You don't have to wish very hard to spot these lumbering giants at Sirena station, though their commonness in Corcovado isn't a true reflection general population figure.

No-Wish List

- **Fer-de-Lance** Known as a *terciopelo* in Costa Rica, the true bushmaster of Corcovado is not to be toyed with.
- **Bullet ant** Sitting alongside the tarantula hawk wasp as one of most pain-inducing biting insects, these enormous ants are best given a wide berth and a lot of respect.
- **Ticks** Approaching megalithic sizes in Corcovado, it's inevitable that you're going to pick up a few dozen, but hopefully they'll stick to where the sun does shine.

Maybe-Yes, Maybe-No Wish List

- **Crocodile** One of nature's oldest and most efficient predators, the crocodile is an amazing sight to behold, given that you're on the land and they're in the water.
- **Peccary** Something akin to a tropical boar, these surly swine are best observed from the lofty heights of a tree, allowing you to view their antics from a safe distance.
- **Army ant** The infamous insect army can be heard crunching its way through the forest, so you'd be wise to give them the right of way.

accommodations and meals, but if you secure a reservation you will be taken care of.

Otherwise, campers must bring all of their own food. Note that ranger stations face a challenge with trash disposal, so all visitors are required to pack out all of their trash.

GETTING THERE & AWAY
From Bahía Drake
From Bahía Drake, you can walk the coastal trail that leads to San Pedrillo station (about four hours from Agujitas), or any lodge can drop you here as a part of their regular tours to Corcovado. Alternatively, you can charter a boat to San Pedrillo (US$80) or Sirena (US$120). If you have a car, most hotels and lodges along Bahía Drake can watch over it for you for a few dollars a day.

From La Palma
From the north, the closest point of access is the town of La Palma, from where you can catch a bus or taxi south to Puerto Jiménez or north to San José.

Heading to Los Patos, you might be able to find a taxi to take you partway; however, the road is only passable to 4WD vehicles (and not always), so be prepared to hike the 14km to the ranger station. The road crosses the river about 20 times in the last 6km. It's easy to miss the right turn shortly before the ranger station, so keep your eyes peeled.

If you have a car, it's best to leave it with a hotel or lodge in La Palma instead of traversing the route to Los Patos, though it certainly is an adventure. Furthermore, once in Los Patos, there is no reliable place to park your car while trekking in the park.

From Carate
In the southeast, the closest point of access is Carate, from where La Leona station is a one-hour, 3.5km hike west along the beach.

IT'S A JUNGLE OUT THERE

The birds are brilliant, the animals are enchanting and the forest is fantastic. But Parque Nacional Corcovado is the real deal, 100% wilderness, and the dangers should not be underestimated. Every season, travelers to Corcovado become injured, sick or even dead; take some precautions to make sure this is not you:

- The number one danger for hikers is heat exhaustion and dehydration. This is the rain forest: it is hot and humid and you are going to sweat more than you realize. Make sure you carry enough water: a 1L or 1.5L bottle (which you can refill at each ranger station) is the bare minimum per person.

- Do not drink untreated water from any stream – this is a surefire way to get a nasty case of giardia. However, prior to setting out for Costa Rica, you should consider investing in a water treatment device, such as a filter and pump system, a UV wand or even a bottle of old-fashioned iodine tablets.

- Wear sunblock and insect repellent. The number two danger for hikers is sunburn and subsequently sunstroke, especially while traveling on the exposed coastal trails. Although malaria and dengue are relatively minor risks in Costa Rica, mosquitoes are a huge nuisance in Corcovado so take precautions and cover up.

- Travel light, as the pleasure of the hike is inversely proportionate to the weight of your pack. Although it's tempting to carry gear for every conceivable type of situation, overloading your pack is a surefire way to succumb to all of the risks we've previously mentioned.

- Always check with the rangers about trail conditions and tide charts before setting out. This is extremely valuable, so that not only are you up-to-date on this information, but also the rangers know the route you are planning to follow and your time of departure. Pay attention to their recommendations as river crossings can be very dangerous.

- If you're hiking without a guide, bring a compass and know how to use it! Also recommended is a topography map or a modern GPS navigation system. If you have limited wilderness experience, hire a guide – you will get your money back many times over in peace of mind.

Carate is accessible from Puerto Jiménez via a poorly maintained, 45km dirt road. This journey is an adventure in itself, and often allows for some good wildlife-spotting along the way. A collective 4WD jeep taxi travels this route twice daily, prices depend on the size of your party, the season (prices increase in the rainy months) and your bargaining skills.

If you have your own car, the *pulpería* in Carate is a safe place to park for a few days, though you'll have some extra piece of mind if you tip the manager before setting out.

By Air

Alfa Romeo Aero Taxi (☎ 2735 5353) offers charter flights connecting Puerto Jiménez, Drake and Golfito to Carate and Sirena. Flights are best booked at the airport in person, and one-way fares are typically less than US$100. Note that long-term parking is not available, so it's best to make prior arrangements if you need to leave your car somewhere.

GOLFO DULCE

While Golfo Dulce is certainly less celebrated than the Península de Osa, an increasing number of travelers are making this arduous journey in search of the world's longest left-hand break at Pavones. The region is also home to Parque Nacional Piedras Blancas, a stunning tract of rain forest that used to be part of Corcovado and still protects the same amazing biodiversity. This far corner of Costa Rica is also home to a significant indigenous population, who live in the Reserva Indígena Guaymí de Conte Burica near Pavones.

GOLFITO

A historic banana port that is slowly fading into obscurity, Golfito is a rough-and-ready town that is struggling to find a purpose beyond yellow gold. Although Golfito has temporarily postponed its demise by implementing duty-free shopping for domestic tourists, the town is slowly being reclaimed by the jungle behind it, and local residents hardly seem concerned. Tellingly, this surreal atmosphere was enough to convince Warner Brothers to choose Golfito as the site to film *Chico Mendes,* the true story of a Brazilian rubber-tapper's efforts to preserve the rain forest.

As the largest town in Golfo Dulce, Golfito is a major transportation hub for hikers heading to Corcovado, surfers heading to Pavones and sportfishers docking for the night. Although it's unlikely that you'll want to stick around for any longer than you have to, there is a certain charm to Golfito that isn't lost on everyone. Indeed, the town is surrounded by the verdant slopes of the Refugio Nacional de Fauna Silvestre Golfito, which provides a picturesque backdrop to the crumbling buildings.

History

From 1938 to 1985, bustling Golfito was the headquarters of United Fruit's operations in the southern part of Costa Rica. In the 1980s, however, declining markets, rising taxes, worker unrest and banana diseases forced its departure. Although some of the plantations now produce oil from the African Oil Palm, the collapse of the banana industry has not alleviated the economic hardship caused by United Fruit's departure.

In an attempt to boost the region's economy, the federal government built a duty-free facility *(depósito libre)* in the northern part of Golfito. This surreal shopping center attracts Ticos from around the country, who descend on the otherwise dying town for 24-hour shopping sprees. The duty-free shopping is for Costa Rica residents only, so you can put away your credit card. Indeed, the primary impact on foreign tourists is that tax-free shoppers are required to spend the night in Golfito, so hotel rooms can be in short supply on weekends and during holiday periods.

Orientation

Golfito is named after a tiny gulf that forms an inlet into the eastern shore of the much larger Golfo Dulce. The town is strung out along a dusty coastal road with a backdrop of steep, thickly forested hills. The southern part of town is where you find most of the bars and businesses, including a seedy red-light district. Nearby is the so-called Muellecito (Small Dock), from where the daily ferry to Puerto Jiménez departs.

The northern part of town was the old United Fruit Company headquarters, and it retains a languid, tropical air, with its large, veranda-decked homes. Now, the so-called *Zona Americana* is home to the airport and the duty-free zone.

Information

Banco Coopealianza (🕑 8am-5pm Mon-Fri, 8am-noon Sat) Has a 24-hour ATM on the Cirrus network and a Western Union office.

Golfito On-line (☎ 2775 2424; Hotel Golfito; per hr US$1.20; 🕑 8am-9pm Mon-Sat, noon-6pm Sun) Speedy Internet connections and delicious air-con.

Hospital de Golfito (☎ 2775 0011) Emergency medical attention.

Land Sea Tours (☎ 2775 1614; www.realestate-costarica.info; Km 2) Books airline tickets, makes hotel reservations and organizes tours.

Migración (☎ 2775 0423; 🕑 8am-4pm) Situated away from the dock, in a 2nd-floor office above the Soda Pavas.

Port captain (☎ 2775 0487; opposite the large Muelle de Golfito; 🕑 7:30-11am & 12:30-4pm Mon-Fri)

Sights

REFUGIO NACIONAL DE FAUNA SILVESTRE GOLFITO

The small, 2810-hectare reserve encompasses most of the steep hills surrounding the Golfito. It was originally created to protect the town's watershed, though it has also had the wonderful side effect of conserving a number of rare and interesting plant species. For example, the reserve is home to several cycads, which are 'living fossils,' and are regarded as the most primitive of plants. The reserve also attracts a

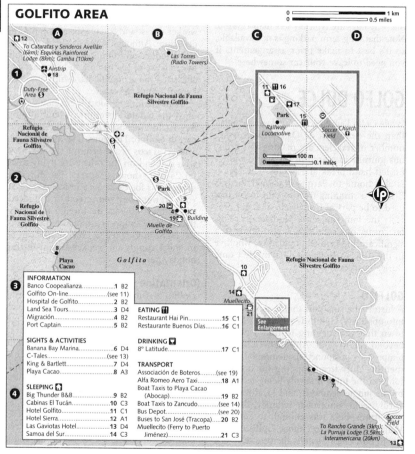

GOLFITO AREA

INFORMATION
Banco Coopealianza..............1 B2
Golfito On-line................(see 11)
Hospital de Golfito..............2 C1
Land Sea Tours..................3 D4
Migración......................4 B2
Port Captain....................5 B2

SIGHTS & ACTIVITIES
Banana Bay Marina..............6 D4
C-Tales......................(see 13)
King & Bartlett.................7 D4
Playa Cacao....................8 A3

SLEEPING
Big Thunder B&B................9 B2
Cabinas El Tucán...............10 C3
Hotel Golfito..................11 C1
Hotel Sierra..................12 A1
Las Gaviotas Hotel.............13 D4
Samoa del Sur.................14 C3

EATING
Restaurant Hai Pin.............15 C1
Restaurante Buenos Días........16 C1

DRINKING
8° Latitude...................17 C1

TRANSPORT
Associación de Boteros........(see 19)
Alfa Romeo Aero Taxi..........18 A1
Boat Taxis to Playa Cacao
  (Abocap)...................19 B2
Boat Taxis to Zancudo.........(see 14)
Bus Depot....................(see 20)
Buses to San José (Tracopa)...20 B2
Muellecito (Ferry to Puerto
  Jiménez)...................21 C3

variety of tropical birds, four species of monkey and several small mammals.

There are no facilities for visitors, save a gravel access road and a few poorly maintained trails. About 2km south of the center of Golfito, a gravel road heads inland, past a soccer field, and winds 7km up to some radio towers (Las Torres) 486m above sea level. This access road is an excellent option for hiking, as it has very little traffic. In any case, you'll probably see more from the cleared road than from the overgrown trails.

A very steep hiking trail leaves from Golfito, almost opposite the Samoa del Sur hotel. A somewhat strenuous hike (allow about two hours) will bring you out on the road to the radio towers. The trail is easier to find in Golfito than at the top.

Another option is to walk along the poor dirt road heading toward Gamba. This road begins a couple of kilometers northwest of the duty-free area and crosses through part of the refuge. The local bus stops at the beginning of this dirt road, from where it is about 10km to Gamba.

Finally, there are several trails off the road to Playa Cacao. Hikers on these routes will be rewarded by waterfalls and views of the gulf. However, the trails are often obscured, so it's worth asking locally about maps and trail conditions before setting off.

As always, be sure that somebody knows when and where you are going before you set off on an independent hike.

PLAYA CACAO
Just a hop, skip and a jump across the bay, this small beach offers a prime view of Golfito stretched out along the coast, with the rain forest as a backdrop. If you're stuck in Golfito for the day, Playa Cacao is perhaps the most appealing spot from which to enjoy the old port. To reach the beach, catch a water taxi from Golfito for about US$2 per person. You can also get to Playa Cacao by walking or driving about 6km along a dirt road west and then south from the airport – a 4WD is recommended.

Activities
CATARATAS Y SENDEROS AVELLÁN
This Tico family-run **reserve and adventure camp** (☎ 8378 7895; admission US$2.50; ☽ 10am-4pm) is an excellent option for adventurers who like a little guidance. Guided hikes (US$18)

and horseback riding tours (US$8 per hour) explore the extensive, rain forest–covered grounds, including three impressive waterfalls. Camping (US$5) and meals (US$2 to US$4) are also available.

SPORTFISHING & BOATING
Golfito is home to several full-service marinas that attract coastal-cruising yachters. If you didn't bring your own boat, you can hire local sailors for tours of the gulf at any of the docks. You can fish year-round, but the best season for the sought-after Pacific sailfish is from November to May.

Banana Bay Marina (☎ 2775 0838; www.bananabaymarina.com) Charters can be arranged, and a full day of all-inclusive fishing on a 6m or 17m boat starts at US$750.
C-Tales (☎ in the USA 772-335 9425; www.c-tales.com) Operating out of Las Gaviotas Hotel, this company offers a three-day package per person from US$1200.
King & Bartlett (☎ 2775 1624; www.kingandbartlettsportfishing.com) This slick new operation offers all-inclusive three-day fishing packages starting at US$1800.

Sleeping
Note that the area around the soccer field in town is Golfito's red-light district, so you'd be best to spend a few more dollars and stay elsewhere.

Cabinas El Tucán (☎ 2775 0553; r per person with/without air-con US$15/10; P ☸) This friendly, family-run hotel is a wonderfully welcoming place to stay, with kids playing in the courtyard and mothers cooking in the kitchen nearby. Clean spacious rooms of varying sizes and shapes are clustered around the shady, tiled courtyard.

Hotel Golfito (☎ 2775 0047; r per person from US$15; P ☸ ▯) This bright yellow building overlooking the gulf is convenient to the Muellecito, and provides one of the best deals in town. Despite the waterside location, the modern rooms do not enjoy water views, though you can sit out back on the shared balcony and watch the sunset.

La Purruja Lodge (☎ 2775 1054; www.purruja.com; 4.5km south of Golfito; s/d/tr incl breakfast US$30/40/50; P ▯ ☖) A delightful Swiss-Tica couple run this secluded lodge, which is home to five simple but sparkling cabins that have all of the necessary comforts. The tranquil and tree-filled grounds are renowned for bird sightings, and the personable owners can organize several unique tours throughout the area.

Las Gaviotas Hotel (☎ 2775 0062; www.resortlas gaviotas.com; s/d/tr/q US$50/60/70/80; P ✷ ☐ ☎) The classiest place to stay in Golfito proper is this mini-resort, complete with stucco cabins set amid a lovely tropical garden. Here, you can pass the time in Golfito by sipping rum on your private porch or doing a few laps in the inviting pool.

Samoa del Sur (☎ 2775 0233, 2775 0264; www.samoa delsur.com; r from US$60, RV US$10; P ✷ ☐ ☎) This French-run facility offers handsome lodgings in 14 spacious rooms that are outfitted with tiled floors and stylish wood furniture. The bar is a popular spot in the evenings, when guests congregate to play pool or darts. The kiddies, meanwhile, seem content to pass the time in the swimming pool, play area and (on rainy days) the onsite shell museum.

Hotel Sierra (☎ 2775 0666, 2775 0336; www.hotel sierra.com; s/d US$60/70; P ✷ ☐ ☎) Appropriate to its location in the *Zona Americana*, this place feels like an American-style motor lodge, though its efficiency and sterility shouldn't deter you from staying here. Far removed from the grit and grime of Golfito, the Hotel Sierra is a mini-island where you can pass the night in relative ease, especially since there is a good restaurant and a small casino on site.

Big Thunder B&B (☎ 2775 9191; www.bigthunder bedandbreakfast.com; opposite Muelle de Golfito; d from US$75; P ✷ ☐ ☎) Colorful depictions of marlin and sailfish adorn the walls of this upscale B&B, which is a pleasant alternative to the more anonymous resorts in town. Backed by the forested hills of the reserve, the property was formerly the home of a banana manager. Six very spacious rooms are equipped with two double beds, a fridge and coffeemaker, and a huge hot-water bathroom.

Eating & Drinking

Most of the midrange hotels have restaurants and bars onsite.

Restaurant Hai Pin (dishes US$3-7) When you tire of *gallo pinto*, you can change it up with some Chinese food. This popular open-air restaurant enjoys views of the main drag, which certainly offers up some interesting people-watching given the nature of the town.

Restaurante Buenos Días (opposite the Muellecito; meals US$5-7; ☽ 6am-10pm) Rare is the visitor who passes through Golfito without stopping at this cheerful spot opposite the Muellecito. Brightly colored booths, bilingual menus and super convenient location ensure a con-stant stream of guests – whether for an early breakfast, a typical Tico casado or a good old-fashioned burger.

Rancho Grande (dishes US$5-12) About 3km south of Golfito, this rustic, thatch-roof place serves country-style Tico food cooked over a wood stove. Margarita, the Tica owner, is famous for her *patacones* (fried plantain chips). Her hours are erratic, so stop in dur-ing the day to let her know you're coming for dinner.

8° Latitude (dishes US$9-15) Northwest of the soccer field, this popular expat bar is fre-quented by Americans seriously into their sportfishing. Its laidback and friendly atmos-phere makes it the perfect place to tipple a few and listen to fish tales.

Getting There & Away

AIR

The airport is 4km north of the town center near the duty-free zone. **NatureAir** (www.natur eair.com) and **Sansa** (www.sansa.com) have daily flights to/from San José (one-way tickets are approximately US$100).

Alfa Romeo Aero Taxi (☎ 2775 1515) has light aircraft (three and five passengers) for char-ter flights to Puerto Jiménez, Carate, Drake, Sirena, Palmar Sur, Quepos and Limón. Prices are dependant on the number of pas-sengers, so it's best to try to organize a larger group if you're considering this option.

BOAT

There are two main boat docks for passenger service: the Muellecito is the main dock in the southern part of town. There is a smaller dock north of the Muelle Bananero (oppo-site the ICE building) where you'll find the **Asociación de Boteros** (Abocap; ☎ 2775 0357), an association of water taxis that can provide service anywhere in the Golfo Dulce area.

Two passenger ferries travel to Puerto Jiménez from the Muellecito (US$2, 1½ hours), departing at 11:30am and 1:30pm daily. The boat taxi for Zancudo (US$4, 45 minutes) departs from the dock at Samoa del Sur at noon, Monday through Saturday. The return trip is at 7:30am the next day (except Sunday). Water taxis to Playa Cacao depart from the Abocap dock (though you can get boatmen to take you from the Muellecito as well) for US$2 per person.

Note that the times listed above may change.

A better option than chugging away on the ferries to Puerto Jiménez is to hire a private water taxi to shuttle you across the bay. You'll have to negotiate, but prices are generally reasonable given that you won't have to rely on the ferry. Waters in the Golfo Dulce are sheltered and generally calm, but it's still best if you feel comfortable with both your captain and ship.

If you're staying at any of the coastal lodges north of Golfito and you've made prior arrangements for transportation, the lodge will send a boat to pick you up at the docks. In the event that your boat doesn't arrive, simply give the name of the lodge to any of the boat captains, and they should be able to get you where you're going.

BUS
Most buses stop at the depot in front of the Muellecito.

Paso Canoas, Panamanian border US$1.50, 2½ hours, departs hourly.

Neily US$1.25, 1½ hours, departs hourly from 6am to 7pm.

Pavones US$2, three hours, 10am and 3pm. This service may be affected by road and weather conditions, especially in the rainy season.

San José, via San Isidro (Tracopa) US$8.50, seven hours, departs from the terminal near Muelle Bananero at 5am and 1:30pm.

Zancudo US$2, three hours, departs 1:30pm.

Getting Around
City buses and collective taxis travel up and down the main road of Golfito. Although the payment system seems incomprehensible to anyone else but the locals, it shouldn't cost you more than a few coins.

PARQUE NACIONAL PIEDRAS BLANCAS
Formerly known as Parque Nacional Esquinas, this national park was established in 1992 as an extension of Corcovado. Currently, Piedras Blancas or 'White Rocks' covers an area of 12,000 hectares of undisturbed tropical primary rain forest, as well as 2000 hectares of secondary forests, pasture land and coastal cliffs and beaches.

As one of the last remaining stretches of lowland rain forest on the Pacific, Piedras Blancas is also home to a vast array of flora and fauna. According to a study conducted at the biological station at Gamba, the biodiversity of trees in Piedras Blancas is the densest in all of Costa Rica, even surpassing Corcovado.

Orientation & Information
Parque Nacional Piedras Blancas borders the Refugio Nacional Fauna Silvestre Golfito in the east. In the west, the Reserva Forestal de Golfo Dulce connects Piedras Blancas with Corcovado, forming an important biological corridor for resident wildlife, especially large mammals and predators that cover vast areas. Unfortunately, the forests around Rincón are threatened by illegal logging, jeopardizing this route.

Parque Nacional Piedras Blancas does not yet have facilities for visitors. However, it is possible to access the park from the Esquinas Rainforest Lodge in Gamba, as well as any of the coastal lodges north of Golfito (see p436).

Wildlife-Watching
Because Piedras Blancas is so remote and so little visited, it is the site for several ongoing animal projects, including the re-introduction of scarlet macaws with the hopes of establishing a self-sustaining population, as well as the re-integration of wild cats like ocelot and margay, which were confiscated from private homes. Look for all of the wildlife that you might see in Corcovado: all five big cats and all four species of monkeys, herds of collared and white-lipped peccary, crocodiles, various species of poison-dart frogs (including the endemic Golfo Dulce dart frog) and more than 330 species of bird.

Sleeping
The **Esquinas Rainforest Lodge** (☎ 2775 0140, 2775 0901; www.esquinaslodge.com; Gamba; s/d/tr incl meals US$135/210/255; P 🏊) was founded by the nonprofit Rainforest for the Austrians, which was also vital in the establishment of Piedras Blancas as a national park. Now, surrounded by the primary and secondary rain forest of the park, Esquinas is integrally connected with the community of Gamba, employing local workers and reinvesting profits in community projects. Accommodations at Esquinas Lodge are in spacious, high-ceilinged cabins with ceiling fans and private porches. The lodge's extensive grounds comprise a network of well-marked trails and a welcoming stream-fed pool. Gamba is 8km north of Golfito and 6km south of the Interamericana.

Getting There & Away

Piedras Blancas is best accessed from the Equinas Rainforest Lodge, which has an extensive trail network onsite and can easily arrange guided hikes deeper into the park. If you don't have your own transportation, any bus heading north from Golfito can drop you off at the lodge.

If you're staying at any of the coastal lodges north of Golfito (see right), you can inquire about transportation to/from the park as well as guided hikes into the interior.

PLAYAS SAN JOSECITO, NICUESA & CATIVO

The northeastern shore of the Golfo Dulce is defined by idyllic deserted beaches, backed by the pristine rain forest of Parque Nacional Piedras Blancas. The appeal of this area is only enhanced by its inaccessibility: part of the charm is that very few people make it to this untouched corner of Costa Rica. If you're looking for a romantic retreat or a secluded getaway, all of the lodges along this stretch of coastline are completely isolated and serve as perfect spots for quiet reflection.

Sights

CASA DE ORQUÍDEAS

This private **botanical garden** (Playa San Josecito; admission & tour US$5; ☻ tours 8:30am Sat-Thu), surrounded on three sides by primary rain forest, is a veritable Eden. The garden's plants have been lovingly collected and tended by Ron and Trudy MacAllister, who have lived in this remote region since the 1970s. Self-taught botanists, they've amassed a wonderful collection of tropical fruit trees, bromeliads, cycads, palms, heliconias, ornamental plants and more than 100 varieties of orchid, after which their garden is named.

The two-hour guided tours stimulate all of the senses: chew on a 'magic' seed that makes lemons taste sweet; smell vanilla beans; see insects trapped in bromeliad pools; or touch ginger in its flower. Casa de Orquídeas is at the west end of Playa San Josecito and can be reached from the lodges on that beach by foot. Otherwise, it's accessible only by boat; **Land Sea Tours** (☎ 2775 1614; www.realestate-costarica.info) in Golfito can make these arrangements.

Activities

The beaches along this stretch are excellent for swimming, snorkeling and sunning.

Lodges also provide kayaks for maritime exploration. Hiking and wildlife-watching opportunities are virtually unlimited, as the lodges provide direct access to the wilds of Piedras Blancas. Miles of trails lead to secluded beaches, cascading waterfalls and other undiscovered attractions.

Sleeping

If you're planning on staying at any of the lodges listed here, advanced reservations via the internet are strongly recommended, especially since it can be difficult to contact them by phone.

All of these lodges are extremely isolated and are all accessible only by boat – you can expect a beach landing, so make sure you're wearing the right kind of shoes! Prices include three meals per day and transportation to/from either Golfito or Puerto Jiménez.

All of the lodges here are also self-sufficient and environmentally sustainable, so you can get a good night's rest while feeling good about the planet.

Dolphin Quest (☎ 2775 8630, 2775 0373; www.dolphinquestcostarica.com; Playa San Josecito; s/d camping US$30/55, cabins US$60/100, houses US$70/120) This jungle lodge offers as much privacy as a mile of beach and 280 hectares of mountainous rain forest can offer. Three round, thatch-roof cabins and one large house are spread out around two hectares of landscaped grounds. Meals – featuring many organic ingredients from the garden – are served communally in an open-air pavilion near the shore. Access to many miles of trails is free after an introductory tour outlining the beauties (and dangers) of the forest.

Golfo Dulce Lodge (☎ 8821 5398; www.golfodulce lodge.com; Playa San Josecito; standard/deluxe 4-day package per person from US$285/315; ☒) Set back from the rocky beach, this Swiss-owned place is on the edge of a 275-hectare property, much of which is primary rain forest. The owners are clued in about local flora and fauna, dedicating their efforts to a nearby wildcat rehabilitation project. The five deluxe units are individual wooden cabins, each with a large veranda containing a rocking chair and hammock; three standard adjoining rooms with smaller verandas surround the spring-fed pool.

Playa Nicuesa Rain Forest Lodge (☎ 2735 5237, in the USA 866-348 7610; www.nicuesalodge.com; Playa Nicuesa; guesthouses/cabins per person US$170/190) Nestled into a 65-hectare private rain forest reserve north of Casa de Orquídeas, this lodge is barely visible from the water (though its dock gives it away). The rustic, natural accommodations are beautifully decorated with canopied beds and indigenous textile spreads; private hot-water bathrooms have garden showers. Meals are served in a thatched rancho, featuring a sparkling, polished wood bar. Electricity is provided by solar power, but the lodge usually uses candlelight to conserve energy and enhance the romantic atmosphere.

Rainbow Adventures Lodge (☎ in the US 503-297 2682; www.rainbowcostarica.com; Playa Cativo; s/d from US$235/355; 🏊) The rustic appearance of the wide wood balconies adorning this lodge belies the elegance within: handmade furniture, silk rugs, early-20th-century antiques and fresh flowers make this a special place. In the 1st-floor library, guests are welcome to relax and peruse one of thousands of natural history publications. Upstairs, the rooms are partially exposed to the elements (but protected by mosquito nets) to allow unimpeded views of the rain forest, beach and gulf.

Getting There & Away
All of the lodges offer boat transportation from Puerto Jiménez and/or Golfito with prior arrangements, though you can always grab a water taxi if plans go awry.

ZANCUDO
Occupying a slender finger of land that juts into the Golfo Dulce, the tiny village of Zancudo is about as laidback of a beach destination as you'll find in Costa Rica. On the west side of town, gentle, warm Pacific waters lap up onto black sands, and seeing another person on the beach means it's crowded. On the east side, a tangle of mangrove swamps attracts birds, crocodiles and plenty of fish, which in turn attract fishers hoping to reel them in. Unlike nearby Pavones, which is slowly developing as a surfing destination, Zancudo is content to remain a far-flung village in a far-flung corner of Costa Rica.

Orientation & Information
Zancudo consists of one dirt road, which leads from the boat dock in the north, past the lodges that are strung along the shore, and out of town south toward Pavones.

The largest shop in town is the **Super Bellavista** (opposite Cabinas Tío Froylan), where there is also a public phone. **Oceano** (☎ 2776 0921;

www.oceanacabinas.com) offers internet access. There is no bank in town and very few places accept credit cards, so bring your cash from Golfito.

Zancudo is a popular destination for Ticos, especially during the annual **Fishing & Blues Festival** held in early February.

Activities
The main activities at Zancudo are undoubtedly swinging on hammocks, strolling on the **beach** and swimming in the aqua blue waters of the Golfo Dulce. Here, the surf is gentle, and at night the water sometimes sparkles with bioluminescence – tiny phosphorescent marine plants and plankton that light up if you sweep a hand through the water. The effect is like underwater fireflies.

The **mangrove swamps** offer plenty of opportunities for exploration: birdlife is prolific, while other animals such as crocodile, caiman, monkey and sloth are also frequently spotted. The boat ride from Golfito gives a glimpse of these waters, but you also paddle them yourself: rent kayaks from any of the accommodation listings following.

Zancudo is a base for inshore and offshore fishing, river fishing (mangrove snapper, snook and corbina) and fly fishing. The best **sportfishing** is from December to May for sailfish and May to September for snook, though many species bite year-round. Trips are best organized through either outfitters in Golfito (see p433) or Roy's Zancudo Lodge (p438).

Sleeping & Eating
Cabinas Tío Froylan (☎ 2776 0128; r per person from US$9; **P**) Plain and cheap whitewashed rooms with fans and private cold showers attract a loyal Tico following, especially since they're the cheapest accommodation in town. There's a shady patio, beach access and an attached restaurant and disco with a pool table. Don't expect any quiet nights here, especially when the disco is pounding.

Cabinas Sol y Mar (☎ 2776 0014; www.zancudo .com; cabins US$20-50; **P**) This popular place offers lodging options for all budgets: smallish economy dwellings that are further from the water, larger standard units with a shared terrace overlooking the beach, and private, deluxe units with fancy tile showers and unobstructed ocean views. Even if you're not staying here, the open-air restaurant and thatched bar is a Zancudo favorite.

MARSHALL & ANGELA MCCARTHY ON THE FUTURE OF GOLFO DULCE

Marshall and Angela McCarthy, the owners and managers of Cabinas La Ponderosa in Pavones (see p440), have respectively spent 19 and 11 years living in Golfo Dulce. Over a hearty breakfast of eggs and potatoes, Marshall and Angela shared their thoughts on the past, present and future of their adopted home.

What was it about this remote corner of the country that made you both want to settle here?
Marshall: Having grown up in the cities throughout North and South America, I immediately fell in love with the nature here. There is so much open space here, and instead of clutter and congestion, you have empty beaches and thick jungles. When I first arrived, Costa Rica was off the tourist map, and I could have easily chosen any part of the country to settle in. However, I chose Golfo Dulce because it was, and still is, the most virgin corner of the country.
Angela: I've traveled throughout all of Central America, but I chose Costa Rica specifically because everything here is so accessible. Even in a place as remote as Golfo Dulce, you literally have the beach, the mountains and the rain forest on your doorstep. Also, I just love the way this place smells! After the rains have fallen, the air here is heavy with the scent of the jungle. It's difficult to describe, but once you spend time here, it's impossible to forget.

Why do you think it is that Golfo Dulce has been spared from hasty development?
Angela: People have always been attracted to Golfo Dulce because of its nature, and fortunately the local government is well attuned to this reality. In fact, tourism officials are actually marketing the pristine beauty of the region, which is attracting the right types of foreign investment. Here in Golfo Dulce, the product is the environment, so the impetus is for developers is to keep everything green.

Cabinas Los Cocos (☎ 2776 0012; www.loscocos .com; cabins from US$50; ℗) This unique beachfront lodge is home to two historic cabins that used to be banana company homes in Palmar but were transported to Zancudo, reassembled and completely refurbished. The other two more spacious cabins are also charming, with loft sleeping areas under palm frond roofs.

Oceano (☎ 2776 0921; www.oceanocabinas.com; s/d US$60/70; ℗) With its back to the beach, this friendly little Canadian-run inn has just two rooms, both spacious and airy with woodbeamed ceilings, tile bathrooms and quaint details like throw pillows and folk art. The open-air restaurant is also inviting for dinner or drinks, especially if the sea has been kind to the local fishers.

Roy's Zancudo Lodge (☎ 2776 0008; www.roys zancudolodge.com; 4- to 7-day packages per person from US$2395; ℗ ✗ 🖳 ⌨) North of the dock you'll find the most established lodge in Zancudo, which caters to a faithful clientele of anglers. The highlight of staying here is clearly the world-class fishing in Golfo Dulce, though the huge pool overlooking the ocean and the luxurious hot tub nearby certainly add a nice touch to this sophisticated lodge.

Getting There & Away

BOAT
The boat dock is near the north end of the beach on the inland, estuary side. A water taxi to Golfito (US$4) departs from this dock at 7am, returning at noon, Monday through Saturday. Inquire locally, however, as times are subject to change, though you can always find a local boat captain willing to take you for a negotiable price.

BUS
A bus to Neily leaves from the *pulpería* near the dock at 5:30am (US$2, three hours). The bus for Golfito (US$2) leaves at 5am for the three-hour trip, with a ferry transfer at the Río Coto Colorado. Service is erratic in the wet season, so inquire before setting out.

CAR
It's possible to drive to Golfito by taking the road south of Río Claro for about 10km. Turn left at the Rodeo Bar and go another 10km to the Río Coto Colorado ferry, which carries three vehicles (US$1.25 per car) and runs all day except during the lowest tides. From there, 30km of dirt road gets you to Golfito. To get to Pavones, take a right at

Marshall: Because the local government has a strict regulatory and development plan, this municipality is growing a lot slower than others. As a direct result, wealthy foreigners who want to come down here and build an enormous condo project or a sprawling resort hotel face intense scrutiny, and eventually decide to invest elsewhere.

Do you think that Golfo Dulce attracts a certain type of person?
Marshall: Simply put, Golfo Dulce is old Costa Rica. The beauty of this area is that it's overgrown and sparsely populated, which tends to attract more educated people who are aware of the broader environmental picture. For the most part, tourists and concerned locals such as ourselves are extremely conscientious about the saving the forest, and are passionate about preserving the natural beauty of the gulf.
Angela: People are attracted to the region by big wildlife and even bigger trees. Although much of Costa Rica is packaged for tourist consumption, the rain forest in Golfo Dulce is as real as it gets. The kind of people who come down here are the kind of people who want to be in the jungle. Almost everyone down here is extremely sensitive to development, and the last thing we want is for the peninsula to develop along the same lines as Cancún.

Are you optimistic about the future of Golfo Dulce?
Angela: Development may be inevitable, but I am optimistic because the market is demanding sustainability. People are coming to the region because they want to see green, and in the end, I believe that developers must always keep this market force in mind.
Marshall: This region is home to one of the last rain forests on the planet, and it is just something that we need to protect. It is a special place, and its value is too much to destroy, though fortunately people are finally starting to catch on to this fact.

the first major intersection, instead of a left. A 4WD is necessary in the rainy season.

PAVONES
Home to what is reportedly the longest left-hand break on the planet, Pavones is a legendary destination for surfers the world over. Although the village remains relatively off the beaten path, both foreigners and Ticos are transforming Pavones from a relative backwater into a hip and happening hot spot. Fortunately, however, development is progressing slowly and sustainably, which means that the palm-lined streets are still not paved, the pace of life is slow and the overall atmosphere remains tranquil.

As this is Costa Rica's southernmost point, you'll need to work hard to get down here. However, the journey is an adventure in its own right, especially since the best months for surfing coincide with the rainy season (think river crossings!).

Orientation & Information
The name Pavones is used to refer to both Playa Río Claro de Pavones and Punta Banco, which is 6km south.

The road into Pavones comes south and dead-ends at the Río Claro, which is where you'll find a small soccer field. About 200m to the east, a parallel road crosses the Río Claro and continues the 6km to Punta Banco.

Pavones has no bank or gas station, so make sure you have plenty of money and gas.

Sights
Set on a verdant hillside between Pavones and Punta Banco, the **Tiskita Jungle Lodge** (☎ in San José 2296 8125; www.tiskita-lodge.co.cr; guided hike US$15) consists of 100 hectares of virgin forest and a huge orchard, which produces more than 100 varieties of tropical fruit from all over the world. Fourteen trails wind through surrounding rain forest, which contains waterfalls and freshwater pools suitable for swimming.

The combination of rain forest, fruit farm and coastline attracts a long list of birds. About 300 species have been recorded here. The fruit farm is particularly attractive to fruit-eating birds such as parrot and toucan. The forest is home to more reticent species such as yellow-billed cotinga, fiery-billed aracari, green honeycreeper and lattice-tailed trogon. Hikes are usually guided by the owners – personable conservationists and conversationalists

Peter and Elizabeth Aspinall – or their son. Reservations are recommended.

Activities

SURFING

Pavones is one of Costa Rica's most famous **surf** breaks: when the surf's up, this tiny beach town attracts hordes of international wave riders and Tico surfer dudes. Conditions are best with a southern swell, usually between April and October. However, because Pavones is inside Golfo Dulce, it is protected from many swells so surfers can go for weeks without seeing any waves.

Pavones has become legendary among surfers for its wicked long left. Some claim it is among the world's longest, offering a two- or three-minute ride on a good day. Legend has it that the wave passes so close to the Esquina del Mar Cantina that you can toss beers to surfers as they zip by. Be warned: when the wave is big, it can deposit surfers on the sharp rocks at the far end of the bay.

Locals know that when Pavones has nothing (or when it's too crowded), they can head south to **Punta Banco**, a reef break with decent rights and lefts. The best conditions are at mid or high tide, especially with swells from the south or west.

YOGA

Yoga Farm (www.yogafarmcostarica.org; dm per night US$35, per week US$175) This yoga retreat center, conservation project and working farm is a unique and welcome addition to Pavones. The price includes accommodation in simple and clean rooms with wood bunk beds; three vegetarian meals, prepared primarily with ingredients from the organic garden; and daily yoga classes, which take place in a fabulous open-air studio overlooking the ocean. This place is a 15-minute walk from Rancho Burica in Punta Banco: take the road going up the hill to the left, go through the first gate on the left and keep walking up the hill. Inquire about volunteer opportunities.

Sleeping

PLAYA RÍO CLARO DE PAVONES

Cabinas Casa Olas (☎ 8826 3693; r per person from US$10; P 🞩) About 100m east of the soccer field, five cabins of varying sizes have wide-plank wood floors, brightly painted walls and an attractive unfinished feel that is appealing if you're one of the laidback surfer set. All

the rooms share access to outdoor kitchen facilities and a covered hammock lounge – an excellent chill-out zone.

Cabinas Mira Olas (☎ 8393 7742; www.miraolas .com; s/d from US$25/45; P) This 4.5-hectare farm is full of wildlife and fruit trees and cabins to suit all tastes. The 'rustic' cabin, incidentally, boasted the first flush toilet in Pavones, though it's quite different from the 'jungle deluxe', a beautiful, open-air lodging with a huge balcony and elegant cathedral ceiling. To find Mira Olas, turn off at the fishing boats and follow the signs up the steep hill: it's worth the climb!

Casa Siempre Domingo (☎ 8820 4709; d/tr US$80/120; www.casa-domingo.com; P) The most unbelievable views of the gulf are from this luxurious bed and breakfast, high in the hills above Pavones. Lodging at the 'Always Sunday House' is elegant and simple, with cathedral ceilings and a wonderful sense of openness. You'll need a car to get here: take the left fork at the Río Claro crossing.

Riviera (☎ 8823 5874; www.pavonesriviera.com; d US$80, additional person US$15; P 🞩) The slickest option in Pavones proper is this clutch of exclusive villas, which have fully equipped kitchens, cool tile floors and attractive hardwood ceilings. Big shady porches overlook the landscaped gardens, which offer a degree of intimacy and privacy found at few other places in town.

PUNTA BANCO

Rancho Burica (www.ranchoburica.com; r per person US$8-22; P) Backpackers can't stop raving about this friendly and youthful Dutch-run outpost, which is literally the end of the road in Punta Banco. All rooms have bathrooms and fans, while the pricier ones have mosquito-netted beds and attractive wood furniture. Hammocks interspersed around the property offer ample opportunity for chilling out. Reservations are not accepted: 'just show up…like everyone else does.'

Cabinas La Ponderosa (☎ 8824 4145, in the USA 954-771 9166; www.cabinaslaponderosa.com; r per person with/without air-con US$55/50; P 🞩) Set on 6 lovely landscaped hectares, these cozy cabins are tenderly cared for by Marshall and Angela McCarthy, who have spent years living in their adopted home of Pavones (see p438). The common lounge offers all kinds of entertainment, including a ping-pong table and a massive video library, but the real appeal of staying here is the warm hospitality of the McCarthys.

Sotavento (☎ 8391 3468; www.sotaventoplantanal .com; houses US$60-80; (P)) These two tropical hardwood, furnished houses are set on a picturesque pepper and cacao plantation perched above Punta Banco. Casa Poinsetta and the larger Casa Vista Grande both have rustic, open-air architecture that takes advantage of the breeze and the views. The houses sleep six to eight people, so they are a great deal if you can get a pack of friends together to split costs. The place is managed by the personable American surfer Harry, who makes his own boards.

ourpick Tiskita Jungle Lodge (☎ in San José 2296 8125; www.tiskita-lodge.co.cr; 2-/5-/7-night packages per person US$735/1020/1120; (P) (R) (c) (Q)) Set amidst extensive gardens and orchards, this lodge is arguably the most beautiful and intimate in all of Golfo Dulce. Accommodation is in a clutch of stunning wooden cabins accented by stone garden showers that allow you to freshen up while you go birding. Daily rates include fresh home-cooked meals and guided walks. Reservations must be made in advance as the lodge fills up quickly. Even if you're not spending the night here, stop by for a guided tour of the property (see p439).

Eating & Drinking

Esquina del Mar Cantina (dishes US$3-6) A Pavones institution that has great views of the left break, this is where you should grab a drink after your last ride.

Café de la Suerte (dishes US$4-8) Animal lovers and the health-conscious will appreciate this open-air vegetarian joint, which serves tropical-fruit smoothies and heart-healthy fare.

La Manta (dishes US$4-15) The best dining in Pavones is at this airy rancho, which catches the breezes off the bay and offers an impressive variety of Mediterranean food.

Restaurante La Piña (dishes US$5-10) Located in Punta Banco, this authentic Italian-run spot has authentic pastas and pizzas from the peninsula (Italy, not Osa).

Getting There & Away

Two daily buses go to Golfito (US$2, three hours): the first leaves at 5:30am and departs from the end of the road at Rancho Burica (but you can pick it up at the bus stop opposite the Riviera); the second leaves at 12:30pm from the Esquina del Mar Cantina. Buses

from Golfito depart at 10am (to Pavones) and 3pm (to Punta Banco via Pavones) from the stop at the Muellecito.

A 4WD taxi will charge about US$50 from Golfito, though you can also take a water taxi for about the same price. If you're driving, follow the directions to Zancudo and look for the signs to Pavones.

PARQUE NACIONAL ISLA DEL COCOS

In the opening minutes of the film *Jurassic Park,* a small helicopter swoops over and around a lushly forested island with dramatic tropical peaks descending straight into clear blue waters. That island is Isla del Cocos, and that scene turned Costa Rica's most remote national park into more than a figment of our collective imaginations.

Isla del Cocos is more than 500km southwest of the mainland in the eastern Pacific and is often referred to as the 'Costa Rican Galapagos.' Because of its remote nature, a unique ecosystem has evolved, earning the island the protective status of national park. More than 70 animal species (mainly insects) and 70 plant species are endemic, and more remain to be discovered. Birders also come here to see the colonies of seabirds, many of which only nest on Cocos.

The island's marine life is varied, with sea turtles, more than 18 species of coral, 57 types of crustacean, three types of dolphin, and tropical fish in abundance. Needless to say, the diving is excellent and is the main attraction of the island. Isla del Cocos also has more than a dozen dive sites and is famous for its huge schools of hundreds of scalloped hammerhead shark.

As it's the most far-flung corner of Costa Rica, you will certainly have to work to get out here, though few other destinations in the country are as exotic and visually stunning as Isla del Cocos. The island is also arguably the most pristine national park in the country and truly one of Costa Rica's great frontier destinations.

History

In 1526, Isla del Cocos was 'discovered' by Spanish explorer Joan Cabezas, though it wasn't noted on maps until its second 'discovery' by French cartographer Nicolas Desliens in 1541. In the centuries that followed, heavy rainfall attracted the attention of sailors, pirates and whalers, who frequently

NEW NATURAL WONDERS OF THE WORLD CANDIDATE: ISLA DEL COCOS

Although you may or may not have agreed with their choices, the **New 7 Wonders** (www.new 7wonders.com) campaign made international headlines in 2007. From the statue of Christ the Redeemer in Rio de Janeiro to the Taj Mahal in Agra, the New 7 Wonders campaign sought to modernize the list of departed ancient wonders – with the sole exception of the Great Pyramids at Giza of course!

Following the extraordinary success of its campaign, the Swiss foundation recently nominated 300 natural wonders of the world, which will be honed down to seven by popular vote in 2009. As this book went to press, Costa Rica's very own Isla del Cocos was proud to stand at number seven in the provisional ranking, just two behind Mount Everest!

Tourism officials in Costa Rica are ecstatic that this little known ecological wonder was given international recognition. Despite the fact that the island has been a Unesco World Heritage Site since 1967, few people know anything about Isla del Cocos – except for the fact that it was the location of the film *Jurassic Park*.

According to a published interview with Danny Gonzalez, the spokesperson for MarViva, the organization that protects the island: 'The island houses great nature and cultural riches. It's home to many endemic species and is, along with the islands of Coiba, Malpelo and the Galapagos, part of the East Pacific Tropical Marine Corridor, which allows the movement of many migratory marine species from North and South America.'

He continues: 'This nomination will also help people learn about serious problems that affect Isla del Cocos' marine ecosystems, such as illegal fishing, shark finning and other human activities that put pressure on natural resources. Protecting these resources is a big challenge, and that's why this year we will do our best to tell people about the importance of knowing about and contributing to the safeguarding of this heritage site.'

stopped by for fresh water, coconuts and fresh seafood.

Between the late 17th and early 19th century, Isla del Cocos became something of a way station for a band of pirates who supposedly hid countless treasures here. The most famous was the storied Treasure of Lima, which consisted of gold and silver ingots, gold laminae scavenged from church domes and a solid-gold, life-size sculpture of the Virgin Mary. Isla del Cocos is so renowned for its hidden treasures that authors have speculated it was the inspiration for Robert Louis Stevenson's *Treasure Island*. Nonetheless, more than 500 treasure-hunting expeditions have found only failure.

In fact, in 1869 the government of Costa Rica organized its own official treasure hunt. No gold or jewels were discovered, but this expedition did result in Costa Rica's unfurling its flag and taking possession of the island, a treasure in itself.

Settlers arrived on the island in the late 19th and early 20th centuries, though their stay on Isla del Cocos was short-lived. However, they did leave behind domestic animals that have since converted into feral populations of pigs, goats, cats and rats.

Today it's the pigs that are the greatest threat to the unique species native to the island: they uproot vegetation, cause soil erosion and contribute to sedimentation around the island's coasts, which damages coral reefs.

Unregulated fishing also poses further, more ominous, threats, especially to populations of shark, tuna and billfish that get caught in logline sets. The Servicio de Parques Nacionales (Sinac) is aware of the problem, but sadly a lack of funding has made regulation of these illegal activities difficult, if not impossible.

Information

In order to protect the conservation status of the island, all visitors must apply for a permit at the **Área de Conservación de la Isla del Cocos** (☎ 2258 7350) in San José. However, unless you're sailing to the island in a private boat, most tour operators will make all of the necessary arrangements for you.

Park fees are US$35 per person per day. On the island, there is also a ranger station, with staff surveillance stations at Wafer Bay and Chatham Bay. Drinking water is available, but there is no camping – visitors must spend the night on their boats.

Sights & Activities

Isla del Cocos is rugged and heavily forested, with the highest point at **Cerro Iglesias** (634m); a network of trails leads to a spectacular viewpoint. The island has two large bays with safe anchorages and sandy beaches: **Chatham** is located on the northeast side and **Wafer Bay** is on the northwest. Just off Cocos are a series of smaller basaltic rocks and islets, which constitute some of the best dive sites. **Isla Manuelita** is a prime spot, home to a wide array of fish, ray and eel. Shark also inhabit these waters, including huge schools of white tip shark and scalloped hammerhead, which are best spotted at night. **Dirty Rock** is another main attraction – a spectacular rock formation that harbors all kinds of sea creatures.

Tours

Even if you're normally a fiercely independent traveler, Cocos is one destination where you will have to join up with an organized tour. Although you may be tempted to visit here on a private sailing vessel, you'll have an easier time getting the government to grant you access to the island's interior if you go with an operator.

The island is serviced by two boats, both of which operate from the Los Sueños Marina near the Marriott Beach & Golf Resort in Playa Herradura. On both tours you are permitted to hike around the island and go on wildlife tours, though you must return to the boat at night to sleep. Diving is the main thrust of any tour as the island is regarded as one of the world's premier dive destinations. Diving and food are included in the tour prices listed below, but daily park fees are not.

Okeanos Aggressor (☎ in the USA 866-653 2667, ext 196; www.okeanoscocosisland.com) Offers eight-day and 10-day land and sea expeditions with room for 21 from US$2695 per person.

Undersea Hunter (☎ 2228 6613, in the USA 800-203 2120; www.underseahunter.com) Offers 10-day and 12-day land and sea expeditions using either their 14- or 18-passenger boat from US$3640.

PENÍNSULA DE OSA & GOLFO DULCE

Caribbean Coast

The thick jungle-lined coastline of Costa Rica's fierce and rugged Caribbean face has historically been a law unto itself. Deemed too wild and impassable by the conquering Spaniards, the area has developed at its own unbothered laidback pace.

However, this isn't your envisioned Caribbean stereotype. Salt-white beaches and gently lapping turquoise waters are replaced by brooding tempestuous seas and black volcanic shores that are skirted by jungle so raw and wild you expect to see a T Rex come roaring out onto the beach at any moment.

While you won't exactly find Jurassic Park (which isn't such a funny gag when you consider the rife rumors of creating Western-styled wildlife parks in the area) there are bountiful amounts of nonextinct animals such as jaguars, sloths, turtles and enough snapping crocodiles to make you skip with haste over any creek and river.

Also to be found are some of the more thriving indigenous tribes in this part of the world. The KéköLdi, Bribrí and Cabécar tribes are strong flavors in the cultural hot pot that has evolved here. But the most obvious ethnic feature is the Afro-Caribbean community. With them comes the heady and colorful Rasta culture known the world over; reggae music, spicy jerk chicken and general *irie* (good) living are found at every turn.

Chinese, Italian and North Americans have more recently emigrated in their droves. The secret is already out about this sloth-paced hotchpotch of people, who live so happily in this wonderfully wild corner of the world. So, best check it out soon, before it's all turned into a theme park.

HIGHLIGHTS

- Taking snaps of snappy crocs on the canals of **Parque Nacional Tortuguero** (p458)

- Beaching it by day and partying by night in **Puerto Viejo de Talamanca** (p477)

- Pedaling through the **Refugio Nacional de Vida Silvestre Gandoca-Manzanillo** (p491) on the scenic cycle route from Puerto Viejo to Manzanillo

- Taking lounging tips from the overhanging sloths and gently rocking the day away in a hammock in **Cahuita** (p468)

- Rolling your sleeves up and searching the beaches to see and save the turtles of **Parismina** (p456)

★ Parque Nacional Tortuguero

★ Parismina

Cahuita ★   Puerto Viejo de ★ Talamanca

Refugio Nacional ★ de Vida Silvestre Gandoca-Manzanillo

History

Despite Columbus first dropping anchor off what is today Limón, and claiming to have witnessed untold riches, the wild jungle of the Caribbean coast was seen as too dense and wild, so the colonization of Costa Rica was done from the Pacific side. The Caribbean coast has its own story, largely as a result of its imposed isolation from the rest of the country. Once the Spanish invaders realized that little wealth was to be found on the alleged 'Rich Coast,' they left the steamy jungle-lined shores and its Indian inhabitants to their own devices. The pre-Columbian Cabécar, KéköLdi and Bribrí tribes still thrived, for the most part unbothered, for centuries after the *conquistadors'* (conquerors') arrival.

In 1867 a port was built on the site of a grand old lemon tree, hence Limón, and the Caribbean coast had an access point to the world. Aside from a small group of cacao farmers in Matina, it wasn't until the 1870s that the first major influx of non-Indian residents arrived. Minor Keith's railroad laborers brought the strong West Indian culture that is the dominant feature of the region's makeup. However, despite a new speedy (for the time) railtrack to unify the country, division would remain. The black people of the Caribbean coast were not granted citizenship until 1949, and until then were not allowed to cross the border to leave the Caribbean provinces. Out of isolation has sprung a unique and independent culture that feels like a country within a country.

Climate

The fact that there is no traditional dry season is a mixed blessing. It pretty much rains all year, but that keeps the crowds away, while the bountiful land remains ocean-green and rich with wildlife. There's a steady year-round temperature of about 27°C/80°F to 8°C/46°F, while the driest months are February, March, September and October. Surfers might note that the biggest swells hit the southern Caribbean from December to March.

Parks & Reserves

Refuges and parks line the Caribbean coast.
Cahuita National Park (p475) In this park mangroves and river banks are home to plenty of point-and-giggle wildlife such as armadillo and sloth, while the protected reef is the most colorful on the coast.
Parque Nacional Tortuguero (p458) Offers kayak safaris around crocodile-infested backwaters, while howler,

spider and capuchin monkeys squawk and holler overhead. But the main draw is the green sea turtles, which come to lay their eggs from June to October.
Refugio Nacional de Vida Silvestre Barra del Colorado (p465) This is where fishing enthusiasts come from all over to hook snook, tarpon and gar. Visitors hole up in luxury fishing lodges and spin lines all day. Wildlife rain-forest trips and deep-sea fishing are also popular.
Refugio Nacional de Vida Silvestre Gandoca-Manzanillo (p491) A rich rain forest and wetland tucked away in the country's southeastern corner. Home to the country's only mangrove oysters, the rivers are full of manatee, caiman and crocodile.

Dangers & Annoyances

The Caribbean coast region has had a bad reputation over the years for being more dangerous than other parts of Costa Rica. In reality, crime levels against tourists are no higher than in any other part of the country. This view has mainly been manifested by the ignorant few who feel threatened in a black environment. Still, as anywhere else, common sense is necessary. A very real problem all along the coast is the sea. Rips can be *very* strong, so make sure you always swim in safe areas (any local will tell you if it's OK to go in the water); if in doubt, just go in for a paddle, or not at all.

Getting There & Around

When traveling to Puerto Limón and the southern Caribbean, it's easy enough to hop on any of the regular buses from San José. Buses also connect up most towns along the coast, from Sixaola, on the Panamanian border, to Puerto Limón. Alternatively, the roads are pretty good, so self-drive is a good option. The north is a little trickier. Much of the area is only linked up by waterways, so boating is the sole means of transport, which essentially rules out self-drive. Both Tortuguero and Barra del Colorado have landing strips, to which there are flights daily from San José.

THE ATLANTIC SLOPE

The idea was simple: build a port on the Caribbean coast and connect it to the Central Valley by railroad, thus opening up important shipping routes for soaring coffee production. In 1867 present-day Puerto Limón was chosen as the site, perhaps not

CARIBBEAN COAST

CARIBBEAN COAST

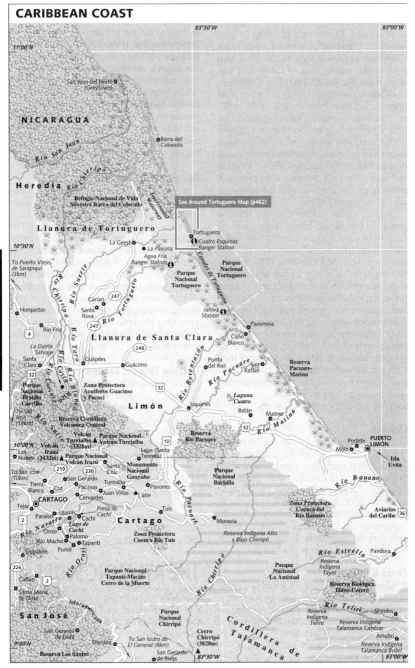

See Around Tortuguero Map (p462)

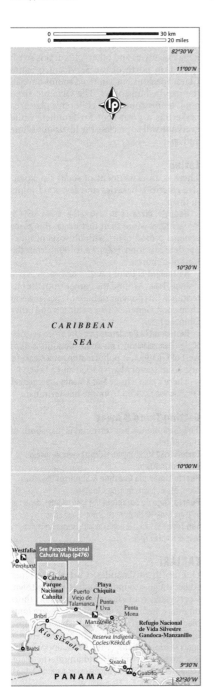

accounting for the 150 unexplored kilometers of dense jungles, malaria-ridden swamps and steep, muddy mountainsides along the Atlantic slope.

Though things did not go exactly according to plan, the Costa Ricans eventually got their port and their railroad. They also got a booming banana business, which dominated this region for 100 years.

The railroad, once the lifeline of the region, is no longer. Today, a cloudy highway links the Central Valley to the Caribbean coast, starting in the foothills of the Cordillera Central, traversing a landscape dominated by banana and pineapple plantations, and ending in the swampy lowlands around Limón.

GUÁPILES & AROUND

This pretty, prosperous town in the northern foothills of the Cordillera Central is the transport center for the Río Frío banana-growing region. Some 60km northeast of San José, Guápiles is a bustling place, its main streets lined with shopping centers and other services. A lively agricultural market takes place on Saturdays.

Guápiles is about 1km north of Hwy 32. The two major streets are one way, running parallel to each other. Most of the services are on the loop these streets make through the busy downtown. The convenient **Café Internet Caribe** (☎ 2771 0631; per hr US$1; ⊙ 8am-10:30pm) is opposite the bus terminal.

Jardín Botánico Las Cusingas

Exhibits at the family-run **Jardín Botánico Las Cusingas** (botanical garden; ☎ 2710 2652; guided tour US$5; ⊙ by appointment) emphasize medicinal plants, rural life, conservation and the ethical use of plants. Eighty medicinal-plant species, 80 orchid species, 30 bromeliad species and more than 100 bird species have been recorded on the flower-filled property. There are several easy trails for walking, as well as courses, research projects and a library on offer.

In the middle of the gardens, a rustic two-room wooden **cabin** (r per person US$5; **P**) houses up to four people. Its cozy living area is equipped with a wood-burning stove; meals are also available. Turn south at the Servicentro Santa Clara (the opposite direction from Cariari), then go 4km by rough paved road to the signed entrance.

CARIBBEAN COAST

Ecofinca Andar

Combining organic agriculture, environmental conservation and community activism, the **Ecofinca Andar** (ecological farm; ☎ 2272 1024; www.andarcr.org; Santa Rosa; 1-day admission US$14, homestays US$17; P) is an impressive educational facility. Demonstrations focus on plants cultivated for medicinal use, sources of renewable energy and the biodiversity of the surrounding rain forest. If you stick around for more than a day you can really get your hands dirty by planting or harvesting in the gardens, fishing and maintaining trails. The farm is 3km northeast of the village of Santa Rosa.

La Danta Salvaje

Make advance arrangements to visit **La Danta Salvaje** (☎ 2750 0012; www.greencoast.com/ladanta /ladantasalvaje.htm; 3-night package per person US$210). On the Caribbean slope at 800m above sea level, this private 410-hectare rain-forest reserve is part of the critical buffer zone that protects Parque Nacional Braulio Carrillo (p146). The rustic lodge hosts small groups for three days of hiking in the jungle, swimming under waterfalls and spotting wildlife like spider monkey and tapir. Prices include three meals a day, as well as transportation (45 minutes by 4WD, followed by a three-hour hike to the lodge).

Sleeping

Hotel Cabinas Lomas del Toro (☎ 2710 2934; d US$10-15; P X) If you'd rather not brave Guápiles proper, this ramp motel off Hwy 32 (about 3km before Guápiles) is efficient and easy to find. Besides the spotless guestrooms, you'll find a good restaurant and a recreation room with table-tennis and pool tables.

Hotel y Cabinas Wilson (☎ 2710 2217; d/tr US$16/24; P X) This clean, comfortable spot is on the left-hand side as you drive into Guápiles north from the highway. A vibrant wall mural brightens up the otherwise nondescript décor of the open-air lobby, which overlooks the busy street.

Cabinas Quinta (☎ 2710 7016; d with fan/air-con US$40/46; P X) Much nicer than the average cabina, these large, spotless rooms have cable TV, hot showers and cold refrigerators. The 19-hectare grounds have private trails, two rivers, horses and a motocross track. It's on the road to Cariari just as you leave Guápiles.

Country Club Suerre (☎ 2710 7551; www.suerre .com; s/d/ste US$75/90/140; P X X X) Join banana executives and other VIPs at this swish spot, 1km north of the Servicentro Santa Clara. Spacious but sanitized rooms have all the required amenities. The Olympic-sized pool, tennis courts and children's play area make this a great spot for families, while everyone will appreciate the luxurious sauna and spa.

Eating

There is an assortment of *sodas* (inexpensive eateries), bakeries and fast-food joints in town.

Happy's Pizza (☎ 2710 2434; mains US$1-5; ⊙ 9am-10pm) More than just pizza, this place anchors a food court with all sorts of independent fast food. Happy's is 100m from the Catholic church.

Restaurant El Unico (☎ 2710 6250; meals US$3-5; ⊙ 10am-11pm) Around the corner from the bus terminal, this popular restaurant specializes in chop suey, General Chau's chicken and other Chinese fare.

Restaurant La Ponderosa (☎ 2710 2075; mains US$3-10; ⊙ 11am-midnight) This roadside joint is 5km west of Guápiles. A popular stop for a steak, or just *bocas* (savory bar snacks) and a beer.

There's also a huge **Más X Menos supermarket** (⊙ 9am-9pm), 200m from the bus terminal.

Getting There & Away

The Guápileños bus terminal is just south of the center.

Cariari US$0.50, 20 minutes, depart every 20 minutes from 6am to 10pm.

Puerto Limón via Guácimo & Siquirres US$2, two hours, depart hourly from 6am to 7pm.

Puerto Viejo de Sarapiquí US$1, 45 minutes, depart at 5:30am, 8am, 10:30am, noon, 2:30pm and 5pm.

San José US$1.75, 1¼ hours, depart every 30 minutes from 6:30am to 7pm.

CARIARI

Due north of Guápiles, Cariari is a blue-collar, rough-around-the-edges banana town. Corrugated-roof shops line the main thoroughfare and look a little like they were jumbled together yesterday and would collapse like dominoes under a slight breeze. There's a gas station, a bank (with ATM, opposite the San José bus terminal) and an internet café, **Compuser** (☎ 2767 8286; Tracopa bus terminal; per hr US$1; ⊙ 7am-10pm Mon-Fri, 11am-8pm Sun).

CARIBBEAN COAST

The reason tourists cruise through Cariari is to catch a boat to Tortuguero (p461), which can usually be accomplished in an hour or two. If you get stuck, you can spend the night at the **Hotel Central** (☎ 2767 6890; r per person US$10; **P**), which is conveniently close to the bus terminals. The proprietor Patricia – known as 'la mama en Cariari' – takes care of her guests, providing breakfast, luggage storage, long-term parking and other services. Plus she used to work in a hospital, so her brightly painted rooms (with shared bathrooms) are spotless.

Getting There & Away

The turnoff for the paved road to Cariari is about 1km east of Guápiles, at the Servicentro Santa Clara. If you are heading to Tortuguero, you can leave your car at the Hotel Central (per day US$2) or at the guarded parking in La Pavona. (Do not drive to La Geest, as parking is not available.)

Cariari has two bus terminals: the one serving San José is at the southern end of town, while the one serving Guápiles and Caribbean destinations is about four blocks closer to the center, behind the police station.

Despite what you might hear from overzealous tour operators, the most common route to Tortuguero is through La Pavona, a private farm on the Río Suerte (La Pavona is not a town, and does not show up on most maps). Buses for La Pavona depart from the central bus terminal behind the police station; buy tickets from the Coopetraca window. Boats from La Pavona to Tortuguero are timed to meet the buses, so you won't have to wait long for your connection.

The private **Bananero** (☎ 2709 8005) boat company also provides transportation from Cariari to Tortuguero via a private plantation called La Geest (also not on maps). Bananero buses leave from the San José bus terminal.

Guápiles US$0.50, 20 minutes, depart every 20 minutes from 6:30am to 10pm.

Puerto Limón US$2.25, 2½ hours, depart at 4:30am, 8:30am, noon and 3pm.

Puerto Lindo (for Barra del Colorado) US$6, depart at noon and 2pm (dry season only).

San José US$2, three hours, depart at 5:30am, 6:30am, 7:30am, 8:30am, 11:30am, 1pm, 3pm and 5:30pm.

Tortuguero via La Geest US$10, three hours, depart at 1:30pm and 3:30pm.

Tortuguero via La Pavona US$10, three hours, depart at 6am, noon and 3pm.

GUÁCIMO

There's not much to this little town, about 12km east of Guápiles, except the expansive campus of the **Escuela de Agricultura de la Región Tropical Húmeda** (Earth; ☎ 2713 0000; www.earth.ac.cr; guided tours US$10). This private, not-for-profit university attracts students from around the world to research sustainable agriculture in the tropics. The university's nontraditional curriculum emphasizes agriculture as a human activity, integrating various academic disciplines and a philosophy of hands-on, active learning. As such, the 3300-hectare campus looks like a college campus at first glance, however, it also contains many hectares of experimental plots, plantations and rain-forest reserves.

A popular destination of the Limón cruise-ship crowd is **Costa Flores** (☎ 2717 6457; guided tour US$15; ☑ by reservation), a huge tropical flower and palm farm, with incredible heliconia gardens. Its 48 hectares include landscaped gardens and fountain-fed ponds (much of it wheelchair accessible). The farm exports 120 varieties of blossoms to the USA and Europe.

Hotel Restaurant Río Palmas (☎ 2760 0330; d with/without air-con US$40/25; **P** ✗ ✗ ✗) This hotel some 600m east of Earth stands out with its lush gardens and hiking trails. Very comfortable rooms have cable TV, hot showers and other amenities, and the restaurant is recommended. It's an excellent deal, in the middle of nowhere.

SIQUIRRES

Siquirres has long served as an important transportation hub as it sits at the intersection of Hwy 32 (the main road that crosses the Atlantic slope to Puerto Limón) with Hwy 10, the old road that connects San José with Puerto Limón via Turrialba.

Even before the roads came, Siquirres administered the most important junction on the San José–Limón railway. And for the first part of the 20th century, the town delineated Costa Rica's segregated interior: without special permission, blacks were barred from traveling west of this internal border. Until the constitution of 1949 outlawed racial discrimination, black conductors and engineers would change places with their Spanish counterparts here, then head back to Limón.

Today, Siquirres still seems to mark the place where Costa Rica proper takes a dip into the Caribbean – and it's not just the

TALLYING THE TRUE COST OF BANANAS *Beth Penland*

Banana cultivation, the second-largest industry (trailing tourism) in Costa Rica, began in 1878 when Minor Keith, the American entrepreneur contracted to build the Atlantic Railway (see p41), planted those first Panamanian cuttings to provide cheap food for his workforce. The sweet crop was a surprise hit in the USA and, after the completion of the Atlantic Railway in 1890, the banana boom began in earnest.

Mostly foreign investors bought and cleared the land that would become the 'banana coast.' In 1909 Keith consolidated his holdings as United Fruit, a banana empire that influenced Central American affairs for the next half century.

The banana industry has created an enormously lucrative monoculture that has been susceptible to a variety of parasites and other diseases, including a series of blights that swept through the region in the early 20th century, decimating banana crops throughout the northern lowlands and Caribbean coast. To combat these diseases and other parasitic organisms that might compromise the bottom line, growers use an arsenal of ecologically destructive methods to guarantee a profitable harvest.

For example, while still on the trees, bananas are wrapped in blue plastic bags impregnated with petrochemicals that shield them from pests, while also inducing the fruit to ripen more quickly. These baggies often end up in streams and canals around the fincas (plantations). The bags can kill wildlife directly by suffocation, or indirectly by contaminating the environment with chemicals. Moreover, runoff from the fincas, which are kept free of weeds and other undergrowth that could naturally stop serious erosion, is enriched with fertilizers that often promote radically increased growth in some plants, potentially denying space and light to organisms less capable of using the fertilizers for themselves.

These synthetic products can also affect humans. At least 280 pesticides are authorized for use in the cultivation of the fruit, including five that the World Health Organization (WHO) ranks as 'extremely hazardous.' Plantation owners and chemical companies have faced lawsuits from more

geography. The lack of infrastructure to the east of Siquirres is subtle, but you'll notice it when you're charged twice as much for painfully slow internet access, then spend half a day locating an ATM to pay for it.

There is little reason to stop in Siquirres, unless you are heading north to Parismina (in which case you should definitely make use of the bank in town). If you need somewhere to crash for the night, head 800m north of Parque Central to **Chito's Lodge** (☎ 2768 9293; per person US$20; 🏊), which also has a lively bar and restaurant, as well as lovely grounds inhabited by many animals. Chito is something of a local celebrity, as he has appeared on TV, wrestling with crocodiles. **Castellana** (Parque Central; meals US$1-3) is a friendly *soda* and bakery serving tasty, typical Tico fare.

Getting There & Away
If you are heading to Parismina, take the **Caño-Aguilar bus** (☎ 2768 8172) to Caño Blanco (US$1.50, two hours) at 4:15am or 12:30pm Monday through Friday, or 7:15am or 3:15pm Saturday and Sunday. Boats to Parismina (US$2, 10 minutes) wait for the buses in Caño

Blanco, departing at 6am and 3pm Monday through Friday, and 9am and 5pm Saturday and Sunday.

Siquirres is a regular stop on the San José–Limón route, so you can catch a bus to either destination every hour between 6am and 7pm.

PUERTO LIMÓN
This is the great city of Costa Rica's Caribbean coast, birthplace of United Fruit (see boxed text, above) and capital of Limón Province. In many ways, it's still removed from San José's sphere of influence. Around here, business is measured by truckloads of bananas, not busloads of tourists, so don't expect much pampering. Cruise ships do deposit passengers between October and May; we can only hope that they weren't expecting to spot a quetzal.

Most travelers simply pass through on their way to more user-friendly destinations, as this hard-working port city doesn't float everyone's boat. Breezes blow in off the Caribbean, but the seaside stretch is underutilized, at best. Only the guests at the Park Hotel and the than 24,000 Latin American workers over the effects of Dibromochloropropane (DBCP), which has been linked to birth defects, tissue damage and sterility in male workers. Although it was banned in 1977 by the USA, where it is manufactured, it was used here until 1990.

In Costa Rica the right to acceptable working conditions is protected under the Declaration of Human Rights, but this does not include protection from hazardous toxins. Workers had to petition US courts to seek recourse against the producers and distributors of DBCP. Although Nicaraguan courts ordered US corporations in 2002 to pay out US$490 million to 583 workers affected by DBCP, most of the 9000 Costa Rican workers who claim to have been rendered sterile are still waiting for a settlement. A Dow Chemical representative called the ruling 'unenforceable.'

Conditions for many Costa Rican banana workers are still poor. Wages are low, particularly among the under-regulated indigenous workforce along the Caribbean coast. Efforts to organize the labor force have reportedly resulted in the blacklisting of union representatives. Paraquat, a chemical that is banned in several European countries because of links to health problems including blurred vision, tissue damage and even death, is still used to the tune of 65kg per worker annually.

In the late 1990s a loose coalition of organizations began certifying bananas as 'Fair Trade'; these labeled, premium-priced fruits are usually grown on smaller farms, and companies must prove that they pay living wages and offer workers minimal protection from agrochemicals. This increased focus on social responsibility is finally moving US corporations to work with auditors to meet labor, human-rights and food-safety standards. However, these auditors have come under scrutiny as some have gained a reputation for loose standards. It has been claimed that some US companies have gained Fair Trade accreditation without ticking all the correct boxes the consumer would expect.

Despite efforts toward change, the long-term ecological damage done by the banana trade will be evident throughout Costa Rica for years to come. Fortunately, socioeconomic and sustainable growth in the industry are roughly on the right track.

workers at the cruise-ship pier can appreciate that this is a coastal city. Further inland, the orderly grid of streets is lined with run-down buildings and overgrown parks, and the sidewalks are crowded with shoppers and street vendors.

If you're the rare traveler inclined to a little urban exploration, Limón is an interesting place. It is the heart of Costa Rica's Afro-Caribbean culture, reflected in the laidback hospitality, a growing music scene and the country's best African cultural festival (see p452). The city's dilapidated charm is giving way to more modern growth, as federal funds are slowly being invested in this side of the country.

Some urban-renewal programs have already been implemented, such as the pedestrian mall from the market to the sea wall and the new bus station. But Limón – both port and province – has a long and difficult history of complications with the capital, and locals don't expect their city to get a full federally funded face-lift anytime soon. (This might not seem such a bad thing to visitors who need a break from the zip-line economy.)

History

Christopher Columbus first dropped anchor in Costa Rica in 1502 at Isla Uvita, just off the coast of Puerto Limón. The Atlantic coast, however, was left largely unexplored by Spanish settlers until the 19th century. In 1867, construction began on an ambitious railroad connecting the highlands to the sea. Limón was chosen as the site of a major port, which would facilitate exports of coffee from the Central Valley.

The railroad project changed Costa Rica in dramatic ways. The freed Jamaican slaves that provided cheap labor for the railroad construction settled on the coast, introducing the English language and Caribbean culture to the previously homogeneous population. The bananas that were planted alongside the tracks as a cheap food source for the workers became the country's number-one export. And the American-owned United Fruit, which controlled the booming business, made Costa Rica a part of its banana empire (see p41).

In 1913 a banana blight shut down many Caribbean fincas, and much of the banana production moved to the Pacific coast.

Afro-Caribbean workers, however, were restricted by visa regulations to Limón Province, so were forbidden from following the employment opportunities. Stranded in the least-developed part of the country, many turned to subsistence farming, fishing or working on cocoa plantations. Others organized and staged bloody strikes against United Fruit.

In 1948 Limón provided key support to José Figueres during the 40-day civil war (see p42). In 1949 the new president enacted a constitution that finally granted blacks the right to work and travel freely throughout Costa Rica.

Orientation

Limón's streets are poorly marked and most do not have signs. Most locals can give you better directions using city landmarks such as the market, the old Radio Casino and Parque Vargas. Av 2 begins as the pedestrian mall, stretching from the sea wall past Parque Vargas to the market, where it becomes a main street. Several banks, bars, restaurants and hotels are within a few blocks, as is the main bus terminal.

Information

Note that banks are a rarity in other parts of the Caribbean coast, so whether you're headed north or south, stock up here with as many colones as you think you're going to need.

Banco de Costa Rica (☎ 2758 3166; cnr Av 2 & Calle 1) Exchanges US dollars cash and has an ATM.

Centro Médico Monterrey (☎ 2798 1723, emergency 2297 1010) Opposite the cathedral.

Hospital Tony Facio (☎ 2758 2222) On the coast at the northern end of town; serves the entire province.

Internet Café (☎ 2798 0128; per hr US$1; ☽ 8am-7pm Mon-Fri, noon-7pm Sat) Ten fairly fast computers, conveniently located upstairs at Terminal Caribeño.

La Casona de Parque (per hr US$1; ☽ 7am-6pm) Another option for internet access, servicing the cruise-ship crowd.

Post office (Calle 4 btwn Avs 1 & 2; ☽ 9am-4pm)

Scotiabank (☎ 2798 0009; cnr Av 3 & Calle 2; ☽ 8:30am-4:30pm Mon-Fri, 8:30am-3:30pm Sat) Exchanges cash and traveler's checks. Also has a 24-hour ATM on the Plus and Cirrus systems that dispenses US dollars.

Dangers & Annoyances

Limón is what you'd call gritty: take precautions against pickpockets during the day, particularly in the market. People do get mugged here, so stick to well-lit main streets at night, avoiding the sea wall and Parque Vargas. Park in a guarded lot and remove everything from the car, as vehicle break-ins are common.

Sights & Activities

The city's main attraction is the waterfront **Parque Vargas**, an incongruous expanse of bench-lined sidewalks beneath a lost little jungle of tall palms and tropical flowers, centered on an appealingly decrepit bandstand.

From here, you can head inland along Avenida 2, the **pedestrian mall** that caters to the cruise-ship traffic. Keep an eye out for vendors selling home-burned CDs by local bands – Limón is getting a reputation for its growing hip-hop and Latin-reggae fusion scenes. You'll end up at the colorful **central market**. Two blocks away, the **Museo Etnohistórico de Limón** (Calle 4 btwn Avs 1 & 2; admission free), on the 2nd floor of the post office, was closed for renovations at press time (and has been for years). Past exhibits of Afro-Caribbean artifacts sound intriguing, so it's worth checking out if it ever opens again.

From the park, it's a pleasant walk north along the **sea wall**, where views of the rocky headland are set to a steady baseline of waves crashing against the concrete. After dark, this is a popular mugging and make-out spot.

Although there are no beaches for swimming or surfing in Limón. If you are keen to get in the water, **Playa Bonita** (p455), 4km northwest of town, has a sandy beach, while **Isla Uvita** (p455), 1km offshore, has one of the country's most powerful lefts.

Festivals & Events

Festival Flores de la Diáspora Africana (Late August) A celebration of Afro-Caribbean culture. While it is centered on Puerto Limón, the festival sponsors events showcasing African heritage throughout the province and San José.

Día de la Raza (Columbus Day; October 12) Columbus' historic landing on Isla Uvita inspires Limón to go all out, with a four- or five-day carnival of colorful street parades and dancing, music, singing and drinking. Book your hotel in advance.

Sleeping

Hotels all along the Caribbean coast are in demand on weekends and during vacations, when prices rise. Reserve ahead if possible during these periods.

CARIBBEAN COAST

PUERTO LIMÓN

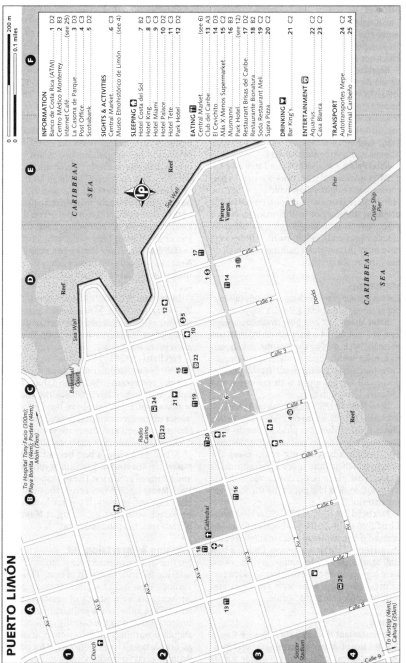

0   200 m
0   0.1 miles

INFORMATION	
Banco de Costa Rica (ATM)	1 D2
Centro Médico Monterrey	2 B3
Internet Café	(see 25)
La Casona de Parque	3 D3
Post Office	4 C3
Scotiabank	5 D2

SIGHTS & ACTIVITIES	
Central Market	6 C3
Museo Etnohistórico de Limón	(see 4)

SLEEPING	
Hotel Costa del Sol	7 B2
Hotel King	8 C3
Hotel Miami	9 C3
Hotel Palace	10 D2
Hotel Tete	11 C3
Park Hotel	12 D2

EATING	
Central Market	(see 6)
Club del Caribe	13 A3
El Cevichito	14 D3
Más X Menos Supermarket	15 C2
Musmanni	16 B3
Park Hotel	(see 12)
Restaurant Brisas del Caribe	17 D2
Restaurante Bionatura	18 B2
Soda Restaurant Meli	19 C2
Supra Pizza	20 C2

DRINKING	
Bar King's	21 C2

ENTERTAINMENT	
Aquarius	22 C2
Casa Blanca	23 C2

TRANSPORT	
Autotransportes Mepe	24 C2
Terminal Caribeño	25 A4

CARIBBEAN SEA

CARIBBEAN COAST

BUDGET

The hotels listed here are at the more wholesome end of the budget spectrum, but they are still pretty gloomy; ask to see a room and check security.

Hotel Costa del Sol (☎ 2798 0909; cnr Calle 5 & Av 5; s/d with shared bathroom US$10/12, with private bathroom US$15/17, with air-con US$18/20; P ☒) Limón's best budget option is this large hotel, staffed by friendly, young employees. Rooms, bearing the distinct odor of disinfectant, have fresh paint and clean sheets, as well as TV, telephones and cold-water showers.

Hotel Palace (☎ 2798 2604; Calle 2 btwn Avs 2 & 3; d US$12) Ornamental stonework adorns the balconies of the bright yellow building, where the Hotel Palace is on the 2nd floor. Potted plants brighten the interior as this woman-owned place, which is otherwise characterized by cracked tiles and peeling paint. All quarters have built-in cold-water bathrooms, which do not offer much privacy.

MIDRANGE

Limón proper offers nothing remotely upscale. Nicer hotels are at Playa Bonita (opposite).

Hotel Miami (☎ 2758 0490; hmiamilimon@yahoo .com; Av 2 btwn Calles 4 & 5; s/d with fan US$14/18, with air-con US$24/32; P ☒) One of the few hotels in Limón with a hint of style, this safe, secure place has rooms with fresh, tasteful décor. All are equipped with cable TV and industrial-strength fans.

Hotel Tete (☎ 2758 1122; Av 3 btwn Calles 4 & 5; s/d/tr with fan US$15/25/29, with air-con US$15/22/30; P ☒) Hotel Tete has dark but pleasant rooms with clean linoleum floors and matching curtains and bedspreads. One big room faces the street, which means more light and more noise. This place is definitely nicer inside than out, so don't be put off by the foreboding exterior.

Park Hotel (☎ 2798 0555, 2758 3476; Av 3 btwn Calles 1 & 2; s/d US$50/60; P ☒ ☒ ☐) Locals will act impressed if you tell them you are staying at the Park Hotel. This is downtown Limón's best stab at upscale, where simple, stylish rooms have high ceilings and attractive wooden furniture. Spacious rooms with sea views and little balconies cost US$5 more.

Eating

Soda Restaurant Meli (Av 3 btwn Calles 3 & 4; meals US$2-4) One of many cheap *sodas* surrounding the central market. It's popular for its cheap prices and big servings of fried rice and casados (set meals).

Restaurante Bionatura (Calle 6 btwn Avs 3 & 4; mains US$2-5; ☺ 8am-8pm Mon-Sat) In a town where everything seems deep-fried, this restaurant stands out with its focus on healthy vegetarian cuisine, from fresh fruit salads to veggie burgers and 'bistek de soya' casados. There's a health-food store next door.

Restaurant Brisas del Caribe (☎ 2758 0138; mains US$3-5; ☺ 7am-11pm Mon-Fri, 10am-11pm Sat & Sun) The best view in town isn't over the waves: right by the Parque Vargas, outdoor tables and a breezy balcony make for excellent people-watching and delicious Caribbean fare.

El Cevichito (Av 2 btwn Calles 1 & 2; mains US$4) The outdoor patio along the pedestrian mall is one of the city's more pleasant spots. You'll find locals gathering here to guzzle beer, discuss soccer and devour tasty garlic fish.

Club del Caribe (Calle 7 btwn Avs 3 & 4; mains US$3-6) Next to a pool hall, this homey eatery is chock-full of Creole flavor. Try a bowl of cow's-foot soup and a cold beer for US$3.

Supra Pizza (☎ 2758 3371; Av 3 btwn Calles 4 & 5; mains US$3-6, large pizza US$10; ☺ 10am-11pm) Upstairs at the Plaza Caribe, this place caters to students and budget travelers with large portions of good pizza and pasta.

Park Hotel (☎ 2798 0555; Av 3 btwn Calles 1 & 2; meals US$6-10; ☺ 6am-10pm) Go upscale at the semi-swanky restaurant attached to Limón's top hotel. With white linen tablecloths and big windows catching Caribbean breezes, it exudes a tropical, colonial ambience. The menu features seafood and many mysterious (but delicious) specialties of the house.

A budget traveler's best bet is the **central market** (☺ 6am-8pm Mon-Sat), with several *sodas* and plenty of groceries. The big supermarket **Más X Menos** (☺ 8am-9pm) across the avenue is useful for self-caterers. If you are looking for breakfast, you can't go wrong at **Musmanni** (☺ 6am-6pm), near the cathedral.

Drinking & Entertainment

No one in Limón need ever go thirsty, considering the wide selection of bars. Those by Parque Vargas and a few blocks west are popular hangouts for a variety of coastal characters: sailors, ladies of the night, entrepreneurs, boozers, losers and the casually curious. The standard warnings for solo women travelers go double here. This is a lousy town for getting drunk – keep your wits about you.

Bar King's (Calle 3 btwn Avs 3 & 4) More Latin and less Carib. Women travelers may feel more comfortable here, as some local señoritas usually make an appearance.

Casa Blanca (cnr Calle 4 & Av 4) On weekends this is the best place to check out the local music scene. On any day of the week it is packed from about 5pm onward with a primarily male clientele. It's easy to find; just follow the reggae beat emanating from the jukebox.

Aquarius (☎ 2758 1010; Av 3 btwn Calles 2 & 3; ☼ 8pm-2am) Inside the Hotel Acon, this is the hottest disco in town, with salsa, reggae and pop spinning on different nights.

Getting There & Away
Puerto Limón is the transportation hub of the Caribbean coast.

AIR
The airstrip is about 4km south of town. There are no regularly scheduled flights, but you can charter a flight to Puerto Jiménez (US$1450) or Golfito (US$1320) through Alfa Romeo Aero Taxi (see p434).

BOAT
Cruise ships occasionally dock in Limón, but most boats providing transportation use the major port at Moín, about 7km west of Limón. For information on boats to Tortuguero, see p456.

BUS
Buses to and from San José, Moín, Guápiles and Siquirres arrive at **Terminal Caribeño** (Av 2 btwn Calles 7 & 8) on the west side and within walking distance from all the hotels. Buses to points south all depart from **Autotransportes Mepe** (Mepe; Av 4 btwn Calles 3 & 4).

Bribrí & Sixaola (Mepe) US$3, three hours, depart at 5am, 7am, 8am, 10am, noon, 1pm, 4pm and 6pm.

Cahuita (Mepe) US$1, 1½ hours, depart at 5am, 6am, 8am, 10am, 1pm, 2:30pm, 4pm and 6pm.

Guápiles via Siquirres & Guácimo (Empresarios Guápileños; Terminal Caribeño) US$2, two hours, depart hourly 6am to 6pm.

Manzanillo (Mepe) US$2, 2½ hours, depart at 6am, 10:30am, 3pm and 6pm.

Moín, for boats to Tortuguero (Tracasa; Terminal Caribeño) US$0.25, 20 minutes, depart hourly 5:30am to 6:30pm.

Puerto Viejo de Talamanca (Mepe) US$1.75, 2½ hours, depart at 5am, 8am, 10am, 1pm, 4pm and 6pm.

San José (Autotransportes Caribeños; Terminal Caribeño) US$3.50, three hours, depart hourly 5am to 8pm.

CAR
There is only one gas station on the coast south of Limón, at the crossroads just north of Cahuita.

AROUND PUERTO LIMÓN
Isla Uvita
The wild green rock just 1km off the coast of Limón is most famous as the site of Columbus' landing on his last trans-Atlantic voyage. It is also a popular destination for surfers, for its thrilling – and often punishing – left that breaks on a reef. Those in the know claim that this is the most powerful left in Costa Rica, with 3m waves on good days. Isla Uvita is a 20-minute boat ride from Limón – ask around the pier to try to hire a boat. Pack a picnic, as there are no facilities on the island.

Playa Bonita
While not the finest beach in the Caribbean, **Playa Bonita** offers sandy stretches of seashore and good swimming convenient to Limón. Surfers make their way to Bonita for its point/ reef break, which makes for a powerful (and sometimes dangerous) left. Just north, **Portete** is a small bay with a wicked right working off the southerly point. Any Limón–Moín bus will drop you at these places.

SLEEPING & EATING
The road between Limón and Moín is home to some decent accommodations. The following are listed in order from Limón (east to west).

Oasys del Caribe (☎ 2795 0024; s/d/tr US$28/32/38; P ⊠) About 3km northwest of Puerto Limón, these cozy pink bungalows are decorated with lace curtains and bamboo furniture, worn sheets and clean towels. They are clustered around a small swimming pool, which is critical, as this place does not have beach access.

Hotel Maribú Caribe (☎ 2795 2543/2553; maribu@ racsa.co.cr; s/d/tr US$55/65/75; P ⊠ ⅏) Just west of Oasys del Caribe, several spacious white stucco bungalows are arranged atop a small hill amid tropical gardens. They all catch ocean breezes and enjoy good views, as does the Afro-Caribbean restaurant.

Cabinas Cocori (☎ 2795 1670; s/d/tr US$35/50/60; P ⊠ ⌨ ⅏) Enjoy your free continental breakfast as you watch the waves crash on the rocks below. This citrus-colored motel is the best deal on the beach, with cute, clean rooms and a breezy restaurant. About 4km out of Limón (2.5km from the Moín dock).

Two side-by-side beach restaurants provide excellent seaside dining, about 5km from Limón. At **Reina's** (☎ 2798 0879; mains US$6-8; ☺ 8am-last guest) loud music and good vibes make for a popular nighttime spot. Next door, **Quimbamba** (☎ 2795 4805; mains US$5-7; ☺ 8am-close) is similar, offering a shady spot to watch the soccer game on the beach. *Mariscos* (seafood) and *cervezas* (beer) are on the menus.

Moín

The reason you're here, no doubt, is to catch a boat through the canals to Parismina, Tortuguero or perhaps Barra del Colorado. There has always been a series of natural waterways between Limón and Barra del Colorado, but they could only be used by small dugouts during the rainy season. In 1974 canals linking the system were completed, eliminating the need for boats to go out to sea when traveling north from Moín.

GETTING THERE & AWAY

The journey by boat to Tortuguero can take anywhere from 1½ to five hours, depending on how often the boat stops to observe the copious wildlife along the way (many tours also stop for lunch). Indeed, it is worth taking your time. As you wind your way through these jungle canals, you are likely to spot howler monkey, morelot's crocodile, both two- and three-toed sloth and an amazing array of waterbird.

While this route is often used by tourist boats, it is not necessarily a regular transportation route to Tortuguero or Parismina (boats rarely go to Barra del Colorado). When canals north of Moín are blocked by water hyacinths or logjams, the route might be closed altogether. Schedules exist in theory only and they change frequently, depending on the boatload. If you are feeling lucky, you can just show up in Moín in the morning and try to get on one of the outgoing tour boats. But you are better off making a reservation in advance.

Associación de Boteros de los Canales de Tortuguero (Abacat; ☎ 8360 7325) In theory, Abacat operates a daily colectivo (small bus; US$30) to Tortuguero at 10am, although it may not run if there are not enough passengers.

Caribbean Tropical Tours (William Guerrero; ☎ 8371 2323; wguerrerotuca@hotmail.com) A highly recommended tour guide, with excellent sloth-spotting skills.

Moín–Parismina–Tortuguero water taxi (☎ 2709 8005) Departs Moín at 11am and Tortuguero at 1:30pm. Reservations are essential, especially if you are requesting a stop in Parismina.

Viajes al Tortuguero (Benjamin Gomez; ☎ 2795 0937; localbenjamin@hotmail.com) One way/round-trip US$30/50, departs from 9:30am to 10am. A member of the association of Boteros Independente de Moín. Again, the schedule is subject to change if there are not enough passengers.

Tracasa buses to Moín from Puerto Limón (US$0.25, 20 minutes) depart from Terminal Caribeño hourly from 5:30am to 6:30pm. Get off the bus before it goes over the bridge. If you are driving, it's worth leaving your car in a guarded lot in Limón.

NORTHERN CARIBBEAN

A vast network of rivers and canals wind their way through this remote region – Costa Rica's wettest. Lush forests, filled with water-birds and sleepy sloths, line the edges of these waterways. The long stretches of otherwise empty beaches are nesting grounds for three kinds of sea turtles, and more green turtles are born here than anywhere else on earth. It's not easy to get here – in fact it's accessible only by boat – but the Amazonian atmosphere is well worth the journey.

PARISMINA

At the southern end of Parque Nacional Tortuguero, and at the mouth of Río Parismina, this friendly village attracts two kinds of travelers: turtle lovers and tarpon lovers. Though not as famed as the beaches of Tortuguero, Parismina is the preferred breeding ground of hundreds of discriminating leatherback, green and hawksbill turtles; and the coastal waters are rife with record-breaking Atlantic tarpon.

Surrounded on all sides by jungle rivers and the Caribbean Sea, Barra de Parismina is accessible only by boat, which has allowed it to preserve a remote 'island' atmosphere. Legend has it that the village was founded by a pregnant woman named Mina, who was traveling down the Caribbean coast. When the time came for her to have her baby, her traveling companion told her, 'Here you give birth, Mina,' or '*Aqui pares, Mina.*' Thus the village was named.

Sportfishing is the traditional tourist draw to Parismina. The top tarpon season is from January to mid-May, while big snook are caught in Río Parismina from September to November.

More recently, with the growth of ecotourism, many travelers come to see (and protect) the endangered sea turtles. Leatherbacks nest on Parismina's beach between late February and early October, with the peak season in April and May. Green turtles begin nesting in June and the peak season is August and September. Hawksbills are not as common, but they are sometimes seen between February and September.

Information

There are no banks or post offices in Parismina. Credit cards and traveler's checks are not accepted, so be sure to bring as much cash as you need.

Asociación Salvemos Las Tortugas de Parismina Information Center (ASTOP; Save the Turtles of Parismina; ☎ 2710 7703; www.costaricaturtles.org; ☑ 9am-8pm daily Mar-Oct, 2-6pm Mon-Sat Nov-Feb) Organizes homestays (US$15), offers internet access (per hour US$1.50) and posts information about local tour guides (US$20), activities and events.

Sights & Activities

ASTOP has built a guarded **turtle hatchery** to deter increasing numbers of poachers and egg thieves. Travelers can volunteer as turtle guards to patrol the beaches alongside local 'turtle guides.' The daily fee of US$20 to US$25 includes three meals a day, lodging with a local family and turtle training (three-night minimum).

This local association is a wonderful way for travelers to get involved with the community; locals also offer Spanish lessons, Latin dance lessons, fishing trips and boat tours into Parque Nacional Tortuguero.

While villagers have traditionally depended on farming and fishing, the turtle project has become a crucial part of the local economy, as families depend on the income they receive from homestays and other activities. As explained in the ASTOP orientation materials, 'If you…support our turtle project, you support not only the turtles, but the whole town.'

The beach near Parismina is very rough, strewn with rubble and dangerous for swimming. However, a nearby lagoon – known as the **Barrita** – is a popular spot for a cooling dip or a picnic. Walk south along the beach or follow the road from the airstrip.

Across the river in Caño Blanco, Don Victor and his wife Isaura run the **Jardin Tropical** (☎ 2200 5567; admission free; ☑ 8am-5pm), an amazing heliconia farm. ASTOP organizes day trips to Caño Blanco, which include visiting a traditional Tico farm and riding horses to the Jardin Tropical (US$20 including transportation from Parismina).

Sleeping & Eating

Besides the options listed here, Soda Parismina, at the boat dock, serves simple meals.

Don Alex (☎ 2710 1892; camping per person with/ without kitchen use US$3/2, cabinas per person US$5) Alex at the hardware store offers sheltered tent sites with access to showers, bathrooms and a kitchen for a small charge, as well as simple cabinas.

Carefree Ranch (☎ 2710 3149; r per person US$10) Opposite the Catholic church, this simple clapboard house – bright yellow with green trim – gives you a lot of charm for your colones. Perks include newish bathrooms with hot water and family-style meals (available for an additional charge).

Iguana Verde (☎ 2710 1528; d with/without air-con US$25/10; ☒) Crazy Rick (or 'Loco Rico' as he is known) and his wife Yenri run this friendly spot, offering three clean rooms with private hot-water bathrooms. Rick is also a popular guide, offering highly entertaining guided hikes and boat tours. Rick and Yenri are both active in the turtle-conservation project, but who is looking out for the poor blue macaw that is caged out front?

Asociación Salvemos Las Tortugas de Parismina (☎ 2710 7703; www.costaricaturtles.com; r per person US$15) Although volunteers get first choice of accommodations, this organization can arrange homestays, including three meals, with a local family. All lodging is in private rooms with locking doors and shared bathroom facilities.

Río Parismina Lodge (☎ 2229 7597, in the USA 800-338 5688, 210-824 4442; www.riop.com; s/d 3 days US$2050/3700, 7 days US$3350/6200; ☒ ☒) Employing many Parismina residents, this deluxe fishing lodge caters to top-end tourists on all-inclusive vacations. Package prices include fishing, lodging in cushy cabins and transfers from San José, as well as three meals a day, which

TORTUGUERO FOR DUMMIES

OK, so you want to get to Tortuguero from San José, but rather than sign up for a package (which arranges transport, accommodations and tours) you'd rather the freedom of going independently. Tour companies, and airline touts will tell you it's very difficult to get there off your own steam. Don't listen to them. Instead follow these simple steps and you'll be in the land of turtles in no time.

- Take the 6:30am, 9am or 10:30am bus from San José's Caribbean terminal to Cariari (two hours).
- Once at Cariari's San José terminal, you need to walk to its other bus station. Turn right down the street in front of the terminal for a few hundred meters and you'll find the town's Caribbean terminal. If you have lots of luggage, take a taxi or any passing vehicle will take you for a hundred colones.
- Jump on any bus for La Pavona, which leave hourly from this terminal.
- The bus ride to La Pavona from Cariari takes about an hour, stopping at a decontamination point where you have to walk through disinfectant before entering the park.
- There should be a boat waiting to collect everyone from the bus to bring you to Tortuguero village. The boat journey (40 minutes) is spectacular and you should have your camera ready to get some snaps of some snappy crocs.

feature plenty of freshly brewed coffee and fabulous seafood.

Getting There & Away

Parismina is only accessible by boat, and the only regular service is to Siquirres, via Caño Blanco.

From Siquirres, take the **Caño-Aguilar bus** (☎ 2768 8172) to Caño Blanco (US$1.50, two hours) at 4:15am or 12:30pm Monday through Friday, 7:15am or 3:15pm Saturday and Sunday. Taxis make this run for about US$40. Boats to Parismina (US$2, 10 minutes) wait for the buses in Caño Blanco, departing at 6am and 3pm Monday through Friday, and 9am and 5pm Saturday and Sunday.

Boats leave from the Parismina dock to Caño Blanco at 5:30am and 2:30pm Monday through Friday, and at 8:30am and 4:30pm on Saturday and Sunday. Again, the buses wait for these water taxis, departing to Siquirres at 6am and 3pm Monday through Friday, and at 10am and 5pm on Saturday and Sunday.

A **water taxi** (☎ 2709 8005) is supposed to travel the route between Moín and Tortuguero every day (one way US$20), and can stop and pick up passengers in Parismina if they make advance arrangements. In theory, the taxi departs Moín at 11am, stopping in Parismina at noon, en route to Tortuguero. The return trip is at 1:30pm, stopping in Parismina at 2:30pm and continuing south to Moín. The boat driver will not stop in Parismina unless he knows passengers are waiting.

Otherwise, if you are trying to get to Tortuguero or Moín, your best bet is to hang around the dock in Caño Blanco and try to snag a spot on one of the tour boats passing through.

PARQUE NACIONAL TORTUGUERO

Parque Nacional Tortuguero is accessible from the village of Tortuguero in the north or from Parismina in the south.

'Humid' is the driest word that could truthfully be used to describe Tortuguero. With annual rainfall of up to 6000mm in the northern part of the park, it is one of the wettest areas in the country. There is no dry season, although it does rain less in February, March and October.

The famed **Canales de Tortuguero** are quite the introduction to this important park. Created to connect a series of naturally lazy lagoons and meandering rivers in 1969, this engineering marvel finally allowed inland navigation between Limón and the coastal villages in something sturdier than a dugout canoe (though you'll still see plenty of those). There are regular flights, sure, but a leisurely ride through the banana plantations and wild jungle is equal parts recreation and transportation.

This 31,187-hectare coastal park (plus about 52,000 hectares of marine area) is the

Caribbean's most important breeding ground for the green sea turtle (Chelonia mydas). Of the world's eight species of sea turtles, six nest in Costa Rica and four lay their eggs right here in Tortuguero.

These black-sand hatching grounds gave birth to the sea turtle-conservation movement. The Caribbean Conservation Corporation (p461), the first program of its kind in the world, has continuously monitored turtle populations here since 1955. Today, green sea turtles are increasing in numbers along this coast, but both the leatherback and hawksbill turtles are in decline (see boxed text, p64).

But Tortuguero is more than just turtles: from sloths and howler monkeys in the treetops, to the tiny frogs and green iguanas that crawl among the roots, to the mighty tarpon and endangered manatee that swim the waters, this place is thick with wildlife.

Orientation & Information

Park headquarters is at **Cuatro Esquinas** (☎ 2709 8086; 1-/3-day admission US$7/10; ☯ 5:30am-6pm with breaks for breakfast & lunch), just north of Tortuguero village. This is an unusually helpful ranger station, with maps, information and access to a 2km-loop nature trail. Wear your boots: it's muddy, even in the dry season.

Jalova Station (☯ 6am-6pm), accessible from Parismina by boat, is on the canal at the south entrance to the national park. Tour boats from Moín often stop here for a picnic; you will find a short nature trail, bathroom, drinking water and camping facilities.

Activities

HIKING

Behind Cuatro Esquinas station, **El Gavilan Land Trail** is the only public trail through the park that is on solid ground. Visitors can hike the muddy, 2km loop that traverses the tropical humid forest and follows a stretch of beach. Green parrots and several species of monkeys are commonly sighted here. The short trail is well marked and does not require a guide.

BOATING

Four aquatic trails wind their way through Parque Nacional Tortuguero, inviting canoe paddlers, kayakers and other boaters to explore the ins and outs of this wild place. **Río Tortuguero** acts as the entrance way to

the network of trails. This wide, beautiful river is often covered with water lilies and frequented by aquatic birds like heron (especially the great blue heron and the night heron), kingfisher and anhinga. The **Caño Chiquero** is thick with vegetation, especially red guacimo trees and epiphytes. Black turtles and green iguana like to hang out here. Caño Chiquero leads to two more waterways. **Caño Mora** is about 3km long but only 10m wide, so it feels like it's straight from Jungle Book. **Caño Harold** is actually an artificially constructed canal, but that doesn't stop the creatures – like Jesus Christ lizard and caiman – from inhabiting its tranquil waters. Canoe rental and boat tours are available in Tortuguero village (p462).

TURTLE-WATCHING

Sea turtles usually nest every two or three years. Depending on the species, a female may nest up to 10 times during one season. She comes ashore about two weeks after mating to lay her eggs on the beach.

Most female turtles share a nesting instinct that drives them to return to the beach of their birth, or natal beach, in order to lay their eggs. Often, a turtle's ability to successfully reproduce depends on the ecological health of this original habitat. Only the leatherback returns to a more general region, instead of a specific natal beach.

The female turtle digs a cavity in the sand using her flippers, and then lays 80 to 120 eggs in the cavity. She diligently covers the nest with sand to protect the eggs, and she may even create a false nest in another location

---

TORTUGUERO BY KAYAK

Unbeknown to many, you can explore Parque Nacional Tortuguero from Parismina, but the only access is by water. The wildlife is just as abundant as at the northern end of the park, and you are unlikely to run into any tour boats in this neck of the woods. Local guides take passengers in dugouts (inquire at ASTOP, p457) for about US$25. The truly adventurous (and experienced) can hire a kayak from Iguana Verde lodgings (p457) and go it alone, but make sure you have a detailed map and a compass. And don't forget to stop at Jalova Station (left) to pay your park admission fee.

DOING TIME FOR THE TURTLES

There are many opportunities to volunteer your time for the greater good of the turtles (and other creatures).

Asociación Nacional de Asuntos Indígenas (ANAI; ☎ 2224 3570, in San José 2277 7549; www.anaicr .org; Gandoca; registration US$35, camping US$8, homestays US$15, cabins US$30) At the other end of the Caribbean coast in the Refugio Nacional de Vida Silvestre Gandoca-Manzanillo (see p493).

Canadian Organization for Tropical Education and Rainforest Conservation (Coterc; ☎ 2709 8052, in Canada 905-831 8809; www.coterc.org; per day US$65) Volunteers help with the upkeep of the station and assist ongoing research projects, including sea turtle conservation, bird banding, and animal- and plant-diversity inventories. The daily fee covers room and board. Lodging is in a brand-new dormitory building, with full access to the facilities and grounds at the research station. Make advance arrangements for transportation from Tortuguero village.

Caribbean Conservation Corporation (CCC; ☎ 2709 8091, in the USA 800-678 7853; www.cccturtle.org) From March through October volunteers can assist scientists with turtle tagging and research on green and leatherback turtles. During bird-migration seasons (March through May and August through October) volunteers can receive training and assist with mist-netting, walking transects and point-counts. Programs range from one week (US$1400 to US$1600) to three weeks (US$2100 to US$2500); prices include dorm lodging, meals and transport from San José.

Asociación Salvemos Las Tortugas de Parismina (ASTOP; Save the Turtles of Parismina; ☎ 2710 5183, in the USA 538 8084; www.costaricaturtles.org; registration fee US$25, per day US$30) Good deeds for the financially challenged. Volunteers assist with turtle patrols and otherwise participate in the community of Parismina. See p457.

---

in an attempt to confuse predators. Then she makes her way back to the sea and the eggs are on their own.

Incubation ranges from 45 to 70 days. Hatchlings break out of their shells with a caruncle, or temporary tooth. Sometimes it takes several days for a group of hatchlings to dig their way up out of the nest cavity. The tiny hatchlings are small enough to fit in the palm of your hand. They crawl to the ocean in small groups, moving as quickly as possible to avoid dehydration and predators. Once they reach the surf, they must swim for at least 24 hours to get to deeper water, away from predators.

Visitors are allowed to check out the turtle rookeries at night from March to October (late July through August is prime time) and observe eggs being laid or hatching. Obviously, turtle sightings are not guaranteed. A licensed guide must accompany all visitors. Local lodges operate these tours for between US$10 and US$30 per person. Local guides charge about US$10. Flashlights and any type of camera or video camera are not allowed on the beach (see boxed text, p270). Dark clothing is strongly recommended.

If you're unable to visit during the peak green turtle-breeding season, the next best time is April, when leatherback turtles nest in small numbers. Hawksbill turtles nest sporadically from March to October, and log-

gerhead turtles are also sometimes seen. For information about volunteering with turtle patrols, see boxed text, above.

OTHER WILDLIFE-WATCHING

Parque Nacional Tortuguero is, without a doubt, one of Costa Rica's top wildlife destinations. To get the best from Tortuguero, be on the water early or go out following rain. As soon as the downpour clears, mammals, birds and reptiles come out into the open to sunbathe and dry out. They're most conspicuous on the rain-forest edges lining the wide main canals.

More than 300 bird species, both resident and migratory, have been recorded in Tortuguero. Due to the wet habitat, the park is especially rich in heron (14 different kinds), kingfisher and wader. In September and October, look for huge flocks of migratory species like eastern kingbird, barn swallow and purple martin. The Caribbean Conservation Corporation (opposite) conducts a biannual monitoring program, in which volunteers can participate. Great green macaw are a highlight. They are most common from December to April, when the almendro trees are fruiting.

Certain species of mammals are particularly evident and relaxed in Tortuguero, especially mantled howler, Central American spider monkey and white-faced capuchin, as well as both two- and three-toed sloth. Normally shy neotropical river otters are reasonably habituated to boats.

Turtles and turtle eggs are one of the favorite foods of jaguar, and turtle-watchers occasionally encounter these big cats, who swim the Laguna del Tortuguero to patrol the beach for nesting turtles. Tortuguero is also possibly Costa Rica's best chance to spot West Indian manatees.

Sleeping

Cuatro Esquinas ranger station has been closed to camping for the foreseeable future, but you can camp at **Jalova Station** (per person US$2) at the southern end of the park. Choose your spot (and season) carefully, as parts of the camping area can become submerged after heavy rainfall.

TORTUGUERO VILLAGE

Wholly surrounded by protected forest and sea, accessible only by air or water, this magical spot is best known for the hordes of hatchling turtles that lurch across its dark sands. Indeed, the name Tortuguero means 'turtle place.' For the 'turtle season,' which peaks from late July through August, make all reservations well in advance.

Once the turtles are safely out at sea, however, both park and village sort of fall off the radar screen. Perhaps it is because these luxuriant jungles rank among the rainiest of all rain forests, and thus are threaded by canals and rivers that are your only way into this place. It's not easy to get to, but it's worth it.

Tortuguero is a quieter destination than others on the Caribbean coast, and the vine-draped trails that weave through the lush, slender peninsula are frequented by a host of wild creatures. This is where the line between sea and dry land is blurred, which may be the reason why so many sea turtles, caught by a trick of evolution between these two worlds, begin their lives here.

It's certainly why so many fishermen originally settled this spot, and the recipes they stirred from the jungle and ocean are still served up faithfully by folks around town.

Information

Small hotels, tour operators and transportation providers compete fiercely for business in Tortuguero. Unfortunately, that means you won't always get a straight answer when you ask for information. Places offering 'Free Tourist Information' are often hawking tours; and friendly 'advice' about lodging and transportation is sometimes outright lies.

Note that there are no banks or ATMs in town. Only a few businesses accept credit cards, so bring all the cash that you will need.

La Casona (☎ 2709 8092; per hr US$2; 🕑 8:30am-9pm) There is a small internet café with two computers behind La Casona restaurant (p463).

Paraíso Tropical Store (☎ 2710 0323) Sells souvenirs and NatureAir airline tickets and cashes traveler's checks.

Tortuguero Info Center (☎ 2709 8055; tortuguero _info@racsa.co.cr; per hr US$3; 🕑 8am-7pm) An independent information center that sells Sansa airline tickets and provides internet access. It is across from the Catholic church.

Sights

About 200m north of Tortuguero village, the **Caribbean Conservation Corporation** (CCC; ☎ 2709 8091, in the USA 800-678 7853; www.cccturtle.org; admission US$1; 🕑 10am-noon & 2-5pm Mon-Sat, noon-5pm Sun) operates a research station that has a small visitor center and museum. Exhibits focus on all things turtle-related, including a video about the history of local turtle conservation. For volunteer opportunities, see boxed text, opposite.

The **Canadian Organization for Tropical Education and Rainforest Conservation** (Coterc; ☎ 2709 8052, in Canada 905-831 8809; www.coterc.org; admission free) is the nonprofit organization that operates the Estación Biológica Caño Palma, 7km north of Tortuguero village. The onsite rancho (thatched-roof or open-air building) houses a museum that contains the station's collection of biological specimens – mainly an impressive though eerie collection of skulls from the area. You can also get up close with some serious insects, and there is a growing display of labeled seeds and fruit. If you'd rather look at live animals, a network of trails leads into the rain forest. This place is surrounded on three sides by water, so you'll have to hire a boat to get here. Coterc also has a volunteer program (again, see boxed text, opposite).

Activities
CANOEING

Signs all over Tortuguero advertise boat tours and boats for hire. This is obviously the best way to explore the waterways of the national park and the surrounding environs (see p459).

CARIBBEAN COAST

For boat tours, see right. You can paddle yourself in a dugout canoe for about US$2 per person per hour, but make sure you have a good map. Rent canoes at accommodations such as Hotel Miss Junie and La Casona or other places around town. This is an excellent way to see nature without disturbing the wildlife and with full access to all the nooks and crannies of the park.

HIKING
Apart from hiking in the park (see p459), hikers can climb the 119m **Cerro Tortuguero**, an extinct volcano about 6km north of the village within the Refugio Nacional de Silvestre Barra del Colorado. You need to hire a boat and guide to get there, and the 45-minute

hike to the top is muddy, steep and strenuous. The trek offers an excellent chance of spotting colorful poison-dart frog. And it is the highest point right on the coast anywhere north of Puerto Limón, so the views of the forest, canals and village are unparalleled. Unfortunately, this trail was closed for maintenance at the time of research; inquire further when you arrive in Tortuguero.

Tours
Guides have posted signs all over town advertising their services for canal tours and turtle walks. Ask at the **Tortuguero Info Center** (☎ 2709 8055; tortuguero_info@racsa.co.cr) or at **Soda El Muellecito** (⏱ 6:30am-8pm), across from Super Morpho Pulpería, to get in touch with a guide. Going rates are about US$10 per person for a two-hour turtle tour, and US$15 for a three- or four-hour hiking or boat excursion. It's also worth noting that many locals blame the big motorboats that herd groups around as a major reason for scaring off the manatees, so it's probably more ethical to take a kayak tour.

Recommended local guides:

Barbara Hartung (☎ 2709 8004) Offers hiking, canoe and turtle tours in German, English, French or Spanish. Also offers a unique tour about Tortuguero history, culture and medicinal plants.

Castor Hunter Thomas (☎ 2709 8050; ask at Soda Doña María, p464)

Chico (☎ 2709 8033; ask at Cabinas Miss Miriam, opposite) Chico's hiking and canoe tours receive rave reviews from readers.

Daryl Loth (☎ 8833 0827, 2709 8011; safari@racsa .co.cr) This knowledgeable Canadian naturalist (formerly of Coterc) offers excellent boat trips in an environmentally friendly, supersilent electric motorboat, as well as turtle tours (in season) and guided hikes to Cerro Tortuguero.

Sleeping
Competition for business is fierce. Unfortunately, it often results in unethical 'touts' trying to lure tourists to an establishment where they will get a commission. Don't make any decisions about where to stay without exploring your options and looking at the rooms being offered.

TORTUGUERO VILLAGE
There is a wide range of budget and midrange options here. The following places are listed in order from south (near the park entrance) to north.

Tropical Lodge (☎ 8826 6246; r per person US$10) This colorful and classically Caribbean setup behind the food store Tienda Bambú has cute yellow cabinas right on the river. While the exterior is bright, the interior is dank concrete.

our pick Cabinas Princesa Resort (☎ 2709 8107; s/d US$15/30) The best of the three Princesa hotels (there are others south of the soccer field and on the river) is the prettiest budget option in town. The lovely clapboard colonial house looks over a trim hammock-strung garden that stretches out to the crashing ocean only meters away.

La Casona (☎ 2709 8092; lacasonadetortuguero@yahoo .com; s/d US$15/25; ☐) Long a favorite for eating, this friendly, family-run spot opposite the main dock is now an excellent sleeping option too. Handsome new rooms have tiled floors and sparkling hot-water bathrooms. Jenny and her sons offer canoe rental, as well as an interesting tour to an ecological finca in Guápiles. This is one of the few places that accepts credit cards.

Cabinas Miss Miriam (☎ 2709 8002, 8821 2037; s/d US$15/30) A top choice, at the soccer field. Miss Miriam's rooms (actually run by her daughter) have tiled floors and firm beds, while those upstairs share a balcony with dramatic sea views. Miss Miriam's restaurant is one of Tortuguero's top spots for Caribbean fare.

Casa Marbella (☎ 8833 0827; http://casamarbella.tripod .com; s/d US$35/40) Filling the void between budget hotels and luxury lodges, this five-room B&B opposite the Catholic church features light-filled rooms with fans suspended from the high ceilings and private hot-water showers. Room rates include a hearty breakfast, perhaps served on the shady riverside patio. Owner Daryl Loth also organizes excellent area tours.

Hotel Miss Junie (☎ 2709 8029, in San José 2709 7102; s/d US$25/40) At the northern end of the village, Miss Junie's place is set on wide, grassy grounds, shaded by palm trees and strewn with hammocks. One side faces the river, while the other looks out to sea, so you can't go wrong. The clean, comfortable rooms smell of disinfectant, so you'll appreciate the big screened windows that let in the breeze. Prices include a full breakfast by Tortuguero's most celebrated cook (see Miss Junie's, p464).

NORTH OF THE VILLAGE

Lodges north of town cater primarily to groups on package deals, usually including transpor-

tation from San José, all meals and a guided tour through the park. Note that lodges on the west side of the lagoon don't have beach – or turtle – access. All these lodges will accept walk-ins if they aren't full, but only Mawamba Lodge can be walked to; others will pick you up. The following are listed from south to north, and all rates are per person, based on double occupancy, including meals.

Pachira Lodge (☎ 2256 7080, in the USA 800-644 7438; www.pachiralodge.com; 2-night package per adult/ child US$269/100; ☒) Rocky, Flintstones-style pathways lead through the landscaped jungle grounds, from the beautiful buffet-style restaurant to your pastel room in the rain forest. This place is right on the Laguna Tortuguero, opposite the CCC visitor center at the north end of the village. Across Laguna Penitencia, the lodge also operates the Evergreen Lodge, which has more privacy but smaller rooms. This is also where you will find the region's only canopy tour (US$25).

Mawamba Lodge (☎ in San José 2293 8181; www .grupomawamba.com; 2-night package per adult/child US$280/144; ☒) Rustic rooms are airy and spacious, with fan and hot shower, all fronted by a veranda with hammocks and rocking chairs. A network of trails leads into the rain forest and to the beach, while the fully equipped recreation room will entertain kids of all ages. But the real draw is that you can walk to town, unlike guests at most of the other lodges.

Samoa Lodge (☎ 2258 6244; www.samoalodge.com; 2-night package US$240; ☒) On the far side of Laguna Penitencia, colorful A-frame bungalows are nestled into tropical gardens. The rooms are simple, but brightly painted in citrus tones and furnished with bamboo and hardwood. The restaurant is recommended for the fusion creations from the kitchen.

Ilan Ilan Lodge (☎ 2296 7378, 2296 7502; www.mi tour.com; r US$40, 2-night package US$215; ☒) Named for the pretty-scented yellow-flowered tree that adorns the grounds. Smallish, fan-cooled rooms are arranged around a rather overgrown courtyard that the birds adore. This hotel is set on 8 hectares between the Lagunas Tortuguero and Penitencia, with a network of trails connecting them. It's a good place to spot poison-dart frogs and other critters.

our pick Tortuga Lodge & Gardens (☎ 2257 0766, 2222 0333; www.costaricaexpeditions.com; s/d US$116/140, 2-night package per person US$379; ☒) This cushy lodge is operated by Costa Rica Expeditions. Superior rooms are spacious and screened, and rocking chairs and hammocks await invitingly in covered walkways outside. Beyond the restaurant, an enticing free-form swimming pool flows serenely by, mirroring the languid movement of the canals. The lodge is on 20 hectares of landscaped gardens, with private trails and a quiet pond.

Turtle Beach Lodge (☎ 2248 0707, after hr 8837 6969; www.turtlebeachlodge.com; 2-night package per adult/child US$275/110; ⊠) Flanked on either side by the beach and the river, this lodge is surrounded by 70 hectares of tropical gardens and rain forest. Spacious, elegant rooms have hardwood furniture and huge screened windows to let in the breezes. You can explore the grounds on the network of jungle trails, or lounge around the turtle-shaped pool or in the thatch-roofed hammock hut.

Eating

One of Tortuguero's unsung pleasures is the cuisine: the homey restaurants lure you in from the rain with steaming platters of Caribbean-style seafood. The following restaurants are listed from south to north.

Soda Doña María (☎ 2709 8050; ⊗ 7am-8pm) Recover from a hike in the park at this riverside *soda*, serving fresh *jugos* (juices) and other cold drinks. Just north of the park entrance.

Miss Miriam's (☎ 2709 8002; mains US$5-8, lobster US$12) It's worth blowing off your lodge's meal plan and getting a boat into town just for this fine food, from delicious *gallo pinto* (rice and beans) to whole lobsters served up by Miss Miriam's friendly and fabulous daughter. It's at the soccer field.

Buddha Cafe (☎ 2709 8084; meals US$4-8; ⊗ 9am-9pm) If the New Age music doesn't lure you inside, the aromas of fresh-from-the-oven pizza certainly will. Peruse the menu before deciding, however, as it features many tempting options: savory crepes, filled with grilled shrimp or chicken and cheese; and the namesake Buddasalata, with avocado, sweet corn and *palmito* (palm hearts). It's just a short walk north of the boat dock.

La Caribeña (meals US$3-5; ⊗ 8am-10pm) A simple enough place that serves up spicy Caribbean fare to tourists and locals alike. It's worth ducking your head in to find out if they're serving *rondón* (an exceptional seafood stew, not to be missed) as a special that day.

Dorling Bakery (☎ 8845 6389; pastries US$1-3; ⊗ 6am-8pm) Outstanding homemade breads

and pastries baked fresh every day get you even more wired when combined with good coffee and espresso beverages. It's cozy.

ourpick Miss Junie's (☎ 2709 8029; dinner US$9-15; ⊗ 6-9pm) The great thing about quality Caribbean-style meals – and this place is Tortuguero's best-known restaurant – is that the longer seafood and veggies simmer in coconut sauce, the better they taste. This is why you should order dinner early in the day. It's worth it.

Grab groceries at the **Super Morpho Pulpería** (☎ 2709 8110; ⊗ 6:30am-9pm Mon-Sat, 8am-8pm Sun).

Drinking

La Taberna (☎ 2710 6716; ⊗ 11:30am-close) Adjacent to Tropical Lodge, and overlooking Laguna Tortuguero, this tavern is Tortuguero's most popular and pleasant spot for a drink. It's particularly enjoyable in the afternoon, when you'll appreciate the cool breezes off the canal, the ice-cold *cerveza* and the sun dropping behind the trees. There's also a karaoke mic, for when things get rowdier.

La Culebra (⊗ 8pm-close) The only nightclub in town is a barren concrete space where thumping music makes for a good dance floor, or you can retire to the waterside bar area for a beer and a *boca*. This place rocks during turtle season. It's next to the boat dock.

Getting There & Away

First of all, it is not *that* hard to get here on your own. However, if you do not care to go it alone, the options for package tours are everywhere, from the moment your airplane lands in San José. Most include meals, lodging, transportation and at least one canal tour. Costs vary widely depending on accommodations and transportation.

Jungle Tom Safaris (☎ 2280 0243; www.jungletom safaris.com) Two-night packages US$119 to US$240. Also offers a one-day trip from San José (US$79) or just round-trip transportation (US$59) – useful for independent travelers who want to be free upon arrival, but don't want the hassle of getting here alone.

Learning Trips (☎ 2258 2293, 8396 1979; www.costa-rica.us) One-/two-night packages US$155/195. Packages include lodging, meals, boat tours and transportation from San José.

Riverboat Francesca Nature Tours (☎ 2226 0986; www.tortugerocanals.com) Two-day packages US$175 to US$190. Highly recommended tours on the riverboat *Francesca*. Prices include food and lodging, canal tours and a nighttime turtle walk (in season).

CARIBBEAN COAST

AIR

The small airstrip is 4km north of Tortuguero village. **NatureAir** (☎ 2220 3054) and **Sansa** (☎ 2709 8055) both have daily flights to and from San José – one way/round-trip US$68/136 with NatureAir, US$63/126 with Sansa. Many of the upscale lodges offer transportation by charter flight as a part of their package tours.

BOAT

Tortuguero is accessible by boat from Cariari or Moín. If you are traveling to Parismina, you should be able to get one of the boats to Moín to drop you off on the way.

To/From Cariari

The most common and least expensive route to/from Tortuguero is through Cariari, from where you can catch buses to San José or Puerto Limón (via Guápiles). Three companies provide transportation along this route for US$10 per person:

Clic Clic (☎ 8844 0463) Via La Pavona, 6am and 11:30am.

Coopetraca (☎ 2767 7137) Via La Pavona, 6am, 11:30am and 3pm.

Viajes Bananeros (☎ 2709 8005) Via La Geest, 7am and 11am.

Buy tickets on the boat or at any of the information centers around Tortuguero. Once you arrive in La Pavona or La Geest, a bus will pick you up and take you to Cariari (buses meet the boats). If you are traveling to San José, you are better off taking a 6am boat because bus connections are better earlier in the day.

If you are coming to Tortuguero through Cariari, you may be greeted by touts luring you onto their buses and boats. Despite what they insist, the common route to Tortuguero is through La Pavona. Coopatreca buses for La Pavona depart from the central bus terminal in Siquirres, behind the police station, at 6am, noon and 3pm. The private Bananero boat company also provides transportation from Cariari to Tortuguero via Geest. Bananero buses leave from the San José bus terminal at 1:30pm and 3:30pm. See also p449.

Transportation schedules and fares for Tortuguero change frequently. For the latest details, see www.geocities.com/tortuguero info/main.html.

To/From Moín

Moín–Tortuguero is primarily a tourist route. While tour boats ply these canals frequently, there is not a reliable, regularly scheduled service.

In theory, **Viajes Bananeros** (☎ 2709 8005; www .tortuguero-costarica.com) offers a daily transfer to Moín at 10am in the high season (US$30).

Otherwise, you can check with the **Tortuguero Info Center** (☎ 2709 8015; tortuguero_info@ racsa.co.cr) to try to find out about tour boats going to Moín that might have space for independent travelers. In any case, call to confirm: schedules change, or they may not run if there are not enough passengers.

BARRA DEL COLORADO

At 90,400 hectares, including the frontier zone with Nicaragua, Refugio Nacional de Vida Silvestre Barra del Colorado, or 'Barra' for short, is the biggest national wildlife refuge in Costa Rica.

It forms a regional conservation unit with the adjacent Parque Nacional Tortuguero, and their landscapes are similar. The refuge has 50km of coastline, and countless square kilometers of canals, lagoons, rivers and marshes. Some hilly areas, none higher than 230m, are ancient volcanic cones (like Cerro Tortuguero). Rain – lots of it – falls year-round.

The Ríos San Juan, Colorado and Chirripó all wind through the refuge and eventually make their way to the Caribbean Sea. The alluvial plain is often flooded, which means the whole place is very marshy, with various islets occasionally appearing and disappearing. The only feasible way to get around is by boat.

Barra is much more remote, more expensive and more difficult to visit than Tortuguero, but adventurous travelers will be rewarded with a wildlife bonanza. The area is home to the endangered West Indian manatee, caiman, crocodile and tarpon. Mammals that live here include four kinds of big cat and two species of monkey, as well as Baird's tapir and three-toed sloth. The bird population includes the colorful keel-billed toucan and the great green macaw, raptor such as osprey and white hawk, as well as many waterbirds.

The northern border of the refuge is the Río San Juan, the border with Nicaragua (many local residents are Nicaraguan nationals). This area was politically sensitive during the 1980s, which contributed to the isolation of the reserve. Since the relaxing of Sandinista-Contra hostilities in 1990, it has become straightforward to journey north along the Río Sarapiquí and east along the San Juan, technically entering Nicaragua (see boxed text, opposite). However, while Costa Ricans have right of use, the Río San Juan is Nicaraguan territory. Other territorial disputes in this area mean that tensions between the countries still exist; carry your passport when you are out fishing.

Orientation & Information

The village of Barra del Colorado lies near the mouth of the Río Colorado and is divided by the river into Barra del Norte and Barra del Sur. There are no roads. The airstrip is on the south side of the river, but more people live on the north side. The area outside the village is swampy and travel is almost exclusively by boat, though some walking is possible around some of the lodges.

The Servicio de Parques Nacionales (SPN) maintains a small **ranger station** (refuge admission US$6) near the village, on the south side of the Río Colorado. However, there are no facilities here. Stop by **Diana's Souvenirs** (☎ 2710 6592), close to the airport, for weather reports, tourist information, internet access or a public telephone.

Activities

FISHING

Despite the incredible wildlife-watching opportunities, fishing is still the bread and butter of most of the area's lodges. Anglers go for tarpon from January to June and snook from September to December. Fishing is good year-round, however, and other tasty catches include barracuda, mackerel and jack crevalle, all inshore; or bluegill, *guapote* (rainbow bass) and machaca in the rivers. There is also deep-sea fishing for marlin, sailfish and tuna, though this sort of fishing is probably better on the Pacific. Dozens of fish can be hooked on a good day, so 'catch and release' is an important conservation policy of all the lodges.

CANOEING & KAYAKING

The best way to explore the rivers and lagoons of the refuge is by boat. If you are not fishing, you can paddle these waterways in a canoe or kayak, available from some of the local lodges. Silver King Lodge rents 5m aluminum canoes, which are used both for fishing and for exploring the backwater lagoons.

Sleeping & Eating

From the airport, only Tarponland Cabinas and Río Colorado Lodge are accessible on foot. All other lodges require a boat ride (a boat operator will be waiting for you at the airport if you have a reservation). Packages include air transfers from San José, all fishing, accommodations, meals and an open bar. Trips of varying lengths can be arranged.

Tarponland Cabinas (☎ 2710 2141; r per person US$25, d with sportfishing US$295; ⛀) This is it as far as budget lodgings go in Barra. Within walking distance from the airport, these basic hardwood rooms are pretty run-down, but there is a good onsite restaurant.

Río Colorado Lodge (☎ 2232 4063, in the USA 800-243 9777; www.riocoloradolodge.com; r per person with/without fishing US$450/120; ⛀ ⛀) Built in 1971, this is the longest-established lodge on the Caribbean coast. The rambling tropical-style buildings near the mouth of the Río Colorado are constructed on stilts, with covered walkways that make a lot of sense in the rain forest. Rooms are breezy and pleasant. For relaxation after a day of fishing the lodge features a happy hour with free rum drinks, a pool table, a breezy outdoor deck and satellite TV. This is the only upscale lodge from which you can walk to the airport; the local crowd it attracts has earned it a reputation as a 'party lodge.' Rates include meals.

Silver King Lodge (☎ 2711 0708, in the USA 800-847 3474; www.silverkinglodge.net; r per person US$135, 3-day package per person US$1875, extra day US$325; ⛀ ⛀ ⛀) This excellent sportfishing lodge caters to couples and families, besides just fishers. Huge hardwood guestrooms have beautiful 3.5m cane ceilings, colorful woven tapestries and plenty of amenities. Outside, covered walkways lead to the waterfall-filled pool, an international buffet-style restaurant and an open-air bar serving tropical drinks (like the specialty 'Funky Monkey'). This lodge closes in July and December.

Casa Mar Lodge (☎ in the USA 800-543 0282; www .casamarlodge.com; 5-night package per person US$2495-3100) When CEOs hang a 'gone fishing' sign on the office door, you can bet this is the type of place they've gone to. Luxurious cabins with nicely tiled hot showers are set in a pleasant 2.8-hectare garden that attracts lots of birds, and meals are home-cooked. But the real drawcards are the big-engine boats and the impressive 75kg tarpon that make the covers of all those sportfishing maga-

---

GETTING TO SAN JUAN DEL NICARAGUA

Day trips along the Río San Juan and some offshore fishing trips technically enter Nicaraguan territory. Carry your passport and US$10, in the unlikely event that you are stopped and checked.

If you are planning to head further into Nicaragua, you can make arrangements with your lodge (or hire a boat independently for about US$300) to take you to the border town of San Juan del Norte – now called San Juan del Nicaragua, in light of the recent border disputes. Though you can get your passport stamped here, you should probably check with immigration officials in San José before doing this independently. (If you are coming from Nicaragua into Costa Rica here, you will need to get your passport stamped in Limón.)

San Juan del Nicaragua, at the mouth of the Río San Juan, is a tranquil village with very few services but an interesting history. Founded in 1549, it became something of a boomtown when English settlers took over in 1847, naming it 'Greytown.' During the gold rush, the Río San Juan became an important transportation route connecting the Atlantic and the Pacific. Huge amounts of cargo, travelers and money passed through this town. Today, the former Greytown is more of a ghost town: only ruins remain from this heyday.

The 'living' (though very wet) village of San Juan del Nicaragua is across the bay. **Río Indio Lodge** (☎ 8381 1549, 2296 0095, in the USA 866-593 3176; www.rioindiolodge.com; s/d US$200/225; 🖳 🖭) has 34 spacious rooms, a gourmet restaurant and a well-stocked bar. Sportfishing is the lodge's forte, but you can also hike on the old railroad track that remains from the Greytown days or kayak on Laguna Silico.

San Juan del Norte is linked with the rest of Nicaragua by irregular passenger boats sailing up the San Juan to San Carlos, on Lago de Nicaragua.

---

zines. Incidentally, you may have seen the owner, Bill Barnes, in one of those magazines, as he currently holds the world record for catching a 12kg snook on a fly rod.

Getting There & Away

By far the easiest way to Barra is by air, and both Sansa (one way/round-trip US$63/126) and NatureAir (US$68/136) will drop you off here on their daily Tortuguero runs.

There is no regular boat service to Barra, although you may be able to arrange a boat ride from Tortuguero (US$50 per boat), Puerto Viejo de Sarapiquí (p518; US$60 per boat) or Moín (p456; for a price). During the dry season, buses run from Cariari (see p449) to Puerto Lindo, from where you can try to hop on a lodge boat or a water taxi continuing on to Barra.

SOUTHERN CARIBBEAN

This is the heart and soul of Costa Rica's Afro-Caribbean community. Jamaicans were brought here by United Fruit to build the backbone of the original banana republic and they learned to call this country home. For more than half a century, the communities of the southern Caribbean existed almost independent of the rest of the country, turning to subsistence farming and fishing when the banana plantations, and later cacao fincas, fell to devastating blights.

These Afro-Caribbean communities had good neighbors among the ancient indigenous groups, now encompassed by the nearby Cocles/KéköLdi, Talamanca Cabécar and Bribrí reserves. The two peoples, isolated from the goings-on of mainstream Costa Rica, exchanged the ancient wisdom of medicinal plants, agriculture and jungle survival, and they thrived.

Although the racial borders fell in 1949, electricity, roads and phones all came late to this perfect stretch of beachfront property. The result of all this isolation is a culture still largely independent of everyday Costa Rica.

Inevitably, however, improved infrastructure and an expanding tourism industry are inexorably wearing away the cultural quirks that many folks come to experience. Puerto Viejo in particular has experienced an influx of North American and European transplants, starting with surfers but now including all kinds of folks looking for a change of pace. (And with this picture-perfect setting and low-key vibe, who can blame them?)

Not to worry, not yet anyway: the music of the islands is everywhere, reggae and calypso pouring from homes and businesses into the streets. The cuisine is extraordinary, where even the simplest rice-and-beans dish conjures flavors of Jamaica. And while most residents speak Spanish, a patois of English remains common, if a little bit difficult to decipher for those unused to it.

Dangers & Annoyances

The southern Caribbean gets a bad rap for being dangerous, with Pacific-coasters warning about hurricanelike weather, prohibitively bad roads and rampant theft and drug use. Most of these warnings are exaggerated. But as in the rest of Costa Rica, it is wise to take the usual precautions: lock your hotel room; don't leave anything in your car; never leave gear unattended on beaches; don't walk the beaches alone at night. While drug use is not uncommon in some places, most residents do not condone or appreciate this activity. Remember that buying drugs is illegal as well as dangerous.

RESERVA BIOLÓGICA HITOY-CERERE

One of the most rugged and rarely visited reserves in the country, **Hitoy-Cerere** (☎ 2795 1446; admission US$6; ⏰ 8am-4pm) is only about 60km south of Limón (half that distance as the crow flies). The 9950-hectare reserve sits on the edge of the Cordillera de Talamanca, characterized by varying altitudes, evergreen forests and rushing rivers. This may be one of the wettest reserves in the parks system; its evergreen forests are inundated with 4000mm to 6000mm of rain annually.

Wildlife is abundant in this moist, humid forest. The most commonly sighted mammals include the woolly opossum, gray four-eyed opossum, tayra, howler monkey and white-faced capuchin. You can hardly miss the Montezuma oropendola, whose nests are suspended from trees like unexpected pendulums. Other ornithological highlights include the keel-billed toucan, spectacled owl and green kingfisher.

The reserve is surrounded by some of the country's most remote indigenous reserves, which you can visit with a local guide (see opposite, and boxed text, p494).

Although there is a ranger station at the reserve entrance, there are no other facilities nearby. A 9km trail leads south from the ranger station, but it is steep, slippery and poorly maintained.

Getting There & Away

By car (4WD recommended), head west on the signed road to Valle de la Estrella and Penshurst (just south of the Río Estrella bridge). Another small sign at the bus stop sends you down a good dirt road about 15km to the reserve.

By public transport, catch a bus from Limón to Valle de la Estrella. From the end of the bus line (Fortuna/Finca 6) you can hire a taxi to take you the rest of the way and pick you up at a prearranged time (US$25).

You can also arrange taxis and guided hikes, including transportation, from Cahuita. **Cahuita Tours** (☎ 2755 0000/0232) offers an all-day guided hike, departing at 6am for optimal wildlife-sighting, for US$100 per person.

CAHUITA

While neighboring Puerto Viejo is rapidly developing into a can't-miss destination on the groovier travel circuit, Cahuita has managed to maintain a more relaxed relationship with folks discovering the Caribbean coast. Most of the businesses are still locally owned and the vibe is still very laidback.

What's more, the place is breathtakingly beautiful. The black sand gives the very swimmable Playa Negra an unusual and ethereal presence.

While the Bribrí and Cabécar Indians were the original inhabitants of this area (see boxed text, p494), Cahuita claims the first Afro-Caribbean settler, one turtle fisherman named William Smith, who moved his family to Punta Cahuita in 1828. Mr Smith's descendents – and the descendents of many other immigrants – are now cooking with coconuts in the kitchen and playing reggae music on the radio, giving this town a decidedly Afro-Caribbean flavor.

Along with excellent meals and quality beach time, an itinerary in this relaxed paradise certainly includes a wander into neighboring Parque Nacional Cahuita, only a five-minute walk from 'downtown.' Here are even more perfect beaches, trails through protected jungle and one of Costa Rica's two living coral reefs.

With the Playa Negra stretching out to the north of town, and the Parque Nacional Cahuita immediately to the south, Cahuita's little center is nestled into a small point that sticks out into the Caribbean Sea. It consists of only two gravel roads, neither of which sees too much traffic. But that doesn't stop the

CARIBBEAN COAST

townsfolk from spending the afternoon sitting in the shade and watching it pass by.

Information

Banco de Costa Rica (9am-4pm Mon-Fri) The ATM here works on Plus and Visa systems.

Centro Turístico Brigitte (2755 0053; www.brigitte cahuita.com; Playa Negra; per hr US$2; 7am-6pm) Internet access.

Internet Palmer (per hr US$2; 9am-8pm)

Mercado Safari (6am-4pm) Changes US and Canadian dollars, euros, Swiss francs, British pounds and traveler's checks but has a steep commission.

Spencer Seaside Lodging (2755 0210/027; per hr US$2; 8am-8pm) Internet access.

Willie's Tours (8843 4700; per hr US$2; 8am-8pm Mon-Sat, 4-8pm Sun) Internet access.

Dangers & Annoyances

Women should know that Cahuita enjoys a free-love reputation and evidently some female travelers do come here for a quick fling. Be prepared to pay your gent's way around town and bring (and use!) your own condoms.

Sights & Activities

SWIMMING & SURFING

At the northwest end of Cahuita, **Playa Negra** is a long, black-sand beach flying the *bandera azul ecológica*, which is a flag that indicates the beach is kept to the highest ecological standards. This is undoubtedly Cahuita's top spot for swimming. Most importantly, it is far enough from town to never be crowded.

Unknown to many surfers, Playa Negra has an excellent beach break. It is not one of the regular stops on the Costa Rica surfer circuit, which means more waves for you. Conditions are best in the early morning, especially with a swell from the south or east. Sign up for a lesson (US$25 for two hours) or just rent a board at the Beach House (p475). Closer to the beach, Centro Turístico Brigitte (below) may also give lessons.

The relatively remote Playa Negra contrasts with the **Playa Blanca** at the entrance to the national park (see p476).

Tours

Snorkeling, sportfishing and horseback riding are standard offerings:

Cahuita Tours (2755 0000/0232) One of the oldest established agencies in town, this place offers guided hikes to the Hitoy-Cerere (opposite) and all-day trips to the Reserva Indígena Talamanca Bribrí (US$55).

Centro Turístico Brigitte (2755 0053; www .brigittecahuita.com) Brigitte specializes in horseback-riding tours (three/five hours per person US$35/45) along the beach or to jungle waterfalls. Also an excellent place to rent a bike (per day US$8).

Roberto's Tours (2755 0117) Arranges snorkeling trips and dolphin tours in the national park, but Roberto's real claim to fame is inshore/offshore sportfishing (per person US$60/300). Bonus: after all your hard work, Roberto can have your haul cooked for dinner in his recommended restaurant.

Willie's Tours (8843 4700; www.willies-costarica -tours.com) Willie's signature tour takes visitors to visit a Bribrí family and a KéköLdi iguana farm (US$35).

Sleeping

There are two possible areas for lodgings in Cahuita – the town center or north of town along the Playa Negra.

CENTER

Within the town, hotels are mostly cheaper and noisier (though there are a few upscale

---

SELVA BANANITO LODGE

At the foot of Cerro Muchito, on the edge of Parque Internacional La Amistad, this family-run **farm and ecolodge** (2253 8118; www.selvabananito.com; 3-day package US$475; P) has about 1200 hectares of pasture, plantation and reforested areas. Conscious of the environmental impact of all their activities, the Stein family employs solar energy, recycled hardwood for construction and biodegradable products. And they are deeply committed to preserving the Limón watershed. While this lodge does not offer beach access, there is plenty to keep the adventurous traveler occupied: tree climbing, tree planting, waterfall hiking and horseback riding. Rates, based on double occupancy, include three meals daily and transportation from San José, as well as the above-mentioned activities.

If you are driving yourself, take the turnoff just south of the Río Vizcaya crossing (about 19km south of Limón). The lodge is about 8km inland. Detailed driving directions are posted on the website.

CARIBBEAN COAST

CAHUITA

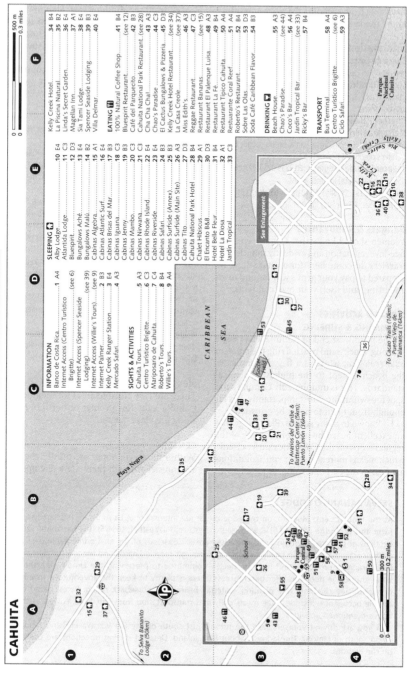

INFORMATION
Banco de Costa Rica	1 A4
Internet Access (Centro Turístico Brigitte)	(see 6)
Internet Access (Spencer Seaside Lodging)	(see 39)
Internet Access (Willie's Tours)	(see 9)
Internet Palmer	2 B3
Kelly Creek Ranger Station	3 E4
Mercado Safari	4 A3

SIGHTS & ACTIVITIES
Cahuita Tours	5 A3
Centro Turístico Brigitte	6 C3
Marposano de Cahuita	7 C4
Roberto's Tours	8 B4
Willie's Tours	9 A4

SLEEPING
Alby Lodge	10 E4
Atlantida Lodge	11 C3
Bluespirit	12 D3
Bungalows Aché	13 E4
Bungalows Malú	14 B2
Cabinas Algebra	15 A1
Cabinas Atlantic Surf	16 E4
Cabinas Brisas del Mar	17 B3
Cabinas Iguana	18 C3
Cabinas Jenny	19 B3
Cabinas Mambo	20 C3
Cabinas Nirwana	21 C3
Cabinas Rhode Island	22 E4
Cabinas Riverside	23 E4
Cabinas Safari	24 B3
Cabinas Surfside (Annex)	25 B3
Cabinas Surfside (Main Site)	26 A3
Cabinas Tito	27 D3
Cahuita National Park Hotel	28 B4
Chalet Hibiscus	29 A1
El Encanto B&B	30 D3
Hotel Belle Fleur	31 B4
Hotel La Diosa	32 A1
Jardín Tropical	33 C3

EATING
Kelly Creek Hotel	34 B4
La Piscina Natural	35 B2
Linda's Secret Garden	36 E4
Magellan Inn	37 A1
Sia Tami Lodge	38 E4
Spencer Seaside Lodging	39 B3
Villa Delmar	40 E4
100% Natural Coffee Shop	41 B4
Bluespirit Restaurant	(see 12)
Café del Parquecito	42 B3
Cahuita National Park Restaurant	(see 28)
Cha Cha Chal	43 A3
Chao's Paradise	44 C3
El Cactus Bungalows & Pizzería	45 D3
Kelly Creek Hotel Restaurant	(see 34)
La Casa Creole	(see 37)
Miss Edith's	46 A3
Reggae Restaurant	47 C3
Restaurant Bananas	(see 15)
Restaurant El Palenque Luisa	48 A3
Restaurant La Fé	49 B4
Restaurant Típico Cahuita	50 A4
Restaurante Coral Reef	51 A4
Roberto's Restaurant	52 B4
Sobre Las Olas	53 D3
Soda Café Caribbean Flavor	54 B3

DRINKING
Beach House	55 A3
Chao's Paradise	(see 44)
Coco's Bar	56 A4
Jardín Tropical Bar	(see 33)
Ricky's Bar	57 B4

TRANSPORT
Bus Terminal	58 A4
Centro Turístico Brigitte	(see 6)
Ciclo Safari	59 A3

CARIBBEAN SEA

Playa Negra

To Selva Bananito Lodge (50km)

To Aviarios del Caribe & Buttercup Center (5km); Puerto Limón (36km)

To Cacao Trails (10km); Puerto Viejo de Talamanca (16km)

Parque Nacional Cahuita

Río Suárez (Kelly Creek)

Kelly Creek

See Enlargement

Soccer Field

School

Parque Central

options). The advantage is being close to many restaurants and to the national park. For more upscale hotels there is greater choice outside of town along Playa Negra.

Budget
Budget accommodations dominate in Cahuita. Most are clean and basic, geared for folks content with a cold shower and décor revolving around mosquito nets.

Cabinas Rhode Island (☎ 2755 0264; r per person US$14; **P**) Good-sized, reasonably clean rooms with comfy chairs and cold showers surround a grassy parking lot. The office is in the yellow house across the street.

Villa Delmar (☎ 2755 0392/75; d with/without aircon US$30/14, extra person US$6; **P** **⚡**) In a quiet, out-of-the-way spot close to the national park, the Villa Delmar has colorful cabins, ranging in size from small singles to more spacious family-sized quarters. Set around a grassy yard, the rooms are dark and musty, brightened only moderately by the pleasant pastel paint job.

Cabinas Riverside (☎ 2553 0153; s/d US$15/20; **P**) Efficient service and superclean rooms are found at this spot near Kelly Creek. With painted wood furniture and colorful woven hammocks strung up around the grounds, this charming place is definitely the best of the budget bunch. Simple rooms have mosquito nets and stone showers with hot water.

Cabinas Safari (☎ 2755 0405; s/d/tr/q US$15/18/22/25; **P**) These basic but well-maintained rooms all have tiled floors and a few frilly details. Be sure to ask the staff for the ocean-view rooms. The helpful owners also provide money-changing services. Big breakfasts are worth the extra US$2.

Cabinas Surfside (☎ 2755 0246; evadarling1930@ yahoo.com; s/d/tr US$20/25/35, d annex US$35; **P**) These concrete-block rooms do not look like much, but they are spotless, from the tiled floor to the wood ceiling. The less expensive cabinas surround a pleasant courtyard, while slightly pricier rooms are in the adjacent annex, facing the waterfront.

Cabinas Bobo Shanti (☎ 2755 0128, 8829 6890; tr US$30; **P**) Come here if you are in a reggae mood. This place is characterized by Rasta colors, plenty of hammocks and *very* laidback service. The rooms are a good deal if you can fill the beds, but single travelers may want to look elsewhere. The outdoor kitchen facilities are useful for self-caterers.

Brigitte at Centro Turístico Brigitte rents a few **cabinas** (s/d/q US$25/30/40). As well, you can camp in Parque Nacional Cahuita (see p477) or just north of town at Reggae Restaurant (p475).

Midrange
The midrange options have private bathrooms with hot water, unless otherwise noted.

Linda's Secret Garden (☎ 2755 0327; d US$20; **P**) The namesake garden really is an enticing retreat, and a lovely setting for Linda's four airy cabins. They all have fresh paint jobs and bamboo furniture, with a wicker screen that separates the bathroom from the rest of the room. The new dorm that sleeps five people, plus communal kitchen facilities, makes this a good option for families.

Spencer Seaside Lodging (☎ 2755 0210; spencer@ racsa.co.cr; s/d downstairs US$16/25, upstairs US$30; **P** **⌨**) A seaside setting makes this the perfect place to take advantage of hammocks strung beneath the coconut palms. The cottages are nothing fancy, but the lizards, turtles and other creatures stenciled on the walls add an element of jungle charm. You'll pay a bit more for the unobstructed view and the hot water in the 2nd-floor rooms.

Cabinas Atlantic Surf (☎ 2755 0116, 8846 4622; www .cabinasatlanticsurf.com; s/d/tr US$20/25/30; **P**) The vibe is definitely cool at this sweet spot, thanks to the manager, Kenneth, and the reggae tunes emanating from within. Attractive hardwood rooms have semiprivate porches, each with a hammock for optimum relaxation. Stone showers – straight out of Bedrock – are hot, unless you choose the cold-water option and save yourself US$5.

Cabinas Brisas del Mar (☎ 2755 0011; s/d US$21/25) Spotless if not stylish, these cabinas are set in overgrown gardens that face the water. Hammocks are conveniently strung to catch the breeze off the sea, as the name promises, but they don't allow for much privacy.

Cahuita National Park Hotel (☎ 2755 0244; s/d/ tr/f US$25/30/35/65; **P** **⚡**) Overlooking the beach at the entrance to the park, this large building looks like a proper hotel. Wood paneling and balconies characterize the rooms, while the family room comes complete with multiple bedrooms and a full kitchen. Views from the upper floors are excellent, and one of Cahuita's favorite restaurants (casados US$3 to US$5, seafood US$8 to US$15, open 11am to 10pm) is just downstairs.

Cabinas Jenny (☎ 2755 0256; d US$25-35, extra person US$7; **P**) A stone's throw from the advancing waves, this straightforward place has great views from the shared porches. Linoleum floors, fresh paint and mosquito nets constitute the décor, but the rooms are functional and offer plenty of storage space. Upstairs, the more private rooms are a few dollars more. Call in advance to make sure that somebody is here when you arrive.

Hotel Belle Fleur (☎ 2755 0283; hotelbellefleur@hot mail.com; d standard/deluxe/king US$25/35/55; **P** 🖥 🖭) Although this hotel is right smack dab in the middle of town, the grounds are completely enclosed, making it a private, peaceful site. The exception is the standard rooms, which are above the Vaz supermarket on the main drag. The pricier rooms are clustered around lovely gardens at the back. A cool hammock hangout and a refreshing swimming pool make it a welcome retreat in a superconvenient locale.

Top End

Bungalows Aché (☎ 2755 0119; www.bungalowsache .com; s/d/tr US$40/45/50; **P** ♿) In Nigeria, *Aché*

means 'Amen,' and you'll likely say the same thing when you arrive at this little piece of paradise. With its back to the national park, it is surrounded by wildlife, and these spacious octagonal bungalows have almost every amenity. High ceilings and spacious woody interiors are brightened by colorful print curtains and linens.

Alby Lodge (☎ 2755 0031; www.albylodge.com; d/tr/q US$40/45/50; **P**) This fine German-run lodge on the edge of the park has spacious landscaped grounds, littered with trees that attract loads of howler monkeys. Four thatch-room bungalows are spread out across the grounds, allowing for plenty of privacy. High ceilings, mosquito nets and driftwood details make for a pleasant jungle décor. A common rancho has excellent communal kitchen facilities.

Kelly Creek Hotel (☎ 2755 0007; www.hotelkelly creek.com; d US$58, extra person US$10; **P** 🗙 🖭) This snazzy hotel is on a busy stretch of beach, right next to the park entrance. The location allows for welcome sea breezes, which blow right into the rooms; it's also not a bad spot for wildlife-watching, as animals sometimes sneak out from the park. Four hardwood

---

GET OUT OF THAT HAMMOCK!

It's easy to let time slip away while you are lounging in a hammock or catching the waves in this tropical paradise. If you need a break from all that relaxation, here are some suggestions:

- **Avarios del Caribe & Buttercup Center** (☎ 2750 0725; www.ogphoto.com/aviaros; ☼ 6am-5pm) About 10km north of Cahuita, this small wildlife sanctuary sits on an 88-hectare island in the delta of the Río Estrella. The now-famous orphaned sloth named Buttercup reigns over the grounds, ever since she was adopted by owners Luis and Judy at the age of five weeks. Their passion for these funny creatures is contagious; informative guided tours (US$20 to US$30) allow visitors to meet some of the resident sloths. The center also offers a variety of excursions through the canals and lagoons of the Estrella delta, where 312 (and counting!) species of birds have been recorded. Besides the prolific birdlife, this lowland rain forest is home to monkey, caiman, river otter and, of course, sloth. The recommended way to explore this lush tropical setting is by canoe (US$30, three hours), but hiking tours are also available. The reserve and research center also contains a restful B&B (doubles US$87 to US$110).

- **Cacao Trails** (☎ 8812 7460; www.cacaotrails.com; Hone Creek; guided tour US$25; ☼ 8am-5pm) Visit this exquisite new botanical garden and outdoor museum, where educational tours demonstrate the various uses of medicinal plants and the workings of a cacao plantation (plus you can see and sample the final product), with plenty of opportunities for wildlife sightings along the way. An additional expedition allows further exploration by kayak. It's midway between Cahuita and Puerto Viejo; any bus between the two can drop you at the entrance. This is a great outing for kids.

- **Mariposario de Cahuita** (☎ 2755 0361; admission US$8; ☼ 9am-4pm) Almost all local tours include a visit to this wonderful garden that's all aflutter with beautiful butterflies. Stroll around the fountain-filled grounds and admire the local residents, including many friendly caterpillars. Descriptions are posted in several languages; guided tours are also available.

rooms each have high ceilings, two double beds with mosquito nets, and two big windows letting in plenty of light. The onsite Spanish restaurant (dishes US$8 to US$10, open 6:30pm Thursday to Tuesday) serves up a mouthwatering paella.

Sia Tami Lodge (☎ 2755 0374; www.siatamilodge .com; d/q US$67/74, extra person US$14; P) A gravel road leads from town, past the other lodges, to this tranquil spot on the edge of the park. This place is ideal for families, as the 10 *casas* (houses) are fully equipped with two bedrooms, living space and kitchen. From each, a terrace overlooks a large private garden. With rain forest all around, this the next best thing to staying in the park itself.

PLAYA NEGRA
Northwest of town, along Playa Negra, you'll find more expensive hotels and a few pleasant cabinas, which offer more privacy and quiet but a limited choice of restaurants and services. All of the options have private bathrooms with hot water.

Budget
Cabinas Algebra (☎ 2755 0057; d US$18, d/tr with kitchen US$25/39; P) This friendly, family-run option is a 2km trek from town. But the owners will pick you up (for free!) if you call in advance. The rooms are cheerful and inviting, as is the onsite Restaurant Bananas (meals US$7 to US$12), serving top-notch Creole food.

Cabinas Nirwana (☎ 2755 0110; nirwana99@racsa .co.cr; d US$35-40; ☒) This good budget choice offers a range of lodging options, from small doubles to larger quarters (sleeping up to four) with kitchenettes. Built by a friendly Italian, the wooden cabins are cool and comfortable, with plenty of windows for cross-ventilation. A wide porch overlooks the grounds, which are perhaps too well maintained.

Midrange
Cabinas Tito (☎ 2755 0286; s/d incl breakfast US$20/25; P) Surrounded by extensive tropical gardens and banana plants, this atmospheric spot offers excellent value. The bright rooms are furnished in wicker, with mosquito nets and jungle accents. If you absolutely love it, there is a furnished house available for long-term rental.

Cabinas Iguana (☎ 2755 0005; www.cabinas-iguana .com; d with shared bathroom US$20, cabins US$35-40; P ☒) Set back from the beach, these cabinas are in the middle of the jungle: agouti and sloth have been sighted on the grounds. Three comfortable, small rooms share warm showers and a small terrace. More spacious cabins have handsome woody interiors, big beds with mosquito nets and hammock-hung porches. One large furnished house with a kitchen sleeps up to six (US$65).

La Piscina Natural (☎ 2755 0146; d US$35; P) This gem is about 2km out of town and 100% worth the walk or cab ride. The comfortable rooms are recently renovated, but what makes this place are the gorgeous grounds fronting a scenic stretch of beach and the neat natural pool for which the complex is named. With drinks available from the breezy bar, you may never feel the need to trek back into town.

Jardín Tropical (☎ 8811 2754; jardintropical@racsa .co.cr; cabins US$35-40, house US$50-60) Deep in the middle of overgrown tropical gardens, two cozy cabins have high ceilings and porch hammocks. It doesn't get more tranquil than this, unless of course there's a rowdy crowd at the popular onsite bar. The same fine folks also run Cabinas Mambo (double/ triple US$30/40) opposite. Inquire at Jardín Tropical about these spacious rooms that share a shady porch.

Bluspirit (☎ 2755 0122; bluspirit_@hotmail.com; d US$50) Three delightful blue A-frame cabins are lined up on this pleasant stretch of waterfront property. They each have a thatch-roofed porch – hung with a hammock, of course – for maximum breeze-catching. The onsite seaside restaurant (pasta US$5 to US$7, seafood US$9 to US$15) is Cahuita's most romantic dining spot.

Top End
Atlantida Lodge (☎ 2755 0115; d US$64-93; P ☒ ☒) The 34 sturdy wood cabins that are spread over resort-feel grounds provide more creature comforts than you'd expect in rough-and-ready Cahuita. The main draws are the large swimming pool and the jungle-like floral gardens. Yoga, reiki and massage are available to ensure your chis and chakras are all in order.

Chalet Hibiscus (☎ 2755 0021; www.hotels.co.cr /hibiscus.html; d/q US$45/55, chalets US$100-120; P ☒) The rooms in the 'principal chalet' are very comfortable, with all the necessary amenities, plus wide balconies and a few artsy touches. The two-story private chalets, however, are fabulous. The balconies, strung with hammocks, overlook private gardens; other practical perks include full kitchens and separate bedrooms. The chalets sleep six to 10 people.

Bungalows Malú (☎ 2755 0114; www.bungalows malu.com; s/d/tr/q US$46/58/64/70; P ⬛ ⬛) At this lodge along Playa Negra, five stone bungalows are scattered across the palm-shaded grounds, surrounding an open-air rancho and a sunken swimming pool. They feature cool Stone Age bathrooms and tropical hardwood interiors, individually decorated with poignant paintings by local artist Alessandra Bucci.

El Encanto B&B (☎ 2755 0113; www.elencantobed andbreakfast.com; s/d US$49/59; P) This B&B, run by French-Canadian artists Pierre and Patricia, is set in lovingly landscaped grounds, with statuettes and nooks reflecting the creative nature of the owners. An Asian-style pavilion has hammocks and lounge chairs – yoga, massage and meditation also take place here. Attractive wooden bungalows have ceiling fans and private patios.

Hotel La Diosa (☎ 2755 0055; www.hotelladiosa.net; s/d US$58/63, with air-con US$76/87, with air-con & Jacuzzi US$88/99; P ⬛ ⬛) Cabins with names like Aphrodite and Isis evoke the feminine energy of La Diosa, or 'the goddess.' This place is designed to please the senses, from the spacious, cool, tiled cabins with king-size beds, to the swimming pool set amid tropical gardens, to the new hardwood yoga and meditation space. Prices include breakfast – with plenty of fresh-brewed coffee – served in the open-air rancho.

Magellan Inn (☎ 2755 0035; www.magellaninn.com; d with fan/air-con US$93/115, extra person US$17; P ⬛ ⬛) At the northern end of Playa Negra, this elegant, upscale inn isn't really within a casual stroll of town, but it is worth the extra effort. Comfortable, classy rooms with king-size beds have beautiful wood furniture, and their private terraces look out into the tropical garden, which is filled with orchids and bromeliads. Prices include breakfast.

Eating
CENTER
A few excellent restaurants in the town center are conveniently attached to hotels, including the Kelly Creek Hotel and Cahuita National Park Hotel.

100% Natural Coffee Shop (☎ 2755 0317; ⏲ 6am-8pm) There is no better place in Cahuita to greet the morning with a cup o' joe or unwind in the afternoon with a refreshing *jugo*. A few tapas

are also on the menu. Rare is the individual who can walk by this place on the main drag without being lured over to the beckoning bar.

Café del Parquecito (☎ 2775 0279; breakfast US$3-5; ⏲ 6:30am-noon) Early risers come for the coffee, but breakfast lovers at any hour of the morning will delight in this menu. The specialty is the huge crepes, wrapped around fresh fruit or other fillings.

Roberto's Restaurant (☎ 2755 0117; seafood dishes US$3-8; ⏲ 7am-10pm) Owned by one of the top fishing guides in the region, you know the seafood is fresh. The restaurant uses organic ingredients and fresh produce whenever possible.

Restaurant El Palenque Luisa (☎ 2755 0400; dishes US$5-8) Tree-trunk beams, bamboo roof and plant-filled interior create quite the jungle décor in this inviting open-air restaurant. It's an ideal spot to feast on tasty vegetarian fare, as well as fish and meat dishes cooked Caribbean Creole style.

Restaurant La Fé (meals US$5-10; ⏲ 7am-11pm) You can't miss this inviting spot on the main drag, draped in swinging oropendola nests. It's particularly atmospheric in the evening, when the open-air terrace is lit by candles. The specialty is anything in coconut sauce, from octopus to marlin to delectable shrimp, served up with a side of plantains.

Cha Cha Cha! (☎ 8394 4153; mains US$6-9; ⏲ noon-10pm Tue-Sun) In a corner veranda of an old blue-painted clapboard house, this attractive eatery offers recommended *cuisine del mundo*. Well-prepared dishes range from Jamaican jerk chicken to Tex-Mex cuisine. There are plenty of vegetarian options, including the 'zen salad' (mandarin oranges with basil, sprinkled with cashews and macadamia nuts). It's all savored against a background of world music and jazz.

Miss Edith's (☎ 2755 0248; mains US$7-12; ⏲ 11am-10pm) As local people earn respect in the community, they are called Miss or Mister, followed by their first name – hence, Miss Edith. Miss Edith's is undoubtedly Cahuita's most famous restaurant, and deservedly so, for mouthwatering, cooked-to-order Caribbean cuisine. Reserve in advance so your dinner has time to simmer.

ourpick Restaurante Coral Reef (☎ 2755 0133; ⏲ 11.30am-10pm) Seafood lovers should come for the best seafood stew in town. This new place has jumped to the top of the heap in Cahuita, and it's often hard to get a table, so book or dine early – it's worth it. Not to mention it's right next to the main bar in town, making post-dinner drinks within easy reach.

You can't really go wrong in Cahuita if you stop for lunch at one of the local *sodas:*

Soda Café Caribbean Flavor (mains US$2-5; ◷ 6am-9pm) Caribbean-style Tico standards, particularly fresh juices, and *gallo pinto.*

Restaurant Típico Cahuita (mains US$4-8, seafood US$5-15; ◷ 8am-close) A spacious spot beneath a *palapa* (shelter with a thatched, palm-leaf roof and open sides) with a wide-ranging menu.

PLAYA NEGRA

Near Playa Negra, you can also head to El Cactus Bungalows y Pizzeria, the restaurant at Bluspirit (p473) and Restaurant Bananas at Cabinas Algebra (p473).

Reggae Restaurant (☎ 2755 0515; mains US$4-9; ◷ 7-11am & noon-9pm) Exuding a friendly, laid-back vibe, this *soda* serves Caribbean-style standards, from inexpensive casados to the house specialty, shrimp in coconut milk. This place also has facilities for camping (per person US$3), plus some comfortable cabins (US$20 to US$30).

Chao's Paradise (☎ 2755 0421; seafood mains US$6-10; ◷ 11am-close) It's worth the short beachside jaunt out of town to enjoy the catch of the day simmered in spicy Chao sauce. The open-air restaurant-bar also has a pool table and live reggae and calypso music some nights.

Sobre Las Olas (☎ 2755 0109; meals US$8-10; ◷ noon-10pm Wed-Mon) Cahuita's top option for waterfront dining. The Italian owners guarantee excellent homemade pasta and an impressively stocked wine cellar, while the location ensures the freshest of ingredients straight from the sea. Vegetarians will also find plenty to sate their appetites.

La Casa Creole (☎ 2755 0035; mains US$7-20; ◷ 6-9pm Mon-Sat) Set in the tropical gardens of the Magellan Inn, this candlelit restaurant serves some of Cahuita's finest fare. The French-fusion cuisine emphasizes seafood and Caribbean flavors. The house specialty is the shrimp Martinique (that's ginger and garlic sauce to make your mouth water). Reservations are required.

Drinking

Though low-key, Cahuita certainly has some fine spots for a few drinks or live music.

Beach House (☎ 8369 4254; cariberen@yahoo.com) 'Eat, Drink and Go Surfing.' So implores

Rennie Leone, owner of this expat hangout. By day, the place rents surfboards; by night, it serves sandwiches (US$5), quesadillas (US$6) and cold beers at the cozy bar or on the breezy terrace. Live calypso music plays Thursday through Saturday.

Coco's Bar (◷ noon-midnight) You can't miss Coco's at the main intersection, painted in Rasta red, yellow and green. It embodies Cahuita's Caribbean atmosphere, so it comes as no surprise that it's famous for fruity rum concoctions and Friday 'reggae night.'

Ricky's Bar (☎ 2755 0228; ◷ 4pm-midnight) Across from Coco's, Ricky's has a jungle vibe, outdoor seating and a nice dance floor. This place really gets hopping on Wednesday and Saturday nights, when live bands sometimes take the stage.

Along Playa Negra, stop by Chao's Paradise restaurant-bar or the bar at Jardín Tropical cabins.

Getting There & Away

Grayline (☎ 2262 3681; www.graylinecostarica.com) runs a daily bus departing at 11am to San José (US$27) and on to Arenal (US$38). All public buses arrive and depart from the terminal half a block southwest of Parque Central.

Puerto Limón/San José (Autotransportes Mepe) US$1/7, 1½/four hours, depart at 7:30am, 8:30am, 9:30am, 11:30am and 4:30pm, additional bus at 2pm on weekends.

Puerto Viejo de Talamanca/Bribrí/Sixaola US$1/2/3, 30 minutes/one hour/1½ hours, depart hourly from 7am to 9pm.

Getting Around

The best way to get around Cahuita – especially if you are staying out along Playa Negra – is by bicycle. In town, rent bikes at **Ciclo Safari** (☎ 2755 0020; per hr/day US$1.50/8; ◷ 7am-6pm). Near the Playa Negra, bikes are available at Centro Turístico Brigitte (see p469) for similar prices. Many lodges also provide bikes for their guests.

PARQUE NACIONAL CAHUITA

This small park – just 1067 hectares – is one of the more frequently visited national parks in Costa Rica. The reasons are simple: the nearby town of Cahuita provides attractive accommodations and easy access; more importantly, the white-sand beaches, coral reef and coastal rain forest are bursting with wildlife.

Declared a national park in 1978, Cahuita is typical of the entire coast (very humid), which

PARQUE NACIONAL CAHUITA

results in dense tropical foliage (mostly coconut palms and sea grapes). The area includes the swampy **Punta Cahuita**, which juts into the sea between two stretches of sandy beach. Often flooded, the point is populated with cativo and mango trees, green ibis, yellow-crowned night heron, boat-billed heron and the rare green-and-rufous kingfisher.

The dark Río Perezoso, or 'Sloth River,' bisects the Punta Cahuita (and sometimes prevents hiking between the ranger stations). This is the discharge for the swamp that covers the point.

Red land and fiddler crab live along the beaches, attracting mammals like crab-eating raccoon and white-nosed coati. White-faced capuchin, southern opossum and three-toed sloth also live in these parts. The mammal you are most likely to see (and hear) is the mantled howler monkey, which makes its presence known. The coral reef represents another rich ecosystem that abounds with life.

Information

The **Kelly Creek ranger station** (☎ 2755 0461; admission by donation; ☯ 6am-5pm) is convenient to the town of Cahuita, while 1km down Hwy 32 takes you to the well-signed **Puerto Vargas ranger station** (☎ 2755 0302; admission US$6; ☯ 8am-4pm).

Technically, you do not have to pay the US$6 admission fee if you enter at Kelly Creek. This is the result of a local stir-up in the 1990s, when locals feared high park fees would deter the tourists. Keep in mind, however, that these fees provide important income for the park service. Tourist dollars support education about and maintenance and conservation of the national park, so it is important to pay the fee, or donate it, as the case may be.

Activities
HIKING

An easily navigable 7km **coastal trail** leads through the jungle from Kelly Creek to Puerto Vargas. At times the trail follows the beach; at other times hikers are 100m or so away from the sand. At the end of the first beach, Playa Blanca, hikers must ford the Río Perezoso. Inquire about river conditions before you set out: under normal conditions, this river can be thigh-deep at high tide. During the rainy season, it is often too dangerous to cross.

The trail continues around Punta Cahuita to the long stretch of Playa Vargas. The trail ends at the southern tip of the reef, where it meets up with a road leading to the Puerto Vargas ranger station. From the ranger station, it is another 2km along a gravel road to the park entrance. From here, you can hike back to Cahuita along the coastal highway, or you can catch a ride going in either direction.

SWIMMING

Almost immediately upon entering the park, you'll see the 2km-long **Playa Blanca** stretching along a gently curving bay to the east. The first 500m of beach may be unsafe for swimming, but beyond that, waves are gentle. These conditions may change, so inquire at the ranger station before diving in. The rocky Punta Cahuita headland separates this beach from the next one, **Playa Vargas**. It is unwise to leave clothing or other belongings unattended when you swim.

SNORKELING

Parque Nacional Cahuita contains one of the last living coral reefs in Costa Rica. The reef is accessible from the beach, but the best way to see the creatures under the sea is to hire a guide with a boat in Cahuita. If you prefer to walk, hike along the beach trail. After about 6km, you will come to a sandy stretch that is cut off from the coastline by a rocky headland of Punta Cahuita. The offshore coral reef represents Cahuita's best snorkeling.

In an attempt to protect the reef from further damage, snorkeling is permitted only with a licensed guide. Local guides include Roberto and Willie (see Tours, p469). The going rate is US$15 to US$25 per person, but prices vary according to the size of your group and the mood of the guide. Cahuita Tours (p469) offers an all-day trip in a glass-bottom boat, which includes snorkeling and hiking (US$35 per person).

Snorkeling conditions vary greatly, depending on the weather and other factors. In general, the drier months in the highlands (from February to April) are best for snorkeling on the coast, as less runoff occurs in the rivers and there is less silting in the sea. Conditions are often cloudy at other times. Indeed, conditions are often cloudy, period.

Sleeping & Eating

Within the park, **camping** (per person US$3; **P**) is permitted at Playa Vargas, less than 1km from the Puerto Vargas ranger station. The limited facilities include cold outdoor showers, drinking water and pit latrines.

After the long, hot hike through the jungle, you may think you are hallucinating when you see the Italian restaurant beckoning at the end of the road. But **Boca Chica** (☎ 2755 0415; meals US$6-12) is not a mirage, just a well-placed eatery, offering cold *jugos*, homemade pasta and fresh *mariscos* (shellfish) to hungry and tired trekkers coming out of the park. If you stop for lunch, they'll spot you the bus fare for your return all the way to Cahuita.

PUERTO VIEJO DE TALAMANCA

Time was that the only disturbances to this sleepy Rasta town were superintrepid surfers who would lazily flip-flop around the dusty streets, board under arm, on their way to ride the infamous Salsa Brava break. While those days are certainly gone, this town has still got a long way to go before it becomes the almost Disneyfied experience you can find on the Pacific coast.

Undoubtedly, Puerto Viejo's sole purpose is tourism, but the one-street town skirts a fine line between providing both local charm and all your traveler amenities. There is still a strong Afro-Caribbean flavor to the place; the dirt streets swing to soca, dancehall and reggae sounds, while the distinct green, gold and red Rastafarian colors are flown from almost every building. Sadly, as more and more expats move in and take over local businesses, it becomes glaringly obvious that the culture is becoming heavily diluted.

But you'll certainly get your fill of local flavor by night. Puerto Viejo is one of the best party towns in the country and the *guaro* (local firewater) and ganja-fueled nightlife is as hedonistic as you'll find in Costa Rica. If that's not your scene you can still escape it all by staying on the outskirts of town, on either of the two dramatically sweeping beaches, Playa Negra or Cocles.

Whether you stay on the beach or in town, it's a great spot for basing yourself and exploring the region. It's possible to trek through rain forest, kayak upstream, surf the Caribbean's best breaks and still be back by sundown for a slap-up meal in any of the town's fantastic eateries.

The easy and amenable touristy nature of the town is unavoidable, but so to is the sleepy slothlike charm of the place. However, you do get that sinking feeling that Puerto Viejo is a hop, skip and a jump from golden arches and soya mocachinos. Thankfully, it's hard to imagine anyone mustering the energy to hop or skip… let alone jump… for the time being.

Dangers & Annoyances

Do keep in mind that as tourism grows, a cottage industry of sketchy drug dealers and irritating touts is growing with it. Stay alert late at night, choose your own accommodations (and use the hotel safe!) and always remember that an ounce of caution is worth more than a pound of weed.

Information

INTERNET ACCESS

Internet access is expensive and slow.

Asociación Talamanqueña de Ecoturismo y Conservación (ATEC; ☎ 2750 0191, 2750 0398; per hr US$2.40; ☽ 8am-9pm) Painfully slow internet access.

books librería y bazar (☎ 2750 2005; per hr US$2.40; ☽ 9am-9pm) Ten machines with decent internet speeds.

Jungle Internet (☎ 2750 2003; per hr US$3.40; ☽ 8am-11pm) Fast computers plus free wireless access.

PUERTO VIEJO MARINA – BEGINNING OF THE END?

Nothing has got the sleepy residents of Puerto Viejo more animated of late than proposed plans to build a marina out on Playa Negra. US and Costa Rican investors want to build a US$40 million dollar, 389-slip marina. The plans include a shopping center, art and craft vendors, yacht maintenance and repair areas, offices, storage areas and two breakwaters. Obviously, if the plans go ahead they will drastically change the face of the town.

Local surfer, Jim Richards said: 'We don't want or need a marina here. This is a special town, with a special vibe. All of that will be lost if we allow this to happen. It won't be good for anyone in the town. No one will make money except the already rich investors, who are building this marina.'

However some disagree. Local businessman, Jorge Ramos said: 'What difference does it make if tourists arrive by boat or by car? The belief that the locals will make no money simply isn't true. Two thousand jobs will be created and the property value of the local-owned land will skyrocket. At present local business in Puerto Viejo is being taken over one-by-one by incoming expats. The locals have already been muscled out of most of the lucrative aspects of tourism and need the jobs. There are a lot of social problems in Puerto Viejo that could be cured by the influx of this business, if it's managed correctly.'

Either way, at the time of research, this development looked as though it was a little way off. Currently, there is only one legal marina in the country, in Jacó, while the government is in the process of considering 21 other marina plans for different parts of the country. Watch this space…

MONEY

Banco de Costa Rica (☙ 9am-4pm Mon-Fri) The ATM here works on the Plus and Visa systems. However, it often runs out of cash after the weekend.

Cabinas Almendras (☎ 2750 0235; ☙ 7:30am-7:30pm) Stop in at the front desk at Cabinas Almendras to change Canadian and US dollars, British pounds and euros at 1% commission, 2.5% on traveler's checks.

Pulpería Manuel León (☙ 8am-8pm) Change US dollars and euros with 'El Chino,' who charges 1.5% commission on cash and more on traveler's checks.

Sights

To the west of town is **Finca La Isla Botanical Garden** (☎ 2750 0046; www.greencoast.com/garden.htm; self-guided/guided tour US$2/5; ☙ 10am-4pm Fri-Mon), a working tropical farm where the owners have been growing local spices, tropical fruits and ornamental plants for more than a decade. Part of the farm is set aside as a botanical garden, which is also good for birding and for wildlife observation (look for sloths and poison-dart frogs). The informative guided tour (in English) includes admission, fruit tasting and a glass of homemade juice to finish, or you can buy a booklet and take yourself on a self-guided tour.

West of Puerto Viejo, the **Jungles of Talamanca** is actually a small tropical nursery and cacao finca. This Bribrí family welcomes visitors to its home, where you can see cacao toasted over an open fire then hand-ground into delicious chocolate or rich cocoa butter. Nutmeg, black pepper or cinnamon, all grown onsite, may be added. The resulting product is truly decadent – it's amazing that something so luscious comes from such humble origins. This place is on the road to Bribrí; look for the sign just past the clinic.

Activities

SURFING

Outside the reef in front of Stanford's Restaurant Caribe, the famed **Salsa Brava** is known as the country's best wave (see boxed text, p480). The reef here is shallow, so if you lose it, you're liable to smash yourself and your board on the reef; this place is not for beginners. Salsa Brava offers both rights and lefts, although the right is usually faster. Conditions are best with an easterly swell.

The waves at **Playa Cocles** are almost as impressive and less-damaging than Salsa Brava. Cocles is about 2km east of town (an area known as 'Beach Break,' which is an accurate description). Lefts and rights both break close to the steep beach. Conditions are usually best early in the day, before the wind picks up.

The waves are generally at their peak here from December to March, and there is a mini-

PUERTO VIEJO DE TALAMANCA

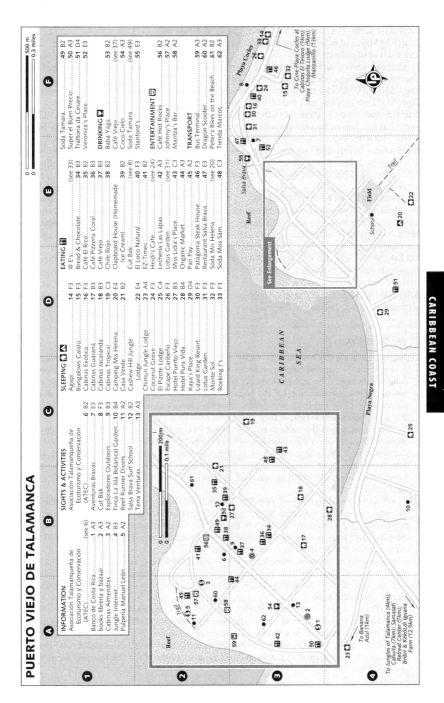

season for surfing in June and July. From late March to May, and in September and October, the sea is at its calmest.

There are several surf schools around town, more or less independent operations charging US$30 to US$35 for two hours of lessons. Note that Puerto Viejo isn't the best spot for true beginners to pick up the sport; the Pacific coast has smaller, more user-friendly waves. Folks with some experience will benefit from local advice before tackling the big breaks. It's not a bad deal as boards rent for about US$10 to US$15 per day. Surf schools around town include:

Caribbean Surf School & Tours (☎ 8357 7703; www.caribbeansurfschoolandtours.com) Run by supersmiley surf instructor, Hershel, who is widely considered the best teacher in the town. Call Hershel to organize a surf (the school has no office).

Cut Bak (☎ 8366 9222, 8885 9688) Also a popular place for surfers to pitch a tent (per person US$3, rent-a-tent US$4) and sleep on the beach.

Salsa Brava Surf School (☎ 2750 0689; salsabrava surfshop@hotmail.com) Opposite Hotel Puerto Viejo.

SWIMMING

The entire southern Caribbean coast – from Cahuita all the way south to Punta Mona – is lined with unbelievably beautiful beaches. Just northwest of town, **Playa Negra** offers the area's safest swimming, as well as excellent body boarding.

But southeast of town is where you will find the region's gems. This is where the jungle meets the sea; stretches of smooth sand (quite slender at high tide) are caressed by waves perfect for swimming and body surfing, all fringed with the requisite swaying coconut palms. Toucans, monkeys and sloths frolic in these treetops, making it all the more exotic. So take your pick: **Playa Cocles** (2km east of town), **Playa Chiquita** (4km east), **Punta Uva** (6km east) and **Manzanillo** (see p492) all offer picture-perfect beach paradises.

Swimming conditions vary and they can be dangerous. Riptides and undertows can be deadly. It is always wise to inquire at your hotel or with local tour operators about current conditions.

SALSA BRAVA

The biggest break in Costa Rica, for expert surfers only and dangerous even then, Salsa Brava is named for the heaping helping of 'sauce' it serves up on the sharp, shallow reef, continually collecting its debt of fun in broken skin, boards and bones. There are a couple of take-off points: newbies waiting around to catch the popular North Peak should keep in mind that there are plenty of people in this town who gave up perks like mom's cooking and Wal-Mart just to surf this wave regularly. Don't get in their way.

In a sense, it was the Salsa Brava that swept Puerto Viejo into the relaxed limelight it enjoys today. Although discrimination against the primarily black residents of the southern Caribbean was officially outlawed in 1949, luxuries such as paved roads, electricity and telephone lines came more slowly here than elsewhere in Costa Rica. Most tourists – nationals and foreigners – still spend most of their beach time on the more accessible and developed Pacific coast.

But surfers are a special breed. Even 30 years ago, they would not be dissuaded by the bumpy bus rides and rickety canoes that hauled them and their boards from San José on the weeklong trip (assuming the bus didn't get stuck in the mud for a night or two) to this once-remote outpost. Bemused locals first opened their homes, then basic cabinas and sodas (cheap eateries), to accommodate those rugged souls on their quest.

In the wake of the wave riders came other intrepid explorers, eager to see those storied sunrises over perfect coastlines and monster curls; residents, who were by this time surfing with the best of them, happily developed a grassroots tourist infrastructure to keep everyone happy – pura vida, baby.

And though today's visitors enjoy internet access, fine dining and a paved route that's shortened travel time by several orders of magnitude, the magnificence of Salsa Brava and its attendant waves still flood Puerto Viejo with tanned troopers on a mission.

So if you find yourself wondering what stirred up this marvelous mix of Caribbean culture and tourist trappings amid all this natural beauty, grab a beer at the Stanford and watch the waves roll in.

SNORKELING

The waters from Cahuita to Manzanillo are protected by Costa Rica's only two living reef systems, which form a naturally protected sanctuary, home to some 35 species of coral and more than 400 species of fish, not to mention dolphin, shark and, occasionally, whale. Generally, underwater visibility is best when the sea is calm, ie when surfing is bad, snorkeling is good.

Just south of **Punta Uva**, in front of the Arrecife restaurant, is a decent spot for snorkeling, when conditions are calm. The reef is very close to the shore and features some stunning examples of reindeer coral, sheet coral and lettuce coral. The reef at **Manzanillo** (p492) is also easily accessible for snorkeling. Rent equipment at Aquamor Talamanca Adventures (p492) in Manzanillo. Most of the tour companies offer snorkeling trips for about US$45 per person.

DIVING

Divers in the southern Caribbean will discover upward of 20 dive sites, from the coral gardens in shallow waters to deeper sites with amazing underwater vertical walls. Literally hundreds of species of fish swim around here, including angelfish, parrotfish, triggerfish, shark and different species of jack and snapper.

The only dive operation in Puerto Viejo is **Reef Runner Divers** (☎ 2750 0480; www.reefrunner divers.net; 1-/2-tank dive US$65/80; ☼ 7am-8pm). If you are not certified, you can use a temporary license for US$65, or spring for the full PADI certification for US$325. Aquamor Talamanca Adventures (p492), in Manzanillo, also coordinates diving trips.

HIKING

The immediate vicinity of Puerto Viejo is not prime hiking territory: the proximity of the Parque Nacional Cahuita (p476) and the Refugio Nacional de Vida Silvestre Gandoca-Manzanillo (p492) means that most trekkers will head to these protected areas to look for toucan and sloth. Getting to the indigenous reserves often requires a pretty serious trek, usually with a guide (see Tours, right).

Still, the edge of town is the edge of the jungle. So, if you are up for some independent exploring, you can discover your own destination. Pack a picnic and follow the town's most southerly road, which goes past the soccer field and the Cashew Hill Jungle Lodge. Once

---

WHITE-WATER RAFTING

Plenty of rafters head straight for Turrialba (see boxed text, p159) but it's also possible to do rafting from the Caribbean. **Exploradores Outdooors** (☎ 2750 2020; www.exploradoresoutdoors.com; trips incl lunch & transport US$95) is one of the best companies in the region that offer one- and two-day rafting trips on the Pacuare, Reventazón and Sarapiquí rivers. They can pick you up and drop you off in either Cahuita, Puerto Viejo, Tortuguero, San José or Arenal, and you're free to mix and match your pick-up and drop-off points. This is particularly useful if you're short on time and don't want to lose days to traveling across the country.

---

out of the village, the road dwindles to a path and leads into the hills.

Festivals & Events

The **South Caribbean Music & Arts Festival** (☎ 2750 0062; www.playachiquitalodge.com) fills weekends in March and April with eclectic offerings, all homegrown on the Caribbean coast. calypso to jazz, reggae to Celtic and classical artists perform; dancing troupes take the stage with Jamaican and African flair; and Costa Rican–produced films are shown. This is a family event, with many programs for kids. Dates for the festival vary but are usually weekends in March and April (for about five weeks before Easter). Most performances are held at the Playa Chiquita Lodge (see p489).

Tours

Tour operators generally require a minimum of two people on any excursion. Rates are per person, but they may be discounted for larger groups.

Asociación Talamanqueña de Ecoturismo y Conservación (ATEC; ☎ 2750 0191, 2750 0398; www .greencoast.com/atec.htm; half-day US$20-25, day trip US$35-55, overnight US$55-70; ☼ 8am-9pm) This nonprofit organization promotes environmentally sensitive local tourism by working with local guides and supporting local communities. Hiking, horseback riding and canoeing trips involve birding, visiting indigenous reserves and visiting local farms.

Aventuras Bravas (☎ 2750 2000, 8849 0626) It now has an office in the town and at Rocking J's (see p482) and works largely as a booking agent arranging almost every tour possible in the region. Popular activities include surf lessons (US$45) as well as kayak (US$20), rafting (US$95) and canopy (US$50) tours.

Terra Venturas (☎ 2750 0750/489; www.terra venturas.com; ⏰ 8am-7pm) Offers overnights in Tortuguero (US$120), hiking (US$38) and snorkeling (US$55) in Cahuita, white-water rafting (US$95), plus its very own 18-platform, 2.1km-long canopy tour (US$50), with a Tarzan swing.

Sleeping
BUDGET
Cold water is the norm in budget places, but you won't miss the hot water.

Camping Mis Helena (☎ 2750 0580; camping US$10, rent-a-tent US$4) Campers who are not interested in the surfer party scene should seek out this family-oriented site off the main drag. It offers covered campsites in the likely event of rain. The onsite Soda Mis Helena (mains US$2 to US$4, open 7am to 6pm Tuesday to Sunday) serves inexpensive Caribbean-Tico standards and daily soup specials made over a wood-burning stove. Cool off with a glass of spicy homemade ginger ale.

our pick Rocking J's (☎ 2750 0657; www.rockingjs .com; pitch-a-tent/rent-a-tent US$4/6, hang-a-hammock/rent-a-hammock US$4/5, dm/d/tr/q US$7/20/30/50; **P**) This truly individual backpacker abode has the personality of J, the boisterous owner, stamped all over it. In the day it feels like a hippy artists' workshop as guests create broken-tile mosaics and splash paint on canvas. When the sun does down, Rocking J's *rocks*. Beachside bonfires, round-the-table drinking games and frivolous flirting are standard. Accommodations fit all budgets, from the 'hammock hotel' to the luxury apartment, fitted with retractable roof (which enables on-the-loo stargazing), king-size bed and private kitchen. J's also rents surfboards (per day US$15), bikes (per day US$5) and other fun stuff. A word of warning: if you are uncomfortable with pot smoking you may feel out of place.

Hotel Puerto Viejo (☎ 2750 0620; r per person with/ without bathroom US$14/10; **P** 🖥) 'No shoes, no shirt, no problem,' dude, and that goes for the clean, functional rooms with hot showers and the shared kitchen. Boards can be hung in the reception area, where talk revolves around surfing big waves, a topic about which owner Kurt Van Dyke is a respected local expert. All the running water in the hotel is taken from giant drums that recycle the great amounts of rain water Puerto Viejo receives.

Chimuri Jungle Lodge (☎ 2750 0119; www.green coast.com/chimurilodge.htm; dm/d/q US$10/30/46; **P**) On the edge of the KéköLdi reserve, this is about as private and peaceful as it gets in Puerto Viejo. Four bungalows mimic the indigenous architecture, with thatched roofs, mosquito nets and private balconies, while one dormitory sleeps eight. All units share a communal kitchen. Follow the 2km walking trail to explore the jungle grounds, which attract an amazing array of birds and wildlife.

Monte Sol (☎ 2750 0098; www.montesol.net, in German; d US$20-30; **P** 🖥) Away from the noise of the main road, this German-run place has a lovely, laidback atmosphere. Simple, stylish cabins have stucco walls and tile bathrooms, with a welcoming hammock-hung terrace. An awesome jungle house, sleeping up to eight, is available for weekly or monthly rental.

Hotel Pura Vida (☎ 2750 0002; www.hotel-puravida .com, in German; s/d/tr with shared bathroom US$20/25/33, with private bathroom US$20/25/30) This place is getting an overhaul, thanks to new German owners. They started with the beautiful, breezy terrace, which has been spruced up with polished-wood floors and furniture, and surrounded with gardens. Comfortable, airy rooms feature high ceilings and big windows; four have brand-new bathrooms with stone floors, elaborate tile work and solar-heated showers.

Coconut Grove (☎ 2750 0093; s/d with shared bathroom US$20/25, with private bathroom US$25/35; **P**) Attentive and efficient Heidi oversees this two-story complex just east of town. Wood-beamed rooms – painted in tropical colors – have mosquito nets, fans and hammocks overlooking the street. Your first stop in the morning should be downstairs at Heidi's Cafe (open 7am to noon), serving pancakes, eggs and terrific smoothies.

Cabinas Jacaranda (☎ 2750 0069; www.cabinas jacaranda.net; s/d/tr/q US$30/45/50/60; **P**) In a beautiful blooming garden woven with mosaic walkways, this colorful spot proves that personal touches and attention to detail are what constitute luxury. Magic inhabits each differently decorated room, with fanciful stenciled designs on the walls, tropical hardwood furniture and mosaic-tiled, hot-water bathrooms. The rooms all have access to a security box – use it!

Several hotels offer camping, including Rocking J's. There's also camping in Manzanillo (see p490).

MIDRANGE

Midrange hotels offer private bathrooms with hot water, unless otherwise indicated.

Kaya's Place (☎ 2750 0690; www.kayasplace.com; s/d/tr/q with shared bathroom US$19/27/35/43, with private bathroom from US$25/35/45/55) This rustic lodge on Playa Negra has been completely renovated and now features inviting lounge areas on two floors, furnished with hammocks and couches and ocean views. The guestrooms facing the ocean are a bit dark and dreary; airy, light-filled rooms facing the garden are more pleasant and more private (thus the price difference).

Cabinas Guaraná (☎ 2750 0244; www.hotelguarana.com; s/d/tr US$25/35/45; P &) A lot of attention has gone into the details in these delightful cabinas, set amid tropical gardens. Painted wood furniture, colorful *molas* (indigenous tapestries made with layers of colorful cloth cut into patterns depicting local flora and fauna) and other local handicrafts decorate each room, while a private terrace with a woven hammock is just outside. On the practical side, all rooms have access to a communal kitchen. Grab a drink and climb up to a perch in the tree house for a spectacular view of the sun setting over the Caribbean Sea.

Lizard King Resort (☎ 2750 0614; lizardkingresort@net.com; s/d/tr/q US$25/35/45/60; 🏊) This slick resort features 15 spacious hardwood cabins overlooking a sweet swimming pool. Rates include a hearty breakfast. If you can't afford these cushy quarters, stop by the laidback lounge upstairs for Mexican food, movie night or – bonus – happy hour.

Cashew Hill Jungle Lodge (☎ 2750 0256; www.cashewhilllodge.co.cr; s/d/tr with shared bathroom US$30/40/52, with private bathroom US$29/40/52, with private patio US$46/58/70; P) Set on a hectare of land in the far southeast corner of town, this lodge is surrounded by jungle gardens. The brightly painted bungalows feature lots of hardwood and whimsical décor, with simple, sturdy beds draped in mosquito nets. Two rooms share kitchen facilities – useful for families – while the pricier rooms boast ocean views in the distance. Daily yoga classes are offered at the studio onsite.

Bungalows Calalú (☎ 2750 0042; www.bungalowscalalu.com; s/d/tr/q US$26/34/42/50, with kitchen US$40/40/50/60; P 🏊) You hear a lot of talk about 'tropical paradise' in Puerto Viejo, but Calalú has actually created it. This hidden gem is set in gardens blooming with exotic flora like heliconia and bromeliads. A rock-formation swimming pool is fed by a gushing waterfall. Breakfast is served at the 'butterfly balcony' with hundreds of the beauties fluttering around. The bungalows themselves are attractive but simple, with tiled floors and wood-beam ceilings, as well as private porches overlooking the gardens.

Cabinas Tropical (☎ 2750 0283; www.cabinastropical.com; s/d US$30/35, tr with kitchen US$45; P ✗ 🏊) Ten spacious rooms – decorated with varnished wood and shiny tiles – surround a primly landscaped garden on the edge of town. The comfortable quarters are just part of the appeal: the biologist owner leads jungle hikes for birders from dawn until about 11am (per person US$40, three minimum, breakfast provided).

Cabinas Exotica (☎ 2750 0542; cabinas_david@yahoo.com; s/d incl breakfast US$30/35; P) Formerly Cabinas David, new owner Gabriel has only recently taken over this row of eight cabins to the east of town. At the time of research they were undergoing a much-needed revamp (with plans to build more rooms and a pool). The formerly dingy cabins have been decluttered, so the newly tiled look is simple enough but bright, airy, spanking clean and very good value. Breakfast, included in the price, is served on the shady terrace.

Casa Verde (☎ 2750 0015; www.cabinascasaverde.com; s/d standard US$32/36, s/d/tr/q deluxe US$60/76/96/110; P 🏊) Tiled walkways wind through gardens showcasing local flora to 14 sparkling rooms, each with spacious interiors decorated with local artwork and dark stained wood furniture, and private terraces with hammocks. The new swimming pool and hot tub are straight out of *Fantasy Island*. Bikes are available (per day US$6) and breakfast is served daily except Monday.

Agapi (☎ 2750 0446; www.agapisite.com; r/ste from US$35/65, apt for 6 from US$100 P) In a prime seaside location east of town, this sweet spot is run by a Greek-Tico couple. All the accommodations are individually decorated, ranging from simple, colorful single rooms to more-spacious multiroom suites with kitchenettes. The pricier rooms have private balconies with ocean views, but all guests have access to lovely beachfront grounds that are sprinkled with gazebos and towering palm trees. The newly built wood-paneled apartments are excellent value if you can fill them.

ourpick Banana Azul (☎ 2750 2035; www.banana azul.com; d incl breakfast US$48-105; **P**) Lost in the jungle at the far end of Playa Negra this wonderfully wild hotel is right on the cusp of a dramatic black-sand beach and sloth-filled rain forest. Each wood-paneled room has a hammock-swinging balcony looking onto the Caribbean only meters away. At night the isolated location means guests are serenaded by howler monkeys, macaws and the crashing surf.

Escape Caribeño (☎ 2750 0103; www.escapecaribeno .com; s/d/tr US$55/65/75, air-con extra US$10; **P** **⊠**) Take your pick from bungalows facing the beach or others surrounded by lush tropical gardens, about 500m east of town. They range in size, but all 14 are equipped with refrigerators and fans and – most importantly – hammocks hanging on the porches.

El Pizote Lodge (☎ 2750 0227; d/q standard US$66/82, bungalows US$82/115; **P** **⊠** **⊠**) On a quiet backroad 1km west of town, this comfortably rustic lodge is a 10-minute walk from town, but just a few steps from the waves lapping at Playa Negra. Spacious but simple standard rooms have shared bathrooms, while the nicer wooden bungalows offer more privacy.

TOP END

Lotus Garden (☎ 2750 0232; www.lotusgarden.net; d US$60-90; **P** **⊠** **⊠**) The luxury suites here feature king-size, four-poster beds, rich varnished wood floors and in-room whirlpools. Set in tropical gardens, the place has a distinctive Asian elegance. To complete the mood, the onsite Lotus Garden restaurant (open 7am to 11pm) offers an impressive menu of pan-Asian cuisine, including an all-you-can-eat sushi special for US$14. Lotus Garden was formerly known as Jordan's.

Samasati Retreat Center (☎ 2750 0315, in the USA 800-563 9643; www.samasati.com; s/d with shared bathroom US$94/150, s/d/tr with private bathroom US$162/230/282) Set on a lush hillside 8km north of Puerto Viejo, this well-built, attractive complex affords lovely sweeping views of the coast and the village far below. Nine private bungalows have cool, wraparound screened walls, while the guesthouse has simple rooms with wood interiors and single beds. Tasty vegetarian meals (included) are served buffet-style on a wooden terrace with ocean views. There are daily yoga classes (US$12) that are open to all guests.

Eating

Cooking up the most impressive restaurant scene on the coast, Puerto Viejo has the cure for casado overkill. Besides the listings here, see also the Lotus Garden Restaurant (left) and Heidi's Cafe at Coconut Grove (p482).

BUDGET

If you can't get enough of the Caribbean flavors, **Soda Miss Sam** (☎ 2750 0108; mains US$2-6) and **Miss Lidia's Place** (☎ 2750 0598; mains US$2-6) are the local favorites for *gallo pinto* and spicy coconut sauce. Both ladies have been around for years, pleasing the palates and satisfying the stomachs of locals and tourists alike.

Café Pizzería Coral (☎ 2750 0051; breakfast US$2-3, pizzas US$4-6; ☺ 7am-noon & 5:30-9:30pm Tue-Sun) Beloved for healthy breakfasts and homemade wholemeal bread, this old stand-by now serves excellent pizza, including lots of vegetarian options.

Pan Pay (☎ 2750 0081; light meals US$2-4; ☺ 7am-7pm) This beachside spot is excellent for strong coffee and freshly baked goods, not to mention delicious sandwiches that are a perfect picnic for a long hike or a beach day. This is a popular spot for tourists and Ticos to meet, post announcements and exchange books.

Bread & Chocolate (☎ 8830 3223; breakfast US$2-4, lunch US$4-8; ☺ 6:30am-2:30pm Wed-Sun) This classy café invites early risers to sit on the spacious, covered porch, sip fresh-brewed coffee and peruse the *Tico Times*. Breakfast favorites include oatmeal like your mom used to make; big, fluffy omelets; and the classic crunchy granola and yogurt.

Soda Tamara (☎ 2750 0148; breakfast US$2-4, seafood dinners US$6-10; ☺ 7am-10pm) With its signature red, green and yellow paint job, this is a popular spot to grab breakfast overlooking the street and watch the village wake up. During the day seafood is the specialty, but don't skip the coconut bread.

Café El Rico (☺ 8am-4pm) Dark, rich coffee – iced, even – is served alongside light breakfasts and lunches. Bonus: you earn yourself a free cappuccino by doing your laundry (US$5 for 4kg) onsite. Bikes are rented here, too.

Veronica's Place (☎ 2750 0132; meals US$3-5; ☺ 7am-9pm Sun-Thu, 7am-4:30pm Fri) This vegetarian café behind Supermercado El Pueblo is a delightful find, and not only for nonmeat-eaters. Veronica offers a fresh, healthy interpretation of Caribbean food, focusing on fresh fruits and vegetables. This is the only place in town where you'll find veggie favorites like soy burgers and soy milk.

EZ-Times (☎ 2750 0663; mains US$5-9; 🕙 10-2:30am) The reggae music and groovy vibe lure in hungry beach bums for pizza, pasta and salads. The outdoor terrace is strewn with colorful cushions, making it a comfy place to sit back and enjoy the fine food, not to mention the live music on Friday nights.

You've got two choices for dessert: homemade ice cream or homemade ice cream. Opposite the Hotel Puerto Viejo, a darling old woman sells creamy concoctions out of her clapboard house (US$0.30). Described by one reader as 'frozen bliss,' this is kind of like a milkshake in a bag, and it hits the spot. For a more traditional *helado,* **Lechería Las Lapas** (🕙 11am-11pm) is in a little kiosk fronting the beach, near the bus stop. The creamy, cool stuff comes in a wide variety of tropical flavors (the macadamia nut is highly recommended), and there is also *arroz con leche* (rice pudding).

The best spot for groceries is **Super el Buen Precio** (🕙 6:30am-8:30pm). Don't miss the weekly **Organic Market** (🕙 6am-6pm Sat), when area vendors and growers sell snacks typical of the region.

MIDRANGE & TOP END

@ E's (☎ 2750 0657; meals US$3-7; 🕙 10am-11pm) The restaurant and bar at Rocking J's is much more than just a travelers hangout. Run by cordon bleu–trained chef, Eric, the food is a fusion of flavors inspired by Thai, Mexican and American cuisine. Each dish, be it the burger and fries or pan-fried shark steak, is as delicious as the next. Cordon bleu food at backpacker prices sounds like a good deal to us.

Chile Rojo (☎ 2750 0025; mains US$7-12; 🕙 noon-10pm) If you are yearning for something spicy, head to this popular spot for excellent Thai and Middle Eastern fare. It's a tiny place, but one whiff of the curry – or whatever daily special is on the menu – and you'll know it's worth whatever wait it takes. The cooked breakfast in the morning is also excellent.

ourpick El Loco Natural (☎ 2750 0263; meals US$8-14; 🕙 6-11pm) This upstairs open-air music café features creative fusion cuisine, combining elements of Italian, Asian and Caribbean cooking. Tropical gazpacho soup and Caribbean fish tacos are some of the delicacies you can enjoy while watching the street scene below. There is live music on Thursday and Saturday,

and local artwork on display every night of the week.

Café Viejo (☎ 2750 0817; mains US$6-15; 🕙 11am-close) Though elegant and a little bit pricey, this fine Italian restaurant gets high marks for its excellently dressed fresh pastas and fancy cocktails. The upscale, romantic ambience makes it a definite date destination if you've got someone to impress. It's also an excellent people-watching spot if you are on your own.

Patagonia Steak House (☎ 8390 5677; meals US$10-15; 🕙 5-11pm) This friendly, family-run restaurant is a real-deal Argentinean-owned steak house. There is not much going on in the basic interior – just plain wooden tables and chairs – and there's an open kitchen, where you can see (and smell) the steaks sizzling on the grill. Washed down with a delicious Malbec from Mendoza, it's a meal you won't forget.

Restaurant Salsa Brava (☎ 2750 0241; meals US$10-15; 🕙 11am-11pm) This well-recommended hot spot specializes in seafood and open-grill cooking in an intimate atmosphere. The ever-popular onsite 'juice joint' is an oasis for thirsty surfers and beachcombers.

Trattoria da Cesare (☎ 2750 0161; meals US$10-15; 🕙 5:30-10pm Thu-Tue) This lovely trattoria west of town features wonderful homemade pastas with fresh cheeses and sauces made from locally grown produce.

Drinking

Restaurants often metamorphose into rollicking bar scenes after the tables are cleared. Try Soda Tamara for some people-watching over a beer, or Café Viejo for being seen over a fancy cocktail. If you want a cool ocean breeze with your frosty mug, stop by the bar at Stanford's during happy hour.

Baba Yaga (☎ 8388 4359) Go on Wednesday for ladies' night, Sunday for reggae night or any day for happy hour.

Coco Cielo (☎ 2750 0263) Restaurant by day/ beach bar by night – this slick new addition is the hippest place in town for margaritas and mojitos.

Entertainment

As you might expect in such a hip town, there is plenty to do after the sun goes down. So put away that surfboard and fluff those dreadlocks – Puerto Viejo is an entirely different sort of paradise after dark.

CINEMA

Café Hot Rocks (☎ 2750 0525; meals US$3-8; ⏱ 11-2:30am) In a big red tent in the center of town, this place shows fine flicks for free most evenings and also hosts live (and often new) calypso, reggae and rock bands. Recommended for fun, not for food.

Cine Playa Cocles (☎ 2750 0128, 2750 0507; Playa Cocles; admission free, minimum purchase US$4.50; ⏱ screenings 7pm Mon-Fri, 5:30pm Sat & Sun) At Cabinas El Tesoro (see opposite), this popular big screen shows a cool selection of camp, cult and classic movies plus plenty of Hollywood blockbusters. Weekend showings are specially for kids.

LIVE MUSIC & DANCING

Maritza's Bar (☎ 2750 0003) This live music bar below a hotel is *the* place to go on Tuesdays. Allegedly it's open-mic, but it seems to be the same bunch of locals who come to play fun reggae every week.

Johnny's Place is a Puerto Viejo institution. DJs spin reggae, hip-hop and salsa, and patrons light beach bonfires outside.

Getting There & Away

Grayline (☎ 2262 3681; www.graylinecostarica.com) runs a daily bus departing at 11am to San José (US$27) and on to Arenal (US$38). Call for a reservation so the bus will pick you up at your hotel. All public buses arrive and depart from the terminal half a block southwest of Maritza's Bar.

TOP REGGAE BARS

Looking to tap into the Caribbean beat? Look no further than these reggae spots:

- **Casa Blanca** (p455) is an authentic reggae bar that is well off the tourist track and the hottest spot to shake your dreadlocks in the city.

- **Johnny's Place** (above) may put off reggae purists with the new reggaetón sound that sneaks into the DJ's play list here, but it's still the most jumping bar on the coast.

- **Maritza's Bar** (above) is a good spot on Tuesdays for open-mic night.

- **Coco's Bar** (p475) is at the heart of Cahuita's chilled night scene and blares out Kingston sounds all week.

Bribrí/Sixaola US$1/2, 30 minutes/1½ hours, depart every hour from 7:30am to 8:30pm.
Cahuita/Puerto Limón US$1/2, 30 minutes/1½ hours, depart every hour on the half-hour from 5:30am to 7:30pm.
Manzanillo US$1.50, 30 minutes, depart at 7:30am, 11:45am, 4:30pm and 7:30pm.
San José US$7.50, five hours, depart at 7am, 9am, 11am and 4pm.

Getting Around

Bicycle is a fine way to get around town, and pedaling out to Manzanillo or to the other beaches east of Puerto Viejo is one of the highlights of this corner of Costa Rica. You'll find bicycle rentals all over town (including at many lodges):

Dragon Scooter (☎ 2750 0728; per 4hr from US$15; ⏱ 8am-late) If you prefer your wheels motorized.
Los Ticos (☎ 2750 0611; ⏱ 7am-6pm) Right next to Rocking J's.
Tienda Marcos (☎ 2750 0303; per day US$3; ⏱ 7am-6pm)

PUERTO VIEJO TO MANZANILLO

The 13km road heading east from Puerto Viejo was paved for the first time in 2003. This dramatically shortened the time that it takes to drive or cycle past the sandy, driftwood-strewn beaches and the rocky points, through the small communities of Punta Uva and Manzanillo, and through sections of Reserva Indígena Cocles/KéköLdi and Refugio Nacional de Vida Silvestre Gandoca-Manzanillo.

The road is still considered the property of folks without internal combustion, and drivers should be particularly careful at night as cyclists and pedestrians make their way between the different bars, restaurants and lodges. Hitching is quite common on this stretch, which does not mean it is risk-free.

This route more or less follows the shoreline, but you usually can't see the beach from the road, once past Playa Cocles. The vegetation is thick – coconut palms and sea grapes protect the coast, while tropical rain forest covers the lowland hills further inland.

If you want to stay close to a nice beach but still have access to restaurants and accommodations, Cocles has a good mix of isolation and amenities. There are wide variety of places to stay and eat that are spread out along the road through Cocles, while there's a small cluster around Punta Uva – the prettiest beach in the region.

It's probably just as easy to head into Puerto Viejo to take care of business, but **Playa Chiquita Services** (☎ 2750 0575; Playa Chiquita; 9am-8pm), across from Miraflores Lodge, has a public phone, internet access (US$2 for 30 minutes) and a small café. Buses heading from Puerto Viejo to Manzanillo will drop you at any of these places along the way.

Sights
MARIPOSARIO PUNTA UVA
The **Mariposario Punta Uva** (butterfly farm; ☎ 2750 0086; Punta Uva; adult/child US$5/free; 8am-4pm) is less a tourist attraction and more a breeding center. Some 70 species of butterfly are bred annually, including four species staff claim exist in captivity nowhere else in the world: Prepona, Filaetinias, Mintorio and Inmanius. What you'll see depends on the time of year. Lydia, the biologist in charge of the project, can lead interesting guided tours in Spanish by request.

CRAZY MONKEY CANOPY TOUR
Affiliated with Punta Uva's Almonds & Corals Lodge (see p490), this is the only **canopy tour** (☎ 2759 9057/56, in San José 2272 2024; www.almondsandcorals.com; tour US$40; 8am-2pm) in the south Caribbean. Set in the heart of Refugio Nacional de Vida Silvestre Gandoca-Manzanillo, this tour starts in the rain forest and ends on the beach, offering plenty of opportunities for wildlife-spotting and adrenaline-rushing.

Activities
The region's biggest draws involve surf, sand, wildlife-watching and attempts to get a decent tan between downpours. Playa Cocles is known for its great **surfing** and organized lifeguard system, which helps offset the dangers of the frequent riptides, while Punta Uva features the best and safest beaches for **swimming**. At the north end of the Punta Uva beach, a footpath leads out to the point, with some interesting rock formations and a wonderful lookout along the way.

Sleeping & Eating
PLAYA COCLES
This stretch begins about 1.5km east of Puerto Viejo. The following places are listed from

west to east and the accommodations have hot water, unless otherwise noted.

Echo Books (desserts US$1-3; 11am-6pm Fri-Tue;) Admittedly, it seems a strange place for a bookstore, but resident expats and tourists alike are overjoyed to drop into this Caribbean-style Borders. It serves coffee and desserts in a deliciously cool, air-conditioned spot, and features thousands (really, thousands) of new and used books. Plus, the homemade chocolates are worth the whole trip to Costa Rica.

Cabinas El Tesoro (☎ 2750 0128; www.puertoviejo .net; dm/s/d/tr US$9/21/28/41; P) Accommodations to suit every budget, from the basic Beach Break hostel with shared bathroom and bunk beds, to the fully loaded 'executive suites' (US$68) with air-con and TV. El Tesoro offers a list of perks a mile long, including free coffee and free internet access to community kitchens. Evening entertainment is also included: movies every night and a fun mobile disco on Saturdays.

La Isla Inn (☎ 2750 0109; islainn@racsa.co.cr; d with/ without air-con US$104/75; P) You can't miss the magical mosaic welcoming guests into La Isla, one of Playa Cocles' upscale options. The elegant lodging features sparkling new bathrooms and unobstructed ocean views. The rooms are furnished with exotic handmade wood pieces, created from the slightly curved outer boards that are discarded during lumber processing. These rates include breakfast, but they are still on the high side.

Totem (☎ 2750 0758; www.totemsite.com; d US$82, extra person US$15, air-con extra US$10; P) Opposite the lifeguard tower at the main hub of the beach you'll find unique modern suites decorated in jewel tones, with terracotta floors and bamboo furniture. This is the Caribbean with a contemporary edge. By day there's the onsite Totem Beach Bar; by night, the Italian restaurant Osteria (mains US$7 to US$10) serves up fresh-baked bread, homemade pasta and fresh seafood prepared by a talented European chef.

Cariblue (☎ 2750 0518; www.cariblue.com; d US$99, bungalows US$128, extra person US$16; P) Set in lovely gardens (plants and trees are labeled for the botanically curious) this complex has nine standard cabins with fans and high ceilings that keep them airy, quiet and cool. Four spacious hardwood bungalows – each decorated with mosaics – have thatched roofs and hammock-hung porches. Prices include breakfast.

Cabinas Garibaldi (☎ 2750 0101; r US$20; P) Many surfers stay at this place, which is among the cheapest along this stretch. The concrete row of reasonably clean cabinas share kitchen facilities and a porch with sea views. The waves are right across the street.

Azania Bungalows (☎ 2750 0540; www.azania-costa rica.com; s/d with breakfast US$76/87; P 🕹) Spacious but dark thatch-roofed bungalows are hidden away in these landscaped jungle grounds. The details here are delectable, including woven bedspreads, elegant bathrooms and wide-plank hardwood floors. A loft allows sleeping space for four people; rates include breakfast. The new free-form swimming pool, fringed with greenery and topped with a hot tub, adds to the exotic ambience.

La Costa de Papito (☎ 2750 0704; www.lacoste papito.com; d US$48-69, extra person US$10; P) Relax in Rasta luxury in sculpture-studded jungle grounds. Hardwood bungalows vary in size, but all feature artistically tiled showers, hand-carved furniture and private porches. For an extra US$6 you can have breakfast delivered to your table (or hammock) on the porch – nice. Set amid these gorgeous grounds is the thoroughly decadent Pure Jungle Spa (☎ 2750 0536; www.purejunglespa.com), which offers a one-hour facial/massage for US$50/60. Indulge in the signature chocolate facial or a 'Rain forest Immersion' massage, using locally grown, hand-mixed natural products.

El Tucán Jungle Lodge (☎ 2750 0026; www.eltucan junglelodge.com; s/d/tr US$25/30/35) You may wonder if you missed your turn, as you follow the signs into the depths of the jungle in search of this little lodge on the banks of the Caño Negro. It's only 1km off the road, but it feels miles from anywhere. Four brand-new wood cabins have balconies that are perfect for bird-watching in the treetops. You are guaranteed to see at least one howler monkey: the orphan, Rubio, who is being raised by the lodge's loving owners.

Hotel Yaré (☎ 2750 0106; www.hotelyare.com; s/d/ tw US$30/41/58, bungalows US$70; P) Somewhere between Playa Cocles, Playa Chiquita and Wonderland is Hotel Yaré. Vine-strewn covered walkways weave through a marshy setting, connecting fanciful citrus-colored cabañas (cabins). Inside, the dark rooms are not as stylish as some of the other options, but they are fully equipped (some with kitchens).

At night, the air is filled with the music of frogs, which drifts across the complex to the pleasant onsite restaurant.

La Pecora Nera (☎ 2750 0490; mains US$10-15; 🕙 11am-close, closed Mon in low season) Arguably the region's finest dining, this recommended spot is marvelously free of pretensions, as you savor delicacies like starfruit-and-shrimp carpaccio, fresh pasta dishes, steak and seafood – all perfectly prepared by the amicable Italian chef Ilario. No menu makes an appearance; the chef or a server will consult about what you'd like and suggest an Italian red to accompany it.

Café Rio Negro (dishes US$3-7; 🕙 9am-11pm; 💻) This pretty little spot at the far end of Cocles serves tasty snacks and juices all day and has live music on Thursdays. Run by cheery Dutch girl, Marleen, the authentic Dutch pancakes are a favorite among the expat community.

PLAYA CHIQUITA

It isn't exactly clear where Playa Cocles ends and Playa Chiquita begins, but conventional wisdom applies the name to a series of beaches 4km to 6km east of Puerto Viejo. The following are listed in order from west to east.

Villas del Caribe (☎ 2750 0202, in San José 2233 2200; www.villascaribe.net; standard with/without air-con US$92/80, ste US$104/92, villa US$115; P 🍴 🕹) Stressing function over form, these 20 motel-style beachside villas offer a comfortable, convenient lodging option. The pricier rooms include kitchens and private terraces with sea views, but even the standard lodgings have king-size beds.

Aguas Claras (☎ 2750 0131; www.aguasclaras-cr.com; 1-/2-/3-room cottages US$70/130/220; P 💻) Five cozy cottages are distinguished by their color of the rainbow, each one brighter than the next. They offer fully equipped kitchens and easy access to the beach. The delightful gazebo out front – this one sea blue with yellow trim – is Miss Holly's Kitchen (open 8am to 4pm), which serves delicious breakfasts, lunches and snacks on the breezy porch.

Cabinas Slothclub (☎ 2750 0358; d US$20, with kitchen US$30, bungalows US$60; P) Five clean wood cabins have great views, beach access and a snorkeling reef out the front. This is the best and only budget option along Playa Chiquita. These little places often attract long-term renters, so call in advance.

Jungle Love Garden Café (☎ 2750 0356; mains US$5-8; 🕙 1-9:30pm Tue-Sat, 3-9:30pm Sun) It's hard to resist this bohemian, Caribbean, cosmopolitan café. The eclectic menu features fusion masterpieces like mango chicken with cilantro (US$7) and Tokyo tuna with tamarind and ginger sauce (US$8). The garden setting is always inviting, but it's particularly romantic after sunset.

Kashá (☎ 2750 0205, in the USA 800-521 5200; www .costarica-hotelkasha.com; s/d/q US$97/105/163; P) These stucco bungalows are pretty basic, for what you are paying, though semiprivate porches and custom-designed furniture are nice perks. Most guests come here on all-inclusive packages. Breakfast is included in the rates quoted; you'll surely want to return for dinner at Magic Ginger (mains US$5 to US$10, open 6pm to 10pm Tuesday to Sunday), the only French restaurant (featuring a chef straight from *la belle France!*) on the Caribbean coast.

Miraflores Lodge (☎ 2750 0038; www.miraflores lodge.com; d US$30-60) Ten rooms with refrigerator, hot water, hammocks and nice décor are tucked away on beautiful grounds. Each one is different and prices vary accordingly. Owner Pamela Carpenter is an expert on local botany and medicinal plants. Breakfast (included) consists of seasonal fruits grown on the grounds.

Bar y Restaurante Elena (☎ 2750 0265; mains US$4-7; ☺ 8am-11pm) The culinary-gifted chef scores high marks with hearty plates of whole red snapper, shrimp dishes and big breakfasts. The *gallo pinto* gets rave reviews. The bar is festive and has a big TV and occasionally live music.

Playa Chiquita Lodge (☎ 2750 0408; www.playa chiquitalodge.com; s/d US$58/70; P) After spending an afternoon at the namesake Playa Chiquita, wind your way through the jungle grounds and stop along the way to rinse off in the funky shower in the roots of a huge sangrillo tree, before retiring to your cozy bungalow. Rooms are simple but elegant, with white stone walls, ceiling fans, big bathrooms and private hammock-hung terraces. Rates include breakfast.

Shawandha Lodge (☎ 2750 0018; www.shawandha lodge.com; d incl breakfast US$116; P ❋) This up-scale lodge has 10 large, airy bungalows, all with fabulous bathroom mosaics – a feature that seems to represent a minor cultural movement along this stretch of coast. The elegant French-Caribbean restaurant (mains US$5 to US$14, open 7am to 9:30pm) adds *flambé panache* and Provençale flavorings to Caribbean classics.

PUNTA UVA

Punta Uva is known for the region's most swimmable beaches, each lovelier than the next. Don't miss the turnoff to the point, about 7km east of Puerto Viejo. The following places are listed in order from west to east.

Itaitá Villas (☎ 2750 0414; labvaco@racsa.co.cr; d incl breakfast US$75; P) Huge, no-nonsense rooms offer festive furnishings and kitchenettes, not to mention the private porches, excellent for catching a coastal breeze. Jungle and beach setting, all in one.

Selvin's Bar (mains US$4-12; ☺ 8am-8pm Wed-Sun) Selvin is a member of the extensive Brown family, noted for their charm and unusual eyes, which have attracted both romantic and scientific attention. His place is considered one of the region's best, specializing in shrimp, lobster and chicken *caribeño*.

Albergue Walaba (☎ 2750 0147; r per person from US$12) This very basic spot has colorful rooms – some dorms and some with private bathroom, but all heavenly hippy havens. The place is tucked away in its own personal jungle. Kitchen facilities, friendly, funky management and a groovy vibe make it a popular spot for budget travelers.

Casa Viva (☎ 2750 0089; www.puntauva.net; d per night/week US$130/800; P ❋) Enormous elegantly constructed and fully furnished hardwood houses, each with tiled shower, kitchen, two bedrooms and wraparound veranda, are set on property that fronts the beach. Hang out on your hammock and spy on the sloths, howler monkeys, hummingbirds and toucans that frequent these tropical gardens.

Chawax (☎ 2750 0219) This friendly spot has good music, original food and a cool vibe. Open for breakfast, lunch and – most importantly – happy hour.

Ranchito Beach Restaurant (☎ 2759 9048; mains US$3-8; ☺ 10am-6pm) Fronting a fine, palm-lined swimming beach, this mellow outpost features a thatch-roofed outdoor bar and a few romantic little tables scattered about beneath their own personal *palapas*. Fruity cocktails, pizzas and seafood are happily served to folks in swimsuits and sandy feet.

Cabinas Angela (☎ 2759 9092; r per person US$10) If you are counting your colones but you still want to be right next to the beach, Angela has the place for you. It could use some maintenance, to say the least, but Angela keeps the cabinas adequately clean and some of them have kitchen facilities. Did we mention it's right next to the beach? Take the turnoff to Punta Uva.

Almonds & Corals Lodge (☎ 2759 9057/56, in San José 2272 2024; www.almondsandcorals.com; s/d/tr US$160/200/280; P 🏊) These 'campsites' are actually huge, fully furnished canvas tents with hardwood floors, big beds draped in mosquito nets and hot-water bathrooms nearby. Set in the middle of the wildlife refuge, it offers all the adventure of camping – including the nighttime serenade of insects and frogs, and the wake-up call from resident howler monkeys – without any of the discomfort. Rates include breakfast and dinner, served family-style in the main lodge.

our pick **Tree House** (☎ 2750 0706; www.costarica treehouse.com; tree or beach house/beach ste US$225/350, extra person US$40; P) The 'tree house' is only one of three ecologically sound and architecturally amazing options on this property (but it *is* our favorite). This bi-level beauty is constructed around a living sangrillo tree, whose roots and branches accentuate the gorgeous hardwood décor. If you prefer to remain closer to the ground – or closer to the ocean – the beautiful 'beach house' is for you. With equally enticing (but nonphotosynthesizing) hardwood construction, the beach house has a wide veranda with a spectacular Caribbean view. All houses offer total seclusion, courtesy of the jungle setting, as well as easy access to a pristine stretch of beach.

MANZANILLO

The idyllic little village of Manzanillo has long been a destination off the beaten track. Until 2003 the 13km road from Puerto Viejo de Talamanca was a rutted, bumpy affair that could take 45 minutes by car or bus. Today, a paved road has cut drive time down to 15 minutes; even better, cycling the gorgeous stretch of perfect, palm-lined beaches is now a relatively smooth option.

Though some worry that the easier access will funnel too many tourists in from Puerto Viejo, this region has remained among the most pristine on the coast, thanks to ecologically minded locals and the 1985 establishment of the Refugio Nacional de Vida Silvestre Gandoca-Manzanillo, which encompasses the village and imposes strict regulations on further development of the region.

The pristine stretch of sandy white beach – protected by a rocky headland – is the focal point of the village. Most of Manzanillo's ac-

tivity takes place right here, including sunning, snorkeling and surfing (see p492). A few simple cabinas and *sodas* are sprinkled along the dusty streets that run parallel to the beach. Beyond that, it's just trees and monkeys.

Wildlife, not nightlife, is the main attraction on this end of the road, where folks wake up early to take advantage of the fog-shrouded beauty of the morning, while those in Puerto Viejo are still rocking out. (Though Manzanillo does have its moments, courtesy of Maxi's.) Beaches are pristine and postcard perfect, but note that the stretch from the Almonds & Coral Lodge all the way to Punta Mona has potentially dangerous riptides. Swimmers are cautioned to inquire locally about conditions before diving in.

The **Casa de Guías** (☎ 2759 9064) provides internet access (per hour US$3), camping facilities (per person US$8) and local tours.

Sleeping & Eating

Most of the facilities for sleeping and eating are concentrated in the village of Manzanillo, with a few additional options scattered along the road to Punta Uva. The following hotels have hot water, unless otherwise noted, and are listed from east to west.

Maxi's Cabinas (☎ 2759 9042; deluxe/basic q US$35/15; P) This family-owned landmark close to the entrance of the park has two sets of cabinas: the older portion with rustic, cold-water, rather ramshackle (but clean and cozy) rooms; the newer, much nicer rooms with TV, hot water and refrigerator, set a bit further back.

Cabinas Something Different (☎ 2759 9014/97; d/tr/q US$35/40/50; P) In a quiet setting one block off the beach, these quaint cabinas are named for local fauna. So, in theory, you could spot a sloth from your porch perch in the 'Sloth.' In reality, the private terraces face the parking lot, so this scenario is unlikely, but it's still a pleasant spot.

Pangea B&B (☎ 2759 9204; r per person incl breakfast US$35; P) Tucked into a corner of the wildlife refuge, this sweet spot has only two rustic rooms that are completely secluded. The wood cabins are equipped with mosquito nets and ceiling fans, and surrounded by extravagant gardens. The included breakfast features organic produce (grown onsite).

Cabinas Las Veraneras (☎ 2759 9050; s/d with fan US$16/26; P) About 100m off the main drag, these 13 simple cabinas smell of fresh paint and disinfectant. They are all equipped with televisions and hot water. The pleasant *soda* (breakfast US$2, other meals US$4 to US$8, open 7am to 9pm), serves Caribbean and Tico standards.

Cabinas Manzanillo (☎ 2759 9033, 8839 8386; d US$20) The ever-helpful Sandra Castrillo and Pablo Bustamante have eight almost-brand-new cabinas at the western end of town. All the rooms have fresh coats of pastel-colored paint, hardworking ceiling fans and spacious bathrooms. Other facilities include bicycle rental, laundry and a recommended restaurant (seafood mains US$4 to US$8, open from 11am).

Congo Bongo (☎ 2759 9016; mvleevwenzegueld@wxs .nl; d/q US$75/120, per week US$450/720; P) On the road between Manzanillo and Punta Uva, four beautiful houses are totally secluded, surrounded by a reclaimed chocolate plantation (now dense forest). They offer fully equipped kitchens and plenty of living space, including open-air terraces and strategically placed hammocks that are perfect for spying on the wildlife. The hardwood construction blends seamlessly with the surroundings, especially the thatch-roofed Bribrí 'Indian rancho.' A network of trails leads through the six hectares of grounds to the beautiful beach.

El Colibrí Lodge (☎ 2759 9036; www.elcolibrilodge .com; d/tr US$75/85; P) Designed with romance in mind, six bright and comfortable rooms open onto a terrace surrounded by gardens alive with interesting insects and colorful birds. Breakfast is included, served on the terrace or in the privacy of your room. A 300m trail winds through the rain forest to the beach.

ourpick Maxi's Restaurant (mains US$2-3, seafood US$4-10; ☺ 6am-close) Maxi's Cabinas' onsite restaurant is generally accepted as serving the best food on the coast. The fare includes inexpensive red snapper, casados and extravagant fresh lobster served by weight. It's all topped off with good mixed drinks, local color and occasional live music, plus it's a fine spot to ask around about trail conditions and local guides.

Soda Miskito (casados US$3; ☺ 7am-9pm) Wood furniture, Indian lamps and lots of greenery and bamboo adorn the terrace of this friendly *soda*. Place your order for a home-cooked casado and sit back and relax, because this place operates on Caribbean time.

Getting There & Away

The most rewarding way to get to and from Manzanillo is to bike along the 13km road. It is paved (though won't be the smoothest ride you ever take) and not heavily trafficked. In Manzanillo, you can rent bikes at Cabinas Manzanillo (see left; per day US$6).

Buses to Manzanillo depart from Puerto Viejo (US$1.50, 30 minutes) at 7:30am, 11:45am, 4:30pm and 7:30pm. They return from Manzanillo to Puerto Viejo at 5am, 8:15am, 12:45pm and 5:15pm, departing from the Sodita La Playa.

REFUGIO NACIONAL DE VIDA SILVESTRE GANDOCA-MANZANILLO

This refuge (called Regama for short) protects nearly 70% of the southern Caribbean coast, extending from Manzanillo southeast to the Panama border. It encompasses 5013 hectares of land plus 4436 hectares of sea, making it the ultimate in surf-and-turf exploration.

The park was created with special provisions for folks already living here, and the dry (well, drier) land portion encompasses various habitats including farmland. This was once a productive cocoa-growing region, but after a devastating blight swept through, the monoculture was replaced by a patchwork of fincas, ranches and encroaching jungle.

The peaceful, pristine stretch of sandy white beach is one of the area's main attractions. It's the center of village life in Manzanillo, and stretches for miles in either direction – from Punta Uva in the west to Punta Mona in the east. Just off the coast, the colorful coral reef comprises almost 5 sq km, providing a nutrient-rich habitat for lobster, sea fan and long-spined urchin.

Besides the farmland and the marine areas, the wildlife refuge is mostly rain forest. Cativo trees form the canopy, while there are many heliconia in the undergrowth. A huge 400-hectare swamp – known as **Pantano Punta Mona** – provides a haven for waterfowl, as well as the country's most extensive collection of holillo palms and sajo trees. Beyond Punta Mona, protecting a natural oyster bank, is the only red mangrove swamp in Caribbean Costa Rica. In the nearby Río Gandoca estuary there is a spawning ground for Atlantic tarpon, and caiman and manatee have been sighted.

The variety of vegetation and the remote location of the refuge attract many tropical birds; sightings of the rare harpy eagle have been recorded here. Other birds to look out for include the red-lored parrot, the red-capped manikin and the chestnut-mandibled toucan, among hundreds of others. The area is also known for incredible raptor migrations, with more than a million birds flying overhead in the fall.

This southeastern corner of Costa Rica is widely considered one of the most scenic spots in the country. Hopefully, this will not change as a result of an ongoing dispute about the status of the wildlife refuge. The federal Ministerio del Ambiente y Energía or Ministry (Minae) and the local municipality are struggling over who has the right and responsibility to administer the refuge – an issue that is currently hung up in a drawn-out court case. In the meantime, nobody seems to be taking the right or the responsibility very seriously, resulting in a lack of signage, no official park entrance and no entrance fee.

Information

Aquamor Talamanca Adventures (☎ 2759 0612; www.greencoast.com/aquamor.htm) An excellent source of general information about the refuge (particularly if you don't speak much Spanish), with an informative display of articles and tips about enjoying the park and reef, as well as the many conservation programs on the coast.

Casa de Guías (☎ 2759 9064) Prominently placed opposite the Minae office, this operation offers internet access (per hour US$3), as well as camping facilities (per person US$8) and local tours.

Minae (☎ 2759 9100; ☽ 8am-noon & 1-4pm) In the green wooden house as you enter town. Offers maps of the refuge and trails. An excellent book of photos featuring local flora and fauna, including the folks who live here, with commentary in Spanish and English, is *Refugio Nacional de Vida Silvestre Gandoca-Manzanillo* by Juan José Pucci, available locally and online.

Activities

HIKING

The trails within the wildlife refuge are not marked, but they are well traveled and easy enough to follow, should you wish to explore independently. However, readers have reported armed robberies in the depths of the reserve, so it is advisable to hire a guide, or at least avoid hiking alone.

There is a coastal trail leading 5.5km from Manzanillo to **Punta Mona**. From the east end of Manzanillo, follow the dirt road until it turns into a path and continue along the coastline all the way. This hike is spectacularly beautiful and rewards hikers with amazing scenery, as well as excellent (and safe) swimming and snorkeling at the end.

Another more difficult 9km trail leaves from just west of Manzanillo and skirts the southern edges of the Pantano Punta Mona, continuing to the small community of **Gandoca**. Again, this trail is fairly easy to follow, but a guide is recommended for enhancing your experience and your knowledge of local flora and fauna. In any case, be sure to pick up the Instituto Geografico Nacional map of the wildlife refuge (available at the Minae office) before you set out.

SNORKELING & DIVING

The undersea portion of the park cradles one of two living coral reefs in the country. Comprising five different types of coral, the reefs begin in about 1m of water and extend 5km offshore to a barrier reef that local fishers have long relied on and researchers have only recently discovered. This colorful undersea world is home to some 400 species of fish and crustaceans. **Punta Mona** is a popular destination for snorkeling, though it's a bit of a trek so you may wish to hire a boat (see opposite). Otherwise, you can snorkel right offshore at **Manzanillo** at the eastern end of the beach (the riptide can be dangerous here; be sure to inquire about conditions).

As at Punta Uva and in Cahuita, conditions vary widely, and clarity can be adversely affected by weather changes. Visit the excellent **coral reef information center** at Aquamore Talamanca Adventures (see left), where you can also rent snorkeling equipment (per day US$8) or organize dive excursions.

KAYAKING

If you prefer to stay dry, you can explore the wildlife refuge in a kayak, also available from Aquamore Talamanca Adventures (per hour US$8). Paddle out to the reef, or head up the **Quebrada Home Wark**, in the west of the village, or the tiny **Simeon Creek**, at the east end of the village.

SPORTFISHING

Manzanillo does not have the same highfalutin facilities that many fishers expect, but it does have the same fish-filled waters that attract them to places like Barra del Colorado, Parismina and Cahuita. If you don't mind more rustic accommodations, the waters off the coast of Manzanillo are filled with tarpon, sailfish, tuna, snook, wahoo, grouper, jacks, barracuda and even blue marlin – all waiting for your hook, line and sinker. **Los Cielos Charters** (☎ 2750 0408; half-/full-day charters from US$300/500) organizes fishing trips, as does the manager at Pangea B&B (see p490) in Manzanillo.

DOLPHIN OBSERVATION
In 1997 a group of local guides in Manzanillo identified tucuxi dolphins, a little-known species previously not found in Costa Rica, and began to observe their interactions with the bottlenose dolphins. A third species – the Atlantic spotted dolphin – is also common in this area. This unprecedented activity has attracted the attention of marine biologists and conservationists, who are following these animals with great interest.

The **Talamanca Dolphin Foundation** (☎ 2759 0715/612; www.dolphinlink.org), housed at Aquamore Talamanca Adventures, is dedicated to the study and preservation of local dolphins through outreach programs. It offers daily dolphin-observation outings, as well as a four-day, all-inclusive tour (US$380 per person).

TURTLE-WATCHING
Marine turtles, especially leatherback but also green, hawksbill and loggerhead – all endangered, nest on the beaches between Punta Mona and Río Sixaola. Leatherbacks nest from March to July, with a peak in April and May. Local conservation efforts are underway to protect these nesting grounds – the growth in the human population of the area has led to increased theft of turtle eggs and contributed to the declining local population.

During turtle season, no flashlights, beach fires or camping are allowed on the beach. All tourists must be accompanied by a local guide (see right) to minimize the disturbance to the nesting turtles.

The **Asociación Nacional de Asuntos Indígenas** (National Association of Indigenous Affairs; ANAI; ☎ 2759 9100, in San José 2277 7549; www.anaicr.org; Gandoca; registration US$30, camping US$7-15, homestays US$15, cabins US$30) is a grassroots organization that works with locals to protect the sea turtles. Volunteers assist efforts to collect nesting and size data, patrol beaches and move eggs that are in danger of being destroyed by high tides or predation. Rates include train-

ing, accommodations and meals; minimum commitment seven days.

Tours
Sure, you can explore the refuge on your own (if you've made it to Manzanillo, you already are). But without a guide you'll probably be missing out on the refuge's incredible diversity of medicinal plants, exotic birds and earth-bound animals. Most guides charge US$20 to US$30 per person for a four- to five-hour trek, depending on the size of the group. Ask around at Maxi's (p491) or at the Casa de Guías (below).

Recommended local guides include **Florentino Grenald** (☎ 2759 9043, 8841 2732), who used to serve as the reserve's administrator; **Ricky Alric** (☎ 2759 9020), a specialist in birding and medicinal plants; and **Abel Bustamonte** (☎ 2759 9043). A local boat captain, Willie Burton, will take you boating and snorkeling from Manzanillo.

Aquamor Talamanca Adventures (☎ 2759 9012; www.greencoast.com/aquamor.htm; 1-/2-tank dives US$45/60, PADI certification US$300) This unique outfit is devoted as much to conservation as recreation. As well as diving packages, it also leads kayak and snorkeling tours (per person US$40) and rents equipment for independent use.

Asociación Talamanqueña de Ecoturismo y Conservación (ATEC; ☎ 2750 0191, 2750 0398; www .greencoast.com/atec.htm) This community organization, based in Puerto Viejo de Talamanca, offers a variety of tours into the refuge, including day and overnight trips on foot, horseback or by boat.

Casa de Guías (☎ 2759 9064) A much-needed though poorly organized initiative to hook up travelers with local guides. Offers guided hikes (four hours US$25), snorkeling (US$25), turtle-watching (US$100) and sportfishing (US$150).

Sleeping & Eating
Many options for sleeping and eating are in the village of Manzanillo, which is contained within the Refugio Nacional de Vida Silvestre Gandoca-Manzanillo and is the easiest access point.

Punta Mona (www.puntamona.org; dm US$30, transportation US$10; 🖳) Five kilometers south of Manzanillo, this organic farm and retreat center is an experiment in permaculture design and sustainable living that covers some 40 hectares. More than 200 varieties of edible fruits and veggies are grown here, which make up about 85% of the huge vegetarian

CARIBBEAN COAST

INDIGENOUS COMMUNITIES IN COSTA RICA

This long-forgotten corner of Costa Rica is one of the few parts of Central America where indigenous culture still thrives. Today the communities can be visited by tourists, but it's always handy to brush up on some local knowledge first:

Bribrí & Cabécar

At least two indigenous groups occupied the territory on the Caribbean side of the country from pre-Columbian times. The Bribrí tended to inhabit lowland areas, while the Cabécar made their home high in the Cordillera de Talamanca. Even today the Bribrí tend to be more acculturated, while the Cabécar remain more isolated.

Over the last century many of these folks migrated across the mountain range to the Pacific side. But many stayed on the coast, intermingling with Jamaican immigrants, and even seeking employment in the banana industry. The most significant populations of Bribrí and Cabécar are still in the Talamanca region, where several indigenous reserves are found today.

The Bribrí and Cabécar have distinct languages, which are preserved to some degree. They share similar architecture, weapons and canoe style.

Tellingly, these indigenous groups share an enlightened spiritual belief that the planet – and the flora and fauna contained therein – are precious gifts from Sibö, or God, and should be conserved and respected. *Taking Care of Sibö's Gifts*, by Juanita Sanchez, Gloria Mayorga and Paula Palmer, is a remarkable record of Bribrí oral history that provides some rare insights into this culture.

Visiting Indigenous Communities

There are several reserves on the Caribbean slopes of the Cordillera de Talamanca, including the Talamanca Cabécar reserve (which is the most remote and difficult to visit) and the Bribrí reserve, where locals are a bit more acculturated and tolerant of visitors.

---

meals that are included in the daily rate. You can visit Punta Mona on a guided day trip (US$35 including transportation). Volunteers (per day/week/month US$15/125/300) work on trail maintenance, community cooking and tending gardens (one-week minimum); advanced arrangements required.

Finca Lomas (☎ 2759 9100, in San José 2277 7549; www .anaicr.org; per month US$90) Besides the turtle conservation project, ANAI has an agroforestry and crop experimentation project at nearby Finca Lomas, where volunteers work on trail maintenance, data recording and caring for species of tropical lowland flora, including fruit, nut and spice trees. The work can be physically demanding and conditions are very basic (no electricity or running water). There's a six-week minimum; a one-time US$160 registration fee covers training.

BRIBRÍ

This small, pleasant town is en route from Cahuita to Sixaola and the Panama border, at the end of the paved (and badly potholed) coastal road. From Bribrí, a 34km gravel road takes the traveler to the border. Bribrí is a lively little town, with little to offer the casual tourist except for a handful of restaurants and a few accommodations options.

Bribrí is the center for the local indigenous communities in the Talamanca mountains, but there's not too much to see here. These indigenous communities are only now starting to welcome tourists and take advantage of the growing interest in their culture. See boxed text, above.

Sleeping & Eating

There are a couple of basic lodging options, a good-sized supermarket and some restaurants, including the requisite Musmanni Bakery. Accommodations tend to fill up on market days (Monday and Tuesday).

Cabinas El Piculino (☎ 2751 0130; d US$12-25; P ☒) Fifteen clean, pleasant rooms have private hot showers; some have TV and air-con. A recommended *soda* (mains US$2 to US$3, open 7am to 10pm Monday to Saturday) run by the same family serves a fine *sopa consomé de pollo* (chicken soup) and good rice dishes.

Complejo Turístico Mango (☎ 2751 0115; s/d/tr/q US$7/10/12/14; P) Various configurations of basic

The most interesting destination is **Yorkín**, in the Reserva Indígena Yorkín (it's a long trip, so it's best to spend the night). While you are there, you can meet with a local women's artisan group, **Mujeres Artesanas Stibrawpa** (☎ 8375 3372). These women offer demonstrations of basket-weaving (with plenty of fine examples you can purchase), roof thatching and cooking, not to mention lots of storytelling. Yorkín is a rewarding trip, but it is not easy to get there: it requires traveling in a traditional dugout canoe from the village of Bambú (midway between Puerto Viejo and Cahuita). To make arrangements contact Stibrawpa or **ATEC** (☎ 2750 0191, 2750 0398; www.greencoast.com/atec.htm; ☽ 8am-9pm).

Alternatively, you can visit the larger village of **Shiroles**, about 20km west of Bribrí. This is one of the most populous indigenous communities in the country and one of the easiest to access. It's a relatively modern place, and so it's very interesting to see how the indigenous people are adapting to outside influences and preserving their traditional customs.

ATEC is a comprehensive source of information about finding local guides to visit the reserves. Note that it is not really recommended to visit the reserves independently, for two reasons: these places are remote and very difficult to reach; and the villages do not have facilities for tourists. A guide will make arrangements for you to visit a local family, participate in daily life and learn about their customs and traditions.

It's wise to be aware of the issues that arise from this form of tourism. Most of the local tribes are very friendly people who welcome outsiders and are keen to show off their proud way of life, hoping that this in turn will encourage international support for them to exist as they do. However, as more tourists come and wave cash around, the more their raison d'être turns into a tourist attraction. As has happened in other parts of the world, increased Western contact and wealth could encourage the indigenous people to abandon their methods of survival, which in turn could drastically change their culture. So, it's worth taking into consideration the possible consequences of visiting these communities before signing up for a trip.

rooms, some with hot water, are adjacent to a large restaurant on the outskirts of town.

Delicias de Mi Tierra (mains US$2-5; ☽ 6am-9pm Mon-Sat) You can't miss this wide-open and popular spot close to the bus terminal, with a steam table and quality local meals.

Restaurante Bribrí (mains US$2-5; ☽ 5am-5pm Mon-Sat) A bit more plush, this restaurant not only serves good casados, *gallos* (tortilla sandwiches) and recommended fried plantains, but is also an excellent place to ask about tours to indigenous villages.

Getting There & Away
Buses to and from Sixaola usually stop in front of Restaurante Bribrí. Buses going north then continue to Puerto Viejo de Talamanca (30 minutes) and Cahuita (one hour), departing at 6:30am, 8:30pm, 10:30am and 3:30pm.

SIXAOLA
This is the end of the road as far as the Costa Rican Caribbean is concerned. Sixaola marks the country's secondary border crossing with Panama, though most foreign tourists travel overland via Paso Canoas on the

Interamericana. Sixaola is a border town, which – by definition – is not a nice place. But the crossing here is more relaxed than Paso Canoas; it's popular among expats without residency visas who take their required 72-hour vacation on the lovely islands of Bocas del Toro, Panama.

Sixaola is centered on the optimistically named Mercado Internacional de Sixaola, a gravelly square where you can find taxis, a handful of *sodas* and several small stores selling a wide selection of rubber boots. The market is about two blocks from the border crossing.

If you need to change money or use the toilet, ask at Restaurante La Prada, just north of the bridge on the main drag. For details on crossing the border at this point, see boxed text, p496.

Sleeping & Eating
While it's not exactly a layover in Tokyo, there are worse places to be stuck if you miss immigration hours. Accommodations and restaurants are basic, but certainly acceptable for any seasoned budget traveler.

GETTING TO GUABITO & BOCAS DEL TORO, PANAMA

With a reputation as one of Costa Rica's most relaxed border crossings, Sixaola is popular among folks embarking on their three-day 'visa vacation' to the islands of Bocas del Toro. The picturesque archipelago of jungle islands has more than a dozen beaches, home to everything from endangered red frogs and leatherback turtles to a dilapidated *Survivor* set, plus a range of accommodations, all accessible by convenient water taxis – paradise.

Get to Sixaola as early as possible. The border is open 7am to 5pm (8am to 6pm in Guabito, Panama, which is an hour ahead of Costa Rica); one or both sides may close for lunch at around 1pm. Begin crossing the high metal bridge over the Río Sixaola, stopping at Costa Rica **migración** (☎ 2754 2044) to process your paperwork. Cars can cross here, but be prepared for a long wait.

Once over the bridge, stop in the small office on the left-hand side which is home to Panama immigration. US citizens will be required to pay an entry fee of US$5. There is no bank, but in a pinch you can change your colones at the market across the street. Guabito has no hotels or banks, but it has plenty of taxis ready to take you further into Panama.

There are two ways to get to Bocas del Toro. The easiest, cheapest route is to take a taxi to Finca 63 near Changuinola (US$5), from where a water taxi goes regularly to Bocas (US$5, 45 minutes). Note that the last water taxi departs at 5:30pm Panama time (so if you are crossing the border at 5pm Costa Rica time you already missed it). Alternatively, you can take a taxi to Almirante (US$20, one hour), where there is another water taxi (US$3, 45 minutes) that runs every hour between 6:30am and 6:30pm.

Cabinas Sanchez (☎ 2754 2196; d US$10) This squat orange building has six clean rooms, offering cracked tiles in the bathroom and mismatched sheets. But it's a clean place to spend the night, about one block west of the main drag.

Hotel Imperio (☎ 2754 2289; d US$16) Cleaner and quieter, this basic motel's biggest selling point is its enviable location, 1km from the border but directly across the street from the police checkpoint.

Soda Navi (mains US$2-4; 6am-9pm) Facing the Mercado Internacional, it's a nice spot with crocheted décor specializing in *gallo pinto* and fried fish casados.

Restaurante Las Cabinas (mains US$2-5; 7am-9:30pm) This is as upscale as it gets in Sixaola, with pretty checkered tablecloths, fried chicken and to-go food.

Getting There & Away

The bus station is one block north of the border crossing, on the east side of the main drag. Buses to either San José or Puerto Limón all stop at Bribrí and Cahuita, but only some go through Puerto Viejo.

Puerto Limón US$3, three hours, depart at 5am, 7am, 8am, 10am, noon, 1pm, 4pm and 6pm.

San José US$9.50, five hours, depart at 6am, 8am, 10am and 3pm.

CARIBBEAN COAST

Northern Lowlands

It's getting harder and harder to get away from it all in Costa Rica – it's only natural for a country this richly blessed with varied gifts to be such a desirable destination. So the saturation point of popular *playas* (beaches) means spillover to the next not-so-secret sliver of coast, and zip lines continue to proliferate over the canopies from Monteverde to Manzanillo. But travelers who stray to the wild rivers and tropical jungle of the northern lowlands, find that in these places, the getting-away is still good.

Tourism has certainly touched the lowlands, creating added revenue for a local economy whose living has historically been made from agriculture. Plantations of banana, sugar cane and pineapple roll across the humid plains from the Cordillera Central to the Nicaraguan border; these plantations are fringed by tropical forest out of which arable soil has been slashed. But green is the color of budding tourism around these parts. Conservationists team with landowners and local governments to make ecotourism work for all parties involved – whether it's the family farmer, the naturalist or the endangered great green macaw.

Birders, hoping to spot this macaw in the wild, flock to remote lodges in the verdant rain forests of the San Juan–La Selva Biological Corridor, while paddlers who are in the know show up to run the fun rapids of the Río Sarapiquí. Wildlife-watchers and fisherfolk alike head to the lagoons of Caño Negro, and travelers of all stripes are hopping launches up the Río Frío for the languid, fauna-rich river crossing to Nicaragua. This is real-life Costa Rica, where the balance of agricultural commerce and ecological conservation converge to create a contemporary work in green progress.

NORTHERN LOWLANDS

HIGHLIGHTS

- Slip-sliding through swampy jungle to spot poison-dart frog and rare green macaw at **Laguna del Lagarto Lodge** (p501)

- Rafting the wildlife-rife **Río Sarapiquí** (p512) near La Virgen

- Keeping your eyes peeled for crocs and sloths as you float to the **Río San Juan** (p515) at the Nicaraguan border

- Motoring via tractor to the luscious rainforest isolation of **Rara Avis** (p520)

- Exploring the lagoons of **Refugio Nacional de Vida Silvestre Caño Negro** (p507) to take a gander at spoonbills or a stab at tarpon

- Traipsing the suspension bridges of **Tirimbina Rainforest Center** (p515)

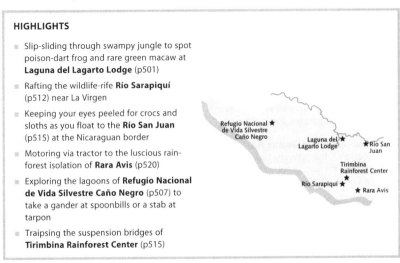

History

Life in the northern lowlands has always followed the rhythms of seasonal rains – when river banks swelled and flooded across the plains the landscape was transformed into a vast swamp that enabled people to subsist on fish, fowl and small game. However, as populations flourished and resources were strained, the earth was altered with the swing of a hoe, and the lowlands were slowly reshaped by farming interests.

In the early 1900s the United Fruit Company planted bananas across Costa Rica and built a railroad from the Caribbean coast to transport them. Many locales in the northern lowlands were originally established by, or branched off from, the banana trade and these settlements continue to make agriculture their business.

Climate

As in most of Costa Rica, the climate varies within this region. From the hot, dry Llanura de Guatusos along the Nicaraguan border, the northern plains roll southward to swampy lowlands and tropical hardwood forests. In the northern lowlands, the dry season runs from April to November. However, the lush jungles surrounding the rivers in the region, such as the Río Frío and the Río Sarapiquí, receive rainfall at almost any time of year.

Parks & Reserves

Several notable refuges and parks are found in the northern lowlands, offering opportunities for low-key, crowd-free boat tours and wildlife-watching.

Parque Nacional Braulio Carrillo (p519) Ecolodges in the Sarapiquí area can arrange rain-forest tours and have accommodations at the northern end of Braulio Carrillo.

Refugio Nacional de Vida Silvestre Caño Negro (p506) The lagoons of Caño Negro attract a wide variety of birds year-round, though prime time for birders is between January and July.

Refugio Nacional de Vida Silvestre Mixto Maquenque (p501) Though there isn't much in the way of infrastructure at this newly formed refuge, local lodges can take you into this remote rain forest.

Getting There & Around

Transport hubs to the lowlands include Puerto Viejo de Sarapiquí and San Miguel to the southeast, and Upala and Los Chiles to the northwest, all of which are served by daily buses from San José. If you're not in a hurry, you can get around with little hassle via public bus, but having your own vehicle will allow you greater ease in getting to the appealingly far-flung reaches of this relatively tourist-free region. In the far north, the border outpost of Los Chiles serves as a launching point for lovely river trips across the border to San Carlos, Nicaragua (see the boxed text Getting to San Carlos, Nicaragua, p510).

HIGHWAY 126 TO SAN MIGUEL

Curving up the slopes of the Cordillera Central, Hwy 126 leaves behind the urban bustle of Heredia and Alajuela and leads to the foot of Volcán Poás before descending again into the bougainvillea-laced greenery of fincas and pastureland.

This is *campesino* (farmer) country, where the plodding hoofbeat of cattle is about the speed of life, as the hard-to-spot rural speed-bumps will remind you if you take those curves too quickly.

The highway passes through a number of small towns and villages before reaching San Miguel, which is the main transport hub in the southeast corner of the region. From San Miguel, you can head northwest towards Los Chiles or northeast towards Puerto Viejo de Sarapiquí. Buses from San José to Puerto Viejo de Sarapiquí follow this route.

VARA BLANCA & AROUND

Hwy 126 climbs to just more than 2000m before reaching the tiny village of Vara Blanca, and, if you are lucky, on a clear day you can see Volcán Poás to the west and Volcán Barva to the east. At the gas station in town, continue straight if you're heading to Poás or make a right turn for San Miguel. A few kilometers past the turnoff, the road starts to descend at a dizzying speed. If you're on a tour or driving your own car, there are numerous viewpoints to stop for a photograph as well as ample opportunities for high- and middle-elevation bird-watching.

About 8km north of Vara Blanca, Río La Paz is crossed by a bridge on a hairpin bend; to your left you will find an excellent view of the absolutely spectacular Catarata La Paz.

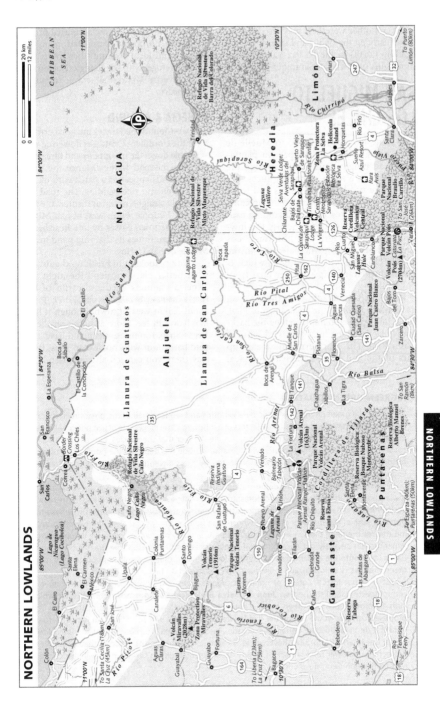

NORTHERN LOWLANDS

Several other waterfalls may also be seen, particularly on the right-hand side (if you are heading north) in the La Paz Valley, which soon joins up with the Sarapiquí Valley.

SAN MIGUEL TO LOS CHILES

The route from San Miguel to Muelle de San Carlos is trimmed by papaya plantations and jungles and winds through the mountains in a series of hairpin turns. But just as the patchwork of fincas and wildflowers gives way entirely to sugar cane, the road opens to a long, straight and usually steaming-hot stretch across the lowlands to Caño Negro and hot, dusty Los Chiles. This is the principal route to the border crossing with Nicaragua, which is a straightforward trip via river boat from Los Chiles.

If, instead of heading northwest, you travel north through the small town of Pital, you'll find yourself bumping along the backroads of one of the least-touristed parts of Costa Rica. This northern zone makes up part of the San Juan–La Selva Biological Corridor, an ongoing collaborative project involving nonprofit conservation organizations and local communities to create a wildlife refuge, with the Refugio Nacional de Vida Silvestre Mixto Maquenque (opposite) at its heart.

VENECIA & AROUND

The westbound road traces the northern limits of the Cordillera Central as flowering vines scramble down the mountains and threaten to overtake the road. In the distance, the northern lowlands appear as a patchwork quilt of cane fields and rice paddies. The road momentarily straightens out as it enters the rural town of Venecia, 14km west of San Miguel, though the town passes by in a heartbeat as the road continues its dizzying wind toward Muelle de San Carlos.

If you're looking to break up the driving, what better place to spend the night than Venecia's famous 'Medieval castle' of **Torre Fuerte Cabinas** (☎ 2472 2424; s/d US$21/29; **P** 🔀), about 2.5km west of town. Though it looks like it would feel more at home on the Las Vegas Strip, rooms are clean and have a private bathroom with hot water. Plus, if you stay there you can tell all your friends and

---

A GREEN-GREEN SITUATION

The gorgeous green plumage, electric-blue wingtips and red forehead of the great green macaw (*Ara ambiguus*) have long attracted collectors of exotic birds. The illegal sale of just one great green macaw can fetch several thousand dollars, despite the fact that the species' nervous personality causes them to fare poorly in captivity. International trade has depleted the population, though fortunately, the great green macaw is protected by the Convention on International Trade in Endangered Species (CITES).

In addition to illegal poaching, deforestation also threatens the great green macaw. The northern lowlands have suffered from heavy deforestation in recent years due to the demand for increased agricultural and pasture land. Furthermore, the almendro tree (*Dipteryx panamensis*), whose nut provides 90% of the macaw's diet and whose high hollows are far and away the preferred nesting tree for breeding pairs, is highly sought after as a luxury hardwood. Extensive logging of the almendro has severely cut back potential nesting sites, and as a result, the great green macaw has made it onto the endangered species list. It's estimated that Costa Rica's population of great green macaws is as low as 200 individuals, with as few as 30 breeding pairs left.

But all is not lost! A coterie of nonprofit organizations and government agencies formed a committee to establish the **San Juan–La Selva Biological Corridor** (www.lapaverde.or.cr), which aims to protect existing green macaw populations as well as other species in the area. The proposed corridor would bridge the gap between the Central Volcanic Mountain Range, Refugio Nacional de Vida Silvestre Barra del Colorado, Parque Nacional Tortuguero and the Indio-Maíz, Punta Gorda and Cerro Silva Reserves in Nicaragua. Eventually, the hope is that all of these protected areas will form a part of a Mesoamerican Biological Corridor that will stretch from Mexico through Central America.

family that you spent the night in a Costa Rican castle.

A great place to relax and rejuvenate your body after a long drive is **Recreo Verde** (☎ 2472 1020; www.recreoverde.com; camping US$15, s/d incl breakfast US$35/55; **P**), which has a number of rustic cabinas near a river bend, all with private bathrooms. Guests have access to four mineral baths featuring a variety of different colored mud, as well as three cold-water pools fed by mountain-spring water. There's also a soccer pitch for a quick pick-up game, and a number of rain-forest trails that you can hike and explore. You can also go spelunking in the Cueva de la Muerte (Cave of Death), though the only real danger is the risk of catching a cold.

Halfway between San Miguel and Venecia is the hamlet of Río Cuarto, from where an unpaved road heads southeast past the beautiful **waterfall** near Bajos del Toro, through Parque Nacional Juan Castro Blanco, and on to Zarcero.

BOCA TAPADA AREA

Don't bother venturing out here if Tico time ticks you off; the rocky roads and lack of signage (even less than usual!) could mean

a few unintended detours. On the roads that pass pineapple fields and packing plants, your fellow travelers will be commuting *caballeros* (cowboys) and *campesinos* going about their day-to-day business. And at the end of the road, you'll be rewarded with a luxuriant bit of rain forest replete with frog songs, rare avian residents and an inkling of the symbiosis that can happen when humans make the effort. Local ecolodges offer rain-forest tours into the Refugio Nacional de Vida Silvestre Mixto Maquenque; for more information, see the boxed text A Green-Green Situation (opposite).

Sleeping & Eating

Laguna del Lagarto Lodge (☎ 2289 8163; www.lagarto-lodge-costa-rica.com; s/d/tr US$52/69/79; **P**) This environmentally sensitive, German-run lodge is surrounded by 1300 hectares of virgin rain forest and is something of a legend among birders. Simple but pleasant screened rooms have private bathrooms, fans and share a large, hammock-strung verandas. Package tours include transportation from San José, all meals and guided tours. Otherwise, breakfast is US$6, lunch US$7.50 and dinner US$14. Room rates include an afternoon guided

In 2005, the **Refugio Nacional de Vida Silvestre Mixto Maquenque** was officially declared by then-President Abel Pacheco. Owing to this victory, Maquenque now protects an estimated 6000 species of vascular plants, 139 mammals, 515 birds, 135 reptiles and 80 amphibians. And as a 'mixed-use' wildlife refuge, the first of its kind in Costa Rica, allows human residents to continue living and working within the boundaries of the refuge. However, most of the refuge's 50,000-odd hectares, which are privately owned, are now bound to certain regulations, such as the drastic reduction of activities like logging. So where does this leave the residents, who depend on forestry and agriculture for subsistence?

Enter the **Costa Rican Bird Route**, a project initiated by the nonprofit Rainforest Biodiversity Group in partnership with several other nonprofit organizations. The Costa Rican Bird Route has been working with and educating communities within these protected areas to help create viable and sustainable ecotourism opportunities, as economic alternatives to habitat-destructive agriculture and logging. While promoting existing locally-owned lodges throughout the region, the Costa Rican Bird Route is also helping to establish new, community-based ecolodges from Río San Juan to Parque Nacional Braulio Carrillo. The hope is that green tourism – a field in which Costa Rica shines – will not only be financially beneficial to these poor communities, but will also be salvation for the great green macaw.

The great news for travelers is that this blossoming birding route offers a rare chance for a wilder birding experience in one of the least-developed regions of Costa Rica. Not only do you get to interact in a real way with the local people and contribute directly to their communities, but traveling way out here may lead you right into the path of a beautiful great green macaw.

We've listed some lodges participating in the Costa Rican Bird Route, in the Boca Tapada area (above) and around Puerto Viejo de Sarapiquí (p514). Check the website (www.costaricanbirdroute.com) for specific lodges, as well as for current volunteer opportunities.

hike through the jungle and a nighttime caiman-feeding walk.

Most of the 500-hectare 'grounds' of the lodge is rain forest, some of which is swamp – as a result the area's 10km of trails can get quite mucky. Canoes are available to explore the surrounding lagoons, where caimans dwell and Jesus Christ lizards make tracks across the water's surface. Horseback trips and boat tours down along the Nicaraguan border can be arranged.

The lodge is about 9km from Boca Tapada, and the staff can also arrange round-trip transportation from San José for US$120 per person (two-person minimum).

Tico-run lodges near Boca Tapada include **Mi Pedacito de Cielo** (☎ 8308 9595; www.pedacitodecielo .net; s/d/tr US$60/70/80; P), whose name charmingly means 'my little piece of heaven.' The lodge has several rustic wooden bungalows built into the semi-wild forest. There is also **Maquenque Eco-Lodge** (☎ 479-8200; www.costarican birdroute.com/sites/maquenque.htm; P), which was under construction at press time. Both lodges offer birding, boating and horseback tours in the Maquenque wildlife refuge.

Getting There & Away

If you're driving, getting to Boca Tapada is an adventure in itself. The nearest town of note is Pital, north of Aguas Zarcas. After passing through Pital, turn right after the church on the right and soccer field on the left and continue through the village of Veracruz. At the Del Huerto pineapple packing plant, hang a left and continue along the paved road. About 10km later where the pavement ends, turn right at the intersection. When you come to the gas station, turn right at the intersection and follow the signs for Mi Pedacito del Cielo to Boca Tapada.

Buses from San José (US$4.30, six hours) depart from the Atlántico Norte terminal at 5:30am and 12:30pm daily, with a connection to Boca Tapada, where most lodges can pick you up by prior request.

MUELLE DE SAN CARLOS

This small crossroads village is locally called Muelle, which means 'dock,' seemingly because 'Cañas' was already taken – this is sugar cane country. Breaks in the sweet scenery include huge sugar cane-processing facilities, always interesting to ponder over a soda, and very slow sugar cane-hauling trucks, so drive carefully. This was, actually, an important dock (hence the shipping infrastructure still here) as it's the most inland spot from which the Río San Carlos is navigable.

The main tourist activity in Muelle is pulling over to have a look at the map. A 24-hour gas station lies at the intersection of Hwy 4 (which connects Ciudad Quesada and Upala) and Hwy 35 (running from San José to Los Chiles). From Hwy 4 you can easily catch Hwy 32, the main artery serving the Caribbean coast. Can't decide? A range of accommodations will let you sleep on it, and they're convenient to just about everything.

Sleeping & Eating

Cabinas Beitzy (☎ 2469 9100; camping US$4, d US$10; P ☂) The cheapest accommodation in town is on the road to Los Chiles. It's perfectly acceptable if you need a place to crash, and the pool is surprisingly well-maintained. Rooms are (not surprisingly) bare and share cold showers. If you're counting every dollar, you can also pitch a tent here and save yourself a few bucks.

La Quinta Lodge (☎ 2475 5260; fax 2475 5921; s/d US$30/35, cabinas per person US$10; P ☂) About 5km south of Muelle in the tiny community of Platanar, this friendly Tico-run inn has a pool with a small waterslide and sauna. Birds have adopted the grounds, and there's a small river behind the inn where fish and caiman can be seen. This is a popular option with Tico families as the atmosphere is warm and inviting.

Hotel La Garza (☎ 2475 5222; www.hotellagarza .com; d/tr incl breakfast US$75/90, additional person US$15; P ✕ ☂) Also near Platanar, this attractive, upscale lodge sits on a 700-hectare working dairy ranch and citrus plantation with views of the Río Platanar and far-off Volcán Arenal. Visitors enter the landscaped reception and restaurant area via a graceful suspension footbridge, and the 12 polished wooden bungalows with big porch, ceiling fan, telephone and good-size private bathroom have a touch of class. Tennis, basketball and volleyball courts are available, as are 4km of private trails, a swimming pool and Jacuzzi. Tours are available, including horseback rides through primary and secondary tropical forest land (US$25/40 for two/four hours).

Tilajari Resort Hotel (☎ 2469 9091; www.tilajari .com; s/d incl breakfast from US$86/96, additional person US$15; P ✕ ☂ ▢ ☂) This former country club turned luxury resort has well-landscaped

---

SUGAR IN THE RAW

The origins of the sugar industry lie in the European colonization of the Americas, particularly on the Caribbean islands. Although it was possible for Europeans to import sugar from the colonies in Asia, the advent of slavery in the New World meant that sugar cane could be grown for a fraction of the cost. This in turn led to lower prices for the European consumer, which took precedent over the lives of the slaves forced to work in the fields.

During the 18th century, European diets started to change dramatically as sugar increased in popularity. Coffee, tea and cocoa were consumed in greater frequency, and processed foods such as candies and jams became commonplace items. The demand for increased production fueled the slave trade, though the actual process of refining sugar became increasingly mechanized.

Today, sugar is one of the most heavily subsidized agricultural products in industrial countries. Sugar prices in the USA, the EU and Japan are on average three times the international market cost as governments maintain elevated price floors by subsidizing domestic production and imposing high tariffs on imports. As a result, sugar-exporting countries are excluded from these markets, and thus receive lower prices than they would under a system of free trade. Brazil, which exports more than a quarter of the world's supply of refined sugar and heads a coalition of sugar-exporting nations, has repeatedly lobbied the World Trade Organization to reform the market.

For countries like Costa Rica, sugar production is mainly a domestic industry because it's not profitable to export sugar to countries that levy a high tariff on imports – true even with the ratification of Cafta (US-Central American Free Trade Agreement), or TLC (Tratado de Libre Comercio), as the US is loathe to open its sugar market to lower-priced imports.

Harvesting sugar cane manually is exhausting work as the stalks can grow to a height of 4m and they are thick, fibrous and difficult to cut down. It's becoming increasingly common in Costa Rica for sugar cane to be harvested using self-propelled harvesting machines, which has made it difficult for rural Ticos to find employment.

The next time you're driving through cane country, support the local industry and look for signs advertising *jugo de caña* – there's nothing quite like a cool glass of fresh sugar-cane juice.

---

grounds overlooking the Río San Carlos, and it offers an impressive number of tours and activities. Comfortable, well-appointed rooms are accented with wood details and have private hot shower, cable TV, refrigerator and private terrace. A few of the rooms and private trails are wheelchair accessible. Other amenities include a lovely pool area, racquetball and tennis courts, a restaurant, sauna, spa and butterfly garden (admission US$3), plus access to the neighboring 400-hectare private rain-forest reserve with several trails. The resort is 800m west of the intersection at Muelle, on the road to Ciudad Quesada.

There are a number of *sodas* (inexpensive eateries) and a small supermarket on the road toward Los Chiles that will do just fine if you're looking for your casado-fix. However, one recommended spot is **Restaurant/Bar La Subasta** (☎ 2467 8087; mains US$3-7; ☺ 11am-11pm), which overlooks a bullpen and is bustling with hungry *campesinos*. It has an expansive menu of local dishes, and it's a great spot for a cold beer. If you speak Spanish, strike up a conversa-tion here as you're bound to meet some interesting characters.

SAN RAFAEL DE GUATUSO AREA

The small town of Guatuso (shown on some maps as San Rafael) is 19km northeast of Nuevo Arenal and 40km east of Fortuna (not to be confused with the town of La Fortuna), and is the main population center of this pre-dominantly agricultural area. Although the town itself is rather unremarkable, it's a good base for exploring the fantastic Venado Caves and Parque Nacional Volcán Tenorio (p205). The area is also home to the few remaining Maleku, one of Costa Rica's indigenous popu-lations, and Guatuso makes a good base for visiting the nearby *palenques* (indigenous set-tlements); see the boxed text A Brief History of the Maleku, p504.

Venado Caves

Four kilometers south of Venado (Spanish for 'deer') along a good dirt road, the **caves** (☎ 2478 8071; admission US$10; ☺ 7am-4pm) are a popular rainy-day attraction that can be organized

NORTHERN LOWLANDS

A BRIEF HISTORY OF THE MALEKU

The Maleku (colloquially referred to as the Guatuso) are one of the few remaining indigenous groups in Costa Rica. Unlike other pre-Columbian populations, the Maleku are closer in stature to Europeans, and their skin tone is comparatively lighter than other groups in Central America. Historically, the Maleku were organized into 12 communities that were scattered around the Tilarán-Guanacaste Range and the San Carlos Plains.

Although their numbers dwindled following the arrival of Spanish colonists, the population survived relatively intact until the early 20th century. With the invention of the automobile, the US rubber industry started searching for new reserves to meet the increasing demand for tires. With the aid of Nicaraguan mercenaries, industry representatives scoured Central America for stable reserves, which were found on Maleku-inhabited land. The resulting rubber war virtually wiped out the population, and confined the survivors to a handful of communities. Today, the Maleku number around 400, and live in the three *palenques* of Sol, Margarita and Tonjibe.

As is the situation with most indigenous groups in Costa Rica, the Maleku are one of the poorest communities in the country, and survive by adhering to a subsistence lifestyle. Their diet revolves around corn and the *tipuisqui* root, a traditional food source that grows wild in the region. Fortunately, since the Maleku have a rich, artisan tradition, they are able to earn a small income by selling traditional crafts to tourists. Although their modern crafts primarily consist of pottery, jewelry, musical instruments and other small trinkets that are desirable to tourists, historically they were renowned for their impressive jade work and arrow craftsmanship.

The Maleku are also famous for their unique style of clothing known as *tana*. Although it's rare to see modern Maleku wearing anything other then Western-style clothing, *tana* articles are often offered to tourists for purchase. *Tana* is actually tree bark that has been stripped of its outer layer, soaked in water and then pounded thin on wooden blocks. After it has been dried and bleached in the sun, it can be stitched together like leather, and has a soft texture similar to suede.

Despite being small in number, the Maleku have held on to their cultural heritage, perhaps more than any other indigenous group in Costa Rica. This is especially evident in their language, which is one of the oldest in the Americas and linguistically unique from the Amazonian and Maya dialects. Today, the Maleku still speak their language to one another, and a local radio station, Radio Sistema Cultural Maleku, airs daily programs in the Maleku language. The Maleku have also maintained their ceremonial traditions, such as the trimonthly custom of crying out to Mother Nature for forgiveness through ritualistic song and dance.

As with all indigenous reservations in Costa Rica, the Maleku welcome tourists as craft sales are vital to their survival. You can access the *palenques* via Rte 143, though it's best to inquire locally for directions as the roads are poorly maintained and unsigned. While you're at the *palenque*, please be sensitive to their situation and buy a few small crafts. If you can, you might also consider bringing some small, useful gifts such as pencils, pens and paper. And of course, avoid giving handouts such as money and candy as this will only create a culture of begging.

as a day trip from La Fortuna, San José and many other cities for US$45 to US$65 per person (including transportation and lunch). It's cheaper to visit by yourself, though bus service is inconvenient.

The caves were discovered by chance in 1945 when a farmer fell through a hole in the ground and found himself in an underground chamber surrounded by stalactites (hanging *tight* to the ceiling) and stalagmites (that *might* reach the ceiling…get it?). The exploration that followed uncovered an eight-chamber limestone labyrinth that extends for almost 3km. The cavern system, composed of soft, malleable limestone, was carved over the millennia by a series of underground rivers.

The caverns get rave reviews from folks fond of giant spiders, swarms of bats and eyeless fish. A guide takes you through the caves, including a few tight squeezes, pointing out various rock formations and philosophizing about what they sort of look like.

Drop-ins are welcome, but it's best to make reservations so you don't need to wait around for a group. You're provided with a guide (some speak English), lights, helmets and showers afterward. You'll definitely want to bring a change of clothes. There's a small *soda* on site, and a few nicer spots for a snack in Venado, but no lodging.

A 1pm bus from Ciudad Quesada drops you off at a steep 4km slog to the cavern entrance at about 2pm, with pick-up at 4pm – hurry! A taxi from Guatuso will cost from US$15 to US$20. If you're driving, the caves are well-signed.

Sleeping & Eating

There are several clean, basic cabinas in San Rafael de Guatuso, sometimes used on a long-term basis by farm workers, as well as a good selection of *sodas* and stores.

Cabinas Milagro (☎ 2464 0037; s/d US$6/10; P) This quiet, family-run place on the edge of town is a tranquil budget option. From the center, go past the church toward the Río Frío bridge and turn right just past the soccer field. Rooms have cold showers and fan.

Cabinas El Bosque (☎ 2464 0335; s/d with fan US$7/11, with air-con US$10/15; P) Just a bit north of town on the road toward Upala, this 10-room hotel is a bit impersonal, though it has clean, simple rooms with private, cold-water showers and optional air-con.

Cabinas Tío Henry (☎ 2464 0344; r per person US$9; P) Big, clean, air-conditioned rooms here are relatively plush, with cable TV and private hot shower. The cabinas are centrally located in town, though the reception is at the vet and feed store next door.

Soda La Macha (☎ 2464 0393; mains US$3; breakfast, lunch & dinner) You don't exactly get a menu at this fine *soda*, on the main road across from the bus stop. Everything here is cooked using a wood-fired oven. Just request your casado or *gallo* (tortilla sandwich) preferences and they'll be made on the spot.

Getting There & Away

Guatuso lies on Hwy 4, about 40km from both Upala, to the northwest, and Muelle, to the southeast. Buses leave about every two hours for either Tilarán or Ciudad Quesada, some of which continue to San José. Ciudad Quesada is the most frequent destination.

UPALA

Just 9km south of the Nicaraguan border in the northwestern corner of the northern lowlands, Upala is a small but thriving town that serves a widespread community of some 15,000 people. A center for the area's cattle and rice industries, Upala enjoys some

apparent affluence. Most visitors are Costa Rican businesspeople, who arrive in town to negotiate for a few dozen calves or a truckload of grain, but travelers who need to stop for the night between Caño Negro and the northwestern coast will find it nice enough.

Sleeping

Rooms fill up quicker than you'd expect, though there are plenty of options in town.

Hotel Buena Vista (☎ 2470 0186; r US$9; P) This cute yellow compound is a steal, with clean but unremarkable rooms that come with private hot-water bathroom and TV. There's a shaded courtyard and secure parking at this family-run spot. Find it 150m south of the metal bridge.

Hotel Upala (☎ 2470 0169; s/d US$12/18; P) The most established hotel in town is always a good choice as all the rooms are spotless and bright, and you can watch the soccer games from your private porch. Rooms have a private cold shower and cable TV.

Cabinas Maleku (☎ 2470 0142; s/d with fan US$12/20, with air-con US$18/24; P) Though it's a few dollars more, this is the best option in town. Big, high-ceilinged rooms with colorful cartoon murals have folksy furniture, including cheery Sarchí-style wooden chairs in front of the rooms. All rooms have a private bathroom and a large TV with cable.

Eating

The busy market, just behind the bus terminal, opens early with several nice *sodas* dishing up good *gallos*, *empanadas* (corn turnovers filled with meat, cheese or fruit) and just about everything else. There are also a few Chinese restaurants and produce vendors.

Soda Norma (☎ 8819 7048; mains US$4-6; 6:30am-9pm) With outdoor tables overlooking the park, this is a seriously top-notch *soda*, serving some of the most beautiful casados, with all the trimmings, you've ever seen.

Restaurant Buena Vista (☎ 2470 0063; mains US$4-6; 11am-9pm) This breezy spot serves a good mix of typical Chinese food. It's also aptly named (Good View) as the river views are wonderful.

Rancho Don Horacio (☎ 2470 0905; mains US$6-9; 11am-10pm) Right off the plaza and far more atmospheric is this romantic restaurant with red tablecloths, mood lighting and a nice bar. The specialty is steak, and chances are it

NORTHERN LOWLANDS

was born, raised and slaughtered right here in Upala.

Getting There & Away

Upala is connected to the Interamericana north of Cañas by Hwy 6, an excellent paved road, and also to La Fortuna and Laguna de Arenal by the somewhat more potholed Hwy 4. A rough, unpaved road, usually passable to all cars, skirts the Refugio Nacional de Vida Silvestre Caño Negro on the way to Los Chiles, the official border crossing with Nicaragua.

Other dirt roads cross the Nicaraguan border, 9km away, but these are not official entry points into either Costa Rica or Nicaragua.

The bus terminal is right off the park; a **ticket booth** (4:30-5:15am, 7:30am-1pm & 6:45-8pm Mon-Sat) has information and can store bags for US$1. Taxis congregate just outside the Upala bus terminal, by the park. The following buses depart from Upala.

Caño Negro US$1, one hour, 11am.

Los Chiles US$2.50, two hours, 5am, 11am and 4pm.

San José, via Cañas US$6, five hours, 10:15am, 3pm and 5:15pm.

San José, via Ciudad Quesada/San Carlos US$6, five hours, 3:45pm.

REFUGIO NACIONAL DE VIDA SILVESTRE CAÑO NEGRO

Because of the region's relative remoteness (although this has changed in recent years with the improvement of roads), this 102-sq-km refuge has long been frequented primarily by two sorts of specialists. Anglers come in search of that elusive 18kg snook, though they abandon ship April through July, when the park is closed to fishing (a good time to get a bargain price on accommodations). Birders alight on the refuge each year from January through March to spot an unequalled assortment of waterfowl. During the dry season water levels drop, with the effect of concentrating the birds (and fish) in photogenically (or tasty) close quarters. From January to March, when migratory birds land in large numbers, avian density is most definitely world class.

The Río Frío defines the landscape – a table-flat, swampy expanse of marsh that is similar in appearance to other famous wetlands such as the Florida Everglades or the Mekong Delta. During the wet season, the river breaks its banks to form an 800-hectare lake, and then contracts during the dry months from January through April,

when water levels drop to the point where the river is barely navigable. By April it has almost completely disappeared – until the May rains begin. This cycle has proceeded without fail for millennia, and the small fishing communities that live around the edges of the reserve have adapted to each seasonal nuance of their environment.

Thanks to improved roads, dozens of tour operators are now able to offer relatively inexpensive trips to Caño Negro from all over the country. However, it's advisable to book your trip through a reputable tour company as it's fairly common practice for operators to save on park fees by taking tourists on a boat ride through swampy private property that is by all accounts lovely, though not Caño Negro. If you're more independently minded, you'll save yourself a little money (and have a much better experience) by heading directly to the park without a tour operator, and hiring a local guide in town. This practice is recommended as it puts money directly in the hands of locals, and encourages communities in the area to protect the wildlife.

Orientation & Information

Caño Negro refuge is part of the Area de Conservación Arenal–Huetar Norte and is accessible primarily by boat. Close to the park entrance (that'd be the dock) is the tiny community of Caño Negro, which has no grocery stores, banks or gas stations, though there is a **Minae office** (2471 1309; 8am-4pm), where you pay your entrance fees (US$6).

You can get all other information and arrange guided tours at the **ranger station** (2471 1309; 8am-5pm), located about 400m from the dock. In addition to administering the refuge, rangers are contact points for local guides and a few community projects, including a butterfly garden put together by a local women's association (Asomucan). You can camp (US$2 per person) by the river, or stay in the rangers' house for US$6 with advance reservations. There are cold showers and meals can be arranged.

Local guides for fishing and ecological tours can also be arranged at most hotels and restaurants in town. You can usually find a guide (US$10 to US$20 per hour) on short notice, but they can get booked up during peak fishing and birding seasons.

THE WEEPING FOREST

Extensive deforestation of the Caño Negro area began in the 1970s in response to an increase in population density and the subsequent need for more farmland. Although logging was allowed to proceed in the area for almost 20 years, the government took action in 1991 with the creation of the Refugio Nacional de Vida Silvestre Caño Negro. Since its creation, Caño Negro has served as a safe habitat for the region's aquatic and terrestrial birds, and has acted as a refuge for numerous migratory birds.

However, illegal logging and poaching have continued around the perimeter of the park, and the wildlife has accordingly suffered. In the last two decades, one-time residents of the park including ocelot, manatee, shark and macaw have vanished. Tarpon and caiman populations are decreasing, and fewer migratory birds are returning to the park each year. Additionally, anglers are reporting record lows in both the size and number of their catches.

Satellite images show that the lake is shrinking each year, and that water levels in the Río Frío are dropping rapidly. It's difficult to say with certainty what is causing these changes, though the farms surrounding Caño Negro require extensive irrigation, and sugar cane is nearly 10 times as water intensive as wheat.

Locals are extremely worried about the stability of the park as entire communities are dependent on fishing and tourism for their survival. In response to the growing need to regulate development in the region, area residents have formed a number of organizations aimed at controlling development in the northern lowlands. If you want to support the Caño Negro community, avoid booking your tour in another town and spend your tourist dollar locally.

Wildlife-Watching

Caño Negro is regarded among birders as one of the premier destinations in Central America. During the dry season, the sheer density of birds in the park is astounding, and you'll be impressed with the number and variety of different species that inhabit the park. In the winter months, migratory duck congregations can be enormous, and very well represented groups include kingfisher, heron, egret, ibis, rail, anhinga, roseate spoonbill and stork. The refuge is also the only reliable site in Costa Rica for olivaceous cormorant, Nicaraguan grackle and lesser yellow-headed vulture.

Reptiles are easily seen in the park, especially spectacled caiman, green iguana and striped basilisk. Commonly sighted mammals in Caño Negro include howler monkey, white-faced capuchin and two-toed sloth. Despite increasing incursions from poachers, puma, jaguar and tapir have also been recorded here in surprising numbers.

Caño Negro also possesses an abundant number of river turtle, which historically were an important part of the Maleku diet (see the boxed text A Brief History of the Maleku, p504). Prior to a hunt, the Maleku would appease the turtle god Javara by fasting and abstaining from sex. If the hunt was successful, the Maleku would later celebrate by feasting on smoked turtle meat and consuming large quantities of *chicha*, an alcohol derived from maize.

Mosquitoes in Caño Negro are huge, abundant and most definitely classifiable as wildlife. Bring bug spray, or suffer the consequences.

Tours

If you don't have your own car or you're not a fan of public transportation, then it's easiest to organize a day trip to Caño Negro from La Fortuna, San José or any hotel within a 150km radius. Tours are geared toward wildlife-watching, though travelers report that a boatload of noisy tourists tends to scare away most animals. If you're looking to do a little sportfishing, it's best to organize your trips through one of the lodges in the park. Fishing licenses, valid for two months, can be arranged through the lodges or at the ranger station for US$30; you will need a photocopy of your passport and a small photo.

Caño Negro is not as difficult to access as it once was, and you'll have a much better experience if you avoid the tour operators and head directly to the park. Hiring a local guide is quick, easy and full of advantages – you'll be supporting the local economy, you'll have more privacy when you're out on the water and, of course, there's the satisfaction of doing things independently. You can

NORTHERN LOWLANDS

TOP WATERWAYS FOR WILDLIFE-WATCHERS

Head to some of the following waterways for an up-close glimpse of the local wildlife.

- Whether you're resting between rapids or traveling up to Trinidad, keep your eyes peeled for somnolent sloth or mud-covered caiman as you float up the **Río Sarapiquí** (p512).
- Wake early to savor a quiet view of breakfasting birds on the lagoons of **Caño Negro** (p507).
- Not only is the **Río Frío** (p510) the kinder, gentler border crossing into Nicaragua, but you'll see trees filled with howler and caiman on the riverbanks along the way.
- Lodges in the Boca Tapada area can get you on the **Río San Carlos** (p501), where the slow flow near the Río San Juan affords good opportunities for birding.
- Float on the **Río Medio Queso** (opposite), which is off the well-trafficked tributaries and where wildlife abounds.

---

usually find indie guides hanging out around the dock during the day.

Either way, the key to Caño Negro is to get there as early in the morning as possible when wildlife is still active, and it's worth paying extra for an overnight adventure that puts you in the water by 7am. Folks staying in town basically have the refuge to themselves at daybreak, with boat-trippers from Puerto Viejo de Sarapiquí and Los Chiles arriving by 9am.

Sleeping & Eating

There are a few budget lodging options in town, plus a handful of nicer accommodations down the road, most of which are geared toward fishing.

Albergue Caño Negro (☎ 2471 2029; r per person US$12; P) There's no sign indicating the cheapest accommodation in the area, a family-run venture of small cabinas overlooking the lagoon. Rooms are simple and share cold-water bathrooms, but the proprietors, Manuel and Isabel, are relaxed and friendly. Look for the stilt cabinas past the bend in the road after the Caño Negro Natural Lodge.

Cabinas Martín Pescador (☎ 2471 1116, 2471 1369; s/d from US$20/45; P) These rustic cabinas are about 100m from the town center and there are a variety of rooms to accommodate travelers of all budgets. They're owned and operated by the Sequera brothers, who are recommended refuge guides and boat captains. Two-hour fishing or naturalist trips for up to five people cost US$50, and you can also arrange horseback riding here. Stop by the pink house with the sign advertising the cabinas to have a look.

Caño Negro Natural Lodge (☎ 2471 1000, 2471 1426; www.canonegrolodge.com; s/d incl breakfast US$65/75;

P X) Perched on land that becomes a virtual island in the Río Frío during the rainy season, this lodge is surprisingly upscale considering its remote location. Well-appointed rooms have hot showers, air-con and satellite TV. The friendly staff can arrange all your trips while you relax in the pleasant pool, Jacuzzi or game room. The onsite restaurant, Jabirú, is open to the public and a great place for breakfast if you're weary of *gallo pinto* (rice and beans).

Hotel de Campo Caño Negro (☎ 2471 1012; www .hoteldecampo.com; s/d incl breakfast US$75/85; P X) Set in an orchard of mango and citrus trees next to one of Caño Negro's lagoons, this Italian-run hotel is a fisherman's paradise. You can rent any combination of boats, guides, kayaks and fishing equipment here at the well-stocked tackle shop. And after angling for gargantuan tarpon all day, relax in comfortable, high-ceilinged rooms with air-con and private hot showers, or soak in the grotto-like Jacuzzi. There's also a restaurant (mains US$7 to US$12, open 7:30am to 9:30pm) specializing in, yep, fish.

Soda La Palmera (☎ 8816 3382; mains US$3-10; 6am-9pm) Right at the entrance to the refuge, this pleasant *soda* serves Tico standards and fresh fish, including your personal catch of the day. The staff can also arrange local guides for fishing and naturalist trips (US$40, two hours, up to three people). Advance reservations are recommended in the high season.

El Caiman Bar & Restaurante (☎ 8399 4164; US$4-10; 10am-10pm Tue-Sun) At the bridge over the Río Frío just outside the village is this pleasant riverside eatery run by Canoa Aventura, a tour operator based in La Fortuna. Sit among the bamboo groves and feast on fresh sea bass or tilapia while you watch the caimans drift idly by, or rent a canoe and paddle into their territory.

Getting There & Away

The village of Caño Negro and the entrance to the park lie on the rough road connecting Upala and Los Chiles, which is passable to all cars during the dry season. However, this road is frequently washed out during the rainy season, when a 4WD is usually required. Two buses daily run past the park entrance from both Upala and Los Chiles.

During the rainy season and much of the dry season, you can also catch a boat here from Los Chiles. This is becoming increasingly popular, especially as more travelers are crossing into and out of Nicaragua on the Río Frío (see the boxed text Getting to San Carlos, Nicaragua, p510).

LOS CHILES

Seventy kilometers north of Muelle on a smooth, paved road through the sugar cane, and just three dusty, red and heavily rutted kilometers south of the Nicaraguan border, lies the sweltering farming and fishing town of Los Chiles. The humid lowland village, arranged with dilapidated grace around a grassy soccer field and along the unmanicured banks of the leisurely Río Frío, is pleasant enough – almost charming by border-town standards. It was originally settled by merchants and fisherfolk who worked on the nearby Río San Juan, much of which forms the Nicaragua–Costa Rica border. In recent history, Los Chiles served as an important supply route for the Contras in Nicaragua, and was home to a strong US military presence throughout the 1980s.

Gringo traffic is on the rise in Los Chiles as it's a great base for enjoying the scenic water route to Caño Negro, and an early-morning excursion by small motorized boat is an adventure in itself. The second big draw is the scenic route to Nicaragua, a one-hour boat ride across the border that is becoming increasingly popular among foreign tourists. Crossing the border via the river is a relaxing, hassle-free way to go.

Although the road continues past Los Chiles to Nicaragua, this border post is closed to pretty much everyone. The police patrolling this line in the sand are heavily armed and extremely bored, so don't waste your time and energy trying your luck there.

Information & Orientation

The last stretch of paved road along Hwy 35 is home to a few restaurants, the post office and a gas station. If you continue north past Los Chiles on the rutted dirt road, you'll find yourself in the dusty no-man's-land en route to a border crossing you won't be allowed to use.

Drivers will want to hang a left (west) off the highway to reach the town center and the docks of the Río Frío. **Banco Nacional** (☎ 2212 2000), close to the central park and soccer field, changes cash and travelers cheques and has a 24-hour ATM. Just down the road, around the side of the pink boutique, is an **Internet café** (☎ 2471 1636; per hr US$1.20; ☺ 8:30am-noon & 2-8pm Mon-Fri). There's a **Cruz Roja** (Red Cross; ☎ 2471 1037, 2471 2025) on the west side of the plaza if you need some basic medical assistance or supplies.

Before hopping the boat to Nicaragua, you must stop at **migración** (immigration; ☎ 2471 1223; ☺ 8am-noon & 1:30-4pm), about 100m east of the park that faces the dock. See the boxed text Getting to San Carlos, Nicaragua, p510 for details on crossing into Nicaragua.

Tours

Los Chiles is a convenient base to organize your tours to Caño Negro. You'll be able to get on the river early, which means you'll probably see more wildlife than folks being shuttled in from La Fortuna and San José. The port is also a good jumping-off point for exploring the islands of Lago de Nicaragua (Lake Nicaragua), and if you miss the early boat, the local tour companies can sometimes arrange private transportation to San Carlos, Nicaragua.

You can arrange tours with Oscar Rojas at **Heliconia Tours & Restaurant** (☎ 2471 2096, 8307 8585), on the road between *migración* and the dock, or at **Rancho Tulipán** (☎ 2471 1414; www.ranchotulipan.com). **Viajes y Excursiones Cabo Rey** (☎ 2471 1251, 8839 7458) provides a boat service to the refuge (from US$45) as well as to El Castillo and the Solentiname Islands in Nicaragua. Cabo himself can usually be found by the dock.

At the boat dock you can also hire individual boat captains to take you up the Río Frío during the dry season and all the way into Lago Caño Negro during the rainy season, as well as to San Carlos, Nicaragua (see the boxed text Getting to San Carlos, Nicaragua,

---

GETTING TO SAN CARLOS, NICARAGUA

Although there's a 14km dirt road between Los Chiles and San Carlos, Nicaragua, using this crossing requires special permission generally reserved for federal employees. Most regular folk go across by boat on the Río Frío, which is easily arranged in Los Chiles. You must first get an exit stamp in your passport at **migración** (☎ 2471 1223; ☾ 8am-noon & 1:30-4pm), about 100m east of the park that faces the dock, which is also your first stop when entering from Nicaragua.

Regular boats (US$10, 45 minutes) leave Los Chiles at 12:30pm and 3:30pm daily, with extra boats at 11am and 2:30pm if demand is high. Boats leave San Carlos for Los Chiles at 10:30am and 4pm, with extra boats scheduled as needed. Of course, the Nicaragua–Costa Rica border is not known for its reliability, so confirm these times before setting out. Nicaragua charges a US$7 entry fee and US$2 exit fee, which can be paid in Nicaraguan córdobas or US dollars. Costa Rica is more gracious (so long as you're not Nicaraguan) as exit and entry are free. Your boat will make a stop at the actual border post about halfway through the trip; note the psychedelic 'camouflage' paint job on the building where your friendly, gun-wielding Nicaraguan border personnel are based.

When you hit the confluence of the Río San Juan, consider keeping your fingers and toes in the boat as there are river sharks (seriously!). Sharks are one of several euryhaline species that are able to survive in both fresh- and salt-water conditions. Every year, sharks that have been tagged by scientists in the Caribbean Sea are later found swimming in Lake Nicaragua. Although the rapids of the Río San Juan are a deterrent for most species of marine fish, sharks are apparently able to negotiate the river without problems, and presumably head for fresh water in search of food.

From San Carlos, which has a similar range of services to Los Chiles, you can arrange bus, boat and plane transportation to Managua, Granada and other destinations in Nicaragua. If you're looking to experience the Nica side of life, here's a quick list of the country's nearby highlights:

- Float down to **El Castillo**, one of Nicaragua's historical fortresses, accessible only by boat and one of the most chill spots.

- Explore the twin volcanoes of **Isla Ometepe**, a strong contender for the world's most beautiful island.

- Visit with the local artists on the **Solentiname Islands**, where art is truly the heartbeat of the community.

See the boxed text Heading North of the Border, p224 for more information on southwestern Nicaragua.

---

above). Three- to four-hour trips cost about US$45 to US$80 for a small group, depending on the size and type of boat.

Festivals & Events

This sleepy little town bursts to life during the October 4 **Feast of San Francisco**. Occasionally, festivities are held in Los Chiles during the irregularly scheduled **Bi-national Green Macaw Festival**, so look out for information.

Sleeping & Eating

Accommodations in town are surprisingly limited, though most people aren't too keen on sticking around anyhow.

No Frills Hotel, Bar & Restaurant (☎ 2471 1200, 2471 1410; r US$20; P ☒) This hotel, about 1km south of Los Chiles just past the gas station, is not, in fact, completely frill-free. Though basic, rooms here are clean and quiet (except for the honking of resident geese) with air-con and TV; some even have a full-size fridge. The restaurant/bar is open for lunch and dinner, and the proprietors can also arrange fishing and boat tours.

Cabinas Jabirú (☎ 2471 1496, 8898 6357; r with/without air-con US$30/25; P ☒) Named for the rare, large jabirú stork *(Jabiru mycteria)* that can sometimes be seen at Caño Negro, this popular spot near the bus terminal has bare rooms and private hot-water bathrooms.

Rancho Tulipán (☎ 2471 1414; www.ranchotulipan .com; s/d US$25/40; P ✗ 🖳) Rancho Tulipán is the most respectable accommodation in town, though it's also the most expensive and home to a very popular (translation: noisy!) bar. All the rooms have air-con, private hot-water bathrooms and cable TV, and it's conveniently located right across from *migración*. The onsite restaurant (mains US$3 to US$7, open 7am to 10pm) will start your day off right with a good breakfast, and the pan-fried sea bass is not to be missed.

Soda Juanita (☎ 2471 1607; mains US$2-5; 🕙 6am-6pm) Right next to the dock, this cheery, bright-green *soda* serves up tasty casados, the usual deep-fried fast foods, *batidos* (fruit shakes) and coffee. Seating at the counter or at one of the thatch-shaded tables makes a sweet spot to watch the world go by and await your boat to Nicaragua.

Restaurant El Parque (☎ 2471 1373, 2471 1090; mains US$3-5; 🕙 6am-9pm) This popular spot has some of the best eats in town, and it's open early if you're looking to get your coffee fix before setting out on the river.

There's a **Palí** two blocks north of the bus stop, and the local **Almacen de Los Chiles** on the west side of the soccer field to meet all of your grocery and bakery needs.

Getting There & Away

Drivers usually get here via Hwy 35 from Muelle, about 70 paved, straight kilometers where you're likely to get passed by big-rig drivers with lead feet. Skid marks and road-kill iguanas do break up the monotony of endless sugar-cane plantations. More scenic, if a little harder on your chassis, is the decent dirt road running for 50km from Upala, through Caño Negro, passable for normal cars throughout the dry season.

Regular boat transport is limited to quick shuttles across the Nicaraguan border (US$10) and various day trips throughout the region.

All buses arrive and leave from the stop on the main street across from the park. Timetables are flexible, so play it safe and inquire locally.

Ciudad Quesada US$3, two hours, depart 12 times daily from 5am to 7:15pm.

San José US$5, five hours, depart 5:30am & 3:30pm.

Upala via Caño Negro US$2.50, 2½ hours, depart 5am & 2pm.

SAN MIGUEL TO PUERTO VIEJO DE SARAPIQUÍ

This flat, steaming stretch of finca-dotted lowlands was once part of the United Fruit Company's cash-cow of banana holdings. Harvests were carried from the plantations to Puerto Viejo de Sarapiquí where they were packaged and shipped down the river on boats destined for the lucrative North American market. However, with the advent of the railway in 1880 that connected most of the country to the new shipping port in Puerto Limón, Puerto Viejo de Sarapiquí became a sleepy backwater.

Banana harvesting continued in the area through most of the 20th century, though in recent years farmers have switched to a more lucrative cash crop – sugar cane. Although Puerto Viejo de Sarapiquí has never managed to recover its faded glory, the area around the town is still one of the premier destinations in Costa Rica for kayakers and rafters. There are also a number of stellar ecolodges in the region that are open to nonguests, and feature everything from rain-forest hiking and suspension bridges to pre-Columbian ruins and chocolate tours.

The road north from San Miguel drops for 12km to the village of La Virgen and then flattens out as it bisects agricultural country for an additional 13km to Bajos de Chilamate. The old port town of Puerto Viejo de Sarapiquí lies 6km further along this road. Buses linking either San José or Ciudad Quesada with Puerto Viejo de Sarapiquí are the primary means of public transportation along this route.

LA VIRGEN

Tucked into the densely jungled shores of the wild and scenic Río Sarapiquí, La Virgen was one of a number of small towns that grew and prospered during the heyday of the banana trade. Although United Fruit has long since packed up and shipped out, the town is still dependent on the river, though most people today earn a living by either mongering fish or guiding gringos through the rapids.

Welcome to one of the premier kayaking and rafting destinations in Costa Rica. Surprisingly, most travelers have never even heard about La Virgen, and those who have would be hard-pressed to find it on a map. But, to the dedicated groups of hard-core rafters and kayakers that spend days running the Río Sarapiquí, La Virgen is a relatively off-the-beaten-path paradise. As an added bonus, the three luxurious lodges east of town feature a number of interesting attractions including museums, private trails and a Maleku archaeological site – so there's plenty to do in the area even on a rest day.

Information

Most of La Virgen's businesses are strung out along the highway, including a gas station, a **Banco Nacional** (☎ 2212 2000) with 24-hour ATM, a couple of small supermarkets and many bars. **Internet Cafe** (☎ 2761 1107; per hr US$1.25; ☽ 8am-9pm Mon-Sat, 2-9pm Sun) has fairly fast connection.

Sights & Activities

WHITE-WATER RAFTING

The Río Sarapiquí isn't as wild as the white water on the Río Pacuare near Turrialba, though it will still get your heart racing, and the dense jungle that hugs the riverbank is lush and primitive. You can run the Sarapiquí year-round, but July through December are considered peak months. Although it's possible to get a rafting trip on short notice, it's far better to make reservations at least two days in advance. Several tour operators in La Fortuna and San José organize trips. You can also call directly to the companies listed in this section.

There are three basic runs offered by several companies, and all have a minimum age of nine or 10; prices and times vary a bit, but the following are average. The Class I-II Chilamate put-in (US$45 per person, three hours) is a gentle float more suited to younger kids and wildlife-watching. The Class III-IV Lower Sarapiquí (US$45 to US$65, three hours) puts in close to La Virgen and is a scenic and challenging trip that's a good choice for healthy people without white-water experience. The Class IV-V Upper Sarapiquí (US$80, five hours) is seven screaming miles of serious white water – perfect for thrill-seekers.

Located just 75m north of the church, **Sarapiquí Outdoor Center** (☎ 2761 1123; sarapaqui outdoor@hotmail.com) is an established, family-run operation that offers top-quality rafting trips, as well as camping and decent budget

accommodations. This should be your first stop if you're an experienced DIY paddler.

In addition to offering rafting trips from La Virgen, San José and La Fortuna, **Aguas Bravas** (☎ 2292 2072; www.aguas-bravas.co.cr) is a safety-oriented, Tico-run outfit that can also arrange horseback rides and bike tours.

Aventuras del Sarapiquí (☎ 2766 6768; www.sara piqui.com) near Chilamate, and **Hacienda Pozo Azul Adventures** (☎ 2761 1360; www.pozoazul.com) are also reputable local professionals who organize rafting trips.

HIKING

For truly rugged do-it-yourself adventurers, it's possible to hike from La Virgen to the southernmost ranger stations in Parque Nacional Braulio Carrillo. For more information on hiking in Parque Nacional Braulio Carrillo, see p147.

KAYAKING

If you're a kayaker, several accommodations in town are directly on the river, which means that you can roll out of bed, brush your teeth and have a quick paddle before breakfast. **Rancho Leona** (☎ 2761 1019; www.rancholeona.com) is something of a meeting spot for kayakers, which isn't surprising as its prime riverside location allows for easy launches and free kayak storage, see opposite for more information. Both here and at **Sarapiquí Outdoor Center** (☎ 2761 1123; sarapaquioutdoor@hotmail.com), staff can provide information regarding launches in the area before you set out on the river.

OTHER ACTIVITIES

Hacienda Pozo Azul Adventures (☎ 2761 1360; www .pozoazul.com) specializes in adventure activities, including horseback riding tours starting from two-hour jaunts (US$35) to multi-day treks. It also runs a canopy tour (US$45) over the lush jungle and river, can take you rappelling (US$28) and lead mountain-bike tours (US$60, one day) and guided hikes (US$15).

SERPENTARIO

A great, locally run attraction is La Virgen's famous **snake garden** (☎ 2761 1059; adult/student US$5/3; ☽ 9am-6:30pm), where you can get face-to-face with more than 60 different species of reptiles and amphibians, including poison-dart frog, anaconda and the star-attraction, an 80kg Burmese python. The owner of the *serpenario*, Lydia, gives impromptu tours and

---

ONE LIFE ON THE RÍO SARAPIQUÍ

Miguel Angel Castillo Espinoza is 21 years old. He works at Rancho Leona (below) during the day and studies at night in this river paradise.

What is it like to live and work on the Río Sarapiquí? The Sarapiquí is one of the most beautiful rivers in all of Costa Rica, with rapids from Class I to Class V. The water is very clean and in all this vegetation it's possible to see animals and many kinds of birds. It's very peaceful here, and those who live here are good people.

I was born in Sarapiquí and I've been here my whole life. I have only my mother; my father died on August 2, 2007. That was a really strong blow that I haven't been able to get over, since before coming to Rancho Leona I lived only with him for the three years that he was ill. I have five brothers who work at a pineapple plantation, and three sisters who are married. My mother lives with four of my brothers. She's a beautiful woman to whom I owe a great deal, and I love her very much.

How would you describe yourself? I'm a chill person; I appreciate natural, unpretentious people and I like to spend time observing everything around me. I'm one of those people who doesn't say much, but I sense when others are feeling bad. I hate seeing people who believe they're better than others, or when I see them fighting about things that aren't worth the trouble. What I enjoy most is listening to music, playing soccer, kayaking and sometimes singing. I want to study physical education, tourism and especially teaching, since I love kids. I'd love to visit the US and to learn new things about the world and all its different cultures.

How did you come to work at Rancho Leona? I used to stay here at the rancho because Frey [former manager] always invited me. We were friends at school, and we hung out all the time, sparring, boxing – a lot of times I wound up pretty beaten up, and him too. That was really fun. [Frey's mother] Leona was an English teacher at my school, and soon she offered to let me stay here, and Frey taught me how to kayak. After that, I started working as a guide, and it's a wonderful experience I wouldn't trade for the world. I've been a kayak guide for a year and a half and it's been great – I love it.

---

takes certain snakes out of their cages for big hugs and memorable photo ops. The mural outside is most definitely tattoo-worthy.

CENTRO BIOLÓGICO SANTUARIO DE MARIPOSAS AGUAS SILVESTRES

You'll need your own wheels, or make arrangements through Rancho Leona (right), to visit this **butterfly sanctuary** (☎ 2761 1095) in the mountains, run by the energetic Edgar Corrales. Guided hikes (in Spanish; US$10) take you through the rain forest along a waterfall trail and include a tour of the butterfly garden. You can also stay overnight in the rustic **bunkhouse** (US$35 per person); the rate includes dinner, breakfast, a half-day tour of the local rain forest with a swim in the lagoon, and lunch on your return. However long your stay, be sure to bring bug repellent, as butterflies are not the only insects living up there.

To get there on your own, turn onto the Pozo Azul road and follow the brown wood signs to the sanctuary, which is about 10km up the mountain, near the village of San Ramon.

Sleeping & Eating

our pick Rancho Leona (☎ 2761 1019; www.rancho leona.com; r per person US$12; P 🖵) This shady, riverside spot is a gem – kayakers congregate here to swap tales of white-water adventure, birders linger over huge breakfasts (US$6) as the local color of avian life flits by, and artistically minded travelers admire the lodge's incredible stained glass, which was handmade by the owners. The handful of simple, spotless rooms in the wood-plank lodge share hot-water bathrooms, and there's a small bathing pool for taking a cool dip; spa services are also available. The super-friendly staff sometimes prepares family-style dinners in the evenings, and they can take you out on inflatable 'ducky' or kayak trips, as well as arrange rafting tours for you.

NORTHERN LOWLANDS

Bar & Cabinas El Río (☎ 2761 0138; r with fan/air-con US$10/15; P ⛄) About 1km from Pozo Azul at the southern edge of town, these seven A-frame bungalows have tile floors, clean hot-water bathrooms and TV – they're cute as heck and bordered with hedges and flowers. About 100m further down the steep hill is the lovely open-air Bar El Río, on rough-hewn stilts high above the river. Though this large treehouse bar has a romantic ambience when it's not karaoke night, beware of the toilet (which doesn't actually contain a toilet but simply is a drain in the corner of the tilted floor).

Sarapiquí Outdoor Center (☎ 2761 1123; sara paquioutdoor@hotmail.com; camping/r US$5/25; P) Riverside campsites here have access to showers and bathrooms. Private rooms are simple and have river views, though they're a bit overpriced for what they are. There's also a communal kitchen and a covered terrace in case of rain. In addition to rafting and kayaking trips, the friendly owners can also arrange horseback rides and guided hikes to a nearby waterfall.

Hacienda Pozo Azul Adventure (☎ 2438 2616, in the USA/Canada 877-810 6903; www.pozoazul.com; s/d/tr luxury tent US$58/93/154; P 🛏 🐴) Beside the bridge over the Río Sarapiquí is, if you've been paying attention, one of the most heavily advertised lodges in the entire region. Accommodation here is in a number of luxury tents scattered on the edge of the treeline, all on raised, polished-wood platforms and outfitted with air mattresses and mosquito nets. For those looking to really get away from it all, there's also the Magsasay Jungle Lodge (single/double/triple luxury tents US$70/112/132) deep in the jungle, perched at the edge of Parque Nacional Braulio Carrillo. All showers at both locations have hot water. Aside from the tent-camping and adventure tours, Pozo Azul also boasts the best restaurant/bar (mains US$5 to US$9) in town, with an outdoor veranda alongside the river.

Restaurante y Cabinas Tía Rosita (☎ 2761 1032, 2761 1125; meals US$3-6; ☺ breakfast, lunch & dinner; P) Tía Rosita is the most highly recommended *soda* in La Virgen, with excellent casados, Costa Rican–style *chiles rellenos* (stuffed fried peppers) and *horchata* (sweet rice shake) and service without a smile. The family also rents several clean, cute cabinas (single/double/triple rooms US$10/15/20)

with private hot shower, TV, fan and plenty of breathing space.

Restaurant La Costa (☎ 2761 1117; mains US$3-7; ☺ 11am-9pm) On the eastern edge of town, La Costa is run by a trio of young Chinese siblings whose specialty is, hey, Chinese-style seafood. The portions are generous, so you know where to go if you're hankering for noodles.

Restaurant Mar y Tierra (☎ 2761 1603; mains US$4-9) La Virgen's favorite fine-dining (but still very relaxed) option is this comfortable seafood and steak restaurant that's popular with both locals and travelers. The specialty here is shrimp, and it's damn good.

Getting There & Away

La Virgen lies on Hwy 126, about 8km from San Miguel, to the south, and 17km from Puerto Viejo de Sarapiquí, to the northeast. Buses originating in either San José, San Miguel or Puerto Viejo de Sarapiquí make regular stops in La Virgen. If you're driving, the curvy road is paved between San José and Puerto Viejo de Sarapiquí, though irregular maintenance can make for a bumpy ride.

LA VIRGEN TO PUERTO VIEJO DE SARAPIQUÍ

This scenic stretch of Hwy 4 is home to a few lovely ecolodges that are extremely popular among well-heeled tourists. However, if you're the kind of traveler that scraps together a few hundred colones every morning to buy a loaf of bread from Palí supermarket, then fear not as these places do allow nonguests to see their unusual attractions and private trails for a small fee. Any bus between La Virgen and Puerto Viejo de Sarapiquí can drop you at the entrances, while a taxi from La Virgen (or Puerto Viejo for Selva Verde) will cost from US$4 to US$6.

Centro Neotrópico Sarapiquís & Tirimbina Rainforest Center

About 2km north of La Virgen is **Centro Neotrópico Sarapiquís** (☎ 2761 1004; www.sarapiquis .org; d/tr US$99/124; P ⛄ 🛏 ✗), a unique ecolodge that aims to foster sustainable tourism by educating its guests about environmental conservation and pre-Columbian history and culture. The entire complex consists of *palenque*-style, thatch-roofed buildings modeled after a 15th-century pre-Columbian village, and contains a clutch of luxuriously appointed hardwood rooms with huge, solar-heated bathrooms

BOATING TO NICARAGUA *Rob Rachowiecki*

Sailing down the Río Sarapiquí to the Río San Juan is a memorable trip. If the water is low, dozens of crocodiles can be seen sunning themselves on the banks. If the water is high, river turtles climb out of the river to sun themselves on logs. Birds are everywhere. North of Puerto Viejo much of the land is cattle pasture with few trees, but as you approach the Nicaraguan border more stands of forest are seen. In trees on the banks you may see monkey, iguana or maybe a snake draped over a branch.

On my trip the boat captain suddenly cut the engine, so I turned around to see what the matter was. He grinned and yelled and it was not until the dugout had gently nosed into the bank beneath the tree that I saw a sloth raise a languid head to see what was going on. How he managed to make out that the greenish-brown blob on a branch (the color is caused by the algae that grows in the fur of this lethargic animal) was a sloth is one of the mysteries of traveling with a sharp-eyed *campesino*.

We continued on down to the confluence of the Sarapiquí with the San Juan, where we stopped to visit an old Miskito Indian fisher named Leandro. He claimed to be 80 years old, but his wizened frame had the vitality of a man half his age. From the bulging woven-grass bag in the bottom of his fragile dugout, Leandro sold us fresh river lobster to accompany that evening's supper.

The official border between Nicaragua and Costa Rica is the south bank of the San Juan, not the middle of the river, so you are technically traveling into Nicaragua when on the San Juan. This river system is a historically important gateway from the Caribbean into the heart of Central America. Today it remains off the beaten tourist track and allows the traveler to see a combination of rain forest and ranches, wildlife and old war zones, deforested areas and protected areas.

and private terraces. However, the main reason guests rave about this ecolodge is the variety of exhibits and attractions located on the grounds.

Even if you're not staying at the lodge, it's worth stopping by just to visit the lodge's real claims to fame, namely the **Alma Ata Archaeological Park**, **Rainforest Museum of Indigenous Cultures** and **Sarapiquís Gardens** (adult/child under 8 US$19/free; 9am-5pm). Admission includes entry to all three places, though alternatively, you can purchase admission for the individual attractions. The archaeological site is estimated to be around 600 years old, and is attributed to the Maleku (see boxed text A Brief History of the Maleku, p504). Currently, about 70 small stone sculptures marking a burial field are being excavated by Costa Rican archaeologists who have revealed a number of petroglyphs and pieces of pottery. Although the site is modest, and is definitely not comparable in size or scope to other Central American archaeological sites, it's one of the few places in Costa Rica where you can get a sense of its pre-Columbian history.

The museum chronicles the history of the rain forest (and of human interactions with it) through a mixture of displays and videos, and also displays hundreds of Costa Rican indigenous artifacts including some superbly crafted musical instruments. Finally, the gardens boast the largest scientific collection of medicinal plants in Costa Rica.

An onsite **restaurant** (mains US$7-20; breakfast, lunch & dinner) serves meals incorporating fruits, vegetables, spices and edible flowers used in indigenous cuisine, many of which are grown on the premises.

As if this wasn't spectacular enough, following the museum tour visitors are invited to enter the **Tirimbina Rainforest Center** (2761 1579; www.tirimbina.org; r incl breakfast US$55), which is a 300-hectare private reserve that is reached by crossing two suspension bridges, 267m and 111m long, that span the Río Sarapiquí. Halfway across, a spiral staircase drops down to a large island in the river. The reserve has more than 6km of trails, some of which are paved or wood-blocked. There are also a number of different guided tours on offer (US$14 to US$20) including birding, 'bat-ing' and a recommended guided chocolate tour, which lets you explore a working cacao plantation and learn about the harvesting, fermenting and drying processes. Student discounts are available. Tirimbina is also directly accessed from the road about 7km north of La Virgen.

La Quinta de Sarapiquí Lodge

About 5km north of La Virgen, this pleasant family-run **lodge** (☎ 2761 1052; www.laquintasara piqui.com; r with fan/air-con US$87/93; 🛏 P 🛁 ♿) is on the banks of the Río Sardinal, which branches off of the Sarapiquí in the north and runs to the west of it. The lodge has covered paths through the landscaped garden connecting thatch-roofed, hammock-strung rooms. All the rooms have a terrace, ceiling fan and private hot shower.

Owner Beatriz Gámez is active in local environmental issues and helps administer the Cámara de Turismo de Sarapiquí (Cantusa), which works to balance conservation and tourism in the area. Activities at the lodge include swimming in the pretty pool or river (there's a good swimming hole nearby), horseback riding, fishing, boat trips, mountain-biking and birding, and you can spend time in the large **butterfly garden** or hike the 'frog land' trail where poison-dart frogs are commonly seen. Fishing and horseback riding are free for lodge guests. You can also get meals in the open-air restaurant (mains US$8 to US$13).

On the hotel grounds, **La Galleria** (admission US$8.50, free for lodge guests) features an eclectic collection of regional ephemera, including an extensive collection of insect specimens such as *la machaca*, a bizarre-looking insect, about 7.5cm long, also known as the lantern bug.

Even more interesting are the unusual exhibits on Costa Rican history. Indigenous artifacts, including some worthwhile copies of the area's more important archaeological finds, are a treat. The collection of Spanish-colonial relics is even more impressive, featuring not only antiques collected by the owners, but interesting family heirlooms as well – Gámez's great-grandmother was pen pals with famed Nicaraguan poet Rubén Darío. The fee also includes access to the lodge's private trails and gardens.

Selva Verde Lodge

In Chilamate, about 7km west of Puerto Viejo, this former finca is now an elegant **lodge** (☎ 2766 6800, in the USA/Canada 800-451 7111; www.selvaverde.com; s/d incl meals US$81/98; 🛏 P 🛁) that protects over 200 hectares of rain forest. Guests can choose to stay in the river lodge, which is elevated above the rain-forest floor on wooden platforms, or in a private bungalow, quietly tucked away in the nearby rain forest. Wood-floored rooms have private hot

shower, screened windows, in-room safes and of course, your very own hammock.

The lodge works closely with a tour company for over-55s called **Elderhostel** (www.elder hostel.org) and offers educational opportunities, guided tours and other interesting diversions, many of which nonguests can enjoy for a fee.

There are several kilometers of walking trails through the grounds and into the premontane tropical wet forest; you can either get a trail map or can hire a bilingual guide from the lodge (US$15 per person, three hours). There's also a garden of medicinal plants, as well as a **butterfly garden** (admission US$5, free for lodge guests). Various boat tours on the Río Sarapiquí are also available, from rafting trips to guided canoe tours; locally guided horseback rides (US$25 for two to three hours) can also be arranged.

The Holbrook family, who own the lodge, funds the nonprofit **Sarapiquí Conservation Learning Center** (www.learningcentercostarica.org), through which guests can participate in cultural exchange activities such as a *charla* (chat) over coffee, homestays or salsa dancing lessons with locals. The center also partners with student groups to serve as a base for conservation and environmental education.

PUERTO VIEJO DE SARAPIQUÍ & AROUND

At the scenic confluence of Río Puerto Viejo and Río Sarapiquí, Puerto Viejo de Sarapiquí was once the most important port in Costa Rica. Boats laden with bananas, coffee and other commercial exports plied the Sarapiquí as far as the Nicaraguan border, then turned east on the Río San Juan to the sea. Today, Puerto Viejo (the full name distinguishes it from Puerto Viejo de Talamanca on the Caribbean coast) is simply a jungle border town – slightly seedy in a film-noir sort of way. There are, however, numerous opportunities in the surrounding area for birding, rafting, boating and jungle exploration.

Migración is near the small wooden dock, sometimes avoided by visiting Nicaraguans who share the river with local fishers and visiting birders. Adventure seekers can still travel down the Sarapiquí in motorized dugout canoes.

There is no dry season, but from late January to early May is the 'less wet' season.

On the upside, when it rains here there are fewer mosquitoes.

Banco Popular (☎ 2766 6815) has an ATM and changes money. **Internet Sarapiquí** (☎ 2766 6223; per hr US$2; ⚅ 8am-10pm) is at the west end of town. **Souvenir Río Sarapiquí** (☎ 2766 6727), on the main street, has tour information on birding, kayaking, white-water rafting and zip lining.

Activities

Grassroots environmental activity is strong in this area. Local guide Alex Martínez, owner of the Posada Andrea Cristina B&B, maintains an **ecotourism center** (☎ 2766 6265; ⚅ 8am-3pm), which focuses on conservation activities and wilderness tours – **birding** trips in particular. You can also arrange transportation and make other reservations here, as well as learn about worthwhile volunteer opportunities in the region.

If you're looking to organize a rafting or kayaking trip, a branch of **Aguas Bravas** (☎ 2292 2072; www.aguas-bravas.co.cr) is across the road from the bank. You can also try **Costa Rica Fun Adventures** (☎ 2290 6015; www.crfunadventures.com), which is 2km north of town and offers a good variety of guided hiking and horseback trips.

Taking the launch trip from Puerto Viejo to the Trinidad Lodge (below), at the confluence of the Río Sarapiquí and the Río San Juan, provides a rich opportunity to see crocodile, sloth, bird, monkey and iguana sunning themselves on the muddy riverbanks and gathering in the trees. This river system is a historically important gateway from the Caribbean into the heart of Central America, and it's still off the beaten tourist track, giving a glimpse of rain forest and ranches, wildlife and old war zones, deforested pastureland and protected areas.

Sleeping

This stretch of jungle boasts quite a range of accommodations, from budget bunks in town, designed for local long-term plantation workers, to several extraordinary lodges on the outskirts, the most exclusive of which are on the road to La Virgen. Lodges in the area north of Puerto Viejo are also listed, including one in the river town of Trinidad, on the Nicaraguan border.

BUDGET

Trinidad Lodge (☎ 2213 0661, 8381 0621; r per person US$10) Situated on the Río San Juan in the com-

munity of Trinidad, this budget lodge is right across from the Nicaraguan border crossing and is pretty much the only gig in town. Though on the rustic side, the bamboo-walled bungalows are charming and very clean, with private cold-water bathrooms. Candle power provides light when the generator shuts off at the end of the night, and meals are available (US$4 to US$8) at the rancho, with a pool table besides. The lodge is accessible only by boat (US$10), which departs once daily at 2pm from the main dock of Puerto Viejo de Sarapiquí (35km away). The motorized launches leave Trinidad daily at (yawn) 5am. Due to the launch schedules, consider staying two nights to fully appreciate a hike, horseback tour or boat trip through this lush, remote sector of jungle.

Mi Lindo Sarapiquí (☎ 2766 6281; s/d US$18/30; ⚅ 🖥 P) On the south side of the soccer field, this is the best budget option in the town center. Rooms here are simple but spacious and clean, and have a private hot shower and fan. The onsite restaurant (mains US$3 to US$10, open 10am to 10pm) is slightly pricey, though it offers some of the freshest seafood in town.

MIDRANGE

Los Cuajipales (☎ 2283 9797, 2766 6608; camping per person US$10, r per person US$20-30; P 🐎) About 3km north of town on a good gravel road, this rustic complex is geared toward Tico tourists. Comfortable thatch-roofed cabinas sleeping up to five were designed according to Huetar Indian techniques that keep them naturally cool (cable TV and private cold showers are, however, less authentic). All rates include meals at the casually elegant restaurant and access to the rather extravagant pool, table-tennis and billiard tables, 4km of private trails and tilapia pond.

Posada Andrea Cristina B&B (☎ 2766 6265; www .andreacristina.com; s/d/tr/q incl breakfast US$25/45/55/65; P) About 1km west of the center, this recommended B&B has eight quiet, immaculate cabins in its garden, each with fan, private hot-water bathroom, hammock and outdoor table and chairs. It's also situated on the edge of the rain forest, so there are plenty of opportunities for birding while you sit outside and eat breakfast. The owner, Alex Martínez, is an excellent, amiable guide as well as a passionate front-line conservationist. He arrived here 30 years ago as a tough young hunter exploring what was virgin forest, and saw the jungle's rapid destruction at the hands of humankind. He changed his philosophy and is now a volunteer game warden – who will abandon a Saturday-night soccer match to chase down poachers on the river. He helped found Asociación para el Bienestar Ambiental de Sarapiquí (ABAS), a local environmental-protection and education agency. Alex, who speaks excellent English, runs an onsite ecotourism center (see p517), and can tell you as much as you want to know about environmental issues in the area. One of Alex's latest projects involves identifying nesting sites of breeding great green macaw, and purchasing living almendro trees from property owners, who are then honor-bound to protect the trees.

Hotel Ara Ambigua (☎ 2766 7101; www.hotelara ambigua.com; s/d/tr incl breakfast from US$45/55/75; 🛏 🖥 🅿 🐾) About 1km west of Puerto Viejo near La Guaíra, this countryside retreat offers cozy rooms that are well equipped with private hot-water showers and cable TV. It's worth up-grading about US$10 for the bungalows, which feature log-style furniture and flagstone floors. The real draw is the varied opportunities for wildlife-watching – you can see poison-dart frogs in the *ranario* (frog pond), caiman in the small lake and the birds that come to feed near the onsite Restaurante La Casona, which is open for breakfast, lunch and dinner.

Hotel El Bambú (☎ 2766 6005; www.elbambu.com; standard/deluxe r incl breakfast US$58/76; 🅿 🛏 🐾) You really can't miss the sign for downtown Puerto Viejo's finest lodging, which caters mostly to package tourists looking for a clean and comfortable base when they're not out on 'adventure tours.' Rooms are all equipped with air-con and hot water, and there's a big, inviting pool and popular restaurant open to the main road. Spring for one of the quieter deluxe rooms out back, whose raised platform paths take you through the trees.

El Gavilán (☎ 2766 6743; www.gavilanlodge.com; d with/without breakfast US$58/64; 🅿) Sitting on a 100-hectare reserve about 4km northeast of Puerto Viejo, this former cattle hacienda is cozy, quaint and a birding haven. All of the spacious rooms have a big hot-water shower and fan; all have porches, some with river views. The grounds feature 5km of private trails and a good restaurant, plus a nice out-door Jacuzzi to relax in after a long hike. Though the accommodations don't quite live up to the price, the birding and boat trips are the draw here. Trips range from short jaunts down the Río Sarapiquí to overnights

in Tortuguero. Multi-day package deals are available that include meals, tours and trans-portation from San José.

A taxi or boat from Puerto Viejo costs US$5. There's a signed turnoff from Hwy 4 about 2km from town.

Eating

Most of the lodgings in and around Puerto Viejo have onsite restaurants or provide meals.

There are several *sodas* in Puerto Viejo de Sarapiquí, including the excellent **Soda Judith** (mains US$2-4; 🕒 6am-7pm), one block off the main road, where early risers grab brewed coffee and big breakfasts or an *empanada* to start their day. **Restaurante La Casona** (meals US$4-10; 🕒 breakfast, lunch & dinner) at the Hotel Ara Ambigua is particularly recommended for its homemade, typical cuisine served in an open-air rancho.

There's also a **Palí supermarket** (🕒 8am-9pm) at the west end of town, and the local Super Sarapiquí on the way to the port.

Getting There & Away

Puerto Viejo de Sarapiquí has been a trans-port center longer than Costa Rica has been a country, and is easily accessed by paved major roads from San José, the Caribbean coast and other population centers. There is a taxi stop across from the bus terminal, and taxis will take you to the nearby lodges and Estación Biológica La Selva for US$4 to US$7.

BOAT

The small port has a regular service to the Trinidad Lodge in Trinidad, and you are able to arrange transportation anywhere along the river (seasonal conditions permit-ting) through independent boat captains. Short trips cost about US$10 per hour per person for a group of four, or US$20 per hour for a single person. Serious voyages to Tortuguero or Barra del Colorado and back cost about US$350 for a boat holding five.

BUS

Right across from the park, the **bus termi-nal** (☎ 2233 4242; 🕒 5am-7pm) sells tickets and stores backpacks (US$1.50).

Ciudad Quesada/San Carlos via La Virgen (Empre-sarios Guapileños) US$1.75, three hours, depart daily at

5:30am, 8:30am, 10:30am, 12:15pm, 2:30pm, 4pm, 6pm and 7:10pm.

Guápiles (Empresarios Guapileños) US$1.40, one hour, 5:30am, 6:45am, 7:10am, 9:40am, 10:30am, 12:10pm, 2:30pm, 3:45pm, 4:45pm and 7pm.

San José (Autotransportes Sarapiquí) US$2.90, two hours, 6:30am, 7:30am, 10am, 11:30am, 1:30pm, 2:30pm, 3:30pm, 4:30pm and 6pm.

SOUTH OF PUERTO VIEJO DE SARAPIQUÍ

South of Puerto Viejo de Sarapiquí, fincas and banana plantations line Hwy 4 and sprawl all the way to the marshes and mangroves of the Caribbean coast. To the west, the rugged hills of the Cordillera Central mark the northeastern boundary of Parque Nacional Braulio Carrillo. Most travelers on this scenic stretch of highway are either heading to the Caribbean coast or to the Central Valley. However, some are pulling off the road to visit the working research center Estación Biológica La Selva, the world-class botanical garden called Heliconia Island, or Rara Avis, one of the most isolated lodges in Costa Rica.

About 12 smoothly paved kilometers from Puerto Viejo de Sarapiquí is the village of Horquetas, around which you'll find the turnoffs for Heliconia Island and Rara Avis. From Horquetas it's another 15km to Hwy 32, which connects San José to the Caribbean coast and bisects Parque Nacional Braulio Carrillo on the way to San José.

ESTACIÓN BIOLÓGICA LA SELVA

Not to be confused with Selva Verde Lodge in Chilamate, **Estación Biológica La Selva** (☎ 2524 0629, 2766 6565; www.ots.ac.cr; s/d US$88/164; **P**) is a working biological research station that is well equipped with laboratories, experimental plots, a herbarium and an extensive library. On any given day, the station is usually teeming with scientists and students, who use the station as a headquarters for researching the nearby private reserve. Although most guests are affiliated with an institution of higher learning, La Selva does welcome drop-ins, though it's best to phone ahead and reserve your accommodation. Rooms are simple but comfortable, and rates include all meals and guided hikes.

La Selva is operated by the **Organization for Tropical Studies** (OTS; ☎ 2524 0607; www.ots.ac.cr), a consortium founded in 1963 to provide leadership in the education, research and wise use of tropical natural resources. In fact, many well-known tropical ecologists have trained at La Selva. Twice a year OTS offers a grueling eight-week course open mainly to graduate students of ecology, along with various other courses and field trips that you can apply for.

The area protected by La Selva is 1614 hectares of pre-montane wet-tropical rain forest, much of which is undisturbed. It's bordered to the south by the 476-sq-km **Parque Nacional Braulio Carrillo** (p146), creating a protected area large enough to support a great diversity of life. More than 445 bird species have been recorded at La Selva, as well as 120 mammal species, 1850 species of vascular plants (especially from the orchid, philodendron, coffee and legume families) and thousands of insect species.

Hiking

Reservations are required for guided hikes (US$36/26 adult/child for a full-day hike, US$28/20 adult/child for half-day; 8am and 1:30pm daily) with a bilingual naturalist guide. You'll head across the hanging bridge and into 57km of well-developed jungle trails, some of which are wheelchair accessible. Unguided hiking is forbidden, although you'll be allowed to wander a bit after your guided tour. Make reservations for the popular guided birding hikes, led at 5:45am and 7pm, depending on demand. Profits from these walks help to fund the research station.

No matter when you visit La Selva, it will probably be raining. Bring rain gear and footwear that's suitable for muddy trails. Insect repellent and a water bottle are also essential.

For the truly rugged do-it-yourself adventurers, it's possible to hike from La Selva to the southernmost ranger stations in Parque Nacional Braulio Carrillo. For more information in hiking in Braulio Carrillo, see p147.

Getting There & Away

Public buses between Puerto Viejo and Río Frío/Horquetas can drop you off 1km from the entrance to La Selva. It's about 4km from Puerto Viejo, where you can catch a taxi for around US$4 to US$6.

OTS runs buses (US$10) from San José on Monday. Make reservations when you arrange your visit, and note that researchers and students have priority.

SUEÑO AZUL RESORT

Yoga retreat groups make up the majority of guests at **Sueño Azul** (☎ 2764 1000; www.sueno azulresort.com; s/d/tr US$94/114/135; P ♻ ♨), a higher-end resort upon a hill. Independent travelers interested in honing their yoga practice will appreciate the appeal of this peaceful place, especially at the secluded bamboo yoga platform if no groups have scheduled a stay. Spacious, airy rooms have hot-water showers and bamboo furnishings, and are nestled on the grounds of this private jungle reserve. Hiking trails offer jungle walks to waterfalls, and the reserve can also be explored on horseback.

HELICONIA ISLAND

This self-proclaimed 'oasis of serenity' is arguably the most beautiful garden in all of Costa Rica. **Heliconia Island** (☎ 2764 5220; www .heliconiaisland.com; s/d incl breakfast US$55/70, d with air-con US$80; P ♻) is a masterpiece of landscape architecture that was started in 1992 by New York City native Tim Ryan, a former professor of art and design. Today, this 2-hectare island is owned by Dutch couple Henk and Carolien, and is home to more than 80 varieties of heliconia, tropical flowers, plants and trees. The grounds are a refuge for 228 species of birds (hummingbirds are the sole pollinators of heliconias). There are also four resident howler monkeys, three species of river otter and a few friendly dogs that will greet you upon arrival.

Henk and Carolien will guide you through the property, showing off a number of memorable plants including the Madagascar traveling palm, rare hybrids of heliconia found only on the island, and the *Phenakospermum guyannense* (Phenomenal sperm), a unique flowering plant native to Guyana. The admission fee (self-guided/guided tours US$10/15) is waived for overnight guests. You can stay in this oasis in immaculate raised cabins, which have stone floors, hot-water showers and breezy balconies.

Heliconia Island is about 5km north of Horquetas, and there are signs along the highway pointing to the entrance. When you arrive at the entrance, park your car, walk across the metal bridge and turn left on the island to reach the gardens.

RARA AVIS

When they say remote, they mean remote: this **private reserve** (☎ 2764 3131; www.rara-avis.com; P), which is comprised of 1335 hectares of high-altitude tropical rain forest, is accessible only to overnight guests willing to make the three-hour tractor ride (seriously!) up a steep, muddy hill to get there.

Rara Avis was founded by Amos Bien, an American who came to Costa Rica as a biology student in 1977. Amos is dedicated to environmental conservation, and has been involved in a number of ongoing sustainability projects since his arrival. The private reserve borders the eastern edge of Parque Nacional Braulio Carrillo and has no real dry season. **Birding** here is excellent, with more than 350 species sighted so far, while mammals including monkeys, coatis, anteaters and pacas are often seen. Visitors can use the trail system alone, or on guided hikes included in the cost of lodging. A popular jaunt is the short trail leading from the lodge to **La Catarata**, a 55m-high waterfall that cuts an impressive swath through the forest.

The accommodations, although lovely, are rustic – most don't have electricity, though the kerosene lamps and starry skies are unforgettable. Room prices, which include all meals, transportation and a guided hike, seem high, but it's because of the remote location – you, the groceries and the guides all have to be hauled up that mountain from Horquetas.

Very basic **cabins** (r per person US$50) in the woods sleep four and have shared cold-water bathrooms, while nicer rooms in the **Waterfall Lodge** (s/d/tr US$85/150/195) have private hot-water shower and a balcony overlooking the rain forest. Even when it's pouring outside you can watch birds from your private balcony. The **River-Edge Cabin** (s/d/tr US$95/170/225) is the nicest spot, with solar-powered electricity, hot water and separate rooms. It's a dark (or romantic, depending on the company) 10-minute hike from the rest of the lodge.

Because access is time consuming and difficult, a two-night stay is recommended. The bus to Puerto Viejo de Sarapiquí leaves San José (US$2, 1½ hours) from the Guápiles-Limón terminal at 6:30am, and you'll need to get off at Horquetas. Here, you'll embark on the famed tractor ride. You can also arrange to be taken by jeep or on horseback, both of which require hiking the last 3km yourself.

Directory

CONTENTS

ACCOMMODATIONS

The hotel situation in Costa Rica ranges from luxurious ecolodges and sparkling all-inclusive resorts to backpacker palaces and I-can't-believe-I'm-paying-for-this barnyard-style quarters. Given this astounding variety of accommodations, it's rare to arrive in a town and find nowhere to sleep.

High or dry season (December to April) prices are provided throughout this book, though many lodges lower their prices during the low or rainy season (May to November). Keep in mind that prices change quickly in Costa Rica, so it's best to see the prices in this book as approximations rather than facts.

> **BOOK YOUR STAY ONLINE**
>
> For more accommodation reviews and recommendations by Lonely Planet authors, check out the online booking service at www.lonelyplanet.com/hotels. You'll find the true, insider lowdown on the best places to stay. Reviews are thorough and independent. Best of all, you can book online.

Throughout this book, sleeping options are listed in order of budget, unless otherwise specified.

B&Bs

Almost unknown in the country in the 1980s, the B&B phenomenon has swept through Costa Rica in the past two decades, primarily fueled by the increasing number of resident European and North American expats. Generally speaking, B&Bs in Costa Rica tend to be midrange to top-end affairs. While some B&Bs are reviewed in this guide, you can also find this type of accommodation on several websites (although they are far from exhaustive):

Bed and Breakfast.com (www.bedandbreakfast.com /costa-rica.html)

Costa Rica Innkeepers Association (www.costarica innkeepers.com)

Pamela Lanier's Worldwide Bed and Breakfasts Directory (www.lanierbb.com)

Camping

Camping is the way that many Ticos (Costa Ricans) can enjoy the more expensive seaside towns, especially since these days most accommodations cater specifically to foreigners. As a result, most major tourist destinations have at least one campsite, and if not, most budget hotels outside San José accommodate campers on their grounds. Although these sites usually include toilets, cold showers and basic self-catering facilities (a sink and a BBQ pit), they can be crowded, noisy affairs.

In most national parks however, camp sites are generally of excellent quality and are rigorously cleaned and maintained by a dedicated

DIRECTORY

staff. As a general rule, you will need to carry in all of your food and supplies, and carry out all of your trash.

Hostels

Although there are still a handful of Hostelling International (HI) hostels left in Costa Rica, the backpacker scene has gone increasingly top end in recent years. Compared to other destinations in Central America, hostels in Costa Rica tend to be fairly expensive affairs, though the quality of service and accommodation is unequalled.

Hotels

It is always advisable to ask to see a room – and a bathroom – before committing to a stay, especially in budget lodgings.

BUDGET

For the most part, this guide's budget category covers lodging in which a typical double costs up to US$20. Cheaper places generally have shared bathrooms, but it's still possible to get a double with a private bathroom for US$10 in some towns off the tourist trail. (Note that 'private' in some low-end establishments consists of a stall in the corner of your hotel room.) On the top end of the budget scale, rooms will frequently include a fan and private bathroom that may or may not have hot water. At the cheapest hotels, rooms will frequently be a stall, with walls that don't go to the ceiling.

Hot water in showers is often supplied by electric showerheads (affectionately termed

---

HOTEL SECURITY

Although hotels give you room keys, it is recommended that you carry a padlock for your backpack or suitcase for extra security. Furthermore, don't invite trouble by leaving valuables, cash or important documents lying around your room or in an unlocked bag. Upmarket hotels will have safes where you can keep your money and passport, so it's advised that you take advantage of them. If you're staying in a basic place, it's probably wise to take your valuables with you at all times. Theft is perhaps the number one complaint of travelers in Costa Rica, so it can't hurt to take a few extra precautions.

---

the 'Costa Rican suicide shower'). Contrary to traveler folklore, they are perfectly safe – provided you don't fiddle with the showerhead while it's on. The electric showerhead will actually dispense hot water if you keep the pressure low.

MIDRANGE & TOP END

Midrange generally covers hotels that charge between US$20 and US$80. These rooms will be more comfortable than budget options, and generally include a private bathroom with gas-heated hot water, a choice between fans and air-con, and cable or satellite TV. The better places will offer tour services, and many will have an onsite restaurant or bar and a swimming pool or Jacuzzi. In this price range, many hotels offer kitchenettes or even full kitchens, and using them is a great way to save money if you're traveling in a large group or as a family.

Anything more than US$80 is considered top end, and includes ecolodges, all-inclusive resorts, business and chain hotels, in addition to a strong network of more intimate boutique hotels, remote jungle camps and upmarket B&Bs. Many such lodging options will include amenities such as hot-water bath tubs, private decks, satellite TV and air-con as well as concierge, tour and spa services.

Most midrange and top-end places charge 16.39% in taxes. This book has attempted to include taxes in the prices listed throughout. Note that many hotels charge per person, rather than per room – read rates carefully. For information on reserving hotels by credit card, see boxed text, opposite.

ACTIVITIES
Bungee Jumping

No vacation appears to be complete without a head-first, screaming plunge off a bridge. **Tropical Bungee** (☎ 2248 2212, 8383 9724; www.bungee .co.cr; 1st/2nd jump US$65/30) in San José has been organizing jumps off the Río Colorado bridge since 1992.

Canopy Tours

Life in the rain forest takes place at canopy level. But with trees extending 30m to 60m in height, the average human has a hard time getting a look at what's going on up there. Enter the so-called 'canopy tour.'

Some companies have built elevated walkways through the trees that allow hikers to stroll

---

RESERVING BY CREDIT CARD

Some of the pricier hotels will require that you confirm your reservation with a credit card. Before doing so, note that some top-end hotels require a 50% to 100% payment upfront when you reserve. Unfortunately, many of them don't communicate this rule clearly.

Sometimes visitors end up 'reserving' a room only to find out that they have actually paid for it in advance. Technically, reservations can be cancelled and refunded with enough advance notice. (Again, ask the hotel about its cancellation policy.) However, in Costa Rica it's a lot easier to make the reservation than to unmake it. In addition, many hotels charge a 7% service fee for credit card use.

Have the hotel fax or email you a confirmation. Hotels often get overbooked, and if you don't have confirmation, you could be out of a room.

---

through. SkyTrek (p179) near Monteverde and Rainmaker (p341) near Quepos are two of the most established operations in the country. A somewhat newer but equally popular operation is Actividades Arboreales (p369) near Santa María de Dota.

You can also take a ski-lift-style ride through the tree tops, such as the Rainforest Aerial Tram (p148) near Braulio Carrillo or the smaller Aerial Adventures & Natural Wonders Tram (p179) in Monteverde.

Diving & Snorkeling

Costa Rica doesn't pretend to rank alongside regional diving and snorkeling heavyweights like Belize, the Cayman Islands and Bonaire. However, Costa Rica's underwater world does offer sheer number and variety of underwater life, and there are few places in the world where you can dive in the Caribbean and the Pacific on the same day.

As a general rule, water visibility is not good during the rainy months, when rivers swell and their outflow clouds the ocean. At this time, boats to locations offshore offer better viewing opportunities.

The water is warm – around 75°F (24°C) to 84°F (29°C) at the surface, with a thermocline at around 20m below the surface where it drops to 73°F (23°C). If you're keeping it shallow, you can skin dive (ie no wetsuit).

For information on the best dive sites in Costa Rica, see p73.

If you want to maximize your diving time, it's advisable to get diving accreditation ahead of time. For more information, check out the **Professional Association of Diving Instructors** (PADI; ☎ in the USA 949-858 7234, 800-729 7234, in Canada 604-552 5969, 800-565 8130, in Switzerland 52-304 1414; www.padi .com). **Divers Alert Network** (☎ in the USA 800-446 2671, 919-684 2948; www.diversalertnetwork.org) is a nonprofit

organization that provides diving insurance and emergency medical evacuation.

If you are interested in diving but are not accredited, you can usually do a one-day introductory course that will allow you to do one or two accompanied dives. If you love it, which most people do, consider getting certified, which takes three to four days and costs around US$350 to US$400.

The following dive companies offer tours to Costa Rica:

JD's Watersports (☎ in the USA 970-356 1028, 800-477 8971; www.jdwatersports.com)

Okeanos Aggressor (☎ in the USA 985-385 2628, in the USA & Canada 800-348 2628; www.aggressor.com)

Undersea Hunter (☎ 2228 6613, in the USA 800-203 2120; www.underseahunter.com)

For snorkelers, many coastal areas have popular reefs. Leading destinations include Cahuita (p476), Manzanillo (p492), Isla del Caño (p406) and Isla Tortuga (p301).

Fishing

Sportfishing is tremendously popular in Costa Rica, though the 'catch-and-release' mantra is strongly encouraged.

Inland, fishing in rivers and lakes is popular. Río Savegre near San Gerardo de Dota is recommended for trout fishing (p372) and Caño Negro for snook (p506). Check with the local operators about closed seasons.

The ocean is always open for fishing. As a general rule, the Pacific coast is best from June and July, though you'll get better fishing on the south coast during that period, while the Caribbean is best during September to November. For more information, see p77.

A good fishing resource is **Costa Rica Outdoors** (☎ 2282 6743, in the USA 800-308 3394; www.costaricaout doors.com), a magazine available online or in

RESPONSIBLE DIVING & SAFETY GUIDELINES

Please consider the following tips when diving and help preserve the ecology and beauty of reefs.

- Never use anchors on the reef, and take care not to ground boats on coral.

- Avoid touching or standing on living marine organisms or dragging equipment across the reef. Polyps can be damaged by even the gentlest contact. If you must hold on to the reef, only touch exposed rock or dead coral.

- Be conscious of your fins. Even without contact, the surge from fin strokes near the reef can damage delicate organisms. Take care not to kick up clouds of sand, which can smother organisms.

- Practice and maintain proper buoyancy control. Major damage can be done by divers descending too fast and colliding with the reef.

- Take great care in underwater caves. Spend as little time within them as possible as your air bubbles may be caught within the roof, creating air pockets that will leave organisms high and dry. Take turns to inspect the interior of a small cave.

- Resist the temptation to collect or buy corals or shells, or to loot marine archaeological sites (mainly shipwrecks).

- Ensure that you take home all your rubbish and any litter you may find as well. Plastics in particular are a serious threat to marine life.

- Do not feed fish.

- Minimize your disturbance of marine animals. Never ride on the backs of turtles.

Before embarking on a scuba diving, skin diving or snorkeling trip, carefully consider the following points to ensure a safe and enjoyable experience.

- Possess a current diving certification card from a recognized scuba diving instructional agency (if scuba diving).

- Be sure you are healthy and feel comfortable diving.

- Obtain reliable information about physical and environmental conditions at the dive site from a reputable local dive operation.

- Be aware of local laws, regulations and etiquette about marine life and the environment.

- Dive only at sites within your realm of experience; if available, engage the services of a competent, professionally trained dive instructor or dive master.

- Be aware that underwater conditions vary significantly from one region, or even site, to another. Seasonal changes can significantly alter any site and dive conditions. These differences influence the way divers dress for a dive and what diving techniques they use.

- Ask about the environmental characteristics that can affect your diving and how local trained divers deal with these considerations.

hardcopy that carries information on adventure travel, with a focus on fishing.

The following companies offer fishing tours in Costa Rica:

Discover Costa Rica (☎ 2257 5780, in the USA 888-484 8227; www.discover-costa-rica.com) Offers six-day fishing packages and is based in Quepos.

JD's Watersports (☎ in the USA 970-356 1028, 800-477 8971; www.jdwatersports.com)

Rod & Reel Adventures (☎ in the USA 800-356 6982; www.rodreeladventures.com)

Hiking & Trekking

With mountains, valleys, jungles, cloud forests and two coastlines, Costa Rica is one of Central America's most varied hiking and trekking destinations. The country also boasts an extensive number of national parks that have well-developed hiking and trekking networks in even the most remote areas.

For long-distance hiking and trekking, it's best to travel in the dry season (December to April). Outside this narrow window, rivers become impassable and trails are prone to flooding. In the highlands, journeys become more taxing in the rain, and the bare landscape offers little protection. And then there are the mosquitoes, which needless to say, are enough to put a damper on your fun.

The following companies offer trekking tours in Costa Rica:

Costa Rica Trekking Adventures (☎ 2771 4582; www.chirripo.com; San Isidro de El General) Offers multiday treks in Chirripó, Corcovado and Tapanti.

Ocarina Expeditions (☎ 2229 4278; www.ocarina expeditions.com) Naturalist-led treks in Corcovado and Chirripó, as well as volcano and cloud-forest hiking.

Osa Aventura (☎ 2735 5670; www.osaaventura.com) Specializes in treks through Corcovado.

Horseback Riding

Wherever you go in Costa Rica, you will inevitably find someone giving horseback-riding trips. Rates vary from US$25 for an hour or two to over US$100 for a full day. Overnight trips with pack horses can also be arranged, and are a popular way of accessing remote destinations in the national parks. Riders weighing more than 100kg (221lb) cannot expect small local horses to carry them very far.

Travelers should continue to recommend good outfitters (and give the heads up on bad ones) by writing to Lonely Planet.

The following companies organize horse riding in Costa Rica:

Sarapiquí Aguas Bravas (☎ 2292 2072; www.aguas -bravas.co.cr) Offers rafting, biking and horse-riding day trips around Puerto Viejo de Sarapiquí and La Virgen.

Serendipity Adventures (☎ 2558 1000, in the USA 734-995 0111, 800-635 2325; www.serendipityadventures .com) Creates quality horse-riding itineraries, including journeys to a Cabécar indigenous reserve.

Mountain Biking & Motorcycling

Outfitters in Costa Rica and the US can organize multiday mountain-biking trips around Costa Rica that cover stretches of highland and beach. Gear is provided on trips organized by local companies, but US outfitters require that you bring your own.

Most international airlines will fly your bike as a piece of checked baggage if you box it (remember to pad it well, because the box is liable to be roughly handled). Some airlines might charge you an extra handling fee.

You can rent mountain bikes in almost any tourist town, but the condition of the equipment varies. Another option is to buy a decent bike and sell it back at a reduced rate at the end of your trip. It is advisable to bring your own helmet and water bottle as the selection of such personalized items may be wider in your home country. For a monthly fee of US$10, **Trail Source** (www.trailsource.com) can provide you with information on trails all over Costa Rica and the world.

The following companies organize bike tours in Costa Rica:

Backroads (☎ in the USA 510-527 1555, 800-462 2848; www.backroads.com) Offers a six-day cycling trip around Arenal and the Pacific coast.

Coast to Coast Adventures (☎ 2280 8054; www.ctoc adventures.com) Everything from short biking excursions to 14-day coast-to-coast multisport trips.

SAFETY GUIDELINES FOR HIKING & TREKKING

Before embarking on a trip, consider the following points to ensure that you have a safe and enjoyable experience:

- Pay any fees and possess any permits required by local authorities.
- Be sure you are healthy and feel comfortable walking for a sustained period.
- Obtain reliable information from park authorities about the physical and environmental conditions along your intended route.
- Be aware of local laws, regulations and etiquette about wildlife and the environment.
- Walk in regions and trails within your realm of experience.
- Be aware that weather conditions and terrain vary significantly from one region, or even from one trail, to another. Seasonal changes can significantly alter any trail. These differences influence the way walkers dress and the equipment they carry.
- Before you set out, ask about the environmental characteristics that can affect your walk and how local, experienced walkers deal with these characteristics.

RESPONSIBLE HIKING & TREKKING

Consider the following tips to help preserve the ecology and beauty of Costa Rica when hiking.

Rubbish

- Carry out all your rubbish. Don't overlook easily forgotten items, such as silver paper, orange peel, cigarette butts and plastic wrappers. Empty packaging should be stored in a dedicated rubbish bag. Make an effort to carry out rubbish left by others.
- Never bury your rubbish – digging disturbs soil and ground cover and encourages erosion. Buried rubbish will likely be dug up by animals, who may be injured or poisoned by it. It may also take years to decompose.
- Minimize waste by taking minimal packaging and no more food than you will need. Take reusable containers or stuff sacks.
- Sanitary napkins, tampons, condoms and toilet paper should be carried out despite the inconvenience. They burn and decompose poorly.

Human Waste Disposal

- Contamination of water sources by human feces can lead to the transmission of all sorts of nasties. Where there is a toilet, please use it. Where there is none, bury your waste. Dig a small hole 15cm deep and at least 100m from any watercourse. Cover the waste with soil and a rock. In snow, dig down to the soil.
- Ensure that the guidelines above are applied to a portable toilet tent if one is being used by a large trekking party. Encourage all party members, including porters, to use the site.

Washing

- Don't use detergents or toothpaste in or near watercourses, even if they are biodegradable.
- For personal washing, use biodegradable soap and a water container (or even a lightweight, portable basin) at least 50m away from the watercourse. Disperse the waste water widely to allow the soil to filter it fully.
- Wash cooking utensils 50m from watercourses using a scourer, sand or snow (not detergent).

Fires & Low-Impact Cooking

- Don't depend on open fires for cooking. The cutting of wood for fires in popular trekking areas can cause rapid deforestation. Cook on a lightweight kerosene, alcohol or Shellite (white gas) stove and avoid those powered by disposable butane gas canisters.

Costa Rica Expeditions (☎ 2257 0766, 2222 0333; www.costaricaexpeditions.com) Multisport itineraries including biking, hiking, rafting and other adventures.

Harley Davidson Rentals (☎ 2289 5552; www.mariaalexandra.com) Motorcycle tours; see p117.

Lava Tours (☎ 2281 2458; www.lava-tours.com) Reader-recommended tours include a bike ride (mostly downhill) from the Cerro de la Muerte to Manuel Antonio. Offers day trips, multiday packages and riding clinics.

MotoDiscovery (☎ in the USA 800-233 6564, 830-438 7744; www.motodiscovery.com) Organizes motorcycle tours through Central America. An annual trip takes riders from the Rio Grande (known locally as Río Bravo del Norte) in Mexico to the Panama Canal on their own motorcycles.

Serendipity Adventures (☎ 2558 1000, in the USA 734-995 0111, 800-635 2325; www.serendipityadventures

.com) Creates custom biking itineraries to fit your schedule and your group.

Western Spirit Cycling (☎ in the USA 800-845 2453; www.westernspirit.com) Offers a few different eight-day biking itineraries.

Wild Rider (☎ 2258 4604; www.wild-rider.com) Motorcycle tours; see San José, p112.

River Rafting & Kayaking

The months between June and October are considered to be the wildest time for river rafting and kayaking, though some rivers offer good trips all year. Rafters and kayakers should bring sunblock, a spare change of clothes, a waterproof bag for a camera, and river sandals for foot protection. The govern-

■ If you are trekking with a guide and porters, supply stoves for the whole team. In alpine areas, ensure that all members are outfitted with enough clothing so that fires are not a necessity for warmth.

■ If you patronize local accommodation, select those places that do not use wood fires to heat water or cook food.

■ Fires may be acceptable below the tree line in areas that get very few visitors. If you light a fire, use an existing fireplace. Don't surround fires with rocks. Use only dead, fallen wood. Remember the adage 'the bigger the fool, the bigger the fire.' Use minimal wood – just what you need for cooking. In huts, leave wood for the next person.

■ Ensure that you fully extinguish a fire after use. Spread the embers and flood them with water.

Wildlife Conservation

■ Do not feed the wildlife as this can lead to animals becoming dependent on handouts, to unbalanced populations and to diseases.

■ Discourage the presence of wildlife by not leaving food scraps behind you. Place gear out of reach and tie packs to rafters or trees.

■ Do not engage in or encourage hunting. It is illegal in all parks and reserves.

■ Don't buy items made from endangered species.

■ Don't attempt to exterminate animals in huts. In wild places, they are likely to be protected native animals.

Erosion

■ Hillsides and mountain slopes, especially at high altitudes, are prone to erosion. Stick to existing trails and avoid short cuts.

■ If a well-used trail passes through a mud patch, walk through the mud so as not to increase the size of the patch.

■ Avoid removing the plant life that keeps topsoil in place.

Camping on & Accessing Private Property

■ Always seek permission to camp from landowners.

■ Always seek permission prior to accessing private property.

ment regulation of outfitters is poor, so make sure that your guide is well versed in safety and has had emergency medical training.

River kayaking can be organized in conjunction with white-water rafting trips if you are experienced; sea kayaking is a popular activity year-round.

The Adventure Travel chapter (p74) has more detailed information on destinations to raft and kayak.

Many companies specialize in kayaking and rafting trips:

Aventuras Naturales (☎ 2225 3939, 2224 0505, in the USA 800-514 0411; www.toenjoynature.com)

BattenKill Canoe Ltd (☎ in the USA 802-362 2800, 800-421 5268; www.battenkill.com) Trips include a six-day canoe journey around Monteverde and an 11-day paddle through Talamanca.

Coast to Coast Adventures (☎ 2280 8054; www.ctoc adventures.com) Trips incorporate rafting, biking and trekking.

Costa Rica Expeditions (☎ 2257 0766, 2222 0333; www.costaricaexpeditions.com) Multisport itineraries including rafting and other adventures.

Costa Rica Sun Tours (☎ 2296 7757; www.crsun tours.com)

Exploradores Outdoors (☎ 2222 6262; www.explora doresoutdoors.com) With offices in San José and Puerto Viejo de Talamanca, offers one- and two-day rafting trips.

Gulf Islands Kayaking (in Canada ☎ 250-539 2442; www.seakayak.ca) Tours on offer include five days of sea kayaking in Corcovado.

H2O Adventures (☎ 2777 4092; www.aventurash2o .com) Two- and five-day adventures on the Río Savegre. Also offers day-long river-rafting and sea-kayaking excursions.

Mountain Travel Sobek (☎ in the USA 510-594 6000, 888-687 6235; www.mtsobek.com) Offers a 10-day adventure that incorporates sea kayaking and river rafting.

Ocarina Expeditions (☎ 2229 4278; www.ocarina expeditions.com)

Ríos Tropicales (☎ 2233 6455; www.riostropicales .com) Offers many day-long river-rafting trips, as well as some two- and three-day adventures on the Río Pacuare and two days of kayaking in Tortuguero.

Safaris Corobicí (☎ 2669 6191; www.nicoya.com) These slow-moving rafting trips are less for adventurers and more for birders.

Sarapiquí Aguas Bravas (☎ 2292 2072; www.aguas -bravas.co.cr) Offers rafting, biking and horse-riding day trips around Sarapiquí and La Virgen.

Surfing

Most international airlines accept surfboards (they must be properly packed in a padded board bag) as one of the two pieces of checked luggage, though this is getting more difficult (and expensive) in the age of higher fuel tariffs.

Domestic airlines offer more of a challenge. They will accept surfboards (for an extra charge), but the board must be under 2.1m in length. If the plane is full, there's a chance your board won't make it on because of weight restrictions.

In recent years, it's becoming more popular to buy a board (new or used) in Costa Rica, and then sell it before you leave. Outfitters in many of the popular surf towns rent short and long boards, fix dings, give classes and organize excursions. Jacó (p330), Tamarindo (p273), Pavones (p440) and Puerto Viejo de Talamanca (p478) are good for these types of activities.

For detailed surfing information, including a comprehensive surf map, see p74. The following companies organize tours and/or courses:

Costa Rica Rainforest Outward Bound (☎ 2278 6058, in the USA 800-676 2018; www.crrobs.org) Multiweek courses cover surf spots in Nicaragua, Panama and Costa Rica.

Discover Costa Rica (☎ 2257 5780, in the USA 888-484 8227; www.discover-costa-rica.com) Budget surf packages center on Tamarindo, Jacó and the Caribbean coast.

Pura Vida Adventures (☎ in the USA 415-465 2162; www.puravidaadventures.com; Mal País) Six-day packages for women and couples.

Tico Travel (☎ in the USA 800-493 8426; www.ticotravel .com) Offers a great variety of surfing packages and camps.

Venus Surf Adventures (☎ 8840 2365, in the USA 800-793 0512; www.venussurfadventures.com; Pavones) Offers a six-day surf camp for women only, including lessons, yoga and other activities.

Wildlife- & Bird-Watching

Costa Rica's biodiversity is legendary, so it should come as no surprise that the country offers unparalleled opportunities for wildlife- and bird-watching.

Any of Costa Rica's national parks are good places for observing wildlife, as are the various private reserves scattered around the country.

Perhaps the single best area for spotting wildlife is the Península de Osa, specifically Parque Nacional Corcovado (p425). Parque Nacional Santa Rosa (p220), Tortuguero (p460) and Caño Negro (p507) all provide good birding and wildlife-watching opportunities. Quetzals can be found in the areas near the Cerro de la Muerte (p373), such as Parque Nacional Los Quetzales (p372). The reserves around Monteverde and Santa Elena (p170) are good for quetzal-watching too. A map of the protected areas of Costa Rica appears p67.

The following Costa Rican-based companies come highly recommended by our readers. These companies can book everything, from gentle hikes to expeditions in remote wilderness.

Aratinga Tours (☎ 2770 6324; www.aratinga-tours .com) Pieter Westra specializes in bird tours in his native Dutch, but he is fluent in English, Spanish and many dialects of bird. His website provides an excellent introduction to birding in Costa Rica.

Birding Costa Rica (☎ 2294 0463; www.birdscostarica .com) Highly recommended agency that creates special birding itineraries or custom adventure and hiking tours.

Condor Journeys & Adventures (☎ in the USA 318-775 0190, in the UK 01700-841 318, in France 06-14 38 63 94)

Costa Rica Expeditions (☎ 2257 0766, 2222 0333; www.costaricaexpeditions.com) Offers custom itineraries and a network of ecolodges.

Expediciones Tropicales (☎ 2257 4171; www.costarica info.com) Offers a variety of one- and two-week itineraries.

Horizontes (☎ 2222 2022; www.horizontes.com) An 11-day itinerary (US$1706) visits Tortuguero, Arenal, Monteverde and Manuel Antonio.

Windsurfing & Kitesurfing

Laguna de Arenal is the nation's undisputed windsurfing (and kitesurfing) center. From

December to April, winds are strong and steady, averaging 20 knots in the dry season, with maximum winds often 30 knots, and windless days are a rarity. The lake has a year-round water temperature of 64°F (18°C) to 70°F (21°C) with 1m-high swells. For more information see boxed text, p250.

For warmer water (but more inconsistent winds), try Puerto Soley in the Bahía Salinas (p227).

BUSINESS HOURS

Restaurants are usually open from 7am and serve dinner until 9pm, though upscale places may open only for dinner. In remote areas, even the small *sodas* (inexpensive eateries) might open only at specific meal times. See other business hours on the inside cover of this book. Unless otherwise stated, count on sights, activities and restaurants to be open daily.

CHILDREN

Generally speaking, Costa Rica is a kid-friendly country, especially since Ticos themselves are extremely family orientated, and will go out of their way to lavish attention on children. Although you will have to take certain precautions to ensure the health and safety of your little ones, Costa Rica is arguably the most popular family destination in Latin America.

For starters, children under the age of 12 receive a discount of 25% on domestic airline flights, while children under two fly free (provided they sit on a parent's lap). Children pay full fare on buses (except for those under the age of three). Infant car seats are not always available at car-rental agencies, so bring your own.

Most midrange and top-end hotels have reduced rates for children under 12, provided the child shares a room with parents. Top-end hotels will provide cribs and usually have activities for children.

If you're traveling with an infant, bring disposable diapers (nappies), baby creams or toiletries, baby aspirin and a thermometer from home, or stock up in San José. In rural areas, supplies may be difficult to find, though cloth diapers are more widespread (and friendlier to the environment).

For a near-infinite number of other travel suggestions, check out Lonely Planet's *Travel with Children*.

CLIMATE

For a small country, Costa Rica's got an awful lot of weather going on. The highlands are cold, the cloud forest is misty and cool, San José and the Central Valley get an 'eternal spring' and both the Pacific and Caribbean coasts are pretty much sweltering year-round. Get ready for some bad-hair days! See below for more information.

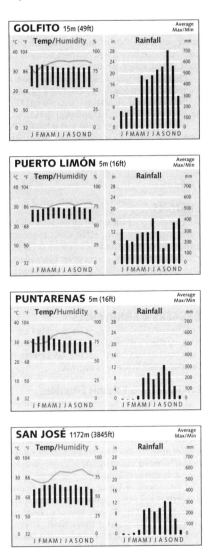

COURSES

Language

Spanish-language schools operate all over Costa Rica and charge by the hour for instruction. Lessons are usually intensive, with class sizes varying from two to five pupils and classes meeting for several hours every weekday.

Courses are offered mainly in central San José and the suburb of San Pedro, which has a lively university and student scene – see boxed text Talk like a Tico, p93. In the Central Valley, there are a number of institutions offering courses – see boxed text Spanish Schools in the Central Valley, p130.

Language schools can also be found in Santa Elena and Monteverde (p179), Playa Sámara (p294), Jacó (p331), Manuel Antonio (p347), La Fortuna (p235) and Dominical (p361).

It is best to arrange classes in advance. A good clearing house is the **Institute for Spanish Language Studies** (ISLS; ☎ 2258 5111, in the USA 800-765 0025, 626-441 3507, 858-456 9268; www.isls.com), which represents half a dozen schools in Costa Rica.

CUSTOMS

All travelers over the age of 18 are allowed to enter the country with 5L of wine or spirits and 500g of processed tobacco (400 cigarettes or 50 cigars). Camera gear, binoculars, and camping, snorkeling and other sporting equipment are readily allowed into the country.

DANGERS & ANNOYANCES

For the latest official reports on travel to Costa Rica see the websites of the **US State Department** (www.travel.state.gov/travel) or the **UK Foreign & Commonwealth Office** (www.fco.gov.uk).

Earthquakes & Volcanic Eruptions

Costa Rica lies on the edge of active tectonic plates, so it is decidedly earthquake prone. Recent major quakes occurred in 1990 (7.1 on the Richter scale) and 1991 (7.4). Smaller quakes and tremors happen quite often – particularly on the Península de Nicoya – cracking roads and knocking down telephone lines. The volcanoes in Costa Rica are not really dangerous as long as you stay on designated trails and don't try to peer into the crater of an active volcano. As a precaution, always check with park rangers before setting out in the vicinity of active volcanoes.

Hiking Hazards

Hikers setting out into the wilderness should be adequately prepared for their trips. Most importantly, don't bite off more than you can chew. If your daily exercise routine consists of walking from the fridge to the TV, don't start your trip with a 20km trek. There are plenty of 3km and 5km trails that are ideally suited to the less active.

In addition, carry plenty of water, even on very short trips. The hiking is hot and dehydration sets in quickly. In Corcovado, at least one hiker dies every year of heat exhaustion on the scorching trail between San Pedrillo and Sirena. Hikers have also been known to get lost in rain forests, so carry maps, extra food and a compass. Let someone know where you are going, so they can narrow the search area in the event of an emergency.

There is also wildlife to contend with. Central America's most poisonous snakes, the fer-de-lance (the 'Costa Rican landmine') and the bushmaster, are quite assertive, and crocodiles are a reality at many estuaries. As if these creatures weren't enough to make you worried, it's also worth mentioning that bull sharks love to lounge at the mouth of Río Sirena in Corcovado.

Ocean Hazards

Approximately 200 drownings a year occur in Costa Rican waters, 90% of which are caused by riptides, which are strong current that pulls the swimmer out to sea. Many deaths in riptides are caused by panicked swimmers struggling to the point of exhaustion. If you are caught in a riptide, do not struggle. Simply float and let the tide carry you out beyond the breakers, after which the riptide will dissipate, then swim parallel to the beach and allow the surf to carry you back in. For more information on riptides see boxed text, p278.

River-Rafting Hazards

River-rafting expeditions may be particularly risky during periods of heavy rain – flash floods have been known to capsize rafts. Reputable tour operators will ensure conditions are safe before setting out; see p526 for a list of operators.

Thefts & Muggings

The biggest danger that most travelers face is theft, primarily from pickpockets. There is a lot of petty crime in Costa Rica so keep your

---

PRACTICALITIES

■ **Electricity** Electrical current is 110V AC at 60Hz; plugs are two flat prongs (same as the USA).

■ **Emergency** The local tourism board, Instituto Costarricense de Turismo (ICT), is located in San José and distributes a helpful brochure with up-to-date emergency numbers for every region.

■ **Magazines** The Spanish-language *Esta Semana* is the best local weekly news magazine.

■ **Newspapers** The most widely distributed newspaper is *La Nación* (www.nacion.co.cr), followed by *Al Día* (a tabloid), *La República* and *La Prensa Libre* (www.prensalibre.co.cr). *Tico Times* (www.ticotimes.net), the English-language weekly newspaper, hits the streets every Friday afternoon.

■ **Radio** 107.5FM is the English-language radio station, playing current hits and providing a regular BBC news feed.

■ **TV** Cable and satellite TV are widely available for a fix of CNN, French videos or Japanese news, and local TV stations have a mix of news, variety shows and *telenovelas* (Spanish-language soap operas).

■ **Video Systems** Videos on sale use the NTSC image registration system (same as the USA).

■ **Weights & Measures** Costa Ricans use the metric system for weights, distances and measures.

---

wits about you at all times and don't let your guard down.

DISABLED TRAVELERS

Independent travel is difficult for anyone with mobility problems. Although Costa Rica has an equal-opportunity law for disabled people, the law applies only to new or newly remodeled businesses and is loosely enforced. Therefore, very few hotels and restaurants have features specifically suited to wheelchair use. Many don't have ramps, while room or bathroom doors are rarely wide enough to accommodate a wheelchair.

Outside the buildings, streets and sidewalks are potholed and poorly paved, making wheelchair use frustrating at best. Public buses don't have provisions to carry wheelchairs and most national parks and outdoor tourist attractions don't have trails suited to wheelchair use. Notable exceptions include Volcán Poás (p139), INBio (p145) and the Rainforest Aerial Tram (p148). Lodges with wheelchair accessibility are indicated in the reviews.

The following organizations offer specially designed trips for disabled travelers:

Accessible Journeys (☎ in the USA 800-846 4537; www.disabilitytravel.com) Organizes independent travel to Costa Rica for people with disabilities.

Vaya con Silla de Ruedas (☎ 2454 2810; www.go withwheelchairs.com) Offers specialty trips for the wheelchair-bound traveler. The company has specially designed vans and its equipment meets international accessibility standards.

DISCOUNT CARDS

Students with an International Student Identity Card (ISIC) or a valid ID from a university offering four-year courses are generally entitled to discounts on museum or guided-tour fees. Cards supplied by language schools are not honored.

EMBASSIES & CONSULATES

Mornings are the best time to go to embassies and consulates, as they are at their quietest. Australia and New Zealand do not have consular representation in Costa Rica; the closest embassies are in Mexico City. For visa information see p537. All of the following are located in San José.

Canada (☎ 2242 4400; Oficentro Ejecutivo La Sabana, Edificio 3, 3rd fl, Sabana Sur) Behind La Contraloría.

El Salvador (☎ 2257 7855) Head 500m north and 25m west of the Toyota dealership on Paseo Colón.

France (☎ 2234 4167) On the road to Curridabat, 200m south and 50m west of the Indoor Club.

Germany (☎ 2232 5533) On the 8th floor of Torre La Sabana, on Sabana Norte, 300m west of the ICE building.

Guatemala (☎ 2283 2555; Curridabat) Casa Izquierda, 500m south and 30m west of Pops.

Honduras (☎ 2291 5147; Urbanización Trejos Montealegre) About 100m west of Banca Promérica, Escazú.

Israel (☎ 2221 6444; Edificio Centro Colón, 11th fl, Paseo Colón)

Italy (☎ 2234 2326; Av Central & Calle 41, Los Yoses)

Mexico (☎ 2257 0633) About 250m south of the Subaru dealership, Los Yoses.

DIRECTORY

Netherlands (☎ 2296 1490; Oficentro Ejecutivo La Sabana, Edificio 3, 3rd fl, Sabana Sur) Behind La Contraloría.
Nicaragua (☎ 2283 8222; Av Central 2540 btwn Calles 25 & 27, Barrio La California)
Panama (☎ 2281 2442) Head 200m south and 25m east from the *antiguo higuerón* (old fig tree), San Pedro.
Spain (☎ 2222 1933; Calle 32 btwn Paseo Colón & Av 2)
Switzerland (☎ 2221 3229; Edificio Centro Colón, 10th fl, Paseo Colón btwn Calles 38 & 40)
UK (☎ 2258 2025; Edificio Centro Colón, 11th fl, Paseo Colón btwn Calles 38 & 40)
USA (☎ 2220 3939; Carretera a Pavas) Opposite Centro Commercial del Oeste.

FESTIVALS & SPECIAL EVENTS

The following events are of national significance in Costa Rica:

JANUARY/FEBRUARY

Fiesta de Santa Cruz (mid-January) Held in Santa Cruz, there is a religious procession, rodeo, bullfight, music, dances and a beauty pageant.
Las Fiestas de Palmares (mid-January) Ten days of beer drinking, horse shows and other carnival events in the tiny town of Palmares.
Fiesta de los Diablitos (December 31 to January 2 in Boruca; February 5 to 8 in Curré) Men wear carved wooden devil masks and burlap masks to re-enact the fight between the Indians and the Spanish. In this one, the Spanish lose.

MARCH

Día del Boyero (second Sunday of the month) A parade is held in Escazú in honor of oxcart drivers.
Día de San José (St Joseph's Day; March 19) This day honors the patron saint of the capital.

JUNE

Día de San Pedro & San Pablo (St Peter & St Paul Day; June 29) Celebrations with religious processions held in villages of the same name.

JULY

Fiesta de La Virgen del Mar (Festival of the Virgin of the Sea; mid-July) Held in Puntarenas and Playa del Coco, it involves colorful regattas and boat parades.
Día de Guanacaste (July 25) Celebrates the annexation of Guanacaste from Nicaragua. There's a rodeo in Santa Cruz on this day.

AUGUST

La Virgen de los Ángeles (August 2) The patron saint is celebrated with an important religious procession from San José to Cartago.

OCTOBER

Día de la Raza (Columbus Day; October 12) Puerto Limón celebrates with gusto the explorer's landing at nearby Isla Uvita. The four-or five-day carnival is full of colorful street parades and dancing, music, singing and drinking.

NOVEMBER

Día de los Muertos (All Souls' Day; November 2) Families visit graveyards and have religious parades in honor of the deceased.

DECEMBER

La Inmaculada Concepción (Immaculate Conception; December 8) An important religious holiday.
Las Fiestas de Zapote (December 25 to January 1) A weeklong celebration of all things Costa Rican (namely rodeos, cowboys, carnival rides, fried food and a whole lot of drinking) in Zapote, southeast of San José.

GAY & LESBIAN TRAVELERS

Let's start with the good news. In Costa Rica, the situation facing gay and lesbian travelers is better than in most Central American countries. Homosexual acts between two consenting adults (aged 18 and over) are legal, though note that travelers may be subject to the laws of their own country in regard to sexual relations. Most Costa Ricans are tolerant of homosexuality only at a 'don't ask; don't tell' level. This is undoubtedly a side effect of the strong role of Catholicism and the persistence of traditionalism in society.

Here's the bad news. In the recent past, there have been an increasing number of outward acts of prejudice. In 1998, a gay-and-lesbian festival planned in San José was cancelled following heavy opposition from Catholic clergy. The church also forced the cancellation of a gay-and-lesbian tour to Manuel Antonio, and encouraged the boycott of a coastal hotel hosting a gay group. Things took an embarrassing turn in 1999 when the tourism minister said that Costa Rica should not be a destination for sex tourism or gays. The gay community made it clear that it was against sex tourism, and that linking gay tourism with sex tourism was untrue and defamatory. The official position in Costa Rica was then modified, stating that gay tourism was neither encouraged nor prohibited.

Although homosexual acts between consenting adults are legal in Costa Rica, gays and lesbians continue to suffer from discrimination in society. Fortunately, discrimination usually takes the role of subtle nonacceptance, as opposed to violence or outright persecution. Homophobia has declined in recent years, especially in heavily touristy areas – one positive result of the influx of foreigners.

Thankfully, Costa Rica's gays and lesbians have made some strides. In the 1990s the Supreme Court ruled against police harassment in gay nightspots and guaranteed medical treatment to people living with HIV/AIDS. And in June 2003 the first ever gay-pride festival in San José drew more than 2000 attendants. Gays and lesbians traveling in Costa Rica are unlikely to be confronted with poor treatment; nonetheless, outside of gay spots, public displays of affection are not recommended.

The undisputed gay and lesbian capital of Costa Rica is Manuel Antonio – for more information see boxed text, p348.

The monthly newspaper *Gayness* and the magazine *Gente 10* (in Spanish) are both available at gay bars in San José (see p106). There are a number of other resources for gay travelers:

Agua Buena Human Rights Association (☎ 2280 3548; www.aguabuena.org, in Spanish) This noteworthy nonprofit organization has campaigned steadily for fairness in medical treatment for people living with HIV/AIDS in Costa Rica.

Cipac (☎ 2280 7821; www.cipacdh.org, in Spanish) The leading gay activist organization in Costa Rica.

Gay Costa Rica (www.gaycostarica.com, in Spanish) Provides up-to-the-minute information on nightlife, travel and many helpful links.

International Gay & Lesbian Travel Association (IGLTA; ☎ in the USA 800-448 8550, 954-776 2626; www .iglta.org) Maintains a list of hundreds of travel agents and tour operators all over the world.

Tiquicia Travel (☎ 2256 9682; www.tiquiciatravel.com) Makes arrangements at gay-friendly hotels.

Toto Tours (☎ in the USA 800-565 1241, 773-274 8686; www.tototours.com) Gay travel specialists who organize regular trips to Costa Rica, among other destinations.

HOLIDAYS

Días feriados (national holidays) are taken seriously in Costa Rica. Banks, public offices and many stores close. During these times, public transport is tight and hotels are heavily booked. Many festivals (see opposite) coincide with public holidays.

New Year's Day January 1

Semana Santa (Holy Week; March or April) The Thursday and Friday before Easter Sunday is the official holiday, though most businesses shut down the whole week. From Thursday to Sunday bars are closed and alcohol sales are prohibited; on Thursday and Friday buses stop running.

Día de Juan Santamaría (April 11) Honors the national hero who died fighting William Walker in 1856; major events are held in Alajuela, his hometown.

Labor Day May 1

Día de la Madre (Mother's Day; August 15) Coincides with the annual Catholic feast of the Assumption.

Independence Day September 15

Día de la Raza Columbus Day; October 12

Christmas Day (December 25) Christmas Eve is also an unofficial holiday.

Last week in December The week between Christmas and New Year is an unofficial holiday; businesses close and beach hotels are crowded.

INSURANCE

No matter where you travel to in the world, getting a comprehensive travel-insurance policy is a good idea. In regards to Costa Rica, a basic theft/loss and medical policy is recommended. Read the fine print carefully as some companies exclude dangerous activities from their coverage, which can include scuba diving, motorcycling and even trekking. You may prefer a policy that pays doctors or hospitals directly rather than you having to pay on the spot and make a claim later.

INTERNET ACCESS

Internet cafés abound in Costa Rica, and you don't have to look very far to find cheap and speedy internet access. The normal access rate in San José and tourist towns is US$1 to US$2 per hour, though you can expect to pay upwards of US$5 per hour in the hard-to-reach places.

Wi-fi access is on the rise in Costa Rica. If you keep your eyes open (and computer on), you'll find wireless hotspots in San José, Alajuela, Jacó, Monteverde and Santa Elena, La Fortuna, Tamarindo, Puerto Jiménez and Puerto Viejo de Talamanca. Furthermore, the majority of top-end hotels and, increasingly, upscale backpacker hostels offer secure wireless networks to their customers.

LEGAL MATTERS

If you get into legal trouble and are jailed in Costa Rica, your embassy can offer limited assistance. This may include an occasional visit from an embassy staff member to make sure your human rights have not been violated,

---

PREVENTING CHILD SEX TOURISM IN COSTA RICA *ECPAT/Beyond Borders*

Tragically, the exploitation of local children by tourists is becoming more prevalent throughout Latin America, including Costa Rica. Various socio-economic factors make children susceptible to sexual exploitation, and some tourists choose to take advantage of their vulnerable position.

Sexual exploitation has serious, lifelong effects on children. Sexual exploitation of children is a crime and a violation of human rights, and Costa Rica has laws against it. Many countries have enacted extraterritorial legislation that allows travelers to be charged as though the exploitation happened in their home country.

Travelers can help stop child sex tourism by reporting it – it is important not to ignore suspicious behavior. **Cybertipline** (www.cybertipline.com) is a website where the sexual exploitation of children can be reported, you can also report it to local authorities, and if you know the nationality of the perpetrator, you can report it to their embassy.

Travelers interested in learning more about how to fight against the sexual exploitation of children can go to **ECPAT International** (End Child Prostitution and Trafficking; www.ecpat.org) or **Beyond Borders** (www.beyondborders.org), the Canadian affiliate of ECPAT. ECPAT aims to advance the rights of children and help them to be free from abuse and exploitation without regard to race, religion, gender or sexual orientation. **ECPAT USA** (☎ in the USA 718-935 9192; www.ecpatusa.org) is part of a global network working on these issues with over 70 affiliate organizations around the world. The US headquarters is located in New York.

---

letting your family know where you are and putting you in contact with a Costa Rican lawyer, who you must pay yourself. Embassy officials will not bail you out and you are subject to Costa Rican laws, not the laws of your own country.

In Costa Rica the legal age for driving, voting and having heterosexual sex is 18 years, and you can get married when you are 15 years old. There is no legal age for homosexual sex but sex with anyone under 18 is not advisable. Travelers may be subject to the laws of their own country in regard to sexual relations.

Drivers & Driving Accidents

Drivers should carry their passport and driver's license at all times. If you have an accident, call the police immediately to make a report (required for insurance purposes) or attend to any injured parties. Leave the vehicles in place until the report has been made and do not make any statements except to members of law-enforcement agencies. The injured should only be moved by medical professionals.

Keep your eye on your vehicle until the police arrive and then call the car-rental company to find out where you should take the vehicle for repairs (do not have it fixed yourself). If the accident results in injury or death, you could be jailed or prevented from leaving the country until legalities are handled.

Emergency numbers are listed on the inside cover of this book.

MAPS

Detailed maps are unfortunately hard to come by in Costa Rica. An excellent option is the 1:330,000 *Costa Rica* sheet produced by **International Travel Map** (ITMB; www.itmb.com; 530 W Broadway, Vancouver, BC, V5Z 1E, Canada), which is waterproof and includes a San José inset.

The **Fundación Neotropica** (www.neotropica.org) publishes a 1:500,000 map showing national parks and other protected areas. These are available in San José bookstores and over the internet.

The Instituto Costarricense de Turismo (ICT; see p82) publishes a 1:700,000 Costa Rica map with a 1:12,500 Central San José map on the reverse. These are free at ICT offices in San José.

Online, **Maptak** (www.maptak.com) has maps of Costa Rica's seven provinces and their capitals.

Don't count on any of the national park offices or ranger stations having maps for hikers. Topographical maps are available for purchase from **Instituto Geográfico Nacional** (IGN; ☎ 2257 7798; Calle 9 btwn Avs 20 & 22, San José; ☼ 7:30am-noon & 1-3pm Mon-Fri). In the USA, contact **Omni Resources** (☎ 336-227 8300; www.omnimap.com).

The *Mapa-Guía de la Naturaleza Costa Rica* is an atlas published by Incafo that includes 1:200,000 topographical sheets, as well as English and Spanish descriptions of Costa Rica's natural areas. It is available at Lehmann's (p79) in San José.

MONEY

ATMs

It's increasingly easy to find *cajeros automáticos* (ATMs) in Costa Rica, even in the smallest towns. The Visa Plus network is the standard, but machines on the Cirrus network, which accepts most foreign ATM cards, can be found in larger cities and tourist towns. In these areas, ATMs also dispense US dollars, which is convenient for payments at top-end hotels and tour agencies. Note that some machines will only accept cards held by their own customers.

Cash & Currency

The Costa Rican currency is the colón (plural colones, ₡), named after Cristóbal Colón (Christopher Columbus). Bills come in 500, 1000, 5000 and 10,000 notes, while coins come in denominations of 5, 10, 20, 25, 50 and 100. Note that older coins are larger and silver, while newer ones are smaller and gold-colored – this is often a source of confusion for travelers fresh off the plane.

Throughout Costa Rica, you can pay for tours, park fees, hotel rooms, midrange to expensive meals and large-ticket items with US dollars. However, local meals, bus fares and small items should generally be paid with colones.

Paying for things in US dollars should be free of hassle, and at times is encouraged since the currency is viewed as being more stable than colones. Newer US dollars (eg big heads) are preferred throughout Costa Rica.

Credit Cards

You can expect a transaction fee on all international credit-card purchases. Holders of credit and debit cards can buy colones and sometimes US dollars in some banks, though you can expect to pay a high transaction fee. Cards are widely accepted at some midrange and most top-end hotels, as well as top-end restaurants and some travel agencies. All car-rental agencies accept credit cards.

Exchanging Money

All banks will exchange US dollars, and some will exchange euros and British pounds; other currencies are more difficult. Most banks have excruciatingly long lines, especially at the state-run institutions (Banco Nacional, Banco de Costa Rica, Banco Popular), though they don't charge commissions on cash exchanges. Private banks (Banex, Banco Interfin, Scotiabank) tend to be faster. Make sure the dollar bills you want to exchange are in good condition or they may be refused.

Taxes

Travelers will notice a 13.39% sales tax at mid-range and top-end hotels and restaurants, while hotels also charge an additional 3% tourist surcharge. Everybody must pay a US$26 airport tax upon leaving the country. It is payable in US dollars or in colones, and credit cards are accepted. Note that some travelers have reported that this fee was charged on their cards as a cash advance, which resulted in a hefty fee.

Tipping

It is customary to tip the bellhop/porter (US$1 to US$3 per service) and the housekeeper (US$1 to US$2 per day) in top-end hotels, less in budget places. On guided tours, tip the guide US$1 to US$10 per person per day. Tip the tour driver about half of what you tip the guide. Naturally, tips depend upon quality of service. Taxi drivers are not normally tipped, unless some special service is provided. Top-end restaurants may add a 10% service charge onto the bill. If not, you might leave a small tip to show your appreciation, but it is not required.

Traveler's Checks

Most banks and exchange bureaus will cash traveler's checks at a commission of 1% to 3%. Some hotels will accept them as payment, but check policies carefully as many hotels do not. US dollar traveler's checks are preferred. It may be difficult or impossible to change checks of other currencies.

PHOTOGRAPHY

Costa Ricans make wonderful subjects for photos. However, most people resent having cameras thrust in their faces, and some attach price tags to their mugs. As a rule, you should ask for permission if you have an inkling your subject would not approve.

Since most people use digital cameras these days, it can be quite difficult to purchase high quality film in Costa Rica. However, most internet cafés in the country can burn your digital pictures on CD, and cheap media is available for purchase in most large towns and cities.

> **BARGAINING**
>
> A high standard of living along with a steady stream of international tourist traffic means that the Latin American tradition of haggling is fast dying out in Costa Rica. In tourist towns especially, fixed prices on hotels cannot be negotiated, and you can expect business owners to be offended if you try. Some smaller hotels in the interior regions still accept the practice.
>
> Negotiating prices at outdoor markets is acceptable, and bargaining is accepted when hiring long-distance taxis. Overall, Ticos respond well to good manners and gentle inquiries. If you demand a service for your price, chances are you won't get it.

POST

Airmail letters cost about US$0.35 for the first 20g. Parcels can be shipped at the rate of US$7 per kilogram. You can receive mail at the main post office of major towns. Mail to San José's central post office should be addressed:

[Name], c/o Lista de Correos, Correo Central, San José, Costa Rica.

Letters usually arrive within a week from North America, longer from more distant places. The post office will hold mail for 30 days from the date it's received. Photo identification is required to retrieve mail and you will only be given correspondence with your name on it.

Note that in addresses, *apartado* means 'PO Box'; it is not a street or apartment address.

SHOPPING

Avoid purchasing animal products, including turtle shells, animal skulls and anything made with feathers, coral or shells. Wood products are also highly suspicious: make sure you know where the wood came from.

Coffee & Alcohol

Coffee is the most popular souvenir, and deservedly so. It is available at gift shops, the Mercado Central (p107) in San José and at any supermarket throughout the country.

The most popular alcohol purchases are Ron Centenario, Café Rica (the coffee liqueur) and *guaro* (the local firewater). All are available at duty-free shops inside the airport, or in supermarkets and liquor stores in every town and city.

Handicrafts & Ceramics

Tropical hardwood items include salad bowls, plates, carving boards, jewelry boxes and a variety of carvings and ornaments. The most exquisite woodwork is available at Biesanz Woodworks (p123) in Escazú. All of the wood is grown on farms expressly for this purpose, so you needn't worry about forests being chopped down for your salad bowl.

Uniquely Costa Rican souvenirs are the colorfully painted replicas of traditional oxcarts (*carretas*) produced in Sarchí (p136).

SOLO TRAVELERS

Costa Rica is a fine country for solo travelers, especially if you get in with the backpacking community. Inexpensive hostels with communal kitchens encourage social exchange, while a large number of language schools, tours and volunteer organizations will provide every traveler with an opportunity to meet others. However, it isn't recommended to undertake long treks in the wilderness by yourself.

TELEPHONE

Public phones are found all over Costa Rica and Chip or Colibrí phonecards are available in 1000, 2000 and 3000 colón denominations. Chip cards are inserted into the phone and scanned. Colibrí cards (the most common) require you to dial a toll-free number (☎ 199) and enter an access code. Instructions are provided in English or Spanish. Colibrí is the preferred card of travelers since it can be used from any phone. Cards can be found just about everywhere, including supermarkets, pharmacies, newsstands, *pulperías* (corner grocery stores) and gift shops.

The cheapest international calls from Costa Rica are direct-dialed using a phonecard. To make international calls, dial '00' followed by the country code and number. Pay phones cannot receive international calls.

Make sure that no one is peeking over your shoulder when you dial your code. Some travelers have had their access numbers pilfered by thieves.

To call Costa Rica from abroad, use the international code (☎ 506) before the eight-digit number. Find other important phone numbers on the inside cover of this book.

Due to the increasing popularity of voice-over IP services like Skype, it's sometimes possible to skip the middle man and just bring a headset along with you to an internet café. Ethernet connections and wireless signals are becoming more common in accommodations, so if you're traveling with a laptop you can just connect and call for pennies.

TIME
Costa Rica is six hours behind Greenwich Mean Time (GMT), so Costa Rican time is equivalent to Central Time in North America. There is no daylight saving time.

TOILETS
Public restrooms are rare, but most restaurants and cafés will let you use their facilities at a small charge – usually between US$0.25 to US$0.50. Bus terminals and other major public buildings usually have bathrooms, also at a charge.

If you're particularly fond of toilet paper, carry it with you at all times as it is not always available. Just don't flush it down! Costa Rican plumbing is often poor and has very low pressure in all but the best hotels and buildings. Dispose of toilet paper in the rubbish bin inside the bathroom.

TOURIST INFORMATION
The government-run tourism board, the Instituto Costarricense de Turismo (ICT), has two offices in the capital (see p82). However, don't expect to be wowed with any particularly insightful travel advice as it's the staff's job to tell you that it's all good in Costa Rica. That said, the ICT can provide you with free maps, a master bus schedule and information on road conditions in the hinterlands. English is spoken.

Consult the ICT's flashy English-language website (www.visitcostarica.com) for information, or in the USA call the ICT's toll-free number (☎ 800-343 6332) for brochures and information.

VISAS
Passport-carrying nationals of the following countries are allowed 90 days' stay with no visa: Argentina, Canada, Israel, Japan, Panama, the USA, and most western European countries.

Citizens of Australia, Iceland, Ireland, Mexico, New Zealand, Russia, South Africa and Venezuela are allowed to stay for 30 days with no visa. Others require a visa from a Costa Rican embassy or consulate. For the latest info on visas, check the websites of the **ICT** (www.visitcostarica.com) or the **Costa Rican embassy** (www.costarica-embassy.org) in Washington, DC.

If you are in Costa Rica and need to visit your embassy or consulate, see p531 for contact information.

Extensions
Extending your stay beyond the authorized 30 or 90 days is a time-consuming hassle. It is far easier to leave the country for 72 hours and then re-enter. Otherwise, go to the office of **migración** (immigration; ☎ 2220 0355; ☾ 8am-4pm) in San José, opposite Channel 6, about 4km north of Parque La Sabana. Requirements for extensions change, so allow several working days.

Onward Tickets
Travelers officially need onward tickets before they are allowed to enter Costa Rica. This requirement is not often checked at the airport, but travelers arriving by land should anticipate a need to show an onward ticket.

WHAT'S THAT ADDRESS?

Though some larger cities have streets that have been dutifully named, signage is rare and finding a Tico who knows what street they are standing on is even rarer. Everybody uses landmarks when providing directions; an address may be given as 200m south and 150m east of a church. A city block is *cien metros* – literally 100m – so '*250 metros al sur*' means 2½ blocks south, regardless of the distance. Churches, parks, office buildings, fast-food joints and car dealerships are the most common landmarks used – but these are often meaningless to the foreign traveler who will have no idea where the Subaru dealership is to begin with. Better yet, Ticos frequently refer to landmarks that no longer exist. In San Pedro, outside San José, locals still use the sight of an old fig tree *(el antiguo higuerón)* to provide directions.

Confused? Get used to it…

DIRECTORY

If you're heading to Panama, Nicaragua or another Central or South American country from Costa Rica, you may need an onward or roundtrip ticket before you will be allowed entry into that country or even allowed to board the plane if you're flying. A quick check with the appropriate embassy – easy to do via the internet – will tell you whether the country that you're heading to has an onward-ticket requirement.

VOLUNTEERING

The sheer number of volunteer opportunities in Costa Rica is mind-blowing. 'Voluntourism' is a great way to travel sustainably and make a positive contribution to the local community. Volunteer work is also an amazing forum for self-exploration, especially if you touch a few lives and meet a few new friends along the way. Generally speaking, you will get as much out of volunteering as you put in and the majority of volunteers in Costa Rica walk away from their experiences content.

The following volunteer opportunities provide a general overview of what is currently available in Costa Rica.

English Teaching

Although most travelers in Costa Rica are extremely keen to learn and/or perfect their Spanish, you can give a lot back by teaching English to kids and adults of all ages. With that said, once class ends and you're outside the school, your students will be happy to swap roles and teach you a bit of Spanish along the way.

Amerispan Unlimited (www.amerispan.com) Offers a variety of educational travel programs in specialized areas.

Cloud Forest School (www.cloudforestschool.org) A bilingual school (kindergarten to 11th grade) in Monteverde offering creative and experiential education.

Institute for Central American Development Studies (www.icadscr.com) Combines month-long Spanish language programs and volunteer placements.

Sustainable Horizon (www.sustainablehorizon.com) Arranges volunteering trips such as guest teaching spots and orphanage placements.

World Language Study (www.worldlanguagestudy.com) Sends volunteers to teach English in kindergartens, primary and secondary schools, and foster homes.

Forestry Management

Despite its relatively small size, Costa Rica is home to an impressive number of national parks, a good number of which protect some of the most pristine rain forest on the planet. If you're interesting in helping to save this threatened ecosystem, and perhaps gaining a valuable skill set in the process, consider a placement in a forest management program.

Bosque Eterno de los Niños (Children's Eternal Forest; www.acmcr.org) Volunteers are needed to help manage the remarkable achievement – a rain forest purchased by children who raised money to buy and protect it.

Cloudbridge Nature Preserve (www.cloudbridge.org) A private reserve where an ongoing reforestation project is being spearheaded by two New Yorkers.

Fundación Corcovado (www.corcovadofoundation.org) An impressive network of people and organizations committed to preserving Parque Nacional Corcovado.

INBio (www.inbio.ac.cr/en/default2.html) A private research center dedicated to biodiversity management throughout Costa Rica's varying ecosystems.

Monteverde Institute (www.mvinstitute.org) A nonprofit educational institute offering training in tropical biology, conservation and sustainable development.

Organic Farming

The entire world is going organic, and Costa Rica is certainly at the forefront of this highly admirable and sustainable movement. Home to virtual living laboratories of self-sufficient farms and plantations, Costa Rica is perfectly suited for volunteers interested in greening their thumbs.

Finca la Flor de Paraíso (www.la-flor-de-paraiso.org) Offers programs in a variety of disciplines from animal husbandry to medicinal-herb cultivation.

Finca Lomas (www.anaicr.org) Home to a crop experimentation project that includes fruit, nut and spice trees.

Punta Mona (www.puntamona.org) An organic farm and retreat center that is based on organic permaculture and sustainable living.

Rancho Margot (www.ranchomargot.org) This self-proclaimed life-skills university offers a natural education emphasizing organic farming and animal husbandry.

Reserva Biológica Dúrika (www.durika.org) A sustainable community that is centered upon a 7500-hectare biological reserve.

Wildlife Conservation

Whether you're interested in sea turtles or rehabilitating rescued animals, Costa Rica is one of the best places in the world to get hands-on experience with wild animals. Whether you're an aspiring veterinarian or just concerned with the plight of endangered species, any of the following programs can help you get a little closer to some of Mother Nature's charismatic creatures.

ANAI (www.anaicr.org) A grassroots organization that is fighting hard to save the sea turtles.

ASCOMOTI (www.ascomoti.org) Protects the squirrel monkey, Costa Rica's most endangered primate.

CCC (www.cccturtle.org) Assist scientists with turtle tagging and research on green and leatherback turtles.

Profelis (www.grafischer.com/profelis) A feline conservation program that takes care of confiscated wild cats, both big and small.

Zoo Ave (www.zooave.org) A wildlife park offering opportunities for domestic and wild animal care.

WOMEN TRAVELERS

Most female travelers experience little more than a *'mi amor'* ('my love') or an appreciative hiss from the local men in Costa Rica. But in general, Costa Rican men consider foreign women to have looser morals and to be easier conquests than Ticas (female Costa Ricans). Men will often make flirtatious comments to single women, particularly blondes. Women traveling together are not exempt from this. The best way to deal with this is to do what the Ticas do – ignore it completely. Women who firmly resist unwanted verbal advances from men are normally treated with respect.

In small highland towns, dress is usually conservative. Women rarely wear shorts, but belly-baring tops are all the rage. On the beach, skimpy bathing suits are ok, but topless and nude bathing are not (see boxed text, p339).

As in any part of the world, the possibilities of rape and assault do exist. Use your normal caution: avoid walking alone in isolated places or through city streets late at night, and skip the hitchhiking. Do not take unlicensed 'pirate' taxis (licensed taxis are red and have medallions) as reports of assaults against women by unlicensed drivers have been reported.

Birth-control pills are available at most pharmacies (without a prescription) and tampons can be difficult to find in rural areas – bring some from home or stock up in San José.

The **Centro Feminista de Información y Acción** (Cefemina; ☎ 2224 3986; www.cefemina.org; San Pedro) is the main Costa Rican feminist organization. It publishes a newsletter and can provide information and assistance to women travelers.

WORK

It's difficult for foreigners to find work in Costa Rica. The government doesn't like anyone taking jobs away from Costa Ricans and the labor laws reflect this sentiment. Basically, the only foreigners legally employed in Costa Rica work for their own businesses, possess skills not found in the country, or work for companies that have special agreements with the government.

Getting a bona fide job necessitates obtaining a work permit – a time-consuming and difficult process. The most likely source of paid employment is as an English teacher at one of the language institutes, or working in the hospitality industry in a hotel or resort. Naturalists or river guides may be able to find work with private lodges or adventure-travel operators, though you shouldn't expect to make more than survival wages from these jobs.

Transportation

CONTENTS

GETTING THERE & AWAY

ENTERING THE COUNTRY

A few people arrive in Costa Rica by sea, either on fishing or scuba charters or as part of a brief stop on a cruise. Others travel in by bus from neighboring countries. But the vast majority of travelers land at the airport in San José, with a growing number arriving in Liberia.

Entering Costa Rica is usually hassle-free (with the exception of some long queues). There are no fees or taxes payable upon entering the country, though some foreign nationals will require a visa. Be aware that those who need visas cannot get them at the border. For information on visas, see p537.

THINGS CHANGE...

The information in this chapter is particularly vulnerable to change. Check directly with the airline or a travel agent to make sure you understand how a fare (and ticket you may buy) works and be aware of the security requirements for international travel. Shop carefully. The details given in this chapter should be regarded as pointers and are not a substitute for your own careful, up-to-date research.

Passport

Citizens of all nations are now required to have a passport that is valid for at least six months beyond the dates of your trip. When you arrive, your passport will be stamped. The law requires that you carry your passport at all times during your stay in Costa Rica.

Onward Ticket

Travelers officially need a ticket out of Costa Rica before they are allowed to enter, but the rules are enforced erratically. Those arriving by land can generally meet this requirement by purchasing an outward ticket from the TICA bus company, which has offices in Managua (Nicaragua) and Panama City.

AIR
Airports & Airlines

International flights arrive at Aeropuerto Internacional Juan Santamaría (p108), 17km northwest of San José, in the town of Alajuela. As a result, an increasing number of travelers are bypassing the capital all together, and choosing instead to strike out into the country from Alajuela instead.

In recent years Aeropuerto Internacional Daniel Oduber Quirós (p214) in Liberia has started receiving international flights from the USA. Although there is a lot of talk about airport expansion, at the time of research only American Airlines, Continental, Delta, Northwest, United Airlines and US Airways were flying into Liberia. It is expected that many international airlines will start to offer flights in and out of this airport, including some flights direct from Europe (eliminating the layover in Miami or Dallas). Daniel Oduber airport is convenient for travelers visiting the Península de Nicoya.

Costa Rica is well connected by air to other Central and Latin American countries, as well as the USA. The national airline, Lacsa (part of the Central American Airline consortium Grupo TACA), flies to numerous points in the USA and Latin America, including Cuba. The Federal Aviation Administration in the USA has assessed Costa Rica's aviation authorities to be in compliance with international safety standards.

Airlines flying to and from Costa Rica include the following companies; see p108 for details of those with offices in San José.

Air Canada (☎ in Canada 514-393 3333; www .aircanada.ca; airline code AC) No office in Costa Rica.

America West (☎ in the USA 480-693 6718; www .americawest.com; airline code HP) No office in Costa Rica.

American Airlines (☎ 2257 1266; www.aa.com; airline code AA)

Continental (☎ 2296 4911; www.continental.com; airline code CO)

COPA (☎ 2222 6640; www.copaair.com; airline code CM)

Cubana de Aviación (☎ 2221 7625, 2221 5881; www.cubana.cu; airline code CU)

Delta (☎ 2256 7909, press 5 for reservations; www.delta.com; airline code DL)

Grupo TACA (☎ 2296 0909; www.taca.com; airline code TA)

Iberia (☎ 2257 8266; www.iberia.com; airline code IB)

KLM (☎ 2220 4111; www.klm.com; airline code KL)

Lacsa (see Grupo TACA)

Mexicana (☎ 2295 6969; www.mexicana.com; airline code MX)

Northwest (☎ in the USA 800-225-2525; www.nwa .com; airline code NW) No office in Costa Rica.

SAM/Avianca (☎ 2233 3066; www.avianca.com; airline code AV)

DEPARTURE TAX

There is a US$26 departure tax on all international outbound flights, payable in cash (US dollars or colones, or a mix of the two). At the Juan Santamaría airport you can pay with credit cards, and Banco de Costa Rica has an ATM (on the Plus system) by the departure-tax station.

United Airlines (☎ 2220 4844; www.united.com; airline code UA)

US Airways (☎ toll-free reservations in Costa Rica 800-011 0793, 800-011 4114; www.usairways.com; airline code US) No office in Costa Rica.

Tickets

Airline fares are usually more expensive during the Costa Rican high season (from December through April), with December and January the most expensive months to travel.

Central & Latin America

American Airlines, Continental, Delta, Northwest, United and US Airways have connections to Costa Rica from many Central and Latin American countries. Grupo TACA usually offers the most flights on these routes.

TRANSPORTATION

CLIMATE CHANGE & TRAVEL

Climate change is a serious threat to the ecosystems that humans rely upon, and air travel is the fastest-growing contributor to the problem. Lonely Planet regards travel, overall, as a global benefit, but also believes we all have a responsibility to limit our personal impact on global warming.

Flying & Climate Change

Pretty much every form of motor travel generates CO_2 (the main cause of human-induced climate change) but planes are far and away the worst offenders, not just because of the sheer distances they allow us to travel, but because they release greenhouse gases high into the atmosphere. The statistics are frightening: two people taking a return flight between Europe and the US will contribute as much to climate change as an average household's gas and electricity consumption over a whole year.

Carbon Offset Schemes

Climatecare.org and other websites use 'carbon calculators' that allow jetsetters to offset the greenhouse gases they are responsible for with contributions to energy-saving projects and other climate-friendly initiatives in the developing world – including projects in India, Honduras, Kazakhstan and Uganda.

Lonely Planet, together with Rough Guides and other concerned partners in the travel industry, supports the carbon offset scheme run by climatecare.org. Lonely Planet offsets all of its staff and author travel.

For more information check out our website: lonelyplanet.com.

BORDER CROSSINGS

There is no fee for travelers to enter Costa Rica. However, the fee for each vehicle entering the country is US$22. For more information on visa requirements for entering Costa Rica, see p537.

Nicaragua – Sapoá to Peñas Blancas

Situated on the Interamericana, this is the most heavily trafficked border station between Nicaragua and Costa Rica. Virtually all international overland travelers from Nicaragua enter Costa Rica through here. The border station is open from 6am to 8pm daily on both the Costa Rican and Nicaraguan sides – though local bus traffic stops in the afternoon. This is the only official border between Nicaragua and Costa Rica that you can drive across.

The **Tica Bus** (☎ in Managua 222 6094), **Nica Bus** (☎ in Managua 228 1374) and **TransNica** (☎ in Managua 278 2090) all have daily buses to Costa Rica. The fare is US$14 and the trip takes nine hours. From Rivas (37km north of the border) twice-hourly buses depart for Sapoá from 5am to 4:30pm. Regular buses depart Peñas Blancas, on the Costa Rican side, for La Cruz, Liberia and San José.

The Costa Rican and Nicaraguan immigration offices are almost 1km apart; most people travel through by bus or private car. Travelers without a through bus will find golf carts (US$2) running between the borders, but walking is not a problem. While Costa Rica does not charge visitors to cross the border, Nicaragua does: people leaving Nicaragua pay US$2, while folks entering Nicaragua will be charged US$7 until noon, after which the fee becomes US$9. All fees must be paid in US dollars.

Note that Peñas Blancas is only a border post, not a town, so there is nowhere to stay. For more information see boxed text Heading North of the Border, p224.

Nicaragua – San Carlos to Los Chiles

International travelers rarely use this route, though it's extremely hassle-free. There is no land crossing and you cannot drive between the two points. Instead, the crossing must be done by boat. Regular boats (US$10, 45 minutes) leave San Carlos and travel the Río Frío to Los Chiles at 10:30am and 4pm, with extra boats scheduled as needed. At other times, boatworkers can usually be found by the ENAP dock in San Carlos, but remember that the border closes at 5pm. Although there is a road that travels from the southern banks of the Río San Juan in Nicaragua to Los Chiles, it is reserved for federal employees. You will not be able to enter Costa Rica this way (and you certainly will not be able to drive in).

If you are entering Costa Rica, don't forget to get the US$2 exit stamp at the San Carlos *migración* (immigration) office, 50m west of the dock. Once you enter Costa Rica, you'll have to stop at Costa Rica *migración* for your entry stamp.

Traveling from Costa Rica to Nicaragua, you will need to pay a US$7 fee when you enter. For more information, see boxed text Getting to San Carlos, Nicaragua, p510.

Recently, the domestic Costa Rican airlines have begun offering a few international flights. **Nature Air** (www.natureaire.com) now flies to Granada from both Liberia (one way/round-trip US$65/130) and San José (one way/round-trip US$120/240) four times a week, and to Bocas del Toro (one way/round-trip US$99/199) two times a week. Note that the prices given here are estimates as rates vary considerably on season and availability.

Grupo TACA offers direct flights to Caracas (US$500, three hours, daily), Guatemala City (US$250, 1½ hours, twice daily) and San Salvador (US$235, 1½ hours, three daily).

TACA and Mexicana have daily flights to Mexico City (US$500, three hours), while both TACA and Copa have several flights a day to Panama City (US$300, 1½ hours, three daily). Round-trip prices are quoted unless otherwise indicated. Again, the prices given here are estimates as rates vary considerably on season and availability.

Other Countries

More than one-third of all travelers to Costa Rica come from the USA, so finding a nonstop flight from Houston, Miami or New York is quite simple. Schedules and prices are com-

Panama – Paso Canoas

This border crossing on the Carretera Interamericana (Pan-American Hwy) is by far the most frequently used entry and exit point with Panama and is open 24 hours a day. The border crossing in either direction is generally straightforward. Be sure to get your exit stamp from Panama at the *migración* office before entering Costa Rica. There is no charge for entering Costa Rica. Travelers without a private vehicle should arrive during the day because buses stop running by 6pm. Travelers in a private vehicle would do better to arrive late in the morning when most of the trucks have already been processed.

Tica Bus (☎ in Panama City 262 2084) travels from Panama City to San José (US$25, 15 hours) daily and crosses this border post. In David, Tracopa has one bus daily from the main terminal to San José (US$18, nine hours). In David you'll also find frequent buses to the border at Paso Canoas (US$2, 1½ hours) that take off every 10 minutes from 4am to 8pm.

If traveling to Panama, you will have to pay US$5 for a tourist card. For further details, see boxed text Getting to Panama, p390.

Panama – Guabito to Sixaola

Situated on the Caribbean coast, this is a fairly tranquil and hassle-free border crossing. Immigration guards regularly take off for lunch and you may have to wait a while to be processed. The border town on the Panamanian side is Guabito.

The border is open from 8am to 6pm in Panama and 7am to 5pm in Costa Rica. (Panama is one hour ahead.) Both sides close for an hour-long lunch at around 1pm, which means that there are potentially two hours each day when you'll be unable to make it across the border quickly. Get to Sixaola as early as possible; while there are a couple of sleeping options, it won't be the highlight of your trip if you have to spend the night. Before crossing the bridge, stop at Costa Rica **migración** (☎ 2754 2044) to process your paperwork. Walking across the bridge is kind of fun, in a vertigo-inducing sort of way.

If you are coming from Bocas del Toro, it's faster and cheaper to take the ferry to Changuinola (US$5, 45 minutes), from where you can take a quick taxi to the border or to the bus station (US$5). One daily bus travels between Changuinola and San José at 10am (US$15, eight hours). Otherwise, you can walk over the border and catch one of the hourly buses that go up the coast from Sixaola. For details, see boxed text Getting to Guabito & Bocas del Toro, Panama, p496.

Panama – Río Sereno to San Vito

This is a rarely used crossing in the Cordillera de Talamanca. The border is open from 8am to 6pm in Panama and 7am to 5pm in Costa Rica. The small village of Río Sereno on the Panamanian side has a hotel and a place to eat; there are no facilities on the Costa Rican side.

Regular buses depart Concepción and David in Panama for Río Sereno. Local buses (four daily) and taxis go from the border to San Vito. See also the boxed text Getting to Panama, p390.

petitive – a little bit of shopping around can get you a good fare.

From Canada, most travelers to Costa Rica connect through US gateway cities, though Air Canada has direct flights from Toronto.

Most flights from the UK and Europe connect either in the USA or in Mexico City, although this may change once the new airport in Liberia starts attracting more flights. High-season fares may still apply during the northern summer, even though this is the beginning of the Costa Rican rainy season.

From Australia and New Zealand, travel routes usually go through the USA or Mexico.

Again, fares tend to go up in June and July even though this is the beginning of the rainy season in Costa Rica.

LAND
Bus

Costa Rica shares land borders with Nicaragua and Panama, and a lot of travelers, particularly shoestringers, enter the country by bus. Furthermore, an extensive bus system links the Central American capitals and it's vastly cheaper than flying.

If crossing the border by bus, note that international buses may cost slightly more than

TRANSPORTATION

DRIVING TO COSTA RICA FROM NORTH AMERICA

Every year, readers send us letters detailing their long-haul road trip across the continent. If you think you're game for a little overland adventure, here is a selection of reader-tested tips for making the most of the big drive:

- **Think it through** Driving yourself through Central America is *not* a cheap option. Having your own car will afford you greater comfort and flexibility, though you will spend more than you expect on petrol, insurance and import fees. Unless you are planning to spend a lot of time off the beaten track or detest the idea of slumming it on local buses, public transport will probably be a cheaper and easier way to go.

- **Buy a Japanese car** Toyotas, Hondas and Nissans are extremely popular in Central America, which makes them substantially easier to service if problems arise.

- **Learn to service your car** A degree of mechanical know-how will allow you to make minor repairs yourself, and help you avoid being ripped off by unscrupulous mechanics. If you do need to repair your vehicle, be advised that mechanics charge much more in Costa Rica than in other Central American countries.

- **Be prepared** It's a good idea to plan for the worst, so make sure that you bring along a good tool kit, an emergency jerry can of petrol, plenty of emergency food and water, and a roll of industrial-strength duct tape for reattaching bits of your battered car. A spare tire or two is also a good idea, especially if you're planning to go off-road or traveling over rough terrain.

- **Know the law** Costa Rican law requires that all vehicles be fitted with a catalytic converter. Bear this in mind if you remove your catalytic converter elsewhere in Central America due to the poorer grades of fuel that can cause the converter to get clogged.

- **And most importantly – drive defensively** As one reader put it, 'Understand that many drivers are clinically insane.' Driving in Costa Rica and the rest of Central America is not for the faint of heart – be smart, be safe and arrive alive.

---

taking a local bus to the border, then another onwards from the border, but they're worth it. These companies are familiar with border procedures and will tell you what's needed to cross efficiently.

There will be no problems crossing, provided your papers are in order. If you are on an international bus, you'll have to exit the bus and proceed through both border stations. Bus drivers will wait for everyone to be processed before heading on.

If you choose to take local buses, it's advisable to get to border stations early in the day to allow time for waiting in line and processing. Note that onward buses tend to wind down by the afternoon. See boxed text Border Crossings, p542.

International buses go from San José to Changuinola (Bocas del Toro), David and Panama City in Panama; Guatemala City in Guatemala; Managua in Nicaragua; San Salvador in El Salvador; and Tegucigalpa in Honduras. For approximate schedules and fares, see p109.

Car & Motorcycle

The cost of insurance, fuel and border permits makes a car journey significantly more expensive than buying an airline ticket. Also, the mountain of paperwork required to drive into Costa Rica from other countries deters many travelers, who prefer to arrive here and then buy or rent a vehicle. To enter Costa Rica by car, you'll need the following items:

- valid registration and proof of ownership
- valid driver's license or International Driving Permit (see p547)
- valid license plates
- recent inspection certificate (not essential, but a good idea)
- passport
- multiple photocopies of all these documents in case the originals get lost.

Sometimes border guards can be overzealous when examining a vehicle, so make sure that it doesn't violate any potential or existing safety regulations or you may have to pay a hefty fee to get it processed. Before departing, check the following elements are present and in working order:

- blinkers, head and tail lights
- spare tire
- jerry can for extra gas (petrol)
- well-stocked toolbox including parts, such as belts, that are harder to find in Central America
- emergency flares, roadside triangles and a fire extinguisher.

Insurance from foreign countries isn't recognized in Costa Rica, so you'll have to buy a policy locally. At the border it will cost about US$15 a month. In addition, you'll probably have to pay a US$22 road tax to drive in.

You are not allowed to sell the car in Costa Rica. If you need to leave the country without the car, you must leave it in a customs warehouse in San José.

For tips on driving to Costa Rica from North America, importing your car and selling it afterwards, see boxed text, opposite.

Another option is to ship a car from Miami to Costa Rica. For specifics, contact

Latii Express International (☎ in the USA 800-590 3789, 305-593 8929; www.latiiexpress.com).

SEA

Cruise ships stop in Costa Rican ports and enable passengers to make a quick foray into the country. Typically, ships dock at either the Pacific port of Caldera (near Puntarenas, p319) or the Caribbean port of Puerto Limón (p450). At the time of writing, plans where already underway to construct a cruise ship dock in the town of Quepos (p341).

It is also possible to arrive in Costa Rica by private yacht.

GETTING AROUND

AIR
Scheduled Flights

Costa Rica's domestic airlines are **NatureAir** (☎ 2220 3054; www.natureair.com) and **Sansa** (☎ 2221 9414; www.flysansa.com); the latter is linked with Grupo TACA.

TRANSPORTATION

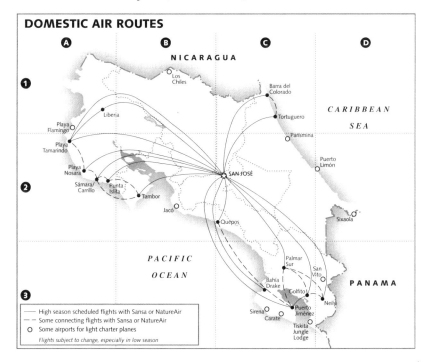

DOMESTIC AIR ROUTES

— High season scheduled flights with Sansa or NatureAir
- - Some connecting flights with Sansa or NatureAir
○ Some airports for light charter planes
Flights subject to change, especially in low season

Both airlines fly small passenger planes, and you're allocated a baggage allowance of no more than 12kg. Space is limited and demand is high in the dry season, so reserve and pay for tickets in advance.

In Costa Rica schedules change constantly and delays are frequent because of inclement weather. Be patient: Costa Rica has small planes and big storms – you don't want to be in them at the same time. You should not arrange a domestic flight that makes a tight connection with an international flight back home.

All domestic flights originate and terminate at San José. High-season fares are listed throughout this book. Destinations reached from San José include Bahía Drake, Barra del Colorado, Golfito, Liberia, Neily, Palmar Sur, Playa Nosara, Playa Sámara/Carrillo, Playa Tamarindo, Puerto Jiménez, Quepos, Tambor and Tortuguero.

Charters

Tobías Bolaños airport in Pavas has small aircraft that can be chartered to fly just about anywhere in the country. Fares start at about US$300 per hour for three- or four-seat planes, and it takes 40 to 90 minutes to fly to most destinations. You also have to pay for the return flight. You should be aware that luggage space is extremely limited.

Many tour agencies can book charters, but you can book directly as well. For a list of companies, see San José (p108), Golfito (p434) and Puerto Jiménez (p412).

BICYCLE

Mountain bikes and beach cruisers can be rented in towns with a significant tourist presence at US$10 to US$15 per day. A few companies organize bike tours around Costa Rica (see p525).

BOAT

Ferries cross the Golfo de Nicoya connecting the central Pacific coast with the southern tip of Península de Nicoya. The **Countermark ferry** (☎ 2661 1069) links the port of Puntarenas with Playa Naranjo four times daily. The **Ferry Peninsular** (☎ 2641 0118) travels between Puntarenas and Paquera every two hours, for a bus connection to Montezuma (see p322).

On the Golfo Dulce, a daily passenger ferry links Golfito with Puerto Jiménez on the Península de Osa and a weekday water taxi travels to and from Playa Zancudo (see p434). On the other side of the Península de Osa, water taxis connect Bahía Drake with Sierpe (see p397).

On the Caribbean coast, there is a bus and boat service that runs several times a day, linking Cariari and Tortuguero (p465), while another links Parismina and Siquirres (p458). Boats also ply the canals that run along the coast from Moín to Tortuguero, although no regular service exists. A daily water taxi connects Puerto Viejo de Sarapiquí with Trinidad on the Río San Juan (p518). The San Juan is Nicaraguan territory, so take your passport. You can try to arrange boat transport in any of these towns for Barra del Colorado.

BUS
Local Buses

Local buses are the best (if rather slow) way of getting around Costa Rica. You can take one just about everywhere, and they're frequent and cheap, with the longest domestic journey out of San José costing less than US$10.

San José is the transportation center for the country (see p109), though there is no central terminal. Bus offices are scattered around the city: some large bus companies have big terminals that sell tickets in advance, while others have little more than a stop – sometimes unmarked.

Normally there's room for everyone on a bus, and if there isn't, someone will squeeze you on anyhow. The exceptions are days before and after a major holiday, especially Easter, when buses are ridiculously full. Note that there are no buses from Thursday to Saturday before Easter Sunday.

There are two types of bus: directo and colectivo. The directo buses should go from one destination to the next with few stops, though it goes against the instincts of most Costa Rican bus drivers to not pick up every single roadside passenger. As for the colectivo, you know you're on one when the kids outside are outrunning your bus.

Trips longer than four hours usually include a rest stop as buses do not have bathrooms. Space is limited on board, so if you have to check luggage watch that it gets loaded and that it isn't 'accidentally' given to someone else at intermediate stops. Keep your day pack with important documents on you at all times. Theft from overhead racks is rampant.

Bus schedules fluctuate wildly, so always confirm the time when you buy your ticket. If you are catching a bus that picks you up somewhere along a road, get to the roadside early. Departure times are estimated and if the bus comes early, it will leave early.

For information on departures from San José, pay a visit to the Instituto Costarricense de Turismo (ICT) office (p82) to pick up the (sort of) up-to-date copy of the master schedule, which is also online at www.visitcostarica.com.

Shuttle Bus

The tourist-van shuttle services (aka the gringo buses) are an alternative to the standard inter-city buses. Shuttles are provided by **Grayline's Fantasy Bus** (☎ 2220 2126; www.graylinecostarica.com) and **Interbus** (☎ 2283 5573; www.interbusonline.com). Both companies run overland transport from San José to the most popular destinations, as well as directly between other destinations (see their websites for the comprehensive list). These services will pick you up at your hotel and reservations can be made online, or through local travel agencies and hotel owners.

CAR & MOTORCYCLE

If you plan to drive in Costa Rica, your driver's license from home is normally accepted for up to 90 days. Many places will also accept an International Driving Permit (IDP), issued by the automobile association in your country of origin. After 90 days

however, you will need to get a Costa Rican driver's license.

Gasoline (petrol) and diesel are widely available, and 24-hour service stations dot the entire stretch of the Interamericana. The price of gas is about US$0.75 per liter, although it can fluctuate to over US$1 per liter. In more remote areas, fuel will likely be more expensive and might be sold from a drum at the neighborhood *pulpería* (corner grocery store); look for signs that say *'Se vende gasolina'* ('We sell gas'). Spare parts may be hard to find, especially for vehicles with sophisticated electronics and emissions-control systems.

Hire

Most car-rental agencies can be found in San José and in popular tourist destinations on the Pacific coast. Car rental is not cheap, but if you are going to be doing even a small amount of driving, invest in a 4WD. Many agencies will insist on 4WD for extended travel, especially in the rainy season, when driving through rivers is a matter of course. In fact, ordinary cars are pointless as soon as you leave the Interamericana.

To rent a car you need a valid driver's license, a major credit card and a passport. The minimum age for car rental is 21. Carefully inspect rented cars for minor damage and make sure that any damage is noted on the rental agreement. If your car breaks down, call the rental company. Don't attempt to get the car fixed yourself – most companies won't reimburse expenses without prior authorization.

ROAD DISTANCES (KM)

	Golfito	Liberia	Monteverde	Puerto Limón	Quepos	San Isidro de El General	San José
Liberia	447						
Monteverde	396	112					
Puerto Limón	449	379	318				
Quepos	194	255	118	334			
San Isidro de El General	180	329	294	294	77		
San José	339	220	160	168	174	134	
Turrialba	364	287	227	136	241	159	67

TRANSPORTATION

DRIVING THROUGH RIVERS

You know all those great ads where 4WD monster trucks splash through rivers full speed ahead? Forget you ever saw them.

Driving in Costa Rica will likely necessitate a river crossing at some point. Unfortunately, too many travelers have picked up their off-road skills from watching TV, and every season Ticos (Costa Ricans) get a good chuckle out of the number of dead vehicles they help wayward travelers fish out of waterways.

If you're driving through water, follow the rules below:

- **Only do this in a 4WD** Don't drive through a river in a car. (It may seem ridiculous to have to say this, but it's done all the time.) Getting out of a steep, gravel riverbed requires a 4WD. Besides, car engines flood very easily – *adiós* rental car.

- **Check the depth of the water before driving through** To accommodate an average rental 4WD, the water should be no deeper than above the knee. In a sturdier vehicle (Toyota 4-Runner or equivalent), water can be waist deep. If you're not sure, ask a local.

- **The water should be calm** If the river is gushing so that there are white crests on the water, do not try to cross. Not only will the force of the water flood the engine, it could sweep your car away.

- **Drive slooooooowly** Taxi drivers all over Costa Rica make lots of money towing tourists who think that slamming through a river at full speed is the best way to get across. This is a huge mistake. The pressure of driving through a river too quickly will send the water right into the engine and you'll be cooking that electrical system in no time. Keep steady pressure on the accelerator so that the tail pipe doesn't fill with water, but take it slow.

- **Err on the side of caution** Car-rental agencies in Costa Rica do not insure for water damage, so if you drown your vehicle, you're paying – in more ways than one.

Prices start at US$450 per week for a 4WD, including *kilometraje libre* (unlimited mileage). Basic insurance will cost an additional US$15 to US$25 per day, and rental companies won't rent you a car without it. The roads in Costa Rica are rough and rugged, meaning that minor accidents or car damage is common. On top of this, you can pay an extra fee (about US$10 to US$15 per day) for a Collision Damage Waiver, or CDW, which covers the driver and a third party with a US$750 to US$1500 deductible.

Above and beyond this, you can purchase full insurance (about US$30 to US$50 per day), which is expensive, but well worth it. Note that if you pay basic ins-urance with a gold or platinum credit card, the company will usually take responsibility for damages to the car, in which case you can forego the cost of the full insurance. Make sure you verify this with your credit card company ahead of time.

Finally, note that most insurance policies do not cover damages caused by flooding or driving through a river (even though this is sometimes necessary in Costa Rica!), so be aware of the extent of your policy.

Rental rates fluctuate wildly, so make sure you shop around before you commit to anything. Some agencies offer discounts if you reserve online or if you rent for long periods of time. Note that rental offices at the airport charge a 12% fee in addition to regular rates.

Thieves can easily recognize rental cars, and many thefts have occurred from them. *Never* leave anything in sight in a parked car – nothing! – and remove all luggage from the trunk overnight. Park the car in a guarded parking lot rather than on the street. We cannot stress enough how many readers write us letters each year detailing thefts from their cars.

Motorcycles (including Harleys) can be rented in San José (p112) and Escazú (p117).

All of the major international car-rental agencies have outlets in Costa Rica, but you can usually get a better deal from one of the local companies:

Adobe (☎ 2259 4242, in the USA 800-769 8422; www.adobecar.com) Reader recommended with offices in Liberia, Tamarindo and Quepos.

Dollar (☎ 2443 2950, in the USA 866-767 8651; www.dollarcostarica.com) One of the cheapest companies in Costa Rica with offices in both airports.

Poas (☎ 2442 6178, in the USA 888-607 POAS; www
.carentals.com) Service centers in Liberia, Tamarindo, La
Fortuna and Guápiles.
Solid (☎ 2442 6000; www.solidcarrental.com) The only
agency with offices in Puerto Jiménez and Golfito.

Road Conditions & Hazards

Overall, driving in Costa Rica is for people
with nerves of steel. The roads vary from
quite good (the Interamericana) to barely
passable (just about everywhere else). Even
the good ones can suffer from landslides,
sudden flooding and fog. Most roads are
single lane and winding, lacking hard shoul-
ders; others are dirt-and-mud affairs that
climb mountains and traverse rivers.

Drive defensively. Always expect to come
across cyclists, a broken-down vehicle, a
herd of cattle, slow-moving trucks or an oxcart around the next bend. Unsigned speed
bumps are placed on some stretches of road
without warning. (The locals lovingly refer
to them as *muertos,* 'dead people.')

Most roads (except around the major
tourist towns) are inadequately signed and
will require at least one stop to ask for directions. Always ask about road conditions
before setting out, especially in the rainy
season; a number of roads become impassable in the rainy season.

Road Rules

There are speed limits of 100km/h or less
on all primary roads and 60km/h or less on
secondary roads. Traffic police use radar
and speed limits are enforced with speeding tickets. You can get a traffic ticket for
not wearing a seat belt. It's illegal to stop
in an intersection or make a right turn on
a red. At unmarked intersections, yield to
the car on your right. Driving in Costa Rica
is on the right and passing is allowed only
on the left.

If you are issued with a ticket, you have to
pay the fine at a bank; instructions are given
on the ticket. If you are driving a rental
car, the rental company may be able to arrange your payment for you – the amount
of the fine should be on the ticket. A portion of the money from these fines goes to
a children's charity.

Police have no right to ask for money and
shouldn't confiscate a car, unless: the driver
cannot produce a license and ownership papers; the car lacks license plates; the driver is
drunk; or the driver has been involved in an
accident causing serious injury. (For more
on what to do in an accident, see p534).

If you are driving and see oncoming cars
with headlights flashing, it often means that
there is a road problem or a radar speed trap
ahead. Slow down immediately.

HITCHHIKING

Hitchhiking is never entirely safe in any
country and Lonely Planet doesn't recommend it. Travelers who hitchhike should
understand that they are taking a small
but potentially serious risk. People who do
hitchhike will be safer if they travel in pairs

THE CASE OF THE FLAT TIRE AND THE DISAPPEARING LUGGAGE

A serious scam is under way on the streets around Aeropuerto Internacional Juan Santamaría.
Many readers have reported similar incidents, so take precautions to ensure this doesn't happen
to you. Here's how it goes...

After picking up a rental car and driving out of the city, you notice that it has a flat tire. You
pull over to try to fix it. Some friendly locals, noticing that a visitor to their fair land is in distress,
pull over to help out. There is inevitably some confusion with the changing of the tire, and everybody is involved in figuring it out, but eventually the car repair is successfully accomplished and
the friendly Ticos (Costa Ricans) give you a wave and drive off. That's when you get back in your
car and discover that your wallet – or your luggage, or everything – is gone.

This incident has happened enough times to suggest that somebody may be tampering with
rental cars to 'facilitate' these flat tires. It certainly suggests that travelers should be very wary –
and aware – if somebody pulls over to help. Keep your wallet and your passport on your person
whenever you get out of a car. If possible, let one person in your party stay inside the car to
keep a watchful eye. In any case, lock your doors – even if you think you are going to be right
outside. There's nothing like losing all your luggage to put a damper on a vacation.

USING TAXIS IN REMOTE AREAS

Taxis are considered a form of public transport in remote areas that lack good public-transportation networks. They can be hired by the hour, the half-day or full day, or you can arrange a flat fee for a trip. Meters are not used on long trips, so arrange the fare ahead of time. Fares can fluctuate due to worse-than-expected road conditions and bad weather in tough-to-reach places.

The condition of taxis varies from basic sedans held together by rust, to fully equipped 4WDs with air-con. In some cases, taxis are pick-up trucks with seats built into the back. Most towns will have at least one licensed taxi, but in some remote villages you may have to get rides from whoever is offering – ask at *pulperías* (corner grocery stores).

and let someone know where they are planning to go. Single women should use even greater discretion.

Hitching in Costa Rica is not common on main roads that have frequent buses. On minor rural roads, hitching is easier. To get picked up, most locals wave to cars in a friendly manner. If you get a ride, offer to pay when you arrive by saying, *¿Cuanto le debo?* (How much do I owe you?). Your offer may be waved aside, or you may be asked to help with money for gas.

LOCAL TRANSPORTATION
Bus
Local buses operate chiefly in San José, Puntarenas, San Isidro, Golfito and Puerto Limón, connecting urban and suburban areas. Most local buses pick up passengers on the street and on main roads. The vehicles in service are usually converted school buses imported from the USA, and they are often packed.

Taxi
In San José taxis have meters, called *marías,* but many drivers try to get out of using them,

particularly if you don't speak Spanish. With that said, it is illegal not to use the meter, so don't be afraid to point this out if you feel as if you're about to be scammed. Outside of San José however, most taxis don't have meters and fares tend to be agreed upon in advance – some bargaining is quite acceptable.

In some towns, there are colectivo taxis that several passengers are able to share. Although colectivo taxis are becoming increasingly difficult to find, the basic principle is that the driver charges a flat fee (usually about US$0.50) to take passengers from one end of town to the other.

In rural areas, 4WD jeeps are often used as taxis and are a popular means for surfers (and their boards) to travel from their accommodation to the break. Prices vary wildly depending on how touristy the area is, though generally speaking a 10-minute ride should cost between US$5 and US$15.

Taxi drivers are not normally tipped unless they assist with your luggage or have provided an above-average service. However, owing to the increasing number of American travelers, don't be surprised if drivers in tourist towns are quick to hold out their palm.

Health Dr David Goldberg

CONTENTS

Travelers to Central America need to be vigilant about food-borne and mosquito-borne infections. Most of these illnesses are not life threatening, but can certainly ruin your trip. Besides getting the proper vaccinations, it's important to use a good insect repellent and exercise care in what you eat and drink.

BEFORE YOU GO

Since most vaccines don't produce immunity until at least two weeks after they're given, visit a physician four to eight weeks before departure. Ask your doctor for an International Certificate of Vaccination (otherwise known as the yellow booklet), which will list all the vaccinations you've received. This is mandatory for countries that require proof of yellow fever vaccination upon entry, but it's a good idea to carry it wherever you travel.

Bring medications in their original containers, clearly labeled. A signed, dated letter from your physician describing all medical conditions and medications, including generic names, is also a good idea. If carrying syringes or needles be sure to have a physician's letter documenting their medical necessity.

INSURANCE

Most doctors and hospitals expect payment in cash, regardless of whether you have travel health insurance or not. If you develop a life-threatening medical problem, you'll probably want to be evacuated to a country with state-of-the-art medical care. As this may cost tens of thousands of dollars, be sure you have insurance to cover this before you leave home. A list of medical evacuation and travel insurance companies is on the website of the **US State Department** (www.travel.state.gov/medical.html).

If your health insurance does not cover you for medical expenses while you are abroad, you should consider supplemental insurance. Check the Travel Services section of the Lonely Planet website at www.lonelyplanet .com/travel_links for more information. It might pay to find out in advance if your insurance plan will make payments directly to providers or if they reimburse you later for any overseas health expenditures.

MEDICAL CHECKLIST

- acetaminophen (Tylenol) or aspirin
- adhesive or paper tape
- antibacterial ointment (eg Bactroban) for cuts and abrasions
- antibiotics
- antidiarrheal drugs (eg loperamide)
- antihistamines for hay fever and allergic reactions
- anti-inflammatory drugs (eg ibuprofen)
- bandages, gauze, gauze rolls
- insect repellent (containing DEET) for the skin
- insect spray (containing permethrin) for clothing, tents and bed nets
- iodine tablets for water purification
- oral rehydration salts
- pocket knife
- scissors, safety pins, tweezers
- steroid cream or cortisone for poison ivy and other allergic rashes
- sunblock
- syringes and sterile needles
- thermometer.

INTERNET RESOURCES

There is a wealth of travel health advice on the internet. For further information, the website of **Lonely Planet** (www.lonelyplanet.com) is a good place to start. A superb book called *International*

Travel and Health, which is revised annually and available online at no cost, is published by the **World Health Organization** (www.who.int/ith). Another website of general interest is **MD Travel Health** (www.mdtravelhealth.com), which provides complete travel health recommendations for every country, updated daily, also at no cost.

It's usually a good idea to consult your government's travel health website before departure, if one is available:

Australia (www.dfat.gov.au/travel)
Canada (www.phac-aspc.gc.ca/tmp-pmv/pub_e.html)
UK (www.dh.gov.uk/PolicyAndGuidance/HealthAdvice ForTravellers/fs/en)
USA (www.cdc.gov/travel)

FURTHER READING

For further information, see *Healthy Travel Central & South America,* also from Lonely Planet. If you're traveling with children, Lonely Planet's *Travel with Children* will be useful. The *ABC of Healthy Travel,* by E Walker et al, is another valuable resource.

IN TRANSIT

DEEP VEIN THROMBOSIS (DVT)

Blood clots (deep vein thrombosis) may form in the legs during plane flights, chiefly because of prolonged immobility. The longer the flight, the greater the risk. Though most blood clots are re-absorbed uneventfully, some may break off and travel through the blood vessels to the lungs, where they could cause life-threatening complications.

The chief symptom of DVT is swelling or pain of the foot, ankle or calf, usually but not always on just the one side. When a blood clot travels all the way to the lungs, it may cause chest pain and difficulty in breathing. Travelers with any of these symptoms should immediately seek out medical attention.

To prevent the development of DVT on long flights you should walk about the cabin, perform isometric compressions of the leg muscles (ie contract the leg muscles while sitting), drink plenty of fluids and avoid alcohol and tobacco.

JET LAG & MOTION SICKNESS

Jet lag is common when crossing more than five time zones, resulting in insomnia, fatigue, malaise or nausea. To avoid jet lag try drinking plenty of fluids (nonalcoholic) and eating light meals. Upon arrival, get exposure to natural sunlight and re-adjust your schedule (for meals, sleep etc) as soon as possible.

Antihistamines such as dimenhydrinate (Dramamine) and meclizine (Antivert, Bonine) are usually the first choice for treating motion sickness. Their main side effect is drowsiness. Ginger is a herbal alternative that works like a charm for some people.

IN COSTA RICA

AVAILABILITY & COST OF HEALTH CARE

Good medical care is available in most major cities, but may be limited in rural areas. For a medical emergency, you should call one of the following numbers:

CIMA San José (☎ 2208 1000; Próspero Fernández Fwy, San José) It's 500m west of the tollbooths on the highway to Santa Ana.
Clínica Bíblica (☎ 2257 0466, 257 5252; www.clinica biblica.com; Av 14 btwn Calles Central & 1)
Hospital Nacional de Niños (☎ 2222 0122; Calle 14, Av Central, San José) Only for children under 12 years.
Poison Center (☎ 2223 1028)
Red Cross Ambulance (☎ 911, in San José 2221 5818)
San Juan de Dios Hospital (☎ 2257 6282; cnr Calle 14 & Av Central, San José)

For an extensive list of physicians, dentists and hospitals go to the US embassy website (usembassy.or.cr). If you're pregnant, be sure to check this site before departure to find the name of one or two obstetricians, just in case.

Most pharmacies are well supplied and the pharmacists are licensed to prescribe medication. If you're taking any medication on a regular basis, be sure you know its generic (scientific) name, since many pharmaceuticals go under different names in Costa Rica. The following pharmacies are open 24 hours:

Farmacia Clínica Bíblica (☎ 2257 5252; cnr Calle 1 & Av 14, San José)
Farmacia Clínica Católica (☎ 2283 6616; Guadalupe, San José)
Farmacia el Hospital (☎ 2222 0985)

INFECTIOUS DISEASES

Chagas' Disease

Chagas' disease is a parasitic infection that is transmitted by triatomine insects (reduviid bugs), which inhabit crevices in the walls and roofs of substandard housing in South and Central America. In Costa Rica most cases occur in Alajuela, Liberia and Puntarenas. The triatomine insect lays its feces on human skin as it bites, usually at night. A person becomes infected when he or she unknowingly rubs the feces into the bite wound or any other open sore. Symptoms of the disease include fever and swelling of the spleen, liver and lymph nodes. Chagas' disease is extremely rare in travelers. However, if you sleep in a poorly constructed house, especially one made of mud, adobe or thatch, you should be sure to protect yourself with a bed net and a good insecticide.

Dengue Fever (Breakbone Fever)

Dengue fever is a viral infection found throughout Central America. In Costa Rica outbreaks involving thousands of people occur every year. Dengue is transmitted by *Aedes* mosquitoes, which prefer to bite during the daytime and are usually found close to human habitations, often indoors. They breed primarily in artificial water containers such as jars, barrels, cans, cisterns, metal drums, plastic containers and discarded tires. As a result, dengue is especially common in densely populated, urban environments.

Dengue usually causes flu-like symptoms including fever, muscle aches, joint pains, headaches, nausea and vomiting, often followed by a rash. The body aches may be quite uncomfortable, but most cases resolve uneventfully in a few days. Severe cases usually occur in children under the age of 15 who are experiencing their second dengue infection.

There is no real treatment for dengue fever except for you to take analgesics such as acetaminophen/paracetamol (Tylenol) and drink plenty of fluids. Severe cases may require hospitalization for intravenous fluids and supportive care. There is no vaccine. The key to prevention is taking insect protection measures (see p555).

Hepatitis A

Hepatitis A is the second most common travel-related infection (after traveler's diarrhea). It's a viral infection of the liver that is usually acquired by ingestion of contaminated water, food or ice, though it may also be acquired by direct contact with infected persons.

The illness occurs throughout the world, but the incidence is higher in developing nations. Symptoms may include fever, malaise, jaundice, nausea, vomiting and abdominal pain. Most cases resolve without complications, though hepatitis A occasionally causes severe liver damage. There is no treatment.

The vaccine for hepatitis A is extremely safe and highly effective. If you get a booster six to 12 months later, it lasts for at least 10 years. You should get vaccinated before you go to Costa Rica or any other developing nation. Because the safety of hepatitis A vaccine has not been established for pregnant women or children under the age of two, they should instead be given a gammaglobulin injection.

Hepatitis B

Like hepatitis A, hepatitis B is a liver infection that occurs worldwide but is more common in developing nations. Unlike hepatitis A, the disease is usually acquired by sexual contact or by exposure to infected blood, generally through blood transfusions or contaminated needles. The vaccine is recommended only for long-term travelers (on the road more than six months) who expect to live in rural areas or have close physical contact with the local population. Additionally, the vaccine is recommended for anyone who anticipates sexual contact with the local inhabitants or a possible need for medical, dental or other treatments while abroad, especially if a need for transfusions or injections is expected.

Hepatitis B vaccine is safe and highly effective. However, a total of three injections are necessary to establish full immunity. Several countries added hepatitis B vaccine to the list of routine childhood immunizations in the 1980s, so many young adults are already protected.

HIV/AIDS

The HIV/AIDS virus occurs in all Central American countries. Be sure to use condoms for all sexual encounters.

Leishmaniasis

Leishmaniasis occurs in the mountains and jungles of all Central American countries. The infection is transmitted by sand flies, which are about one-third the size of mosquitoes. Most cases occur in newly cleared forest or areas of secondary growth. The highest incidence is in Talamanca. In Costa Rica it is generally limited to the skin, causing slow-growing ulcers over exposed parts of the body, but more severe infections may occur in those with HIV. There is no vaccine for leishmaniasis. To protect yourself from sand flies, follow the same precautions as for mosquitoes (opposite), except that netting must be finer mesh (at least 18 holes to the linear inch).

Leptospirosis

Leptospirosis is acquired by exposure to water contaminated by the urine of infected animals. Whitewater rafters are at particularly high risk. In Costa Rica most cases occur in Limón, Turrialba, San Carlos and Golfito. Cases have been reported among residents of Puerto Limón who have bathed in local streams. Outbreaks can occur at times of flooding, when sewage overflow may contaminate water sources. The initial symptoms, which resemble a mild flu, usually subside uneventfully in a few days, with or without treatment, but a minority of cases are complicated by jaundice or meningitis. There is no vaccine. You can minimize your risk by staying out of bodies of fresh water that may be contaminated by animal urine. If you're engaging in high-risk activities, such as river rafting, in an area where an outbreak is in progress, you can take 200mg of doxycycline once weekly as a preventative measure. If you actually develop leptospirosis, the treatment is 100mg of doxycycline twice daily.

Malaria

Malaria occurs in every country in Central America. It's transmitted by mosquito bites, usually between dusk and dawn. The main symptom is high spiking fevers, which may be accompanied by chills, sweats, headache, body aches, weakness, vomiting or diarrhea. Severe cases may involve the central nervous system and lead to seizures, confusion, coma and death.

Taking malaria pills is recommended for the provinces of Alajuela, Limón (except for Puerto Limón), Guanacaste and Heredia. The risk is greatest in the cantons of Los Chiles (Alajuela Province), and Matina and Talamanca (Limón Province).

For Costa Rica the first-choice malaria pill is chloroquine, taken once weekly in a dosage of 500mg, starting one to two weeks before arrival and continuing through the trip and for four weeks after departure. Chloroquine is safe, inexpensive and highly effective. Side effects are typically mild and may include nausea, abdominal discomfort, headache, dizziness, blurred vision or itching. Severe reactions are uncommon.

Protecting yourself against mosquito bites (see opposite) is just as important as taking malaria pills, since no pills are 100% effective.

If you may not have access to medical care while traveling, you should bring along additional pills for emergency self-treatment, which you should take if you can't reach a doctor and you develop symptoms that suggest malaria, such as high spiking fevers. One option is to take four tablets of Malarone once daily for three days. If you start self-medication, you should try to see a doctor at the earliest possible opportunity.

If you develop a fever after returning home, see a physician as malaria symptoms may not occur for months.

Rabies

Rabies is a viral infection of the brain and spinal cord that is almost always fatal. The rabies virus is carried in the saliva of infected animals and is typically transmitted through an animal bite, though contamination of any break in the skin with infected saliva may result in rabies.

Rabies occurs in all Central American countries. However, in Costa Rica only two cases have been reported over the last 30 years. Rabies vaccine is therefore recommended only for those at particularly high risk, such as spelunkers (cave explorers) and animal handlers.

All animal bites and scratches must be promptly and thoroughly cleansed with large amounts of soap and water. Local health authorities should be contacted to determine whether or not further treatment is necessary (see Animal Bites, opposite).

Typhoid

Typhoid fever is caused by ingestion of food or water contaminated by a species of *Salmonella* known as *Salmonella typhi*. Fever occurs in virtually all cases. Other symptoms may include headache, malaise, muscle aches, dizziness, loss of appetite, nausea and abdominal pain. Either diarrhea or constipation may occur. Possible complications include intestinal perforation, intestinal bleeding, confusion, delirium or (rarely) coma.

Unless you expect to take all your meals in major hotels and restaurants, a typhoid vaccine is a good idea. It's usually given orally, but is also available as an injection. Neither vaccine is approved for use in children under the age of two.

The drug of choice for typhoid fever is usually a quinolone antibiotic such as ciprofloxacin (Cipro) or levofloxacin (Levaquin), which many travelers carry for treatment of traveler's diarrhea. However, if you self-treat for typhoid fever, you may also need to self-treat for malaria, since the symptoms of the two diseases may be indistinguishable.

TRAVELER'S DIARRHEA

To prevent diarrhea, you should avoid tap water unless it has been boiled, filtered or chemically disinfected (iodine tablets); only eat fresh fruits or vegetables if cooked or peeled; be wary of dairy products that might contain unpasteurized milk; and be highly selective when eating food from street vendors.

If you develop diarrhea, be sure to drink plenty of fluids, preferably an oral rehydration solution containing lots of salt and sugar. A few loose stools don't require treatment, but if you start having more than four or five stools a day you should begin taking an antibiotic (usually a quinolone drug) and an antidiarrheal agent (such as loperamide). If diarrhea is bloody or persists for more than 72 hours, or is accompanied by fever, shaking chills or severe abdominal pain, you should seek medical attention.

ENVIRONMENTAL HAZARDS
Animal Bites

Do not attempt to pet, handle or feed any animal, with the exception of domestic animals known to be free of any infectious disease. Most animal injuries are directly related to a person's attempt to touch or feed the animal.

Any bite or scratch by a mammal, including bats, should be promptly and thoroughly cleansed with large amounts of soap and water, followed by application of an antiseptic such as iodine or alcohol. The local health authorities should be contacted immediately for possible postexposure rabies treatment, whether or not you've been immunized against rabies. It may also be advisable to start an antibiotic, since wounds caused by animal bites and scratches frequently become infected. One of the newer quinolones,

such as levofloxacin (Levaquin), which many travelers carry in case of diarrhea, would be an appropriate choice.

Insect Bites

No matter how much you safeguard, getting bitten by mosquitoes is part of every traveler's experience in the country. While there are occasional outbreaks of dengue (see p553) in Costa Rica, for the most part the greatest worry you will have with bites is the general discomfort that comes with them, namely itching.

The best prevention is to stay covered up – wearing long pants, long sleeves, a hat and shoes (rather than sandals). Unfortunately, Costa Rica's sweltering temperatures might make this a bit difficult. Therefore, the best measure you can take is to invest in a good insect repellent, preferably one containing DEET. (These repellents can also be found in Costa Rica.) This should be applied to exposed skin and clothing (but not to eyes, mouth, cuts, wounds or irritated skin).

In general, adults and children over 12 can use preparations containing 25% to 35% DEET, which usually lasts about six hours. Children between two and 12 years of age should use preparations containing no more than 10% DEET, applied sparingly, which will usually last about three hours. Neurologic toxicity has been reported from DEET, especially in children, but appears to be extremely uncommon and generally related to overuse. Compounds containing DEET should not be used on children under age two.

Insect repellents containing certain botanical products, including eucalyptus and soybean oil, are effective but last only 1½ to two hours.

A particularly good item for every traveler to take is a bug net to hang over beds (along with a few thumbtacks or nails with which to hang it). Many hotels in Costa Rica don't have windows (or screens) and a cheap little net will save you plenty of nighttime aggravation. The mesh size should be less than 1.5mm.

Dusk is the worst time for mosquitoes, so it's best to take extra precautions once the sun starts to set.

Snake Bites

Costa Rica is home to all manner of venomous snakes and any foray into forested areas will put you at (a very slight) risk for snake bite.

HEALTH

The best prevention is to wear closed, heavy shoes or boots and to keep a watchful eye on the trail. Snakes like to come out to cleared paths for a nap, so watch where you step. (For more on Costa Rica's fer-de-lance and bushmaster, see p195).

In the event of a bite from a venomous snake, place the victim at rest, keep the bitten area immobilized and move the victim immediately to the nearest medical facility. Avoid tourniquets, which are no longer recommended.

Sun

To protect yourself from excessive sun exposure you should stay out of the midday sun, wear sunglasses and a wide-brimmed sun hat, and apply sunblock with SPF 15 or higher, with both UVA and UVB protection. Sunblock should be generously applied to all exposed parts of the body approximately 30 minutes before sun exposure and should be reapplied after swimming or vigorous activity. Travelers should also drink plenty of fluids and avoid strenuous exercise when the temperature is high.

Water

It's generally safe to drink the tap water everywhere in Costa Rica, other than in the most rural and undeveloped parts of the country. However, if you prefer to be cautious, buying bottled water is your best bet. If you have the means, vigorous boiling for one minute is the most effective means of water purification. At altitudes greater than 2000m, boil for three minutes. Another option is to disinfect water with iodine pills: add 2% tincture of iodine to 1L of water (five drops to clear water, 10 drops to cloudy water) and let stand for 30 minutes. If the water is cold, longer times may be required.

TRAVELING WITH CHILDREN

In general, it's safe for children and pregnant women to go to Costa Rica. However, because some of the vaccines listed previously are not approved for use by children or during pregnancy, these travelers should be particularly careful not to drink tap water or consume any questionable food or beverage. Also, when traveling with children, make sure they're up-to-date on all routine immunizations. It's sometimes appropriate to give children some of their vaccines a little early before visiting a developing nation. You should discuss this with your pediatrician.

Lastly, if pregnant, you should bear in mind that should a complication such as premature labor develop while abroad, the quality of medical care may not be comparable to that in your home country.

See p529 for some general information on traveling with children.

Language

CONTENTS

Spanish is the official language of Costa Rica and the main language the traveler will need. Every visitor to the country should attempt to learn some Spanish, the basic elements of which are easily acquired.

A month-long language course taken before departure can go a long way toward facilitating communication and comfort on the road. Alternatively, language courses are also available in all parts of Costa Rica (see p530). Even if classes are impractical, you should make the effort to learn a few basic phrases and pleasantries. Don't hesitate to practice your new skills – in general, Latin Americans meet attempts to communicate in the vernacular, however halting, with enthusiasm and appreciation.

PHRASEBOOKS & DICTIONARIES

Lonely Planet's *Costa Rica Spanish Phrasebook* will be very helpful during your trip. If you're traveling outside of Costa Rica, LP's *Latin American Spanish Phrasebook* is another worthwhile addition to your backpack. Another really useful little number is the University of Chicago *Spanish-English, English-Spanish Dictionary*. It's small, light and has thorough entries, making it ideal

---

SPANISH IN COSTA RICA

The following colloquialisms and slang *(tiquismos)* are frequently heard, and are for the most part used only in Costa Rica.

¡Adiós! – Hi! (used when passing a friend in the street, or anyone in remote rural areas; also means 'farewell,' but only when leaving for a long time)
bomba – gas station
Buena nota – OK/Excellent (literally 'good note')
chapulines – a gang, usually of young thieves
chunche – thing (can refer to almost anything)
cien metros – one city block
¿Hay campo? – Is there space? (on a bus)
machita – blonde woman (slang)
mae – buddy (pronounced 'ma' as in 'mat' followed with a quick 'eh'; it's mainly used by boys and young men)
mi amor – my love (used as a familiar form of address by both men and women)
pulpería – corner grocery store
¡Pura vida! – Super! (literally 'pure life,' also an expression of approval or even a greeting)
sabanero – cowboy, especially one who hails from Guanacaste Province
Salado – Too bad/Tough luck
soda – café or lunch counter
¡Tuanis! – Cool!
¡Upe! – Is anybody home? (used mainly in rural areas at people's homes, instead of knocking)
vos – you (informal, same as *tú*)

---

for travel. It also makes an excellent gift to give to any newfound friends upon your departure.

LATIN AMERICAN SPANISH

The Spanish of the Americas comes in a bewildering array of varieties. Depending on the areas in which you travel, consonants may be glossed over, vowels squashed into each other, and syllables, even words, dropped entirely. Slang and regional vocabulary, much of it derived from indigenous languages, can further add to the bewilderment. The boxed text above gives you a few insights into the local lingo of Costa Rica.

Throughout Latin America, the Spanish language is referred to as *castellano* more often than *español*. Unlike in Spain, the plural of the familiar *tú* form is *ustedes* rather than *vosotros;* the latter term will sound quaint and archaic in the Americas. Another notable difference is that the letters **c** and **z** are never lisped in Latin America; attempts to do so could well provoke amusement.

OTHER LANGUAGES

Travelers will find English is often spoken in the upmarket hotels, airline offices and tourist agencies, and some other European languages are encountered in hotels run by Europeans. On the Caribbean coast, many of the locals speak some English, albeit with a local Creole dialect.

Indigenous languages are spoken in isolated areas, but unless travelers are getting off the beaten track they'll rarely encounter them. The indigenous languages Bribrí and Cabécar are understood by an estimated 18,000 people living on both sides of the Cordillera de Talamanca.

PRONUNCIATION

Spanish spelling is phonetically consistent, meaning that there's a clear and consistent relationship between what you see in writing and how it's pronounced. Also, most Spanish sounds have English equivalents, so English speakers shouldn't have too much trouble being understood. The words and phrases in this language guide are all accompanied by guides to pronunciation, so the task of getting your message across is made even simpler.

Vowels

a	as in 'father'
e	as in 'met'
i	as in 'marine'
o	as in 'or' (without the 'r' sound)
u	as in 'rule'; the 'u' is not pronounced after **q** and in the letter combinations **gue** and **gui**, unless it's marked with a diaeresis (eg *argüir*), in which case it's pronounced as English 'w'
y	at the end of a word or when it stands alone, **y** is pronounced as the Spanish **i** (eg *ley*); between vowels within a word it's as the 'y' in 'yonder'

Consonants

As a rule, Spanish consonants resemble their English counterparts, with the odd exceptions listed below. While the consonants **ch**, **ll** and **ñ** are generally considered distinct letters, **ch** and **ll** are now often listed alphabetically under **c** and **l** respectively. The letter **ñ** is still treated as a separate letter and comes after **n** in dictionaries.

b	similar to English 'b,' but softer; referred to as 'b larga'
c	as in 'celery' before **e** and **i**; otherwise as English 'k'
ch	as in 'church'
d	as in 'dog,' but between vowels and after **l** or **n**, the sound is closer to the 'th' in 'this'
g	as the 'ch' in the Scottish 'loch' before **e** and **i** ('kh' in our guides to pronunciation); elsewhere, as in 'go'
h	invariably silent. If your name begins with this letter, listen carefully if you're waiting for public officials to call you.
j	as the 'ch' in the Scottish 'loch' (written as 'kh' in our guides to pronunciation)
ll	as the 'y' in 'yellow'
ñ	as the 'ni' in 'onion'
r	a short **r** except at the beginning of a word, and after **l**, **n** or **s**, when it's often rolled
rr	very strongly rolled
v	similar to English 'b,' but softer; referred to as 'b corta'
x	usually pronounced as **j** above; in some indigenous place names **x** is pronounced as the 's' in 'sit'; in other instances, it's as in 'taxi'
z	as the 's' in 'sun'

Word Stress

Rules for word stress are quite simple. In general, words ending in vowels or the letters **n** or **s** have stress on the next-to-last syllable, while those with other endings have stress on the last syllable. Thus *vaca* (cow) and *caballos* (horses) both carry stress on the next-to-last syllable, while *ciudad* (city) and *infeliz* (unhappy) are both stressed on the last syllable.

Written accents will almost always appear in words that don't follow the rules above, eg *sótano* (basement), *América* and *porción* (portion). Stressed syllables are marked in italics in the guides to pronunciation included in this language guide.

GENDER & PLURALS

In Spanish, nouns are either masculine or feminine, and there are rules to help determine gender (there are of course some exceptions). Feminine nouns generally end with -**a** or with the groups -**ción**, -**sión** or -**dad**. Other endings typically signify a masculine noun. Endings for adjectives also change to agree with the gender of the noun they modify (masculine/feminine -**o**/-**a**). Where both masculine and feminine forms are included in this language guide, they are separated by a slash, with the masculine form first, eg *perdido/a*.

If a noun or adjective ends in a vowel, the plural is formed by adding **s** to the end. If it ends in a consonant, the plural is formed by adding **es** to the end.

ACCOMMODATIONS

I'm looking for ...	*Estoy buscando ...*	e·stoy boos·kan·do ...
Where is ...?	*¿Dónde hay ...?*	don·de ai ...
a cabin	*una cabina*	oo·na ca·bee·na
a camping ground	*un camping/ campamento*	oon kam·ping/ kam·pa·men·to
a guesthouse	*una casa de huespedes*	oo·na ka·sa de wes·pe·des
a hostel	*un hospedaje/ una residencia*	oon os·pe·da·khe/ oon·a re·see·den·sya
a hotel	*un hotel*	oon o·tel
a youth hostel	*un albergue juvenil*	oon al·ber·ge khoo·ve·neel

Are there any rooms available?
¿Hay habitaciones libres?
ay a·bee·ta·syon·es lee·bres

I'd like a ... room.	*Quisiera una habitación ...*	kee·sye·ra oo·na a·bee·ta·syon ...
double	*doble*	do·ble
single	*individual*	een·dee·vee·dwal
twin	*con dos camas*	kon dos ka·mas

How much is it per ...?	*¿Cuánto cuesta por ...?*	kwan·to kwes·ta por ...
night	*noche*	no·che
person	*persona*	per·so·na
week	*semana*	se·ma·na

full board	*pensión completa*	pen·syon kom·ple·ta
private/shared bathroom	*baño privado/ compartido*	ba·nyo pree·va·do/ kom·par·tee·do

too expensive	*demasiado caro*	de·ma·sya·do ka·ro
cheaper	*más económico*	mas e·ko·no·mee·ko
discount	*descuento*	des·kwen·to

MAKING A RESERVATION
(for phone or written requests)

To ...	*A ...*
From ...	*De ...*
Date	*Fecha*
I'd like to book ...	*Quisiera reservar ...*
(see the list under 'Accommodations' for bed and room options)	
in the name of ...	*en nombre de ...*
for the nights of ...	*para las noches del ...*
credit card ...	*tarjeta de crédito ...*
number	*número*
expiry date	*fecha de vencimiento*
Please confirm ...	*Puede confirmar ...*
availability	*la disponibilidad*
price	*el precio*

Does it include breakfast?
¿Incluye el desayuno? een·kloo·ye el de·sa·yoo·no
May I see the room?
¿Puedo ver la habitación? pwe·do ver la a·bee·ta·syon
I don't like it.
No me gusta. no me goos·ta
It's fine. I'll take it.
Está bien. La tomo. es·ta byen la to·mo
I'm leaving now.
Me voy ahora. me voy a·o·ra

CONVERSATION & ESSENTIALS

In their public behavior, Latin Americans are very conscious of civilities. You should never approach a stranger for information without extending a greeting, such as *buenos días* or *buenas tardes*, and you should use only the polite form of address, especially with the police and public officials.

Central America is generally more formal than many of the South American countries. The polite form *usted* (you) is used in all cases in this guide; where options are given, the form is indicated by the abbreviations 'pol' and 'inf.'

Hi.	*Hola.*	o·la (inf)
Good morning.	*Buenos días.*	bwe·nos dee·as
Good afternoon.	*Buenas tardes.*	bwe·nas tar·des
Good evening/ night.	*Buenas noches.*	bwe·nas no·ches

The three most common greetings are often abbreviated to simply *buenos* (for *buenos días*) and *buenas* (for *buenas tardes* and *buenas noches*).

Bye/See you soon.	*Hasta luego.*	*as-ta lwe-go*
Goodbye.	*Adiós.*	*a-dyos*
(see also the boxed text, p557)		
Yes.	*Sí.*	*see*
No.	*No.*	*no*
Please.	*Por favor.*	*por fa-vor*
Thank you.	*Gracias.*	*gra-syas*
Many thanks.	*Muchas gracias.*	*moo-chas gra-syas*
You're welcome.	*De nada.*	*de na-da*
Excuse me.	*Con permiso.*	*kon per-mee-so*
(to get past or when reaching over to take something)		
Excuse me.	*Perdón.*	*per-don*
(when apologising or before asking directions/advice)		
I'm sorry.	*Disculpe.*	*dees-kool-pe*
(when apologizing)		

How are things?
¿Qué tal?   *ke tal*
What's your name?
¿Cómo se llama usted?   *ko-mo se ya-ma oo-sted* (pol)
¿Cómo te llamas?   *ko-mo te ya-mas* (inf)
My name is ...
Me llamo ...   *me ya-mo ...*
It's a pleasure to meet you.
Mucho gusto.   *moo-cho goos-to*
The pleasure is mine.
El gusto es mío.   *el goos-to es mee-o*
Where are you from?
¿De dónde es/eres?   *de don-de es/er-es* (pol/inf)
I'm from ...
Soy de ...   *soy de ...*
Where are you staying?
¿Dónde está alojado?   *don-de es-ta a-lo-kha-do* (pol)
¿Dónde estás alojado?   *don-de es-tas a-lo-kha-do* (inf)
May I take a photo?
¿Puedo sacar una foto?   *pwe-do sa-kar oo-na fo-to*

DIRECTIONS

How do I get to ...?
¿Cómo llego a ...?   *ko-mo ye-go a ...*
Is it far?
¿Está lejos?   *es-ta le-khos*
Go straight ahead.
Siga/Vaya derecho.   *see-ga/va-ya de-re-cho*
Turn left.
Voltée a la izquierda.   *vol-te-e a la ees-kyer-da*
Turn right.
Voltée a la derecha.   *vol-te-e a la de-re-cha*
Can you show me (on the map)?
¿Me lo podría señalar   *me lo po-dree-a se-nya-lar*
(en el mapa)?   *(en el ma-pa)*

Entrada	Entrance
Salida	Exit
Información	Information
Abierto	Open
Cerrado	Closed
Prohibido	Prohibited
Comisaria	Police Station
Servicios/Baños	Toilets
Hombres/Varones	Men
Mujeres/Damas	Women

north	*norte*	*nor-te*
south	*sur*	*soor*
east	*este*	*es-te*
west	*oeste*	*o-es-te*
here	*aquí*	*a-kee*
there	*ahí*	*a-ee*
avenue	*avenida*	*a-ve-nee-da*
block	*cuadra*	*kwa-dra*
street	*calle/paseo*	*ka-lye/pa-se-o*

EMERGENCIES

Help!	*¡Socorro!*	*so-ko-ro*
Fire!	*¡Fuego!*	*fwe-go*
I've been robbed.	*Me han robado.*	*me an ro-ba-do*
Go away!	*¡Déjeme!*	*de-khe-me*
Get lost!	*¡Váyase!*	*va-ya-se*

Call ...!	*¡Llame a ...!*	*ya-me a*
the police	*la policía*	*la po-lee-see-a*
a doctor	*un médico*	*oon me-dee-ko*
an ambulance	*una ambulancia*	*oo-na am-boo-lan-sya*

It's an emergency.
Es una emergencia.   *es oo-na e-mer-khen-sya*
Could you help me, please?
¿Me puede ayudar,   *me pwe-de a-yoo-dar*
por favor?   *por fa-vor*
I'm lost.
Estoy perdido/a.   *es-toy per-dee-do/a*
Where are the toilets?
¿Dónde están los baños?   *don-de es-tan los ba-nyos*

HEALTH

I'm sick.
Estoy enfermo/a.   *es-toy en-fer-mo/a*
I need a doctor.
Necesito un médico.   *ne-se-see-to oon me-dee-ko*
Where's the hospital?
¿Dónde está el hospital?   *don-de es-ta el os-pee-tal*

I'm pregnant.
  Estoy embarazada.   es·*toy* em·ba·ra·*sa*·da
I've been vaccinated.
  Estoy vacunado/a.   es·*toy* va·koo·*na*·do/a

I'm allergic	*Soy alérgico/a*	soy a·*ler*·khee·ko/a
to ...	*a ...*	a ...
antibiotics	*los antibióticos*	los an·tee·*byo*·tee·kos
nuts	*las nueces*	las *nwe*·ses
peanuts	*los cacahuates*	los ka·ka·*khwa*·tes
penicillin	*la penicilina*	la pe·nee·see·*lee*·na

I'm ...	*Soy ...*	soy ...
asthmatic	*asmático/a*	as·*ma*·tee·ko/a
diabetic	*diabético/a*	dya·be·tee·ko/a
epileptic	*epiléptico/a*	e·pee·*lep*·tee·ko/a

I have ...	*Tengo ...*	*ten*·go ...
a cough	*tos*	tos
diarrhea	*diarrea*	dya·*re*·a
a headache	*un dolor de*	oon do·*lor* de
	cabeza	ka·*be*·sa
nausea	*náusea*	*now*·se·a

11	*once*	*on*·se
12	*doce*	*do*·se
13	*trece*	*tre*·se
14	*catorce*	ka·*tor*·se
15	*quince*	*keen*·se
16	*dieciséis*	dye·see·*says*
17	*diecisiete*	dye·see·*sye*·te
18	*dieciocho*	dye·see·o·cho
19	*diecinueve*	dye·see·*nwe*·ve
20	*veinte*	*vayn*·te
21	*veintiuno*	vayn·tee·*oo*·no
30	*treinta*	*trayn*·ta
31	*treinta y uno*	*trayn*·ta ee *oo*·no
40	*cuarenta*	kwa·*ren*·ta
50	*cincuenta*	seen·*kwen*·ta
60	*sesenta*	se·*sen*·ta
70	*setenta*	se·*ten*·ta
80	*ochenta*	o·*chen*·ta
90	*noventa*	no·*ven*·ta
100	*cien*	syen
101	*ciento uno*	syen·to *oo*·no
200	*doscientos*	do·*syen*·tos
1000	*mil*	meel
5000	*cinco mil*	*seen*·ko meel

LANGUAGE DIFFICULTIES
Do you speak English?
  ¿Habla/Hablas inglés?   a·bla/a·blas een·*gles* (pol/inf)
Does anyone here speak English?
  ¿Hay alguien que hable   ai al·*gyen* ke a·ble
  inglés?   een·*gles*
I (don't) understand.
  (No) Entiendo.   (no) en·*tyen*·do
How do you say ...?
  ¿Cómo se dice ...?   ko·mo se *dee*·se ...
What does ...mean?
  ¿Qué significa ...?   ke seeg·*nee*·fee·ka ...

Could you	*¿Puede ..., por*	*pwe*·de ... por
please ...?	*favor?*	fa·vor
repeat that	*repetirlo*	re·pe·*teer*·lo
speak more	*hablar más*	a·*blar* mas
slowly	*despacio*	des·*pa*·syo
write it down	*escribirlo*	es·kree·*beer*·lo

NUMBERS
1	*uno*	*oo*·no
2	*dos*	dos
3	*tres*	tres
4	*cuatro*	*kwa*·tro
5	*cinco*	*seen*·ko
6	*seis*	says
7	*siete*	*sye*·te
8	*ocho*	o·cho
9	*nueve*	*nwe*·ve
10	*diez*	dyes

PAPERWORK
birth certificate	*certificado de nacimiento*
border (frontier)	*la frontera*
car-owner's title	*título de propiedad*
car registration	*registración*
customs	*aduana*
driver's license	*licencia de manejar*
identification	*identificación*
immigration	*migración*
insurance	*seguro*
passport	*pasaporte*
temporary vehicle	*permiso de importación*
import permit	*temporal de vehículo*
tourist card	*tarjeta de turista*
visa	*visado*

SHOPPING & SERVICES
I'd like to buy ...
  Quisiera comprar ...   kee·*sye*·ra kom·prar ...
I'm just looking.
  Sólo estoy mirando.   so·lo es·*toy* mee·*ran*·do
May I look at it?
  ¿Puedo verlo/a?   pwe·do ver·lo/a
How much is it?
  ¿Cuánto cuesta?   kwan·to kwes·ta
That's too expensive for me.
  Es demasiado caro   es de·ma·*sya*·do *ka*·ro
  para mí.   *pa*·ra mee
Could you lower the price?
  ¿Podría bajar un poco   po·*dree*·a ba·*khar* oon *po*·ko
  el precio?   el *pre*·syo

I don't like it.
No me gusta.   no me *goos*·ta
I'll take it.
Lo llevo.   lo *ye*·vo

Do you   *¿Aceptan ...?*   a·sep·*tan* ...
accept ...?
  American   *dólares*   *do*·la·res
  dollars   *americanos*   a·me·ree·*ka*·nos
  credit cards *tarjetas de*   tar·*khe*·tas de
                crédito   *kre*·dee·to
  traveler's *cheques de*   *che*·kes de
  checks   *viajero*   vya·*khe*·ro

less   *menos*   *me*·nos
more   *más*   mas
large   *grande*   *gran*·de
small   *pequeño/a* (m/f) pe·*ke*·nyo/a

I'm looking   *Estoy*   es·*toy*
for the ...   *buscando ...*   boos·*kan*·do...
  ATM   *un cajero*   oon ka·*khe*·ro
             automático   ow·to·*ma*·tee·ko
  bank   *un banco*   oon *ban*·ko
  bookstore *la librería* la lee·bre·*ree*·a
  exchange house *una casa de* *oo*·na *ka*·sa de
             cambio   *kam*·byo
  general store *la tienda* la *tyen*·da
  laundry *la lavandería* la la·van·de·*ree*·a
  market   *el mercado*   el mer·*ka*·do
  pharmacy/ *la farmacia* la far·*ma*·sya
  chemist
  post office *el correo*   el ko·*re*·o
  supermarket *el supermercado* el soo·per·
                       mer·*ka*·do
  tourist office *la oficina de* la o·fee·*see*·na de
             turismo   too·*rees*·mo

What time does it open/close?
¿A qué hora abre/cierra?
a ke *o*·ra *a*·bre/*sye*·ra
I want to change some money/traveler's checks.
Quisiera cambiar dinero/cheques de viajero.
kee·*sye*·ra kam·*byar* dee·*ne*·ro/*che*·kes de vya·*khe*·ro
What is the exchange rate?
¿Cuál es el tipo de cambio?
kwal es el *tee*·po de *kam*·byo
I want to call ...
Quisiera llamar a ...
kee·*sye*·ra lya·*mar* a ...

airmail   *correo aéreo*   ko·*re*·o a·*e*·re·o
letter   *carta*   *kar*·ta
registered (mail) *certificado* ser·tee·fee·*ka*·do
stamps   *timbres*   *teem*·bres

TIME & DATES
What time is it? *¿Qué hora es?* ke *o*·ra es
It's one o'clock. *Es la una.*   es la *oo*·na
It's ten o'clock. *Son las diez.* son las dyes
Half past two.   *Dos y media.*   dos ee *me*·dya

midnight   *medianoche*   me·dya·*no*·che
noon   *mediodía*   me·dyo·*dee*·a
now   *ahora*   a·*o*·ra
today   *hoy*   oy
tonight   *esta noche*   es·ta *no*·che
tomorrow   *mañana*   ma·*nya*·na
yesterday *ayer*   a·*yer*

Monday   *lunes*   *loo*·nes
Tuesday   *martes*   *mar*·tes
Wednesday *miércoles*   *myer*·ko·les
Thursday   *jueves*   *khwe*·ves
Friday   *viernes*   *vyer*·nes
Saturday   *sábado*   *sa*·ba·do
Sunday   *domingo*   do·*meen*·go

January   *enero*   e·*ne*·ro
February   *febrero*   fe·*bre*·ro
March   *marzo*   *mar*·so
April   *abril*   a·*breel*
May   *mayo*   *ma*·yo
June   *junio*   *khoo*·nyo
July   *julio*   *khoo*·lyo
August   *agosto*   a·*gos*·to
September *septiembre*   sep·*tyem*·bre
October   *octubre*   ok·*too*·bre
November   *noviembre*   no·*vyem*·bre
December   *diciembre*   dee·*syem*·bre

TRANSPORT
Public Transport
What time does *¿A qué hora ...* a ke *o*·ra ...
... leave/arrive? *sale/llega?*   *sa*·le/*ye*·ga
  the bus *el bus/autobús* el bus/ow·to·*boos*
  the ferry *el barco*   el *bar*·ko
  the minibus *el colectivo/* el ko·lek·*tee*·vo/
             la buseta/   la boo·*se*·ta/
             el microbus   el *mee*·kro·boos
  the plane *el avión*   el a·*vyon*
  the train *el tren*   el tren

  the airport *el aeropuerto* el a·e·ro·*pwer*·to
  the bus station *la estación de* la es·ta·*syon* de
             autobuses   ow·to·*boo*·ses
  the bus stop *la parada de* la pa·*ra*·da de
             autobuses   ow·to·*boo*·ses
  the train station *la estación de* la es·ta·*syon* de
             ferrocarril   fe·ro·ka·*reel*

| the luggage locker | *la consigna para el equipaje* | la kon·*see*·nya para el e·kee·*pa*·khe |
| the ticket office | *la boletería/ ticketería* | la bo·le·te·*ree*·ya/ tee·ke·te·*ree*·ya |

A ticket to ..., please.
Un boleto a ..., por favor.
oon bo·*le*·to a ... por fa·*vor*

What's the fare to ...?
¿Cuánto cuesta hasta ...?
kwan·to *kwes*·ta *a*·sta ...

student's	*de estudiante*	de es·too·*dyan*·te
1st class	*primera clase*	*pree*·me·ra *kla*·se
2nd class	*segunda clase*	se·*goon*·da *kla*·se
one-way	*de ida*	de *ee*·da
round trip	*de ida y vuelta*	de *ee*·da e *vwel*·ta
taxi	*taxi*	*tak*·see

Private Transport

I'd like to hire a ...	*Quisiera alquilar ...*	kee·*sye*·ra al·kee·*lar* ...
4WD	*un todo terreno*	oon *to*·do te·*re*·no
car	*un auto/carro*	oon *ow*·to/*ka*·ro
motorcycle	*una motocicleta*	*oo*·na *mo*·to·see·*kle*·ta
bicycle	*una bicicleta*	*oo*·na bee·see·*kle*·ta

pick-up (truck)	*camioneta*	ka·myo·*ne*·ta
truck	*camión*	ka·*myon*
hitchhike	*pedir un aventón*	pe·deer oon a·ven·*ton*

Where's a petrol station?
¿Dónde hay una gasolinera/bomba?
don·de ai oo·na ga·so·lee·*ne*·ra/*bom*·ba

How much is a liter of gasoline?
¿Cuánto cuesta el litro de gasolina?
kwan·to *kwes*·ta el *lee*·tro de ga·so·*lee*·na

Please fill it up.
Lleno, por favor.
ye·no por fa·*vor*

I'd like (2000 colones) worth.
Quiero (dos mil colones) en gasolina.
kye·ro (dos meel ko·*lo*·nes) en ga·so·*lee*·na

diesel	*diesel*	*dee*·sel
gas (petrol)	*gasolina*	ga·so·*lee*·na
leaded (regular)	*gasolina con plomo*	ga·so·*lee*·na kon *plo*·mo
unleaded	*gasolina sin plomo*	ga·so·*lee*·na seen *plo*·mo
oil	*aceite*	a·*say*·te
tire	*llanta*	*yan*·ta
puncture	*agujero*	a·goo·*khe*·ro

Is this the road to ...?
¿Por aquí se va a ...?
por a·*kee* se va a ...

(How long) Can I park here?
¿(Por cuánto tiempo) Puedo estacionar aquí?
(por *kwan*·to *tyem*·po) pwe·do ess·ta·syo·*nar* a·*kee*

Where do I pay?
¿Dónde se paga?
don·de se *pa*·ga

I need a mechanic/tow truck.
Necesito un mecánico/remolque.
ne·se·*see*·to oon me·*ka*·nee·ko/re·*mol*·ke

Is there a garage near here?
¿Hay un garaje cerca de aquí?
ai oon ga·*ra*·khe ser·ka de a·*kee*

The car has broken down in ...
El carro se ha averiado en ...
el *ka*·ro se a a·ve·*rya*·do en ...

The motorbike won't start.
La moto no arranca.
la *mo*·to no a·*ran*·ka

I have a flat tire.
Tengo una llanta desinflada.
ten·go *oo*·na *yan*·ta des·een·*fla*·da

I've run out of petrol.
Me quedé sin gasolina.
me ke·*de* seen ga·so·*lee*·na

I've had an accident.
Tuve un accidente.
too·ve oon ak·see·*den*·te

LANGUAGE

TRAVEL WITH CHILDREN

I need ...
Necesito ...
ne·se·*see*·to ...
Do you have ...?
¿Hay ...?
ai ...

a car baby seat
un asiento de seguridad para bebés
oon a·*syen*·to de se·goo·ree·*da* pa·ra be·*bes*
a child-minding service
oon club para niños
oon kloob pa·*ra* nee·nyos
a children's menu
un menú infantil
oon me·*noo* een·fan·*teel*
a crèche
una guardería
oo·na gwar·de·*ree*·a
(disposable) diapers/nappies
pañales (de usar y tirar)
pa·*nya*·les (de oo·*sar* ee tee·*rar*)

an (English-speaking) babysitter
una niñera (que habla inglesa)
oo·na nee·*nye*·ra (ke *a*·bla een·*gle*·sa)
formula (milk)
leche en polvo
le·che en *pol*·vo
a highchair
una silla para bebé
oo·na *see*·ya *pa*·ra be·*be*
a potty
una bacinica
oo·na ba·see·*nee*·ka
a stroller
una carreola
oona ka·re·o·la

Do you mind if I breast-feed here?
¿Le molesta que dé el pecho aquí?
le mo·*les*·ta ke de el *pe*·cho a·*kee*
Are children allowed?
¿Se admiten niños?
se ad·*mee*·ten nee·nyos

Also available from Lonely Planet:
Costa Rican Spanish Phrasebook

Glossary

See p58 for useful words and phrases dealing with food and dining. See the Language chapter (p557) for other useful words and phrases.

adiós – means goodbye universally, but used in rural Costa Rica as a greeting
alquiler de automóviles – car rental
apartado – post-office box
artesanía – handicrafts
ATH – *a toda hora* (open all hours); used to denote automatic teller machines
automóvil – car
avenida – avenue
avión – airplane

bahía – bay
barrio – district or neighborhood
biblioteca – library
bocas – small savory dishes served in bars
bomba – short, funny verse; also means gas station; also means bomb
bosque – forest
bosque nuboso – cloud forest
buena nota – excellent/OK; literally 'good note'

caballo – horse
cabaña – cabin; see also *cabina*
cabina – cabin; see also *cabaña*
cajero automático – ATM
calle – street
cama/cama matrimonial – bed/double bed
campesino – peasant, farmer or person who works in agriculture
carretas – colorfully painted wooden oxcarts, now a form of folk art
carretera – road
casado – set meal; also means married
casita – cottage or apartment
catedral – cathedral
caverna – cave; see also *cueva*
cerro – mountain or hill
cerveza – beer
ceviche – local dish of raw, marinated seafood
Chepe – affectionate nickname for José; also used when referring to San José
cine – cinema
ciudad – city
cocina – kitchen or cooking

colectivo – buses, minivans or cars operating as shared taxis
colibrí – hummingbird
colina – hill
colón – Costa Rican unit of currency; plural colones
comida típica – typical food
cordillera – mountain range
correo – mail service
Costarricense – Costa Rican; see also *Tico*
cruce – crossing
cruda – often used to describe a hangover; literally 'raw'
cueva – cave; see also *caverna*
culebra – snake; see also *serpiente*

Dios – God
directo – direct; refers to long-distance bus with few stops

edificio – building
estación – station, as in ranger station or bus station; also means season

farmacia – pharmacy
fauna silvestre – wildlife
fiesta – party or festival
finca – farm or plantation
floresta – forest
frontera – border
fútbol – football (soccer)

gallo pinto – rice and beans
garza – cattle egret
gasolina – gas or petrol
gracias – thanks
gringo/a – male/female US or European visitors; can be affectionate or insulting, depending on the tone used
guaro – local firewater

hacienda – rural estate
hielo – ice

ICT – Instituto Costarricense de Turismo; Costa Rica Tourism Board, which provides tourist information
iglesia – church
indígena – indigenous
Interamericana – the Pan-American Hwy; the nearly continuous highway running from Alaska to Chile (it breaks at the Darién Gap between Panama and Colombia)
invierno – winter; the rainy season in Costa Rica
isla – island

jardín – garden
josefino – resident of San José

lago – lake
lavandería – laundry facility, usually offering dry-cleaning services
librería – bookstore
llanuras – tropical plains

machismo – an exaggerated sense of masculine pride
macho – a virile figure, typically a man
marías – local name for taxi meters
mercado – market
Meseta Central – Central Valley or central plateau
mestizo – person of mixed descent, usually Spanish and Indian
metate – flat stone platform, used by Costa Rica's pre-Columbian populations to grind corn
migración – immigration
Minae – Ministerio de Ambiente y Energía; Ministry of Environment and Energy, in charge of the national park system
mirador – lookout point
mono – monkey
mono tití – squirrel monkey
motocicleta – motorcycle
muelle – dock
museo – museum

niño – child
normal – refers to long-distance bus with many stops

ola(s) – wave(s)
OTS – Organization for Tropical Studies

pájaro – bird
palapa – shelter with a thatched, palm-leaf roof and open sides
páramo – habitat characterized by highland shrub and tussock grass
parque – park

parque central – central town square or plaza
parque nacional – national park
perezoso – sloth
perico – mealy parrot
playa – beach
posada – country-style inn or guesthouse
puente – bridge
puerto – port
pulpería – corner grocery store
punta – point
pura vida – super; literally 'pure life'

quebrada – stream
queso – cheese

rana – frog or toad
rancho – small house or house-like building
refugio nacional de vida silvestre – national wildlife refuge
río – river

sabanero – cowboy from Guanacaste
selva – jungle
Semana Santa – the Christian Holy Week that precedes Easter
sendero – trail or path
serpiente – snake; see also *culebra*
soda – lunch counter or inexpensive eatery
supermercado – supermarket

Tico/a – male/female Costa Rican; see also *Costarricense*
tienda – store
tortuga – turtle

valle – valley
verano – summer; the dry season in Costa Rica
vino – wine
volcán – volcano

zoológico – zoo

The Authors

MATTHEW D FIRESTONE Coordinating Author: Central Pacific Coast, Southern Costa Rica, Península de Osa & Golfo Dulce

Matt is a trained biological anthropologist and epidemiologist who is particularly interested in the health and nutrition of indigenous populations. His first visit to Costa Rica in 2001 brought him deep into the rain forests of Parque Nacional Chirripó, where he performed a field study on the modern diet of the Cabécar. Unfortunately, Matt's promising academic career was postponed due to a severe case of wanderlust, though he has traveled to over 65 different countries in a relentless search for a cure. Matt is hoping that this book will help ease the pain of other individuals bitten by the travel bug, though he fears that there is a growing epidemic on the horizon.

GUYAN MITRA   San José, Central Valley & Highlands, Caribbean Coast

Guyan is one of those lucky people who fell straight from university into a dream job. Having graduated from Cardiff University with a BA in Ancient History, he elbowed his way into the offices of the *Sunday Times Travel Magazine*, where he cut his teeth as a budding travel journalist. He has since worked as a freelance travel journalist contributing to the *Sunday Times*, *Esquire* and various inflight magazines. He has written two books, and works and lives in his hometown, London. Guyan has been hopping back-and-forth to Latin America for over a decade. He always promises the next trip will be the one where he finally masters salsa, merengue or some other Latin step. Despite his best efforts, he only has the chicken dance perfected.

WENDY YANAGIHARA   Northwestern Costa Rica, Península de Nicoya, Northern Lowlands

Born in a bucolic paradise in southern California, Wendy was raised on white rice and wanderlust, which she owes to her late mom. Childhood trips led to study abroad and then a brief expat life. Occupational stints have included farmer's marketer, espresso puller, jewelry pusher, graphic designer and ESL teacher. She has worked on over a dozen guidebooks for Lonely Planet, including *Mexico, Indonesia, Tokyo, Vietnam, Grand Canyon National Park*, and most recently, *Costa Rica*. For the time being, she's based in beautiful Boulder, Colorado.

THE AUTHORS

CONTRIBUTING AUTHORS

Dr David Goldberg wrote the Health chapter (p551). He completed his training in internal medicine and infectious diseases at Columbia-Presbyterian Medical Center in New York City, where he has also served as voluntary faculty. At present he is an infectious diseases specialist in Scarsdale, New York, and the editor-in-chief of the website MDTravelHealth.com.

David Lukas wrote the Environment chapter (p61) and Wildlife Guide (p193). He is an avid student of natural history who has traveled widely to study tropical ecosystems in locations such as Borneo and the Amazon. He has also spent several years leading natural history tours to all corners of Costa Rica, Belize and Guatemala.

Behind the Scenes

THIS BOOK

This 8th edition of Costa Rica was written by Matthew D Firestone (coordinating author), Guyan Mitra and Wendy Yanagihara. David Lukas penned the Wildlife Guide and Environment chapters and Dr David Goldberg wrote the Health chapter. Mara Vorhees and Matthew D Firestone wrote the 7th edition of Costa Rica. The first five editions were written by Rob Rachowiecki, and the 6th edition was written by Paige R Penland and Carolina Miranda. This guidebook was commissioned in Lonely Planet's Oakland office, and produced by the following:

Commissioning Editor Catherine Craddock
Coordinating Editor Anna Metcalfe
Coordinating Cartographer Julie Dodkins
Coordinating Layout Designer Katherine Marsh
Managing Editor Bruce Evans
Managing Cartographers Alison Lyall, Adrian Persoglia
Managing Layout Designers Adam McCrow, Celia Wood
Assisting Editors Simone Egger, Justin Flynn, Amy Karafin, Anne Mulvaney, Kristin Odijk
Assisting Cartographers Owen Eszeki, Andy Rojas
Assisting Layout Designer Jacqui Saunders
Cover Designer Pepi Bluck
Project Manager Fabrice Rocher
Language Content Coordinator Quentin Frayne

Thanks to Helen Christinis, Jay Cooke, Eoin Dunlevy, Rachel Imeson, Laura Jane, Lisa Knights, Katie Lynch, Katy Murenu, Wayne Murphy, Trent Paton, Glenn van der Knijff

THANKS
MATTHEW D FIRESTONE

First and foremost, I'd like to thank my family for their tireless patience and continued support. This time around, I'd like to extend a special thanks to my fearless mother, who braved cold showers, unpaved roads and a few onions here and there. Needless to say, you were a true backpacker from the very start! Second, I'd like to thank Catherine for giving me the opportunity to have a second go at this massive travel tome. And of course, I'd like to give a shout out to my wonderful co-authors Wendy and Guyan, for their great work and warm vibes throughout the research and writing process. Finally, I can't forget my roommate, hermano and all-round partner in crime, Tac, for keeping me sane throughout the writing process. 本当にありがとうございました.

GUYAN MITRA

Firstly, I'd like to thank Catherine for trusting me with this project. I'd like to also thank Matt for being such a fantastic support throughout the process. You've been such good help and I

THE LONELY PLANET STORY

Fresh from an epic journey across Europe, Asia and Australia in 1972, Tony and Maureen Wheeler sat at their kitchen table stapling together notes. The first Lonely Planet guidebook, Across Asia on the Cheap, was born.

Travelers snapped up the guides. Inspired by their success, the Wheelers began publishing books to Southeast Asia, India and beyond. Demand was prodigious, and the Wheelers expanded the business rapidly to keep up. Over the years, Lonely Planet extended its coverage to every country and into the virtual world via lonelyplanet.com and the Thorn Tree message board.

As Lonely Planet became a globally loved brand, Tony and Maureen received several offers for the company. But it wasn't until 2007 that they found a partner whom they trusted to remain true to the company's principles of traveling widely, treading lightly and giving sustainably. In October of that year, BBC Worldwide acquired a 75% share in the company, pledging to uphold Lonely Planet's commitment to independent travel, trustworthy advice and editorial independence.

Today, Lonely Planet has offices in Melbourne, London and Oakland, with over 500 staff members and 300 authors. Tony and Maureen are still actively involved with Lonely Planet. They're traveling more often than ever, and they're devoting their spare time to charitable projects. And the company is still driven by the philosophy of Across Asia on the Cheap: 'All you've got to do is decide to go and the hardest part is over. So go!'

greatly appreciate your time and patience. I'd like to thank all the people in Costa Rica who helped me: Nealan, Dan, Martijn, Sitsi, Caroline, Mariella, Andres, Adrian, Eric, J, Philip, Anton, Yolanda, John and Miguel. *Gracias por todo*. X

WENDY YANAGIHARA
So many people buoyed my journey from river to ocean to volcano and back, it would be impossible to thank them all, but here's a start: huge thanks and a toast of Flor de Caña to Fred and Luisa, Polar Bear, Miguel Angel Castillo Espinoza, Mario Tulio Brenes, Andres Vargas, Andrew Rothman, Mariana in Liberia, Ranger Lupita at Parque Nacional Santa Rosa, Luis at Las Hornillas, Wander *'gracias pero no,'* Gracie and Cody, Manuel in Montezuma, butterfly-man Josh, Eyal and Coryn, Kenn and Trish, Cheney Wells, Edwin in Santa Cruz, Joe and Mari, Thisbe and Mark, Carolyn, Paige, Jimmy for safe passage, Matt for being so good to work with and Cat for offering me this most wonderful chance to return to Costa Rica.

OUR READERS
Many thanks to the travelers who used the last edition and wrote to us with helpful hints, useful advice and interesting anecdotes:

A Mariem Aameyri, Sherron Abernethy, Simi Aboutboul, Marla Abrolat, Ashima Aggarwal, Patricia Aguilera, Claire Allen, Eric Allen, William Alvarado, Leif Andersson, Mike Andrews, Victor Anysimiv, Milly Anz, Silvia Argerich, Rachel Arnold, Deneice Arthurton, Nina Auer, Fiorentina Azizi **B** Alexandra Baackes, Elisabeth Babich, Martin Backman, Matthew Barendse, Beverly Bean, Danielle Beckham, David Bekhor, Steven Bernd, William Berry, Sean Besser, Kristyn Bishop, Tea Biteznik, William Blaettler, Amir Blumenthal, Jeramy Boik, Alex Boladeras, Michael Boller, Christopher Booth, Silke Bork, Ian Boroughs, Michael Bowers, Tad Brady, Suzanne Braun, Dana Breen, Remo Britschgi, Matt Brockwell, Jay Brodell, Lindsey Brown, David Bruhowzki, Kevin Bryant, Patricia Buschor, Tammie Buxton **C** Mark Cannalte, Gregory Casillas, Robert Chatfield, Roni Chernin, Maureen Chorney, Joseph Christie, Hsiao-Yun Chu, Elsa Citeau, Casey Clark, Erin Cleary, John Clode, Shannon Cobb, Jim Cohen, Karen Coker, Michelle Collins, Christopher Conatser, Ann Conroy, Sharla Cooper, Hernan Cordero, Sarah Corkill, Sara Cote, Ann Cowles, Janna Crabb, Simon Crosbie, Rachel Crosier, Peter Crossley **D** Raymond Danner, Chris Davis, Paul Davis, Carolyn De Groot, Ineke De Weerdt, Sander De Wit, Cathy Deeley, Diane Dejoannis, Noel Dekking,

SEND US YOUR FEEDBACK
We love to hear from travelers – your comments keep us on our toes and help make our books better. Our well-traveled team reads every word on what you loved or loathed about this book. Although we cannot reply individually to postal submissions, we always guarantee that your feedback goes straight to the appropriate authors, in time for the next edition. Each person who sends us information is thanked in the next edition – and the most useful submissions are rewarded with a free book.

To send us your updates – and find out about Lonely Planet events, newsletters and travel news – visit our award-winning website: **www.lonelyplanet.com/contact**.

Note: we may edit, reproduce and incorporate your comments in Lonely Planet products such as guidebooks, websites and digital products, so let us know if you don't want your comments reproduced or your name acknowledged. For a copy of our privacy policy visit www.lonelyplanet.com/privacy.

Linda Derfiny, Nicole Diamond, Anne Dias, John Dillard, Jennifer Dominique, Judy Donie, Dustin Donovan, William Douglas, Craig Dowle, Frank Driscoll, Florian Dünner **E** Leisl Ellis, Laura Emmett, Steven Engler, Kamyar Eshraghi, Jaco Expert **F** Elizabeth Fabbre, Bliss Fago, Gregory Falkenstein, Geoffroy Fauchet, Laura Faulkner, Nadia Ferrari, Federico Fileti, Elodie Fish, Melissa Fishburne, Lee Fitzgerald, Julia Flood, Brian Flores, Patrick Foster, Eva Fuchs **G** Sarah Garber, Andy Garcia, Aurora Garcia, Becky Garrod, Mari Gasiorowicz, Bill Gasteyer, Iris Gat, Otto Geesink, Clinton Gilliland, Lucy Gillon, Deborah Goldman, Justine Grajski, Ray Granade, Kate Gregory, Carrie Griffin, Meghan Grosscup, Thomas Grund, Susanne Grütter, Saul Guerrero **H** Daniel Haesen, Taili Hardiman, Linda Harleman, Corinne Hartmann, Sabine Hein, Cristin Hendrickson, Erik Henricsson, Jim Herdman, Lia Hesseling, Kevin Hill, Louise Hockley, Esmé Hoekstra, Michele Hoopes, Cassandra Hoover, Zohar Hoshen, Hi Howard, Kenneth Hoyt, Verena Hrovat, Frans Huber, Hans Huisman, Diana Hüchelbach **I** Nadine Imhasly **J** Sara J, Henriette Jacob, Goeran Jaeger, Jeannie Jarnot, Lauren Jawer, JD, Rachel Jensen, Duncan Jodrell, Milena Johnson, Michael Jones, Nicole Ellen Jones, Claudia Joos, Paul Jorgensen, Anne Junius, Tomi Jylhä **K** Jessica Kagle, Carly Kim, Leah Kirkpatrick, Elaine Klemmensen,

Kimberly Klootwyk, Christina Ko, Jasmin Köhler, Margot Kokke, Jesper Konig, Helga Krammer, Ron Kreisman, Anthony Kremski, Ronald Kuegler, Lesley Kunikis, Lucie Kyselova **L** Jane-Anne Lee, Pascala Leff, Jose Ignacio Leguina, Marguerite H Leishman, Laureline Lesselingue-Belair, Marian Klein Leugemors, Shira Lev-Ami, Diana Levengood, Lisa Levine, Suzanne Lew, Catherine Lewis, Jean Lewis, Jan Lim, Fernando Lizano, Amy Lodge, Torge Löding, John Lofy, Parker Love, Mauricio Luna, Diego Lynch, Kari Lyons **M** Aimée Machiels, Erika Malitzky, Patrick Mannens, Oren Marciano, James Martin, John Martin, Kathleen Martin, Laszlo Mathe, Esther Matute, Scott Mcintyre, Jessica Mcquade, David Mcsherry, Jennifer Medley, Patty Meier, Chris Mellen, Martin Merkle, Klaus Meyer-Arendt, Jean-Louis Michels, Lee Milner, Mark Douglas Minor, Susie Minson, Chris Mitchell, Sílvia Martín Molina, Marianne Mongillo, Pete Mooney, Adrian Moreno, Melanie Mueller-Jensen, Nancy Muir, Anne Mulcair, Paloma Muñoz, Gerri Myles **N** Alexandra Nadler, Kellee Napieralski, Melissa Nettles, Terry Newton, Sabrina Nichols, Lesley Noble, Mariana Nogaro, Camie Noll, Eka Norris, Christina Noz, Clara Nussbaum, Jens Nyman **O** Jasmine O'Brien, Jack Ocarroll, Jacquo Odemaere, Anne Olson, Caprice Olsthoorn, Smadar Oren, Daniele Oudinot **P** Dutch Pablo, Elizabeth Parker, Julia Patrick, Peter Peeters, Sarah Pelot-Hobbs, James Peters, Tom Pfyffer, Susan Phares, Peter Phillips, Joan Piazza, Suzanne Pincus, Max Pitman, Geoff Polci, Gretchen Powers, John Pratt, Shirley Price, Anthony Primozich, Angela Prior, Jean Prominski, John Puricelli **R** Dion Ramos, Kamini Rangappan, Juliette Ranson, Al Rapaport, Jim Ratti, Anna Ravensbergen, Nick Rayman, Cheryl Reed, Jennifer Reed, Alistair Reeves, Susan Register, Christina Reichel, Cynthia Renaud, Elisa Renda, Stefanie Reska, Kon Rhyu, Marci Richards, Esther Rietveld, Rod and June Ririe, Karen Robacker, Cigi Robert, Mike Roberto, Regina Rosa, Jess Rose, Tracy Rosecrans, Joyce and Nick Rouy, Maggie Roy, Mark Rutherford, Amatierra Hotel and Retreat Ruttenberg **S** Anne Karin Sæther, Gideon Saroufiem, Sarah Sattin, Milena Schmidt, P Schneider, Danette Schwab, Kim Schwartz, Todd Schwebel, Jody Seasonwein, Yolanda Senders, Carrie Serwetnyk, Stephen Shaw, Chun Jui Shen, Jacob Silber, Patricia Simpson, Anthony Smith, Brian Smith, Cayenne Smith, Chad Smith, Gill Smith, Lynne Smith, Stacey Sowards, Paige Spencer, Krista Spiro, Arlene Stanton, David Stanton, Danny Steinman, Igor Sterk, Dustin Stucki, Susana Susana, Mardi Swatek, Antje Szymendera **T** Maud Taillard, Humberto Takara, Stefan Tanamal, Emanuela Tasinato, Amber Tatum, Elly Taylor, Francesca Taylor, Carl Tera, June Terry, Lotti Tetteroo, Sian Thomas, Barbara Tilford, Sam Tomlinson, Francoise Touboul, Micha Tranchida, Rita Treiber, Martin Tremblay, Carolyn Trend, Monika Trojan, Robby Tucker, Sarah Turgon **V** Maritza Valenzuela, Maria Valerio, Luisa Valfre, Peter G van Jensen, Rick van Klaveren, Peter van Laere, Vicky van Loock, Jan and Charlotte van Oostrum, Hijmen van Twillert, Anne Vanderschueren, Josh Vanek, Raymond Venner, Laura Vernoy, Sigrid Verweij, Cristina Viray **W** Tali Waisel, David Walker, Sara Walsh, Dave Warner, Maerle Wasmann, Kerstin Wasson, Cara Waters, Mazey Watson, Stéphanie Weber, Michèle Wegmann, R Weinzweig, Cheney Wells, Sabrina Wendorff, Lauren West, Valerie Wezran, Stephanie White, Tracey Whybrow, Jo Ann Wichmann, Amy Widmer, Damon Willaman, Irene Williams, Joris Wind, Melissa Wolf, Patti Wolf, Kenneth Wood, Charlie Woodall, Alex Woodcraft, Marieke Wright, Michelle Wright **Z** Cathryn Zommer, Tal Zoucker

ACKNOWLEDGMENTS

Many thanks to the following for the use of their content:

Globe on title page ©Mountain High Maps 1993 Digital Wisdom, Inc.

Internal photographs p5 Neil McAllister/Alamy; p10 (#6), 12 (#1) Yadid Levy/Alamy; p9 (#3) Ellen McKnight/Alamy; p14 (#2) R1/Alamy; p15 (#5), p16 REUTERS/Juan Carlos Ulate. All other photographs by Lonely Planet Images, and by Johnny Haglund p6 (#5), p12 (#6); Luke Hunter p6 (#3), p7 (#6); Corey Wise p7 (#4); Christian Aslund p13; Ralph Hopkins p9 (#2); Tom Boyden p8; Christian Aslund p10 (#3); Mark Newman p10 (#4); Stephen Saks p14 (#1); Christer Fredriksson p15 (#3).

All images are the copyright of the photographers unless otherwise indicated. Many of the images in this guide are available for licensing from Lonely Planet Images: www.lonelyplanetimages.com.

Index

INDEX

000 Map pages
000 Photograph pages

INDEX

GreenDex

GOING GREEN

It seems like everyone's going 'green' these days, but how can you know which businesses are actually ecofriendly and which are simply jumping on the sustainable bandwagon?

The following organizations have been selected by Lonely Planet authors because they demonstrate an active sustainable-tourism policy. Some are involved in conservation or environmental education, and many are owned and operated by local and indigenous people, thereby maintaining and preserving regional identity and culture. Some of the listings below have also been certified by the **Costa Rica Tourism Board** (ICT; www.visitcostarica.com), which means they meet high standards of environmental sustainability, business ethics and cultural sensitivity.

We want to keep developing our sustainable-tourism content. If you think we've omitted someone who should be listed here, or if you disagree with our choices, email us at www.lonely planet.com/contact. For more information about sustainable tourism and Lonely Planet, see www .lonelyplanet.com/responsibletravel.

12am 1am 2am 3am 4am 5am 6am 7am 8am 9am 10am 11am 12pm

International Date Line
Mon / Sun

ARCTIC OCEAN

CHUKCHI SEA
Russia
Alaska (US)
BEAUFORT SEA
Banks Is (Can)
Victoria Is (Can)
Queen Elizabeth Is (Can)
Ellesmere Is (Can)
BAFFIN BAY
Greenland (Denmark)
9am
11am
GREENLAND SEA
NORWEGIAN SEA
Iceland
NORTH SEA

3am
2am
BERING SEA
GULF OF ALASKA
4am
5am
Baffin Is (Can)
HUDSON BAY
Canada
6am
7am
LABRADOR SEA
8am
8.30am
Bermuda (UK)
NORTH ATLANTIC OCEAN
Azores (Port)
Portugal
Spain
Morocco
Canary Is (Sp)
United Kingdom
Ireland

2am
1am
Midway Is (US)
NORTH PACIFIC OCEAN
Hawaii (US)
United States
Mexico
GULF OF MEXICO
The Bahamas
Cuba
Haiti
Eastern Caribbean Islands
CARIBBEAN SEA
Guatemala
Nicaragua
Panama
Cape Verde
Mauritania
Mali
Senegal
Guinea
Burkina Faso
Liberia
Ghana
GULF OF GUINEA

EQUATOR
Samoa
Kiribati
Galapagos Is (Ecuador)
Venezuela
Guyana
Colombia
Suriname
Ecuador
Peru
8am
Brazil
9am
Ascension (UK)

Tonga
12am
Cook Is (NZ)
Tahiti
French Polynesia (Fr)
2.30am
2am
Pitcairn Is (UK)
Easter Is (Chile)
Bolivia
Paraguay
7am
SOUTH ATLANTIC OCEAN

1am
New Zealand
12.45am
Chatham Is (NZ)
SOUTH PACIFIC OCEAN
Chile
Argentina
Uruguay
Tristan da Cunha (UK)
Gough Is (UK)

Falkland Is (UK)
South Georgia & South Sandwich Is (UK)
Bouvet Is (Norway)

12am 1am 2am 3am 4am 5am 6am 7am 8am 9am 10am 11am 12pm

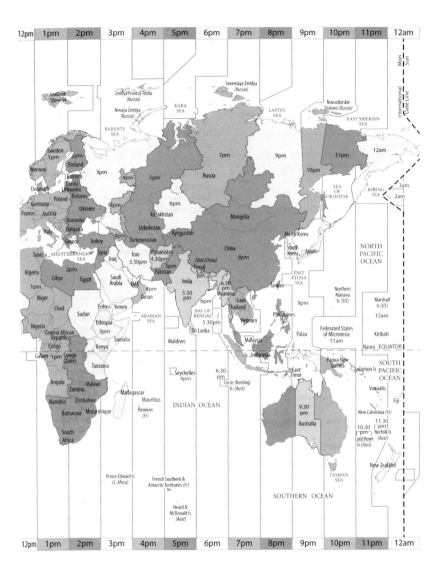

MAP LEGEND

ROUTES

Primary	Tunnel
Secondary	Pedestrian Overpass
Tertiary	Walking Tour
Lane	Walking Tour Detour
Under Construction	Walking Trail
Unsealed Road	Walking Path
One-Way Street	Track
Mall/Steps	

TRANSPORT

Ferry	Rail (Underground)
Metro	Tram
Rail	

HYDROGRAPHY

River, Creek	Reef
Intermittent River	Canal
Swamp	Water
Mangrove	Mudflats

BOUNDARIES

International	Regional, Suburb
State, Provincial	Ancient Wall
Marine Park	Cliff

AREA FEATURES

Airport	Land
Area of Interest	Mall
Beach, Desert	Market
Building	Park
Campus	Reservation
Cemetery, Christian	Sports
Forest	Urban

POPULATION

✪	CAPITAL (NATIONAL)	◉	CAPITAL (STATE)
●	Large City	○	Medium City
○	Small City	○	Town, Village

SYMBOLS

Sights/Activities
- Beach
- Canoeing, Kayaking
- Castle, Fortress
- Christian
- Golf
- Monument
- Museum, Gallery
- Point of Interest
- Pool
- Ruin
- Surfing, Surf Beach
- Trail Head
- Zoo, Bird Sanctuary

Eating
- Eating

Drinking
- Drinking
- Café

Entertainment
- Entertainment

Shopping
- Shopping

Sleeping
- Sleeping
- Camping

Transport
- Airport, Airfield
- Border Crossing
- Bus Station
- Gas Station
- General Transport
- Parking Area
- Taxi Rank

Information
- Bank, ATM
- Hospital, Medical
- Information
- Internet Facilities
- Police Station
- Post Office, GPO
- Telephone
- Toilets

Geographic
- Lookout
- Mountain, Volcano
- National Park
- Spot Height
- Waterfall

LONELY PLANET OFFICES

Australia
Head Office
Locked Bag 1, Footscray, Victoria 3011
☎ 03 8379 8000, fax 03 8379 8111
talk2us@lonelyplanet.com.au

USA
150 Linden St, Oakland, CA 94607
☎ 510 250 6400, toll free 800 275 8555
fax 510 893 8572
info@lonelyplanet.com

UK
2nd fl, 186 City Rd,
London EC1V 2NT
☎ 020 7106 2100, fax 020 7106 2101
go@lonelyplanet.co.uk

Published by Lonely Planet Publications Pty Ltd
ABN 36 005 607 983

© Lonely Planet Publications Pty Ltd 2008

© photographers as indicated 2008

Cover photograph: White-faced capuchin (Cebus capucinus) laying on a branch in a tropical rainforest, Ralph Hopkins/Lonely Planet Images. Many of the images in this guide are available for licensing from Lonely Planet Images: www.lonelyplanetimages.com.

Printed by SNP Security Printing Pte Ltd, Singapore.